wwnorton.com/nawr

The StudySpace site that accompanies *The Norton Anthology of World Religions* is FREE, but you will need the code below to register for a password that will allow you to access the copyrighted materials on the site.

WRLD—RLGN

THE NORTON ANTHOLOGY OF

WORLD

RELIGIONS

THE NORTON ANTHOLOGY OF

WORLD RELIGIONS

BUDDHISM

Donald S. Lopez, Jr.

JACK MILES, *General Editor*
DISTINGUISHED PROFESSOR OF ENGLISH AND
RELIGIOUS STUDIES
UNIVERSITY OF CALIFORNIA, IRVINE

W · W · NORTON & COMPANY

NEW YORK · LONDON

W. W. Norton & Company has been independent since its founding in 1923, when William Warder Norton and Mary D. Herter Norton first published lectures delivered at the People's Institute, the adult education division of New York City's Cooper Union. The firm soon expanded its program beyond the Institute, publishing books by celebrated academics from America and abroad. By midcentury, the two major pillars of Norton's publishing program—trade books and college texts—were firmly established. In the 1950s, the Norton family transferred control of the company to its employees, and today—with a staff of four hundred and a comparable number of trade, college, and professional titles published each year—W. W. Norton & Company stands as the largest and oldest publishing house owned wholly by its employees.

Manufacturing by RRDonnelley Crawfordsville
Composition by Westchester Book
Book design by Jo Anne Metsch
Production Manager: Sean Mintus

LIBRARY OF CONGRESS CATALOGING-IN-PUBLICATION DATA

The Norton anthology of world religions / Jack Miles, General Editor, Distinguished Professor of English and Religious Studies, University of California, Irvine; Wendy Doniger, Hinduism; Donald S. Lopez, Jr., Buddhism; James Robson, Daoism. — First Edition.
    volumes cm
  Includes bibliographical references and index.
  ISBN 978-0-393-91259-3 (hardcover)
  1. Religions. 2. Religions—History—Sources. I. Miles, Jack, 1942– editor.
II. Doniger, Wendy, editor. III. Lopez, Donald S., 1952– editor. IV. Robson, James, 1965 December 1– editor.
  BL74.N67 2014
  208—dc23

                                                                            2014030756

Buddhism (978-0-393-91259-3): Jack Miles, General Editor; Donald S. Lopez, Jr., Editor

W. W. Norton & Company, Inc.
500 Fifth Avenue
New York NY 10110
wwnorton.com

W. W. Norton & Company Ltd.
Castle House, 75/76 Wells Street, London W1T 3QT

1 2 3 4 5 6 7 8 9 0

Contents

GENERAL INTRODUCTION

How the West Learned to Compare Religions   3

JACK MILES

BUDDHISM   43

Introduction: In the World of the Buddha   45

DONALD S. LOPEZ, JR.

Buddhism in Korea   581

Buddhism in Japan   603

Buddhism in Tibet   677

Modern Buddhism   735

Maps and Illustrations

Preface

Welcome to *The Norton Anthology of World Religions.* The work offered to you here is large and complex, but it responds to a simple desire—namely, the desire that six major, living, international world religions should be allowed to speak to you in their own words rather than only through the words of others about them. Virtually all of the religious texts assembled here are primary texts. Practitioners of Hinduism, Buddhism, Daoism, Judaism, Christianity, and Islam have written and preserved these texts over the centuries for their own use and their own purposes. What is it like to read them, gathered as they are here like works of religious art in a secular museum?

For practitioners of any of these six religions, who number in the hundreds of millions, this anthology is likely to provide some of the surprise and fascination of a very large family album: some of one's religious ancestors trigger an immediate flash of recognition, while others look very distant and perhaps even comical. For an army of outsiders—those whose religion is not anthologized here, those who practice no religion, those who are "spiritual but not religious," and those who count themselves critics or antagonists of religion—the experience will be rewarding in different ways. No propaganda intrudes here on behalf either of any given religion or of religion in general. The goal at every point is not conversion, but exploration. The only assumptions made are that the most populous and influential of the world's religions are here to stay, that they reward study best when speaking to you in their own words, and that their contemporary words make best sense when heard against the panoramic background of the words they have remembered and preserved from their storied pasts.

Many of the texts gathered here have been translated from foreign languages, for the religions of the world have spoken many different languages over the course of their long histories. A few of the works—the Bhagavad Gita, the *Daode jing*, the Bible, the Qur'an—are readily available. Many more are available only in the libraries of a few major research universities or, though physically available, have not been intellectually available without detailed guidance that was impossible for the lay reader to come by. Bibliographic information is always provided for previously published translations, and a number of translations have been made especially for this anthology. A central concern throughout has been that the anthologized texts should be not just translated but also framed by enough editorial explanation to make them audible and intelligible across the barriers of time and space even if you are coming to them for the first time. When those explanations require the use of words in a foreign language with a non-Roman writing system, standard academic modes of transliteration have sometimes been simplified to enhance user-friendliness.

Globalization, including international migration in all its forms, has brought about a large-scale and largely involuntary mingling of once-separate religious communities, and this historic change has created an urgent occasion for a deeply grounded effort at interreligious understanding. Yes, most of the world's Hindus still live in India, yet the Hindu Diaspora is enormous and influential. Yes, many Jews have migrated to Israel, but half of the world's Jews still live in deeply rooted Diaspora communities around the world. Conventionally, Islam is thought of as a Middle Eastern religion, yet the largest Muslim populations are in South and Southeast Asia, while the Muslim minority in Europe is growing rapidly. By the same token, Christianity is not thought of as an African religion, yet the Christian population of sub-Saharan Africa is growing even more rapidly than the Muslim population of Europe. In a bygone era, the six religions treated here might have been divided geographically into an "Eastern" and a "Western" trio, but we do not so divide them, for in our era they are all everywhere, and none is a majority. Religiously, we live and in all likelihood will continue to live in a world of large and mingling minorities.

This involuntary mingling has created a state of affairs that can be violently disruptive. Terrorism in the name of religion, more often within national borders than across them, has turned many minds against religion in all forms. And yet, paradoxically, religious violence during the twenty-first century has persuaded many that, contrary to innumerable past predictions, religion is by no means fading from modern life. And though the threat of religious violence is a dark challenge of one sort, the bright new opportunities for cross-cultural and interreligious learning present an unprecedented challenge of a different and, in the end, a more consequential sort. On the one hand, whatever some of us might have wished, religious violence has made religion a subject that cannot be avoided. On the other, for those who engage the subject in depth, the study of religion across cultural and political borders builds a uniquely deep and subtle form of cosmopolitan sophistication.

In all its formal features—the format of its tables of contents; its use of maps and illustrations; its handling of headnotes, footnotes, glossaries, and bibliographies; its forty-eight pages of color illustration in six inserts—*The Norton Anthology of World Religions* announces its membership in the venerable family of Norton anthologies. As was true of *The Norton Anthology of English Literature* upon its first publication more than half a century ago, this anthology is both larger and more rigorously realized than any prior anthology published in English for use by the general reader or the college undergraduate. It opens with a generous introduction addressing a set of basic questions not linked to any single tradition but affecting all of them. Each of the six religious traditions is then presented chronologically from its origins to the present (the Buddhism volume also uses a geographical organizing principle). Each presentation begins with a substantial overview of the tradition being anthologized. Each is also punctuated by period introductions tracing the history of the tradition in question. And yet this work is not a history merely enlivened by the inclusion of original texts. No, history here is simply the stage. The texts themselves are the performance, displaying as only they can the perennial and subversive power of religious literature. The difference might be compared to the difference between English history with a bit of Shakespeare and Shakespeare with a bit of English history. The histories come and go, but Shakespeare is irreplaceable. Shakespeare is, to use a term that originated in the church, *canonical*.

Derived from the Greek word for a ruler or measuring rod, *canon* came to mean a rule or criterion of any kind. By extension, the same word came to mean the church rule or "canon" law governing the contents of the Bible: which books were to be included and which excluded. And by yet a further extension, canon came to refer to the understood list of acknowledged masterpieces in English or some other literature. So, the Bible has a canon. English literature has a canon (however endlessly contested). But what works of religious literature constitute the world religious canon?

Aye, dear reader, there was the rub as plans were laid for this anthology. In 2006, when the editorial team began work in earnest, no canons existed for the literatures of the world's major religions. There were limited canons within that vast expanse of written material, the Bible itself being the paradigmatic example. But the literature of Christianity is larger than the Bible, and the situation grows only more complicated as one ranges farther afield into traditions whose concentric canons are more implicit than explicit. Even though more than one canon of the Bible exists, Bible scholars can easily handle that limited variety and still quite literally *know what they are talking about*: they can deal with a clearly delimited body of material within which evidence-based historical interpretation can go forward. But what canon of religious texts exists to help define the entire field of religious studies for religion scholars? The field has never had an agreed-upon answer to that question, and some of the most sweeping theoretical statements about religion turn out, as a result, to rest on an astonishingly small and vague empirical base.

Granted that no master canon in the original religious sense of that term can ever be devised for the religions of the world, the lack of a limited but large and serious study collection of texts is one major indication that the study of religion remains at an early stage of its development as a discipline. For the religions of Asia, especially, it has been as if the Elizabethan theater were being studied without ready access by students to the plays of Shakespeare or with, at most, access to *Hamlet* alone. This lack has been particularly glaring in the United States for reasons that deserve a brief review. Until the early 1960s, the study of religion was largely confined to private colleges and universities, where, thanks to the country's Protestant intellectual heritage, it consisted overwhelmingly of biblical studies and Christian theology. Often, the department of religion was a department of philosophy and religion. Often, too, there was a close relationship between such departments and the college chaplaincy. In public colleges and universities, meanwhile, the situation was quite different. There, the traditional constitutional separation of church and state was understood to preclude the formal study of religion, perhaps especially of the very religions that the student body and the faculty might turn out to be practicing.

But then several events, occurring at nearly the same moment in both the public and the private spheres, created a new climate for the study of religion, and "religious studies" emerged as a new academic discipline distinct from philosophy or theology, on the one hand, and even more distinct from the chaplaincy, on the other. We are still reckoning with the consequences of this shift.

In 1963, Associate Justice Arthur Goldberg wrote for the Supreme Court of the United States in a concurring opinion in *Abington v. Schempp* (374 U.S. 203, 306): "It seems clear to me . . . that the Court would recognize the propriety of . . . the teaching *about* religion, as distinguished from the teaching *of* religion, in the public schools," language that seemed to clear a path for the study of religion in tax-supported schools. Significantly, Goldberg was a Jew; just three years earlier, Americans had elected John F. Kennedy as their first Roman Catholic president. American religious pluralism was becoming increasingly inescapable at the highest levels in American public life; and as it came to be understood that university-level religious studies was to be the study of various religions at once, including but by no means confined to the religions of the United States, the Founding Fathers' fear of an imposed, national religion began to recede from the national consciousness. American pluralism was now as powerful a factor in American religious life as the Constitution itself.

This anthology is published on the fiftieth anniversary of an event little noticed in the cultural ferment of the 1960s but of great importance for the study of religion—namely, the 1964 reincorporation of the National Association of Biblical Instructors (NABI), the principal association of college professors teaching these subjects, as the American Academy of Religion (AAR), whose current mission statement focuses pointedly on "the understanding of religious traditions, issues, questions, and values"—all in the plural. The formal incorporation of the AAR was intended first as a quiet but magnanimous gesture of invitation by a Protestant academic establishment toward the scholars of America's Catholic and Jewish communities, but this was just the beginning. Others would soon be drawn into a conversation whose animating academic conviction is well captured in a dictum of the great nineteenth-century scholar Max Müller: "He who knows one religion knows none."

Catholics and Jews had had their own seminaries and their own institutions of higher learning, but scholarship produced in them tended to remain in them—partly, to be sure, because of Protestant indifference but also because of defensive or reactively triumphalist habits of mind among the residually embattled minorities themselves. But this was already changing. Optimism and openness in the Roman Catholic community had been much assisted in the earlier 1960s by the Second Vatican Council, whose byword was the Italian *aggiornamento*—roughly, "updating"—as employed by the benignly bold Pope John XXIII. American Jews, meanwhile, profoundly traumatized as they had been during and after World War II by the Shoah, or Holocaust, Nazi Germany's attempted genocide, breathed a collective (if premature) sigh of relief in 1967 after Israel's stunning victory over its Arab opponents in the Six-Day War. During the same period, the Reverend Dr. Martin Luther King, Jr., had spearheaded a revolution in American race relations, as segregation ended and the social integration began that would lead to the election of a black president, Barack Obama, in 2008. In short, the mood in the early 1960s was in every way one of barred doors swung open, locked windows flung up, and common cause undertaken in moral enterprises like the interfaith campaign to end the war in Vietnam.

One influential scholar saw the shift occurring in the study of religion as cause for academic jubilation. Writing in 1971 in the *Journal of the American Academy of Religion* (which had been, until 1966, *The Journal of Bible and*

Religion), Wilfred Cantwell Smith clearly welcomed the change that was taking place:

> Perhaps what is happening can be summed up most pithily by saying that the transition has been from the teaching of religion to the study of religion. Where men used to instruct, they now inquire. They once attempted to impart what they themselves knew, and what they hoped (of late, with decreasing expectation) to make interesting; now, on the contrary, they inquire, into something that both for them and for their students is incontrovertibly interesting, but is something that they do not quite understand.

And yet there was a shadow across this scene. The newborn American Academy of Religion had bitten off rather more than it could chew. The spread of religious studies to the state university campuses that were proliferating in the late 1960s and the 1970s was vigorously pluralist. Jewish studies experienced an enormous growth spurt, and so did Hindu studies, Buddhist studies, Islamic studies, and so forth. Smith, a scholar of comparative religion who had made his first mark as a specialist in Islam, could only welcome this in principle. But others, writing later, would be troubled by growth that seemed to have spun out of control.

Recall that in 1971, *globalization* was not the byword that it has since become. The Hindu Diaspora in the United States was still tiny. Christian Pentecostalism, though well established, had not yet achieved critical mass in Africa. Europe's Muslim minority, if already substantial, was relatively dormant. Mainland China's population was still in Maoist lockdown. And in the United States, Americans had not yet begun to grasp the coming effects of the passage of the Immigration and Nationality Act of 1965, which removed quotas that had been in place since the 1920s; the resulting explosive growth in Hispanic and Asian immigration would by 1990 make non-Hispanic Caucasians a minority in Los Angeles, America's second-largest city. Americans still saw themselves as a colonized people who had achieved independence, rather than as a colonizing people. The rhetoric of European postcolonialism had not yet been applied to the United States, a superpower whose world hegemony was quasi-imperial in its reach and neocolonialist in its effects. Worldwide, the transformative interrogation of religious traditions by women and about women had barely begun.

While all of these changes, as they have brought about the multiplication and intensification of religious encounters, have made the study of world religions more important than ever, they have not made it easier. They have not, in particular, lent it any internal intellectual coherence. They have not created for it a new study canon to replace the narrowly Protestant study canon, as the founding of the AAR seemed in principle to require. The creation of religious studies as a field had been an academic gamble on a barely perceived religious future. Had the bet paid off? An eminent senior scholar, Jonathan Z. Smith, wrote in 1995 of the change that had taken place: "The field made a decision to give up a (limited) coherence for a (limitless) incoherence."

That limitless incoherence was the context in which we took up the challenge to produce *The Norton Anthology of World Religions*. How ever were we to begin?

There came first the recognition that we would be creating for the field of religious studies a first draft of the very canon that it lacked—a canon covering nearly four thousand years of history in a score of different languages, aspiring not to be authoritative regarding belief or practice but to be plausibly foundational for the study of the subject.

There came second the recognition that though canons, once achieved, are anonymous, they do not begin anonymously. They begin with somebody who declares this in and that out and defends his or her choice. This realization shifted the decision to be made from *What?* to *Who?*

There came third the question of whether the answer to the question *Who?* would come in the singular or in the plural and if in the plural, how multitudinously plural. For each of the traditions to be anthologized, would a large board of specialist advisers be assembled to determine what would be included? Would the selections be formally approved by some kind of plebiscite, as in the verse-by-verse ratification by translators of the language included in the King James Version of the Bible? Would the work of annotating the resulting selections be divided among committees and subcommittees and so forth? Would some governing board formulate a set of topics that each editor or team of editors would be required to address so as to confer a sturdy structure upon the whole? Would there be, for example, a different board of consultants for each period in the long history of Judaism or each language across the geographic breadth of Buddhism?

Our decision was to reject that kind of elaboration and gamble instead on six brilliant and creative individuals, each with a distinct literary style and a record of bold publication, and then to impose no common matrix of obligatory topics or categories on them, nor even a common set of chronological divisions. (Does China have its own Middle Ages? When does modernity begin in Turkey?) It was understood, however, playing to an institutional strength at W. W. Norton & Company, that the prose of these editors, formidable though they were, would be edited very heavily for explanatory clarity even as we second-guessed very lightly indeed their actual anthological choices. To what end this blend of laxity and severity? Our aim has been simply to enhance the intelligent delight of students in religious literature both as literature and as religion. "Intelligent" delight does not mean the delight of intelligent people. The reference is rather to the delight that a strange and baffling ancient text can provide when a great scholar, speaking in his or her own voice, renders it intelligible for you and you recognize, behind it, a human intelligence finally not all that unlike your own.

If that has been our aim for students, our aim for professors has been rather different. Professors of religious studies often find themselves called upon to teach insanely far beyond their area of trained academic competence. For them, we hope to have provided both an invaluable reference tool and a rich reservoir of curricular possibilities. For their graduate students, we hope to have provided breadth to complement the depth of doctoral study at its best. A student studying in depth and probably in the original language some particular religious text can discover here what *else* was being written in the same tradition at the same time. What preceded that text in the life of the religious tradition? What followed it? Who celebrated it? Who attacked it? The fine art of page flipping, crucial to the unique operating system of an ink-on-paper anthology, enables just this kind of exploratory learning. Over time, by repeated forays backward and forward in the evolution of a religious tradition, a serious student can come to know its literature like the interior of a large residence. But this is just the beginning. Comparable forays into the development of other traditions can by degrees situate the target religious tradition in the global religious context. Finally, to further aid all users, the companion website to *The Norton Anthology of World Religions* will provide, over time, both supplementary substantive content—other religious traditions, to begin with—not included in the print anthology and an array of aids for the use of teachers and students.

Beyond these conventional services, however, lies something riskier. We acknowledge that we have provided the professoriate a target to shoot at: "How could you *possibly* omit X?" some will exclaim. And others: "Why on *earth* did you ever bother with Y?" We welcome all such objections. They betray nothing more than the real, existential condition of a field still in many ways struggling to be born. Disciplines do not spring into existence overnight. They are negotiated into existence over time through trial and error. The more vigorously our colleagues find fault with this first draft of a canon for their field, the more productive will be the ensuing negotiation.

Intuition based on deep scholarship and teaching experience has surely played a role in the choices made by the six associate editors responsible, respectively, for anthologizing the six religious literatures covered: Wendy Doniger (Hinduism), Donald S. Lopez, Jr. (Buddhism), James Robson (Daoism), David Biale (Judaism), Lawrence S. Cunningham (Christianity), and Jane Dammen McAuliffe (Islam). They have all sought to include those incipiently canonical texts that few of their colleagues would dare exclude. More intuitively, they have sought to include neglected works of beauty and power whose very appearance here might help them become canonical. The editors have even included occasional attacks on the religious traditions anthologized—for example, excerpts from Kancha Ilaiah, "Why I Am Not a Hindu," in the Hinduism anthology and from Bertrand Russell, "Why I Am Not a Christian," in the Christianity anthology. As these two contrarian entries nicely demonstrate, the canon of texts regarded as permanent and irreplaceable in a religious tradition does not coincide exactly with the canon of texts arguably crucial for the study of the tradition. Coping with all these complications, the editors have coped in every case as well with the painful space limitations that we have had to impose on them even after allowing the anthology to grow to nearly twice its originally envisioned size.

One large question remains to be addressed in this brief preface: *By what criteria did you choose to anthologize these and only these six religions?* This question has a theoretical as well as a practical dimension. How, to begin with, do we distinguish that which is religious from that which is not? Is atheism a religion, or at least a "religious option"? Whatever atheism is, it is certainly no modern novelty. *The Cambridge Companion to Atheism* (2007) begins with a substantial chapter, "Atheism in Antiquity," by the distinguished Dutch classicist Jan Bremmer. Whether atheism in a given ancient or modern form should be considered a strictly religious option may depend on how a given atheist "plays" it. The novelist Alain de Botton, nothing if not playful, dreams or artfully feigns dreaming of a floridly religious enactment of atheism in his *Religion for Atheists: A Non-believer's Guide to the Uses of Religion* (2012). Meanwhile, a 2010 survey by the Pew Forum suggests that the religiously unaffiliated might actually be both more interested in and better informed about religion than the affiliated. But back to the question at hand: If we cannot clearly distinguish religion from irreligion or the "strictly" from the "casually" religious, how can we be sure that we are choosing six versions of the same thing? Arcane and obscure as this question may sound, it did bear rather directly on one of our six key choices, as will be explained below.

In the end, in making our choices, we fell back to an infra-theoretical, practical, or "working" criterion for inclusion: we required that the religions anthologized should be the six most important *major, living, international* religions, a rubric in which each of the three italicized words counted.

Because we anthologize only *living* religions, we do not anthologize the religions of ancient Mesopotamia, Greece, and Rome, despite the fact that these religious traditions loom large in the history of the study of religion in the West, thanks to the dominance of the Bible and of the Greco-Roman classics in Western higher education.

Because we anthologize only *international* religions, we do not anthologize folkloric or indigenous religions, which are typically and symbiotically confined to a single locale, despite the fascination that these religions have had for the sociological or anthropological study of religion, from Johann Gottfried Herder and Émile Durkheim in the late eighteenth and nineteenth century to Clifford Geertz in the twentieth.

Geography, except as the difference between national and international, is not the principle of organization in this anthology. One consequence, however, of our anthologizing only literary religions and then applying a mostly demographic criterion in choosing among them has been the omission of indigenous African religion. While it is true that Yoruba religion is now international and that some texts for it are now available, no such text has become canonical even for practitioners themselves. Rather than saying anything about the limitations of African or other indigenous religious traditions, notably the rich array of Amerindian religions, our decision says something about the inherent limitations of any text-based approach to the study of religion. Texts can indeed teach much, but they cannot teach everything about everybody.

As for the key criterion *major*, we apply it demographically with one glaring exception. Religious demography tends to overstate or understate the size of a religion depending on whether and how that religion counts heads. Roman Catholicism, which counts every baptized baby as a member, probably ends up with somewhat overstated numbers. Daoism, by contrast, probably ends up with its adherents undercounted because formal affiliation is not a recognized criterion for basic participation in it.

Yet even after these difficulties have been acknowledged, there can be no quarrel that Christianity and Islam are demographically major as well as living and international. The same goes at almost equal strength for Hinduism and Buddhism. The obvious exception is Judaism, whose numbers worldwide, though far from trivial, are small even when the question "Who is a Jew?" is given its most broadly inclusive answer. Too small to be reckoned major by a head count, Judaism is too important on other counts to be reckoned less than major. It is the exception that breaks the rule. Its categories, its legends, and many of its practices have been decisive not only for Christianity and Islam but also, arguably, for Western secularism.

As many readers will have noticed by now, this grid of six does not stray very far from the textbook areas of religious studies, as is only right and proper in a reference work, yet this claim of relative "normality" calls for qualification in two final regards if only to provide the occasion for a pair of disclaimers.

First, this anthology does not deal with several religious traditions that, though fully literary and indeed of great intrinsic interest, do not meet its stated criteria. Three that might be named among these are Sikhism, Jainism, and Shinto, but several other traditions commonly enough included in textbooks might easily be added to the list. No judgment of intrinsic worth or importance should be inferred from their exclusion, just as none should be inferred from the omission of indigenous African or Amerindian religion. A less ample presentation of a larger number of religious traditions would always have been possible. Our choice, and all such choices come at a cost, has been to produce ampler presentations of plausibly canonical texts for those most populous religions traditions that the world citizen is likeliest to encounter in the new religious environment that we all inhabit.

To name a second perhaps surprising choice, our grid of six, though generally familiar, has "Daoism" where most textbooks have "Chinese religion." The usual textbook grid resorts to geography or ethnicity as a naming criterion in and only in the Chinese case. Why so? Though, as noted, the designations "Eastern" and "Western" do still have some textbook currency, no one speaks of Christianity as "European religion" or of Islam as "Afro-Asiatic religion." Why proceed otherwise in the Chinese case alone?

Our decision, breaking with this practice, has been, in the first place, to anthologize Chinese Buddhism within the Buddhism anthology, allowing that sub-anthology to become, by the inclusion of its Chinese material, the longest of the six. Our decision, in the second place, has been not to anthologize Chinese Confucianism at all. We have a secondary and a primary reason for this second decision.

The secondary reason not to anthologize Confucianism is that the People's Republic of China does not regard it as a religion at all. The government recognizes only five religions: Buddhism, Daoism, and Islam plus (as separate religions) Catholicism and Protestantism. Confucianism it simply defines as altogether out of the category *religion*.

Properly so? Is Confucianism a religion, or not? This question is notoriously one that "the West has never been able to answer and China never able to ask," and we do not presume to give a definitive answer here. It is true, on the one hand, that at many points during its long history, Confucianism has seemed to be neither a religion nor quite a philosophy either but rather a code of wisdom and conduct for the Chinese gentleman scholar—or, perhaps better, the aspiring Chinese statesman. Yet at other points in Confucian history, it must be noted, Confucius has been accorded the honor of a virtual god. We choose to leave that question in abeyance.

Our primary reason, in any case, to set Confucianism aside and dedicate our limited space to Daoism is that while the Confucian canon has been widely translated and, as ancient religious texts go, is relatively accessible, the Daoist canon has only recently been rescued from near death and has never before been presented for the use of nonspecialists in an overview of any historical completeness.

While two pre-Daoist classics—the gnomic *Daode jing* of Laozi and the tart wisdom of Zhuangzi—have been endlessly translated and are in no danger of disappearance, their relationship to the Daoist canon as a whole is, to borrow from an observation quoted in James Robson's introduction to the Daoism anthology, like the real but distant relationship of Plato and Aristotle to the Christian canon. What would we know of Christianity if Paul, Augustine,

Dante, Luther, Milton, and so on down the hallowed list had all been lost and only Plato and Aristotle survived?

Such a fate did indeed very nearly befall Daoism. In the nineteenth century, leading up to the establishment of the first Republic of China in 1912, Qing dynasty authorities systematically confiscated Daoist temples and turned them into schools and factories. Having begun as an underground movement in the second century, Daoism—long out of official favor—was largely forced underground only again and more deeply so after the establishment of the Republic, which condemned it as superstition.

For the Daoist canon, the cost of this persecution was nearly outright extinction. By the early twentieth century, few copies of Daoism's canon of eleven hundred religious texts survived in all of China. But then, remarkably, circumstances eased enough to permit the reprint in 1926 of a rare surviving copy of the full 1445 Ming dynasty canon. This had been the last great effort at canon formation in Daoist history before Daoism's long decline commenced. As this reprint reached the West, scholarship on the history of Daoism and the interpretation of its texts slowly began. Nonetheless, particularly after the establishment of the Communist People's Republic of China in 1949, with its aggressive early persecution of all religions, many in the West believed that the actual practice of Daoism had finally died out in its birthplace.

They were mistaken. Over the past few decades, reliable reports have made it clear that Daoism is still alive and indeed is growing steadily stronger, having survived as if by taking Mao Zedong's advice to his guerrillas that they "move among the people as a fish swims in the sea." Just as the fish in the sea are not easily counted, so the Daoists of China escape the usual forms of Western quantification and Communist surveillance alike. But the Daoist fish are numerous, even if they have reason to swim deep.

Meanwhile, the work of translating and contextualizing the recovered texts has attracted a growing corps of Western scholars—initially in France and more recently in other Western countries, including the United States. As their work has gone forward, the world has begun to hear of Daoist messiahs and utopian dreams of peace; Daoist confession rituals and community liturgies; Daoist alchemy and proto-scientific experimentation; Daoist medicine, bodily cultivation (as distinct from asceticism), and sexual practices; Daoist prayer, including Daoist letter-writing to the gods; and Daoist pageantry, costume, magic, and music. In short, a lost religious world—the central, popular, indigenous, full-throated religious world of China—has been brought back to textual life. Our decision was to bring our readers a major sampling from this remarkable recovery.

The major religions of the world are probably better grasped, many scholars now insist, as a set of alternative customs and practices in loose organization—worship liturgies, pilgrimages, dietary restrictions, birth and burial practices, art, music, drama, dance, and so forth—than as a set of contending ideologies. Millions of men and women, even when they practice religions that we rightly regard as literary, are themselves illiterate. Yet when writing remade the world, it did remake religion as well. The major religious traditions of the world would not be major today had they not become literary traditions as well.

Because it is *written*, religious literature can be and has been shared, preserved through wars and persecutions, transmitted over time and space, and, most important of all, *taught* with ease and delight. When all else perishes, the written word often survives. The work before you is a self-contained, portable library of religious literature. You may read it on a plane, in the park, or in a waiting room and trust that every foreign or otherwise strange term will be explained on or near the page where it occurs. No foreign alphabets are used. Transliterations have been simplified to serve pedagogical utility rather than philological perfection. Diacritical marks have been kept to the absolute minimum. Though, as noted, a few of the large theoretical considerations that religion raises as a subject for human inquiry will be addressed in the general introduction, the emphasis in this work is overwhelmingly pragmatic rather than theoretical. For in this domain, more perhaps than in any other, outsiders have historically been as important as insiders, and beginners as welcome as veterans. So, to conclude where we began, whether you are an outsider or an insider, a beginner or a veteran, we welcome you to the pages of *The Norton Anthology of World Religions.*

JACK MILES
IRVINE, CALIFORNIA

Acknowledgments

*T**he Norton Anthology of World Religions* would not have been possible without the help of many generous and able friends. We are grateful for the help of those named below as well as of others too numerous to list.

From W. W. Norton & Company, we wish to thank Roby Harrington, head of the college division, who conceived this volume; Pete Simon, its first editor, who contributed its title; Carly Fraser Doria, who has managed the assembly of illustrations and ancillary materials with intelligence and taste; developmental editors Alice Falk, Carol Flechner, and Kurt Wildermuth, who have tamed its prose to the demanding Norton standard; Adrian Kitzinger, who created the beautiful maps; Megan Jackson and Nancy Rodwan, permissions experts; art directors Debra Morton Hoyt and Ingsu Liu, designer Chin-Yee Lai, and artist Rosamond Purcell; production managers Sean Mintus and Julia Druskin; managing editor Marian Johnson, whose project-editorial wisdom is quietly evident on every page; and, most of all, Julia Reidhead, editorial director, whose taste and managerial finesse have preserved and advanced this work sagaciously for fully seven years.

Wendy Doniger wishes to thank Velcheru Narayana Rao for finding "Sita Lost in Thought" for her, and for finding and translating "Kausalya in Fury"; Vasudha Naranayan and Richard Fox for the Southeast Asian materials; Eleanor Zelliot, Gail Omvedt, and Dilip Chitre for the Dalit materials; her student assistants, Jeremy Morse and Charles Preston, for assembling all the texts; and Anne Mocko for help with the pronouncing glossaries.

James Robson wishes to thank Stephen R. Bokenkamp, for helping to get this project started; Alice Falk, for helping to get it completed; and Billy Brewster, for help with the pronouncing glossaries.

David Biale wishes to thank Ariel Evan Mayse and Sarah Shectman for research assistance beyond the call of duty.

Lawrence S. Cunningham wishes to thank his beloved wife, Cecilia, and their two daughters, Sarah and Julia.

Jane Dammen McAuliffe wishes to thank her splendid research associates, Carolyn Baugh, Sayeed Rahman, Robert Tappan, and Clare Wilde, and to recognize with appreciation both Georgetown University and Bryn Mawr College for their support of this work.

For generous financial support of this project, Jack Miles wishes to thank the John T. and Catherine D. MacArthur Foundation, the Getty Research Institute, and the University of California, Irvine. He thanks, in addition, for early editorial consultation, his publishing colleague John Loudon; for generous technical assistance, Steve Franklin and Stan Woo-Sam of UCI's information technology office; for invaluable assistance with the initial enormous delivery of texts, his former student Matthew Shedd; for helpful counsel on Asian Christianity, his colleague Tae Sung; for brilliant assistance in editorial rescue and rewrite, his irreverent friend and colleague Peter Heinegg; and for her sustaining and indomitable spirit, his irreplaceable Catherine Montgomery Crary.

This work is dedicated—in gratitude for all that they have preserved for our instruction—to the scribes of the world's great religions.

THE NORTON ANTHOLOGY OF

WORLD
RELIGIONS

BUDDHISM

The relation of the various peoples of the earth to the supreme interests of life, to God, virtue, and immortality, may be investigated up to a certain point, but can never be compared to one another with absolute strictness and certainty. The more plainly in these matters our evidence seems to speak, the more carefully must we refrain from unqualified assumptions and rash generalizations.

—JACOB BURCKHARDT,
The Civilization of
the Renaissance in Italy (1860)

GENERAL INTRODUCTION

How the West Learned to Compare Religions

BY JACK MILES

How to Read This Book: A Poetic Prelude

The *Norton Anthology of World Religions* is designed to be read in either of two ways. You may read it from start to finish, or you may pick and choose from the table of contents as in a museum you might choose to view one gallery rather than another or one painting rather than another.

Imagine yourself at the entrance to a large museum containing a great many strange works of religious art. If you enter, what will you do? Will you devote equal time or equal intensity of attention to every work in the huge museum? Or will you skip some works, linger over others, and shape as you go a kind of museum within the museum? In the latter case, what will be your criteria? Those, too, you may well shape as you go. You may not entirely know even your own mind as you begin. You may not know exactly what you're after. You may be detached, and yet—disinterested? No, you are not exactly disinterested. You're looking around, waiting for something to reach you, some click, some insemination, a start. Entering is sometimes enough. You do not need a briefing by the curator to begin your visit.

So it is with this anthology. Take the works assembled here as lightly as you wish. You will still be taking them properly: you will be taking them for what they are. A new path begins to open into the consideration of religion when it is regarded as unserious, un-adult—but only in the way that art, poetry, and fiction in all its forms (including the theatrical and the cinematic) are so regarded. They all deal with made-up stuff. And yet will we ever be so adult as to outgrow them?

The Western cast of mind has undeniably had an intrusive and distorting effect in many parts of the world as Western culture has become a world culture, and yet that cast of mind has also had a liberating and fertilizing effect. It has opened a space in which the once incomparable has become comparable. Looking at the religions of others even from the outside but with a measure of openness, empathy, and good will can enable those of any religious tradition or none to see themselves from the outside as well, and that capacity is the very foundation of human sympathy and cultural wisdom.

In church one morning in the eighteenth century, the poet Robert Burns spotted a louse on a proper lady's bonnet and started thinking: If only she could see herself as he saw her! He went home and wrote his wonderfully earthy and witty "To a Louse, On Seeing One on a Lady's Bonnet, at Church 1786." The fun of the poem is that it is addressed to the louse in a mock "How dare you!" tone almost all the way to the end. At that point, however, it becomes suddenly reflective, even wistful, and Burns concludes, in his Scots English:

> O wad some Pow'r the giftie gie us
> To see oursels as ithers see us!
> It wad frae monie a blunder free us,
>   An' foolish notion:
> What airs in dress an' gait wad lea'e us,
>   An' ev'n Devotion!

Burns dreams, or half-prays, that some power would "the giftie gie us" (give us the gift) to see "oursels" (ourselves) as others see us—to see, as it were, the lice on our bonnets. Our fine and flouncing airs then "wad lea'e us" (would leave us). But it might not be simply vanity that would depart. The last words in the poem are "an' ev'n Devotion!" (and even devotion). Even our religious devotions might be affected if we could see ourselves at that moment just as others see us. So many of the cruelest mistakes in religion are made not out of malice but out of simple ignorance, blunders we would willingly avoid could we but see ourselves as others see us. Looking at other traditions, you need to see the bonnet and not just the louse. Looking at your own, however you define it, you need to see the louse as well as the bonnet.

Can Religion Be Defined?

What is religion? The word exists in the English language, and people have some commonsense notion of what it refers to. Most understand it as one kind of human activity standing alongside other kinds, such as business, politics, warfare, art, law, sport, or science. Religion is available in a variety of forms, but what is it, really? What makes it itself?

Simple but searching questions like these may seem to be the starting point for the study of religion. Within the study of religion, they are more precisely the starting point for the *theory* of religion. And readers will not be surprised to learn that academic theoreticians of religion have not been content with the commonsense understanding of the subject.

The theoretical difficulties that attend any basic element of human thought or experience are undeniable. What is mathematics? What is art? What is law? What is music? Books have been written debating number theory, aesthetic theory, legal theory, and music theory. It should come as no surprise then that the theory of religion is no less actively debated than are those other theories. Some definitions of religion are so loose as to allow almost anything to qualify as a religion. Others are so strict as to exclude almost everything ordinarily taken to be a religion (prompting one recent contributor to the *Journal of the American Academy of Religion* to give his article the wry or rueful title "Religions: Are There Any?").[1]

The inconvenient truth is that no definition of religion now enjoys general acceptance. In *The Bonobo and the Atheist* (2013), the primatologist Frans de Waal writes:

> To delineate religion to everyone's satisfaction is hopeless. I was once part of a forum at the American Academy of Religion, when

someone proposed we start off with a definition of religion. However much sense this made, the idea was promptly shot down by
another participant, who reminded everyone that last time they
tried to define religion half the audience had angrily stomped out
of the room. And this in an academy named after the topic![2]

A survey of competing theories, if we were to attempt one here, could quickly
jump to twenty-three entries if we simply combined the contents of two
recent handbooks—the eight in Daniel L. Pals's *Eight Theories of Religion*
(2006) and the fifteen in Michael Stausberg's *Contemporary Theories of
Religion: A Critical Companion* (2009).[3]

Though no one writing on religion can entirely escape theoretical commitments, *The Norton Anthology of World Religions* is foremost an anthology of primary texts. By the term *primary* we understand texts produced by
the practitioners of each of the anthologized religions for their fellow practitioners. Such an anthology does not collect theories of religion, for the simple
reason that such theories are secondary texts. They belong not to the creation and practice of religion but, retrospectively, to its study and analysis.
Accordingly, they have rarely been of much interest to religious practitioners themselves.

Religious practitioners are far from unique in this regard. "Philosophy of
science is about as useful to scientists as ornithology is to birds," Richard
Feynman (1918–1988), a Caltech physicist, famously quipped.[4] The philosophy (or theory) of religion is of as little use to, say, the Buddhist as philosophy of science is to the scientist. Just as the scientist is interested in her
experiment rather than in the philosophy of science and the painter in his
painting rather than in the philosophy of art, so the Buddhist is interested
in the Buddha rather than in the philosophy of religion. The term *religion*
itself, as an academic term comprising—as indeed it does in this work—
many different religious traditions, may not be of much practical utility to
the practitioner of any one of the traditions.

And yet we who have assembled this work may not excuse ourselves
altogether from addressing the question "What is religion?" simply on the
grounds that our pages are filled with primary texts, for introducing, framing, and contextualizing these texts are the words of our six anthologizing
editors as well as the general editor. The seven of us speak in these pages not
as practitioners of the religions anthologized here but as scholars writing
about those religions. Scholarship at its most empirical cannot escape theory,
because, to quote a dictum from the philosophy of science, all data are
theory-laden. A theory of some sort will be found operative even when no
explicit theoretical commitment has been made.

If, then, some tacit theory or theories of religion must necessarily have
informed the choices made by our associate editors, given the general
editor's decision to impose no single theory, has any silent theoretical convergence occurred? Now that the results are in and the editors' choices
have actually been made, do they reflect a working answer to the question
"What is religion?"

As general editor, I believe that they do, though it would take some rather
elaborate spelling out to explain just *how* they do. Something more modest
but more readily discernible must suffice for this introduction—namely,
the claim that the choices made by the respective associate editors reflect a

common method or, more modestly still, a common approach to the task of presenting a major religious literature with some coherence. In brief, the six associate editors have approached the six religions whose texts they anthologize as six kinds of practice rather than as six kinds of belief. In common usage, religious and unreligious people are divided into "believers" and "unbelievers." The editors have departed from this common usage, proceeding instead on the silent and admittedly modest premise that religion is as religion *does*. Even when speaking of belief, as they do only occasionally, they generally treat it as embedded in practice and inseparable from practice. Monotheism in the abstract is a belief. "Hear, O Israel, the Lord is our God, the Lord alone" as sung by a cantor in a synagogue is a practice.

When religion is approached as practice, what follows? Clearly, Daoist practice, Muslim practice, Christian practice, and so on are not identical, but the substantial differences *within* each of them can loom as large as the differences from one to another among them. *The goal of this anthology is to present through texts how this variety has developed and how the past continues to shape the present.* Thus, the body of material put on exhibit here serves less to answer the question "What is religion?" in any theoretically elaborate or definitive way than to question the answers others have given to that question—answers such as those offered by, for example, the twenty-three theories alluded to above. Whatever fascinating questions a given theory of religion may have posed and answered to its own satisfaction, it must also, we submit, be able to account for the complexity of the data that these primary texts exhibit. Rather than serving to illustrate some fully developed new theory of religion, in other words, the texts gathered here constitute the empirical evidence that any such theory must cope with. In the meantime, the working focus is squarely on practice.

Each of the religions anthologized here has contained multiple versions of itself both over time and at any given time, and the anthology does not attempt to drive past the multiplicity to the singular essence of the thing. Practitioners, of course, have not always been so neutral. Many have been or still are prepared to deny the legitimacy of others as Hindu, Muslim, Christian, Jewish, and so on. But for the purposes of this anthology, those denials themselves simply become a part of the broader story.

Syncretism, moreover—namely, the introduction of a feature from one religion into the life of another—is in itself an argument that the borrower and the lender are, or can be, related even when they are not, and never will be, identical. Multiple religious belonging—double or triple affiliation—sometimes takes syncretism a step further. And while borrowings across major borders are an additive process, adjustments within borders can often be a subtractive process, as seen in many statements that take the form "I am a Buddhist, but . . . ," "I am a Catholic, but . . . ," "I am a Muslim, but . . . ," and so forth. In such statements, the speaker takes the broad term as a starting point and then qualifies it until it fits properly.

Yet we do not claim anything more than practical utility for this default approach to the subject, knowing as we do that a great many scholars of religion decline to define the essence of religion itself but do not find themselves inhibited by that abstention from saying a great deal of interest about one religious tradition or another. Rather than name at the outset the one feature that establishes the category *religion* before discussing the particular religion that interests them, they make the usually silent assumption that the full range of beliefs and practices that have been conventionally thought of as religious is vast and that each religion must be allowed to do as it does, assembling its subsets from the vast, never-to-be-fully-enumerated roster of world religious practices. Having made that assumption, the scholars take a deep breath and go on to talk about what they want to talk about.

Twenty-first-century religion scholars are prepared to acknowledge coherence when they find it but determined never to impose it. They are aware that the entries made under the heading *religion* may not all be versions of just the same thing, but they are equally aware that the overlaps, the innumerable ad hoc points of contact, are also there and also real—and so they find the continued use of the collective term *religion* justified for the enriching and enlightening comparisons that it facilitates. All knowledge begins with comparison.

In telling the life stories of six major, living, international religions through their respective primary texts, the editors of *The Norton Anthology of World Religions* have neither suppressed variability over time in service to any supposedly timeless essence of the thing nor, even when using the word *classical*, dignified any one age as truly golden. Each of the stories ends with modernity, but modernity in each case is neither the climax nor the denouement of the story. It is not the last chapter, only the latest.

How Christian Europe Learned to Compare Religions

Most people, we said earlier, understand religion as "one kind of human activity standing alongside other kinds, such as business, politics, warfare, art, law, sport, or science." Another way to say this is that they understand religion to be one domain among many, each separate from the others. Broadly compatible with this popular understanding is a widely influential definition of religion formulated by the anthropologist Clifford Geertz (1926–2006).

In "Religion as a Cultural System," first published in 1966, Geertz defined religion as

> (1) *a system of symbols which acts to* (2) *establish powerful, pervasive, and long-lasting moods and motivations in men by* (3) *formulating conceptions of a general order of existence and* (4) *clothing these conceptions with such an aura of factuality that* (5) *the moods and motivations seem uniquely realistic.*[5]

Geertz does not claim that all cultures are equally religious. In fact, toward the end of his essay he observes that "the degree of religious articulateness is not a constant even as between societies of similar complexity."[6] However, he does tacitly assume that religion is if not universal then at least extremely widespread and that it is a domain separate from others, such as—to name two that he explores—science and ideology.[7]

But just how widespread is religion, and is it truly a domain separable from the rest of culture? Can religion really be distinguished from ideology? In Geertz's terms, wouldn't Marxism qualify as a religion? In recent decades, some have argued that even a thoroughly secular anthropologist like Geertz, in whose definition of religion neither God nor Christ is mentioned, can be seen as carrying forward an ideological understanding of religion that originated in the Christian West and has lived on in Western academic life as a set of inadequately examined assumptions. That religion is a domain separate from either ethnicity or culture is one of two key, historically Christian assumptions. That religion is a universal phenomenon—in some form, a part of every human society and even every human mind—is the other key assumption.

Perhaps the most widely cited historical critique of these assumptions is Tomoko Masuzawa's revealing *The Invention of World Religions, Or, How European Universalism Was Preserved in the Language of Pluralism* (2005). Masuzawa's book is not about the invention of the world's religions themselves but about the invention of *world religions* as a phrase used in the West to talk about them, postulating their parallel existence as separable and separate realities, available as an indefinitely expandable group for academic discussion.[8]

When and how, she asks, did this omnibus-phrase *world religions* come into the general usage that it now enjoys? She concludes her influential investigation with the candid confession that the invention and, especially, the very widespread adoption of the phrase remain something of a puzzle—but her analysis traces the usage back only to the nineteenth century. Our claim below is that though the phrase *world religions* may be recent, its roots run much deeper than the nineteenth century, as deep in fact as early Christianity's peculiar and unprecedented self-definition.

To say this is not to undercut the strength of the criticism. Christian explorers, traders, missionaries, and colonists encountering non-Western societies, especially after the discovery of the Americas and the colonial expansion of the West into Asia, have often isolated and labeled as "religions" behaviors that they took to be the local equivalents of what they knew in the West as Christianity. This process of isolating and labeling was a mistake when and if the societies themselves did not understand the behaviors in question as constituting either a separate domain or merely one instance of a more general phenomenon called religion. Moreover, when those purporting to understand non-Western societies in these historically Christian terms were invaders and imperialists, a perhaps unavoidable theoretical mistake could have grievous practical consequences. And when, in turn, ostensibly neutral, secular theories of religion—not imposed by conquerors or missionaries but merely proffered by Western academics—are alleged to make the same historically Christian assumptions, the entire project of comparative religious study may be faulted as Christian imperialism.

Because the viability and indeed the enormous value of such study are premises of this anthology, the challenge calls for a significant response, one that necessarily includes substantial attention to just how Christianity influenced the study of what the West has defined as world religions. The intention in what follows, however, is by no means to make a case for Christianity as inherently central or supreme among the world's religions. We intend rather, and only, to trace how, in point of fact, Christianity began as central to the Western *study* of religions and then, by degrees, yielded its position as more polycentric forms of study emerged.

Let us begin by stipulating that Christians did indeed acquire very early and thereafter never entirely lost the habit of thinking of their religion as a separate domain. Once this is conceded, it should come as no great surprise that as a corollary of this habit, they should have adopted early and never entirely lost the habit of thinking of other religions, rightly or wrongly, as similarly separate domains. This would be simply one more instance of the human habit of beginning with the known and with the self and working outward to the unknown and to the others.

But we must stipulate further that Christians made a second assumption—namely, that theirs should become humankind's first-ever programmatically "world" religion. The idea of universally valid religious truth was not new in itself. Ancient Israel had long since been told that its vocation was to be the light of the world. In the book of Isaiah, God says to his people through the prophet (49:6):

> It is too light a thing that you should be my servant to raise up the tribes of Jacob and to restore the preserved of Israel; I will give you as a light to the nations, that my salvation may reach to the end of the earth.[9]

In the Gospel of Matthew, Jesus turns this latent potential into a radically intrusive program for action. His final words to his apostles are

> Go therefore, and make disciplines of *all nations*, baptizing them in the name of the Father and of the Son and of the Holy Spirit, teaching them to observe all that I have commanded you; and, lo, I am with you always, even to the close of the age. (Matthew 28:19–20; emphasis added)

How ever did this instruction, as the first Christians put it into practice, lead to the secular study of "world religions" as we know it today?

The Social Oddity of the Early Church

In the earliest centuries of its long history, the Christian church defined its belief as different from the official polytheism of the Roman Empire, on the one hand, and from the monotheism of Rabbinic Judaism, on the other, inasmuch as the rabbinic Jews did not recognize Jesus as God incarnate. But if the church was thus, to borrow a convenient phrase from contemporary American life, a faith-based organization, it was not just a school of thought: it was also an *organization*. As faith-based, it undeniably placed unique and unprecedented stress on belief (and indeed set the pattern by which today all those religiously active in any way are routinely called *believers*, even when not all regard belief as central to their practice). Yet as an organization, the church depended not just on a distinct set of beliefs but also on a social identity separate, on the one hand, from that of the Roman Empire (or any other empire) and equally separate, on the other, from that of the Jewish nation (or any other nation). As a faith-based, voluntary, nonprofit, multiethnic, egalitarian, nongovernmental organization, the Christian church was a social novelty: nothing quite like it had ever been seen before. And as Christians, growing steadily in number, projected their novel collective self-understanding upon Roman and Jewish social reality alike, the effect was profoundly disruptive. Though many others would follow, these were the first two instances of Christian projection, and an analysis of how they worked is especially instructive.

By encouraging Roman polytheists to *convert* to Christianity while maintaining that they did not thereby cease to be Romans, the Christians implicitly invented religious conversion itself as an existential possibility. The term *religion* did not exist then in Greek, Latin, or Aramaic as a fully developed universal category containing both Roman polytheism and Christianity, but in the very action of conversion the future category was already implicit. By seeking to convert Roman polytheists to Christianity, the early Christians implied that Roman religiosity was a domain both separate from the rest of Roman life and replaceable. You could exchange your Roman religiosity for this modified Jewish religiosity, as the very act of conversion demonstrated, while bringing the rest of your Roman identity with you.

In the first century, conversion thus defined was an unprecedented and socially disruptive novelty. Until the destabilizing intrusion of Christianity, respect for the Roman gods had always been inseparable from simply being Roman: religious identity and civic identity had always constituted an unbroken whole. Christianity encouraged Romans to split that single identity into a double identity: religion, on the one hand; culture and ethnicity, on the other. In this sequestration of the religiously meaningful from the religiously neutral or meaningless was born the very possibility of secular culture, as well as religion as Western modernity has come to understand it—religion as involving some semblance of faith and some form of collective identity separable from ethnicity or culture.

In by far the most important instance of this division of social identity, the original Christian Jews, having adopted a minority understanding of Jewish tradition, denied that they were any less Jewish for that reason. Writing of his Jewish critics, St. Paul fumed (2 Corinthians 11:22): "Are they Israelites? So am I!" Much of first-century Jewry would not have disagreed with him had the matter stopped there, for there were many peacefully coexisting Jewish views about Jewish belief and practice. As no more than the latest variation on the old themes, the Christian Jews would not have created anything structurally new. But they did create something new by taking the further step of bringing themselves, with their recognizably Jewish religious views (views indeed unrecognizable as anything except Jewish), into an unprecedented social relationship with non-Jews—namely, into the Christian church. By linking themselves to non-Jews in this way, without renouncing their Jewish identity, the Christian Jews—enjoying particular success in the Roman Diaspora—demonstrated that as they conceived their own Jewish religiosity to be distinguishable from the rest of what was then the Jewish way of life, so they conceived the same two components of identity to be likewise distinguishable for all other Jews.

Rabbinic Judaism, dominant in Palestine and the Mesopotamian Diaspora, would eventually repudiate this Christian projection and reassert that Jewish religiosity and Jewish identity are one and indistinguishable. In the rabbinic view that became and has remained dominant in world Judaism, there are no "Judaists," only Jews. But this reassertion did not happen overnight: it took generations, even centuries. Neither the Romans nor the Jews nor the Christians themselves immediately understood the full novelty of what was coming into existence.

Through most of world history, in most parts of the world, what we are accustomed to call religion, ethnicity, culture, and way of life have been inextricable parts of a single whole. How did Christianity begin to become an exception to this general rule? On the one hand, it appropriated a set of Jewish religious ideas—including monotheism, revelation, covenant, scripture, sin, repentance, forgiveness, salvation, prophecy, messianism, and apocalypticism—without adopting the rest of the highly developed and richly nuanced Jewish way of life. On the other hand, it universalized these Jewish religious ideas, creating a new social entity, the church, through which non-Jews could be initiated into an enlarged version of the ancestral Jewish covenant with God. The Jews had believed for centuries God's declaration, "I am the LORD your God, who have separated you from the peoples" (Leviticus 20:24) and "you are a people holy to the LORD your God" (Deuteronomy 7:6). In effect, the Christian Jews split the idea of covenanted separateness and holiness from what consequently became the relatively secularized idea of nationality. The Jews were still a people, they maintained, but God had now revised and universalized the terms of his covenant. In the words of Jesus' apostle Peter, "Truly I perceive that God shows no partiality, but in every nation any one who fears him and does what is right is acceptable to him" (Acts 10:34–35).

The original Greek word for church, *ekklēsia*, suggests a collective understanding of church members as "called out" from other kinds of religious, ethnic, or political membership into this new—and now, in principle, universal—"people set apart as holy." The *ekklēsia* offered its members a sense of sacred peoplehood, but it tellingly lacked much else that ordinarily maintains a national identity. It had no ancestral land, no capital city, no language of its own, no literature at the start other than what it had inherited from the Jews, no distinct cuisine, no standard dress, and no political or governmental support beyond the organizational management of the church itself. Moreover, this ethnically mixed and socially unpromising group was atheist in its attitude toward all gods except the God of Israel as they had come to understand him—God as incarnate in Jesus the Messiah. Within the political culture of the Roman Empire, this rejection of the empire's gods was a seditious and rebellious rejection of Roman sovereignty itself. When, unsurprisingly, the empire recognized it as such and began intermittently to persecute the church, the Christian sense of separateness only grew.

In this form, and despite intermittent persecution, the church grew quietly but steadily for more than three centuries. At that point, with perhaps a fifth of the population of the Roman Empire enrolled in separate local Christian churches under relatively autonomous elected supervisors (bishops), the emperor Constantine (r. 312–37) first legalized Christianity and then stabilized its doctrine by requiring the Christian bishops—ordered to convene for the first time as a council at Nicaea, near his eventual capital city of Constantinople—to define it. In 381, the emperor Theodosius (r. 379–95) made this newly defined Christianity the official religion of the Roman Empire, and the new religion—no longer persecuted but now operating under a large measure of imperial control—began a fateful reversal of course. It began to fuse with the political governance and the Hellenistic culture of imperial Rome, compromising the character of the *ekklēsia* as a domain separate from nationality or culture. In a word, it began to normalize.

The establishment of Christianity as the state religion of the Roman Empire ushered in a period of rapid growth, pushed by the government, within the borders of the empire. Beyond them, however, most notably in the Persian Empire just to the east, its new status had the opposite effect.

Once relatively unhindered as a social movement taken to be as compatible with Persian rule as with Roman, Christianity now became suspect as the official religion of the enemy.

Meanwhile, in Rome itself—the "First Rome," as historically prior to the Eastern Empire's capital, Constantinople—and in the western European territories that it administered, a partial but significant return to the original separation of domains occurred just a century later. In 476, Odoacer, king of an invading Germanic tribe, deposed the last Roman emperor, Romulus Augustulus, without effectively assuming authority over the Christian church. Instead, the power of the bishop of Rome—the highest surviving official of the old imperial order—over the church in western Europe began to grow, while the power of kings and feudal lords over all that was not the church steadily grew as well. The nominally unified imperial authority over the empire and its established religion thus split apart. To be sure, for centuries the pope claimed the authority to anoint kings to their royal offices, and at certain moments this was a claim that could be sustained. But gradually, a sense that civilian and religious authority were different and separate began to set in. At the same time, the identity of the church as, once again, detached or disembedded from the state and from culture alike—the church as a potentially universal separate domain, a holy world unto itself—began to consolidate.

The Four-Cornered Medieval Map of Religion

Wealth, power, and population in the world west of India were concentrated during the sixth century in the Persian Empire and in the Eastern Roman or Byzantine Empire. Western Europe during the same century—all that had once been the Western Roman Empire—was far poorer, weaker, more sparsely populated, and culturally more isolated than the empires to its east. Then, during the seventh and eighth centuries, a third major power arose. Arabia had long provided mercenary soldiers to both of the then-dominant empires; but religiously inspired by the Islam newly preached by Muhammad (ca. 570–632) and militarily unified under his successors, it became a major world power in its own right with stunning speed. Arab armies conquered the entirety of the Persian Empire within a generation. Within a century, they had taken from the Eastern Roman Empire its Middle Eastern and North African possessions (half of its total territory) as well as the major Mediterranean islands. From what had been the Western Roman Empire, they had subtracted three-quarters of Spain and penetrated deep into France until driven back across the Pyrenees by the unprecedented European alliance that defeated them in the 732 Battle of Poitiers.

The political map of the world had been redrawn from India to the Atlantic, but what of the religious map? How did western European Christians now understand themselves among the religions of the world? The symbolic birth date of Europe as Christendom has long been taken to be Christmas Day of the year 800. On that date, Pope Leo III crowned Charles the Great, better known as Charlemagne—the grandson of Charles Martel, who had unified the European forces at Poitiers—as the first "Holy Roman Emperor." The Muslim invasion from distant Arabia had shocked an isolated and fragmented region into an early assertion of common religious and geographical identity. As a result, there was a readiness to give political expression to a dawning collective self-understanding. The lost Western Roman Empire was by no means reconstituted: Charlemagne was an emperor without much of an empire, his coronation expressing a vision more than a reality. But the vision itself mattered decisively in another way, for what came into existence at about this time was an understood quadripartite map of the world of religion that would remain standard in Europe for centuries.

There was, first and foremost for Christians, Christianity itself: the Christian church understood to be the same single, separate domain wherever it was found, with the same distinct relationship to national and cultural identity. To the extent that it rested on common faith, the church could be divided by heresy; but even heretical Christians, of whom there would be fewer in the early ninth century than there had been in earlier Christian centuries, were still understood to be Christians. They were practicing the right religion in a wrong way, but they were not practicing another religion altogether.

There was, second, Judaism: the Jews of Europe, a population living among Christians, disparaged but well known, whose relationship to Christianity was well remembered and whose religious authenticity rested on a recognized if more or less resented prior relationship with the same God that the Christians worshipped. Christian understanding of Jewish religious life as the Jews actually lived it was slender, and Christian knowledge of the vast rabbinic literature that had come into existence between the second and the ninth century, much of it in far-off Mesopotamia, was virtually nonexistent. Knowledge of Greek had been lost in Latin Europe, and knowledge of the Hebrew and Aramaic that the Jews of Europe had managed to preserve (despite recurrent persecution) was confined to them alone. Yet, this ignorance notwithstanding, Christian Europe was well aware that the Jews practiced a religion different from their own. And the implicit Christian understanding of religion as a separate domain of potentially universal extent was reinforced by the fact that from the outside, Jewish religious practice appeared to be at least as deeply divorced from national and cultural practices as was Christian religious practice: the Jews, who had lost their land and were dispersed around the world, lived in Europe much as Europe's Christians lived.

The third corner of Europe's four-cornered understanding of world religion was Islam, though the terms *Islam* and *Muslim* would not come into European usage until centuries later. Even the term *Arab* was not standard. The multinational religious commonwealth that we now call world Islam has been traditionally referred to by the Muslims themselves with the Arabic expression *dar al-islam*, the "House of Islam" or the "House of Submission" (because *islam* means "submission"—that is, submission to God). Whether it was *Saracen, Moor, Turk, or Arab*, the ethnic terms used by Christians to refer to the Muslims who faced them in the south and the east depended on time and place. Christendom as the Holy Roman Empire had become a domain geographically separate from the House of Islam. Similarly, Christianity as distinct from Christendom was evidently a domain of belief and practice separate from that of Islam. But among Christians, the further inference was that as Christian identity was separate from Bavarian or Florentine identity, so Muslim identity must be separate from Arab or Turkish identity. To some extent, this was a false inference, for obligatory Arabic in the Qur'an and obligatory pilgrimage to Mecca did much to preserve the originally Arab identity of Islam. Yet the tricontinental distribution and ethnic variability of the House of Islam fostered among Europeans an understanding of Islam as, like Christianity, a potentially universal religion separable from the ethnicity of any one of its component parts.

As Christian anxiety mounted that the year 1000 might mark the end of the world (an outcome that some Christians saw predicted in the New Testament book of Revelation), Muhammad came to be seen by some as the Antichrist, a destructive figure whose appearance during the last apocalyptic period before the end had been foretold (again in the book of Revelation). Yet gradually, albeit as "Mohammedanism," Islam came to be differentiated from Christianity in theological rather than in such floridly mythological terms. The Qur'an was translated into Latin in 1142. The High Middle Ages began to witness various forms of religious and cultural encounter—some as an unintended consequence of the Crusades; others through the influence of large Christian minorities living under Muslim rule and, over time, substantial Muslim minorities living under Christian rule, notably in Spain and Sicily. Finally, there was the mediating influence of a cross-culturally significant Jewish population residing on either side of the Muslim–Christian border and communicating across it. One result of these minglings was a gradually growing overlap in the techniques in use in all three communities for the exegesis of the sacred scriptures that for each mattered so much.

As Muslim monotheism came gradually into clearer focus, medieval Christianity came to recognize Muslims as worshippers of the same God that Jews and Christians worshipped. Meanwhile, Islam was, like Christianity, a religion that actively sought converts who were then made part of a separate quasi-national, quasi-familial, yet potentially universal social entity. The genesis of the Western understanding of religion as such—religion as a separate but expandable social category—was thus significantly advanced by Christianity's encounter with another social entity so like itself in its universalism and its relative independence from ethnic or cultural identity.

The fourth corner of the world religion square was occupied by a ghost—namely, the memory of long-dead Greco-Roman polytheism. Christianity was born among the urban Jews of the Roman Empire and spread gradually into the countryside. Even in largely rural Europe, monasteries functioned as surrogate cities and Christianity spread outward from these centers of structure and literacy. *Pagus* is the Latin word for "countryside," and in the countryside the old polytheisms lingered long after they had died out in the cities. Thus, a rural polytheist was a *paganus*, and *paganismus* (paganism) became synonymous with polytheism. In England, pre-Christian polytheism lingered in the inhospitable heath, and so *heathenism* became an English synonym for *paganism*. Though polytheism is not necessarily idolatrous (one may believe in many gods without making a single idol), polytheistic belief and idolatrous practice were generally conflated. More important for the centuries that lay ahead, the increasingly jumbled memory of what Greco-Roman polytheism—remembered as "paganism"—had been in the Christian past was projected upon the enormous and almost entirely unknown world beyond the realms occupied by Christians, Muslims, and Jews.

The quadripartite typology just sketched was only one long-lived stage in the development of the comparative study of religion in Christian Europe. We may pause to note, however, that as of the year 800 Judaism and Islam were operating under similar typologies. The Qur'an, definitive for all Islamic thought, takes frequent and explicit note of Judaism and Christianity, while the place occupied by the memory of Greco-Roman polytheism in Christianity is occupied in the Qur'an by the memory of polytheism as it existed in Arabia at the time when Muhammad began to receive his revelations. World Jewry, as a minority maintaining its identity and its religious practice in both Christendom and the House of Islam, had a richer experience of both Christians and Muslims than either of those two had of the other. Yet what functioned for Jews in the way that the memory of Greco-Roman polytheism functioned for Christians and the memory of Arabian polytheism functioned for Muslims was the memory of ancient Canaanite, Philistine, and Babylonian polytheism as recorded in the Bible and used thereafter as a template for understanding all those who were the enemies of God and the persecutors of his Chosen People.

Now, the comparison of two religions on terms set by one of them is like the similarly biased comparison of two nationalities: the outcome is a predictable victory for the side conducting the comparison. In fact, when religion and ethnicity are fused, religious comparison is commonly stated in ethnic terms rather than in what we would consider religious terms. Thus, in the Hebrew Bible, apostasy from the religion of Israel is called "*foreign worship*" ('*avodah zarah*) rather than simply false worship, though falsehood or worse is unmistakably implied. To the extent that ethnicity is taken to be a matter of brute fact, and therefore beyond negotiation, religion bound to ethnicity has seemed a nonnegotiable matter of fact as well.

In this regard, however, the condition of medieval Christian Europe was interestingly unstable. Demographically, the two largest religious realities it knew—Islam and Christianity itself—were consciously and ideologically multinational in character, and both actively sought converts from all nations. Judaism was not evangelistic in this way, but world Jewry was uniquely the world's first global nation: the bulk of its population was distributed internationally in such a way that Jews were accustomed in every place to distinguish their ethnicity from the ethnicity of the locale and their religion from its religion. Christian prejudice often prevented Jewish acculturation (not to suppose that Jews always wished to acculturate), but it did not always do so. And so during extended periods of Christian toleration, even the generally firm Jewish sense that religion, ethnicity, and culture were a seamless whole may have become more difficult to sustain. This three-sided—Christian, Muslim, and Jewish—embrace of the notion that religion was a separate domain set the stage in Europe for the comparison of the three on terms derived from a neutral fourth entity that was not to be equated with any one of them.

This fourth entity was Aristotelian philosophy as recovered in Europe during the eleventh and twelfth centuries. Of course, the philosophical discussions that began to be published—such as Abelard's mid-twelfth-century *Dialogue among a Philosopher, a Jew, and a Christian*, in which the philosopher of the title often appears to be a Muslim—always ended in victory for the imagined Christian. Yet Abelard (1079–1142) was eventually condemned by the church because his dialogue clearly recognized reason, mediated by philosophy, as independent of the religions being discussed and as capable of rendering judgments upon them all. Philosophy as that fourth, neutral party would be joined over time by psychology, sociology, anthropology, economics, evolutionary biology, cognitive science, and other analytical tools. But these enlargements lay centuries in the future. As the Middle Ages were succeeded by the Renaissance, philosophy had made a crucial start toward making neutral comparisons, even though Europe's quadripartite map of the world's religions was still quite firmly in place, with most comparisons still done on entirely Christian and theological terms.

The Renaissance Rehearsal of Comparative Religion

The Italian Renaissance—beginning in the fourteenth century and flourishing in the fifteenth and sixteenth—is commonly taken to be more important as a movement in art and literature than in philosophy or religion. To be sure, it did not attempt a transformation of European Christianity comparable to that of the Protestant Reformation of the sixteenth century. But the kind of religious comparison that began in the early eighteenth century, in the aftermath of Europe's devastating seventeenth-century Protestant–Catholic Wars of Religion, was foreshadowed during the Renaissance by the revival of classical Greek and Latin and by the recovery of masterpieces of world literature written in those languages.

First of all, perfected knowledge of Latin and the recovered knowledge of Greek enabled Italian scholars to publish critical editions of the texts of classical antiquity as well as philologically grounded historical criticism of such later Latin texts as the Donation of Constantine, exposed as a papal forgery by the Italian humanist Lorenzo Valla (1407–1457). It was in Renaissance Italy, too, that Christian Europe first recovered knowledge of biblical Hebrew. The earliest chair of Hebrew was established late in the fifteenth century at the University of Bologna. Despite repeated persecutions, ghettoizations, and expulsions, the Jewish population of Italy grew substantially during the Renaissance, enthusiastically embracing the then-new technology of printing with movable type. The first complete publication of the Hebrew Bible in the original, with Jewish commentaries, appeared in Venice in 1517 and proved highly instructive to Christian Europe; by the end of the following century, Italian scholars were even starting to read both the post-biblical rabbinic literature and the Kabbalah, writings in a later extra-rabbinic Jewish mystical tradition that fascinated some of them. Little by little, Christian Europe was beginning to learn from Europe's Jews.

As the Renaissance began to introduce Christian Europe by slow degrees to the critical examination of ancient texts as well as to the inner religious life of Judaism, it accomplished something similar in a more roundabout way for the lost religions of Greece and Rome. The humanists of the Renaissance did not believe in the gods and goddesses of Olympus as they believed in God the Almighty Father of Christianity, but even as they read the classical literature only as literature, they nonetheless were taken deep inside the creedal, ritual, imaginative, and literary life of another religion—namely, the lost Greco-Roman polytheism. During the Italian Renaissance, the term *humanist* (Italian *umanista*), we should recall, was not used polemically, as if in some sort of pointed contrast to *theist*. Rather, it was a declaration of allegiance to the humanizing, civilizing power of art and imaginative literature. Renaissance humanism's imaginative engagement with the religions of classical Greece and Rome thus constituted an unplanned rehearsal for the real-world, real-time imaginative engagements with non-Christian religions and cultures that lay immediately and explosively ahead for Europe. When the Spanish *conquistadores* encountered the living polytheism of Aztec Mexico, their first interpretive instinct was to translate the gods of Tenochtitlán into their nearest Greek and Roman equivalents. This was an intellectually clumsy move, to be sure, but less clumsy than interpreting them exclusively in mono-theist Christian terms would have been. Moreover, because neither classical paganism nor Aztec polytheism was taken to be true, the two could be com-pared objectively or, if you will, humanistically—and from that early and fumbling act of comparison many others would follow.

In the study of philosophy, the Renaissance added Plato and various ancient Neoplatonists to the Aristotle of the medieval universities. More important, perhaps, it began to read late-classical moral philosophies—notably Stoicism and Epicureanism—whose frequent references to the gods made them in effect lost religions. Sometimes inspiring, sometimes scandal-ous, these recovered moral philosophies introduced personality and inner complexity into the inherited category of paganism. Philosophical recover-ies of this sort could remain a purely academic exercise, but for that very reason their influence might be more subtly pervasive. Often, those who studied these texts professed to be seeking only their pro forma subordina-tion to the truth of Roman Catholic Christianity. Nonetheless, the ideas found their way into circulation. To be sure, the few who took the further step of propagating pagan worldviews as actual alternatives to Christian faith or Aristotelian cosmology could pay a high price. The wildly specula-tive Neoplatonist Giordano Bruno (1548–1600) was burned at the stake as a heretic. But others, scarcely less speculative, spread their ideas with little official interference and in response to widespread popular curiosity.

Comparative Christianity in the Protestant Reformation

Important as the Renaissance was to the development in Europe of a capac-ity for religious comparison, the Protestant Reformation was surely even more important, for it forced Europeans in one region after another to com-pare forms of Christianity, accept one, and reject the others. Frequently, this lacerating but formative experience required those who had rejected Catholi-cism to reject one or more contending forms of Protestantism as well. This was clearly the case during the English Civil War (1642–51), which forced English Christians to side either with the Anglican king or with the Puritan rebels who beheaded him; but there were other such choices, some of them much more complicated.

Tentative moves toward tolerance during these struggles were far less frequent than fierce mutual persecution and, on either side, the celebration of victims as martyrs. The Catholics tried to dismiss and suppress the Prot-estants as merely the latest crop of Christian heretics. The Protestants commonly mythologized Rome as Babylon and compared Catholics to the ancient Babylonians, viewing them as pagans who had taken the New Israel, the Christian church, into exile and captivity. The century and a half of the reformations and the Wars of Religion certainly did not seem to promise a future of sympathetic, mutually respectful religious comparison. And yet within the religious game of impassioned mutual rejection then being played, each side did develop formidable knowledge of the practices, beliefs, and arguments of the other. To the extent that the broader religious comparison initiated during the Enlightenment of the late seventeenth and the eighteenth centuries called for close observation, firsthand testimony, logical analysis, and preparatory study of all kinds, its debt to both the Protestant Reformation and the Catholic Counter-Reformation is enormous.

Particularly important was the historical awareness that the Protestant Reformation introduced into Christian thought. Protestantism took the New Testament to be a historically reliable presentation of earliest Christianity and, using that presentation as a criterion, proceeded to reject the many aspects of Roman Catholic practice that appeared to deviate from it. To be sure, the Roman church had been reading, copying, and devotedly commenting on the Bible for centuries, but it had not been reading it as history. Here the Renaissance paved the way for the Reformation, for the Bible that Rome read was the Bible in a Latin translation; and the Renaissance, as it recovered the knowledge of Hebrew and Greek, had recovered the ability to read the original texts from which that Latin translation had been made. In 1516, the Dutch humanist Desiderius Erasmus published a bilingual, Greek-Latin edition of the New Testament, correcting the received Latin to bring it into conformity with the newly recovered Greek. Armed with this new tool, the many educated Europeans who knew Latin but not Greek could immediately see that the Latin on which the church had relied for a thousand years was at many points unreliable and in need of revision. In this way, Erasmus, a child of the Renaissance, took a first, fateful step toward historicizing the Bible.

The Reformation, launched just a year later with the publication by Martin Luther of "Ninety-Five Theses on the Power and Efficacy of Indulgences," would take the further, explosive step of historicizing the church itself. To quote a famous line from Reformation polemics, Erasmus "laid the egg that Luther hatched." Thus, two epoch-making historical tools of Protestantism as it would dynamically take shape became integral parts of the later comparative study of non-Christian religions as undertaken by Christian scholars: first, the reconstruction of the composition history of the original texts themselves by scholars who had mastered the original languages; and second, the comparison of later religious practice to earlier through the study of the recovered and historically framed original texts.

In one regard, finally, Protestantism may have indirectly contributed to the comparative study of religion by setting in motion a gradual subversion of the very understanding of religion as a domain separate from ethnicity and culture that had been constitutive of Christian self-understanding almost from its start. Mark C. Taylor argues brilliantly in *After God* (2007) that what is often termed the disappearance of God or the disappearance of the sacred in modernity is actually the integration of that aspect of human experience with the rest of modern experience—a process whose onset he traces to Martin Luther's and John Calvin's sanctification of all aspects of human life as against medieval Christianity's division of the religious life of monks and nuns from the worldly (secular) life of laypeople.[10]

This progressive modern fusion of once separate domains would explain the spread in the West of the experience of the holy in ostensibly secular contexts and of the aesthetic in ostensibly religious contexts. Clearly the earlier Christian sense of religion as a separate domain has lingered powerfully in the West. Yet if Taylor is right, then post-Protestant religious modernity in the West, though deeply marked by Protestantism, may be a paradoxical correction of Christianity to the world norm. Or, to put the matter more modestly, the diffuse post-Christian religiosity of the modern West may bear a provocative similarity to the much older but equally diffuse religiosity of South and East Asia or indeed of pre-Christian world Jewry.

Toleration, Science, Exploration, and the Need for a New Map

After decades of controversy climaxing in all-out war, it became clear to exhausted Protestants and Catholics alike that neither could dictate the religious future of Europe. The Wars of Religion came to a close in 1648 with the Peace of Westphalia, which, though it by no means established individual freedom of religion, did end international religious war in Europe. Its key principle—*Cuius regio, eius religio* (literally, "Whose the rule, his the religion")—allowed the king or the government of each nation to establish a national religion, but effectively banned any one nation from attempting to impose its religion upon another. At the international level, in other words, there was agreement to disagree. Christian religious fervor itself—at least of the sort that had burned heretics, launched crusades, and so recently plunged Europe into civil war—fell into relative disrepute. The latter half of the seventeenth century saw what Herbert Butterfield (1900–1979), a major historian of Christianity in European history, once called "the Great Secularization." [11]

The old religious allegiances remained, but by slow degrees they began to matter less, even as national allegiance and national devotion—patriotism, as it came to be called—began to take on the moral gravity and ceremonial solemnity of religious commitment and the fallen soldier began to supplant the martyr. In 1689, John Locke published *A Letter Concerning Toleration*, in which he advanced the idea that a state would better guarantee peace within its borders by allowing many religions to flourish than by imposing any one of them. Locke favored a division of the affairs of religion as essentially private from the affairs of state as essentially public, capturing an attitudinal shift that was already in the air during the Enlightenment and would significantly mark the comparative study of religion as it took lastingly influential shape in the following century.

More intensely than by nascent toleration, the mood of the late seventeenth century was marked by wonder at the discoveries of natural science, above all those of Isaac Newton, whose major work establishing the laws of motion and universal gravitation was published in 1687. The poet Alexander Pope captured the popular mood in a famous couplet, written as Newton's epitaph (1730): "Nature, and Nature's Laws lay hid in Night. / God said, *Let Newton be!* and All was *Light*." Light was the master image of the Enlightenment—light, light, and "more light" (the legendary last words of Johann Wolfgang von Goethe [1749–1832]). Though the notion of natural law did not begin with Newton, his vision of the vast, calm, orderly, and implicitly benign operation of the laws of motion and gravity was unprecedented and gave new impetus to the search for comparable natural laws governing many other phenomena, including religion. Was there such a thing as a natural religion? If so, how did Christianity or any other actual religion relate to it? This idea, too, was pregnant with the promise of a future comparative study of religion.

While northern European Christianity was fighting the Wars of Religion, southern European Christianity had been transforming both the demography of Christendom and its understanding of the physical geography of the planet. The globe-spanning Portuguese and Spanish empires came into existence with speed comparable only to the Arab conquests of the seventh and eighth centuries. In evangelizing the Americas, the Portuguese and the Spaniards may have made Christianity for the first time the world's largest religion. In any case, their success in establishing colonial trading outposts along the African, Indian, Japanese, and Chinese coasts as well as founding the major Spanish colony of the Philippine Islands (named for the king of Spain) meant that European trade with India and China, above all the lucrative spice trade, no longer needed to pass through Muslim Central Asia or the Muslim Middle East.

Catholic missionaries did not have the success in Asia that they enjoyed in the Americas, yet the highly educated and culturally sophisticated Jesuit missionaries to Asia and the Americas became a significant factor in the evolving religious self-understanding of Europe itself. As extensive reports on the religions of Mexico, Peru, and above all India, China, and Japan reached Europe, they were published and read by many others besides the religious superiors for whom they had been written. Portugal and Spain had opened Europe's doors to a vastly enlarged world. The centuries-old quadripartite European division of the world's religions—Christianity, Judaism, Islam, and Paganism—was still generally in place in European minds. But from that point forward, as the sophistication of the religions of Asia and the Americas as well as the material and social brilliance of their civilizations came into focus, the inadequacy of *paganism* as a catchall term became evident, as did the need for new ways to speak of the newly recognized reality.

A New Reference Book Defines a New Field of Study

If any occasion can be singled out as the juncture when all these factors coalesced and produced a powerful new engagement with *world religions* in a way that approached the modern understanding of that phrase, it is the publication in Amsterdam between 1723 and 1737 of an epochal reference work, one that should indeed be seen as a direct ancestor of *The Norton Anthology of World Religions*. Appearing in seven sumptuous volumes comprising more than 3,000 pages with 250 pages of engravings, this encyclopedic production was *Religious Ceremonies and Customs of All the Peoples of the World* (*Cérémonies et coutumes religieuses de tous les peuples du monde*) by Jean Frédéric Bernard and Bernard Picart. Here, for the first time, was a presentation in one large work of all the religions of the world then known to Europe. Here, for the first time, was an attempt to reckon with how Europe's religious self-understanding would have to change in light of the previous two centuries of exploration, far-flung evangelization, and colonization.

It is important to note that this work, which was an immediate success and went through many editions and translations (and plagiarizations and piracies) over the next two hundred years, did not begin in the academic world and spread outward to the general public. Its address was directly to the general literate public—to the French public first, but quickly to other publics reading other languages. Jean Frédéric Bernard, brilliant but far from famous, was not just its behind-the-scenes research director, editor, and author: he was also its entrepreneurial publisher. It was a masterstroke on his part to secure the collaboration of Bernard Picart, already famous as an engraver producing reproductions of masterpiece paintings in an era before public art museums and long before photography, when what the public knew about art was limited to what they saw in church or what they acquired as engravings. By enabling the European public to see Picart's depictions of Aztec and Asian temples, costumes, and ceremonies, reconstructed from missionaries' descriptions, Bernard and Picart introduced the stimulating possibility of visual comparison. Where visual comparison led, philosophical and other critical comparison were intended to follow—and did.

As noted above, in the latter decades of the seventeenth century and the first of the eighteenth John Locke and a few other thinkers began to argue forcefully for religious toleration. Like Locke, Bernard and Picart were radical Calvinists as well as early "freethinkers," and the Netherlands was unique in their lifetimes as a haven for refugee dissidents and minorities of various kinds. Locke himself took refuge in the Netherlands during a turbulent and threatening period in England. Bernard's Huguenot (French Calvinist) family had fled to the Netherlands when Jean Frédéric was a boy. Picart, having abandoned Catholicism, moved there permanently as an adult, joining a large émigré French or French-speaking population in Amsterdam. The Peace of Westphalia, though it had imposed mutual forbearance in religious matters at the international level, had not done so at the national level. Protestants were still severely persecuted in France, as were Catholics in England. In the Netherlands, by contrast, though Calvinists were overwhelmingly dominant in public life, the private practice of Catholicism was indulged, while Jews were allowed public worship, and even deists or atheists had little to fear from the government. So it happened that though their great work was written in French, Bernard and Picart had good reason to publish it in the Netherlands.

In their magisterial account of the making of this work, *The Book That Changed Europe: Picart and Bernard's "Religious Ceremonies of the World,"* the historians Lynn Hunt, Margaret C. Jacob, and Wijnand Mijnhardt speculate about another possible consequence of its publication in the Netherlands—namely, the relative oblivion that overtook it in the twentieth century. The most populous European nations have tended to understand the intellectual history of the West through the minds of their own most influential thinkers, then through those of their major rivals, and only then through authors, however important, whose works were written or published in the smaller nations. Be that as it may, "Picart," as the work was commonly called, had two lasting effects far beyond the borders of the Netherlands. First, by discussing and illustrating the religions of Asia and of the Americas at length, it ended forever the quadripartite division of the world's religions that had structured European thought for eight hundred years. Second, it further solidified the conception of religion as a domain separable from culture and ethnicity. To quote *The Book That Changed Europe*, "This global survey of religious practices effectively *disaggregated and delimited* the sacred, making it specific to time, place, and institutions."[12]

There was now a greatly enlarged universe of religions to reckon with, to be sure, and Christian "teach ye all nations" missionary universalism had already mobilized to engage it. But also now, more strongly than ever, there was "religion" as an incipiently secular category capable of growth: it had lately been expanded by several new members and conceivably could be expanded further as further reports came in. The universalism of this emergent understanding of religion explains in part why the French Revolution, at the end of the eighteenth century, could presume to declare the "Rights of Man" rather than merely "of the [French] Citizen."

Bernard's and Picart's personal libraries suggest two favorite areas of reading: the ancient classics and travel books. The three historians note that 456 travel books were published in Europe in the fifteenth century, 1,566 in the seventeenth, and 3,540 in the eighteenth.[13] The co-creators' reading in the classics put them in touch with that pluralism of the mind made possible by the Renaissance recovery of classical moral philosophy and by the humanists' imaginative participation in the beliefs that figure so largely in classical literature. Their avid reading of travel reports gave them the enlarged geographical awareness made possible by the age of exploration.

As an early theorist of religion in this transformed mise-en-scène, Bernard blended elements of deist "natural religion" with classic Protestantism. His discussion of the religious customs of the world was scholastically Protestant in its combination of meticulous footnotes and sometimes-strenuous argumentation. More important for its later influence, Bernard's discussion was structurally Protestant in that it cast contemporary religious practice, wherever it was observed around the world, as the corruption of an earlier purity. But where sixteenth-century Protestantism had seen the purity of primitive Christianity, Bernard, writing in the full flush of eighteenth-century enthusiasm for natural science, saw the purity of an early, universal, natural, and "true" religion corrupted by the variously scheming priests of the religions reviewed. Despite this structural Calvinism in their philosophy of religion, Bernard and Picard were indebted to John Locke as well as to John Calvin; and especially when the non-Christian religions were under discussion, their manner was more often expository than forensic.

There is no doubt that Bernard discusses and Picart illustrates the religious customs and ceremonies of the world on the assumption both that each religion is, like Christianity, a separate, practice-defined domain and that these domains are all comparable. For better and for worse, the two of them contributed massively to the establishment of "religion" as a category projecting elements of Christian identity upon the vast, newly discovered worlds that lay beyond Christendom. Discussing Bernard and Picart's treatment of indigenous American religion, Hunt, Jacobs, and Mijnhardt declare:

> In short, Picart's images, especially when read alongside Bernard's text, *essentially created the category "religion."* Whereas the text sometimes wandered off on tangents about the sources of particular ceremonies, the similarities between rituals across space (Jewish and Catholic) and time (Roman antiquity and American Indian), or the disputes between scholars on the origins of different peoples, the images kept the focus on the most commonly found religious ceremonies—birth, marriage, death rituals, and grand processions—or on the most strikingly different practices,

which could range from the arcane procedures for the election of popes in Rome to human sacrifice in Mexico. Implicitly, the images transformed religion from a question of truth revealed to a select few of God's peoples (the Jews, the Catholics, and then the Protestants) to an issue of comparative social practices.[14]

The charge of Christian projection can plausibly be lodged against Picart and Bernard's interpretation of particular non-Christian rituals through their nearest equivalents in Christianity or Western antiquity. And yet if such habits of mind were limiting, they were scarcely crippling; and for Picart and Bernard themselves, they were evidently enabling and energizing. Is it true to say that between them, these two "essentially created the category 'religion'"? If they did so, we would claim, they did so largely through the convergence in their work and in themselves of the complex heritage that we have tried to sketch above.

Picart and Bernard carry forward the age-old, often suppressed, but never entirely forgotten understanding of the church as a thing in itself, not to be confounded with any nation or any set of cultural habits or practices. They carry forward the relatively subversive late medieval assumption that philosophy provides a neutral standpoint from which all religions may be compared. When considering religions remote from them in space rather than in time, they carry forward the Renaissance habit of drawing freely on classical paganism interpreted with textual sophistication and literary sympathy. They collate, as no one before them had yet done, the reports streaming into Europe about the religions of Asia and the Americas and, in their most brilliant stroke, they make these the basis for a major artistic effort to *see* what had been reported. They apply to their undertaking a distinct blend of moral seriousness, commercial enterprise, and erudite documentary attention to the particulars of religious practice that is their legacy from French Calvinist Protestantism. Finally, as sons of the Enlightenment, they bring a pioneering openness and breadth of vision to what they study.

Bernard can seem genuinely and intentionally prophetic when he writes:

> All religions resemble each other in something. It is this resemblance that encourages minds of a certain boldness to risk the establishment of a project of universal syncretism. How beautiful it would be to arrive at that point and to be able to make people with an overly opinionated character understand that with the help of charity one finds everywhere *brothers*.[15]

The place of good will—the sheer *novelty* of good will—in the study of religion has received far less attention than it deserves. Bernard's dream may seem commonplace now, when courteous interfaith dialogue is familiar enough in much of the West, but it was far from commonplace when he dreamed it.

Like *The Norton Anthology of World Religions*, Bernard and Picart's great work attended first and foremost to rituals and practices, considering beliefs only as expressed or embedded in these. Their work was path-breaking not just as a summary of what was then known about the religions of the world but also as an early demonstration of what sympathetic, participative imagination would later attain in the study of religion.

In painting their portraits of the religions of the world and in dreaming Bernard's dream ("How beautiful it would be . . . !"), Bernard and Picart were at the same time painting their own intellectual self-portrait as representative Europeans—neither clerics nor philosophers but thoughtful professionals—avid to engage in the comparison of the religions of the world on the widest possible scale. Religious comparison did not begin with them, nor had they personally created the intellectual climate in Europe that welcomed religious comparison once they so grandly attempted it. But it is not too much to say that in their day and to some significant degree because of them, Christian Europe finally learned how to compare religions.

Broadening the Foundation, Raising the Roof: 1737–1893

In 1737, when Picart and Bernard completed their work, Europe had barely discovered Australia. The peoples of the Arctic and of Oceania were living in nearly unbroken isolation. And even among peoples well-known to Europe, Japan was a forbidden kingdom, while China's first engagement with the West had only recently come to a xenophobic close. India was becoming relatively familiar, yet the doors of many smaller nations or regions remained barred. Europe had not yet lost its North and South American colonies to revolution; its later, nineteenth-century colonialist "scramble for Africa" had not yet begun. Russia had not yet expanded eastward to the Pacific. The English colonies in North America had not yet become the United States or expanded westward to the Pacific. The enlarged world that Bernard and Picart had sought to encapsulate in their illustrated reference work had many enlargements ahead, with corresponding consequences for the study of religion.

Though the intellectual framework for a global and comparative study of religion was essentially in place among an intellectual elite in Europe by the middle of the eighteenth century, much of even the known religious world remained culturally unexplored because the local languages were not understood. The accepted chronology within which Europeans situated new cultural and religious discoveries did not extend to any point earlier than the earliest events spoken of in the Old Testament. All this was to change during the century and a half that separates the publication of Picart from the convocation of the first World's Parliament of Religions at the 1893 Columbian Exposition in Chicago. That date may serve to mark the entrance of the United States of America into the story we have been telling and will bring us to the more immediate antecedents of *The Norton Anthology of World Religions*.

Broadening the Textual Base

Of special relevance for our work as anthologists is the enormous broadening of the textual foundation for religious studies that occurred during this long period. To review that transformation, we will consider the pivotal roles played by four European linguistic prodigies: F. Max Müller (1823–1900), James Legge (1815–1897), Sir William Jones (1746–1794), and Eugène Burnouf (1801–1852). One may grasp at a glance the scope of the documentary change that took place during the 150 years that followed the publication of Bernard and Picart's *Religious Ceremonies and Customs of All the Peoples of the World* by looking forward to the London publication between 1879 and 1910 of *The Sacred Books of the East* in no fewer than fifty volumes.

This enormous reference work, a superlative and in some regards still unsurpassed academic achievement, was produced under the general editorship of F. Max Müller, a German expatriate long resident in England. Müller's role in the nineteenth-century evolution of the disciplines of both comparative linguistics and comparative religious studies is large, but for the moment what concerns us is the sheer scope of the landmark reference work that he edited: two dozen volumes on Hinduism and Jainism translated into English from Sanskrit; nine on Buddhism alike from Sanskrit, from Pali (the canonical language of Indian Buddhism), and from other Asian languages; seven from Chinese on Confucianism, Daoism, and Chinese Buddhism; eight from Persian on Zoroastrianism; and two from Arabic on Islam. The range is astonishing, given that at the time when Bernard and Picart were writing and engraving, knowledge of *any* of these languages, even Arabic, was rare to nonexistent in Europe. How did Europeans learn them over the intervening century and a half? What motivated them to do so? The story blends missionary daring, commercial ambition, and sheer linguistic prowess in different proportions at different times.

Let us begin with Chinese. The first two modern Europeans known to have mastered Chinese were the Italian Jesuit missionaries Michele Ruggieri (1543–1607) and the preternaturally gifted Matteo Ricci (1552–1610), who entered China from the Portuguese island colony of Macao. Over time, as French Jesuits largely succeeded their Italian brethren in the Jesuit mission to China, the reports that they sent back to France about Qing dynasty (1644–1912) culture and the Confucian scholars they encountered stimulated French and broader European curiosity both about China itself and about the Chinese language. Though the Vatican terminated the Jesuits' Chinese mission on doctrinal grounds and though the Qing dynasty suppressed further Christian missionary work and expelled the missionaries themselves in 1724, a seed had been planted. In retirement on Macao, the French Jesuit Joseph Henri Marie de Prémare would compose the first-ever Chinese grammar in 1729. Later, during the nineteenth century, as Britain forced a weakening Qing dynasty to sign a treaty establishing coastal enclaves or "treaty ports" under British control, British Protestants commenced a new round of missionary activity in China, including the first attempt to translate the Bible into Chinese.

James Legge, originally a Scottish missionary to China, building on de Prémare's grammar and working with the help of Chinese Christians, undertook a major effort to translate the principal Confucian, Daoist, and Chinese Buddhist classics into English, always with the ultimate intention of promoting Christianity. Meanwhile, in 1814, Europe's first chair of Chinese and Manchu was established at the Collège de France. In 1822, Jean-Pierre Abel-Rémusat published in France a formal grammar of Chinese intended not for missionaries alone but for all interested European students. Legge himself became Oxford University's first professor of Chinese in 1876, and near the end of his life he was F. Max Müller's principal collaborator for Chinese texts in *The Sacred Books of the East*.

European penetration into China proceeded almost entirely from off-shore islands or coastal enclaves under European colonial control; China as a whole never became a Western colony. India, by contrast, did indeed become a Western colony—specifically, a British colony—and the West's acquisition of the Indian languages and first encounter with the Indian religious classics is largely a British story. From the sixteenth through the early eighteenth century, Portuguese, Dutch, French, and British commercial interests vied for primacy in the lucrative Indian market. By late in the eighteenth century, however, Britain had overtaken all European rivals and established India, including what is now Pakistan, as its most important future colony—more lucrative at the time than the thirteen North American colonies that would become the United States of America. Britain's colonial motives were originally commercial rather than either evangelical or academic, but after British commercial and political control was firmly established in the Indian subcontinent, first cultural and linguistic explorations and then Christian missionary activity would follow.

In the launch of Sanskrit studies in the West, no figure looms larger than Sir William Jones, an Anglo-Welsh jurist in Calcutta who was at least as prodigiously gifted in language study as Matteo Ricci or James Legge. Fascinated by all things Indian, Jones founded an organization, the Asiatic Society, to foster Indian studies; and in 1786, on its third anniversary, he delivered a historic lecture on the history of language itself. In it, he expounded the thesis that Sanskrit, Greek, Latin, most of the European vernacular languages, and probably Persian were all descendants of a vanished common ancestor. Today, linguistic scholarship takes for granted the reality of "Proto-Indo-European" as a lost ancient language whose existence is the only conceivable explanation for the similarities that Jones may not have been the very first to chart but was certainly the first to bring to a large European public.

Jones's lecture detonated an explosion of European interest in studying Sanskrit and in tracing the family tree of the Indo-European, or "Aryan," languages, including all the languages mentioned in the previous paragraph but notably excluding Hebrew and Arabic—descendants of a different linguistic ancestor, later postulated as Proto-Semitic. (In the Bible, it is from Noah's son Shem—*Sēm* in Greek—that the peoples of the Middle East are descended—whence the term *Sem*-itic.) Now, the New Testament had been written in Greek rather than Hebrew or Aramaic, and Western Christianity had quickly left its Aramaic-speaking Palestinian antecedents behind and become a Greek-speaking Mediterranean religion. Did that mean that Christianity was actually Indo-European, or "Aryan," rather than Semitic, even though Jesus and Paul were Jews? This became one cultural strand within the European enthusiasm for Sanskrit studies, as further discussed below. Suffice it to say for now that it was during this period that *Semitic* and *Semitism* were coined as linguistic terms and the anti-Jewish *anti-Semitic* and *anti-Semitism* were coined as prejudicial, pseudo-anthropological counterterms.

Of greater immediate importance for the broadening of the study of religion was the window that Sanskrit opened on an almost unimaginably vast Indian literature whose most ancient and venerated texts, the Vedas, may be as old as, or even older than, the oldest strata of the Old Testament. Sanskrit is the classical language of India, no longer spoken and perhaps artificially perfected as a sacred language at some unrecoverable point in the past. But India has in addition a great many vernacular languages, more of them than Europe has, and in a number of these languages, other extensive Hindu literatures exist. These, too, gradually came to light in the nineteenth and the early twentieth century as knowledge of the relevant languages gradually spread to Europe.

India, for all its immense internal variety, did and does have a sense of itself as a single great place and of its gods as the gods of that place. Siddhartha Gautama, the Buddha, was born in India, and Indian Buddhism was the first Buddhism. Buddhist texts in Sanskrit are foundational for all students of Buddhism. But after some centuries had passed, Buddhism largely died out in India, living on in Sri Lanka, Southeast Asia, China, Korea, Japan, Mongolia, and Tibet. The linguistic and cultural variety of these countries was enormous. The Buddha was not called by the same name in all of them (in China, for example, he was called "Fo"). Western travelers, not knowing the languages of any of the countries where Buddhism was dominant, were slow to recognize even such basic facts as that the Buddha himself was a historical personage and not simply one among the many deities and demons whose statues they saw in their travels.

Donald S. Lopez, Jr., Buddhism editor for *The Norton Anthology of World Religions*, has written or edited several books telling the fascinating tale of how the puzzle of international Buddhism slowly yielded to the painstaking Western acquisition of several difficult languages and the related gradual recovery of a second, astoundingly large multilingual religious literature standing alongside that of Hinduism. In his *From Stone to Flesh: A Short History of the Buddha* (2013), Lopez allows what we might call the statue story—the gradual realization that sculptures of the Buddha represented a man, not a god—to become the human face on this much larger and less visible story of literary and historical recovery.[16]

In the story of how a broad textual foundation was laid for the study of Buddhism, a third linguistic genius stands between the Anglo-Welsh William Jones and the expatriate German F. Max Müller—namely, the French polymath Eugène Burnouf, the last of the four gifted linguists mentioned near the start of this section. Because of the enthusiasm for Sanskrit studies that Jones had touched off in Europe, copies of texts in Sanskrit began reaching European "orientalists" during the first decades of the nineteenth century. Those that arrived from India itself, as they were translated, would enable the assembly of the twenty-one volumes of Hindu texts that open Müller's *Sacred Books of the East*. Initially, however, no Sanskrit texts dealing with Buddhism were forthcoming from the Indian subcontinent. This situation would change, thanks to the fortuitous posting of an energetic and culturally alert English officer, Brian Houghton Hodgson (1801?–1894), to Nepal, where Buddhism thrived. Hodgson collected dozens of Nepalese Buddhist texts in Sanskrit, including the crucially important *Lotus Sutra*, and arranged for copies to be shipped to Europe.

Burnouf had been appointed to the Sanskrit chair at the Collège de France five years before the first shipment from Hodgson arrived. Thanks in part to earlier work he had done in the study of Pali, the Indian language in which the oldest Buddhist texts survive, Burnouf seems to have quickly grasped that what he had before him was the key to the historical roots of Buddhism in India. But this recognition was father to the further insight that Buddhism was the first true world religion (or, as he was inclined to think, the first internationally embraced moral philosophy) in human history. Burnouf was among the first, if not the very first, to see Buddhism whole. His 1844 *Introduction à l'histoire du Buddhisme indien* (*Introduction to the History of Indian Buddhism*) was the first of a projected four volumes that, had he lived to write them, would surely have been his greatest work. The one lengthy volume that he did bring to completion was already of epoch-making importance, particularly in light of his influence on his student F. Max Müller.

What the discovery and European importation of the classical religious literatures of India and China meant for the comparative study of religion in the West can be signaled concisely in the terms *Confucianism, Daoism* (earlier, *Taoism*), *Hinduism,* and *Buddhism.* They are all Western coinages, hybrids combining an Asian word at the front end and the Greek morpheme *–ism* at the back end, and each represents the abstraction of a separate domain of religious literature and religious practice from the cultural and ethnic contexts in which it originated. The coinage of these terms themselves may not coincide exactly with the recovery of the respective literatures; but to the extent that nineteenth-century Western scholarship viewed the texts as the East's equivalent of the Bible, it all but unavoidably engaged them on structurally Christian and even Protestant terms, thereby furthering the European conception of each related *–ism* as a religion in Europe's now consolidated and universalist sense of the word.

Structurally, Protestant influence was apparent again whenever, in the manner of Bernard and Picart, the great nineteenth-century linguist-historians judged the early texts to be superior to the later ones. Thus, in the interpretation of newly available Chinese texts, the earlier, more interior or "philosophical" versions of Daoism and Confucianism were often judged superior to the later, more ceremonial or "religious" versions, in which Laozi or Kongzi (Confucius) seemed to be deified or quasi-deified. Similarly, in the nineteenth-century interpretation of Hindu literature, India's British colonial rulers celebrated the supposed nobility and purity of the early Vedas and Upanishads while disparaging later Hindu religious texts and especially actual nineteenth-century Hindu practice. In the Buddhist instance, Eugène Burnouf set the early, human, historical Indian Buddha—whom he understood to have preached an ethics of simplicity and compassion—against the later, superhuman metaphysical Buddha. Consciously or unconsciously, Burnouf's contrast of the historical and the metaphysical Buddha coincided strikingly with the contrast then being drawn for a wide Christian audience between the historical Jesus of Nazareth and the divine God incarnate of Christian faith.

In short, as this new, broadened textual foundation was laid for the documentary study of Hinduism, Buddhism, and Daoism, a Christian theology of scripture and a post-Protestant philosophy of history were often projected upon it by the brilliant but Eurocentric scholars who were shaping the field. However, once primary texts are in hand, their intrinsic power can exert itself against any given school of interpretation. Thus, for example, late twentieth-century scholarship began to foreground and valorize the late and the popular over the early and the elite in several traditions, dignifying texts and practices once thought unworthy of serious scholarly attention.

Though nineteenth-century scholars might shudder at such a shift, it is essentially to them that we owe the availability of the key texts themselves. To be sure, the full recovery and the translation of these literatures are works in progress; nonetheless, knowledge of their great antiquity and their scope—barely even dreamed of by Picart and Bernard—was substantially complete by the end of the nineteenth century. The literary foundation had been put in place for an enormously enlarged effort at comparative study.

Enlarging the Chronological Frame

As already noted, Europeans as late as the early nineteenth century situated new cultural and religious discoveries, including all the texts whose recovery we have been discussing, in a chronology of religion understood to commence no earlier than the earliest events spoken of in the Old Testament. This framework led to efforts, comical in retrospect, to link newly discovered places and newly encountered legends or historical memories in Asia and the Americas to place-names in the book of Genesis, to the Noah story of Genesis 6–9, and to legends about the eastward travels of the apostles of Christ. All this would change with a discovery that might be described as blowing the roof off recorded history.

During Napoleon Bonaparte's occupation of Egypt in 1798–99, a French soldier stationed near the town of Rosetta in the Nile delta discovered a large stone bearing an inscription in three scripts: first, ancient Egyptian hieroglyphics, a script that no one then could read; second, another unknown script, which turned out to represent a later form of the Egyptian language; and finally, a third script, Greek. It took two decades of work, but in 1822, Jean-François Champollion deciphered this "Rosetta Stone." In the ensuing decades, his breakthrough enabled later scholars to translate hundreds of ancient Egyptian hieroglyphic inscriptions recovered from the ruins of ancient Egypt's immense tombs and temples and to discover, as they did so, that the Egyptians had maintained a remarkably complete chronology stretching back millennia before the oldest historical events recorded in the Bible. Decades of archaeological excavation in Egypt further enabled the construction of a chronological typology of Egyptian pottery. And then, since Egyptian pottery and pottery fragments are found all over the ancient Near East in mounds (tells) left by the repeated destruction and reconstruction of cities on the same sites, Egyptian pottery could be used to date sites far removed from Egypt. Over time, the Egyptian chronology would become the anchor for a chronological reconstruction of the entire lost history of the Near East, much of it written on thousands of archaeologically recovered clay tablets inscribed in the Mesopotamian cuneiform script that at the start of the eighteenth century was as undecipherable as Egyptian hieroglyphic.

The cuneiform (literally, "wedge-shaped") writing system was used as early as the late fourth millennium B.C.E. for the representation of Sumerian, a mysterious language without known antecedents or descendants. Sumeria, the oldest civilization of the ancient Near East—situated near the southern tip of Iraq, just north of the Persian Gulf—appears to have invented cuneiform writing. Most extant cuneiform texts, however, survive as small tablets representing several ancient Semitic languages rather than Sumerian. Starting in the mid-nineteenth century, hundreds of thousands of cuneiform tablets were recovered by archaeological excavations nearly as important as those in Egypt.

Cuneiform was deciphered thanks to the discovery in Persia in 1835 of a trilingual set of incised cuneiform wall inscriptions in Behistun (Bisitun, Iran) that, like the Rosetta Stone, included one already-known language—in this case ancient Persian—that scholars were eventually able to recognize behind the mysterious script. The challenge lay in going beyond the Persian of that inscription to decipher the language—now known to be the Mesopotamian Semitic language Akkadian—represented by one of the other two inscriptions. Though Eugène Burnouf played almost as important a role in this decipherment as he played in the recovery of Indian Buddhism, it is Henry Rawlinson, the British East India Company officer who first visited the Behistun inscriptions in 1835, whose name is usually linked to the recovery for European scholarship of the lost cuneiform literatures of Mesopotamia.

None of the now-extinct religions whose literatures survive in cuneiform is anthologized in *The Norton Anthology of World Religions*; we have chosen only major, living international religions. But the recovery of these lost literatures significantly affected the evolving historical context for all religious comparison. What these texts made clear was that recorded history had not dawned in Athens and Jerusalem. The religion of ancient Israel, in particular, was relocated from the dawn of history to a late morning hour, and thus could no longer be seen as in any sense the ancient ancestor of all the religions of the world. On the contrary, it now became possible to study the Bible itself comparatively, as a text contemporaneous with other texts, produced by a religion contemporaneous with and comparable to other ancient Semitic religions. And since the Bible is an anthology produced over a millennium, it became possible and even imperative to study each stratum within the Bible as contemporaneous with differing sets of non-Israelite religions and their respective texts.

European Protestantism, accustomed since the Reformation to employing the Bible as a historically reliable criterion for criticizing and revising the inherited practices of Christianity, was deeply affected by the discovery of both prebiblical and contemporaneous extrabiblical literatures, for they were clearly a way to deepen the historical understanding of the Bible. But the recovery of these literatures, set alongside related evidence from archaeological excavation, was a threat as well as an opportunity. It was an opportunity because it enabled illuminating comparisons of key motifs in Hebrew mythology with their counterparts in other ancient Near Eastern mythologies; it was a threat because though it corroborated the historicity of some biblical events, it undermined that of others.

Arguably, religious truth can be conveyed as well through fiction as through history. Patristic and medieval Christianity had been content for centuries to search the Bible for moral allegories rather than for historical evidence. Where history was not a central concern, comparative Semitic studies could and did enrich the linguistic and literary interpretation of the Bible without impugning its religious authority. But because Protestantism, rejecting allegorical interpretation, had consistently emphasized and valorized the historical content of the Bible, Protestant Christianity had particular trouble entertaining the notion that the Bible could be historically false in some regards and yet still religiously valid. A desire to defend the Old Testament as historically valid thus arose as a second motivation for Semitic studies. In the process, the prestige of the study of history itself as an intellectual discipline able to produce authoritative judgments about religion was significantly enhanced if not indeed somewhat inflated.

The discovery of the Rosetta Stone and the Behistun inscriptions affected the comparative study of Islam as well, though less directly. The recovery of lost Semitic languages and their lost literatures invited comparative linguistic study of the now-increased number of languages clearly related to Aramaic, Hebrew, and Arabic—the three principal languages of this family that were already known at the end of the eighteenth century. This study led to the postulated existence of a lost linguistic ancestor, Proto-Semitic, from which they were all plausibly descended. Proto-Semitic then began to play a role in the study of the religions practiced by the peoples who spoke these languages, somewhat like the role that Proto-Indo-European was playing in the study of the religions practiced by the peoples who spoke Sanskrit, Greek, Latin, German, and the other languages of that linguistic family.

As Proto-Semitic was reconstructed, moreover, it became clear to scholars that classical Arabic, the Arabic of the Qur'an, resembled it very closely and thus was an extremely ancient language that preserved almost the entire morphology of the lost ancestor of all the Semitic languages. Classical Hebrew, by contrast, was shown to be a much younger Semitic language. In an era of so much speculation about the relationship between ancient religions and ancient languages, the near-identity of classical Arabic and Proto-Semitic suggested to some that Islam might have preserved and carried forward ancient features of a Semitic proto-religion that was the lost ancestor of all the Semitic religions, just as Proto-Semitic was the lost ancestor of all the Semitic languages.

Orientalism, Neo-Hellenism, and the Quest for the Historical Jesus

The emergence of "Semitic languages" and "Semitic religions" as groups whose members were identifiable through comparison meant that biblical studies and Qur'anic studies—or more generally the study of ancient Israel and that of pre- and proto-Islamic Arabia—were more closely linked in the nineteenth century than they usually are in the twenty-first. Julius Wellhausen (1844–1918), a major German biblical scholar, reconstructed the formative stages of both. Historical linguists in Wellhausen's day who engaged in such comparative study of languages and history were called "orientalists." Orientalism is a term now associated with cultural condescension to the peoples of a region extending from Turkey through Persia to the borders of Afghanistan; but when first coined, it connoted primarily a stance of neutral comparison across that large cultural realm, a realm that the study of the languages, ancient and modern, had now thrown open for historical study as never before.

Interest in the language and history of classical Greece also grew enormously in nineteenth-century Europe, fed both by Hellenic revivalism and by Christian anxiety. The upper class generally celebrated Greek literature and thought as expressing a humane ideal distinct from and even superior to that of Christianity. In the late eighteenth century, in his *The History of the Decline and Fall of the Roman Empire* (1776–88), the English historian Edward Gibbon had already presented the emergence of Christianity as in itself the key factor in the decline of a superior classical civilization; Gibbon elevated the nobility and civic virtue of republican Rome above the faith, hope, and charity of Pauline Christianity as celebrated by classic Protestantism.

In the nineteenth century, it was Greece rather than Rome that defined the cultural beau ideal for an intellectual elite across western Europe. The German philosopher Friedrich Nietzsche (1844–1900), a classicist by training, was steeped in this philo-Hellenic tradition and drew heavily upon it for his well-known critique of Christianity. In its devout classicism, nineteenth-century European culture thus continued and intensified a celebration of an idealized and indeed a more or less mythologized Greece that had begun during the Renaissance and continued during the Enlightenment.

This European cultural identification with Greece, whether or not tinged with antipathy toward Christianity, sometimes worked symbiotically with a larger geographical/cultural identification already mentioned—namely, Europe's identification with the larger world of the Indo-European peoples as distinct from and superior to the disparaged Semitic peoples, most notably the Jews. Religiously motivated Christian prejudice against Jews had by no means disappeared, but it was now joined by a form of pseudo-scientific racism that made more of national than of religious difference. Because nationalist self-glorification linked to invidious anti-Semitism had a seriously distorting effect on the comparative study of religion in nineteenth-century Europe, the full enfranchisement of Europe's Jews as fellow scholars would have, as we will see, a comparably important corrective effect.

A second motivation for classical studies, especially in Lutheran Germany, was Christian: an urgently felt need to write the still-unwritten history of the New Testament in the context of first-century Hellenistic Judaism. The historical reliability of the New Testament had been the foundation of the Lutheran critique of sixteenth-century Catholicism. But nineteenth-century New Testament scholars now claimed to recognize adulterations by the church within the Gospels themselves. To exaggerate only slightly, the challenge that nineteenth-century Protestant scholars saw themselves facing was to recover the historical Jesus from the church-corrupted Gospels in the same way that they understood the sixteenth-century reformers to have recovered the historical practice of Christianity from the corrupted church practice of their day.

"Historical Jesus" scholarship of this sort grew enormously in scope and erudition during the first decades of the nineteenth century, fed by the growing prestige of history as a social science and climaxing with the publication in 1835–36 of David Friedrich Strauss's massive, learned, sensationally successful, but scandalously skeptical *Life of Jesus, Critically Examined*, a German work that appeared in English in 1846 in an anonymous translation by the aspiring English novelist George Eliot (Marian Evans). Decades of further scholarship followed, some of it indirectly stimulated once again by archaeology. As the excavations by Heinrich Schliemann (1822–1890) proved that there was a Troy and that a great war had occurred there, thus allegedly proving the historical reliability of the *Iliad*, so, it was hoped, further archaeological and historical research might yet demonstrate the historical reliability of the New Testament.

A denouement occurred in 1906 with the publication of the German first edition of Albert Schweitzer's epoch-making *The Quest of the Historical Jesus*.[17] Schweitzer believed that the quest for the historical Jesus had actually succeeded as history. Yet the recovered historical Jesus was more a problem for contemporary Christianity than a solution, the renowned scholar ruefully concluded. Schweitzer's work continues to haunt historical Jesus scholarship, even though fresh quests and fresh alleged recoveries of the lost historical Jesus, both learned and popular, have continued to appear.

In sum, narrowly Christian though the quest for the historical Jesus may seem, it did much to establish historical study as the default mode of religious study. Its shadow lies across studies of the historical Buddha, the historical Laozi, and the historical Muhammad, among others, stamping them all with the assumption that in the study of any religious tradition, historical truth will prove the indisputable form of truth.

The Haskalah and Its Impact on the Comparative Study of Religion

The character of the literature of religious studies is determined as much by who is writing as by what is written about. So far, we have concentrated on changes in what was available as subject matter to be written about, thanks to the recovery of religious literatures either lost in time or remote in place. We turn now to a new line of inquiry and a new question: Who was to be commissioned to conduct the study, to do the writing, to tell the story of the religions of the world? In the late eighteenth and the nineteenth centuries, above all in Germany, a Jewish religious, cultural, and intellectual movement called the *Haskalah* emerged, one of whose effects would be the historic enfranchisement of Jews as, for the first time, full participants in Europe's comparative study of religion. Before saying more about the impact of the Haskalah upon secular religious studies in Europe, we should briefly review its direct and complex impact upon the Jews of Europe themselves.

Religiously, thanks in good measure to the pathbreaking work of the Jewish-German philosopher Moses Mendelssohn (1729–1786), the Haskalah gave rise to Reform Judaism as a revised form of Jewish belief and practice more attentive to the Tanakh, or Hebrew Bible (Christianity's Old Testament), than to the Talmud. However uncontroversial it may seem in the twenty-first century for the reformers to honor the biblical prophets rather than the Talmudic sages as the ethical pinnacle of the Jewish tradition, the shift was highly disruptive in the late eighteenth and the nineteenth centuries, for the emphasis in Jewish religious practice until then had been squarely on the Talmud and on the rabbinical sages whose debates, preserved in the Talmud, had made the rabbinate the final authority in Jewish religious observance. In the rabbinic tradition, the Talmud is the heart of the "Oral Torah" that Moses, the original rabbi (teacher), received from God and conveyed in speech to his first (rabbinical) students, beginning a teacher-to-student chain that legitimated the rabbinate as authoritative. To undercut the Talmud, Rabbinic Judaism's foundational second scripture, was thus to undercut the rabbis themselves.

Reform Judaism was religiously unsettling in another way because by going back to the Bible, thereby setting aside centuries of venerable Jewish tradition and subverting established rabbinical religious authority, its founders, beginning with Moses Mendelssohn, delivered a critique that bore a striking structural resemblance to German Lutheranism's back-to-the-Bible critique of Roman Catholicism. The Jewish reformation looked rather like the Christian, to the exhilaration of many Jews at the time in Lutheran northern Germany but to the consternation of others.

Religiously disruptive in these ways, the Haskalah—often referred to as the Jewish Enlightenment—represented as well a major turning point in Jewish European cultural life, away from oppressive and once inescapable social restriction and confinement. The *Maskilim*, as the leaders of the Haskalah were called, recognized that the dawn of a culture of toleration in Christian Europe might just light the path to an escape for Jews who were willing to acculturate in certain manageable ways. Mendelssohn himself, for example, became an acknowledged master of literary German as written by the intellectual elite of Berlin. German culture was then entering its most brilliant century. In an earlier century, German Jews would have had to become Christians to exit the ghetto and take part. But absent the requirement to convert, perhaps German Jews could become Jewish Germans. Such was the tacit hope of the Haskalah.

As Reform Judaism grew in popularity, thousands of Jews gambled that the ghetto walls were indeed coming down, and ultimately they were not mistaken. Despite the murderous anti-Semitism that would rise in the later nineteenth century and the genocide that would so profoundly scar the twentieth, a page had been turned for good in Western academic life—not least in the comparative study of religion.

For this anthology, the Haskalah mattered in one further, only slightly narrower regard: while no longer deferring to the immense corpus of rabbinic literature as authoritative, the Maskilim did not ignore it. On the contrary, they began to apply to it the same techniques of critical scholarship that the Renaissance had pioneered and that Protestantism and the Enlightenment had further developed for the interpretation of the Bible and other classical texts. The process of critically editing and translating the rabbinic literature, which placed yet another major religious literature within the reach of secular study, began very slowly and approached completion only in the twentieth century. Yet were it not for the Maskilim, that great work would not have been undertaken.

Most important of all, however, was the inclusion of Christianity's original "other" in the corps of those attempting in the West to make comparative sense of the religions of the world. This inclusion was truly a watershed event, for it foreshadowed a long list of subsequent, cumulatively transformative inclusions of the previously excluded. Religious studies in the twenty-first century is open to all qualified participants, but such has not always been the case. Broadening the textual basis for religious studies and exploding the temporal frame around it were important nineteenth-century developments. Broadening the composition of the population that would engage in religious studies was even more important.

The gradual inclusion of non-Christian scholars in the Western discussion of world religions has not entailed retiring the historically Christian but now secularized concept of religion (or the related concept of world religions), but Christian or Western scholars have lost any presumptive right to serve as moderators or hosts of the discussion. The overcoming of insufferable condescension, not to speak of outright prejudice, has played a part, but so too, and more importantly, have matters of perception, perspective, and the "othering" of Christianity: the rest had long been accustomed to see themselves through the eyes of the West; now the West has begun to see itself through the eyes of the rest.

The dynamic entry of Europe's Jews not just into the European study of religion but also into many other areas of European life brought about a massive backlash in the late nineteenth century, then the Nazi genocide in the twentieth, the post–World War II triumph of Zionism, and belatedly, among other consequences, a distinct mood of remorse and repentance in late twentieth-century European Christianity.[18] Somewhat analogous emotions accompanied the end of European colonialism during the same late twentieth-century decades amid exposés of the exploitation and humiliation suffered by the colonized. The comparative study of religion has both influenced and been influenced by these ongoing revisionist shifts of mood and opinion, but, to repeat, the first steps down this long path were taken by and during the Haskalah.

Evolution and the Comparative Study of Religion

While the decipherment of Egyptian hieroglyphic and Mesopotamian cuneiform were still throwing new light on the earliest centuries of recorded history, Charles Darwin's *On the Origin of Species by Means of Natural Selection* in 1859 and *The Descent of Man, and Selection in Relation to Sex* in 1871 shone a beam into the deeper darkness of the unrecorded, biological prehistory of the human species. At the time, no one, including Darwin, knew just how old *Homo sapiens* was as a species; the technique of absolute dating by the measurement of radioactive decay would not be developed until the mid-twentieth century. What Darwin could already demonstrate from the fossil record, however, was that the human species had evolved from earlier species in a process that antedated recorded history. The implications of this discovery for all forms of scientific and historical investigation were enormous and are still being explored. For the study of religion, the discovery meant that behind the religions of recorded history, there now stood in principle all the religions of human prehistory. At what point in human evolution did religion first appear, or was that even the right question? Should the question rather be about precursors to religion—earlier behaviors that would evolve into what we now call religion? How, if at all, could the practitioners of these prehistoric proto-religions or precursors to religion be studied?

Answers to that question are still being devised, but none involves their texts, for they left none. Tempting as it would be to explore new work being done on the evolution of religion before the invention of writing, such work is not properly a part of the study of religion to which *The Norton Anthology of World Religions* contributes, for ours is, after all, a collection of texts. We know that the human species emerged some two hundred thousand years ago in southwest Africa and migrated from there eastward and then northward through the Great Rift Valley in what appear to be two noteworthy spikes. One spike proceeded by way of Lake Victoria up the Nile River to where its delta empties into the Mediterranean Sea. The other spike crossed from Africa to Arabia at the Strait of Bab el Mandeb and then proceeded along the southeast coast of Arabia to the Strait of Hormuz, where it crossed into Asia. From there, one stream of human migrants veered northward to the delta of the Tigris River at the upper end of the Persian Gulf, while the other moved southward to the delta of the Indus River. The Indus delta and the river system above it cradled the civilization that, as it moved south into the Indian subcontinent, would produce the Vedas, written in Sanskrit, the earliest scriptures of ancient India. The Nile and the Tigris deltas and the river systems that lay above them would together define the "Fertile Crescent" within which ancient Israel would produce the earliest Hebrew scriptures. The invention of writing in the Tigris delta (Sumer) and the Nile Valley (Egypt) does not antedate the late fourth millennium B.C.E. The oldest works honored as scripture by Hinduism or by Judaism may be a full millennium younger than that. As recoverable from surviving texts, the story of the world's major, living, international religions can reach no further back in time than this.

To concede this much is not to concede that the earlier evolution of religion cannot be reconstructed at all or indeed even reconstructed in a way that would link it to the story told here. It is to concede only that that reconstruction would call for another kind of book than this one, assembling very different kinds of evidence than are assembled here.

The First World's Parliament of Religions

We may close this review of the development of religious studies between 1737 and 1893 with a visit to the World's Parliament of Religions at the World's Columbian Exposition in Chicago in 1893. The vast exposition, which ran for six months and attracted millions of visitors, was a celebration of progress—scientific, political, and cultural—during the five hundred years since Columbus had discovered America. (The exposition missed its intended 1892 opening by a few months.) Though the organizers often seemed to tacitly assume that the latest and greatest chapter in world progress was the American chapter and that thriving, optimistic Chicago was the epitome of American progress, nonetheless an exuberant, generally benevolent and inclusive curiosity characterized much on display. And though there was condescension in the presentation of model villages from "primitive" societies as natural history exhibits, there was also an acknowledgment that many fascinating and once entirely unknown societies were now no longer unknown and could be presented for the instruction of the interested.

As for the World's Parliament of Religions, it seemed to reflect a contemporary, enlightened, Protestant American view that there existed—or there could come into existence—something like a generic religion whose truth all specific religions could acknowledge without renouncing their respec-

tive identities. This view may have owed something to the many translations and plagiarizations of *The Religious Ceremonies and Customs of All the
Peoples of the World* that for a century and a half had been steadily propagating Bernard and Picart's confidence that a pure, "natural" religion underlay
the variously corrupted historical religions of the world. It may have owed
something as well to the 1890 publication of James Frazer's *The Golden
Bough*, a romantic and enormously popular work that marshaled classical
mythology and selected early anthropological studies of primitive tribes in
a grand evolutionary march from magic to science.[19] It may have reflected
in addition the gradual influence on American Protestants of the Enlightenment ideas underpinning the United States Constitution. Under the Constitution, since there was no "religious test" for public office, a Muslim or even
an atheist could legally become president.[20] The legal leveling explicit in the
Constitution implicitly encouraged a comparable leveling in American society, first among Protestants but later extended to Catholics and Jews, and
gradually to the adherents of other religions. The process was slow, but its
direction was unmistakable.

What is most remarkable about the Parliament, however, is the simple fact
that when the organizers invited representatives of Hinduism, Buddhism, Daoism, Confucianism, Shinto, Jainism, Islam, and Zoroastrianism to come
together and deliberate with Christians and Jews, everyone accepted the
invitation. Swami Vivekananda (1863–1902) accepted both the invitation
and the idea behind it—namely, that Hinduism was a world religion. He did
not object that there was no such thing as "Hinduism," that the religious life
of India was not a separate province within a postulated empire named "religion," that Indians who honored the Vedas did not see themselves as en route
to any brighter collective religious future, and so forth and so on. Objections
like this are legitimate, but Vivekananda agreed to attend anyway, gave a
sensationally well-received speech, and went on to found the Vedanta Society as an American branch of Hinduism. Plainly enough, he had begun to
construe Hinduism as potentially a global religion, separable from Indian
ethnicity. The Sri Lankan Buddhist Anagarika Dharmapala (1864–1933)
did something similar. In the real world of religious practice, these were
important ratifying votes for a vision of world religious pluralism.

"How beautiful it would be," Jean Frédéric Bernard had written, "to arrive
at that point and to be able to make people with an overly opinionated character understand that with the help of charity one finds everywhere *brothers*." If the organizers of the World's Parliament of Religions thought that
they had arrived at that blessed point when Swami Vivekananda thrilled his
American audience with the opening words of his oration, "Sisters and
Brothers of America," they were mistaken. And yet something was happening. A change was taking place. In various related European and American
venues, a subtle but distinct shift of attitude was under way.

Is it possible to contemplate beliefs that one does not share and practices
in which one does not engage and to recognize in them the shaping of a life
that one can recognize as human and even good? When attitudes shift on a
question as basic as that one, novelists and poets are often the first to
notice. The novelist Marcel Proust wrote as follows about the Hindu and
Buddhist concepts of *samsara* and *karma*—though without ever using those
words—in his early twentieth-century masterpiece *In Search of Lost Time*
(1913–27):

He was dead. Dead for ever? Who can say? . . . All that we can say is that everything is arranged in this life as though we entered it carrying a burden of obligations contracted in a former life; there is no reason inherent in the conditions of life on this earth that can make us consider ourselves obliged to do good, to be kind and thoughtful, even to be polite, nor for an atheist artist to consider himself obliged to begin over again a score of times a piece of work the admiration aroused by which will matter little to his worm-eaten body, like the patch of yellow wall painted with so much skill and refinement by an artist destined to be for ever unknown and barely identified under the name Vermeer. All these obligations, which have no sanction in our present life, seem to belong to a different world, a world based on kindness, scrupulousness, self-sacrifice, a world entirely different from this one and which we leave in order to be born on this earth, before perhaps returning there to live once again beneath the sway of those unknown laws which we obeyed because we bore their precepts in our hearts, not knowing whose hand had traced them there[.][21]

Marcel Proust was not a Hindu, he was a Frenchman of Jewish descent. Like not a few writers of his day, he may have been influenced by Frazer's *The Golden Bough*, but *In Search of Lost Time* is in any case a novel, not a work of science, philosophy, or theology. And yet we might say that in the words quoted, Proust is a Hindu by sympathetic, participative imagination and thus among the heirs of Jean Frédéric Bernard and Bernard Picart. This kind of imaginatively participant sympathy was taking hold in a new way.

In the United States, the World's Parliament of Religions reflected the same *Zeitgeist* and heralded, moreover, an organizational change that would occur in the latter third of the following century, building on all that had transpired since Bernard dreamed his dream. That change—the decision of the National Association of Biblical Instructors to reincorporate in 1964 as the American Academy of Religion—reflected the emergent conviction that some knowledge of the world's religions was properly a part of every American's education.[22]

If American intellectual culture is distinctive in any regard, it is distinctive in its penchant for popularization or for the democratization of knowledge. The intellectual leadership of the country has generally assumed that the work of intellectual discovery is not complete until everybody has heard the news. But judgment about what constitutes "news"—that is, what subjects constitute the core of education for all people—has changed over time, and knowledge of the world's religions has not always been on the list. It was during the twentieth century that it made the list, and so for the study of religion we may regard the World's Parliament of Religions as opening the twentieth century.

In the comparative study of religion, Europe was America's teacher until the end of World War II. The secular, neutral comparative study of religion was a European inspiration. The heavy lifting necessary to assemble linguistic and archaeological documentary materials for such study—the story we have been reviewing here—was almost entirely a European achievement as well. But a distinctive aspect of the American contribution to the story has been the impulse to share inspirations, achievements, and knowledge gained in the study of religion with the general public. A work like *The Norton Anthology of World Religions*, intended for the college undergraduate or the willing general reader, is a work entirely in the American grain. If you find the texts assembled in the collection that now follows surprising, if you find the editorial frame around them instructive, please know that you are cordially invited to explore the remaining five anthologies that with this one constitute the full *Norton Anthology of World Religions*.

Notes

The intellectual debts incurred in the foregoing introduction are far greater than could be registered even in a far longer list of footnotes than appears here. The subject matter touched upon could obviously command a far longer exposition than even so lengthy an introduction as this one has allowed. I beg the indulgence alike of the students I may have overburdened and of the scholars I have failed to acknowledge. JM

1. Kevin Schilback, "Religions: Are There Any?" *Journal of the American Academy of Religion* 78.4 (December 2010): 1112–38.
2. Frans de Waal, *The Bonobo and the Atheist: In Search of Humanism among the Primates* (New York: Norton, 2013), p. 210.
3. Daniel L. Pals, *Eight Theories of Religion*, 2nd ed. (New York: Oxford University Press, 2006); Michael Stausberg, ed., *Contemporary Theories of Religion: A Critical Companion* (London: Routledge, 2009). Strikingly, they do not overlap on a single entry.
4. Feynman is quoted in Dennis Overbye, "Laws of Nature, Source Unknown," *New York Times*, December 18, 2007.
5. Clifford Geertz, "Religion as a Cultural System," in *The Interpretation of Cultures: Selected Essays* (New York: Basic Books, 1973), p. 90 (emphasis his).
6. Ibid., p. 125.
7. Ibid., pp. 193–233.
8. Tomoko Masuzawa, *The Invention of World Religions, Or, How European Universalism Was Preserved in the Language of Pluralism* (Chicago: University of Chicago Press, 2005).
9. All Bible quotations in this introduction are from *The Holy Bible, Revised Standard Version* (New York: Thomas Nelson & Sons, 1952).
10. Mark C. Taylor, *After God* (Chicago: University of Chicago Press, 2007).
11. Herbert Butterfield, *The Englishman and His History* (Cambridge: The University Press, 1944), p. 119.
12. Lynn Hunt, Margaret C. Jacob, and Wijnand Mijnhardt, *The Book That Changed Europe: Picart and Bernard's "Religious Ceremonies of the World"* (Cambridge, Mass.: Belknap Press of Harvard University Press, 2010), p. 2 (emphasis added).
13. Ibid., p. 5.
14. Ibid., pp. 155–57 (emphasis added).
15. Jean Frédéric Bernard, quoted in ibid., p. 241 (emphasis in original).
16. Donald S. Lopez, Jr., *From Stone to Flesh: A Short History of the Buddha* (Chicago: University of Chicago Press, 2013).
17. *The Quest of the Historical Jesus* is the colorful title of the English translation first published in 1910; Schweitzer's sober German title was *Von Reimarus zu Wrede: Eine Geschichte der Leben-Jesu-Forschung* (From Reimarus to Wrede: A History of Research into the Life of Jesus). Hermann Reimarus and William Wrede were earlier scholars.
18. For the background in World War II and its aftermath, see John Connelly, *From Enemy to Brother: The Revolution in Catholic Teaching on the Jews, 1933–1965* (Cambridge, Mass.: Harvard University Press, 2012).
19. James Frazer, *The Golden Bough: A Study in Magic and Religion: A New Abridgment from the Second and Third Editions* (Oxford: Oxford University Press, 2009). Frazer's extravaganza eventually grew to twelve volumes, now out of print. For a more recent and more richly informed account of the evolution of religion, see Robert M. Bellah, *Religion in Human Evolution: From the Paleolithic to the Axial Age* (Cambridge, Mass.: Belknap Press of Harvard University Press, 2011).
20. See Denise A. Spellberg, *Thomas Jefferson's Qur'an: Islam and the Founders* (New York: Knopf, 2013).
21. Marcel Proust, *In Search of Lost Time*, vol. 5, *The Captive; The Fugitive*, trans. C. K. Scott Moncrieff and Terence Kilmartin, rev. D. J. Enright (New York: Random House, 1993), 5:245–46.
22. See Preface, xviii.

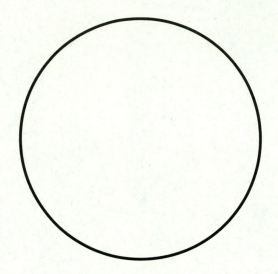

BUDDHISM

EDITED BY

Donald S. Lopez, Jr.

INTRODUCTION
In the World of the Buddha

Among all the world religions, Buddhism enjoys a particularly positive reputation, widely respected for its teachings of love and compassion, its promotion of nonviolence and commitment to a vegetarian diet, and its renunciation of war. In fact, Buddhism does teach love and compassion and it does promote nonviolence. But the Buddha himself ate meat and he did not forbid his monks from doing so. And wars have been fought by Buddhists in the name of Buddhism. Thus, there is some dissonance between the commonly held view of Buddhism and its history, a dissonance that may have much to do with Western yearnings for a religion founded by a man who declared that there is no God, a religion whose primary practice is to sit cross-legged on the ground and calm the passions.

When the term "world religion" was first coined by European scholars in the nineteenth century, only two were deemed worthy of the name: Christianity and Buddhism. They were called world religions because European scholars believed that their teachings had spread around the world by the force of their truths, not by the force of their armies. All the other religions were somehow local. Indeed, Buddhism has been so highly regarded that it is often claimed that Buddhism is not a religion at all—it is rather a philosophy or simply a way of life, one whose tenets can be selectively adopted regardless of religious affiliation, or lack of one.

Yet, as we will see in what follows, Buddhism is a religion, regardless of how one might seek to define that indefinable term. Some 350 million people around the world are counted, either by themselves or by others, as Buddhists. But what makes someone a Buddhist? The traditional answer is that a Buddhist is someone who "takes refuge" in what are called "the three jewels": the Buddha, the dharma (which here means his teachings), and the sangha (or community, a term that we will consider in more detail below). Someone who says three times, "I go for refuge to the Buddha. I go for refuge to the dharma. I go for refuge to the sangha," is a Buddhist. "Refuge" here means protection from the sufferings of life, and a Buddhist is thus someone who has concluded that the best protection from those sufferings is provided by the Buddha, his teachings, and the community of his disciples. But as is so often true of religions, affiliation is not always a matter of conscious reflection and logical conclusion. And in the case of Buddhism, even this classical definition of a Buddhist does not preclude one from seeking assistance from other quarters on matters less weighty than liberation from suffering. Buddhism has a long history of accommodating the religious traditions of the cultures it encounters, making it rarely an all-or-nothing proposition.

"Going for refuge" does not make one a Buddhist monk or nun; although monks and nuns also go for refuge, they achieve their monastic status through an ordination ceremony and the taking of vows. Over the course of Buddhism's long history in Asia, kings and emperors have often tried, with mixed success, to count the number of monks and nuns in their nations. With rare exceptions, they have not tried to count the much larger number of lay Buddhists. Indeed, counting Buddhists has always been difficult, long before the twentieth century and proclamation of a Buddhist identity in Europe and North America by Christians and Jews. How this came to be the case is something we will consider in due course, but we should begin at the beginning.

Buddhism began in India in the fifth century before the Common Era (B.C.E.), spreading throughout the Indian subcontinent and into what is today Pakistan and Afghanistan. It was introduced into the island of Sri Lanka in the third century B.C.E., into China in the first century of the Common Era (C.E.), then into Southeast Asia in the second century, Korea in the fourth century, Japan in the sixth century, Tibet in the seventh century, and Mongolia in the thirteenth century.

Each nation has its own myth of the arrival of Buddhism. In the case of China, it is said that the emperor Ming of the Han Dynasty (who reigned from 58 to 75 C.E.) had a dream in which he saw a golden spirit outside his palace, emitting rays of light from the top of its head. When he told his ministers about the dream, they reported that they had heard of a sage called "Buddha" who was able to fly. The emperor dispatched a party of envoys, who journeyed westward into Central Asia and the eastern end of the vast and vague region that the Greeks called "Scythia," returning with a copy of the *Scripture in Forty-two Sections* (p. 1496).

In Tibet, the king received a Chinese princess in marriage as part of a treaty between the two nations. As part of her dowry, she brought a large statue of the Buddha, said to have been made during his lifetime. As the cart that carried the statue entered Tibetan territory, its wheels repeatedly became stuck in the sandy terrain. The princess, skilled in the arts of geomancy, determined that the landscape of Tibet was in fact a huge demoness, lying on her back. Dismayed at the prospect of Buddhism entering her domain, the demoness kept shifting her body to impede its progress. The statue eventually arrived safely in the capital of Lhasa, where the king then undertook a royal construction project: he built temples at key sites across his kingdom, each located at a particular point on the demoness's body. The temples were designed to pin her down and prevent further interference. The Jokhang, the so-called Cathedral of Lhasa, is said to be located directly over her heart.

In Burma, they tell the story of Bhallika and Tapussa, two merchants who happened upon the Buddha near the Bodhi tree not long after his enlightenment. They offered him some honey cakes, the first food he had received since achieving buddhahood. In return, the Buddha offered them the first of his relics: some of his hair and parings from his nails. The merchants went on their way, continuing, it is said, all the way to Burma, where these relics of the Buddha were enshrined in the Shwedagon Pagoda in Rangoon, the holiest site in the nation.

Knowledge of Buddhism in the West came by different routes. Perhaps the first reference to Buddhism in European sources is that of Clement of Alexandria in the third century C.E. In describing the Indian gymnosophists, Clement writes, "Some of the Indians obey the precepts of Boutta; whom, on account of his extraordinary sanctity, they have raised to divine honors." After Clement of Alexandria, not much is heard about the Buddha in Greek or Latin until the eighth century, when, in works ascribed to St. John of Damascus, we find the story of two Christian saints, Barlaam and Josaphat—a story that is clearly drawn from the life of the Buddha (the name Josaphat derives from the Buddhist term *bodhisattva*), though this was not recognized for many centuries. References to the Buddha in Europe began to increase in the thirteenth century, when European emissaries and missionaries came into contact, not always by choice, with the westward-advancing Mongol horde. During the colonial period that began in the eighteenth century, Western knowledge of Buddhism grew significantly, owing to increased contact with Buddhist cultures and the learning of Buddhist languages by European scholars. They were the ones who coined the term Buddhism—according to the Oxford English Dictionary, the word *Boudhism* first appeared in English in 1801; it has no terminological equivalent in the languages of the various Buddhist canons. In Sanskrit, what we call Buddhism is *buddhadharma*, the "teaching of the Buddha." In Tibetan, what we call Buddhism is *nang pa'i chos*, the "religion of the insiders."

Chinese Buddhists came to California in the nineteenth century to work on the railroads, to be followed by Japanese Buddhist laborers, but the American fascination with Buddhism did not begin in earnest until the late nineteenth century, following on a wave of similar interest in Europe propelled by such figures as Schopenhauer, Nietzsche, and Wagner. In the January 1844 issue of *The Dial: A Magazine for Literature, Philosophy, and Religion*, Henry David Thoreau, then twenty-six years old, included a piece called "The Preaching of the Buddha"; it was in fact a translation of the fifth chapter of the *Lotus Sutra* (see the *Saddharmapundarika*, or *White Lotus of the True Dharma*, p. 278). Madame Blavatsky sometimes described her new religion of Theosophy, particularly popular among poets and painters, as "Esoteric Buddhism." In 1958, Jack Kerouac published *The Dharma Bums*, a roman à clef about his and his fellow Beats' dabblings in Buddhism. The following year, the Dalai Lama, today the most famous Buddhist monk in the world, left his native Tibet and went into exile in India. He made his first visit to America in 1979 and won the Nobel Peace Prize in 1989 (see "The Nobel Evening Address," p. 781).

What we call Buddhism was founded by a person known to history not by his name but by his title: the Buddha, the "Awakened One." Like Jesus, the Buddha never wrote anything himself and, unlike Moses and Muhammad, he never wrote down divine words that were spoken to him. Instead, he spoke himself, and others remembered his words. His words typically occur in a text called a *sutra*, often translated as "discourse." Buddhist sutras begin with the phrase "Thus did I hear."

The words of Jesus were written down, although most scholars place the earliest of the four gospels after the destruction of the Second Temple in Jerusalem in 70 C.E., some four decades after the crucifixion. Perhaps time moves more quickly now, yet we still might wonder about the accuracy of the words attributed to Jesus after such a time span. The Buddhist case is much more extreme. We do not know precisely when the Buddha lived, or how long he lived. The traditional "long chronology," accepted in Sri Lanka and Southeast Asia, gives the date of the Buddha's death as 486 B.C.E. There is only one canonical Buddhist text that mentions the length of the Buddha's life. Called the *Great Discourse on the Final Nirvana* (*Mahaparinibbana Sutta*; see p. 158), it says that the Buddha passed into nirvana when he was eighty. If this figure is correct and not simply a round number indicating old age, he would have been born in 566 B.C.E. These dates were later adjusted by scholars to produce the well-known dates, found in many reference works, of 563–483 B.C.E. But another chronology, the "short chronology," places the death of the Buddha more than a century later, in 368 B.C.E. In Japan and Korea, a traditional date is 949 B.C.E.; in Tibet it is 881 B.C.E. After much research, and some contention, most scholars today place the death of the Buddha at 400 B.C.E., plus or minus twenty years, and accept that he lived a long life.

What is not disputed is that what the Buddha taught remained only an oral tradition for a very long period of time, and was finally written down not in India but on the island of Sri Lanka to the south. There, the king, fearing that the words of the Buddha might be lost if the monks who had memorized them died in a famine or a war, ordered that they be inscribed onto dried palm leaves, the paper of the day—a relatively fragile medium for the preservation of the truth. That king reigned from 29 to 17 B.C.E. Thus, some four centuries passed between the death of the Buddha and the first recording of his discourses. But those texts do not survive; the oldest extant Pali manuscripts date from around 800 C.E. The oldest Buddhist manuscripts, some of which date from the first century B.C.E., were recently discovered in Afghanistan; they were written in a form of Sanskrit, in a script called Kharoshthī. Does this mean that there is nothing we can say with certainty about what the Buddha taught? Not necessarily. In ancient India—in Hinduism, Buddhism, and Jainism—there was a deep reverence for the power of speech; a standard term for a learned person literally means "one who has heard much." Writing was not unknown, but it was used for more mundane matters, such as record-keeping and commerce. What we would regard as religious teachings were preserved orally. And thus the traditions of ancient India developed sophisticated mnemonic devices to maintain the word accurately. In the case of the Vedas, priests were recite the text literally forward and backward. monks do not seem to have gone to the same lengths, but we have references to monks called "reciters of the long discourses,"

Head of the Buddha from Gandhara, 4th–5th century.

"reciters of the middle-sized discourses," and "reciters of the short discourses," indicating that from an early date, the monastic community included memory specialists whose job it was to preserve the teachings of the Buddha.

The Order of Monks and Nuns

The teachings that they preserved are often called in the early sources the *dharmavinaya*, a compound made up of two words, *dharma* and *vinaya*. The first is notoriously difficult to translate. A celebrated fourth-century commentator gives ten meanings, including "phenomenon," "path," "nirvana," and "virtue." Nineteenth-century translators rendered it as "law," but in this context it appears to refer to the discourses of the Buddha and might best be translated as "doctrine." The *vinaya* is the "discipline": that is, the ethical code, especially the ethical code followed by monks and nuns. Thus, the term *dharmavinaya* would mean "the doctrine and the discipline." The teachings of the Buddha, on a variety of topics, would be "the doctrine," and the code of monastic conduct would be "the discipline." That the discipline makes up half of this famous compound suggests the centrality of monastic life to the tradition.

It is said that the Buddha in the early years of his teaching did not have a formal system for the selection and ordination of monks, and no formal system of rules existed. When someone sought to join the order, the Buddha would say simply, "Come, monk," and the person was ordained. In later centuries, this moment was described as something of a magical transformation. Accounts of an ordination by the Buddha commonly resemble the following: "No sooner had the Lord pronounced these words than he found himself shaved, dressed in the religious mantle, and provided with the begging bowl and the pitcher whose spout is shaped like the beak of a bird, having a beard and hair of seven days; he appeared with the decent aspect of a monk who would have received investiture one hundred years ago." There was no code of conduct, because almost all the early disciples quickly attained enlightenment, rendering their behavior naturally ethical. But as the community of monks grew, it became necessary to establish rules. The Buddha did not do so preemptively. When he heard that a monk had done something untoward, he made a rule that henceforth such deeds were prohibited but did not punish the initial transgressor. Thus, at first, there was no vow of celibacy, until the parents of a monk who had left his wife begged him to return home long enough to produce an heir. He obeyed, not out of lust but out of filial devotion. When the Buddha learned what had happened, he made a rule against sexual intercourse. Thus, each of the rules of the monastic code—253, according to one version—has a story about the circumstances that led to its imposition; those stories, like the hadith in Islam, provide a wealth of insights into Buddhist monastic life in India. According to the account of his final days (see the *Great Discourse on the Final Nirvana*, p. 158), the Buddha tells the monks that they can ignore the minor precepts after his death. But no one remembers to ask him which precepts are minor, and so the entire code has remained in place over the centuries, with no rules added or subtracted. However, as Buddhism spread beyond India, monasteries formulated additional local rules to govern monastic life more effectively than could a set of regulations that reflected the cultural mores of ancient India.

In the early tradition, men could be ordained when they were twenty years old; the minimum age was later reduced to "old enough to scare away a crow," meaning that boys could also be ordained. One would begin as a novice, with a limited set of vows that included the five precepts, which Buddhist laypeople may also take but are not required to do so: not to kill humans, not to steal, not to engage in sexual misconduct, not to lie about spiritual attainments, and not to use intoxicants. Novices took an additional five vows: not to eat after noon, not to handle gold and silver, not to adorn their bodies, not to attend musical performances, and not to sleep on high beds. After spending some time as a novice, one would decide whether to go on to become a fully ordained monk (*bhikshu*, literally "beggar" in Sanskrit). It was the full monk who took and kept the full set of more than two hundred vows, confessing transgressions in a ceremony every two weeks.

Those vows defined a certain way of life conducive to the practice of the path. But in addition, the vows—especially to remain celibate and not to kill any creature—bestowed a certain purity on monks and nuns, making them suitable recipients of the alms of the laity, who garnered good karma by their gifts. This symbiosis of monk and layperson has been central to the Buddhist traditions across Asia: the monk offers the layperson a kind of spiritual sustenance in the form of merit that will fructify as happiness in the future, while the layperson provides the monk with the physical sustenance necessary for one who has renounced a life of labor in the world. Thus there must always be both monks and laity, in proportions that vary in different Buddhist cultures at different moments in their history. Tibet is generally regarded as having had the largest monastic population, sometimes as high as 15 percent of males. The vows of the fully ordained monk are expected to be kept for life, and a certain stigma clings to those who return to lay life. The novitiate, in contrast, could be temporary. In Thailand, for example, most males are ordained as novices for a period of one rainy season (sometimes extending to three years) and then return to lay life.

Women have played an important role in Buddhism in all Asian cultures, despite the tradition's ambivalent attitude toward them. The Buddha's mother is extolled as the Buddhist *theotokos* (mother of God), but died seven days after his birth; the commentaries explain that after the birth of a buddha, nothing may ever enter his mother's womb. She was reborn as a (male) god, and after his enlightenment the Buddha preached the dharma to her in heaven. The Buddha abandoned his wife on the day of his firstborn's birth in order to seek enlightenment. In a famous scene, his resolve to leave his palace is steeled when he surveys the sleeping women of his harem and sees a charnel ground of corpses.

The Buddha was raised by his stepmother, who urged him to allow women also to renounce the world to seek nirvana. He conceded that women are capable of following the path to enlightenment, but only grudgingly permitted the founding of an order of nuns. He is said to have established an additional set of rules for nuns (including the rule that the most senior nun must always defer to the most junior monk) and to have predicted that as a consequence of his allowing women to enter the order, his teaching would remain in the world only for five hundred years. If he had not admitted women, it would have lasted for one thousand years.

Among the women who joined the order, many achieved enlightenment (see *Songs of the Female Elders*, p. 232), including his stepmother and his wife. Moreover, the Buddha had a number of important lay female disciples, including queens and courtesans; he sometimes used the aging bodies of the latter to illustrate the truth of impermanence. Perhaps reflecting the impediments faced by women in traditional Indian society, in the prayer that concludes his *Introduction to the Practice of the Bodhisattva Path* (see the *Bodhicharyavatara*, p. 395), Shantideva writes, "May all women in the world be reborn as men." Yet women, in the form of female bodhisattvas, would become objects of devotion in the Mahayana, receiving prayers from both women and men (see "In Praise of the Twenty-One Taras" and *Dharani Sutra of Five Mudras of the Great Compassionate White-Robed One*, pp. 486 and 571).

Nuns eventually appeared in Sri Lanka, Burma, China, Vietnam, Korea, and Japan. However, it was difficult for the order to survive periods of social upheaval and declines in patronage; the rules of discipline required that ten fully ordained nuns be present to confer ordination on a new nun, followed by a second ordination ceremony at which ten monks were present. If those conditions could not be met, ordination was not permitted. Indeed, as a result of Sri Lanka's protracted war with a south Indian king in the late tenth century, Buddhist institutions were devastated to the point that new monks could not be ordained. The king brought monks from Burma to revive the order, but he did not make similar efforts for the order of nuns. Thus, although the order of nuns survives in China, Korea, and Vietnam, it died out in Sri Lanka and the other Theravada countries of Southeast Asia. In Tibet, all ordained women were novices. The right to full ordination for women in all Buddhist cultures became an important, and controversial, topic in the late twentieth century.

As noted above, a Buddhist, whether female or male, is traditionally defined as someone who seeks refuge from suffering through the "three jewels" of the Buddha, the dharma, and the sangha, saying three times, "I go for refuge to the Buddha. I go for refuge to the dharma. I go for refuge to the sangha." The Buddha is said to be the teacher of refuge; the dharma, or his teaching, is said to be the actual refuge; the sangha is said to be those who help one to find refuge. In one of the medical metaphors so common in Buddhism, the Buddha is the physician, the dharma is the medicine, the sangha are the nurses. These three are called "jewels," because like a jewel, they are difficult to find in this world and, when they are found, they are of great value.

Exactly what constitutes the sangha, the dharma, and even the Buddha would become points generating considerable commentary. In the practice of going for refuge, it is said that the sangha consists only of the Buddha's enlightened disciples—those who have advanced far on the path to nirvana that he set forth. That is the most restrictive meaning of the term. More generally, in Asia the sangha means the community of monks and nuns. In American Buddhism, it has taken on a much broader sense, functioning as a kind of Buddhist correlate to a Christian "congregation."

The Vehicles to Enlightenment

At around the time that the teachings of the Buddha were being committed to palm leaf in Sri Lanka, the words of the Buddha were also being recorded in India. But these were words that the historical Buddha never spoke, in works known as the Mahayana ("Great Vehicle") sutras. They include some of the most famous and influential Buddhist texts—some of the very few Buddhist works that would come to be well-known by their English title, such as the *Lotus Sutra*, the *Diamond Sutra*, and the *Heart Sutra* (each of which appears here). Exactly what the Mahayana was and how it evolved continues to be explored and debated by scholars, but its importance is difficult to overstate; for Mahayana Buddhism, first appearing in India in the first centuries of the Common Era, would become the dominant form of Buddhism in China, Korea, Japan, Tibet, Mongolia, and parts of Vietnam. Because of its geographical distribution, Victorian scholars called it Northern Buddhism. It seems to have begun as a disparate group of cults; composed of both monastic and lay followers, they were devoted to a single text, which purported to be the word of the Buddha and promised all manner of rewards to those who regarded it as the word of the Buddha and revered it above all others. The fundamental claim of this text was not universally accepted. Indeed, a standard element of Mahayana treatises in India, from the rise of the Mahayana in the first century to the demise of Buddhism in India in the twelfth century, is the defense of the Mahayana as the word of the Buddha. Apparently, this claim remained a point of contention and, despite its subsequent fame, the Mahayana remained a minority movement in India.

The Mahayana sutras sometimes called the majority form of Buddhism the Hinayana, a Sanskrit pejorative often euphemistically rendered in English as "Lesser Vehicle." In fact, it means "Vile Vehicle." Scholars have long struggled with this term, often using it as a convenient designation for the many non-Mahayana schools (traditionally counted as eighteen, although there were many more). Only a Sinhalese offshoot of one of these remains today: the Theravada ("Way of the Elders") of Sri Lanka and Southeast Asia. Thus, it is historically inaccurate to speak only of Mahayana Buddhism and Theravada Buddhism. Scholars tend to refer to the non-Mahayana as "Nikaya Buddhism" (*nikaya* means "school" or "group"), covering the eighteen traditional schools, or simply as "mainstream Buddhism," in recognition of its majority status in India. In this volume, I have called it the "shared tradition," because it consists of those elements that the various forms of Buddhism, both across time and across Asia, have tended to accept as canonical. Developments in Buddhism have generally taken the form of augmentations to or reinterpretations of this shared tradition.

Regardless of which texts a school of Buddhism considers to be the word of the Buddha, those words contain rather little biographical information. One of the most detailed accounts of the Buddha's quest for enlightenment occurs in the *Ariyapariyesana Sutta*, or *The Noble Search* (see p. 119). It is interesting to note that none of the familiar details about the Buddha's sheltered youth—the four chariot rides outside the palace, his departure from the palace and his wife and newborn son—are found there. Those stories appear much later in works like the *Nidanakatha* or *Account of the Beginning* (see p. 131), the first biography of the Buddha in Pali, the canonical language of the Buddhist traditions of Sri Lanka and Southeast Asia. It dates from the fifth century C.E., some eight centuries after the Buddha's passing. In the *Ariyapariyesana*, the description is much more spare; the Buddha says simply, "Later, while still young, a black-haired young man endowed with the blessing of youth, in the prime of life, though my mother and father wished otherwise and wept with tearful faces, I shaved off my hair and beard, put on the yellow robe, and went forth from the home life into homelessness." In ancient India, the shaved head and the ochre robe were signs that one had left the world in search of a condition beyond it. The Buddha was not the first to seek such a state, but he would become the most famous of those who claimed to find it. In this text, and in other accounts, the Buddha's description of his enlightenment is brief. Over the centuries, commentators across the Buddhist world would seek to recover the meaning of that moment in widely different ways, attempting to understand what it means to be the Buddha.

A vast body of teachings would come to be ascribed to the Buddha in the centuries after his death, with considerable disagreement among the Buddhist traditions of Asia as to what is authentic—what should be considered *buddhavachana*, the "word of the Buddha." As more texts were added to the corpus, they needed to be placed within the chronology of his life, with pride of place given to the first words that he spoke after he achieved enlightenment at the age of thirty-five. Most of the traditional sources, however, agree that in his first sermon he first proclaimed the famous "four noble truths" (see *Setting the Wheel of the Dharma in Motion*, p. 177). They are worth reviewing briefly here because they set the terms for much of the tradition that would follow.

Although the four truths are certainly comprehensible when set forth simply, much of their power, and indeed the power of all Buddhist teachings, derives from their context, the world in which the four truths are true. Thus, before outlining the four truths, it is useful to describe the Buddhist universe, which, although locally modified, has been generally accepted across the history of Buddhism.

The Buddhist Universe

In one sense, the Buddhist world is our world, taking the personal pronoun in the broadest possible terms. For though the teachings of the Buddha were directed to humans, humans were not the only members of the Buddha's audience. A common closing of a discourse by the Buddha declares, "The entire world, the gods, humans, demigods, and *gandharvas*, admired and praised the speech of the Bhagavan [the 'Blessed One,' an epithet of the Buddha]." Also present are *nagas*, a kind of water spirit that was identified with a dragon when Buddhism was transmitted from India to China. One of the most important genres of Buddhist literature is the *abhidharma* (see the *Abhidharmakosha*, or *Treasury of Higher Doctrine*, p. 267), sometimes translated as "metaphysics": the detailed analysis of the constituents of experience and the functions of consciousness. The Buddha is said to have first imparted these teachings not to humans but to the gods, specifically to his mother.

After her death she had been reborn in heaven, so during the rainy season in the seventh year after his enlightenment, he went there to teach her. The most famous of all Buddhist festivals in East Asia, called Obon in Japan, commemorates another maternal visitation—this time by the eminent monk Maudgalyayana, who went in search of his dead mother and found her in hell. Thus, the Buddhist universe includes not just the world of humans but celestial and infernal realms as well.

For Buddhists, the universe has no beginning. Various world systems come into existence and eventually cease to be, but other worlds precede and follow them. The Buddha is said to have discouraged speculation about the origin of the universe; the question of whether the world has a beginning is one of fourteen questions that the Buddha refused to answer. He also remained silent when asked whether the universe will ever come to an end. Individual worlds are destroyed, incinerated by the fire of seven suns; but no apocalypse, no final end time, is foretold. Individual beings put an end to their individual existence, one that also has no beginning, by traversing the path to nirvana.

This does not mean that Buddhists do not have creation myths. One is offered in the *Agganna Sutta* (p. 92), which describes how beings first came to populate a newly formed world system and how gender, sexuality, private property, labor, and government came into existence. The place that they inhabit—and which we inhabit, according to the Buddhists—is an island continent called Jambudvipa, "Rose Apple Island," in a great sea. It is the southern continent, one of four continents in a flat world, situated in the four cardinal directions around a central mountain called Mount Meru. The mountain is in the shape of a great cube, each of its four faces composed of a different kind of precious stone. The southern face of the mountain is made of lapis lazuli and so when the light of the sun reflects off Meru's south face, it turns the color of our sky blue. Gods live on the slopes of the mountain and on the summit. It was in the heaven on the summit on Mount Meru that the Buddha taught the *abhidharma* to his mother.

The Buddha, like other teachers of his day, believed in rebirth—a process of birth and death called *samsara*, literally "wandering." According to the Buddha, this process has no beginning and will not end unless one brings it to an end. Until then, each being is born in lifetime after lifetime into one of six, and only six, realms: as a god, demigod, human, animal, ghost, or denizen of hell. This is not a process of evolution but rather very much an aimless wandering from realm to realm, up and down, for aeons, a process that on the surface appears entirely random. The gods live above our world, some on the surface of the central mountain, some in the heavens above it. Their lives there are long but not eternal. For the gods who live on the summit of Mount Meru, the life span is a thousand years, and every day of those years is equal in length to one hundred human years. In the heavens arrayed above the summit of Mount Meru, the life spans are longer. These heavens, as well as the realms of demigods, humans, animals, ghosts, and the denizens of hell, together constitute what is called the Realm of Desire, because the beings there desire the pleasures that derive from the five senses, constantly seeking beautiful things to see, hear, smell, taste, and touch. Above the Desire Realm are the heavens of the Realm of Form, where the gods have bodies made of a subtle matter invisible to humans; having no need for food or drink, these gods only have the senses of sight, hearing, and touch. The highest Buddhist heavens are located in what is called the Formless Realm. There the gods have no bodies but exist only as consciousness, and the names of its four heavens are derived from the object in which the minds of the gods of that heaven are absorbed: Infinite Space, Infinite Consciousness, Nothingness, Neither Perception nor Nonperception. But these heavens remain within the cycle of birth and death, and when the karmic effect has run its course, each inhabitant is reborn elsewhere.

In general, it is said that one is reborn as a god as a result of acts of generosity and charity in a former life; charity directed toward the community of Buddhist monks and nuns is considered particularly efficacious. However, one is reborn in these heavens of the Formless Realm by achieving their deep levels of concentration in meditation while a human. Yet even these profound states of bliss, states that last for millennia, are not eternal. Indeed, Buddhist texts sometimes consign the saints of other religions to these heavens, explaining that they have mistaken such states, which lie within samsara, as liberation from it.

Below the gods in the hierarchy of beings are the demigods (excluded in some lists), a kind of catchall category of all manner of spirits and sprites, some malevolent and some benign; one of the words for "plant" or "tree," which Buddhist monks are prohibited from uprooting or cutting down, literally means "abode of a being." The demigods are less potent than the gods but have powers that exceed those of humans and can cause all manner of mischief if not properly propitiated. In the category of demigod, one finds the *gandharvas* mentioned above, a class of celestial musicians who, according to their name, subsist on fragrances; a crude translation of their name would be "odor eaters." One also finds a kind of half-human half-horse creature called the *kimnara*, literally "is that a man?"

The third realm is the world of humans, regarded as the ideal state for the practice of the Buddhist path. The realms of the gods above are too pleasurable; those of the animals, ghosts, and denizens of hell below are too painful. The world of humans is said to have sufficient suffering to cause one to wish to escape from it, but not so much as to cause paralysis and thereby block such an attempt. Among the sufferings of humans, the Buddha enumerated eight: birth, aging, sickness, death, losing friends, gaining enemies, not getting what you wish for, and getting what you do not wish for. As we consider, as we always must, the extent to which the doctrines of a religion reflect, on the one hand, the concerns of a distant time and place and, on the other hand, more general elements of the human condition, this list, set forth in ancient India more than two millennia ago, seems to fall on the universal side of the spectrum.

It is said that one is reborn as a human as a result of being an ethical person, generally understood as keeping vows. As mentioned above, for the Buddhist laity, there are five traditional vows: to abstain from killing humans, from stealing, from sexual misconduct, from lying, and from intoxicants. Laypeople could take any one, two, three, four, or all five of these vows, whether for life or for a more limited period. The vows kept by monks and nuns number in the hundreds. They govern all elements of monastic life, including possessions (especially robes), hygiene, and general comportment. The vows are categorized by the weight of the infraction they seek to prevent. Four transgressions result in permanent expulsion from the order: murder, sexual intercourse, theft (of anything above a specified value), and lying about spiritual attainments. Lesser infractions may require probation, confession, or simply a verbal acknowledgment.

Vows play a central role in Buddhist practice. They are not commandments from God, nor do they represent a covenant, but instead are a mechanism for making merit, the good karma that leads to happiness in this life and the next. It is sometimes said that one of the Buddhist innovations in Indian karma theory was to introduce the element of intention. A misdeed was no longer a ritual mistake, a sacrifice poorly performed, as it was in Vedic times, but an intentional action—whether physical, verbal, or mental—motivated by desire, hatred, or ignorance. A vow represented not a situational decision for good over evil but a lifetime commitment to refrain from a particular negative act. It was said that one accrued greater good karma by taking a vow not to kill humans than by simply happening not to commit murder over the course of one's life. Conversely, one accrued greater negative karma if one took and then broke a vow to avoid a particular misdeed than if one simply happened to commit that misdeed. The scholastic tradition would later explain why this was the case. In the act of taking a vow, a kind of "subtle matter" was created in one's body. As long as the vow was kept, this subtle matter caused good karma to accrue in every moment throughout one's life. For this reason, taking a vow was a much more efficient means to generate the seeds of future happiness than simply being occasionally ethical.

The realms of gods and humans are considered the "good" or "fortunate" realms within the cycle of rebirth, because rebirth there is the result of virtuous actions and because the sufferings undergone by the beings in these realms are far less horrific than those of the beings reborn in the three lower realms.

The realm of animals (which includes all birds, mammals, amphibians, fish, and insects, but not plants) is familiar enough, as are their various sufferings. Buddhist texts say that the particular suffering of animals is that they always must go in search of food while avoiding themselves becoming food; unlike humans, animals are killed not because of something that they did or said, but because of the taste of their flesh or the texture of their skin. One is said to be reborn as an animal as a result of past actions that were motivated by ignorance.

The next realm is that of the ghosts—often called "hungry ghosts," the translation of the Chinese term for the denizens of this realm. Their primary form of suffering is indeed hunger and thirst, and they are constantly seeking to fill their bellies. As they do so, they encounter all manner of obstacles. In Buddhist iconography, ghosts are depicted as baleful beings with huge distended bellies and emaciated limbs, not unlike the victims of famine. But beyond this affliction so familiar in human history, the other sufferings of ghosts are more fantastic. Some have knots in their throats, making it impossible for food and drink to pass. For others, who are able to swallow, the food they eat is transformed into sharp weapons and molten lead when it reaches their stomach. Still others find that when they finally come upon a stream of flowing water, it turns into blood and pus as they kneel down to drink. Ghosts live in a world located five hundred leagues beneath the surface of the earth, but they sometimes venture into the

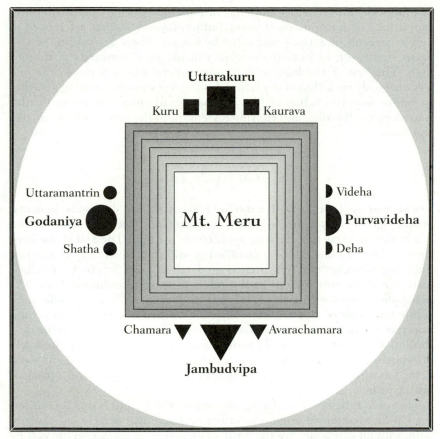

A diagram of the Buddhist cosmos, with Mount Meru in the center, surrounded by four island continents.

human world, where they can be seen by monks with supernormal powers. Indeed, the feeding of ghosts is a special responsibility of Buddhist monks. The Sanskrit term translated as "ghost" is *preta*, which means "departed" or "deceased," suggesting that they are the spirits of the dead who have not received the proper ritual offerings from their families and thus are doomed to starvation. Buddhist monks and nuns, who also have left family life behind, have a special responsibility to feed the hungry ghosts, who appear often in Buddhist stories. It is said that one is reborn as a ghost as a result of actions motivated by greed in a former life.

In the Buddhist cosmology, the most elaborate of the realms are the most desired—the heavens—and the most feared—the hells. There are eight hot hells and eight cold hells, four neighboring hells, and a number of trifling hells. They are stacked beneath the surface of the earth—the deeper below, the greater the intensity and duration of the suffering. The cold hells are desolate lands of ice where snow is always falling, without a sun or moon, or any source of light and heat. The beings there are naked, and the names of some of the hells describe the shape of the blisters that form on their bodies: for example, "Split Like a Blue Lotus." The hot hells are lands of burning iron where beings undergo various forms of torture during lifetimes that last for millions of years, but not forever. Beings are reborn in hell as a result of actions motivated by hatred. There are said to be five deeds that result in immediate rebirth in the most torturous of the hot hells. The first of the four of these seems particularly heinous, the last less obviously so: killing one's father, killing one's mother, killing an arhat (someone who has achieved liberation and will enter nirvana at death), wounding the Buddha, and causing dissension in the community of monks and nuns.

The Four Noble Truths

The six realms of samsara—the dwelling places of gods, demigods, humans, animals, ghosts, and denizens of hell—constitute the Buddhist universe, and it is in this universe that the four noble truths are true. The first of the four, then, is the truth that all life is qualified by suffering, in one way or another. Suffering (*duhkha*) is a term that is analyzed at great length in Buddhist texts, but at its most obvious level it refers to physical and mental pain. As noted above, each of the six realms has its specific sufferings, some more subtle than others. But all the realms are marked by impermanence and uncertainty, the ever-present possibility that suffering may occur in the next instant. Thus, one of the fundamental tenets of Buddhism is that the world of rebirth, a world in which each being has already been born and each being has already died countless times in the past, can never be a place of lasting peace.

The world is flawed by suffering; the second noble truth is that this suffering has an identifiable origin. According to Buddhist doctrine, all cases of pain, without exception, are the result of an action performed in the past by the person who undergoes the pain. This is their cause, this is their origin (*samudaya*), the name of the second noble truth. Thus, Buddhism recognizes no suffering as truly "innocent." The origins or causes of suffering are only two, called *karma* and *klesha* in Sanskrit. Let us consider each in turn.

First is the famous doctrine of *karma*, a Sanskrit word that simply means "action." According to the religious traditions of ancient India, good actions— good karma—result in feelings of pleasure in the future, and evil actions— bad karma—result in feelings of pain, with the meanings of "good" and "evil" (a more literal translation would be "virtuous" and "nonvirtuous") specified and enumerated. Typically, ten negative actions are listed. Much might be said about these ten and how they compare to the ethical systems of other religions; here it suffices to simply observe that each represents a form of harm to others, whether physical, verbal, or mental. They are thus divided into three groups, depending on their source. The three negative actions done with the body are killing, stealing, and committing sexual misconduct. The four negative actions done with the voice are lying, speaking divisively, speaking harshly, and speaking senselessly. The three negative actions done with the mind—and it is important to note that thoughts also have karmic effects—are coveting, wishing that harm come to others, and holding wrong views (variously described, but here referring specifically to the mistaken view that actions do *not* have consequences). As the Indian master Naropa remarked, "Samsara is blaming others." He likely meant that as long as one continues to imagine that something (like bad luck) or someone (like an enemy) is the cause of one's suffering, one will continue to be reborn in the cycle of birth and death called samsara. In fact, nothing, and no one, is to blame but oneself. When one realizes that all suffering is the result of one's own decisions and one's own actions, one will seek to understand how to put an end to actions and their effects, and hence an end to suffering and rebirth.

These ten negative actions plant a seed in the mind of their agent, and that seed will one day—perhaps tomorrow, perhaps a thousand lifetimes in the future—fructify as an experience of pain. Since the cycle of rebirth has no beginning, the number of past lives of each being in the universe is limitless, and thus the number of deeds done in the past is boundless. These deeds, whether positive or negative, create the future. They create the environment, they create the beings that inhabit that environment, they create the experiences of those beings. And those experiences are ultimately unsatisfactory because they are unpredictable, shaped by factors beyond one's control. There is a Buddhist saying, "All that is independent is a form of happiness; all that is dependent is a form of suffering."

If samsara were simply a matter of good deeds and bad deeds, of positive and negative karma, then liberation from samsara would be impossible, because it is impossible to cease all action. It is therefore necessary to seek the cause of the negative actions that in turn give rise to all manner of pain. We now come to the second of the causes or origins of suffering that constitute the second noble truth. According to the Buddha, these are states of mind that he called *kleshas*, "afflictions" (or, less literally, "negative emotions"). In a sense, the afflictions are not a second cause of suffering. Rather, karma is the cause of suffering, and klesha is the cause of karma—the cause of the cause. The afflictions are variously specified, but three, called the "three poisons," are particularly important: desire, hatred, and ignorance. When one considers what motivates the ten negative actions above, desire and hatred are their prime drivers: people kill because of hatred, they steal because of desire, they wish harm to others because of hatred, they covet because of desire. But desire and hatred also have a cause, and that cause is ignorance. Here, ignorance has an active meaning: not so much the absence of knowledge as a misunderstanding of the true nature of things. The Sanskrit term is *avidya*, literally "nonknowledge," but one of its synonyms is *moha*, denoting a dark and deluded state of mind. In Buddhism, ignorance most commonly is a false belief—in particular, the belief that in each being in the universe, there is a permanent, partless, and independent self or soul, a self that is the agent of actions, a self that goes from lifetime to lifetime. It is the Buddha's fundamental claim that such a self does not exist and has never existed; instead there is only the illusion of self, the false belief that there is something real and enduring located somewhere in the mind or body—the thinker of thoughts, the doer of deeds, the enjoyer of pleasures—something that must be soothed with desire and protected with hatred, something that lasts more than an instant. But such a self is an illusion, and the belief in such a self is the cause of all the suffering in the universe. If ignorance is the false belief in self, then wisdom is the confident knowledge that there is no self.

The Buddhist claim is that the collection of physical and mental constituents that we call the person consists entirely of perishable parts—arising, abiding, and disintegrating in each instant. This does not mean that the person does not exist, or that there is no agency or action, or that rebirth is impossible. Rather, rebirth is simply another of the endless changes that this impermanent process called the person undergoes, changes that occur every instant. The only difference is that at the end of one lifetime, this impermanent person is blown to the next lifetime by the winds of karma. The second of the four truths is thus called origin (*samudaya*). The first two truths—suffering and origin—describe the predicament.

The last two truths provide the solution. Ignorance is the cause of desire and hatred, and desire and hatred are the cause of negative actions, and negative actions cause suffering. Thus, the Buddha argued, if ignorance can be destroyed, then all that follows from it will come to an end. The third truth is therefore called "cessation" (*nirodha*). Suffering will cease if ignorance can be destroyed by wisdom. And because the root cause of the entire cycle of rebirth is this ignorance, wisdom will bring the entire edifice that is samsara tumbling down—at least for that individual. On the night of his enlightenment, the Buddha declared, "All your beams are broken. The ridgepole is shattered." The goal of the path, then, is to bring about the cessation of each of the accumulated causes of future suffering and rebirth. The state of their collective cessation is called *nirvana*. Perhaps the most famous of Buddhist terms, it literally means "blown out" or "extinguished," like a flame. The fuel that feeds the fire is gone, and the fire goes out. Here, the fuel of ignorance has been destroyed, and that destruction is so complete that it not only stops the production of future karma but also incinerates all the unripened seeds of past deeds accumulated over countless lifetimes in the past. In the case of the Buddha, and those who followed the path he set forth, nirvana occurs in two phases. The first occurs when all the causes for future rebirth are destroyed; this might be called "seeing nirvana" and is not followed by death. The Buddha saw nirvana at the age of thirty-five; he did not die until he was eighty. Since the causes of the present lifetime have already been set in motion at birth, what is destroyed is the causes for future lives. And so, the Buddha lived out his life, and when the cause of that life was spent, he experienced nirvana in the second sense of the term: he entered nirvana. Hence, the third truth postulates a state of freedom from suffering and its causes, a state that is entered at the only death that is not followed by rebirth. But exactly what that state is like is difficult to say, because, at least as conceived early in the history of Buddhism, nirvana is also the state of the cessation of mind and body, making it a state of freedom that is literally inconceivable.

The fourth truth is the truth of the path, the path to the cessation of all suffering. In his first sermon (see *Setting the Wheel of the Dharma in Motion*, p. 177), the Buddha characterizes this path as eightfold— right view, right intention, right speech, right action, right livelihood, right effort, right mindfulness, right meditation—and each aspect receives considerable commentary. However, a somewhat more straightforward, and shorter, list describes the path to nirvana in terms of three trainings under which the eightfold path is often subsumed: the training in ethics, the training in meditation, and the training in wisdom. Here, ethics refers to the restraint of negative deeds of body and speech, especially through the taking and keeping of vows, whether the five vows of the layperson or the 253 vows (as enumerated in one of the major orders) of a monk. It is only when body and speech have been controlled through ethics that one can begin to control the mind through meditation. In this context, meditation (*samadhi*) is the practice of bringing the wild elephant of the mind under control and developing powers of concentration that enable one to focus single-mindedly on one object for a prolonged period of time. Such a concentrated mind is necessary to undertake the third training, the training in the wisdom that will destroy the seeds of ignorance. That is, a simple intellectual understanding that there is no self is necessary but not sufficient to achieve liberation from suffering. One must understand the reality of no-self with a mind that has developed strong powers of concentration. It is said that the ax may be sharp, but a strong arm is required to uproot the tree of suffering. That is, in order to destroy suffering at its root, one needs both the sharp insight of wisdom and the power of concentration.

This, in broad paraphrase, is how the Buddha's first teaching after his achievement of enlightenment has been generally understood across the various Buddhist traditions of Asia. Though these have been long known in English as the "four noble truths," the traditional commentaries indicate that a better translation might be the "four truths for the noble"—that is, the four truths for those on the path to enlightenment. Benighted beings would not agree that all life is characterized by suffering and that the root cause of that suffering is their own ignorance. One must understand this truth about suffering in order to successfully end it. One must understand that suffering is produced by its origin, that cessation results from following the path. Indeed, one sees immediately a strong emphasis on causation: suffering is caused by negative actions, which in turn are caused by desire and hatred, which are themselves caused by ignorance; by destroying the cause one can destroy the effect; and through the practice of the path, one can achieve nirvana.

Not long after his enlightenment, one of the Buddha's disciples was asked to summarize what he learned from his teacher. The monk said, "For those things that have causes, he has set forth the causes. And he has also set forth their cessation. The great renunciant has so spoken." According to the story, by simply hearing these words, the person who requested the summary reached the first stage of insight into nirvana. This statement is the most famous in all of Buddhism; when it was written down it served as a substitute for a relic of the Buddha's body.

The Presence of the Buddha

But who was the Buddha, the great renunciant? As noted above, we do not know precisely what he taught, yet we do know what teachings the various traditions of the Buddhist world attribute to him. When one gathers together the various canons—the Pali canon, the Tibetan canon, the Chinese canon—his teachings exceed anything that a single person could produce. Regardless of which particular tradition one might consider to be the most authentic, the most faithful to his teachings, its canonical texts fill thousands of pages. Unlike Judaism, Christianity, and Islam, Buddhism does not have a single sacred text. But if Buddhism is not a "religion of the book," it is a "religion of the books." The Buddha is said to have taught the dharma for forty-five years, during which he was renowned for his "skillful methods" in teaching what was appropriate to particular disciples and what was appropriate to the moment. This motif of adaptation remained powerful in the tradition, providing an important impetus for the production of texts over many centuries and in many lands. Texts that represent "the word of Buddha" not only served to transmit Buddhism across Asia but were themselves objects of devotion, to be worshipped, recited, copied, translated, studied, and commented upon.

Only a tiny sampling from these canons is provided in this volume, providing just a glimpse of the scope and complexity of the Buddhist tradition. In reading through the sixty-seven selections from Buddhist texts here, one might continue to ponder the question: Who is the Buddha?

This is a question that Buddhists themselves have long sought to answer. In one sense, the answer is easy: The Buddha was an Indian prince who lived sometime around the fifth century B.C.E. He claimed to achieve enlightenment (*bodhi*, literally "awakening" in Sanskrit)—the salvific insight into the nature of reality that bestows liberation at death—at the age of thirty-five. He spent the rest of his life teaching others the path to that state of liberation, a state he called nirvana. But this account in fact tells us very little. One of the things left unmentioned is that all Buddhist traditions believe that there is more than one buddha. Multiple buddhas populate the pages of this book.

Regardless of one's perspective—whether it be that of the scholar of Buddhist history or that of the adherent of any of the schools of Buddhism—the Buddha did not come out of nowhere. As is clear from some of the readings here (e.g., see the *Tevijja Sutta*, p. 181), the Buddha rejected the authority of the Vedas, the sacred texts of Hindus, as well as the authority of the brahmin priests who recited them. Those priests declared that the Vedas were eternal, preexistent sound—sound not produced by either gods or humans; the authority of the Vedas derived in part from their antiquity. Innovation is rarely lauded in religion; when innovation occurs, it must be sanctified by the past. And thus it is not surprising that the Buddha did not claim to teach something new. Instead, he maintained that he discovered a truth, indeed a preexistent truth, that had been forgotten. Previous buddhas had come in the past, had discovered the path to nirvana, and had taught it to others. But with the passage of time, oblivion had set in; the path had become so overgrown that it was no longer visible and was eventually lost. And so another buddha had come who discovered the same path and taught the same truth. But that discovery had also been forgotten, and so another buddha—our buddha, "the historical Buddha"—had appeared in the world. According to some accounts, he was the seventh; according to others, he was the twenty-fifth. Indeed, the main concern of the early tradition seems to be describing the lives of the buddhas who had come before our Buddha, explaining not how he differed from his predecessors but how he was exactly like them. All buddhas are said to be remarkably similar in word and deed; they differ from each other in just a few ways, one of which is the circumference of their auras.

The appearance of a buddha in the world is a rare moment of profound significance, for when the world is bereft of the teachings of a buddha, there is no escape from suffering. In a famous scene after the Buddha's enlightenment, the god Brahma descends from his heaven and implores the Buddha to teach. Such a request might at first seem surprising. But from the perspective of Buddhist doctrine, there is no God, no eternal creator of the universe; there are only gods—beings who were once humans, animals, ghosts, and denizens of hell—who, through their practice of charity in the past, are reborn as gods in the future. Their lifetimes in heaven are long and blissful, but they come to an end. Thus, even Brahma, the powerful god of creation in the Hindu tradition, is also bound in the cycle of rebirth and does not know how to escape. He therefore asks the Buddha to teach him. The story also represents an attempt to portray the Buddha as superior to Hindu deities and to incorporate those deities, already in existence at the time of the rise of Buddhism in India, into a Buddhist pantheon. According to tradition, there are thirty-three gods in the Rig Veda, the most ancient of the Hindu scriptures. In Buddhism, one of the heavens of the gods—that is, those reborn as gods, who will one day be reborn as humans, animals, ghosts, or in hell—is called the Heaven of the Thirty-three. Thus, the gods of India were retained in Buddhism, but they were made subservient to the Buddha.

Yet another indication of the relations between the early Buddhist and Hindu communities was the Buddha's caste. Traditional Indian society was divided into four castes: the brahmins, or priests; the kshatriyas, or warriors; the vaishyas, or merchants; and the shudras, or servants. Only the first three "twice-born" castes were granted access to the sacred Veda. The brahmins were the Buddhist monks' chief competitors for both alms and patronage, and thus they receive particular criticism in the early literature (see the *Agganna Sutta* and *Tevijja Sutta*). Further evidence of this competition and sometimes antipathy is found in the Buddhist doctrine that prior to his final birth, the future buddha selects both his parents and his caste. A buddha, it is said, is always born as either a brahmin or kshatriya, choosing whichever is more highly respected at the time. The buddha of our age was born as a kshatriya.

The appearance of a buddha is said to be the culmination of a long process of perfection. The Buddha decided to set out on the path to enlightenment not during his youth as a prince but billions of lifetimes before. Over the course of the succeeding millennia, he had accumulated the great stores of virtue that would make it possible for him to discover the path to enlightenment without the instructions of a teacher, for buddhas appear only in a world in which the teachings of the previous buddha have been completely forgotten. He had vowed aeons ago to become a buddha in the far distant future, and from the time that he made that vow, he was called a *bodhisattva*: a being intent on *bodhi*, enlightenment.

Many reference books state that a bodhisattva is someone who "postpones his enlightenment." This definition is somewhat misleading. It is said that a person who vows to achieve buddhahood vows to do so in the presence of a previous buddha. At the time of the vow, the person understands that should he become a disciple of that buddha, he would quickly complete the path in that same lifetime to become an *arhat*, one who has destroyed the causes for future rebirth and who enters nirvana at death. But an arhat is not a buddha; an arhat must rely on the teachings of a buddha to achieve liberation, whereas a buddha does not. And so, out of compassion for the world, the bodhisattva decides not to become an arhat, vowing instead to become a buddha at a time in the far distant future when the path to liberation from suffering has been forgotten. The bodhisattva then sets out on the path to buddhahood at full speed, postponing nothing. But the path is very long, requiring billions of lifetimes.

Over the course of those lifetimes the bodhisattva who would become "our buddha"—known to the tradition as Gautama Buddha or Shakyamuni Buddha—practiced virtues called the perfections: giving, ethics, patience, effort, concentration, and wisdom, in the most famous list. After his enlightenment, he told stories of his previous lives, each of which he remembered, recounting his practice of virtue sometimes as an animal, sometimes as a human (see the *Shibi Jataka* and *Vessantara Jataka*, pp. 100 and 109). These are the famous jataka or "birth" stories, as well-known in some Buddhist cultures as the story of Prince Siddhartha. When he emerged from his mother to be born as that prince (exiting from under her right arm rather than by the usual route), he took seven steps and announced, "This is my final birth."

Much, then, is made of the birth of a buddha, and of the many births leading up to it. And much is made of his death. The story of the Buddha's passage into nirvana is told in the *Great Discourse on the Final Nirvana* (the *Mahaparinibbana Sutta*), a long section of which appears below. There, in a scene not included in that excerpt, the Buddha tells his attendant Ananda that a buddha is able to extend his life "for an aeon or until the end of the aeon" if one of his disciples asks him to so. But Ananda somehow does not take the hint, a sin of omission for which he was tried after the Buddha's death. To live in a time when a buddha walks the earth is considered fortunate beyond value, and Buddhists have long lamented the mistake of kind Ananda, who, blinded by the illusion of permanence, somehow imagined that the person he loved most would live forever.

And so the Buddha died. Before he died, he gave instructions on how his body should be burned. He said that what remained in the ashes should be buried within a hemispherical tomb built at a crossroads. Such a tomb or reliquary is called a *stupa*. As the sutra explains, there was a dispute over who deserved the relics, and they were eventually divided into ten parts, with a stupa erected for each. Later it is said that the Emperor Ashoka (see the *Ashokavadana*, or *Legend of Ashoka*, p. 238) broke open the existing stupas, gathered the relics together, and enshrined them in 84,000 others. These stupas took many shapes, from the domes of India to the spires of Cambodia to the pagodas of Japan. The Buddha was said to be alive within each stupa, and they became important places of pilgrimage. When there were not enough relics to be held by more stupas, they would instead enshrine the words of the Buddha, making use of a different kind of corpus (see the *Perfection of Wisdom That Rends Like a Thunderbolt* [the *Diamond Sutra*], p. 325).

Yet despite the continued presence of the Buddha in stupas erected to sanctify the landscape, his death marks the beginning of the disappearance of his teaching from the world. Indeed, the so-called First Council was said to have been convened shortly after the Buddha's death so that the monks could collectively remember what he had taught them before it was forgotten. The Buddha is said to have taught for forty-five years, from the time of his enlightenment to the time of his death, and there was much to remember. The Buddha himself is said to have predicted how his dharma would

The great stupa, or reliquary, of the Buddha at Sanchi in India. The stupa dates to the 3rd century B.C.E.

disappear in the centuries after his passage. Although often referred to as "the decline of the dharma," the decline is less in the dharma than in the ability of his followers to put it into practice. Eventually it will be completely forgotten. In the final stages of its disappearance, all Buddhist texts will vanish, the saffron robes of the monks will turn white (the color of the robes of laymen), all of the stupas will break open, and the relics of the Buddha will fly through the air to Bodh Gaya, the site of his enlightenment, where they will reassemble beneath the tree under which he had sat millennia ago. They will be worshipped one last time by the gods and then they will burst into flames.

But what is one to do until then? It is standard Buddhist doctrine that as the nirvana of the last buddha recedes further into the past, it becomes more difficult to practice the dharma, to the point that some have claimed that now no one can follow the path to nirvana. Attempts to deal with the problem of living in a time between two buddhas have been made across the Buddhist world. One approach is simply to wait. The next buddha, whose name is Maitreya ("Kindness"), has all but completed the long path of the bodhisattva and now abides in the Tushita ("Joyous") heaven, awaiting the appropriate moment to appear in the world. Buddhists have long prayed to be reborn as one of his disciples in the far distant future, or they have practiced alchemy to extend their life span until his advent.

In the form of Buddhism called the Mahayana, the "Great Vehicle," the consequence of the death of the Buddha has been confronted in a variety of ways. Proponents of one solution say that in fact the Buddha never died, he only pretended to do so in order to illustrate the truth of impermanence to his disciples. Indeed, the entire life story of the Buddha had been something of a pretense. In a famous scene from the *Lotus Sutra* (a selection from which is found on p. 278), a host of bodhisattvas rise out of the earth to pay homage to the Buddha. The Buddha explains that these are bodhisattvas that he himself had set on the path to enlightenment. But knowing the length of the bodhisattva path, a member of the audience points out the impossibility of the Buddha's having inspired so many in the few years since his enlightenment, saying, "Suppose a handsome man with dark hair, twenty-five years of age, were to point to a hundred-year-old man and say, 'He is my son.'" In response, the Buddha reveals that he achieved buddhahood aeons earlier and that his life span is beyond measure. The Buddha had pretended to agonize about leaving the palace, the Buddha had pretended to practice austerities for six years, the Buddha had pretended to achieve enlightenment under the tree, the Buddha had pretended to pass into nirvana. In fact, he had been a buddha for ages. In fact, he had not died and his life span is immeasurable.

In the early tradition, there was only one buddha per universe; there needed to be only one, for he taught the path to nirvana to all the gods and humans who had the good fortune to encounter him. Salvation was dispensed sequentially by a single teacher who appears in the universe once per age. The appearance of a buddha was considered a rare and momentous event in the history of the universe; indeed, it was an epochal moment, requiring all the resources of the entire universe to sustain his brief and majestic presence.

But in the Mahayana, the bodhisattva was no longer that rare individual who makes the remarkable vow to free all beings in the universe from suffering. The vow remains remarkable, but the bodhisattva became the ideal, and the norm. If, as the Buddha stated in the *Lotus Sutra*, all beings in the universe would set out on the bodhisattva path and become buddhas (a statement that some other Mahayana sutras did not make), then many beings were achieving buddhahood. They were not appearing in our world—Shakyamuni Buddha was still the buddha of our world—but they were achieving buddhahood in other realms, for there are multiple worlds. And thus, those who have been reborn in this world after the Buddha is gone, or at least appears to be gone, need not spend aeons waiting for Maitreya. It is possible for them to be reborn in their very next lifetime in a different world where a different buddha is presently teaching the dharma.

It is this possibility that motivates what is referred to as "Pure Land Buddhism" in the West, a form of Buddhism—or more accurately, a form of Buddhist practice—typically associated with Japan but with a long history in India and China. The most famous of those "pure lands" is Sukhavati, the Land of Bliss of the buddha Amitabha (see the *Sukhavativyuha Sutra*, p. 316). But the Mahayana sutras name many other buddhas and many other lands, and they explain how to be reborn in those lands and into the presence of those buddhas.

The simultaneous presence of multiple buddhas in multiple worlds meant that many teachings were being dispensed, with each buddha employing his skillful methods to set forth what was most appropriate for his time, his place, and his disciples. And thus, much as the teachings of the Mahayana came to be ascribed to the Buddha in texts that began to be composed some four centuries after his death, another genre of Buddhist literature called the *tantras* began to appear some ten centuries after his death—sometimes ascribed to Shakyamuni Buddha, sometimes ascribed to other buddhas from other worlds (see the *Tantra on the Complete Enlightenment of Vairo-chana*, p. 471). These texts did not simply teach the path to buddhahood but presented all manner of techniques for achievements both sacred and pro-fane (see the *Sarvadurgatiparishodhana Tantra*, p. 464); Victorian scholars condemned them as magic.

However, many of the tantras set forth techniques by which the long path of the bodhisattva—described both in the mainstream schools and in the Mahayana as requiring billions of lifetimes—could be radically curtailed; indeed, it was said that the bodhisattva path could be undertaken and com-pleted in a single lifetime. Various initiations, rituals, and vows were required; one must make mandalas and recite mantras. One also had to imagine one-self as now being a buddha, by—as an important Tibetan tradition describes it—"taking the result as the path" (see *Heart of the Practice*, p. 701).

In some ways, the idea was not new. Some of the most famous Mahayana sutras had proclaimed the existence of the *tathagatagarbha*, the "essence of the *tathagata*," the Buddha nature (see the *Tathagatagarbha Sutra*, p. 340). According to these sutras, all beings possessed within them, at least in an obscured form, the buddha that they were destined to become. From this point on, one sees a tension in the tradition, in India, Tibet, and East Asia alike, as questions arose about the nature of the Buddhist path. If each person possesses the buddha nature, what does it mean to be mired in igno-rance and what does it mean to be enlightened? Is the path a slow purging of pollution, accumulated lifetime after lifetime, the gradual lifting of the layers of obscurations that have prevented the mind from seeing things as they are? Or is the path a moment of recognition of an enlightenment that has always been the mind's true nature?

The great eleventh-century Bengali scholar Atisha often walked by an old woman who was alternately crying and laughing. Finally, he asked her why. She said, "I think about the terrible sufferings that sentient beings undergo. And so I cry. But then I realize that all of these sufferings result from one tiny error, and when this error is understood, they are freed from all suffer-ing. And so I laugh."

The Buddhist Canon

This story is not included in the selections that follow, but many works from the vast Buddhist canons are. When we consider the Buddhist canons, perhaps the first question we might ask is, "What language did the Buddha speak?" Like so many other things about his life, no one knows for sure. In ancient India, languages were divided into two categories. The first was San-skrit, a term that literally means "constructed, refined, perfected." It was originally considered not a separate language but rather a refined form of expression, especially suited for liturgical, philosophical, and literary pur-poses and used by cultured elites, including members of the brahmin caste. The other category was Prakrit, a term that literally means "natural, ordi-nary" and was used to refer to vernaculars, not a single language. The partic-ular Prakrit or vernacular that was likely spoken in the region and period of the Buddha is called Magadhi. However, discourses of the Buddha are not preserved in that language, much as the teachings of Jesus are not preserved in his native Aramaic. Instead, the teachings of the Buddha come to us largely in two other Indian languages, Pali and Sanskrit.

It is said that after the Buddha had assembled sixty disciples and guided each of them to enlightenment, he gave them these instructions:

> I am free, O monks, from all shackles, human and divine. You, O monks, are also free from all fetters, human and divine. Go forth, O monks, and wander, for the welfare of the many, for the happiness of the many, out of compassion for the world, for the benefit, welfare, and happiness of gods and humans. Let no two take the same road. Teach, O monks, the dharma that is of benefit in the beginning, of benefit in the middle, and of benefit in the end, with the meaning and the letter. Make known the holy life, which is utterly perfect and pure. There are beings with little dust in their eyes, who will be lost unless they hear the dharma. Some will understand.

It is largely on the basis of this statement that Buddhism is sometimes described as a "missionary religion." Yet Buddhism never developed the missionary apparatus of Christianity, nor was the failure of nonbelievers to convert said to lead to punishment in this life or damnation in the next. According to Buddhist doctrine, one encountered the dharma because of virtuous deeds done in the past; those reborn in Buddhist cultures, and hence with access to the dharma, were considered more karmically fortunate than those bereft of it. Because of future rebirths, there was the possibility, and in Buddhist lands the fervent hope, that one would encounter the dharma in future lives. Yet this relatively relaxed attitude toward conversion did not mean that Buddhists have ever believed that all paths take believers to the same mountaintop. Other religions offer, through their teachings of an ethical life, the possibility of favorable rebirth within the six realms of rebirth. But the path to liberation from the cycle of birth and death is set forth only in Buddhism. In effect, all paths lead to Everest Base Camp, but Buddhism is the sole route to the summit.

And so, in keeping with the Buddha's exhortation, the dharma was carried around the world, not as a disembodied truth descending on another culture from above but as a more material movement—of monks (sometimes in groups of two or more, despite the Buddha's instruction), and of Buddhist texts, relics, and icons—along trade routes and across deserts, mountains, and seas. In addition, monks also conveyed elements of Indian culture more generally that would be highly valued at their destinations, elements such as writing, medicine, and forms of art. Tibet, for example, did not have a written language until the introduction of Buddhism in the seventh century.

The Buddha is said not to have spoken in Sanskrit, the learned language of the priests of his day, but in the vernacular, and he is said to have forbidden monks from composing his teachings in formal verses for chanting. This prohibition implies that the content was more important than the form, and led to the notion that the dharma that the monks were to convey "for the benefit, welfare, and happiness of gods and humans" could be translated from one language to another. Thus, Buddhism has no sacred language comparable to Sanskrit for Hinduism, Hebrew for Judaism, or Arabic for Islam. Over the centuries, therefore, the act of translation (together with the sponsorship of translation) has been regarded throughout Asia as one of the most pious and meritorious acts that a Buddhist could perform. It was common for Buddhist kings to sponsor the translation of texts from one language into another: from Sanskrit into Chinese, from Sanskrit into Tibetan, from Tibetan into Manchu, from Pali into Burmese, and so on. Adding to Buddhism's ease of dissemination was that the primary objects of Buddhist devotion—texts, relics, icons—were all portable; stories of the transportation and enshrinement of a particularly potent image of the Buddha figure in the histories of almost all Buddhist cultures.

For the Theravada tradition of Sri Lanka and Southeast Asia, the language of the canon is Pali, one of the Indian vernaculars spoken at the time that Buddhism spread to Sri Lanka. (Despite claims to the contrary, it was not the language of the Buddha himself.) Pali functions for Theravada Buddhism much as Latin has traditionally done for Roman Catholicism: it is the language of the canon and the liturgy, but not the language spoken every day, even by learned monks. The various Theravada countries render Pali in their own script.

Most of the Mahayana texts, including the Mahayana sutras and treatises as well as the tantras, were composed in Sanskrit or some version of it (including something called Buddhist Hybrid Sanskrit); and from Sanskrit, these texts were translated into Chinese and into Tibetan. For the Buddhist traditions of East Asia, whether in China, Korea, or Japan, the Chinese translations became their canon; and exegetes, regardless of their nationality, first read these works and composed commentaries on them in Chinese. In the Tibetan Buddhist cultural domain, which included Mongolia, Tibetan was the canonical language. Thus, when scholars of Buddhism refer to the canonical languages of Buddhism, they typically have four in mind: Pali, Sanskrit, Chinese, and Tibetan. There is considerable overlap in the texts preserved in these languages, but one very significant divide.

The largest, and in many ways the most significant, overlap is the texts shared, in one form or another, by all traditions of Buddhism. In organizing this anthology, I have called these texts "the shared tradition" and placed them first. They include descriptions of the formation and structure of the universe; the collections of stories about the Buddha's past lives, called the jataka or "birth" stories; the biographies of the Buddha, from his birth to his death; the accounts of his teachings to his first disciples; and the *abhidharma*, technical works on psychology and epistemology. All of these works originated in India, and versions of them were translated from Indian languages into Chinese and Tibetan, and eventually into the vernaculars of the many other Buddhist cultures of Asia. Thus, although scholars often like to speak of "Buddhisms" rather than "Buddhism," it is important to recall how much the various Buddhist traditions share. The works placed in "The Shared Tradition" provide both the foundation for all forms of Buddhism and the touchstone for all subsequent developments. This, therefore, is the largest section of the anthology.

The great divide in the canon appears in the question of the Mahayana sutras. Composed in India beginning some four centuries after the death of the Buddha, they purported to be records of his words. Because these works went on to be so important in China and Tibet, one might imagine that they somehow carried the day. However, the influence of a religious tradition cannot always be measured by the size of its corpus. Indeed, it appears that most Buddhist monks in India regarded the Mahayana sutras as spurious. But many did accept them as authentic, and they continued to be composed in Sanskrit over the course of several centuries. Just as importantly, monks who regarded the Mahayana sutras as the word of the Buddha took those sutras to China, where the previous history of the tradition in India was unknown. Thus, the second section of this anthology is devoted to several of the most famous of the Mahayana sutras—works that were important in India, especially to those who accepted them, but were of much greater importance in East Asia, following their translation into Chinese.

With a few exceptions, the works presented in the initial two sections of the anthology are anonymous, works that begin with the standard line that opens all sutras: "Thus did I hear"; the rapporteur is unnamed but usually is assumed by the tradition to be the Buddha's personal attendant, the monk Ananda. However, there is a large body of Indian texts—works of philosophy, devotion, counsel, and polemic—by some of the leading figures in the history of Indian Buddhism. The third section of the anthology provides a selection of these writings, some of which went on to become important in China and all of which became important in Tibet.

Whether an Indian work went on to become important in China (and hence Korea and Japan) depended in large part on when it was written. Buddhism began to be transmitted to China in the first century of the Common Era, and by the end of the seventh century most of the texts that would define East Asian Buddhism had been translated into Chinese. Tibet received Buddhism from India much later, beginning in the seventh century, just as the transmission of Buddhism from India to China was drawing to a close. Following a lapse of almost two centuries, the transmission of Buddhism from India to Tibet resumed in earnest in the eleventh century. As a consequence, Tibet received a much fuller corpus of Indian works than China did; some works that would be very important in Tibet were less significant or even unknown in China. This was especially the case for the Mahayana treatises and the Buddhist tantras. Early treatises, such as those of Nagarjuna (see the *Madhyamakakarika* or *Verses on the Middle Way*, p. 366), were highly influential in both East Asia and Tibet, but later treatises, such as those of Shantideva (see *Introduction to the Practice of the Bodhisattva Path*, p. 395), were important only in Tibet. Some of the early tantras (such as the *Tantra on the Complete Purification of All Negative Places of Rebirth*, p. 464) were central to the development of Esoteric Buddhism in East Asia, while the accounts of the lives of many of the tantric saints (e.g., the *Lives of the Eighty-Four Siddhas*, p. 478), compiled rather late, were largely unknown in China, Korea, and Japan.

In selecting works for this volume, I have chosen to provide fewer and longer selections, rather than more and shorter ones, offering the text in full whenever possible. I have done so with the conviction that the power of the text derives at least in part from its development and its structure. Longer selections also provide the reader with the opportunity to identify the many shared themes and tropes that appear across Buddhist texts of all traditions. The section on Indian Buddhism, organized more or less chronologically, is followed by sections on China, Korea, Japan, and Tibet—the order in which Buddhism came to those countries. In all cases, however, the Indian

tradition must be assumed as an integral part of their Buddhism. For example, perhaps the most influential of all Buddhist texts in China and Japan
was the *Lotus Sutra*, which inspired both philosophical schools and a wide
range of popular practice. Indeed, each of the Mahayana sutras that appears
here was of great importance for East Asian Buddhism. Thus, all of the
works listed under China, Korea, Japan, and Tibet were composed by natives
of those lands on the Indian foundation.

Among Buddhist nations, China, Korea, and Japan form one group and
Tibet, Mongolia, and Nepal—a geographically contiguous region—form a
second. China received its Buddhism from India, and Korea and Japan received
their Buddhism from China (in Japan's case, initially via Korea). Thus, all the
works in the China section would go on to be important in Korea and Japan,
whereas the works in the Korea and Japan section remained largely limited in
influence to their respective homelands. Tibet, as already mentioned, is in
many ways a different case, having received Buddhism directly from India
and much later than did China, Korea, and Japan. Tibet inherited traditions
from the last centuries of Buddhism in India, as did Nepal, and these would
form the foundation for the Tibetan Buddhism that would spread to Mongolia, Bhutan, and other regions of the Himalayas. In the twentieth century,
Buddhism was brought from Asia to the West not by European travelers and
scholars, as had been the case in the eighteenth and nineteenth centuries,
but by Asian Buddhists themselves, both monks and laypeople from China,
Tibet, Vietnam, and Cambodia, often driven across the sea by the winds of
revolution and war.

Even though each Buddhist tradition claims to teach only what the Buddha himself taught, the nations touched by Buddhism have each made their
own contributions to its theory and practice. Just as the Vedic gods of India
were incorporated into the Buddhist pantheon and housed in the Heaven of
the Thirty-three, so the local gods of other Asian cultures would become
Buddhist deities, whether they were originally the mountain spirits of Tibet
or the *kami* of Japan. Rather than simply commenting on the sutras received
from India, Buddhist authors would sometimes write their own, presenting
them as originally Indian works spoken by the Buddha himself and beginning "Thus did I hear." This genre of "Buddhist apocrypha" constitutes an
important form of Buddhist literature, one that even spread to the United
States when the Zen poet Gary Snyder wrote the "Smokey the Bear Sutra"
(see p. 777), in which the Buddha manifests himself in the form of a local
deity of the American West and teaches that "all true paths lead through
mountains."

The need to present new works in the ancient voice of the Buddha suggests that Buddhism is a profoundly retrospective tradition. And indeed,
from one perspective, all Buddhist texts are commentaries, each attempting
to articulate the silent content of the Buddha's enlightenment so many centuries ago. It is also the case, in a more prosaic sense, that commentary is one
of the most important genres of Buddhist literature; the idea of the "root text"
with layers of commentary and subcommentary abounds throughout the
Buddhist world. Each of the Buddhist traditions of Asia has its own "golden
age" (variously identified), but by the seventeenth century, much Buddhist
literature across Asia was taking the form of commentary (with some notable
exceptions, as in Tibet). Therefore, few works from that period are represented

in this anthology, which moves ahead to the nineteenth century and the formation of what has been called "modern Buddhism."

Buddhism and the West

The encounter of Buddhism with the West is a long and fascinating story, told here by five works under the heading "Modern Buddhism"—one from the end of the nineteenth century and four from the twentieth. Only in the nineteenth century did Westerners remove Buddhism from the catch-all category of paganism to view it as a world religion, a shift that largely reflected European scholars' new ability to read Buddhist texts in the original, especially in Sanskrit and Pali. This ability was gained just around the time that philologists were discovering the existence of a language family that they called Aryan and is today called Indo-European or Indo-Iranian, which includes Sanskrit, Persian, Russian, French, Italian, German, English, and, importantly, Greek and Latin. The Aryan language family did not include Chinese, Turkish, Arabic, or Hebrew. European scholars thus discovered a kinship between the classical language of India and the classical languages of Europe.

This discovery, which occurred at the end of the eighteenth century, coincided with the British East India Company's gaining control over much of India; India would become a colony of the United Kingdom in 1858. Britain's was not the first European interaction with India; Alexander the Great had led his troops across the Indus in 326 B.C.E., when Buddhism was just beginning. Modern contact is generally dated to 1498, when four ships under the command of Vasco da Gama landed on the western coast of India. By that time Buddhism had disappeared from India, the land of its birth, although it was flourishing almost everywhere else in Asia.

Buddhism came under assault early in India, in ways both direct and indirect. For example, during the first millennium C.E., Buddhism's holy of holies, the Bodhi tree under which the Buddha sat on the night of his enlightenment, was repeatedly cut down at the order of various Hindu kings—only to miraculously return. A more subtle attack sought to redefine the nature of Buddhism, incorporating the Buddha into the Hindu pantheon in a way that undercut his authority.

According to Hindu belief, the great god Vishnu appears in the world at crucial moments in different avatars, or incarnations, usually numbered at nine. The most famous are the seventh and eighth, Rama and Krishna, but long after his death the Buddha was named as the ninth. Each appearance of Vishnu, it is said, is intended to right a particular wrong, and the specific purpose of his incarnation as the Buddha was variously portrayed in the Hindu scriptures. In one well-known version, demons gain so much power through the recitation of the sacred Veda and the practice of asceticism that they challenge the supremacy of the gods. In order to deprive the demons of their power, Vishnu appears as a sage who condemns the practice of Vedic sacrifice, ignores caste distinction, and denies the existence of a creator deity. The demons become disciples of this new teacher, the Buddha, and embrace his teachings. As a consequence, they not only lose their power but are reborn in hell. Vishnu thus appears as the Buddha to deceive the demons, convincing them that important truths—Vedic sacrifice, caste distinction, and a creator god—are instead false. But in the Buddhist tradition, the Buddha did in fact reject these elements of Hinduism (though his attitude toward caste was more nuanced than modern accounts suggest). This story of the Buddha's incarnation as Vishnu—hardly an ecumenical embrace, as it is often portrayed—is not accepted by any of the Buddhist schools or reported with anything but condemnation in any Buddhist text.

It is important to note, however, that in conflicts between Buddhists and Hindus, even the more violent ones, the Buddhists were not always the victims. According to the *Great Chronicle* (Mahavamsa) of Sri Lanka, the Buddhist prince Dutthagamani defeated the righteous but Hindu king Elara in 164 B.C.E., killing him in a bloody battle in which each monarch was mounted on a war elephant. After his victory, the Buddhist prince is troubled by all the carnage he has caused. But a delegation of eight monks, all arhats (those who will enter nirvana at death), reassure him: "From this deed arises no hindrance to the way to heaven. Only one and half human beings have been slain here by thee, O Lord of Men. . . . Unbelievers and men of evil life were the rest, not more to be esteemed than beasts." The *Great Chronicle* explains their odd calculation: among the "millions" slain in battle (an obviously hyperbolic number), one person had taken refuge in the Buddha, dharma, and the sangha (making him half a human) and another who had done so had also taken the five vows of a Buddhist layman (making him a full person). The story of Dutthagamani continues to be told, and was offered in the late twentieth century in defense of the violence of Sinhalese Buddhists against Hindu Tamils in Sri Lanka. Dutthagamani is also remembered for building important stupas and for granting sovereignty over the island of Sri Lanka not to any king but to the relics of the Buddha.

Although Buddhism continued to thrive in Sri Lanka, it died out in India for reasons beyond theological polemics. Buddhism had been in decline in India, or at least certain regions of India, for centuries; the famous seventh-century Chinese pilgrim Xuanzang (see his *Great Tang Dynasty Record of the Western World*, p. 511) reports seeing stupas in ruins. The religious life of India, especially the life cycle rituals at its center, was increasingly controlled by Hindu priests, depriving Buddhist monks of the lay support they relied on for their survival. The intellectual vitality of the monastic tradition came to depend on large monastic universities, whose fortunes rose and fell with the level of royal patronage. Without these monasteries, Buddhism had little chance to survive in India.

The monastic universities of northern India became favored targets of Muslim troops. In 1193 they attacked Nalanda, the most famous of all the celebrated monasteries of India. At its height it housed some ten thousand monks and was considered the greatest center of Buddhist learning in the world, drawing students from across Asia. Its library was said to contain hundreds of thousands of manuscripts. The Muslim forces apparently mistook it for a fortress. Buddhists clearly regarded the Muslim armies with a combination of fear and contempt, blaming them for the decline of the dharma in India. An eleventh-century text, the *Kalachakra Tantra*, describes barbarians who drink camel blood and cut off the ends of their penises (i.e., practice circumcision), followers of one Madhumati (a Sanskrit approximation of "Muhammad"). The same text foretold an apocalyptic war in which

Buddhist armies would sweep south out of the Himalayas to defeat the barbarians and restore the dharma to India. Instead, Buddhism had essentially disappeared from India by the time Vasco da Gama arrived in 1498. In the nineteenth century, a new form of Buddhism would arise, originating not in India but in Europe.

Two factors—the European discovery of Sanskrit with its kinship to Greek and Latin, on the one hand, and the conquest of India by the British long after Buddhism had disappeared, on the other—were key to the development of Modern Buddhism. A common feature of colonialism is the denigration of the colonized culture, and in India the British condemned Hinduism as a form of polytheistic idolatry, filled with multiheaded and multiarmed gods, and overseen by a corrupt class of priests. For early European scholars, many of whom never traveled to Asia and knew it only from a relatively random group of texts, Buddhism offered an alternative. Here was a religion, or perhaps it was a philosophy, in which there was no God. The founder was a prince who had set out in search of life's meaning; having found it, he condemned the priests and their caste system (many of the British, German, and French scholars of Buddhism were for varying reasons strongly anti-Catholic), opening his new religion to all. Through their selective reading of Buddhist texts, unconstrained by contact with any living Buddhists, they painted a portrait of the Buddha as a man of (the) Enlightenment who was able to set forth a rational philosophy and an ethical way of life without a jealous God. And this founder taught in an Aryan language. Over the course of the nineteenth century, the verbal roots of the Aryan language turned into bloodlines: race science was born, as the creation of the category of Semitic languages and the Semites who spoke them gave an apparently natural foundation to centuries of prejudice against Jews and Muslims. In the process, the Buddha some two millennia after his death somehow became an ancient kinsman—an Aryan like the Europeans, not a Semite like Moses, Jesus, and Muhammad. At the time of the quest for the historical Jesus, European scholars set out on their own quest for the historical Buddha and discovered someone who taught what they called "original Buddhism," sometimes "pure Buddhism"—a Buddhism long dead in India (and thus all the easier to control from Europe), a Buddhism against which the other still living Buddhisms of Asia could be judged, and found to be lacking. The Buddhism that was known in Europe from such best-selling works as Sir Edwin Arnold's *The Light of Asia* (a favorite of Queen Victoria) derives from this process, as does the positive portrayal of Buddhism that persists in the West to this day.

But European and North American views of the Buddha were not uniformly positive. For the Christian missionaries who fanned out across the Buddhist world, Buddhism, like Hinduism, was a form of idolatry, and the Buddha was an atheist who taught a life-denying philosophy. During the latter half of the nineteenth century, Buddhist leaders in Asia responded to this criticism by importing to Asia, and sending into battle against the Christian missionaries, the ethical and human Buddha who had been invented in Europe. They were able to claim that Buddhism, rather than Christianity, was the religion most suited to the modern world. The reasons for its superiority were many, including what they saw as its compatibility with science: the mechanistic universe described by the Buddha seemed to anticipate the science of the day. This claim, used to defend Buddhism in Asia during the nineteenth century, would be used to promote Buddhism in the West during the twentieth century. And so Modern Buddhism was born.

The earlier Buddhist traditions of Asia had developed regionally, as contact with other forms of Buddhism usually occurred across local borders. The lineage of monastic ordination in the Theravada had been established in Burma by monks from Sri Lanka, and from Burma moved eventually to Thailand. When that lineage became threatened in Sri Lanka as a result of wars, a delegation of monks was invited from Burma around 1070, and another from Thailand in 1753, to come back to Sri Lanka and ordain Sinhalese monks. In the early centuries of Japanese Buddhism, monks would often make the perilous sea voyage to China to retrieve texts and teachings. Korean monks would travel to Chinese monasteries. Tibetans invited Indian Buddhist masters to Tibet, and Indian monks would sail to Sumatra to study there. Sometimes the journey was longer. The lineage of fully ordained Buddhist nuns was introduced to China in the fifth century C.E. by a delegation of nuns from Sri Lanka. However, the importance placed on foreign contacts waned as each local tradition developed and began to present itself as the repository of the true teaching with its own sacred sites. This pattern became increasingly common after India, once the place of pilgrimage shared by all Buddhists, lost its own Buddhist tradition. The development of modern travel, made possible in part by colonialism, encouraged greater contact between Buddhists; such contacts would be a key element in the development of Modern Buddhism. For example, heeding the claim of European scholars that the Pali tradition of Sri Lanka was the fullest remnant of original Buddhism, some Japanese monks traveled there to be ordained.

A central feature of Modern Buddhism was the belief that centuries of cultural and clerical ossification around the teachings of the Buddha could be reversed to reveal a Buddhism that was neither Theravada nor Mahayana; neither monastic nor lay; neither Sri Lankan, Japanese, Chinese, nor Thai. As a consequence, many of the distinctions important to Asian forms of Buddhism faded. For example, it was traditionally held that Buddhism could not exist without the presence of ordained monks, yet many of the leaders of Modern Buddhism were laypeople. Another tradition set aside was the sexism that has pervaded the Buddhist monastic orders, as women played key roles in the development of Modern Buddhism.

Two young monks, Sonada Monastery in Darjeeling, India, 1989.

However, Modern Buddhism did not dispense with monastic concerns. Rather, it blurred the boundary between monk and layperson, as laypeople claimed for themselves vocations of the traditionally elite monks such as the study and interpretation of scriptures and the practice of meditation.

Over the course of Buddhism's long history, most of its adherents have not meditated. Even in the twentieth century, the Buddhist monks and priests who accompanied refugee communities to America did not teach them how to meditate; instead they performed the rituals, especially funerals, that had long been among the central responsibilities of Buddhist monks. Yet when these monks came to America, those whose families had immigrated in the decades and centuries before—the so-called white Buddhists—wanted to learn how to meditate. And so the essential practice of Modern Buddhism is meditation. In keeping with the quest to return to the origin, Modern Buddhists looked back to the primary image of the tradition: the Buddha seated in silent meditation, contemplating the ultimate nature of the universe. An emphasis on this silent practice allowed Modern Buddhism generally to dismiss the rituals of consecration, purification, and expiation so common throughout Buddhist Asia as extraneous elements that had crept into the tradition to address the needs of those unable to follow the true path. Silent meditation enabled Modern Buddhism to transcend local expressions, which required form and language. And this same silence made it possible to move beyond sectarian concerns of institutional and doctrinal formulations by making Buddhism, above all, an experience.

This is not to say that Modern Buddhism has displaced or even overshadowed all other forms of Buddhism. Rather, it is useful to consider Modern Buddhism as itself a Buddhist sect of a distinctly new and international kind, unlike the previous national forms of Buddhism in that embracing it does not require the rejection of all other forms. For example, one may be a Chinese Buddhist and also be a Modern Buddhist. Yet one may also be a Chinese Buddhist without being a Modern Buddhist.

Asia is a vast continent of many nations, peoples, and languages. There is one element—whether labeled a religion or a culture—that has linked its inhabitants together. That common possession is Buddhism. Born in India, it is no longer widely practiced there or in adjacent Muslim Central and South Asia, where it had flourished for many centuries. Over those centuries it also evolved into undeniably many, undeniably different, undeniably local forms, each with its own language, in the broadest sense of the term. Yet through these transformations, Buddhism has traveled further and lasted longer than any other cultural creation in Asian history.

At this point, readers may still be asking themselves, "What does it mean to be a Buddhist?" As noted at the beginning of this introduction, the traditional answer is that a Buddhist is a person who seeks refuge in the three jewels: the Buddha, the dharma, and the sangha. But as the following chapters will make clear, it is difficult to say exactly who the Buddha was, and who the Buddha is. The word *dharma* remains resistant even to translation into English. The membership of the sangha is at once limited and vast. Each question leads to another, like an object placed between two mirrors. And even this analogy is a Buddhist allusion: Indra's net has a jewel at each knot in the pattern, each jewel reflecting all the others, just as everything in the universe arises in dependence on everything else.

I cannot promise that after reading the following sixty-seven selections, readers will have a definitive answer to the question "What does it mean to be a Buddhist?" But those who read these classic texts will find that question to be refined, deepened, and enriched. After two and a half millennia, the story of this endlessly fascinating, often surprising, sometimes shocking, sometimes profoundly calming engagement with the human condition continues to touch us, and never more deeply than in the words of those whom Buddhists revere as their greatest teachers, teachers who themselves struggled with this very question.

NOTE ON TRANSLITERATION

The Norton Anthology of World Religions policy for representing words from Indian languages and alphabets in the characters of the Roman (Latin) alphabet is to simplify as much as possible, since the text is designed for the general reader rather than the scholar. To enable consistent public pronunciation of key names and terms in the texts anthologized here, ś = sh, c = ch, and no macrons or other diacritics are employed to modify the Roman characters. Thus, "Śākyamuni" appears as "Shakyamuni," "bodhicitta" as "bodhichitta," and "Mahāyāna" as "Mahayana" (without macrons) in all texts in Sanskrit and Pali. In addition, all Chinese terms are transliterated in pinyin rather than Wade-Giles. In this way, besides enabling consistent classroom and other public pronunciation, we obviate the confusion that might arise from citing several texts in a given language, each from a scholar who uses a different system of transliteration.

Chronology

566 B.C.E. Birth of the Buddha, according to the "long chronology"

551–479 B.C.E. Life of Confucius

539 B.C.E. Conquest of Babylon by Cyrus the Great

486 B.C.E. Death of the Buddha, according to the "long chronology"

486 or 368 B.C.E. First Council at Rajagriha, India

448 B.C.E. Birth of the Buddha, according to the "short chronology"

386 or 268 B.C.E. Second Council at Vaishali, India

368 B.C.E. Death of the Buddha, according to the "short chronology"

327 B.C.E. Alexander the Great invades India

265–232 B.C.E. Reign of Ashoka, emperor of India and patron of Buddhism

ca. 250 B.C.E. Buddhism established in Kathmandu Valley, Nepal
Third Council at Pataliputra in India under Ashoka
Buddhism established in Sri Lanka with mission of Ashoka's son Mahinda

247–207 B.C.E. Reign of Sri Lankan king Devanampiya Tissa, first royal patron of Buddhism

221 B.C.E. Earliest linking of fortifications into Great Wall of China

162 B.C.E. The Buddhist king Dutthagamani defeats the Hindu king Elara in Sri Lanka

ca. 155–130 B.C.E. Reign of Indo-Greek King Menander (Milinda), patron of Buddhism

ca. 25 B.C.E. Recording of Pali canon under King Vattagamani of Sri Lanka

1st century B.C.E. Emergence of Mahayana Buddhism in India
Bharhut and Sanchi stupas established in India
Earliest phase of construction at Ajanta cave temples in India

ca. 4 B.C.E. Birth of Jesus in Bethlehem

early 1st century C.E. Karli cave temple complex in Maharashtra, India, established

1st century C.E. Buddhism spreads from Bactria (modern Afghanistan) throughout Central Asia

67 C.E. Indian Buddhist monks said to arrive at the court of Emperor Ming of China

70 C.E. Destruction of the Second Temple in Jerusalem

1st–2nd centuries C.E. Earliest Buddha images in Mathura and Gandhara, India

ca. 100 C.E. *Lotus Sutra* composed in India

ca. 127–51 Reign of Indian king Kanishka, patron of Buddhism

148 Parthian translator An Shigao arrives at Chinese capital of Luoyang

ca. 2nd century Life of Nagarjuna

2nd–3rd centuries Development of Mathura art in India

ca. 200 Spread of Buddhism to Burma, Cambodia, Laos, and Vietnam
Construction of pagodas at Luy-lau in Vietnam

286 *Lotus Sutra* translated from Sanskrit into Chinese

3rd–5th centuries Construction of caves and images at Bamiyan in Afghanistan

312 Emperor Constantine converts to Christianity

4th century Lives of Asanga and Vasubandu

ca. 362 Arrival of the relic of the Buddha's tooth in Sri Lanka

366 Beginning of Dunhuang cave construction in China

372 Chinese monk Shundao arrives in Korean state of Koguryo, formally introducing Buddhism into the Korean Peninsula

399–414 Chinese monk Faxian's travels to India

4th–5th centuries Height of Anuradhapura period in Sri Lanka

401 The translator Kumarajiva arrives at the Chinese capital

ca. 425 Indian monk Buddhaghosa composes the *Visuddhimagga* and edits the Pali canon

ca. 450 Founding and flourishing of Nalanda University in India

477–495 Construction of Sigiriya rock-cut monastery in Sri Lanka

484 Monk Nagasena's embassy from Cambodia to China

ca. 5th century Bronze Buddha of Sungai Kolok and Korat in Thailand
Mahabodhi Temple constructed at Bodhgaya in India

ca. 5th–6th centuries Buddha statues in South Indian style made in Cambodia

5th–6th centuries Development of major cave temples at Yun'gang and Longmen in China

5th–11th centuries Thaton kingdom, center of Mon and Buddhist culture in Burma

ca. 500 Buddhist rock carvings made at Ajanta, Ellora, in India

ca. 500–700 Buddhist paintings at Qizil caves in China

520 Bodhidharma said to arrive in China with Chan teachings

538–597 Life of Tiantai Zhiyi, founder of the Tiantai sect of Buddhism in China

552 Buddhism officially adopted in Japan from Korean state of Paekche

ca. 570–632 Life of Muhammad

574–622 Life of Prince Shotoku in Japan

ca. 580 Indian monk Vinitaruci brings Chan Buddhism to Vietnam

ca. 6th century Gupta influence from northern India seen in Buddhist statuary in Thailand
Buddhist monuments at Nakhon, Panthom, Ku Bua, and U Thong in Thailand

6th–7th centuries Rise of Buddhism in Indonesia
Buddhist art flourishes in Korean states

7th century Buddhist communities established in Indonesia
Beginnings of Shrivijaya kingdom in Sumatra, Indonesia
Spread of Mahayana in Southeast Asia

ca. 600 C.E. First datable use of the term "Mahayana" in Indian inscriptions

605–647 Reign of Indian king Harsha Vardhana, patron of Buddhism

607 Horyuji temple founded in Japan

617–686 Life of Korean monk Wonhyo

629–45 Xuanzang's visit to India

638–713 Life of Huineng, sixth Chan patriarch, in China

ca. 640 Foundation laid for Jokhang Temple in Lhasa, Tibet

671–95 Yijing's visit to India

699 Fazang lectures on the *Avatamsaka-sutra* and builds Huayan sect in China

8th century Spread of Vajrayana in India
Odantapuri Monastery founded in Bihar, India
Shantideva composes *Bodhicharyavatara* in India
Borobudur Temple constructed in Java

710–784 Nara period in Japan, during which Buddhism became firmly established

711–718 Muslim Arabs conquer much of Spain

720 Tantric masters Vajrabodhi and Amoghavajra arrive in Chinese capital

745 Chan monk Shenhui extols the teachings of the Chan patriarch Huineng in the *Platform Sutra*

ca. 750 Pala dynasty established in India

767–822 Life of Saicho, founder of the Tendai sect of Japanese Buddhism

ca. 770 Indian tantric master Padmasambhava invited to Tibet and construction of Samye Monastery begins

774–835 Life of Kukai, founder of the Shingon sect of Japanese Buddhism

777–797 Buddhist establishments at Anuradhapura and Polonnaruwa in Sri Lanka

ca. 797 Debate at Samye Monastery in Tibet between the Chan monk Moheyan and the Indian monk Kamalashila over sudden vs. gradual enlightenment

ca. 798 Sailendra dynasty established in Java; patronage of Mahayana

ca. 8th century Life of tantric master Saraha in India

late 8th century Mahayana spreads in Vietnam

9th century Mahabodhi Temple at Bodhgaya in India restored
Surge of Mahayana Buddhism in Southeast Asia

ca. 800 Vikramashila Monastery founded in India

828 First mountain site of Nine Mountain School of Son founded in Korea

ca. 840 South Indian invasion of Sri Lanka, sack of Anuradhapura

842 Assassination of Tibetan king Lang Darma, ending the Tibetan monarchy

842–845 Huichang persecution of Buddhism by Emperor Wuzong in China

866 Death of Chan master Linji

868 *Diamond Sutra*, oldest extant printed book, printed in China

875 Great Mahayana temple of Dong-duong founded in Champa, Vietnam

10th century Decline of Mahayana Buddhism in Maenam Basin in Thailand

958–1055 Life of translator Rinchen Zangpo, who helped reestablish Buddhism in Tibet

983 First printing of Chinese Buddhist canon completed in China

985 Copy of Udayana Buddha image produced for Chonen at Seiryoji, Japan

988–1069 Life of tantric master Tilopa in India

996 Founding of Tabo Monastery in western Tibet

late 10th century Mahayana renaissance in Cambodia

11th century Life of tantric master Naropa in India

1010 Koryo dynasty Korean king orders carving of complete Buddhist canon; destroyed in 1232 by Mongols

1028/40–1111/23 Life of Milarepa, the famous hermit-saint of Tibet

1042 Atisha arrives in Tibet from India

1044–1077 Reign of King Anawartha in Burma and construction of Shwezigon pagoda

1044–1287 Kingdom of Pagan in Burma

1063 Founding of the Great Relic Monastery at Lamphun in Thailand

1073 Founding of Sakya Monastery in Tibet

1089–1163 Life of Chan master Dahui in China

1096–1099 First crusades

ca. 1100 Mahabodhi Temple in India restored by Burmese

1113–ca. 1145 Reign of Suryavarman II in Cambodia; Angkor Wat founded as Vaishnavite temple

1118–ca. 1220 Khmer expansion into the Vientiane area of Laos

1133–1212 Life of Honen in Japan, founder of the Jodoshu or Pure Land sect

1141–1215 Life of Eisai in Japan; Rinzai sect of Zen established

1153–1186 Reign of Parakramabahu I in Sri Lanka

1158–1210 Life of Buddhist monk Chinul in Korea

1173–1262 Life of Shinran in Japan, founder of the Jodo Shinshu or True Pure Land sect

1181–ca. 1218 Reign of Jayavarman VII in Cambodia; state support of Mahayana Buddhism, construction of Bayon and other Buddhist monuments

1187–1196 Reign of Nissankamalla in Sri Lanka, patron of Buddhism

1193 Nalanda Monastery in India sacked by Muslim troops

1200–1253 Life of Dogen in Japan; establishment of Soto Zen sect of Japanese Buddhism

ca. 1220–1250 Thai kingdom of Sukhothai founded; promotion of Theravada Buddhism

1222–1282 Life of Nichiren in Japan; Nichiren sect established

1236 Korean court orders carving of second set of woodblocks of the Buddhist canon, the Koryo taejanggyong

1236–1270 Reign of Parakramabahu II in Sri Lanka

1247 Meeting of Sakya Pandita of Tibet and Mongol Godan Khan, leading to Mongol patronage of Tibetan Buddhism

1279 Latest extant inscriptions of any Theravada nunnery in Burma

1279–1316 Sukhothai kingdom expands into Vientiane region of Laos

14th century Editing of Tibetan canon by Buton

1327 King Jayavarman Paramesvara establishes Theravada Buddhism in Cambodia

1350 Thai kingdom of Ayutthaya founded

1353–1373 Theravada promoted as state religion in Laos by Fa Ngum, who brings Prabang Buddha statue from Angkor

1357–1419 Life of Tsong kha pa, founder of the Geluk sect of Tibetan Buddhism

1360 Theravada adopted as state religion of Thailand

1392 Choson dynasty established in Korea, leading to persecution of Buddhism

1394–1481 Life of Zen master Ikkyu in Japan

15th–16th centuries Buddhist temples and monasteries at Pegu in Burma

1412–1467 Reign of Parakramabahau VI in Sri Lanka

1475 Buddhist council at Chieng Mai in Thailand

1523–1596 Life of Mangtho Ludrup Gyatso, Tibetan master of the Sakya sect

1532–1612 Life of Buddhist monk Yunqi Zhuhong, Chinese critic of Christianity

1570 Japanese general Oda Nobunaga launches campaign against Buddhism

1570–1662 Life of the First Panchen Lama in Tibet

1592–1598 Korean monks Ch'ongho Hyujong and Samyong Yujong help defeat Japanese Hideyoshi invasions

1600 East India Company charter granted by Elizabeth I

1617–1682 Life of Fifth Dalai Lama in Tibet

1642 Beginning of political rule by Dalai Lamas

1686–1768 Life of Zen master Hakuin in Japan

1687 Temple of the Tooth Relic established at Kandy in Sri Lanka

18th century King Kirti Rajasimha reinstates Buddhism by inviting Thai monks to his court
"Emerald Buddha" installed in Bangkok, Thailand
Expansion of European empires and colonies throughout Asia

1717–1786 Life of Jang-gya, Tibetan monk of the Geluk sect

1749 Mongolian canon completed

1808–1887 Life of Patrul Rinpoche, Tibetan monk of the Nyingma sect

1829 Prince Mongkut founds the Thammayut sect in Thailand

1846–1923 Life of Burmese monk Ledi Sayadaw

1864–1933 Life of Anagarika Dharmapala, Sinhalese advocate of Buddhism

1868 Meiji reforms of Buddhism begin in Japan, separating Shinto from Buddhism

1871 Fifth Theravada Council held at Mandalay, Burma

1870–1966 Life of D. T. Suzuki, Japanese Zen scholar

1873 Panadure Debate between Buddhist monk and Methodist minister in Sri Lanka

1875 Founding of the Theosophical Society by Helena Blavatsky and Henry Steel Olcott, supporters of Buddhism

1881 Founding by Thomas W. Rhys-Davids of the Pali Text Society, which sponsored the editing and translation of many Buddhist scriptures

1891 Founding of Maha Bodhi Society

1890–1947 Life of Chinese monk Taixu

1891–1956 Life of B. R. Ambedkar, an Indian untouchable leader who converted to Buddhism

1904–1971 Life of Shunryu Suzuki, Japanese Zen priest and founder of San Francisco Zen Center

1904–1982 Life of Burmese monk Mahasi Sayadaw

1906–2005 Life of Chinese monk Yin Shun

1910–1945 Japanese occupation of Korea

1924–1929 Taisho Shinshu Daizokyo edition of Chinese Buddhist canon printed in Tokyo

1935 Birth of Fourteenth Dalai Lama in Tibet

1937 Birth of Chinese nun Cheng Yen, founder of the Buddhist Compassion Relief Tzu Chi Foundation

1942 Founding of World Fellowship of Buddhists

1946 Founding of Soka Gakki, a sect based on the *Lotus Sutra*, in Japan

1955 Korean monks launch purification campaign to purge Japanese colonial influence

1959 Fourteenth Dalai Lama goes into exile in India

1989 Fourteenth Dalai Lama awarded Nobel Peace Prize

2006 In the United States, two Buddhists are elected for the first time to Congress

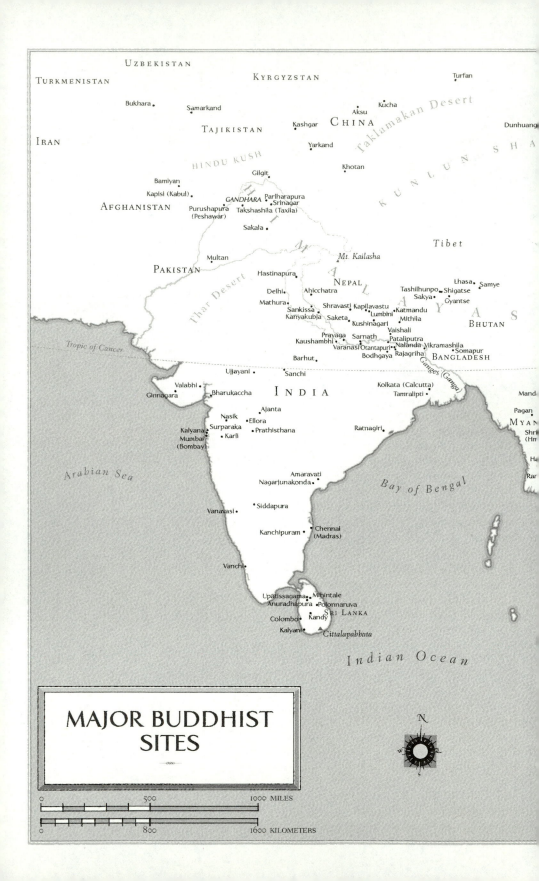

MAJOR BUDDHIST
SITES

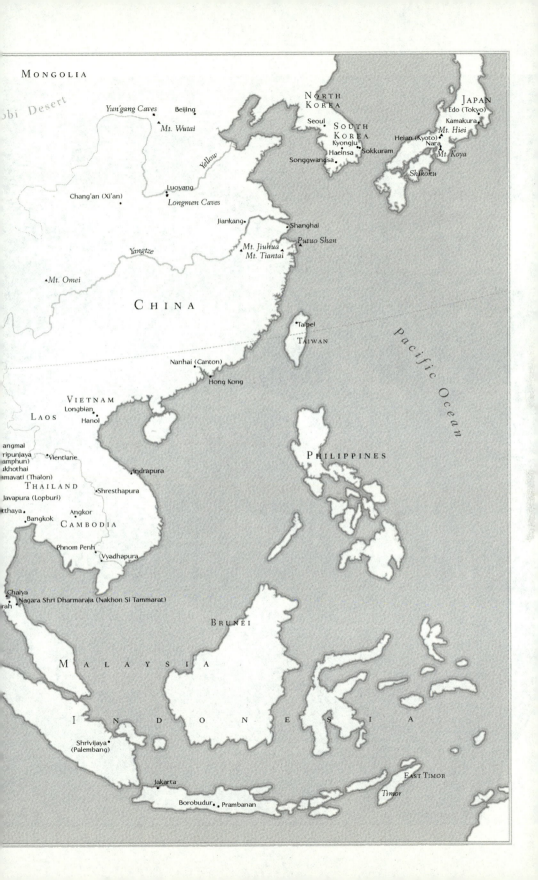

MONGOLIA

Gobi Desert

Yun'gang Caves   Beijing

Mt. Wutai

NORTH
KOREA

Seoul

SOUTH
KOREA   Kyongju
Haeinsa   Sokkuram
Songgwangsa

JAPAN
Edo (Tokyo)
Kamakura
Heian (Kyoto)   Mt. Hiei
Nara
Mt. Koya

Yellow

Luoyang

Chang'an (Xi'an)

Longmen Caves

Jiankang

Shanghai
Putuo Shan

Mt. Jiuhua
Mt. Tiantai

Shikoku

Yangtze

Mt. Omei

CHINA

Taipei

TAIWAN

Pacific Ocean

Nanhai (Canton)

Hong Kong

VIETNAM
Longbian

LAOS   Hanoi

PHILIPPINES

angmai
ripunjaya
amphun)   Vientiane
akhothai
amavati (Thalon)   Indrapura
THAILAND
Javapura (Lopburi)   Shresthapura
tthaya.
Bangkok   Angkor
CAMBODIA

Phnom Penh
Vyadhapura

Chaiya
Nagara Shri Dharmaraja (Nakhon Si Tammarat)
rah

BRUNEI

M A L A Y S I A

I N D O N E S I A

Shrivijaya
(Palembang)

EAST TIMOR

Jakarta   Timor

Borobudur   Prambanan

Buddhism in India

Buddhists traditionally trace what is called the *buddhadharma*, the teaching of the Buddha, back to buddhas of the ancient past; from the perspective of modern history, however, what we call Buddhism began with the historical Buddha, who, according to the most recent research, lived in northern India sometime in the fifth century B.C.E. He is said to have lived for eighty years. Relatively little is known about his life with historical accuracy, but his life, and his former lives, are recounted in detail by the tradition.

How much of what the Buddha taught was original to him is a question that scholars still ponder. Some was obviously borrowed from the religious milieu of the day, yet how much he borrowed from that milieu and how much he contributed to it remains an open question. It is clear from the Buddhist sources that he was but one of many teachers in northern India during this period. An early text called the *Discourse on Brahma's Net* (*Brahmajala Sutta*) lists sixty-two wrong views held by various ascetic groups in the Buddha's day. Also commonly mentioned are the "six heterodox teachers," who hold various wrong opinions: for example, one argues that positive and negative actions had no effect on the person who performed them, thereby denying the law of karma, while another is a materialist, denying the existence of rebirth.

The Buddha with his disciples. Gandhara, ca. 2nd century.

Although the Buddha famously denied the existence of a permanent self (*atman*), it is unclear whether he had any direct contact with the teachings of the Upanishads, the Vedic writings in which this self, and its identity with Brahman, the ultimate reality, is set forth. Early Buddhism and the Upanishads share a similar view of the law of karma and of the cycle of birth and death, called *samsara*, but the term does not appear in pre-Buddhist Upanishads, again raising the question of influence. The Buddha's most pointed criticism of his various opponents is directed at Vedic religion and its brahmin priests, with whom the community of Buddhist monks competed for alms and patronage. The Buddha was a member of the kshatriya caste, and much of his support came from regional kings of his caste, as well as from wealthy merchants in the burgeoning urban culture of northern India. These patrons contributed the dwelling places for monks that would evolve into the viharas, or monasteries, that were so central to Buddhism in India. The most famous of the Indian kings to propagate Buddhism was Ashoka in the third century B.C.E., though the depth of his devotion and extent of his support was likely less than Buddhist sources suggest.

According to the tradition, shortly after the Buddha's death, a group of arhats (enlightened monks) gathered for the first council. The word translated as "council" is *sangiti* in Sanskrit—literally, "singing together," and by extension "recitation." This term reminds us of the oral nature of Buddhist teaching in the first centuries following the master's death. And so it is said that at that first council, the monks gathered to recite everything that the Buddha had taught—both the sutras, or his discourses, and the vinaya, or the "discipline" (the code of monastic conduct). Additional councils would be held in the following centuries, usually to settle various matters of monastic conduct. Indeed, the interpretation of what was and was not permitted to monks, even regarding such apparently minor questions as whether a sitting mat could have fringe, led eventually to the formation of many Buddhist nikayas (sects), traditionally numbered at eighteen; the actual count seems to have been higher. One of those sects was called the Sthavira Nikaya ("Sect of the Elders," in Sanskrit), which is claimed to be a forerunner of the Theravada ("Way of the Elders," in Pali) tradition of modern Sri Lanka and Southeast Asia. (It is important to note that "Theravada" was not used as a term of self-identification in Southeast Asia until the early twentieth century.) These sects differed from each other more on monastic discipline than on doctrine, and each sect had its own monasteries. Buddhist monasteries were soon established throughout the Indian subcontinent, some growing to house thousands of monks. Although the architectural style of these monasteries varied by region and period, a common element was a stupa, or reliquary, said to hold a relic of the Buddha or another Buddhist saint.

Despite the ongoing emphasis on orality, a new genre of writing appeared in India some four centuries after the Buddha's death: texts that purported to be the "word of the Buddha." These were the Mahayana sutras, works that would become the most important Buddhist scriptures in East Asia. The origins of the Mahayana, or "Great Vehicle," remain unclear, but they seem to have involved groups of monks and nuns devoted to a single text, regarded by them as the word of the Buddha, who extolled the ideal of the bodhisattva, one who seeks buddhahood for the welfare of all beings, over that of the arhat, one who seeks his or her own liberation from suffering.

The arhat had been the ideal of the early tradition, but the Mahayana sutras described it as an expedient teaching and disparaged the path of the arhat as the Hinayana, or "Low Vehicle."

Because of the supremacy of the Mahayana in East Asia and Tibet, it is sometimes assumed that the earlier tradition was subsumed under it, as the Mahayana sutras themselves claimed. However, the reports of Chinese pilgrims indicate that the Mahayana remained a minority movement in India and that the pre-Mahayana sects, the texts that they considered canonical, and the doctrines they held to be orthodox remained prominent. The difference between this mainstream Buddhism and Mahayana Buddhism consisted largely in the former's rejection of the new sutras held to be canonical by followers of the Mahayana. In addition, the Mahayana added bodhisattva vows to the monastic code that was followed by the mainstream tradition. Although elements of the Mahayana were influential in Sri Lanka and Southeast Asia, it was the Theravada—which saw itself as a descendant of one of the mainstream schools and which viewed the Mahayana sutras as spurious—that would become dominant there. Thus, this anthology contains no separate geographical section for Sri Lanka and Southeast Asia, though works by authors from that region do appear. The works grouped here in "The Shared Tradition" are central to Pali Buddhism, and its tradition of exegesis and commentary on them is long and venerable.

The final major genre of Buddhist literature in India was the tantras, which began to appear in the seventh century C.E. These works set forth rituals and practices to produce all manner of supernatural powers, including the power to achieve buddhahood. Some of the tantras would make their way to China, whence they eventually came to Japan in the Shingon school of Kukai (see his "Treatise Distinguishing the Two Teachings of Exoteric and Esoteric Methods," p. 606). However, it was in Tibet that a more substantial canon of Indian tantric texts, and a tradition of Indian tantric exegesis, would prove most influential.

As Buddhism became institutionalized around monasteries, especially large monasteries that served as centers for the study of Buddhist doctrine, the fortunes of the tradition waxed and waned, largely in step with royal patronage. The last great period of royal support for Buddhism occurred in the Pala Dynasty (750–1174), which at its peak ruled much of northern and central India. After the collapse of this dynasty and the invasion of northern India by Muslim armies, the great monastic universities fell into decline and Buddhism eventually disappeared from the Indian subcontinent, with the exception of the Newars, a community that survived in the Kathmandu Valley of Nepal. It would return only in the latter half of the twentieth century, with efforts to convert members of the Dalit, or untouchable, community to Buddhism, and with the influx of Tibetan Buddhist refugees after their country became part of the People's Republic of China.

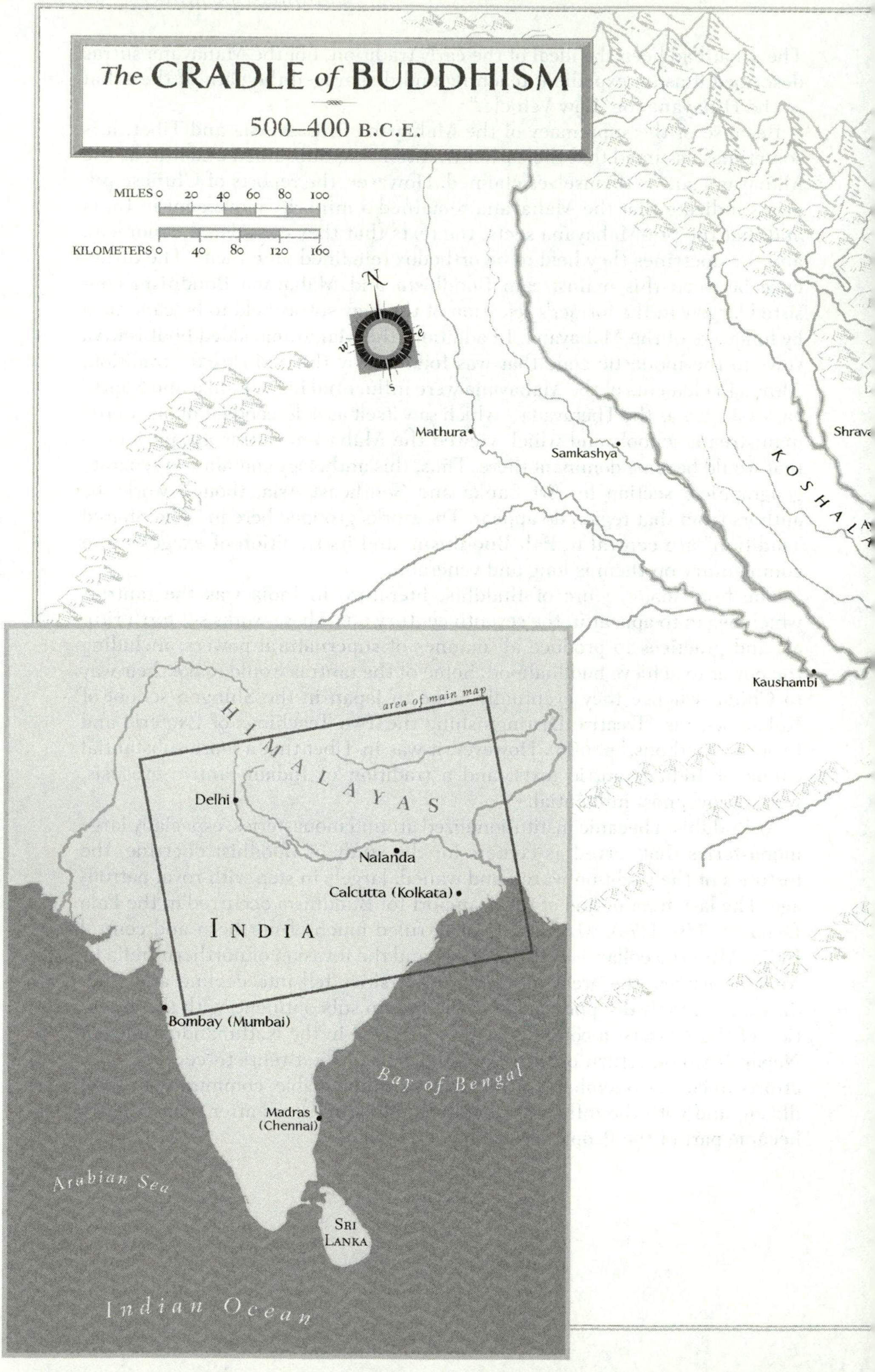

The CRADLE of BUDDHISM

500–400 B.C.E.

MILES 0 20 40 60 80 100

KILOMETERS 0 40 80 120 160

N

W E

S

Mathura

Samkashya

Shrava

K O S H A L A

Kaushambi

area of main map

H I M A L A Y A S

Delhi

Nalanda

Calcutta (Kolkata)

I N D I A

Bombay (Mumbai)

Madras (Chennai)

Bay of Bengal

Arabian Sea

SRI LANKA

Indian Ocean

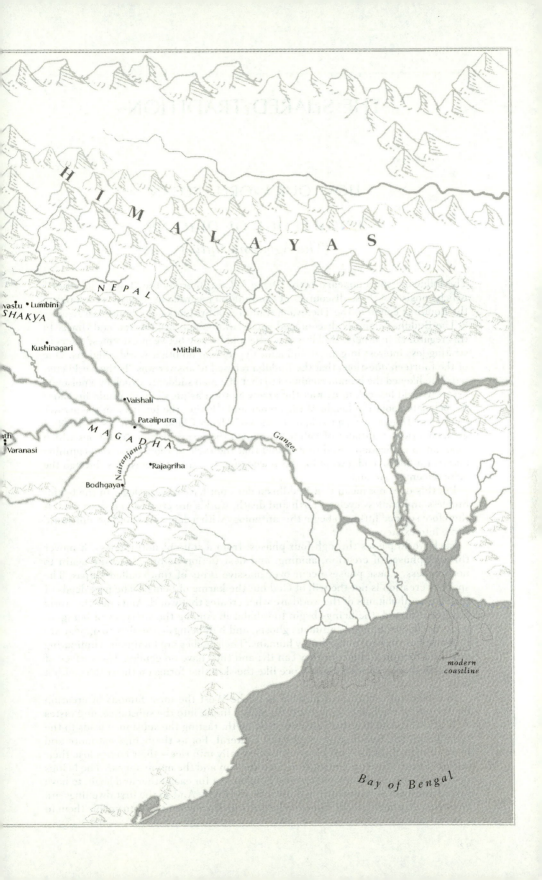

THE SHARED TRADITION

HOW OUR WORLD BEGAN

KNOWLEDGE OF ORIGINS
(*The Agganna Sutta*)

The following sutra appears in the *Digha Nikaya*, literally the "Long Collection," which consists of those discourses of the Buddha regarded as lengthy. It belongs to the Buddhist canon in the Theravada tradition of Sri Lanka and Southeast Asia.

The Buddha famously discouraged speculation about origins and end times. In this regard, as in others, Buddhism is "the middle way between extremes," demonstrating less interest in genesis and apocalypse than do other world religions. One of the fourteen questions that the Buddha refused to answer was "Is the world eternal?" He likened the human condition to that of a man suddenly struck by a poisoned arrow. Would he seek to extract the arrow as soon as possible, or would he pause to speculate about the height of the archer and whether the feathers on the arrow's shaft came from a stork, a hawk, or a peacock? Henry Clarke Warren (1854–1899), a great American translator of Pali texts, named these speculations "questions which tend not to edification." And so it is said that the cycle of rebirth has no beginning and that it has no end, except for those who put an end to it themselves through the achievement of nirvana.

But this does not mean that Buddhism does not have a cosmology. In the beginningless and endless cycle of birth and death, worlds are created and destroyed. It therefore seemed fitting to begin this anthology with a description of how our world came into existence.

Each world passes through four phases; from a state of nothingness, it moves through phases of creation, abiding, and destruction before returning again to nothingness. These phases occur over massive units of time, called *kalpas*. The spark of creation is not the will of God but the karma of beings. The past deeds of the future inhabitants of the world are what creates that world. And once the world has been formed, the beings begin to inhabit it. Among the six types of beings—gods, demigods, humans, animals, ghosts, and hell beings—the first to appear are humans, but they are not ordinary humans. Their bodies are luminous, eliminating any need for sun and moon; they can fly; and they have no gender. The surface of the earth is covered with a substance like the skin that forms on the surface of hot milk.

In a moment reminiscent of what is in the West the most famous of creation myths, one of the beings grows curious, dips a finger into the substance, and tastes it. It is sweet. And like that other creation myth, tasting the substance leads to the fall—but in the Buddhist story, the fall is literal. For as the beings eat more and more of the substance—which evolves eventually into rice—their bodies lose their natural luster, they can no longer fly, and the sun and the moon appear. The beings develop sex organs. Males and females develop lust for each other and begin to have sexual intercourse, scandalizing those who see them. And so the first dwellings are constructed, not to provide humans shelter from the elements but to enable them to have sex without being observed by others. They also begin hoarding the naturally growing rice, being too lazy to reap it in the morning and the evening. Eventually, the rice has to be cultivated, plots are assigned, private property established. Soon, theft occurs, requiring that the thief be punished, which in turn requires that a king be appointed to administer justice. And so from a single taste on the tip of a finger came human society.

The context of the Buddha's description of the origin of the world is noteworthy: it occurs as part of a polemic against the brahmin priests of Vedic Hinduism, with whom the Buddha and his monks competed for alms and patronage. The text begins with two recent converts from the brahmin caste approaching the Buddha. Before they can pose a question, the Buddha asks whether they have been reviled for joining the order of monks. They reply that they have indeed been abused for leaving the high class of brahmin priests to join "the base class of shaveling petty ascetics." The brahmins, following the Vedas, believed that they had emerged from the mouth of the god Brahma, whereas the warriors or kshatriyas (here, Khattiya) emerged from his arms, the merchants from his legs, and the servant class from his feet. Part of the Buddha's motivation in describing the origin of the world is to dispute the Hindu creation myth, making clear that all beings are born into the world as a result of their karma and that none is naturally more noble than another. At the end of the text, he explains that the original brahmins were those who left human society behind to meditate in the forest (as Buddhist monks do), but some of these brahmins were incapable of such practice and settled in villages where they "compiled books." It is these lesser brahmins who were the forebears of the brahmin caste. The Buddha concludes by declaring that true ascetics can come from any of the four castes.

We note, then, that in Buddhism, as in all religions, even the account of the beginning of time arises from a particular moment in history, and the elements of the creation myth reflect the concerns of that historical moment.

PRONOUNCING GLOSSARY

Abhassara: *ah-bas-sa-ra*
Agganna Sutta: *a-ga-nya soot-ta*
Ajjhayaka: *aj-jah-ya-ka*
arahant: *a-ra-hant*
Bharadvaja: *bah-ra-dvah-ja*
Brahma: *bra-mah*
deva: *day-va*
Dhamma: *dam-ma*
Digha Nikaya: *dee-ga-ni-kah-ya*
Gotama: *goh-ta-ma*
Jhayaka: *jah-ya-ka*

Khattiya: *kat-ti-ya*
mara: *mah-ra*
Migara: *mi-gah-ra*
parinibbana: *pa-rih-nib-bah-na*
Pasenadi: *pa-say-na-di*
Sakyan: *sa-kyan*
Sanankumara: *sa-nan-ku-mah-ra*
tathagata: *ta-tah-ga-ta*
Vasettha: *vah-sayt-ta*
Vessa: *vay-sa*

Thus have I heard. Once the Lord was staying at Savatthi, at the mansion of Migara's mother in the East Park. And at that time Vasettha and Bharadvaja were living among the monks, hoping to become monks themselves. And in the evening, the Lord rose from his secluded meditation and came out of the mansion, and started walking up and down in its shade.

TRANSLATED FROM the Pali by Maurice Walshe.

Vasettha noticed this, and he said to Bharadvaja: 'Friend Bharadvaja, the Lord has come out and is walking up and down. Let us approach him. We might be fortunate enough to hear a talk on Dhamma[1] from the Lord himself.' 'Yes, indeed', said Bharadvaja, so they went up to the Lord, saluted him, and fell into step with him.

Then the Lord said to Vasettha: 'Vasettha, you two are Brahmins born and bred, and you have gone forth from the household life into homelessness from Brahmin families. Do not the Brahmins revile and abuse you?' 'Indeed, Lord, the Brahmins do revile and abuse us. They don't hold back with their usual flood of reproaches.' 'Well, Vasettha, what kind of reproaches do they fling at you?' 'Lord, what the Brahmins say is this: "The Brahmin caste is the highest caste, other castes are base; the Brahmin caste is fair, other castes are dark; Brahmins are purified, non-Brahmins are not, the Brahmins are the true children of Brahma,[2] born from his mouth, born of Brahma, created by Brahma, heirs of Brahma. And you, you have deserted the highest class and gone over to the base class of shaveling petty ascetics, servants, dark fellows born of Brahma's foot! It's not right, it's not proper for you to mix with such people!" That is the way the Brahmins abuse us, Lord.'

'Then, Vasettha, the Brahmins have forgotten their ancient tradition when they say that. Because we can see Brahmin women, the wives of Brahmins, who menstruate and become pregnant, have babies and give suck. And yet these womb-born Brahmins talk about being born from Brahma's mouth . . . These Brahmins misrepresent Brahma, tell lies and earn much demerit.

'There are, Vasettha, these four castes: the Khattiyas,[3] the Brahmins, the merchants and the artisans. And sometimes a Khattiya takes life, takes what is not given, commits sexual misconduct, tells lies, indulges in slander, harsh speech or idle chatter, is grasping, malicious, or of wrong views. Thus such things as are immoral and considered so, blameworthy and considered so, to be avoided and considered so, ways unbefitting an Ariyan[4] and considered so, black with black result and blamed by the wise, are sometimes to be found among the Khattiyas, and the same applies to Brahmins, merchants and artisans.

'Sometimes, too, a Khattiya refrains from taking life, . . . is not grasping, malicious, or of wrong views. Thus such things as are moral and considered so, blameless and considered so, to be followed and considered so, ways befitting an Ariyan and considered so, bright with bright results and praised by the wise, are sometimes to be found among the Khattiyas, and likewise among Brahmins, merchants and artisans.

'Now since both dark and bright qualities, which are blamed and praised by the wise, are scattered indiscriminately among the four castes, the wise do not recognise the claim about the Brahmin caste being the highest. Why is that? Because, Vasettha, anyone from the four castes who becomes a monk, an Arahant[5] who has destroyed the corruptions, who has lived the life, done what had to be done, laid down the burden, reached the highest

---

1. Pali for *dharma*.
2. The god who persuaded the Buddha to teach (in Hinduism, the god of creation).
3. Pali for *kshatriyas*, members of the second of four castes of ancient India, sometimes called the warrior caste. The Buddha was himself a kshatriya.

4. Pali for "Aryan" (*arya* means "noble" in Sanskrit), an ethnic self-designation by the Vedic Hindus. The Buddha reinterpreted it to mean a spiritual nobility acquired through the practice of the Buddhist path.
5. Pali for *arhat*, one who enters nirvana at death.

goal, destroyed the fetter of becoming, and become emancipated through super-knowledge—he is proclaimed supreme by virtue of Dhamma and not of non-Dhamma.

> Dhamma's the best thing for people
> In this life and the next as well.

'This illustration will make clear to you how Dhamma is best in this world and in the next. King Pasenadi of Kosala[6] knows: "The ascetic Gotama has gone forth from the neighbouring clan of the Sakyans." Now the Sakyans are vassals of the King of Kosala. They offer him humble service and salute him, rise and do him homage and pay him fitting service. And, just as the Sakyans offer the King humble service . . . , so likewise does the King offer humble service to the Tathagata,[7] thinking: "If the ascetic Gotama is well-born, I am ill-born; if the ascetic Gotama is strong, I am weak; if the ascetic Gotama is pleasant to look at, I am ill-favoured; if the ascetic Gotama is influential, I am of little influence." Now it is because of honouring the Dhamma, making much of the Dhamma, esteeming the Dhamma, doing reverent homage to the Dhamma that King Pasenadi does humble service to the Tathagata and pays him fitting service:

> Dhamma's the best thing for people
> In this life and the next as well.

'Vasettha, all of you, though of different birth, name, clan and family, who have gone forth from the household life into homelessness, if you are asked who you are, should reply: "We are ascetics, followers of the Sakyan." He whose faith in the Tathagata is settled, rooted, established, solid, unshakeable by any ascetic or Brahmin, any deva or mara[8] or Brahma or anyone in the world, can truly say: "I am a true son of Blessed Lord, born of his mouth, born of Dhamma, created by Dhamma, an heir of Dhamma." Why is that? Because, Vasettha, this designates the Tathagata: "The Body of Dhamma", that is, "The Body of Brahma", or "Become Dhamma", that is, "Become Brahma".

'There comes a time, Vasettha, when, sooner or later after a long period, this world contracts. At a time of contraction, beings are mostly born in the Abhassara Brahma[9] world. And there they dwell, mind-made, feeding on delight, self-luminous, moving through the air, glorious—and they stay like that for a very long time. But sooner or later, after a very long period, this world begins to expand again. At a time of expansion, the beings from the Abhassara Brahma world, having passed away from there, are mostly reborn in this world. Here they dwell, mind-made, feeding on delight, self-luminous, moving through the air, glorious—and they stay like that for a very long time.

'At that period, Vasettha, there was just one mass of water, and all was darkness, blinding darkness. Neither moon nor sun appeared, no constellations or stars appeared, night and day were not distinguished, nor months

---

6. An ancient kingdom of northern India, in what is now south-central Uttar Pradesh.
7. A title of a buddha; it is the one most often used by the Buddha, Siddhartha Gautama (in Pali, Siddattha Gotama), to refer to himself.

8. Personification of evil and desire. "Deva": inhabitant of the heavenly realms (literally, "shining one").
9. The "Heaven of Radiant Light," one of the heavens in the Buddhist cosmology.

and fortnights, no years or seasons, and no male and female, beings being reckoned just as beings. And sooner or later, after a very long period of time, savoury earth spread itself over the waters where those beings were. It looked just like the skin that forms itself over hot milk as it cools. It was endowed with colour, smell and taste. It was the colour of fine ghee or butter, and it was very sweet, like pure wild honey.

'Then some being of a greedy nature said: "I say, what can this be?" and tasted the savoury earth on its finger. In so doing, it became taken with the flavour, and craving arose in it. Then other beings, taking their cue from that one, also tasted the stuff with their fingers. They too were taken with the flavour, and craving arose in them. So they set to with their hands, breaking off pieces of the stuff in order to eat it. And the result of this was that their self-luminance disappeared. And as a result of the disappearance of their self-luminance, the moon and the sun appeared, night and day were distinguished, months and fortnights appeared, and the year and its seasons. To that extent the world re-evolved.

'And those beings continued for a very long time feasting on this savoury earth, feeding on it and being nourished by it. And as they did so, their bodies became coarser, and a difference in looks developed among them. Some beings became good-looking, others ugly. And the good-looking ones despised the others, saying: "We are better-looking than they are." And because they became arrogant and conceited about their looks, the savoury earth disappeared. At this they came together and lamented, crying: "Oh that flavour! Oh that flavour!" And so nowadays when people say: "Oh that flavour!" when they get something nice, they are repeating an ancient saying without realising it.

'And then, when the savoury earth had disappeared, a fungus cropped up, in the manner of a mushroom. It was of a good colour, smell, and taste. It was the colour of fine ghee or butter, and it was very sweet, like pure wild honey. And those beings set to and ate the fungus. And this lasted for a very long time. And as they continued to feed on the fungus, so their bodies became coarser still, and the difference in their looks increased still more. And the good-looking ones despised the others . . . And because they became arrogant and conceited about their looks, the sweet fungus disappeared. Next, creepers appeared, shooting up like bamboo . . . , and they too were very sweet, like pure wild honey.

'And those beings set to and fed on those creepers. And as they did so, their bodies became even coarser, and the difference in their looks increased still more . . . And they became still more arrogant, and so the creepers disappeared too. At this they came together and lamented, crying: "Alas, our creeper's gone! What have we lost!" And so now today when people, on being asked why they are upset, say: "Oh, what have we lost!" they are repeating an ancient saying without realising it.

'And then, after the creepers had disappeared, rice appeared in open spaces, free from powder and from husks, fragrant and clean-grained. And what they had taken in the evening for supper had grown again and was ripe in the morning, and what they had taken in the morning for breakfast was ripe again by evening, with no sign of reaping. And these beings set to and fed on this rice, and this lasted for a very long time. And as they did so, their bodies became coarser still, and the difference in their looks became even greater. And the females developed female sex-organs, and the males developed male organs. And the women became excessively preoccupied with men, and the men with women. Owing to this excessive preoccupation with each other, passion was aroused, and their bodies burnt with lust. And later, because of this burning, they indulged in sexual activity. But those who saw them indulging threw dust, ashes or cow-dung at them, crying: "Die, you filthy beast! How can one being do such things to another!" Just as today, in some districts, when a daughter-in-law is led out,[1] some people throw dirt at her, some ashes, and some cow-dung, without realising that they are repeating an ancient observance. What was considered bad form in those days is now considered good form.

'And those beings who in those days indulged in sex were not allowed into a village or town for one or two months. Accordingly those who indulged for an excessively long period in such immoral practices began to build themselves dwellings so as to indulge under cover.

'Now it occurred to one of those beings who was inclined to laziness: "Well now, why should I be bothered to gather rice in the evening for supper and in the morning for breakfast? Why shouldn't I gather it all at once for both meals?" And he did so. Then another one came to him and said: "Come on, let's go rice-gathering." "No need, my friend, I've gathered enough for both meals." Then the other, following his example, gathered enough rice for two days at a time, saying: "That should be about enough." Then another being came and said to that second one: "Come on, let's go rice-gathering." "No need, my friend, I've gathered enough for two days." (*The same for 4, then 8, days*). However, when those beings made a store of rice and lived on that, husk-powder and husk began to envelop the grain, and where it was reaped it did not grow again, and the cut place showed, and the rice grew in separate clusters.

'And then those beings came together lamenting: "Wicked ways have become rife among us: at first we were mind-made, feeding on delight . . . (*all events repeated down to the latest development, each fresh change being said to be due to* 'wicked and unwholesome ways') . . . and the rice grows in separate clusters. So now let us divide up the rice into fields with boundaries." So they did so.

'Then, Vasettha, one greedy-natured being, while watching over his own plot, took another plot that was not given to him, and enjoyed the fruits of it. So they seized hold of him and said: "You've done a wicked thing, taking another's plot like that! Don't ever do such a thing again!" "I won't", he said, but he did the same thing a second and a third time. Again he was seized and rebuked, and some hit him with their fists, some with stones, and some with sticks. And in this way, Vasettha, taking what was not given, and censuring, and lying, and punishment, took their origin.

'Then those beings came together and lamented the arising of these evil things among them: taking what was not given, censuring, lying and punishment. And they thought: "Suppose we were to appoint a certain being who would show anger where anger was due, censure those who deserved it, and banish those who deserved banishment! And in return, we would grant him a share of the rice." So they went to the one among them who

1. That is, in marriage.

was the handsomest, the best-looking, the most pleasant and capable, and asked him to do this for them in return for a share of the rice, and he agreed.

'"The People's Choice" is the meaning of Maha-Sammata, which is the first regular title to be introduced. "Lord Of The Fields" is the meaning of Khattiya, the second such title. And "He Gladdens Others With Dhamma" is the meaning of Raja, the third title to be introduced. This, then, Vasettha, is the origin of the class of Khattiyas, in accordance with the ancient titles that were introduced for them. They originated among these very same beings, like ourselves, no different, and in accordance with Dhamma, not otherwise.

> Dhamma's the best thing for people
> In this life and the next as well.

'Then some of these beings thought: "Evil things have appeared among beings, such as taking what is not given, censuring, lying, punishment and banishment. We ought to put aside evil and unwholesome things." And they did so. "They Put Aside Evil And Unwholesome Things" is the meaning of Brahmin, which is the first regular title to be introduced for such people. They made leaf-huts in forest places and meditated in them. With the smoking fire gone out, with pestle cast aside, gathering alms for their evening and morning meals, they went away to a village, town or royal city to seek their food, and then they returned to their leaf-huts to meditate. People saw this and noted how they meditated. "They Meditate" is the meaning of Jhayaka, which is the second regular title to be introduced.

'However, some of those beings, not being able to meditate in leaf-huts, settled around towns and villages and compiled books. People saw them doing this and not meditating. "Now These Do Not Meditate" is the meaning of Ajjhayaka, which is the third regular title to be introduced. At that time it was regarded as a low designation, but now it is the higher. This, then, Vasettha, is the origin of the class of Brahmins in accordance with the ancient titles that were introduced for them. Their origin was from among these very same beings, like themselves, no different, and in accordance with Dhamma, not otherwise.

> Dhamma's the best thing for people
> In this life and the next as well.

'And then, Vasettha, some of those beings, having paired off, adopted various trades, and this "Various" is the meaning of Vessa,[2] which came to be the regular title for such people. This, then, is the origin of the class of Vessas, in accordance with the ancient titles that were introduced for them. Their origin was from among these very same beings . . .

'And then, Vasettha, those beings that remained went in for hunting. "They Are Base Who Live By The Chase", and that is the meaning of Sudda,[3] which came to be the regular title for such people. This, then, is the origin of the class of Suddas in accordance with the ancient titles that

---

2. Pali for *vaishya*, the third of the four castes of ancient India, sometimes called the merchant caste.

3. Pali for *shudra*, the fourth of the four castes of ancient India, sometimes called the servant caste.

were introduced for them. Their origin was from among these very same beings . . .

'And then, Vasettha, it came about that some Khattiya, dissatisfied with his own Dhamma, went forth from the household life into homelessness, thinking: "I will become an ascetic." And a Brahmin did likewise, a Vessa did likewise, and so did a Sudda. And from these four classes the class of ascetics came into existence. Their origin was from among these very same beings, like themselves, no different, and in accordance with Dhamma, not otherwise.

> Dhamma's the best thing for people
> In this life and the next as well.

'And, Vasettha, a Khattiya who has led a bad life in body, speech and thought, and who has wrong view will, in consequence of such wrong views and deeds, at the breaking-up of the body after death, be reborn in a state of loss, an ill fate, the downfall, the hell-state. So too will a Brahmin, a Vessa or a Sudda.

'Likewise, a Khattiya who has led a good life in body, speech and thought, and who has right view will, in consequence of such right view and deeds, at the breaking-up of the body after death, be reborn in a good destiny, in a heaven-state. So too will a Brahmin, a Vessa or a Sudda.

'And a Khattiya who has performed deeds of both kinds in body, speech and thought, and whose view is mixed will, in consequence of such mixed views and deeds, at the breaking-up of the body after death, experience both pleasure and pain. So too will a Brahmin, a Vessa or a Sudda.

'And a Khattiya who is restrained in body, speech and thought, and who has developed the seven requisites of enlightenment, will attain to Parinibbana[4] in this very life. So too will a Brahmin, a Vessa or a Sudda.

'And, Vasettha, whoever of these four castes, as a monk, becomes an Arahant who has destroyed the corruptions, done what had to be done, laid down the burden, attained to the highest goal, completely destroyed the fetter of becoming, and become liberated by the highest insight, he is declared to be chief among them in accordance with Dhamma, and not otherwise.

> Dhamma's the best thing for people
> In this life and the next as well.

'Vasettha, it was Brahma Sanankumara who spoke this verse:

> "The Khattiya's best among those who value clan;
> He with knowledge and conduct is best of gods and men."

This verse was rightly sung, not wrongly, rightly spoken, not wrongly, connected with profit, not unconnected. I too say, Vasettha:

> "The Khattiya's best among those who value clan:
> He with knowledge and conduct is best of gods and men."'

Thus the Lord spoke, and Vasettha and Bharadvaja were delighted and rejoiced at his words.

---

4. Pali for *parinirvana*, the passage into nirvana that occurs at the death of a buddha or an arhat.

KING SHIBI RESCUES A DOVE

THE SHIBI JATAKA

The Buddha's path to enlightenment began not when Prince Siddhartha left his palace at the age of twenty-nine, culminating in his achievement of buddhahood six years later, but billions of years earlier. All Buddhist schools assert that in order to achieve buddhahood, it is necessary to perfect oneself over countless lifetimes. A person takes the first step by vowing to achieve buddhahood for the welfare of all beings. Such a vow—which according to some schools must be made under specific circumstances—makes one a bodhisattva. Scholars are unsure of the precise etymology of this term, but it clearly refers to a person who has vowed to become a buddha.

From the making of that vow until the attaining of buddhahood, the bodhisattva is said to accumulate merit, the karmic power that will propel him forward on the long path. Such merit is produced through the practice of virtues called perfections (*paramita*): there are six in the Mahayana traditions (giving, ethics, patience, effort, concentration, and wisdom) and ten in the Theravada tradition (giving, ethics, renunciation, wisdom, effort, patience, truthfulness, determination, love, and equanimity).

The biography of the Buddha is recounted across the Buddhist world, but narratives of his former lives as a bodhisattva—his prebiography—constitute one of the most important genres of Buddhist literature. These are the *jataka* or "birth" stories, accounts of his former rebirths prior to his achievement of buddhahood. They are typically called "tales" in English because of their fabulous nature. They tell of the marvelous feats of the bodhisattva, whether he is a fish, a rabbit, a deer, a monkey, or a human. Regardless of his species, the bodhisattva is often a king, and the virtue that he most commonly displays is giving, as he sacrifices his own welfare for that of his subjects. The story that follows is the *Shibi Jataka*: that is, the story of the bodhisattva when he was born as King Shibi. It is perhaps the most famous of the stories—the often quite gruesome stories—that recount his "gift of the body."

Here, Indra, the king of the gods, is told by an ascetic that there is no such thing as perfect enlightenment. However, he is told by another deity, Vishvakarman, the divine architect, that there is a king named Shibi who is determined to attain enlightenment. In order to test the king's dedication to the welfare of others, Vishvakarman transforms himself into a dove (pigeon in the translation) and Indra transforms himself into a hawk. The hawk then pursues the dove, who flies under King Shibi's arm seeking protection. The king promises to protect the bird, but the hawk (who can speak) protests that the king is depriving him of food, and that his compassion should extend not only to the hunted but also to the hunter. The king agrees and decides to cut a piece of flesh from his own thigh, equal in weight to the dove. The divine hawk uses his magical powers to keep the scale tipped on the side of the dove, no matter how much of his flesh the king piles into the other pan. Eventually, the king, reduced to a skeleton connected by sinews, climbs onto the scale himself.

The hawk, now convinced of the king's compassionate resolve to achieve buddhahood, assumes his true form and pays his respects. But he cannot believe that the king did not feel a twinge of regret at the thought of giving up his life for the sake of a dove. The king proclaims the purity of his dedication, saying, "If this be true, may my body be restored as it was before, and may I soon attain enlightenment, that I may bring salvation to all beings!" Such a declaration is called an "act of truth": a statement that, if true, makes the speaker's wish come true. Acts of truth are common in the jataka stories. In this case, the king's body is restored, the songs of the gods resound through the heavens, and flowers, garments, and jewels fall from the sky.

PRONOUNCING GLOSSARY

bodhisattva: *boh-di-saht-tva*   Sumeru: *su-may-ru*
paramita: *pah-ra-mi-tah*   Sutra: *soo-tra*
Shibi Jataka: *shi-bi jah-ta-ka*   Vishva-karman: *vish-va-kar-man*

There was an heretical teacher who expounded his false doctrine to Indra
[king of the gods]. This heretical teacher, destitute of true knowledge, pretended to possess omniscience, and denied the existence of a being possessed of Perfect and Supreme Enlightenment. When Indra heard these
words, he experienced displeasure, and became very sad. Then Indra proceeded to explore the universe, to discover whether there was an ascetic who
had arrived at omniscience, at the end of his desires—even as it is said in
the stanzas of the Sutras of the *Questions of Indra:*

> My spirit seeks, but cannot find contentment;
> Day and night, doubts agitate me;
> I cannot distinguish the true from the false.
>
> From afar am I come
> With anxious desire never-ceasing
> To complete my inquiries:
>
> I know not in what place
> The great and true Saviour is now to be found.

Vishva-karman [Vulcan[1]] said to Indra: "A denizen of heaven should not
give himself over to sadness. In the world of men, in the kingdom of Kushinagara, dwells a king named Shibi. He devotes himself with zeal to macera-
tions and to the quest of Supreme Enlightenment. Men of intelligence who
have watched him, believe that this king will presently attain the condition
of a Buddha. Let us approach him!" Indra replied: "Is it perfectly certain that
he will not be shaken in his resolution?" Then he uttered these stanzas:

> Although the little fishes
> Be very numerous, few among them grow big;
> And among the fruits of the mango-tree,
> Those that attain maturity are rare.
>
> So also is it with Future Buddhas:
> Those who utter the vow to attain Enlightenment
>   are numerous;
> Those who attain it are few indeed.
>
> Those who practice austerities
> Without ever flinching,
> May be looked upon as Future Buddhas;
> Those who desire to become Buddhas
> Should show a heart full of constancy.

TRANSLATED FROM the Pali by Eugene Watson Burlingame. All bracketed additions are the translator's.

1. That is, the craftsman god (Vulcan was the Roman god of fire and metalworking).

Vishva-karman said: "Let us make a journey and find out for ourselves. If, in reality, he has formed an unshakable resolution, we will pay our respects to him."

Then Indra, with the intention of sounding the heart of the Future Buddha, changed himself into a hawk, and said to Vishva-karman: "Change yourself into a pigeon!" Immediately Vishva-karman changed himself into a pigeon with a body as blue as the sky and eyes like red pearls, and took his place near Indra. At this moment Indra, filled with pity, said to Vishva-karman: "Why do we seek to increase the troubles of the Future Buddha? We shall cause the king of the Shibis to endure sufferings; it is true that he will suffer. But when one is selecting a precious jewel, one examines it repeatedly in order to make sure that it is not artificial. The way to examine a jewel is to cut it, to break it, to expose it to the fire, and to strike it; then alone does one know whether it is not artificial."

Then the pigeon, pursued by the hawk, displayed great fear, and in the presence of a great crowd, came and sought refuge under the arm-pit of the king of the Shibis. The pigeon had the blue color of a lotus-leaf, and his brightness shone like a rain-bow in the midst of a dark cloud; he gleamed with pure lustre. Thereat all the people were filled with wonderment, and uttered these stanzas:

> In truth, he ought to be full of mercy,
> In order that all living beings may have entire
>   confidence in him.
>
> Thus [the birds], when the sun disappears,
> Fly away towards their nest.
>
> But at this moment the hawk says:
> "O king, give me back my prey!"

The king heard the words of the hawk, and saw the fright of the pigeon. Straightway he pronounced these stanzas:

> This pigeon, seized with fear,
> Has come towards me with wings outspread.
>
> Although his mouth cannot speak,
> His eyes are filled with tears.
>
> It becomes me, therefore,
> To grant him aid and protection.

Then the great king, in order to reassure the pigeon, uttered these stanzas further:

> Have no fear!
> Never will I permit your death.
>
> Even should it become my duty to save you at the risk of my life,
> In no wise will I refuse you my assistance.
>
> Not only will I give you aid and help,
> But I will protect also all living beings.

> For the good of all living beings
> I lavish my efforts.
>
> The inhabitants of my kingdom pay heavy taxes to me;
> Of six parts of their goods, they pay one to me.
>
> Upon me [in return] rests the obligation, towards all living
>   beings
> To show myself a benevolent patron.
>
> It is just for me to protect them,
> And on no account to permit any to injure them.

Then the hawk said again to the king: "Great king! Deign to release the pigeon, for he is my food!" The king replied to the hawk: "Long ago I conceived pity towards all living beings, and I owe them all the assistance and protection I can give them." The hawk asked the king: "Why did you conceive long ago [pity towards all living beings]?" The king replied to him by pronouncing these stanzas:

> When I uttered the vow to attain Enlightenment,
> I granted my protection
> To all living beings:
> All shall win my profound compassion.

The hawk replied with these stanzas:

> If your words are true,
> Give me back the pigeon quickly;
>
> For if you make me die of hunger,
> You show no more compassion.

When the king had heard that, he reflected thus: "I am in an extremely difficult position. What expedient ought I to employ?" Having thus thought, he replied to the hawk and said: "Then you have no other meat to sustain your life?" The hawk replied to the king: "I can sustain my life only with fresh flesh and with blood." Then the king said to himself: "What means ought I to employ?" Then he pronounced these stanzas:

> Towards all creatures
> I have always shown profound compassion.
>
> Blood and fresh flesh
> Cannot be obtained without committing murder.

Having thus reflected, he found that it would be very easy to give his own flesh to feed the hawk. And he pronounced these stanzas further:

> I will cut a piece of my own flesh
> And give it to the hawk.
>
> Even if it becomes my duty to sacrifice myself,
> It is incumbent on me to protect the life of this frightened
>   being.

When the great king had pronounced these verses, he said to the hawk: "Will my flesh be proper food for you?" The hawk said: "Yes! Let the king deign to cut out of his body a piece of flesh equal [in weight] to that of the pigeon! Let him give it to me, and I will eat it." When the great king had heard these words, he became joyful. He ordered a servant: "Bring quickly a pair of scales! I am going to cut a piece of my flesh to redeem this pigeon. It is a fortunate day for me to-day! And why is it a fortunate day?" He uttered these stanzas:

> This flesh is the seat of old age and of maladies,
> Of numerous perils and of disgusting substances.
>
> It is fitting that for the good of the Law
> I sacrifice this flesh, vile and corrupt.

In the meantime the king's servant had executed the order, and brought a pair of scales. When the king saw the pair of scales coming, he showed no feeling. Immediately he bared the white flesh of his thigh, smooth as a tala-leaf.[2] He called the servant and recited these stanzas to him:

> Take a sharp knife, and cut the flesh of my thigh!
> Do as I tell you, without any fear!
>
> For without submitting oneself to severe austerities,
> One obtains not Omniscience.
>
> For Omniscience,—
> Is there aught more sublime in the three worlds?
>
> Never, without sufficient cause,
> Does one obtain Enlightenment.
> Hence I ought to act with unshakable firmness.

At this moment the servant's eyes were filled with tears. Joining the palms of his hands, he spoke thus: "Have mercy on me! I cannot do it! I have always received good things from the king. How could I, with a knife, cut a piece of flesh from the thigh of the king?" He uttered these stanzas:

> The king is the saviour and protector of all.
> If I cut the flesh of the king,
> Certainly, I myself, with the knife,
> Should be overwhelmed, and should fall to the earth.

Then the great king took the knife in his own hand to cut the flesh from his thigh. The ministers and the great dignitaries, lamenting and weeping, made remonstrances to him without being able to stop him. All the inhabitants of the city pressed close to him. But he heard them not, and cut the flesh from his thigh. Those who were near him, turned their eyes away and dared not look. The Brahmans turned their eyes away and dared not look. The women of the palace uttered cries and wept. The deities, the dragons, the demons, the heavenly minstrels, the spirits, the fairies, and the great serpents said to each other throughout space: "It is not probable that the

2. The leaves of the palmyra palm, which can be almost six feet long, were used as a writing surface.

like of this deed has ever been done before." The king had a body that was feeble and tender. Born and reared at the palace, he had never been able to endure any pain. Now his body was tortured with pains, and he suffered intensely. But he exhorted himself, and pronounced these stanzas:

> O my Heart, preserve thy firmness
> Against this slight pain!
>
> Why art thou cast down?
> Only see how the whole universe
>
> Is entangled in hundreds and thousands of evils!
> Living beings are deprived of refuge and assistance;
>
> They have no shelter and protection;
> They live in utter dependence.
>
> THOU ALONE, O MY HEART,
> ART CALLED TO BE THE SAVIOUR OF ALL!
>
> Art thou not ashamed of thyself
> To yield thus to pain?

Then Indra reflected thus: "Will the great king preserve his constancy in the midst of the greatest sufferings?" And desiring to put him to the test, he said: "You have just endured sufferings difficult to endure. Why do you not stop torturing yourself? You have suffered enough. Leave off, and release the pigeon!" The Future Buddha smiled feebly, and replied to him: "Never will sufferings make me break my word. Even if I am destined to suffer yet more, I will not flinch. These insignificant sufferings cannot be compared with the sufferings of hell. Therefore it is incumbent upon me that I lift up my thought, and that even in the midst of these sufferings I increase my compassion [for living beings]." When he had made this reflection, he pronounced these stanzas:

> I suffer now from my bodily wound.
> But let not my heart be cast down!
>
> Let it know the extent to which the irresolute and the
>   heedless
> Endure sufferings in hell,—
>
> Tortures which never cease,—
> Eternal and unending.
>
> Who would wish to endure them?
> Because I am filled with compassion for living beings,
>
> I must make haste
> To attain Enlightenment quickly.
>
> All those who suffer from these miseries,—
> Them will I save, and for them will I procure Deliverance.

Then Indra made this further reflection: "What the great king has just done, is not yet sufficiently painful. Will he preserve his constancy if I cause him to increase his sufferings? I will put him to the test!" Having made this reflection, he preserved silence and left off speaking.

In the meantime the great king had taken the piece of flesh which he had cut, and had placed it on one pan of the scales; he placed the pigeon on the other pan. It so happened that the pigeon made the scales tip. Then the king cut the two pi^3 and placed this flesh in the scales. But it was still lighter than the pigeon. At this the great king was much surprised, and failed to understand what was the cause. Immediately he arose to place himself in the scales.

At this moment the hawk asked him: "Why do you fidget? Are you beginning to have regrets?" The great king replied to him: "I regret nothing. I wish to place myself whole and entire in the scales to save this pigeon." When the great king was on the point of ascending the scales, his face remained calm. The servants and the assistants dared look no more; all the members of his entourage turned their eyes away.

At this moment the king said: "Look freely!" *He cut off all of his flesh.* There remained no more anything but his bones and his joints. He was like a statue, which, when exposed to the rain, becomes dismembered and difficult to recognize.

Then cried aloud the great king as follows:

"IF I SACRIFICE MY BODY, IT IS NOT TO OBTAIN TREASURES, NOR FOR PLEASURE, NOR FOR LOVE OF MY WIFE AND MY CHILDREN AND MY KINSFOLK. WHAT I COVET IS ENLIGHTENMENT, THAT THEREBY I MAY BE ABLE TO PROCURE SALVATION FOR ALL LIVING BEINGS!"

Then he pronounced these stanzas:

> Deities and spirits, heavenly musicians and ogres,
> Dragons and demons,—all classes of living beings,

> Seeing me in this state,
> Will be incited to imitate my constancy.

> Because I covet Supreme Enlightenment,
> I make my body suffer, and I wound it.

> He that would win Enlightenment,
> Must prove himself possessed of compassion unshakable.

> If one does not possess constancy that is proof against
>   everything,
> One should renounce the thought of winning Enlightenment.

At the instant when the great king, sacrificing his body, ascended the scales, the great earth trembled six times, like a blade of grass or a leaf, agitated in all the directions. In the sky, the deities expressed their wonderment at this extraordinary spectacle, and cried out: "Bravo! bravo! Thou dost deserve to be called zealous and of resolution unshakable."

---

3. The meaning of this term is unknown.

And the great king uttered these stanzas:

> To save the life of this living being,
> I have cut my flesh to pieces.
>
> I have acted from a heart that is sincere and full of
>   compassion,
> With a firm and unshakable resolution.
>
> The whole company of the deities
> Is filled with wonderment thereat.

At this moment the hawk expressed his wonderment at the sight of this extraordinary act: "His resolution is firm and sincere; he will soon become a Buddha; all living beings will put their confidence in him." Then Indra showed himself to the king under his true form, and told Vishva-karman to resume his true form also. And he added: "Let us pay him our respects! For this Future Buddha is imbued with resolution firm and unshakable, like Mount Sumeru,[4] which lies in mid-ocean without ever being shaken. Such is the heart of this Future Buddha." Then he added these stanzas:

> Let us pay our respects to this valiant and resolute man!
> Let us lift up our voices and spread his praises abroad!
> Let all that are harassed with cares seek shelter with him!
> Let them unite closely with him whose conduct is unshakable!
>
> He has planted in the ground of Compassion
> The tree of Supreme Enlightenment.
> His shoots begin to sprout,
> And prudent men will seek a shelter under him.

Vishva-karman then addressed himself to Indra and said: "The great king has shown his compassion for all living beings. His body should be restored as it was before. May all living beings be able to seek after Enlightenment without faltering [as the king has done]!" Then Indra asked the king: "Had you no regret over sacrificing yourself for a pigeon?" The king replied to him with these stanzas:

> This body is destined to perish;
> It is like a piece of wood, or a rock:
> It shall be thrown to the birds and to the beasts of prey;
> It shall be burned, or it shall rot in the earth.
>
> If, then, by means of this worthless body,
> I can obtain great advantage,
> I have only to rejoice over it;
> It would not befit me to sorrow over it.
>
> Where, then, is the prudent man,
> Who would give this body, exposed to all dangers,
> In exchange for the Law, stable and firm,
> Without rejoicing?

4. According to Buddhist cosmology, the mountain at the center of the world.

Indra said to the king: "Such words are difficult to believe. Never has an act equal to it been seen. Who could give credence to it?" The great king replied: "I know myself. Were there in the world a great sage capable of fathoming my heart, he would see that it is pure and without duplicity." Indra replied: "You have spoken the truth." At this moment the great king made this declaration: "If I have no regret [for having done what I have just done], may my body become once more as it was before!" And the king surveyed his mutilated body and uttered these stanzas:

> When I mutilated my body,
> I was free from sorrow and joy,
> From anger and grief;
> I experienced no sadness.
>
> IF THIS BE TRUE,
> MAY MY BODY BE RESTORED AS IT WAS BEFORE,
> AND MAY I SOON ATTAIN ENLIGHTENMENT,
> THAT I MAY BRING SALVATION TO ALL LIVING BEINGS!

When the great king had pronounced these stanzas, his mutilated body was transformed, and became as it was before. Here follow the stanzas:

> The mountains, and the great earth as well,
> Were all shaken;
> The trees and the ocean
> Began to stir, and lost their calm,
> Like a timorous man
> Who loses his confidence in battle.
>
> The deities sang with joy,
> And from the sky fell a rain of fragrant flowers.
> Bells and drums were heard,
> Mingling their sounds together.
>
> The deities expressed their joy,
> And all sang together.
>
> All living beings were affected;
> The ocean itself lifted up its voice;
> From heaven fell fragrant dust,
> Covering all the roads.
>
> The sky was full of flowers
> Which fell, some slowly, others quickly.
>
> The celestial nymphs, assembled in heaven,
> Covered the earth with flowers.
>
> Garments of all colors,
> Adorned with gold and precious stones,
> Fell in a rain from heaven,
> And caskets too, filled with heavenly robes,
> Resounding as they clashed together.

In everybody's dwelling
Appeared spontaneously urns filled with precious stones,
Giving out, without a touch, sounds
Like the music of the heavenly musicians.

No cloud covered the heavens;
The four directions shone resplendent.

A gentle wind exhaled perfumes;
The streams flowed clear and noiseless.

The demons, ardently desirous to obtain the Law,
Once more redoubled zeal:
"Soon he will attain Enlightenment,"—
Thus they sang in praise of him.

All the heavenly musicians
Sang and made their music heard;
Their notes harmonious were sometimes soft, sometimes
      low.
And thus they sang the praises of the king:

"Soon he will obtain the condition of a Buddha;
"He will cross the ocean of his vow;
"Right quickly will he reach the place auspicious:
"When he shall attain the object of his desire,
"He will remember us, to win Salvation for us."

Then Indra and Vishva-karman paid their respects to the Future Buddha,
and returned in their heavenly mansions.

PRINCE VESSANTARA GIVES AWAY HIS CHILDREN

THE VESSANTARA JATAKA

Among the hundreds of jataka stories, none is more famous than that of Prince
Vessantara. Immediately prior to his birth as Prince Siddhartha, the future Buddha
had been reborn as a god in the Tushita Heaven, where he awaited the appropriate
moment to descend to the world. But before that divine existence, he had been a
human, Prince Vessantara. Having practiced the perfections over billions of lives,
the bodhisattva was very close to enlightenment in his last human rebirth before
his birth as Prince Siddhartha. It is noteworthy, then, that in this penultimate
human existence, the bodhisattva once again practices the perfection of giving. He
has already given away various body parts, and his own life, many times in the past.
But as Prince Vessantara, the bodhisattva does something even more difficult: he
gives away his own children.

  Here, briefly, is the story. Vessantara is married to a beautiful princess named
Maddi, who bears him two children: a boy, Jali, and a girl, Kanhajina (or Kanha).
One day a delegation arrives from a nearby kingdom that is suffering from drought.
They ask that Vessantara give them a white elephant that brings rain wherever it
goes. Known for his generosity, Vessantara gives them the elephant, but the people

Prince Vessantara gives away the elephant, Central Thailand, ca. 1800–1850.

of his own kingdom soon complain that the source of their prosperity has been lost. They complain to the king, Vessantara's father, who reluctantly agrees that his son be banished. Before his departure, Vessantara makes a lavish gift of clothing, food, and drink to the people. En route to their forest hermitage, Vessantara, accompanied by his wife and children, gives away their carriage and horses. They find a hut on Crooked Mountain, where they live happily in a beautiful sylvan setting for seven months. But—and here the excerpt below begins—one night Maddi has a terrible prophetic dream. In perhaps the most heartrending passage in all of Buddhist literature, Vessantara gives his children to an evil brahmin, Jujuka.

The story concludes as follows. Maddi is overcome with despair when she returns to find her children missing. She searches for them all night, finally fainting at Vessantara's feet. When she regains consciousness, she asks where the children have gone. He replies that he gave them to a brahmin as slaves, telling her that she is young enough to have more children. Soon, another brahmin arrives, asking that Vessantara give him Maddi. Vessantara agrees, and Maddi is led away without complaint. But in this case, the brahmin is Indra, the king of the gods, in disguise. As in the *Shibi Jataka,* he has come to test the limits of the prince's generosity. He returns Maddi to the prince and grants him eight wishes. Vessantara asks, among other things, that his father be glad to see him upon his return to the kingdom, that he ascend to the throne to become a compassionate king, that he have a son, and that he never regret a gift. Because he never regrets a gift, he does not wish for the return of his children.

The children are still slaves of the evil brahmin, made to serve him by day and sleep on the ground at night. One day, he takes them to the kingdom of Vessantara's father, who recognizes his grandchildren and purchases them from the brahmin. The king regrets having banished Vessantara, and leads a procession to invite him to return. Vessantara and Maddi are overcome with joy to be reunited with their children. The prince agrees to return home and assume the throne, insisting that his gift of the elephant long ago had been proper, despite all that it set in motion. As king, his first act is to free all captives, human and animal. Indra causes a rain of jewels that soon become waist deep. Vessantara distributes some of the jewels and saves the rest, to be used as gifts in the future.

The story of Vessantara, far more elaborate than can be recounted here, is immensely popular in Southeast Asia, where it is as well-known as the life of the Buddha. It is retold in elaborate poems and depicted in painting and sculpture, including in the famous murals at Angkor Wat in Cambodia. According to a Thai tradition, if one wishes to be reborn in the retinue of the coming buddha, Maitreya, one should listen to the *Vessantara Jataka* over the course of a single day and night.

PRONOUNCING GLOSSARY

Bodhisatta: *boh-di-sat-ta*

brahmin: *bra-min*

Jali: *jah-li*

Jetuttara: *jay-tut-ta-ra*

Jujaka: *joo-ja-ka*

Kanhajina: *kan-hah-ji-nah*

kapitthana: *kah-peet-tah-nah*

kasumari: *kah-su-mah-ri*

Maddi: *mad-dee*

madhuka: *ma-doo-ka*

piyala: *pi-yah-la*

Siddhartha: *sid-dahr-ta*

sinduvara: *sin-du-va-ra*

tinduka: *tin-du-ka*

vedisa: *vay-di-sa*

Vessantara Jataka: *vays-san-ta-ra jah-ta-ka*

During that night, at dawn, Maddi had a dream, and the dream was like this: A dark man wearing two saffron robes and with red garlands adorning his ears came threatening her with a weapon in his hand. He entered the leaf-hut, and grasping Maddi by the hair, dragged her out and threw her flat on the ground. Then, as she shrieked, he dug out her eyes, cut off her arms, and splitting her breast took her heart, dripping blood, and went off. She woke up, terrified, and thinking, 'I have had a nightmare. No one can interpret dreams for me like Vessantara. I shall ask him about it,' she went to the leaf-hut of the Great Being and knocked at the door. The Great Being said, 'Who is it?' 'My lord, it is I, Maddi,' she replied. 'Why have you broken our agreement, my lady, and come at an improper time?' 'My lord, it is not improper desires which bring me here, but I have had a nightmare.' 'Well then, tell me about it, Maddi.' When she had told him, just as she had experienced it, the Great Being understood the dream, and knew that he would fulfil the Perfection of giving, and that a suppliant would on the next day come and beg his children from him. He decided to console Maddi and send her away. 'Your mind must have been agitated because you were lying uncomfortably, or because of something you had eaten, Maddi. Do not be frightened.'

So he deceivingly consoled her, and sent her away. In the morning, when she had done all her chores, she embraced her two children and kissed them on the head, and warned them to be careful, since she had had a bad dream that night. Then, leaving them in the charge of the Great Being, with the words, 'Take good care of the children, my lord', she took her basket and other implements, and went into the forest in search of roots and fruit, wiping away her tears.

Jujaka, sure she would by then be gone, came down from the mountain ridge and set off for the hermitage along the narrow footpath. The Great Being came out of the leaf-hut and sat down on a stone slab, looking like a golden statue. There he sat, thinking, 'The suppliant will come now,' looking at the path by which he would come, like a drunkard eager for a drink, while his children played at his feet. As he watched the path he saw the brahmin coming, and almost visibly taking up the yoke of liberality, which had been laid aside for seven months, he cried, 'Come then, brahmin!' and with great happiness addressed Prince Jali in this verse:

TRANSLATED FROM the Pali by Margaret Cone and Richard F. Gombrich.

'Up now, Jali; stand firm! I think I see a sight from the past. I think I see a brahmin, and joy floods over me.'

To this the boy replied:

'I too see a man who looks like a brahmin, daddy. He comes like a suppliant, and he will be our guest.'

And then the boy paid him respect, and rising from his seat went to meet the brahmin and offered to take his baggage. When the brahmin saw him he thought, 'This must be Vessantara's son, the prince Jali. I shall speak roughly to him straightaway.' So he snapped his fingers at him saying, 'Be off, be off!' Thinking that the brahmin was terribly rough, and wondering what was the matter, the boy looked at his body and saw the eighteen human deformities. The brahmin approached the Bodhisatta[1] and greeted him:

'I hope you are well, sir; I hope you are in health, sir. I hope you can live by gathering food and that there are roots and fruit in plenty.
'I hope there are few gadflies and mosquitoes and creepy-crawlies. I hope you meet with no harm in this forest thronged with wild beasts.'

The Bodhisatta answered him in a friendly spirit:

'We are well, brahmin; we are in health, brahmin. We can live by gathering food and there are roots and fruit in plenty.
'There are few gadflies and mosquitoes and creepy-crawlies, and we meet with no harm in the forest thronged with wild beasts.
'We have lived a life of sorrow in the forest for seven months, and you are the first godlike brahmin with vilva stick[2] and sacred fire and water-pot that we have seen.
'Welcome, great brahmin, and very welcome. Come inside, sir, and wash your feet.
'Eat, brahmin, of the very best: of honey-like fruit, tindukas and piyalas, madhukas and kasumaris.[3]
'Here too is cool water brought from a mountain cavern. Drink from it, great brahmin, if you wish.'

Realizing that the brahmin would not have come to the great jungle without having a purpose in view, the Great Being determined to ask him straightaway the reason for his coming, and so spoke this verse:

'For what reason, for what purpose have you come to the great jungle? Tell me what I ask you.'

Jujaka answered:

'As a full river never runs dry, I have come to beg from you. I ask you to give me your children.'

When he heard this the Great Being was filled with happiness, and as if putting a purse of a thousand gold coins in an outstretched hand, he cried out, making the mountain resound,

---

1. Pali for *bodhisattva*.
2. From the bel tree.

3. All plants whose fruits are associated with ayurvedic medicine.

'I give, I do not hesitate. Take them as their master, brahmin. The princess went off in the morning, and she will return from gathering food in the evening.

'Stay for one night and go in the morning, brahmin, when she will have washed them and anointed them with scent, and adorned them with garlands.

'Then when you go you will take them hung about with many kinds of flowers, anointed with every fragrance, and carrying a plentiful variety of roots and fruit.'

But Jujaka replied:

'I do not wish to stay, I would rather go. There may be trouble for me. I am going, lord of charioteers.

'Women are not open-handed; they are trouble-makers. They know spells; they take everything the wrong way.

'You are resolved to give the gift, so do not let me meet their mother. She would cause trouble. I am going, lord of charioteers.

'Call your children; do not let them see their mother. In that way the merit you gain by giving a gift with resolve is increased.

'Call your children; do not let them see their mother. It is by giving treasure to someone like me, O prince, that a man goes to heaven.'

Vessantara answered:

'If you do not wish to see my devoted wife, let their grandfather see Jali and Kanhajina.

'When he sees these children, sweetly chattering in their dear voices, he will be glad and pleased, and delighted to give you much money.'

But Jujaka said:

'Listen to me, O prince. I am afraid of robbery. The king might have me beaten, or might sell me, or kill me. Deprived of both wealth and slaves I should be an object of contempt to my brahmin wife.'

Vessantara said:

'Full of joy and gladness when he sees the children, sweetly chattering in their dear voices, the great king of the Sivis, who causes his kingdom to prosper and who always does what is right, will give you much money.'

Jujaka answered:

'I shall not do what you urge. I shall take the children as servants for my wife.'

When the children heard his rough words, they rushed behind the leaf-hut, and then ran away from there and hid in a clump of bushes. But imagining Jujaka coming and dragging them out even from there, they ran trembling this way and that, unable to keep still in any one place. When they reached the square lotus pond, putting on their strong bark clothes they slipped into the water and stood there, covered by the water with a lotus leaf over their heads.

In explanation the Teacher said:

> When they heard the words of that cruel man, the children Jali
> and Kanhajina ran trembling this way and that.

As Jujaka could not see the children, he said to the Bodhisatta in reproach, 'Vessantara, just now you agreed to give me the children, but when I said I would not go to the city of Jetuttara, but would take them as servants for my wife, you gave them a signal to run away, while you sit here, all innocent. You must be the biggest liar in the world.' The Great Being was shaken by this, and realized that they must have run off. 'Do not worry, brahmin,' he said, 'I will fetch the children.' He rose and went to the back of the leaf-hut, and knowing they had entered the forest thicket, followed their footprints to the shore of the lotus pond. When he saw that these continued into the water he knew that they must have gone down into the pond and be standing there, so he called out, 'Jali dear,' and spoke these two verses:

> 'Come, my dear son, fulfil my Perfection. Consecrate my heart;
> do what I say.
> 'Be a steady boat to carry me on the sea of becoming. I shall cross to
> the further shore of birth, and make the world with its gods cross also.'

'Jali dear!' he called out. The boy heard his father's voice and thought, 'Let the brahmin do with me what he will; I will not argue with my father,' and raising his head and removing the lotus leaves, he climbed out of the water and fell at the Great Being's right foot, clutching him tightly by the ankle and sobbing. The Great Being asked him, 'Where is your sister, my son?' But the boy answered, 'When they are in danger, daddy, people look after themselves.' The Great Being realized that the children must have made a pact with each other, so calling out, 'Come, Kanha, my precious!' he spoke these two verses:

> 'Come, my dear daughter, fulfil my Perfection. Consecrate my
> heart; do what I say.
> 'Be a steady boat to carry me on the sea of becoming. I shall cross
> to the further shore of birth, and deliver the world with its gods.'

And she too, thinking, 'I will not argue with my father,' climbed out as the boy had done and fell at the Great Being's left foot, clutching him tightly by the ankle and sobbing. Their tears fell on to the Great Being's feet, which were the colour of a lotus in bloom,[4] and his tears fell onto their backs, which were like slabs of gold. Then the Great Being made them get up, and said to comfort them, 'Dear Jali, do you not know that giving brings me gladness? Help me to realize my aspiration.' And like someone valuing oxen, he put a price on his children just as he stood there, with these instructions to his son: 'Dear Jali, when you wish to be free, you can gain your freedom by paying the brahmin one thousand gold coins. Your sister, however, is very lovely, and if someone of low birth were able to buy her freedom by paying a certain amount to the brahmin, there would result a great differ-

---

4. Probably a creamy white.

ence of rank in the marriage. But since no one but a king can give one hundred of everything, when your sister wishes to be free, she can buy her freedom by giving to the brahmin one hundred of everything, that is, one hundred male slaves, one hundred female slaves, one hundred elephants, one hundred horses, one hundred bullocks, and one hundred gold coins.' So he put a price on his children and comforted them, and took them to the hermitage. There he took water in a pot, and calling the brahmin to him, he formed an aspiration for omniscience; and as he poured out the water he made the earth resound with the words, 'Omniscience is a hundred times, a thousand times, a hundred thousand times more precious to me than my son!' and so made the gift of his dear children to the brahmin.

In explanation the Teacher said:

> Then he who brought prosperity to the kingdom of the Sivis gave the children Jali and Kanhajina as a gift to the brahmin.
> Gladly he gave his son and daughter, the children Jali and Kanhajina, as the best of gifts to the brahmin.
> Then there was a frightening thing, then there was something to make your hair stand on end, for when he gave away the children, the earth shook.
> Then there was a frightening thing, then there was something to make your hair stand on end, when the prince, who brought prosperity to the Sivis' kingdom, raising his folded hands, gave those luckless children as a gift to the brahmin.

After he had given this gift, full of joy because he had given so good a gift, the Great Being stood still, watching his children. Jujaka went into a forest thicket, and biting off a creeper, used it to bind together the boy's right hand and the girl's left hand. Beating him with the ends of the creeper, he went off with them.

In explanation the Teacher said:

> Then that cruel brahmin bit off a creeper. With the creeper he bound their hands, with the creeper he thrashed them.
> Then, holding a rope and a stick, the brahmin led them away, beating them while the Sivi prince looked on.

Where they were beaten the skin broke and blood flowed, and as they were beaten they pressed back to back. The brahmin tripped on an uneven piece of ground, and fell, and the stiff creeper slipped off the soft hands of the children. In tears they ran right back to the Great Being.

In explanation the Teacher said:

> Then the children broke free from the brahmin, and ran off. With eyes full of tears the boy gazed at his father.
> Trembling like a leaf on a holy fig tree, he made obeisance at his father's feet, and having made obeisance he spoke these words:
> 'Mummy is out, and you are giving us away, daddy. When we have seen our mummy, then give us away.
> 'Mummy is out, and you are giving us away, daddy. Do not give us away until mummy comes back. Then let this brahmin sell us or kill us as he will.

'He is splay-footed; his nails are filthy; his calves are rolls of fat. He has a long upper lip; he slavers and his teeth stick out. He has a broken nose.

'He is pot-bellied, hunch-backed, and cross-eyed. His beard is red and his hair is yellow, and he is covered with wrinkles and freckles.

'With his red eyes, with massive hands, bent and deformed, wearing an antelope skin, he is horrible, he is not human.

'Is it a man, or a ghoul who feeds on flesh and blood, who has come from the village to the jungle to ask you for money, daddy? How can you just look on as we are taken off by an ogre?

'Your heart must be made of stone or strongly bound with iron, if you do not care that we have been tied up by a brahmin greedy for money, excessive and ferocious, who drives us along like cattle.

'Let Kanha stay here anyway; she does not understand. She cries like a fawn who has strayed from the herd and longs for its mother's milk.'

But the Great Being made no reply to these words. The boy then, grieving for his mother and father, said:

'This is not so painful—for a man can bear it—but that I will not see my mother again, that is much more painful.

'This is not so painful—for a man can bear it—but that I will not see my father again, that is much more painful.

'My poor mother will weep for a long time, when she cannot see her daughter, pretty Kanhajina.

'My poor father will weep for a long time, when he cannot see his daughter, pretty Kanhajina.

'My poor mother will weep for a long time in the hermitage when she cannot see her daughter, pretty Kanhajina.

'My poor father will weep for a long time in the hermitage when he cannot see his daughter, pretty Kanhajina.

'My poor mother will cry for a long time, at midnight, through the night. Her tears will run dry, like a river.

'My poor father will cry for a long time, at midnight, through the night. His tears will run dry, like a river.

'All these different trees, these rose-apples and vedisas and sinduvaras—these we leave today.

'All these different fruits, these figs and bread-fruits, banyans and kapitthanas—these we leave today.

'Here are gardens, here a river with cool water, where we used to play: these we leave today.

'All these different flowers growing up on the hill, which we used to wear—these we leave today.

'All these different fruits growing up on the hill, which we used to eat—these we leave today.

'These toy elephants and horses, and these oxen of ours, with which we used to play: these we leave today.'

As he mourned like this with his sister, Jujaka came up and took them off, beating them.

In explanation the Teacher said:

> As they were driven away, the children said to their father, 'Wish
> our mummy well, and may you be happy, daddy!
>   'If you give these toy elephants and horses and oxen of ours to
> mummy, she will console herself with them.
>   'When mummy sees these toy elephants and horses and oxen of
> ours, she will restrain her sorrow.'

Overpowering grief rose up in the Great Being for his children, and his
heart grew hot. Trembling like a rutting elephant seized by a maned lion, or
like the moon caught in the jaws of Eclipse, his feelings unable to bear it,
he went into the leaf-hut with eyes full of tears, and wept bitterly.

In explanation the Teacher said:

> Then Vessantara, prince of noble birth, having given that gift,
> went into the leaf-hut and wept bitterly.

These are the verses of the Great Being's lament:

> 'Where will the children cry today in hunger and thirst at evening,
> at bedtime: "Who will give us food?"
>   'Where will the children cry today in hunger and thirst at eve-
> ning, at bedtime: "Mummy, we are hungry. Give us food."
>   'How will they manage to walk along the road, with no shoes,
> tired on their swollen feet? Who will hold their hands?
>   'How could he not be ashamed, beating those innocent children
> in front of my face? That brahmin is shameless!
>   'Who with any idea of shame would beat even one of my slaves,
> or some other servant, even the lowest?
>   'Yet he scolds and beats my dear children, now that I am out of
> sight, as helplessly restricted as a fish caught in a net.'

The Great Being, feeling in his affection for his children that the brahmin was treating them too cruelly, and unable to bear the grief, considered
running after the brahmin and killing him, and so bringing back the children. But a second thought convinced him that this was impossible. 'For to
wish to redeem a gift once offered, because the suffering of children is too
painful, is not the way of good men.'

In explanation of this matter, there are these two verses of inner debate:

> 'No! with my bow and my sword girded on my left side, I shall
> bring back my children; for I suffer when they are struck.
>   'Certainly it is painful to me that my children are beaten. But
> who, knowing what is expected of good men, regrets a gift once it
> has been made?'

Jujaka drove on the children, beating them. And the boy sobbed this lament:

> 'Indeed men speak the truth when they say: "He who has not his
> own mother is as good as dead."
>   'Come, Kanha, let us die, we have no reason for living. We have
> been given away by the prince of men to a brahmin greedy for
> money, excessive and ferocious, who drives us along like cattle.

'All these different trees, these rose-apples and vedisas and sinduvaras—these we leave, Kanha.

'All these different fruits, these figs and bread-fruits, banyans, and kapitthanas—these we leave, Kanha.

'Here are gardens, here a river with cool water, where we used to play: these we leave, Kanha.

'All these different flowers growing up on the hill, which we used to wear—these we leave, Kanha.

'All these different fruits growing up on the hill, which we used to eat—these we leave, Kanha.

'These toy elephants and horses, and these oxen of ours, with which we used to play: these we leave, Kanha.'

Then the brahmin stumbled on an uneven piece of ground and fell, and the strap slipped from the children's hands. Trembling like chickens who have been struck, they ran off with a single impulse back to their father.

In explanation the Teacher said:

As they were led away, the children, Jali and Kanhajina, escaped from the brahmin and ran this way and that.

Jujaka got up quickly, and spitting like the fire at the end of an aeon,[5] the stick and creeper in his hand, he caught up with them, and shouting, 'You are too clever at getting away!' he bound their hands and led them off again.

In explanation the Teacher said:

Then, holding a rope and a stick, the brahmin led them away, beating them, while the Sivi prince looked on.

As they were led away like this Kanhajina turned round to look at her father and cried out to him.

In explanation the Teacher said:

Then Kanhajina called out to him, 'O daddy, this brahmin beats me with a switch, as though I were a slave who had been born in his house.

'This is not a real brahmin, daddy, for brahmins are good men. This is a ghoul, disguised as a brahmin, who is leading us away to eat us. How can you just watch as we are driven away by an ogre?'

At the sight of his little daughter going off sobbing and trembling, overpowering grief rose up in the Great Being, and his heart grew hot. His breath came from his mouth in gasps, for he could not breathe through his nose, and tears that were drops of blood poured from his eyes. Realizing that such pain overcame him because of a flaw in him, his affection, and for no other reason, and certain that that affection must be banished and equanimity developed, he plucked out that dart of grief by the power of his knowledge, and sat down in his usual position.

The girl sobbed aloud as she walked, before they even reached the mountain pass:

---

5. In Buddhist cosmology, each age ends in all-consuming fire.

'Our feet hurt, the path is long and hard; the sun hangs so low, and the brahmin hurries us on.

'We cry out to the spirits of the mountains and of the forest; we salute with bowed head the spirits of the lake and the accessible rivers.

'Grass and creepers, plants, mountains, and woods, please wish our mummy well. This brahmin is taking us away.

'Please, sirs, tell our mummy, our mother Maddi, "If you want to catch us up, you must follow us quickly.

'"This narrow path leads straight to the hermitage. If you follow it you will see us easily."

'Alas, when you bring fruit and roots from the forest, and see the hermitage empty, lady ascetic, you will be so sad.

'Gathering a lot of food is surely making mummy late, and she does not know that we have been tied up by a brahmin who is greedy for money, excessive and ferocious, who drives us along like cattle.

'If only we could see mummy today, back from her gathering in the evening, mummy would give the brahmin fruit mixed with honey.

'Then, satisfied after his meal, he would not make us hurry so much. Our feet are swollen, the brahmin makes us hurry so much.'

In this way, fretting for their mother, the children wept.

THE BUDDHA REMEMBERS HIS MOTHER'S TEARS

THE NOBLE SEARCH
(*The Ariyapariyesana Sutta*)

Biographies of the Buddha—that is, accounts of his life that begin with his birth and end with his death—did not begin to appear until some five hundred years after his passage into nirvana. However, biographical elements occur in earlier texts. For example, the Buddha recounts individual events in his life that occurred from the time that he renounced his life as a prince until he achieved enlightenment six years later. The *Great Discourse on the Final Nirvana* (p. 840) describes the Buddha's last days, his passage into nirvana, his funeral, and the distribution of his relics. Another category of early Buddhist literature, the vinaya (the rules of monastic discipline), contains accounts of numerous incidents from the Buddha's life, but rarely in the form of a continuous narrative. Instead, the stories tended to feature the Buddha's previous lives, leading to his momentous final birth; the circumstances in which he gave a particular teaching or formulated a particular rule for the monastic code; a particular miraculous deed; or his death and the disposition of his relics.

The text presented here, called the *Ariyapariyesana* (*The Noble Search*), is one of the best-known autobiographical narratives from the sutra collections. It is found in the *Majjhima Nikaya*, or *Middle-sized Collection*, a group of discourses of the Buddha regarded as being of medium length. The text begins with an appealing human moment. The Buddha and his personal attendant Ananda have taken their evening bath in the river. Ananda then suggests that they go to a nearby hermitage, where a number of monks have gathered. Upon arriving, the Buddha hears the monks discussing the dharma and waits patiently for a break in the conversation, at which point he coughs to indicate his presence and knocks on the door. The monks of course invite him in, and when he asks what they were discussing, they reply that they were in fact talking about him: "Our discussion on the Dhamma that was interrupted was about the Blessed One himself."

He begins by saying that there are two kinds of searches, one ignoble and one noble. In the former case, someone who is subject to birth, aging, sickness, and death goes in search of what is also subject to birth, aging, sickness, and death. In the latter, someone who is subject to birth, aging, sickness, and death goes in search of what is beyond birth, aging, sickness, and death—that is, in search of nirvana.

This declaration provides the occasion for the Buddha to recount his own noble search, "while I was still only an unenlightened Bodhisatta" (Pali for *bodhisattva*). Here the Buddha recounts his departure from the home in search of the truth, his instruction by other teachers, his enlightenment, and his first sermon, ending with directions for achieving the various levels of deep concentration. One notes immediately the understated tone of the narrative, devoid of the rich detail so familiar from the biographies. There is no mention of the opulence of his youth, no mention of his wife, no mention of chariot rides, no description of his departure from the palace in the dead of night—all points featured in the next selection. Instead, he simply says, "Later, while still young, a black-haired young man endowed with the blessing of youth, in the prime of life, though my mother and father wished otherwise and wept with tearful faces, I shaved off my hair and beard, put on the yellow robe, and went forth from the home life into homelessness." Although the descriptions of his study with other meditation masters and of levels of concentration at the end of the chapter assume a sophisticated system of meditative states, his account of the most momentous event in the history of Buddhism, his enlightenment, is set forth in sober tones, portrayed as the outcome of long reflection rather than as an ecstatic moment of revelation.

This is not to say that the passage somehow lacks the divine. Familiar elements of the enlightenment narrative are found here, including the reluctance to teach and the famous pleadings by the deity Brahma. But the emphasis is on the human. The group of five—the ascetics who, shortly before his enlightenment, abandoned him when he gave up his practice of austerities—are initially very skeptical about the Buddha's claim that he has attained the deathless state. And on the way to the Deer Park in Sarnath, where he will deliver his first sermon, the newly enlightened Buddha encounters another mendicant, who asks him who his teacher is. The Buddha responds in triumphant verse, saying that he has no teacher because there is no one else as enlightened as he is. The mendicant responds, "May it be so, friend"—in more modern parlance, "Whatever"—shakes his head, and continues on his way.

PRONOUNCING GLOSSARY

Ajivaka Upaka: *ah-jee-va-ka u-pa-ka*
Alara Kalama: *ah-lah-ra kah-lah-ma*
Ananda: *ah-nan-da*
Anathapindika: *a-nah-ta-pihn-di-ka*
Ariyapariyesana Sutta: *a-ri-ya-pa-rih-yay-sa-nah soot-ta*
Benares: *ba-nah-ras*
bhikkhu: *bik-ku*
Brahma Sahampati: *bra-mah sa-ham-pa-ti*
Dhamma: *dam-ma*
Gaya: *ga-yah*

Gotama: *goh-ta-ma*
Isipatana: *ih-sih-pa-ta-na*
Jeta: *jay-ta*
jhana: *jah-na*
Kasi: *kah-sih*
Magadha: *ma-ga-da*
Majjhima Nikaya: *maj-ji-ma nih-kah-ya*
Mara: *mah-ra*
Migara: *mih-gah-ra*
Nibbana: *nib-bah-na*
Rammaka: *ram-ma-ka*

Savatthi: *sah-vat-tee*

Senanigama: *say-nah-ni-ga-ma*

Tathagata: *ta-tah-ga-ta*

Uddaka Ramaputta: *ud-da-ka rah-ma-put-ta*

Uruvela: *u-ru-vay-la*

Thus have I heard. On one occasion the Blessed One was living at Savatthi in Jeta's Grove, Anathapindika's Park.

Then, when it was morning, the Blessed One dressed, and taking his bowl and outer robe, went into Savatthi for alms. Then a number of bhikkhus went to the venerable Ananda[1] and said to him: "Friend Ananda, it is long since we heard a talk on the Dhamma[2] from the Blessed One's own lips. It would be good if we could get to hear such a talk, friend Ananda."—"Then let the venerable ones go to the brahmin Rammaka's hermitage. Perhaps you will get to hear a talk on the Dhamma from the Blessed One's own lips."—"Yes, friend," they replied.

Then, when the Blessed One had wandered for alms in Savatthi and had returned from his almsround, after his meal he addressed the venerable Ananda: "Ananda, let us go to the Eastern Park, to the Palace of Migara's Mother, for the day's abiding."—"Yes, venerable sir," the venerable Ananda replied. Then the Blessed One went with the venerable Ananda to the Eastern Park, the Palace of Migara's Mother, for the day's abiding.

Then, when it was evening, the Blessed One rose from meditation and addressed the venerable Ananda: "Ananda, let us go to the Eastern Bathing Place to bathe."—"Yes, venerable sir," the venerable Ananda replied. Then the Blessed One went with the venerable Ananda to the Eastern Bathing Place to bathe. When he was finished, he came up out of the water and stood in one robe drying his limbs. Then the venerable Ananda said to the Blessed One: "Venerable sir, the brahmin Rammaka's hermitage is nearby. That hermitage is agreeable and delightful. Venerable sir, it would be good if the Blessed One went there out of compassion." The Blessed One consented in silence.

Then the Blessed One went to the brahmin Rammaka's hermitage. Now on that occasion a number of bhikkhus were sitting together in the hermitage discussing the Dhamma. The Blessed One stood outside the door waiting for their discussion to end. When he knew that it was over, he coughed and knocked, and the bhikkhus opened the door for him. The Blessed One entered, sat down on a seat made ready, and addressed the bhikkhus thus: "Bhikkhus, for what discussion are you sitting together here now? And what was your discussion that was interrupted?"

"Venerable sir, our discussion on the Dhamma that was interrupted was about the Blessed One himself. Then the Blessed One arrived."

"Good, bhikkhus. It is fitting for you clansmen who have gone forth out of faith from the home life into homelessness to sit together to discuss the Dhamma. When you gather together, bhikkhus, you should do either of two things: hold discussion on the Dhamma or maintain noble silence.

TRANSLATED FROM the Pali by Bhikkhu Ñāṇamoli; translation revised and edited by Bhikkhu Bodhi.

1. The Buddha's cousin and personal attendant.   2. That is, the dharma.
"Bhikkhus": Pali for *bhikshus*, monks.

"Bhikkhus, there are these two kinds of search: the noble search and the ignoble search. And what is the ignoble search? Here someone being himself subject to birth seeks what is also subject to birth; being himself subject to ageing, he seeks what is also subject to ageing; being himself subject to sickness, he seeks what is also subject to sickness; being himself subject to death, he seeks what is also subject to death; being himself subject to sorrow, he seeks what is also subject to sorrow; being himself subject to defilement, he seeks what is also subject to defilement.

"And what may be said to be subject to birth? Wife and children are subject to birth, men and women slaves, goats and sheep, fowl and pigs, elephants, cattle, horses, and mares, gold and silver are subject to birth. These objects of attachment are subject to birth; and one who is tied to these things, infatuated with them, and utterly committed to them, being himself subject to birth, seeks what its also subject to birth.

"And what may be said to be subject to ageing? Wife and children are subject to ageing, men and women slaves, goats and sheep, fowl and pigs, elephants, cattle, horses, and mares, gold and silver are subject to ageing. These objects of attachment are subject to ageing; and one who is tied to these things, infatuated with them, and utterly committed to them, being himself subject to ageing, seeks what is also subject to ageing.

"And what may be said to be subject to sickness? Wife and children are subject to sickness, men and women slaves, goats and sheep, fowl and pigs, elephants, cattle, horses, and mares are subject to sickness. These objects of attachment are subject to sickness; and one who is tied to these things, infatuated with them, and utterly committed to them, being himself subject to sickness, seeks what is also subject to sickness.

"And what may be said to be subject to death? Wife and children are subject to death, men and women slaves, goats and sheep, fowl and pigs, elephants, cattle, horses, and mares are subject to death. These objects of attachment are subject to death; and one who is tied to these things, infatuated with them, and utterly committed to them, being himself subject to death, seeks what is also subject to death.

"And what may be said to be subject to sorrow? Wife and children are subject to sorrow, men and women slaves, goats and sheep, fowl and pigs, elephants, cattle, horses, and mares are subject to sorrow. These objects of attachment are subject to sorrow; and one who is tied to these things, infatuated with them, and utterly committed to them, being himself subject to sorrow, seeks what is also subject to sorrow.

"And what may be said to be subject to defilement? Wife and children are subject to defilement, men and women slaves, goats and sheep, fowl and pigs, elephants, cattle, horses, and mares, gold and silver are subject to defilement. These objects of attachment are subject to defilement; and one who is tied to these things, infatuated with them, and utterly committed to them, being himself subject to defilement, seeks what is also subject to defilement. This is the ignoble search.

"And what is the noble search? Here someone being himself subject to birth, having understood the danger in what is subject to birth, seeks the unborn supreme security from bondage, Nibbana;[3] being himself subject to

3. Pali for *nirvana*.

ageing, having understood the danger in what is subject to ageing, he seeks the unageing supreme security from bondage, Nibbana; being himself subject to sickness, having understood the danger in what is subject to sickness, he seeks the unailing supreme security from bondage, Nibbana; being himself subject to death, having understood the danger in what is subject to death, he seeks the deathless supreme security from bondage, Nibbana; being himself subject to sorrow, having understood the danger in what is subject to sorrow, he seeks the sorrowless supreme security from bondage, Nibbana; being himself subject to defilement, having understood the danger in what is subject to defilement, he seeks the undefiled supreme security from bondage, Nibbana. This is the noble search.

"Bhikkhus, before my enlightenment, while I was still only an unenlightened Bodhisatta,[4] I too, being myself subject to birth, sought what was also subject to birth; being myself subject to ageing, sickness, death, sorrow, and defilement, I sought what was also subject to ageing, sickness, death, sorrow, and defilement. Then I considered thus: 'Why, being myself subject to birth, do I seek what is also subject to birth? Why, being myself subject to ageing, sickness, death, sorrow, and defilement, do I seek what is also subject to ageing, sickness, death, sorrow, and defilement? Suppose that, being myself subject to birth, having understood the danger in what is subject to birth, I seek the unborn supreme security from bondage, Nibbana. Suppose that, being myself subject to ageing, sickness, death, sorrow, and defilement, having understood the danger in what is subject to ageing, sickness, death, sorrow, and defilement, I seek the unageing, unailing, deathless, sorrowless, and undefiled supreme security from bondage, Nibbana.'

"Later, while still young, a black-haired young man endowed with the blessing of youth, in the prime of life, though my mother and father wished otherwise and wept with tearful faces, I shaved off my hair and beard, put on the yellow robe, and went forth from the home life into homelessness.

"Having gone forth, bhikkhus, in search of what is wholesome, seeking the supreme state of sublime peace, I went to Alara Kalama and said to him: 'Friend Kalama, I want to lead the holy life in this Dhamma and Discipline.' Alara Kalama replied: 'The venerable one may stay here. This Dhamma is such that a wise man can soon enter upon and abide in it, realising for himself through direct knowledge his own teacher's doctrine.' I soon quickly learned that Dhamma. As far as mere lip-reciting and rehearsal of his teaching went, I could speak with knowledge and assurance, and I claimed, 'I know and see'—and there were others who did likewise.

"I considered: 'It is not through mere faith alone that Alara Kalama declares: "By realising for myself with direct knowledge, I enter upon and abide in this Dhamma." Certainly Alara Kalama abides knowing and seeing this Dhamma.' Then I went to Alara Kalama and asked him: 'Friend Kalama, in what way do you declare that by realising for yourself with direct knowledge you enter upon and abide in this Dhamma?' In reply he declared the base of nothingness.

"I considered: 'Not only Alara Kalama has faith, energy, mindfulness, concentration, and wisdom. I too have faith, energy, mindfulness, concentration,

---

4. Pali for *bodhisattva*.

and wisdom. Suppose I endeavour to realise the Dhamma that Alara Kalama declares he enters upon and abides in by realising for himself with direct knowledge?'

"I soon quickly entered upon and abided in that Dhamma by realising for myself with direct knowledge. Then I went to Alara Kalama and asked him: 'Friend Kalama, is it in this way that you declare that you enter upon and abide in this Dhamma by realising for yourself with direct knowledge?'—'That is the way, friend.'—'It is in this way, friend, that I also enter upon and abide in this Dhamma by realising for myself with direct knowledge.'—'It is a gain for us, friend, it is a great gain for us that we have such a venerable one for our companion in the holy life. So the Dhamma that I declare I enter upon and abide in by realising for myself with direct knowledge is the Dhamma that you enter upon and abide in by realising for yourself with direct knowledge. And the Dhamma that you enter upon and abide in by realising for yourself with direct knowledge is the Dhamma that I declare I enter upon and abide in by realising for myself with direct knowledge. So you know the Dhamma that I know and I know the Dhamma that you know. As I am, so are you; as you are, so am I. Come, friend, let us now lead this community together.'

"Thus Alara Kalama, my teacher, placed me, his pupil, on an equal footing with himself and awarded me the highest honour. But it occurred to me: 'This Dhamma does not lead to disenchantment, to dispassion, to cessation, to peace, to direct knowledge, to enlightenment, to Nibbana, but only to reappearance in the base of nothingness.' Not being satisfied with that Dhamma, I left it and went away.

"Still in search, bhikkhus, of what is wholesome, seeking the supreme state of sublime peace, I went to Uddaka Ramaputta and said to him: 'Friend, I want to lead the holy life in this Dhamma and Discipline.' Uddaka Ramaputta replied: 'The venerable one may stay here. This Dhamma is such that a wise man can soon enter upon and abide in it, himself realising through direct knowledge his own teacher's doctrine.' I soon quickly learned that Dhamma. As far as mere lip-reciting and rehearsal of his teaching went, I could speak with knowledge and assurance, and I claimed, 'I know and see'—and there were others who did likewise.

"I considered: 'It was not through mere faith alone that Rama[5] declared: "By realising for myself with direct knowledge, I enter upon and abide in this Dhamma." Certainly Rama abided knowing and seeing this Dhamma.' Then I went to Uddaka Ramaputta and asked him: 'Friend, in what way did Rama declare that by realising for himself with direct knowledge he entered upon and abided in this Dhamma?' In reply Uddaka Ramaputta declared the base of neither-perception-nor-non-perception.

"I considered: 'Not only Rama had faith, energy, mindfulness, concentration, and wisdom. I too have faith, energy, mindfulness, concentration, and wisdom. Suppose I endeavour to realise the Dhamma that Rama declared he entered upon and abided in by realising for himself with direct knowledge.'

"I soon quickly entered upon and abided in that Dhamma by realising for myself with direct knowledge. Then I went to Uddaka Ramaputta and asked him: 'Friend, was it in this way that Rama declared that he entered upon and abided in this Dhamma by realising for himself with direct knowledge?'—

5. The father of Uddaka Ramaputta.

'That is the way, friend.'—'It is in this way, friend, that I also enter upon
and abide in this Dhamma by realising for myself with direct knowledge.'—
'It is a gain for us, friend, it is a great gain for us that we have such a venerable one for our companion in the holy life. So the Dhamma that Rama
declared he entered upon and abided in by realising for himself with direct
knowledge is the Dhamma that you enter upon and abide in by realising for
yourself with direct knowledge. And the Dhamma that you enter upon and
abide in by realising for yourself with direct knowledge is the Dhamma that
Rama declared he entered upon and abided in by realising for himself with
direct knowledge. So you know the Dhamma that Rama knew and Rama
knew the Dhamma that you know. As Rama was, so are you; as you are, so
was Rama. Come, friend, now lead this community.'

"Thus Uddaka Ramaputta, my companion in the holy life, placed me in
the position of a teacher and accorded me the highest honour. But it occurred
to me: 'This Dhamma does not lead to disenchantment, to dispassion, to
cessation, to peace, to direct knowledge, to enlightenment, to Nibbana, but
only to reappearance in the base of neither-perception-nor-non-perception.'
Not being satisfied with that Dhamma, I left it and went away.

"Still in search, bhikkhus, of what is wholesome, seeking the supreme
state of sublime peace, I wandered by stages through the Magadhan country until eventually I arrived at Senanigama near Uruvela.[6] There I saw an
agreeable piece of ground, a delightful grove with a clear-flowing river with
pleasant, smooth banks and nearby a village for alms resort. I considered:
'This is an agreeable piece of ground, this is a delightful grove with a clear-
flowing river with pleasant, smooth banks and nearby a village for alms
resort. This will serve for the striving of a clansman intent on striving.' And
I sat down there thinking: 'This will serve for striving.'

"Then, bhikkhus, being myself subject to birth, having understood the danger in what is subject to birth, seeking the unborn supreme security from
bondage, Nibbana, I attained the unborn supreme security from bondage,
Nibbana; being myself subject to ageing, having understood the danger in
what is subject to ageing, seeking the unageing supreme security from bondage, Nibbana, I attained the unageing supreme security from bondage, Nibbana; being myself subject to sickness, having understood the danger in what
is subject to sickness, seeking the unailing supreme security from bondage,
Nibbana, I attained the unailing supreme security from bondage, Nibbana;
being myself subject to death, having understood the danger in what is subject
to death, seeking the deathless supreme security from bondage, Nibbana, I
attained the deathless supreme security from bondage, Nibbana; being
myself subject to sorrow, having understood the danger in what is subject to
sorrow, seeking the sorrowless supreme security from bondage, Nibbana, I
attained the sorrowless supreme security from bondage, Nibbana; being
myself subject to defilement, having understood the danger in what is subject to defilement, seeking the undefiled supreme security from bondage,
Nibbana, I attained the undefiled supreme security from bondage, Nibbana.
The knowledge and vision arose in me: 'My deliverance is unshakeable; this
is my last birth; now there is no renewal of being.'

6. A village in Magadha, a kingdom in northeastern India.

"I considered: 'This Dhamma that I have attained is profound, hard to see and hard to understand, peaceful and sublime, unattainable by mere reasoning, subtle, to be experienced by the wise. But this generation delights in worldliness, takes delight in worldliness, rejoices in worldliness. It is hard for such a generation to see this truth, namely, specific conditionality, dependent origination. And it is hard to see this truth, namely, the stilling of all formations, the relinquishing of all attachments, the destruction of craving, dispassion, cessation, Nibbana. If I were to teach the Dhamma, others would not understand me, and that would be wearying and troublesome for me.' Thereupon there came to me spontaneously these stanzas never heard before:

> 'Enough with teaching the Dhamma
> That even I found hard to reach;
> For it will never be perceived
> By those who live in lust and hate.
>
> Those dyed in lust, wrapped in darkness
> Will never discern this abstruse Dhamma
> Which goes against the worldly stream,
> Subtle, deep, and difficult to see.'

Considering thus, my mind inclined to inaction rather than to teaching the Dhamma.

"Then, bhikkhus, the Brahma Sahampati knew with his mind the thought in my mind and he considered: 'The world will be lost, the world will perish, since the mind of the Tathagata,[7] accomplished and fully enlightened, inclines to inaction rather than to teaching the Dhamma.' Then, just as quickly as a strong man might extend his flexed arm or flex his extended arm, the Brahma Sahampati vanished in the Brahma-world[8] and appeared before me. He arranged his upper robe on one shoulder, and extending his hands in reverential salutation towards me, said: 'Venerable sir, let the Blessed One teach the Dhamma, let the Sublime One teach the Dhamma. There are beings with little dust in their eyes who are wasting through not hearing the Dhamma. There will be those who will understand the Dhamma.' The Brahma Sahampati spoke thus, and then he said further:

> 'In Magadha there have appeared till now
> Impure teachings devised by those still stained.
> Open the doors to the Deathless! Let them hear
> The Dhamma that the Stainless One has found.
>
> Just as one who stands on a mountain peak
> Can see below the people all around,
> So, O Wise One, All-seeing Sage,
> Ascend the palace of the Dhamma.
> Let the Sorrowless One survey this human breed,
> Engulfed in sorrow, overcome by birth and old age.

7. A title of a buddha; it is the one most often used by the historical Buddha to refer to himself.

8. The heavens, which are presided over by the god Brahma.

> Arise, victorious hero, caravan leader,
> Debtless one, and wander in the world.
> Let the Blessed One teach the Dhamma,
> There will be those who will understand.'

"Then I listened to the Brahma's pleading, and out of compassion for beings I surveyed the world with the eye of a Buddha. Surveying the world with the eye of a Buddha, I saw beings with little dust in their eyes and with much dust in their eyes, with keen faculties and with dull faculties, with good qualities and with bad qualities, easy to teach and hard to teach, and some who dwelt seeing fear in blame and in the other world. Just as in a pond of blue or red or white lotuses, some lotuses that are born and grow in the water thrive immersed in the water without rising out of it, and some other lotuses that are born and grow in the water rest on the water's surface, and some other lotuses that are born and grow in the water rise out of the water and stand clear, unwetted by it; so too, surveying the world with the eye of a Buddha, I saw beings with little dust in their eyes and with much dust in their eyes, with keen faculties and with dull faculties, with good qualities and with bad qualities, easy to teach and hard to teach, and some who dwelt seeing fear in blame and in the other world. Then I replied to the Brahma Sahampati in stanzas:

> 'Open for them are the doors to the Deathless,
> Let those with ears now show their faith.
> Thinking it would be troublesome, O Brahma,
> I did not speak the Dhamma subtle and sublime.'

Then the Brahma Sahampati thought: 'I have created the opportunity for the Blessed One to teach the Dhamma.' And after paying homage to me, keeping me on the right, he thereupon departed at once.

"I considered thus: 'To whom should I first teach the Dhamma? Who will understand this Dhamma quickly?' It then occurred to me: 'Alara Kalama is wise, intelligent, and discerning; he has long had little dust in his eyes. Suppose I taught the Dhamma first to Alara Kalama. He will understand it quickly.' Then deities approached me and said: 'Venerable sir, Alara Kalama died seven days ago.' And the knowledge and vision arose in me: 'Alara Kalama died seven days ago.' I thought: 'Alara Kalama's loss is a great one. If he had heard this Dhamma, he would have understood it quickly.'

"I considered thus: 'To whom should I first teach the Dhamma? Who will understand this Dhamma quickly?' It then occurred to me: 'Uddaka Ramaputta is wise, intelligent, and discerning; he has long had little dust in his eyes. Suppose I taught the Dhamma first to Uddaka Ramaputta. He will understand it quickly.' Then deities approached me and said: 'Venerable sir, Uddaka Ramaputta died last night.' And the knowledge and vision arose in me: 'Uddaka Ramaputta died last night.' I thought: 'Uddaka Ramaputta's loss is a great one. If he had heard this Dhamma, he would have understood it quickly.'

"I considered thus: 'To whom should I first teach the Dhamma? Who will understand this Dhamma quickly?' It then occurred to me: 'The bhikkhus of the group of five who attended upon me while I was engaged in my striving were very helpful. Suppose I taught the Dhamma first to them.' Then I thought: 'Where are the bhikkhus of the group of five now living?' And with the divine eye, which is purified and surpasses the human, I saw that they were living at Benares[9] in the Deer Park at Isipatana.

"Then, bhikkhus, when I had stayed at Uruvela as long as I chose, I set out to wander by stages to Benares. Between Gaya and the Place of Enlightenment the Ajivaka Upaka saw me on the road and said: 'Friend, your faculties are clear, the colour of your skin is pure and bright. Under whom have you gone forth, friend? Who is your teacher? Whose Dhamma do you profess?' I replied to the Ajivaka Upaka in stanzas:

> 'I am one who has transcended all, a knower of all,
> Unsullied among all things, renouncing all,
> By craving's ceasing freed. Having known this all
> For myself, to whom should I point as teacher?
>
> I have no teacher, and one like me
> Exists nowhere in all the world
> With all its gods, because I have
> No person for my counterpart.
>
> I am the Accomplished One in the world,
> I am the Teacher Supreme.
> I alone am a Fully Enlightened One
> Whose fires are quenched and extinguished.
>
> I go now to the city of Kasi
> To set in motion the Wheel of Dhamma.
> In a world that has become blind
> I go to beat the drum of the Deathless.'

'By your claims, friend, you ought to be the Universal Victor.'

> 'The victors are those like me
> Who have won to destruction of taints.
> I have vanquished all evil states,
> Therefore, Upaka, I am a victor.'

"When this was said, the Ajivaka Upaka said: 'May it be so, friend.' Shaking his head, he took a bypath and departed.

"Then, bhikkhus, wandering by stages, I eventually came to Benares, to the Deer Park at Isipatana, and I approached the bhikkhus of the group of five. The bhikkhus saw me coming in the distance, and they agreed among themselves thus: 'Friends, here comes the recluse Gotama[1] who lives luxuriously, who gave up his striving, and reverted to luxury. We should not pay homage to him or rise up for him or receive his bowl and outer robe. But a seat may be prepared for him. If he likes, he may sit down.' However, as I approached, those bhikkhus found themselves unable to keep their pact. One came to meet me and took my bowl and outer robe, another prepared a seat, and another set out water for my feet; however, they addressed me by name and as 'friend.'

9. That is, Varanasi (also called Kasi), a city on the Ganges in northeastern India.   1. That is, Gautama.

"Thereupon I told them: 'Bhikkhus, do not address the Tathagata by name and as "friend." The Tathagata is an Accomplished One, a Fully Enlightened One. Listen, bhikkhus, the Deathless has been attained. I shall instruct you, I shall teach you the Dhamma. Practising as you are instructed, by realising for yourselves here and now through direct knowledge you will soon enter upon and abide in that supreme goal of the holy life for the sake of which clansmen rightly go forth from the home life into homelessness.'

"When this was said, the bhikkhus of the group of five answered me thus: 'Friend Gotama, by the conduct, the practice, and the performance of austerities that you undertook, you did not achieve any superhuman states, any distinction in knowledge and vision worthy of the noble ones. Since you now live luxuriously, having given up your striving and reverted to luxury, how will you have achieved any superhuman states, any distinction in knowledge and vision worthy of the noble ones?' When this was said, I told them: 'The Tathagata does not live luxuriously, nor has he given up his striving and reverted to luxury. The Tathagata is an Accomplished One, a Fully Enlightened One. Listen, bhikkhus, the Deathless has been attained . . . from the home life into homelessness.'

"A second time the bhikkhus of the group of five said to me: 'Friend Gotama . . . how will you have achieved any superhuman states, any distinction in knowledge and vision worthy of the noble ones?' A second time I told them: 'The Tathagata does not live luxuriously . . . from the home life into homelessness.' A third time the bhikkhus of the group of five said to me: 'Friend Gotama . . . how will you have achieved any superhuman states, any distinction in knowledge and vision worthy of the noble ones?'

"When this was said I asked them: 'Bhikkhus, have you ever known me to speak like this before?'—'No, venerable sir.'—'Bhikkhus, the Tathagata is an Accomplished One, a Fully Enlightened One. Listen, bhikkhus, the Deathless has been attained. I shall instruct you, I shall teach you the Dhamma. Practising as you are instructed, by realising for yourselves here and now through direct knowledge you will soon enter upon and abide in that supreme goal of the holy life for the sake of which clansmen rightly go forth from the home life into homelessness.'

"I was able to convince the bhikkhus of the group of five. Then I sometimes instructed two bhikkhus while the other three went for alms, and the six of us lived on what those three bhikkhus brought back from their almsround. Sometimes I instructed three bhikkhus while the other two went for alms, and the six of us lived on what those two bhikkhus brought back from their almsround.

"Then the bhikkhus of the group of five, thus taught and instructed by me, being themselves subject to birth, having understood the danger in what is subject to birth, seeking the unborn supreme security from bondage, Nibbana, attained the unborn supreme security from bondage, Nibbana; being themselves subject to ageing, sickness, death, sorrow, and defilement, having understood the danger in what is subject to ageing, sickness, death, sorrow, and defilement, seeking the unageing, unailing, deathless, sorrowless, and undefiled supreme security from bondage, Nibbana, they attained the unageing, unailing, deathless, sorrowless, and undefiled supreme security from bondage, Nibbana. The knowledge and vision arose in them: 'Our deliverance is unshakeable; this is our last birth; there is no renewal of being.'

"Bhikkhus, there are these five cords of sensual pleasure. What are the five? Forms cognizable by the eye that are wished for, desired, agreeable and likeable, connected with sensual desire, and provocative of lust. Sounds cognizable by the ear . . . Odours cognizable by the nose . . . Flavours cognizable by the tongue . . . Tangibles cognizable by the body that are wished for, desired, agreeable and likeable, connected with sensual desire, and provocative of lust. These are the five cords of sensual pleasure.

"As to those recluses and brahmins who are tied to these five cords of sensual pleasure; infatuated with them and utterly committed to them, and who use them without seeing the danger in them or understanding the escape from them, it may be understood of them: 'They have met with calamity, met with disaster, the Evil One may do with them as he likes.' Suppose a forest deer who was bound lay down on a heap of snares; it might be understood of him: 'He has met with calamity, met with disaster, the hunter can do with him as he likes, and when the hunter comes he cannot go where he wants.' So too, as to those recluses and brahmins who are tied to these five cords of sensual pleasure . . . it may be understood of them: 'They have met with calamity, met with disaster, the Evil One may do with them as he likes.'

"As to those recluses and brahmins who are not tied to these five cords of sensual pleasure, who are not infatuated with them or utterly committed to them, and who use them seeing the danger in them and understanding the escape from them, it may be understood of them: 'They have not met with calamity, not met with disaster, the Evil One cannot do with them as he likes.' Suppose a forest deer who was unbound lay down on a heap of snares; it might be understood of him: 'He has not met with calamity, not met with disaster, the hunter cannot do with him as he likes, and when the hunter comes he can go where he wants.' So too, as to those recluses and brahmins who are not tied to these five cords of sensual pleasure . . . it may be understood of them: 'They have not met with calamity, not met with disaster, the Evil One cannot do with them as he likes.'

"Suppose a forest deer is wandering in the forest wilds: he walks without fear, stands without fear, sits without fear, lies down without fear. Why is that? Because he is out of the hunter's range. So too, quite secluded from sensual pleasures, secluded from unwholesome states, a bhikkhu enters upon and abides in the first jhana,[2] which is accompanied by applied and sustained thought, with rapture and pleasure born of seclusion. This bhikkhu is said to have blindfolded Mara,[3] to have become invisible to the Evil One by depriving Mara's eye of its opportunity.

"Again, with the stilling of applied and sustained thought, a bhikkhu enters upon and abides in the second jhana, which has self-confidence and singleness of mind without applied and sustained thought, with rapture and pleasure born of concentration. This bhikkhu is said to have blindfolded Mara . . .

"Again, with the fading away as well of rapture, a bhikkhu abides in equanimity, and mindful and fully aware, still feeling pleasure with the body, he enters upon and abides in the third jhana, on account of which

---

2. Pali for *dhyana*, a meditative state.   3. The personification of evil and desire.

noble ones announce: 'He has a pleasant abiding who has equanimity and is mindful.' This bhikkhu is said to have blindfolded Mara . . .

"Again, with the abandoning of pleasure and pain, and with the previous disappearance of joy and grief, a bhikkhu enters upon and abides in the fourth jhana, which has neither-pain-nor-pleasure and purity of mindfulness due to equanimity. This bhikkhu is said to have blindfolded Mara . . .

"Again, with the complete surmounting of perceptions of form, with the disappearance of perceptions of sensory impact, with non-attention to perceptions of diversity, aware that 'space is infinite,' a bhikkhu enters upon and abides in the base of infinite space. This bhikkhu is said to have blindfolded Mara . . .

"Again, by completely surmounting the base of infinite space, aware that 'consciousness is infinite,' a bhikkhu enters upon and abides in the base of infinite consciousness. This bhikkhu is said to have blindfolded Mara . . .

"Again, by completely surmounting the base of infinite consciousness, aware that 'there is nothing,' a bhikkhu enters upon and abides in the base of nothingness. This bhikkhu is said to have blindfolded Mara . . .

"Again, by completely surrounding the base of nothingness, a bhikkhu enters upon and abides in the base of neither-perception-nor-non-perception. This bhikkhu is said to have blindfolded Mara, to have become invisible to the Evil One by depriving Mara's eye of its opportunity.

"Again, by completely surmounting the base of neither-perception-nor-non-perception, a bhikkhu enters upon and abides in the cessation of perception and feeling. And his taints are destroyed by his seeing with wisdom. This bhikkhu is said to have blindfolded Mara, to have become invisible to the Evil One by depriving Mara's eye of its opportunity, and to have crossed beyond attachment to the world. He walks without fear, stands without fear, sits without fear, lies down without fear. Why is that? Because he is out of the Evil One's range."

That is what the Blessed One said. The bhikkhus were satisfied and delighted in the Blessed One's words.

THE LIFE OF THE BUDDHA

ACCOUNT OF THE BEGINNING
(*The Nidanakatha*)

In the previous selection, we read what scholars consider to be one of the early accounts of the Buddha's noble search for enlightenment. It lacked many details that, added over the centuries in retellings of the story, became standard features of biographies produced across the Buddhist world. The text presented here contains many of these familiar elements: Queen Maya's dream of the white elephant, the birth of the future Buddha from her right side, the predictions of the astrologers, the confinement in the palace of pleasures, the chariot rides outside the city.

The text is titled *Nidanakatha*, the *Account of the Beginning*. It was composed in Pali in the fifth century c.e.—that is, some eight centuries after the Buddha's death—and is the earliest Pali work to link the events of the life of the Buddha into a coherent biographical account (although it ends long before his death). It is traditionally ascribed to the great scholar Buddhaghosa (see his *Visuddhimagga*, p. 249). Before we turn to its content, it is important to briefly consider its structure.

The *Nidanakatha* is itself a preface to the Pali collection of jataka stories, in a sense providing a frame for all of those stories of the Buddha's previous lives. To that end, it is divided into three sections. The first section is titled "The Distant Epoch." It tells the story of Sumedha, the yogin who, billions of years ago, made a vow in the presence of the Buddha Dipamkara to one day become a buddha himself. It was Sumedha who eventually would be reborn as Prince Siddhartha and achieve enlightenment under the Bodhi tree. Thus, the jataka stories begin when Sumedha becomes a bodhisattva and they end when Siddhartha becomes the Buddha; each intervening life is a past birth of a future buddha. This first section also tells of the bodhisattva's encounters with twenty-three other buddhas of the past as he proceeds toward enlightenment, and it describes the ten perfections that he practices.

The second part of the *Nidanakatha*, presented in full here, is called literally "The Not Distant Epoch," and it might seem to belong not before the jataka collection but after it, for it is the story of his last lifetime as bodhisattva. It recounts the life of the Buddha from his penultimate life as a god in Tushita Heaven, where he surveys the world to choose the circumstances of his birth, through his birth, his youth, the chariot rides, the departure from the palace, and the practice of asceticism, all presented in rather baroque detail. It concludes with his attainment of enlightenment and the first words that he spoke afterward, words spoken by all the buddhas:

> Seeking the builder of the house I sped along many births in Samsara but
> to no avail; ill is birth again and again.
> O builder of the house, you are seen. Do not build the house again! All your
> beams are broken, and the ridgepole is shattered.
> The mind that has gone beyond things composite has attained the destruction
> of the cravings.

The final section (not included here), "The Recent Epoch," begins by describing the events of the first seven weeks after the Buddha's enlightenment, his decision to teach, his first sermon, the conversion of the first disciples, his return to his home city of Kapilavastu, and the ordination of his son, Rahula. It ends with the donation to the Buddha of Jetavana Monastery by Anathapindika, the Buddha's most famous lay disciple and patron.

Although this particular text comes from the Pali tradition of Sri Lanka and Southeast Asia, the story of the Buddha presented here is widely known, and loved, across the Buddhist world.

PRONOUNCING GLOSSARY

ammana: *am-ma-na*

anicca: *a-nich-cha*

Asalhi: *ah-sahl-hi*

Avici: *a-vee-chi*

Bhoja: *boh-ja*

Bodhisatta: *boh-di-sat-ta*

Brahmana: *brah-ma-na*

Citralata: *chi-tra-la-tah*

Culamani: *choo-lah-ma-ni*

deva: *day-va*

Devadaha: *day-va-da-ha*

devaputta: *day-va-pu-ta*

Dhanapalaka: *da-na-pah-la-ka*

Digha-nikaya: *dee-ga-ni-kah-ya*

Ghatikara: *ga-ti-kah-ra*

Girimekhala: *gi-ri-meh-ka-la*

Isipatana: *i-si-pa-ta-na*

Jambudipa: *jam-bu-dee-pa*

jhana: *jah-na*

Kajangala: *ka-jan-ga-la*

Kaladevala: *kah-la-day-va-la*

Kaludayi: *Kah-lu-dah-yee*

Kanthaka: *kan-ta-ka*

Kapilavatthu: *ka-pi-la-vat-tu*

khattiya: *kat-ti-ya*

Kisagotami: *ki-sah-goh-ta-mee*

Kondanna: *kohn-dan-nya*
Kutumbaka: *ku-tum-ba-ka*
Kuyyaka: *ku-ya-ka*
Lakkhana: *lak-ka-na*
Lokabyuha: *loh-ka-byoo-ha*
Magadha: *mah-ga-da*
Mahakala: *ma-hah-kah-la*
Mahamaya.: *ma-hah-mah-yah*
Mahapadana: *ma-hah-pa-dah-na*
Mahasala: *ma-hah-sah-la*
Mahosadha: *ma-hoh-sa-da*
Mandarava: *man-dah-ra-va*
Manjerika: *man-jay-ri-ka*
Neranjara: *nay-ran-ja-rah*
Nibbana: *nib-bah-na*
Nidanakatha: *ni-dah-na-ka-thah*
Osadha-daraka: *oh-sa-da-dah-ra-ka*
Pacceka: *pach-cheh-ka*
Pancavaggiya: *pan-cha-vag-gi-ya*
Paranimmita: *pa-ra-nim-mi-ta*
Paricchattaka: *pah-rich-cha-ta-ka*
Salalavati: *sa-la-la-va-tee*

Santusita: *san-tu-si-ta*
Sarabhanga Jataka: *sa-ra-ban-ga jah-ta-ka*
Setakannika: *seh-ta-kan-ni-ka*
Siddhattha: *sid-dat-ta*
Sotthiya: *soh-ti-ya*
Suddhodhana: *sud-doh-da-na*
Tathagata: *ta-tah-ga-ta*
Tavatimsa: *tah-va-tim-sa*
Thuna: *too-na*
Uddaka Ramaputta: *ud-da-ka rah-ma-put-ta*
uposatha: *u-poh-sa-ta*
Uruvela: *u-ru-vay-lah*
usabha: *u-sa-ba*
Vasavatti: *va-sa-vat-ti*
Vedanga: *vay-dan-ga*
Vesakha: *vay-sah-ka*
Vessantara: *vays-san-ta-ra*
Vijayuttara: *vi-ja-yut-ta-ra*
Vissakamma: *vi-sa-kam-ma*
Yugandhara: *yu-gan-da-ra*

It was when the Bodhisatta[1] was living in the City of Tusita that the tumultuous proclamation of the Buddha arose. For, in the world three tumultuous proclamations take place, namely, that of the æon, of a Buddha, and that of a Universal Monarch.[2] Herein, a class of deities called Lokabyuha (World Array), who belong to the realm of sensuous existence, having come to know that a new æon would dawn on the elapse of another hundred thousand years, go about in the world of men, with their hair loosened and dishevelled, with sorrowful faces, wiping away their tears with their hands, wearing red clothes and presenting an exceedingly disorderly appearance. They proclaim, "Friends, a hundred thousand years from now there will be the dawn of a new æon. This world will perish. Even the great ocean will become dry. This great earth and the mighty mountain Sineru[3] will be burnt up and will perish. The destruction of the world will extend as far as the realm of Brahma.[4] Friends, develop love, compassion, sympathy and equanimity. Friends, cherish mother and father and be respectful towards the elders of the family." This is called the tumultuous proclamation of the æon.

The guardian deities of the world having come to know that a Buddha, an Enlightened One, would appear in the world on the elapse of another thousand years go about proclaiming, "Friends, a thousand years from now a

---

TRANSLATED FROM the Pali by N. A. Jayawickrama. All bracketed additions are the translator's.

1. Pali for *bodhisattva*.
2. The ideal ruler. "Æon": a complete cosmic cycle, from the beginning to the end of a universe.
3. According to Buddhist cosmology, the mountain at the center of the world; it stands in the

middle of a vast ocean, with an island continent located to its north, south, east, and west.
4. The god who presides over the heaven called the world of Brahma; he persuaded the Buddha to teach.

Buddha will appear in the world." This is called the tumultuous proclamation of a Buddha.

The deities themselves having come to know that a Universal Monarch would appear on the elapse of another hundred years go about proclaiming, "Friends, a hundred years from now a Universal Monarch will appear in the world." This is called the tumultuous proclamation of a Universal Monarch.

These three tumultuous proclamations are great. The deities of all the ten thousand world spheres having heard, among these three proclamations, the tumultuous proclamation of the Buddha, assemble all together, ascertain the being who will become a Buddha and go to him and beg of him [to do so]. When they request, they do so at the first appearance of the signs. On this occasion all of them, together with the four Guardian Deities, Sakkas, the deities of the Suyama, Santusita, Paranimmita, and Vasavatti heavens and the Great Brahmas of each world system assembled in one world and went to the Bodhisatta in the Tusita heaven and begged of him, "Sire, when you were fulfilling the Ten Perfections, you did not do so with a view to attain the state of a Sakka or a Mara,[5] a Brahma or a Universal Monarch; but you have fulfilled them with the intention of gaining Omniscience in order to save mankind. Now Sire, the moment has come for your Buddhahood. Sir, it is now the time for your Buddhahood."

Then the Great Being, even before giving an assurance to the deities looked for the Five Great Considerations which consist of the time, the country, the district, the family, and the mother and her age-limit. Of these he first considered the time, reflecting whether the time was ripe or not. In this respect, if the normal expectation of life exceeds a hundred thousand years, it is not the time. Why? Because, at such a time, birth, decay, and death are not noticed by beings. Besides, the teachings of the Buddhas are never devoid of the threefold characteristics (*aniccha, dukkha,* and *anatta*).[6] When transiency, ill, and non-ego are preached to them, they will not think it worth listening to and believing in, but question, "What is it that they talk about?" With the result, it will not be understood. In the absence of this [realization] the dispensation will not lead to Salvation. Therefore this is not the time. When the expectation of life is less than a hundred years, then also it is not the time. Why? Because at such time, beings have defilements to an excessive degree; and admonition given to those whose defilements are acute does not serve the purpose of advice, but like a line drawn with a stick on water it soon disappears. Therefore this too is not the time. But, when the expectation of life is under a hundred thousand years and over a hundred years, that is the proper time. At that time [the span of] life stood at a hundred years; hence the Great Being saw that it was the time to seek birth [on earth].

Next, considering the country, he looked at the four continents with their surrounding islands and saw that in three of the continents Buddhas are not born, but only in Jambudipa; thus he beheld the country. Again considering the region, he thought, "Jambudipa is indeed large, it is ten thousand *yojanas*[7]

5. The personification of evil and desire; Sakka is the king of the gods. "The Ten Perfections": giving, ethics, patience, effort, concentration, wisdom, skillful means, prayer, force, and exalted awareness.
6. The three qualities of all things: imperma-

nence, suffering, and no self.
7. A *yojana* was the standard measurement of distance in ancient India, said to be how far a yoked team of oxen can pull a royal cart in one day (estimated to be between five and nine miles).

in extent. In which district are Buddhas born?", and he beheld the Middle Country. The Middle Country is the region described in the Vinaya[8] with the words: "To the East is the township of Kajangala, and beyond it is Mahasala, after that on the near side are the frontier districts; in the middle of the South Eastern region is the river Salalavati, beyond it are the frontier districts as far as which the Middle Country extends; to the South is the township of Setakannika, beyond it are the frontier districts up to which the Middle Country extends; to the West is the brahmin village of Thuna, beyond it are the frontier districts up to which the Middle Country extends." It is three hundred *yojanas* in length, two hundred and fifty *yojanas* in breadth and nine hundred *yojanas* in circumference. It is within this region that Buddhas and Pacceka Buddhas, the chief disciples and other leading disciples, the eighty great disciples, Universal Monarchs and other powerful khattiya[9] and brahmin householders of great wealth are born. And he came to the decision, "The city of Kapilavatthu is situated here, and I should be born there."

Considering the family next he thought, "Buddhas are not born in a Vessa or Sudda[1] family, but are born in either a Khattiya or Brahmana family, whichever the people consider as superior at the time. At this time Khattiya families are held in greater esteem; I will be born in one, and the king Suddhodhana will be my father"; and foresaw the family.

Considering the mother next he thought, "The mother of the Buddha is neither wanton nor addicted to drink, she has fulfilled the Perfections for a hundred thousand æons and her observance of the five moral vows[2] has remained unbroken from birth. And this queen Mahamaya is such a one; she will be my mother."

And further considering how long she will live he saw that it was ten months and seven days.

Having thus reflected on the fivefold considerations he honoured the deities by assuring them, "Friends, it is now the time for me to become a Buddha"; and dismissing them by asking them to go he entered the Nandana Gardens in the City of Tusita in the company of the deities of Tusita. In every heaven there is a park called Nandana, and there the deities go about reminding one another of the opportunities one has had in the past for doing good deeds, repeatedly saying, "Passing away from here you go to a better state." He too being thus surrounded by the deities who reminded him of his good deeds, as he went about there, passed away and took conception in the womb of the queen Mahamaya.

Here follows the story from the beginning which recounts it fully: At that time, it is said, the festival of the asterism of Asalhi[3] was proclaimed in the city of Kapilavatthu. The people were merrymaking at the festival. Queen Mahamaya took part from the seventh day prior to the full moon in the festivities which involved no indulgence in spirituous liquors, but were gay with a profusion of garlands and perfumes; she rose early in the morning on the seventh day and bathed herself in scented water, gave great alms

8. The monastic code.
9. Pali for *kshatriya*, the second of the four castes of ancient India, sometimes called the warrior caste.
1. Pali for *vaishya* and *shudra*, the third and fourth of the four castes of ancient India, sometimes called the merchant and the servant caste, respectively.

2. That is, the vows to abstain from killing humans, from stealing, from sexual misconduct, from lying, and from intoxicants.
3. The conjunction of stars in the month of Asalhi (Asalha), the fourth month of the Indian calendar (correponding to June/July).

spending four hundred thousand [pieces] and partook of delicious food, decked in all her finery, and entered her decorated bed-chamber having set her mind firmly upon the *uposatha* [fast] vows. Falling asleep as she lay on the royal couch she dreamt the following dream:

She felt as though the four Guardian Deities of the world lifted her up with the bed and taking her to the Himalaya mountain placed her beneath a great Sala tree seven *yojanas* in height growing on a plateau of red arsenic sixty *yojanas* in extent, and stood on one side. Then their consorts came forth and taking the

Queen Maya's dream of the elephant. Relief from stupa for Bharhut, Madhya Pradesh, India, 2nd century B.C.E.

queen to the lake Anotatta bathed her to rid her of her human stains, and clothed her in heavenly garments, anointing her with divine perfumes and decking her with heavenly flowers. Not far from that place there is a silver mountain and within it is a golden abode. In it they prepared a heavenly couch with its head towards the East and made her lie upon it. Then the Bodhisatta, who in the form of a lordly white elephant was wandering there on the neighbouring golden mountain, descended from it and climbed the silver mountain; and coming from the northern direction carrying a white lotus in his trunk which has the lustre of a silver chain, trumpeted. Then entering the golden abode he went reverentially round the mother's bed thrice and appeared as though to have entered the womb making an opening on the right side. Thus did he take conception under the descendant asterism of Asalha.

The queen woke up on the following day and told the king of her dream. The king summoned sixty-four eminent brahmins and prepared costly seats for them on the floor made ready for the ceremonial occasion, smeared with yellow dung and strewn with *laja*[4] and other articles; he offered them as they were seated there gold and silver bowls, covered with gold and silver trays and filled with delicious milk rice prepared with clarified butter, honey and molasses. He delighted them with other gifts such as unbleached cloth and tawny cattle. He then told the brahmins whose every desire was satisfied of the dream and asked them what it all meant. The brahmins replied, "Be not anxious, great king, a fœtus has formed in your queen's womb; and that too is of a male child and not of a female: a son will be born. If he leads the household life he will become a Universal Monarch, but if he renounces home and takes to the life of a recluse he will become a Buddha who will unfurl the covering in this world."

4. Puffed grain [translator's note].

The moment the Bodhisatta took conception in his mother's womb the entire ten thousand world systems quaked, trembled and and shook violently with one accord. Thirty-two portents made themselves manifest. An unlimited radiance spread in the ten thousand world spheres. And the blind regained their sight as though to behold this wonder. The deaf regained hearing. The dumb spoke to one another. The hunchbacks stood erect. Cripples were able to walk on their feet. Creatures in bondage were released from imprisonment and fetters. The fire in all the hells was extinguished. Hunger and thirst in the realm of the departed was allayed. Fear among beasts vanished. Disease amongst creatures subsided. All beings became affable. Horses neighed gently and so did elephants trumpet. All musical instruments echoed forth their music. Bracelets and other ornaments of human beings resounded even without striking against each other. All the directions became calm. A cool and gentle breeze blew refreshing every one. Rain fell out of season. Water spouted out from the earth and flowed around. Birds gave up their flight in the sky. The rivers stopped flowing. The great ocean turned into sweet water. Everywhere the surface was covered with the five kinds of lotuses. All varieties of flowers bloomed on land and water; flowers that bloom on creepers—all of them bloomed forth. Lotuses on stalks burst out in clusters of seven, one upon the other, breaking through slabs of rock on dry land. Hanging lotuses appeared in the sky. Showers of flowers came down on every side. Heavenly music resounded in the sky. The entire ten thousand world systems bearing one mass of garlands and fanned vigorously with yak-tail whisks, were impregnated with the fragrance of flowers and incense and attained the highest splendour, like a ball of flowers spun round and released, or like a wreath of garlands tied firmly together, or like a well decorated flower altar.

When the Bodhisatta had thus taken conception, four deities with swords in hand stood guard from the time of conception over the Bodhisatta and his mother to ward off any danger. No lustful thoughts towards men arose in the Bodhisatta's mother; and she spent the time in great comfort and glory. She was happy and underwent no physical hardship; and the Bodhisatta who lay in her womb was clearly visible like a yellow thread passed through a clear crystal. Since the womb in which a Bodhisatta has lain is like the relic chamber of a shrine, and no other being can lie in it or occupy it, the mother of the Bodhisatta dies seven days after the Bodhisatta's birth and is reborn in the City of Tusita. Unlike other women who give birth before or after the completion of the tenth month, some seated, others lying down, the Bodhisatta's mother cherishes him for ten months in her womb and gives birth to him standing. This is the general rule with the mother of the Bodhisatta.

And Queen Mahamaya having cherished the Bodhisatta in her womb for ten months, like oil in a vessel, and being in an advanced stage of pregnancy informed King Suddhodana of her desire to visit her parents' home: "Your majesty, I wish to go to Devadaha, the city over which my family reigns." The king consented, saying, "Very well," and had the road from Kapilavatthu to the city of Devadaha made even, and decorated with plantain trees, pots filled with water, and with banners and streamers and the like; and he seated the queen in a golden palanquin, and entrusting a thousand officers with the task of carrying it, sent her away with a large retinue. Now, between the two towns there is a pleasure grove of Sala trees, called the Lumbini Park, belonging to the citizens of both towns. At that time all the trees were one mass of blossoming flowers from the root to the topmost branches. In between the branches and among the flowers swarms of bees of five varieties and flocks of birds of many species moved about warbling in sweet tones. The entire Lumbini Grove was like the Citralata forest or like the well-arranged banqueting hall of a mighty king. The queen who saw this felt inclined to besport herself in the Sala grove. The officers bearing the queen entered the park. Having walked up to the foot of the hallowed Sala tree she wished to take hold of a branch. The branch bent low like the tip of a well-seasoned cane and came within reach of the queen's hand. She stretched out her hand and held it. At that very instant labour pains seized her. Then the people drew a curtain round her and withdrew. As she stood there clinging to the branch of the Sala-tree she was delivered of her Child.

Almost immediately the four Great Brahmas of pure mind drew near with a golden net and received the Bodhisatta in this net; and placing the Child in front of the mother they said, "O queen, be joyful; to you is born a great son." Unlike other beings who are smeared with loathsome impurities when they leave their mother's womb, the Bodhisatta left his mother's womb like a preacher descending from his pulpit or a man descending from a stairway, stretching out his hands and feet, in an erect posture, unsmeared with any impurity arising from the mother's womb, pure and clear and shining like a precious gem placed on a silken cloth.

Even though this was so two streams of water came down from the sky to do honour to the Bodhisatta and his mother and allayed the heat in their bodies. Then from the hands of the Brahmas who remained there, having received him in a golden net, the Four Guardian Deities of the world received him on a cloth of antelope skins [sewn together], soft to the touch and considered suitable for ceremonial occasions. From them the people received him in a cushion of soft cloth.

Releasing himself from their hands he stood upon the earth and looked towards the East. Many thousands of world spheres became like a courtyard to him. The deities and men there honoured him with perfumes and garlands and said, "O Great Being, there is no other like you here, how can there be one superior to you?" In this manner he surveyed the ten directions consisting of the four quarters, the four subdirections, the nadir and the zenith, and without seeing any one to equal him he took seven strides saying, "Here lies the northern direction," while the Great Brahma held the white parasol above him, Suyama the yak-tail whisk, and the other deities followed carrying the other insignia of royalty in their hands. Then at the seventh step he stopped and roared the lion's roar proclaiming the victorious utterance beginning with, "I am the chief of the world."

And the Bodhisatta made a proclamation in three births immediately after leaving his mother's womb: in his birth as Mahosadha, as Vessantara, and in this birth. In his birth as Mahosadha, as he left the mother's womb, Sakka the king of the deities came and placed a piece of sandalwood core in his hand and departed. He held it in his fist and came forth. Then his mother asked:

"What have you brought with you, dear, as you come?"

"A medicine, mother."

On account of the fact that he came into the world bringing with him a medicine they named him Osadha-daraka (Medicine-child). Taking that medicine they placed it in an earthenware vessel. It alone served as a drug for removing the ailments of all the blind and the deaf and others who came there. On account of the reputation that arose, "Great is this medicine, great is this medicine," he received the name Mahosadha.[5] On the other hand, in his birth as Vessantara, as he left the mother's womb he came forth saying, "Mother, is there anything in the house? I wish to give away in charity."[6] Then his mother took his hand in hers and placed in it a purse containing a thousand saying, "You are born in a rich family, dear." And it is said that in this birth he roared this lion's roar. Thus did the Bodhisatta make his proclamation in three births as he left his mother's womb.

The thirty-two portents appeared at the time of his birth as on the occasion of his conception. At the same time as our Bodhisatta was born in the Lumbini Grove, Rahula's mother the queen, Channa the minister, Kaludayi the minister, the lordly elephant of high breed, the royal horse Kanthaka, the great Bodhi tree, and the four treasure urns, also came into being. Of these [four] one was a *gavuta*[7] in size, one half a *yojana*, one three *gavutas* and the other a *yojana*. These seven are called the Sahajatas (of simultaneous appearance). The inhabitants of both cities went to Kapilavatthu taking with them the Bodhisatta.

On that very day hosts of deities in Tavatimsa, joyful and delighted that a son was born to the great king Suddhodana of the city of Kapilavatthu and that he would become a Buddha seated at the foot of the Bodhi tree, were rejoicing waving garments above their heads. At that time the hermit named Kaladevala, a frequent visitor to the palace of the great king Suddhodana and master of the eight attainments, had gone to the Tavatimsa abode to spend the noon-day heat after his repast; seated there resting himself he saw those deities and asked them, "What is the reason for your great rejoicing and your being so joyful and delighted? Tell me also the reason for it." The deities replied, "Sir, a son is born to king Suddhodana; seated at the foot of the Bodhi tree he will become a Buddha and set rolling the wheel of the Dhamma.[8] The reason why we are glad is that we will get an opportunity to see his infinite Buddha splendour and listen to the doctrine."

The ascetic who heard their words immediately descended from the world of the deities and entered the royal palace; seated in the seat made ready for him he said, "Great King, a son is born to you, they say; I wish to see him." The king had the child brought decked in all splendour, and carried it up to salute the ascetic. The Bodhisatta's feet having turned around planted themselves on the matted locks of the ascetic. For, in that birth there is no one who can receive worship from the Bodhisatta. Had they through ignorance placed the Bodhisatta's head at the feet of the ascetic, his [the latter's] head would have split in seven. The ascetic, who realized that he should not bring about his self-destruction, rose from his seat and clasped his hands in homage to the Bodhisatta. The king who saw this miracle himself paid homage to his son. The ascetic was able to call to mind [events in] eighty æons, forty in the past and forty in the future. On seeing the characteristic

---

5. Literally, "Great Medicine."
6. See the *Vessantara Jataka*, p. 109.

7. One-fourth the length of a yojana.
8. Pali for *dharma*.

marks of the Bodhisatta, he investigated, reflecting whether he would become a Buddha or not; and when he perceived that without doubt he would, he smiled thinking what a wonderful being he was. Further, investigating whether he would get an opportunity to see him when he became a Buddha, he perceived that he would not; but that he would die before that time and be born in a formless existence, in which he would not be able to receive awakening even while a hundred or a thousand Buddhas appeared. Lamenting the great loss that was to come upon him, he wept. People saw him and asked: "Our master smiled just now, but again he has begun to weep. What is it, Sir? Will any misfortune befall our little master?"

"No misfortune will befall him; he, for certain, will become a Buddha."

"Then why did you weep?"

He said, "I will not get the opportunity to see a person his like when he becomes a Buddha. Great will be my loss. Bewailing my condition I weep."

Then, reflecting whether there was anyone among his kinsmen who would get an opportunity to see him or not when he became a Buddha, he saw his nephew, the child Nalaka. He went to his sister's house and asked: "Where is your son Nalaka?"

"In the house, brother."

"Call him."

He told him as he came to him, "Dear boy, a son is born in the palace of the great king Suddhodana; he is a Buddha-to-be. He will become a Buddha thirty-five years hence. You will get an opportunity to see him. Renounce household life this very day." The child, who was born in a rich family owning eighty-seven crores,[9] thought that his uncle would not urge him on without a purpose and ordered yellow robes and an earthenware bowl brought from the market-place immediately; and shaving off his hair and beard he donned the yellow robes saying, "My renunciation has him who is the noblest person on earth as its aim"; and clasping his hands with reverence in the direction of the Bodhisatta he worshipped him falling prostrate; he next placed his bowl in a bag and hanging it on his shoulder entered the Himalaya region and fulfilled the duties of a monk.

He visited the Tathagata[1] after his attainment of the highest Enlightenment and requested him to preach the Nalaka Discourse; then returning to the Himalayas he reached Arahantship; treading his noble path he lived for seven months longer and standing beside a golden mountain passed away in the element of Nibbana[2] free from clinging to the material substratum.

On the fifth day they anointed the Bodhisatta saying, "Let us perform the rite of choosing a name"; they sprinkled the royal palace with the four kinds of perfumes and strewed it with five kinds of flowers with *laja* as the fifth; having had thick milk rice prepared they invited one hundred and eight brahmins who had mastered the three Vedas, and seating them in the king's palace, fed them with the best food, and showed them great honour and requested them to examine the signs, asking them what the child would become. Among them,

---

9. A large sum (*crore* means "10 million").
1. A title of a buddha; it is the one most often used by the historical Buddha to refer to himself.

2. Pali for *nirvana*. "Arahantship": the status of an arhat, one who enters nirvana at death.

Rama, Dhaja, Lakkhana and Manti, Kondanna and Bhoja, Suyama and Sudatta—these were the eight brahmins adept in the six [Vedangas³] who then expounded the science [of reading the signs].

These eight brahmins alone were to interpret the marks. On the day of the conception, the dream too was interpreted by them. Seven of them raised two fingers and explained in a two-fold manner: "A person who is endowed with these characteristics, will become a Universal Monarch if he leads the household life; but if he renounces the world he will become a Buddha"; and declared the glory and prosperity of a Universal Monarch. The youngest of them all, Kondanna by clan, a brahmin still in his youth, examined the perfection of the noble characteristics of the Bodhisatta and prophesied categorically raising one finger only: "There is no reason for him to live amidst the household cares; assuredly he will become a Buddha who unfurls the covering [of this world]". As he had reached his final existence having made previous resolutions he surpassed the other seven in wisdom, and foresaw one path only open to him. Therefore, he raised one finger and prophesied thus: "There is no occasion for one possessed of these characteristics to remain amidst household cares. Without doubt, he will become a Buddha."

Thereupon those brahmins returned to their homes and addressed their sons: "Dear sons, we are old. We may or may not get the opportunity to meet the great king Suddhodana's son after his attainment of Omniscience. When that prince attains Enlightenment will you seek ordination in his Dispensation?" And the seven of them remained till their span of life was over and followed their destiny. The young brahmin Kondanna remained in good health. He heard that the Great Being had become a mendicant friar, having gone forth in the Great Renunciation on reaching the years of discretion, and had taken up his residence at Uruvela,⁴ whither he had gone in due course and made up his mind, saying, "This is a delightful spot, it is indeed suitable for exertion to a clansman in quest of striving"—Kondanna then went to the sons of those brahmins and said: "I have heard that prince Siddhattha has become a mendicant. It is certain that he will become a Buddha. Had your fathers remained alive [in good health] they would have gone forth in renunciation. If you wish to accompany me, come; I will follow him in his renunciation." They were not able to arrive at a unanimous decision. Three of them did not renounce the world. The other four became recluses appointing the brahmin Kondanna as their leader. All five of them came to be known as the Pancavaggiya Theras (the Elders of the Group of Five).

In the meantime, the king asked: "Seeing what will my son renounce the world?"

"The Four Omens."

"What are they?"

"A person struck down with old age, a sick man, a dead body and a mendicant."

The king said: "From now on let not any one of these come within sight of my son. My son has no need of Buddhahood. I wish to see him reigning with sovereign powers over the four continents with the two thousand islands surrounding them, and holding sway over the vast [ærial] regions, attended

3. The sections of the Vedas.
4. A village in Magadha, a kingdom in northeastern India.

by a retinue filling a circumference of thirty-six *yojanas*." Having said this he placed guards at intervals of a *gavuta*, in order to prevent these four types of individuals coming within the prince's sight. A member from each of the eighty thousand families of kinsmen who foregathered there on that day at the place of the ceremony promised a son each, saying, "Whether he becomes a Buddha or a king we will give a son each. If he were to become a Buddha he will wander forth attended by a retinue of Khattiya monks; and if he were to become a king he will go about followed by a train of Khattiya princes."

The king, for his part, appointed for the Bodhisatta nurses of great beauty who were free from all faults. The Bodhisatta grew up amidst great comforts attended by an innumerable retinue. Then one day, the king's ploughing festival was to take place. On that day they decorated the whole city like a divine abode. All slaves, servants, and others assembled at the royal palace wearing new garments and adorned with perfumes and garlands. A thousand ploughs were used for the king's work. On that day, eight hundred ploughs less one, together with oxen, reins and cords were ornamented with silver. But the plough that was to be driven by the king was ornamented with red gold. The horns of the oxen, the reins and goad were also ornamented with gold. The king who set out with a large retinue took his son along with him.

At the place of work there was a rose-apple tree with thick foliage affording pleasant shade. The king had a couch spread for the prince under it, a canopy decorated with golden stars set up above it, and an enclosure of curtains made around it; he placed guards and went to the place of ploughing, decked in all ornaments and followed by his band of ministers. Thereat the king took the golden plough, the ministers the seven hundred and ninety-nine silver ploughs, and the ploughmen the remaining ploughs. They took those ploughs and ploughed in every direction. The king continued to plough from the near side to the far side and back. And here was a great display of splendour. The nurses who were seated round the Bodhisatta came out of the enclosure of curtains wishing to witness the success the king met with. The Bodhisatta who saw no one about as he looked around got up in all haste and sat cross-legged and evolved the first *jhana* (ecstasy arising from meditation) controlling his inward and outward breath. The nurses went about [enjoying themselves with] food and drink, and delayed a while. The shadows of other trees moved away but the shade of this tree remained spreading out in a circle. The nurses, realizing that their young master was alone, lifted the curtain hurriedly and entered within. They saw the Bodhisatta seated cross-legged on the couch, and also that miracle [of the shadow]; they went up to the king and told him, "Your majesty, your son is thus seated. The shadows of all other trees have moved away, but that of the rose-apple tree remains spread out in a circle." The king returned in all haste and saw that miracle and worshipped his son, saying, "This is the second time, dear, I pay homage to you."

Then in due course the Bodhisatta became sixteen years of age. The king built for the Bodhisatta three palaces suitable for the three seasons: one nine storeys high, one seven, and the other five. He also provided forty thousand dancing women. Surrounded by gaily dressed dancing women, the Bodhisatta was like a deity surrounded by bands of heavenly nymphs, being entertained with the music of an all-female orchestra; he lived in these three mansions in rotation with the seasons enjoying immense luxuries. The queen, mother of Rahula, was his chief consort.

Whilst he was thus enjoying this great prosperity, one day the following talk arose amongst a group of his kinsfolk: "Siddhattha passes his days in the enjoyment of pleasures. He does not learn any of the arts. What will he do if war breaks out?" The king sent for the Bodhisatta and said, "My son, your kinsmen say, 'Siddhattha spends his time in the enjoyment of pleasures without learning any of the arts.' What do you think of it when this [accusation] is made?"

"Sire, it is not necessary for me to learn the arts. Proclaim in the city by beat of drum that I will display my skill in the arts. Seven days hence I will show my skill in the arts to my kinsmen." The king did so. The Bodhisatta assembled such archers as would shoot at their targets during a flash of lightning or split a horse's hair, and in the midst of the assembly displayed to his kinsmen his skill in twelve ways not shared in common with other archers. This should be understood as handed down in the Sarabhanga Jataka. Then did his kinsfolk dispel their doubts.

Then one day the Bodhisatta who wished to go to the pleasure-grove ordered the charioteer to harness the chariot. He said, "Very well," and decking a glorious chariot of priceless worth with all the paraphernalia, yoked to it four state horses of Sindhu breed, of the colour of the petals of the white water lily, and announced it to the Bodhisatta. The Bodhisatta climbed in the chariot, which resembled a heavenly abode, and set out for the park. The deities thought, "Prince Siddhattha's time for Enlightenment is drawing near; let us show him the Omens," and presented one of the deities in the form of an old man overcome by decay, with decayed teeth, grey hair, bent and broken-down in body, leaning on a staff and trembling. The Bodhisatta and the charioteer only were able to see him. Thereupon the Bodhisatta asked the charioteer, as is narrated in the Mahapadana,[5] "Friend, what kind of man is he? His hair is not at all like that of others." On hearing the other's reply he said, "Alas, friend, shame on this existence wherein old age makes its appearance to the born!"; and with agitated heart he turned back from there and went up into his mansion. The king asked, "What is the reason for my son to return so soon?"

"At the sight of an old man, your majesty."

The king said, "They have declared that he will renounce the world on seeing an old man. Hence, do not bring ruin upon me. Quickly arrange dramatic performances for my son [to see]. So long as he enjoys pleasures he will not think of renunciation." Saying this he increased the guards and placed them at a distance of half a *yojana* in all the directions.

When the Bodhisatta likewise went to the park on the following day, he beheld a sick man presented by the deities, and having questioned as before turned back with agitated heart and went up into his mansion. The king too investigated into it and made the same arrangements as stated earlier; and again increased the guards stationing them in an area extending three *gavutas* all around.

And further, one day when the Bodhisatta was making a similar visit to the park he saw a dead body likewise presented by the deities, and having

5. A sutra in the *Digha Nikaya* (Long Collection).

questioned as before he again turned back with agitated heart and went up into his mansion. And the king investigated into it and made arrangements as mentioned before and further increased the guard, stationing them in an area extending a *yojana* all round.

Once again, one day when the Bodhisatta again went to the park he beheld an ordained monk, well clad and well draped, presented by the deities, and asked his charioteer, "Friend, who is he?" Even though the charioteer was ignorant as to what a monk was or what his distinctive features were as it was not a time when a Buddha had appeared on earth, by the supernatural power of the deities he was prompted to say, "Sire, this is a mendicant friar"; and he extolled the virtues of recluseship. The Bodhisatta, cherishing a desire for renunciation, continued his journey to the park that day. But the Reciters of the Digha[-nikaya] say: "He saw the Four Omens on the same day and went [forth]".

Then he disported himself in the park during the remaining hours of daylight and bathed in the royal pond; and when the sun had set he sat on the stone slab meant for the use of royalty, wishing to have himself dressed. Then his attendants stood around waiting on him with garments of many colours, with various kinds of many makes of ornaments and garlands, perfumes, and ointments ready at hand. At that instant the seat on which Sakka was seated became warm. He investigated, "Who is it that wishes to make me leave this seat?", and saw that it was the time to adorn the Bodhisatta. He addressed Vissakamma,[6] "Friend Vissakamma, this day at midnight Prince Siddhattha will go forth in his Great Renunciation. This is the last time he will adorn himself. Go to the park and deck the Great Being with all divine ornaments." He agreed, saying, "Very well," and instantaneously by his supernatural divine power went up to him in the guise of his own valet; taking from the valet's hand the cloth used for his headdress, he draped it round the Bodhisatta's head. At the very touch of his hand the Bodhisatta knew that he was not a human being but a *devaputta* (divinity). No sooner the turban was draped round his head than did a thousand layers stand upright, taking the form of jewels and precious gems in the crown on his head. As he continued to drape the thousand layers ten times over, ten thousand layers stood upright. The head is but small, but one should not begin to doubt how so many folds of cloth could remain upon it. However, the largest [fold] among them was of the size of the flower of a Sama creeper, and the others were only of the size of Kutumbaka flowers.[7] The Bodhisatta's head was now like a Kuyyaka flower with its intertwined filaments. When he had been thus decked in all splendour, he mounted his exquisitely decorated royal chariot; the musicians in his retinue were displaying each one his particular skill; the brahmins were honouring him with words of victory and joy; and Sutas, Magadhas,[8] and others were singing panegyrics in unison uttering festive cries.

At that time the great king Suddhodana, hearing that the queen, mother of Rahula, had given birth to a son, sent a message saying, "Convey my felicitations to my son." The Bodhisatta on hearing it, said, "An impediment (*rahula*) has come into being, a bond has arisen." The king, who came to hear of it on enquiring what his son had said, ordered that thenceforth his grandson should be known as Prince Rahula.

---

6. Pali for Vishvakarman, the craftsman god.
7. That is, tiny; the flowers of the creeper are also small.
8. Singers, bards.

The Bodhisatta, riding in his stately chariot, entered the city in all pomp and glory and dazzling splendour. At that time the Khattiya maiden Kisagotami, who had gone up to the terrace of her mansion, beholding the majestic beauty of the Bodhisatta as he paraded the city streets, gave utterance to the following statement of joy, being exceedingly pleased with his appearance:

> Tranquilled indeed is the mother, tranquilled is the father and tranquilled is the woman who has a lord like him.

The Bodhisatta heard these words and reflected, "She says that by beholding this physical form such as it is, a mother's heart is pacified, a father's, a wife's. But what should first be extinguished for the heart to become pacified?" As his mind was detached from the defilements, it then occurred to him, "When the fires of attachment, hatred and delusion are extinguished, and the cares of all the defilements such as those arising from arrogance and dogmatic beliefs are allayed, then only is one tranquilled. A worthy saying has she put into my hearing; and I go about seeking Nibbana. It is meet that this very day I should give up household life, go forth, and become a religious mendicant in order to seek Nibbana." He then unfastened from his neck a string of pearls worth a hundred thousand and sent it to Kisagotami, saying, "Let this go to her as a teacher's fee." And she was delighted with it, thinking that prince Siddhattha had fallen in love with her and had sent her a present.

As for the Bodhisatta, he returned to his mansion in great splendour, ascended it and lay on his couch of state. Almost immediately, women decked with all manner of ornaments, proficient in dancing and singing and other arts, as enchanting as heavenly maidens, stood around with their diverse musical instruments, and engaged themselves in dancing, singing and playing their instruments to entertain him. As the Bodhisatta's mind was detached from the defilements he took no delight in the dance and so forth, and fell asleep for a while. And those women themselves lay down to sleep discarding the musical instruments they held saying, "He, for whose benefit we engage ourselves in dancing and so forth has gone to sleep. Why need we tire ourselves now?" Lamps fed with perfumed oil were burning. As the Bodhisatta woke up and sat cross-legged upon the couch he saw those women who had lain aside their musical instruments and were sleeping, some of them with saliva pouring out of their mouths, some with their bodies wet with saliva, some grinding their teeth, some talking in their sleep, some groaning, some with gaping mouths and some others with their clothes in disorder revealing plainly those parts of the body which should be kept concealed for fear of shame. He saw the disorder in which they were and became all the more detached from sensual pleasures. The large terrace of his mansion, magnificently decorated and resembling the abode of Sakka appeared to him as a charnel ground full of corpses scattered here and there. The three states of existence seemed to him as a house in flames. He made the inspired utterance, "Alas, this is beset with obstacles! Alas, it is constricted!" His mind was greatly drawn towards renunciation.

He rose from his bed, resolving, "It is meet that I go forth in the Great Renunciation this very day," and went up to the door and called out, "Who is there?" Channa, who was reclining with his head resting on the threshold, replied, "Sire, it is I, Channa." [He commanded:] "I wish to set out on my Great Renunciation today. Prepare a horse for me." He said, "Very well," and taking the trappings for a horse went to the stable and saw the stately horse Kanthaka standing on a delightful spot beneath a silken canopy with jasmine flowers on it; and while lamps fed with scented oil were burning he saddled Kanthaka, saying, "This is the very horse I should saddle today." Even while he was being caparisoned the horse knew, "This caparisoning is very elaborate; it is quite unlike that on other days such as that on the visits to the park for pleasure. It may be that my master wishes to set out on his Great Renunciation today." Then, glad at heart, he neighed very loud. The sound of it would have spread through the entire city; but the deities silenced that sound and allowed no one to hear it.

And the Bodhisatta having dismissed Channa, thought of first looking at his son; he rose from where he was seated and going up to the apartments of Rahula's mother opened the door of the bedchamber. At this time a lamp fed with scented oil was burning inside the room. Rahula's mother was sleeping in her bed strewn with an *ammana*[9] of flowers such as the large jasmine and the Arabian jasmine; and she was resting her hand on her son. Stepping upon the threshold and standing there the Bodhisatta looked at him and thought, "If I remove the queen's hand and take my son into my arms she will wake up, and that will prevent my journey. I will come back after gaining Enlightenment and then see him". With these thoughts he descended from the upper storey. The statement made in the Jataka Commentary that at that time Prince Rahula was seven days old is not found in the other commentaries. Therefore this version alone should be accepted.

In this manner the Bodhisatta descended from the upper storey of his mansion; he went near his horse and said, "My good Kanthaka, today take me across in one night, and I will, with your assistance, become a Buddha and take across the inhabitants of the world together with the deities." Then he leapt upon Kanthaka's back. Kanthaka was eighteen cubits in length starting from his neck, and was of proportionate height; he was strong and fleet of foot, all-white as a cleansed chank[1] [shell]. If he were to neigh or kick his heels its sound would spread through the whole city. For that reason, the deities by their supernatural power muffled the sound of his neighing so that none could hear it and placed under his hooves, at each step, the palms of their hands. The Bodhisatta, making Channa cling on to the tail and himself mounted on the middle of the back of the stately horse, reached the great gate [of the city] at midnight. At this time the king had so fixed the doors on the gateways that a thousand men were required to open each door, so that the Bodhisatta would not, at any time, be able to open the city gate and go away. The Bodhisatta was endowed with great physical strength; reckoned in terms of elephants he possessed the strength of a thousand crores of them, and in terms of men that of ten thousand crores. He thought, "If the door does not open by itself, I will now, seated as I am on Kanthaka's back with Channa clinging to the tail, press Kanthaka hard with my thighs and jump the rampart eighteen cubits high and depart." Channa too thought, "If the door does not open itself I will leap over the rampart seating my master upon my shoulder, and keeping Kanthaka under my armpit taking him firmly round his belly with my right hand, and [so] depart." And Kanthaka

9. A unit of measure (5 or 6 bushels).   1. A conch shell.

too thought, "If the door does not open by itself I will carry my master upward, seated as he is upon my back, with Channa as well clinging to my tail, and [so] leap over the rampart and depart." Had the door not opened by itself, one or another of the three would have accomplished what he had thought of. But the residing deity of the gate opened it.

At the selfsame moment, Mara came there with the intention of making the Bodhisatta turn back; and remaining in the sky he said, "Friend, do not depart; on the seventh day from today the wheel of empire will manifest itself to you. You will reign over the four great continents with their surrounding islands numbering two thousand. Turn back, O hero."

"Who are you?"

"I am Vasavatti."

"Mara, I know full well of the wheel of empire manifesting itself, but of sovereignty I have no use. I will become a Buddha causing the ten thousand world systems to resound."

Then Mara said, "Whenever a reflexion of lust, hatred, or malice arises in your mind from now on, I will know of it"; and followed him closely like his shadow without going away from his side, waiting for an opportunity to seize him.

As for the Bodhisatta, he forsook the universal sovereignty which lay within his reach, like a blob of spittle, without any yearning for it; he set out from the city in great glory on the full moon day of Asalhi under the descendant asterism of Asalha; he then wished to look at the city once again. When this thought arose in his mind the great earth revolved like a potter's wheel that had broken loose, as if it were saying, "O Great Being, once you have done what you have accomplished, it does not require you to turn back and gaze." The Bodhisatta stood in front of the city, gazed upon it, and indicated on that spot the site of the shrine commemorating the place where Kanthaka halted; leading Kanthaka in the direction of the route to be taken, he set out with great honour and in supreme splendour. At that time, it is said, the deities bore sixty thousand torches ahead, sixty thousand behind and a sixty thousand each on his right and on his left. Other deities carried innumerable torches on the ridge of the universe; still other deities, *nagas*, *supannas*,[2] and others followed honouring him with heavenly perfumes, garlands, powders, and incense. The sky was completely overcast with Paricchattaka and Mandarava flowers, just as it is with heavy showers when thick rain clouds gather. Heavenly music prevailed. On every side resounded six million eight hundred thousand musical instruments, consisting of the eight and the sixty varieties; and it seemed like a time when thunder roared from the depths of the ocean or the ocean rumbled from the heart of Yugandhara.[3] Proceeding with such splendour, the Bodhisatta traversed three kingdoms in one night and arrived at the bank of the river Anoma covering a distance of thirty *yojanas*. Why was the horse not able to go beyond that? It is not that he was not able; for he was capable of traversing from end to end the confines of one universe, as though treading on the rim of a wheel lying on its hub, and then return in time for his morning meal to eat the food prepared for him. But on this occasion his progress was greatly impeded by his having to extricate himself and

2. Bird creatures. "*Nagas*": water deities, often depicted with the torso of a human and the tail of a snake.

3. One of the mountain ranges around Sineru.

cut his way through the tangled mass of perfumes and garlands which rose to the height of his flanks as a result of the deities, *nagas* and *supannas*, and others who remained in the sky showering down perfumes and garlands. That was why he covered thirty *yojanas* only. Then the Bodhisatta, halting on the river bank, asked Channa, "What is the name of this river?"

"Sire, it is called Anoma."

Saying, "And *anoma* (not-of-little-consequence) will be our renunciation," he signalled to the horse by pressing it with his heel. The horse sprang forward and stood on the further bank of the river, which was eight *usabhas*[4] in width.

The Bodhisatta alighted from horse-back, and standing on the sandy bank which resembled a sheet of silver, addressed Channa: "Channa, my friend, you go back taking with you my ornaments and Kanthaka. I will become a religious mendicant."

"Sire, I too wish to renounce the world."

The Bodhisatta refused him thrice, saying, "It is not meet that you become a religious mendicant now; you go back." Entrusting the ornaments and Kanthaka to him he thought, "These locks of mine do not become a monk. And besides, I see no-one who is fit to cut a Bodhisatta's locks. Therefore, I myself will cut them with my sword." And taking the sword in his right hand and holding the topknot with the diadem in his left he cut it off. The stumps of hair that were left on his head were two inches in length and curling to the right. They remained of that length as long as he lived and the beard too was in keeping with the hair. It was not necessary for him to shave off his hair and beard again. The Bodhisatta took his topknot together with the diadem and threw it into the air, saying, "If I am to become a Buddha let it remain in the sky; if not, let it fall to the ground". The topknot, which was plaited with gems, rose to the height of a *yojana* and remained in mid-air. Sakka, the king of the deities, beheld this with his divine eye and received it in a jewel casket the size of a *yojana*, and founded the Culamani (Crest Gem) Shrine in Tavatimsa heaven.[5]

> The highest of men cut off his topknot made fragrant with the best of perfumes and threw it into the sky. The thousand-eyed Sakka, the descendant of Vasu, received it with head bent low in a precious casket of gold.

Again the Bodhisatta thought, "These silken garments of mine are not suitable for a monk." Then the Great Brahma Ghatikara, his erstwhile companion in Kassapa Buddha's time, with his friendship not grown cold during one whole Buddha-period, thought, "Today my friend has gone forth in the Great Renunciation. I will go to him taking with me the requisites of a monk."

> The three robes, the bowl, the razor, the needle, the girdle together with the water-strainer—these are the eight [requisites] of a monk who is devoted to religious exertion.

He brought these eight requisites of a monk and gave them to him. The Bodhisatta donned the banner of the Worthy Ones [the yellow robes], and

---

4. Bulls.
5. The "Heaven of the Thirty-three," one of the Buddhist heavens; it is located on the summit of Sineru.

appearing in the garb of the noble life of recluseship dismissed Channa [with the words], "Channa, tell my parents on my behalf, that I am well." Channa saluted the Bodhisatta, went round him reverentially and departed. But Kanthaka who stood nearby listening to the Bodhisatta's conversation with Channa, was unable to endure the grief at the thought that he would no longer be able to see his master. And going out of their sight he died broken hearted and was reborn in Tavatimsa heaven as the deity Kanthaka. At first Channa had only one cause for sorrowing, but with Kanthaka's death he was overcome by a second sorrow, and he returned to the city weeping and lamenting.

And the Bodhisatta, who thus became a religious mendicant, spent a week at the mango grove called Anupiya, situated there in that region, enjoying the bliss of renunciation; and covering a distance of thirty *yojanas* on foot he reached Rajagaha in one day. He entered the city and went begging alms from door to door. The whole city was thrown into a state of excitement at the very sight of the Bodhisatta as though at the entry of Dhanapalaka to Rajagaha or the entry of the chief of the Asuras to the city of the Devas.[6] The king's officers went before the king and announced, "Your majesty, a person of this description goes on his begging round in the city. We do not know who he is, whether a deity, a human being, a *naga* or a *supanna*." Standing on the terrace of his mansion the king espied the Great Being, and overcome with wonder and amazement he commanded his men, "Go, fellows, and ascertain it; if he is a non-human he will disappear on leaving the city; if he is a deity he will go through the air; if he is a *naga* he will dive into the earth and disappear and if he is a human being he will partake of the alms he has gathered." As for the Great Being, he collected a mixed meal, and when he knew that it was sufficient for his sustenance he left the city by the gate through which he had entered it; and seating himself with his face towards the East, in the shadow of the mountain Pandava, began to eat his food. Then his intestines began to turn and were about to come out of his mouth. Being disgusted with that loathsome food the like of which he had not set his eyes upon before, he then began to admonish himself, "Siddhattha, though you have sprung from a family in which food and drink is found in plenty and are accustomed to eating food prepared from perfumed *sali* rice[7] kept in storage for three years, and with various delicacies, you were wondering when you would be able to collect scraps of food and eat them like the mendicant dressed in robes made of rags whom you had seen. You have gone forth reflecting whether such a time would come to you. And now see what you are doing!" Having thus admonished himself he overcame his disgust and ate his food. The king's officers saw what took place and went back and informed the king of it. Having listened to the words of his emissaries the king set out from his city in all haste, and arriving at the Bodhisatta's presence was so pleased with the composure of his movements that he offered him all prosperity. The Bodhisatta replied, "O Great King, of material wealth or sensual enjoyments I have no need. I have gone forth resolving on the highest Enlightenment." When the king was not able to gain his consent even though he requested him in many ways he said at last, "Assuredly you

---

6. Demigods (as are the Asuras). "Dhanapalaka": a great elephant in the royal stalls at Rajagaha.　　7. Winter rice.

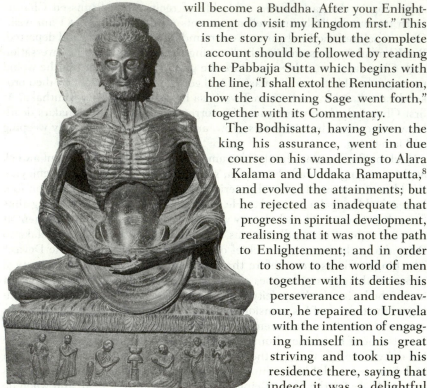

The fasting bodhisattva. Pakistan, 2nd–3rd century.

will become a Buddha. After your Enlightenment do visit my kingdom first." This is the story in brief, but the complete account should be followed by reading the Pabbajja Sutta which begins with the line, "I shall extol the Renunciation, how the discerning Sage went forth," together with its Commentary.

The Bodhisatta, having given the king his assurance, went in due course on his wanderings to Alara Kalama and Uddaka Ramaputta,[8] and evolved the attainments; but he rejected as inadequate that progress in spiritual development, realising that it was not the path to Enlightenment; and in order to show to the world of men together with its deities his perseverance and endeavour, he repaired to Uruvela with the intention of engaging himself in his great striving and took up his residence there, saying that indeed it was a delightful spot, and began practising his great exertion.

And those five religious mendicants with Kondanna as their leader came across the Bodhisatta there on their wanderings in quest of alms through villages, townships, and capital cities. And they became his constant companions during the six years he was engaged in his great striving, and they served him attending to various duties such as sweeping the cell and so forth, saying, "Now he will become a Buddha! Now he will become a Buddha!" And the Bodhisatta himself, who was determined to practise austerities in their most extreme form began to subsist on one grain of sesamum[9] or rice a day. He even took to complete fasting. He dissuaded the deities from infusing divine energy through the pores of his skin. Then his body which was once golden in colour turned black from the great emaciation it had reached as a result of that fasting. The thirty-two characteristics of a Great Being were obliterated. And one day overcome by severe pain whilst engaged in the *jhana* of the suppression of breath he fell down unconscious at the edge of the cloister. Then some deities said, "The recluse Gotama[1] is dead"; while others said, "This is only a mode of abiding of the Worthy Ones." Those of them there who thought that he was dead went to the great king Suddhodana and announced to him, "Your son is dead."

---

8. Two of the Buddha's teachers.
9. Sesame.

1. That is, Gautama.

"Did he die before his Enlightenment or after?"

"He was not able to become a Buddha. He fell down on the scene of his exertions and died."

Hearing this the king refused to believe their words, saying, "I do not believe it. Death cannot come upon him before his attainment of Enlightenment."

Why did the king not believe it? Because he had seen the miracles on the day he took him to worship Kaladevala and also at the foot of the Jambu tree.

When the Bodhisatta regained his consciousness and stood up, those deities came back and told him, "Great King, your son is well." And the king replied, "I know very well that my son cannot die like that." When the Great Being was practising severe austerities for six years it was to him like a time of intertwining the sky with knots. Realizing that the practice of such austerities was not the path to Enlightenment he went about gathering alms in villages and townships in order to revert to solid food, and he subsisted on it. Then his thirty-two characteristics of a Great Being reappeared in their natural form, and the body regained its golden hue. The monks of the Group of Five (Pancavaggiya) left the Great Beings, saying, "Even though he has practised severe austerities for six years he has not been able to realize Omniscience. How will he be able to do so now that he has begun to take solid food, going about begging alms in the villages? He now leads a life of indulgence and he has swerved from his exertions. Our expecting spiritual attainments under him is like a man who wishes to bathe thinking of using dew drops. Of what use is he to us?" They took each his begging bowl and robes and went away; covering a distance of eighteen *yojanas* they entered Isipatana.

And at that time a maiden named Sujata, born in the family of the householder Senani of the hamlet of Senani in Uruvela, had reached her years of discretion and made a wish at a Banyan tree: "If I marry a member of a family of equal rank and succeed in obtaining a son as my first child I will make an annual sacrifice to you spending a hundred thousand." Her wish was fulfilled. Wishing to perform the sacrifice on the full-moon day of the month of Vesakha, on the completion of the six years of the Great Being's practice of austerities, she had first of all sent a thousand cows to pasture in a grove of liquorice. She then made five hundred cows drink their milk, and two hundred and fifty theirs. In this manner she brought the number down to the last sixteen, whose milk eight cows were made to drink; and she made the milk go in this rotation in order to obtain its correct thickness, sweetness, and strength. Thinking that she would perform the sacrifice early in the morning on the full-moon day of Vesakha, she rose at early dawn and milked those eight cows. The calves did not go near the cows' udders. The moment new vessels were placed under the udders streams of milk poured into them of their own accord. Seeing this miracle Sujata herself took the milk and poured it into a new pot, and with her own hands built a fire and began to boil it. When that milk rice was boiling, large bubbles rose and ran around turning to their right. Not a drop fell outside. Not even a faint smoke rose from the hearth. At that time the four Guardian Deities of the world came there and mounted guard over the fireplace, and the Great Brahma held his parasol. Sakka brought the pieces of firewood together and kindled the fire. The deities by their divine power, as though they were extracting honey by squeezing out a honeycomb formed on a stick, brought together the beneficial energy of the deities and men of the four great continents and their two thousand surrounding islands and placed it there. At other times the deities infuse energy at each mouthful, but on the day of the Enlightenment and on the day of passing away in Nibbana they infuse it into the vessel itself.

Sujata, who saw the numerous wonders that appeared to her on one and the same day, said to Punna her slave girl, "Dear Punna, our deity is greatly pleased today. All these days I have not seen a miracle like this. Go with all haste and prepare the seat of the divinity." Saying, "Very well, lady," and obeying her command she hastened to the foot of the tree. Meanwhile the Bodhisatta, who had dreamt the five great dreams that night, arrived at the conclusion, on examining their significance, that without doubt he would become a Buddha that day; and having attended to his bodily ablutions, on the elapse of that night he went early in the morning and sat at the foot of that tree, illuminating the whole tree with his bodily radiance, awaiting the time of setting out for alms. Thereupon the slave girl Punna who came there saw the Bodhisatta seated at the foot of the tree surveying the eastern quarter, and also saw the whole tree turned golden in colour with the radiance issuing forth from his body; and having seen all this she thought, "Today our divinity has descended from the tree and is seated there, methinks, to receive the sacrificial offering in his own hand." Overcome with fervour she ran to Sujata and told her about it.

On hearing her words Sujata was delighted in mind; and telling her, "From now on you will be in the station of my eldest daughter," she gave her all the ornaments as became her daughter. Since it is fit that he should receive on the day of his attainment of Enlightenment a golden bowl worth a hundred thousand, she conceived the idea of serving the milk rice in a golden vessel and had a golden bowl worth a hundred thousand brought to her, and wishing to put the milk rice into it she tilted the vessel in which the food was cooked. All the milk rice rolled out into the bowl like water from a lotus leaf. The bowl was full to the brim with it. She covered the bowl with another golden vessel and wrapped it with a cloth; and having adorned herself with all ornaments she placed that bowl on her head and went in all her splendour to the foot of the Banyan tree. Overcome with great joy on beholding the Bodhisatta, thinking him to be the tree god she went up to him bowing in a humble manner from the place where she first espied him, and taking down the bowl from her head she uncovered it; and taking in a golden water pot water perfumed with sweet-smelling flowers she walked up to the Bodhisatta and stood near him. The earthenware vessel given by the Great Brahma Ghatikara, which had remained with the Bodhisatta so long, disappeared at this moment. Not being able to find the bowl the Bodhisatta stretched out his right hand and accepted the water offered to him. Sujata placed in the hand of the Great Being the milk rice together with the bowl which contained it. The Great Being looked at Sujata. She understood what it meant and worshipped him saying, "Lord, accept what I have offered you and depart wherever you please. Even as my wish has been fulfilled may yours as well be fulfilled!" And she went away with no more desire for the golden bowl worth a hundred thousand than for a withered leaf.

And the Bodhisatta rose from where he was seated and went reverentially round the tree, and taking the bowl with him he proceeded to the bank of the river Neranjara. There is a ford of easy access, the bathing place at which many hundred thousands of Bodhisattas go down into the river on the day of their attainment of Enlightenment. Leaving his bowl on its bank he went down into the river and bathed, and donning the banner of the Worthy Ones, the inner robe worn by many hundred thousand Buddhas, he sat down facing the East and ate all the honeyed milk rice which had been prepared without using water, after having divided it up into forty-nine balls of the size of a single-seeded palmyra fruit. That was all the food he had for the forty-nine days of the seven weeks he spent after his Enlightenment at the foot of the Bodhi tree. During this period he took no other food, he did not bathe nor wash his face nor rid himself of waste matter. He spent the time in the bliss of the ecstasy of *jhana*-meditation, in the bliss of the Path and its Fruits. Having partaken of that milk rice he took the golden bowl and sent it adrift saying, "If I succeed in becoming a Buddha this day let this bowl go upstream; if not, let it go down with the current." Cutting its way through the current it went to the middle of the river and proceeded against the current for a distance of eighty cubits, keeping to a central course, as fast as a swift horse. And sinking at a whirlpool it went to the abode of the *naga* king Kala, and making a clanging noise striking against the bowls used by the three previous Buddhas placed itself as the bottommost among them. The *naga* king Kala heard that sound and began to sing songs of praise in many hundred verses, saying, "A Buddha was born yesterday, and again another today." For to him all this interval during which the great earth rose filling the sky to the extent of a *yojana* and three *gavutas* was like yesterday and today. And the Bodhisatta having spent his noonday rest [in meditation] in the blossoming Sala grove on the bank of the river, wended his way in the direction of the Bodhi tree at eventide, the time flowers drop off from their stems, along the path which was eight *usabhas* wide and decorated by the deities, like a lion shaking off his drowsiness. *Nagas, yakkhas,*[2] *supannas,* and others honoured him with heavenly perfumes, flowers and so forth, playing divine music. The ten thousand world systems were filled alike with perfumes and garlands as well as with shouts of joy.

At that time a grass seller named Sotthiya, who was coming from the opposite direction carrying a bundle of grass, offered the Great Being eight handfuls of grass, impressed with his bearing. Taking the grass the Bodhisatta ascended the platform at the foot of the Bodhi tree and stood on the southern side facing the North. At that moment the southern ridge of the universe sank low and appeared to have reached Avici[3] below. The northern ridge of the universe was raised upward and appeared to have reached the vault of heaven above. The Bodhisatta thought that perhaps it was not the place for the attainment of Enlightenment, and going round in a clockwise direction he went and stood on the western side facing the East. Then the western ridge of the universe sank low and appeared to have reached Avici below and the eastern ridge rose and appeared to have reached the vault of heaven above. Wherever he stood the mighty earth was bent downward on one side and raised upward on the other like a wheel of a wagon lying on its hub with the edge of its rim trodden on on one side. The Bodhisatta thought

2. Pali for *yaksha*, a class of nonhuman beings that are a kind of nature spirit. 3. The worst of the Buddhist hells.

that that too perhaps was not the place for the attainment of Enlightenment and going round in a clockwise direction he went and stood on the northern side facing the South. Then the northern ridge of the universe sank low and appeared to have reached Avici below. The southern ridge rose and appeared to have reached the vault of heaven above. The Bodhisatta thought that that too perhaps was not the place for the attainment of Enlightenment and going round in a clockwise direction he went and stood on the eastern side facing the West. The seat of meditation of all Buddhas is on the eastern side, it trembles not and shakes not.

The Great Being, having realised that that was the stable place, never forsaken by any of the Buddhas, the seat for the destruction of the aggregate of defilements, held those blades of grass at their tips and shook them. And immediately there sprang a seat fourteen cubits in extent. And those blades of grass placed themselves in a manner that even the ablest painter or sculptor would not have been able to design. The Bodhisatta with his back to the trunk of the Bodhi tree and facing the East, made the firm resolve, "Let only my skin, sinews and bones remain and let the flesh and blood in my body dry up; but not until I attain the supreme Enlightenment will I give up this seat of meditation"; and he sat down cross-legged in his invincible seat, from which he could not be dislodged even if thunderbolts were hurled at him in their hundreds.

At that time the *devaputta* Mara, thinking, "Prince Siddhattha wishes to go beyond my control: but I will not give him the opportunity of doing so," went and announced it to his forces and marched forward with them uttering the characteristic battle cry of Mara. Mara's army in battle array was a column twelve *yojanas* long in front of him and twelve *yojanas* each on either flank [to the right and left of him]; behind him it extended as far as the edge of the universe, and upward to the height of nine *yojanas*. As it rent the air with its war cry it was heard like the rumbling of an earthquake progressing from a distance of thousand *yojanas*. Thereupon the *devaputta* Mara mounted on the elephant called Girimekhala, which was a hundred and fifty *yojanas* in height, and armed himself with diverse weapons creating a thousand hands. No two people of the rest of the army of Mara carried the same type of weapon. They came in diverse forms assuming various guises to overwhelm the Great Being.

And at this time the deities of the ten thousand world spheres stood around the Great Being singing songs in praise of him. Sakka the king of the deities stood there blowing his conch shell Vijayuttara. And this shell was two thousand cubits in circumference. When it is sounded once by blowing air into it, its blast lasts four months before the sound finally dies down. The *naga* king Mahakala stood singing his praises with over a hundred verses. The Great Brahma stood there bearing the white parasol. When the army of Mara was fast approaching the foot of the Bodhi tree, not one among them was able to remain; they fled in whichever direction they were facing. The *naga* king Kala dived into the earth and fled to his *naga* abode Manjerika, which was five hundred *yojanas* in extent, and lay down covering his face with both hands. Sakka stood at the ridge of the universe dangling his conch shell Vijayuttara on his back, the Great Brahma left his white parasol on the edge of the universe and went straight to the Brahma world. Not a single deity was able to remain there. The Great Being sat there all alone. And Mara then said to his followers, "My men, there is no man to equal Siddhattha the son of Suddhodana. We are not equal to the task of giving him battle face to face. Let us attack him from behind." And the Great Being looked at the three sides and saw the whole place deserted as all the deities had fled. And again beholding the forces of Mara swooping down upon him from the North he continued to sit there reflecting thus on the Ten Perfections: "Such a large force makes a great effort and displays much prowess against me, single handed as I am. In this place there is neither my mother, father, brother, nor any other relative. But these Ten Perfections are like retainers whom I have maintained for a long time. Therefore it behoves me to rout this army making the Perfections themselves my shield as well as the weapon of attack."

Then the *devaputta* Mara raised a tornado wishing to drive away Siddhattha with it. Instantaneously such gales rose from the East and other directions as would have shattered to bits mountain peaks of the height of half a *yojana*, two *yojanas* or three *yojanas*, or could have uprooted shrubs and trees of the forest, or could have reduced to fragments the villages and townships in the neighbourhood; but by the virtue and majesty of the Great Being they lost their force, and on reaching the Bodhisatta they were not able to shake even the hem of his robe. Wishing to engulf him in water and slay him, he next caused a heavy downpour of rain. By his great miraculous power clouds gathered in their hundreds and thousands, layer upon layer, and poured forth rain. The earth was hollowed out by the violence of the torrential downpour. A great flood came submerging the tree tops of the forest: but it could not moisten his robe even to the extent of the little space on which a dewdrop would fall. Next he raised a shower of rocks. Large mountain peaks came swirling through the air issuing smoke and flames; but on reaching the Bodhisatta they turned into wreaths of heavenly garlands. Next he raised a storm of missiles. Swords, daggers, darts, and other weapons, single edged and double edged, came hurtling through the sky, smoking and flaming; but on reaching the Bodhisatta they turned into heavenly flowers. Next he raised a shower of burning coals; embers of the hue of Kimsuka flowers[4] came flying through the sky and were scattered at the feet of the Bodhisatta turning into heavenly flowers. Next he raised a storm of ashes; red hot ashes, glowing like fire came flying through the air, fell at the feet of the Bodhisatta and turned into sandalwood powder. Next he raised a sandstorm; fine particles of sand came smoking and flaming through the sky, fell at the feet of the Bodhisatta and turned into heavenly flowers. Next he raised a storm of mud; the mud came smoking and flaming through the air, fell at the feet of the Bodhisatta and turned into heavenly ointments. He next created a gloom which was as thick as when four conditions are found in combination; on reaching the Bodhisatta it disappeared as darkness that vanishes with the oncoming radiance of the sun.

Mara was thus unable to put the Bodhisatta to flight with these nine storms: of wind, rain, rocks, missiles, embers, ashes, sand, mud and darkness. He ordered his followers, "My men, why do you stand still? Capture this prince or smite him or put him to flight." He himself advanced upon the Bodhisatta, mounted on the back of the elephant Girimekhala armed with a disc-weapon, and cried out, "Rise, Siddhattha, from that seat. It is not meant

4. That is, red.

for you. It goes to me." On hearing his words the Great Being answered, "Mara, you have neither practised the Ten Perfections, the Sub-Perfections, and the Supreme Perfections, nor made the five great sacrifices, nor have you fulfilled the quest of knowledge, the quest of the weal of the world and the quest of wisdom. This seat is not meant for you. I alone have the right to it."

Enraged at this, Mara, being unable to restrain the vehemence of his temper, hurled his discus at the Great Being. But it turned into a canopy of garlands and remained above him while he was reflecting on the Ten Perfections. It is said that this razor-edged disc weapon, when it is hurled with rage at other times, careers along cleaving asunder pillars of solid rock as though they were bamboo shoots, but now it turned into a canopy of garlands and remained there. Others of Mara's army hurled huge masses of rock, thinking that it would make him rise from his seat and take to flight. But even these turned into wreaths of garlands and fell upon the ground, while the Great Being continued to reflect on the Ten Perfections.

The deities who stood at the ridge of the universe continually raised their heads and craning their necks looked out, saying, "Alas, ruined indeed is the handsome physical frame of Prince Siddhattha! What will he do?" Then the Great Being told Mara, as he stood there claiming the throne accruing on the day of their Enlightenment to Bodhisattas who fulfil their Perfections, "Mara, who will testify to your having given away in charity?" Mara stretched forth his hand in the direction of his army saying, "All these are my witnesses." Instantaneously the cry of one accord, "I am witness, I am his witness," coming from the followers of Mara resounded like an earthquake. Then said Mara to the Great Being, "Siddhattha, who will testify to your having given in charity?" The Great Being answered, "You have sentient beings as witnesses to your having given away in charity, but here in this place I have no living being whatever as my witness. Let alone the generosity I have practised in all other existences, let this great and solid earth, nonsentient as it is, be my witness to the seven hundredfold great alms I gave when I was born as Vessantara"; and extricating his right hand from underneath the folds of his robe he stretched it out towards the earth saying, "Are you or are you not witness to my having given the seven hundredfold alms in my birth as Vessantara?" And the great earth resounded with a hundred, a thousand, or a hundred thousand echoes as though to overwhelm the forces of Mara, and saying as it were, "I was your witness to it then."

Then as the Great Being continued to reflect on the alms he had given as Vessantara, saying to himself, "O Siddhattha, you have given away vast charities and made the highest sacrifice," the elephant Girimekhala which was a hundred and fifty *yojanas* in height went down on its knees. The followers of Mara fled in every direction. No two fled by the same path. They ran in whichever direction that lay before them discarding their head ornaments and the clothes they were wearing.

When the heavenly hosts beheld the army of Mara taking to flight, the *nagas* among them sent messengers to the *naga* realm, the suppannas to their kingdom, the deities to heaven, and the Brahmas to the Brahma world, saying, "Mara has been defeated, Prince Siddhattha has triumphed, let us honour him at his victory," drew near the Great Being, going up to his Bodhi seat. And they thus advanced [singing]:

For this is the victory to the illustrious Buddha, and defeat to Mara the Evil One. So did the hosts of *nagas* overcome with joy then proclaim at the foot of the Bodhi tree the victory of the Great Sage.

For this is the victory to the illustrious Buddha, and defeat to Mara the Evil One. So did the bands of *supannas* overcome with joy then proclaim at the foot of the Bodhi tree the victory of the Great Sage.

For this is the victory to the illustrious Buddha, and defeat to Mara the Evil One. So did the hosts of deities overcome with joy then proclaim at the foot of the Bodhi tree the victory of the Great Sage.

For this is the victory to the illustrious Buddha, and defeat to Mara the Evil One. So did the hosts of Brahmas overcome with joy then proclaim at the foot of the Bodhi tree the victory of the Steadfast Sage.

The remaining deities of the ten thousand world systems stood there honouring him with garlands, perfumes, and ointments and singing his praises in diverse ways. While the sun was still shining above, the Great Being thus dispersed Mara's army; being honoured with the offerings in the form of the young leaves from the Bodhi tree falling on his robe, as though with shoots of red coral, he entered into the knowledge of previous existences in the first watch of the night; in the second watch he purified his divine eye; and in the final watch gained an insight into the knowledge of the interdependent causal origins. As he continued to reflect on the nature of the causal antecedents which consist of twelve constituents, in their direct and inverse relations in progressive and regressive evolution, the ten thousand world systems quaked twelve times up to the very limits of the ocean. When the Great Being gained penetrative insight into omniscient knowledge at dawn, making the ten thousand world systems resound, the entire ten thousand worlds assumed a festive garb.

The radiance of the banners and streamers hoisted on the eastern ridge of the world sphere spread as far as the western ridge. Similarly, the radiance of the banners and streamers hoisted on the western ridge, the northern ridge, and the southern ridge spread as far as the eastern, southern, and northern ridges respectively. And the radiance of the banners and streamers hoisted on the surface of the earth remained in constant contact with the world of Brahma, and that of those held aloft in the world of Brahma penetrated to the surface of the earth. Flowering trees in the ten thousand world spheres blossomed forth. Fruit-bearing trees were weighted down with clusters of fruit. Flowers that bloom on tree trunks, branches and creepers blossomed in their respective places. Lotuses on stalks sprang in clusters of seven, breaking through rocky surfaces, and were heaped layer upon layer. The ten thousand world systems revolved and remained like a wreath of garlands tossed about or like a well-arranged spread of flowers. The intervening regions of eight thousand *yojanas* between the world spheres which had not been lit before even with the radiance of seven suns shining together became one mass of light. The great ocean eighty-four thousand *yojanas* deep turned into sweet water. Rivers ceased to flow. Those blind from birth were able to see objects, those deaf from birth were able to hear sounds, and those crippled from birth walked on their feet. Bonds and fetters broke loose and fell apart.

Being thus honoured with unlimited glory and splendour, whilst manifold wondrous happenings were taking place, he gained penetrative insight into the knowledge of omniscience and made the ecstatic utterence customary with all Buddhas:

> Seeking the builder of the house I sped along many births in Samsara but to no avail; ill is birth again and again.
> O builder of the house, you are seen. Do not build the house again! All your beams are broken, and the ridgepole is shattered. The mind that has gone beyond things composite has attained the destruction of the cravings.

All the incidents commencing with his departure from the heaven of Tusita and ending with the attainment of Omniscience should be known as the Intermediate Epoch.

THE BUDDHA'S FINAL DAYS

GREAT DISCOURSE ON THE FINAL NIRVANA
(The Mahaparinibbana Sutta)

The accounts of the life of the Buddha in the two previous selections stop long before his death, ending in the first years after his enlightenment, when he was still in his late thirties. But the Buddha is said to have lived until the age of eighty. In fact, only one canonical text tells us how long the Buddha lived, recounting his last days, his death, his funeral, and the distribution of his relics, each a momentous event in the history of the tradition. That text is titled the *Mahaparinibbana Sutta*. *Nibbana* is "nirvana" in Pali, and *parinibbana* (or *parinirvana*) is usually translated as "final nirvana." It is the term that is used to describe the passage into nirvana that occurs at the death of a buddha or an arhat, often in contradistinction to the achievement of nirvana or realization of nirvana that is the moment of enlightenment and that may occur many years before the individual finally passes away. *Maha* means "great," either in quantity or quality. Here, it likely refers to the length of the text, which is found in the *Digha Nikaya*, or "Long Collection," of the discourses of the Buddha. Indeed, it is the longest text in the Pali canon. There are Sanskrit versions of this text, with the title *Mahaparinirvana Sutra*. Another sutra of the same title, a text often referred to simply as the *Nirvana Sutra*, is a very different work: it narrates a number of the same events from the Buddha's final days, but it also contains influential expositions of the Mahayana doctrine of the buddha nature (see the *Tathagatagarbha Sutra*, p. 340).

Stories of the death of the founder of a religion are commonly imbued with profound significance. In the case of Buddhism, it is said that buddhas appear in the world only at rare moments in the beginningless round of rebirth. And when a buddha passes into nirvana, he does not appear in the world again. Thus, the death of a buddha is a momentous event in the universe, attended with all manner of signs, and each event and statement in his last days is subject to contemplation and commentary. It is therefore appropriate to provide a fairly detailed summary of this great work.

The text is divided into six chapters, the last three of which appear here. The Buddha and his attendant Ananda travel from Rajagaha, the capital of Magadha, to the town of Kusinara (in Sanskrit, Kushinagara) in fourteen stages, and along the way the Buddha gives teachings to different audiences on a variety of topics. He is eighty years old and describes his body as being like an old cart held together by straps. Becoming progressively more frail, the Buddha decides to spend his final retreat with Ananda meditating in the forest, using his powers of concentration to control his illness. When Ananda asks him who will lead the order after his death, the Buddha replies with the oft-quoted instruction, "You should live as islands unto yourselves, being your own refuge, with no one else as your refuge, with the dharma as an island, with the dharma as your refuge, with no other refuge." This is taken to mean that the Buddha has taught everything necessary to traverse the path to nirvana; no other teacher is needed, nor is anyone else required to lead the order of monks.

While meditating in the forest, the Buddha mentions to Ananda three times that a buddha has the power to live for an aeon or until the end of an aeon if he is asked to do so. Ananda, however, fails to make that request. The deity of death and desire, Mara, then appears to the Buddha, reminding him of his promise long ago to enter nirvana when he had trained monks and disciples who were able to teach the dharma, something that he has now done. The Buddha informs Mara that he will pass away in three months. The earth then quakes, causing the Buddha to explain to Ananda the eight reasons for an earthquake, one of which is that a buddha has renounced his life force. Ananda implores the Buddha to remain until the end of the aeon, but the Buddha scolds him, saying that the time for that request has passed. In fact, the Buddha recalls the numerous occasions on which he had told Ananda of this power; each time Ananda failed to ask him to extend his life span. Ananda's failure would long be lamented. Indeed, after the Buddha's passing he would be tried by the community of arhats for this and other misdeeds.

The question of where authority will reside after the Buddha's death, already raised by Ananda, is an important theme in the text. The section of the sutra excerpted here begins with the Buddha explaining to a group of monks what he calls the four great authorities: the means of determining the authenticity of a particular doctrine after the death of the Buddha. He then receives his last meal from a blacksmith named Chunda. The dish that the Buddha requests is called "pig's delight." Scholars have much debated whether this is a pork dish or something eaten by pigs, such as truffles. The Buddha was not a vegetarian, and commentators in the Pali tradition from which the sutra derives have generally believed it was pork. During the meal, the Buddha gave instructions that only he should be served the dish, and the rest should be buried. Interpretations of this puzzling instruction have varied widely, and some modern commentators see in it evidence of poison. But the traditional commentators explain that the final meal of a buddha is something so potent that no one else could survive it. Shortly after the meal, the Buddha suffers an attack of dysentery, a remarkable manifestation of human suffering in an account that abounds in divine signs and portents.

The Buddha then converts a layman named Pukkusa, who offers him gold robes. When the Buddha puts them on, Ananda notices that the color of the robes appears dull next to the Buddha's skin. The Buddha explains that the skin of a buddha is particularly bright on two occasions: the night when he achieves enlightenment and the night when he passes into nirvana.

Proceeding to the outskirts of the town of Kusinara, the Buddha lies down on his right side between twin sal trees, which immediately blossom out of season. This is one of the most famous scenes in Buddhist art. The frequently seen statues of the Buddha lying on his right side, his head propped on his right hand, do not depict him relaxing; they show him about to die. In paintings of this scene, many in attendance, not monks alone but also gods and animals, are weeping. At one point, the Buddha instructs the monk who is fanning him to stand to the side; he is blocking the view of the gods who have come from far away to see the Buddha one last time.

The Buddha next provides a series of final instructions, on matters great and small. He tells Ananda to visit the blacksmith Chunda and assure him that he was in no way responsible for the Buddha's death. Indeed, he should rejoice at the great merit he earned in offering the Buddha his last meal. Ananda asks how monks can pay respect to the Buddha after he has passed away. The Buddha explains that monks, nuns, and laypeople should visit four places of pilgrimage: the site of his birth, the site of his enlightenment, the site of his first teaching, and this, the site of his *parinirvana*. Anyone who dies while on pilgrimage to one of these four places, the Buddha says, will be reborn as a god in heaven. Scholars have taken these instructions as a sign of the relative late date of this sutra (or at least this portion of the sutra), arguing that this assertion by the Buddha was added to promote pilgrimage to four already well established shrines.

The Buddha then gives instructions on how his body should be cremated, saying that his remains should be enshrined in a stupa, to which the faithful should offer flowers and perfumes in order to gain happiness in the future. The Buddha comforts Ananda, telling him that all things must pass away and praising him to the other monks for his devotion, predicting that he will soon become an arhat. When Ananda is distressed that the Buddha will pass away in such a "miserable little town of wattle-and-daub" rather than a great city, the Buddha tells him that Kusinara was once the capital of a great king. The wanderer Subhadda then becomes the last person to be ordained by the Buddha. When Ananda laments that the monks will soon have no teacher, the Buddha explains that henceforth the dharma and the vinaya will be their teacher. He makes some modifications to the rules of discipline, saying that after he has passed away, the monks may abolish the minor rules. (At his trial, Ananda was chastised for not having asked which rules were minor; because the Buddha did not specify, no rules were abolished.) As his last disciplinary act, the Buddha orders that Channa, his former charioteer, be completely shunned by his fellow monks for having sided with nuns in a dispute between monks and nuns.

Finally, the Buddha asks three times whether any of the five hundred monks in attendance has any doubt or uncertainty for him to address; hearing none, the Buddha speaks his last words: "All conditioned things are of a nature to decay—strive on untiringly." The Buddha's mind then passed upward through the eight levels of concentration, back down through the same eight levels to the first, and back up to the fourth concentration, when he died—at which point the earth quaked.

Seven days later, his body was prepared for cremation. However, the funeral pyre could not be ignited until the arrival of his chief disciple, Mahakassapa, who had been away at the time of the Buddha's death. After he arrived and paid his respects, the funeral pyre ignited spontaneously. The relics of the Buddha that remained after the cremation were taken by the local people, the Mallas of Kusinara, but seven other groups of the Buddha's former patrons also came to claim the relics to carry back to their home kingdoms for veneration; the members of the Buddha's immediate family were either dead themselves or had joined the order of monks and nuns. In order to avoid an altercation, the brahmin Dona was called upon to divide up the remains among the eight claimants. Dona kept for himself the urn that had held the relics; a ninth group was given the embers that remained from the funeral pyre. These ten—the eight portions of relics, the urn, and the embers—were each then enshrined in stupas. The emperor Ashoka (see the *Ashokavadana*, p. 238) is said to have broken open these original stupas, gathered the relics, and distributed them among 84,000 new stupas.

PRONOUNCING GLOSSARY

Ajatasattu: *a-jah-ta-sat-tu*

Ajita Kesakambali: *a-jih-ta kay-sa-kam-ba-lee*

Ajivika: *ah-jee-vi-ka*

Alakamanda: *ah-la-ka-man-dah*

Alara Kalama: *ah-lah-ra kah-lah-ma*

Allakappa: *al-la-kap-pa*

Ambagama: *am-ba-gah-ma*

Anuruddha: *a-nu-rud-da*

Arahant: *a-ra-hant*

Bhandagama: *ban-da-gah-ma*
Bhoganagara: *boh-ga-na-ga-ra*
Brahma Sahampati: *bra-mah sa-ham-pa-ti*
deva: *day-va*
Hatthigama: *hat-ti-gah-ma*
Hirannavati: *hi-ran-nya-va-tee*
Jambudipa: *jam-bu-dee-pa*
Jambugama: *jam-bu-gah-ma*
jhana: *jah-na*
Kakuttha: *ka-kut-tah*
Kapilavatthu: *ka-pi-la-vat-tu*
Kassapa: *kahs-sa-pa*
Khattiya: *kat-ti-ya*
Kusavati: *ku-sah-va-tee*
Kusinara: *ku-si-nah-rah*
Licchavi: *li-cha-vi*
Mahaparinibbana Sutta: *ma-hah-pa-ri-nib-bah-na sut-ta*
Mahasudassana: *ma-hah-su-das-sa-na*
Makkhali Gosala: *mak-kali goh-sah-la*
Makuta-Bandhana: *ma-ku-ta-ban-da-na*
Nibbana: *ni-bah-na*

Nigantha Nataputta: *ni-gan-ta na-ta-pu-ta*
Paccheka: *pach-chay-ka*
Pakudha Kacchayana: *pa-ku-da kach-cha-ya-na*
Pipphalavana: *pip-pa-la-va-na*
Pukkusa: *puk-ku-sa*
Purana Kassapa: *poo-ra-na kahs-sa-pa*
Ramagama: *rah-ma-gah-ma*
Saketa: *sah-kay-ta*
Samadhi: *sa-mah-dee*
Sangha: *san-ga*
Sanjaya Belatthaputta: *san-ja-ya bay-lat-ta-put-ta*
Savatthi: *sah-vat-tee*
Subhadda: *su-bad-da*
Sutta: *soot-ta*
Tathagata: *ta-tah-ga-ta*
Upavana: *u-pa-vah-na*
Vasettha: *vah-sayt-ta*
Varanasi: *vah-rah-na-see*
Vesali: *vay-sah-lee*
Vethadipa: *vay-ta-dee-pa*

4.1. Then the Lord, having risen early and dressed, took his robe and bowl and went into Vesali for alms. Having returned from the alms-round and eaten, he looked back at Vesali with his 'elephant-look' and said: 'Ananda,[1] this is the last time the Tathagata[2] will look upon Vesali. Now we will go to Bhandagama.' 'Very good, Lord', said Ananda, and the Lord proceeded with a large company of monks to Bhandagama, and stayed there.

4.2. And there the Lord addressed the monks: 'It is, monks, through not understanding, not penetrating four things that I as well as you have for a long time fared on round the cycle of rebirths. What are the four? Through not understanding the Ariyan[3] morality, through not understanding the Ariyan concentration, through not understanding the Ariyan wisdom, through not understanding the Ariyan liberation, I as well as you have for a long time fared on round the cycle of rebirths. And it is by understanding and penetrating the Ariyan morality, the Ariyan concentration, the Ariyan wisdom and the Ariyan liberation that the craving for becoming has been cut off, the tendency towards becoming has been exhausted, and there will be no more rebirth.'

4.3. Thus the Lord spoke. The Well-Farer having thus spoken, the Teacher said this:

TRANSLATED FROM the Pali by Maurice Walshe. All bracketed additions are the translator's.

1. The Buddha's cousin and personal attendant. "Elephant-look": turning around completely, rather than looking over his shoulder.
2. A title of a buddha; it is the one most often used by the historical Buddha to refer to himself.

3. Pali for "Aryan" (*arya* means "noble" in Sanskrit), an ethnic self-designation by the Vedic Hindus. The Buddha reinterpreted it to mean a spiritual nobility acquired through the practice of the Buddhist path.

'Morality, samadhi, wisdom and final release,
These glorious things Gotama[4] came to know.
The Dhamma he'd discerned he taught his monks:
He whose vision ended woe to Nibbana's[5] gone.'

4.4. Then the Lord, while staying at Bhandagama, delivered a comprehensive discourse: 'This is morality, this is concentration, this is wisdom. Concentration, when imbued with morality, brings great fruit and profit. Wisdom, when imbued with concentration, brings great fruit and profit. The mind imbued with wisdom becomes completely free from the corruptions, that is, from the corruption of sensuality, of becoming, of false views and of ignorance.'

4.5. And when the Lord had stayed at Bhandagama for as long as he wished, he said: 'Ananda, let us go to Hatthigama . . . , to Ambagama . . . , to Jambugama . . .' giving the same discourse at each place. Then he said: 'Ananda, let us go to Bhoganagara.'

4.6. 'Very good, Lord', said Ananda, and the Lord went with a large company of monks to Bhoganagara.

4.7. At Bhoganagara the Lord stayed at the Ananda Shrine. And here he said to the monks: 'Monks, I will teach you four criteria. Listen, pay close attention, and I will speak.' 'Yes, Lord', replied the monks.

4.8. 'Suppose a monk were to say: "Friends, I heard and received this from the Lord's own lips: this is the Dhamma, this is the discipline, this is the Master's teaching", then, monks, you should neither approve nor disapprove his words. Then, without approving or disapproving, his words and expressions should be carefully noted and compared with the Suttas and reviewed in the light of the discipline. If they, on such comparison and review, are found not to conform to the Suttas or the discipline, the conclusion must be: "Assuredly this is not the word of the Buddha, it has been wrongly understood by this monk", and the matter is to be rejected. But where on such comparison and review they are found to conform to the Suttas or the discipline, the conclusion must be: "Assuredly this is the word of the Buddha, it has been rightly understood by this monk." This is the first criterion.

4.9. 'Suppose a monk were to say: "In such and such a place there is a community with elders and distinguished teachers. I have heard and received this from that community", then, monks, you should neither approve nor disapprove his words . . . (as verse 4.8). That is the second criterion.

4.10. 'Suppose a monk were to say: "In such and such a place there are many elders who are learned, bearers of the tradition, who know the Dhamma, the discipline, the code of rules . . ." (as verse 4.8). This is the third criterion.

4.11. 'Suppose a monk were to say: "In such and such a place there is one elder who is learned . . . I have heard and received this from that elder . . ." (as verse 4.8). But where on such comparison and review they are found to conform to the Suttas and the discipline, then the conclusion must be: "Assuredly this is the word of the Buddha, it has been rightly understood by this monk."

4.12. Then the Lord, while staying at Bhoganagara, delivered a comprehensive discourse: 'This is morality, this is concentration, this is wisdom . . .'

---

4. That is, Gautama. "Samadhi": meditative concentration.

5. Pali for *nirvana*. "Dhamma": Pali for *dharma*.

4.13. And when the Lord had stayed at Bhoganagara for as long as he wished, he said: 'Ananda, let us go to Pava.' 'Very good, Lord', said Ananda, and the Lord went with a large company of monks to Pava, where he stayed at the mango-grove of Chunda the smith.

4.14. And Chunda heard that the Lord had arrived at Pava and was staying at his mango-grove. So he went to the Lord, saluted him and sat down to one side, and the Lord instructed, inspired, fired and delighted him with a talk on Dhamma.

4.15. Then Chunda said: 'May the Lord accept a meal from me tomorrow with his order of monks!' And the Lord consented by silence.

4.16. And Chunda, understanding his consent, rose from his seat, saluted the Lord and, passing by to the right, departed.

4.17. And as the night was ending Chunda had a fine meal of hard and soft food prepared with an abundance of 'pig's delight',[6] and when it was ready he reported to the Lord: 'Lord, the meal is ready.'

4.18. Then the Lord, having dressed in the morning, took his robe and bowl and went with his order of monks to Chunda's dwelling, where he sat down on the prepared seat and said: 'Serve the "pig's delight" that has been prepared to me, and serve the remaining hard and soft food to the order of monks.' 'Very good, Lord', said Chunda, and did so.

4.19. Then the Lord said to Chunda: 'Whatever is left over of the "pig's delight" you should bury in a pit, because, Chunda, I can see none in this world with its devas, maras[7] and Brahmas, in this generation with its ascetics and Brahmins, its princes and people who, if they were to eat it, could thoroughly digest it except the Tathagata.' 'Very good, Lord', said Chunda and, having buried the remains of the 'pig's delight' in a pit, he came to the Lord, saluted him and sat down to one side. Then the Lord, having instructed, inspired, fired and delighted him with a talk on Dhamma, rose from his seat and departed.

4.20. And after having eaten the meal provided by Chunda, the Lord was attacked by a severe sickness with bloody diarrhoea, and with sharp pains as if he were about to die. But he endured all this mindfully and clearly aware, and without complaint. Then the Lord said: 'Ananda, let us go to Kusinara.' 'Very good, Lord', said Ananda.

> Having eaten Chunda's meal (this I've heard),
> He suffered a grave illness, painful, deathly;
> From eating a meal of 'pig's delight'
> Grave sickness assailed the Teacher.
> Having purged, the Lord then said:
> 'Now I'll go to Kusinara town.'

4.21. Then turning aside from the road, the Lord went to the foot of a tree and said: 'Come, Ananda, fold a robe in four for me: I am tired and want to sit down.' 'Very good, Lord', said Ananda, and did so.

4.22. The Lord sat down on the prepared seat and said: 'Ananda, bring me some water: I am thirsty and want to drink.' Ananda replied: 'Lord, five hundred carts have passed this way. The water is churned up by their wheels

6. See the introduction to this selection.
7. Personifications of evil and desire. "Devas": gods; inhabitants of the heavenly realms (literally, "shining ones").

and is not good, it is dirty and disturbed. But, Lord, the River Kakuttha nearby has clean water, pleasant, cool, pure, with beautiful banks, delightful. There the Lord shall drink the water and cool his limbs.'

4.23. A second time the Lord said: 'Ananda, bring me some water . . .', and Ananda replied as before.

4.24. A third time the Lord said: 'Ananda, bring me some water: I am thirsty and want to drink.' 'Very good, Lord', said Ananda and, taking his bowl, he went to the stream. And that stream whose water had been churned up by the wheels and was not good, dirty and disturbed, as Ananda approached it began to flow pure, bright and unsullied.

4.25. And the Venerable Ananda thought: 'Wonderful, marvellous are the Tathagata's great and mighty powers! This water was churned up by wheels . . . , and at my approach it flows pure, bright and unsullied!' He took water in his bowl, brought it to the Lord and told him of his thought, saying: 'May the Lord drink the water, may the Well-Farer drink!' And the Lord drank the water.

4.26. At that moment Pukkusa the Malla, a pupil of Alara Kalama,[8] was going along the main road from Kusinara to Pava. Seeing the Lord sitting under a tree, he went over, saluted him and sat down to one side. Then he said: 'It is wonderful, Lord, it is marvellous how calm these wanderers are!

4.27. 'Once, Lord, Alara Kalama was going along the main road and, turning aside, he went and sat down under a nearby tree to take his siesta. And five hundred carts went rumbling by very close to him. A man who was walking along behind them came to Alara Kalama and said: "Lord, did you not see five hundred carts go by?" "No, friend, I did not." "But didn't you hear them, Lord?" "No, friend, I did not." "Well, were you asleep, Lord?" "No, friend, I was not asleep." "Then, Lord, were you conscious?" "Yes, friend." "So, Lord, being conscious and awake you neither saw nor heard five hundred carts passing close by you, even though your outer robe was bespattered with dust?" "That is so, friend."

'And that man thought: "It is wonderful, it is marvellous! These wanderers are so calm that though conscious and awake, a man neither saw nor heard five hundred carts passing close by him!" And he went away praising Alara Kalama's lofty powers.'

4.28. 'Well, Pukkusa, what do you think? What do you consider is more difficult to do or attain to—while conscious and awake not to see or hear five hundred carts passing nearby or, while conscious and awake, not to see or hear anything when the rain-god streams and splashes, when lightning flashes and thunder crashes?'

4.29. 'Lord, how can one compare not seeing or hearing five hundred carts with that—or even six, seven, eight, nine or ten hundred, or hundreds of thousands of carts to that? To see or hear nothing when such a storm rages is more difficult . . .'

4.30. 'Once, Pukkusa, when I was staying at Atuma, at the threshing-floor, the rain-god streamed and splashed, lightning flashed and thunder crashed, and two farmers, brothers, and four oxen were killed. And a lot of people went out of Atuma to where the two brothers and the four oxen were killed.

8. One of the Buddha's two meditation teachers after he left the palace and before he achieved enlightenment.

4.31. 'And, Pukkusa, I had at that time gone out of the door of the threshing-floor and was walking up and down outside. And a man from the crowd came to me, saluted me and stood to one side. And I said to him:

4.32. '"Friend, why are all these people gathered here?" "Lord, there has been a great storm and two farmers, brothers, and four oxen have been killed. But you, Lord, where have you been?" "I have been right here, friend." "But what did you see, Lord?" "I saw nothing, friend." "Or what did you hear Lord?" "I heard nothing, friend." "Were you sleeping, Lord?" "I was not sleeping, friend." "Then, Lord, were you conscious?" "Yes, friend." "So, Lord, being conscious and awake you neither saw nor heard the great rainfall and floods and the thunder and lightning?" "That is so, friend."

4.33. 'And, Pukkusa, that man thought: "It is wonderful, it is marvellous! These wanderers are so calm that they neither see nor hear when the rain-god streams and splashes, lightning flashes and thunder crashes!" Proclaiming my lofty powers, he saluted me, passed by to the right and departed.'

4.34. At this, Pukkusa the Malla said: 'Lord, I reject the lofty powers of Alara Kalama as if they were blown away by a mighty wind or carried off by a swift stream or river! Excellent, Lord, excellent! It is as if someone were to set up what had been knocked down, or to point out the way to one who had got lost, or to bring an oil lamp into a dark place, so that those with eyes could see what was there. Just so the Blessed Lord has expounded the Dhamma in various ways. And I, Lord, go for refuge to the Blessed Lord, the Dhamma and the Sangha. May the Blessed Lord accept me from this day forth as a lay-follower as long as life shall last!'

4.35. Then Pukkusa said to one man: 'Go and fetch me two fine sets of robes of cloth-of-gold, burnished and ready to wear.' 'Yes, Lord', the man replied, and did so. And Pukkusa offered the robes to the Lord, saying: 'Here, Lord, are two fine sets of robes of cloth-of-gold. May the Blessed Lord be graciously pleased to accept them!' 'Well then, Pukkusa, clothe me in one set and Ananda in the other.' 'Very good, Lord', said Pukkusa, and did so.

4.36. Then the Lord instructed, inspired, fired and delighted Pukkusa the Malla with a talk on Dhamma. Then Pukkusa rose from his seat, saluted the Lord, passed by to the right, and departed.

4.37. Soon after Pukkusa had gone, Ananda, having arranged one set of the golden robes on the body of the Lord, observed that against the Lord's body it appeared dulled. And he said: 'It is wonderful, Lord, it is marvellous how clear and bright the Lord's skin appears! It looks even brighter than the golden robes in which it is clothed.' 'Just so, Ananda. There are two occasions on which the Tathagata's skin appears especially clear and bright. Which are they? One is the night in which the Tathagata gains supreme enlightenment, the other is the night when he attains the Nibbana-element without remainder at his final passing. On these two occasions the Tathagata's skin appears especially clear and bright.

4.38. 'Tonight, Ananda, in the last watch, in the *sal*-grove of Mallas near Kusinara, between two *sal*-trees, the Tathagata's final passing will take place. And now, Ananda, let us go to the River Kakuttha.' 'Very good, Lord', said Ananda.

Two golden robes were Pukkusa's offering:
Brighter shone the Teacher's body than its dress.

4.39. Then the Lord went with a large number of monks to the River Kakuttha. He entered the water, bathed and drank and, emerging, went to the mango grove, where he said to the Venerable Chundaka: 'Come, Chundaka, fold a robe in four for me. I am tired and want to lie down.' 'Very good, Lord', said Cundaka, and did so.

4.40. Then the Lord adopted the lion-posture, lying on his right side, placing one foot on the other, mindfully and with clear awareness bearing in mind the time of awakening. And the Venerable Chundaka sat down in front of the Lord.

4.41.   The Buddha having gone to Kakuttha the river
          With its clear, bright and pleasant waters,
          Therein the Teacher plunged his weary body.
          Tathagata—without an equal in the world.
          Surrounded by the monks whose head he was.
          The Teacher and Lord, Preserver of Dhamma,
          To the Mango Grove the great Sage went,
          And to Chundaka the monk he said:
          'On a fourfold robe I'll lie down.'
          And thus adjured by the great Adept,
          Chundaka placed the fourfold robe.
          The Teacher laid his weary limbs to rest
          While Chundaka kept watch beside him.

4.42. Then the Lord said to the Venerable Ananda: 'It might happen, Ananda, that Chunda the smith should feel remorse, thinking: "It is your fault, friend Chunda, it is by your misdeed that the Tathagata gained final Nibbana after taking his last meal from you!" But Chunda's remorse should be expelled in this way: "That is your merit, Chunda, that is your good deed, that the Tathagata gained final Nibbana after taking his last meal from you! For, friend Chunda, I have heard and understood from the Lord's own lips that these two alms-givings are of very great fruit, of very great result, more fruitful and advantageous than any other. Which two? The one is the alms-giving after eating which the Tathagata attains supreme enlightenment, the other that after which he attains the Nibbana-element without remainder at his final passing. These two alms-givings are more fruitful and profitable than all others. Chunda's deed is conducive to long life, to good looks, to happiness, to fame, to heaven and to lordship." In this way, Ananda, Chunda's remorse is to be expelled.'

4.43. Then the Lord, having settled this matter, at that time uttered this verse:

          'By giving, merit grows, by restraint, hatred's checked.
          He who's skilled abandons evil things.
          As greed, hate and folly wane, Nibbana's gained.'

5.1. The Lord said: 'Ananda, let us cross the Hirannavati River and go to the Mallas' sal-grove in the vicinity of Kusinara.' 'Very good, Lord', said Ananda, and the Lord, with a large company of monks, crossed the river and went to the sal-grove. There the Lord said: 'Ananda, prepare me a bed between these twin sal-trees with my head to the north. I am tired and want to lie down.' 'Very good, Lord', said Ananda, and did so. Then the Lord lay down on his right side in the lion-posture, placing one foot on the other, mindful and clearly aware.

5.2. And those twin *sal*-trees burst forth into an abundance of untimely blossoms, which fell upon the Tathagata's body, sprinkling it and covering it in homage. Divine coral-tree flowers fell from the sky, divine sandal-wood powder fell from the sky, sprinkling and covering the Tathagata's body in homage. Divine music and song sounded from the sky in homage to the Tathagata.

5.3. And the Lord said: 'Ananda, these *sal*-trees have burst forth into an abundance of untimely blossoms . . . Divine music and song sound from the sky in homage to the Tathagata. Never before has the Tathagata been so honoured, revered, esteemed, worshipped and adored. And yet, Ananda, whatever monk, nun, male or female lay-follower dwells practising the Dhamma properly, and perfectly fulfils the Dhamma-way, he or she honours the Tathagata, reveres and esteems him and pays him the supreme homage. Therefore, Ananda, "We with dwell practising the Dhamma properly and perfectly fulfil the Dhamma-way"—this must be your watchword.'

5.4. Just then the Venerable Upavana was standing in front of the Lord, fanning him. And the Lord told him to move: 'Move aside, monk, do not stand in front of me.' And the Venerable Ananda thought: 'This Venerable Upavana has for long been the Lord's attendant, keeping close at hand, at his beck and call. And now in his last hour the Lord tells him to stand aside and not stand in front of him. Why ever does he do that?'

5.5. And he asked the Lord about this. 'Ananda, the devas from ten world-spheres have gathered to see the Tathagata. For a distance of twelve yojanas[9] around the Mallas' *sal*-grove near Kusinara there is not a space you could touch with the point of a hair that is not filled with mighty devas, and they are grumbling: "We have come a long way to see the Tathagata. It is rare for a Tathagata, a fully-enlightened Buddha, to arise in the world, and tonight in the last watch the Tathagata will attain final Nibbana, and this mighty monk is standing in front of the Lord, preventing us from getting a last glimpse of the Tathagata!"'

5.6. 'But, Lord, what kind of devas can the Lord perceive?' 'Ananda, there are sky-devas whose minds are earth-bound, they are weeping and tearing their hair, raising their arms, throwing themselves down and twisting and turning, crying: "All too soon the Blessed Lord is passing away, all too soon the Well-Farer is passing away, all too soon the Eye of the World is disappearing!" And there are earth-devas whose minds are earth-bound, who do likewise. But those devas who are free from craving endure patiently, saying: "All compounded things are impermanent—what is the use of this?"'

5.7. 'Lord, formerly monks who had spent the Rains in various places used to come to see the Tathagata, and we used to welcome them so that such well-trained monks might see you and pay their respects. But with the Lord's passing, we shall no longer have a chance to do this.'

5.8. 'Ananda, there are four places the sight of which should arouse emotion in the faithful. Which are they? "Here the Tathagata was born" is the first. "Here the Tathagata attained supreme enlightenment" is the second. "Here the Tathagata set in motion the Wheel of Dhamma" is the third. "Here

9. A yojana was the standard measurement of distance in ancient India, said to be how far a yoked team of oxen can pull a royal chariot in one day (estimated to be between five and nine miles).

the Tathagata attained the Nibbana-element without remainder" is the fourth. And, Ananda, the faithful monks and nuns, male and female lay-followers will visit those places. And any who die while making the pilgrimage to these shrines with a devout heart will, at the breaking-up of the body after death, be reborn in a heavenly world.'

5.9. 'Lord, how should we act towards women?' 'Do not see them, Ananda.' 'But if we see them, how should we behave, Lord?' 'Do not speak to them, Ananda.' 'But if they speak to us, Lord, how should we behave?' 'Practise mindfulness, Ananda.'

5.10. 'Lord, what shall we do with the Tathagata's remains?' 'Do not worry yourselves about the funeral arrangements, Ananda. You should strive for the highest goal, devote yourselves to the highest goal, and dwell with your minds tirelessly, zealously devoted to the highest goal. There are wise Khattiyas,[1] Brahmins and householders who are devoted to the Tathagata: they will take care of the funeral.'

5.11. 'But, Lord, what are we to do with the Tathagata's remains?' 'Ananda, they should be dealt with like the remains of a wheel-turning monarch.'[2] 'And how is that, Lord?' 'Ananda, the remains of a wheel-turning monarch are wrapped in a new linen-cloth. This they wrap in teased cotton wool, and this in a new cloth. Having done this five hundred times each, they enclose the king's body in an oil-vat of iron, which is covered with another iron pot. Then having made a funeral-pyre of all manner of perfumes they cremate the king's body, and they raise a stupa at a crossroads. That, Ananda, is what they do with the remains of a wheel-turning monarch, and they should deal with the Tathagata's body in the same way. A stupa should be erected at the crossroads for the Tathagata. And whoever lays wreaths or puts sweet perfumes and colours there with a devout heart, will reap benefit and happiness for a long time.'

5.12. 'Ananda, there are four persons worthy of a stupa. Who are they? A Tathagata, Arahant, fully-enlightened Buddha is one, a Paccheka Buddha[3] is one, a disciple of the Tathagata is one, and a wheel-turning monarch is one. And why is each of these worthy of a stupa? Because, Ananda, at the thought: "This is the stupa of a Tathagata, of a Paccheka Buddha, of a disciple of the Tathagata, of a wheel-turning monarch", people's hearts are made peaceful, and then, at the breaking-up of the body after death they go to a good destiny and rearise in a heavenly world. That is the reason, and those are the four who are worthy of a stupa.'

5.13. And the Venerable Ananda went into his lodging and stood lamenting, leaning on the door-post: 'Alas, I am still a learner with much to do! And the Teacher is passing away, who was so compassionate to me!'

Then the Lord enquired of the monks where Ananda was, and they told him. So he said to a certain monk: 'Go, monk, and say to Ananda from me: "Friend Ananda, the Teacher summons you."' 'Very good, Lord', said the monk, and did so. 'Very good, friend', Ananda replied to that monk, and he went to the Lord, saluted him and sat down to one side.

---

1. Pali for *kshatriyas*, members of the second of the four castes of ancient India, sometimes called the warrior caste.
2. The *chakravartin*, a figure of Indian mythology who possesses a magical wheel that rolls around the world; every land that it reaches becomes part of his domain.
3. One who is enlightened but does not proclaim the truth to the world. "Arahant": Pali for *arhat*, one who enters nirvana at death.

5.14. And the Lord said: 'Enough, Ananda, do not weep and wail! Have I not already told you that all things that are pleasant and delightful are changeable, subject to separation and becoming other? So how could it be, Ananda—since whatever is born, become, compounded is subject to decay—how could it be that it should not pass away? For a long time, Ananda, you have been in the Tathagata's presence, showing loving-kindness in act of body, speech and mind, beneficially, blessedly, whole-heartedly and unstintingly. You have achieved much merit, Ananda. Make the effort, and in a short time you will be free of the corruptions.'

5.15. Then the Lord addressed the monks: 'Monks, all those who were Arahant fully-enlightened Buddhas in the past have had just such a chief attendant as Ananda, and so too will those Blessed Lords who come in the future. Monks, Ananda is wise. He knows when it is the right time for monks to come to see the Tathagata, when it is the right time for nuns, for male lay-followers, for female lay-followers, for kings, for royal ministers, for leaders of other schools, and for their pupils.

5.16. 'Ananda has four remarkable and wonderful qualities. What are they? If a company of monks comes to see Ananda, they are pleased at the sight of him, and when Ananda talks Dhamma to them they are pleased, and when he is silent they are disappointed. And so it is, too, with nuns, with male and female lay-followers. And these four qualities apply to a wheel-turning monarch: if he is visited by a company of Khattiyas, of Brahmins, of householders, or of ascetics, they are pleased at the sight of him and when he talks to them, and when he is silent they are disappointed. And so too it is with Ananda.'

5.17. After this the Venerable Ananda said: 'Lord, may the Blessed Lord not pass away in this miserable little town of wattle-and-daub, right in the jungle in the back of beyond! Lord, there are other great cities such as Champa, Rajagaha, Savatthi, Saketa, Kosambi or Varanasi. In those places there are wealthy Khattiyas, Brahmins and householders who are devoted to the Tathagata, and they will provide for the Tathagata's funeral in proper style.'

'Ananda, don't call it a miserable little town of wattle-and-daub, right in the jungle in the back of beyond!

5.18. 'Once upon a time, Ananda, King Mahasudassana was a wheel-turning monarch, a rightful and righteous king, who had conquered the land in four directions and ensured the security of his realm, and who possessed the seven treasures. And, Ananda, this King Mahasudassana had this very Kusinara, under the name of Kusavati, for his capital. And it was twelve yojanas long from east to west, and seven yojanas wide from north to south. Kusavati was rich, prosperous and well-populated, crowded with people and well-stocked with food. Just as the deva-city of Alakamanda is rich, prosperous and well-populated, crowded with yakkhas[4] and well-stocked with food, so was the royal city of Kusavati. And the city of Kusavati was never free of ten sounds by day or night: the sound of elephants, horses, carriages, kettle-drums, side-drums, lutes, singing, cymbals and gongs, with cries of "Eat, drink and be merry!" as tenth.

---

4. Pali for *yakkha*, a category of nonhuman beings, a kind of nature spirit (sometimes kindly, but usually viewed as evil and violent).

5.19. 'And now, Ananda, go to Kusinara and announce to the Mallas of Kusinara: "Tonight, Vasetthas,[5] in the last watch, the Tathagata will attain final Nibbana. Approach him, Vasetthas, approach him, lest later you should regret it, saying: 'The Tathagata passed away in our parish, and we did not take the opportunity to see him for the last time!'"' 'Very good, Lord', said Ananda and, taking robe and bowl, he went with a companion to Kusinara.

5.20. Just then the Mallas of Kusinara were assembled in their meeting-hall on some business. And Ananda came to them and delivered the Lord's words.

5.21. And when they heard Ananda's words, the Mallas, with their sons, daughters-in-law and wives were struck with anguish and sorrow, their minds were overcome with grief so that they were all weeping and tearing their hair . . . Then they all went to the *sal*-grove where the Venerable Ananda was.

5.22. And Ananda thought: 'If I allow the Mallas of Kusinara to salute the Lord individually, the night will have passed before they have all paid homage. I had better let them pay homage family by family, saying: "Lord, the Malla so-and-so with his children, his wife, his servants and his friends pays homage at the Lord's feet."' And so he presented them in that way, and thus allowed all the Mallas of Kusinara to pay homage to the Lord in the first watch.

5.23. And at that time a wanderer called Subhadda was in Kusinara, and he heard that the ascetic Gotama was to attain final Nibbana in the final watch of that night. He thought: 'I have heard from venerable wanderers, advanced in years, teachers of teachers, that a Tathagata, a fully-enlightened Buddha, only rarely arises in the world. And tonight in the last watch the ascetic Gotama will attain final Nibbana. Now a doubt has arisen in my mind, and I feel sure that the ascetic Gotama can teach me a doctrine to dispel that doubt.'

5.24. So Subhadda went to the Mallas' *sal*-grove, to where the Venerable Ananda was, and told him what he had thought: 'Reverend Ananda, may I be permitted to see the ascetic Gotama?' But Ananda replied: 'Enough, friend Subhadda, do not disturb the Tathagata, the Lord is weary.' And Subhadda made his request a second and a third time, but still Ananda refused it.

5.25. But the Lord overheard this conversation between Ananda and Subhadda, and he called to Ananda: 'Enough, Ananda, do not hinder Subhadda, let him see the Tathagata. For whatever Subhadda asks me he will ask in quest of enlightenment and not to annoy me, and what I say in reply to his questions he will quickly understand.' Then Ananda said: 'Go in, friend Subhadda, the Lord gives you leave.'

5.26. Then Subhadda approached the Lord, exchanged courtesies with him, and sat down to one side, saying: 'Venerable Gotama, all those ascetics and Brahmins who have orders and followings, who are teachers, well-known and famous as founders of schools, and popularly regarded as saints, like Purana Kassapa, Makkhali Gosala, Ajita Kesakambali, Pakudha Kacchayana, Sanjaya Belatthaputta and the Nigantha Nataputta—have they all realised the truth as they all make out, or have none of them realised it, or have some realised it and some not?' 'Enough, Subhadda, never mind whether all, or none, or some of them have realised the truth. I will teach you Dhamma, Subhadda. Listen, pay close attention, and I will speak.' 'Yes, Lord', said Subhadda, and the Lord said:

5. The name of a local clan.

5.27. 'In whatever Dhamma and discipline the Noble Eightfold Path is not found, no ascetic is found of the first, the second, the third or the fourth grade.[6] But such ascetics can be found, of the first, second, third and fourth grade in a Dhamma and discipline where the Noble Eightfold Path is found. Now, Subhadda, in this Dhamma and discipline the Noble Eightfold Path *is* found, and in it are to be found ascetics of the first, second, third and fourth grade. Those other schools are devoid of [true] ascetics; but if in this one the monks were to live the life to perfection, the world would not lack for Arahants.

> Twenty-nine years of age I was
> When I went forth to seek the Good.
> Now over fifty years have passed
> Since the day that I went forth
> To roam the realm of wisdom's law
> Outside of which no ascetic is
> [First, second, third or fourth degree].
> Other schools of such are bare,
> But if here monks live perfectly,
> The world won't lack for Arahants.'

5.28. At this the wanderer Subhadda said: 'Excellent, Lord, excellent! It is as if someone were to set up what had been knocked down, or to point out the way to one who had got lost, or to bring an oil lamp into a dark place, so that those with eyes could see what was there. Just so the Blessed Lord has expounded the Dhamma in various ways. And I, Lord, go for refuge to the Blessed Lord, the Dhamma and the Sangha. May I receive the going-forth in the Lord's presence! May I receive ordination!'

5.29. 'Subhadda, whoever, coming from another school, seeks the going-forth and ordination in this Dhamma and discipline, must wait four months on probation. And at the end of four months, those monks who are established in mind may let him go forth and give him ordination to the status of a monk. However, there can be a distinction of persons.'

'Lord, if those coming from other schools must wait four months on probation, . . . I will wait four years, and then let them give me the going-forth and the ordination!' But the Lord said to Ananda: 'Let Subhadda go forth!' 'Very good, Lord', said Ananda.

5.30. And Subhadda said to the Venerable Ananda: 'Friend Ananda, it is a great gain for you all, it is very profitable for you, that you have obtained the consecration of discipleship in the Teacher's presence.'

Then Subhadda received the going-forth in the Lord's presence, and the ordination. And from the moment of his ordination the Venerable Subhadda, alone, secluded, unwearying, zealous and resolute, in a short time attained to that for which young men of good family go forth from the household life into homelessness, that unexcelled culmination of the holy life, having realised it here and now by his own insight, and dwelt therein: 'Birth is destroyed, the holy life has been lived, what had to be done has been done, there is nothing further here.' And the Venerable Subhadda became another of the Arahants. He was the last personal disciple of the Lord.

6. The four stages of the path are Stream Enterer (or Stream-Winner), Once Returner, Never Returner, and Arhat.

6.1. And the Lord said to Ananda: 'Ananda, it may be that you will think: "The Teacher's instruction has ceased, now we have no teacher!" It should not be seen like this, Ananda, for what I have taught and explained to you as Dhamma and discipline will, at my passing, be your teacher.

6.2. 'And whereas the monks are in the habit of addressing one another as "friend", this custom is to be abrogated after my passing. Senior monks shall address more junior monks by their name, their clan or as "friend", whereas more junior monks are to address their seniors either as "Lord" or as "Venerable Sir".

6.3. 'If they wish, the order may abolish the minor rules after my passing.

6.4. 'After my passing, the monk Channa is to receive the Brahma-penalty.' 'But, Lord, what is the Brahma-penalty?' 'Whatever the monk Channa wants or says, he is not to be spoken to, admonished or instructed by the monks.'[7]

6.5. Then the Lord addressed the monks, saying: 'It may be, monks, that some monk has doubts or uncertainty about the Buddha, the Dhamma, the Sangha, or about the path or the practice. Ask, monks! Do not afterwards feel remorse, thinking: "The Teacher was there before us, and we failed to ask the Lord face to face!"' At these words the monks were silent. The Lord repeated his words a second and a third time, and still the monks were silent. Then the Lord said: 'Perhaps, monks, you do not ask out of respect for the Teacher. Then, monks, let one friend tell it to another.' But still they were silent.

6.6. And the Venerable Ananda said: 'It is wonderful, Lord, it is marvellous! I clearly perceive that in this assembly there is not one monk who has doubts or uncertainty . . .' 'You, Ananda, speak from faith. But the Tathagata knows that in this assembly there is not one monk who has doubts or uncertainty about the Buddha, the Dhamma or the Sangha or about the path or the practice. Ananda, the least one of these five hundred monks is a Stream-Winner,[8] incapable of falling into states of woe, certain of Nibbana.'

6.7. Then the Lord said to the monks: 'Now, monks, I declare to you: all conditioned things are of a nature to decay—strive on untiringly.' These were the Tathagata's last words.

6.8. Then the Lord entered the first jhana.[9] And leaving that he entered the second, the third, the fourth jhana. Then leaving the fourth jhana he entered the Sphere of Infinite Space, then the Sphere of Infinite Consciousness, then the Sphere of No-Thingness, then the Sphere of Neither-Perception-Nor-Non-Perception, and leaving that he attained the Cessation of Feeling and Perception.

Then the Venerable Ananda said to the Venerable Anuruddha: 'Venerable Anuruddha, the Lord has passed away.' 'No, friend Ananda, the Lord has not passed away, he has attained the Cessation of Feeling and Perception.'

6.9. Then the Lord, leaving the attainment of the Cessation of Feeling and Perception, entered the Sphere of Neither-Perception-Nor-Non-Perception, from that he entered the Sphere of No-Thingness, the Sphere of Infinite Consciousness, the Sphere of Infinite Space. From the Sphere of Infinite Space he

---

7. Channa, the Buddha's former charioteer, is punished for having sided with nuns in their dispute with monks.
8. The first of the four stages of the path: one who has entered the stream to nirvana and will achieve it in seven lifetimes or less.
9. Pali for *dhyana* (concentration), referring here to a particular level of deep concentration. The Buddha's mind passes up and down through all of these levels before he enters nirvana.

entered the fourth jhana, from there the third, the second and the first jhana. Leaving the first jhana, he entered the second, the third, the fourth jhana. And, leaving the fourth jhana, the Lord finally passed away.

6.10. And at the Blessed Lord's final passing there was a great earthquake, terrible and hair-raising, accompanied by thunder. And Brahma Sahampati[1] uttered this verse:

> 'All beings in the world, all bodies must break up:
> Even the Teacher, peerless in the human world,
> The mighty Lord and perfect Buddha's passed away.'

And Sakka, ruler of the devas, uttered this verse:

> 'Impermanent are compounded things, prone to rise and fall,
> Having risen, they're destroyed, their passing truest bliss.'

And the Venerable Anuruddha uttered this verse:

> 'No breathing in and out—just with steadfast heart
> The Sage who's free from lust has passed away to peace.
> With mind unshaken he endured all pains:
> By Nibbana the Illumined's mind is freed.'

And the Venerable Ananda uttered this verse:

> 'Terrible was the quaking, men's hair stood on end,
> When the all-accomplished Buddha passed away.'

And those monks who had not yet overcome their passions wept and tore their hair, raising their arms, throwing themselves down and twisting and turning, crying: 'All too soon the Blessed Lord has passed away, all too soon the Well-Farer has passed away, all too soon the Eye of the World has disappeared!' But those monks who were free from craving endured mindfully and clearly aware, saying: 'All compounded things are impermanent—what is the use of this?'

6.11. Then the Venerable Anuruddha said: 'Friends, enough of your weeping and wailing! Has not the Lord already told you that all things that are pleasant and delightful are changeable, subject to separation and to becoming other? So why all this, friends? Whatever is born, become, compounded is subject to decay, it cannot be that it does not decay. The devas, friends, are grumbling.'

'Venerable Anuruddha, what kind of devas are you aware of?' 'Friend Ananda, there are sky-devas whose minds are earth-bound they are weeping and tearing their hair . . . And there are earth-devas whose minds are earth-bound, they do likewise. But those devas who are free from craving endure patiently, saying: "All compounded things are impermanent. What is the use of this?"'

6.12. Then the Venerable Anuruddha and the Venerable Ananda spent the rest of the night in conversation on Dhamma. And the Venerable Anuruddha said: 'Now go, friend Ananda, to Kusinara and announce to the Mallas: "Vasetthas, the Lord has passed away. Now is the time to do as you think fit." 'Yes, Lord', said Ananda, and having dressed in the morning and taken his robe and bowl, he went with a companion to Kusinara. At that time the

1. The god who had asked the Buddha to make the teaching known to all.

Mallas of Kusinara were assembled in their meeting-hall on some business. And the Venerable Ananda came to them and delivered the Venerable Anuruddha's message. And when they heard the Venerable Ananda's words, the Mallas . . . were struck with anguish and sorrow, their minds were overcome with grief so that they were all tearing their hair . . .

6.13. Then the Mallas ordered their men to bring perfume and wreaths, and gather all the musicians together. And with the perfumes and wreaths, and all the musicians, and with five hundred sets of garments they went to the *sal*-grove where the Lord's body was lying. And there they honoured, paid respects, worshipped and adored the Lord's body with dance and song and music, with garlands and scents, making awnings and circular tents in order to spend the day there. And they thought: 'It is too late to cremate the Lord's body today. We shall do so tomorrow.' And so, paying homage in the same way, they waited for a second, a third, a fourth, a fifth, a sixth day.

6.14. And on the seventh day the Mallas of Kusinara thought: 'We have paid sufficient honour with song and dance . . . to the Lord's body, now we shall burn his body after carrying him out by the south gate.' Then eight Malla chiefs, having washed their heads and put on new clothes, declared: 'Now we will lift up the Lord's body', but found they were unable to do so. So they went to the Venerable Anuruddha and told him what had happened: 'Why can't we lift up the Lord's body?' 'Vasetthas, your intention is one thing, but the intention of the devas is another.'

6.15. 'Lord, what is the intention of the devas?' 'Vasetthas, your intention is, having paid homage to the Lord's body with dance and song . . . to burn his body after carrying him out by the south gate. But the devas' intention is, having paid homage to the Lord's body with heavenly dance and song . . . , to carry him to the north of the city, bring him in through the north gate and bear him through the middle of the city and out through the eastern gate to the Mallas' shrine of Makuta-Bandhana, and there to burn the body.' 'Lord, if that is the devas' intention, so be it!'

6.16. At that time even the sewers and rubbish-heaps of Kusinara were covered knee-high with coral-tree flowers. And the devas as well as the Mallas of Kusinara honoured the Lord's body with divine and human dancing, song . . . ; and they carried the body to the north of the city, brought it in through the north gate, through the middle of the city and out through the eastern gate to the Mallas' shrine of Makuta-Bandhana, where they set the body down.

6.17. Then they asked the Venerable Ananda: 'Lord, how should we deal with the body of the Tathagata?' 'Vasetthas, you should deal with the Tathagata's body as you would that of a wheel-turning monarch.' 'And how do they deal with that, Lord?'

'Vasetthas, the remains are wrapped in a new linen-cloth. This they wrap in teased cotton-wool . . . ; then having made a funeral-pyre of all manner of perfumes, they cremate the king's body and they raise a stupa at a cross roads . . .'

6.18. Then the Mallas ordered their men to bring their teased cotton-wool. And they dealt with the Tathagata's body accordingly . . .

6.19. Now just then the Venerable Kassapa the Great[2] was travelling along the main road from Pava to Kusinara with a large company of about five

2. Mahakassapa.

hundred monks. And leaving the road, the Venerable Kassapa the Great sat down under a tree. And a certain Ajivika chanced to be coming along the main road towards Pava, and he had picked a coral-tree flower in Kusinara. The Venerable Kassapa saw him coming from afar, and said to him: 'Friend, do you know our Teacher?' 'Yes, friend, I do. The ascetic Gotama passed away a week ago. I picked this coral-tree flower there.' And those monks who had not yet overcome their passions wept and tore their hair . . . But those monks who were free from craving endured mindfully and clearly aware, saying: 'All compounded things are impermanent—what is the use of this?'

6.20. And sitting in the group was one Subhadda, who had gone forth late in life, and he said to those monks, 'Enough, friends, do not weep and wail! We are well rid of the Great Ascetic. We were always bothered by his saying: "It is fitting for you to do this, it is not fitting for you to do that." Now we can do what we like, and not do what we don't like.'

But the Venerable Kassapa the Great said to the monks: 'Friends, enough of your weeping and wailing! Has not the Lord already told you that all things that are pleasant and delightful are changeable, subject to separation and becoming other? So why all this, friends? Whatever is born, become, compounded is subject to decay, it cannot be that it does not decay.'

6.21. Meanwhile four Malla chiefs, having washed their heads and put on new clothes, said: 'We will light the Lord's funeral pyre', but they were unable to do so. They went to the Venerable Anuruddha and asked him why this was. 'Vasetthas, your intention is one thing, but that of the devas is another.' 'Well, Lord, what is the intention of the devas?' 'Vasetthas, the devas' intention is this: "The Venerable Kassapa the Great is coming along the main road from Pava to Kusinara with a large company of five hundred monks. The Lord's funeral pyre will not be lit until the Venerable Kassapa the Great has paid homage with his head to the Lord's feet.' 'Lord, if that is the devas' intention, so be it!'

6.22. Then the Venerable Kassapa the Great went to the Mallas' shrine at Makuta-Bandhana to the Lord's funeral pyre and, covering one shoulder with his robe, joined his hands in salutation, circumambulated the pyre three times and, uncovering the Lord's feet, paid homage with his head to them, and the five hundred monks did likewise. And when this was done, the Lord's funeral pyre ignited of itself.

6.23. And when the Lord's body was burnt, what had been skin, under-skin, flesh, sinew, or joint-fluid, all that vanished and not even ashes or dust remained, only the bones remained. Just as when butter or oil is burnt, no ashes or dust remain, so it was with the Lord's body . . . , only the bones were left. And all the five hundred garments, even the innermost and the outermost cloth, were burnt up. And when the Lord's body was burnt up, a shower of water from the sky, and another which burst forth from the *sal*-trees extinguished the funeral pyre. And the Mallas of Kusinara poured perfumed water over it for the same purpose. Then the Mallas honoured the relics for a week in their assembly hall, having made a lattice-work of spears and an encircling wall of bows, with dancing, singing, garlands and music.

6.24. And King Ajatasattu Vedehiputta of Magadha heard that the Lord had passed away at Kusinara. And he sent a message to the Mallas of Kusinara: 'The Lord was a Khattiya and I am a Khattiya. I am worthy to receive

a share of the Lord's remains. I will make a great stupa for them.' The Licchavis of Vesali heard, and they sent a message: 'The Lord was a Khattiya and
we are Khattiyas. We are worthy to receive a share of the Lord's remains, and
we will make a great stupa for them.' The Sakyas of Kapilavatthu heard,
and they sent a message: 'The Lord was the chief of our clan. We are worthy
to receive a share of the Lord's remains, and we will make a great stupa for
them.' 'The Bulayas of Allakappa and the Koliyas of Ramagama replied
similarly. The Brahmin of Vethadipa heard, and he sent a message: 'The
Lord was a Khattiya, I am a Brahmin . . .', and the Mallas of Pava sent a message: 'The Lord was a Khattiya, we are Khattiyas. We are worthy to receive
a share of the Lord's remains, and we will make a great stupa for them.'

6.25. On hearing all this, the Mallas of Kusinara addressed the crowd, saying: 'The Lord passed away in our parish. We will not give away any share of the
Lord's remains.' At this the Brahmin Dona addressed the crowd in this verse:

> 'Listen, lords, to my proposal.
> Forbearance is the Buddha's teaching.
> It is not right that strife should come
> From sharing out the best of men's remains.
> Let's all be joined in harmony and peace,
> In friendship sharing out portions eight:
> Let stupas far and wide be put up,
> That all may see—and gain in faith!'

'Well then, Brahmin, you divide up the remains of the Lord in the best and
fairest way!' 'Very good, friends', said Dona. And he made a good and fair division into eight portions, and then said to the assembly: 'Gentlemen, please give
me the urn, and I will erect a great stupa for it.' So they gave Dona the urn.

6.26. Now the Moriyas of Pipphalavana heard of the Lord's passing, and
they sent a message: 'The Lord was a Khattiya and we are Khattiyas. We are
worthy to receive a portion of the Lord's remains, and we will make a great
stupa for them.'

'There is not a portion of the Lord's remains left, they have all been divided
up. So you must take the embers.' And so they took the embers.

6.27. Then King Ajatasattu of Magadha built a great stupa for the Lord's
relics at Rajagaha. The Licchavis of Vesali built one at Vesali, the Sakyans
of Kapilavatthu built one at Kapilavatthu, the Bulayas of Allakappa built one
at Allakappa, the Koliyas of Ramagama built one at Ramagama, the Brahmin
of Vethadipa built one at Vethadipa, the Mallas of Pava built one at Pava, the
Mallas of Kusinara built a great stupa for the Lord's relics at Kusinara,
the Brahmin Dona built a great stupa for the urn, and the Moriyas of Pipphalavana built a great stupa for the embers at Pipphalavana. Thus, eight
stupas were built for the relics, a ninth for the urn, and a tenth for the embers.
That is how it was in the old days.

6.28.   Eight portions of relics there were of him,
         The All-Seeing One. Of these, seven remained
         In Jambudipa with honour. The eighth
         In Ramagama's kept by naga[3] kings.
         One tooth the Thirty Gods have kept,

---

3. A water deity, often depicted with the torso of a human and the tail of a snake.

Kalinga's kings have one, the nagas too.
They shed their glory o'er the fruitful earth.
Thus the Seer's honoured by the honoured.
Gods and nagas, kings, the noblest men
Clasp their hands in homage, for hard it is
To find another such for countless aeons.

THE BUDDHA'S FIRST SERMON

SETTING THE WHEEL OF THE DHARMA IN MOTION
(The Dhammachakkappavattana Sutta)

After achieving enlightenment, the Buddha is said to have been reluctant to teach. But the god Brahma descended from his heaven to implore him to do so, arguing that though there are some beings with much dust in their eyes (who thus would be unable to perceive the truth the Buddha had seen), there are also beings with little dust in their eyes (and thus able to perceive that truth). The Buddha agreed, deciding that his two old meditation teachers would be most worthy to be the first to hear his dharma. But they had recently died, and so he chose instead "the group of five" (also encountered in *Account of the Beginning*, p. 131), the five ascetics with whom he had practiced austerities and who had abandoned him in disgust when he gave up their regimen of controlled starvation and accepted a meal. He determined that they were staying in an animal sanctuary called Deer Park outside the great city of Banaras, or Varanasi. The Buddha walked there, a distance of about 150 miles. When they saw him approaching, they agreed among themselves to ignore him, still holding him in contempt for his weakness. But when he came into their presence they were moved, as if against their will, to greet him and offer him a seat.

The text that follows is what he taught them, renowned in the West as his "first sermon" after his achievement of buddhahood. The traditional title in Pali is "Dhammachakkappavattana"—literally, "Setting the Wheel of the Dharma in Motion." The Buddha's teaching is called the dharma and is represented as a wheel, like the wheel of a chariot, with eight spokes. Despite the great fame of the term, its symbolism is not entirely clear. It likely is related to the wheel of the universal monarch (*chakravartin*), a figure of Indian mythology: this king possesses a magical wheel that rolls around the world, and every land that it reaches becomes part of his domain. When the Buddha teaches, he is said to turn the wheel of the dharma to set it rolling. This brief text is dense with the key terms of Buddhism, expressed here for the first time: middle way, four noble truths, eightfold path.

The middle way is the path between the two extremes that the Buddha himself had fallen into earlier in his life, the self-indulgence that he had known as prince and the self-mortification that he had practiced with the group of five as an ascetic. Neither of these leads to peace; only a middle way between them leads to nirvana. That middle way is the famous eightfold path of right view, right intention, right speech, right action, right livelihood, right effort, right mindfulness, and right meditation (*samadhi*, translated in the passage below as "concentration"). Each aspect receives extensive comment in the tradition. In brief, they are summarized under the three trainings necessary for liberation from rebirth: the training in ethics (right speech, right action, right livelihood), the training in meditation (right effort, right mindfulness, right meditation), and the training in wisdom (right view, right intention).

The Buddha turning the wheel of the dharma. India, 5th century.

The four truths are suffering, origin, cessation, and path (the last translated here as "way"). In the standard English rendering, they are called the four noble truths. The term translated as noble is *aryan* in Sanskrit, a common term meaning "noble" or "superior" in ancient India that was ruined forever by race theorists in the nineteenth and twentieth centuries. In fact, a more accurate translation might be the "four ennobling truths" or the "four truths for the spiritually noble," as these four things are said to be true only for those with insight into the nature of reality. For the benighted, they are not true.

In presenting the first truth, the Buddha identifies the sufferings as eight: birth, aging, sickness, death, meeting with the unpleasant, separation from the pleasant, not finding what one wants, and "the five aggregates subject to clinging"—that is, the physical and mental constituents of the person. The second truth is the truth of the cause or origin of those sufferings. Here, in the first sermon, the Buddha names craving—whether it be for pleasure, for continued existence, or for the end of existence—as the source of suffering. Elsewhere, he would identify ignorance as the root cause of suffering. The origin of suffering is to be abandoned. The third truth is the truth of the cessation of suffering and the craving that is its cause, not temporarily but permanently: "remainderless fading away," as the text says. The cessation of all forms of suffering and their causes is called nirvana. Finally, there is a path or way leading to that state of cessation. This is the fourth truth, the truth of the path—that is, the eightfold path described above.

The Buddha makes three statements about each of the four truths. The first is the knowledge or recognition of each truth ("This is the truth of suffering"). The second statement is what must be done with regard to each truth. Specifically, suffering is to be recognized, its origin is to be abandoned, its cessation is to be realized, the path to cessation is to be followed. The third statement for each truth is a declaration that the goal for each truth has been accomplished: suffering has been recognized, its origin has been abandoned, and so on. Hence, the Buddha explains that he understood the four truths in three phases and twelve aspects (the three phases for each of the four truths). When he had done so, he was enlightened.

The text ends with a fairly standard expression of joy and delight from various deities. But before that, something important takes place: one of the group of five, named Kondanna, achieves enlightenment based simply on the Buddha's discourse.

In the words of the text, he achieved "stainless vision of the Dhamma." This is a key moment in the history of the tradition, because the dharma, that which the Buddha initially felt was too difficult to be understood by others, had indeed been conveyed. The Buddha had successfully taught the truth to one other person. Soon it would be learned by many more.

PRONOUNCING GLOSSARY

Anna: *a-nyah*

Baranasi: *bah-rah-na-si*

bhikkhu: *bik-ku*

Brahma: *bra-mah*

deva: *day-va*

Dhammachakkappavattana Sutta: *dam-ma-chak-ka-pa-va-ta-na soot-ta*

Isipatana: *i-si-pa-ta-na*

Kondanna: *kohn-dany-nya*

Mara: *mah-ra*

Nibbana: *nib-bah-na*

Nimmanarati: *nim-mah-na-ra-ti*

Paranimmitavasavatti: *pa-ra-ni-mi-ta-va-sa-va-ti*

Tathagata: *ta-tah-ga-ta*

Tavatimsa: *tah-va-tim-sa*

Tusita: *tu-si-ta*

Thus have I heard. On one occasion the Blessed One was dwelling at Baranasi[1] in the Deer Park at Isipatana. There the Blessed One addressed the bhikkhus[2] of the group of five thus:

"Bhikkhus, these two extremes should not be followed by one who has gone forth into homelessness. What two? The pursuit of sensual happiness in sensual pleasures, which is low, vulgar, the way of worldlings, ignoble, unbeneficial; and the pursuit of self-mortification, which is painful, ignoble, unbeneficial. Without veering towards either of these extremes, the Tathagata[3] has awakened to the middle way, which gives rise to vision, which gives rise to knowledge, which leads to peace, to direct knowledge, to enlightenment, to Nibbana.[4]

"And what, bhikkhus, is that middle way awakened to by the Tathagata, which gives rise to vision . . . which leads to Nibbana? It is this Noble Eightfold Path; that is, right view, right intention, right speech, right action, right livelihood, right effort, right mindfulness, right concentration. This, bhikkhus, is that middle way awakened to by the Tathagata, which gives rise to vision, which gives rise to knowledge, which leads to peace, to direct knowledge, to enlightenment, to Nibbana.

"Now this, bhikkhus, is the noble truth of suffering: birth is suffering, aging is suffering, illness is suffering, death is suffering; union with what is displeasing is suffering; separation from what is pleasing is suffering; not to get what one wants is suffering; in brief, the five aggregates[5] subject to clinging are suffering.

"Now this, bhikkhus, is the noble truth of the origin of suffering: it is this craving which leads to renewed existence, accompanied by delight and lust, seeking delight here and there; that is, craving for sensual pleasures, craving for existence, craving for extermination.

TRANSLATED FROM the Pali by Bhikkhu Bodhi.

1. That is, Varanasi, in modern-day Uttar Pradesh.
2. Bhikkhu is Pali for *bhikshu*, a monk or ascetic.
3. A title of a buddha; it is the one most often used by the historical Buddha to refer to himself.

4. Pali for *nirvana*.
5. The five elements of existence that come together to temporarily constitute the mind and body.

"Now this, bhikkhus, is the noble truth of the cessation of suffering: it is the remainderless fading away and cessation of that same craving, the giving up and relinquishing of it, freedom from it, nonreliance on it.

"Now this, bhikkhus, is the noble truth of the way leading to the cessation of suffering: it is this Noble Eightfold Path; that is, right view . . . right concentration.

"'This is the noble truth of suffering': thus, bhikkhus, in regard to things unheard before, there arose in me vision, knowledge, wisdom, true knowledge, and light.

"'This noble truth of suffering is to be fully understood': thus, bhikkhus, in regard to things unheard before, there arose in me vision, knowledge, wisdom, true knowledge, and light.

"'This noble truth of suffering has been fully understood': thus, bhikkhus, in regard to things unheard before, there arose in me vision, knowledge, wisdom, true knowledge, and light.

"'This is the noble truth of the origin of suffering': thus, bhikkhus, in regard to things unheard before, there arose in me vision, knowledge, wisdom, true knowledge, and light.

"'This noble truth of the origin of suffering is to be abandoned': thus, bhikkhus, in regard to things unheard before, there arose in me vision, knowledge, wisdom, true knowledge, and light.

"'This noble truth of the origin of suffering has been abandoned': thus, bhikkhus, in regard to things unheard before, there arose in me vision, knowledge, wisdom, true knowledge, and light.

"'This is the noble truth of the cessation of suffering': thus, bhikkhus, in regard to things unheard before, there arose in me vision, knowledge, wisdom, true knowledge, and light.

"'This noble truth of the cessation of suffering is to be realized': thus, bhikkhus, in regard to things unheard before, there arose in me vision, knowledge, wisdom, true knowledge, and light.

"'This noble truth of the cessation of suffering has been realized': thus, bhikkhus, in regard to things unheard before, there arose in me vision, knowledge, wisdom, true knowledge, and light.

"'This is the noble truth of the way leading to the cessation of suffering': thus, bhikkhus, in regard to things unheard before, there arose in me vision, knowledge, wisdom, true knowledge, and light.

"'This noble truth of the way leading to the cessation of suffering is to be developed': thus, bhikkhus, in regard to things unheard before, there arose in me vision, knowledge, wisdom, true knowledge, and light.

"'This noble truth of the way leading to the cessation of suffering has been developed': thus, bhikkhus, in regard to things unheard before, there arose in me vision, knowledge, wisdom, true knowledge, and light.

"So long, bhikkhus, as my knowledge and vision of these Four Noble Truths as they really are in their three phases and twelve aspects was not thoroughly purified in this way, I did not claim to have awakened to the unsurpassed perfect enlightenment in this world with its devas, Mara, and Brahma,[6] in this generation with its ascetics and brahmins, its devas and

---

6. The god who persuaded the Buddha to teach. "Devas": gods; inhabitants of the heavenly realms (literally, "shining ones"]. "Mara": personification of evil and temptation.

humans. But when my knowledge and vision of these Four Noble Truths as they really are in their three phases and twelve aspects was thoroughly purified in this way, then I claimed to have awakened to the unsurpassed perfect enlightenment in this world with its devas, Mara, and Brahma, in this generation with its ascetics and brahmins, its devas and humans. The knowledge and vision arose in me: 'Unshakable is the liberation of my mind. This is my last birth. Now there is no more renewed existence.'"

This is what the Blessed One said. Elated, the bhikkhus of the group of five delighted in the Blessed One's statement. And while this discourse was being spoken, there arose in the Venerable Kondanna the dust-free, stainless vision of the Dhamma: "Whatever is subject to origination is all subject to cessation."

And when the Wheel of the Dhamma had been set in motion by the Blessed One, the earth-dwelling devas raised a cry: "At Baranasi, in the Deer Park at Isipatana, this unsurpassed Wheel of the Dhamma has been set in motion by the Blessed One, which cannot be stopped by any ascetic or brahmin or deva or Mara or Brahma or by anyone in the world." Having heard the cry of the earth-dwelling devas, the devas of the realm of the Four Great Kings raised a cry: "At Baranasi . . . this unsurpassed Wheel of the Dhamma has been set in motion by the Blessed One, which cannot be stopped . . . by anyone in the world." Having heard the cry of the devas of the realm of the Four Great Kings, the Tavatimsa devas . . . the Yama devas . . . the Tusita devas . . . the Nimmanarati devas . . . the Paranimmitavasavatti devas . . . the devas of Brahma's company raised a cry: "At Baranasi, in the Deer Park at Isipatana, this unsurpassed Wheel of the Dhamma has been set in motion by the Blessed One, which cannot be stopped by any ascetic or brahmin or deva or Mara or Brahma or by anyone in the world."

Thus at that moment, at that instant, at that second, the cry spread as far as the brahma world,[7] and this ten thousandfold world system shook, quaked, and trembled, and an immeasurable glorious radiance appeared in the world surpassing the divine majesty of the devas.

Then the Blessed One uttered this inspired utterance: "Kondanna has indeed understood! Kondanna has indeed understood!" In this way the Venerable Kondanna acquired the name "Anna Kondanna—Kondanna Who Has Understood."

7. The heaven of the god Brahma.

THE BUDDHA BELITTLES THE BRAHMINS

THE THREE KNOWLEDGES
(The Tevijja Sutta)

Buddhism arose within a well-established religious milieu. Victorian scholars referred to the dominant religion as "Brahmanism," because it was controlled by priests of the brahmin caste; the chief form of religious practice was sacrifice. Today, scholars usually call this system of religious practice Vedic Hinduism, since the chief texts of the period (preserved only orally) were the Vedas, traditionally counted as three: the Rig Veda, Yajur Veda, and Sama Veda (a fourth, the Atharva Veda, was added later). At the time of the Buddha, there were dozens of smaller competing traditions, only two of which, Buddhism and Jainism, survive to the present day. In order to survive, the early Buddhist community required support in the form of followers, alms, and patronage; and to garner this support, it had to demonstrate its superiority to the Brahmanical system in a competition made more consequential as an urban economy developed in India. Here, as elsewhere, the truth claims of religions had both philosophical and material foundations.

The Buddha's attitude toward the caste system, the hierarchical fourfold division of society, is far more nuanced than Western enthusiasts of Buddhism have generally realized. He did not reject it. And although he did accept members of all four castes into the order of monks and nuns, the majority came from the two highest castes: the brahmin or priestly caste and the kshatriya or warrior caste (of which the Buddha himself was a member). Rather than criticizing the caste system as a whole, the Buddha reserves most of his condemnation of the religions of his day for the brahmins, repeatedly calling their inborn superiority into question. This attack is not surprising, since the brahmins were at once his chief antagonists and his chief competitors.

One of the most famous critiques of the brahmins and their religion is the *Tevijja Sutta*. The text occurs in the *Digha Nikaya,* or "Long Collection," the section of the Pali canon that contains the longer discourses of the Buddha. The title literally means "three knowledges" in Pali, but it also means "three Vedas." Here, the Buddha provides a sharp criticism of brahmins learned in the three Vedas.

Two young brahmins are arguing about which of the brahmin teachers correctly sets forth the path to union with the god Brahma. Brahma is one of the Vedic deities, and they seem to be referring not to a mystical union in the sense described in the Upanishads but rather to rebirth in his heaven. They go to the Buddha to settle their argument. He points out that none of the brahmins, from the teachers of the present day to the great seers of the past, has ever seen Brahma. Using a number of similes, the Buddha convinces them that it is therefore impossible for them to know how to find him. Furthermore, these brahmins are prevented from seeing Brahma because they are addicted to the five sense objects (pleasing sights, sounds, fragrances, flavors, and objects of touch) and they are afflicted with the five hindrances (desire, anger, sloth, worry, and doubt). These two lists figure prominently in the Buddha's instructions on what to avoid in order to achieve various meditative states. The Buddha then compares brahmins who claim to know the way to Brahma to a man who wants to cross a river but lies chained and bound on the shore. "Crossing to the other shore" is a standard Buddhist metaphor for achieving nirvana.

But here, the Buddha is talking not about seeing nirvana but about seeing Brahma, a less exalted attainment in the Buddhist universe. The Buddha tells his interlocutors that unlike the brahmins, he has seen Brahma, and he thus knows the way to reach his heaven. (It was Brahma who descended from his heaven after the Buddha's enlightenment to implore the Buddha to teach the dharma.) He explains that the god Brahma (whose name means "purity") is unencumbered with wives and wealth, that he is free of ill will and hate, that he is pure and disciplined. Thus, in order to reach him, one should be like him. The Buddha then sets forth the four *brahmaviharas*, which can mean either "abodes of Brahma" or "pure abidings," which would become among the most famous of the many objects of meditation in Buddhism: loving-kindness, compassion, sympathetic joy, and equanimity. (The technique for cultivating loving-kindness is described in the *Visuddhimagga,* or *Path of Purification*, p. 249) It is by meditating on these that one is reborn in the heaven of Brahma in the next lifetime. Convinced that only the Buddha knows the path to Brahma, the two young brahmins ask to be accepted by him not as monks, although the Buddha has clearly recommended that path, but as lay followers.

PRONOUNCING GLOSSARY

Achiravati: *a-chi-ra-va-tee*
Addhariya: *ad-da-ri-ya*
Angirasa: *an-gi-ra-sa*
Arahant: *a-ra-hant*
Atthaka: *a-ta-ka*
Bhagu: *ba-gu*
Bharadvaja: *bah-ra-dva-ja*
Brahmacariya: *brah-ma-cha-ri-ya*
Chanki: *chan-kee*
deva: *day-va*
Janussoni: *jah-nus-soh-ni*
jhana: *jah-na*
Kassapa: *kahs-sa-pa*

Mahiddhi: *ma-hid-di*
Manasakata: *ma-na-sah-ka-ta*
Pokkharasati: *pohk-ka-ra-sah-ti*
Pajapati: *pa-jah-pa-ti*
Sangha: *san-ga*
Tarukkha: *tah-ruk-ka*
Tevijja Sutta: *tay-vij-ja soot-ta*
Tittiriya: *tit-ti-ri-ya*
Todeyya: *toh-day-ya*
Vamadeva: *vah-ma-day-va*
Vasettha: *vah-say-ta*
Vessamitta: *vays-sa-mit-ta*
Yamataggi: *ya-ma-tag-gi*

---

1. Thus have I heard. Once the Lord was touring Kosala with a large company of some five hundred monks. He came to a Kosalan Brahmin village called Manasakata, and stayed to the north of the village in a mango-grove on the bank of the River Achiravati.

2. And at that time many very well-known and prosperous Brahmins were staying at Manasakata, including Chanki, Tarukkha, Pokkharasati, Janussoni, and Todeyya.

3. And Vasettha and Bharadvaja went strolling along the road, and as they did so, an argument broke out between them on the subject of right and wrong paths.

4. The young Brahmin Vasettha said: 'This is the only straight path, this is the direct path, the path of salvation that leads one who follows it to union with Brahma, as is taught by the Brahmin Pokkharasati!'

5. And the young Brahmin Bharadvaja said: '*This* is the only straight path . . . as taught by the Brahmin Tarukkha!'

6. And Vasettha could not convince Bharadvaja, nor could Bharadvaja convince Vasettha.

7. Then Vasettha said to Bharadvaja: 'This ascetic Gotama[1] is staying to the north of the village, and concerning this Blessed Lord a good report has been spread about: "This Blessed Lord is an Arahant,[2] a fully-enlightened Buddha, perfected in knowledge and conduct, a Well-Farer, Knower of the worlds, unequalled Trainer of men to be tamed, Teacher of gods and humans, a Buddha, a Blessed Lord." Let us go to the ascetic Gotama and ask him, and whatever he tells us, we shall accept.' And Bharadvaja agreed.

8. So the two of them went to see the Lord. Having exchanged courtesies with him, they sat down to one side, and Vasettha said: 'Reverend Gotama, as we were strolling along the road, we got to discussing right and wrong paths. I said: "This is the only straight path . . . as is taught by the Brahmin Pokkharasati", and Bharadvaja said: "*This* is the only straight path . . . as is taught by the Brahmin Tarukkha." This is our dispute, our quarrel, our difference.'

TRANSLATED FROM the Pali by Maurice Walshe.

1. That is, Gautama.
2. Pali for *arhat* (literally, "worthy one" in San-skrit), someone who has destroyed all causes for future rebirth and will enter nirvana at death.

9. 'So, Vasettha, you say that the way to union with Brahma is that taught by the Brahmin Pokkharasati, and Bharadvaja says it is that taught by the Brahmin Tarukkha. What is the dispute, the quarrel, the difference all about?'

10. 'Right and wrong paths, Reverend Gotama. There are so many kinds of Brahmins who teach different paths: the Addhariya, the Tittiriya, the Chandoka, the Chandava, the Brahmacariya Brahmins—do all these ways lead to union with Brahma? Just as if there were near a town or village many different paths—do all these come together at that place? And likewise, do the ways of the various Brahmins . . . lead the one who follows them to union with Brahma?'

11. 'You say: "They lead", Vasettha?' 'I say: "They lead", Reverend Gotama.'
'You say: "They lead", Vasettha?' 'I say: "They lead", Reverend Gotama.'
'You say: "They lead", Vasettha?' 'I say: "They lead", Reverend Gotama.'

12. 'But, Vasettha, is there then a single one of these Brahmins learned in the Three Vedas who has seen Brahma face to face?' 'No, Reverend Gotama.'
'Then has the teacher's teacher of any one of them seen Brahma face to face?' 'No, Reverend Gotama.'
'Then has the ancestor seven generations back of the teacher of one of them seen Brahma face to face?' 'No, Reverend Gotama.'

13. 'Well then, Vasettha, what about the early sages of those Brahmins learned in the Three Vedas, the makers of the mantras, the expounders of the mantras, whose ancient verses are chanted, pronounced and collected by the Brahmins of today and sung and spoken about—such as Atthaka, Vamaka, Vamadeva, Vessamitta, Yamataggi, Angirasa, Bharadvaja, Vasettha, Kassapa, Bhagu—did they ever say: "We know and see when, how and where Brahma appears"?' 'No, Reverend Gotama.'

14. 'So, Vasettha, not one of these Brahmins learned in the Three Vedas has seen Brahma face to face, nor has one of their teachers, or teacher's teachers, nor even the ancestor seven generations back of one of their teachers. Nor could any of the early sages say: "We know and see when, how and where Brahma appears." So what these Brahmins learned in the Three Vedas are saying is: "We teach this path to union with Brahma that we do not know or see, this is the only straight path . . . leading to union with Brahma." What do you think, Vasettha? Such being the case, does not what these Brahmins declare turn out to be ill-founded?' 'Yes indeed, Reverend Gotama.'

15. 'Well, Vasettha, when these Brahmins learned in the Three Vedas teach a path that they do not know or see, saying: "This is the only straight path . . .", this cannot possibly be right. Just as a file of blind men go on, clinging to each other, and the first one sees nothing, the middle one sees nothing, and the last one sees nothing—so it is with the talk of these Brahmins learned in the Three Vedas: the first one sees nothing, the middle one sees nothing, the last one sees nothing. The talk of these Brahmins learned in the Three Vedas turns out to be laughable, mere words, empty and vain.

16. 'What do you think, Vasettha? Do these Brahmins learned in the Three Vedas see the sun and moon just as other people do, and when the sun and moon rise and set do they pray, sing praises and worship with clasped hands?' 'They do, Reverend Gotama.'

17. 'What do you think, Vasettha? These Brahmins learned in the Three Vedas, who can see the sun and moon just as other people do, . . . can they point out a way to union with the sun and moon, saying: "This is the only

straight path . . . that leads to union with the sun and moon"?' 'No, Reverend Gotama.'

18. 'So, Vasettha, these Brahmins learned in the Three Vedas cannot point out a way to union with the sun and moon, which they have seen. And, too, none of them has seen Brahma face to face, . . . nor has even the ancestor seven generations back of one of their teachers. Nor could any of the early sages say: "We know and see when, how and where Brahma appears." Does not what these Brahmins declare turn out to be ill-founded?' 'Yes indeed, Reverend Gotama.'

19. 'Vasettha, it is just as if a man were to say: "I am going to seek out and love the most beautiful girl in the country." They might say to him: ". . . Do you know what caste she belongs to?" "No." "Well, do you know her name, her clan, whether she is tall or short . . . , dark or light-complexioned . . . , or where she comes from?" "No." And they might say: "Well then, you don't know or see the one you seek for and desire?" and he would say: "No." Does not the talk of that man turn out to be stupid?' 'Certainly, Reverend Gotama.'

20. 'Then, Vasettha, it is like this: not one of these Brahmins . . . has seen Brahma face to face, nor has one of their teachers . . .' 'Yes indeed, Reverend Gotama.'

'That is right, Vasettha. When these Brahmins learned in the Three Vedas teach a path that they do not know and see, this cannot possibly be right.

21. 'Vasettha, it is just as if a man were to build a staircase for a palace at a crossroads. People might say: "This staircase for a palace—do you know whether the palace will face east or west, north or south, or whether it will be high, low or of medium height?" and he would say: "No." And they might say: "Well then, you don't know or see what kind of a palace you are building the staircase for?" and he would say: "No." Does not the talk of that man turn out to be stupid?' 'Certainly, Reverend Gotama.'

22–23. (as verse 20)

24. 'Vasettha, it is just as if this River Achiravati were brimful of water so that a crow could drink out of it, and a man should come along wishing to cross over, to get to the other side, to get across, and, standing on this bank, were to call out: "Come here, other bank, come here!" What do you think, Vasettha? Would the other bank of the River Achiravati come over to this side on account of that man's calling, begging, requesting or wheedling?' 'No, Reverend Gotama.'

25. 'Well now, Vasettha, those Brahmins learned in the Three Vedas who persistently neglect what a Brahmin should do, and persistently do what a Brahmin should not do, declare: "We call on Indra, Soma, Varuna, Isana, Pajapati, Brahma, Mahiddhi, Yama." But that such Brahmins who persistently neglect what a Brahmin should do, . . . will, as a consequence of their calling, begging, requesting or wheedling, attain after death, at the breaking-up of the body, to union with Brahma—that is just not possible.

26. 'Vasettha, it is just as if this River Aciravati were brimful of water so that a crow could drink out of it, and a man should come wishing to cross over, . . . but he was bound and pinioned on this side by a strong chain, with his hands behind his back. What do you think, Vasettha? Would that man be able to get to the other side?' 'No, Reverend Gotama.'

27. 'In just the same way, Vasettha, in the Ariyan[3] discipline these five strands of sense-desire are called bonds and fetters. Which five? Forms seen by the eye which are agreeable, loved, charming, attractive, pleasurable, arousing desire; sounds heard by the ear . . . ; smells smelt by the nose . . . ; tastes savoured by the tongue . . . ; contacts felt by the body which are agreeable, . . . arousing desire. These five in the Ariyan discipline are called bonds and fetters. And, Vasettha, those Brahmins learned in the Three Vedas are enslaved, infatuated by these five strands of sense-desire, which they enjoy guiltily, unaware of danger, knowing no way out.

28. 'But that such Brahmins learned in the Three Vedas, who persistently neglect what a Brahmin should do, . . . who are enslaved by these five strands of sense-desire, . . . knowing no way out, should attain after death, at the breaking-up of the body, to union with Brahma—that is just not possible.

29. 'It is just as if this River Achiravathi were brimful of water so that a crow could drink out of it, and a man should come along wishing to cross over . . . and were to lie down on this bank, covering his head with a shawl. What do you think, Vasettha? Would that man be able to get to the other side?' 'No, Reverend Gotama.'

30. 'In the same way, Vasettha, in the Ariyan discipline these five hindrances are called obstacles, hindrances, coverings-up, envelopings. Which five? The hindrance of sensuality, of ill-will, of sloth-and-torpor, of worry-and-flurry, of doubt. These five are called obstacles, hindrances, coverings-up, envelopings. And these Brahmins learned in the Three Vedas are caught up, hemmed in, obstructed, entangled in these five hindrances. But that such Brahmins learned in the Three Vedas, who persistently neglect what a Brahmin should do . . . and who are caught up, . . . entangled in these five hindrances, should attain after death, at the breaking-up of the body, to union with Brahma—that is just not possible.

31. 'What do you think, Vasettha? What have you heard said by Brahmins who are venerable, aged, the teachers of teachers? Is Brahma encumbered with wives and wealth, or unencumbered?' 'Unencumbered, Reverend Gotama.'

'Is he full of hate or without hate?' 'Without hate, Reverend Gotama.'

'Is he full of ill-will or without ill-will?' 'Without ill-will, Reverend Gotama.'

'Is he impure or pure?' 'Pure, Reverend Gotama.'

'Is he disciplined or undisciplined?' 'Disciplined, Reverend Gotama.'

32. 'And what do you think, Vasettha? Are the Brahmins learned in the Three Vedas encumbered with wives and wealth, or unencumbered?' 'Encumbered, Reverend Gotama.'

'Are they full of hate or without hate?' 'Full of hate, Reverend Gotama.'

'Are they full of ill-will or without ill-will?' 'Full of ill-will, Reverend Gotama.'

'Are they impure or pure?' 'Impure, Reverend Gotama.'

'Are they disciplined or undisciplined?' 'Undisciplined, Reverend Gotama.'

---

3. Pali for "Aryan" (*arya* means "noble" in Sanskrit), an ethnic self-designation by the Vedic Hindus. The Buddha reinterpreted it to mean a spiritual nobility acquired through the practice of the Buddhist path.

33. 'So, Vasettha, the Brahmins learned in the Three Vedas are encumbered with wives and wealth, and Brahma is unencumbered. Is there any communion, anything in common between these encumbered Brahmins and the unencumbered Brahma?' 'No, Reverend Gotama.'

34. 'That is right, Vasettha. That these encumbered Brahmins, learned in the Three Vedas, should after death, at the breaking-up of the body, be united with the unencumbered Brahma—that is just not possible.

35. 'Likewise, do these Brahmins learned in the Three Vedas and full of hate . . . , full of ill-will . . . , impure . . . , undisciplined, have any communion, anything in common with the disciplined Brahma?' 'No, Reverend Gotama.'

36. 'That is right, Vasettha. That these undisciplined Brahmins should after death be united with Brahma is just not possible. But these Brahmins learned in the Three Vedas, having sat down on the bank, sink down despairingly, thinking maybe to find a dry way across. Therefore their threefold knowledge is called the threefold desert, the threefold wilderness, the threefold destruction.'

37. At these words Vasettha said: 'Reverend Gotama, I have heard them say: "The ascetic Gotama knows the way to union with Brahma."'

'What do you think, Vasettha? Suppose there were a man here born and brought up in Manasakata, and somebody who had come from Manasakata and had missed the road should ask him the way. Would that man, born and bred in Manasakata, be in a state of confusion or perplexity?' 'No, Reverend Gotama. And why not? Because such a man would know all the paths.'

38. 'Vasettha, it might be said that such a man on being asked the way might be confused or perplexed—but the Tathagata,[4] on being asked about the Brahma world and the way to get there, would certainly not be confused or perplexed. For, Vasettha, I know Brahma and the world of Brahma, and the way to the world of Brahma, and the path of practice whereby the world of Brahma may be gained.'

39. At this Vasettha said: 'Reverend Gotama, I have heard them say: "The ascetic Gotama teaches the way to union with Brahma." It would be good if the Reverend Gotama were to teach us the way to union with Brahma, may the Reverend Gotama help the people of Brahma!'

'Then, Vasettha, listen, pay proper attention, and I will tell you.' 'Very good, Reverend Sir', said Vasettha. The Lord said:

40. 'Vasettha, a Tathagata arises in the world, an Arahant, fully-enlightened Buddha, endowed with wisdom and conduct, Well-Farer, Knower of the worlds, incomparable Trainer of men to be tamed, Teacher of gods and humans, enlightened and blessed. He, having realised it by his own superknowledge, proclaims this world with its devas, maras[5] and Brahmas, its princes and people. He preaches the Dhamma[6] which is lovely in its beginning, lovely in its middle, lovely in its ending, in the spirit and in the letter, and displays the fully-perfected and purified holy life.

41. 'This Dhamma is heard by a householder or a householder's son, or one reborn in some family or other. Having heard this Dhamma, he gains faith

---

4. A title of a buddha; it is the one most often used by the historical Buddha to refer to himself.
5. Personifications of evil and temptation. "Devas":
gods; inhabitants of the heavenly realms (literally, "shining ones").
6. Pali for *dharma*.

in the Tathagata. Having gained this faith, he reflects: "The household life is close and dusty, the homeless life is free as air. It is not easy, living the household life, to live the fully-perfected holy life, purified and polished like a conch-shell. Suppose I were to shave off my hair and beard, don yellow robes and go forth from the household life into homelessness!" And after some time, he abandons his property, small or great, leaves his circle of relatives, small or great, shaves off his hair and beard, dons yellow robes and goes forth into the homeless life.

42. 'And having gone forth, he dwells restrained by the restraint of the rules, persisting in right behaviour, seeing danger in the slightest faults, observing the commitments he has taken on regarding body, deed and word, devoted to the skilled and purified life, perfected in morality, with the sense-doors guarded, skilled in mindful awareness and content.

43. 'And how, Vasettha, is a monk perfected in morality? Abandoning the taking of life, he dwells refraining from taking life, without stick or sword, scrupulous, compassionate, trembling for the welfare of all living beings. Thus he is accomplished in morality. Abandoning the taking of what is not given, he dwells refraining from taking what is not given, living purely, accepting what is given, awaiting what is given, without stealing. Abandoning unchastity, he lives far from it, aloof from the village-practice of sex.

44. 'Abandoning false speech, he dwells refraining from false speech, a truth-speaker, one to be relied on, trustworthy, dependable, not a deceiver of the world. Abandoning malicious speech, he does not repeat there what he has heard here to the detriment of these, or repeat here what he has heard there to the detriment of those. Thus he is a reconciler of those at variance and an encourager of those at one, rejoicing in peace, loving it, delighting in it, one who speaks up for peace. Abandoning harsh speech, he refrains from it. He speaks whatever is blameless, pleasing to the ear, agreeable, reaching the heart, urbane, pleasing and attractive to the multitude. Abandoning idle chatter, he speaks at the right time, what is correct and to the point, of Dhamma and discipline. He is a speaker whose words are to be treasured, seasonable, reasoned, well-defined and connected with the goal.

45. 'He is a refrainer from damaging seeds and crops. He eats once a day and not at night, refraining from eating at improper times. He avoids watching dancing, singing, music and shows. He abstains from using garlands, perfumes, cosmetics, ornaments and adornments. He avoids using high or wide beds. He avoids accepting gold and silver. He avoids accepting raw grain or raw flesh, he does not accept women and young girls, male or female slaves, sheep and goats, cocks and pigs, elephants, cattle, horses and mares, fields and plots; he refrains from running errands, from buying and selling, from cheating with false weights and measures, from bribery and corruption, deception and insincerity, from wounding, killing, imprisoning, highway robbery, and taking food by force.

46. 'Whereas some ascetics and Brahmins, feeding on the food of the faithful, are addicted to the destruction of such seeds as are propagated from roots, from stems, from joints, from cuttings, from seeds, he refrains from such destruction.

47. 'Whereas some ascetics and Brahmins, feeding on the food of the faithful, remain addicted to the enjoyment of stored-up goods such as food, drink, clothing, carriages, beds, perfumes, meat, he refrains from such enjoyment.

48. 'Whereas some ascetics and Brahmins . . . remain addicted to attending such shows as dancing, singing, music, displays, recitations, hand-music, cymbals and drums, fairy-shows, acrobatic and conjuring tricks, combats of elephants, buffaloes, bulls, goats, rams, cocks and quail, fighting with staves, boxing, wrestling, sham-fights, parades, manoeuvres and military reviews, he refrains from attending such displays.

49. 'Whereas some ascetics and Brahmins remain addicted to such games and idle pursuits as eight- or ten-row chess, "chess in the air", hopscotch, spillikins, dicing, hitting sticks, "hand-pictures", ball-games, blowing through toy pipes, playing with toy ploughs, turning somersaults, playing with toy windmills, measures, carriages, and bows, guessing letters, guessing thoughts, mimicking deformities, he refrains from such idle pursuits.

50. 'Whereas some ascetics and Brahmins remain addicted to high and wide beds and long chairs, couches adorned with animal figures, fleecy or variegated coverlets, coverlets with hair on both sides or one side, silk coverlets, embroidered with gems or without, elephant-, horse- or chariot-rugs, choice spreads of antelope-hide, couches with awnings, or with red cushions at both ends, he refrains from such high and wide beds.

51. 'Whereas some ascetics and Brahmins remain addicted to such forms of self-adornment and embellishment as rubbing the body with perfumes, massaging, bathing in scented water, shampooing, using mirrors, ointments, garlands, scents, unguents, cosmetics, bracelets, headbands, fancy sticks, bottles, swords, sunshades, decorated sandals, turbans, gems, yak-tail fans, long-fringed white robes, he refrains from such self-adornment.

52. 'Whereas some ascetics and Brahmins remain addicted to such unedifying conversation as about kings, robbers, ministers, armies, dangers, wars, food, drink, clothes, beds, garlands, perfumes, relatives, carriages, villages, towns and cities, countries, women, heroes, street- and well-gossip, talk of the departed, desultory chat, speculations about land and sea, talk about being and non-being, he refrains from such conversation.

53. 'Whereas some ascetics and Brahmins remain addicted to disputation such as: "You don't understand this doctrine and discipline—I do!" "How could *you* understand this doctrine and discipline?" "Your way is all wrong—mine is right!" "I am consistent—you aren't!" "You said last what you should have said first, and you said first what you should have said last!" "What you took so long to think up has been refuted!" "Your argument has been overthrown, you're defeated!" "Go on, save your doctrine—get out of that if you can!" he refrains from such disputation.

54. 'Whereas some ascetics and Brahmins remain addicted to such things as running errands and messages, such as for kings, ministers, nobles, Brahmins, householders and young men who say: "Go here—go there! Take this there—bring that from there!" he refrains from such errand-running.

55. 'Whereas some ascetics and Brahmins remain addicted to deception, patter, hinting, belittling, and are always on the make for further gains, he refrains from such deception.

56. 'Whereas some ascetics and Brahmins, feeding on the food of the faithful, make their living by such base arts, such wrong means of livelihood as palmistry, divining by signs, portents, dreams, body-marks, mouse-gnawings, fire-oblations, oblations from a ladle, of husks, rice-powder, rice-grains, ghee or oil, from the mouth or of blood, reading the finger-tips, house- and garden-lore,

skill in charms, ghost-lore, earth-house lore, snake-lore, poison-lore, rat-lore, bird-lore, crow-lore, foretelling a person's life-span, charms against arrows, knowledge of animals' cries, he refrains from such base arts and wrong means of livelihood.

57. 'Whereas some ascetics and Brahmins make their living by such base arts as judging the marks of gems, sticks, clothes, swords, spears, arrows, weapons, women, men, boys, girls, male and female slaves, elephants, horses, buffaloes, bulls, cows, goats, rams, cocks, quail, iguanas, bamboo-rats, tortoises, deer, he refrains from such base arts.

58. 'Whereas some ascetics and Brahmins make their living by such base arts as predicting: "The chiefs will march out—the chiefs will march back", "Our chiefs will advance and the other chiefs will retreat", "Our chiefs will win and the other chiefs will lose", "The other chiefs will win and ours will lose", "Thus there will be victory for one side and defeat for the other", he refrains from such base arts.

59. 'Whereas some ascetics and Brahmins make their living by such base arts as predicting an eclipse of the moon, the sun, a star; that the sun and moon will go on their proper course—will go astray; that a star will go on its proper course—will go astray; that there will be a shower of meteors, a blaze in the sky, an earthquake, thunder; a rising, setting, darkening, brightening of the moon, the sun, the stars; and "such will be the outcome of these things", he refrains from such base arts and wrong means of livelihood.

60. 'Whereas some ascetics and Brahmins make their living by such base arts as predicting good or bad rainfall; a good or bad harvest; security, danger; disease, health; or accounting, computing, calculating, poetic composition, philosophising, he refrains from such base arts and wrong means of livelihood.

61. 'Whereas some ascetics and Brahmins make their living by such base arts as arranging the giving and taking in marriage, engagements and divorces; [declaring the time for] saving and spending, bringing good or bad luck, procuring abortions, using spells to bind the tongue, binding the jaw, making the hands jerk, causing deafness, getting answers with a mirror, a girl-medium, a deva; worshipping the sun or Great Brahma, breathing fire, invoking the goddess of luck, he refrains from such base arts and wrong means of livelihood.

62. 'Whereas some ascetics and Brahmins, feeding on the food of the faithful, make their living by such base arts, such wrong means of livelihood as appeasing the devas and redeeming vows to them, making earth-house spells, causing virility or impotence, preparing and consecrating building-sites, giving ritual rinsings and bathings, making sacrifices, giving emetics, purges, expectorants and phlegmagogues,[7] giving ear-, eye-, nose-medicine, ointments and counter-ointments, eye-surgery, surgery, pediatry, using balms to counter the side-effects of previous remedies, he refrains from such base arts and wrong means of livelihood. A monk refrains from such base arts and wrong means of livelihood. Thus he is perfected in morality.

63. 'And then, Vasettha, that monk who is perfected in morality sees no danger from any side owing to his being restrained by morality. Just as a duly-anointed Khattiya[8] king, having conquered his enemies, by that very

---

7. A medicine for expelling phlegm.
8. Pali for *kshatriya*, the second of the four castes of ancient India (to which the Buddha belonged), sometimes called the warrior caste.

fact sees no danger from any side, so the monk, on account of his morality, sees no danger anywhere. He experiences in himself the blameless bliss that comes from maintaining this Ariyan morality. In this way, Vasettha, he is perfected in morality.

64. 'And how, Vasettha, is he a guardian of the sense-doors? Here a monk, on seeing a visible object with the eye, does not grasp at its major signs or secondary characteristics. Because greed and sorrow, evil unskilled states, would overwhelm him if he dwelt leaving this eye-faculty unguarded, so he practises guarding it, he protects the eye-faculty, develops restraint of the eye-faculty. On hearing a sound with the ear, . . . on smelling an odour with the nose, . . . on tasting a flavour with the tongue, . . . on feeling an object with the body, . . . on thinking a thought with the mind, he does not grasp at its major signs or secondary characteristics, . . . he develops restraint of the mind-faculty. He experiences within himself the blameless bliss that comes from maintaining this Ariyan guarding of the faculties. In this way, Vasettha, a monk is a guardian of the sense-doors.

65. 'And how, Vasettha, is a monk accomplished in mindfulness and clear awareness? Here a monk acts with clear awareness in going forth and back, in looking ahead or behind him, in bending and stretching, in wearing his outer and inner robe and carrying his bowl, in eating, drinking, chewing and swallowing, in evacuating and urinating, in walking, standing, sitting, lying down, in waking, in speaking and in keeping silent he acts with clear awareness. In this way, a monk is accomplished in mindfulness and clear awareness.

66. 'And how is a monk contented? Here, a monk is satisfied with a robe to protect his body, with alms to satisfy his stomach, and having accepted sufficient, he goes on his way. Just as a bird with wings flies hither and thither, burdened by nothing but its wings, so he is satisfied . . . In this way, Vasettha, a monk is contented.

67. 'Then he, equipped with this Ariyan morality, with this Ariyan restraint of the senses, with this Ariyan contentment, finds a solitary lodging, at the root of a forest tree, in a mountain cave or gorge, a charnel-ground, a jungle-thicket, or in the open air on a heap of straw. Then, having eaten after his return from the alms-round, he sits down cross-legged, holding his body erect, and concentrates on keeping mindfulness established before him.

68. 'Abandoning worldly desires, he dwells with a mind freed from worldly desires, and his mind is purified of them. Abandoning ill-will and hatred . . . and by compassionate love for the welfare of all living beings, his mind is purified of ill-will and hatred. Abandoning sloth-and-torpor, . . . perceiving light, mindful and clearly aware, his mind is purified of sloth-and-torpor. Abandoning worry-and-flurry . . . and with an inwardly calmed mind his heart is purified of worry-and-flurry. Abandoning doubt, he dwells with doubt left behind, without uncertainty as to what things are wholesome, his mind is purified of doubt.

69. 'Just as a man who had taken a loan to develop his business, and whose business had prospered, might pay off his old debts, and with what was left over could support a wife, might think: "Before this I developed my business by borrowing, but now it has prospered . . .", and he would rejoice and be glad about that.

70. 'Just as a man who was ill, suffering, terribly sick, with no appetite and weak in body, might after a time recover, and regain his appetite and bodily

strength, and he might think: "Before this I was ill . . .", and he would rejoice and be glad about that.

71. 'Just as a man might be bound in prison, and after a time he might be freed from his bonds without any loss, with no deduction from his possessions. He might think: "Before this I was in prison . . .", and he would rejoice and be glad about that.

72. 'Just as a man might be a slave, not his own master, dependent on another, unable to go where he liked, and after some time he might be freed from slavery, able to go where he liked, might think: "Before this I was a slave . . ." And he would rejoice and be glad about that.

73. 'Just as a man, laden with goods and wealth, might go on a long journey through the desert where food was scarce and danger abounded, and after a time he would get through the desert and arrive safe and sound at the edge of a village, might think: "Before this I was in danger, now I am safe at the edge of a village", and he would rejoice and be glad about that.

74. 'As long, Vasettha, as a monk does not perceive the disappearance of the five hindrances in himself, he feels as if in debt, in sickness, in bonds, in slavery, on a desert journey. But when he perceives the disappearance of the five hindrances in himself, it is as if he were freed from debt, from sickness, from bonds, from slavery, from the perils of the desert.

75. 'And when he knows that these five hindrances have left him, gladness arises in him, from gladness comes delight, from the delight in his mind his body is tranquillised, with a tranquil body he feels joy, and with joy his mind is concentrated. Being thus detached from sense-desires, detached from unwholesome states, he enters and remains in the first jhana,[9] which is with thinking and pondering, born of detachment, filled with delight and joy. And with this delight and joy born of detachment, he so suffuses, drenches, fills and irradiates his body that there is no spot in his entire body that is untouched by this delight and joy born of detachment.

76. 'Then, with his heart filled with loving-kindness, he dwells suffusing one quarter, the second, the third, the fourth. Thus he dwells suffusing the whole world, upwards, downwards, across, everywhere, always with a heart filled with loving-kindness, abundant, unbounded, without hate or ill-will.

77. 'Just as if a mighty trumpeter were with little difficulty to make a proclamation to the four quarters, so by this meditation, Vasettha, by this liberation of the heart through loving-kindness he leaves nothing untouched, nothing unaffected in the sensuous sphere. This, Vasettha, is the way to union with Brahma.

78. 'Then with his heart filled with compassion, . . . with sympathetic joy, with equanimity he dwells suffusing one quarter, the second, the third, the fourth. Thus he dwells suffusing the whole world, upwards, downwards, across, everywhere, always with a heart filled with equanimity, abundant, unbounded, without hate or ill-will.

79. 'Just as if a mighty trumpeter were with little difficulty to make a proclamation to the four quarters, so by this meditation, Vasettha, by this liberation of the heart through compassion, . . . through sympathetic joy, . . . through equanimity, he leaves nothing untouched, nothing unaffected in the sensuous sphere. This, Vasettha, is the way to union with Brahma.

---

9. Pali for *dhyana*, state of deep concentration attained through meditation.

80. 'What do you think, Vasettha? Is a monk dwelling thus encumbered with wives and wealth or unencumbered?' 'Unencumbered, Reverend Gotama. He is without hate . . . , without ill-will . . . , pure and disciplined, Reverend Gotama.'

81. 'Then, Vasettha, the monk is unencumbered, and Brahma is unencumbered. Has that unencumbered monk anything in common with the unencumbered Brahma?' 'Yes indeed, Reverend Gotama.'

'That is right, Vasettha. Then that an unencumbered monk, after death, at the breaking-up of the body, should attain to union with the unencumbered Brahma—that is possible. Likewise a monk without hate . . . , without ill-will . . . , pure . . . , disciplined . . . Then that a disciplined monk, after death, at the breaking-up of the body, should attain to union with Brahma—that is possible.'

82. At this the young Brahmins Vasettha and Bharadvaja said to the Lord: 'Excellent, Reverend Gotama, excellent! It is as if someone were to set up what had been knocked down, or to point out the way to one who had got lost, or to bring an oil-lamp into a dark place, so that those with eyes could see what was there. Just so the Reverend Gotama has expounded the Dhamma in various ways.'

'We take refuge in the Reverend Gotama, in the Dhamma, and in the Sangha. May the Reverend Gotama accept us as lay-followers having taken refuge from this day forth as long as life shall last!'

THE BENEFITS OF MINDFULNESS

THE ESTABLISHMENT OF MINDFULNESS
(The Satipatthana Sutta)

It is sometimes said that meditation is to Buddhism what prayer is in Christianity. If this statement means that Buddhists meditate as often as Christians pray, or even that Buddhists are supposed to meditate as often as Christians pray, then it is false. In fact, prayer is also an important element of Buddhist practice, and most Buddhists over the course of Asian history have not meditated. But what is true is that meditation is regarded as the form of practice par excellence in Buddhism and is the preferred practice of the religious virtuoso, whether monastic or lay. There are detailed instructions on the practice of meditation in all the Buddhist traditions of Asia. One of the most famous, especially for the Pali tradition of Sri Lanka and Southeast Asia, appears here.

One of the first questions to be considered, however, is what is meant by "meditation." The Sanskrit term that the word typically translates, *bhavana*, literally means "causing to be" or "cultivation," and encompasses far more than what is meant by "meditation" in the West. The myriad types of meditation are sometimes classified under two broad headings, based on the practice's goal: concentration and insight.

Concentration involves developing the ability to focus the mind on a single object for an extended period of time, without distraction. In the Pali tradition, forty objects of concentration are enumerated. The development of concentration, in and of itself, does not necessarily entail the development of wisdom, nor does it result in liberation from rebirth. Instead, attaining a particular level of concentration in one's lifetime as a human will lead to rebirth as a god in one of the heavens. The minds of gods are more powerful than those of humans, and it is said that developing a mind with the powers of concentration of a god in this lifetime will enable one to be reborn as a god with such powers in the next lifetime. Thus, in the previous selection, the Buddha recommended the development of concentration on four objects—loving-kindness, compassion, sympathetic joy, and equanimity—in order to be reborn in the heaven of Brahma.

The other major category of meditation seeks insight as its goal—insight into the nature of the person, the nature of the world, the nature of reality. Whereas the development of concentration involves stabilizing the mind by placing it on the chosen object and holding it there, often with particular effort, insight meditation is typically more discursive, marked by controlled reflection and analysis. The most famous form of such meditation is the search for a permanent and autonomous self among the physical and mental elements that constitute the person, a search that is supposed to fail.

Just as "meditation" fails to convey the full meaning of the original Buddhist term, so also the key English term in the text presented here falls short. The Pali word *sati* (*smriti* in Sanskrit) most often means "memory," but it also has connotations of "awareness" and "attention." The Victorian scholar Thomas W. Rhys Davids translated it "mindfulness," which since has become the standard English rendering. In the context of meditation practice, mindfulness is that factor which keeps the mind on its chosen object. A famous dictum is "Tie the wild elephant of the mind to the post of the object with the rope of mindfulness." Mindfulness is therefore generally associated with the development of concentration.

However, it is also central to a technique in which concentration and insight are developed together, as set forth in the *Satipatthana Sutta*, or *Discourse on the Establishment of Mindfulness*. One of the most widely commented-upon texts in the Pali canon, it continues to hold a central place in the modern *vipassana*, or "insight meditation," movement; although the Buddha's instructions are offered to bhikkhus, or monks, since the twentieth century they have been adopted by the laity, especially in Southeast Asia (see Mahasi Sayadaw's "Practical Vipassana Exercises," p. 761).

The Buddha sets forth what he calls the *ekayana magga*, translated here as "direct path"; other possible renderings are "the only path" and "the one way." Four objects of mindfulness are prescribed. The first is the mindfulness of the body. The second is the mindfulness of feelings—physical and mental experiences of pleasure, pain, and neutrality. The third is the mindfulness of the mind, or the observation of the mind when influenced by different positive and negative emotions. The fourth is the mindfulness of dharmas, which involves the contemplation of several key categories, including the five aggregates (the constituents of mind and body) and the four truths.

The first of the four, the mindfulness of the body, involves fourteen exercises, beginning with the mindfulness of the inhalation and exhalation of the breath. Next is mindfulness of the four physical postures of walking, standing, sitting, and lying down, which is then extended to a full awareness of all activities. Thus, mindfulness is meant to accompany all activities in the course of the day, and is not restricted to formal sessions of seated meditation. The mindfulness of the various components of the body—a rather unsavory list that includes fingernails, bile, spittle, and urine—is followed by the mindfulness of the body as composed of the four elements: earth (the solid), water (the liquid), fire (the warm), and air (the empty). These exercises end with what are known as the "charnel ground contemplations": mindfulness of the body in nine successive stages of decomposition.

The practice of the mindfulness of the body is intended to result in the understanding that the body is a collection of impure elements that arise and cease in rapid succession, utterly lacking any kind of permanent self. That is, the body and indeed all conditioned things are marked by three qualities: impermanence, suffering, and no self. Understanding of this fact leads to nirvana.

The second of the four kinds of mindfulness, the mindfulness of feeling, observes the various feelings of pleasure, pain, and neutrality that occur in the mind and body, noting when and where they arise and when and where they vanish. The third of the four gives similar attention to the various types of mental states and emotions that occur, such as lust, hate, delusion, and distraction.

The fourth and final kind of mindfulness takes dharmas as its object. Here the term *dharma* (*dhamma* in Pali) means "phenomena," or the constituents of the world. In the translation below, it is rendered as "mind-objects." This section takes up some of the standard lists of Buddhist philosophy: the five hindrances, the five aggregates, the six bases, the seven enlightenment factors, and the four truths. In each case, the meditator recognizes each for what it is: its presence, its absence, how it arises, how it disappears. In the case of virtuous states such as the seven enlightenment factors, the meditator comes to understand how to cultivate them and then how to sustain them.

At the end of the text, the Buddha makes a powerful claim for the efficacy of the practice, which he calls "the direct path for the purification of beings"—a path that leads to nirvana in as little as seven days.

PRONOUNCING GLOSSARY

bhikkhu: *bik-ku*

Kammasadhamma: *kam-mah-sad-dam-ma*

Nibbana: *nib-bah-na*

Satipatthana Sutta: *sa-ti-pat-tah-na soot-ta*

Thus have I heard. On one occasion the Blessed One was living in the Kuru country at a town of the Kurus named Kammasadhamma. There he addressed the bhikkhus[1] thus: "Bhikkhus."–"Venerable sir," they replied. The Blessed One said this:

"Bhikkhus, this is the direct path for the purification of beings, for the surmounting of sorrow and lamentation, for the disappearance of pain and grief, for the attainment of the true way, for the realisation of Nibbana[2]—namely, the four foundations of mindfulness.

"What are the four? Here, bhikkhus, a bhikkhu abides contemplating the body as a body, ardent, fully aware, and mindful, having put away covetousness and grief for the world. He abides contemplating feelings as feelings, ardent, fully aware, and mindful, having put away covetousness and grief for the world. He abides contemplating mind as mind, ardent, fully aware, and mindful, having put away covetousness and grief for the world. He abides contemplating mind-objects as mind-objects, ardent, fully aware, and mindful, having put away covetousness and grief for the world.

"And how, bhikkhus, does a bhikkhu abide contemplating the body as a body? Here a bhikkhu, gone to the forest or to the root of a tree or to an empty

---

TRANSLATED FROM the Pali by Bhikku Ñāṇamoli; translation edited and revised by Bhikkhu Bodhi.

1. Pali for *bhikshus*, monks. 2. Pali for *nirvana*.

hut, sits down; having folded his legs crosswise, set his body erect, and mind-fulness in front of him, ever mindful he breathes in, mindful he breathes out. Breathing in long, he understands: 'I breathe in long'; or breathing out long, he understands: 'I breathe out long.' Breathing in short, he under-stands: 'I breathe in short'; or breathing out short, he understands: 'I breathe out short.' He trains thus: 'I shall breathe in experiencing the whole body [of breath]'; he trains thus: 'I shall breathe out experiencing the whole body [of breath].' He trains thus: 'I shall breathe in tranquillizing the bodily formation'; he trains thus: 'I shall breathe out tranquillizing the bodily for-mation.' Just as a skilled turner or his apprentice, when making a long turn,[3] understands: 'I make a long turn'; or, when making a short turn, understands: 'I make a short turn'; so too, breathing in long, a bhikkhu understands: 'I breathe in long' . . . he trains thus: 'I shall breathe out tranquillizing the bodily formation.'

"In this way he abides contemplating the body as a body internally, or he abides contemplating the body as a body externally, or he abides con-templating the body as a body both internally and externally. Or else he abides contemplating in the body its arising factors, or he abides contem-plating in the body its vanishing factors, or he abides contemplating in the body both its arising and vanishing factors. Or else mindfulness that 'there is a body' is simply established in him to the extent necessary for bare knowledge and mindfulness. And he abides independent, not cling-ing to anything in the world. That is how a bhikkhu abides contemplating the body as a body.

"Again, bhikkhus, when walking, a bhikkhu understands: 'I am walking'; when standing, he understands: 'I am standing'; when sitting, he understands: 'I am sitting'; when lying down, he understands: 'I am lying down'; or he understands accordingly however his body is disposed.

"In this way he abides contemplating the body as a body internally, exter-nally, and both internally and externally . . . And he abides independent, not clinging to anything in the world. That too is how a bhikkhu abides contem-plating the body as a body.

"Again, bhikkhus, a bhikkhu is one who acts in full awareness when going forward and returning; who acts in full awareness when looking ahead and looking away; who acts in full awareness when flexing and extending his limbs; who acts in full awareness when wearing his robes and carrying his outer robe and bowl; who acts in full awareness when eating, drinking, con-suming food, and tasting; who acts in full awareness when defecating and urinating; who acts in full awareness when walking, standing, sitting, falling asleep, waking up, talking, and keeping silent.

"In this way he abides contemplating the body as a body internally, exter-nally, and both internally and externally . . . And he abides independent, not clinging to anything in the world. That too is how a bhikkhu abides contemplating the body as a body.

"Again, bhikkhus, a bhikkhu reviews this same body up from the soles of the feet and down from the top of the hair, bounded by skin, as full of many kinds of impurity thus: 'In this body there are head-hairs, body-hairs, nails, teeth, skin, flesh, sinews, bones, bone-marrow, kidneys, heart, liver, dia-

---

3. That is, of a lathe.

phragm, spleen, lungs, large intestines, small intestines, contents of the stomach, feces, bile, phlegm, pus, blood, sweat, fat, tears, grease, spittle, snot, oil of the joints, and urine.' Just as though there were a bag with an opening at both ends full of many sorts of grain, such as hill rice, red rice, beans, peas, millet, and white rice, and a man with good eyes were to open it and review it thus: 'This is hill rice, this is red rice, these are beans, these are peas, this is millet, this is white rice'; so too, a bhikkhu reviews this same body . . . as full of many kinds of impurity thus: 'In this body there are head-hairs . . . and urine.'

"In this way he abides contemplating the body as a body internally, externally, and both internally and externally . . . And he abides independent, not clinging to anything in the world. That too is how a bhikkhu abides contemplating the body as a body.

"Again, bhikkhus, a bhikkhu reviews this same body, however it is placed, however disposed, as consisting of elements thus: 'In this body there are the earth element, the water element, the fire element, and the air element.' Just as though a skilled butcher or his apprentice had killed a cow and was seated at the crossroads with it cut up into pieces; so too, a bhikkhu reviews this same body . . . as consisting of elements thus: 'In this body there are the earth element, the water element, the fire element, and the air element.'

"In this way he abides contemplating the body as a body internally, externally, and both internally and externally . . . And he abides independent, not clinging to anything in the world. That too is how a bhikkhu abides contemplating the body as a body.

"Again, bhikkhus, as though he were to see a corpse thrown aside in a charnel ground, one, two, or three days dead, bloated, livid, and oozing matter, a bhikkhu compares this same body with it thus: 'This body too is of the same nature, it will be like that, it is not exempt from that fate.'

"In this way he abides contemplating the body as a body internally, externally, and both internally and externally . . . And he abides independent, not clinging to anything in the world. That too is how a bhikkhu abides contemplating the body as a body.

"Again, as though he were to see a corpse thrown aside in a charnel ground, being devoured by crows, hawks, vultures, dogs, jackals, or various kinds of worms, a bhikkhu compares this same body with it thus: 'This body too is of the same nature, it will be like that, it is not exempt from that fate.'

". . . That too is how a bhikkhu abides contemplating the body as a body.

"Again, as though he were to see a corpse thrown aside in a charnel ground, a skeleton with flesh and blood, held together with sinews . . . a fleshless skeleton smeared with blood, held together with sinews . . . a skeleton without flesh and blood, held together with sinews . . . disconnected bones scattered in all directions—here a hand-bone, there a foot-bone, here a shin-bone, there a thigh-bone, here a hip-bone, there a back-bone, here a rib-bone, there a breast-bone, here an arm-bone, there a shoulder-bone, here a neck-bone, there a jaw-bone, here a tooth, there the skull—a bhikkhu compares this same body with it thus: 'This body too is of the same nature, it will be like that, it is not exempt from that fate.'

". . . That too is how a bhikkhu abides contemplating the body as a body.

"Again, as though he were to see a corpse thrown aside in a charnel ground, bones bleached white, the colour of shells . . . bones heaped up, more than a year old . . . bones rotted and crumbled to dust, a bhikkhu compares this same body with it thus: 'This body too is of the same nature, it will be like that, it is not exempt from that fate.'

"In this way he abides contemplating the body as a body internally, or he abides contemplating the body as a body externally, or he abides contemplating the body as a body both internally and externally. Or else he abides contemplating in the body its arising factors, or he abides contemplating in the body its vanishing factors, or he abides contemplating in the body both its arising and vanishing factors. Or else mindfulness that 'there is a body' is simply established in him to the extent necessary for bare knowledge and mindfulness. And he abides independent, not clinging to anything in the world. That too is how a bhikkhu abides contemplating the body as a body.

"And how, bhikkhus, does a bhikkhu abide contemplating feelings as feelings? Here, when feeling a pleasant feeling, a bhikkhu understands: 'I feel a pleasant feeling'; when feeling a painful feeling, he understands: 'I feel a painful feeling'; when feeling a neither-painful-nor-pleasant feeling, he understands: 'I feel a neither-painful-nor-pleasant feeling.' When feeling a worldly pleasant feeling, he understands: 'I feel a worldly pleasant feeling'; when feeling an unworldly pleasant feeling, he understands: 'I feel an unworldly pleasant feeling'; when feeling a worldly painful feeling, he understands: 'I feel a worldly painful feeling'; when feeling an unworldly painful feeling, he understands: 'I feel an unworldly painful feeling'; when feeling a worldly neither-painful-nor-pleasant feeling, he understands: 'I feel a worldly neither-painful-nor-pleasant feeling'; when feeling an unworldly neither-painful-nor-pleasant feeling, he understands: 'I feel an unworldly neither-painful-nor-pleasant feeling.'

"In this way he abides contemplating feelings as feelings internally, or he abides contemplating feelings as feelings externally, or he abides contemplating feelings as feelings both internally and externally. Or else he abides contemplating in feelings their arising factors, or he abides contemplating in feelings their vanishing factors, or he abides contemplating in feelings both their arising and vanishing factors. Or else mindfulness that 'there is feeling' is simply established in him to the extent necessary for bare knowledge and mindfulness. And he abides independent, not clinging to anything in the world. That is how a bhikkhu abides contemplating feelings as feelings.

"And how, bhikkhus, does a bhikkhu abide contemplating mind as mind? Here a bhikkhu understands mind affected by lust as mind affected by lust, and mind unaffected by lust as mind unaffected by lust. He understands mind affected by hate as mind affected by hate, and mind unaffected by hate as mind unaffected by hate. He understands mind affected by delusion as mind affected by delusion, and mind unaffected by delusion as mind unaffected by delusion. He understands contracted mind as contracted mind, and distracted mind as distracted mind. He understands exalted mind as exalted mind, and unexalted mind as unexalted mind. He understands surpassed mind as surpassed mind, and unsurpassed mind as unsurpassed mind. He understands concentrated mind as concentrated mind, and unconcentrated mind as unconcentrated mind. He understands liberated mind as liberated mind, and unliberated mind as unliberated mind.

"In this way he abides contemplating mind as mind internally, or he abides contemplating mind as mind externally, or he abides contemplating mind as mind both internally and externally. Or else he abides contemplating in mind its arising factors, or he abides contemplating in mind its vanishing factors, or he abides contemplating in mind both its arising and vanishing factors. Or else mindfulness that 'there is mind' is simply established in him to the extent necessary for bare knowledge and mindfulness. And he abides independent, not clinging to anything in the world. That is how a bhikkhu abides contemplating mind as mind.

"And how, bhikkhus, does a bhikkhu abide contemplating mind-objects as mind-objects? Here a bhikkhu abides contemplating mind-objects as mind-objects in terms of the five hindrances. And how does a bhikkhu abide contemplating mind-objects as mind-objects in terms of the five hindrances? Here, there being sensual desire in him, a bhikkhu understands: 'There is sensual desire in me'; or there being no sensual desire in him, he understands: 'There is no sensual desire in me'; and he also understands how there comes to be the arising of unarisen sensual desire, and how there comes to be the abandoning of arisen sensual desire, and how there comes to be the future non-arising of abandoned sensual desire.'

"There being ill will in him . . . There being sloth and torpor in him . . . There being restlessness and remorse in him . . . There being doubt in him, a bhikkhu understands: 'There is doubt in me'; or there being no doubt in him, he understands: 'There is no doubt in me'; and he understands how there comes to be the arising of unarisen doubt, and how there comes to be the abandoning of arisen doubt, and how there comes to be the future non-arising of abandoned doubt.

"In this way he abides contemplating mind-objects as mind-objects internally, or he abides contemplating mind-objects as mind-objects externally, or he abides contemplating mind-objects as mind-objects both internally and externally. Or else he abides contemplating in mind-objects their arising factors, or he abides contemplating in mind-objects their vanishing factors, or he abides contemplating in mind-objects both their arising and vanishing factors. Or else mindfulness that 'there are mind-objects' is simply established in him to the extent necessary for bare knowledge and mindfulness. And he abides independent, not clinging to anything in the world. That is how a bhikkhu abides contemplating mind-objects as mind-objects in terms of the five hindrances.

"Again, bhikkhus, a bhikkhu abides contemplating mind-objects as mind-objects in terms of the five aggregates affected by clinging. And how does a bhikkhu abide contemplating mind-objects as mind-objects in terms of the five aggregates affected by clinging? Here a bhikkhu understands: 'Such is material form, such its origin, such its disappearance; such is feeling, such its origin, such its disappearance; such is perception, such its origin, such its disappearance; such are the formations, such their origin, such their disappearance; such is consciousness, such its origin, such its disappearance.'

"In this way he abides contemplating mind-objects as mind-objects internally, externally, and both internally and externally . . . And he abides independent, not clinging to anything in the world. That is how a bhikkhu abides contemplating mind-objects as mind-objects in terms of the five aggregates affected by clinging.

"Again, bhikkhus, a bhikkhu abides contemplating mind-objects as mind-objects in terms of the six internal and external bases. And how does a bhikkhu abide contemplating mind-objects as mind-objects in terms of the six internal and external bases? Here a bhikkhu understands the eye, he understands forms, and he understands the fetter that arises dependent on both; and he also understands how there comes to be the arising of the unarisen fetter, and how there comes to be the abandoning of the arisen fetter, and how there comes to be the future non-arising of the abandoned fetter.

"He understands the ear, he understands sounds . . . He understands the nose, he understands odours . . . He understands the tongue, he understands flavours . . . He understands the body, he understands tangibles . . . He understands the mind, he understands mind-objects, and he understands the fetter that arises dependent on both; and he also understands how there comes to be the arising of the unarisen fetter, and how there comes to be the abandoning of the arisen fetter, and how there comes to be the future non-arising of the abandoned fetter.

"In this way he abides contemplating mind-objects as mind-objects internally, externally, and both internally and externally . . . And he abides independent, not clinging to anything in the world. That is how a bhikkhu abides contemplating mind-objects as mind-objects in terms of the six internal and external bases.

"Again, bhikkhus, a bhikkhu abides contemplating mind-objects as mind-objects in terms of the seven enlightenment factors. And how does a bhikkhu abide contemplating mind-objects as mind-objects in terms of the seven enlightenment factors? Here, there being the mindfulness enlightenment factor in him, a bhikkhu understands: 'There is the mindfulness enlightenment factor in me'; or there being no mindfulness enlightenment factor in him, he understands: 'There is no mindfulness enlightenment factor in me'; and he also understands how there comes to be the arising of the unarisen mindfulness enlightenment factor, and how the arisen mindfulness enlightenment factor comes to fulfilment by development.

"There being the investigation-of-states enlightenment factor in him . . . There being the energy enlightenment factor in him . . . There being the rapture enlightenment factor in him . . . There being the tranquillity enlightenment factor in him . . . There being the concentration enlightenment factor in him . . . There being the equanimity enlightenment factor in him, a bhikkhu understands: 'There is the equanimity enlightenment factor in me'; or there being no equanimity enlightenment factor in him, he understands: 'There is no equanimity enlightenment factor in me'; and he also understands how there comes to be the arising of the unarisen equanimity enlightenment factor, and how the arisen equanimity enlightenment factor comes to fulfilment by development.

"In this way he abides contemplating mind-objects as mind-objects internally, externally, and both internally and externally . . . And he abides independent, not clinging to anything in the world. That is how a bhikkhu abides contemplating mind-objects as mind-objects in terms of the seven enlightenment factors.

"Again, bhikkhus, a bhikkhu abides contemplating mind-objects as mind-objects in terms of the Four Noble Truths. And how does a bhikkhu abide contemplating mind-objects as mind-objects in terms of the Four Noble Truths? Here a bhikkhu understands as it actually is: 'This is suffering'; he understands as it actually is: 'This is the origin of suffering'; he understands as it actually is: 'This is the cessation of suffering'; he understands as it actually is: 'This is the way leading to the cessation of suffering.'

"In this way he abides contemplating mind-objects as mind-objects internally, or he abides contemplating mind-objects as mind-objects externally, or he abides contemplating mind-objects as mind-objects both internally and externally. Or else he abides contemplating in mind-objects their arising factors, or he abides contemplating in mind-objects their vanishing factors, or he abides contemplating in mind-objects both their arising and vanishing factors. Or else mindfulness that 'there are mind-objects' is simply established in him to the extent necessary for bare knowledge and mindfulness. And he abides independent, not clinging to anything in the world. That is how a bhikkhu abides contemplating mind-objects as mind-objects in terms of the Four Noble Truths.

"Bhikkhus, if anyone should develop these four foundations of mindfulness in such a way for seven years, one of two fruits could be expected for him: either final knowledge here and now, or if there is a trace of clinging left, non-return.

"Let alone seven years, bhikkhus. If anyone should develop these four foundations of mindfulness in such a way for six years . . . for five years . . . for four years . . . for three years . . . for two years . . . for one year, one of two fruits could be expected for him: either final knowledge here and now, or if there is a trace of clinging left, non-return.

"Let alone one year, bhikkhus. If anyone should develop these four foundations of mindfulness in such a way for seven months . . . for six months . . . for five months . . . for four months . . . for three months . . . for two months . . . for one month . . . for half a month, one of two fruits could be expected for him: either final knowledge here and now, or if there is a trace of clinging left, non-return.

"Let alone half a month, bhikkhus. If anyone should develop these four foundations of mindfulness in such a way for seven days, one of two fruits could be expected for him: either final knowledge here and now, or if there is a trace of clinging left, non-return.

"So it was with reference to this that it was said: 'Bhikkhus, this is the direct path for the purification of beings, for the surmounting of sorrow and lamentation, for the disappearance of pain and grief, for the attainment of the true way, for the realisation of Nibbana—namely, the four foundations of mindfulness.'"

That is what the Blessed One said. The bhikkhus were satisfied and delighted in the Blessed One's words.

EARLY APHORISMS

VERSES OF THE DHARMA
(*The Dhammapada*)

The Buddha wrote nothing; for the first four centuries of the tradition, his teachings were preserved orally. According to tradition, they were first written down in Sri Lanka, during the reign of a king who ruled from 29 to 17 B.C.E. But that version did not survive. The texts of the Pali canon as we have them today were edited in the fifth century C.E. by the monk Buddhaghosa (see the *Path of Purification*, p. 249), also in Sri Lanka. Faced with a gap of some eight centuries between author and text, scholars have limited resources available to determine what is "early" in the Pali canon. One approach is linguistic, as certain features, especially of poetry, seem to preserve archaic forms. Another is textual; when verses appear in a variety of different texts, scholars speculate that those verses may derive from a shared early source. A third approach is semantic; passages that remain cryptic, for which generations of commentators offer particularly forced and unconvincing readings, are sometimes regarded as ancient.

On the basis of these criteria, the *Dhammapada*, or *Verses of the Dharma*—among the most popular texts in the Pali canon—contains a number of early verses. It is composed of 423 aphorisms in verse form, said to have been spoken by the Buddha himself, which are arranged in twenty-six sections ("chapters"). In addition to the Pali version, there are similar but hardly identical collections in other Indic languages, including Sanskrit and Gandhari, suggesting the possible existence of an earlier corpus from which these works all borrowed. Of the 423 verses in the Pali version, more than half also appear elsewhere in the canon; chapter 11, verse 154, is renowned as the first words of the Buddha after he achieved enlightenment and thus occurs in later biographies (see *Account of the Beginning*, p. 131). Some verses appear in non-Buddhist works, such as the Hindu epic the *Mahabharata*; indeed, they lend themselves to a range of uses, since they are largely concerned with ethics and in most cases are not particularly "Buddhist" in meaning. Another sign of their broad applicability in different contexts is that the same verse sometimes occurs in different chapters in the various recensions. Whatever the textual issues that surround the *Dhammapada*, it is one of the most beloved of Buddhist texts, memorized by many. One of its most famous verses is chapter 14, verse 183, which can be simply translated as follows:

> To avoid all evil.
> To do good.
> To purify the mind.
> This is the teaching of the Buddhas.

The *Dhammapada* is found in the *Khuddaka Nikaya*, or "Minor Collection," a section of the Pali canon that contains a number of short and popular works. Chapters 1–5 and 11 are provided here.

PRONOUNCING GLOSSARY

bhikkhu: *bik-ku*
Dhammapada: *dam-ma-pa-da*
Maghavan: *ma-ga-van*
mallika: *mal-li-kah*

Mara: *mah-ra*
samsara: *sam-sah-ra*
sankhara: *san-kah-ra*
vassiki: *vas-si-kee*

Chapter I. The Pairs

1. Preceded by perception are mental states,
    For them is perception supreme,
    From perception have they sprung.
    If, with perception polluted, one speaks or acts,
    Thence suffering follows
    As a wheel the draught ox's foot.

2. Preceded by perception are mental states,
    For them is perception supreme.
    From perception have they sprung.
    If, with tranquil perception, one speaks or acts,
    Thence ease follows
    As a shadow that never departs.

3. "He reviled me! He struck me!
    He defeated me! He robbed me!"
    They who gird themselves up with this,
    For them enmity is not quelled.

4. "He reviled me! He struck me!
    He defeated me! He robbed me!"
    They who do not gird themselves up with this,
    For them is enmity quelled.

5. Not by enmity are enmities quelled,
    Whatever the occasion here.
    By the absence of enmity are they quelled.
    This is an ancient truth.

6. Others do not realize
    "We here are struggling."
    Those who realize this—for them
    Are quarrels therefore quelled.

7. Whoever dwells seeing the pleasurable, in senses unrestrained,
    Immoderate in food, indolent, inferior of enterprise,
    Over him, indeed, Mara[1] prevails,
    Like the wind over a weak tree.

8. Whoever dwells seeing the nonpleasurable, in senses well-restrained,
    And moderate in food, faithful, resolute in enterprise,
    Over him, indeed, Mara prevails not,
    Like the wind over a rocky crag.

9. One not free of defilements,
    Who will don a yellow robe,[2]

TRANSLATED FROM the Pali by John Ross Carter and Mahinda Palihawadana. All bracketed additions are the translators'.

1. The Buddhist deity of death and desire who attacked the Buddha under the Bodhi tree and who seeks to impede those on the path to enlightenment.

2. Thereby becoming a monk.

That one, devoid of control and truth,
Is not worthy of a yellow robe.

10. But one who, well placed in virtues,
Would be with defilements ejected,
Endowed with control and truth,
That one is worthy of a yellow robe.

11. Those who consider the nonessential as the essential,
And see the essential as the nonessential,
They do not attain the essential,
Being in the pastures of improper intentions.

12. Having known the essential as the essential,
And the superficial as the superficial,
They attain the essential
Who are in the pastures of proper intentions.

13. As rain penetrates
The poorly thatched dwelling,
So passion penetrates
The untended mind.

14. As rain does not penetrate
The well-thatched dwelling,
So passion does not penetrate
The well-tended mind.

15. Here he grieves; having passed away, he grieves;
In both places the wrongdoer grieves.
He grieves; he is afflicted,
Having seen the stain of his own action.

16. Here he rejoices; having passed away he rejoices.
In both places he who has done wholesome deeds rejoices.
He rejoices; he is delighted,
Having seen the purity of his own action.

17. Here he is tormented; having passed away he is tormented.
In both places, the wrongdoer is tormented.
He is tormented, thinking, "I have done wrong."
Gone to a state of woe, he is tormented all the more.

18. Here he rejoices; having passed away he rejoices.
In both places he who has done wholesome deeds rejoices.
He rejoices, thinking, "I have done wholesome deeds."
Gone to a state of weal, he rejoices all the more.

19. If one, though reciting much of texts,
Is not a doer thereof, a heedless man;
He, like a cowherd counting others' cows,
Is not a partaker in the religious quest.

20. If one, though reciting little of texts,
     Lives a life in accord with dhamma,[3]
     Having discarded passion, ill will, and unawareness,
     Knowing full well, the mind well freed,
     He, not grasping here, neither hereafter,
     Is a partaker of the religious quest.

Chapter II. Awareness

21. The path to the Deathless is awareness;
     Unawareness, the path of death.
     They who are aware do not die;
     They who are unaware are as dead.

22. Having known this distinctly,
     Those who are wise in awareness,
     Rejoice in awareness,
     Delighted in the pasture of the noble ones.

23. Those meditators, persevering,
     Forever firm of enterprise,
     Those steadfast ones touch Nibbana,[4]
     Incomparable release from bonds.

24. By standing alert, by awareness,
     By restraint and control too,
     The intelligent one could make an island
     That a flood does not overwhelm.

25. Fame increases for the one who stands alert,
     Mindful, and of pure deeds;
     Who with due consideration acts, restrained,
     Who lives dhamma, being aware.

26. People deficient in wisdom, childish ones,
     Engage in unawareness.
     But the wise one guards awareness
     Like the greatest treasure.

27. Engage not in unawareness,
     Nor in intimacy with sensual delight.
     Meditating, the one who is aware
     Attains extensive ease.

28. When the wise one by awareness expels unawareness,
     Having ascended the palace of wisdom,
     He, free from sorrow, steadfast,
     The sorrowing folk observes, the childish,
     As one standing on a mountain
     [Observes] those standing on the ground below.

3. Pali for *dharma*.   4. Pali for *nirvana*.

29. Among those unaware, the one aware,
    Among the sleepers, the wide-awake,
    The one with great wisdom moves on,
    As a racehorse who leaves behind a nag.

30. By awareness, Maghavan[5]
    To supremacy among the gods arose.
    Awareness they praise;
    Always censured is unawareness.

31. The bhikkhu[6] who delights in awareness,
    Who sees in unawareness the fearful,
    Goes, burning, like a fire,
    The fetter subtle and gross.

32. The bhikkhu who delights in awareness,
    Who sees in unawareness the fearful—
    He is not liable to suffer fall;
    In Nibbana's presence is such a one.

Chapter III. The Mind

33. The quivering, wavering mind,
    Hard to guard, hard to check,
    The sagacious one makes straight,
    Like a fletcher, an arrow shaft.

34. Like a water creature
    Plucked from its watery home and thrown on land,
    This mind flaps;
    [Fit] to discard [is] Mara's sway.

35. Commendable is the taming
    Of mind, which is hard to hold down,
    Nimble, alighting wherever it wants.
    Mind subdued brings ease.

36. The sagacious one may tend the mind,
    Hard to be seen, extremely subtle,
    Alighting wherever it wants.
    The tended mind brings ease.

37. They who will restrain the mind,
    Far-ranging, roaming alone,
    Incorporeal, lying ahiding—
    They are released from Mara's bonds.

38. For one of unsteady mind,
    Who knows not dhamma true,
    Whose serenity is adrifting,
    Wisdom becomes not full.

5. An epithet of Indra, the king of the gods in
heaven on the summit of Sumeru, the mountain
at the center of the universe.
6. Pali for *bhikshu*, a monk.

39. No fear is there for the wide-awake
    Who has mind undamped
    And thought unsmitten—
    The wholesome and the detrimental left behind.

40. Knowing this body as a pot of clay,
    Securing this mind as a citadel,
    One may fight Mara with wisdom's weapon,
    Guard what has been gained—and be unattached.

41. Soon indeed
    This body on the earth will lie,
    Pitched aside, without consciousness,
    Like a useless chip of wood.

42. What a foe may do to a foe,
    Or a hater to a hater—
    Far worse than that
    The mind ill held may do to him.

43. Not mother, father, nor even other kinsmen,
    May do that [good to him—]
    Far better than that
    The mind well held may do to him.

Chapter IV. Flowers

44. Who shall conquer this earth and the realm of Yama,[7]
    This [human realm] together with [the realm of] gods?
    Who shall pluck a well-taught dhamma word
    Like an expert, a flower?

45. A learner shall conquer this earth and the realm of Yama,
    This [human realm] together with [the realm of] gods.
    A learner shall pluck a well-taught dhamma word
    Like an expert, a flower.

46. Knowing this body to be like foam,
    Awakening to its mirage nature,
    Cutting out Mara's flowers, one may go
    Beyond the sight of the King of Death.

47. Death takes away
    The man with attached mind,
    Plucking only flowers,
    Like a great flood, a sleeping village.

48. The End-Maker overpowers
    The man with attached mind,
    Insatiate in sensual pleasures,
    Plucking only flowers.

7. Death.

49. Even as a bee, having taken up nectar
    From a flower, flies away,
    Not harming its color and fragrance,
    So may a sage wander through a village.

50. Let one regard
    Neither the discrepancies of others,
    Nor what is done or left undone by others,
    But only the things one has done oneself or left undone.

51. Just as a brilliant flower,
    Full of color, [but] scentless,
    So is a well-spoken word fruitless
    For one who does not do it.

52. Just as a brilliant flower,
    Full of color and fragrance,
    So is a well-spoken word fruitful
    For one who does it.

53. Just as many garland strands
    One could make from a mass of flowers,
    So, much that is wholesome ought to be done
    By a mortal born [into this world].

54. No flower's fragrance moves against the wind
    Neither sandalwood, *tagara*, nor *mallika*,[8]
    But the fragrance of the good ones moves against the wind;
    All directions a good person pervades.

55. Among these kinds of perfume,
    Such as sandalwood, *tagara*,
    Also waterlily and *vassiki*,[9]
    The fragrance of virtue is incomparable.

56. Slight is this fragrance—
    The *tagara* and sandalwood—
    But the fragrance of one who is virtuous
    Wafts among the gods, supreme.

57. Mara does not find the path
    Of those who have virtue abounding,
    Who are living with awareness,
    Liberated through realization.

58. Just as in a heap of rubbish
    Cast away on a roadside,
    A lotus there could bloom,
    Of sweet fragrance, pleasing the mind,

8. Two fragrant plants.   9. A kind of jasmine.

59. So amid the wretched, blinded ordinary folk,
    Among them who have turned to rubbish,
    The disciple of the Fully Awakened One
    Shines surpassingly with wisdom.

Chapter V. The Childish

60. Long is the night for one awake,
    Long is a league to one exhausted,
    Long is *samsara* to the childish ones
    Who know not dhamma true.

61. If while moving [through life], one were not to meet
    Someone better or like unto oneself,
    Then one should move firmly by oneself;
    There is no companionship in the childish.

62. A childish person becomes anxious,
    Thinking, "Sons are mine! Wealth is mine!"
    Not even a self is there [to call] one's own.
    Whence sons? Whence wealth?

63. A childish one who knows his childishness
    Is, for that reason, even like a wise person.
    But a childish one who thinks himself wise
    Is truly called a childish one.

64. Even though, throughout his life,
    A childish one attends on a wise person,
    He does not perceive dhamma,
    As a ladle, the flavor of the dish.

65. Even though, for a brief moment,
    An intelligent one attends on a wise person,
    He quickly perceives dhamma,
    As the tongue, the flavor of the dish.

66. Childish ones, of little intelligence,
    Go about with a self that is truly an enemy;
    Performing the deed that is bad,
    Which is of bitter fruit.

67. That deed done is not good,
    Having done which, one regrets;
    The consequence of which one receives,
    Crying with tear-stained face.

68. But that deed done is good,
    Having done which, one does not regret;
    The consequence of which one receives,
    With pleasure and with joy.

69. The childish one thinks it is like honey
    While the bad [he has done] is not yet matured.
    But when the bad is matured,
    Then the childish one comes by suffering.

70. Month by month a childish one
    Might eat food with a *kusa*[1] grass blade.
    He is not worth a sixteenth part
    Of those who have understood dhamma.

71. For a bad act done does not coagulate
    Like freshly extracted milk.
    Burning, it follows the childish one,
    Like fire concealed in ashes.

72. Only for his detriment
    Does knowledge arise for the childish one.
    It ruins his good fortune,
    Causing his [very] head to fall.

73. He would desire unreal glory
    And preeminence among bhikkhus,
    Authority, too, concerning dwellings,
    And offerings in other families.

74. "Let both householders and those who have gone forth
    Think that it is my work alone;
    In whatever is to be done or not done,
    Let them be dependent on me alone!"
    Such is the thought of the childish one;
    Desire and pride increase.

75. The means of acquisition is one,
    And another the way leading to Nibbana.
    Having recognized this as so,
    Let a bhikkhu who is a disciple of the Buddha
    Not delight in [receiving] esteem;
    Let him cherish disengagement.

Chapter XI. Old Age

146. Oh, what laughter and why joy,
    When constantly aflame?
    In darkness enveloped,
    You do not seek the lamp.

147. Oh, see this beautified image;
    A mass of sores erected.
    Full of illness, highly fancied,
    Permanence it has not—or constancy.

1. A kind of grass with a narrow blade.

148. Quite wasted away is this form,
A nest for disease, perishable.
This putrid accumulation breaks up.
For life has its end in death.

149. Like these gourds
Discarded in autumn,
Are gray-hued bones.
Having seen them, what delight?

150. Of bones the city is made,
Plastered with flesh and blood,
Where decay and death are deposited,
And pride and ingratitude.

151. Even well-decked royal chariots wear away;
And the body too falls into decay.
But the dhamma of the good ones goes not to decay,
For the good speak [of it] with the good.

152. This unlearned person
Grows up like an ox.
His bulk increases,
His wisdom increases not.

153. I ran through *samsara*, with its many births,
Searching for, but not finding, the house-builder.
Misery is birth again and again.

154. House-builder, you are seen!
The house you shall not build again!
Broken are your rafters, all,
Your roof beam destroyed.
Freedom from the *sankharas*[2] has the mind attained.
To the end of cravings has it come.

155. Not having lived the higher life,
Nor having acquired wealth in youth,
They wither away like old herons
In a lake without fish.

156. Not having lived the higher life,
Nor having acquired wealth in youth,
Like [arrows] discharged from a bow they lie
Brooding over the things of yore.

2. Pali for *samskaras*, conditioned things, which are marked by impermanence, suffering, and no self.

THE BEGINNINGS OF BUDDHIST PHILOSOPHY

THE CHAPTER ON THE GOAL
(*The Atthakavagga*)

Scholars of religion are interested in origins, seeking evidence of how things began, before institutions and their often self-serving histories were created. Since the nineteenth century, scholars of Buddhism have sought to describe what has been termed "original Buddhism" or "primitive Buddhism"—that is, the Buddhism of the Buddha. As has already been noted, this is a difficult task, for a number of historical and linguistic reasons.

The Pali canon contains a work called the *Sutta Nipatta* or *Section of Discourses*, a collection of 1,149 verses (with some prose). One of its chapters, the "Atthakavagga" or "Chapter on the Goal" (presented in its entirety here), is believed by a number of scholars to contain some of the oldest extant Buddhist verse, which perhaps goes back to the time of the Buddha himself. Indeed, it has been suggested that some of the more "radical" statements regarding the rejection of all views derive from an ascetic group at the time of the Buddha that came to be incorporated into the monastic community. Evidence for the text's antiquity, in addition to various linguistic and metrical clues, includes its mention by name in three other canonical texts, as well as the existence of an early commentary on it.

But many questions remain about the chapter and its meaning, questions that add to its fascination. One basic question has to do with its title, which in the Pali tradition means "The Octet," reflecting its structure: the first four of the sixteen poems that constitute the work have eight verses. But the rendering into Chinese treats the first part of the title as *artha*, meaning "goal" or "aim," a reading followed by our translator. The work is largely free of the technical terminology and lists familiar to the tradition, suggesting to some that it predates them. The sage (*muni*) and the "true brahmin" are extolled more often than is the monk (*bhikkhu*).

The primary theme of the sections of the work (which may have been composed in different periods) is non-attachment—specifically, non-attachment to sensual pleasure, to views and beliefs generally, and to belief in the self. In the ninth poem, for example, the Buddha explains to Magandiya why he rejected his daughter when she was offered to him in marriage. Here, the misogyny of the text is quite consistent with the later tradition. However, scholars have paid most attention to the rejection of views, with some seeing an anticipation of the philosophical position of Nagarjuna (see the *Madhyamakakarika*, p. 366). The dangers of attachment to philosophical views and their disputation are indeed stated in stark terms at several points in the text, and commentators both ancient and modern have struggled with how to harmonize such statements with the importance of "right view," one of the constituents of the eightfold path. The commentary to the text, attributed to the Buddha's wisest disciple, Shariputra, seeks to resolve these apparent paradoxes.

PRONOUNCING GLOSSARY

Atthakavagga: *at-ta-ka-vag-ga*

brahmana: *brah-ma-na*

Magandiya: *mah-gan-di-ya*

Mara: *mah-ra*

Pasura: *pa-su-ra*

Sariputta: *sah-ri-put-ta*

shramana: *shra-ma-na*

Tissa Metteyya: *ti-sa may-tay-ya*

1. On Desire

If someone pursues the object of his desires and succeeds, that mortal being will truly rejoice, having found what he was seeking.

But, if that same person that was so desirous of this object when excited by desire should lose the object he seeks, he will be as if wounded by his own arrow.

A person who avoids desires, like someone stepping to the side to avoid a viper, he, ever mindful, will overcome this clinging to the world.

A person craving for land, property, gold, cattle, slaves and servants, wives and family, and all other objects of desire

will be overcome by his own weaknesses, crushed by his anguish; therefore, suffering will follow him, like water rushing into a broken ship.

Therefore, let him remain always mindful, avoiding desires. Having abandoned them he will cross the flood waters, like someone reaching the other shore after bailing out the water from his ship.

2. Eight Stanzas on the Cave

Stuck to his cave, he hides every which way, this human being sinking into darkness; for someone like this is far from detached solitude, for desire in this world is not easily abandoned.

Those imprisoned by desire, bound by the sweet tastes of existence, are not easily released, for no one but themselves could release them; they have their sight on the past and the future, on the object of their present desires, longing for the object of his desires here or beyond.

Greedy, clinging, confused, and miserly in all that they desire, they are bogged down in an uneven path; dragged into misery, they cry out, wondering, "What will become of us when we have left this life?"

A human being should therefore train here and now so that anything that he knows in this world to be uneven or crooked will not be a cause for uneven and crooked conduct; for life is short, as the resolute sages have declared.

I see living things in this world quivering, overcome by their thirst for existence. These abject humans cry out from within the jaws of death, unable to go beyond this thirst for coming to be this and stopping to be that.

Look at how they quiver like fish in a drying riverbed, obsessed with the thought of "mine, mine." Once you have seen this state of things, you should seek to act free of this "mine," no longer clinging to this coming to be this or that.

He should restrain and tame this wanting to be one thing or the other, free of self-seeking greed, having understood fully the nature of contact, he will do nothing that he should have to hide. This resolute sage will not cling to anything seen or heard.

Having understood thoroughly concept and perception, he should cross the torrent; the sage does not cling to possessions and possessing; having pulled out the barb, he lives undistracted, he does not yearn for anything in this life, or in any life to come.

TRANSLATED FROM the Pali by Luis O. Gómez.

3. Eight Stanzas on the Impure

Some speak with a tainted and clouded mind, others speak with a mind packed with truths. The sage, however, does not join in where these arguments arise, therefore the sage is nowhere hard or stubborn.

For, someone led by desire and firmly set in his preferences—one who labors seeking gain and success—how could he ever escape his own views and beliefs? Because, he can only speak of what he knows.

Those skilled in the teaching declare that someone who only speaks of himself, proclaiming to others his own moral conduct and vows, even when he is not asked about this, is not a person who follows a noble practice.

But, those skilled in the teaching declare, the calm mendicant who is at peace within himself will not go about talking up his good moral habits, saying, "I am like this" or like that; he is one following a practice that makes him noble, he who is not puffed up with conceit about anything in the world.

The one who dreams up and constructs truth and principle, preferring a truth not truly limpid, keeping an attentive eye on what he sees as self-interest, such a one leans on an unstable sense of peace.

For, it is not easy to overcome this setting root in views and beliefs—one should discern the grasping and holding that is in all things; therefore a person set in his deeply rooted ways will drop one truth only to take up another one.

For the one who is truly pure does not dream up views and beliefs about becoming or ceasing to be anywhere in the world; he is pure because he has abandoned deceit and conceit. Where would he go, he who does not seek a place to moor in?

For, one who seeks a place to moor in, joins in disputes; the one who seeks no such place, with whom and how would he enter into an argument? For he neither takes up nor rejects anything; he has cleansed himself even here in this life from opinions and beliefs.

4. Eight Stanzas on the Pure

Some rely on this conviction: "I now see the pure, supreme state of health. A person who has perceived this state gains complete purity. Having deeply understood this, knowing that this is the ultimate truth, one is an observer of the pure."

But, if a person can become pure by mere views and beliefs, and if one could leave suffering behind by mere knowledge, then, while still seeking to acquire something or other, one can be made pure by something outside oneself. For, if someone speaks this way, he merely speaks of views and beliefs.

The true brahmin does not proclaim that purity is possible by something other than himself, whether it is in something seen or heard, by moral habits and vows, or by something imagined or conceived. He does not cling to good or evil; having left behind all possessiveness, he is not here engaged in constructing more of it.

They let go of this only to take up that, obediently following their excitement, they do not cross the swampland; they grasp at something, then let it go, like a monkey who lets go a branch only to hold on to the next.

A person taking up his own vows goes up and down, still trapped in concept and imagination. But understanding this, a person who discerns deeply does not go up and down, having approached his practice with full knowledge.

He gives up all things and ideas, be it those that are seen, or heard, or those that are thought or felt. He who sees things in this way, who behaves openly, what would he use to conceive notions about this world?

They fashion no preconceptions, they have no preferences, they never declare: "This is the highest purity." They have undone the ropes that were tied with the knots of grasping, they form no longing for anything in the world.

He is a true brahmin who has crossed beyond all limitations; he possesses nothing, having once known and seen the nature of grasping and holding. He feels no excitement in passion, nor does he delight in dispassion. For him nothing more remains for him to grasp and hold.

5. *Eight Stanzas on the Ultimate*

The person who settles into views, thinking "this is supreme," when he conceives something as "better" than anything else in the world, he will call everything else "inferior." Therefore he has not gone beyond allegations and disputes.

When he sees in himself something praiseworthy, or something of value in what he has seen, or heard, or in moral habit or vows, or in what he thinks or feels, he clings to this and only this, and considers everything else as worthless.

Those who truly know also call "bondage" that which, when one relies on it, leads to thinking that everything else is inferior. Therefore, the mendicant should not lean on things seen or heard, thought or imagined, or on moral habit and vows.

Let him not fashion any views or beliefs about the world, by following his knowledge, his moral habits, or his vows. Let him not conform to thoughts of being equal; let him not think of "inferior" or "superior."

Having given up gain and achievement, grasping no more, he does not lean even on knowledge; he does not take sides among those holding divergent views, and he does not rely even on any view or belief.

The person who does not aim at either one of these two extremes—becoming this or that, here or beyond—that person does not set roots anywhere, discerning what is grasping and holding in any and all things.

About what he has seen, heard, thought, or felt, he does not fashion even the most infinitesimal concept. This brahmin who does not hold on to any views or beliefs, how could anyone understand what distinguishes him in this world?

They fashion no preconceptions, they establish no preferences, they form no belief even about what is true. The true brahmin will not be led by moral habits or vows. Having crossed over to the other shore, only being the way he is, he does not rely on beliefs about anything.

6. *On Aging*

Short indeed is this life of ours! We die before we reach a hundred, and even those who can live more than this will also die of old age.

They grieve over what they have considered "mine," for nothing can be held on to constantly. Understanding that separation is inevitable, give up the household life.

With death will fade away whatever this human person has regarded with the thought of "this is mine." The wise person who has seen this is not one obsessed with himself, who would be inclined to imagine anything as "mine."

As a person awakening from sleep no longer sees those he had met in his dreams, in the same way, once dead and departed, one will not see everything that is dear to us.

These very people we now see and hear, whose names we here call upon, from them only the names will remain for us to pronounce once they have died.

Those greedily longing for that which they regard as "mine" will not leave behind grief, lamentation, and envy. This is why sages abandon all grasping at possession and depart on the wandering life, they who know where the true resting place lies.

The mendicant who, living in a secluded dwelling, enjoys a well-collected mind, for him, they say, the highest point in life is reached when he no longer displays himself in his own dwelling.

The sage does not lean on anything anywhere, he does not imagine anything as dear nor does he imagine anything as hateful; neither regret nor envy adhere to him, as water does not stick to a leaf.

As a water bead does not cling to a lotus leaf or rainwater to a lotus blossom, the sage does not hold on to whatever he sees or hears, or to things thought or felt.

For, the truly cleansed does not hold thoughts about things seen or heard, thought or felt. He does not seek purity from anything outside himself, for he is neither excited by passion nor made indifferent by dispassion.

7. *Dialogue with Tissa Metteyya*

Tissa Metteyya asked,

"Tell me, respected teacher, which impediments are faced by one attached to sexual desire. Upon receiving your teachings, we will train ourselves in the life of seclusion."

The Blessed One replied,

"Metteyya, a person attached to sexual desire will only neglect the teaching, and will follow the wrong path, and in him will be absent the noble conduct.

"Someone who used to wander alone and now surrenders to sexual pleasure, he becomes like a carriage swerving off the road; the world regards him as lost, one more among common people.

"The honor and reputation he enjoyed in the past will be squandered away. Having understood this, you should train so that you may abandon sexual contact and desire.

"Overcome by the fantasy of his desires, he broods like a miserable wretch, hearing the scornful words of others. Someone like this lives troubled and confused.

"Then he readies his weapons, piqued by the censure of others; because he still has an intense longing, he sinks into mendacity.

"Regarded as wise when he followed a life of seclusion, once he engages in sexual contact he is despised as a fool.

"Once he has understood the risks and troubles found in this desire, the sage should consistently engage in the life of the lonely wanderer; he will not engage in sexual contact.

"He should train in a life of seclusion, the highest state of noble ones. But he will not because of this think himself better than anyone, even if he is already close to the cool and calm state.

"The wandering sage, in every way free, indifferent to desires, the one who has crossed the flood—he is envied by those who are tied down in desires."

8. *Discourse with Pasura*

Some say, "Purity is this and only this, and in the teachings of others you will find no purity." Whichever teaching they hold to, they regard as the best, so that each separately holds a different truth.

These glib debaters descend on the assembly hall and engage in arguments, taking each other as an adversary and a fool; because they still depend on something other than themselves, they bandy words about, hoping to win praise, calling themselves the experts.

In the midst of these assemblies, such a person engages in disputation, longing for praise and fearing defeat. In defeat he becomes downcast. He seeks flaws in others, and quivers in rage when criticized by others.

When those judging the question say his argument is faulty, refuted, he laments, he grieves, feeling his arguments are worthless, wailing, "They have defeated me!"

Such are the disputes we find among wandering mendicants, causing them now elation, now dejection. Understanding this, avoid arguments. For they have no other purpose than to gain praise.

On the one hand, he who is praised right there in the midst of the assembly for presenting a successful argument will feel elated and thrilled, for he has achieved the goal he so much desired.

But elation itself proves his downfall, for he talks on, with pride and arrogance. Understanding this, do not engage in disputes, for the true experts do not call this purity.

Like a brave champion fighter, goaded by his kingly lord, these shramanas[1] rush on, roaring, looking for a rival. But, you, true hero, go to where you will find one who has nothing to provoke a fight.

Those who argue over their chosen views maintain that this or that alone is the truth. If you engage them in conversation, you may tell them: "There is no opponent here to do battle with you."

From those who walk on, leaving all this behind, who do not counter one view with another, Pasura, what do you expect to gain from them? For them there is nothing left to accept or possess.

You came to me in deep reflection, in your mind pondering different views and opinions, in such a state you cannot walk along in the company of one who is truly pure.

9. *Dialogue with Magandiya*

"No sensual desire arose in me even when I saw those maidens called Thirst, Displeasure, and Passion. How would I then wish to touch this bag full of excrement and urine, even with the tip of my foot?"

"But, if you do not want this jewel of a woman, desired by so many princes and monarchs, then what sort of views, what kind of moral conduct, vows, and lifestyle do you propose, aspiring to what kind of rebirth?"

---

1. Austere wandering monks.

The Blessed One replied,

"Magandiya, it does not occur to him to propose anything, to him who would discern that there is grasping and holding in any and all things. Looking among views and beliefs for what is free of grasping, I realized and saw that peace is within me."

Magandiya replied,

"Oh sage, you speak of freedom from grasping and holding by clearly discerning everything that is constructed by the imagination. But, as regards what you call the 'peace within me,' tell me, how do resolute sages explain the meaning of this?"

The Blessed One replied,

"Magandiya, they teach that purity is not attained by things seen or heard, or by knowledge, or moral habit and vows. Nor is it attained by not seeing, not hearing, not knowing, or the absence of moral habit and vows. Discarding all of this, not grasping and holding, relying on nothing, at peace, he would not desire to become anything."

Magandiya replied,

"But, if one says that purity is not attained by things seen or heard, or by knowledge, or moral habit and vows, and that it is also not attained by not seeing, not hearing, not knowing, or the absence of moral habit and vows—this seems to me a teaching of confusion. There are others who accept and rely on a sense of purity that they understand through their views and beliefs."

The Blessed One replied,

"Magandiya, because you put your trust in views and beliefs even as you ask this question, you sink into the confusion of all things grasped and held. This is why you are unable to see even an atom of this notion; therefore it seems confused to you.

"He who imagines himself as equal, better, or even inferior, he is the one who will be willing to enter into a dispute with you; the thought of equal or superior does not occur to one who is not shaken by any of these conditions.

"What would the true brahmin call the true, what the false, and with whom would he enter into disputes? One for whom there is neither 'the same' nor 'not the same,' against whom would he initiate an argument?

"Leaving behind life at home, wandering without a dwelling, the sage does not form bonds among village folk; separated from objects of sense desire, free of preferences, he would not engage in quarrelsome disputes with anyone.

"He who is like the noble elephant does not argue about all that he no longer grasps, what he has left behind to live the life of the wanderer in this world. Like the lotus blossom rises on its stalk above muddy waters unsoiled by soggy water, thus the sage who speaks of peace hankers after neither sensual desire nor the world, and remains unstained by the world.

"One who has attained to wisdom will not fall into pride because of his views or beliefs, or because of his ideas; for he is not shaped by these beliefs; he will not be led by past actions or acquired knowledge, he has not been led to anything where he could grow roots.

"No knots or fetters remain for the one who abstains from generating perceptions and concepts; no delusion remains for the one released by discernment. Those who hold on to conceptions and views and beliefs wander this world from one confrontation to another."

10. Before the Body Breaks Down

"Tell me, oh Gotama,[2] how it is that the one called 'completely calm' sees things, how does he behave? This I ask of the best of humans."

The Blessed One replied,

"One who before the breakdown of his body is already free from craving thirst, who does not rely on the past or the future, and does not build up a present, he holds no preferences.

"Free from anger and fear, never boastful, free from regret indeed is the sage, of wise words, placid when giving counsel.

"He holds no expectations for the future, he does not regret anything in the past; in the midst of contact with sense objects he perceives with collected discernment, and he is not led into views and beliefs.

"Withdrawn in solitude, without duplicity, free of ambitions, free of envy, modest and temperate, never contemptuous, he is not one to slander.

"He is not addicted to pleasurable tastes, not given to pride; soft-spoken but eloquent and alert; he is not credulous, nor is he indifferent.

"He does not engage in training with the hope of gain, nor is he disturbed when he gains nothing; craving thirst does not get in his way; he is not greedy for any pleasurable tastes.

"Observing with equanimity, mindful, he does not see anyone in this world as equal, superior, or inferior; he is not swollen with pride.

"One who does not seek support in anything, having known how things are does not support himself on anything; one free from the thirst that craves becoming or ceasing to become,

"This is the person I call 'completely calm.' Remaining uninterested among sense pleasures, for him no tied knots remain; he has crossed beyond all clinging.

"He has neither children, nor cattle, nor land or property; in him you will not find any accepting or rejecting.

"He gives no weight to those opinions that would find blame in him, those of common people as well as those of shramanas and brahmanas;[3] therefore, he is not perturbed in the midst of their arguments and disputes.

"He has left greed behind, he is free of envy; the sage does not speak of himself as being among the superior, or among equals or being among the inferior.

"He who has nothing of his own in the world, who does not regret the loss of anything, who does not pursue any thing or doctrine, he is said to be truly at peace."

11. Contentions and Disputes

"Whence arise contentions and disputes, grief and lamentation, together with envy, and conceit and arrogance, with grudges and slander to go with them? Please explain where they all come from."

"From holding things dear arise contentions and disputes, grief and lamentation, together with envy, and conceit and arrogance, with grudges and slander to go with them. Contentions and disputes are linked to envy; and slanderous words are born amid disputes."

---

2. That is, Gautama.

3. Brahmins, in the literal sense of "holy men."

"What is the cause of holding things dear in this world, and all the possessiveness that roams the world? And all the expectations and achievements that give humans a goal beyond, what is their cause?"

"Holding things dear in this world and all the possessiveness that roams the world are caused by wanting, so too are all the expectations and achievements that give humans a goal beyond."

"What is the cause of wanting in this world? And judgments and convictions, whence do they arise? And what of all the other conditions explained by the Shramana:[4] anger, falsehood, and bewilderment?"

"When people think 'this is pleasurable' or 'this is not pleasurable'—on the basis of this conviction arises wanting. And, when they see the arising and ceasing of body and sense objects, people in this world fashion judgments and convictions.

"And, as to anger, falsehood, and bewilderment, they too arise whenever this same twofold division exists. The bewildered should train in the path of knowledge—taught by the Shramana who understands it well."

"But what is the cause from which arise what is pleasurable and what is not pleasurable, and in the absence of what, do these two cease? And, likewise, the matter of coming to be and ceasing to be, explain to me where is its cause."

"What is pleasurable and what is not pleasurable have their origin in contact. If contact is absent, they do not arise at all. And, likewise, coming to be and ceasing to be, I declare to you, also come from this same source."

"But, what is the cause of contact in this world? And grasping and holding, from what does it arise? In the absence of what is there no more sense of 'mine'? When what ceases are contacts no longer touched?"

"Contact arises by dependence on name and form, and grasping and holding is caused by wishing. If there were no wishing, there would be no 'mine.' When body and sense objects cease, contacts are no longer touched."

"The person for whom body and sense objects would cease, what need he attain? And how will pleasure and sorrow cease? Tell me how this ceasing takes place—this we all want to know; this is my heart's desire."

"When one no longer perceives any notion or idea, and does not have a perception of the absence of notions and ideas, and yet is not without perception, nor have one's perceptions ceased, then, with this practice, body and sense objects cease for him. For, the perception of notions and ideas is the cause of mental calculation and mental dispersion."

"You have given an answer to all our questions; but we still have one more question to ask—please tell us: Is it not the case that some wise men declare this to be the highest purification of the spirit, or do they say there is still something else beyond this?"

"Indeed there are some wise men who declare that this is the highest purification of the spirit, yet others who are regarded as experts on the state without remainder say it is to pass away;

"but the sage knows that these experts 'still depend'—he knows them and understands that on which they depend. Knowing this, he has become free. He enters no arguments. The resolute sage seeks not to become this or that."

---

4. That is, the Buddha.

12. *Shorter Discourse on Taking Sides in Disputes*

"Those who call themselves experts declare as they quarrel, each one stuck in his own views and beliefs: 'Whoever knows this knows the true state of things; whoever rejects this has not reached liberation.'

"In this way they quarrel and argue, declaring: 'He is a fool, he is not an expert.' Who among them speaks the truth? For they all declare themselves experts.

"If rejecting another person's truth makes a person a fool, a nitwit, short on discernment, then all are equally foolish, and equally lacking in discernment; for all are stuck in their own views and beliefs.

"And if each one would become perfectly pure by dint of holding their own views and beliefs, thus becoming a clear-sighted, insightful expert, then no one among them would be lacking in discernment, for the opinion of each and everyone would be equally valid.

"With regards to what foolish rivals will say to each other, I do not say, 'This is the truth.' Each one has decided that his own opinion is true and therefore brands his opponent a fool."

"What some call 'true, the truth,' others call, 'vanity, a lie.' In this way they argue, confronting each other. Why is it that shramanas do not speak with one voice?"

"Indeed truth is one, and not split into two, so that a discerning person could argue about it with another discerning person. The multiple truths they praise are only each one's own; this is why shramanas do not speak with one voice."

"Why is it then that those who call themselves experts defend so many different truths? Are truths indeed so many and diverse, or is it that they each follow their own reasoning?"

"Indeed truths are not so many and diverse, other than what follows from the idea of unchanging things in the world; and, when they direct and apply their own discursive faculties to opinions and beliefs, then they speak of teachings as split into 'true or false.'

"Relying on what he has seen, or heard, on his moral habits and his vows, and on what he has felt or thought, he haughtily looks down on others; unmoving in his conviction he mocks them: 'They are fools, they are not true experts,' he will say.

"He declares himself an expert merely by branding others as 'fools.' He proclaims himself an expert, despises all others, and thus promotes himself.

"Adopting the most absurd opinions, drunk with his own pride, he thinks himself accomplished, he bestows upon himself the title 'talented,' for this is how right and correct are his views and beliefs.

"For, if another person's pronouncement declares him worthless, then with him the other is also lacking completely in discernment. But, if this same person has attained true knowledge and is resolute in his wisdom, then no one is a fool among the shramanas.

"'Those who promote any doctrine other than this one fail to reach purity, they are not liberated,' thus, everywhere the teachers of the various schools declare, for they have become intoxicated with a zeal for their own views.

"Some argue, 'Only here will you find purity,' they say there is no purity in any other teaching. In this way, everywhere the teachers of the various schools grow deep roots in these, their very own ways, obstinately defending them.

"And even if a person obstinately speaks of only his own way, why would he brand the other person here a fool? He will only bring conflict upon himself, by calling the other 'a fool, a follower of an impure teaching.'

"Unmoving in his convictions, he takes himself as the measure of everything else; for time to come he will be involved in polemics in this world. If he abandons this judging to form convictions, he will not be a person to initiate conflict in this world."

13. Longer Discourse on Taking Sides in Disputes

"Those who settle into views and beliefs, arguing 'only this is true,' will they all bring upon themselves only sneers, or will they also gain praise in the assembly?"

"Indeed all this struggle is insignificant, it is of no use in attaining peace. These two, praise and blame, I say, are the only fruits of disputes. Once having seen this, one will not engage in disputes, with one's eyes on tranquillity, that land that is free of strife.

"Whichever opinions might be held by consensus among the common folk, the person who has understood will not turn to any one among these. What would he seek, this person who seeks no more, who seeks nothing to accept in what is seen or heard?

"Those who regard moral practice as the highest practice declare that purity is attained through self-control. They take care to observe the vows they adopt: 'With these we shall train, for only here is found purity.' Dragged back into existence, they proclaim themselves experts.

"If one of them stumbles and falls from his moral rules and vows, he will tremble in anguish for the actions that he sees as his failings. He pines, yearning for his goal of purity—like the traveler when the caravan has departed and left him at home alone.

"Passing beyond all moral rules and vows, and those actions that are blameworthy as well as those that are praiseworthy, he will not seek what is thought to be purity or impurity, wandering without a stopping place, not holding on to peace.

"Some rely on extreme austerities, or on loathsome ascetic practices, or on something seen or heard, or thought or felt; they give out loud cries, wailing over purity, not free yet from the thirst of craving for one or another form of existence.

"For, as long as one holds to design and ambition one is either trapped by longing or likewise anguished by those things he constructs in his mind; but the person who in this world is free from passing away and being reborn, what would make him tremble in anguish, what would he long for?

"The very same doctrine that some call supreme, others will call inferior. Who among them then is speaking the truth? For they all proclaim 'I am the expert'."

"For they regard their own doctrine as perfect, but the teachings of others they call despicable. Quarreling in this way, they continue their contending disputes. Each one among them calls his own opinion the truth.

"If the opponent's views become contemptible simply by being despised, then would none among these teachings be superior to any other? For usually they will call the teaching of others contemptible, and will obstinately defend their own as the highest.

"They also pay homage to their own doctrines, as much as they praise their own ways. All these teachings must be true, for each and all claim purity for themselves.

"The brahmin is not one to follow others, he has discerned what is grasping and holding in any and all things. Therefore, he has gone well beyond disputes, because he does not see any other teaching that is better than this.

"Thinking, 'I know, I perceive that this is just so,' some put their trust in purity attained by views and beliefs. But even if he perceives something, of what use is this for him? They proclaim purity, still relying completely on something other than themselves.

"Even as he sees, this man will see name and form, and having seen, he will only know these two; even if he has seen much or little, the truly adept say this is indeed not the way to purity.

"For, a person who speaks for his deeply settled views is not easily led in the right direction, one who follows his preferences for the views and beliefs he fashions, will declare excellent only that upon which he leans and relies; he will claim that this is purity, that in it he has seen things as they are.

"The true brahmin does not turn to conceptions and ideations, he is not one going about seeking views and beliefs, he does not seek the support of knowledge. Knowing the beliefs generated by the consensus of common people, he observes others with an even mind as they grasp and hold.

"The sage has undone all the knots found in this world; he will not join parties engaged in disputes. Calm among those who are flustered, he observes them with an even mind, not grasping and holding what others grasp and hold.

"He has left behind whatever flows from his past actions, and he does not create them anew. He is not moved by wants, he is not one to speak for deeply seated views; firm in his wisdom, he is completely free from the ways of opinions and beliefs. He does not cling to the world, he has nothing to reproach in himself.

"He has cast aside all things, whether they are seen, heard, thought, or felt, he is a sage who has laid down the load, has undone his ties, he will not fashion further notions, does not stop anywhere and seeks nothing."

14. The Quick Way

"I ask the Great Rishi,[5] Descendant of the Sun, about solitude and the state of peace. With what manner of insight does the mendicant cool down, grasping at nothing in the world?"

The Blessed One replied,

"He should cut out the whole root of mental calculation and dispersion, the thought of 'I am.' He should train, ever mindful, to cast aside whatever form the thirst of craving may take in him.

"Whatever condition or state of being he may perceive, inwardly or outwardly, he will not use it as a point of pride—for good men do not call this the cool, calm state.

---

5. That is, the Buddha (a rishi is a holy sage or seer).

"Therefore, he should not think of anything or anyone as better, worse, or even comparable. Touched by multiple sense images, he will not dwell in them forming ideas about himself.

"The mendicant should become calm within himself, and seek peace nowhere else. For when one is inwardly placid and still, nothing is taken up, much less is anything rejected.

"As in the depths of the ocean arise no waves, but all stays still, so let it be with him—still, composed, the mendicant will not swell up with feelings of superiority with respect to anything."

"Your eyes open and clear, you have explained the truth that you have seen with your own eyes, which drives away all dread. Tell me, Venerable One, the path, the rules of restraint, and the practice of mental concentration to be practiced."

"A mendicant keeps his eyes from wandering wantonly, and his ears are deaf to village chatter. He is not greedy for new tastes in food; nor does he think of anything in the world as his own.

"When touched by sense contact, the mendicant finds nothing to regret in anything. And he will not wish for existence elsewhere, nor will he tremble when among fearful things.

"The mendicant would not store what is given to him—solid food, soft food, drink, or clothes to wear. And he will not be anxious if he does not get any of them.

"Rapt in meditation, he will not loiter, he will not be idle, he will not fret or feel regret, he will not behave heedlessly. The mendicant will dwell in a place with few noises, and there he will have his lodging and his bed.

"He should not sleep excessively. When he is awake he will ever be intently watchful. He will refrain from laughter, sloth, deception, games, sexual intercourse, and ornaments.

"He will not use the spells of the Atharva Veda,[6] nor will he foretell things using dreams or omens, or the movement of heavenly bodies in the zodiac. My follower will not spend time interpreting bird cries or curing infertility, or dispensing medicines and cures.

"The mendicant should not be perturbed by blame or become conceited with praise. He will expel possessiveness, and envy as well, together with anger and slander.

"He does not engage in buying or selling. The mendicant will find fault in no one anywhere. When he meets people in the village, he is never brash, nor does he talk to them desiring gain.

"The mendicant should not boast, nor should he speak out of self-interest, he should not teach himself impudence, and he will not speak contentious words.

"He will not be drawn to falsehood. He would not willfully do anything that is a sham or that is dishonest. He should not look down upon another, feeling proud of his livelihood, his wisdom, or his observance of moral rules or vows.

---

6. A Hindu sacred text that consists largely of spells and incantations.

"Even if he is vexed listening to the excessive talk of other wandering mendicants and ordinary people, he does not reply with harsh words; for men of calm do not retaliate.

"Understanding this teaching, the discerning mendicant should train himself, constantly mindful. When he realizes that being calm is peace, he will not be remiss in practicing the teaching of Gotama.

"For the undefeated conqueror did see this state of things, with his own eyes, not from lore handed down to him. Thus, diligently, without distraction, and with constant respect, should one apply oneself to train in the teachings of the Blessed One."

—Thus spoke the Blessed One.

15. The Violent Way

"From violence comes fear. Observe human beings in strife. I shall now tell you how I found myself disturbed by this anguish."

"I saw living beings thrashing about like fish in a drying riverbed, I saw how they assaulted each other, and I was overtaken by fear."

"Seeing how the whole world lacked safety and substance, and how it shook in every direction, I sought shelter for myself, but found no place that was not already inhabited."

"In the end, I saw only strife, nothing to give me pleasure; then, I saw in this a barb hidden, deeply lodged in the heart."

"A person pierced by this thorn will run about from one place to another; but if one were only to extract this thorn, one would no more need to run and would come to rest."

(Here one recites the rules of training:)

"Let him not be tied in the knotted ropes of the world. Penetrating in all their aspects the objects of desire, he will train in the attainment for himself of the cool and calm state."

"He should be truthful, modest and respectful, free of guile, not engaging in slander, free from anger; the sage will cross beyond greediness and the taint of possessiveness."

"This man, his thoughts focused in the cool and calm state, will not live in sleepiness, indolence, lassitude, and heedlessness, and will not rise in arrogance."

"He is not misled into falsehood, he does not generate affection for sense objects; he understands well the nature of conceit, he will live abstaining from violence."

"He will not hanker after the past, or seek things to accept in what is new; he will not grieve over what has been lost; he will not tie himself down with longing."

"Greed I call a flash flood, the agitation of desire I call an overflowing torrent. Yearning is an overflowing lake. The swamp of desires is difficult to cross."

"The sage does not stray from truth, the true brahmin stands firm, having renounced everything, he is indeed the one called 'truly calm.'"

"A master of knowledge who has thoroughly understood, he knows the true state of things and need not settle on anything; as he walks the path of right conduct he feels no envy toward anyone."

"He who crosses beyond desire and the bonds, so difficult to surmount, he neither grieves nor pines over anything, he has stopped the torrent, has broken the chains."

"What happened in the past, let it wither away; let there be nothing in the future for you, and if you cling to nothing in the present, you will live perfectly calm."

"He who nowhere thinks of something that has name or form as 'my own,' and grieves not over what no longer is, he will suffer no loss in this world."

"He for whom with respect to anything whatsoever there is no thought of 'this is mine,' nor is there the thought 'this belongs to others,' who finds nothing to call 'my own,' never grieves thinking 'this is not mine.'"

"Free of envy, craving nothing, unperturbed, the same under all circumstances. These are, to answer your question, the many blessings enjoyed by those who remain unshaken by the world.

"For the one remaining unperturbed, understanding fully, there is nothing he needs to do, abstaining from ambitious effort, everywhere he finds a safe and tranquil home.

"The sage does not speak about equals, inferiors, superiors. Perfectly calm he has left envy behind, he does not seek to acquire or reject anything."

—Thus spoke the Blessed One.

16. Dialogue with Sariputta[7]

The venerable Sariputta said,

"Before today I had never seen, nor had I ever heard of anyone like the Master, with such a soothing voice, who has come down to us from the Heaven of the Tusita deities,[8]

"so that he, possessed of clear sight, removing all darkness, he alone having reached true satisfaction, now appears before the world, with its gods.

"He, the awakened one, in this way released, not hiding anything, having arrived to guide his followers, him I now approach asking a question for the benefit of all those who are here still bound.

"A mendicant who, disgusted by the world betakes himself to an isolated place to live, the root of a tree, a charnel ground, or a cave in the mountains,

"making his bed on lowlands or highlands—in such places, which terrible dangers will he face, dangers before which the mendicant will not tremble in his silent dwelling place?

"What are the tribulations to be conquered in this world by one who has set out toward the state that is beyond dying, the mendicant who makes his home in a secluded place?

"For the resolute mendicant, what shall be his daily activities, what should be here his mode of conduct, his moral habits and vows?

"Which form of training will he, prudent, mindful, adopt single-mindedly so as to cleanse all taint from himself, as a silversmith removing dross from silver?"

7. That is, Shariputra, one of the Buddha's chief disciples.
8. The heaven in which all buddhas are reborn in their last life before appearing on earth as the next buddha.

The Blessed One replied,

"Sariputta, all that is most beneficial for one averse to the world, once he has chosen to dwell in a secluded spot, seeking to awaken, all that is beneficial according to the right doctrine and practice, this I will now explain to you as I have come to discern it:

"The resolute sage should not fear these five fears, this mindful mendicant who practices within the limits of the rule: gadflies, mosquitos, reptiles, human contact, and wild beasts.

"Nor should he fear those who hold a different doctrine, although he may have seen that they can bring many fearsome troubles. The one who seeks his own true welfare should conquer these and other fears.

"When illness afflicts him, or if he is afflicted by hunger, or in cold or heat, he will endure all of this. As many times as he is met by these conditions in his homeless state, he will redouble his energy and his courage.

"He will not steal, he will speak no falsehood, he will approach kindly both the weak and the strong. When he becomes aware of mental confusion, he will expel it, thinking, 'This is the fruit of Mara's[9] darkness.'

"He will not give in to the power of anger and arrogance; he will remain firm, having dug out the root of these attitudes. And whether he comes across something dear or, likewise, across something that repels him, he will be the master who will conquer it.

"Letting himself be guided by discernment, full of the joy of goodness, he will defeat these dangers. He should overcome the discontents of life in seclusion, and he should overcome these four common causes of complaint:

"What shall I eat? Where will I eat? How poorly did I sleep! Where shall I sleep tonight? The disciple leading the homeless life will restrain this kind of rumination, which only leads to lamentations.

"When he is given food and shelter at the appropriate time, he will know in each case the exact measure necessary to satisfy his needs. Well guarded before the stream of sense impressions, he walks well restrained through the village. He will not pronounce harsh words even when he is provoked.

"He will walk with downcast eyes and will not loiter, engaged in intent meditation, fully awake and attentive; by being engaged in even-minded observation his whole self will become well concentrated, free of pondering and scrupulous regret.

"Let him mindfully accept counsel when admonished by others, let him soften any hardness or stubbornness toward those who follow the acetic life with him. Anytime he speaks, let his words be pertinent and timely. He will not worry about teachings and instructions bandied about among people.

"But, even more, he will learn to lead away from himself the five worldly dusts, ever mindful of them: he will overcome passion for objects of sight, sound, taste, smell, and touch.

"Let him restrain this wanting directed at things and doctrines; the mendicant, mindful, with a fully liberated mind, observing and pondering what is real as time passes by, he will dispel darkness with focused attention."

—Thus spoke the Blessed One.

9. The personification of evil and temptation.

WANDER SOLITARY AS A RHINOCEROS HORN

THE RHINOCEROS HORN SUTTA
(*The Khaggavisana Sutta*)

According to traditional accounts, the early community of Buddhist monks, led by the Buddha, wandered throughout the year, without a fixed abode. However, the lay supporters of the community complained that during the rainy season (occurring in late summer in ancient India), the monks were damaging their crops. In addition, by stepping on many worms and insects as they walked from town to town, the monks were creating negative karma. The Buddha thus instituted the "rains retreat," a period in which groups of monks would remain together during the monsoon. Laypeople provided shelters for the monks. Scholars speculate that these shelters eventually evolved into monasteries, where monks could dwell throughout the year.

But a certain nostalgia for the homeless life remained, and it appears that some monks continued to live it. One of the most famous celebrations of the life of the solitary wanderer is a poem known as the "Rhinoceros Horn Sutta." It is the third sutra in the *Sutta Nipata*, the same collection of 1,149 verses that contains the *Atthakavagga* or, *The Chapter on the Goal* (p. 212). Some scholars believe that the poem originated in the early community, for whom the homeless life remained the ideal.

The title of the text derives from its refrain, "One should wander solitary as a rhinoceros horn." Some translators have found this phrase puzzling, choosing to render it more poetically as "One should wander solitary like a rhinoceros." However, the commentaries make it clear that the horn is indeed the object of the simile. Unlike the African rhinoceros, the Indian rhinoceros has only one horn, and it was perhaps unique in this regard among the animals of India. The horn of the rhinoceros was thus a symbol of that which stands alone, without companions.

The speaker of the text is unidentified, but early commentaries name him as a *pratyekabuddha* (in Pali, *pacchekabuddha*); literally, a "solitary enlightened one." This term seems to apply to a particular type of monk who preferred not to live among the community with other monks, instead practicing in solitude, often in silence. As the tradition developed, the pratyekabuddha became doctrinally defined in distinction from the *shravaka*—literally, "listener"—a disciple of the Buddha who remained in his presence. It was said that the pratyekabuddhas passed through the same stages as the other disciples of the Buddha and likewise achieved nirvana, but (according to some accounts) they did not rely on the teachings of the Buddha during their last lifetime. They were also said to gain enlightenment during times when the teachings of a buddha were not present in the world. Yet, having gained enlightenment, they did not speak of the path to others. Thus, they seem to have been renowned for their solitude even in a tradition that extolled the virtues of the solitary life.

That Buddhist monks attributed this text so early to a representative of this rather mysterious group identified with the more reclusive elements of the brotherhood suggests that even they found the solitude recommended in the text to be somewhat extreme. In the later monastic code, monks who were not affiliated with a particular monastery were regarded with suspicion.

If one accepts the traditional story of the origins of monastic life, then the "Rhinoceros Horn Sutta" may offer some insight into the practice, or at least the theory, of that early community of wandering mendicants.

PRONOUNCING GLOSSARY

Khaggavisana Sutta: *kag-ga-vi-sah-na*   Kovilara: *koh-vi-lah-ra*
  soot-ta

Laying aside violence in respect of all beings, not harming even one of them, one should not wish for a son, let alone a companion. One should wander solitary as a rhinoceros horn.

Affection comes into being for one who has associations; following on affection, this misery arises. Seeing the peril (which is) born from affection, one should wander solitary as a rhinoceros horn.

Sympathising with friends (and) companions one misses one's goal, being shackled in mind. Seeing this fear in acquaintance (with friends), one should wander solitary as a rhinoceros horn.

The consideration which (exists) for sons and wives is like a very wide-spreading bamboo tree entangled (with others). Like a (young) bamboo shoot not caught up (with others), one should wander solitary as a rhinoceros horn.

As a deer which is not tied up goes wherever it wishes in the forest for pasture, an understanding man, having regard for his independence, should wander solitary as a rhinoceros horn.

In the midst of companions, whether one is resting, standing, going (or) wandering, there are requests (from others). Having regard for the independence (which is) not coveted (by others), one should wander solitary as a rhinoceros horn.

In the midst of companions there are sport, enjoyment, and great love for sons. (Although) loathing separation from what is dear, one should wander solitary as a rhinoceros horn.

One is a man of the four quarters[1] and not hostile, being pleased with whatever comes one's way. A fearless bearer of dangers, one should wander solitary as a rhinoceros horn.

Even some wanderers are not kindly disposed, and also (some) householders dwelling in a house. Having little concern for the children of others, one should wander solitary as a rhinoceros horn.

Having removed the marks of a householder, like a Kovilara tree whose leaves have fallen, a hero, having cut the householder's bonds, should wander solitary as a rhinoceros horn.

If one can obtain a zealous companion, an associate of good disposition, (who is) resolute, overcoming all dangers one should wander with him, with elated mind, mindful.

If one cannot obtain a zealous companion, an associate of good disposition, (who is) resolute, (then) like a king quitting the kingdom (which he has) conquered, one should wander solitary as a rhinoceros horn.

Assuredly let us praise the good fortune of (having) a companion; friends better (than oneself) or equal (to oneself) are to be associated with. If one

---

TRANSLATED FROM the Pali by K. R. Norman.

1. That is, of the whole world.

does not obtain these, (then) enjoying (only) blameless things, one should wander solitary as a rhinoceros horn.

Seeing shining (bracelets) of gold, well-made by a smith, clashing together (when) two are on (one) arm, one should wander solitary as a rhinoceros horn.

'In the same way, with a companion there would be objectionable talk or abuse for me.' Seeing this fear for the future, one should wander solitary as a rhinoceros horn.

For sensual pleasures, variegated, sweet (and) delightful, disturb the mind with their manifold form. Seeing peril in the strands of sensual pleasure, one should wander solitary as a rhinoceros horn.

'This for me is a calamity, and a tumour, and a misfortune, and a disease, and a barb, and a fear.' Seeing this fear in the strands of sensual pleasure, one should wander solitary as a rhinoceros horn.

Cold and heat, hunger (and) thirst, wind and the heat (of the sun), gadflies and snakes, having endured all these, one should wander solitary as a rhinoceros horn.

As an elephant with massive shoulders, spotted, noble, may leave the herds and live as it pleases in the forest, one should wander solitary as a rhinoceros horn.

It is an impossibility for one who delights in company to obtain (even) temporary release. Having heard the word of the sun's kinsman, one should wander solitary as a rhinoceros horn.

Gone beyond the contortions of wrong view, arrived at the fixed course (to salvation), having gained the way, (thinking) 'I have knowledge arisen (in me); I am not to be led by others', one should wander solitary as a rhinoceros horn.

Being without covetousness, without deceit, without thirst, without hypocrisy, with delusion and faults blown away, without aspirations in the whole world, one should wander solitary as a rhinoceros horn.

One should avoid an evil companion, who does not see the goal, (who has) entered upon bad conduct. One should not oneself associate with one who is intent (upon wrong views, and is) negligent. One should wander solitary as a rhinoceros horn.

One should cultivate one of great learning, expert in the doctrine, a noble friend possessed of intelligence. Knowing one's goals, having dispelled doubt, one should wander solitary as a rhinoceros horn.

Not finding satisfaction in sport and enjoyment, nor in the happiness (which comes) from sensual pleasures in the world, (and) paying no attention (to them), abstaining from adornment, speaking the truth, one should wander solitary as a rhinoceros horn.

Leaving behind son and wife, and father and mother, and wealth and grain, and relatives, and sensual pleasures to the limit, one should wander solitary as a rhinoceros horn.

'This is an attachment; here there is little happiness, (and) little satisfaction; here there is very much misery; this is a hook.' Knowing this, a thoughtful man should wander solitary as a rhinoceros horn.

Having torn one's fetters asunder, like a fish breaking a net in the water, not returning, like a fire (not going back) to what is (already) burned, one should wander solitary as a rhinoceros horn.

With downcast eye and not foot-loose, with sense-faculties guarded, with mind protected, not overflowing (with defilement), not burning, one should wander solitary as a rhinoceros horn.

Having discarded the marks of a householder, like a coral tree whose leaves have fallen, having gone out (from the house) wearing the saffron robe, one should wander solitary as a rhinoceros horn.

Showing no greed for flavours, not wanton, not supporting others, going on an uninterrupted begging round, not shackled in mind to this family or that, one should wander solitary as a rhinoceros horn.

Having left behind the five hindrances of the mind,[2] having thrust away all defilements, not dependent, having cut off affection and hate, one should wander solitary as a rhinoceros horn.

Having put happiness and misery behind oneself, and joy and dejection already, having gained equanimity (which is) purified calmness, one should wander solitary as a rhinoceros horn.

Resolute for the attainment of the supreme goal, with intrepid mind, not indolent, of firm exertion, furnished with strength and power, one should wander solitary as a rhinoceros horn.

Not giving up seclusion (and) meditation, constantly living in accordance with the doctrine in the world of phenomena, understanding the peril (which is) in existences, one should wander solitary as a rhinoceros horn.

Desiring the destruction of craving, not negligent, not foolish, learned, possessing mindfulness, having considered the doctrine, restrained, energetic, one should wander solitary as a rhinoceros horn.

Not trembling, as a lion (does not tremble) at sounds, not caught up (with others), as the wind (is not caught up) in a net, not defiled (by passion), as a lotus (is not defiled) by water, one should wander solitary as a rhinoceros horn.

Wandering victorious, having overcome like a strong-toothed lion, the king of beasts, one should resort to secluded lodgings, one should wander solitary as a rhinoceros horn.

Cultivating at the right time loving-kindness, equanimity, pity, release and (sympathetic) joy, unimpeded by the whole world, one should wander solitary as a rhinoceros horn.

Leaving behind passion, hatred, and delusion, having torn the fetters apart, not trembling at (the time of) the complete destruction of life, one should wander solitary as a rhinoceros horn.

(People) associate with and resort to (others) for some motive; nowadays friends without a motive are hard to find. Wise as to their own advantage, men are impure. One should wander solitary as a rhinoceros horn.

---

2. Desire, anger, sloth, worry, and doubt.

NUNS ACHIEVE NIRVANA

SONGS OF THE FEMALE ELDERS
(*The Therigatha*)

In ancient India, women did not participate in religious rituals except in their roles as wives. The various schools of philosophy and yogic practice in the sixth century B.C.E. saw some involvement by women (a woman is an interlocutor in a famous Upanishad, for example). However, these movements were overwhelmingly male. The Buddhist order was also exclusively male in the early days until, as the story goes, the Buddha visited his home city of Kapilavastu after his enlightenment.

During his visit, the Buddha was approached by his aunt and stepmother, Mahapajapati. She asked him to allow women to go forth from the worldly life and enter the order, but the Buddha refused. Shortly thereafter, he and his monks—most of whom were newly ordained men, leaving their families behind—departed from the city. Looking back, they saw that they were being followed by five hundred women, led by Mahapajapati. The women had shaved their heads and donned monk's robes. Unused to the demands of the ascetic life, their bare feet were bleeding. The Buddha's cousin, the monk Ananda, approached him and asked that the women be allowed to enter the order. When the Buddha refused, Ananda asked him whether women were capable of following the path to enlightenment. The Buddha said that they are. Ananda persisted, and after his third request, the Buddha relented, but only after establishing a set of eight rules for nuns. Called the eight "heavy rules" (*gurudharma*), they are meant to codify the inferiority of nuns to monks in the life of the order. For example, although seniority within the order of monks was based on how long each individual had been ordained, these rules required a nun who had been ordained for one hundred years to rise and pay respect to all monks, even those who had been ordained that day. Other rules stated that although a monk may criticize a nun, a nun may not criticize a monk.

The account of the establishment of the order of nuns ends on an ominous note, as the Buddha predicts that his admission of women into the order will drastically curtail the length of time that his teaching will remain in the world. Had he not been compelled to admit them, his teaching would have lasted for one thousand years; now it will remain only five hundred before it disappears. The Buddha's views on the dangers of women seem not to have changed over the course of his life. As he was about to pass into nirvana, Ananda asked him how monks should behave toward women. The Buddha replied, "Do not look at them." Ananda asked how monks should behave if they happen to see women. The Buddha replied, "Do not speak to them." "But if they speak to us?" Ananda asked. The Buddha said, "Practice mindfulness, Ananda." This negative view seems to have been held by other monks as well.

After the death of the Buddha, the order of monks brought five charges against Ananda: (1) the Buddha had said that after his passing, the monks could disregard the minor precepts, but because Ananda failed to ask him which those were, all the precepts had to be followed; (2) Ananda had once stepped on the Buddha's robe when sewing it; (3) Ananda had allowed women to honor the Buddha's naked body after his death, and their tears had fallen on his feet; (4) Ananda had failed to ask the Buddha to live on for an aeon; and (5) Ananda had urged the Buddha to admit women to the order. Ananda responded that he saw no fault in any of these deeds, but agreed to confess them.

In traditional Indian society, a woman is said to be protected by her father in her youth, protected by her husband in midlife, and protected by her son in old age.

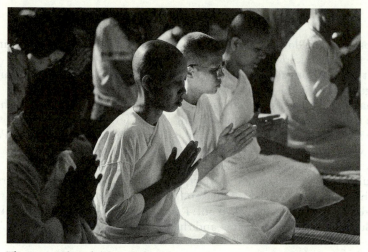

Thai nuns. Photo by Don Farber.

According to the rules of ordination, men required the consent of their parents, but not of their wives, to enter the order. Women, however, required the consent of their husbands. Thus, most of the illustrious female disciples of the Buddha are women who lack the protection of father, husband, or son: widows, courtesans, and unwed daughters of kings, as well as the abandoned wives of monks. When the Buddha's wife demands that he bestow upon their son Rahula his birthright, the Buddha ordains him as a monk; this is his inheritance. When the Buddha's recently widowed stepmother turns to her son for protection, he (eventually) ordains her as a nun.

Despite the burden of the heavy rules, Mahapajapati and many other women went on to achieve enlightenment. Their experiences are recounted in a work titled the *Therigatha, the Songs of the (Female) Elders* or, in its somewhat more poetic 1909 rendering, *Psalms of the Sisters*. It consists of seventy-three poems, and the eight presented here make up the chapter of poems that have six verses. The commentaries provide the context for each. For example, the first song is the advice of the nun Patachara, offered to a woman whose son has died. The second song is that of a woman whose son died when he was a toddler; she is driven almost mad with grief until she meets the Buddha. The third and fourth songs present one of the common themes of the collection: the fleeting nature of youth and beauty. The sixth song is a hymn of praise to the Buddha, spoken by his stepmother Mahapajapati herself.

PRONOUNCING GLOSSARY

Anjana: *an-ja-na*
Anopama: *a-noh-pa-mah*
bhikkhuni: *bik-ku-nee*
Khema: *kay-mah*
Mahapajapati Gotami: *ma-hah-pa-jah-pa-tee goh-ta-mee*
Majjha: *maj-ja*
Mara: *mah-ra*
Maya: *mah-yah*

Mithila: *mi-ti-lah*
Panchasata Patachara: *pan-cha-sa-tah pa-tah-chah-rah*
Sujata: *su-jah-tah*
Therigatha: *tay-ree-gah-tah*
Vasitthi: *vah-sit-tee*
vihara: *vi-hah-ra*
Vijaya: *vi-ja-yah*

Panchasata Patachara

"Whose way you do not know, either coming or going, that being you lament, come from who knows where, crying 'My son.'

But you do not grieve for him whose way you do know, either coming or going; for such is the nature of living creatures.

Unasked he came from there, unpermitted he went from here, surely having come from somewhere or other, having lived a few days.

He went from here by one road, he will go from there by another. Passed away with the form of a man he will go journeying-on. As he came, so he went. What lamentation is there in that?"

Truly she has plucked out my dart, hard to see, nestling in my heart; she has thrust away that grief for my son for me, overcome by grief.

Today I have my dart plucked out; I am without hunger, quenched. I go to the Buddha-sage, the doctrine, and the Order, as a refuge.

Vasitthi

Afflicted by grief for my son, with mind deranged, out of my senses, naked, and with dishevelled hair, I wandered here and there.

I dwelt on rubbish heaps in the streets, in a cemetery, and on highways; I wandered for three years, consigned to hunger and thirst.

Then I saw the well-farer who had gone to the city of Mithila,[1] the tamer of the untamed, the enlightened one, who has no fear from any quarter.

Regaining my mind, I paid homage to him, and sat down. In pity Gotama[2] taught me the doctrine.

I heard the doctrine from him, and went forth into the houseless state. Applying myself to the teacher's utterance, I realized the blissful state.

All griefs have been cut out, eliminated, ending in this way; for I have comprehended the grounds, from which is the origin of griefs.

Khema

"You are young and beautiful; I also am young and in my prime. Come, Khema, let us delight ourselves with the 5-fold music."[3]

I am afflicted by and ashamed of this foul body, diseased, perishable. Craving for sensual pleasures has been rooted out.

Sensual pleasures are like swords and stakes; the elements of existence are a chopping block for them; what you call "delight in sensual pleasures" is now "non-delight" for me.

Everywhere love of pleasure is defeated; the mass of darkness (of ignorance) is torn asunder; in this way know, evil one, you are defeated, death.

Revering the lunar mansions, tending the fire in the wood, not knowing it as it really is, fools, you thought it was purity.

But revering the enlightened one, best of men, I am indeed completely released from all pains, doing the teacher's teaching.

TRANSLATED FROM the Pali by C. A. F. Rhys Davids and K. R. Norman.

1. The capital of the kingdom of Videha, in modern-day Nepal and northern India.

2. That is, Gautama.

3. Music from five instruments.

Sujata

Ornamented, well-dressed, wearing a garland smeared with sandalwood-paste, covered with all my ornaments, attended by a crowd of slave-women, taking food and drink, food hard and soft, in no small quantity, going out from the house I betook myself to the pleasure garden.

Having delighted there, having played, coming back to my own house, I saw a vihara.[4] I entered the Anjana wood at Saketa.[5]

I saw the light of the world. I paid homage to him and sat down. In pity the one with vision taught me the doctrine.

And hearing the great seer, I completely pierced the truth. In that very place I attained the stainless doctrine, the state of the undying.

Then knowing the true doctrine, I went forth into the houseless state. I have obtained the three knowledges;[6] the Buddha's teaching was not in vain.

Anopama

I was born in an exalted family, which had much property and much wealth. I possessed a good complexion and figure, being Majjha's own daughter.

I was sought after by kings' sons, longed for by merchants' sons; one sent my father a messenger, saying "Give me Anopama.

However much that daughter of yours Anopama weighs, I will give you eight times that amount of gold and jewels."

I saw the enlightened one, who was supreme in the world, unsurpassed. I paid homage to his feet, and sat down on one side.

In pity Gotama taught me the doctrine. Seated on that seat I attained the third fruit.[7]

Then I cut off my hair and went forth into the houseless state. Today is the seventh night since my craving was dried up.

Mahapajapati Gotami

Buddha, hero, homage to you, best of all creatures, who released me and many other people from pain.

All pain is known; craving as the cause is dried up; the noble eight-fold way[8] has been developed; I have attained cessation.

Formerly I was mother, son, father, brother, and grandmother; not having proper knowledge, I journeyed-on without expiation.

I have indeed seen that blessed one; this is the last body; journeying-on from rebirth to rebirth has been completely eliminated; there is now no renewed existence.

I see the disciples all together, putting forth energy, resolute, always with strong effort; this is homage to the Buddhas.

Truly Maya[9] bore Gotama for the sake of many. He has thrust away the mass of pain of those struck by sickness and death.

---

4. A monastery or nunnery.
5. A city in northern India.
6. Knowledge that she is an arhat, knowledge of the form of the dharma, and knowledge of the meaning of the dharma.
7. That is, the third stage of the path (see p. 171, n. 6).

8. Right view, right intention, right speech, right action, right livelihood, right effort, right mindfulness, and right meditation; see *Setting the Wheel of the Dharma in Motion*, p. 177 and its introduction.
9. The sister of Mahapajapati.

Gutta

Gutta, give up your son, and those who are equally dear to you, and devote yourself to that very thing for the sake of which you went forth. Do not go under the influence of mind.

Creatures, deceived by mind, delighting in Mara's[1] realm, run through the journeying-on of numerous rebirths, ignorant.

Desire for sensual pleasures, and malevolence, and the false view of individuality, misapprehension about rules of virtuous conduct and vows, and uncertainty fifth—

bhikkhuni,[2] abandoning these fetters, which lead to the lower-world, you will not come to this again.

Avoiding desire, pride, and ignorance, and conceit, cutting the fetters, you will put an end to pain.

Annihilating journeying-on from rebirth to rebirth, comprehending and giving up renewed existence, you will wander in the world of phenomena, without hunger, stilled.

Vijaya

Four or five times I went forth from my cell, not having obtained peace of mind, being without self-mastery over the mind.

I approached a bhikkhuni, honoured her, and questioned (her). She taught me the doctrine, and the elements, and sense-bases,

the four noble truths,[3] the faculties, and the powers, the constituents of enlightenment and the eight-fold way for the attainment of the supreme goal.

I heard her utterance, took her advice, and in the first watch of the night I recollected that I had been born before.

In the middle watch of the night I purified the divine eye. In the last watch of the night I tore asunder the mass of darkness (of ignorance).

And I then dwelt suffusing the body with joy and happiness. On the seventh day I stretched forth my feet, having torn asunder the mass of darkness (of ignorance).

---

1. The Buddhist deity of evil and desire who seeks to impede those on the path to enlightenment.
2. Pali for *bhikshuni*, a nun.
3. Suffering, origin, cessation, and path; see *Setting the Wheel of the Dharma in Motion*, p. 177 and its introduction.

THE LIFE WELL LIVED

DISCOURSE ON GOOD FORTUNE
(*The Mangala Sutta*)

Only twelve verses long, the *Mangala Sutta* or *Discourse on Good Fortune* is one of the shorter texts in the Pali canon. But it is also one of the most popular texts of Theravada Buddhism, often known by heart and widely commented upon in Sri Lanka and the countries of Southeast Asia; a famous Thai work from the sixteenth century offers five hundred pages of commentary on these twelve verses. It also has an important ritual function, being one of the texts chanted by monks as part of the protective rituals (*paritta*) to ward off misfortune.

The term *mangala* appears frequently in Indian literature. It has no direct translation into English, encompassing good luck, auspiciousness, welfare, happiness, and prosperity. In the text, the Buddha is approached near dawn by a radiant deity. After noting that both humans and gods long for good fortune but do not know what it is, the deity asks the Buddha to describe true good fortune. The Buddha responds not by describing good fortune itself but rather by enumerating those practices and virtues that lead to good fortune. The list appears to be a fairly conventional recitation of social virtues found in many cultures. As such, it offers an important insight into the ideals of Buddhists. Far from calling for a renunciation of the world to devote one's life to meditation, the Buddha counsels hard work, humility, gratitude, and respect for one's parents. Those things that we most commonly associate with Buddhism— teachings like the four noble truths—are not mentioned until the very end. The *Discourse on Good Fortune* thus offers a broad view of the life well lived, one that applies equally to monks, nuns, and laypeople. This breadth may account in part for its great fame.

PRONOUNCING GLOSSARY

Anathapindika: *a-nah-ta-pin-di-ka* Mangala Sutta: *man-ga-la soot-ta*
deva: *day-va* Savatthi: *sah-va-tee*

Thus have I heard. Once the Blessed One was staying at Savatthi, in the Jeta-vana[1] in Anathapindika's park. Then, as night was passing away, a deity of surpassing radiance, illuminating the whole Jetavana, came up to the Blessed One and stood on one side after saluting him. Standing there that deity addressed the Blessed One with a verse.

'Many devas[2] and men have thought about good fortunes, longing for well-being. Tell (me) the good fortune (which is) supreme.'

'Not associating with fools, but associating with the wise, and honouring those who deserve honour—this is supreme good fortune.

Living in suitable regions, the previous performance of merit, and proper self-application—this is supreme good fortune.

Great learning and craft, and a discipline well-instructed, and what(ever) utterance is well-spoken—this is supreme good fortune.

Service to mother and father, support of wife and sons, and straightforward work—this is supreme good fortune.

Giving, and living the just life, and support of relatives, (and) blameless deeds—this is supreme good fortune.

Aversion to and abstinence from evil, complete restraint from intoxicating drink, and vigilance in respect of mental phenomena—this is supreme good fortune.

Reverence, and humility, and contentment, (and) gratefulness, (and) hearing the doctrine at the right time—this is supreme good fortune.

TRANSLATED FROM the Pali by K. R. Norman.

1. A monastery; Savatthi (Sravasti) was the capital of the kingdom of Kosala, in present-day Uttar Pradesh.

2. Gods; inhabitants of the heavenly realms (literally, "shining ones").

Forbearance, and meekness when corrected, and seeing ascetics, and discussion of the doctrine at the right time—this is supreme good fortune.

Penance, and living the holy life, and seeing the noble truths, and the realisation of quenching[3]—this is supreme good fortune.

Whose mind is not shaken when he is touched by the phenomena of the world, being without grief, unpolluted, secure—this is supreme good fortune.

Having done such things, (being) unconquered everywhere, they go everywhere in safety—this is their supreme good fortune.'

3. That is, the cessation of suffering. The (four) noble truths are suffering, origin, cessation, and path; see *Setting the Wheel of the Dharma in Motion*, p. 177, and its introduction.

KUNALA LOSES HIS EYES

LEGEND OF ASHOKA
(*The Ashokavadana*)

The most famous king in the history of Buddhism is the emperor Ashoka of the Mauryan dynasty of India. He lived around 300–232 B.C.E., ruling from 268 B.C.E. until his death. If we accept 480–400 B.C.E. as the approximate dates of the Buddha, Ashoka was born a century after the Buddha's passing.

There is no doubt that Ashoka was a historical figure. He left more than thirty inscriptions, known as his "rock edicts," carved on pillars, large boulders, and cave walls. They provide a wealth of information about his reign, including the extent of his empire (they are found in India, Pakistan, Nepal, and Afghanistan) and his relations with foreign powers, among them Greek kings. These edicts, several of which are located at such important sites as the place of the Buddha's birth and the place of his enlightenment, make specific mention of the Buddha and his teachings. They therefore represent the earliest evidence of Buddhism.

In one of his most famous edicts, Ashoka expresses his profound regret at the carnage resulting from his conquest of Kalinga (the region of Orissa in modern India). He renounces war and dedicates himself to the dharma. Buddhists over the centuries have interpreted the term *dharma* here to mean Buddhism, and it is clear that Ashoka was a patron of the Buddhist order and that he visited Buddhist pilgrimage sites such as Bodh Gaya, where the Buddha achieved enlightenment. But some scholars have noted that he also supported other religious groups and that in this context *dharma* may instead refer to a more generalized policy of ethical government, based on religious tolerance and social welfare.

Regardless of the true extent of Ashoka's commitment to Buddhism, Buddhists have had no doubt about his piety, writing extensive accounts of his reign, and even of his former lives, and telling how, as a little boy, he offered a handful of dirt into the begging bowl of the Buddha. As a result, he came to rule the earth, but was very ugly. He is said to have made a pilgrimage to the sites of the major events in the Buddha's life, making prodigious offerings to the Bodhi tree. Moreover, he is said to have broken open the stupas built at the time of the Buddha's death, gathering the relics and then redistributing them among 84,000 other stupas. According to the Theravada tradition, his own son and daughter became ordained and were sent by their father to take the dharma to the island of Sri Lanka.

The story below comes from the *Legend of Ashoka* (*Ashokavadana*). It is the story of Kunala, Ashoka's beloved son, so named because his eyes were as beautiful as those of a *kunala* bird. When he resists the sexual advances of his evil stepmother, she responds with a gruesome act of revenge. We have already encountered stories of human mutilation (see the *Shibi Jataka*), but these are often formulaic. Here, there is a poignancy in Kunala's conversations with his captors and particular poetry in his attitude toward his beautiful eyes. Like most Buddhist stories of this type, this one has a happy ending. Readers will delight that Ashoka, who had long ago renounced all violence, makes an exception in this case.

The story of Kunala appears in the first European language translation of Buddhist Sanskrit texts, Eugène Burnouf's 1844 *Introduction à l'histoire du Buddhisme indien*. In tribute to this pathbreaking work, the story is translated here from Burnouf's elegant French.

PRONOUNCING GLOSSARY

Ashoka: *a-shoh-ka*
Ashokavadana: *a-sho-ka-ah-va-dah-na*
Dharmavivardhana: *dar-ma-vi-var-da-na*
Kanchanamala: *kan-cha-na-ma-la*
Krakuchanda: *kra-ku-chan-da*
Kunala: *ku-nah-la*

Padmavati: *pad-mah-va-tee*
Pataliputra: *pah-ta-li-pu-tra*
Shakyamuni: *shah-kya-mu-ni*
Takshashila: *tak-sha-shee-lah*
Tishyarakshita: *ti-shya-rak-shi-tah*

The day when the king promulgated his edicts, the queen Padmavati gave birth to a beautiful, pleasant to see, graceful son; the eyes of this child shone with most sparkling radiance. One went to announce the news to the king: "Happiness to the king; a son is born to him." Enraptured with joy, Ashoka exclaimed: "An extreme joy, a limitless joy fills my heart; the splendor of the Mauryan race[1] is at its height; it is because I govern according to the law that a son was born to me; may he also make the law blossom!" This is why the name Dharmavivardhana[2] was given to him. The child was then brought to the king, who, seeing him, was overjoyed and exclaimed:

"How pure are the beautiful eyes of this child, these eyes resemble a blue lotus in full bloom! His face, adorned with beauty, shines like the disc of the full moon."

Then, the king said to his ministers: "Do you see, lords, whose eyes the eyes of this child resemble?" "We do not know a man," replied the ministers, "who has such eyes; but, there is, in the Himavat,[3] this king [of mountains], a bird named kunala, whose eyes resemble the eyes of your son." This is what this stanza expresses:

"On the summit of one of the mountain peaks, king of snow, rich in shrubs, in flowers, and in waters, lives a bird named kunala; the eyes of your son resemble those of this bird."

"Bring a kunala," exclaimed the king. Thus, the yakshas heard the orders he gave at a distance of one yojana in the sky, and the nagas[4] heard them at

---

Translated from the Sanskrit by Eugène Burnouf; translated from the French by Katia Buffetrille and Donald S. Lopez, Jr. All bracketed additions are the translators'.

1. That is, the dynasty founded ca. 325 B.C.E. by Ashoka's grandfather, Chandragupta Maurya.
2. Literally, "Increase of the Dharma."
3. The Himalayas.
4. Water deities, often depicted with the torso of a human and the tail of a snake. "Yakshas": one

of the varieties of nonhuman beings; a yaksha is a kind of nature spirit. "Yojana": the standard measurement of distance in ancient India, said to be how far a yoked team of oxen can pull a royal chariot in one day (estimated to be between five and nine miles).

a distance of one yojana beneath the earth. So, the yakshas brought a kunala to him at that very instant. The king, after having examined the eyes of the bird for a long time, could not discover any difference between its eyes and those of his son. This is why he said to his ministers: "The prince has eyes like those of a kunala; thus, give him the name Kunala." This is what this stanza expresses:

"Struck by the charm of his eyes, the king of the earth exclaimed: 'My son must be called Kunala.' This is how the name of this prince who had the virtues of an arya[5] was celebrated on earth."

When the prince was grown, he was given a young girl named Kanchanamala as his wife. One day, the king went with his son to the hermitage of Kukkuta. At this moment, Yashas, the sthavira of the assembly, who possessed the five supernatural knowledges,[6] saw that Kunala would not be long without losing his eyes, and he made it known to the king. "Why?" [replied Ashoka]. "It is that Kunala does not fulfill his duties." "Kunala," the king said to him, "take good care to do what the sthavira of the assembly commands you to do." Immediately throwing himself at the feet of the sthavira, Kunala said to him: "Lord, what do you command me?" "Convince yourself well, O Kunala, that the eye is something perishable." And he added this stanza:

"Reflect constantly, O prince, that the eye is by its nature perishable, that it is the source of a thousand sorrows; becoming too attached to it, many ordinary men commit actions that make their misfortune."

Kunala began to reflect on this maxim and he had it ceaselessly in mind. He liked only solitude and repose. Seated at the back of the palace, in a solitary place, he imagined the eye and the other senses as perishable. One day Tishyarakshita, the foremost of the wives of Ashoka, passed through this place and saw Kunala, who was alone. Seduced by the beauty of his eyes, she clasped him in her arms and said to him:

"At the sight of the ravishing look in your eyes, of your beautiful body, of your charming eyes, all my body burns like dried straw that the forest fire consumes."

At these words, Kunala, covering his ears with his two hands, responded to her: "Do not pronounce such culpable words in front of a son, for you are like a mother to me; renounce licentious passion; this love would be the path to hell for you." But Tishyarakshita, seeing that she could not seduce him, said to him in anger: "Since you push me away here, at the moment when, enraptured with love, I come to offer myself to you, in a short time, insane one, you will cease to live." "O my mother," responded Kunala, "it is better to die persisting in duty and remaining pure; I have nothing to do with a life that would be an object of blame for good people, a life that, in closing the path to heaven to me, would become the cause of my death and would be scorned and condemned by the sages." From this moment, Tishyarakshita dreamed only of finding the occasion to harm Kunala.

It happened that the city of Takshashila, which was located in the North and which obeyed king Ashoka, began to revolt. At this news, the king wished to go there himself, but his ministers said to him: "O king, send the prince

5. Noble one; someone who has achieved at least the first of the four stages on the path to nirvana.
6. Clairvoyance, clairaudience, telepathy, memory of one's past lives, and yogic powers. "Sthavira": elder monk.

there; he will bring the city back to duty." Consequently, the king, having called Kunala, spoke to him in this way: "My dear son, go to Takshashila and subdue this city." "Yes, Lord, I will go," responded Kunala. [This is what this stanza expresses:]

"The king, having learned thereby the desire of the one he called his son and knowing in his heart what he could expect from his affection, himself renounced the journey and destined Kunala for it."

Ashoka, having the city and the road ornamented and having the old, the sick, and the destitute moved to a distance, mounted a chariot with his son and left Pataliputra.[7] At the moment of leaving his son to retrace his steps, he threw his arms around his neck, and contemplating his eyes, he said to him while bursting into tears: "The eyes are fortunate and the eyesight happy for mortals who will constantly see the prince's lotus face." But a brahman astrologer predicted that in a short time Kunala would lose his sight. Therefore, king Ashoka, unable to tire of contemplating the eyes of his son, exclaimed when he looked at them:

"The eyes of the prince are perfect," and the king felt an extreme attachment for him. "Today, I contemplate these eyes whose radiance is so pure, which spread happiness; these eyes destined to perish.

"This city, happy as heaven itself, is overjoyed because it sees the prince; but when he has lost his eyes, all the hearts of the city will plunge into grief."

The young prince soon arrived in the vicinity of Takshashila. At the news of his approach, the inhabitants, having ornamented the city and the main road to a distance of two and a half yojanas, went out to meet him with bowls [full of offerings]. This is what this stanza expresses:

"At this news, the inhabitants of Takshashila went out in respect to meet the son of the king, carrying bowls filled with jewels in their hands."

When they had arrived in his presence, they said, with hands joined in a sign of respect: "We are not revolting against the prince and king Ashoka; there are evil ministers who have come to heap outrage on us." Thus, Kunala entered the city of Takshashila with great pomp.

Meanwhile, king Ashoka was affected by a terrible malady. His excrement came out of his mouth; an impure humor escaped from all his pores and nothing could cure him. He then said: "Let Kunala come, I wish to put him on the throne."

When the king was cured, full of joy, he asked Tishyarakshita which favor she desired: "What gift will I make to you?" he said to her. "May the king," she responded, "grant me the monarchy for seven days." "And I, what will I become?" "After seven days," said the queen, "the king will again take royal power." Thus, Ashoka ceded the monarchy to Tishyarakshita for seven days. The first thing the queen thought of was to satisfy her hatred against Kunala. She wrote a false letter [in the name of the king] that ordered the inhabitants of Takshashila to tear out the eyes of Kunala. And she added this stanza:

"For Ashoka, this strong and violent king, has ordered the inhabitants of Takshashila to tear out the eyes of this enemy; he is the shame of the Mauryan race."

---

7. The capital of the Mauryan emperors, in northeast India (modern-day Patna).

When king Ashoka gave an order that must be carried out promptly, he sealed it with an ivory seal. Tishyarakshita said to herself: "I will seal this letter with the ivory seal when the king is asleep"; and she went near Ashoka. But at that moment the king awakened, quite afraid. "What is there?" the queen said to him, "I just had a sad dream," the king responded. "I saw two vultures who wanted to tear out Kunala's eyes." "Happiness to the prince!" exclaimed the queen. A second time, the king again awakened, quite afraid. "O queen," he said, "I just had a sad dream." "And what dream?" the queen asked him. "I saw Kunala," said the king, "who had entered the city with long hair, nails, and beard." "Happiness to the prince!" exclaimed the queen. Finally, the king having fallen asleep again, Tishyarakshita sealed her letter with the ivory seal and had it sent to the city of Takshashila.

Meanwhile the king saw his teeth fall out in a dream. As soon as it was day, he called the soothsayers and said to them: "What does the dream I just had foretell?" "O king," answered the soothsayers, "he who has such dreams, he who during his sleep sees his teeth fall out and be destroyed, will see his son deprived of his eyes and will learn of his death." At these words, king Ashoka rose with all possible speed from his seat and, pointing his joined hands to the four sides of the horizon in a sign of respect, began to beseech the divinity, and he pronounced this stanza:

"May the divinity who is benevolent to the preceptor, to the law and to the assembly, the foremost of troops, may the rshis[8] who are foremost in the world, protect our son Kunala."

During this time, the letter of the queen reached Takshashila. At the sight of this missive, the inhabitants of Takshashila, those of the city and of the country who were happy with the numerous virtues of Kunala, did not have the courage to make known to him the inhuman order it contained; but after having reflected for a longtime, they said to themselves: "The king is violent; he is naturally hot-tempered; if he does not forgive his son, all the more reason for him not to spare us." And they pronounced this stanza:

"He who could conceive hatred against a prince so calm, whose mores are those of a recluse, and who desires only the welfare of all beings, how will he be for others?"

Finally, they decided to inform him of this news, and handed the letter to him. Kunala, having read it, exclaimed: "The order is worthy of confidence. Do what you are commanded." Chandalas[9] were thus made to come and the order was given to them to tear out the eyes of Kunala, but the torturers, joining their hands in a sign of respect, exclaimed: "We do not have the courage for it. And why?

"Only an insane man capable of wiping out the radiance of the moon could tear out the eyes of your face, which resembles the star of the night."

The prince gave them the crown that covered his head and said to them: "Do your duty for the price of this gift"; [but they refused, saying:] "This action must necessarily lead to misfortune." Then, a man with a deformed aspect and covered with eighteen marks of a repulsive color appeared, who offered to tear out the eyes of the prince. He was thus led to Kunala. At this

---

8. Sages, saints.　　　　　　　　　9. Members of the lowest caste.

moment, the words of the sthaviras came to the young man's mind; the prince, recalling them, pronounced this stanza:

"It is because they predicted this misfortune that these sages who know the truth have said: 'See, this entire world is perishable; no one remains in a permanent situation.'

"Yes, they were virtuous friends to me who sought my advantage and wished for my happiness, these magnanimous sages, free from passion, who have taught me the law.

"When I consider the fragility of all things and reflect on the counsel of my masters, I no longer tremble, friend, at the idea of this torture; for I know that my eyes are something perishable.

"Let them be torn out or preserve them for me, according to what the king commands; I have taken in with my eyes the best that they could give me, since I have seen that objects are perishable."

Then, addressing himself to this man: "Go on," he said, "tear out one eye first and place it in my hand." The torturer proceeded to perform his duty; and at this moment, thousands of men uttered lamentable cries: "Ah! misfortune!

"Here is this moon of pure splendor that falls from the sky; a beautiful lotus is torn from the clump of the white water lilies."

While this multitude of people made these lamentations heard, the eye of Kunala was torn from him and he received it in his hand. Taking it, the prince said:

"Why thus do you not see shapes as you did a little while ago, crude globe of flesh? How mistaken and how blameworthy, the insane who become attached to you, saying: 'It is me.'

"Those who, always attentive, know to recognize in you an organ that resembles a ball which one cannot grab, which is pure but dependent, those will be sheltered from misfortune."

While the prince reflected in this way on the instability of all beings, he acquired the reward of the state of shrotapatti[1] at the sight of the multitude of people. Then, Kunala, who saw the truths, said to the torturer: "Now the second eye; tear it out." Indeed, the man tore it out and put it in the hand of the prince. At this moment, Kunala, who had just lost the eyes of flesh but in whom those of science had been purified, pronounced this stanza:

"The eye of flesh, although difficult to seize, has just been taken from me; but I have acquired the perfect and irreproachable eyes of wisdom.

"If I am abandoned by the king, I become the son of the magnanimous king of the law, whose child I am called.

"If I am deposed from the supreme grandeur that brings so much grief and suffering in its wake, I have acquired the sovereignty of the law that destroys suffering and grief."

Some time later, Kunala knew that his torture was not the work of his father Ashoka but that it was the effect of the intrigues of Tishyarakshita. At this news, he exclaimed:

"May queen Tishyarakshita, who has here put to use this means to ensure me such a great advantage, preserve her happiness, life, and power for a long time."

---

1. Stream enterer, the first stage of the path to nirvana.

However, Kanchanamala learned that the eyes of Kunala had been torn out. Immediately, using her right as spouse, she rushed through the multitude to go to meet Kunala and saw him deprived of his two eyes and his body completely covered with blood. At this sight, she fainted and fell to the ground. One hastened to throw water on her and to revive her. When she began to regain her senses, she exclaimed while shedding tears:

"These ravishing and beloved eyes, which looking at me made my happiness, now that they are thrown to the ground and deprived of the faculty of sight, I feel life abandoning my body."

Then, Kunala, wishing to soothe his wife, replied in this way: "Cease your tears; you must not give yourself over to grief. Each collects the recompense of the actions he has done in this world"; and he pronounced this stanza:

"Recognizing that this world is the fruit of deeds and that creatures are condemned to misfortune; knowing that men are made to see their dear ones taken from them, you must not, dear friend, shed tears."

Then, Kunala departed from Takshashila with his wife. Since the time he had been conceived in the womb of his mother, the prince always had a very delicate body. He thus could not engage in any profession, and he only knew how to sing and play the vina. He went begging for his food and shared what he gathered with his wife. Kanchanamala, returning on the route by which she had been brought from Pataliputra, followed it accompanied by the prince; and once arrived in the city, she proceeded to enter the residence of Ashoka. But they were stopped by the guard at the door. Meanwhile, they were ushered into the place where the chariots of the king were kept. At the break of day, Kunala began to play his vina and to sing of how his eyes had been torn out and how the view of the truths had appeared to him. And he pronounced this stanza:

"The sage who sees the eye and the other senses with the pure torch of science is free from the law of transmigration.

"If your mind, indulged in sin, is tormented by the sufferings of existence and if you desire happiness in this world, hasten to renounce forever the objects of the senses."

King Ashoka heard the songs of the prince, and he said with a feeling of joy:

"It is to me that are addressed the songs of Kunala and the sounds of this vina that I have not heard for so long. The prince has returned to my residence, but he does not want to see anyone."

Immediately calling one of the guards, the king said to him: "Do you not find some resemblance between this song and that of Kunala? It seemed that this performance betrayed some trouble. This voice has strongly moved my soul; I am like the elephant who, having lost its young, would come to hear its voice. Thus go and bring me Kunala." The guard immediately went to the place where the chariots were kept; and there he found Kunala, deprived of his eyes and whose body was burned by the ardor of the sun and by the wind; but not having recognized him, he returned to king Ashoka and said to him: "O king, it is not Kunala; it is a blind mendicant with his wife in the place where the chariots of the king are kept." At these words, the king, quite troubled, had this reflection: "Here is the effect of the disastrous dreams I have had; certainly, it is Kunala whose eyes have been torn out." And he pronounced this stanza:

"According to the omens I saw in times past in a dream, no, there is no more doubt, the eyes of Kunala have been torn out."

Bursting into tears, he exclaimed: "Quickly bring this mendicant into my presence; for my heart cannot find calm while thinking about the misfortune that could have struck my son." The guard, having returned to the hall of the chariots, said to Kunala: "Of whom are you the son and what is your name?"

"Ashoka," replied Kunala, "this king who increases the glory of the Mauryas, whose authority the entire earth obeys with submission, this king is my father, and my name is Kunala. But today, I am the son of the Buddha, this descendant of the solar race who established the law." Immediately Kunala was conducted with his wife into the presence of king Ashoka. On seeing Kunala, who was deprived of his eyes, whose body, burned by the ardor of the sun and by the wind, was covered with a shabby robe drained of color by water during his travels, the king to whom the crime was unknown, gazed at his son several times without being able to recognize him, and seeing only a human form before his eyes, he said: "Are you Kunala?" "Yes," responded the prince. "I am Kunala." At these words, the king fainted and fell on the ground. This is what this stanza expresses:

"Seeing the face of Kunala, whose eyes had been torn out, king Ashoka, ripped by suffering, fell to the ground, consumed by the fire of grief at the sight of his son's misfortune."

Water was thrown on the king, he was helped back up, placed again on his seat. When he had regained a little of his senses, he clasped his son in his arms. This is what this stanza says:

The king, after some moments, returning to himself, threw his arms around his son's neck; and caressing the face of Kunala several times, many moans were heard, his voice broken with sobs:

"In the past, at the sight of these eyes like those of the kunala, I called my son Kunala; today these eyes are extinguished, how could I continue to give him this name?"

Then, he said to him: "Tell me, tell me, my dear son, how this face with beautiful eyes has been deprived of its light and has come to be like the sky where the setting of the moon had taken away its splendor.

"He has a merciless heart, O my son, the spiteful one who, driven by his hatred against a good man, stranger to all feelings of hatred, has destroyed the eyes of the best of men, of the very image of the recluse, cruel act that is a source of sorrows for me.

"Speak quickly to me, O you whose face is so beautiful. Consumed by the grief that the loss of your eyes causes in me, my body perishes like a forest devoured by the thunderbolt thrown by the nagas."

Then, Kunala, having thrown himself at his father's feet, spoke to him in this way:

"O king, you need not lament so over an event that has past; have you not heard quoted the words of the recluse who has said that the jinas themselves, or the pratyekabuddhas,[2] cannot escape the inevitable influence of deeds?

---

2. Solitary buddhas, who do not teach the dharma to others (see *The Rhinoceros Horn Sutta*, p. 228). "Jinas": buddhas.

"They collect, like all ordinary men, the fruit of bad deeds committed here below; it is in this world that one finds the reward for what one has done; how could I call the treatment that I have experienced the deed of another?

"I committed some fault [long ago], O great king, and it is under the influence of this fault that I have returned [to this world], I whose eyes have been the cause of my unhappiness.

"Sword, thunderbolt, fire, poison, birds, nothing injures the ether, whose nature is inalterable; it is on the body in which souls are enveloped, O king, that cruel sufferings that somehow take it as a target fall."

But Ashoka, whose heart was ripped by grief, replied in this way: "Who thus has deprived my son of his eyes? Who thus has resolved to renounce [for the price of this crime] life, this good so dear? Anger descends into my heart devoured by the fire of grief; tell me quickly, O my son, on whom must I make punishment fall." In the end, the king learned that this crime was the work of Tishyarakshita. Immediately, having the queen called, he said to her:

"How, cruel one, are you not swallowed into the earth? I will make your head fall under the sword or under the axe. I renounce you, woman covered by crimes, unjust woman, just as the sage renounces fortune."

Then, looking at her with a face blazing with the fire of anger, he added:

"Why would I not break her limbs after having torn out her eyes with my sharp nails? Why would I not place her alive on the execution post? Why would I not cut off her nose?

"Why would I not cut out her tongue with a razor or would I not make her die by poison?" Such were the tortures with which the king of men threatened her.

The magnanimous Kunala, full of compassion, having heard these words, said to his father: "It would not be honorable for you to put Tishyarakshita to death; act in conformity with honor and do not kill this woman.

"There is indeed no reward superior to that of benevolence; patience, Lord, has been celebrated by the Sugata."[3] Then, throwing himself again at his feet, the prince made his father hear these truthful words:

"O king, I experience no suffering and despite this cruel treatment, I do not feel the fire of anger; my heart has only benevolence for my mother, who gave the order to tear out my eyes.

"In the name of the truth of these words, may my eyes become again as they were before." Hardly had he pronounced these words than his eyes reappeared with their original radiance.

However, king Ashoka, incensed at Tishyarakshita, had her thrown into a place of torture where she died by fire; and he had the inhabitants of Takshashila massacred.

The monks who conceived some doubts questioned in this way the respectable sthavira Upagupta, who settles all doubts: "What action had Kunala thus committed so that his eyes had been torn out?" The sthavira responded: "Listen, respectable personages. Long ago, in times past, there was in Benares[4] a certain hunter who went to the Himavat and killed wild animals there. One day when he went to the mountain, at the end of a cave, he came upon

---

3. That is, the Buddha. 4. That is, Varanasi, in modern-day Uttar Pradesh.

five hundred gazelles that had gathered there, and he caught them all in a net. He then had this reflection: 'If I kill them, I will be encumbered with all this meat.' This is why he put out the eyes of the five hundred gazelles. These animals deprived of sight were unable to escape. It is in this way that he put out the eyes of several hundred gazelles.

"What do you think about that, O monks? This hunter was Kunala himself. Because at that time, he put out the eyes of several hundred gazelles, he has undergone the sufferings of hell during several hundred thousand years as the price for this action. Then, to complete the expiation of the remainder of his fault, he has had the eyes torn out during five hundred existences in the form of a human." "But what action had he done to merit rebirth in a high family, to have a pleasant outward appearance, and to know the truths?" "Listen, respectable personages:

"Long ago, in times past, when the lifespan of humans was forty-four thousand years, there appeared in the world a perfect buddha called Krakuchanda. When he had completely fulfilled the duties of a buddha, he entered into the domain of nirvana, where nothing remains of the elements of existence. A king named Ashoka had built for him a stupa made of four kinds of precious stones. But, after the death of Ashoka, his throne was occupied by a monarch who had no faith. The precious stones were stolen by thieves who left only earth and wood. The people who had gathered in this place, seeing the stupa destroyed, burst into tears. Now, the son of a chief of artisans was at that time [among the people]. This young man asked: 'Why are you crying?' 'The stupa of Krakuchanda the buddha was made of four kinds of precious stones,' the multitude responded to him. 'Now it is destroyed.' The young man [raised it again]. There was, moreover, in this place a statue of the perfect buddha Krakuchanda that was of natural size; it had been destroyed. The young man restored it also and pronounced this prayer: 'May I make myself agreeable to a master like Krakuchanda! May I not be disagreeable to him!'

"What do you think about that, respectable personages? This son of the chief of the artisans was Kunala himself. It is he who at that time had the stupa of Krakuchanda raised again, and it is in recompense for this action that he was born into an illustrious family. Because he restored the statue of the buddha, as recompense for this good deed he was reborn with an agreeable outward appearance. Because he pronounced the prayer reported above, he had the privilege of pleasing a master similar to Shakyamuni, the perfect buddha, he was not displeasing to him, and he knew the truths."

THE MEANING OF LOVE

DISCOURSE ON LOVING-KINDNESS
(*The Metta Sutta*)

In the *Tevijja Sutta* (p. 181), the Buddha advised two young brahmins to develop four virtues in order to be reborn in the heaven of the god Brahma: loving-kindness, compassion, sympathetic joy, and equanimity. The standard elucidation of the first of these virtues is the short text below. The term *metta* is variously translated as love, loving-kindness, friendliness, benevolence, and good will. Later commentators would define it as the wish that someone, either oneself or another, be happy.

This short text occurs in a collection called the *Sutta Nipata*, which contains a number of works that scholars believe, judging largely from grammatical criteria, to be early. The text is short enough for easy memorization, and it is one of the works (like the *Mangala Sutta*, or, *Discourse on Good Fortune*, p. 236) that is said to have apotropaic powers—that is, the power to ward off evil. According to the framing story, a group of monks went into the forest to meditate during the rains retreat, which took place each year during the monsoon. However, the spirits who inhabited the trees were disturbed by the monks' presence and sought to drive them away by harassing them in the night. The monks went to the Buddha for help, and he is said to have offered these instructions. Following his advice, the monks filled the forest with thoughts of loving-kindness and the tree spirits were subdued. The sutra is thus traditionally recited to ward off various dangers, including snakes and tigers.

The text is in two parts. The first two and a half verses describe the qualities of one who seeks "the peaceful state"—that is, nirvana. The remainder of the text, beginning with "Let all creatures indeed be happy and secure; let them be happy-minded," contains the instructions on the cultivation of loving-kindness. The next-to-last stanza describes the practice as "the holy state." This phrase is the translator's rendering of the term *brahmavihara*, literally "abode of Brahma," discussed in other selections, the *Tevijja Sutta* and the *Visuddhimagga* or, *Path of Purification* (p. 249). The discourse concludes with the Buddha's assurance that one who abandons wrong views, is virtuous, has developed insight, and is not attached to the objects of the senses "does not come to lie again in a womb"—that is, will never be reborn again.

――――――――

This is what is to be done by one who is skilful in respect of the good, having attained the peaceful state. He should be capable, straight, and very upright, easy to speak to, gentle and not proud,

contented and easy to support, having few duties and of a frugal way of life, with his sense-faculties calmed, zealous, not impudent, (and) not greedy (when begging) among families.

And he should not do any mean thing, on account of which other wise men would criticize him. Let all creatures indeed be happy (and) secure; let them be happy-minded.

Whatever living creatures there are, moving or still without exception, whichever are long or large, or middle-sized or short, small or great,

whichever are seen or unseen, whichever live far or near, whether they already exist or are going to be, let all creatures be happy-minded.

TRANSLATED FROM the Pali by K. R. Norman.

One man should not humiliate another; one should not despise anyone anywhere. One should not wish another misery because of anger or from the notion of repugnance.

Just as a mother would protect with her life her own son, her only son, so one should cultivate an unbounded mind towards all beings,

and loving-kindness towards all the world. One should cultivate an unbounded mind, above and below and across, without obstruction, without enmity, without rivalry.

Standing, or going, or seated, or lying down, as long as one is free from drowsiness, one should practise this mindfulness. This, they say, is the holy state here.

Not subscribing to wrong views, virtuous, endowed with insight, having overcome greed for sensual pleasures, a creature assuredly does not come to lie again in a womb.

HOW TO MEDITATE ON LOVE

PATH OF PURIFICATION
(*The Visuddhimagga*)

BUDDHAGHOSA

In the history of the Theravada tradition of Sri Lanka and Southeast Asia, there is no monk more important than Buddhaghosa, a fifth-century scholar whose name means "Voice of the Buddha." According to his traditional biography, he was born to a brahmin family living in the vicinity of Bodh Gaya, the site of the Buddha's enlightenment. He became well versed in the Vedas and gained a reputation as a skillful debater. However, he was defeated in debate by the monk Revata and converted to Buddhism. Seeking commentaries on the Pali suttas, he traveled to Sri Lanka. The monks there were initially reluctant to provide the commentaries; as a test, they asked him to compose a commentary on two verses. A deity asks the Buddha:

> The inner tangle and the outer tangle—
> This generation is entangled in a tangle.
> And so I ask of Gotama this question:
> Who succeeds in disentangling the tangle?

To which the Buddha replies:

> When a wise man, established well in virtue,
> Develops consciousness and understanding,
> Then as a bhikkhu [monk] ardent and sagacious
> He succeeds in disentangling this tangle.

To explain these two verses, Buddhaghosa composed the *Visuddhimagga*, or the *Path of Purification*. It is a massive work, some nine hundred pages in its English translation. Satisfied with his answer, the monks gave him the Sinhalese commentaries he sought. He translated these into Pali and went on to write his own commentaries on many of the most important works in the Pali canon, including the *vinaya*, or rules of monastic discipline; the collections of *suttas*, or discourses of the Buddha; and the *abhidhamma*, or philosophical works. The glosses of key terms

The Cambodian monk Maha Ghosananda, a renowned meditator on love.

provided by Buddhaghosa's commentaries would become orthodox readings for subsequent generations, defining the way that the canon was understood.

The *Visuddhimagga* is the single most influential compendium of Buddhist doctrine for the Theravada tradition. It treats the practice of the Buddhist path in the framework of the three trainings—the training in ethics (which includes observance of the monastic code), the training in meditation (which includes developing various levels of concentration), and the training in wisdom (which includes the development of insight into the three marks of existence: impermanence, suffering, and no self).

The selection below comes from the second section, the training in meditation. The Buddha is said to have set forth forty topics that monks could employ to develop the various levels of deep concentration, called *jhana* here. These objects of concentration include everything from one's own breath to a decaying human corpse. Four among the forty are the four "divine abidings" or "abodes of Brahma"—loving-kindness, compassion, sympathetic joy, and equanimity—recommended by the Buddha in the *Tevijja Sutta* (p. 181). The Buddha's simple and straightforward instructions for the cultivation of loving-kindness are given in the *Metta Sutta* (p. 248).

Here, we have Buddhaghosa's far more systematic and detailed instructions on how to go about developing loving-kindness. It is a discussion that one might describe as Talmudic in style, with Buddhaghosa asking and answering questions, citing the appropriate scripture at every turn, and frequently alluding to the jatakas, or "birth stories" (see selections from the *Shibi Jataka* and *Vessantara Jataka*, pp. 100 and 109), in which the Buddha displays loving-kindness in his previous lives as a bodhisattva (here, in Pali, spelled *bodhisatta*).

PRONOUNCING GLOSSARY

abhinibbattatta: *a-bi-nib-bat-tat-ta*
abyabajjha: *a-byah-baj-ja*
akkhara-cintaka: *ak-ka-ra-chin-ta-ka*
atta-samata: *at-ta-sa-ma-tah*
attabhava: *at-ta-bah-va*
attata: *at-ta-tah*
bhikkhu: *bik-ku*
Bhuridatta: *boo-ri-da-ta*
bhuta: *boo-ta*
bhutatta: *boo-tat-ta*
Bodhisatta: *boh-dih-sat-ta*
byabadha-rahita: *byah-bah-da-ra-hi-ta*
Champeyya: *cham-pay-ya*
Chittalapabbata: *chit-ta-la-pab-ba-ta*
Chula-Dhammapala: *choo-la-dam-ma-pah-la*

Chula-Siva: *choo-la-si-va*
Jambudipa: *jam-bu-dee-pa*
jhana: *jah-na*
Khantivadin: *kan-ti-vah-din*
Mahavihara Anuradhapura: *ma-hah-vi-hah-ra a-nu-rah-da-pu-ra*
Matuposaka: *mah-tu-poh-sa-ka*
Metta Sutta: *meh-ta soot-ta*
nibbana: *nih-bah-na*
pananata: *pah-na-na-tah*
pariyapanna: *pa-rih-yah-pa-na*
Pataliputta: *pah-ta-li-put-ta*
Patisambhida: *pa-tih-sam-bih-dah*
Pavarana: *pa-vah-ra-nah*
sabbasattavant: *sab-ba-sat-ta-vant*
sabbattataya: *sab-bat-ta-tah-ya*

sabbavant: *sab-bah-vant*
sambhutatta: *sam-boo-tat-ta*
Sankhapala: *san-ka-pah-la*
Sankiccha: *san-kich-cha*
sima: *see-mah*

Tambapanni: *tam-ba-pan-ni*
Uposatha: *u-poh-sa-ta*
Visakha: *vih-sah-ka*
Visuddhimagga: *vi-soo-dee-mag-ga*

The four divine abidings were mentioned next to the recollections as meditation subjects. They are lovingkindness, compassion, gladness and equanimity. A meditator who wants to develop firstly lovingkindness among these, if he is a beginner, should sever the impediments and learn the meditation subject. Then, when he has done the work connected with the meal and got rid of any dizziness due to it, he should seat himself comfortably on a well-prepared seat in a secluded place. To start with, he should review the danger in hate and the advantage in patience.

Why? Because hate has to be abandoned and patience attained in the development of this meditation subject, and he cannot abandon unseen dangers and attain unknown advantages.

Now the danger in hate should be seen in accordance with such suttas as this: 'Friends, when a man hates, is a prey to hate and his mind is obsessed by hate, he kills living things, and . . .' And the advantage in patience should be understood according to such suttas as these:

> 'No higher rule, the Buddhas say, than patience,
> And no nibbana higher than forbearance';

> 'Patience in force, in strong array:
> 'Tis him I call a brahman';

> 'No greater thing exists than patience'.

Thereupon he should embark upon the development of lovingkindness for the purpose of secluding the mind from hate seen as a danger and introducing it to patience known as an advantage.

But when he begins, he must know that some persons are of the wrong sort at the very beginning and that lovingkindness should be developed towards certain kinds of persons and not towards certain other kinds at first.

For lovingkindness should not be developed at first towards the following four kinds of persons: an antipathetic person, a very dearly loved friend, a neutral person, and a hostile person. Also it should not be developed specifically towards the opposite sex, or towards a dead person.

What is the reason why it should not be developed at first towards an antipathetic person and the others? To put an antipathetic person in a dear one's place is fatiguing. To put a very dearly loved friend in a neutral person's place is fatiguing; and if the slightest mischance befalls the friend, he feels like weeping. To put a neutral person in a respected one's or a dear one's place is fatiguing. Anger springs up in him if he recollects a hostile

TRANSLATED FROM the Pali by Bhikkhu Ñāṇamoli. All bracketed additions are the translator's; the translator's parenthetical citations for quotations from canonical Buddhist texts have been deleted.

person. That is why it should not be developed at first towards an antipathetic person and the rest.

Then, if he develops it specifically towards the opposite sex, lust inspired by that person springs up in him. An elder supported by a family was asked, it seems, by a friend's son, 'Venerable sir, towards whom should lovingkindness be developed?' The elder told him, 'Towards a person one loves'. He loved his own wife. Through developing lovingkindness towards her he was fighting against the wall all the night.[1] That is why it should not be developed specifically towards the opposite sex.

But if he develops it towards a dead person, he reaches neither absorption nor access. A young bhikkhu,[2] it seems, had started developing lovingkindness inspired by his teacher. His lovingkindness made no headway at all. He went to a senior elder and told him, 'Venerable sir, I am quite familiar with attaining jhana[3] through lovingkindness, and yet I cannot attain it. What is the matter?'. The elder said, 'Seek the sign, friend, [the object of your meditation]'. He did so. Finding that his teacher had died, he proceeded with developing lovingkindness inspired by another and attained absorption. That is why it should not be developed towards one who is dead.

First of all it should be developed only towards oneself, doing it repeatedly thus: 'May I be happy and free from suffering' or 'May I keep myself free from enmity, affliction and anxiety and live happily'.

If that is so, does it not conflict with what is said in the texts? For there is no mention of any development of it towards oneself in what is said in the Vibhanga:[4] 'And how does a bhikkhu dwell pervading one direction with his heart filled with lovingkindness? Just as he would feel lovingkindness on seeing a dearly loved person, so he pervades all beings with lovingkindness'; and in what is said in the Patisambhida:[5] 'In what five ways is the mind-deliverance of lovingkindness [practised] with unspecified pervasion? May all beings be free from enmity, affliction and anxiety and live happily. May all breathing things . . . all who are born . . . all persons . . . all those who have a personality be free from enmity, affliction and anxiety and live happily'; and in what is said in the Metta Sutta:[6] 'In joy and safety may all beings be joyful at heart'. [Does it not conflict with those texts?]

It does not conflict. Why not? Because that refers to absorption. But this [initial development towards oneself] refers to [making oneself] an example. For even if he developed lovingkindness for a hundred or a thousand years in this way, 'I am happy' and so on, absorption would never arise. But if he develops it in this way: 'I am happy. Just as I want to be happy and dread pain, as I want to live and not to die, so do other beings, too', making himself the example, then desire for other beings' welfare and happiness arises in him. And this method is indicated by the Blessed One's saying:

> 'I visited all quarters with my mind
> Nor found I any dearer than myself;

---

1. Overcome by lust, he was trying to get to his wife in the next room.
2. Pali for *bhikshu*, a monk.
3. Pali for *dhyana*, a state of deep concentration attained through meditation.

4. A collection of texts focusing on the code of monastic conduct.
5. "Analytical Understanding."
6. "Discourse on Loving-Kindness" (p. 248).

> Self is likewise to every other dear;
> Who loves himself will never harm another'.

So he should first, as example, pervade himself with lovingkindness. Next after that, in order to proceed easily, he can recollect such gifts, kind words, etc., as inspire love and endearment, such virtue, learning, etc., as inspire respect and reverence met with in a teacher or his equivalent or a preceptor or his equivalent, developing lovingkindness toward him in the way beginning 'May this good man be happy and free from suffering'. With such a person, of course, he attains absorption.

But if this bhikkhu does not rest content with just that much and wants to break down the barriers, he should next, after that, develop lovingkindness towards a very dearly loved friend, then towards a neutral person as a very dearly loved friend, then towards a hostile person as neutral. And while he does so, he should make his mind malleable and wieldy in each instance before passing on to the next.

But if he has no enemy, or he is of the type of a great man who does not perceive another as an enemy even when the other does him harm, he should not interest himself as follows: 'Now that my consciousness of lovingkindness has become wieldy towards a neutral person, I shall apply it to a hostile one'. Rather it was about one who actually has enemy that it was said above that he should develop lovingkindness towards a hostile person as neutral.

If resentment arises in him when he applies his mind to a hostile person because he remembers wrongs done by that person, he should [get] rid of the resentment by entering repeatedly into lovingkindness [jhana] towards any of the first-mentioned persons and then, after he has emerged each time, directing lovingkindness towards that person.

But if it does not die out in spite of his efforts, then:

> Let him reflect upon the saw
> With other figures of such kind,
> And strive, and strive repeatedly,
> To leave resentment far behind.

He should admonish himself in this way: 'Now, you who get angry, has not the Blessed One said this: "Bhikkhus, even if bandits brutally severed limb from limb with a two-handled saw, he who entertained hate in his heart on that account would not be one who carried out my teaching"? And this:

> "To repay angry men in kind
> Is worse than to be angry first;
> Repay not angry men in kind
> And win a battle hard to win.

> "The weal of both he does promote,
> His own and then the other's too,
> Who shall another's anger know
> And mindfully maintain his peace"?

And this: "Bhikkhus, there are seven things gratifying and helpful to an enemy that happen to one who is angry, whether woman or man. What seven? Here, bhikkhus, an enemy wishes thus for his enemy, 'Let him be ugly!'. Why is that? An enemy does not delight in an enemy's beauty. Now this angry person is a prey to anger, ruled by anger; though well bathed, well anointed, with hair and beard trimmed and clothed in white, yet he is ugly, being a prey to anger. This is the first thing gratifying and helpful to an enemy that befalls one who is angry, whether woman or man. Furthermore, an enemy wishes thus for his enemy, 'Let him lie in pain!' . . . 'Let him have no good fortune!' . . . 'Let him not be wealthy!' . . . 'Let him not be famous!' . . . 'Let him have no friends!' . . . 'Let him not on the breakup of the body, after death, reappear in a happy destiny in the heavenly world!'. Why is that? An enemy does not delight in an enemy's going to a happy destiny. Now this angry person is a prey to anger, ruled by anger; he misconducts himself in body, speech and mind. Misconducting himself thus in body, speech and mind, on the breakup of the body, after death, he reappears in a state of loss, in an unhappy destiny, in perdition, in hell, being a prey to anger"? And this: "As a log from a pyre, burnt at both ends and fouled in the middle, serves neither for timber in the village nor for timber in the forest, so is such a person as this I say"? If you are angry now, you will be one who does not carry out the Blessed One's teaching; by repaying an angry man in kind you will be worse than the angry man and not win the battle hard to win; you will yourself do to yourself the things that help your enemy; and you will be like a pyre log'.

If his resentment subsides when he strives and makes effort in this way, it is good. If not, then he should remove irritation by remembering some controlled and purified state in that person, which inspires confidence when remembered.

For one person may be controlled in his bodily behaviour with his control in doing an extensive course of duty known to all, though his verbal and mental behaviour are not controlled. Then the latter should be ignored and the control in his bodily behaviour remembered.

Another may be controlled in his verbal behaviour, and his control known to all—he may naturally be clever at welcoming kindly, easy to talk with, congenial, open-countenanced, deferential in speech, and he may expound the Dhamma[7] with a sweet voice and give explanations of Dhamma with well-rounded phrases and details—though his bodily and mental behaviour are not controlled. Then the latter should be ignored and the control in his verbal behaviour remembered.

Another may be controlled in his mental behaviour, and his control in worshipping at shrines, etc., evident to all. For when one who is uncontrolled in mind pays homage at a shrine or at an Enlightenment Tree[8] or to elders, he does not do it carefully, and he sits in the Dhamma-preaching pavilion with mind astray or nodding, while one whose mind is controlled pays homage carefully and deliberately, listens to the Dhamma attentively, remembering it, and evincing the confidence in his mind through his body or his speech. So another may be only controlled in his mental behaviour, though his bodily and verbal behaviour are not controlled. Then the latter should be ignored and the control in his mental behaviour remembered.

---

7. Pali for *dharma*.
8. A tree that is directly descended from the one under which the Buddha achieved enlightenment.

But there may be another in whom not even one of these three things is controlled. Then compassion for that person should be aroused thus: 'Though he is going about in the human world now, nevertheless after a certain number of days he will find himself in [one of] the eight great hells or the sixteen prominent hells'. For irritation subsides too through compassion. In yet another all three may be controlled. Then he can remember any of the three in that person, whichever he likes; for the development of lovingkindness towards such a person is easy.

And in order to make the meaning of this clear the following sutta from the Book of Fives should be cited in full: 'Bhikkhus, there are five ways of dispelling annoyance whereby annoyance arisen in a bhikkhu can be entirely dispelled'.

But if irritation still arises in him in spite of his efforts, then he should admonish himself thus:

'Suppose an enemy has hurt
You now in what is his domain,
Why try yourself as well to hurt
Your mind?—That is not his domain.

'In tears you left your family.
They had been kind and helpful too.
So why not leave your enemy,
The anger that brings harm to you?

'This anger that you entertain
Is gnawing at the very roots
Of all the virtues that you guard—
Who is there such a fool as you?

'Another does ignoble deeds,
So you are angry—How is this?
Do you then want to copy too
The sort of acts that he commits?

'Suppose another, to annoy,
Provokes you with some odious act,
Why suffer anger to spring up,
And do as he would have you do?

'If you get angry, then maybe
You make *him* suffer, maybe not;
Though with the hurt that anger brings
You certainly are punished now.

'If anger-blinded enemies
Set out to tread the path of woe,
Do you by getting angry too
Intend to follow heel to toe?

'If hurt is done you by a foe
Because of anger on your part,

Then put your anger down, for why
Should you be harassed groundlessly?

'Since states last but a moment's time
Those aggregates, by which was done
The odious act, have ceased, so now
What is it you are angry with?

'Whom shall he hurt, who seeks to hurt
Another, in the other's absence?
Your presence is the cause of hurt;
Why are you angry, then, with *him*?'

But if resentment does not subside when he admonishes himself thus, then he should review the fact that he himself and the other are owners of their deeds (*kamma*).[9]

Herein, he should first review this in himself thus: 'Now what is the point of your getting angry with him? Will not this kamma of yours that has anger as its source lead to your own harm? For you are the owner of your deeds, heir of your deeds, having deeds as your parent, deeds as your kin, deeds as your refuge; you will become the heir of whatever deeds you do. And this is not the kind of deed to bring you to full enlightenment, to undeclared enlightenment or to the disciple's grade, or to any such position as the status of Brahma or Sakka, or the throne of a Wheel-turning Monarch[1] or a regional king, etc.; but rather this is the kind of deed to lead to your fall from the Dispensation,[2] even to the status of the eaters of scraps, etc., and to the manifold suffering in the hells, and so on. By doing this you are like a man who wants to hit another and picks up a burning ember or excrement in his hand and so first burns himself or makes himself stink'.

Having reviewed ownership of deeds in himself in this way, he should review it in the other also: 'And what is the point of his getting angry with you? Will it not lead to his own harm? For that venerable one is owner of his deeds, heir of his deeds . . . he will become the heir of whatever deeds he does. And this is not the kind of deed to bring him to full enlightenment, to undeclared enlightenment or to the disciple's grade, or to any such position as the status of Brahma or Sakka, or to the throne of a Wheel-turning Monarch or a regional king, etc.; but rather this is the kind of deed to lead to his fall from the Dispensation, even to the status of the eaters of scraps, etc., and to the manifold suffering in the hells, and so on. By doing this he is like a man who wants to throw dust at another against the wind and only covers himself with it'. For this is said by the Blessed One:

'When a fool hates a man that has no hate,
Is purified and free from every blemish,
Such evil he will find comes back on him,
As does fine dust thrown up against the wind'.

---

9. Pali for *karma*.
1. A universal monarch, a figure of Indian mythology who possesses a magic wheel that rolls around the world—every land that it reaches becomes part of his domain. "Brahma": the god who persuaded the Buddha to teach. "Sakka": king of the gods.
2. The Buddha's teaching.

But if it still does not subside in him when he reviews ownership of deeds in this way, then he should review the special qualities of the Master's former conduct.

Here is the way of reviewing it: 'Now you who have gone forth, is it not a fact that when your Master was a Bodhisatta[3] before discovering full enlightenment, while he was still engaged in fulfilling the perfections during the four incalculable ages and a hundred thousand aeons, he did not allow hate to corrupt his mind even when his enemies tried to murder him on various occasions?

'For example, in the Silavant Birth Story when his friends rose to prevent his kingdom of three hundred leagues being seized by an enemy king who had been incited by a wicked minister in whose mind his own queen had sown hate for him, he did not allow them to lift a weapon. Again when he was buried, along with a thousand companions, up to the neck in a hole dug in the earth in a charnel ground, he had no thought of hate. And when, after saving his life by a heroic effort helped by jackals scraping away soil when they had come to devour the corpses, he went with the aid of a spirit to his own bedroom and saw his enemy lying on his own bed, he was not angry but treated him as a friend, undertaking a mutual pledge, and he then exclaimed:

> "The brave aspire, the wise will not lose heart;
> I see myself as I had wished to be".

'And in the Khantivadin Birth Story he was asked by the stupid king of Kasi (Benares[4]), "What do you preach, monk?", and he replied, "I am a preacher of patience"; and when the king had him flogged with scourges of thorns and had his hands and feet cut off, he felt not the slightest anger.

'It is perhaps not so wonderful that an adult who had actually gone forth into homelessness should have acted in that way; but also as an infant he did so. For in the Chula-Dhammapala Birth Story his hands and feet were ordered to be lopped off like four bamboo shoots by his father, King Mahapatapa, and his mother lamented over him thus:

> "Oh, Dhammapala's arms are severed
> That had been bathed in sandalwood;
> He was the heir to all the earth:
> O king, my breath is choking me!"

'Then his father, still not satisfied, commanded that his head be cut off as well. But even then he had not the least trace of hate, since he had firmly resolved thus: "Now is the time to restrain your mind; now, good Dhammapala, be impartial towards these four persons, that is to say, towards your father who is having your head cut off, the man who is beheading you, your lamenting mother, and yourself".

'And it is perhaps not so wonderful that one who had become a human being should have acted in that way; but also as an animal he did so. For while the Bodhisatta was the elephant called Chaddanta he was pierced in the navel by a poisoned shaft. But even then he allowed no hate towards the hunter who had wounded him to corrupt his mind, according as it is said:

---

3. Pali for *bodhisattva*.

4. That is, Varanasi, in modern-day Uttar Pradesh.

"The elephant, when struck by the stout shaft,
Addressed the hunter with no hate in mind:
'What is your aim? What is the reason why
You kill me thus? What can your purpose be?'"

'And when the elephant had spoken thus and was told, "Sir, I have been sent by the king of Kasi's queen to get your tusks", in order to fulfil her wish he cut off his own tusks whose gorgeous radiance glittered with the flashes of the six-coloured rays and gave them to him.

'And when he was the Great Monkey, the man whom he had pulled out of a rocky chasm thought:

"Now this is food for human kind
Like other forest animals,
So why then should a hungry man
Not kill the ape to eat? [I ask.]
I'll travel independently
Taking his meat as a provision;
Thus I shall cross the waste, and that
Will furnish my viaticum".

Then he took up a stone and dashed it on his head. But the monkey looked at him with eyes full of tears and said:

"Oh, act not so, good sir, or else
The fate you reap will long deter
All others from such deeds as this
That you would do to me today".

And with no hate in his mind and regardless of his own pain he saw that the man reached his journey's end in safety.

'And while he was the royal naga (serpent) Bhuridatta, when he had undertaken the Uposatha precepts[5] and was lying on the top of an ant-hill, though he was [caught and] sprinkled with medicinal charms resembling the fire that ushers in the end of an aeon, and was put into a box and treated as a plaything throughout the whole of Jambudipa,[6] yet he had no trace of hate for that brahman, according as it is said:

"While being put into the coffer
And being crushed down with his hand,
I had no hate for Alambana
Lest I should break my precept vow".

'And when he was the royal naga Champeyya he let no hate spring up in his mind while he was being cruelly treated by a snake charmer, according as it is said:

"While I was living in the Law
Observing the Uposatha
A snake charmer took me away
To play with at the royal gate.
Whatever hue he might conceive,

---

5. Precepts that monks communally recite on the 14th or 15th day of the lunar fortnight.

6. The continent on which ordinary human beings dwell.

Blue and yellow, and red as well,
So in accordance with his thought
I would become what he had wished;
I would turn dry land into water,
And water into land likewise.
Now had I given way to wrath
I could have seared him into ash,
Had I relaxed mind-mastery
I should have let my virtue lapse;
And one who lets his virtue lapse
Cannot attain the highest goal".

'And when he was the royal naga Sankhapala, while he was being carried along on a carrying pole by the sixteen village boys after they had wounded him in eight places with sharp spears and inserted thorn creepers into the wounds' orifices, and while, after threading a strong rope through his nose, they were causing him great agony by dragging him along bumping his body on the surface of the ground, though he was capable of turning those village boys to cinders with a mere glance, yet he did not even show the least trace of hate on opening his eyes, according as it is said:

"On the fourteenth and the fifteenth too, Alara,
I regularly kept the Holy Day,
Until there came those sixteen village boys
Bearing a rope and a stout spear as well.
The hunters cleft my nose, and through the slit
They passed a rope and dragged me off like that.
But though I felt such poignant agony,
I let no hate disturb my Holy Day".

'And he performed not only these wonders but also many others too such as those told in the Matuposaka Birth Story. Now it is in the highest degree improper and unbecoming to you to arouse thoughts of resentment, since you are emulating as your Master that Blessed One who reached omniscience and who has in the special quality of patience no equal in the world with its deities'.

But if, as he reviews the special qualities of the Master's former conduct, the resentment still does not subside in him, since he has long been used to the slavery of defilement, then he should review the suttas that deal with the beginninglessness [of the round of rebirths]. Here is what is said: 'Bhikkhus, it is not easy to find a being who has not formerly been your mother . . . your father . . . your brother . . . your sister . . . your son . . . your daughter'. Consequently he should think about that person thus: 'This person, it seems, as my mother in the past carried me in her womb for ten months and removed from me without disgust, as if it were yellow sandalwood, my urine, excrement, spittle, snot, etc., and played with me in her lap, and nourished me, carrying me about on her hip. And this person as my father went by goat paths and paths set on piles, etc., to pursue the trade of merchant, and he risked his life for me by going into battle in double array, by sailing on the great ocean in ships and doing other difficult things, and he nourished me by bringing back wealth by one means or another thinking to feed his children.

And as my brother, sister, son, daughter, this person gave me such and such help. So it is unbecoming for me to harbour hate for him in my mind'.

But if he is still unable to quench that thought in this way, then he should review the advantages of lovingkindness thus: 'Now you who have gone forth into homelessness, has it not been said by the Blessed One as follows: "Bhikkhus, when the mind-deliverance of lovingkindness is cultivated, developed, much practised, made the vehicle, made the foundation, established, consolidated, and properly undertaken, eleven blessings can be expected. What are the eleven? A man sleeps in comfort, wakes in comfort, and dreams no evil dreams, he is dear to human beings, he is dear to non-human beings, deities guard him, fire and poison and weapons do not affect him, his mind is easily concentrated, the expression of his face is serene, he dies unconfused, if he penetrates no higher he will be reborn in the Brahma-world".[7] If you do not stop this thought, you will be denied these advantages'.

But if he is still unable to stop it in this way, he should try resolution into elements. How? 'Now you who have gone forth into homelessness, when you are angry with him, what is it you are angry with? Is it head hairs you are angry with? Or body hairs? Or nails? . . . Or is it urine you are angry with? Or alternatively, is it the earth element in the head hairs, etc., you are angry with? Or the water element? Or the fire element? Or is it the air element you are angry with? Or among the five aggregates[8] or the twelve bases or the eighteen elements with respect to which this venerable one is called by such and such a name, which then, is it the materiality aggregate you are angry with? Or the feeling aggregate, the perception aggregate, the formations aggregate, the consciousness aggregate you are angry with? Or is it the eye base you are angry with? Or the visible-object base you are angry with? . . . Or the mind base you are angry with? Or the mental-object base you are angry with? Or is it the eye element you are angry with? Or the visible-object element? Or the eye-consciousness element? . . . Or the mind element? Or the mental-object element? Or the mind-consciousness element you are angry with?' For when he tries the resolution into elements, his anger finds no foothold, like a mustard seed on the point of an awl or a painting on the air.

But if he cannot effect the resolution into elements, he should try the giving of a gift. It can either be given by himself to the other or accepted by himself from the other. But if the other's livelihood is not purified and his requisites are not proper to be used, it should be given by oneself. And in the one who does this the annoyance with that person entirely subsides. And in the other even anger that has been dogging him from a past birth subsides at the moment, as happened to the senior elder who received a bowl given to him at the Chittalapabbata Monastery by an almsfood-eater elder who had been three times made to move from his lodging by him, and who presented it with these words: 'Venerable sir, this bowl worth eight ducats was given me by my mother who is a lay devotee, and it is rightly obtained; let the good lay devotee acquire merit'. So efficacious is this act of giving. And this is said:

'A gift for taming the untamed,
A gift for every kind of good;

7. The heaven of the god Brahma.
8. The five elements that constitute the mind and body.

Through giving gifts they do unbend
And condescend to kindly speech'.

When his resentment towards that hostile person has been thus allayed, then he can turn his mind with lovingkindness towards that person too, just as towards the one who is dear, the very dear friend, and the neutral person. Then he should break down the barriers by practising lovingkindness over and over again, accomplishing mental impartiality towards the four persons, that is to say, himself, the dear person, the neutral person and the hostile person.

The characteristic of it is this. Suppose this person is sitting in a place with a dear, a neutral, and a hostile person, himself being the fourth; then bandits come to him and say, 'Venerable sir, give us a bhikkhu', and on being asked why, they answer, 'So that we may kill him and use the blood of his throat as an offering'; then if that bhikkhu thinks, 'Let them take this one, or this one', he has not broken down the barriers. And also if he thinks, 'Let them take me but not these three', he has not broken down the barriers either. Why? Because he seeks the harm of him whom he wishes to be taken and seeks the welfare of the others only. But it is when he does not see a single one among the four people to be given to the bandits and he directs his mind impartially towards himself and towards those three people that he has broken down the barriers. Hence the Ancients said:

'When he discriminates between
The four, that is himself, the dear,
The neutral, and the hostile one,
Then "skilled" is not the name he gets,
Nor "having amity at will",
But only "kindly towards beings".

'Now when a bhikkhu's barriers
Have all the four been broken down,
He treats with equal amity
The whole world with its deities;
Far more distinguished than the first
Is he who knows no barriers'.

Thus the sign and access are obtained by this bhikkhu simultaneously with the breaking down of the barriers. But when breaking down of the barriers has been effected, he reaches absorption in the way described under the earth kasina[9] without trouble by cultivating, developing, and repeatedly practising that same sign.

At this point he has attained the first jhana, which abandons five factors, possesses five factors, is good in three ways, is endowed with ten characteristics, and is accompanied by lovingkindness. And when that has been obtained, then by cultivating, developing, and repeatedly practising that same sign, he successively reaches the second and third jhanas in the fourfold system, and the second, third and fourth in the fivefold system.

9. A device to develop one's concentration.

Now it is by means of one of these jhanas beginning with the first that he 'Dwells pervading (intent upon) one direction with his heart endued with lovingkindness, likewise the second direction, likewise the third direction, likewise the fourth direction, and so above, below, and around; everywhere and equally he dwells pervading the entire world with his heart endued with lovingkindness, abundant, exalted, measureless, free from enmity, and free from affliction'. For this versatility comes about only in one whose consciousness has reached absorption in the first jhana and the rest.

And here *endued with lovingkindness* means possessing lovingkindness. *With his heart (chetasa)*: with his mind *(chittena)*. *One direction*: this refers to any one direction in which a being is first discerned and means pervasion of the beings included in that one direction. *Pervading*: touching, making his object. *He dwells (viharati)*: he causes the occurrence of an abiding *(vihara—* dwelling or continuation) in postures that is devoted to the divine abidings. *Likewise the second*: just as he dwells pervading any one direction among those beginning with the eastern one, so he does with the next one, and the third and the fourth, is the meaning.

So above: in that same way in the upper direction is what is meant. *Below, around*: so too the lower direction and the direction all round. Herein, *below* is underneath, and *around* is in the intermediate directions. So he sends his heart full of lovingkindness back and forth in all directions like a horse in a circus ground. Up to this point specified pervasion with lovingkindness is shown in the discernment of each direction separately.

Everywhere, etc., is said for the purpose of showing unspecified pervasion. Herein, *everywhere* means in all places. *Equally (sabbattataya)*: to all classed as inferior, medium, superior, friendly, hostile, neutral, etc., just as to oneself *(attata)*; equality with oneself *(atta-samata)* without making the distinction 'This is another being', is what is meant. Or alternatively, *equally (sabbattataya)* is with the whole state of the mind; not reserving even a little, is what is meant. *Entire (sabbavant)*: possessing all beings *(sabbasattavant)*; associated with all beings, is the meaning. *World* is the world of beings.

Endued with lovingkindness is said again here in order to introduce the synonyms beginning with *abundant*. Or alternatively, *endued with lovingkindness* is repeated because the word *likewise* or the word *so* is not repeated here as it was in the case of the [preceding] specified pervasion. Or alternatively, it is said as a way of concluding. And *abundant* should be regarded here as abundance in pervading. But it is *exalted* in plane [from the sensual-sphere plane to the fine-material-sphere plane], *measureless* through familiarity and through having measureless beings as its object, *free from enmity* through abandonment of ill will and hostility, and *free from affliction* through abandonment of grief; without suffering, is what is meant. This is the meaning of the versatility described in the way beginning 'With his heart endued with lovingkindness'.

And just as this versatility is successful only in one whose mind has reached absorption, so too that described in the Patisambhida should be understood to be successful only in one whose mind has reached absorption, that is to say: 'The mind-deliverance of lovingkindness is [practised] with unspecified pervasion in five ways. The mind-deliverance of lovingkindness is [practised] with specified pervasion in seven ways. The mind-deliverance of lovingkindness is [practised] with directional pervasion in ten ways'.

And herein, the mind-deliverance of lovingkindness is [practised] with unspecified pervasion in these five ways: 'May all beings be free from enmity, affliction and anxiety, and live happily. May all breathing things . . . all creatures . . . all persons . . . all those who have a personality be free from enmity, affliction and anxiety, and live happily'.

The mind-deliverance of lovingkindness is [practised] with specified pervasion in these seven ways: 'May all women be free from enmity, affliction and anxiety and live happily. May all men . . . all noble ones . . . all not noble ones . . . all deities . . . all human beings . . . all in states of loss be free from enmity, affliction and anxiety, and live happily'.

The mind-deliverance of lovingkindness is [practised] with directional pervasion in these ten ways: 'May all beings in the eastern direction be free from enmity, affliction and anxiety, and live happily. May all beings in the western direction . . . northern direction . . . southern direction . . . eastern intermediate direction . . . western intermediate direction . . . northern intermediate direction . . . southern intermediate direction . . . downward direction . . . upward direction be free from enmity, affliction and anxiety, and live happily. May all breathing things in the eastern direction . . . May all creatures in the eastern direction . . . May all persons in the eastern direction . . . May all who have a personality in the eastern direction . . . [etc.] . . . in the upward direction be free from enmity, affliction and anxiety, and live happily. May all women in the eastern direction . . . May all men in the eastern direction . . . May all noble ones in the eastern direction . . . May all not noble ones in the eastern direction . . . May all deities in the eastern direction . . . May all human beings in the eastern direction . . . May all those in states of loss in the eastern direction . . . [etc.] . . . be free from enmity, affliction and anxiety, and live happily'.

Herein, *all* signifies inclusion without exception. *Beings (satta)*: they are held *(satta)*, gripped *(visatta)* by desire and greed for the aggregates beginning with materiality, thus they are beings *(satta)*. For this is said by the Blessed One: 'Any desire for matter, Radha, any greed for it, any delight in it, any craving for it, has held *(satta)* it, has gripped *(visatta)* it, that is why "a being" *(satta)* is said'. But in ordinary speech this term of common usage is applied also to those who are without greed, just as the term of common usage 'palm fan' *(talavanta)* is used for different sorts of fans [in general] even if made of split bamboo. However, [in the world] etymologists *(akkhara-chintaka)* who do not consider meaning have it that it is a mere name, while those who consider meaning have it that a 'being' *(satta)* is so called with reference to the 'bright principle' *(satta)*.

Breathing things (pana): so called because of their state of breathing *(pananata)*; the meaning is, because their existence depends on in-breaths and out-breaths. *Creatures (bhuta)*: so called because of being *(bhutatta* = become-ness); the meaning is, because of their being fully become *(sambhutatta)*, because of their being generated *(abhinibbattatta)*. *Persons (puggala)*: 'pum' is what hell is called; they fall *(galanti)* into that, is the meaning. *Personality (attabhava)* is what the physical body is called; or it is just the pentad of aggregates, since it is actually only a concept derived from that pentad of aggregates. [What is referred to is] included (*pariyapanna*) in that personality, thus it 'has a personality' (*attabhava-pariyapanna*). 'Included in' is delimited by; 'gone into' is the meaning.

And all the remaining [terms] should be understood as synonyms for 'all beings' used in accordance with ordinary speech as in the case of the term 'beings'. Of course, there are other synonyms too for all 'beings', such as all 'folks', all 'souls', etc.; still it is for clarity's sake that 'The mind-deliverance of lovingkindness is [practised] with unspecified pervasion in five ways' is said and that only these five are mentioned.

Those who would have it that there is not only a mere verbal difference between 'beings', 'breathing things', etc., but also an actual difference in meaning, are contradicted by the mention of unspecified pervasion. So instead of taking the meaning in that way, the unspecified pervasion with lovingkindness is done in any one of these five ways.

And here, *may all beings be free from enmity* is one absorption; *free from affliction* is one absorption—free from affliction (*abyabajjha*) is free from afflictedness (*byabadha-rahita*); *free from anxiety* is one absorption—free from anxiety is free from suffering; *may they live happily* is one absorption. Consequently he should do his pervading with lovingkindness according to whichever of these phrases is clear to him. So with the four kinds of absorption in each of the five ways, there are twenty kinds of absorption in unspecified pervasion.

In specified pervasion, with the four kinds of absorption in each of the seven ways, there are twenty-eight kinds of absorption. And here 'woman' and 'man' are stated according to sex; 'noble ones' and 'not noble ones' according to noble ones and ordinary people; 'deities' and 'human beings' and 'those in states of loss' according to the kind of rebirth.

In directional pervasion, with twenty kinds of absorption in each of the directions beginning with 'all beings in the eastern direction', there are two hundred kinds of absorption; and with twenty-eight kinds in each of the directions beginning with 'all woman in the eastern direction' there are two hundred and eighty kinds; so these make four hundred and eighty kinds of absorption. Consequently all the kinds of absorption mentioned in the Patisambhida amount to five hundred and twenty-eight.

So when this meditator develops the mind-deliverance of lovingkindness through any one of these kinds of absorption, he obtains the eleven advantages described in the way beginning 'A man sleeps in comfort.'

Herein, *sleeps in comfort* means that instead of sleeping uncomfortably, turning over and snoring as other people do, he sleeps comfortably, he falls asleep as though entering upon an attainment.

He *wakes in comfort*: instead of waking uncomfortably, groaning and yawning and turning over as others do, he wakes comfortably without contortions, like a lotus opening.

He *dreams no evil dreams*: when he sees dreams, he sees only auspicious ones, as though he were worshipping a shrine, as though he were making an offering, as though he were hearing the Dhamma. But he does not see evil dreams as others do, as though being surrounded by bandits, as though being threatened by wild beasts, as though falling into chasms.

He is dear to human beings: he is as dear to and beloved by human beings as a necklace worn to hang on the chest, as a wreath adorning the head.

He is dear to non-human beings: he is just as dear to non-human beings as he is to human beings, as in the Elder Visakha's case. He was a landowner, it seems, at Pataliputta (Patna). While he was living there he heard this: 'The Island of Tambapanni (Ceylon[1]), apparently, is adorned with a diadem of shrines and gleams with the yellow cloth, and there a man can sit or lie wherever he likes; there the climate is favourable, the abodes are favourable, the people are favourable, the Dhamma to be heard is favourable, and all these favourable things are easily obtained there'.

He made over his fortune to his wife and children and left his home with only a single ducat (*kahapana*) sewn into the hem of his garment. He stopped for one month on the sea coast in expectation of a ship, and meanwhile by his skill in trading he made a thousand during the month by buying goods here and selling them there in lawful enterprise.

Eventually he came to the Great Monastery [(Mahavihara) in Anuradhapura[2]], and there he asked for the going forth into homelessness. When he was being conducted to the chapter house (*sima*) for the going-forth ceremony, the purse containing the thousand pieces dropped out from under his belt. When asked 'What is that?', he replied, 'It is a thousand ducats, venerable sirs'. They told him, 'Lay follower, it is not possible to distribute them after the going forth. Distribute them now'. Then he said, 'Let none who have come to the scene of Visakha's going forth depart empty-handed', and opening [the purse] he strewed them over the chapter house yard, after which he received the going forth and the full admission.

When he had acquired five years' seniority and had become familiar with the two Codes, he celebrated the *Pavarana* at the end of the Rains,[3] took a meditation subject that suited him, and set out to wander, living for four months in each monastery and doing the duties on a basis of equality with the residents. While he was wandering in this way:

> The elder halted in a wood
> To scan the tenor of his way;
> He thundered forth this roundelay
> Proclaiming that he found it good:

> 'So from your full-admission day
> Till in this place you paused and stood
> No stumbling mars your bhikkhuhood;
> Be thankful for such grace, I say'.

On his way to Chittalapabbata[4] he came to a road fork and stood wondering which turn to take. Then a deity living in a rock held out a hand pointing out the road to him.

---

1. Sri Lanka. Patna is in northeast India.
2. The ancient capital of Sri Lanka.
3. The ceremony held by monks at the end of the rains retreat during the monsoon season. "The

two Codes": that is, the codes for monks and nuns.
4. A mountain that was an important monastic center in Sri Lanka.

He came to the Chittalapabbata Monastery. After he had stayed there for four months he lay down thinking, 'In the morning I depart'. Then a deity living in a *manila* tree at the end of the walk sat down on a step of the stair and burst into tears. The elder asked, 'Who is that?'.—'It is I, Maniliya, venerable sir.'—'What are you weeping for?'—'Because you are going away.'—'What good does my living here do you?'—'Venerable sir, as long as you live here non-human beings treat each other kindly. Now when you are gone, they will start quarrels and loose talk.' The elder said, 'If my living here makes you live at peace, that is good', and so he stayed there another four months. Then he again thought of leaving, but the deity wept as before. And so the elder lived on there, and it was there that he attained nibbana.[5]

This is how a bhikkhu who abides in lovingkindness is dear to non-human beings.

Deities guard him: deities guard him as a mother and father guard their child.

Fire, poison and weapons do not affect him: they do not affect, do not enter into, the body of one who abides in lovingkindness, like the fire in the case of the lay woman devotee Uttara, like the poison in the case of the Samyutta reciter the Elder Chula-Siva, like the knife in the case of the novice Sankiccha;[6] they do not disturb the body, is what is meant.

And they tell the story of the cow here too. A cow was giving milk to her calf, it seems. A hunter, thinking 'I shall shoot her', flourished a long-handled spear in his hand and flung it. It struck her body and bounced off like a palm leaf—and that was owing neither to access nor to absorption, but simply to the strength of her consciousness of love for her calf. So mightily powerful is lovingkindness.

His mind is easily concentrated: the mind of one who abides in lovingkindness is quickly concentrated, there is no sluggishness about it.

The expression of his face is serene: his face has a serene expression, like a palmyra fruit loosed from its stem.

He dies unconfused: there is no dying deluded for one who abides in lovingkindness. He passes away undeluded as if falling asleep.

If he penetrates no higher: if he is unable to reach higher than the attainment of lovingkindness and attain Arahantship,[7] then when he falls from this life, he reappears in the Brahma-world as one who wakes up from sleep.

This is the detailed explanation of the development of lovingkindness.

5. Pali for *nirvana*.
6. These stories are all recounted elsewhere in the canon.

7. The status of an arhat, one who enters nirvana at death.

THE WORKINGS OF THE LAW OF KARMA

TREASURY OF HIGHER DOCTRINE
(*The Abhidharmakosha*)

VASUBANDHU

The teachings of the Buddha are traditionally organized into three groups, called the *tripitaka*, the "three baskets." They are the *sutras*, or discourses of the Buddha; the *vinaya*, or code of monastic discipline; and the *abhidharma*, a term that resists easy definition. It combines *dharma*—a famously untranslatable term, which in Buddhism most commonly means "doctrine" or "phenomenon"—with the prefix *abhi*, which can mean either "superior" or "pertaining to." Traditional commentators have thus glossed the term as "special doctrine" or "advanced doctrine," or simply as "pertaining to the doctrine."

In its style and content, the *abhidharma* is the most sober section of the canon, consisting of prose presentations, often quite technical in nature, on the various elements and processes that constitute both the external world and the inner domains of consciousness. In a sense, the *abhidharma* takes the various statements made by the Buddha to various audiences in various contexts, and seeks to derive from them a consistent philosophical system through a process of exegesis. Thus, scholars speculate that the *abhidharma* reflects an effort to systematize the many lists that occur in the sutras.

The *abhidharma* literature treats a wide range of topics, including epistemology, cosmology, psychology, and the function of the law of karma and mechanisms of rebirth, as well as specific processes by which the practice of the path leads to liberation from rebirth. The texts of the *abhidharma* do not have the dialogical form of the sutras, dispensing with the pretense that they were taught by the Buddha. According to one traditional account, the Buddha taught the *abhidharma* to his mother (who had died shortly after his birth) after her rebirth as a deity. He spent one rains retreat teaching the *abhidharma* to the gods in the Heaven of the Thirty-three on the summit of Mount Meru, returning to earth each day to repeat those teachings to the monk Shariputra.

Perhaps the most famous of the many texts on the *abhidharma* is a later independent work, the *Abhidharmakosha*, by the great fourth-century scholar Vasubandhu. Although Vasubandhu would later write Mahayana works (after his conversion, according to tradition, by his brother Asanga), the *Abhidharmakosha* presents positions held by two of the mainstream philosophical schools of Indian Buddhism, the Sarvastivada and the Sautrantika. The book is written in verse, with a prose commentary supplied by Vasubandhu himself. It is divided into eight chapters, and has an important appendix on the nature of the person. Vasubandhu's work was especially influential in East Asia and Tibet; in Tibet, it served as the primary source on the *abhidharma* in the monastic curriculum.

The passage here is drawn from the fifth chapter, which deals with karma, the law of the cause and effect of actions. The specific causes of suffering are said to be ten types of negative deeds, called, literally, the ten "nonvirtues": killing, stealing, sexual misconduct ("illicit sexuality," in this translation), lying, malicious speech, inconsiderate words (specifically, divisive talk), frivolous speech, greed, harmful intent (called "wickedness" here), and wrong views. Such deeds are said to be motivated by the "three poisons": the negative emotions of desire, hatred, and ignorance. The passage begins by considering which of the three poisons motivates which of the nonvirtues. Thus, Vasubandhu explains that killing may be motivated by desire, as when murder is committed in the course of a robbery; by hatred; and by ignorance, as when sacrifice is considered a virtuous deed.

Vasubandhu goes on to consider other questions. He examines what constitutes a "principal cause of action," that is, an action that is carried to completion and thereby can serve as the cause of an entire future lifetime. For example, if a murderer happens to die before his or her victim, the deed, though negative, does not constitute a complete act of murder. In addition, he affirms that an act of murder committed by one member of the group taints each member of the group.

Buddhism famously teaches that there is no self and that skandhas, the constituents of mind and body, are all impermanent, coming into existence and passing out of existence in each moment. If this is the case, what does it mean to murder someone? Vasubandhu says that it is when the life force, itself an impermanent process, is intentionally stopped by another person. He notes that he will consider the nature of the person further in the final chapter.

Following this discussion of the nature of killing, the remainder of the chapter considers what constitutes the other nine types of negative deeds.

PRONOUNCING GLOSSARY

Abhidharmakosha: *a-bee-dar-ma-ko-sha*
abhidhya: *a-bi-dyah*
adhyaropa: *a-dyah-roh-pa*
arthabhijna: *ar-tah-bij-nya*
avijnapti: *a-vij-nyap-ti*
Bhikshu: *bik-shu*
bhinnapralapita: *bin-na-pra-lah-pi-tah*
Chakravartin: *cha-kra-var-tin*
drishta: *drish-ta*
dvaha: *dvah-ha*
kamacchanda: *kah-mach-chan-da*
Kamadhatu: *kah-ma-dah-tu*
karmavachana: *kar-ma-vah-cha-na*
Malakimatar: *mah-la-kee-mah-tar*
matamatram bhavishyati: *ma-ta-mah-tram ba-vish-ya-ti*
mritakalpa: *mri-ta-kal-pa*
namakaya: *nah-ma-kah-ya*
namarupa: *nah-ma-roo-pa*
nanavasa: *nah-nah-va-sa*
nikayasabhaga: *nih-kah-ya-sa-bah-ga*

Nirgrantha: *nir-gran-ta*
Nivarana: *nee-va-ra-na*
parityaga: *pa-ri-tyah-ga*
prandtipata: *prahnd-ti-pah-ta*
prayoktar: *pra-yohk-tar*
Pudgala: *pud-ga-la*
sambhinnapralapa: *sam-bin-na-pra-lah-pa*
samutthapaka: *sa-mut-tah-pa-ka*
Sangha: *san-ga*
Sautrantika: *sau-trahn-ti-ka*
shruta: *shru-ta*
skandha: *skan-da*
Stupa: *stoo-pa*
Sutra: *soo-tra*
tryambuka: *tryam-bu-ka*
Vaibhashika: *vai-bah-shi-ka*
Vibhasha: *vi-bah-shah*
vijnapti: *vij-nyap-ti*
vijnata: *vij-nyah-ta*
vivaha: *vi-vah-ha*
Vrisalas: *vri-sa-las*

The Sutra says, "There are, Oh Bhikshus,[1] three types of killing: killing arisen from desire, killing arisen from hatred, and killing arisen from ignorance," and thus following to, "There are, Oh Bhikshus, three types of false views." What are these different killings, etc.?

TRANSLATED FROM the Chinese into French by Louis de La Vallée Poussin; trans. from the French and Sanskrit by Leo M. Pruden. The translator's parenthetical citations for quotations from canonical Buddhist texts have been deleted.

1. Monks. "The Sutra": the discourse of the Buddha being commented on here.

All the courses of action are not indifferently achieved by desire, hatred, or ignorance; but

Preparatory action arises from three roots.

The preparatory action of all of the courses of action can indifferently arise from the three roots. The Blessed One, by expressing himself as we have seen, refers to the first cause, the cause which gives rise (*samutthapaka*) to the course of action.

Killing arisen from desire: killing in order to seize a certain part of an animal; killing in order to seize some goods; killing for pleasure; killing in order to defend oneself, or one's friends.

Killing arisen from hatred, in order to satiate hostility.

Killing arisen through ignorance. To consider the sacrifice as a pious action and so to kill; when a king, according to the authority of the legalists kills through duty, "The first of the meritorious actions of the king is to punish evil-doers"; when the Persians say, "One should kill one's aged and sick parents"; when one says, "One should kill serpents, scorpions, and *tryambuka* flies, etc., because these creatures are poisonous; one must kill game, cattle, birds, and buffalos in order to nourish oneself."

And finally killing which is provoked by false views: murder committed by a person who denies a future life and whom nothing can stop.

Stealing arisen from desire. Either one steals the object desired, or one steals in order to then gain possession of another object, to acquire honor and respect, or in order to defend oneself and one's friends.

Stealing arisen from hatred, in order to satiate hostility.

Stealing arisen from ignorance. A king, upon the authority of the legalists, seizes the goods of evil-doers. The Brahmins say, "All things have been given to the Brahmins by Brahma, and it is through the weakness of the Brahmins that the Vrisalas[2] enjoy it. Consequently, when a Brahmin steals, he takes that which belongs to him; he eats what is his, wears what is his, and gives what is his." And yet, when Brahmins take, they indeed have the notion of the goods of another.

Stealing provoked through false views is also stealing from ignorance.

Illicit sexuality arisen from desire. Sexual intercourse with the wife of another, either through love, or in order to obtain honor and respect, or in order to defend oneself and one's friends.

Illicit sexuality arisen through hatred, in order to satiate hostility.

Illicit sexuality arisen from ignorance. The Persians, etc., have intercourse with their mothers and other forbidden women. In the *gosava* sacrifice, a Brahmin drinks water in the manner of an animal, grazes through the grass, has intercourse with his mother, his sister, or a woman of his *gotra;*[3] he must copulate with them wherever he finds them: in this manner this bull will triumph over the world. And such too are those that say, "Women are like rice mortars, flowers, fruits, cooked food, ladders, roads, and ferryboats: they are there to be used."

Lying and other vocal transgressions arisen from ignorance and from hatred, as above.

---

2. Those of lowest caste, the shudras. "Brahma": in Hindu theology, the creator god.   3. Lineage.

Lying arisen from ignorance. "Oh King, playful lying, lying to women, in marriage, or in danger of death, does not hurt: one says that these five lies are not transgressions." This is lying provoked by false views.

Malicious words and other vocal transgressions arisen from ignorance. These are provoked through false views. Further, the false discourses of the *Vedas*,[4] etc., are frivolous words arisen from ignorance.

How do greed, wickedness and false views arise out of desire, etc.? Since they are not preparatory action, this creates a difficulty:

> Greed and the other two mental courses arise from the three roots because they appear subsequent to these roots.

When they appear immediately after desire, they arise from desire; the same for the other two roots.

We have explained the bad courses of action in their relationship with the roots. As for the good courses of action,

> Good actions, with their preparatory and consecutive actions, arise from non-desire, non-hatred, and non-ignorance.

Good courses of action, with their preparatory and consecutive actions, have a good mind for their originating (*pravartaka*) cause. This good mind, being necessarily associated with the three roots, arises from the three roots.

The renouncing of a preparation of a bad course of action is a preparation of a good course of action; the renouncing of the action proper which constitutes a bad course of action is itself a good course of action; the renouncing of a consecutive action of a bad course of action is a consecutive action of a good course of action.

Let us give as an example: the ordination of a novice. From the moment when the novice enters into the *nanavasa*, salutes the Sangha, addresses his request to the Upadhyaya, until the first or second *karmavachana*,[5] this is the preparatory action. At the achievement of the third *karmavachana* there takes place a *vijnapti*, and an *avijnapti*[6] simultaneous to this *vijnapti*, which constitute the course of action itself. After this moment, when one notifies the new monk of the *nishrayas*,[7] when he makes known that he accepts them, and as long as the series of the *avijnapti* created by the principal action continues—that is to say, as long as the monk does not lose the Pratimoksha discipline[8]—this is the consecutive action.

We have seen that bad courses of action were not indifferently "achieved" by the three roots.

> Killing, wickedness, and injurious words are achieved through hate.

4. Four canonical texts of Hinduism.
5. "Stating of the matter": a proposition—e.g., that a man should be ordained—that is placed before the order of monks and to which they must assent. "*Nanavasa*": the place where the ordination of a monk occurs. "Upadhyaya": "preceptor," the monk who performs the ordination ceremony.
6. "Non informative" [event], a subtle and invisible karmic force created when an action is performed. "*Vijnapti*": "informative" [event], an action that is communicative.
7. The requisites allowed to a monk, typically listed as four: eating alms food, wearing a robe made from rags, dwelling at the foot of a tree, and using cow's urine for medicine.
8. The code of monastic conduct.

Solely by hate. They are achieved when one thought of murder, or one thought of violence (concerning wickedness and injurious words) manifests itself.

Adultery, greed, and stealing are achieved through desire.

"Adultery" is illicit sexuality.

False views, through ignorance.

Through an extreme ignorance.

The others, by the three.

The other courses of action,—lying, malicious words, and inconsiderate words,—are achieved either through desire, hatred, or ignorance.

The courses of action, which have just been divided into four sections, three, three, one and three, have respectively for their

Object: living beings, objects of enjoyment, *namarupa*, and *naman*.[9]

Living beings are the objects of killing, wickedness and injurious speech; the objects of enjoyment are the objects of adultery, greed and stealing; *namarupa,* that is, the five *skandhas*,[1] are the object of false views; *naman*, that is, the *namakaya* is the object of lying and the other two transgressions of the voice.

When one has decided to kill someone, and if the murderer dies either before the intended victim, or if he dies at precisely the same moment as the victim, is there a principal course of action for the author of the murder?

If one dies before or at the same time, there is no principal course of action.

This is why the *Vibhasha*[2] says, "Question: When a person has made the preparation for killing, can it be that, at the moment when the result of this preparation is achieved, this person is not touched by the transgression of killing? Answer: Yes, when the murderer dies before or at the same time [as the victim]." The reason is clear: as long as the victim is living, the murderer is not touched by the transgression of murder; and when the victim dies, he (=the murderer) no longer exists if he died at the same time or before.

Because a new body has come into existence.

The body—the personality—by whom the preparation had been accomplished, the body of the murderer, is destroyed; the murderer takes up a new body which belongs to another *nikayasabhaga*: this body did not make the preparation, is not *prayoktar*[3] and, as a consequence, cannot be touched by the transgression of murder.

9. Literally, "name," the immaterial components of the person. *"Namarupa"*: literally, "name and form," a term for the mind and body.
1. The five "aggregates," a standard division of the constituents of mind and body into five groups: form, feeling, discrimination, compositional factors, and consciousness.

2. The Mahavibhasha, a famous commentary on the *abhidharma* (see the introduction to this selection).
3. The agent of an action. *"Nikayasabhaga"*: literally, "similarity of type," in this case a new rebirth or existence.

When many persons are united with the intention to kill, either in war, or in the hunt, or in banditry, who is guilty of murder, if only one of them kills?

As soldiers, etc., concur in the realization of the same effect, all are as guilty as the one who kills.

Having a common goal, all are guilty exactly as he who among them kills, for all mutually incite one another, not through speech, but by the very fact that they are united together in order to kill.

But is the person who has been constrained through force to join the army also guilty?

Evidently so, unless he has formed the resolution, "Even in order to save my life, I shall not kill a living being."

What does he do in order that he who kills should commit the course of action? Same question for the other transgressions up to and including false views.

Murder is to kill another, consciously, without making an error.

When a person kills by thinking, "I am killing such a one," and kills this same person, and not another through error, then there is murder.

But is there murder when a person kills, doubting if he hits a living being or a thing, or if he hits another?

This person possesses the certitude, "This is certainly him"; he hits him; and as a consequence, there is the thought of *parityaga*.[4]

How can there be murder, or destruction of the *prana* (*pranatipata*), since the *skandhas* are momentary?

Prana, the "vital breath", is a wind whose existence depends on the body and the mind. This *prana* is annihilated by a murderer in the same way in which one annihilates a flame or a sound of a bell, that is to say, by obstructing the continuation of its reproducing itself.

Or rather, *prana* is the vital organ (*jivitendriya*): when a person creates an obstacle to the arising of a new moment of the vital organ, he annihilates it, and is touched by the transgression of killing.

But to whom do you attribute the vital organ? Who do you say is dead when life is absent?

The true value of the pronoun "to whom" or "of whom" will be examined in the chapter on the Refutation of the Pudgala.[5] Let us observe that the Blessed One said, "When life, heat and consciousness leave the body, it lies abandoned, like a piece of wood, deprived of feeling." One says that the body lives when it is endowed with the organs; and that the body is dead when it is devoid of them.

According to the Nirgranthas,[6] a transgression (*adharma*) results for the doer from killing, even committed without knowing it, or without desiring it, in the way that contact with fire results in burning.

But if this is the case, then one is guilty when one sees, or touches, without wanting to, the wife of another; he who trims the hair of the Nirgranthas

4. Killing.
5. The Person.

6. Jains.

is guilty; the master of the Nirgranthas is guilty since he preaches terrible austerities; he who gives the Nirgranthas food which provokes cholera and death is also guilty. The mother and the embryo which are both the cause of suffering, are guilty; guilty also is the person killed, for he is bound to the action of killing as the object killed: and fire burns its own support. But on the other hand, he who has murder committed by another is not guilty, for one is not himself burned when one has another person touch the fire. Since you do not take intention into consideration, wood and other materials, even though lacking consciousness, are guilty of murder when a house collapses and living beings perish. If you would avoid these consequences, recognize that but one example—the example of the fire—and it alone, not accompanied by any argument, cannot prove your thesis.

> Stealing—taking what is not given—is to appropriate to oneself
> the goods of another through force or in secret.

The reservation above holds: "with the condition that there has been no error."

To appropriate to oneself, through force or in secret, that which is possessed by another, when one does not confuse the person from whom one wants to steal with another person, constitutes stealing.

The plunder of a Stupa is to take a thing that has not been given by the Buddha: for, at the moment of Nirvana, the Blessed One accepted, appropriated to himself all the gifts made to Stupas. According to others, this is to take a thing which has not been given by the guardians of the Stupa.

To take a thing that does not have an owner is to take what is not given by the ruler of the country.

To take the goods, the robes, etc, of an deceased monk, is to take what is not given by the Sangha of the parish, in the case when an ecclesiastical action has not been done; in the opposite case, this is to take what is not given by all the disciples of the Buddha.

> Illicit sexuality, fourfold, is intercourse with a woman with whom
> one should not have intercourse.

Intercourse with a forbidden woman, that is, the wife of another, one's mother, one's daughter, or one's paternal or maternal relations; Intercourse with one's own wife through a forbidden way; in an unsuitable place: an uncovered spot, a *chaitya*, an *aranya*;[7] at an unsuitable time: when the wife is pregnant, when she is nursing, or when she has taken a vow. Some say: when she has taken a vow only with the consent of her husband.

The reservation relative to killing, "with the condition that there has been no error," also extends to illicit sexuality, and there is no course of action when one has intercourse with the wife of another if one thought that he was with his own wife.

Opinions differ on whether there is a course of action when one takes the wife of a certain one for the wife of another one. For some, yes, for it is the wife of another who was the object of the preparatory action; it is also the wife of another that one enjoys. For others, no, as in the case of killing with an

---

7. A forest, often one inhabited by ascetics. *"Chaitya"*: a shrine.

error of person: the object of the preparatory action is not the object of the enjoyment.

With regard to whom is intercourse with Bhikshunis[8] illicit sexuality?

With regard to the master of the land, who is not disposed to tolerate it. As for the master of the country himself, if his spouse, when she has undertaken a vow, is forbidden to him, all the more reason are nuns so forbidden.

Intercourse with a young girl is illicit with regard to the man to whom she is engaged, and, if she is not engaged, with regard to her guardian; if she has no guardian, then with regard to the king.

> Lying is discourse held, with differing thoughts, with a person who understands the meaning.

Lying is discourse held, with thoughts different from the sense expressed, with a person who understands the meaning. When the person addressed does not understand, such discourse is only frivolous words.

Discourse is sometimes made up of numerous syllables. Which will be the course of action? Which will be lies?

The last syllable, which is *vijnapti* and which is accompanied by *avijnapti*. Or rather, the syllable whose hearing causes the meaning to be understood. The preceeding syllables are a preparation for the lie.

How should one interpret the expression *arthabhijna*, "a person who understands the meaning?" Does this refer to the moment when the person addressed understands the meaning? Does it refer to a person addressed capable of understanding the meaning? In the first hypothesis, you admit that the course of action takes place when the person addressed has understood the meaning; it follows then that the course of action is solely *avijnapti*: for the person addressed understood the meaning through mental consciousness, which is consecutive to auditory consciousness; and the *vijnapti*, or vocal action, perishes at the same time as the auditory consciousness. There is no longer any *vijnapti* at the moment when the person addressed understands. In the second hypothesis, this difficulty is not present. But what must one do in order that the person addressed is "capable of understanding the meaning?"

The person who knows the language and in whom auditory consciousness has arisen is "capable of understanding the meaning."

One must interpret the text in a manner in which it will not give rise to criticism.

The Sutra teaches that there are sixteen "vocal actions," eight of which are bad: to say that one has seen what one has not seen, to say that one has heard, cognized, or known what one has not heard, cognized, or known; to say that one has not seen when one has seen; and to say that one has not heard, cognized, or known when one has heard, cognized, or known; and eight are good: to say that one has not seen when one has not seen . . .

What is the meaning of the words seen (*drishta*), heard (*shruta*), cognized (*vijnata*), and known (*mata*)?

> What is perceived through the visual consciousness, through the auditory consciousness, through the mental consciousness, and

8. Nuns.

through three consciousnesses, is called, in order, seen, heard, cognized, and known.

What is perceived through the visual consciousness receives the name of seen, . . . what is perceived through the consciousness of smell, taste, and touch, receives the name of known.

How do you justify this last interpretation?

The Vaibhashikas[9] say that odors, tastes and tangible things, being morally neutral, are as dead (*mritakalpa*); this is why they are called *mata*.

The Sautrantikas:[1] According to what authority do you maintain that the expression *mata* refers to what is smelled, tasted, and touched?

The Vaibhashikas: According to the Sutra, and by virtue of reasoning.

The Sutra says, "What do you think, Oh Malakimatar, the visible objects that you have not seen, that you have not seen formerly, that you do not see, about which you do not think 'Would that I could see them,' do you have, by reason of them, any longing, lust, desire, affection, attachment, appetite, or searching out? No, Lord. Oh Malakimatar, with regard to the subject seen, you will only think, 'it is seen,' with regard to the subject heard, cognized, and known, you will only think, 'it is heard, cognized, known (*matamatram bhavishyati*).'"

The words "seen," "heard," and "cognized," certainly refer to visible things, to sounds, and to the *dharmas*: hence the word *mata* refers to smells, tastes, and tangible things. If it were otherwise, the experience relative to smells, tastes and tangible things would not be referred to in this teaching of the Blessed One.

The Sautrantikas: This Sutra does not have the meaning that you believe it does, and it does not confirm your interpretation of the word *mata*. The Blessed One does not aim to define the characteristics of the four experiences, having seen, having heard, having cognized, having *mata*. His mind is evidently, "In the fourfold experience, seeing, etc.,—each of which bears on the sixfold objects, visible things, sounds, smells, tastes, tangible things and *dharmas*,—you maintain only that this experience takes place, that you see, etc., without attributing (*adhyaropa*) to the object the characteristic of disagreeable or agreeable."

Then what should one thus understand by seen, heard, *mata* (known) and cognized?

According to the Sautrantikas, that which is immediately perceived by the five material organs, is seen, *drishta*; that the consciousness of which is transmitted to us by another, is heard, *shruta*; what is admitted by reason of correct reasoning, is *mata*, known; and what is perceived by the mental organ is cognized, *vijnata*. Thus five categories of objects—visible matter, sounds, odors, tastes, and tangible things—are seen, heard, known, and cognized; the sixth category—*dharmas*—is not seen: such is the fourfold experience that the Sutra refers to. It is thus false that, in the hypothesis where *mata* does not designate odors, tastes, and tangible matter, the experience relative to these objects would be omitted in the Sutra: thus the argument of the Vaibhashikas does not hold.

9. A school of Buddhist philosophy. 1. A school of Buddhist philosophy.

According to former masters, "seen" is what is perceived by the organ of seeing; "heard" is what is perceived by the organ of hearing and what one learns from another: "known" is what is personally accepted or experienced; and "cognized" is what one feels in and of oneself (i.e., agreeable sensation, etc., or an intuition that one has in an absorption).

Does he who, by means of his body and not by means of speech, causes to be understood what is not in his mind, commit lying?

Yes. The Shastra[2] says in fact, "Question: Can one be touched by the transgression of killing, without acting, without attacking bodily? Answer: Yes, when one acts vocally. Question: Can one be touched by the transgression of lying without vocal action? Answer: Yes, when one acts bodily. Question: Can one be touched by the transgression of murder, by the transgression of lying, without either bodily or vocal action? Answer: Yes, for example the Rishis,[3] guilty of murder through their anger, and a Bhikshu, guilty of lying through his silence in the confession ceremony."

But, we would say, how could one admit that Rishis and a Bhikshu accomplish a course of action which is at one and the same time *vijnapti* and *avijnapti*? Neither the Rishis nor a Bhikshu have bodily or vocal action: hence there is no *vijnapti*; and *avijnapti* of the sphere of Kamadhatu[4] cannot exist where *vijnapti* is absent. This is a difficulty that must be resolved.

> Malicious or slanderous speech is the discourse of a person with a defiled mind with a view to dividing.

The discourse that one has, with a defiled mind, with a view to dividing others and creating enmity, is malicious speech.

The restrictions formulated above, "when the person addressed understands, when there is no confusion of persons," applies here.

> Injurious words are abusive discourse.

Discourse pronounced with a defiled mind, outraging, understood by him whom one addresses, addressed to him whom one wants to address, is injurious speech.

> All defiled discourse is inconsiderate speech.

The Karika[5] has "all defiled . . ."; but it refers here to discourse.

All defiled discourse is inconsiderate speech; one who utters it is thus an "inconsiderate speaker"; but the Karika has *bhinnapralapita* in place of *sambhinnapralapa*.[6]

> According to others, inconsiderate speech is the defiled discourse which differs from the others.

> Lying, malicious and injurious speech and defiled discourse: the name "inconsiderate speech" is reserved for the defiled speech which is neither lying, nor malicious, nor injurious.

---

2. Commentary.
3. Sages.
4. Realm of desire.

5. Verse.
6. The more common term for "senseless speech."

For example, boasting, singing, declamations; for example, bad commentaries.

For example, a monk boasts about himself in order to obtain alms, etc; through frivolity some others sing; in the course of plays or dances, the dancers, in order to entertain the public, hold inconsiderate discourse; adopting the doctrines of bad philosophers, non-Buddhists read bad commentaries. And in addition, there are lamentations and loquaciousness, carried out with a defiled mind but which differ from lying, malicious speech and injurious speech.

But is it not true that, in the period of a Chakravartin King,[7] there are songs that do not have inconsiderate words?

In this period, songs are inspired by a spirit of detachment, not by sensuality. Or, according to another opinion, there is, in this period, inconsiderate words, since one speaks of *avaha*, of *vivaha*,[8] etc.; but this inconsiderate speech does not constitute the course of action of this name.

> Greed is the desire to appropriate to oneself, by illegitimate means, the goods of another.

To desire to appropriate to oneself the goods of another in an illegitimate manner, in an unjust manner, by force or secretly—"Would that the goods of another were mine!"—is the course of action called greed, *abhidhya*.

According to another opinion, *abhidhya* means all desire of the sphere of Kamadhatu, for the *Sutra of the Five Nivaranas*,[9] on the subject of *kamacchanda*, expresses itself thusly, "Having abandoned *abhidhya* . . ."

But, say other masters, Chakravartin Kings and the Uttarakurus[1] are not guilty of the course of *abhidhya* action, and yet they are not delivered from desire of the sphere of Kamadhatu.

Let us admit that all desire of the sphere of Kamadhatu is *abhidhya*; but all *abhidhya* is not a course of action. Only the most notable among the bad practices are included among the courses of action.

> Wickedness is a hatred of living beings.

It is a hatred of living beings, by which one desires to harm the person of another.

> False view is the opinion that there is neither good nor bad.

As it is said in the Sutra, "There is no gift, no sacrifice, no oblation, no good action, no bad action . . . there are no Arhats in the world." False view, as this Sutra shows, consists of negating action, its results, and the existence of Aryans.[2] The Karika only indicates the beginning.

Such is the definition of the ten bad courses of action.

---

7. A wheel-turning monarch: a figure of Indian mythology who possesses a magic wheel that rolls around the world—every land that it reaches becomes part of his domain.

8. The leading of the bride away by the bridegroom's family. "*Avaha*": the leading of a bride by the bride's family.

9. Hindrances, the five qualities that obstruct the development of concentration. One of them is sensual desire (*kamacchanda*).

1. Inhabitants of the northern continent in Buddhist cosmology.

2. The Buddha reinterpreted "Aryan," originally an ethnic self-designation by the Vedic Hindus, to mean a spiritual nobility acquired through the practice of the Buddhist path.

MAHAYANA SUTRAS

THE LOTUS SUTRA

WHITE LOTUS OF THE TRUE DHARMA
(*The Saddharmapundarika*)

On a full moon night in May, more than 2,500 years ago, the Buddha is said to have gained full knowledge of the nature of reality. The Buddha understood everything there is to know. How, then, has Buddhism evolved in the subsequent centuries? How has the tradition changed? And how has it understood innovation? In some sense, there can be nothing new, nothing that the Buddha did not know. Thus, if innovation is to occur, it must be backdated, and added to the contents of the Buddha's capacious enlightenment so long ago.

One of the most important innovations in the history of Buddhism is what has come to be known by a single Sanskrit word: *Mahayana,* the "Great Vehicle." Scholars have debated how new the Mahayana really was, how much of a break it represented from what had come before. But one text clearly saw a break and felt compelled to explain it. That text is the *White Lotus of the True Dharma* (*Saddharmapundarika*), better known simply as the *Lotus Sutra*. It is the most important of the Mahayana sutras, and arguably the most influential single text in the history of Buddhism. It was also the first Buddhist sutra to be translated from Sanskrit into a European language, published in French in 1852 by Eugène Burnouf as *Le Lotus de la bonne loi.*

As is true of all Mahayana sutras, the author of the *Lotus Sutra* is unknown. Its date of composition cannot be specified with much precision; it cannot have been written later than the date of its earliest translation into Chinese, 267 C.E. On the basis of internal evidence, scholars speculate that the sutra dates from the latter half of the first century C.E. Like many sutras, it developed in stages, beginning with verses that were then supplemented with prose paraphrases, elaborations, and frames. Into this core text a number of freestanding chapters were interpolated (some of which went on to become important texts in their own right), resulting in a sutra of twenty-eight chapters. The sutra in this final form was likely complete by around 150 C.E.

Just as the author of the sutra is unknown, so is the audience for which it was originally intended. However, scholars speculate that the *Lotus Sutra* had a devoted following of monks, nuns, and laypeople, who believed, as the sutra declares, that the Buddha did not suffer doubts as a prince, did not mortify his flesh through the practice of austerities, and did not achieve enlightenment under the Bodhi tree at the age of thirty-five (as described in the *Ariyapariyesana Sutta* and *Nidanakatha,* pp. 119 and 131); instead, he had been enlightened long ago and only pretended to do these things in order to offer inspiration to the world. Furthermore, the sutra proclaims that the Buddha did not die and disappear into nirvana (as described in the *Great Discourse on the Final Nirvana,* p. 158); instead, his lifespan is immeasurable, and he only pretended to die to spur his disciples in their practice of the path. The original audience of the *Lotus Sutra* was likely centered around one or more stupas, the famous reliquaries that contain ashes of the Buddha. But because the Buddha did not die, the stupa is said to contain not his desiccated remains but the living Buddha: in the eleventh chapter of the sutra, a stupa opens to reveal the Buddha seated within.

Like other Mahayana sutras, the *Lotus Sutra* was regarded not as simply a component of a large canon but rather as an independent work, sufficiently rich to serve as the single foundation for the practice of the "true dharma." And the anonymous author is not reluctant to declare this superior status, though in such a way that the text seems to take on a life of its own and to speak for itself. In a device common to the Mahayana sutras, the *Lotus Sutra* repeatedly extols its own virtues, and the rewards assured to its devotees. It is as if in reading the Bible one found the statement, "Whoever recites, copies, or offers flowers to this Gospel of Mark is certain to enter the kingdom of heaven." Such declarations were taken quite literally by generations of readers, as the stories in the *Accounts in Dissemination and Praise of the* Lotus Sutra (p. 518) attest.

The sutra was translated into Chinese again in 406 by the great Kumarajiva (344–413), a monk of Indian ancestry known for his fluent rendering of Sanskrit texts into Chinese. His translation would become highly influential in East Asia. As the Chinese sought to organize the vast amount of Buddhist literature being translated from Indic languages, they developed classification systems that arranged various sutras hierarchically. One of the most significant of these was that of the Tiantai school (named after the mountain where its chief temple was located), which declared that the *Lotus Sutra* represented the fullest exposition of the Buddha's enlightenment. This school would become important in both Japan (as Tendai) and Korea (as Cheontae). In Japan, Nichiren (1222–1282), a Tendai monk who became the founder of his own sect, would declare that during the current degenerate age, devotion to the *Lotus Sutra* was the only acceptable and effective form of Buddhist practice (see his *Treatise on the Establishment of the Orthodox Teaching and the Peace of the Nation*, p. 637).

The section of the *Lotus Sutra* presented here, perhaps the most famous of the many powerful moments in this renowned sutra, offers a solution to a dilemma mentioned above: how to accommodate innovation when there is nothing that the Buddha did not reveal. The Buddha said that he did not teach "with a closed fist." About four centuries after the death of the Buddha, new texts began to appear in India, texts referred to as the "discourses of the Great Vehicle." These Mahayana sutras, which purported to be records of teachings of the historical Buddha, open, as all sutras do, with the statement, "Thus did I hear." Yet they were previously unknown to the monastic community of Buddhist India, and they presented doctrines that likewise were unknown. Among the most important of these doctrines was that all beings would one day achieve buddhahood.

In the mainstream tradition, in each historical age only one person followed the long path of the bodhisattva to achieve buddhahood. That buddha then taught the dharma to the world, and those who followed his teachings—called either "listeners" (*shravaka*) or the "individually enlightened" (*pratyekabuddha*)—followed the path set forth by the buddha to achieve the same state of the cessation of rebirth (*nirvana*) that he had achieved. Those who completed that path were known as *arhats* (literally "worthy ones"), but they did not achieve buddhahood, nor did they need to. The path to liberation had already been set forth; they had merely followed it. Thus, in the mainstream tradition, there were three paths to liberation: the path of the shravaka, the path of pratyekabuddha (both of which led to the state of the arhat) and the path of the bodhisattva, reserved for that rare person who will become the buddha for a historical age far in the future.

The *Lotus Sutra* declares that the nirvana of the arhat is but an illusion, that all beings should forgo the path of the shravaka and the pratyekabuddha and follow the path of the bodhisattva to buddhahood. All beings will become buddhas one day. An inspiring thought—but one that did not seem to appear anywhere in the teachings attributed to the Buddha. The authors of the *Lotus Sutra* thus faced a double challenge. They had both to declare a new teaching and to explain that it was in fact old. This they did by presenting the new teaching as the word of the Buddha. Hence, the *Lotus Sutra*, like all Mahayana sutras, follows the traditional form, beginning with the setting of the scene (specifying where the Buddha was staying and who was in the audience) and the asking of a question, which the Buddha answers. But there was a further challenge: the sutra had to account for the old teaching it was now rejecting. The Buddha had clearly set forth the three vehicles to enlightenment in the mainstream texts. Now he declares that in fact there is but one vehicle, the vehicle that transports all beings to buddhahood. If that is the case, why did he speak of three vehicles in the first place? Had he been wrong? Had he been lying?

This is the question that stands at the center of the chapter below. As it begins, Shariputra, the wisest of the Buddha's disciples and himself already an arhat, expresses his delight at receiving this new teaching of the Buddha. Apparently aware of the charge of innovation, the Buddha explains that the teaching of the single vehicle is not new: he had

Statue of the monk Shariputra.

taught it to Shariputra in a previous lifetime ages ago, but Shariputra had forgotten it. The Buddha then predicts that Shariputra will himself become a buddha in the future, and describes the circumstances of his buddhahood. Shariputra rejoices in his destiny, but tells the Buddha that the other members of the assembly are wondering why the Buddha had not explained to them earlier that there is in fact but one vehicle to enlightenment. The Buddha responds with the most famous parable in Buddhist literature, the parable of the burning house.

The children of a kind and wealthy father are playing in his decaying mansion (described in frightening detail) when a fire breaks out. The father sees the flames and calls out to his children to escape, but they are so absorbed in their games that they pay him no heed. Fearing that they will perish in the conflagration, he calls out again, telling them that he has special gifts awaiting them outside: there are carts, some drawn by a sheep, some drawn by a deer, some drawn by an ox. The children give up their games and run out of the house. But when they reach their father, there is only one kind of cart: large and beautiful, with jeweled cords and red pillows, it is drawn by a powerful white ox of steady gait. The father is so wealthy that there are enough of these magnificent carts for each of the children, who happily climb on.

The Buddha then asks Shariputra whether the father had deceived his children, and Shariputra immediately answers, "No": he had used a skillful method in order to save their lives. This term, "skillful means" (*upayakaushalya* in Sanskrit, also translated "skillful methods," "skill in means," and "expedient means"), would become a key concept for the Mahayana. In the early tradition, the Buddha was sometimes compared to a physician, who does not prescribe the same medicine for every malady but gives each person what is appropriate. And thus the Buddha was known to adapt his teaching to the needs of the audience. In the Mahayana, this notion develops into a central tenet, one that allows for significant innovation by having the Buddha explain (away) a previous teaching as something intended for a particular audience.

The Buddha next spells out the meaning of the parable. The burning house is the cycle of rebirth, the children are all sentient beings, the father is the Buddha. Sentient beings are so attached to the distractions of samsara that they are unaware of the dangers all around them: they live in a world ablaze with birth, old age, sickness, and death, a world burning with greed, hatred, and ignorance. The Buddha knows that were he simply to declare this truth to sentient beings they would not be able to understand. He therefore offers them three different conveyances to match their capacities and dispositions. To some he offers the vehicle of the shravaka, to some he offers the vehicle of the pratyekabuddha, to some he offers the vehicle of the bodhisattva. But in fact, there is only one vehicle, the buddha vehicle, and each sentient being, regardless of his or her capacity of disposition, will eventually mount it and proceed down the path of the bodhisattva to the state of perfect buddhahood.

This is a message that is deeply appealing, as it offers universal salvation and erases gradations in the goal of liberation. Yet it also serves a polemical purpose, making clear that the conception of the Buddhist path that up to that point had been held by the tradition—and that had been maintained by the monastic institution—was in fact wrong. The Buddha hadn't really meant it. Indeed, the sutra's full title, the *White Lotus of the True Dharma*, suggests that its dharma or doctrine supersedes that found in earlier sutras. The chapter ends with a disquieting catalogue of horrors that will befall those who reject the *Lotus Sutra*—a clear sign that at the time that the sutra appeared in India, there were many who did reject it.

Its doctrine of skillful means, reiterated in other parables in the sutra, proved to be powerful but also dangerous. By this device, innovation could be established as tradition, at the expense of earlier tradition. But by the same device, later innovation could replace earlier innovation. After the *Lotus Sutra*, there would be other sutras that also claimed to express, as never before, the inexpressible content of the Buddha's enlightenment.

PRONOUNCING GLOSSARY

Bhagavat: *ba-ga-vat*
bodhisattva: *boh-di-sat-tva*
deva: *day-va*
devaputra: *day-va-pu-tra*
Dhritiparipurna: *drih-ti-pa-ri-poo-rna*
gandharva: *gan-dar-va*
kumbhanda: *kum-bahn-da*
Maharatnapratimandita: *ma-hah-rat-na-prat-ti-man-di-ta*
mahasattva: *ma-hah-sat-tva*
Mahayana: *ma-hah-yah-na*
mahoraga: *ma-hoh-ra-ga*
mandarava: *mahn-dah-ra-va*
Padmaprabha: *pad-ma-pra-ba*
Padmavrishabhavikrama: *pad-ma-vrih-sha-ba-vi-kra-ma*

parinirvana: *pa-ri-nir-vah-na*
pishacha: *pi-shah-cha*
Prabhutaratna: *pra-boo-ta-rat-na*
pratyekabuddha: *prat-yay-ka-bud-da*
preta: *pray-ta*
Saddharmapundarika: *sad-dar-ma-poon-da-ree-ka*
Shariputra: *shah-ri-pu-tra*
shramana: *shrah-ma-na*
shravaka: *shrah-va-ka*
Tathagata: *ta-tah-ga-ta*
Varanasi: *vah-rah-na-see*
Viraja: *vi-ra-ja*

TRANSLATED FROM the Chinese of Kumārajiva by Tsugunari Kubo and Akira Yuyama. All bracketed additions are the translators'.

Chapter III. A Parable

Thereupon Shariputra stood up ecstatic and joyful, pressed his palms together and, gazing at the Buddha, the Bhagavat,[1] said: "Now, hearing the words of this Dharma from the Bhagavat, my heart is full of joy for I have experienced something unprecedented. What is the reason for this? In the past when I heard this Dharma from the Buddha and saw the bodhisattvas receive their predictions, I was not included. I grieved because I thought I had been deprived of the immeasurable wisdom and insight of the Tathagata.[2]

"O Bhagavat! While I was dwelling alone under forest trees, whether sitting or walking, I was constantly thinking this: 'Since we have also realized the true nature of the Dharma, why has the Tathagata tried to save us with the teachings of the inferior vehicle?'[3]

"The fault is ours, not the Bhagavat's. Why is this? If we had waited for your explanation about the way to achieve highest, complete enlightenment, we certainly would have been able to save ourselves by means of the Mahayana. However, we did not understand that you were teaching with skillful means, according to what is appropriate to us. When we first heard the Buddha's teaching, we immediately accepted, contemplated, and understood it.

"O Bhagavat! Since long ago I have reproached myself incessantly day and night. But now from the Buddha we have heard the unprecedented Dharma that we have never heard before, and it has removed all our doubts.

"I have obtained peace and tranquility in body and mind. Today I have finally realized that I am truly the heir of the Buddha, born from the mouth of the Buddha, incarnated from the Dharma, and that I have inherited a part of the Buddha-Dharma."

Then Shariputra, wanting to elaborate this meaning, spoke again in verse:

> When I heard the words of this Dharma,
> Experiencing something unprecedented,
> My heart overflowed with joy,
> And I was rid of all my doubts.
> From long ago, ever since I heard
> The teaching of the Buddha,
> I have not lost the Mahayana.
> The words of the Buddhas are extremely rare
> And are capable of ridding sentient beings
> Of their suffering.
> Although I had already attained
> Freedom from corruption,
> By hearing the Buddha's voice,
> I have also been rid of my anxiety.
> Whether I was dwelling
> In mountain valleys or under forest trees,
> Whether I was sitting or walking,

---

1. The Blessed One (the Lord).
2. A title of a buddha; it is the one most often used by the historical Buddha to refer to himself.

3. On "the inferior vehicle" (Hinayana), as distinguished from the "great vehicle" (Mahayana), see p. 655.

Grieving and blaming myself deeply,
I thought incessantly:

How have I deceived myself!

I am also the heir of the Buddhas,
Having entered the same incorruptible Dharma.
Nevertheless, in the future,
I shall not be able to explain the highest path.
The golden color, the thirty-two marks,
The ten powers,[4] and the liberations
Are all in the same Dharma;
And yet I have not attained any of these.
Moreover, such qualities as
The eighty excellent and eighteen special characteristics[5]
Are completely lost to me.
When I was wandering alone,
I saw the Buddha in the great assembly
Filling the ten directions[6] with his fame
And greatly benefiting sentient beings.
I then thought:

I have lost all these benefits
Because I have been deceiving myself.

I thought about this constantly day and night
And wanted to ask the Bhagavat:

Have I or have I not lost these?

I always saw the Bhagavat
Praising the bodhisattvas.
That is why I pondered over such matters
As these both day and night.
Now I have heard the words of the Buddha,
Explaining to sentient beings
The incorruptible Dharma,
Which is difficult to comprehend,
And making them enter
The terrace of enlightenment.
Formerly, I was attached to false views
And was a teacher of brahmans.
The Bhagavat, knowing my mind,
Removed the false views and taught nirvana.
I got rid of false views completely
And attained the teaching of emptiness.
At that time I considered myself
To have attained nirvana.
But now I have become aware
That this was not the real nirvana.
When I become a Buddha

4. All aspects of a buddha: his skin is golden, he has thirty-two physical characteristics, and he has ten mental powers.
5. Specific attributes of a buddha.

6. That is, all directions (north, south, east, west, northeast, northwest, southeast, southwest, the nadir, and the zenith).

I shall be endowed with the thirty-two marks,
And be honored by *devas*, humans, *yakshas*, and *nagas*.[7]
Only then can it be said that I have
Permanently attained nirvana without residue.[8]
Before the great assembly
The Buddha has proclaimed
That I will become a Buddha.
After hearing these words of the Dharma,
I was immediately rid of all my doubts.
When I first heard this teaching of the Buddha's,
I was greatly startled and thought:

> I wonder if Mara,[9] acting like the Buddha,
> Is confusing me!

But the Buddha, who teaches skillfully
By means of various explanations and illustrations,
Has made my mind tranquil like the ocean.
While listening to him
I was freed from the web of my doubts.
The Buddha has said that immeasurable Buddhas
Who have attained *parinirvana*[1] in the past,
Established in the use of skillful means,
Have also taught this Dharma.
Immeasurable Buddhas in the present and future
Will also teach this Dharma
With various skillful means.
The present Bhagavat,
From the time he was born
And renounced household life
Until he obtained the path
And turned the wheel of the Dharma,
Has also taught through skillful means.
The Bhagavat teaches the real path,
But the Wicked One does not.
Therefore I know definitely
That it was not Mara acting like the Buddha.
Because I fell into a web of doubt,
I thought that Mara was impersonating the Buddha.
When I heard the voice of the Buddha,
Profound and very subtle,
Fluently explaining the pure Dharma,
I became full of great joy.
My doubts are completely and forever exhausted,
And I have achieved the true wisdom.
I will definitely become a Buddha,
Honored by *devas* and humans.
I will turn the wheel of the highest Dharma
And lead and inspire the bodhisattvas.

7. Water deities, often depicted with the torso of a human and the tail of a snake. "*Devas*": gods; inhabitants of the heavenly realms (literally, "shining ones"). "*Yakshas*": one of the varieties of non-human beings, a kind of nature spirit.

8. The nirvana entered into by a buddha or arhat at death.
9. The personification of evil and desire.
1. Final nirvana.

At that time the Buddha said to Shariputra: "I will now reveal to you before the great assembly of *devas*, humans, *shramanas*, and brahmans that in the past, in the presence of two hundred thousand *kotis*[2] of Buddhas, I led and inspired you constantly for the sake of the highest path. You have followed my instructions for a long time. Because I led you with skillful means, you were born in my Dharma.

"O Shariputra! In the past I inspired you to seek the Buddha path. Yet just now you had completely forgotten this and considered yourself to have attained nirvana. Now, because I want you to remember the path that you practiced according to your original vow in the past, I will teach the *shravakas* the Mahayana sutra called the *Lotus Sutra*, the instruction for the bodhisattvas and treasured lore of the Buddhas.

"O Shariputra! In the future after immeasurable, limitless, and inconceivable *kalpas*,[3] you will have paid homage to thousands of myriads of *kotis* of Buddhas, preserved the True Dharma, and mastered the path practiced by the bodhisattvas. You will become a Buddha called Padmaprabha, a Tathagata, Arhat, Completely Enlightened, Perfect in Knowledge and Conduct, Well-Departed, Knower of the World, Unsurpassed, Tamer of Humans, Teacher of Devas and Humans, Buddha, Bhagavat.

"Your land will be called Viraja. Its earth will be level and pure, ornamented, peaceful, and rich. The *devas* and humans will prosper. The earth will be made of lapis lazuli with a well-planned network of roads like a chessboard bordered with golden cords. Rows of seven-jeweled trees, which are always full of flowers and fruits, will line the borders of these roads. The Tathagata Padmaprabha will also lead and inspire sentient beings by means of the three vehicles.[4]

"O Shariputra! When that Buddha appears, even though his will not be a troubled world, he will teach the three vehicles because of his original vow. This *kalpa* will be called Maharatnapratimandita, meaning 'Adorned with Great Jewels.' Why will it be called Maharatnapratimandita? Because in that world the bodhisattvas will be like great jewels. The number of these bodhisattvas will be immeasurable, limitless, inconceivable, and beyond all comparison, known only by those with the power of the Buddha's wisdom.

"When they want to walk they will step on jeweled flowers. And these bodhisattvas will not be those who are just setting out. Over a long time they will have planted roots of good merit and practiced the pure path of discipline and integrity in the presence of immeasurable hundreds of thousands of myriads of *kotis* of Buddhas. They will always be praised by the Buddhas and continually practice the Buddha wisdom. They will be endowed with transcendent powers and know well all the teachings of the Dharma. They will be honest, without falsity, and firm in recollection. That world will be filled with bodhisattvas like these.

"O Shariputra! The lifespan of this Buddha Padmaprabha will be twelve intermediate *kalpas*, not including the period after he becomes a prince and before he becomes a Buddha; and the lifespan of the people in that world will be eight intermediate *kalpas*.

2. One *koti* equals 10,000,000. "*Shramaṇas*": religious ascetics.
3. Aeons.

4. The paths of the *shravakas* ("hearers," or disciples), *pratyekabuddhas* (individually enlightened ones), and bodhisattvas (future buddhas).

"After these twelve intermediate *kalpas* have passed, the Tathagata Pad-maprabha will predict Bodhisattva Dhritiparipurna's attainment of highest, complete enlightenment and will address the monks, saying:

> This Bodhisattva Dhritiparipurna will become the next Buddha after me. His name will be Padmavrishabhavikrama, a Tathagata, Arhat, Completely Enlightened. His Buddha world will also be like this one.

"O Shariputra! After the *parinirvana* of the Buddha Padmaprabha the True Dharma will remain in the world for thirty-two intermediate *kalpas* and the Semblance Dharma will also remain in the world for thirty-two intermediate *kalpas*."

Then the Bhagavat, wanting to elaborate on the meaning of this again, spoke these verses:

> O Shariputra! In the future
> You will become a Buddha of universal wisdom
> Named Padmaprabha,
> Who will save innumerable sentient beings.
> Having paid homage to innumerable Buddhas,
> Perfected the bodhisattva practice,
> And the qualities, including the ten powers,
> You will attain the highest path.
> After immeasurable *kalpas* have passed,
> The *kalpa* will be called Prabhutaratna,
> And the world will be called Viraja,
> Pure and without dirt.
> The earth will be made of lapis lazuli
> And the roads, bordered with golden cords,
> Will be lined with variegated trees of the seven treasures
> Which are always full of flowers and fruits.
> The bodhisattvas in that world
> Will be always firm in recollection.
> All of them will be completely endowed
> With transcendent powers and the perfections
> And will have properly practiced the bodhisattva path
> In the presence of innumerable Buddhas.
> Such *mahasattvas*[5] as these
> Will be led and inspired by the Buddha Padmaprabha.
> When this Buddha becomes a prince
> He will abdicate his kingship
> And give up his worldly fame.
> Bearing his last body,
> He will renounce household life
> And attain the path of the Buddha.
> This Buddha Padmaprabha will live in the world
> For twelve intermediate *kalpas*.
> And the lifespan of the people in this world
> Will be eight intermediate *kalpas*.
> After the *parinirvana* of this Buddha,

5. Great beings; an honorific title for bodhisattvas.

The True Dharma will last in the world
For thirty-two intermediate *kalpas,*
During which time many sentient beings
Will be saved.
After the extinction of the True Dharma,
The Semblance Dharma will last
For thirty-two intermediate *kalpas.*
The relics of the Buddha
Will be distributed widely
And *devas* and humans will pay them homage.
All that the Buddha Padmaprabha does
Will be exactly like this.
That very Best of Humans,
Who will be foremost and without comparison,
Is none other than you.
You should be delighted to hear this!

At that time the fourfold assembly of monks, nuns, laymen, and laywomen and the great assembly of *devas, nagas, yakshas, gandharvas, asuras, garudas, kimnaras,* and *mahoragas*[6] saw Shariputra receive his prediction of highest, complete enlightenment in the presence of the Buddha. They rejoiced greatly and became immeasurably happy. All of them removed their outer garments and proffered them to the Buddha as offerings.

Shakra, the lord of *devas,* and Brahma, together with innumerable *devaputras*[7] also made offerings to the Buddha of their heavenly beautiful garments, heavenly *mandarava* flowers, and great *mandarava* flowers. Their heavenly garments floated and fluttered in the air, while in the sky the *devas* played hundreds of thousands of myriads of kinds of music together at one time. They rained down various heavenly flowers and said: "In the past the Buddha turned the wheel of the Dharma for the first time in Varanasi. Now he has turned the wheel of the utmost and greatest Dharma again."

Thereupon the *devaputras* spoke these verses in order to explain this again:

In the past you turned the wheel of the Dharma
Of the Four [Noble] Truths[8] in Varanasi;
And you illuminated and explained the Dharma
Of the origination and extinction of the five aggregates.[9]
You have now again turned the wheel
Of the subtlest, utmost, and greatest Dharma.
This Dharma is extremely profound;
Only a few will be able to believe it.
Since long ago we have frequently heard
The teaching of the Bhagavat,
Yet we have never before heard
Such a profound and supreme teaching.
When the Bhagavat taught this Dharma
We were all delighted.

6. Varieties of nonhuman beings: *gandharvas* are heavenly musicians; *asuras,* demigods; *garudas,* mythical birds; *kimnaras,* singers and dancers who are half-horse, half-human; and *mahoragas,* great serpents.
7. Gods. "Brahma": the god who persuaded the Buddha to teach.
8. Suffering, origin, cessation, and path, as discussed on p. 178.
9. A standard division of the constituents of mind and body into five groups: form, feeling, discrimination, compositional factors, and consciousness.

And now Shariputra, possessed of great wisdom,
Has received his prediction from the Bhagavat.
In the same way, we too,
Shall certainly become Buddhas.
We shall become peerless,
Unrivaled in all the world.
The path of the Buddha,
Which is difficult to understand,
Is taught with skillful means
According to what is appropriate for sentient beings.
May the merits of our beneficial acts,
Whether of the past or the present,
And those acquired in meeting the Buddha,
Be completely transferred to the Buddha path.

At that time Shariputra said this to the Buddha: "O Bhagavat! I now have no further doubts. I have received the prediction of the highest supreme enlightenment in the presence of the Buddha.

"When all those twelve hundred who have attained complete mental discipline were still under training in the past, the Buddha constantly led and inspired them, saying: 'My teaching overcomes birth, old age, illness, and death and it leads to nirvana.' Both those who were still in training and those who were not thought that they were free from false views about the self, existence and nonexistence, and declared that they had attained nirvana. Yet now, in the presence of the Bhagavat, they have heard what they have never heard before and have fallen into doubt.

"Splendid, O Bhagavat! I entreat you to explain to the fourfold assembly the reason why, and free them from their doubts!"

Then the Buddha said to Shariputra: "Did I not previously tell you that all the Buddha Bhagavats explain the Dharma with various explanations and illustrations using skillful means, all for the sake of highest, complete enlightenment!? All of these teachings are for leading and inspiring the bodhisattvas.

"Moreover, Shariputra, I will now clarify what I mean with illustrations. Those with wisdom will be able to understand through these illustrations.

"O Shariputra! Suppose there were an aged and extremely affluent man, either in a town, city, or country, who has immeasurable wealth, abundant estates, mansions, and servants. He has a spacious house, yet it only has a single entrance. Suppose many people live there, as many as one, two, or even five hundred people. The buildings are in poor repair, the fences and walls are crumbling, the pillar bases are rotten, and the beams and framework are dangerously tilted.

"Suddenly and unexpectedly, fires break out everywhere, setting the house swiftly aflame. The children of this man, ten, twenty, or thirty in number are in the house.

"The affluent man, seeing the fire breaking out everywhere, becomes alarmed and terrified. He thinks:

I am capable of escaping through the burning entrance in safety,
but my children are absorbed in play within the burning house and
are not aware [of the fire], do not know, are not alarmed or terrified,

and the fire is approaching them! They are not troubled about their suffering nor do they intend to leave the house.

"O Shariputra, this affluent man thought:

Since I am still physically strong I could take the children out of the house in the folds of my garment or on top of a desk.

"He further thought:

There is only one entrance to this house and it is very narrow. The children, who are immature and still unaware, are attached to their place of play. They may fall into danger and be burned by the fire. I should now tell them of the danger; this house is already burning! They must escape as quickly as they can to avoid being burned by the fire!

"After considering this he urged the children according to his thought:

Children! Run out immediately!

"Although their father in his concern has given them the proper advice, the children are immersed in their play and do not accept it; they are neither alarmed nor afraid and have no intention of leaving [the burning house]. Moreover, they do not even know what a fire is, the condition of the house, or what they may lose. They merely run about, back and forth, looking at their father.

"Thereupon the affluent man thought:

This house is already engulfed in flames. If my children and I do not get out, we shall perish in the fire. I will now use skillful means to help my children escape from this disaster.

"Since the father already knew that his children were attached to various rare toys and unusual things that each of them liked, he said to them:

The toys you are fond of are rare and hard to obtain. If you do not take them you will certainly regret it later. Right now, outside the house, there are three kinds of carts. One is yoked to a sheep, one to a deer, and one to an ox. Go play with them. Children! Run out of this burning house immediately and I will give you whatever you want!

"The children, hearing what their father had said about the rare toys, became excited and, in their eagerness to get to them they pushed each other out of the way in a mad rush out of the burning house.

"Then the affluent man saw that his children had got out safely and were sitting unharmed in an open area at a crossroad. He was relieved, happy, and joyful. The children said to their father:

Father, please give us the toys you promised: those [three] carts, one yoked to a sheep, one to a deer, and one to an ox!

"O Shariputra, the affluent man then gave each child the same kind of large cart. These carts were tall and spacious, adorned with various jewels, and encircled with railings full of hanging bells. On the tops of the carts were canopies also decorated with various kinds of jewels. These carts were draped with jeweled cords and hung with flower garlands. They were thickly piled with fabrics, and red pillows had been placed about. These carts were each yoked to an ox with a spotlessly white hide. These oxen had beautiful bodies with powerful muscles, even gaits, and were as swift as the wind; and there were many attendants guarding them. Why did the affluent man give these carts? Because the man had great and immeasurable wealth and his abundant storehouses were full. He thus thought further:

> Since my treasure has no limit, I should not give my children inferior carts. These are my children and I love them all equally. I have an immeasurable number of large carts such as these, decorated with the seven treasures. I should equally distribute them to each child without discrimination. Why is this? Even if I gave carts like these to everyone in the country, their number would not be exhausted. Why should I not give them to my own children?

"At that time, the children each climbed into a great cart and had an unprecedented experience, one beyond their original expectations.

"O Shariputra! What do you think about this? This affluent man gave to his children equally a large cart decorated with precious treasures. Has he deceived them or not?"

Shariputra replied: "No Bhagavat! The affluent man only tried to help his children escape from the disastrous fire. He saved their lives and did not deceive them. This is by no means a deception. Why? Because by saving their lives they obtained marvelous toys. Moreover, they were saved from the burning house by skillful means.

"O Bhagavat! If this affluent man had not given them even the smallest cart, it still would not have been a deception. Why is this? Because this affluent man thought before:

> I will help my children escape with skillful means.

"This is why it was not a deception. How much more so, since the affluent man, knowing that he had immeasurable wealth and wanting to benefit them equally, gave each of his children a large [ox]cart."

The Buddha said to Shariputra: "Splendid, splendid! It is exactly as you have said. O Shariputra, the Tathagata is also just like this. That is to say, as the father of the entire world, he permanently dispels fear, distress, anxiety, ignorance, and blindness. He has attained immeasurable wisdom, insight, power, and fearlessness, as well as great transcendent powers and the power of wisdom. He has attained the perfection of skillful means and of wisdom. With his great mercy and compassion he incessantly and indefatigably seeks the welfare of all beings and benefits them all.

"The Tathagata appears in the triple world,[1] which is like a decaying old house on fire, to rescue sentient beings from the fire of birth, old age, illness, and death, anxiety, sorrow, suffering, distress, delusion, blindness, and the three poisons of greed, hatred, and ignorance. Thus he leads and inspires sentient beings and causes them to attain highest, complete enlightenment.

---

1. The Realm of Desire, the Realm of Form, and the Formless Realm; see pp. 54–55.

"The Tathagatas see all sentient beings burning in the fire of birth, old age, illness, and death, anxiety, sorrow, suffering, and distress. Because of the desires of the five senses and the desire for monetary profit they also experience various kinds of suffering. Because of their attachment and pursuits they experience various kinds of suffering in the present; and in the future they will suffer in the states of existence of hell, animals, and hungry ghosts (*pretas*). If they are born in the heavens or in the human world they will experience a variety of sorrows such as suffering from poverty and destitution, separation from loved ones, or suffering from encounters with those they dislike.

"Although sentient beings are immersed in such sorrows, they rejoice and play. They are not aware, shocked, startled, or disgusted nor do they seek release. Running around in the burning house of the triple world, they experience great suffering and yet they do not realize it.

"O Shariputra! Seeing these things the Buddha thought:

> Since I am the father of sentient beings I must rid them of their immeasurable suffering and distress. I will cause them to rejoice through the immeasurable and limitless pleasure of the Buddha wisdom.

"O Shariputra! The Tathagata further thought:

> If I proclaim the Tathagata's wisdom, insight, power, and fearlessness to sentient beings with my transcendent powers and the power of my wisdom alone, without using skillful means, it will be impossible to save them. Why is this? Because these sentient beings have not escaped from birth, old age, illness, and death; anxiety, sorrow, suffering, and distress; and are being burned in the blazing house of the triple world. How would they be able to understand the Buddha's wisdom?

"O Shariputra! Although that affluent man had physical strength he did not use it. He only earnestly employed skillful means to save his children from the disaster of the burning house, and later he gave each of them a large cart decorated with precious treasures. The Tathagata is exactly like this.

"Although the Tathagata has power and fearlessness he does not use them, but rescues sentient beings from the burning house of the triple world only through wisdom and skillful means, teaching the three vehicles to the *shravakas*, *pratyekabuddhas*, and the Buddhas, saying:

> Do not take pleasure in living in this burning house of the triple world. And do not thirst after inferior objects, sounds, smells, flavors, and tangibles. If you are attached to these objects and have desires, then you will be burned. Leave the triple world in haste and you will obtain the three vehicles—the vehicles for the *shravakas*, *pratyekabuddhas*, and Buddhas. I definitely guarantee this to you. In the end it will come true. You should be diligent and persistent!

"The Tathagata attracts sentient beings through this skillful means, saying further:

You should know that the Noble Ones praise the teachings of these three vehicles that are self-directed, unrestricted, and independent. When they ride in them, sentient beings will enjoy faculties free from corruption and also powers, paths to enlightenment, meditation, liberation, and concentration. And they themselves will attain immeasurable ease and pleasure.

"O Shariputra! Those beings, wise by nature, who accept the Dharma from the Buddha Bhagavat, who are diligent, persistent, and wish to escape from the triple world quickly, and who are seeking nirvana, are all practicing the *shravaka* vehicle. They are like those children who left the burning house seeking the cart yoked to a sheep.

"Those beings who accept the Dharma of the Buddha Bhagavat, who are diligent and persevere in seeking the wisdom of the Self-generated One and enjoy tranquility for themselves, who profoundly know the causes of and reasons for existence, are all practicing the *pratyekabuddha* vehicle. They are just like those children who left the burning house seeking the cart yoked to a deer.

"Those beings who accept the Dharma of the Buddha Bhagavat, who are diligent and persevere in seeking the wisdom of the Omniscient One, the wisdom of the Buddha, the wisdom of the Self-generated One, the wisdom acquired without a teacher, the wisdom and insight, powers, and fearlessness of the Tathagata; who are compassionate, put immeasurable sentient beings at ease, benefit *devas* and humans, and save all beings, are all practicing the Mahayana. Bodhisattvas are called *mahasattvas* (great beings) because they seek this vehicle. They are just like those children who left the burning house seeking the cart yoked to an ox.

"O Shariputra! That affluent man saw his children leave the burning house safely and arrive at a safe place. Knowing that he had immeasurable wealth, he gave a large cart equally to each child. The Tathagata is exactly like this. As the father of all sentient beings he sees that immeasurable thousands of *kotis* of sentient beings escape from the dangers, sufferings, and fears of the triple world through the gates of the Buddha's teaching and attain the pleasure of nirvana.

"Then the Tathagata thought:

> Because I possess the treasure house of the Dharma of all the Buddhas, which contains immeasurable limitless wisdom, power, and fearlessness, and because all sentient beings are my children, I will give them equally the Mahayana. I will not allow anyone to attain nirvana merely for himself but will cause everyone to attain it through the Tathagata's nirvana.
>
> I will give sentient beings who have escaped from the triple world all the toys of the Buddha's meditations and liberations, which are of one character and one kind, are praised by the Noble Ones, and which produce pure and supreme pleasure.

"O Shariputra! At first that affluent man attracted his children with three kinds of carts, then later gave them only the safest and best large [ox]cart, adorned with jewels. Moreover, that affluent man was never accused of telling a lie. The Tathagata is exactly like this. He tells no lies.

"In the beginning the Tathagata teaches the three vehicles in order to lead sentient beings. And later he saves them through only the Mahayana. Why is this? Because the Tathagata possesses the treasure house of the Dharma, which contains immeasurable wisdom, power, and fearlessness. And although he is able to give the teaching of the Mahayana to all sentient beings, not all of them can accept it.

"O Shariputra! You should know that the Buddhas, with the power of skillful means, teach the single Buddha vehicle, dividing and teaching it as three."

Then the Buddha, wanting to elaborate on the meaning of this again, spoke these verses:

Suppose there were an affluent man
Who had a large house,
And this house was very old,
On the verge of collapsing.
The halls were extremely dangerous,
The pillar bases rotten and disintegrating,
The beams and framework dangerously tilted,
And the stairways were falling apart.
The fences and walls were cracked,
The plaster was peeling off,
The thatched roof was falling down,
The rafters and eaves were coming apart,
The partitions were everywhere askew,
And the whole place was covered with filth.
Five hundred people lived there,
And moving around helter-skelter were
Kites, owls, hawks, eagles, crows, magpies,
Doves, pigeons, lizards, snakes, vipers,
Scorpions, centipedes, millipedes,
Newts, myriapods, ferrets, badgers, mice,
Rats, and other harmful creatures.
It was filled with stench,
And there were places overflowing with excrement.
All kinds of bugs
Had gathered there.
There were foxes, wolves, and vermin
Devouring, trampling, and gnawing on corpses,
Scattering bones and flesh about;
And a pack of dogs,
Forcing each other out of the way,
Rushed to the spot—
Frightened and exhausted from hunger,
They were searching everywhere for food,
Fighting among themselves, snatching at food,
Biting, snarling, and barking at each other.
This house was terrifying,
Corrupted to this grotesque condition:
Ogres of the mountains and valleys,
Yakshas, and demons were everywhere
Devouring human flesh.
There were various poisonous insects,

All kinds of harmful birds of prey,
And beasts who were producing, rearing,
And protecting their offspring.
Yakshas were scrabbling and fighting to devour them.
And after sating themselves,
Evil thoughts would arise in them.
The sound of their fighting
Was terrifying.
The *kumbhanda* demons were crouching on the ground,
Sometimes rising up a foot or two.
Roaming about, pleasing themselves as they liked,
They would catch two legs of a dog,
Beat it until it could not bark
And grabbing the dog's neck with their legs,
Terrify it for their own amusement.
There were also other demons living there
With large bodies, naked, dark, and gaunt.
They were screaming horrifying howls,
Crying out while searching for food.
Other demons were there,
Some with needlelike throats,
While others had necks
Like a cow's head;
Some had those of human flesh-eaters or dog-devourers.
Their hair was disheveled like rank weeds
And they were destructive and malicious.
Driven by hunger and thirst,
They were crying and scurrying about.
Yakshas, hungry ghosts,
And various malicious birds and beasts
Were peering out of the windows
And running frantically in all directions,
Driven by hunger.
In this house, with its immeasurable terrors,
There were many such horrendous things as these.
Now suppose this old and decaying house
Belonged to a man,
And this man came out from it a short distance.
Soon after, the house suddenly
Burst into flames behind him.
The fire instantly spread in all directions.
The frame, beams, rafters, and pillars exploded,
And shaking, split and crashed,
While the fences and walls collapsed.
All the demons screamed out loudly.
The hawks, eagles, other birds,
And *kumbhanda* demons, panicked and terrified,
Could not get out.
Malicious beasts and poisonous insects
Concealed themselves in holes.
There were also *pishacha* demons[2] dwelling there

2. Demons who haunt places where violent deaths have occurred.

Who, because of little merit,
Were chased by the flames.
They were tearing at each other,
Drinking blood and eating flesh.
A horde of vermin had already died off,
And the large malicious beasts
Raced to devour them,
While the smoke of the stench flowed
And filled everywhere.
As the centipedes, millipedes,
And poisonous snakes rushed,
Burning, out of their holes
The *kumbhanda* demons devoured them
One after another.
The hungry ghosts, with their hair on fire,
Ravenous, thirsty, and suffering from the heat,
Frantically scurried about.
In this way, the house was extremely terrifying
With poison and fire,
And disasters more than one.
Then the householder, who was standing
Outside the entrance of the house,
Heard someone say:

> Just a moment ago,
> In the midst of their play,
> Your children entered this house.
> Being young and ignorant,
> They are attached to playing games.

Hearing this, the affluent man was startled
And went into the burning house
To save them from the disaster of the fire.
As he thought fit, he warned the children
And explained the various dangers:

> There are malicious demons, poisonous insects,
> And the fire is raging everywhere.
> There are endless horrors,
> One right after another.
> There are poisonous snakes, lizards, vipers,
> *Yakshas*, *kumbhanda*, demons, vermin,
> Foxes, dogs, hawks, eagles, kites,
> Owls, and centipedes, all acutely suffering
> From hunger and thirst
> And all extremely terrifying.
> These horrors are difficult to deal with,
> How much more so the conflagration!

But the children, being ignorant,
Would not listen to their father's warning.
Still attached to their games,
They kept right on playing.
Thereupon the affluent man thought:

My children by doing this
Increase my distress!
There is nothing to enjoy now in this house.
Nevertheless, my children who are absorbed in play
Will not accept my instructions
And so will be hurt by the fire.

Then he immediately thought
That he should advise his children
Using various skillful means, and said:

I have a variety of unusual toys
Such as fine carts adorned with beautiful treasures,
Yoked to sheep, deer, and oxen.
They are just outside the gate.
O children! Come out of the house!
I had these carts made for you.
Play with them as you like!

Hearing about these carts,
The children immediately started
To push each other out of the way
To get out of the house.
Arriving at an open area,
They escaped from the disaster.
The affluent man, seeing that his children
Had escaped from the burning house
And were standing at the crossroads,
Sat down on his lion seat.
Then he joyously said:

Now I am happy!
It is extremely difficult to raise these children.
Foolish and ignorant,
They entered a dangerous house
Full of various poisonous insects,
Terrifying ogres from mountains and valleys,
And a raging fire that broke out in all directions.
In spite of this,
These children were attached to playing their games.
But by causing them to escape from the disaster,
I have saved them.
Therefore, my people, I now feel at ease.

Thereupon the children,
Seeing their father sitting in peace,
Approached him saying:

Please, father,
Give us the three kinds of carts
Adorned with treasures
That you just promised us,
When you said that if we, your children, came out
You would give us three kinds of carts
Just as we like.

Now is the right time.
Give them to us right away!

This affluent man,
Who was extremely wealthy,
Had an abundance of treasures.
He had a number of great carts made,
Adorned with various precious things
Like gold, silver, lapis lazuli,
Mother-of-pearl, and agate.
They were beautifully decorated,
Encircled with railings,
And were covered with hanging bells
Attached to golden cords.
Over them was hung a net of pearls
With golden flower tassels
Hanging down everywhere.
They were all completely
Decorated in a variety of colors.
The bedding was made of soft silk
That was covered with
An extremely fine carpet of spotless white
Which cost thousands of *kotis*.
There were large white oxen,
Healthy and powerful with beautiful bodies,
Yoked to the jeweled carts,
And they were guarded by many attendants.
When they were given these fine carts,
The children were joyful and excited.
They got on the carts
And drove delightedly all about.
Amusing themselves in play,
They mastered them without difficulties.

The Buddha said to Shariputra:

I am also like this.
I am the father of the world,
The best of the sages.
All sentient beings are my children.
They are deeply attached to worldly pleasures
And have no wisdom.
There is no peace in the triple world,
Just like in the burning house,
Which is full of various suffering
And which is extremely terrifying.
There are always the sufferings
Of birth, old age, illness, and death.
Such fires as these burn endlessly.
The Tathagata, who has already left
The burning house of the triple world,
Lives in tranquility
And dwells at ease in the forest.

Now this triple world is my property
And the sentient beings in it are my children.
There are now many dangers here
And I am the only one who can protect them.
Although I give them advice,
They do not accept it,
Because they are tainted with desires
And have deep attachments.
On this occasion
I teach the three vehicles
Using skillful means.
Realizing the sufferings of the triple world,
I reveal and explain it
To cause sentient beings to
Escape from the mundane path.
If these children are resolute,
They are endowed with the three knowledges
And six transcendent powers.
Or they can become *pratyekabuddhas* or
Bodhisattvas who have reached
The stage of nonretrogression.[3]
O Shariputra!
I explain the single Buddha vehicle
To sentient beings, using this illustration.
If you are able to accept what I say,
You will all attain the Buddha path.
This vehicle is subtle, pure, and peerless.
There is nothing superior to it
In all the worlds.
This is what the Buddha enjoys.
All the sentient beings should praise,
Honor, and revere it.
There are immeasurable thousands of *kotis*
Of powers, liberations, meditations,
Wisdoms, and other attributes of the Buddha.
I cause my children to obtain such a vehicle
And let them play continuously,
Day and night, for *kalpas*.
I cause the bodhisattvas as well as the shravakas
To board this jeweled vehicle,
And lead them directly
To the terrace of enlightenment.
For this reason,
There is no other vehicle but
The skillful means of the Buddhas,
Even if one seeks in all the ten directions.
I tell you, O Shariputra:
All of you are my children,
And I am thus your father.

3. The stage at which bodhisattvas are assured of reaching enlightenment and not regressing to being a shravaka or pratyekabuddha.

Since you were burned by the fire
Of various sufferings for many *kalpas*,
I saved you all
By leading you out of the triple world.
Although I have previously told you
About your *parinirvana*,
You have only extinguished birth and death
And have not actually attained nirvana.
You should now seek only
The wisdom of the Buddha.
If there are any bodhisattvas in this assembly,
They should listen singlemindedly
To the real teaching of all the Buddhas.
Those sentient beings
Whom the Buddha Bhagavats
Lead and inspire with skillful means
Are all bodhisattvas.
Because people have little knowledge
And are deeply attached to pleasures,
I teach them the truth of suffering (i.e., the First Noble Truth).
And those sentient beings rejoice,
Having attained
Such an unprecedented experience.
The truth of suffering taught by the Buddha
Is nothing but the truth.
To those who do not know the origin of suffering (i.e., the Second
     Noble Truth),
Who are deeply attached to its causes
And unable to abandon them even for a while,
I teach the truth about the path to its cessation
Using skillful means.
All the causes of suffering
Originate from excessive craving.
When this craving is extinguished,
The source is removed.
The cessation of suffering
Is called the Third [Noble] Truth.
One practices the path leading to its cessation (i.e., the Fourth
     Noble Truth)
In order to attain the truth of cessation.
Removing the bonds of sufferings is called liberation.
In what sense have these people attained liberation?
They have merely removed false views
And called that liberation.
But actually, they have not yet completely attained it.
The Buddha has explained that these people
Have not actually attained nirvana:
I do not intend to lead them to nirvana
Because they have not yet attained the highest path.
I am the Lord of the Dharma
And have mastered the Dharma.
I appear in the world

To cause sentient beings to be at peace.
O, you, Shariputra!
Teach this my Dharma sign
To benefit the world!
Wherever you may go,
Never propagate it recklessly.
You should know that those who hear,
Rejoice, and fully accept it
Have reached the stage of nonretrogression.
Those who accept the teaching of this sutra
Have formerly seen the Buddhas in the past,
Honored, and paid homage to them,
And also heard this teaching.
Those who are able to accept what you teach,
Will see me, you, the monks and the bodhisattvas.
This very *Lotus Sutra* shall be taught
Only to the profoundly wise.
Those of superficial awareness who hear it
Will become confused and will not comprehend it.
This sutra is beyond the comprehension
Of all the *shravakas* and *pratyekabuddhas*.
O, you, Shariputra!
Even you understood this sutra only through faith;
It is no wonder that the other disciples cannot.
They accept this sutra
Because they believe the Buddha's teaching,
But it is beyond their intellectual comprehension.
O Shariputra!
Never teach this sutra
To those who are arrogant and lazy,
Or to those who hold
False views about the self.
Never teach it to those people
Of superficial awareness,
Who are deeply attached
To the desires of the five senses,
Since even if they heard it,
They would not understand.
Those people who will not accept
And who disparage this sutra,
Will consequently destroy the seed of the Buddha
In the entire world.
Now listen to what I teach
About the results of the errors of those people
Who frown upon and have doubts about this sutra.
Listen also to what I teach
Concerning the results of the errors of those people,
Who, whether at the time
Of the Buddha's presence in this world
Or after his *parinirvana*, disparage this sutra,
And despise, hate, and hold grudges
Against the people who recite, copy, and preserve it.

When such people die,
They will go to the Avichi Hell,[4]
And after spending a *kalpa* there,
Will be born in the same way
Again and again for innumerable *kalpas*.
After coming out of this hell,
They will be reborn as animals.
If born as dogs or vermin,
Their bodies will be emaciated, dark-spotted,
Devoid of hair, with scabies and leprosy.
Tormented, hated, and despised by people,
They will constantly suffer from hunger and thirst.
With withered bones and flesh,
They will be in anguish while living
And covered with stones after death.
Because they destroyed
The seed of the Buddha,
They will suffer the consequences
Of their errors.
If they are born as camels or mules,
They will always have heavy burdens to carry.
They will be whipped repeatedly
And think of nothing but water and grass.
It is because they disparaged this sutra
That they suffer the consequences of their errors in this way.
If they are born as vermin and enter a village,
Children will beat them because they have scabies,
Leprosy, and perhaps a missing eye.
At times they will be tortured even to death.
After dying,
They will be reborn as giant snakes
With great bodies as long as five hundred *yojanas*.[5]
Deaf, dumb, legless, slithering on their bellies,
Eaten at by small insects,
They will suffer day and night without respite.
They suffer the consequences of their errors in this way,
Because they disparaged this sutra.
If they are born as humans,
They will have dull faculties
And be runts who twitch and are crippled,
Blind, deaf, and humpbacked.
No matter what they may say
People will not believe them.
Their breath will always be foul.
They will be snatched at by demons.
Being poor and degraded and enslaved by others,
They will be emaciated from many illnesses
And will have nowhere to turn.
When they approach others,

4. The most painful of the Buddhist hells.
5. A yojana was the standard measurement of distance in ancient India, said to be how far a yoked team of oxen can pull a royal chariot in one day (estimated to be between five and nine miles).

They will be disdained.
Even if they manage to get something
They will immediately lose it.
Even if they study medicine
And cure themselves according to the correct method,
They will suffer from other illnesses again
And may even die.
When they get sick
No one will tend to them;
And even if they take the proper medicine
Their pain will increase.
Every hand will be turned against them,
Threatening them, pilfering and stealing from them.
They will fall helplessly into this plight
Because of their transgressions.
Such erring people will never see
The Buddha, the king of seers,
Preaching the Dharma and leading and inspiring people.
Such people will always be born
Into difficult circumstances.
Crazed, unheeding, and unthinking,
They will never hear the teaching.
They will be born deaf and dumb,
With defective faculties
For as many immeasurable *kalpas*
As the sands of the Ganges River.
Though they will always find themselves in hell,
They will feel as if they were playing
In a pleasure garden.
Although they are in other troubled states of being,
They will feel as if they were in their own home.
They will live among camels, mules, boars, and dogs.
These are the results of their error
In disparaging this sutra.
If they are born as human beings,
They will be deaf, blind, mute,
Impoverished, and decrepit.
Such will be their adornments.
They will have dropsy, gonorrhea,
Scabies, leprosy, and tumors.
Such diseases as these will be their clothing.
Their bodies will always be foul, filthy, and impure.
Their deep attachment to false views
About the self will cause
Their anger and passion to increase.
Their sexual desires will be insatiable,
With either birds or beasts as their objects.
These are the results of their
Errors in disparaging this sutra.

The Buddha said to Shariputra:

If one were to explain
The consequences of the errors

Of those who disparage this sutra,
It would take more than a *kalpa*.
For that reason I am now telling you
Never to expound this sutra
To those who have little wisdom.
You should teach it
Only to those people of sharp faculties
Who are wise, learned, and understanding,
Who have good memories and erudition,
And are seeking the Buddha path.
You should teach it to those who have seen
Hundreds of thousands of *kotis* of Buddhas,
Who have planted good roots, and are resolute.
Teach it to those who strive,
Always practice compassion,
And give unsparingly of their bodies and lives.
You should teach it to those who are respectful
And devoid of hypocrisy,
Who are living alone
In mountains and valleys away from fools.
O Shariputra!
You should teach it
To those who have left their bad companions
And made friends with virtuous people.
Teach it to the heirs of the Buddha
Who have good conduct, are as pure as jewels,
And who are seeking the Mahayana sutras.
You should teach it
To those who are free of anger,
Honest, flexible, always sympathetic to everyone,
And who honor all the Buddhas.
Teach it to the heirs of the Buddha
In the great assembly,
Who have pure thoughts
And who teach the Dharma without doubts,
Using various reasonings,
Illustrations, and explanations.
You should teach it to those monks
Who, always and everywhere in search of the Dharma,
Seek the Omniscient One,
To whom they joyfully press their palms together,
Touch their heads, and preserve
Only the Mahayana sutras with pleasure,
Who never preserve even a single verse
Of any other sutra.
Teach it to those who seek this sutra
As intently as they seek for the relics of the Buddha,
Who after obtaining it will accept it
Respectfully, with bowed heads;
And will not seek any other sutra
And will never think about heretical scriptures.
O Shariputra! I say to you:
I have described the characteristics of those

Who seek the Buddha path,
Though a *kalpa* would not suffice to do so in full.
You should teach the *Lotus Sutra*
To those who are able to accept it.

A LAYMAN HUMBLES THE MONKS

THE VIMALAKIRTI SUTRA

The *Vimalakirti Sutra*, also known as the *Instructions of Vimalakirti (Vimalakir-tinirdesha)*, was composed in India, likely in the late first or early second century C.E. It was first translated from Sanskrit into Chinese around 180, but its most famous Chinese rendering was that of Kumarajiva in 406. That is the text translated here. Apart from the teachings it contains, the sutra is known for its literary qualities, especially its repartee marked with both paradox and humor.

The sutra can be briefly summarized as follows. The Buddha requests that his leading monk disciples visit his lay disciple Vimalakirti, who is ill. In this Mahayana sutra, these monks, called *shravakas* or "disciples" in Sanskrit (hence the title of chapter 3), would be recognized as belonging to what the Mahayana pejoratively called the Hinayana or "Low Vehicle"—that is, those who seek only their own liberation from suffering and who do not accept the Mahayana sutras as the word of the Buddha. Thus, here, as in other Mahayana sutras, historical figures who lived before the composition of those sutras become characters in them, in this case serving as straight men for the potent ripostes of the layman Vimalakirti. Each of the monks politely declines the Buddha's request, while recounting an earlier encounter with Vimalakirti in which he had scolded the monk for his limited understanding of the dharma. The Buddha then turns to his leading bodhisattva disciples, the heroes of the Mahayana, and makes the same request. Again, each declines and recounts the story of his meeting with Vimalakirti. Finally, the Buddha asks Manjushri, the bodhisattva of wisdom, who agrees to visit Vimalakirti. Upon arriving, the bodhisattva asks Vimalakirti about the nature of his ailment, and he replies that his sickness is the sickness of all sentient beings; he goes on to describe how a sick bodhisattva should understand his sickness, emphasizing the necessity of both wisdom and method, or "skillful means." A large number of monks and bodhisattvas enter Vimalakirti's house, whose small room is magically able to accommodate them all. He delivers a sermon on "inconceivable liberation." Present in the audience is Shariputra, renowned as the wisest of the Buddha's arhat disciples—that is, those who have achieved liberation and will enter nirvana at death. To demonstrate the superiority of the Mahayana over the Hinayana, this wisest of monks is made to play the fool who fails to understand how all dichotomies are resolved in emptiness. In a famous scene, a goddess momentarily transforms Shariputra into a female. Later, various bodhisattvas take turns describing various forms of duality and how they are overcome in nonduality. Vimalakirti is the last to be invited to speak. He remains silent and is praised for this teaching of the entrance into nonduality. The sutra became particularly famous in East Asia, not only because of the literary merits of Kumarajiva's translation but also because the protagonist is a layman. A sutra in which a householder repeatedly demonstrates that his wisdom is superior to that of a monk had special appeal in a culture like that of China, which upheld the importance of the family and at times condemned the monk who left his familial duties behind to join the Buddhist order.

Chapters 2 and 3 are presented here. Chapter 2 begins with the famous description of Vimalakirti and how he embodied the virtue of "skillful means": the ability to make use of various expedient devices in order to convey the truth in such a way that it can be comprehended by a particular audience. The chapter continues with Vimalakirti's homily that compares the ordinary body of humans to the extraordinary body of the Buddha. Chapter 3 recounts the reluctance of the monks and bodhisattvas to visit Vimalakirti on his sickbed.

PRONOUNCING GLOSSARY

Ajita Keshakambala: *a-ji-ta kay-sha-kam-ba-la*

Aniruddha: *a-nih-rud-da*

anuttara samyaksambodhi: *an-ut-ta-rah sam-yak-sam-boh-di*

bhikshu: *bik-shu*

Brahma: *bra-mah*

chakravartin: *cha-kra-var-tin*

dharani: *dah-ra-nee*

Hinayana: *hee-na-yah-na*

Kakuda Katyayana: *ka-ku-da kaht-yah-ya-na*

Kashyapa: *kah-shya-pa*

Katyayana: *kaht-yah-ya-na*

kshatriya: *ksha-tri-ya*

Mahakashyapa: *ma-hah-kahsh-ya-pa*

Mahakatyayana: *ma-hah-kahty ah-ya-na*

Mahamaudgalyayana: *ma-hah-maud-gal-yah-ya-na*

Mahayana: *ma-hah-yah-na*

Maskarin Goshaliputra: *ma-ska-rin goh-shah-lee-pu-tra*

Nirgrantha Jnatiputra: *nihr-gran-ta jnyah-ti-pu-tra*

pratyekabuddha: *prat-yay-ka-bud-da*

Purana Kashyapa: *poo-rah-na kahsh ya-pa*

Purnamaitrayaniputra: *poor-na-mai-trah-ya-nee-pu-tra*

samadhi: *sa-mah-di*

Samjayin Vairatiputra: *sam-ja-yin vai-ra-tee-pu-tra*

samsara: *sam-sah-ra*

Shariputra: *shah-ri-pu-tra*

shramana: *shrah-ma-na*

shravaka: *shrah-va-ka*

skandha: *skan-da*

srota-apanna: *sroh-ta-ah-pan-na*

Subhuti: *su-boo-ti*

Tathagata: *ta-tah-ga-ta*

Vaishali: *vai-shah-li*

Vimalakirti: *vih-ma-la-keer-ti*

Chapter II. Skillful Means

At that time there was within the great city of Vaishali[1] an elder named Vimalakirti. He had already made offerings to immeasurable Buddhas, deeply planting the foundation of goodness. He had attained forbearance of the nonarising [of *dharmas*], and his eloquence was unhindered. He disported in the numinous penetrations and had achieved all the *dharanis*.[2] He had attained fearlessness and had subjugated the troubling vengeance of the Maras.[3] Entering into [all the] gates of profound Dharma, he was excellent at the perfection of wisdom. Having penetrated skillful means, his great vows had been accomplished. Understanding the tendencies of the minds of sentient beings, he was also able to discriminate between those of sharp and dull faculties. Long [a practitioner of] the path of Buddhahood, his mind was already pure, and he was definitively [dedicated to] the Mahayana. He considered well the activities of the realms of existence, and, residing in the deportment of the Buddha, his mind was great as the ocean. The Buddhas

TRANSLATED FROM the Chinese by John R. McRae. All bracketed additions are the translator's.

1. A city in northeast India on the Ganges, in present-day Bihar.

2. Extended mantras.

3. Personifications of evil and desire.

praised him [as their] disciple, and the Indras, Brahmas,[4] and world lords (i.e., heavenly kings) revered him.

Wanting to save people, [Vimalakirti] used his excellent skillful means to reside in Vaishali, where with wealth immeasurable he attracted the poor, with the purity of his morality he attracted the miscreants, with the moderation of his forbearance he attracted the angry, with great exertion he attracted the indolent, with singleminded concentration he attracted the perturbed, and with definitive wisdom he attracted the foolish.

Although he was a white-robed [layman], he maintained the pure Vinaya conduct of a *shramana*;[5] although he resided in the home, he was not attached to the triple world.[6] He manifested the existence of wife and sons, but always cultivated chastity. He revealed the existence of subordinates, but always enjoyed transcendence. Although his clothing was richly decorated, it was with the marks and features [of a Tathagata[7]] that he adorned his body. Although he drank and ate, the joy of concentration was his [favorite] flavor. If he went to gambling houses or theaters it was only to save people. He hosted those of the heretic paths without breaking his correct faith. Although he illuminated the profane classics he always took pleasure in the Buddha-Dharma. He was revered by all as the one most worthy of offerings.

In supporting the correct Dharma he attracted both old and young. In all of his business dealings, although he made worldly profits he never took joy in them. In wandering the crossroads, he dispensed benefit to sentient beings. In entering into government administration, he safeguarded everyone. In entering into the lecture halls, he led people by means of the Mahayana. In entering the schools, he inspired the children. In entering the brothels, he revealed the transgressions [that arise from] desire. In entering the wine shops, he was able to maintain (lit., "establish") his [good] intention.

When he was with the elders, as the most honored of the eminent he explained the excellent Dharma for them. When he was among retired scholars, as the most honored of the retired scholars he eradicated their attachments. When he was among *kshatriyas*,[8] as the most honored among *kshatriyas* he taught them forbearance. When he was among brahmans, as the most honored among brahmans he eliminated their arrogance. When he was among the ministers, as the most honored among ministers he taught them the correct Dharma.

When he was among princes, as the most honored among princes he instructed them with loyalty and filiality.

When he was among palace officials, as the most honored among palace officials he converted the palace women.

When he was among the common people, as the most honored among the common people he had them generate the power of blessings.

When he was among Brahma gods, as the most honored of the Brahma gods he taught with superior wisdom.

---

4. Gods. Indra was the ruler of the Heaven of the Thirty-three.
5. An ascetic or mendicant. "Vinaya": the code of monastic conduct.
6. The Realm of Desire, the Realm of Form, and the Formless Realm; see pp. 54–55.
7. A title of a buddha; it is the one most often used by the historical Buddha to refer to himself.
8. Members of the second of the four castes of ancient India, sometimes called the warrior caste.

When he was among Indras, as the most honored among Indras he manifested impermanence.

When he was among world-protector [gods], as the most honored among world-protectors he protected sentient beings.

The Elder Vimalakirti used immeasurable skillful means such as these to benefit sentient beings.

Using skillful means he manifested becoming ill himself. Because he was ill, the king, ministers, elders, retired scholars, brahmans, the princes and the other palace retainers, and innumerable thousands of people all came to inquire about his illness.

To those who came, Vimalakirti used the occasion of his illness to make extensive explanations of the Dharma.

"Sirs, the body is impermanent, without strength, without power, without solidity. Given the way it rapidly disintegrates, it cannot be trusted (i.e., relied upon). Alternately suffering and vexatious, it accumulates a host of illnesses. Sirs, the wise do not rely on such a body.

"This body is like a bit of foam that cannot be grasped. This body is like bubbles that do not last very long. This body is like a mirage, generated from thirst. This body is like a banana tree, with nothing solid within. This body is like a phantasm arising from confused [views]. This body is like a dream, an illusory view. This body is like a shadow, manifested through karmic conditions. This body is like an echo, dependent on causes and conditions. This body is like a cloud, which changes and disappears in an instant. This body is like lightning, unstable from one moment to another.

"This body is without master, like the earth. This body is without self, like fire. This body is without lifespan, like the wind. This body is without person, like water.

"This body is insubstantial, being housed in the four elements. This body is empty, transcending self and the qualities of self. This body is ignorant, like plants and rocks. This body is inactive, being turned by the power of the wind. This body is impure, replete with defilements. This body is untrustworthy, since even though one washes, clothes, and feeds it it will necessarily disintegrate. This body is a disaster, vexed by a hundred and one illnesses. This body is like a well on a hill, pressed by age. This body is unreliable, dying in spite of being needed. This body is like a poisonous snake, a vengeful bandit, an empty aggregation. It is the composite of the *skandhas*,[9] sensory realms, and sensory capacities.

"Sirs, this [body] being so calamitous and repugnant, you should wish for the body of the Buddha. Why?

"The body of the Buddha is the body of the Dharma. It is generated through immeasurable wisdom and merit. It is generated through morality, meditation, wisdom, emancipation, and the knowledge and vision of emancipation. It is generated through sympathy, compassion, joy, and equanimity (i.e., the four unlimiteds). It is generated through the perfections of charity, morality, forbearance and adaptability, energetic exertion, meditation, emancipation,

---

9. The "aggregates," a standard Buddhist list of five categories that together constitute mind and body: form, feeling, discrimination, compositional factors, and consciousness.

samadhi,[1] and learned wisdom. It is generated from skillful means; it has been generated from the six penetrations; it is generated from the three illuminations; it is generated from the thirty-seven factors of enlightenment; it has been generated from concentration and contemplation; it is generated from the ten powers, the four fearlessnesses, and the eighteen exclusive attributes; it is generated from the eradication of all the *dharmas* that are not good and accumulation of all the good *dharmas*; it is generated from the truth; it is generated from the absence of negligence.

"The Tathagata's body is generated from immeasurable pure *dharmas* such as these. Sirs, if you wish to attain the body of the Buddha and eradicate all the illnesses of sentient beings, you should generate the intention to achieve *anuttara samyaksambodhi*!"[2]

Thus did the Elder Vimalakirti explain the Dharma for those who inquired about his illness, causing innumerable thousands of people to all generate the intention to achieve *anuttara samyaksambodhi*.

Chapter III. Disciples

At that time the Elder Vimalakirti thought to himself, "I am lying sick in bed. How can the World-honored One, He of Great Sympathy, not take pity on me?"

Knowing what [Vimalakirti] was thinking, the Buddha immediately told Shariputra, "Go visit Vimalakirti and inquire about his illness."

Shariputra addressed the Buddha, "World-honored One, I dare not accept your instruction to go inquire about his illness. Why? I remember once in the past, when I was sitting in repose beneath a tree. At the time Vimalakirti came and said to me,

"'O Shariputra, you need not take this sitting [in meditation] to be sitting in repose. Sitting in repose is to not manifest body and mind in the triple world—this is sitting in repose. To generate the concentration of extinction[3] while manifesting the deportments—this is sitting in repose. Not to relinquish the Dharma of enlightenment and yet manifest the affairs of [ordinary] sentient beings—this is sitting in repose. To have the mind neither abide internally nor locate itself externally—this is sitting in repose. To be unmoved by the [sixty-two mistaken] views yet cultivate the thirty-seven factors of enlightenment—this is sitting in repose. Not to eradicate the afflictions yet enter into nirvana—this is sitting in repose.

"'Those who are able to sit in this fashion [will receive] the Buddha's seal of approval.'

"At the time, World-honored One, I simply listened to this explanation in silence and was unable to respond. Therefore, I cannot accept your instruction to go inquire about his illness."

The Buddha told Mahamaudgalyayana,[4] "You go inquire about Vimalakirti's illness."

Maudgalyayana addressed the Buddha, "World-honored One, I dare not accept your instruction to go inquire about his illness. Why? I remember

---

1. A state of deep meditation.
2. "Unsurpassed complete perfect enlightenment"; that is, buddhahood.
3. The most advanced level of concentration, a temporary suspension of all consciousness and mental activity.
4. The prefix *Maha* means "Great."

once in the past, I had entered the great city of Vaishali and was explaining the Dharma to the retired scholars of a certain neighborhood. At the time Vimalakirti came and said to me,

"'O Mahamaudgalyayana, when you explain the Dharma to white-robed retired scholars, you should not explain it as you are now doing. In explaining the Dharma, you should explain according to the Dharma.

"'The Dharma is without sentient beings because it transcends the defilements of sentient beings; the Dharma is without self because it transcends the defilements of self; the Dharma is without lifespan because it transcends birth and death (samsara); and the Dharma is without person because it eradicates the threshold between previous and subsequent [moments].

"'The Dharma is permanently serene because it extinguishes the characteristics; the Dharma transcends characteristics because it is without conditions; the Dharma is without names because it eradicates words; the Dharma is without explanation because it transcends discursive thought and reasoning; the Dharma is without the characteristics of form because it is like space; the Dharma is without hypotheses because it is ultimately empty; the Dharma is without the sense of personal possession because it transcends personal possession; the Dharma is without discrimination because it transcends the consciousnesses; and the Dharma is incomparable because there is nothing to match it; the Dharma is divorced from causation because it is not located in conditionality.

"'The Dharma is identical to Dharma-nature because it inheres in the *dharmas*;[5] Dharma accords with suchness because it is without anything that accords with it; the Dharma abides in the actual because it is unmoved by the extremes; the Dharma is motionless because it is not dependent on the six types of sensory data; and the Dharma is without past and future because it is constantly nonabiding.

"'The Dharma concurs with emptiness, accords with the absence of characteristics, and responds to inactivity. The Dharma transcends good and ugly, the Dharma is without gain and loss, the Dharma is without generation and extinction, and the Dharma is without refuge. The Dharma surpasses eye, ear, nose, tongue, body, and mind. The Dharma is without high and low, the Dharma abides constantly without moving, and the Dharma transcends all practices of contemplation.

"'O Mahamaudgalyayana, with characteristics such as these, how can the Dharma be explained? Explaining the Dharma should be without explaining and without indicating. Listening to the Dharma should be without listening and without attaining.

"'It is like a magician explaining the Dharma to conjured people.

"'One should have such a mindset in explaining the Dharma; one should comprehend that the faculties of sentient beings [include both] sharp and dull. You would do well to be without hindrance in your knowledge and vision. Use the mind of great compassion and praise the Mahayana. Remember to recompense the kindness of the Buddha and do not cut off the Three Jewels.[6] Thus should you explain the Dharma.'

5. In this context, "phenomena."
6. That is, the Buddha, the dharma, and the sangha.

"When Vimalakirti explained this Dharma, eight hundred retired scholars generated the intention to achieve *anuttara samyaksambodhi*. I lack this eloquence. Therefore I cannot accept [your instruction] to go inquire about his illness."

The Buddha told Mahakashyapa, "You go inquire about Vimalakirti's illness."

Kashyapa addressed the Buddha, "World-honored One, I dare not accept your instruction to go inquire about his illness. Why? I remember once in the past, when I was begging in a poor neighborhood, Vimalakirti came and said to me,

"'O Mahakashyapa, you have the mind of sympathy and compassion but are unable [to apply it] universally. You have abandoned the wealthy to beg from the poor.

"'Kashyapa, while abiding in the Dharma of universal sameness, you should proceed in sequence in your begging.

"'It is because of not eating that you should practice begging.

"'It is because of the destruction of one's physical integrity that you should take that lump of food. It is because of not receiving that you should receive that food.

"'You should enter a village with the idea that it is an empty aggregation.

"'The forms you see are equivalent to [what] the blind [see]; the sounds you hear are equivalent to echoes; the fragrances you smell are equivalent to the wind; the flavors you eat should not be discriminated; your tactile sensations are like the realizations of wisdom; and you should understand that the *dharmas*[7] are like phantasms. That which is without self-nature and without other-nature originally was not burning and will not become extinguished now.

"'Kashyapa, if you are able to enter the eight emancipations without renouncing the eight perversions, using the characteristic of perversion to enter into the correct Dharma, and using a single meal to give to all, making offerings to the Buddhas and the assembly of worthies and sages—only then should you eat.

"'To eat in this fashion is neither to have the afflictions nor to transcend the afflictions, it is neither to enter into concentration nor to arise from concentration, it is neither to abide in the world nor to abide in nirvana.

"'Where there is charity, there are neither great nor small blessings, neither benefit nor harm. This is the correct entry into the path of Buddhahood, without relying on the *shravaka* [vehicle].[8]

"'Kashyapa, if you can eat according to this [understanding] then you will not render void the charity of those who feed you.'

"At the time, World-honored One, the explanation I heard was unprecedented to me, and I immediately generated a profound sense of reverence for all bodhisattvas. I also thought, 'This householder's eloquence and wisdom being as they are, how could anyone who hears him not generate the intention to achieve *anuttara samyaksambodhi*? From now on I will never exhort anyone to undertake the practices of *shravaka* or *pratyekabuddha*.'[9] Therefore I cannot accept [your instruction] to go inquire about his illness."

---

7. Phenomena.
8. That is, the path of the "hearer" (disciple).

9. "Solitary enlightened one," the second vehicle.

The Buddha told Subhuti, "You go inquire about Vimalakirti's illness."

Subhuti addressed the Buddha, "World-honored One, I dare not accept your instruction to go inquire about his illness. Why? I remember once in the past, I entered into his home to beg. At the time Vimalakirti filled my bowl full of food and said to me,

"'O Subhuti, if you are able to be universally same about eating, then the *dharmas* are also universally same; if the *dharmas* are universally same, you should also be universally same about eating. If you can practice begging like this, you may accept the food.

"'If, Subhuti, you refrain from eradicating licentiousness, anger, and stupidity, yet are not equipped with them; if you do not destroy the body, yet accord with the single characteristic; if you do not extinguish stupidity and affection, yet generate wisdom and emancipation; if you use the characteristics of the five transgressions to attain emancipation, without either emancipation or bondage; if you do not perceive the four noble truths, yet do not fail to perceive the truths; neither attaining the results [of becoming a stream-enterer (*srota-apanna*),[1] and so on,] nor not attaining the results; neither being an ordinary [unenlightened] person nor transcending the state (lit., "*dharma*") of ordinary person; neither being a sage nor not being a sage; accomplishing all the *dharmas* yet transcending the characteristics of the *dharmas*—then you can accept this food.

"'Subhuti, you should only accept this food if you can neither see the Buddha nor hear the Dharma, nor the six teachers of heterodox paths—Purana Kashyapa, Maskarin Goshaliputra, Samjayin Vairatiputra, Ajita Keshakambala, Kakuda Katyayana, and Nirgrantha Jnatiputra, who were your teachers, following whom you left home, [so that] at the defeat of those teachers you were also defeated—then you can accept this food.

"'If, Subhuti, you can enter into the heterodox views and not reach the other shore; abide in the eight difficulties and not attain the absence of difficulty; identify with the afflictions and transcend the pure *dharmas*; attain the *samadhi* of noncontention; if all sentient beings generate this concentration; if the donors do not name you their field of blessings; if those making offerings to you fall into the three evil destinations; if you join hands with the host of Maras and make them your co-workers; if you do not differentiate yourself from the host of Maras and the sensory troubles; if you bear resentment toward all sentient beings; if you revile the Buddhas, denigrate the Dharma, and do not enter the Sangha; and if you never attain extinction— if you are like this then you can accept the food.'

"When I heard these words, World-honored One, I was bewildered and did not understand what he had said. I did not know how to answer, so I put down the bowl and tried to leave his house. Vimalakirti then said,

"'O Subhuti, do not be afraid to take your bowl. What is the meaning of this? If a [phantasmagorical] person whom the Tathagata has created through the transformation [of conjury] is criticized for this, should he be afraid?' I said, 'No.' Vimalakirti said, 'All the *dharmas* have the characteristic of being like phantasmagorical transformations. You should not have any fear now. Why? All verbal explanations do not transcend this characteristic. The wise

1. Also translated as "stream-winner," the first of the four stages of progress on the path to nirvana (the other three are once-returner, never- returner, and arhat). A stream-enterer has entered the stream to nirvana and will achieve it in seven or fewer lifetimes.

are not attached to letters, and therefore they have no fear. Why? The nature of letters transcends [their characteristics]; there are no letters. This is emancipation, and the characteristic of emancipation is the *dharmas*.'

"When Vimalakirti explained this Dharma, two hundred gods attained purification of their Dharma eyes. Therefore I cannot accept [your instruction] to go inquire about his illness."

The Buddha told Purnamaitrayaniputra, "You go inquire about Vimalakirti's illness."

Purna addressed the Buddha, "World-honored One, I dare not accept your instruction to go inquire about his illness. Why? I remember once in the past, when I was beneath a tree in the forest explaining the Dharma to novice *bhikshus*.[2] At the time Vimalakirti came and said to me,

"'O Purna, you should only explain the Dharma after first entering into concentration and contemplating the minds of these people—do not put defiled food in a jeweled vessel. You should understand what these *bhikshus* are thinking—do not put lapis lazuli together with crystal.

"'You are unable to understand the fundamental sources of sentient beings—do not inspire them with the Hinayana Dharma. Other and self are without flaw, so do not harm them. If someone wants to travel the great path (i.e., practice the Mahayana), do not show them a small pathway. The ocean cannot be contained within the hoofprint of an ox; the radiance of the sun cannot be equaled by that of a firefly.

"'Purna, these *bhikshus* have long since generated the aspiration for the Mahayana but in the midst [of many rebirths] they have forgotten this intention.

"'Why would you teach them with the Hinayana Dharma? When I consider the Hinayana, its wisdom is as minute as a blind man's, [and with it you are] unable to discriminate the sharp and dull faculties of all sentient beings.'

"Then Vimalakirti entered into *samadhi* and made the *bhikshus* aware of their previous lives. They had planted virtuous roots under five hundred Buddhas and had rededicated them to their [eventual achievement of] *anuttara samyaksambodhi*. [Learning this], they immediately experienced a suddenly expansive reacquisition of that original inspiration. At this the *bhikshus* bowed their heads in reverence to Vimalakirti's feet. Then Vimalakirti explained the Dharma for them, and they never again retrogressed from [their progress to] *anuttara samyaksambodhi*.

"I thought, '*Shravakas* do not consider the faculties of people and therefore should not explain the Dharma.'

"Therefore, I cannot accept [your instruction] to go inquire about his illness."

The Buddha told Mahakatyayana, "You go inquire about Vimalakirti's illness."

Katyayana addressed the Buddha, "World-honored One, I dare not accept your instruction to go inquire about his illness. Why? I remember once in the past, when the Buddha briefly explained the essentials of the Dharma to some *bhikshus*, and immediately afterward I expanded upon your meaning, discussing the meanings of impermanence, suffering, emptiness, no-self, and extinction. At the time Vimalakirti came and said to me,

2. Monks.

"'O Katyayana, do not explain the Dharma of the true characteristic using the mental processes of generation and extinction (i.e., samsara).

"'Katyayana, the *dharmas* are ultimately neither generated nor extinguished: this is the meaning of impermanence.

"'The five *skandhas* are empty throughout, with no arising: this is the meaning of suffering.

"'The *dharmas* ultimately do not exist: this is the meaning of emptiness.

"'There is no self in the self, yet no duality: this is the meaning of no-self.

"'The *dharmas* were originally not burning and will not become extinguished now: this is the meaning of extinction.'

"When [Vimalakirti] explained this Dharma, the *bhikshus'* minds attained emancipation. Therefore, I cannot accept [your instruction] to go inquire about his illness."

The Buddha told Aniruddha, "You go inquire about Vimalakirti's illness."

Aniruddha addressed the Buddha, "World-honored One, I dare not accept your instruction to go inquire about his illness. Why?

"I remember once in the past I was walking quietly in a certain location. At the time a Brahma king named Adorned Purity, in the company of ten thousand Brahmas generating pure radiance, proceeded to where I was. He bowed to my feet in reverence and asked me, 'How much, Aniruddha, can you see with your divine eye?'

"I answered, 'Sir, I see the trimegachiliocosm of Shakyamuni's[3] Buddha land as if I were looking at a mango in the palm of my hand.'

"Then Vimalakirti came and said to me, 'O Aniruddha, is the seeing of the divine eye a constructed characteristic, or is it an unconstructed characteristic? If it is a constructed characteristic, then it is equivalent to the five supernormal powers of the heterodox paths. If it is an unconstructed characteristic then it is unconditioned[4] and should be without seeing (i.e., "views").' World-honored One, at the time I remained silent.

"Hearing his words, the Brahmas attained something unprecedented, immediately reverenced [Vimalakirti], and asked him, 'Who in this world has the true divine eye?' Vimalakirti said, 'There is the Buddha, the World-honored One, who has attained the true divine eye. Always in *samadhi*, he sees all the Buddha lands without any characteristic of duality.'

"At this Adorned Purity Brahma King and his attending five hundred Brahma kings all generated the intention to achieve *anuttara samyaksambodhi*. They bowed to Vimalakirti's feet, then instantly disappeared. Therefore, I cannot accept [your instruction] to go inquire about his illness."

The Buddha told Upali, "You go inquire about Vimalakirti's illness."

Upali addressed the Buddha, "World-honored One, I dare not accept your instruction to go inquire about his illness. Why?

"I remember once in the past, there were two *bhikshus* who had violated the practice of the Vinaya but from their shame did not dare ask you about it. They came to ask me: 'O Upali, we have violated the Vinaya and are sincerely ashamed, not daring to ask the Buddha about it. We want you to explain our doubts and the [need for] repentance, so that we may be relieved of the

---

3. Literally, "Sage of the Shakyas"; a title of the Buddha, who was born into the Shakya clan. "Trimegachiliocosm": great billion-world universe (i.e., the whole universe).
4. That is, unconditioned by impermanence.

transgressions.' I immediately explained [the matter] to them according to the Dharma.

"At the time Vimalakirti came and said to me,

"'O Upali, do not increase these two *bhikshus*' transgressions. You should just remove [the transgressions] and not disturb their minds. Why?

"'The nature of those transgressions does not reside within, it does not reside without, and it does not reside in the middle.

"'As the Buddha has explained, when their minds are defiled, sentient beings are defiled. When their minds are purified, sentient beings are purified. The mind likewise does not reside within, does not reside without, and does not reside in the middle. Just so is the mind, and just so are transgression and defilement. The *dharmas* are also likewise, in not transcending suchness.

"'Just so, Upali, when one attains emancipation using the characteristics of the mind, is it (i.e., the mind) defiled or not?' I said, 'It is not.'

"Vimalakirti said, 'The characteristics of the minds of all sentient beings are likewise, in being without defilement.

"'O Upali, to have false concepts is defilement; to be without false concepts is purity.

"'Confusion is defilement, and the absence of confusion is purity.

"'To grasp the self is defilement, and not to grasp the self is purity.

"'Upali, all the *dharmas* are generated and extinguished, without abiding. Like phantasms or lightning bolts, the *dharmas* do not depend on each other. They do not abide even for a single instant. The *dharmas* are all false views, like a dream, like a mirage, like the moon [reflected] in water, like an image in a mirror—[all] generated from false conceptualization. Those who understand this are called 'upholders of the Vinaya.' Those who understand this are said to 'understand well.'"

"At this the two *bhikshus* said, 'Such superior wisdom! Upali cannot match this! There could be no better explanation of upholding the Vinaya!'

"I then answered, 'Excluding the Tathagata, there has never been a *shravaka* or bodhisattva able to command the eloquence for such a felicitous explanation—such is the brilliance of his wisdom!'

"At the time, the doubts and [need for] repentance of the two *bhikshus* were eliminated. They generated the intention to achieve *anuttara samyaksambodhi*, speaking this vow: 'Let all sentient beings attain this [level of] eloquence!' Therefore, I cannot accept [your instruction] to go inquire about his illness."

The Buddha told Rahula, "You go inquire about Vimalakirti's illness."

Rahula addressed the Buddha, "World-honored One, I dare not accept your instruction to go inquire about his illness. Why?

"I remember once in the past, the elders' sons of Vaishali came to where I was, bowed their heads to me in reverence, and asked, 'O Rahula, you are the son of the Buddha, who forsook the position of universal ruler (*chakravartin*)[5] and left home for the path (i.e., enlightenment). What benefits are there to leaving home?'

"I then explained to them, according to the Dharma, the benefits of the merits of leaving home. At that point Vimalakirti came and said to me,

---

5. Wheel-turning monarch: a figure of Indian mythology who possesses a magic wheel that rolls around the world—every land that it reaches becomes part of his domain.

"'O Rahula, you should not explain the benefits of the merits of leaving home. Why? To be without benefit and without merits—this is leaving home. One may explain that there are benefits and merits in the conditioned *dharmas*, but leaving home is an unconditioned *dharma* and there are no benefits and merits in unconditioned *dharmas*.

"'Rahula, to leave home is to be without that and this, and without intermediate. It is to transcend the sixty-two views and be located in nirvana.

"'[Leaving home] is accepted by the wise and practiced by the sagely. It subjugates the host of Maras and [allows one to] transcend the five destinations, purify the five eyes, attain the five powers, and establish the five faculties. It is to be without vexation over "that," to transcend the host of heterogeneous evils, and to demolish the heterodox paths. It is to transcend provisional names and emerge from the muck [of samsara]. It is to be without attachments, without any sense of personal possession. It is to be without experience, without turmoil. It is to harbor joy within and defend the intentions of others. It is to accord with meditation and transcend the host of transgressions. If one can be like this, then this is true leaving home.'

"At this Vimalakirti said to those elders' sons, 'You would do well to leave home together in the correct Dharma. Why? It is difficult to encounter a time when a Buddha is in the world.'

"The elders' sons said, 'O retired scholar, we have heard that the Buddha has said one may not leave home without first receiving permission from one's parents.'

"Vimalakirti said, 'So it is. You should immediately generate the intention to achieve *anuttara samyaksambodhi*, and this is to "leave home." This is sufficient.'

"Then thirty-two elders' sons all generated the intention to achieve *anuttara samyaksambodhi*. Therefore, I cannot accept [your instruction] to go inquire about his illness."

The Buddha told Ananda,[6] "You go inquire about Vimalakirti's illness."

Ananda addressed the Buddha, "World-honored One, I dare not accept your instruction to go inquire about his illness. Why? I remember once in the past, the World-honored One had a slight illness requiring cow's milk [as medicine]. I took my bowl and proceeded to the gateway of a great brahman home.

"While I was standing there Vimalakirti came and said to me, 'O Ananda, why are you standing here with your bowl so early in the morning?'

"I said, 'O retired scholar, the World-honored One has a slight illness requiring cow's milk, and so I have come here.'

"Vimalakirti said, 'Stop, stop, Ananda! Do not speak thus. The Tathagata's body is the essence of *vajra*.[7] [In it] the evils are already eradicated and the host of goods universally assembled. What illness could it have, what vexation could there be?

"'Go silently, Ananda—do not revile the Tathagata, and do not let anyone else hear such coarse talk. Do not allow the gods of awesome power and virtue and the bodhisattvas who have come from pure lands in other directions to hear these words.

---

6. The Buddha's cousin and personal attendant.
7. Translated either as "diamond" or as "thunderbolt"; something unbreakable.

"'Ananda, even a small degree of blessings (i.e., merit) allows the wheel-turning sage king (*chakravartin*) to be without illness—how could the immeasurable blessings of the Tathagata fail to exceed his in every regard?!

"'Go, Ananda—do not make us experience this shame. If brahmans in the heterodox paths hear this, they will think, "Who is this teacher, who is unable to save himself from illness but would save others of their ills?" Sir, go in secret haste and do not let anyone hear this.

"'You should understand, Ananda, the bodies of the Tathagatas are bodies of the Dharma, not bodies of longing. The Buddha is the World-honored One, who has transcended the triple world. The Buddha's body is without flaws, the flaws having been extinguished. The Buddha's body is unconditioned and does not fit the [conventional] analytic categories. A body such as this—how could it be ill, how could it be vexed?'

"At the time, World-honored One, I was really ashamed that I might have mistakenly heard what the Buddha had said in spite of being so close.

"'I then heard a voice from space saying, 'Ananda, it is as the retired scholar has said. It is just that the Buddha has appeared in this evil age of the five corruptions[8] and manifests this Dharma to emancipate sentient beings. Go, Ananda. Take the milk without shame.'

"World-honored One, the eloquence of Vimalakirti's wisdom is like this. Therefore, I cannot accept [your instruction] to go inquire about his illness."

In similar fashion all of the Buddha's five hundred great disciples each explained their original encounters and related what Vimalakirti had said, and each said he was unable to accept [the Buddha's instruction] to go inquire about [Vimalakirti's] illness.

8. Corruptions of life span, views, afflictions, sentient beings, and time.

THE PURE LAND

DISCOURSE ON THE LAND OF BLISS
(*The Sukhavativyuha Sutra*)

The Buddha taught the path to liberation from rebirth, but he also taught the path to rebirth in heaven. It is sometimes said that he taught this latter path to those who were incapable, at least in the present lifetime, of following the former. Rebirth in heaven is the result of the practice of virtue, especially the virtue of charity, while liberation from rebirth requires an insight into reality so powerful that it destroys the causes for all future rebirth. Nirvana is a permanent state, whereas heaven (unlike in Christianity) is temporary; after a long sojourn as a god in one of the several celestial realms, one is reborn someplace else, and less desirable, within the cycle of birth and death. Still, over the course of the history of Buddhism, the practice of laypeople—that is, the majority of Buddhists—has been directed not toward the goal of nirvana but instead toward rebirth in heaven, after which an individual will eventually die and be reborn in another realm within samsara. With the rise of the Mahayana, a third alternative developed, one that combined nirvana's security with heaven's relative ease of entry. Such a place is called a "pure land."

The Buddha Amitabha. Japan, late 13th century.

The Mahayana sutras describe a universe filled with numerous world systems, generally similar to our own. These worlds differ in such things as the length of the life span of their inhabitants, as well as the degree of their happiness and suffering. Worlds also differed in whether they were "fortunate": that is, whether a buddha was present in the world during a given aeon. In such a fortunate time and fortunate place, that world became a "buddha-field," a site for the deeds of a buddha. The purpose of the buddha was to purify the world, both by teaching the dharma and by performing miraculous deeds. Such worlds existed in various degrees of purity, generally measured by whether they contained realms of denizens of hell, hungry ghosts, or animals as well as the realms of humans and gods. The three unfortunate realms were absent from the pure buddha-fields. The Mahayana sutras envisioned the simultaneous presence of many buddhas in many worlds, throughout a vast universe, and rebirth could be gained in any of these worlds, under the care of one of these buddhas. Thus, birth in a buddha-field became a popular goal of Buddhist practice in the Mahayana, first in India and then in East Asia and Tibet.

The most famous of those buddha-fields was called Sukhavati, the "Land of Bliss." Its existence is proclaimed and its qualities described in two sutras from the third century C.E—one considerably longer than the other—with the same title, *Sukhavativyuha*: literally, the "Sutra Displaying [the Land of] Bliss." These two sutras, together with a text unknown in India but important in China, the *Sutra on the Contemplation of Amitayus (Guan Wuliangshou Jing)*, constitute the main texts of the Pure Land tradition of East Asia.

The longer *Sukhavativyuha Sutra*, an excerpt from which appears here, begins with Ananda noticing that the Buddha looks especially serene and asking why. The Buddha replies that he was thinking back many millions of aeons to the time of a buddha named Lokeshvararaja. The Buddha then tells the following story, in the form of a flashback.

In the audience of this buddha was a monk named Dharmakara ("Treasury of the Dharma"), who approached Lokeshvararaja and announced his aspiration to become a buddha himself. Dharmakara then requested that the buddha describe all of the qualities of a buddha-field. Lokeshvararaja agreed, but because the myriad buddha-fields of the myriad buddhas have many qualities, the discourse lasted for a million years. Having listened intently throughout, the monk Dharmakara then retired and entered into a state of deep meditation, which lasted for five aeons. The goal of his meditation was to synthesize all of the marvelous qualities of the millions of buddha-fields that Lokeshvararaja had described to him into a single pure buddha-field.

When he had completed his meditation, he returned to describe his imagined land to Lokeshvararaja, promising to turn this dream into reality by creating a place of birth for fortunate beings. He vowed to traverse the long bodhisattva path and become the buddha of this new buddha-field. He then went on to describe the land that he would create and, importantly, he expressed that description in the form of a series of vows, stating that unless specific conditions in his pure land were met, he would not become a buddha. For example, he said, "If in my pure land there are animals, ghosts, or denizens of hell, may I not become a buddha." He made forty-eight such vows. These included the vow that all of the beings in his pure land will be the color of gold; that beings in his pure land will have no conception of private property; that no bodhisattva will have to wash, dry, sew, or bleach his own robes; that bodhisattvas in his pure land will be able to hear the dharma in whatever form they wish to hear it and whenever they wish to hear it; and that any woman who hears his name, creates the aspiration to enlightenment in her mind, and feels disgust at the female form will not be reborn as a woman again. Two of these vows would become the focus of particular attention. In the eighteenth vow (the seventeenth in the East Asian versions), Dharmakara promises that when he is a buddha, he will appear at the moment of death to anyone who creates the aspiration to enlightenment, hears his name, and remembers him with faith. In the following vow, he promises that all those who hear his name, wish to be reborn in his pure land, and dedicate their merit to that end will be reborn there, even if they make such a resolution as few as ten times during the course of their life. Only those who have committed one of the five sins of immediate retribution (killing one's father, killing one's mother, killing an arhat, wounding a buddha, or causing schism in the sangha) would be excluded.

The flashback ends and the scene shifts back to the present. Ananda asks the Buddha whether Dharmakara was successful, whether he was in fact able to complete the long path of the bodhisattva to become a buddha. The Buddha replies that he did indeed succeed and that he became the buddha called Amitabha, "Infinite Light." The buddha-field that he created is called Sukhavati. And because Dharmakara became a buddha, all of the things that he promised to create in his buddha-field have become realities. The Buddha proceeds to describe Sukhavati; a portion of his description appears here.

Some of the inhabitants sit cross-legged on lotus blossoms while others are enclosed within the calyx of a lotus. The latter do not feel imprisoned, because the calyx of the lotus is so large that it holds a palace similar to those of the gods. Persons who in their previous life dedicated their merit toward rebirth in the buddha-field of Amitabha, yet who still harbor doubts, are reborn inside lotuses where they must remain for 500 years, enjoying visions of the buddha-field but unable to hear the dharma. Those who are free from doubt are reborn immediately on open lotuses, with unlimited access to the dharma. Rebirth in Amitabha's buddha-field, his "pure land," would become a common goal of Buddhist practice, for monks and laity alike, in India, Tibet, and throughout East Asia (see Shinran's *Lamenting the Deviations*, p. 611).

PRONOUNCING GLOSSARY

Ananda: *ah-nan-da*

bodhisattva: *boh-dih-sat-tva*

Maudgalyayana: *maud-gal-yah-ya-na*

samadhi: *sa-mah-di*

Sangha: *san-ga*

Sukhavativyuha Sutra: *soo-kah-va-tee-vyu-ha soo-tra*

tathagata: *ta-tah-ga-ta*

"Moreover, regarding the disciples and bodhisattvas in that land, it is difficult to measure their number. One cannot estimate or express the degree of their thorough command of supernormal knowledge or of their majestic

TRANSLATED FROM the Chinese by Luis O. Gómez.

power and total mastery. They are able to hold all world systems in the palm of the hand."

The Buddha said to Ananda:[1] "The number of disciples in the first of the four assemblies of this buddha cannot be calculated. And, likewise, one cannot express the number of bodhisattvas in his land.

"Hundreds, thousands, tens of thousands, millions, measureless, numberless persons equal in supernormal powers to Maudgalyayana the Great[2] would not be able to comprehend fully the number of the disciples, even if these persons went on counting together for countless trillions of cosmic ages, even until the time they attained liberation.

"It is like the great ocean; its depth and breadth cannot be measured. If, for example, someone should split one strand of his hair into a hundred slivers, and he should dip one of these slivers in the ocean, picking up one drop of water—what do you think? That drop of water that he has taken up—what part is it of all the water in the great ocean?"

Ananda replied to the Buddha: "One can know the proportion of this drop to the water in the great ocean neither by estimation, nor by calculation, nor by description, nor by comparison."

The Buddha said to Ananda: "Those persons equal in supernormal powers to someone like Maudgalyayana cannot determine the number of disciples and bodhisattvas in the first assembly of the Buddha of Measureless Life, even counting for countless trillions of cosmic ages, any more than one could know the amount of water in the great ocean by means of one single drop."

"Furthermore, that buddha-land is a world system surrounded on all sides by trees made of the seven precious substances. There are trees of gold, trees of silver, trees of lapis-lazuli, trees of rock crystal, trees of coral, trees of agate, and trees of mother-of-pearl. Some trees are made of two precious substances, some are made of three, and so on, up to trees made of the seven precious substances.

"Some golden trees have silver leaves, flowers, and fruits. Some silver trees have gold leaves, flowers, and fruits. Some lapis-lazuli trees have leaves, flowers, and fruits made of crystal, and so forth. Some crystal trees have leaves, flowers, and fruits made of lapis-lazuli, and so forth. Some coral trees have leaves, flowers, and fruits made of agate. Some agate trees have leaves, flowers, and fruits made of lapis-lazuli. Some mother-of-pearl trees have their leaves, flowers, and fruits made of all sorts of gems.

"Some jewel trees have roots made of purple gold, trunks of white silver, branches of lapis-lazuli, boughs of crystal, leaves of coral, flowers of agate, and fruits of mother-of-pearl. Some jewel trees have roots made of white silver, trunks of lapis-lazuli, branches of crystal, boughs of coral, leaves of agate, flowers of mother-of-pearl, and fruits of purple gold. Some jewel trees have roots made of lapis-lazuli, trunks of crystal, branches of coral, boughs of agate, leaves of mother-of-pearl, flowers of purple gold, and fruits of white silver. Some jewel trees have roots made of crystal, trunks of coral, branches of agate, boughs of mother-of-pearl, leaves of purple gold, flowers of white silver, and fruits of lapis-lazuli. Some jewel trees have roots made of coral, trunks of agate, branches of mother-of-pearl, boughs of purple gold, leaves

1. The Buddha's cousin and personal attendant.   2. One of the Buddha's closest disciples.

of white silver, flowers of lapis-lazuli, and fruits of crystal. Some jewel trees have roots made of agate, trunks of mother-of-pearl, branches of purple gold, boughs of white silver, leaves of lapis-lazuli, flowers of crystal, and fruits of coral. Some jewel trees have roots made of mother-of-pearl, trunks of purple gold, branches of white silver, boughs of lapis-lazuli, leaves of crystal, flowers of coral, and fruits of agate.

"These trees all stand in neat rows next to each other, the trunks facing each other, the branches following one after the other, the leaves facing each other, the flowers following one after the other, and the fruits touching each other. Their blazing colors and lights shine so that one can barely look at them directly. Occasionally, pure breezes blow among these trees, producing the five tones of the musical scale, and these delicate and mysterious tunes harmonize spontaneously.

"Furthermore, the tree under which the Buddha of Measureless Life practiced the Way of awakening is four million leagues high, its roots spread out for five thousand leagues, its branches and leaves extend in the four directions for two million leagues. All kinds of jewels combine naturally in this tree—the jewel called Moonbeam Pearl, the jewel called Bearing the Circle of the Sea, and other monarchs among the jewels. And between its boughs covered with ornaments hang jeweled garlands with hundreds of thousands of myriad colors of different and varying hues, shining with numberless dazzling lights. Extraordinarily rare and precious jeweled nets hang over the tree. Every ornament appears in response to a person's desire.

"And a subtle breeze stirs, so that marvelous sounds of Dharma flow from that tree into all the buddha-realms in the ten regions of the universe. Those who hear these sounds attain the serene acceptance of the Deepest Dharma and remain in the condition of not falling back from awakening; they will attain the Way of a buddha without ever again encountering pain or sorrow. The eyes that have seen the colors of this tree, the ears that have heard its sounds, the nose that has smelled its fragrance, the tongue that has tasted its tastes, the body that has been touched by its light, as well as the mind with all its thoughts and mental states—they all attain the serene acceptance of the Deepest Dharma, they will continue on the Path without ever falling back until they attain the Way of a buddha, and their six sense organs[3] remain pure and serene, free from all pain and sorrow.

"Ananda, when humans and gods in this realm see this tree, they attain the three levels of serene acceptances of the Dharma: first, serene acceptance of the word, second, serene acceptance of compliance, and third, serene acceptance of nonarising. All this comes from the majestic power of the Buddha of Measureless Life, from the power of his former vows, from the fulfillment of his vows, from the full realization of his vows, from the establishment of his vows, from the completion of his vows."

The Buddha said to Ananda: "Earthly kings enjoy a hundred thousand varieties of music. From the musical tunes enjoyed by wheel-turning emperors,[4] up to those enjoyed in the Sixth Heaven, each surpasses the preceding by ten thousand billion times. The ten thousand kinds of musical

---

3. Eye, ear, nose, tongue, body, and mind.   4. Universal monarchs.

melodies of the Sixth Heaven, even if they were a hundred million times better than they are, cannot be compared to any one of the varieties of tunes produced among these trees in this country of the Buddha of Measureless Life—trees made of the seven precious substances. Moreover, in this realm there are ten thousand varieties of spontaneous music. Furthermore, these musical tunes consist only of the sounds of Dharma heard in a clear, soft, and exquisite symphony, which is the first and foremost among all the sounds in all the world systems in the ten regions of the universe.

"And again the lecture halls, the monks' quarters, the palaces, and the watchtowers are all adorned with the seven precious substances, created miraculously. And curtains studded with genuine pearls, the Bright Moon jewel, and other gems hang over and envelop these buildings.

"Inside and outside, on the left and on the right, are bathing ponds— some measuring ten leagues, some twenty, thirty, and so on, up to a hundred thousand leagues. In width, length, and depth each measures the same and is filled to the brim with water possessing the eight good qualities.[5] Pure, clean, and fragrant is the water, and most sweet to taste, like ambrosia. The floor of those ponds that are made of yellow gold is spread with white silver sands; the floor of ponds made of white silver is spread with yellow gold sands. The floor of crystal ponds is spread with lapis-lazuli sands; the floor of lapis-lazuli ponds is spread with crystal sands. The floor of coral ponds is spread with amber sands; the floor of amber ponds is spread with coral sands. The floor of mother-of-pearl ponds is spread with agate sands; the floor of agate ponds is spread with mother-of-pearl sands. The floor of white jade ponds is spread with purple gold sands; the floor of purple gold ponds is spread with white jade sands. Some are adorned with sands of two precious substances, others with sands of three precious substances, and so forth, so that some are adorned with sands made of all seven precious substances.

"On the banks of these ponds grow sandalwood trees: their leaves and flowers spread perfume all over the sky. And various blossoms spread on the surface of the water—the blue water lily, the lotus, the white water lily, and the white lotus—shining with their various colors. If the bodhisattvas and disciples enter these jeweled ponds and wish that the water cover only their feet, the water will only cover them up to the feet. If they wish that the water reach only to their knees, the water will reach up only to the knees. If they wish that the water reach only to their waist, the water will reach only up to the waist. If they wish that the water reach only as high as their neck, the water will reach only as high as the neck. If they wish that the water bathe all their body, the water will spontaneously and naturally bathe their whole body. If they wish to make the water recede, it will recede at once. How warm or cool the water will be is regulated spontaneously, naturally, and exactly as they may wish it to be. It opens the mind, delights the body, and washes away all impurities from the heart. It is pure, clear, and limpid—so pure that it is imperceptible. The sands made of precious substances are so brilliant that there is no depth that they will not illuminate. Gentle waves ripple back and

5. Purity, refreshing coolness, sweetness, softness, calmness, power to fertilize, power to prevent famine, and productiveness.

forth on the surface, flowing into each other softly as they slowly fade, never too slowly, never rushed—yet these ripples miraculously produce endless marvelous sounds.

"There is no sound in that land that one will not be able to hear if one so desires. One will hear the sound of the word 'Buddha,' or one will hear the sound of the word 'Dharma,' or one will hear the sound of the word 'Sangha'; or one will hear the sound 'calm,' the sound 'empty and without a self,' the sound 'great compassion,' the sound 'perfect virtues,' or the sounds 'ten powers, ten conditions of fearlessness, eighteen unique qualities of a buddha,' or the sound 'supernormal powers and knowledges,' the sound 'unconditioned,' or the sound 'neither arising nor ceasing,' or the sound 'serene acceptance of nonarising,' and so forth, even up to the sound of the words 'bodhisattvas anointed with the ambrosia of Dharma,' and the sound of the words for all kinds of other sublime truths, virtues, and states of spiritual advancement.

"The joy of anyone listening to such sounds has no limits. It is a joy that reflects purity, freedom from desire, calm, and truth. It is the joy associated with the Three Treasures,[6] the ten powers, the ten conditions of fearlessness, and the eighteen unique qualities of buddhas. It is the joy found in the path of the supernormal powers and knowledges, which is followed by bodhisattvas and disciples.

"In this land the names of the three impure realms,[7] of suffering, and of the difficult forms of rebirth are not to be found. On the contrary, the sound of the word 'bliss' occurs spontaneously. This is why this realm is called 'Land of Peace and Happiness.'"

"Ananda, all the living beings that go to be reborn in this buddha's land possess the following qualities: bodies of pure color, marvelous voices, supernormal powers, and merits. The palaces in which they reside, the clothing they wear, and the food they eat, the flowers that adorn them, the perfumes and ornaments they wear are like the possessions of the gods of the Sixth Heaven, which appear spontaneously. If they wish to eat, vessels made of the seven precious substances appear spontaneously before them according to their wish. According to each one's desires, there will appear different vessels made of gold, silver, lapis-lazuli, mother-of-pearl, agate, coral, and amber, as well as genuine Moonbeam pearls. Many vessels such as these, if one so desires, are filled spontaneously with food and drink of a hundred different flavors. But, even though their meals appear before them in this manner, these living beings do not consume the food; rather, they look at the color, taste the flavor, and, by merely thinking of eating, their hunger is sated miraculously. Their bodies and minds become supple and tender, and the taste of this food does not cling to them. When the vessels have served their purpose, they disappear; as time passes, they reappear.

"That buddha's land is pure and peaceful, blessed with the exquisite and rare joys found in the unconditioned Way[8] of nirvana.

"As for the disciples, bodhisattvas, humans, and gods in that land, their wisdom is high and clear, their supernormal powers are far-reaching, and of the same kind for all. There is no difference among them in their bodily

---

6. That is, the three jewels: the Buddha, the dharma, and the sangha.
7. The realms of animals, hungry ghosts, and denizens of hell.
8. That which is unconditioned by impermanence.

forms. It is only in buddha-fields in other regions of the universe that such names as humans and gods are used. Their visage is well proportioned, surpassing the faces we see in this world, rare. Their countenance is wonderful and exquisite. They are neither gods nor humans. They miraculously have acquired bodies like empty space, bodies that are not surpassed anywhere."

The Buddha said to Ananda: "In our own world, this would be like a destitute beggar standing next to a sovereign emperor. Could one ever compare the two in appearance and demeanor?"

Ananda replied to the Buddha: "If one compares this man to a sovereign emperor, one can only say that his miserable and disgraceful condition, even if improved a hundred times, a thousand times, ten thousand times, or a hundred thousand times, would not measure up to the emperor's condition. The reason is that this destitute beggar is in an extremely lowly and miserable condition: his clothing barely covers his body, his food is the nourishment of famine, and he spends his life in cold, fatigue, and suffering.

"This man finds himself in a situation so miserable because, during all of his previous lives, he did not cultivate the roots of virtue. Whenever he was able to acquire wealth, he did not give of it. Whenever he was able to become rich, he only thought of his own profit and became a miser. He sought only to increase his wealth—always more and more—without ever being content, and he did not have faith in the cultivation of the good. He accumulated a mountain of evil actions, and, at the end of his life, his riches and his treasures were dispersed. He brought pain upon his own body and piled misery on himself. He did nothing to benefit others. Without good actions what could he rely on? Without merit where could he place his trust?

"This is why, when he died, this beggar fell into the unfortunate rebirths, where he experienced the long torments of those rebirths. Finally, he has managed to be reborn as this person, so low and stupid that he barely seems a human being.

"On the other hand, in this world, a sovereign emperor is the one most revered by human beings. If he has reached this condition it is because of the merits he has accumulated during all his past lives. Compassionate and generous, he has given with largesse. Humane, he has offered his assistance to others. He has lived with faith. He has cultivated the good. He did not feel animosity towards those who have resisted him. This is why, when his life came to its end in a previous rebirth, he entered one of the fortunate rebirths according to his merits, and he was born high above in the heavens and there enjoyed great happiness. The virtues he has accumulated have added further to his bliss. Now he has obtained the human condition and has obtained birth in a royal house. He receives honors as a matter of course. His appearance is perfect, and he receives many signs of respect. At his very whim and command, he can enjoy marvelous garments and exquisite foods. If he has come to such a condition it is only because of the merits he has accumulated in the past."

The Buddha said to Ananda: "What you say is true. Yet, consider this other comparison: an emperor can be noble among men and his demeanor irreproachable, but he can appear petty and mean when compared to a universal emperor, the most august wheel-turning emperor. This sovereign emperor will look like a beggar standing next to this monarch, the august wheel-turning emperor. Yet, again, even though the wheel-turning emperor may thus look august, wonderful, and the foremost under Heaven, if he is compared to the King of the Heaven of the Thirty-Three,[9] he will appear so low and mean that he cannot stand comparison to that heavenly monarch, even if his merits were increased tens of thousands of millions of times. Yet, again, when this heavenly king is himself compared to the King of the Sixth Heaven, the difference will be hundreds of thousands of millions of times. But even the radiant face and bodily form of this heavenly king will be no match, by hundreds of thousands of trillions of times, to the bodhisattvas and disciples born in the country of the Buddha of Measureless Life."

The Buddha said to Ananda: "As to the gods and humans in the country of the Buddha of Measureless Life, the clothing, the meals, the flowers, the incense, the strings of gems, the parasols and banners, the wonderful sounds they enjoy, and the mansions, palaces, and towers where they live are in shape and size variously high or low, large or small. Or, again, these gods and humans obtain one precious substance, or two, or even as many as countless different kinds of precious substances the moment the wish comes to mind and exactly as they want them to be. And wonderful tapestries, studded with all kinds of gems, are spread on the ground all over, and every human and god walks on these. Nets studded with countless gems are stretched all over this buddha-land. All are decorated with golden laces, genuine pearls, and hundreds of thousands of various kinds of gems that are rare, wonderful, and unique. These ornaments extend everywhere into the four corners of that land, with jeweled bells, perfumes, and bright colors shining splendidly, in the most charming way.

"Breezes blow spontaneously, gently moving these bells, which swing gracefully. The breezes blow in perfect harmony. They are neither hot nor cold. They are at the same time calm and fresh, sweet and soft. They are neither fast nor slow. When they blow on the nets and the many kinds of jewels, the trees emit the innumerable sounds of the subtle and sublime Dharma and spread myriad sweet and fine perfumes. Those who hear these sounds spontaneously cease to raise the dust of tribulation and impurity. When the breezes touch their bodies they all attain a bliss comparable to that accompanying a monk's attainment of the samadhi of extinction.[1]

"Moreover, when they blow, these breezes scatter flowers all over, filling this buddha-field. These flowers fall in patterns, according to their colors, without ever being mixed up. They have delicate hues and strong fragrance. When one steps on these petals the feet sink four inches. When one lifts the foot, the petals return to their original shape and position. When these flowers stop falling, the ground suddenly opens up, and they disappear as if by magic. They remain pure and do not decay, because, at a given time, the breezes blow again and scatter the flowers. And the same process occurs six times a day.

"Moreover, many jewel lotuses fill this world system. Each jewel blossom has a hundred thousand million petals. The radiant light emanating from their petals is of countless different colors. Blue colored flowers give out a blue light. White colored flowers give out a white light. Others have a deep color and light, and some are of yellow, red, and purple color and light. But the splendor of each of these lights surpasses the radiance of the sun and

9. One of the heavens of the gods, located on the summit of Mount Meru.
1. The most advanced level of concentration, a temporary suspension of all consciousness and mental activity.

the moon. From every flower issue thirty-six hundred thousand million rays of light. From each one of these rays issue thirty-six hundred thousand million buddhas. Their bodies have the color of purple gold and in them the major marks and minor signs that adorn buddhas and bodhisattvas are rare and extraordinary. Moreover, each one of those buddhas emits hundreds of thousands of rays of light that spread out everywhere in the ten quarters and proclaim the subtle and sublime Dharma. In this way, each of these buddhas firmly establishes innumerable living beings in the Buddha's True Way."

The Buddha said to Ananda: "The living beings who have been born in this land all are firmly established among those who are assured of certain success in the Path. Why is this so? In this buddha-land there is no group of people that has fallen astray, nor a group of those with an indeterminate future in the Path.

"All the buddhas, tathagatas,[2] in the ten regions of the universe, as many as the sands in the Ganges, together praise the august presence and the virtues of the Buddha of Measureless Life, which are inconceivable.

"Any living beings who hear his name and vow to be reborn in his realm, with a trusting mind, rejoicing even if only for a single moment of thought, single-mindedly dedicating their thoughts with the resolution to be reborn there, immediately gain rebirth there and dwell in the condition of not falling back—except only those who have committed the five abominable sins[3] or have reviled the True Dharma."

2. "Tathagata" is the title of a buddha most often used by the historical Buddha to refer to himself.

3. That is, killing one's father, killing one's mother, killing an arhat, wounding a buddha, or causing schism in the sangha.

THE DIAMOND SUTRA

THE PERFECTION OF WISDOM THAT RENDS LIKE A THUNDERBOLT
(The Vajracchedika Prajnaparamita)

Some scholars mark the rise of the Mahayana with the appearance of a genre of texts that call themselves the "perfection of wisdom" (prajnaparamita), which began to circulate in India in the first century of the Common Era. These texts are generally identified by their length; the oldest is likely the Perfection of Wisdom in Eight Thousand Stanzas. Others include the Perfection of Wisdom in Eighteen Thousand Stanzas, and the Perfection of Wisdom in Twenty-five Thousand Stanzas. The longest is the Perfection of Wisdom in One Hundred Thousand Stanzas; the shortest is the Perfection of Wisdom in One Letter (that letter is the letter a). However, the two perfection of wisdom sutras most celebrated in the West, presented here and on p. 362 (the Heart Sutra), are not known by their length. These works are renowned in the West for their proclamation of the emptiness of all phenomena in the universe, a doctrine made famous in the works of Nagarjuna (see the Madhyamakakarika, p. 366), the founder of the Madhyamaka or "Middle Way" school of Buddhist philosophy. But as profound as this philosophy is, the significance of these sutras extends far beyond it.

Despite their ability to inspire philosophies, the perfection of wisdom sutras do not themselves set forth philosophical positions in a straightforward manner. The perfection of wisdom that they repeatedly praise is often identified as the knowledge of emptiness, the knowledge necessary to become a buddha. This emptiness was frequently presented in a series of negations, such as "that which is a world, that is said by the Tathagata not to be a world. In that sense [the term] 'world' is used." The precise meaning of such statements would be explored by generations of commentators in India, East Asia, and Tibet.

Only three Buddhist sutras are widely known by English titles. One is the *Lotus Sutra* (see the *Saddharmapundarika*, p. 278). The other two are perfection of wisdom sutras: the *Heart Sutra* and the *Diamond Sutra*, the present selection. And in each case, the English title is not quite right. A more accurate rendering of the title of the *Lotus Sutra* would be the *White Lotus of the True Dharma*, emphasizing the term "true dharma" (*saddharma*) over the flower. The *Heart Sutra*, more properly, is the *Essence of the Perfection of Wisdom*. The *Diamond Sutra* is perhaps the least accurate rendering of the three. *Vajra* is a Sanskrit term for a mythical weapon wielded by the god Indra, a kind of thunderbolt in the shape of a discus, capable of cutting through anything. A diamond is called a *vajra* because it is said to be made from a thunderbolt. The title of the sutra, *Vajracchedika Prajnaparamita*, thus might best be translated as the *Perfection of Wisdom That Rends Like a Thunderbolt*. Probably composed in Sanskrit sometime between the second and fourth centuries C.E., it was to become one of the most famous, and most commented upon, of the Mahayana sutras.

The sutra (presented in its entirety here) opens, as many sutra do, with the Buddha (here called, "Realized One") residing in the Jetavana grove with 1,250 monks and a large number of bodhisattvas. After returning from his begging round and eating his meal, the Buddha is approached by the great arhat Subhuti, who asks him about the practice of the bodhisattva. The Buddha replies that a bodhisattva must vow to lead all beings in the universe into nirvana, while knowing full well that there are in fact no beings to be led into nirvana: "If, Subhuti, the idea of a living being occurs to a bodhisattva, he should not be called a bodhisattva." This is one of many famous statements in the sutra, regarded by commentators as setting forth the doctrine of emptiness (although the term *shunyata* does not appear in the text), the claim that all phenomena are falsely imagined to have a self, a soul, an "own-being," a reality that they in fact lack. Any meritorious deed, from the giving of a gift to the vow to free all beings, is not a deed of a bodhisattva if it is tainted with this misconception of self. The Buddha asks Subhuti whether the Buddha is to be seen by the possession of the thirty-two physical marks of a superman that adorn his body. Subhuti says that he is not, because what the Buddha has described as the possession of marks is in fact the non-possession of no-marks. This formula of question and response, in which the correct answer is "A is in fact not A, therefore it is called A," is repeated throughout the sutra.

However, the *Diamond Sutra* is not simply a radical challenge to ordinary conceptions of the world, of language, and of thought, as Western readers have often viewed it. It is also a Mahayana sutra, seeking, like other Mahayana sutras, to declare its supremacy and to promise rewards to those who exalt it. It is noteworthy that here, as in many other perfection of wisdom sutras, the Buddha's interlocutor is not a bodhisattva but an arhat, the wise Subhuti, suggesting that even those who have completed the path to nirvana still have more to learn. The Buddha predicts that this sutra will be understood far into the future, into the period of the last 500 years that the Buddha's teaching remains in the world. At that time, anyone who has even a moment of faith in this sutra will be honored by millions of buddhas. Indeed, even now, long before that point in the distant future, anyone who would teach just four lines of it to others would win incalculable merit. The Buddha makes a statement that appears in other perfection of wisdom sutras: "Subhuti, on whatever piece of ground one elucidates this discourse, that piece of ground will become worthy of worship, that piece of ground will become worthy of veneration and reverential circumambulation for the whole world with its gods, human beings and anti-gods, that piece of ground will become a shrine." In this declaration, scholars have seen the possibility that the perfection of wisdom sutras were part of something of a "cult of the book," in which the sutra itself was worshipped in place of more traditional objects of veneration, such as stupas. The sutra suggests that such practices were not always condoned by others; the Buddha goes on to say that those who worship the sutra will be mocked, but by suffering ridicule they will destroy the great stores of negative karma accumulated over many lifetimes. Miracle tales of the benefits of reciting and copying the sutra were also recounted across Asia.

And indeed the sutra was widely recited and copied. Many texts of the *Diamond Sutra* were discovered in the caves at Dunhuang in western China—including the world's oldest copy of a printed book, created in China from carved wooden blocks centuries before the Gutenberg Bible was set from movable type.

PRONOUNCING GLOSSARY

Anathapindada: *a-nah-ta-pin-da-da*
anuttara: *a-nut-ta-rah*
bodhisattva: *boh-di-sat-tva*
Dipankara: *dee-pan-ka-ra*
gandharva: *gan-dar-va*
Jetri: *jay-tri*
Kshantivadin: *kshahn-ti-vah-din*
mahasattva: *ma-hah-sat-tva*

Shakyamuni: *shah-kya-mu-ni*
Shravasti: *shrah-vas tee*
Subhuti: *su-boo-ti*
Sumeru: *su-may-ru*
tathagata: *ta-tah-ga-ta*
tathata: *ta-ta-tah*
Vajracchedika Prajnaparamita: *vaj-ra-chay-di-kah praj-nyah-pah-ra-mi-tah*

Hail to Shakyamuni, the Realized, Worthy and Perfectly Awakened One!

This is the word as I heard it once when the Lord was staying in Shravasti,[1] in Jetri's Grove, at the monastery of Anathapindada, together with a large community of monks, 1,250 monks strong.

Then the Lord got dressed in the morning, took his bowl and robe, and entered the great city of Shravasti for alms. Then, after walking around the great city of Shravasti for alms, the Lord returned in the afternoon after eating the almsfood, washed his feet, and sat down on the seat set out for him with legs crossed, body held erect and attention directed in front of him. Then a great many monks approached the Lord, and after approaching him they prostrated themselves at the Lord's feet, circumambulated the Lord three times, and sat down to one side.

Moreover, on that occasion the Venerable Subhuti had joined that particular assembly and was seated with it. Then the Venerable Subhuti rose from

---

TRANSLATED FROM the Sanskrit of the Schøyen text and the Gilgit text by Paul Harrison; all bracketed additions are the translator's. For a fully annotated translation, see Paul Harrison, "Vajracchedikā Prajñāpāramitā: A New English Translation of the Sanskrit Text Based on Two Manuscripts from Greater Gandhāra," in *Buddhist Manuscripts*, ed. Jens Braarvig, et al., Buddhist Manuscripts in the Schøyen Collection 3 (Oslo: Hermes, 2006).
The translation begins from the Schøyen text, which is joined by the Gilgit where indicated below.

1. An important city in what is now northeast Uttar Pradesh.

his seat, arranged his cloak over one shoulder, went down on his right knee, saluted the Lord with his hands placed together, and said this to the Lord: "It is a marvelous thing, Lord, just how much bodhisattvas and mahasatt-vas[2] have been favored with the highest of favors by the Realized, Worthy and Perfectly Awakened One, just how much bodhisattvas have been entrusted with the greatest of trusts by the Realized One.[3] How, Lord, should one who has set out on the bodhisattva path take his stand, how should he proceed, how should he control the mind?"

At these words the Lord said this to the Venerable Subhuti: "Well done, Subhuti, well done! Quite so, Subhuti. Bodhisattvas have been favored with the highest of favors by the Realized One, bodhisattvas have been entrusted with the greatest of trusts by the Realized One. Therefore listen, Subhuti, and pay attention closely and carefully. I will tell how one who has set out on the bodhisattva path should take his stand, how he should proceed, how he should control the mind." "Yes, Lord," replied the Venerable Subhuti, signifying his assent to the Lord.

The Lord said this to them: "In this regard, Subhuti, those who have set out on the bodhisattva path should have the following thought, 'However many living beings are comprised in the total aggregation of living beings, be they born from eggs, or born from wombs, or born from moisture, or aris-ing spontaneously, whether having physical form or being non-material, whether having apperception, or lacking apperception, or neither having apperception nor lacking apperception—however the realm of living beings is defined when one defines it—I should bring all of them to final extinction in the realm of extinction without substrate remaining.[4] But after I have brought immeasurable living beings to final extinction in this way, no living being whatsoever has been brought to extinction.' What is the reason for that? If, Subhuti, the idea of a living being occurs to a bodhisattva, he should not be called a bodhisattva. Why is that? Subhuti, anybody to whom the idea of a living being occurs, or the idea of a soul or the idea of a person occurs, should not be called a bodhisattva.

"However, a bodhisattva should not give a gift while fixing on an object, Subhuti. He should not give a gift while fixing on anything. He should not give a gift while fixing on physical forms. He should not give a gift while fixing on sounds, smells, tastes or objects of touch, or on *dharmas*. For this is the way, Subhuti, a bodhisattva should give a gift, so that he does not fix on the idea of the distinctive features (of any object). Why is that? Subhuti, it is not easy to take the measure of the quantity of merit, Subhuti, of the bodhisattva who gives a gift without fixation. What do you think, Subhuti, is it easy to take the measure of space in the east?"

Subhuti said, "Indeed not, Lord."

"Similarly, is it easy to take the measure of space in the south, west, north, nadir, zenith, all the intermediate directions and any direction besides them, in the ten directions?"

Subhuti said, "Indeed not, Lord."

2. "Great beings," a common epithet of bodhi-sattvas.
3. That is, the Buddha.

4. The "nirvana without remainder": the nirvana entered at death by a buddha or an arhat.

The Lord said, "Quite so, Subhuti. Quite so, Subhuti. It is not easy to take the measure of the quantity of merit of the bodhisattva who gives a gift without fixation. However, this is the way a bodhisattva should give a gift, Subhuti, as an instance of the meritorious activity which consists in giving.

"What do you think, Subhuti, can a Realized One be seen by virtue of the possession of distinctive features?"

Subhuti said, "A Realized One cannot be seen by virtue of the possession of distinctive features. Why is that? The very thing which the Realized One has preached as the possession of distinctive features lacks any possession of distinctive features."

At these words the Lord said this to the Venerable Subhuti, "Subhuti, as long as there is any distinctive feature there is falsehood, and as long as there is no distinctive feature there is no falsehood. Accordingly it is by virtue of the featurelessness of his distinctive features that a Realized One can be seen."

At these words the Venerable Subhuti said this to the Lord, "Can it be, Lord, that there will be any living beings at a future time, when the final five hundred years come to pass, who, when the words of such discourses as these are being spoken, will conceive the idea that they are the truth?"

The Lord said, "Subhuti, you must not say things like 'Can it be that there will be any living beings at a future time, when the final five hundred years come to pass, who, when the words of such discourses as these are being spoken, will conceive the idea that they are the truth?'! On the contrary, Subhuti, there will be bodhisattvas and mahasattvas at a future time, when in the final five hundred years the destruction of the true *dharma* is coming to pass, who will be endowed with moral conduct, good qualities, and insight. Moreover it is not the case, Subhuti, that the bodhisattvas will have served a single Buddha, or that they will have planted the roots of goodness under a single Buddha. On the contrary, Subhuti, they will have served many Buddhas, they will have planted the roots of goodness under many Buddhas. As for those who, when the words of such discourses as these are being spoken, will experience the serenity of faith, even if it is for no more than a single thought, the Realized One knows them, Subhuti, the Realized One sees them, Subhuti. They will all generate and come to be endowed with an immeasurable quantity of merit. Why is that? Because, Subhuti, the idea of a self will not occur to those bodhisattvas, nor will the idea of a living being, or the idea of a soul, or the idea of a person occur to them. Not even the idea of a *dharma* will occur to those bodhisattvas, Subhuti, nor the idea of a non-*dharma*; not even an idea or a non-idea will occur to them. Why is that? If, Subhuti, the idea of a *dharma* should occur to those bodhisattvas, for them that would constitute seizing upon a self, it would constitute seizing upon a living being, seizing upon a soul, seizing upon a person. If the idea of a non-*dharma* should occur, for them that would constitute seizing upon a self, seizing upon a living being, seizing upon a soul, seizing upon a person. Why is that? One should moreover not take up any *dharma*, Subhuti, or any non-*dharma*. It was therefore with this in mind that the Realized One said that those who understand the round of teachings of the Simile of the Raft[5] should let go of the *dharmas* themselves, to say nothing of the non-*dharmas*."

5. The dharma is like a raft, in that it is used for crossing over and then left behind.

Furthermore, the Lord said this to the Venerable Subhuti, "What do you think, Subhuti? Is there anything whatsoever that the Realized One has fully awakened to, or any *dharma* whatsoever that the Realized One has taught, as supreme and perfect awakening?"

Subhuti said, "Lord, as I understand the meaning of what the Lord has preached, there is no *dharma* whatsoever that the Realized One has fully awakened to, nor any *dharma* whatsoever that the Realized One has taught, as supreme and perfect awakening. Why is that? The *dharma* which the Realized One has taught is ungraspable, it is ineffable, it is neither a *dharma* nor a non-*dharma*. Why is that? Because the Noble Persons are distinguished by the power they derive from the unconditioned."[6]

"What do you think, Subhuti? If someone were to fill this trigalactic megagalactic world-system with the seven treasures[7] and give it as a gift, then what do you think, Subhuti, would that gentleman or lady generate a lot of merit on that basis?"

Subhuti said, "A lot, Lord, a lot, Blessed One. That gentleman or lady would generate a lot of merit on that basis. Why is that? It is indeed, Lord, quantityless. For that reason the Realized One preaches that a quantity of merit is quantityless."

The Lord said, "If, however, some gentleman or lady were to fill this trigalactic megagalactic world-system with the seven treasures and give it as a gift, Subhuti, and if someone else were to do no more than learn just one four-lined verse from this round of teachings and teach and illuminate it for others, then the latter would on that basis generate a lot more merit, an immeasurable, incalculable amount. Why is that? Because it is from this, Subhuti, that the supreme and perfect awakening of the Realized Ones is born, it is from this that the Buddhas and Lords are born. What is the reason for that? The so-called '*dharmas* of a Buddha,' Subhuti, are indeed devoid of any *dharmas* of a Buddha.

"What do you think, Subhuti? Does it occur to a Stream-enterer[8] that he has obtained the fruit of Stream-entry?"

Subhuti said, "No indeed, Lord. Why is that? Because, Lord, he has not entered anything. That is why he is called a Stream-enterer. He has not entered form, nor has he entered sounds, smells, tastes, objects of touch, or *dharmas*. That is why he is called 'a Stream-enterer.'"

The Lord said, "What do you think, Subhuti? Would it occur to a Once-returner[9] that he has obtained the fruit of a Once-returner?"

Subhuti said, "No indeed, Lord. It does not occur to a Once-returner that he has obtained the fruit of a Once-returner. What is the reason for that? Because there is no *dharma* whatsoever which enters the state of being a Once-returner. That is why one is called 'a Once-returner.'"

The Lord said, "What do you think, Subhuti? Does it occur to a Non-returner[1] that he has obtained the fruit of a Non-returner?"

6. That which is unconditioned by impermanence.
7. Seven precious things. "Trigalactic megagalactic world-system": that is, the entire universe.
8. Someone in the first of the four stages on the path to nirvana, who will enter nirvana in seven lifetimes or less.
9. Someone in the second of the four stages on

the path to nirvana, who will be reborn one more time in this world prior to the lifetime in which he or she enters nirvana.
1. Someone in the third of four stages on the path to nirvana, who will not be reborn in this world prior to the lifetime in which he or she enters nirvana.

Subhuti said, "No indeed, Lord. It does not occur to a Non-returner that he has obtained the fruit of a Non-returner. Why is that? There is no *dharma* whatsoever which observes that it is a Non-returner. That is why one is called 'a Non-returner.'"

The Lord said, "What do you think, Subhuti? Does it occur to a Worthy One[2] that he has obtained the state of a Worthy One?"

Subhuti said, "No indeed, Lord. Why is that? Because there is no *dharma* whatsoever, Lord, which is called a Worthy One. If, Lord, it should occur to a Worthy One that he has obtained the state of a Worthy One, then for him that would indeed constitute seizing upon a self, it would constitute seizing upon a living being, seizing upon a soul, seizing upon a person.

"I am the one, Lord, who was designated by the Realized, Worthy and Perfectly Awakened One as the foremost of those who live in peace, and I am, Lord, a Worthy One free of passion, but it does not occur to me, Lord, that I am a Worthy One. If it were to occur to me, Lord, that I have attained the state of a Worthy One, the Realized One would not have declared of me 'As the foremost of those who live in peace, the gentleman Subhuti does not live anywhere. That is why he is the so-called "one who lives in peace."'"

The Lord said, "What do you think, Subhuti? Did the Realized One learn any *dharma* at all from the Realized, Worthy and Perfectly Awakened One Dipankara?"

Subhuti said, "No indeed, Lord. There is no *dharma* at all which the Realized One learned from the Realized, Worthy and Perfectly Awakened One Dipankara."

The Lord said, "Any bodhisattva, Subhuti, who says 'I will make the dispositions of a field perfect!' would be telling a lie. Why is that? Because these so-called 'dispositions of a field,' Subhuti, have been preached by the Realized One as dispositionless. That is why they are called 'dispositions of a field.'

"For that reason, then, Subhuti, a bodhisattva should conceive an aspiration in such a way that it is unfixed. He should not conceive an aspiration which is fixed in form, he should not conceive an aspiration which is fixed in sounds, smells, tastes, objects of touch, or *dharmas*, he should not conceive an aspiration which is fixed in anything at all. Subhuti, it is as if, say, there were a man, whose personal presence was such that it was like, say, Sumeru,[3] the king of all mountains. What do you think, Subhuti? Would his personal presence be substantial?"

Subhuti said, "His personal presence would be substantial, Lord, it would be substantial, Blessed One. Why is that, Lord? The Realized One has described it as an absence. That is why it is called 'a personal presence.' For it is not a presence. That is why it is called 'a personal presence.'"

The Lord said, "What do you think, Subhuti? If there were just as many Ganges Rivers as there are grains of sand in the Ganges River, would the grains of sand in them be numerous?"

Subhuti said, "That many Ganges Rivers alone would be numerous, Lord, to say nothing of the grains of sand in them."

2. The arhat, who is in the fourth of the four stages on the path to nirvana and will enter nirvana at death.

3. According to Buddhist cosmology, Sumeru is the mountain at the center of the world.

The Lord said, "I'll tell you, Subhuti, I'll have you know—if there were as many world-systems as there would be grains of sand in those Ganges Rivers, and some woman or man were to fill them with the seven treasures and make a gift of them to the Realized, Worthy and Perfectly Awakened Ones, what do you think, Subhuti, would that woman or man generate a lot of merit on that basis?"

Subhuti said, "A lot, Lord, a lot, Blessed One. That woman or man would generate a lot of merit on that basis."

The Lord said, "If, however, someone were to fill that many world-systems with the seven treasures and make a gift of them, Subhuti, and if someone were to do no more than learn just a four-lined verse from this round of teachings and teach it to others, the latter would generate from that a lot more merit, an immeasurable and incalculable amount.

"However, Subhuti, the piece of ground where one might do no more than recite or teach just a four-lined verse from this round of teachings would become a veritable shrine for the whole world with its gods, humans and anti-gods, so it goes without saying, Subhuti, that those who will memorize this round of teachings will come to be endowed with the most marvelous thing, and on that piece of ground the Teacher himself dwells, or one or another of his venerable lieutenants."

At these words, the Venerable Subhuti said this to the Lord, "What is the name, Lord, of this round of teachings, and how should I memorize it?"

At these words, the Lord said this to the Venerable Subhuti, "This round of teachings, Subhuti, is called the perfection of insight, and this is how you should memorize it. Why is that? The very perfection of insight, Subhuti, which the Realized One has preached is itself perfectionless.

"What do you think, Subhuti? Is there any *dharma* at all which the Realized One has preached?"

Subhuti said, "No indeed, Lord. There is no *dharma* at all, Lord, which the Realized One has preached."[4]

"Would all the dust of the earth, Subhuti, that there is in the trigalactic megagalactic world-system be a lot?"

Subhuti said, "Lord, the dust of that much earth would be a lot. Any dust of the earth preached by the Realized One, Lord, has been preached by the Realized One as dustless. Thus it is called 'the dust of the earth.' Any world-system there is has been preached by the Realized One as systemless. Thus it is called 'a world-system.'"

The Lord said, "What do you think, Subhuti? Can a Realized, Worthy, and Perfectly Awakened One be seen by virtue of the thirty-two distinctive features of a great man?"

Subhuti said, "No indeed, Lord. Why is that? Whatever thirty-two distinctive features of a great man have been preached by the Realized One, Lord, have been preached by the Realized One as featureless. Therefore they are called 'the thirty-two distinctive features of a great man.'"

The Lord said, "If, however, some woman or man were to sacrifice as many of their own bodies as there are grains of sand in the Ganges River, Subhuti, and if someone were to learn just a four-lined verse from this

4. After this point the Gilgit text begins, and the Schøyen text continues.

round of teachings and teach it to others, the latter would on that basis generate a lot more merit, an immeasurable and incalculable amount."

Then the Venerable Subhuti burst into tears at the impact of the *dharma*. Wiping his tears away as he continued to shed them, he said this to the Lord, "It is a marvelous thing, Lord, it is a most marvelous thing, Blessed One, that this round of teachings has been preached by the Realized One. Since knowledge arose for me, Lord, I have never heard a round of teachings of this kind before. They will come to be endowed with a most marvelous thing, Lord, who, when this discourse is being preached, conceive the idea that it is the truth. But any such idea of truth, Lord, is indeed idealess. Therefore the Realized One preaches the so-called 'idea of truth.'

"For me it is no great marvel, Lord, that I believe and have faith in the round of teachings when it is being preached. Those, Lord, who will learn, master, and memorize this round of teachings will come to be endowed with a most marvelous thing.

"However, Lord, the idea of a self will not occur to them, nor will the idea of a living being, the idea of a soul, or the idea of a person occur. Why is that? Any such idea of a self is indeed idealess, any idea of a living being, idea of a soul, or idea of a person is indeed idealess. Why is that? Because the Buddhas and Lords are free of all ideas."

At these words the Lord said this to the Venerable Subhuti, "Quite so, Subhuti! Quite so, Subhuti! Those living beings will come to be endowed with a most marvelous thing who, when this discourse is being preached, do not become afraid, frightened or fearful on hearing it. Why is that? This has been preached by the Realized One as the supreme perfection. And what the Realized One preaches as the supreme perfection is preached by innumerable Buddhas and Lords. That is why it is called 'the supreme perfection.'

"However, Subhuti, any perfection of acceptance the Realized One has is indeed perfectionless. Why is that? When, Subhuti, King Kalinga cut off my limbs and extremities,[5] I did not have at that time any idea of a self or idea of a living being or idea of a soul or idea of a person. I had no idea whatsoever, nor any non-idea. Why is that? If, Subhuti, I had had the idea of a self at that time, I would also have had the idea of ill-will at that time. I remember, Subhuti, 500 rebirths in the past when I was the sage Kshantivadin, and then too I had no idea of a self, no idea of a living being, no idea of a soul, and no idea of a person.

"For that reason, then, Subhuti, a bodhisattva and mahasattva should conceive the aspiration for supreme and perfect awakening after eliminating all ideas, he should not conceive an aspiration which is fixed on forms, he should not conceive an aspiration which is fixed on sounds, smells, tastes, or objects of touch, he should not conceive an aspiration which is fixed on *dharmas*, he should not conceive an aspiration which is fixed on non-*dharmas*, he should not conceive an aspiration which is fixed on anything. What is the reason for that? Whatever is fixed is indeed unfixed. For that very reason the Realized One preaches that a gift should be given by one without fixing on form.

5. That is, in a previous life.

"However, Subhuti, this is the way in which a bodhisattva should engage in the giving away of gifts for the benefit of all living beings, but any idea of a living being is indeed idealess. All living beings of whom the Realized One has preached are indeed beingless. The Realized One, Subhuti, speaks truly, the Realized One tells the truth, he tells things as they are, the Realized One does not tell lies.

"However, Subhuti, in that *dharma* which the Realized One has awakened to and taught there is no truth and no falsehood. Subhuti, one should regard a bodhisattva who has sunk to the level of objects and who gives away a gift which has sunk to the level of objects as being like, say, a man who has been plunged into darkness. Subhuti, one should regard a bodhisattva who gives a gift which has not sunk to the level of objects as being like, say, a man endowed with sight, who would see shapes of various kinds when dawn breaks and the sun comes up.

"However, Subhuti, those gentlemen or ladies who will learn, memorize, recite, and master this round of teachings, the Realized One knows them, Subhuti, the Realized One sees them, Subhuti, the Realized One comprehends them. All those living beings will generate an immeasurable quantity of merit.

"If, however, some woman or man were to sacrifice in the morning as many of their own bodies as there are grains of sand in the Ganges River, Subhuti, were to sacrifice in the middle of the day and in the evening as many of their own bodies as there are sands in the Ganges River, were to sacrifice their own bodies in this manner for a hundred thousand million billion aeons, and if someone were to hear this round of teachings and not reject it, the latter would on that basis generate a much larger quantity of merit, an immeasurable and incalculable amount, to say nothing of someone who after copying it would learn it, memorize it, recite it, master it, and elucidate it in full for others.

"However, Subhuti, this round of teachings is inconceivable and incomparable. The Realized One has preached this round of teachings for the benefit of living beings who have set out on the highest path, for the benefit of living beings who have set out on the best path. Those who will learn, memorize, recite, and master this round of teachings, the Realized One knows them, Subhuti, the Realized One sees them, Subhuti. All those living beings will come to be endowed with an immeasurable quantity of merit, they will come to be endowed with an inconceivable, incomparable, unreckonable, measureless quantity of merit. Why is that? This *dharma*, Subhuti, cannot be heard by those of inferior inclinations, nor can it be heard, or learned, or memorized, or recited, or mastered by those who hold the false view of a self, who hold the false view of a living being, who hold the false view of a soul, or who hold the false view of a person. That is an impossibility.

"However, Subhuti, on whatever piece of ground one elucidates this discourse, that piece of ground will become worthy of worship, that piece of ground will become worthy of veneration and reverential circumambulation for the whole world with its gods, human beings and anti-gods, that piece of ground will become a shrine.

"Those gentlemen and ladies, Subhuti, who will learn, memorize and master such discourses as these will be despised, they will be roundly despised. Whatever acts leading to perdition those living beings have done in former rebirths, through being despised they will in this life exhaust the demeritorious acts of their former rebirths, and they will attain the awakening of a Buddha.

"I remember, Subhuti, that in the past, an incalculable aeon ago and more incalculable still, back before the Realized, Worthy and Perfectly Awakened One Dipankara and back further still, there were 84 hundred thousand million billion Buddhas with whom I found favor and with whom, after finding favor, I did not lose favor. However, Subhuti, that previous quantity of merit from when I found favor with the Buddhas and Lords, and after finding favor with them, I did not lose favor, does not approach even a hundredth part, even a thousandth part, even a hundred-thousandth part, even a hundred-thousand-millionth part, it does not even permit of any calculation, or reckoning in fractions, or computation, or comparison, or analogy, Subhuti, in relation to the quantity of merit from when, in the last time, as the final five hundred years come to pass, they will learn, memorize, recite and master this discourse.

"If, Subhuti, one were to describe the quantity of merit of those gentlemen and ladies, of as many of those gentlemen or ladies as acquire a quantity of merit at that time, those living beings would go mad or become mentally disturbed.[6] However, Subhuti, this round of teachings is inconceivable, and the effect it has is truly inconceivable."

He said, "How, Lord, should one who has set out on the bodhisattva path take his stand, how should he proceed, how should he control the mind?"

The Lord said, "In this regard, Subhuti, one who has set out on the bodhisattva path should have the following thought, 'I should bring all living beings to final extinction in the realm of extinction without substrate remaining. But after I have brought living beings to final extinction in this way, no living being whatsoever has been brought to extinction.' Why is that? If, Subhuti, the idea of a living being were to occur to a bodhisattva, or the idea of a soul or the idea of a person, he should not be called a bodhisattva. Why is that? There is no *dharma* called 'one who has set out on the bodhisattva path.'

"What do you think, Subhuti? Is there any *dharma* which the Realized One had from the Realized One Dipankara by which he fully awakened to supreme and perfect awakening?"

He said, "There is no *dharma* whatsoever which the Realized One had from the Realized One Dipankara by which he fully awakened to supreme and perfect awakening."

He said, "Therefore the Realized One Dipankara predicted of me, 'At a future time, young man, you will become a Realized, Worthy and Perfectly Awakened One by the name of Shakyamuni!'[7]

"Why is that? The word 'Realized' (*tathagata*), Subhuti, is a synonym for reality (*tathata*).

"Should anyone say, Subhuti, that the Realized One has fully awakened to supreme and perfect awakening, there is no *dharma* whatsoever to which the Realized One has fully awakened as supreme and perfect awakening. In the *dharma* to which the Realized One has fully awakened, there is no truth and no falsehood. Therefore the Realized One preaches, 'All *dharmas*

---

6. Here the Schøyen text ends; from this point on, only the Gilgit text is translated.

7. Literally, "Sage of the Shakyas"; a title of the Buddha, who was born into the Shakya clan.

are Buddha-*dharmas*.' As far as 'all *dharmas*' are concerned, Subhuti, all of them are *dharma*-less. That is why they are called 'all *dharmas*.'

"Subhuti, it is as if there were, say, a man who was full-bodied and big-bodied."

Subhuti said, "That man whom the Realized One has described as full-bodied and big-bodied has, Lord, been described by the Realized One as bodiless. That is why he is called full-bodied and big-bodied."

The Lord said, "Quite so, Subhuti. Any bodhisattva who would say such things as 'I will bring living beings to final extinction' should not be called a bodhisattva. Why is that? Does any *dharma* at all exist called 'a bodhisattva,' Subhuti?"

He said, "No indeed, Lord."

The Lord said, "Therefore the Realized One preaches that all *dharmas* are devoid of a living being, devoid of a soul, devoid of a person.

"The bodhisattva, Subhuti, who would say such things as 'I shall make the dispositions of a field perfect' should also be described in just that way. Why is that? The Realized One has preached, Subhuti, that the so-called 'dispositions of a field' are dispositionless. That is why they are called 'dispositions of a field.'

"The bodhisattva who has faith, Subhuti, in the oft-repeated saying '*dharmas* are selfless' has been declared by the Realized, Worthy and Perfectly Awakened One to be a bodhisattva, a bodhisattva indeed.

"What do you think, Subhuti? Does the Realized One have the eye of the flesh?"

He said, "It is so, Lord, the Realized One has the eye of the flesh."

The Lord said, "What do you think, Subhuti? Does the Realized One have the eye of the gods, the eye of insight, the eye of *dharma*, the eye of the Awakened?"

He said, "It is so, Lord, the Realized One has the eye of the gods, the eye of insight, the eye of *dharma*, the eye of the Awakened."

The Lord said, "What do you think, Subhuti? If there were as many Ganges Rivers as there are grains of sand in the Ganges River, and if there were just as many world-systems as there would be grains of sand in them, would those world-systems be numerous?"

He said, "Quite so, Lord, those world-systems would be numerous."

The Lord said, "Subhuti, as many living beings as there might be in those world-systems, I would know their manifold streams of thought. Why is that? Those so-called 'streams of thought,' Subhuti, have been preached by the Realized One as streamless. That is why they are called 'streams of thought.' Why is that? Subhuti, one cannot apprehend a past thought, one cannot apprehend a future thought, one cannot apprehend a present [thought].

"What do you think, Subhuti? If someone were to fill this trigalactic megagalactic world-system with the seven treasures and give it as a gift, would that gentleman or lady engender a lot of merit on that basis?"

He said, "A lot, Lord. A lot, Blessed One."

The Lord said, "Quite so, Subhuti, quite so. It is a lot. That gentleman or lady would engender a lot of merit on that basis. If there were a quantity of merit, Subhuti, the Realized One would not have preached the so-called 'quantity of merit.'

"What do you think, Subhuti? Can a Realized One be seen by virtue of the perfection of his physical body?"

He said, "No, Lord, a Realized One cannot be seen by virtue of the perfection of his physical body. Why is that? The so-called 'perfection of the physical body' has been preached by the Realized One as perfectionless. That is why it is called the 'perfection of the physical body.'"

The Lord said, "What do you think, Subhuti? Can a Realized One be seen by virtue of the possession of distinctive features?"

He said, "No, Lord, a Realized One cannot be seen by virtue of the possession of distinctive features. Why is that? What the Realized One has preached as the possession of distinctive features has been preached by the Realized One as lacking the possession of distinctive features. That is why it is called the possession of distinctive features."

The Lord said, "What do you think, Subhuti? Does it occur to the Realized One that he has taught the *dharma*? Subhuti, anybody who would say such things as 'The Tathagata has taught the *dharma*' would misrepresent me, Subhuti, on account of wrong learning. Why is that? As for the so-called 'teaching of the *dharma*,' Subhuti, there exists no *dharma* whatsoever which can be apprehended called the teaching of the *dharma*."

He said, "Can it be, Lord, that there will be be any living beings at a future time who will hear such *dharmas* as these being preached and have faith in them?"

The Lord said, "Subhuti, they are not beings, nor are they non-beings. Why is that? 'All beings,' Subhuti, have been preached by the Realized One as beingless. That is why they are called 'all beings.'"

"What do you think, Subhuti? Does any *dharma* at all exist to which the Realized One became fully awakened as supreme and perfect awakening?"

He said, "No *dharma* whatsoever exists to which the Realized One became fully awakened as supreme and perfect awakening."

The Lord said, "Quite so, Subhuti, quite so. Not even a fine or minute (*anu*) *dharma* is to be found or apprehended in it. That is why it is called 'superfine or supreme (*anuttara*) and perfect awakening.'

"However, Subhuti, that *dharma* is the same as any other (*sama*), and there is nothing at all different (*vishama*) about it. That is why it is called 'supreme and perfect (*samyak*) awakening.' By virtue of being devoid of a soul, being devoid of a living being and being devoid of a person, that supreme and perfect awakening is fully awakened to as being the same as all wholesome *dharmas*. These so-called 'wholesome *dharmas*,' Subhuti, have been preached by the Realized One as being indeed *dharma*-less. That is why they are called 'wholesome *dharmas*.'

"If, however, someone were to amass piles of the seven treasures as high as all the Sumerus, kings of all mountains, in the trigalactic megagalactic world-system and give them as a gift, Subhuti, and if someone else were to do no more than learn just a four-lined verse from this perfection of insight and teach it to others, then the former quantity of merit, Subhuti, does not approach even a hundredth part of the latter quantity of merit *and so on, until* nor does it even permit of any analogy.

"What do you think, Subhuti? Does it occur to the Realized One that he has liberated living beings? This is again not the way one should see things, Subhuti. Why is that? There is no living being whatsoever who has been liberated by the Realized One. If moreover there were any living being who was liberated by the Realized One, Subhuti, that would constitute seizing upon a self on his part, seizing upon a living being, seizing upon a soul, seizing upon a person. This 'seizing upon a self,' Subhuti, has been preached by the Realized One as devoid of seizing, but it is learned by foolish ordinary people. These 'foolish ordinary people,' Subhuti, have been preached by the Realized One as peopleless. That is why they are called 'foolish ordinary people.'

"What do you think, Subhuti? Can a Realized One be seen by virtue of the possession of distinctive features?"

He said, "Quite so, Lord, a Realized One can be seen by virtue of the possession of distinctive features."

The Lord said, "If, however, a Realized One could be seen by virtue of the possession of distinctive features, Subhuti, a wheel-turning king[8] would also be a Realized One."

He said, "As I understand the meaning of what the Lord has preached, a Realized One cannot be seen by virtue of the possession of distinctive features."

Then on that occasion the Lord uttered these verses:

"Whoever saw me through my physical form,
Whoever followed me through the sound of my voice,
Engaged in the wrong endeavors,
Those people will not see me.

"A Buddha is visible through the *dharma*,
A Realized One has the *dharma* for a body,
But the nature of *dharma* being unknowable by sensory consciousness,
It cannot be known by sensory consciousness."

"What do you think, Subhuti? Did the Realized One awaken fully to supreme and perfect awakening through the possession of distinctive features? This is again not the way one should see things, Subhuti. The Realized One did not awaken fully to supreme and perfect awakening through the possession of distinctive features.

"Moreover, Subhuti, if it should be thought that those who have set out on the bodhisattva path assert the destruction of any *dharma* or its annihilation, then once again, Subhuti, this is not the way one should see things. Those who have set out on the bodhisattva path do not assert the destruction or annihilation of any *dharma* whatsoever.

"If, however, some gentleman or lady were to fill as many world-systems as there are grains of sand in the Ganges River with the seven treasures and give them as a gift to the Realized, Worthy and Perfectly Awakened Ones, Subhuti, and if some bodhisattva were to attain acceptance with regard to the fact that *dharmas* are devoid of self, the latter would generate from that a lot more merit. However, Subhuti, the quantity of merit should not be acquired by the bodhisattva."

He said, "Lord, should the quantity of merit be acquired?"

The Lord said, "It should be acquired, Subhuti, but should not be taken up. That is why one says 'It should be acquired.'

8. A universal monarch.

"However, Subhuti, if someone were to say that the Realized One goes or comes or stands or sits or lies down, he does not understand the meaning of what I have preached. Why is that? He who is called 'the Realized One' (*tathagata*), Subhuti, has not come (*agata*) from anywhere, nor has he gone (*gata*) anywhere. That is why he is called 'the Realized, Worthy and Perfectly Awakened One.'

"If, however, some gentleman or lady were to take as many world-systems as there are dust-particles of earth in the trigalactic megagalactic world-system, Subhuti, and grind them to powder, so that they were like, say, a pile of the most minute atoms, what do you think, Subhuti? Would that pile of the most minute atoms be considerable?"

He said, "Quite so, Lord, that pile of the most minute atoms would be considerable. Why is that? If, Lord, there were a pile, the Lord would not say 'pile of the most minute atoms.' Why is that? Any pile of the most minute atoms which has been preached has been preached as pileless by the Lord. That is why it is called 'a pile of the most minute atoms.'

"And whenever the Realized One preaches about a 'trigalactic megagalactic world-system,' that has been preached by the Realized One as systemless. That is why it is called 'a trigalactic megagalactic world-system.' Why is that? If, Lord, there were a system, that, Lord, would indeed constitute seizing upon a solid mass, yet what the Realized One has preached of as seizing upon a solid mass, that has been preached by the Realized One as devoid of any seizing. That is why it is called 'seizing upon a solid mass.'"

The Lord said, "And yet seizing upon something solid is a *dharma* which is beyond linguistic expression, Subhuti, which is ineffable. It has been taken up by foolish ordinary people.

"Why is that? If someone were to say, Subhuti, that the Realized One preached the view of a self, the view of a living being, the view of a soul, the view of a person, would he be saying the right thing by saying that, Subhuti?"

He said, "No, Lord. Why is that? Any view of a self, Lord, preached of by the Realized One has been preached by the Realized One as viewless. That is why it is called 'a view of a self.'"

The Lord said, "It is in this way, Subhuti, that one who has set out on the bodhisattva path should know all *dharmas* and have faith in them. But he should have faith in them in such a way that even the idea of a *dharma* does not come to be present. Why is that? This so-called 'idea of a *dharma*,' Subhuti, has been preached by the Realized One as idealess. That is why it is called the 'idea of a *dharma*.'

"If, however, any bodhisattva and mahasattva were to fill immeasurable and incalculable world-systems with the seven treasures and make a gift of them, Subhuti, and if some gentleman or lady were to do no more than learn just a four-lined verse from this perfection of insight and memorize it, teach it, and master it, the latter would generate from that a lot more merit, an immeasurable and incalculable amount. And how should he elucidate it? So as not to throw light on it. That is why one says 'he should elucidate it.'

> "A shooting star, a clouding of the sight, a lamp,
> An illusion, a drop of dew, a bubble,
> A dream, a lightning's flash, a thunder cloud—
> This is the way one should see the conditioned."

This is what the Lord said. Delighted, the elder Subhuti, those monks, nuns, male lay followers, female lay followers, and the whole world with its gods, humans, anti-gods and gandharvas[9] rejoiced at what the Lord had preached.

The Vajracchedika Prajnaparamita is concluded.

9. Heavenly musicians.

THE BUDDHA NATURE LIES HIDDEN WITHIN

DISCOURSE ON THE BUDDHA NATURE
(*The Tathagatagarbha Sutra*)

The *Lotus Sutra* famously declared that all beings would one day become buddhas. This was a radical claim. No longer were there three vehicles—the vehicle of the shravaka, or disciple; the vehicle of the pratyekabuddha, or individually enlightened one; and the vehicle of the bodhisattva. No longer was the bodhisattva the rare being who decided to forgo the enlightenment of the arhat to follow the much longer path to buddhahood. Now, everyone would follow the bodhisattva path and everyone would become a buddha. But how was that possible? What was it that allowed a benighted sentient being to become a buddha?

One answer set forth in a number of Mahayana sutras was the "buddha nature," a quality naturally and eternally present in all beings (or almost all beings) called the *tathagatagarbha*. The word *tathagatagarbha* has been widely translated. *Tathagata*, one of the most common epithets of the Buddha, means either "one who has thus come" or "one who has thus gone." It was a name that he often used when referring to himself. *Garbha* has a wide range of meanings in Sanskrit, including element, inner chamber (and by extension "treasure room"), husk, and the calyx of a flower. It was translated into Chinese as *zang*, which means "storehouse." This buddha nature is often described with similes involving something whose great value remains unrecognized until the arrival of a person with the eyes to see what is hidden. Many of the most famous of these comparisons appear in the text below.

As the Mahayana philosophical schools developed, the doctrine of the *tathagatagarbha*, a pure buddha nature eternally present in all sentient beings, became subject to exegesis and controversy. Some scholars of the Yogachara school argued that the *tathagatagarbha* is not a universal quality but instead is one of four spiritual destinies, almost a genetic disposition. Some beings had the shravaka seed and would eventually follow that path to achieve the nirvana of the arhat; others had the pratyekabuddha seed and would follow that somewhat longer path to the same nirvana. Still others were endowed with the bodhisattva seed, entering the Mahayana and following the bodhisattva path to buddhahood. Finally, there were those who had an indeterminate seed and, depending on the teachings they encountered over the course of their births, would enter either the Hinayana or Mahayana. One of the great controversies in Mahayana Buddhism arose over the question of whether there were certain beings—called *icchantikas*, beings of great desire—that had no enlightenment seed of any kind and thus were doomed to eternal rebirth in samsara.

The idea of the buddha nature raised other problems in a tradition whose philosophical hallmark was the doctrine of no self, for the buddha nature sounded very much like a self. For this reason, some exegetes of the Madhyamaka school argued that the *tathagatagarbha* was a provisional teaching, something intended by the Buddha for a given audience and for a specific purpose, and not a statement of his final position. These authors saw the *tathagatagarbha*, the buddha nature, as the emptiness of the mind, with which all beings were indeed endowed. It was this emptiness than made possible all transformation and would eventually become the omniscience of a buddha. Knowing that any direct mention of emptiness would have been mistaken by many in his audience for nihilism, the Buddha compassionately spoke in more positive terms, declaring that all are endowed with the *tathagatagarbha*.

The *tathagatagarbha* continued to spark both controversy and inspiration. In seventh-century China, the members of the Three Levels school believed that in the degenerate age in which we live, it is impossible to take refuge in a particular buddha, because humans are incapable of knowing who is the enlightened and who is not. If we cannot discriminate between a benighted sentient being and a buddha, how could we choose one buddha over another—Amitabha over Shakyamuni, for example—as a source of refuge? Those in the Three Levels school argued that the Buddha encompasses all living beings, because all beings are equally endowed with the *tathagatagarbha*. Thus, in Tang China they were renowned for bowing down at the feet of stray dogs.

Such practices were inspired by works like the one below. The *Tathagatagarbha Sutra* is one of the most influential of all the Mahayana sutras, and the earliest to set forth the doctrine of *tathagatagarbha*. It was probably composed in the second half of the third century C.E. Set ten years after the Buddha's enlightenment, it opens with the Buddha seated on Vulture Peak surrounded by 100,000 monks and by bodhisattvas equal in number to the sands of the Ganges. The Buddha causes myriad lotuses to fill the sky, each enclosing a buddha who is emitting rays of light—a scene that appears in a number of Mahayana sutras. But then something very strange occurs: the petals of the lotuses open and then wilt and finally become rotten, while the buddhas seated upon them remain pristine. The bodhisattva Vajramati next asks the Buddha to explain what has occurred. In the most famous section of the sutra, the Buddha responds by setting forth nine similes of the *tathagatagarbha*.

PRONOUNCING GLOSSARY

Achalapadavikramin: *a-cha-lah-pa-da-vih-krah-min*

Ajnatakaundinya: *ah-jnyah-ta-kaun-din-ya*

Amoghadarshin: *a-moh-ga-dar-shin*

Anantarashmi: *a-nan-ta-rash-mi*

Anantaratnayashti: *a-nan-ta-rat-na-yash-ti*

Anantavikramin: *a-nan-ta-vih-krah-min*

Aprameyabhigarjitasvara: *a-pra-may-yah-bi-gar-ji-ta-sva-ra*

Aprameyavikramin: *a-pra-may-ya-vi-krah-min*

Arthamati: *ar-ta-ma-ti*

Avalokiteshvara: *a-va-loh-ki-taysh-va-ra*

Bodhisamutthapana: *boh-di-sa-mu-tah-pa-na*

bodhisattva-mahasattva: *boh-di-sat-tva-ma-hah-sat-tva*

Chandanagarbha: *chan-da-na-gar-ba*

Chandraprabha: *chan-dra-pra-ba*

Dharanimdhara: *da-ra-neem-da-ra*

Dharanishvararaja: *dah-ra-neesh-va-rah-ja*

Dharmamati: *dar-ma-ma-ti*

Gaganaganja: *ga-ga-na-gan-ja*

Gandhahastin: *gan-da-ha-stin*

Gandharati: *gan-da-ra-ti*

Gandharatishri: *gan-da-ra-ti-shree*

Gayakashyapa: *ga-yah-kahsh ya-pa*

Gunaratnaloka: *gu-na-rat-nah-loh-ka*

Ihavivartana: *ee-ha-vi-var-ta-na*

Jyotishkara: *jyoh-ti-shka-ra*

Khinnamanas: *ki-na-ma-nas*

Mahakashyapa: *ma-hah-kah-shya-pa*

Mahakatyayana: *ma-hah-kaht-yah-ya-na*

Mahakaushthila: *ma-hah-kaush-ti-la*

Mahaketu: *ma-hah-kay-tu*

Mahamaudgalyayana: *ma-hah-maud-gal-yah-ya-na*

Mahameru: *ma-hah-may-ru*

Mahasthamaprapta: *ma-hah-stah-ma-prah-pta*

Mahavikramin: *ma-hah-vi-krah-mihn*

Maitreya: *mai-tray-ya*

Manjushri: *man-ju-shree*

Nadikashyapa: *na-dee-kahsh ya-pa*

parinirvana: *pa-ri-nihr-vah-na*

Pramodyamanas: *prah-mo-dya-ma-nas*

Pramodyaraja: *prah-moh-dya-rah-ja*

Pravaramati: *pra-va-ra-ma-ti*

Purnachandraprabha: *poor-na-chan-dra-pra-ba*

Purnamaitrayaniputra: *poor-na-mai-trah-ya-nee-pu-tra*

Ratna-chandraprabha: *rat-na-chan-dra-pra-ba*

Ratnacchattra: *rat-na-cha-tra*

Ratnamati: *rat-na-ma-ti*

Ratnapani: *rat-na-pah-ni*

Sadapramudita: *sa-dah-pra-mu-di-ta*

Sadapramuktarashmi: *sa-dah-pra-muk-ta-rash-mi*

Sarvadharmavashavartin: *sar-va-dar-ma-va-sha-var-tin*

Sarvasattvaroganivartana: *sar-va-sat-tva-roh-ga-ni-var-ta-na*

Shakyaprabha: *shah-kya-pra-ba*

Shariputra: *shah-ri-pu-tra*

shravaka: *shrah-va-ka*

Shrigarbha: *shree-gar-ba*

Simhadhvaja: *sim-ha-dva-ja*

Simhamati: *sim-ha-ma-ti*

Surya-garbha: *soo-rya-gar-ba*

Tathagatagarbha Sutra: *ta-tah-ga-ta-gar-ba soo-tra*

Trailokyavikramin: *trai-loh-kya-vih-krah-min*

Tyaktaratnayashti: *tyak-ta-rat-na-yash-ti*

Uruvilvakashyapa: *u-ru-vil-vah-kahsh ya-pa*

Vajramati: *vaj-ra-ma-tih*

Vimalaketu: *vi-ma-la-kay-tu*

Vimalaratnayashti: *vih-ma-la-rat-na-yash-ti*

Vyaghramati: *vyah-gra-ma-ti*

Ye shes sde: *yeh sheh deh*

Homage to all buddhas and bodhisattvas!

At one time I heard the following: In the hot months ten years after [his] complete awakening, the Exalted One was staying on the mountain Vulture Peak near Rajagriha,[1] in the Chandanagarbha pavilion of Ratnacchattra palace, together with a great community of monks, fully a hundred thousand [in number]. The monks [were both] *shravakas*[2] under training and [those] no [longer in] need of training; almost all [of them were] honorable ones (*arhat*) [whose] contaminations were stopped, [who were] free of defilements, [who] had attained mastery, [with] completely liberated minds and insight, of noble race, [powerful like] great elephants, [whose] duties were done, [whose] tasks were performed, [who had] laid down [their] burden, [who had] reached their own goal, [in whom all] the fetters to existence were eliminated, [whose] minds were completely liberated by perfect knowledge, and [who had] attained excellent supremacy in the control over the whole mind.

[Among] the fully hundred thousand monks were the venerable Mahakashyapa, the venerable Uruvilvakashyapa, the venerable Nadikashyapa, the venerable Gayakashyapa, the venerable Mahakatyayana, the venerable

TRANSLATED FROM the Tibetan by Michael Zimmerman. All bracketed additions are the translator's.

1. The capital of the kingdom of Magadha, in northeast India, where the Buddha lived for many years.

2. Disciples.

Mahakaushthila, the venerable Vakula, the venerable Revata, the venerable Subhuti, the venerable Purnamaitrayaniputra, the venerable Vagisha, the venerable Shariputra, the venerable Mahamaudgalyayana, the venerable Ajnatakaundinya, the venerable Udayin, the venerable Rahula, the venerable Nanda, the venerable Upananda, the venerable Ananda, and others.

Also accompanying him were bodhisattva-mahasattvas who had come together from various buddha-fields[3]—as many as the sands of sixty Ganges Rivers. [They were] all of them [only] one lifetime away [from perfect awakening] and had attained the [five] great supernatural faculties, the [ten] powers and the [four kinds of] self-assurance, [had] venerated many myriads of buddhas and had set in motion the wheel of the dharma [which] never regresses. It happened that sentient beings of immeasurable, innumerable world systems attained non-regression in [their striving after] supreme and perfect awakening from hearing their names only.

[Among them were] the bodhisattva-mahasattvas Dharmamati, Simhamati, Vyaghramati, Arthamati, Ratnamati, Pravaramati, Chandraprabha, Ratnachandraprabha, Purnachandraprabha, Mahavikramin, Aprameyavikramin, Anantavikramin, Trailokyavikramin, Achalapadavikramin, Mahasthamaprapta, Avalokiteshvara, Gandhahastin, Gandharati, Gandharatishri, Shrigarbha, Surya-garbha, Ketu, Mahaketu, Vimalaketu, Anantaratnayashti, Tyaktaratnayashti, Vimalaratnayashti, Pramodyaraja, Sadapramudita, Ratnapani, Gaganaganja, Meru, Sumeru, Mahameru, Gunaratnaloka, Dharanishvararaja, Dharanimdhara, Sarvasattvaroganivartana, Pramodyamanas, Khinnamanas, Akhinna, Jyotishkara, Chandana, Ihavivartana, Aprameyabhigarjitasvara, Bodhisamutthapana, Amoghadarshin, Sarvadharmavashavartin, the bodhisattva-mahasattva Maitreya, Manjushri as a young man, and other bodhisattva-mahasattvas, as many as the sands of sixty Ganges Rivers.

Also accompanying [him] were an immeasurable [number of] divinities, snake-gods, spirits, celestial musicians, demons, man-birds, man-horses, serpent-beings, human beings and [further] non-human beings.

Then, after the Exalted One had been surrounded and honored by many hundreds of thousands of assemblies, [he] was honored, venerated, worshipped, and revered by kings, chief ministers, guild leaders, noblemen, ministers, citizens, and country folk.

At that time, after having been served food, the Exalted One withdrew for meditation in that same Chandanagarbha pavilion, whereupon through the power of the Buddha appeared myriads of lotuses [coming out] from the Chandanagarbha pavilion, with myriads of petals, as large as the wheels of carts, colorful and not [yet] open. The [lotuses] then rose into the sky, covered this whole buddha-field, and remained [there] like a jewel canopy.

---

3. Particular buddhas' spheres of influence and activity. In Buddhist cosmology, each buddha arises in a particular world system. *Mahasattva* means "great being," a common epithet of bodhisattvas.

In each calyx of the lotuses was seated, cross-legged, the body of a tatha-gata,[4] emitting hundreds of thousands of rays of light and visible everywhere. And all the lotuses were opened up in blossom.

Then, by the supernatural power of the Buddha all the petals of the lotuses, without exception, became dark, deep-black, putrid and disgusting, and no [longer] pleasing. But in the calyxes of the lotuses the bodies of the tatha-gatas sitting cross-legged and emitting hundreds of thousands of rays of light were [still] visible everywhere.

Further, this whole buddha-field became filled with the [rays of light from] the bodies of the tathagatas sitting in the calyxes of the lotuses. This buddha-field became extremely beautiful [during] that time. Then at that time the whole multitude of bodhisattvas and the four assemblies were extremely astonished and filled with pleasurable excitement.

[But] after seeing that supernatural display of the Exalted One, [they] became uncertain [and questioned themselves]:

> "What is the reason that the petals of all these myriads of lotuses became so unsightly, and that the[ir] stalks too became unsightly, disgusting and not pleasing, whereas in the calyxes of the lotuses each body of the tathagatas is [still] sitting cross-legged, and in that [they] emit hundreds of thousands of rays of light visible everywhere as [something] extremely beautiful?"

Thereupon, [the Exalted One] motioned to the entire multitude of bodhisatt-vas and the four assemblies who had become uncertain to come closer. At that time there was a [certain] bodhisattva-mahasattva named Vajramati [who had also] gathered [with the others] in the Chandanagarbha pavilion.

Then the Exalted One said to the bodhisattva-mahasattva Vajramati:

> "Son of good family, venture to question the Tathagata, the Honor-able One and Perfectly Awakened One, with reference to an expo-sition on the dharma!"

At the Exalted One's permission, the bodhisattva-mahasattva Vajramati, real-izing that the world with [its] gods, humans and demons, and all the bod-hisattvas and the four assemblies were anxious with doubts, then asked him the following:

> "Exalted One, what is the reason this entire world system is covered with these myriads of such unsightly and putrid lotuses, yet in their centers sit cross-legged bodies of tathagatas emitting hundreds of thousands of rays of light and visible everywhere, and now myriads of living beings, seeing the bodies of the tathagatas, raise their joined palms in homage?"

4. That is, a buddha.

Then at that time the bodhisattva Vajramati uttered these verses:

"Myriads of buddhas are seated motionless in the center of
    lotuses; [with] such supernatural powers you display [them].
    Never before have I seen [anything like] this!
"The [sight] of the leaders emitting thousands of rays of light,
    covering this entire buddha-field [with their splendor, and]
    wonderfully displaying a facile mastery of the dharmas, [is]
    constantly beautiful.
"There, in the center of unsightly lotuses [with] disgusting petals
    and stalks, sit [tathagatas], as if they [had] the nature of a jewel.
    Why have [you with your] supernatural powers created these
    [manifestations]?
"I see buddhas equal in number to the sands of the Ganges River,
    [and] I see the exquisite [manifestations] of the [Tathagata's]
    supernatural powers. Never before have [I] witnessed such a
    miracle like this one existing right now.
"[I] implore the Highest among Humans, the Divine, to teach. [I]
    implore [him] to explain the reason [for this miraculous
    display]. [I] implore [him] to speak [with] solicitude [in order
    to] benefit the world. [I] implore [him] to remove the doubts of
    all embodied [beings]."

Then the Exalted One said to the whole multitude of bodhisattvas, [includ-
ing] the bodhisattva mahasattva Vajramati and others:

"Sons of good family, there is a sutra of great extent called *A Tathagata Within*. In order to teach it the Tathagata has produced these
signs [which] appeared [to you]; Listen therefore closely, be attentive, and [I] will teach [you]."

"Just so!" replied the bodhisattva-mahasattva Vajramati and the whole multitude of bodhisattvas to the Exalted One, thereby acquiescing, and the
Exalted One spoke:

"Sons of good family, just as these unsightly, putrid, disgusting, and
no [longer] pleasing lotuses, supernaturally created by the Tathagata, and the pleasing and beautiful form of a tathagata sitting cross-
legged in [each of] the calyxes of these lotuses, emitting hundreds of
thousands of rays of light, [are such that when they are] recognized
by gods and humans, [these latter] then pay homage and also show
reverence [to them], in the same way, sons of good family, also the
Tathagata, the Honorable One and Perfectly Awakened One, [per-
ceives] with his insight, knowledge and tathagata-vision that all the
various sentient beings are encased in myriads of defilements, [such
as] desire, anger, misguidedness, longing, and ignorance.
    "And, sons of good family, [he] perceives that inside sentient beings
encased in defilements sit many tathagatas, cross-legged and motionless, endowed like myself with a [tathagata's] knowledge and vision.
And [the Tathagata], having perceived inside those [sentient beings]
defiled by all defilements the true nature of a tathagata motionless
and unaffected by any of the states of existence, then says: 'Those
tathagatas are just like me!'

"Sons of good family, in this way a tathagata's vision is admirable, [because] with it [he] perceives that all sentient beings have a tathagata within."

"Sons of good family, it is like the example of a person endowed with divine vision [who] would [use this] divine vision to look at such unsightly and putrid lotuses, not blooming and not open, and would [owing to his vision] recognize that there are tathagatas sitting cross-legged in their center, in the calyx of [each] lotus, and [knowing that, he] would then desire to look at the forms of the tathagatas; [he would] then peel away and remove the unsightly, putrid, and disgusting lotus petals in order to thoroughly clean the forms of the tathagatas.

"In the same way, sons of good family, with the vision of a buddha, the Tathagata also perceives that all sentient beings have a tathagata within, and [therefore] teaches the dharma [to them] in order to peel away the sheaths of those sentient beings [encased in such] defilements [as] desire, anger, misguidedness, longing, and ignorance. And after [those sentient beings] have realized the [dharma, their] tathagatas [inside] are established in the perfection [of the tathagatas]."

"Sons of good family, the essential law of [all] things is this: whether or not tathagatas appear in the world, all these sentient beings at all times have a tathagata within.

"Sons of good family, in view of [this fact and] because [sentient beings] are encased in the disgusting sheaths of defilements, the Tathagata, the Honorable One and Perfectly Awakened One, teaches the dharma to bodhisattvas and also leads [them] to put faith in this [revelatory] activity in order to destroy their sheaths of defilements and [thereby] also completely purify the tathagata-knowledge [contained within]. When in this [connection] the bodhisattva-mahasattvas [who] assiduously apply [themselves] to these dharmas have completely become free from all defilements and impurities, then [they] will be designated 'tathagata, honorable one and perfectly awakened one,' and [they] will also perform all the tasks of a tathagata."

Then at that time the Exalted One uttered these verses:

"It is as if [there were] a disgusting lotus whose [unsightly] sheath-[like] petals were not opened out, yet [whose] inside [containing a] tathagata, were unpolluted [by the petals], and a person with divine vision perceived [this].
"If this [person] peeled away its petals, in the center the body of a victorious one would appear, and no impurity would then arise any longer [from this] victorious one. He would appear as a victorious one [in] the whole world.
"In the same way, I also see bodies of victorious ones placed in the midst of all living beings, encased in myriads of defilements [that are] just like the disgusting sheaths of a lotus.

"[And] because I also desire to remove [the defilements] of those [sentient beings, I] am continually teaching the dharma to the wise, thinking,

'May these sentient beings become awakened!
'[And I] purify [their] defilements, so that [they may become] victorious ones.'

"My buddha-vision is like that [person's divine vision]: with the [vision of a buddha I] see that in all these sentient beings the body of a victorious one is established, and in order to purify them [I] preach the dharma."

"Sons of good family, again it is as if there were, for example, a round honeycomb hanging from the branch of a tree, shielded on all sides by a hundred thousand bees and filled with honey. And a person desiring honey, [and knowing of the honey within,] would then with skill [in the application of appropriate] means expel all the living beings, the bees, and then use the honey [in the way] honey is to be used.

"In the same way, sons of good family, all sentient beings without exception are like a honeycomb; with a tathagata's mental vision [I] realize that [their] buddhahood within is 'shielded on all sides' by myriads of defilements and impurities.

"Sons of good family, just as a skillful person by [his] knowledge realizes that there is honey inside a honeycomb shielded on all sides by myriads of bees, in the same way [I] realize with [my] tathagata's mental vision that buddhahood is without exception 'shielded on all sides' in all sentient beings by myriads of defilements and impurities."

"And, sons of good family, just like the [person who] removed the bees, also the Tathagata, with skill in [the application of appropriate] means, removes sentient beings' defilements and impurities [from their buddhahood] within, [such as] desire, anger, misguidedness, pride, insolence, jealous disparagement, rage, malice, envy, avarice, and so on. [He] then teaches the dharma in such a way so that those sentient beings will not again become polluted and harmed by the defilements and impurities.

"[When their] tathagata's mental vision has become purified, [they] will perform the tasks of a tathagata in the world. Sons of good family, this is how I see all sentient beings with my completely pure vision of a tathagata."

Then at that time the Exalted One uttered these verses:

"It is as if there were a honeycomb here, shielded on all sides and hidden by bees, [but] a person desiring honey would perceive the [honey within] and expel the bees.
"Also here in the same way, all sentient beings [in] the triple states of existence are like the honeycomb. The many myriads of

defilements are [like] the [bees, yet I] see that inside the
defilements there exists a tathagata.

"Also, in order to clean [this] buddha, I remove the defilements,
just as [the person desiring honey] expels the bees. [Using
appropriate] means, [I] teach here so that myriads of
defilements will be eradicated.

"[I do this] in order to induce those [sentient beings], after becoming
tathagatas, to continually perform the tasks [of a tathagata]
throughout the world, and with readiness in speech to teach
the dharma, [which is] like a pot of honey from bees."

"Sons of good family, again it is like the example of winter rice, barley, millet, or monsoon rice [whose] kernel is shielded all around by a
husk: as long as the [kernel] has not come out of its husk, [it can]not
serve the function of solid, soft and delicious food. But, sons of good
family, [it can serve this function very well once] some men or women,
desiring that [these grains serve their] function as food and drink in
hard, soft, or other [forms], after having it reaped and threshed,
remove the [coarse] sheath of the husk and the [fine] outer skin."

"Sons of good family, in the same way [that people are aware of
the precious kernel within the husk, so] too the Tathagata perceives with [his] tathagata-vision that tathagatahood, buddhahood,
awakening-by-one's-own-power—wrapped in the skin of the sheaths
of defilements—is [always] present in every sentient being. Sons of
good family, the Tathagata also removes the skin of the sheaths
of defilements, purifies the tathagatahood in them and teaches the
dharma to sentient beings, thinking:

'How [can] these sentient beings become free from all the skins
of the sheaths of defilements [so that they] will be designated
in the world as "tathagata, honorable one and perfectly awakened one"?'"

Then at that time the Exalted One uttered these verses:

"[It is] like monsoon rice or winter rice, or [like] millet or barley,
[which,] as long as they are in the husk, [can]not serve [their]
function.

"[But] having been pounded [and their] husks having been removed,
they [can] serve all [their] various functions. [However,] the
kernels in the husks [can]not serve [any] function for sentient
beings.

"In the same way [that people are aware of the precious kernel
within the husk,] I see that the ground of buddha[hood of]
all sentient beings is covered by defilements. And then I
teach the dharma in order to purify them and let [them]
attain buddha[hood] quickly. In order that [they] may quickly
become victorious ones, [I] teach the dharma so that, like
mine, [their] true nature, which, [though] wrapped in
hundreds of defilements, is in all sentient beings, becomes
purified [in] all [of them]."

"Sons of good family, again it is like the example of a round nugget of gold [belonging to] someone [who] had walked [along] a narrow path, [and whose nugget] had fallen into a place of decaying substances and filth, [a place] full of putrid excrement. In that place of decaying substances and filth full of putrid excrement, the [gold nugget], having been 'overpowered' by various impure substances, would have become invisible, [and would have remained] there for ten, twenty, thirty, forty, fifty, a hundred, or a thousand years, [but it would, though surrounded] by impure substances, [never be affected by them, owing to] its imperishable nature. [Because of the covering of impure substances, however, it could] not be of use to any sentient being."

"Sons of good family, [if] then a divinity with divine vision looked at that round gold nugget, [the divinity] would direct a person:

'O man, go and clean that gold of excellent value [t]here, [which is only externally] covered with all sorts of decaying substances and filth, and use the gold [in the way] gold is to be used!'

In [this simile], sons of good family, [what] is called 'all sorts of decaying substances and filth' is a designation for the different kinds of defilements. [What] is called 'gold nugget' is a designation for [what] is not subject to perishability [i.e., the true nature of living beings]. [What] is called 'divinity [with] divine vision' is a designation for the Tathagata, the Honorable One and Perfectly Awakened One.

"Sons of good family, in the same way also the Tathagata, the Honorable One and Perfectly Awakened One, teaches the dharma to sentient beings in order to remove the defilements—[which are like] all sorts of decaying substances and mud—[from] the imperishable true nature of a tathagata found in all sentient beings."

Then at that time the Exalted One uttered these verses:

"It is just like [the example of some] man's nugget of gold [that] has fallen into all sorts of filth: though it remained there in such a state for not a few years, [yet it would never be affected owing to its] imperishable nature.
"[And] a divinity perceiving it with divine vision, in order to clean [it], would tell somebody:

'Here is gold of excellent value! Clean [it] and use it [in the way gold] is to be used!'

"In the same way I [can] see that also all sentient beings have for a long time been constantly overpowered by defilements, [but] knowing that their defilements [are only] accidental, [I] teach the dharma with [appropriate] means in order to purify [their] intrinsic nature."

"Sons of good family, again it is as if in the earth beneath a storeroom in the house of some poor person, under a covering of earth seven fathoms deep there were a great treasure, full of money and gold, [of the same] volume as the storeroom. But the great treasure—

not being, of course, a sentient being, given [its lack of] a mental essence—[could] not say to the poor [man]:

'O man, I am a great treasure, but [I am] buried [here], covered under earth.'

[In his] mind the poor man, the owner of the house, would consider [himself] poor, and even though [he] walked up and down directly above the [treasure], he [could] not hear of, know of, or perceive the existence of the great treasure beneath the earth.

"Sons of good family, in the same way, [in] all sentient beings, beneath the[ir] thinking, [which is based on] clinging—[and] analogously to the house—there is a great treasure, [namely] the treasury of a tathagata within, [including the ten] powers, [the four kinds of] self-assurance, [the eighteen] specific [qualities of a buddha], and all [other] qualities of a buddha.

"And yet sentient beings cling to color and shape, sound, odor, flavor, and tangible objects, and therefore wander in samsara, [caught in] suffering. And as a result of not having heard of that great treasure of [buddha] qualities [within themselves, they] in no way apply [themselves] to taking possession [of it] and to purifying [it]."

"Sons of good family, then the Tathagata appears in the world and manifests a great treasure of such [buddha] qualities among the bodhisattvas. The [bodhisattvas] then acquire confidence in that great treasure of [buddha] qualities and dig [it] out. Therefore in the world [they] are known as 'tathagatas, honorable ones and perfectly awakened ones,' because having become [themselves] like a great treasure of [buddha] qualities, [they] teach sentient beings the aspects of [this] unprecedented argument [of buddhahood in all of them], similes [illustrating this matter], reasons for actions, and [tasks] to fulfill. [They] are donors [who give from] the storeroom of the great treasure, and having unhindered readiness of speech, [they are] a treasury of the many qualities of a buddha, including the [ten] powers and the [four kinds of] self-assurance.

"Sons of good family, in this way, with the completely pure vision of a tathagata, the Tathagata, the Honorable One and Perfectly Awakened One, also perceives that all sentient beings are like the [poor owner of the house with the hidden treasure] and then teaches the dharma to the bodhisattvas in order to clean the treasury [in all sentient beings, which contains such qualities as] the tathagata-knowledge, the [ten] powers, the [four kinds of] self-assurance, and the [eighteen] specific qualities of a buddha."

Then at that time the Exalted One uttered these verses:

"[It is] as if beneath the house of a poor [man] there was a treasure full of gold and money, in which neither motion nor thinking was existent and [which could] not say: 'I am yours!'
"At the same time a sentient being, the owner of the house, had become poor. But because [he] would not know [of the treasure] and [because] there was nobody [who] had informed

him, the poor [man] would remain above the [treasure without
digging it out].

"In the same way, with the vision of a buddha I see that in all
sentient beings—though [from the outside] they resemble poor
[men]—there is a great treasure; and [I see this treasure] as
the motionless body of a well-gone [buddha].

"I see that [treasure and] teach [the following] to the bodhisattvas:

'O you [bodhisattvas], take the treasury of my knowledge! Act
[so that you may] become treasures of the supreme dharma,
being free of poverty and becoming protectors of the world!'

"Whoever acquires confidence in [this] my teaching—in each of
those sentient beings is a treasure. Whoever, having acquired
confidence, exerts himself will quickly attain excellent
awakening."

"Sons of good family, again it is like the example of a fruit of a mango
tree, a rose apple tree, a palmyra palm or of cane: inside the sheaths of
the outer peel there is a seed of imperishable nature [containing] a
sprout, [a seed] which, thrown on soil, will become a great king of trees.

"Sons of good family, in the same way also the Tathagata perceives
that [sentient beings who are] dwelling in the world are completely
wrapped in the sheaths of the outer peel of [such] defilements [as]
desire, anger, misguidedness, longing, and ignorance."

"In this [connection] the true nature of a tathagata, being in the
womb inside the sheaths of [such] defilements [as] desire, anger, misguidedness, longing, and ignorance, is designated 'sentient being.'
When it has become cool, it is extinct. And because [it is then] completely purified [from] the sheaths of defilements of ignorance, [it]
becomes a great accumulation of knowledge [in the] realm of sentient beings. The world with [its] gods, having perceived that supreme,
great accumulation of knowledge [in the] realm of sentient beings
speaking like a tathagata, recognizes [him] as a tathagata.

"Sons of good family, in this [connection] the Tathagata perceives
that [all sentient beings] are like the [seed containing a sprout],
and then propounds the matter to the bodhisattva-mahasattvas in
order that [they] might realize the tathagata-knowledge [within
themselves]."

Then at that time the Exalted One uttered these verses:

"Just as all the fruits of cane have a cane sprout inside [their
seeds], and [just as a sprout] is also in all the [fruits of]
palmyra palms and rose apple trees: when the result, [which
is already perfectly] contained within [the fruit's outer peel,]
is made to germinate, [a great tree will] grow.

"In the same way also the Master of the Dharma, the Leader,
perceives with the supreme, uncontaminated vision of a
buddha that in all sentient beings without exception—
similarly to the cane seed—there is the body of a well-gone
[buddha].

"The [being in the state when] the sheaths [of defilements] have not been destroyed is called 'sentient being.' Even though [the essence of this sentient being, namely the body of a well-gone buddha,] dwells [hidden] in ignorance, there is no illusory imagining. [It] dwells in mental absorption, is completely calm, and there is no motion whatsoever.

"Thinking:

'How may these sentient beings become awakened—just as a great tree has grown from a seed—and [thus become] refuges for the world with [its] gods?'

"I speak the dharma in order to completely purify [sentient beings]."

"Sons of good family, again it is like the example of a poor man [who] has a tathagata image the size of the palm of a hand [and] made of seven kinds of jewels. It then so happened that the poor man wished to cross a [dangerous] wilderness carrying the tathagata image [with him]. And in order that it might not be discovered by anybody else, or stolen by robbers, he then wrapped it in some rotten, putrid rags.

"Then the man died owing to some calamity in that same wilderness, and his tathagata image, made of jewels [and] wrapped in rotten rags, then lay around on the footpath. [But] travelers, unaware [of the precious tathagata image in the rags], repeatedly stepped over [it] and passed by. And [they would] even point [at it] as something disgusting [and question]: 'Where has the wind brought this wrapped bundle of rotten, putrid rags from?' And a divinity dwelling in the wilderness, having looked [at the situation] with divine vision, would show [it to] some people and direct [them]:

'O men, [here] inside this bundle of rags is a tathagata image made of jewels, worthy to be paid homage by all worlds. So [you] should open [it]!'"

"Sons of good family, in the same way also the Tathagata perceives that all sentient beings are wrapped in the wrappings of defilements and that [they are like something] disgusting, wandering around for ages throughout the wilderness of samsara. And, sons of good family, [the Tathagata] perceives that also within sentient beings [who] are wrapped in the wrappings of various defilements—and even though [they] may have come into existence as animals—there is the body of a tathagata of the same [kind] as my own.

"Sons of good family,

'How does the mental vision of a tathagata [in all sentient beings] become free and completely purified from impurities so that [sentient beings] become worthy of the homage of all worlds, as I am now?'

"Thus thinking, the Tathagata teaches in this [connection] the dharma to all bodhisattvas in order to cause [such beings] to become free from the wrappings of defilements [in which they] are wrapped."

Then at that time the Exalted One uttered these verses:

"It is as if an image of a well-gone [buddha] were wrapped in putrid, disgusting [materials]—made of jewels [and yet] wrapped in rags—[and] had been left on a path and lay around [there].

"And the divinity, having perceived it with divine vision, had said to some [people]:

'Here is a tathagata [image made of] jewels. Open quickly this bundle of rags!'

"My [vision] is like this divinity's vision: with that [vision I] see that without exception all these sentient beings, wrapped in the wrappings of defilements, are suffering severely [and] are continuously tormented by [this] suffering of samsara.

"I perceive that inside the wrappings [consisting of] defilements the body of a victorious one is firmly established, that that [body] is without motion and change, and that yet there is nobody setting that [body] free.

"Having seen [this], I then urged [the bodhisattvas]:

'[O you] who have entered excellent awakening, listen! Thus [is] the essential law [regarding] sentient beings: here [within each sentient being] always dwells a victorious one, wrapped around [with defilements].

'When the knowledge of a well-gone [buddha within] has been set free and all defilements are pacified, then this [sentient being] is called 'awakened' and the hearts of gods and humans are full of joy.'"

"Sons of good family, again it is like the example of a woman without a protector, of unsightly complexion, having a bad smell, disgusting, frightening, ugly, and like a demoness, [and this woman] had taken up residence in a poorhouse. While staying there she had become pregnant. And though the life that had entered into her womb was such as to be destined to reign as a world emperor, the woman would neither question herself with reference to the sentient being existing in her womb, 'Of what kind is this life [that] has entered my womb?,' nor would she [even] question herself in that [situation]: 'Has [some life] entered my womb or not?' Rather, thinking herself poor, [she would be] depressed, [and] would think thoughts [like] '[I am] inferior and weak,' and would pass the time staying in the poorhouse as somebody of unsightly complexion and bad smell."

"Sons of good family, in the same way also all sentient beings [think of themselves as] unprotected and are tormented by the suffering of samsara. [They, too,] stay in a poorhouse: the places of [re]birth in the states of being. Then, though the element of a tathagata has entered into sentient beings and is present within, those sentient beings do not realize [it].

"Sons of good family, in order that sentient beings do not despise themselves, the Tathagata in this [connection] teaches the dharma with the [following] words:

'Sons of good family, apply energy without giving in to despondency! It will happen that one day the tathagata [who has] entered [and] is present within you will become manifest. Then you will be designated "bodhisattva," rather than "[ordinary] sentient being." [And] again in the [next stage you] will be designated "buddha," rather than "bodhisattva."'"

Then at that time the Exalted One uttered these verses:

"It is as if a simple woman without a protector, of bad complexion and ugly disposition would [go to] stay in a poorhouse, [and] after a time would there have become pregnant,

"[and yet] the [life] that had entered her womb would be such that the [embryo] was destined [to become] a world emperor king, elevated by [his] magnanimity [and his seven] jewels, and ruling [over all] four continents.

"[But] that simple woman would [behave] like this: [she] would not know if [some life] had entered [her] womb; rather [she] would [continue to] stay in the poorhouse and pass the time in the belief that [she] was poor.

"In the same way, I see that all sentient beings also [think of themselves as] unprotected and are distressed by things, [which lead to] suffering, remaining [caught up] in the lesser pleasures of the three spheres,[5] [even though] inside [them] there is the true nature—like [the world emperor in] the womb [of the woman].

"Having seen thus [I] taught the bodhisattvas:

'As all sentient beings do not know about the true nature within [their own] wombs [which] grants benefit [to] the world, [take care of them and let them] not consider themselves inferior!

'Apply energy firmly! Soon you yourselves will become victorious ones. At some point [you will] attain the essence of awakening. Then [you] will proceed to liberate myriads of living beings.'"

"Sons of good family, again it is like the example of figures of horses, elephants, women, or men being fashioned out of wax, then encased in clay [so that they are completely] covered [with it and finally, after the clay has dried,] melted [in fire]; and after [the wax] has been made to drip out, gold is melted. And when [the cavity inside the mold] is filled with the melted [gold], even though all the figures, having cooled down step-by-step [and] arrived at a uniform state, are [covered with] black clay and unsightly outside, [their] insides are made of gold.

"Then, when a smith or a smith's apprentice [uses] a hammer [to] remove from the [figures] the outer [layer of] clay [around] those figures which he sees have cooled down, then in that moment the golden figures lying inside become completely clean."

5. That is, the three realms: the Realm of Desire, the Realm of Form, and the Formless Realm; see pp. 54–55.

"Sons of good family, likewise also the Tathagata perceives with the vision of a tathagata that all sentient beings are like figures [in] clay; the cavity inside the sheaths of outer defilements and impurities is filled with the qualities of a buddha [and with] the precious uncontaminated knowledge; inside, a tathagata exists in [all] magnificence.

"Sons of good family, having then perceived that all sentient beings are like this, the Tathagata goes among the bodhisattvas and perfectly teaches [them] these [nine] dharma discourses of that kind [i.e., on the tathagata-knowledge within all sentient beings]. [Using] the diamond[-like] hammer of the dharma, the Tathagata then hews away all outer defilements in order to entirely purify the precious tathagata-knowledge of those bodhisattva-mahasattvas who have become calm and cool.

"Sons of good family, what is called 'smith' is a designation for the Tathagata. Sons of good family, after the Tathagata, the Honorable One and Perfectly Awakened One, has perceived with [his] buddha-vision that all sentient beings are like this, [he] teaches the dharma in order to establish [them] in buddha-knowledge, having let [them] become free from the defilements."

Then at that time the Exalted One uttered these verses:

"It is like [the example of casting golden images: first, wax] figures
     are covered outside with clay; [then, after the wax has been
     melted and so drips out,] the inside [of the clay] has a cavity
     and is empty; [finally,] when [these cavities] are filled with
     precious melted materials, [they] turn into many hundreds of
     thousands [of golden figures].
"[Then] a smith, realizing that [the figures in the clay] have
     thoroughly cooled down, hews away the coverings of clay
     around the figures, thinking:

'What can [I] do so that these [black molds with their insides]
     made of precious materials may turn into clean figures?'

"In the same way I see that all sentient beings, without exception,
     are like golden figures covered with clay: [their] outside
     crusts are the sheaths of defilements, but inside there is the
     buddha-knowledge.
"[Using] the tool of the dharma, [the Tathagata] then hews away
     the [defilements of those] bodhisattvas who have become
     calm and cool, so that their defilements are expelled
     without any remainder.
"[Living beings' internal] child of a victorious one who has become
     clean in this [world is] just like the beautiful precious figure:
     [living beings'] bodies are filled with the ten powers [of a
     buddha], and [they] are venerated here [by] the world with
     [its] gods.
"Thus I see all living beings; thus I see also the bodhisattvas.
     Thus purified [by the Tathagata they] become well-gone
     [buddhas]. [Having become] pure well-gone [buddhas],
     [they] then teach the rule of the buddhas."

Then the Exalted One said to the bodhisattva-mahasattva Vajramati:

"Vajramati, sons and daughters of good family, whoever—whether a layman or ordained—learns this dharma discourse [called] *A Tathagata Within*, preserves [it], recites [it], understands [it], arranges [it] into a book, explains [it] also to others in detail, and teaches [it], [that person] will produce much merit."

"Vajramati, a certain bodhisattva might apply [himself] to realize the tathagata-knowledge, and for the purpose of venerating all buddhas without exception in every single world system, [he] would, after achieving supernatural powers, attain such a mental absorption that through the power created by [this] absorption [he could] day by day present pavilions to every single existing tathagata among the buddhas, the exalted ones, even more [numerous] than the sands of the Ganges River, in myriads of buddha-fields even more [numerous] than the sands of the Ganges River, together with [their] bodhisattvas and the communities of *shravakas*. [To reside in these pavilions would be] pleasant in [every] season. [Their] width [and length would each be] one mile, [their] height ten miles. [They] would be made of all [kinds of] jewels, [and would be] heavenly fragrant, being strewn with a variety of fallen blossoms and furnished with all immaculate object of enjoyment. [The number of pavilions would be] as many as fifty [times] the sands of a hundred thousand Ganges Rivers. For fully a hundred thousand cosmic cycles [he] would show reverence in this way.

"If [on the contrary] a certain son or daughter of good family should forge the resolution to [strive for] awakening, and internalize or arrange into a book only one simile from this dharma discourse [called] *A Tathagata Within*, [then], Vajramati, the previously [described bodhisattva's] accumulation of merit does not come near by even a hundredth, a thousandth, a hundred thousandth—any number, any tiny part, any calculation, or any resemblance—to his accumulation of merit; nor does [it] bear any comparison."

"Then, Vajramati, [suppose] a bodhisattva, in searching for the dharma of the buddhas, strewed four hundred thousand triple-bushels of flowers of the coral tree for every single tathagata among the buddhas, the exalted ones, for fully a hundred thousand cosmic cycles.

"Vajramati, if [on the contrary] any monk, nun, layman, or lay woman should decide [to strive] for awakening, and after listening to this dharma discourse [called] *A Tathagata Within* raised [their] joined palms and said [just] the single phrase 'I joyfully approve [what I have heard]!,' [then] Vajramati, the previously [described bodhisattva's] accumulations of merit and benefit, connected with the offering of flowers and flower garlands, planted among the tathagatas [as fields of merit], do not come near by even a hundredth, a thousandth, a hundred thousandth—any number, any tiny part, any calculation, or any resemblance—to those accumulations of merit and benefit; nor do [they] bear any comparison."

Then at that time the Exalted One uttered these verses:

"[Suppose], having brought forth the wish for awakening, some
sentient being listened to this [discourse and] learned [it],
copied [it], or arranged [it] into a book and explained [even
just] a single verse with appreciation;
"or if after listening to this [text called] *A Tathagata Within*
somebody searched for this excellent awakening: listen to [my
description of] the benefit [accruing] to him in these cases—
[a description of] what amount of merit is produced!
"[Suppose] a hero abiding in these excellent supernatural powers
worshipped for a thousand cosmic cycles the highest of
humans and [their] *shravakas* in the ten directions.
"[He] would present to each teacher of the world without exception
excellent palaces made of jewels—in number several myriad
[times the sands of] the Ganges [and] more, unimaginably
many.
"The [palaces] would be ten miles high and one mile wide and
long, be excellently furnished with fragrances and incense,
and inside be provided with thrones made of jewels.
"[These] thrones, and palanquins too, [would be] spread with silk
and calico a hundred [times], as innumerable as [the sands of
the] Ganges River; [he] would present [these palaces with
thrones] to each victorious one.
"Upon the victorious ones who reside in world systems—those
victorious ones more [numerous] than the sands of the
Ganges River—[he] would thus bestow [these palaces, and]
would venerate [them] all with appreciation.
"If [on the contrary] some wise [person], having listened to this
sutra, learns only one single simile correctly, or having learnt
[it], explains [it] to somebody [else, then] he will [produce] a
greater amount of merit thereby [than the previous person].
"Regarding the [former] merit seized by the hero [who worshipped
the tathagatas, it] does not come near by any tiny part or
resemblance [to the merit of this wise person]. [The wise
person therefore] becomes a refuge for all living beings, and
he quickly attains excellent awakening.
"The wise bodhisattva who reflects upon [the following]:

'A tathagata within exists in the same way [in all beings]! This
is the true nature of all sentient beings,'

will quickly become an awakened one [through] his own power."

"Vajramati, again, by way of this [following] kind [of exposition],
[one] should know thus: namely, that this dharma discourse is
extremely beneficial for bodhisattva-mahasattvas [because it] will
lead to the realization of the knowledge of an omniscient one.
  "Vajramati, formerly, in the past, innumerable, vast, measureless,
unimaginable, unparalleled, and [quantitatively] inexpressible cosmic
cycles [ago], [and] even more beyond the other side of that [time]—
then, at that time—there appeared in the world the tathagata, the
honorable one and perfectly awakened one, named Sadapramuk-

tarashmi, realized in wisdom and conduct, a well-gone [buddha], a world-knowing one, a charioteer of human beings to be tamed, unsurpassable, a teacher of gods and men, a buddha, an exalted one."

"Vajramati, why is that tathagata called Sadapramuktarashmi? Vajramati, immediately after the exalted one, the tathagata Sadapramuktarashmi, then a bodhisattva, had entered the womb of [his] mother, light was emitted from [his] body, while [he was still] within the womb of his mother, [so that] in the east hundreds of thousands of world systems, as many as the atomic-sized dust of ten buddha-fields, came to be constantly filled with brightness. In the same way, in the [other nine of the] ten directions, [namely] the south, the west, the north, the southeast, southwest, northwest, and northeast, along with the nadir and the zenith, hundreds of thousands of world systems, as many as the atomic-sized dust of ten buddha-fields, came to be constantly filled with brightness. And owing to the pleasant and beautiful light from the body of that bodhisattva, [which] caused [sentient beings] to rejoice [and] led [them] to delight, as many as hundreds of thousands of world systems constantly came to be filled with brightness."

"Vajramati, all sentient beings in the hundreds of thousands of world systems who were touched by the light from that bodhisattva within the womb of [his] mother attained strength, beauty, mindfulness, comprehension, understanding, and readiness of speech.

"All sentient beings in the hundreds of thousands of world systems who had been born in hells, in animal existences, in the world of Yama[6] and [as] demons immediately [could] abandon their birth by virtue of being touched by the light from that bodhisattva, and were [re]born among gods and men.

"Those [born as gods and men] by virtue of being touched [by the light], immediately became incapable of turning back from supreme and perfect awakening.

"In addition, all those incapable of turning back who had been touched by the light immediately, when touched by the light, attained intellectual receptivity [to the truth that] dharmas [have] no origination. [They] also obtained the efficacious formulas called 'Chapter of the Five Hundred Qualities.'"

"All those hundreds of thousands of world systems which had been touched by the light from the body of the bodhisattva within the womb of [his] mother came to be established as made of beryl, laid out in [the form of] a chessboard with golden threads, [with] jewel trees coming out of each square, [the trees] having blossoms, fruits, fragrances, and colors.

"When the jewel trees were shaken and moved by the wind, such pleasant [and] charming [sounds] came up as there are: the sound 'Buddha,' the sound 'dharma,' the sound 'religious community' [and]

6. The god of death.

the sound 'bodhisattva,' along with the sounds '[five] powers of a bod-hisattva,' '[five spiritual] faculties,' '[seven] branches of awakening,' 'liberation,' 'mental absorption,' and 'attainment.' Because of those sounds of the jewel trees, sentient beings in all of the hundreds of thousands of world systems became and remained satisfied and joy-ful. In all the buddha-fields the hells, animal existences, the world of Yama, and the world of the demons disappeared.

"The bodhisattva within the womb of [his] mother emitted light like the disk of the moon for all those sentient beings. Three times a day and three times a night [they] raised their joined palms [to pay homage] while [he] was still in the womb."

"Vajramati, when that bodhisattva had been born, had set out for ascetic life and [finally] completely awakened to buddhahood, light continued to be emitted in such a way from the body of that bodhisat-tva. Even after [his] complete awakening, light continued to be emit-ted from the body of that exalted one. Even when the exalted one entered into *parinirvana*,[7] that light [from] his body continued to be emitted in the same way. [And] even after that tathagata had entered *parinirvana* and [his body] remained [as] relics in a stupa, the light [from his] body [still] continued to be emitted. For this reason, Vajramati, that exalted one is named the 'Always Light-Emitting One' (Sadapramuktarashmi) by gods and men."

"Vajramati, under the rule of that exalted one, the tathagata, the honorable one and perfectly awakened one, Sadapramuktarashmi— right after [he had become] completely awakened—there appeared a certain bodhisattva named Anantarashmi. [He was accompanied] by a retinue of a thousand [bodhisattvas]. And, Vajramati, that bo-dhisattva Anantarashmi questioned the exalted one, the tathagata, the honorable one and perfectly awakened one, Sadapramukta-rashmi, with reference to this dharma discourse [called] *A Tatha-gata Within*."

"In order to benefit the bodhisattvas and to win [them] over [to his side], the exalted one, the tathagata, the honorable one and perfectly awakened one, Sadapramuktarashmi thereupon perfectly explained this dharma discourse [called] *A Tathagata Within* for five hundred great cosmic cycles, remaining in the same seat. And because he per-fectly explained to the bodhisattvas this dharma discourse [called] *A Tathagata Within* in intelligible words [and by employing] various means [with regard to the] dharma, explanations and hundreds of thousands of similes, [the bodhisattvas] in all world systems in the ten directions, as many as the atomic-sized dust of ten buddha-fields, understood [this dharma] easily."

"Vajramati, in this [connection] the roots of virtue [of] all the bod-hisattvas who heard this dharma discourse [called] *A Tathagata*

7. Final nirvana.

Within, [or] even only the title *A Tathagata Within*, successively came to maturity. Then, in such a way that the marvelous manifestation of the excellent qualities [of their buddha-fields] conformed to their [roots of virtue, these bodhisattvas] attained supreme and perfect awakening—apart from four bodhisattva-mahasattvas.

"Vajramati, if you think that then, at that time, the bodhisattva Anantarashmi was somebody other [than yourself, you] should not see it this way! Vajramati, you yourself were then, at that time, the bodhisattva Anantarashmi! Who are the four bodhisattvas who under the rule of that exalted one have not attained supreme and perfect awakening to buddhahood up until today? The four are the bodhisattvas Manjushri, Mahasthamaprapta, Avalokiteshvara, and you yourself, Vajramati!

"Vajramati, this dharma discourse [called] *A Tathagata Within* is thus of great benefit, since listening [to it leads] immediately to the realization of buddha-knowledge for bodhisattva-mahasattvas."

Then at that time the Exalted One uttered these verses:

"In the past, endless cosmic cycles ago, the exalted one [Sada]
     pramuktarashmi appeared. From such light being emitted
     from his body, myriads of [buddha-]fields came to be
     illuminated.
"At that time, right after [that] victorious one had attained
     complete awakening, the bodhisattva Anantarashmi asked
     that well-gone [buddha], victorious one and master [for this
     discourse, and the latter then] perfectly [and] without pause
     explained this sutra.
"All those who happened to hear this sutra personally from the
     leader, under the rule of that [same] victorious one, quickly
     attained noble awakening—apart from four bodhisattvas:
"Mahasthamaprapta, Avalokiteshvara, [and], third, the
     bodhisattva Manjushri. And you yourself, Vajramati, are the
     fourth! At that time they [all] heard this sutra.
"The bodhisattva Anantarashmi, who at that time had questioned
     the victorious one [about this text called *A Tathagata Within*
     and who] had been tamed by that [same victorious one]—[this]
     son of a well-gone [buddha], Vajramati, was at that time
     yourself!
"I, too, when [I] formerly practiced the path [of a bodhisattva],
     happened to hear the title of this sutra from the well-gone
     [buddha] Simhadhvaja. [And] having heard [it] with
     appreciation [I] raised my joined palms.
"By those well-done deeds I quickly attained noble awakening.
     Therefore wise bodhisattvas should always learn this
     excellent sutra!"

"Vajramati, [when] sons and daughters of good family who are restricted by obstacles [caused by their] deeds listen to this dharma discourse [called] *A Tathagata Within*, [and when they] show, recite, or teach [it, then]—with regard to listening to this dharma discourse, showing [it], reciting [it], explaining [it], and copying [it]—they will all, seeing the dharma before their eyes, easily become purified [from] the obstacles [caused by their] deeds."

Then the venerable Ananda asked the Exalted One the following:

"Exalted One, [as for] those sons and daughters of good family who are not restricted by obstacles [caused by their] deeds and [who] apply [themselves] to this dharma discourse, from how many buddhas, exalted ones, [do they preserve] expositions of the dharma as [persons of] great learning so that [they] become perfected?"

The Exalted One said:

"Ananda, there are sons and daughters of good family as well who are [already] perfected on account of having preserved expositions of the dharma from a hundred buddhas."

"Ananda, [but] there are also sons and daughters of good family who are [only] perfected on account of having preserved expositions of the dharma from two hundred buddhas, three hundred, four hundred, five hundred, one thousand, two thousand, three thousand, four thousand, five thousand, six thousand, seven thousand, eight thousand, nine thousand, ten thousand, or a hundred thousand buddhas, [or] even myriads of buddhas.

"Ananda, a bodhisattva who preserves this dharma discourse, recites [it], perfectly teaches [it] in detail also to others and preserves [it] as a book should bring forth this thought: 'I [wish to] attain supreme and perfect awakening already now!' He is worthy of the homage and veneration of the world with [its] gods, humans and demons, as I [am] now."

Then at that time the Exalted One uttered these verses:

"When a bodhisattva has heard this sutra, [he] thinks:

'I [wish to] attain the noble awakening!'

"He in whose hands this sutra is found is worthy of the homage of the world, as I [am now].
"[Being himself] a protector of the world [and] training [sentient beings], he is worthy of the praise [of] the leaders [and] trainers. Thus he in whose hands this sutra is found should be called 'king of the dharma.'
"He in whose hands this sutra is found is worthy of being looked upon [as] the best of men, [as] bearer of the lamp of the dharma [and] like the full moon. Like a protector of the world, [he is] a foundation [worthy] of being paid homage."

After the Exalted One had spoken thus, the bodhisattva Vajramati, the entire multitude of bodhisattvas, the great *shravakas*, the four assemblies, and the world with [its] gods, humans, demons, and celestial musicians were delighted, and praised [what] the Exalted One had said.

[Here] ends the Holy Mahayana sutra called *A Tathagata Within*.

The Indian master Shakyaprabha and the venerable great reviser and translator Ye shes sde have executed [this] translation and revised and established [it] definitively.[8]

8. This sentence is the Tibetan colophon.

THE HEART SUTRA

DISCOURSE ON THE HEART OF THE PERFECTION OF WISDOM
(*The Prajnaparamitahridaya Sutra*)

The *Heart Sutra* is the most commonly recited of all Buddhist texts, renowned as the "heart" or essence of the perfect wisdom. The Sanskrit title of the text is *Prajnaparamitahridaya Sutra*, the *Discourse on the Heart of the Perfection of Wisdom*. The label "sutra" is reserved for texts said to have been spoken by the Buddha or, more rarely, spoken with his sanction. The *Heart Sutra* is perhaps the most famous work in the latter category, for the Buddha says very little, remaining in meditation until the very end of the text. The presence of the phrase "perfection of wisdom" in the title signals its membership in a famous genre of texts crucial to the development of Mahayana Buddhism, whose names typically reflect their length: for example, the *Perfection of Wisdom in Eight Thousand Lines*, the *Perfection of Wisdom in Twenty-five Thousand Lines*, the *Perfection of Wisdom in One Hundred Thousand Lines*, and the *Perfection of Wisdom in One Letter* (the letter *a*, the first letter of the Sanskrit alphabet). The two most famous works of the genre are named differently, the *Heart Sutra* and the *Diamond Sutra* (see *The Perfection of Wisdom That Rends Like a Thunderbolt*, p. 325). Whatever their titles, these works set forth, among many other things, the wisdom by which a bodhisattva becomes a buddha. The *Heart Sutra* is said to be the essence of all the perfection of wisdom sutras.

The sutra, like all sutras, begins with the statement "Thus did I hear," indicating that it was heard by a direct witness, often said to be the Buddha's attendant, Ananda. The scene is then set: as in so many sutras, it is Vulture Peak, not far from where the Buddha had achieved enlightenment. At this point in most sutras, a member of the audience asks the Buddha a question, to which he responds. But here, the Buddha enters samadhi, a state of deep meditation. Another figure is immediately introduced. He is Avalokiteshvara (literally, "the lord who looks down"), the bodhisattva regarded as the embodiment of all the compassion of all the buddhas. Although mentioned in the *Lotus Sutra* (see the *Saddharmapundarika*, p. 276) and the subject of an entire chapter there (probably an interpolation; see *Dharani Sutra of Five Mudras of the Great Compassionate White-Robed One*, p. 571), his appearance in a perfection of wisdom sutra is unusual, leading some scholars to attribute a late date to the text. Here, he is described as seeing "that those five aggregates also are empty of intrinsic existence."

"Emptiness" (*shunyata* in Sanskrit) is a key term in the perfection of wisdom sutras. The Sanskrit adjective (*shunya*) has the same denotations that "empty" does in English;

for example, a vessel without liquid is described as *shunya*. But because the Sanskrit has none of the connotations of despair found in the English noun "emptiness," a literal translation can be slightly misleading. Some translators therefore prefer the term "voidness." In the sutra, Avalokiteshavara understands that the physical and mental constituents of the person (the "aggregates") are devoid of self: they lack any kind of essence or enduring nature. They are, in fact, empty; they do not exist in and of themselves; and their emptiness, their absence of any kind of essence, is what a bodhisattva must perceive in order to become a buddha.

The sutra next introduces Avalokiteshvara's interlocutor, Shariputra. In the Mahayana sutras, he often plays the questioner (and sometimes even the fool), a role suggesting that even the monk renowned in the early tradition as the wisest of the Buddha's "Hinayana" disciples requires tutelage in order to acquire the profound wisdom set forth in the Mahayana (see the *Vimalakirti Sutra*, p. 304). Indeed, here he cannot even ask a question himself but must rely on "the power of the Buddha." When the monk asks the bodhisattva how one should practice the perfection of wisdom, his response is one of the most famous statements in all of Buddhist literature: "Form is empty; emptiness is form." Many palm leaves have been incised with metal styluses and many calligraphy brushes have been dipped into pots of black ink in an effort to explain the meaning of those six words. In brief, one might say that the true nature of the physical world, including our own bodies, is emptiness, an absence, the lack of any intrinsic nature. And this emptiness, this natureless nature of reality, is not to be found in the heavens; it exists right here as what is most fundamental about the objects of the conventional world, about our everyday experience.

The bodhisattva then provides a litany of negations, going through the standard categories of Buddhist thought—the five aggregates, the twelve sources, the eighteen elements, the twelve links of dependent origination, the four noble truths—declaring that each does not exist: "no eye, no ear, no nose, no tongue, no body." These stark denials are generally interpreted to mean that the elements named are also empty of any intrinsic nature; they do not exist as they appear. Avalokiteshvara explains that all the buddhas have understood this: "All the buddhas who abide in the three times [past, present, and future] have fully awakened into unsurpassed, complete, perfect enlightenment in dependence on the perfection of wisdom."

What follows is something of a non sequitur, as the bodhisattva introduces a mantra—that is, a kind of spell, the embodiment in sound of a particular principle (or deity) whose invocation brings about a particular effect. Mantras are often a string of syllables with no apparent semantic value, but "the mantra of the perfection of wisdom," does make sense: *gate gate paragate parasamgate bodhi svaha*; it means "gone, gone, gone beyond, gone completely beyond, enlightenment, *svaha*" (*svaha* is a capping word in many mantras, not unlike the Hebrew interjection *amen*). The mantra, which has also drawn much commentary, seems to suggest a progression along the path of enlightenment, a movement from samsara to the other shore of nirvana.

With this, the Buddha rises from his meditation to endorse the words that Avalokiteshvara has spoken and, in a stock conclusion, the audience praises the words of the Buddha (who has in fact said almost nothing).

Although the *Heart Sutra* is one of the most famous of Buddhist texts (it is recited daily by Chinese, Japanese, Korean, and Tibetan monks), and for centuries has inspired profound exegesis, its origins remain obscure. Some have viewed it as an early Mahayana sutra, from which later perfection of wisdom sutras derive. Others see it as a summary of an already extant literature. And one scholar has argued that it is not of Indian origin at all but was composed by the Tang dynasty Chinese monk Xuanzang (see his *Great Tang Dynasty Record of the Western World*, p. 511) in the seventh century C.E.; Xuanzang himself reports copying the sutra from the wall of a cave in Loyang. Regardless of its date of composition, it was accepted as the word of the Buddha throughout East Asia and Tibet. Even in India, it was the subject of more extant commentaries than any other Mahayana sutra; but the earliest of these commentaries was not written until the eighth century C.E.

There is also a short version of the sutra, which starts with Avalokiteshvara perceiving the perfection of wisdom and ends with the mantra. But even the long version, translated here, is brief, and its concision clearly heightens the sutra's appeal as it itself becomes something of a magic spell, recited in Tibet prior to a discourse on the dharma to dispel any demons that might be loitering nearby. The sutra's brevity also enables it to be easily copied and turned into a talisman; at Buddhist temples in Japan one can purchase coffee mugs, fans, and neckties bearing the text of the *Heart Sutra*. These offer perhaps the most famous reminder that Buddhist sutras are potent objects of the senses, to be seen, heard, and touched, as well as pondered.

PRONOUNCING GLOSSARY

Avalokiteshvara: *a-va-loh-ki-taysh-va-ra*
Bhagavan: *ba-ga-van*
bodhisattva: *boh-di-sat-tva*
gandharva: *gan-dar-va*
gate: *ga-tay*
mahasattva: *ma-hah-sat-tva*
paragate: *pah-ra-ga-tay*
parasamgate: *pah-ra-sam-ga-tay*

Prajnaparamitahridaya Sutra: *pra-nya-pah-ra-mee-tah-hri-da-ya soo-tra*
Rajagriha: *rah-ja-gri-ha*
Shariputra: *shah-ri-pu-tra*
tathagata: *ta-tah-ga-ta*
samadhi: *sa-mah-di*
svaha: *svah-hah*

Thus did I hear. At one time the Bhagavan was residing at Vulture Peak in Rajagriha[1] with a great assembly of monks and a great assembly of bodhisattvas. At that time, the Bhagavan entered into a samadhi[2] on the categories of phenomena called "perception of the profound." Also at that time, the bodhisattva, the mahasattva, the noble Avalokiteshvara beheld the practice of the profound perfection of wisdom and saw that those five aggregates[3] also are empty of intrinsic existence. Then, by the power of the Buddha, the venerable Shariputra said this to the bodhisattva, the mahasattva, the noble Avalokiteshvara, "How should a son of good lineage who wishes to practice the profound perfection of wisdom train?" He said that and the bodhisattva, the mahasattva, the noble Avalokiteshvara said this to the venerable Shariputra, "Shariputra, a son of good lineage or a daughter of good lineage who wishes to practice the profound perfection of wisdom should perceive things in this way: form is empty; emptiness is form. Emptiness is not other than form; form is not other than emptiness. In the same way, feeling, discrimination, conditioning factors, and consciousnesses are empty. Therefore, Shariputra, all phenomena are empty, without characteristic, unproduced, unceased, stainless, not stainless, undiminished, unfilled. Therefore, Shariputra, in emptiness there is no form, no feeling, no discrimination, no conditioning factors, no consciousness, no eye, no ear, no nose, no tongue, no body, no

TRANSLATED FROM the Tibetan by Donald S. Lopez, Jr.

1. The capital of the kingdom of Magadha, in northeast India, where the Buddha lived for many years.
2. A state of deep meditation.
3. A standard division of the constituents of mind

and body into five groups: form, feeling, discrimination, compositional factors, and consciousness. "Mahasattva": "great being," a common epithet of bodhisattvas.

mind, no form, no sound, no odor, no taste, no object of touch, no phenomena, no eye constituent up to and including no mental consciousness constituent, no ignorance, no extinction of ignorance, no aging and death up to and including no extinction of aging and death. In the same way, no suffering, origin, cessation, path, no wisdom, no attainment, no non-attainment. Therefore, Shariputra, because bodhisattvas have no attainment, they rely on and abide in the perfection of wisdom; because their minds are without obstruction, they have no fear. They pass completely beyond error and go to the fulfillment of nirvana. All the buddhas who abide in the three times[4] have fully awakened into unsurpassed, complete, perfect enlightenment in dependence on the perfection of wisdom. Therefore, the mantra of the perfection of wisdom is the mantra of great wisdom, the unsurpassed mantra, the mantra equal to the unequaled, the mantra that completely pacifies all suffering. Because it is not false, it should be known to be true. The mantra of the perfection of wisdom is stated thus: *[om] gate gate paragate parasamgate bodhi svaha*.[5] Shariputra, a bodhisattva mahasattva should train in the profound perfection of wisdom in that way." Then the Bhagavan rose from samadhi and said, "Well done" to the bodhisattva, the mahasattva, the noble Avalokiteshvara. "Well done, well done, child of good lineage, it is like that. It is like that; the practice of the profound perfection of wisdom is just as you have taught it. Even the tathagatas[6] admire it." The Bhagavan having so spoken, the venerable Shariputra, the bodhisattva, mahasattva, the noble Avalokiteshvara, and all those surrounding, and the entire world, the gods, humans, demigods, and gandharvas,[7] admired and praised the speech of the Bhagavan.

4. The past, the present, and the future.
5. See the introduction to this selection.
6. Buddhas; *tathagata* is the title of a buddha most often used by the historical Buddha to refer to himself.
7. Divine beings known as heavenly musicians.

MAHAYANA TREATISES

ON THE MEANING OF EMPTINESS

VERSES ON THE MIDDLE WAY
(*The Madhyamakakarika*)

NAGARJUNA

After the Buddha himself, the most famous figure in the history of Indian Buddhism is Nagarjuna. We know little about his life. Prophecies about him by the Buddha, obviously inserted into texts after Nagarjuna's death, state that he would appear in the world four hundred years after the Buddha passed into nirvana, which would place him near the beginning of the Common Era. Scholars speculate that he lived sometime between 150 and 250 C.E., and perhaps was born in south India. Traditional accounts say that he lived for six hundred years through the practice of alchemy, identifying him with a later tantric master of the same name (see Abhayadatta's *Lives of the Eighty-Four Siddhas*, p. 478). The first Nagarjuna was the first major exponent—after the anonymous authors of the earliest Mahayana sutras—of the Mahayana in India. He is especially associated with the Perfection of Wisdom corpus (see *The Perfection of Wisdom That Rends Like a Thunderbolt*, p. 325, and *Discourse on the Heart of the Perfection of Wisdom*, p. 362). According to one legend, he retrieved the *Perfection of Wisdom in One Hundred Thousand Stanzas* from the bottom of the sea, where it had been left by the Buddha in the safekeeping of aquatic deities called *nagas*.

Though scholars question the authorship of many of the large number of works attributed to Nagarjuna, by even a conservative calculation his oeuvre is impressive in size and significance, ranging from philosophical treatises to letters of advice to kings, an anthology of sutra passages, and hymns of praise to the Buddha (see the Four Hymns, p. 375). By far the most famous of those texts is the *Verses on the Middle Way* (also known as the *Treatise on the Middle Way*), four chapters of which appear here. Indeed, its fame has led to a somewhat one-sided portrayal of the great master, and this anthology includes a second work by Nagarjuna in the hope of providing more balance.

"Middle way" is a phrase particularly associated with Nagarjuna, but it originated not with him but with the Buddha. In his very first sermon after his enlightenment (see *Setting the Wheel of the Dharma in Motion*, p. 177), the Buddha spoke of a middle way between the extremes of self-indulgence and self-mortification. The various philosophical schools that developed over the following centuries each claimed to present a middle way between extremes, variously defined. All schools would steer between the extreme of permanence, manifest in the view that each sentient being has a permanent, partless, independent self that goes from lifetime to lifetime, and the extreme of nihilism, manifest in the view that nothing lies beyond this life, that former and future lives do not exist. But no other school stressed the concept as much as the Madhyamaka, which Nagarjuna is credited with founding: the Sanskrit word *madhyamaka* literally means "middle-ist." Nagarjuna defined the middle way more radically than did his predecessors. For him, the middle way lay between the extremes of existence and nonexistence, between the position that everything exists and the position that nothing exists.

Two terms are particularly important for Nagarjuna. *Pratityasamutpada*, usually translated as "dependent origination," had appeared in the early tradition to describe a twelvefold chain of causation, but he applied it more generally. In his view, it describes the dependence of everything, from ordinary material forms to the omni-scient mind of the Buddha, on something else—an effect exists in dependence on its cause, a whole exists in dependence on its parts, anything exists in dependence on the consciousness that perceives it—nothing is independent, nothing exists in and of itself. Indeed, everything lacks any kind of independent existence or intrin-sic nature; and because everything is devoid or empty of such a nature, the other key term for Nagarjuna is *shunyata*, "emptiness." It is clear that by emptiness Nagarjuna means not nothingness (a charge leveled against him by his opponents over the centuries) but rather the absence of a specific quality—called in Sanksrit *svabhava*, literally "own being"—that is falsely imagined to inhere in all the objects of our experience. For Nagarjuna, because everything is dependently arisen, everything is empty. But emptiness does not negate function; rather, it makes function possible. As he famously declared, "All is possible when emptiness is possible." Thus, the middle way between the extremes of existence and nonexistence is that nothing exists ultimately (i.e., independently), but everything exists conventionally (i.e., depend-ently). Nagarjuna draws out the philosophical implications of the doctrine of causa-tion so central to the early teachings of the tradition.

His most thoroughgoing exposition of the implications of dependent origination occurs in the *Verses on the Middle Way*. The work is composed of 448 verses in twenty-seven chapters, which respectively analyze (1) conditions, (2) motion, (3) the eye and the other sense faculties, (4) the aggregates, (5) elements, (6) passion and the passionate, (7) the conditioned, (8) action and agent, (9) prior existence, (10) fire and fuel, (11) the past and future limits of samsara, (12) suffering, (13) disposition, (14) contact, (15) intrinsic nature, (16) bondage and liberation, (17) action and effect, (18) self, (19) time, (20) assemblage, (21) arising and dissolving, (22) the Tathagata, (23) error, (24) the four noble truths, (25) nirvana, (26), the twelve branches of dependent origination, and (27) views.

Nagarjuna's target audience for this work has been discussed at length, and scholars generally agree that it was intended for Buddhist monks well versed in the *abhidharma* (the detailed analysis of the constituents of experience and the func-tions of consciousness)—especially those of the Sarvastivada school, who posited a certain reality for the constituents of experience. The tone of the work is set in the famous homage to the Buddha with which it opens: "I bow down to the perfect Bud-dha, the best of teachers, who taught that what is dependency arisen is without cessation, without production, without annihilation, without permanence, without coming, without going, without difference, without sameness, pacified of elabora-tion, at peace." *The Verses on the Middle Way* subjects many of the most important categories of Buddhist thought to a relentless examination that reveals the impos-sibility and the absurd consequences of imagining any of them to be real in the sense of possessing an independent and intrinsic nature.

Nagarjuna usually proceeds by considering the various ways in which a given entity could exist, and then demonstrating that each entails absurdities. In the case of something regarded as the effect of a cause, he shows that the effect cannot be produced from itself (because an effect is the product of a cause), from something other than itself (because there must be a link between cause and effect), from something that is both the same as and different from itself (because neither option is possible), or from something that is neither the same as nor different from itself (because no such thing exists). This, he believes, is what the Perfection of Wisdom sutras mean when they state that all phenomena are "unproduced." The purpose of such an analysis is to destroy misconceptions and encourage the abandonment of all views.

Nagarjuna demonstrates repeatedly that these various categories exist only relationally and function only heuristically in a worldly and conventional sense. His thoroughgoing negative critique leads to charges of nihilism, which he anticipates and directly confronts in the text—especially in chapter 24, on the four noble truths (included here). There, introducing the topic of the two truths—ultimate and conventional—he declares the importance of both in correctly understanding the doctrine of the Buddha; he also discusses the danger of misunderstanding emptiness, and the relation between emptiness and dependent origination.

All four chapters included in this anthology—the others focus on the self; on the Buddha, or Tathagata; and on dependent origination—were selected on the advice of the fourteenth Dalai Lama.

PRONOUNCING GLOSSARY

Madhyamakakarika: *mad-ya-ma-ka-kah-ree-kah*
namarupa: *nah-ma-roo-pa*
pratyekabuddha: *prat-yay-ka-bud-da*

sangha: *san-ga*
skandha: *skan-da*
Tathagata: *ta-tah-ga-ta*

XVIII. An Analysis of the Self

1. If the self were the *skandhas*,[1] it would participate in coming to be and passing away.
If it were something other than the *skandhas*, it would be something having the defining characteristic of a non-*skandha*.

2. The self not existing, how will there be 'what belongs to the self'?
There is no 'mine' and no 'I' because of the cessation of self and that which pertains to the self.

3. And who is without 'mine' and 'I'-sense, he is not found.
One who sees that which is without 'mine' and 'I'-sense does not see.

4. The senses of 'mine' and 'I' based on the outer and the inner being lost,
Appropriation is extinguished; because of losing that, there is the cessation of birth.

5. Liberation is attained through the destruction of actions and defilements; actions and defilements arise because of falsifying conceptualizations;
Those arise from hypostatization; but hypostatization is extinguished in emptiness.

6. 'The self' is conveyed, 'non-self' is taught
By buddhas, as well as that neither self nor non-self is the case.

TRANSLATED FROM the Sanskrit by Shoryu Katsura and Mark Siderits. All bracketed additions are the translators'.

1. The "aggregates," a standard division of the constituents of mind and body into five groups: form, feeling, discrimination, compositional factors, and consciousness.

7. The domain of objects of consciousness having ceased, what is to be named is ceased.
The nature of things is to be, like nirvana, without origination or cessation.

8. All is real, or all is unreal, all is both real and unreal,
All is neither unreal nor real; this is the graded teaching of the Buddha.

9. Not to be attained by means of another, at peace, not populated by hypostatization,
Devoid of falsifying conceptualization, not having many separate meanings—this is the nature of reality.

10. When something exists dependent on something [as its cause], that is not on the one hand identical with that [cause],
But neither is it different; therefore that [cause] is neither destroyed nor eternal.

11. Not having a single goal, not having many goals, not destroyed, not eternal,
This is the nectar of the teachings of the buddhas, lords of the world.

12. Though the completely enlightened ones do not arise, though the Hearers disappear,
The knowledge of the *pratyekabuddhas*[2] arises independently.

XXII. An Analysis of the Tathagata

1. The Tathagata[3] is neither identical with the *skandhas* nor distinct from the *skandhas*; the *skandhas* are not in him nor is he in them.
He does not exist possessing the *skandhas*; what Tathagata, then, is there?

2. If the Buddha is dependent on the *skandhas*, then he does not exist intrinsically.
But how can someone who does not exist intrinsically exist extrinsically?

3. It is possible that one who is dependent on an other-existent is without an essence.
But how will one who is devoid of essence become the Tathagata?

4. And if there is no intrinsic nature, how will there be an extrinsic nature?
Besides intrinsic nature and extrinsic nature, what Tathagata is there?

5. If there were some Tathagata not dependent on the *skandhas*,
Then he could attain dependence (on the *skandhas*); thus he would be dependent.

2. Individually enlightened ones; these followers of the Buddha are distinguished from the *shra-vakas* (literally, "hearers"), or disciples.

3. A title of a buddha (literally, "one who has thus come/gone"); it is the one most often used by the historical Buddha to refer to himself.

6. But there is no Tathagata whatever without dependence on the *skandhas*. And how will one who does not exist without dependence come to depend [on them]?

7. Something cannot be what is depended upon without having been depended upon [by someone].
Nor can it be that the Tathagata somehow exists devoid of what he depends on.

8. Being something that does not exist as either identical with or distinct from (the *skandhas*) when investigated in any of the five ways [mentioned in v. 1],[4]
How is the Tathagata conceptualized by means of what he depends on?

9. Moreover, that on which he depends does not exist by virtue of intrinsic nature.
And how can what does not exist intrinsically exist extrinsically?

10. Thus both that on which he depends and the one who is dependent are altogether empty.
And how is an empty Tathagata to be conceptualized by means of something empty?

11. 'It is empty' is not to be said, nor 'It is non-empty',
Nor that it is both, nor that it is neither; ('empty') is said only for the sake of instruction.

12. How can 'It is eternal', 'It is non-eternal', and the rest of this tetra-lemma[5] apply to (the Tathagata) who is free from hypostatization?
And how can 'It has an end', 'It does not have an end', and the rest of this tetralemma apply to (the Tathagata) who is free from hypostatization?

13. But one who has taken up a mass of beliefs such as that the Tathagata exists,
So conceptualizing, that person will also imagine that (the Tathagata) does not exist when extinguished.

14. And the thought does not arise, with reference to this (Tathagata) who is intrinsically empty,
That the Buddha either exists or does not exist after cessation.

15. Those who hypostatize the Buddha, who is beyond hypostatization and unwavering,
They all, deceived by hypostatization, fail to see the Tathagata.

16. What is the intrinsic nature of the Tathagata, that is the intrinsic nature of this world?
The Tathagata is devoid of intrinsic nature, this world is devoid of intrinsic nature.

4. The Buddha is not the same as the skandhas, he is not different from them, the skandhas are not in him, he is not in the skandhas, he does not possess the skandhas.
5. An argument that presents four alternatives.

XXIV. An Analysis of the Noble Truths

1. [Objection:] If all this is empty, there is neither origination nor cessation.
It follows for you that there is the non-existence of the four noble truths.[6]

2. Comprehension [of the truth of suffering], abandonment [of attachment, the cause of suffering], practice [of the path to the cessation of suffering] and personal realization [of the cessation of suffering, i.e., nirvana]—
None of these is possible due to the non-existence of the four noble truths.

3. And due to the non-existence of those, the four noble fruits [of stream-winner, once-returner, never-returner, and *arhat*[7]] do not exist.
If the fruits are non-existent, then there are neither the strivers for nor the attainers of those fruits.

4. The sangha does not exist if the eight kinds of person[8] do not exist.
And because of the non-existence of the noble truths, the true dharma does not exist either.

5. Dharma and sangha[9] being non-existent, how will a buddha come to be?
In this way you deny all three jewels when you proclaim

6. Emptiness; you deny the real existence of the [karmic] fruit, both good and bad [actions],
And all worldly modes of conduct.

7. [Reply:] Here we say that you do not understand the point of [teaching] emptiness,
Emptiness itself, and the meaning of emptiness; thus you are frustrated.

8. The dharma-teaching of the buddhas rests on two truths:
Conventional truth and ultimate truth.

9. Who do not know the distinction of the two truths,
They do not understand the profound reality in the teachings of the buddhas.

10. The ultimate [truth] is not taught independently of customary practice.
Not having acquired the ultimate [truth], nirvana is not attained.

11. Emptiness misunderstood destroys the slow-witted,
Like a serpent wrongly held, or a spell wrongly executed.

12. Hence the Sage's intention to teach the dharma was turned back,
Realizing the difficulty, for the slow, of penetration of this dharma.

13. Moreover, the objection which you make concerning emptiness
Cannot be a faulty consequence for us or for emptiness.

---

6. These truths are given in the following verse.
7. The four stages on the path to nirvana.
8. A person who either is entering one of the four

stages of the previous note or is abiding in one of those stages.
9. The Buddhist community.

14. All is possible when emptiness is possible.
Nothing is possible when emptiness is impossible.

15. You, throwing your own faults on us,
Are like the person who, being mounted on a horse, forgets the horse.

16. If you look upon existents as real intrinsically,
In that case you regard existents as being without cause and conditions.

17. Effect and cause, as well as agent, instrument and act,
Arising and ceasing, and fruit—all these you [thereby] deny.

18. Dependent origination we declare to be emptiness.
It is a dependent concept, just that is the middle path.

19. There being no dharma whatever that is not dependently originated,
It follows that there is no dharma whatever that is non-empty.

20. If all this is non-empty, there is neither origination nor cessation.
It follows for you that there is the non-existence of the four noble truths.

21. How will suffering come to be if it is not dependently originated?
Indeed what is impermanent was declared to be suffering; it does not exist
if there is intrinsic nature.

22. How will something that exists intrinsically arise again?
Therefore the arising [of suffering] does not exist for one who denies
emptiness.

23. There is no cessation of a suffering that exists intrinsically.
You deny cessation through your maintaining intrinsic nature.

24. There is no practice of a path that exists intrinsically.
But if this path is practiced, then there is none of your intrinsic nature.

25. When there is neither suffering nor the arising and cessation (of suffering),
Then because [nirvana] is the cessation of suffering, what path will lead to it?

26. If the non-comprehension [of suffering] is intrinsic, how will there
later be its
Comprehension? Isn't an intrinsic nature said to be immutable?

27. In the same manner abandonment, personal realization and practice,
Like comprehension, are impossible for you; so too the four fruits.

28. For those holding that there is intrinsic nature, if the lack of acquisition
of the fruit is intrinsic,
how would it be possible to acquire it later?

29. If the fruits are non-existent, then there are neither the strivers after
nor the attainers of those fruits.
The sangha does not exist if the eight kinds of person do not exist.

30. And because of the non-existence of the noble truths, the true dharma does not exist either.
Dharma and sangha being non-existent, how will a buddha come to be?

31. And it follows for you that there can even be a buddha not dependent on enlightenment.
It follows for you as well that there can even be enlightenment not dependent on a buddha.

32. One who is unenlightened by intrinsic nature, though they strive for enlightenment,
Will not attain enlightenment in the course of the bodhisattva's practice.

33. Moreover, no one will ever perform either good or bad [actions].
What is there that is to be done with regard to the non-empty? For [what has] intrinsic nature is not done.

34. For you, indeed, there is fruit [even] without good or bad [actions],
For you there is no fruit conditioned[1] by good or bad [actions].

35. Or if, for you, the fruit is conditioned by good or bad [actions],
How is it that for you the fruit, being originated from good and bad [actions], is non-empty?

36. You also deny all worldly modes of conduct
When you deny emptiness as dependent origination.

37. There would be nothing whatever that was to be done, action would be uncommenced,
The agent would not act, given the denial of emptiness.

38. The world would be neither produced nor destroyed, and unchangeable,
It would be devoid of its manifold appearances if there were intrinsic nature.

39. The obtaining of that which is not yet obtained, activity to end suffering,
The abandonment of all the defilements, none of these exists if all this is non-empty.

40. He who sees dependent origination sees this:
Suffering, arising, cessation and the path.

XXVI. An Analysis of the Twelve-Fold Chain[2]

1. One who is enveloped in ignorance forms three kinds of volitions [viz., toward the good, bad and neutral, or toward physical, verbal and mental actions] that lead to rebirth;
And by means of these actions one goes to one's (next) mode of existence.

1. That is, created by karma.
2. The traditional chain of causation: ignorance, compounded formations, consciousness, name and form, the six senses, contact, feeling, attachment, grasping, existence, birth, and old age and death.

2. Having volitions as its conditions, consciousness enters into the [new] mode of existence.
Then, consciousness having entered (into the new mode of existence), *namarupa* [the five *skandhas*] becomes infused [with life].

3. But *namarupa* having become infused [with life], the six sense organs[3] occur.
[The infused *namarupa*] having attained the six sense organs, contact takes place.

4. Dependent on the eye, color-and-shape, and attention,
Dependent thus on *namarupa*, (eye-)consciousness occurs.

5. The conjunction of three things—color-and-shape, consciousness and the eye—
That is contact; and from that contact there occurs feeling.

6. Dependent on feeling is desire, for one desires the object of feeling.
Desiring, one takes up the four kinds of appropriation [viz., that connected with pleasure, with views, with rituals and vows, and with belief in a self].

7. There being appropriation, there is the existence of the appropriator,
For if there were non-appropriation, one would be liberated, there would be no (further) existence.

8. And this existence is the five *skandhas*; from existence results birth;
The suffering of old age, death, etc., grief accompanied by lamentations,

9. Frustration, despair, these result from birth;
Thus is the arising of this entire mass of suffering.

10. Thus does the ignorant one form the volitions that are the roots of *samsara*.
The ignorant one is therefore the agent, not so the wise one, because of having seen reality.

11. Upon the cessation of ignorance there is the non-arising of volitions.
But the cessation of ignorance is due to meditation on just the knowledge of this.

12. By reason of the cessation of one [link in the twelve-fold chain], another [successor link] fails to arise;
Thus does this entire mass of suffering completely cease.

3. Eye, ear, tongue, nose, body, and mind.

IN PRAISE OF THE EMPTY BUDDHA

FOUR HYMNS
(The Chatuhstava)

NAGARJUNA

The great Indian Buddhist philosopher Nagarjuna, who lived in the second or third century C.E., is best known for his *Verses on the Middle Way* (see the previous selection). But he also wrote hymns in praise of the Buddha. Yet if everything is empty, including the Buddha, how can one praise him? Nagarjuna asks this very question in "Hymn to the Ultimate":

> How shall I praise you, the protector, unborn, without foundation, who has passed beyond all comparison with the world, whose domain is beyond the path of speech?

> Nevertheless, whatever you may be in the domain of the true reality, I, having resorted to the world of conventional designations, shall praise the Master out of devotion.

Among Nagarjuna's most famous works is a collection known simply as the *Four Hymns (Chatuhstava)*, each in praise of the Buddha. They are "Hymn to the Incomparable One" ("Niraupamyastava"), "Hymn to the Ultimate" ("Paramarthastava"), "Hymn to the One Beyond the World" ("Lokatitastava"), and "Hymn to the Inconceivable One" ("Achintyastava"). They differ in style and intent, and there is no evidence that among all the hymns by Nagarjuna—he is credited with eighteen hymns in the Tibetan canon, and arguably at least half of the ascriptions are accurate—these four were composed as a set. But around the tenth century, they began to be considered as a group.

Despite their differences, they are all works of a devotee of the Buddha, an adherent of the Mahayana who is seeking to understand the Buddha from the perspective of emptiness while using the conventions of language. Knowing that his audience is well aware of the famous statement that from the night of his enlightenment to the night he entered nirvana, the Buddha never stopped preaching the dharma, Nagarjuna writes in the "Hymn to the Incomparable One":

> Not a single syllable has been uttered by you, o Lord,
> [yet] all people fit to be trained have been gladdened by the rain of your doctrine.

Mahayana works like the *Lotus Sutra* often deal with the seeming contradictions between the Buddha's perfected state and his humanity by claiming that his appearance in the world, his quest for buddhahood, his enlightenment, and his passage into nirvana were but a magical display, that the Buddha in fact was enlightened long before, and that he never died. Nagarjuna makes a similar point in this same hymn:

> There is no disease or impurity in your body, no arising of hunger or thirst either, [but],
> for the sake of conforming yourself to the world, you have shown worldly behaviour.

> In no way do you have the faults [caused by] the obstacles of actions, o faultless one,
> [but] because of the pity for the world you have shown [yourself] as submersed in action.

Although all is empty, there is also activity, and no activity is more praiseworthy than the Buddha's appearance in the world and his preaching of the dharma, especially the dharma of emptiness. And thus, although all is empty, there is also merit—merit that once made is to be dedicated to the welfare of all beings in the universe. Each of these four hymns ends with such a dedication.

PRONOUNCING GLOSSARY

Chatuhstava: *cha-too-sta-va*
dharmadhatu: *dar-ma-dah-tu*

Hymn to the Incomparable One

O incomparable one, homage to you who knows the meaning of
    inexistence of own-being,
[homage to] you intent on the benefit of this world gone wrong by views.

Nothing has been seen by you with your Buddha eye,
but your supreme vision, o protector, perceives the truth.

There is neither knower nor thing to be known from the standpoint of the
    ultimate truth, o,
you know the reality most difficult to know.

No dharma has been caused to rise nor caused to cease by you.
By perceiving the universal sameness of everything the supreme station
    has been reached by you.

Nirvana has not been desired by you through elimination of *samsara*.
You have realised peace, o protector, through non-perceiving of *samsara*.

You know the sameness in taste (nature) of impurity and purity.
Because there is no differentiation in the reality, you are completely pure.

Not a single syllable has been uttered by you, o Lord,
[yet] all people fit to be trained have been gladdened by the rain of your
    doctrine.

You are not attached to the aggregates,[1] elements and sensory spheres; [with
    your] mind the same as space, you are independent of all dharmas.

Perception of beings [as anything other than empty] in no way occurs in
    you, o protector, and
[yet], you are exceedingly compassionate towards all beings tortured by
    suffering.

"Happiness, suffering, self, absence of self, eternal, not-eternal," etc.—
your mind, o splendid one, is not attached to those various mental notions.

"For the dharmas there is no going nor coming at all"—thus you think.

TRANSLATED FROM the Sanskrit by Drasko Mitrikeski. All bracketed additions are the translator's.

1. A division of the constituents of mind and body into five groups: form, feeling, discrimination, compositional factors, and consciousness.

Nowhere is there existence of conglomerates. Therefore, you are the
 knower of the ultimate truth.

You arrive everywhere but you are born nowhere.
In terms of the two bodies of birth and dharma, you are inconceivable,
 o great sage.

You who are beyond reproach know the world as without unity or multiplicity,
resembling an echo, subject to neither change nor destruction.

Devoid of eternity and destruction, lacking characterised and characteristic,
samsara, you know, is similar to dream and illusion, o splendid one.

The defilements up to the roots, the subliminal impulses have been,
 o faultless one, subdued [by you]. And, indeed from the original
 nature of defilements you have obtained immortality.

By you, o sage, form has been seen as without characteristics, as not
 possessing form.
But you are seen in the realm of form, your body resplendent.

You are not declared "seen" because your form is seen.
When *dharma* is seen you are properly seen. The reality, however, is not
 visible.

In your body there are no holes, flesh, bones or blood;
You manifested a body like a rainbow in the sky.

There is no disease or impurity in your body, no arising of hunger or thirst
 either, [but],
for the sake of conforming yourself to the world, you have shown worldly
 behaviour.

In no way do you have the faults [caused by] the obstacles of actions, o
 faultless one, [but]
because of the pity for the world you have shown [yourself] as submersed
 in action.

Since the *dharmadhatu*[2] cannot be differentiated, there are no different
 vehicles, o Lord. [But]
the three vehicles[3] have been preached by you for the sake of ushering the
 beings into [the path].

Your body made out of dharma is eternal, imperishable, auspicious, victorious.
But, for the sake of the people who need to be trained, [entering into the
 final] cessation has been shown by you.

---

2. The "sphere of dharma," the infinite domain in
which the activity of all phenomena takes place
(that is, the universe). This also serves as one of
several terms for ultimate reality.

3. The paths of the *shravakas* ("hearers," or disciples), *pratyekabuddhas* (individually enlightened
ones), and bodhisattvas (future buddhas).

But in the countless worlds you are seen anew by your devotees
eagerly longing [for] your descent, birth, perfect enlightenment, teaching
 and [entering into the final] cessation.

In you, o protector, there is no thought, no mental creation, no motion.
Without any effort on your part, in this world your Buddha-deeds occur.

Thus, I have spread the flowers of his good qualities over
the well-gone, the unthinkable, the immeasurable.
Through the merit I have obtained [by doing so]
may all beings participate in the profound doctrine of the best of sages.

Hymn to the Ultimate

How shall I praise you, the protector, unborn, without foundation,
who has passed beyond all comparison with the world, whose domain is
 beyond the path of speech.

Nevertheless, whatever you may be in the domain of the true reality,
I, having resorted to the world of conventional designations, shall praise
 the Master out of devotion.

Of you there is no origination since your nature is un-arisen.
Not going or coming, o protector, I salute you, the one without inherent
 existence.

You are not an existent being nor a non-existent, not [subject to]
 destruction nor everlasting,
you are not eternal nor impermanent. I salute you, the one without duality.

Your color is not perceived as red, green, brown, yellow,
not pale, dark or bright. I salute you, the one without color.

You are neither big nor small, neither long nor round;
You have reached the immeasurable state. I salute you, the one without
 measure.

Neither far nor near, neither in the space nor on the earth,
not in *samsara* nor in *nirvana*. I salute you, who are without place.

Not located in any *dharmas*, you have gone to the state of *dharmadhatu*;
you have arrived at the highest profundity. I salute you, the profound one.

Thus praised, praised again, but what, indeed, has been praised?
All *dharmas* being empty, who has been praised and by whom has he been
 praised?

Who can praise you, devoid of arising and passing away,
of whom there is no end or middle, no perception or perceptible object?

Having praised the well-gone, neither gone nor come, devoid from going,
By that merit [accumulated from such praises], may this world go to the
 state of the well-gone.

Hymn to the One Beyond the World

O you who are beyond the world, salutations to you, versed in
discriminative knowledge!
You, solely for the benefit of the world, have suffered distress with
compassion for a long time.

You are convinced that apart from mere constituents no being exists,
but for the sake of beings you went to great pain, o great sage.

And, o wise one, you have explained to the wise ones that these
constituents are like
illusions, mirages, cities in clouds, dreams.

Those whose arising is from causes and which do not occur in absence of
that,
how, pray tell, can they not be clearly considered the same as a reflection
by you?

"[Since] elements are not graspable by the eye, how can what is visible be
made of them?"—
By you, who speaks thus about the form, the apprehension of form was
rejected.

Feeling does not exist without what is to be felt. Hence, it is without self.
And, you consider
that that which is to be felt does not exist by own being, that is your declaration.

"If perception and the object were non-different, then the mouth would
be burnt by the [word/concept] 'fire.' If they were different, there
would be no comprehension," is stated by you, speaker of truth.

That "The agent is self-dependent and so is the action" is stated by you
conventionally. But, dependent on each other they are established,
you maintained.

No doer is there, no experiencer is there, merit and demerit are
dependently born. What is dependent that is not [really] born, you
have declared, o lord of words.

There is no object of knowledge without its being known and there is
no consciousness [i.e., knower] without that [object of knowledge].
Therefore, the knowledge and the object of knowledge do not exist by
own being, you have said.

If the characteristics were different from the characterized then that
characterized would be without characteristics. If they were not
different, there would be non-existence of both—this has been
clearly declared by you.

Devoid of characterized and characteristics, free from utterances of words,
(and) peaceful this world has been seen by you with your eye of wisdom.

An existent being does not arise, nor does non-existent, nor does [both] existent and non-existent, not from itself, nor from another, nor from both. How would it be born?

The destruction of an existent endowed with endurance is not fitting. How can a non-existent [thing] like the horns of a horse be extinguished?

Destruction is not different from the being nor can be thought to be non-different. If it was something different it would have been permanent; nor can it exist as non-different.

For, if there were unity, destruction of being would not be fitting.
If there were separateness, destruction of being would not be fitting.

In the first place, through a cause which is destroyed, the arising of an effect is not logical.
Nor from one that is not destroyed. Origination is the same as a dream, you maintain.

Not from a destroyed nor from un-destroyed seed a sprout arises. Every origination is like the origination of an illusion, you say.

Therefore, you have understood that this world has arisen due to imagination: unreal, un-arisen, it is not destroyed.

There is no being in *samsara* [i.e., no migration] of a permanent [self], there is no being in *samsara* [i.e., no migration] of an impermanent self. Being in *samsara* [i.e., migrating beings] is like a dream, you, o best of knowers of truth, have declared.

Caused by itself, by other, by both, without cause—this is what dialecticians have maintained about the suffering. But, you have stated that it is dependently originated.[4]

What is dependent origination, that itself is emptiness, you maintain.
There is no independently existent being, that is your incomparable lion's roar.

The teaching of the nectar of emptiness is for destruction of all conceptions. Whoever holds even to that (emptiness) is censured by you.

Inactive, controlled (by others), empty, like illusion, dependently existent, all dharmas are without existence by own being, [thus] o protector, you have explained.

Nothing has been put forward by you and nothing denied. Just as before, just so afterwards, you are aware of suchness.

For, unless one resorts to cultivation practiced by the noble ones, the consciousness would in no way become signless.

4. On Nagarjuna's concept of dependent origination, see the introduction to *Verses on the Middle Way*, p. 367.

Without arriving at the signless, there is no liberation, you said.
Hence, that has been taught by you in full in the Mahayana.

By the merit that I have obtained praising you, worthy of praise, may the
 whole world be free from the bondage of signs.

Hymn to the Inconceivable One

I salute him, the one with unequal cognition, the inconceivable, the
 indescribable,
who taught that all dependency born beings are without inherent existence.

Just as you in Mahayana personally understood the selflessness of
 phenomena,
just so you taught that to the wise ones out of compassion.

What has arisen from conditions is un-arisen, was said by you.
That is not born with inherent existence, thus it was declared empty.

In the same way as echo is [produced] dependent on the sound,
and, as an illusion and a mirage [are produced], thus is the origination of
 existence [produced].

If illusion, mirage, cities in the clouds, reflections, as well as dreams are
 unborn, there can be no vision, etc. of them.

Just as those arising from causes and conditions are considered to be
 created, in that way all conditioned [things][5] you declared, o
 protector, are conventional[ly existent].

[To say that] this created thing exists as a whole—that is immature talk
 similar to an empty fist, declared to be false.

If a created thing is not born, how, then, [can it be] present?
From destruction of what can it be past? How can it be related to the future?

An existent thing is not born from itself, from other, or both,
not existent, non-existent, both existent-and-non-existent. Then, what
 arises from what?

The unborn has no inherent existence. How can it arise from itself?
Since it is established that there is no inherent existence, how can it arise
 from something else?

If there is selfhood, otherness may be. If there is otherness based on
 another, selfhood is maintained.
The establishment of these two is said to be correlative like far and close.

When it is not related to anything, how could something exist?
When it is not related to anything [considered to be] long, how could
 something be short?

5. Things conditioned by impermanence.

If there is existence, [then] there is non-existence; if there is long, [then] there is short. And, if there is non-existence, [then there is] existence. Therefore, the two do not exist [independently].

Unity as well as multiplicity, and that which has gone by and that which has not come yet, etc., affliction and purification, correct and incorrect, how [can they exist] by themselves?

Since there is no thing that exists by itself, then, [how] can it exist as a whole? That which is called "other" does not exist without own inherent existence.

When there is neither self-existent nor other-existent, then how can one hold to the understanding that there [really] is existence dependent on other?

Originally born the same and extinguished of inherent existence, and [therefore] in truth non-arisen—that is how the phenomena are—you said.

It was shown by you, o wise one, that form, etc. [the remaining aggregates] are without inherent existence; they are the same as foam, bubbles, illusions, clouds, mirages, plantain tree.

If that which is grasped by the senses were truth, fools would have been born with the knowledge of truth. Then, what [good would be the] knowledge of truth?

Senselessness, trivialisation, even indistinctness; Inverted knowledge [all of the above] belongs to senses—you said.

Because of being obstructed by ignorance, the world does not properly understand [the truth] as it is—this has been thought and declared by you.

"Exists" is the view of eternalism, "does not exist" is the view of annihilationism. Therefore, the doctrine free from the two extremes is shown by you.

Phenomena are liberated from [any of] the four alternatives[6]—[thus] has been said by you. Not knowable even by consciousness, how much less are they [within] the sphere of words.

Like what is arisen as illusion in a dream, like seeing a double moon, thus, this world has been seen by you as existing and non-existing thing.

As a son born, present and destroyed in a dream, thus this world is not truly born, present and destroyed, you have declared.

Just as arising is seen as in a dream because of a cause, so is the opposite [i.e., destruction in a dream].

6. That something is, is not, both is and is not, and neither is nor is not.

The arising and destruction is thus of all beings everywhere—this is what you thought.

As suffering born from passion, etc., as affliction [and] transmigration, so liberation through completing the accumulation [of wisdom and merit] is like a dream, you have said.

One who thus cognizes [i.e., sees things as] born, unborn, come, gone, bound or liberated, maintains duality; a knower of truth does not [maintain duality].

That which does not arise, how can it be extinguished?
Because it appears like an illusory elephant [it is], in reality, originally calm.

As we think of the illusory elephant as born but it is not born,
In the same way [we think of] all [as] born [but] in reality it is unborn.

By the immeasurable world protectors (buddhas) the liberation of immeasurable beings has been accomplished one by one. But [in reality], not a single one has been set free by them.

Those beings are not born and not extinguished—[this is] your clear statement. No one is set free by anyone—thus you announced, o great sage.

Just as the things made by illusion-making are empty,
the whole world is empty, and likewise the creator, you have said.

The maker [is] also made by another, [he] cannot pass the state of being created. Or otherwise that action as the maker of the maker is a consequence.

That the whole world is merely name—has been loudly declared by you.
What is named is not found separate from the name.

Because of this all phenomena have been explained as "mere conceptualisations."
Also the imagination through which the emptiness is conceived is declared [to be] unreal.

That [which has] gone beyond the duality of being and non-being and has not passed over to some place,
[that which is] not knowledge nor knowable, does not exist and does not not exist,

That which is not one nor not-one, not both nor not-both,
Without foundation, un-manifest, unthinkable, indescribable,

That which does not arise, does not disappear, cannot be annihilated and is not permanent;
that which is like space, [that is] not within the range of words or knowledge.

What is dependent origination, that itself is emptiness, you maintain.
Of that kind is the true doctrine and same as that is the Tathagata.[7]

That is also regarded as truth, ultimate, suchness, and real.
That is indisputable fact. [Through] understanding that one is called
"buddha."

Really, [the fundament] of buddhas and the fundament of living beings
are identical. Hence, you maintain the sameness between yourself
and others.

Emptiness is no different from things, nor there is a thing without it.
Therefore, dependently born things were declared by you to be empty.

Convention arises from causes and conditions and is dependent
(on another).
Thus, the dependent on another has been spoken by you. The ultimate,
however, is not artificial.

[The ultimate is] also [named]: "own-existence," "nature," "truth," "real,"
"actual existent," "true." Imagined existence does not exist but the
relative is found.

[To say:] "it exists" [about the] imagined existent thing is called by you
superimposition. [To say:] "It does not exist" because of the
annihilation of what is created is explained as annihilation.

Through the knowledge of truth you maintain that there is no annihilation
and no permanence. The whole world is empty of actual existence,
like a mirage, you maintain.

As the water of a mirage is not annihilated nor permanent,
So is the whole world not annihilated or permanent, you declared.

For him for whom the "real substance" is born, for him there is
annihilation, etc.;
For him it follows that the world has ending as well as that it has no ending.

Just as there is the knowable when there is knowledge, so there is
knowledge when there is the knowable. When it is understood that
both are unborn [i.e., without independent existence], then what does
[independently] exist?

Thus, having spoken clearly, through analogies of the magical illusion and
so on, the best of physicians has shown the true doctrine that heals
all dogmatic views.

This is the supreme truth, the teaching for the sake of instructing the
absence of inherent existence. For those obsessed by the obsession
of being (i.e., view of positivism), this is unsurpassed medicine.

7. A title of a buddha (literally, "one who has thus come/gone"); it is the one most often used by the
historical Buddha to refer to himself.

For this reason, o sacrificial priest of the doctrine, the supreme sacrifice of
  the doctrine has been constantly offered by you in all three worlds,[8]
  without obstacles, without impediments.

You have roared the marvellous lion's roar of non-self which annihilates
  the fear [arisen from] grasping existent things and frightens the deer,
  the heretical teachers.

With the deep law of emptiness, you have beaten the dharma-drum;
With the loud sound of non-inherent existence you have blown the
  dharma-conch.

The gift of dharma, the nectar of the teaching of the buddhas, has been
  declared.
The emptiness of dharmas has been indicated as the definite meaning.

But, the teaching about birth, cessation, etc., beings, living things, etc.,
  has been declared as of provisional meaning, o Lord, and as
  conventional.

He who has gone finally to the other shore of the ocean of the perfection
  of wisdom,
He, endowed with jewels of merit and good qualities, has crossed [into]
  the ocean of your qualities.

By the merit which I have obtained having praised you, the protector of
  the world,
The inconceivable, the indescribable, may the world become the same
  as you.

8. The Realm of Desire, the Realm of Form, and the Formless Realm; see pp. 54–55.

ADVICE TO A KING

LETTER TO KANISHKA
(The Kanishkalekha)

MATRICHETA

Kings were always important in the history of Buddhism. The Buddha was himself
the son of a king, and at the time of his birth, the astrologers predicted that he would
become either a universal monarch or a great sage. Shortly after he left the palace in
search of enlightenment, Prince Siddhartha encountered King Bimbisara, who
offered him half his kingdom. The prince politely declined. Bimbisara, together with
several other rulers of the kingdoms of northeast India, would become an important
patron of the Buddha.

The Buddhist community of monks and nuns came to rely on kings for patronage
and protection, the most famous of those patrons being the emperor Ashoka (see
the *Ashokavadana*, p. 238). In return, Buddhist monks served as a virtuous object

of the king's offering, allowing him to accumulate merit. They performed rituals for the protection of the king, his family, and his kingdom. And they offered religious instruction and advice. The great philosopher of emptiness, Nagarjuna (see the previous two selections), composed two treatises of advice to a king who probably ruled in south India: the *Garland of Jewels* (*Ratnavali*) and the *Letter to a Friend* (*Suhrillekha*).

After Ashoka, perhaps the most renowned of the Buddhist kings of India was Kanishka, ruler of the Kushan empire, who lived in the second century C.E. His realm stretched from Bactria in the west through much of northern India. In his capital, located at the city of modern Peshawar, in Pakistan, he built a great stupa said to contain three relics of the Buddha. Some of the surviving coins from his reign depict Shakyamuni Buddha, others the future buddha Maitreya.

One of Kanishka's early advisers was the monk Matricheta, regarded as one of the great Sanskrit poets of the Buddhist tradition. Two long hymns to the Buddha were particularly renowned: a Chinese pilgrim who visited India five hundred years after Matricheta's death commented on their beauty and noted that all monks were taught them. It was said that at the time of the Buddha he was an oriole who, upon seeing the Buddha, sang a beautiful song; the Buddha then predicted that he would be reborn as a great poet in the future. In his human lifetime, Matricheta was initially a devotee of the Hindu god Shiva; according to one account, he embraced Buddhism after being defeated in debate by Aryadeva, Nagarjuna's one-eyed disciple. His letter to King Kanishka begins:

> That I, though invited, did not come to you,
> one so worthy to be approached,
> was not due to lack of reverence or to disrespect,
> but because I am hindered by old age and illness.

Too frail to journey to the young king, the old monk wrote, in a clear and rather simple style, his advice on how to rule with wisdom and compassion, exhorting the king to always remember that death can come at any moment.

PRONOUNCING GLOSSARY

Kanishka: *ka-ni-shka*   Tathagata: *ta-tah-ga-ta*
Kushana: *ku-sha-na*

Homage to All the Tathagatas[1]

> That I, though invited, did not come to you,
> one so worthy to be approached,
> was not due to lack of reverence or to disrespect,
> but because I am hindered by old age and illness.
>
> Although the love I feel for you
> is similar to what I feel toward all beings,
> because of your virtues,
> I feel especially intimate and close to you.

TRANSLATED FROM the Tibetan by Michael Hahn.

1. Buddhas; "Tathagata" (literally, "one who has thus come/gone") is the title of a buddha most often used by the historical Buddha to refer to himself.

What I have to teach, I have already largely taught,
and who can advise on everything?
Yet because of your many virtues,
I have become loquacious once more.

The fragrance of your irresistible qualities
has imbued every corner of the world,
so that even the greatest men,
fully confident in their own abilities,
do not shun your friendship.

Therefore, please lend me your ear and
for your own sake, listen well to what I have to say,
so that out of the two opposites—
what should be done and what should be given up—
you may take the right one to heart.

Sense objects that give rise to pleasure, *Desire*
youth swelling with pride, *Ignorance*
and acting just as one likes without regard for others— *hatred*
these are the gates to what is entirely harmful.

Avoid these three things leading to ruin.
For a wise man must act to diminish these three faults
by relying upon the noble, controlling the senses,
and using the power of wisdom.

These three things have become
the foundation of your failings;
having remedied them with discipline
and lawful behavior,
turn them into virtues.

Is it not especially appropriate for the king
and his ministers,
their hearts filled with vast compassion,
to exert their sovereign power
through deeds always free of emotional taint?

In this world, those who are weak-minded
and without a protector
will certainly become involved in doing
actions that should not be done.

Therefore, so long as you have not yet
passed beyond that stage,
cheerfully endeavor to gather wise men around you
in order to gain strength of mind.

Have the code of laws recited
and listen to the way it is explained.

Examine the laws you hear
and be wise in your judgments.

Nothing seems impossible to a mind
free from the torment of sorrow
and characterized by
youth, health, and self-confidence.

Here in this life, whenever you can, listen
to even little things said by noble people.
Even if you accumulate knowledge a little at a time,
it will certainly not be long
before it becomes considerable.

Is there any vessel
that would not become full
when an uninterrupted chain of water droplets
falls into it constantly?

Therefore, Your Majesty, take as conclusively valid
what has been shown in this clear example,
and always take delight in
listening to the holy dharma.

For your own sake, keep around you good men
who assist you in seeking a wealth of virtue,
who are wise and full of compassion,
who show gratitude and open-handedness.

You should not allow
the stupid, stingy, greedy,
ungrateful, garrulous, cruel,
and evil even to remain in your realm.

You should always get to know
the particular merits of each individual person;
your welfare and prosperity depend solely
on knowing these distinctive qualities.

Those who accomplish difficult tasks,
who give up what is difficult to give up,
who tolerate what is difficult to bear,
who accept what is difficult to accept;

who turn you away from what is inappropriate,
and take care to turn you toward what is appropriate;
whose devotion matches their thoughts,
who desire your happiness
and regard you with affection—

these are friends,
relatives, and allies.

Others who follow you only in their own interest
are nothing but very ordinary beings.

Please take to heart the words of a friend
who intends your benefit.
Even when not sweet to hear,
these words are useful, tender, and true.

But do not take to heart
the sweet words of wicked people,
which are harmful,
and neither tender nor true.

May you accept with an open heart
one who gives useful advice, even if wrathful,
but take no pleasure in one
who gives harmful advice,
even though full of praise.

Just as access to a crystal clear lake should be
easy for the king of geese and difficult for flood,
let access to you be easy for the good,
and difficult for the wicked.

Consider it more important to please the wise
than to strive for wealth;
in order to rejoice in virtues,
become insatiable for virtues.

In conducting your life,
whether enjoying yourself,
or feeling happy or sad,
or being engaged in ordinary or higher pursuits,
you should adhere to the good;

when you surround yourself with mindful friends,
you will remain alert and watchful.
O good monarch,
you will then be embraced by good fortune
as the sal tree is embraced by creepers.

You should bestow gifts upon those who are mild,
truthful, and especially worthy;
examine your desires without dwelling on them;
never use punishment.

But those who use deceit to cultivate quarrels and strife,
who look down upon the poor,
who do not delight in moral beings,
and who distract ascetics from their vows—

these four types of people are not desirable.
They destroy the root of moral behavior.

Take great care to ensure that such people
do not stay here in your realm.

You must see to it that there is no contempt or disdain
among the strong toward the weak,
among benefactors toward those
who have nothing to give,
among the honored toward the unworthy,

among intimate friends toward those they do not know,
or for anyone at all toward anyone.
Conducting all business with honesty,
may you regard everyone as equal.

See to it that everyone fulfills his own dharma,
and that all live according to the law.
May you make all happy,
even the disagreeable, if they are free from fault.

If you love your retinue
as a father loves his son,
your subjects will want to please you
as a son would please his father.

When the general populace is good-natured,
they will become what you intend;
when the people are bad-natured,
they will not become what you intend.

If you adopt good thoughts and views,
you will be lifted higher and higher,
but if you practice bad behavior,
you will fall lower and lower.

If you abide by good works,
all the people, whose lives depend upon you,
will follow you
as a flock follows its leader.

If you become involved in duplicity,
and follow nothing but intrigue,
then all the people,
the subjects who follow your example,
will be polluted.

Therefore, in order to protect yourself and others,
please apply yourself fully
and establish anew the declining
tradition of the ancient kings and seers.

From the practice of the ancient kings,
take whatever is good and put it into practice.

But whatever is not appropriate
you must revile and abandon.

Break the hold of former laws that were enacted in error,
even when they exist as of old,
and make a new code of law
marked by the name of King Kanishka.

Your Majesty—you who are like a god—
intent on virtue, practice only virtues, like a god.
Your Majesty—you who are like a god—
as one who knows fault,
do only what is faultless, like a god.

Be like the waning moon,
and dim the hosts of evil;
be like the waxing moon,
and ever adorn yourself with virtues.

Like your fathers before you, wholeheartedly
rule the earth according to the law.
Like your fathers before you, increase
the ceremonies in the temples.

For the sake of (gaining) the matchless ladder
that leads to heaven and liberation,
always gather together in the temples
the great works of art that merit produces.

Be apprehensive of old age and death.
Having enjoyed the glory of lawful sovereignty,
in your old age retire into a hermitage
and let your life become fruitful
through the teachings of the holy dharma.

You who were born into the lineage of the Kushanas[2]
and instructed according to the (teaching of the)
self-arising Buddhas
must see to it that the religious system
of the solar race, your noble lineage,
does not degenerate.

Given the absolute certainty that those who are born
will grow old, fall ill, and die,
of what use is it even to pray: "May you not
become old, not become sick, not die."

Any life form whatsoever
by its very nature grows old and dies.
Gradual transformation is the nature of old age;
instantaneous destruction is the nature of death.

2. That is, the Kushans, a Central Asian people who formed a dynasty late in the 1st century B.C.E. and founded an empire in the 1st century C.E. that eventually stretched from Central Asia across the northern Indian subcontinent and Afghanistan.

If people say, "May I not grow old,
not become sick, not die"—
since this world will be completely consumed by fire,[3]
what choice is left but not to exist again at all?

Where is the place where nothing is unpleasant?
Where will composite things not decay?
Where is the place of happiness alone?
Where can you go where you will not die?

Do not defilement and suffering
inevitably arise in the phenomenal world?
Therefore, noble one, meditate extensively
on the non-existence of the phenomenal world.

This alone is what you should do here in samsara—
do not seek to do anything other than that.
Having done what you should do,
you will avoid doing what you should not do.

While revolving in the circle of existence
again and again, like a rosary,
what have you not already done in the world
a hundred times, or even thousands?

Believing that we have not done something,
we foolishly try again and again to do it.
Thus, since beginningless time,
we have not reversed direction up to now.

The Lord of Death, who is no man's friend,
will descend upon you suddenly.
Therefore, with great effort turn to the holy dharma
and do not say, "I will do it tomorrow."

"I will do this tomorrow, not today"
is not good for a man to say.
Without any doubt, that tomorrow will come
when you no longer exist.

When the heartless Lord of Death,
who destroys men's powers without rhyme or reason,
approaches with the intent to kill,
what wise man can remain at ease?

Therefore, so long as that extremely impatient one
has not loosed that unbearable arrow
which cannot be avoided,
give heed to your own welfare.

When your former karma,
having brought forth its fruit, has abandoned you,

---

3. In Buddhist cosmology, each age ends in all-consuming fire.

you will be dragged away by the Lord of Death,
bound to new karma.

Then all beings will turn away and
nothing at all will follow you,
save for your virtuous and evil actions.
Knowing this, conduct your life well.

Pray listen for a while to
my lamentation, which is overwhelmed by compassion
and soaked through and through
with the moisture of melancholy.

Unfortunate beings that have fallen low,
who are unprotected and blameless,
who live mostly on plain
grass, water, and fruit—

relying on truth, you yourself should say
whether it is right or wrong
for a king to kill or be involved in killing
birds, game, and cattle.

They say that you never become very angry
and that you forgive even those
who have done you harm.
Alas, who has obstructed
your compassion toward animals?

Since you pardon those who harm you,
but put to death those who have done you no harm,
there are clearly two bases for
your kindness and unkindness.

When even someone in your position harms those
who have become a target
because of deeds committed in the past,
tell me, in whom will they take refuge?

When others harm you
but still you offer your own hand to raise them up,
and then openly harm those to whom you give shelter—
has not the whole world turned dark?

All beings take pleasure in being alive;
life is dear to all.
All are subject to death;
all are tormented by suffering.

Thus anything we do not want
leads to suffering.
What wise man would, like a smith,
put fire again on what is already burned?

If you do not take pleasure in taking life
and turn away from pleasure in killing,
will your kingdom come to ruin?
Tell me, what kind of custom is this killing?

If you, who are skilled in the use of weapons,
see with your own eyes what they can do in battle,
why do you, at other times,
commit such harm against animals?

You who have the eyes of a young deer,
why do you not feel compassion
for the deer who are like your eyes
when they are wild-eyed with fright?

How could you not rejoice
when you give joy even to the deer
who give pleasure to you
because their eyes are like your eyes?

That they are fallen beings,
that their eyes are similar to yours,
that they live in a place where there is no protection—
these facts, even taken singly,
should be valid reasons for not killing deer.

I entreat you to act toward animals,
who are sorely troubled by sorrow,
with even greater compassion than
you have shown toward human beings.

I do not fold my hands
in order to ask for your protection, but
to make a request on behalf of the lives of others.
Therefore, with all respect, may you consider it well.

To refine your studies, begin with the main points—
this is known as the custom of the noble.
In light of this, I make my request to the king
as would a beloved son.

If I request what is not beneficial,
then sentence me to death!
But if I request only what has benefit,
then act in accord with my request.

If I have not displeased you,
I would repeat my request again and again.
But if you scorn my words,
please ignore what I have said.

If you are pleased, then henceforth do not kill.
If you are displeased, may you have some misgivings.

Because doing harm like the sun is something
you simply cannot do, act like the moon,
O moon among kings!

O king, like honey from a thorny bush,
accept words well said even from an enemy,
but like a poisonous stream from the Golden Mountain,[4]
reject the evil words of a congenial person.

Supreme among men,
if this royal splendor—achieved
by practicing good works in former lives
and having the power to ward off the harm
enemies would do—
is ornamented by virtue in this life, then such glory,
even though intrinsically fickle and unreliable,
through being somehow linked to virtuous behavior,
cannot help but be faithful to you for a long time to come.

4. Mount Meru or Sumeru, which according to Buddhist cosmology is the mountain at the center of the world.

HOW TO BE A BODHISATTVA

INTRODUCTION TO THE PRACTICE OF THE BODHISATTVA PATH
(*The Bodhicharyavatara*)

SHANTIDEVA

Among the treatises of late Indian Buddhism, none is more beloved than the *Introduction to the Practice of the Bodhisattva Path* (*Bodhicharyavatara*) by the eighth-century monk Shantideva. It was the subject of numerous commentaries in India and became especially important in Tibet. Despite its length, it was commonly memorized, and almost all discussions of the bodhisattva contain verses from it.

As is true of so many Indian works, almost nothing can be said with certainty about its author. Only two works by him survive; the other is an anthology of sutra passages titled the *Compendium for Training* (*Shikshasamucchaya*), organized around the elements of a bodhisattva's practice. An entertaining story about the origins of the text presented here has also been passed down.

According to the legends, Shantideva was of royal birth but renounced the world before his investiture as king, as the Buddha had done. He was ordained and entered Nalanda, a monastery in north India renowned as a great center of learning. However, he remained for the most part in his cell and became known as an indolent monk, earning the nickname *bhusuku*, which meant that he was engaged in only three activities: eating, sleeping, and defecating. In order to humiliate him, one day his fellow monks challenged him to recite scriptures before the assembly, preparing a throne for him to sit on. Shantideva agreed, but asked whether the monks wished to hear him recite a well-known scripture or something new. They opted for something new, and he recited the *Introduction to the Practice of the Bodhisattva Path*. He eventually reached the thirty-fourth stanza of the ninth chapter—the chapter on wisdom—which reads, "When one no longer apprehends an entity that one could conceive as not existing, then all being has lost its ground. How could it appear before the mind again?" At that point, he began to rise into the air, making it difficult for everyone to hear how the recitation ended (and thus there are two recensions of the text, of different lengths).

There are of course a great many expositions and extolments of the bodhisattva in the Mahayana sutras, commentaries, treatises, and poems. We have seen an example of the bodhisattva's extreme charity in the *Shibi Jataka* (p. 100), which describes King Shibi cutting the flesh from his own body to save the life of a dove. Poetic evocations of the bodhisattva's various virtues appear in the *Avatamsaka Sutra*. But what sets Shantideva's work apart from these other classics is its humanity. To vow "I will free all beings in the universe from suffering" is a noble but insane sentiment. How could a single person ever possibly do that? Shantideva's text, written largely in the first person, represents the most powerful attempt in Indian Buddhist literature to take the profound difficulties of the bodhisattva's vow seriously, treating it not simply as words spoken in a prayer but as the guiding principle of the ordinary activities of one's life. Particularly famous are his arguments for patience in the sixth chapter, his argument for "the exchange of self and other" at the end of the eighth chapter, and the prayer that concludes the work, which is often recited alone.

Because of its remarkable appeal, all of the text is presented here—except for some highly technical sections of the ninth chapter, which remain difficult to grasp, just as they were for those who watched Shantideva disappear into the sky.

PRONOUNCING GLOSSARY

Akashagarbha: *ah-kah-sha-gar-ba*
Avalokita: *a-va-loh-ki-ta*
Avalokiteshvara: *a-va-loh-ki-taysh-va-ra*
Avichi: *a-vee-chih*
Bodhicharyavatara: *bo-dee-char-yah-va-tah-ra*
bodhisattva: *boh-di-sat-tva*
dakini: *dah-ki-nee*
Gaganaganja: *ga-ga-na-gan-ja*
Gandavyuha: *gan-da-vyoo-ha*
Indra: *in-dra*
Jambudvipa: *jam-bu-dvee-pa*
Kshitigarbha: *kshi-ti-gar-ba*
Lokeshvara: *loh-kaysh va-ra*
Maitreya: *mai-tray-ya*
Mandakini: *man-dah-ki-nee*
Manjugosha: *man-ju-goh-sha*

Manjushri: *man-ju-shree*
Mayadevi: *mah-yah-day-vee*
Meru: *may-ru*
Nagarjuna: *nah-gahr-ju-na*
rakshasa: *rahk-sha-sa*
Samantabhadra: *sa-man-ta-ba-dra*
Shikshasamucchaya: *shik shah-sa-mu-cha-ya*
Shrisambhavavimoksha: *shree-sam-ba-va-vih-mohk-sha*
Sudhana: *su-da-na*
Supushpachandra: *su-push-pa-chan-dra*
Sutrasamucchaya: *soo-tra-sa-mu-cha-ya*
tathagata: *ta-tah-ga-ta*
Uttarakuru: *u-ta-ra-ku-ru*
Vaitarani: *vai-ta-ra-nee*
Vajrapani: *vaj-ra-pah-nih*

Chapter I. The Power of a Commitment to Awakening

(1) Reverently prostrating myself before the sugatas,[1] their sons, and their bodies of dharma, and before all those who are worthy of reverence, I will offer, according to scriptural tradition and in succinct form, an introduction to the principles guiding the life of bodhisattvas, true sons of the sugatas.

(2) Now, I will not say anything new. Besides, since I have no skill in writing, I have not composed this work with others in mind, but only as a way to cultivate my own mind. (3) By writing this work at the very least faith and the impulse to cultivate the good will grow in me. But if someone else, with a disposition similar to mine, should read it, it might then be of use to others.

(4) This unique opportunity, so difficult to obtain, once it has been obtained can bring to realization all human aspirations. If then one does not set the mind on what is beneficial, how will this opportunity come again?

(5) Only through the inspiration of the awakened ones occasionally arises in a human being, for one instant, a thought directed toward the good, as lightning flashes for only an instant in clouded night skies. (6) Therefore, virtue is always the weaker, whereas the force of evil is powerful and terrifying. What other good could overcome this evil if the thought of awakening never arose?

(7) This is the same good that the monarchs among the sages perceived after meditating for countless cosmic ages. The growing bliss that easily comes from this thought makes the endless flood of living beings overflow with happiness. (8) Whether you seek to cross beyond the hundreds of pains of existence, or to free living beings from their torments, or to enjoy superabundant happiness in heaven, you should never abandon this thought of awakening.

(9) From the moment when the thought of awakening arises in him, a wretched being chained in the prison of existence becomes the son of the sugatas in an instant, and becomes worthy of the veneration of the whole world, men and gods. (10) This impure image is transformed into the priceless image of the jewel of a victorious conqueror. Hold on firmly, therefore, to this powerful elixir called "thought of awakening"! (11) The immeasurably wise guides of the world's caravan have assessed its great value—hold on firmly to this jewel of the thought of awakening, you who travel through the marketplaces of human destinies. (12) Truly, all other goods perish after bearing fruit, like a plantain tree; but the tree of the thought of awakening never perishes after bearing its fruit, and remains fruitful thereafter. (13) Even someone who has committed the most abominable sins overcomes them all in an instant when he takes refuge in this thought, as he who takes refuge in a great hero overcomes the greatest dangers. How can it be that there are insensible beings who do not take refuge in this thought? (14) It consumes in an instant the gravest sins, like the fire that puts an end to the

TRANSLATED FROM the Sanskrit by Luis O. Gómez.

1. *Sugata* is an epithet of a buddha, meaning "he who has gone well."

cosmic cycle. The sagely protector Maitreya explained to Sudhana[2] the endless virtues of this thought.

(15) In short, the thought of enlightenment is twofold: the thought of the vow of awakening and the thought of setting out toward awakening. (16) The wise should distinguish the two in the same way that one distinguishes someone who only wishes to depart from someone who has already set out, respectively.

(17) The thought of the vow of awakening produces great fruits, even in the realm of becoming, but it is not a source of uninterrupted merit, as is the thought of setting out. (18) From the moment in which you take possession with unwavering mind of this determination to free the whole unlimited sphere of living beings, (19) uninterrupted currents of merit, endless like space, continue to flow, even if one is asleep or if one neglects this thought repeatedly.

(20) For the benefit of beings of inferior aspiration, the Tathagata[3] himself has explained this resolution with detailed reasons in the sutra *The Questions of Subahu*.

(21) If a person, endowed with a good disposition, resolved to allay merely headaches among living beings, that person would gain immeasurable merit.

(22) How much more would he not gain if he sought to free them, one by one, from infinite pain, and endow each of them with immeasurable virtues? (23) Who has a father or a mother with a wish for the well-being of his son that would be comparable to this desire of the bodhisattva? Could there be such a desire among gods, rishis,[4] or brahmins? (24) What is more, none of these, not even in dreams, have ever desired, even for themselves, something like this. How could it be possible then that they would desire it for others? (25) How is it that the bodhisattva, this sublime jewel among living beings, is born, without precedent—he whose disposition to do good to others is not found in anyone else, even as a wish for their own personal benefit?

(26) How is one to assess the merit of this jewel of the thought of awakening, which is the seed for all the world's bliss, a balm for all its pains?

(27) By simply desiring to benefit others one goes beyond the merit that can be derived from worshipping the Awakened ones; how much more will arise then from the actual effort to bring all happiness to all living beings?

(28) Because they seek to escape suffering, ordinary sentient beings run to meet that same suffering; even when they seek happiness, their delusion is such that they destroy their own happiness, as if they were their own enemies.

(29) The bodhisattva is the one who would satiate with all happiness all these beings, who are tormented in so many different ways, and go about begging for happiness. The bodhisattva is the one who will put an end to

2. A young bodhisattva whose pilgrimage is described in the *Avatamsaka Sutra*. "Maitreya": the buddha who will succeed Gautama.
3. A title of a buddha (literally, "one who has thus come/gone"); it is the one most often used by the historical Buddha to refer to himself.
4. Sages.

their torments, (30) and heal their blindness. Where will one find someone with kindness equal to his? Where will one find such a friend, such merit?

(31) People praise someone who returns a favor, but what will we say of the bodhisattva, whose kindness is not due to any request? (32) They respect a man of good when he offers a public meal to a handful of people, because at one particular point in time he offers disdainfully a meagre mouthful that sustains these persons for half a day. (33) What must one say, then, of him who offers to a limitless number of living beings, during limitless time, the satisfaction of all their desires, a gift that remains inexhaustible as long as all living beings and endless space do not come to an end?

(34) This is why the Protector[5] has said that whoever conceives a thought of ill will toward the bodhisattva—the host of this inexhaustible meal, the son of the victorious conquerors—will suffer in hell for as many cosmic ages as ill thoughts arise in his mind. (35) But one who produces a thought of goodwill gains for himself a fruit that will be even more powerful; for one needs great effort to incur a fault against the sons of the victorious conquerors, but it is easy to derive merit from them.

(36) I bow before these bodies in which is born the jewel of the sublime thought. I take refuge in these mines of bliss, from which one receives happiness even when one offends them.

Chapter II. Confession of Sins

(1) To acquire the jewel that is this thought, I worship duly the tathagatas, the pure gem of the true dharma, and those oceans of virtue, the legitimate sons of the Awakened One.

(2) For an offering I will avail myself of all the flowers, fruits, and medicinal plants, all the treasures that there are in the universe: of whatever waters flow, clear and sweet, (3) of mountains rich in fine gems, forests that charm with calm, their creepers shining with loads of flowers, their trees bent by the weight of fruit. (4) From the world of the gods and the other celestial beings I will take perfumes and incenses, the wish-fulfilling tree and the gem-bearing trees. I will take ponds adorned by lotus flowers, made more lovely by the song of the swan. (5) I will take the grains of the fields— wild and cultivated. And I will take any other treasure I may find in the immeasurable ends of space, that I may use to adorn the venerable buddhas. All these treasures that have no owner (6ab) I make my own in thought, and I offer them to the bulls among the sages, together with their sons.

(6cd) May they, who deserve the best offerings and are endowed with the greatest pity, accept this offering of mine, out of compassion for me. (7) I have no merit of my own, I am only a poor beggar. Apart from this universe of ownerless treasures I have nothing with which to adore them. Therefore, may the protectors, who only desire the good of others, accept this offering through their own powers and for my sake.

(8) I also offer myself without constraints to the victorious conquerors and their sons. "Take me as your property, o sublime beings. Devoutly, I

5. That is, the Buddha.

become your slave. (9) Therefore, having become your property, I will, without hesitation or fear, dedicate myself to the well-being and benefit of living beings. In this way I free myself from my past faults and do not commit any further evil."

(10) In perfumed bathing halls, beautified by columns that shine with encrusted pearls, with awnings that shine with garlanded pearls, and with floors of shining pure crystal, (11) full of urns inlaid with fine gems, full of delicate flowers and perfumed waters, there will I prepare a bath for the tathagatas and their sons, accompanied by music and song. (12) With incomparable and pure garments, impregnated with the smell of incense, I wipe clean their bodies, and then give them select, perfumed tunics, dyed in exquisite colors. (13) With delicate heavenly satin clothing, of many colors, and with fine ornaments, I cover Samantabhadra, Ajita, Manjughosha, Lokeshvara, and the other bodhisattvas. (14) With the best perfumes that fill a billion worlds with their scent I anoint the monarchs among the sages, whose bodies shine with the brightness of well-purified, burnished, and polished gold.

(15) With all kinds of lovely and sweet-smelling flowers—such as Mandarava,[6] blue lotus, or jasmine—and with gracefully woven garlands I worship the monarchs among the sages, who are most worthy of worship. (16) I cense them with clouds of incense that charm the senses with thick, penetrating scent. And I offer them food—hard and soft—and the most varied drinks. (17) On golden, lotus-shaped trays I present to them lamps inlaid with precious stones. On floors sprinkled with perfumed waters and powders I strew delicate flowers.

(18) I also offer these benevolent ones heavenly chapels arrayed in shining clouds adorning the heavenly directions, bedecked with festoons of pearls and rubies, embellished by hymn and song. (19) Over the heads of these great sages I spread out tall and beautiful parasols made of precious stones, strung together with pearls, with graceful golden handles.

(20) May these pleasing clouds of offerings rise, these clouds of music and song, which delight all living beings. (21) May flowers, jewels, and other offerings rain without interruption upon the three jewels[7] of the true dharma, and upon their shrines and images.

(22) As Manjughosha[8] and the other bodhisattvas adore the victorious conquerors, so do I adore the tathagatas, protectors, and their sons. (23) With hymns that are oceans of melody I praise these oceans of virtue. May these clouds of hymn and song reach them directly.

(24) I bow before the awakened ones of the three times, the dharma and the sublime order, with as many prostrations as there are atoms in all the buddha-fields.[9] (25) I pay homage to all the shrines and sacred sites associated with the lives of the bodhisattvas. I bow before all teachers, and before all venerable ascetics as well.

(26) I take refuge in the awakened, until I have attained the heart of awakening. I take refuge in the dharma, and in the community of the bodhisattvas.

6. The flower of the coral tree.
7. That is, the Buddha, the dharma, and the sangha (the Buddhist community).
8. Another name for Manjushri, the bodhisattva of wisdom.

9. Particular buddhas' spheres of influence and activity; in Buddhist cosmology, each buddha arises in a particular world system. "The three times": the past, the present, and the future.

(27) I address with joined palms the perfectly awakened who dwell in all the directions of the universe, and the bodhisattvas of great compassion.

(28) All the evil that I, like a beast, have committed or have had someone else commit in my beginningless transmigrations, or in this very same life, (29) and the evil that I have approved of, all this that I have done out of delusion for my own harm, all this evil, I now confess burning with remorse. (30) Every violation of body, word, or thought that out of negligence I have committed against the three jewels, or against my mother, or father, or others who are equally deserving of my respect—(31) every grave sin that I, a sinner corrupted by various vices, have committed—all I confess now, O guides!

(32) How will I ever escape from this? I live in constant fear, O guides, that the hour of death might come soon, before I have erased this mass of sins. (33) How will I ever escape from this? Save me at once, that death may not reach me suddenly before I have erased this mass of sins. (34) Death does not look into what has been done and what remains to be done. It destroys the overconfident. The strong and healthy, as well as the sick, should not trust it. Always unexpected, it is a bolt of lightning.

(35) What I love and what I hate have been many times cause for my sins. I did not examine this: that one day I will have to depart and leave everything behind. (36) What I love will cease to be, what I hate will be no more. I too will cease to be. Everything will cease to be. (37) What I now experience will be nothing but a memory; like the experiences of dreams all things pass to be seen no more. (38) In the brief time I have spent in this life, many times what I love and what I hate have departed, yet the evil that I committed on their account remains, terrifying, before my eyes. (39) I had not realized that I am a stranger in this life. Out of delusion, attachment, hatred, I have committed innumerable sins.

(40) Day and night, without respite, my life is spent, with no possibility of restitution. How could it be that I would not die? (41) Right here in this bed, surrounded by my friends and relatives, I will have to suffer the pain of agony by myself. (42) When the messengers of Yama[1] take hold of me, where will I find a relative or friend? Then, merit will be the only protection; but I have not gathered any.

(43) Because of my clinging to this transient life, unaware of the danger, heedless, I have accumulated many sins, O protectors.

(44) When a prisoner is led to be maimed, his throat parched, afflicted by thirst, the world appears different to his weak eyes. (45) How will I feel when the terrible messengers of Yama take hold of me, consumed by fever and fear, sunken in my own excrement? (46) My terrified eyes will look in vain in all directions for a means of escape. Which kind being will then become my savior from this terrifying danger? (47) I will see no salvation anywhere and I will sink deeper in confusion. What will I do then before this terrifying danger?

REFUGE

(48) Right away I must take refuge in the powerful world protectors, the victorious conquerors who are devoted to caring for the world, those who keep away all causes of fear. (49) I also take refuge in the dharma that they have

1. The Lord of Death and overseer of the hells.

understood, which destroys all danger in the sphere of transmigration. I likewise take refuge with sincere faith in the community of the bodhisattvas.

(50) Confused with fear, I turn to Samantabhadra. I also surrender myself to Manjughosha. (51) Terrified, I call with anguished voice upon the protector Avalokita whose actions are all moved by pity. Let him protect this sinner! (52) Searching for my salvation, I call with true faith upon the Noble Akashagarbha, Kshitigarbha,[2] and all the greatly compassionate ones.

(53) I pay homage to Vajrapani, the one who holds the vajra,[3] whose mere presence is enough to scatter away in terror Yama's messengers and other beings of hell.

(54) I have transgressed against your precepts, and now, terrified by these dangers, I seek refuge in you. Hasten to destroy this threat!

(55) One would not disobey the instructions of a physician, even if it is for fear of a common and short illness; how much less should one ignore them when one is afflicted by the four hundred four diseases! (56) For a single one of them would exterminate all the human beings on Jambudvipa,[4] and in the whole universe there is no cure for any of them. (57) Yet I ignore the advice of the all-knowing physician who cures all these pains. How pitiful is this endless delusion of mine!

(58) I am careful when I stand on the edge of a cliff. How could I be less careful, then, as I walk along this precipice of rebirth, extending for thousands of miles, along which one walks for so long.

(59) "Death will not come today"—I have no reason for feeling so smug. The time when I will cease to be most surely will come. (60) Who will give me shelter? How will I escape? Surely I will cease to be. How can my mind be at ease? (61) Is it perhaps that something of value remains of those things that perished after I enjoyed them—attachment to which led me to ignore the advice of the teachers? (62) When I will have left the world of the living, as well as friends and relatives, and when I depart alone to I know not where, what good will come from those things that I have loved and those that I have hated?

(63) Therefore I must day and night remain mindful of this reflection: from evil necessarily follows suffering, how will I escape from it?

(64) Whatever faults I, deluded fool that I am, have committed, be they shunned by a natural sense of the right or by prescription of the monastic code, (65) I confess them all before the protectors, palms joined in prayer, with repeated prostrations. For I fear the pains that will arise from my sins. (66) Let the guides recognize my faults as faults. It was not noble conduct, protectors. I will not repeat this conduct.

Chapter III. Taking Possession of the Thought of Awakening

(1) With delight I rejoice that all living beings acquire the merit that quells the pains of the evil destinies. May all suffering beings reach happiness!

---

2. Other bodhisattvas who are principal Mahayana disciples of the Buddha (as is Avalokita, or Avalokiteshvara).
3. A kind of mythical thunderbolt, a weapon capable of cutting through anything. Vajrapani is the bodhisattva who embodies power.
4. In Buddhist cosmology, the southern continent (or "island," *dvipa*) on which ordinary human beings live.

(2) I rejoice that living beings can become free from the suffering of transmigration and I celebrate the attainment of the state of a buddha or a bodhisattva by those who are exemplars of perfection. (3) I rejoice in the arising of the thought of awakening in those who adopt the teaching, for this thought is an ocean whose tide brings bliss, whose depths hold the treasure of everything that is beneficial to all sentient beings.

(4) Palms joined in prayer, I entreat all awakened ones in all the directions that they light the lamp of dharma for those who, in the darkness of their own delusion, fall into the abyss of suffering.

(5) Palms joined in prayer, I plead with the victorious conquerors who seek the final rest of nirvana, that they remain in the world of transmigration for an infinite number of cosmic ages.

(6) With the merit that I have achieved through these acts of devotion may I relieve all living beings from every form of suffering.

(7) Let me be medicine, physician and nurse for the sick, until I have put an end to all illness. (8) May I bring an end to the torments of hunger and thirst with rivers of food and drink, and may I myself become food and drink when the minor cosmic cycle ends with a great famine. (9) May I become inexhaustible wealth for the poor. May I remain at their side ready to satisfy each one of their needs. (10) All bodies, property, and merit that I have acquired in the past, the ones I have now, and the ones that I may acquire in the future, I surrender them all with indifference for the benefit of all living beings. (11) Nirvana means renunciation of all things, and my mind seeks this peace. If I must renounce all, it would be better to surrender it to living beings.

(12) I relinquish my person to the whims of all embodied beings; let them hurt me, insult me, cover me with dust without ceasing, (13) let them use my body as their toy, let them laugh at it and enjoy themselves with it. I have given them my body, why should it be my concern any more? (14) Let them have it to do whatever is pleasing to them, but let them never suffer any harm on my account. (15) Rather, if because of me their hearts are driven to anger or anxiety, let these same feelings become in every occasion the cause for their attainment of all merit. (16) May all those who slander me, injure me, or scoff at me, and all other beings share in awakening.

(17) May I become protector for those who have no protection, caravan leader for travelers, a ship, bridge, or ford for those who seek to reach the other shore, (18) a lamp for those who seek light, a bed for the tired, a slave for those embodied beings who need slaves. (19) May I become a wish-fulfilling jewel to all embodied beings, a horn of plenty, a powerful magical formula, the universal remedy, the tree of desires, the cow of plenty. (20) Just as earth and the other elements render service, in multiple ways, conforming to their desires, to the numberless living beings that inhabit infinite space, (21) may I in the same manner, in numberless ways, serve as sustenance for this universe of living beings filling the breadth of space, for as long as they have not reached satisfaction and peace.

(22) "Just as the sugatas in the past took possession of the thought of awakening and established themselves progressively in the discipline of the bodhisattvas, (23) today I give rise the thought of awakening for the good of the world. In this way I will train successively in the various levels of the discipline."

(24) Once the man of wisdom has taken possession of the thought of enlightenment in this manner, he will exalt that same thought repeatedly in the following manner, in order to secure its subsequent growth:

(25) "Today my birth bears fruit, and my human existence becomes profitable; today I have been born in the family of the tathagatas, now I become a son of the awakened. (26) From today on I must act according to the customs of my family, so that no stain will fall on this immaculate lineage." (27) It is as if a blind man were to find a jewel in a pile of dung. In the same way, I know not how, this thought of awakening has arisen in me.

(28) This elixir has arisen to vanquish death in the world. It is the inexhaustible treasure that will alleviate thirst in the world. (29) It is the unsurpassable medicine that will allay the sufferings of the world. It is the tree under which the tired world can rest from its wandering through the roads of existence. (30) It is like a bridge open to all travelers that they may cross beyond the evil destinies. This moon of the thought of awakening has arisen to freshen with its light the heat of the afflictions of the world. (31) It is an immense sun that dissipates the darkness of worldly ignorance. It is the fresh butter produced by the churning of the ocean of milk of the true dharma. (32) The caravan of men, which travels through the roads of existence, hungering for pleasure and happiness, finds here the banquet of bliss, in which all those who come to it become satiated.

(33) "Today, before the perfect ones, I invite the whole world to the condition of awakening, and, at the same time, to happiness. May gods, asuras,[5] and all living beings rejoice."

Chapter IV. Vigilance in Preserving the Thought of Awakening

(1) After a son of the victorious conquerors takes a firm hold of the thought of enlightenment in the way explained above, he should exert himself constantly and tirelessly in avoiding any transgression of the precepts.

(2) If something is begun rashly, without carefully examining the consequences, one should reconsider whether it is worth carrying to completion or not, even if one has promised to do it. (3) However, an enterprise that has been examined by beings of great discernment—the buddhas and their sons— and also by myself, to the extent of my capacity, how could I neglect it? (4) Having made this promise of the vow, if I do not fulfill it with action, I will have broken my word with all beings. What future state would await me then?

(5) It is said that the person who does not give, even if in thought he has the best of intentions, will become a hungry ghost—no matter how insignificant the intended gift may have been. (6) How much worse would it be then to proclaim openly and with great conviction the highest bliss for all living beings, only to break my word with the whole world? What future state will await me then?

(7) Only the All-knowing One knows the unfathomable course of actions and their fruits. He alone brings to liberation even those who have abandoned the thought of awakening.

(8) Therefore every lapse of the bodhisattva is extremely grave, for, every time he lapses he reduces the welfare of all living beings. (9) Likewise, any

5. Demigods.

other who hinders the good works of the bodhisattva, even if it is only for an instant, will never see the end of his evil destinies, for he keeps all beings away from their goal. (10) For, someone who destroys the good of a single living being is himself destroyed; how much more serious would it be if he harmed all embodied beings inhabiting the confines of space?

(11) If one is moved to and fro, now by the ebb of his faults, now by the flow of the thought of enlightenment, a long time will have to pass before he reaches firm ground. (12) Therefore, whatever I have promised I should carry out zealously. If today I do not make effort I will have sunk from the low to the lowest.

(13) Countless awakened ones have come through this world in search of all living beings, and I, by my own fault, have not been within reach of their medicine. (14) If today too I should do what I have done repeatedly in the past, again I will suffer disease and death, I will be cut to pieces and hacked to death in the evil destinies. (15) When will I obtain again things so difficult to obtain as to be reborn in a world where a tathagata has appeared, as faith in the dharma, as this human condition, as the capacity to practice good, and (16) as this peaceful day of today when I am in good health and I have food to eat? Life lasts only one instant, it disappoints us. The body is like only borrowed property.

(17) By conduct such as mine I will not reach again the human condition. If I do not attain again human birth, I will only meet sin; whence would arise then what is meritorious? (18) If I do not practice good while I have the capacity to do so, what will I do when the torments of evil destinies blind me? (19) For him who does not practice the good and accumulates evil conduct, the word "good destiny" has perished for hundreds of millions of cosmic ages.

(20) This is why the Blessed One has said that to obtain human birth is as difficult as having a sea turtle pass its head through a yoke drifting in the ocean. (21) For the sin of one instant one falls into the Avichi[6] hell for one cosmic age; but if it is about sin accumulated since beginningless time, how can you speak of good destinies? (22) What is more, you will not escape this merely by suffering the pains of the evil destinies, for even as you suffer you commit new sins.

(23) There is, therefore, no greater self-deception, no greater delusion, than this one of not practicing good when one has attained the unique opportunity to do so. (24) But if, in spite of having reflected in this way, out of sheer delusion I give in to inertia, then I will wail for an even longer time, chased by Yama's messengers. (25) My body will burn for a long time in the unbearable fires of hell; for a long time will burn my unbending mind in the fire of remorse.

(26) Though I do not know how, I have attained the firm ground of good which is so difficult to obtain, yet, though I am aware of this, I let myself be dragged again into hell.

(27) I know not what to think of this. Like someone who falls under the influence of a magical spell, I know not the cause of my delusion, I know not what is within me. (28) Craving, hatred, and the other afflictions are enemies without hands, feet, or any other faculty, they are not courageous or astute, how could they enslave me then? (29) Residing in my own mind they smite

6. Literally, "unrelenting," the worst of the Buddhist hells.

me at their own pleasure, yet I do not become angry at them. How pitiful is this misplaced forbearance!

(30) If all the gods and all the human beings were my enemies, all of them together could not force me into the fires of Avichi hell. (31) But my powerful enemies, the afflictions in an instant throw me into that fire which will upon contact turn Mount Meru[7] into ashes. (32) There is not one enemy of mine with a life so long as that of my foes the afflictions, whose life knows no beginning or end.

(33) Whoever is well treated or receives some service will show some interest in the well-being of those who serve him; but the afflictions bring even greater evil upon those who serve them. (34) If their hatred is so lasting and constant, if they are the only cause of this torrent of suffering, if they hide in my own mind, how can I remain unperturbed, delighting in this world of transmigration? (35) How could I know happiness as long as these guards of the prison of existence, the executioners of those who are condemned to hell and the other evil destinies, lodge in the house of my mind, in the cage of my desires?

(36) Therefore, I will not rest until these enemies are slain before my eyes. There are some who, victims of their own anger, mad with pride, do not sleep until they have destroyed the most insignificant of those who offend them. (37) In the battlefield violent men attack fiercely those blind fools who are destined to die. Ignoring the pain of arrows and spears, they do not retreat until they have achieved their goal. (38) How much more should I persevere then, I who have set out to destroy my natural enemies, the constant cause of all suffering! What reason is there to give in to despair and dejection, even among hundreds of difficulties?

(39) Warriors show off, like ornaments, the fruitless scars that enemies have left on their bodies; why then should I become discouraged by suffering, I who am seeking a greater purpose? (40) Those whose minds can only show eagerness for earning a livelihood—fishermen, pariahs and laborers— withstand heat, cold, any vexation. How could I not withstand them too, if it is for the sake of the world?

(41) When I promised that I would free from the afflictions this world, extending to the limits of space in the ten directions,[8] while I was myself not free from these same afflictions, (42) I did not recognize my limitations. I spoke like a madman. Therefore, I will not turn back from the destruction of the afflictions. (43) I will attack them and furiously oppose them all—except for that affliction which leads to the destruction of the afflictions. (44) They may scatter my bowels, they may cut my head off, never will I stoop to these enemies of mind, the afflictions.

(45) An enemy after being repelled may retreat and occupy a different position whence he may return with new strength; but the enemy which are the afflictions has no such sanctuary. (46) If this enemy were expelled from its dwelling place in my mind, where could it go to again plot my destruction? He depends only on my lack of fortitude, on my sluggish mind. The wretched afflictions could be conquered merely by seeing with the eye of wisdom.

---

7. In Buddhist cosmology, the mountain at the center of the world.
8. That is, everywhere (north, south, east, west, northeast, northwest, southeast, southwest, the nadir, and the zenith).

(47) The afflictions do not dwell in the objects of the senses or in the senses themselves, or in between the senses and their objects, or elsewhere; where do they dwell, then, that they can batter the whole world? They are only magical illusions. Fear no more, oh my mind, and strive unceasingly for discernment! Why should you submit yourself to the tortures of hell for no reason at all?

(48) Having made this resolution, I will make effort to put into practice the precepts, exactly as they have been taught. Medicine can cure him, but how will the patient recover if he does not follow the physician's instructions?

Chapter V. Protecting the Thought of Awakening

(1) He who would keep the precepts should watch the mind diligently; a person who does not watch the unstable mind cannot keep the precepts.

(2) Wild elephants in rut do not cause in this world the damage that the elephant of an unrestrained mind will cause in the Avichi hell and all the other hells. (3) However, if the elephant of the mind is well tied with the rope of mindfulness, all danger vanishes, all good is within our reach. (4) Tigers, lions, elephants, bears, poisonous snakes, and all human enemies, and in addition all the jailers of hell, as well as dakinis and rakshasas,[9] (5) all of them become restrained by merely restraining the mind, and by merely taming the mind they all become tame. (6) For he who speaks the truth has said that all the dangers and the countless sorrows of the world arise from the mind.

(7) Who fashioned so carefully the swords of hell, the pavement of red-hot iron? Whence are born the women that tempt and punish men in hell? (8) The Sage has explained that all and each of these arise from sinful thoughts. Therefore, in the three worlds[1] there is nothing more frightful than mind itself.

(9) If the perfection of generosity meant freeing the whole world from poverty, then, since there still is poverty in the world today, how could it have been that the perfect ones of the past attained this perfect virtue? (10) It is said that the perfection of generosity is the result of the will to surrender to all living beings everything that is yours, including the fruit of such surrender. Therefore, this perfection is only a mental act.

(11) Where could I lead all fish and other living beings, so that I could avoid killing them? But the moment one acquires a dispassionate thought, there is agreement that there is perfection of morality.

(12) How many men of evil, endless like the skies, would I have to bring to death to get rid of my enemies? But if my thoughts of hatred are brought to death, all my enemies will be dead.

(13) Where will you find enough leather to cover the whole earth? Merely by wearing a pair of leather shoes you will cover the earth. (14) In the same way, since I cannot control external objects, I will control my own mind. What is there to gain by controlling the rest?

---

9. Demons who eat human flesh. A *dakini* is here a kind of female demon.

1. The Realm of Desire, the Realm of Form, and the Formless Realm; see pp. 54–55.

(15) Even with the help of body and speech an indolent mind will not achieve the fruits that a keen mind will gain by itself—fruits such as the state of the Brahma gods,[2] and other fortunate rebirths.

(16) The All-knowing One has declared that all prayers and ascetic exercises, even if they are practiced for a long time, will be in vain if the mind is distracted or indolent.

(17) In vain they wander through the vast open spaces of the universe seeking to put an end to sorrow and reach happiness—these beings who do not cultivate the mysterious mind that contains all dharmas.

(18) Therefore, I should focus my mind correctly, and keep a careful watch over it. What good will it do to keep many vows, if one neglects the vow of watching over the mind?

(19) An injured person carefully protects his wound if he is in the midst of a disorderly crowd. In the same way one should always keep watch over the wound that is the mind when one is among evil persons. (20) Fearing a slight bruise to a healing wound, one protects it carefully; why not protect with the same care the wound of the mind for fear of the crushing mountains of hell? (21) For, by following this course of action the firm ascetic will not break his vows even if he finds himself among evil people or loose women.

(22) Better that my fortune perish! Better that I lose my reputation, my life and limb! Better that any other good perish, lest my own mind be lost!

(23) You who wish to protect your minds, I beg of you: "Protect mindfulness and discerning awareness with all your might!" (24) Just as a man afflicted by fever is incapable of any action, a mind lacking these two is incapable of action.

(25) As a broken jar cannot hold water, so a mind lacking awareness cannot retain what has been acquired through study, reflection, and cultivation. (26) Numberless persons, though they are properly trained and committed, even though they make earnest efforts, acquire the stains of transgression, because of their unawareness. (27) Unawareness is a thief who roams about watching for neglect in mindfulness. The victims of this thief end up in evil destinies, no matter how much merit they may otherwise possess.

(28) The afflictions are a band of robbers in search for an open door. If they find it, they steal and destroy your chances of rebirth in a good destiny. (29) Therefore, mindfulness should never leave the door of the mind. If it does, one should bring it back by remembering the torments of the evil destinies.

(30) Mindfulness arises easily from the company of a teacher for those blessed ones who act with fear and respect, according to the instructions of their preceptor.

(31) "The eye of buddhas and bodhisattvas sees everywhere without hindrance, everything stands before them, and I too stand before them." (32) If one reflects in this way, one will remain in possession of respect and fear, and will remember the buddhas at every moment.

(33) If mindfulness stands watch at the door of the mind, discerning awareness will arrive and leave no more.

---

2. Gods of one of the heavens.

(34) First of all one should restrain the mind constantly in this manner: "I must always remain as if I had no sense organs, like a piece of wood."

(35) Never should there be pointless movements of the eyes here and there. The eyes should always look down, as is done in meditation. (36) However, one may occasionally look toward the horizon, to rest his eyes. Also, if he perceives the shadow of someone approaching, he may raise his eyes and look up in order to greet that person. (37) Moreover, in country roads he may look in the four directions to watch for any danger; but he should first come to a complete stop if he is going to examine the four cardinal points. And to look behind, he should turn his whole body.

(38) He should advance or retreat only after examining his thoughts and actions very carefully. In this way he should act in every circumstance with full awareness of his actions. (39) Whenever he begins to move he thinks: "The body should be held thusly." And while moving he should be attentive to his bodily demeanor.

(40) One should observe with the greatest care the elephant of the mind, so that, bound to the post that is reflection on dharma, it will not break loose. (41) One should examine the mind by asking, "Where is my mind," so that it will not throw away the yoke of concentration even for an instant.

(42) Under special circumstances—as in cases of danger, or when there is a festival—he acts freely, because it has been declared that at the time of practicing generosity one may neglect strict morality.

(43) One should consider that enterprise that has been carefully considered and begun, before considering another one. One should bring this enterprise to completion by committing oneself wholeheartedly to it. (44) For in this manner both tasks, the one begun and the one to follow, will be completed successfully. Otherwise, neither will be successful, and the perturbation of unawareness will continue to grow.

(45) One should put an end to excitement arising from the many kinds of frivolous talk and from the many extraordinary events that occur in the world. (46) Fearful of the consequences of distraction, and remembering the precepts of the tathagatas, one should at once give up fruitless actions such as idly pounding the ground, tearing up grass, or scribbling.

(47) If he feels like moving or speaking, he should first examine his own mind and keep it steadfast. (48) If he perceives that his own mind is attracted or repelled by something, he will not act or speak; rather, he will remain still like a piece of wood.

(49) If the mind is arrogant, jeering, proud, infatuated, derisive, devious and deceiving, (50) boastful, slanderous, disdainful, or aggressive, he will remain still like a piece of wood.

(51) "My mind seeks only wealth, honors and fame, a large retinue, homage and service; therefore, I will remain still like a piece of wood." (52) "My mind, while being indifferent to the well-being of others, concerned only with my own interests, and merely seeking the attention of an audience, feels like speaking; therefore, I will remain still like a piece of wood." (53) "My thoughts are intolerant, sluggish, fearful, rash, inclined to prattling, partial to those I consider my own; therefore, I will remain still like a piece of wood." (54) When he perceives that the mind is disturbed in this way, or that it is intent on carrying out fruitless activities, the hero should constantly restrain it firmly with an opposing force—the proper antidote.

(55) "I will remain resolved, peaceable, steadfast, deferent and respect-ful, modest and fearful, calm, dedicated to pleasing others, (56) unwearied by the way the wishes of childish and foolish beings contradict each other, full of pity for them, knowing that their desires arise from their perturba-tions. (57) This mind I will hold firmly. Always subject to living beings and to me, I will hold this mind free from reproach, with no sense of egotism, like a magical creation. (58) By remembering again and again, at every moment, that I have obtained this unique opportunity only after a long time, I will keep such a state of mind, unshakable like Mount Meru."

(59) When vultures, eager to devour your carrion, will pull at your body from every direction, why will it not do anything to prevent this? (60) Why do you protect this frame as if it were your own self? If it is something dif-ferent from yourself, why should its end matter to you? (61) You fool, you would not consider part of yourself a clean wooden doll; why do you take such good care of this impure machine, which will end up in rot?

(62) First remove the covering of skin with your mind. Then remove the flesh from its bony frame with the scalpel of discernment. (63) Break open these bones and observe the marrow. Ask yourself what is there in here that is a substantial core. (64) After examining it carefully in this manner, you have found nothing that is substantial; tell me then, why do you still persist in protecting your body so much?

(65) You cannot eat the body's excretions, nor can you drink its blood or suck its innards; of what use is the body to you then? (66) Of course, one could preserve it in order to offer it as food for vultures and jackals; also, this body is the instrument for action. (67) But even if you preserve it with these purposes in mind, what will you do when unremitting death smites it and gives it to the vultures? (68) One does not give clothing and other necessities to a servant who is not to remain with his master. This servant, the body, will depart after its meal is finished; why do you waste so much on it? (69) Pay it its due wage and see to your own interests, for a hireling does not receive all that he produces.

(70) Conceive of your body as a ship, for it should be a vessel for those who cross the ocean of transmigration. So that sentient beings may reach their destination, let your body move at their will.

(71) When one becomes in this manner self-possessed, he always has a smile and never shows a frown on his face, he is the first one to speak to greet someone, a friend to the world. (72) He does not throw chairs or other objects noisily or rashly, nor does he knock at doors in such a manner; rather, he will always delight in silence. (73) The crane, the cat, and the thief move about quietly and silently, and thus achieve their goal. The ascetic should constantly act in the same manner.

(74) He should accept with a bow the instruction of those who are skillful in advising others and are ready to help without being asked to do so. He should always be the disciple of everyone. (75) He should express his enthu-siastic approval for all words that are appropriate and correct, and encourage with words of praise any person he sees doing meritorious works. (76) Let him praise in private the virtue of others, and repeat their praise in public with great joy. When one's own virtue is being praised, however, one should consider it a simple acknowledgment of virtue generally. (77) All human endeavors have as their aim satisfaction, and this is difficult to obtain even

through wealth. Therefore, I will enjoy to the utmost this joy, born from being satisfied by the virtues that others obtain through their efforts. (78) In this way I will have no loss in this life, and will have a greater happiness in the next. Resenting the virtue of others, on the other hand, will bring dissatisfaction in this world, and even greater sufferings in the next.

(79) One should speak with reassuring and precise words, conveying the meaning clearly, in a manner that is delighting to the spirit, pleasant to hear, and rooted in compassion, with a sweet and calm tone. (80) He should always look directly at other beings as if he drank from them with his eyes, thinking: "Only because of them will I reach the state of a buddha."

(81) The greatest merit arises from constant dedication, from the cultivation of the opposing forces, and a practice focused on the fields of merit that are those that lead a virtuous life, our benefactors, and suffering living beings.

(82) Let him always be ready, energetic, capable of doing things for himself; he would not let anybody else take his place in any task.

(83) The perfections, beginning with generosity, are presented in the order of their excellence. One should not give up a superior virtue for another, inferior one, except in the case of the dam that holds the reservoir of good conduct. (84) Having understood this, one should devote himself constantly to the well-being of others. Even what is normally forbidden is permitted to the compassionate person if he sees in it something of benefit to others.

(85) He should eat moderately after sharing his food with those who have fallen on misfortune, those who have no one to take care of them, and those who have taken religious vows. He should renounce all but his three robes.[3]

(86) His body is the servant of true dharma. He should not cause this body any pain for any other, inferior purpose. For by taking care of his body he will rapidly fulfill the aspirations of living beings. (87) Therefore, he should not sacrifice his life for someone who has not the pure intentions of compassion; but he should do it for someone whose intentions are comparable to his own—in this way nothing will be lost.

(88) He should not preach the dharma to a person who does not show the proper respect, to someone who wears a turban though he is in good health, to someone holding a parasol, a cane, or a sword, if he has his head covered. (89ab) He will not teach the profound and sublime dharma to men of inferior virtue, or to unaccompanied women.

(89cd) He behaves with equal respect toward the inferior and the higher dharmas. (90) He should not impart the inferior dharma to someone who is worthy of the sublime one. Nor should he try to win him over to the Great Vehicle[4] only with sutras and mantras, neglecting practical conduct.

(91) It is not permitted to throw away one's toothpick or spit in public places. It is forbidden to excrete in water or usable land. (92) One should not eat with the mouth full, or make noise or open one's mouth while eating. One should not sit with the feet dangling down. One should not scratch both arms at the same time. (93ab) One should not travel alone with the wife of another man, nor should one lie or sit with her.

3. A monk's only clothing.   4. That is, the Mahayana.

(93cd) After observing and inquiring about everything that is scandalous to the world, he should avoid it.

(94) He should not point at anything with the finger; rather, he should politely do so with his whole right hand, even when pointing the right way on the road. (95) He should not beckon anyone by waving his arms in cases of little importance; rather, let him snap the fingers or the like. Otherwise, he will lose his composure. (96) He should lie down as the Protector lay when he entered nirvana, his head in the most auspicious direction, attentive, ready to rise early, without hesitation, according to the rules.

(97) Numberless forms of proper conduct have been declared for the bodhisattva, but above all one should follow rigorously the practice of purifying the mind. (98) Three times a day and three times a night one should practice the three elements of ritual. In this way, through the thought of awakening and with the aid of the victorious conquerors one will extinguish the last residue of sin.

(99) In whatever circumstance he may find himself, either through his own will or that of another, he will diligently practice the precepts that are relevant to the case. (100) For there is nothing in them that should not be practiced by the sons of the victorious conquerors. For someone who acts in this way there is nothing that will not result in merit. (101) He should act only for the sake of living beings, directly or indirectly; everything he must dedicate only to the benefit of living beings, and to awakening.

(102) He should never abandon, even for his own life, a good friend who is well established in the bodhisattva vows and well versed in the meaning of the Great Vehicle. (103ab) He should study, in the Shrisambhavavi-moksha of the *Gandavyuha Sutra*,[5] the way one should behave toward his teacher.

(103cd) These and other teachings of the buddhas should be understood according to statements in the sutras. (104) The precepts are found in the sutras. Therefore, he should read them. One should also consider the fundamental transgressions as presented in the *Akashagarbha Sutra*.[6]

(105) One should by all means look into the *Shikshasamucchaya*,[7] again and again, for in it one finds a detailed explanation of the proper conduct of the bodhisattva. (106) Or, if one prefers, one should at least consult diligently, as a second possibility, and for brevity's sake, the *Sutrasamucchaya*[8] composed by the venerable Nagarjuna. (107) Having understood the precepts, one will follow in practical conduct whatever is proscribed and whatever is prescribed in these works, for the sake of preserving this thought of concern for the whole world.

(108) In brief, discerning awareness can be defined accurately as the uninterrupted observation of all states and attitudes of body and mind.

(109) With my body I will proclaim the dharma; of what use is its recitation with words? What will the patient get from reciting the physician's prescription?

---

5. A text in the *Avatamsaka Sutra* that details the conversations of Sudhana with fifty-three masters as he seeks enlightenment. Shrisambhavavi-moksha is one of its chapters.
6. A Mahayana sutra that sets forth the vows of a

boddhisattva.
7. A compendium of Buddhist doctrine composed by Shantideva.
8. Literally, "Compendium of Scriptures."

Chapter VI. The Virtue of Patience

(1) Ill will destroys all of these good deeds, as well as generosity and worship of the sugatas, even if one has practiced them for thousands of cosmic cycles. (2) There is no evil like hatred, no ascetic discipline like patience. Therefore, cultivate patience actively by all means possible.

(3) As long as the barb of hatred is in your heart, your mind will find no rest, no joy or happiness, it will have no rest or steadfastness. (4) The same who have been honored with his gifts and attentions, the same whom he has sheltered under his own roof, wish to bring death to the landlord who is cursed with an angry character. (5) His own friends fear him; though he gives generously he receives no recognition or favors. In brief, there is nothing that can bring well-being to a wrathful man. (6) Whoever sees that anger is the one enemy that brings upon him these and other evils, and attacks it tenaciously, will be happy in this and the next life.

(7) Discontent arises whenever our desire is contradicted or the undesirable occurs. When hatred receives its nourishment from discontent, it gathers strength and destroys me. (8) Therefore, I will destroy this enemy's nourishment, since (9) the most unpleasant event will not perturb my satisfaction. In discontent I do not find the object of my desires, rather it makes me neglect meritorious action. (10) If there is a solution, what good is discontent? If there is no solution, what good is it anyway?

(11) No one wishes pain, humiliation, insult and disgrace for himself or for those whom he loves, yet he wishes them for his enemies.

(12) One is hardly ever able to reach happiness, even with great difficulty, but sorrow recurs effortlessly. But liberation is only passing through sorrow. Therefore, keep your spirit steadfast!

(13) The people of Karnata, who believe they are the children of Durga,[9] vainly undergo the pains of fire and mutilation with the hope of liberation. How can I be so cowardly then? (14) There is nothing that will remain difficult after practice; therefore, if one first practices with less severe afflictions, even the greatest torments will become bearable. (15) Why is it that you ignore as useless the sting of mosquitoes, wasps, and gnats, hunger and thirst, and other painful sensations, or violent itch and similar miseries? (16) Cold, heat, rain, wind, travel, disease, imprisonment, beatings—do not become tender in the face of these, otherwise your torments will multiply.

(17) Some attack with even greater valor at the sight of their own blood, others faint by the mere sight of the blood of others. (18) This is due respectively to the valor and cowardice of their spirits. Therefore, he who does not let himself be conquered by sorrow will vanquish all afflictions.

(19) Even in pain the wise man will not allow the serenity of his mind to be disturbed; for he is at war with the perturbations, and in the battlefield pain abounds. (20) Only those who defeat their adversaries by welcoming on their bare chests the enemy's blows are true conquering heroes, the rest are merely slayers of the dead.

(21) Sorrow has another advantage, and it is that the shock of pain can bring about the downfall of pride, compassion for beings in transmigration, fear of sin, and love for the Victorious Conqueror.[1]

9. A Hindu warrior goddess. Karnata is a region of south India.

1. An epithet of the Buddha.

(22) I do not feel anger toward bile and the other humors, though they are the cause of great pains to me. Why should I become angry at conscious beings, they too are moved to anger by conditions they are not aware of. (23) As physical pain arises without being sought, anger also arises by force, even when not desired. (24) A human being does not become angry by freely deciding, "I will become angry," and anger itself does not come into existence by willing, "I will arise." (25) All the manifold transgressions and sins are due to the force of causes and conditions, they do not exist as independent acts or entities. (26) And the conjunction of conditions does not have the will to think, "I will bring about this effect," and the product also does not have the will to think, "I will be produced."

(27) The primordial substance proposed by some, or the self conceived by others, indeed could not be born by deciding, "I will be." (28) For, as long as the primordial substance has not arisen, it exists not. Who would be there to want to come into existence then? Moreover, once it came into existence it would not be able to cease from its active involvement with the objects of the senses.

(29) Indeed, if the self is eternal, unconscious, then, like the sky, it is evidently inactive. Even if it could come into contact with other conditions, what sort of activity could the unchanging have? (30) Anything that at the time of an effect being produced remains the same as it was before the effect was produced, what part of the act of production did it perform? In the relation between this thing and the effect, which one of the two is the actual locus of change?

(31) Thus, everything depends on something else, and that on which it depends is also dependent. Under these circumstances, among entities that, like magical creations, lack self-activity, what should be the object of our anger?

An Objector Interjects: (32ab) Then, it is also absurd to practice self-control, for who could restrain what?
The Author Replies: (32cd) It is reasonable to practice self-control, because there is causality. We thus accept that there is an end to suffering.

(33) Therefore, when one sees that a friend or a foe has done wrong, one must remain at peace, reflecting, "Such and such conditions are the cause for his actions."

(34) But if only by one's own wish one could attain the object of his desire, there would be no sorrow among all living beings, for no one desires sorrow.

(35) As a result of their own thoughtlessness some human beings will torture themselves with thorns, hunger, and other tribulations, due to their anger, and their desire for women or other things that are not theirs to have. (36) Others will kill themselves by hanging or jumping from a cliff, by taking poison or eating excessively, and through demeritorious conduct. (37) If, enslaved by the perturbations, they thus destroy their own selves, so dear to them, then how could they be expected to refrain from bringing down these same torments upon the bodies of others? (38) Maddened by the afflictions, they act for their own destruction, they inspire only pity; how could there arise any anger for them?

(39) If harming others is intrinsically natural to the foolish, it makes no more sense to feel anger toward them than it would be to be angry with fire

because it is in its nature to burn. (40) On the other hand, if this defect is accidental, and living beings are by nature kind, still it would be as absurd to feel anger toward them as it would be to be angry with air when it carries fetid smoke.

(41) If one forgets the stick, which is the nearest cause of pain, and feels anger toward the one who moved the stick, then it would be better to hate hatred, since it is hatred that moves the one who brandishes the stick.

(42) I myself during my past lives brought similar torments upon other beings. Therefore it is only fitting that this same tribulation should fall upon me, who am the cause of injury to other living beings.

(43) His sword and my body are the twofold cause of my pain. He bears the sword, I, the body, with which one should I feel angry? (44) In the shape of a body I adopted this open sore, sensitive to the slightest touch. If I myself, blinded by thirst, bring upon it further affliction, what should be the object of my anger?

(45) I do not desire suffering, yet I foolishly seek the causes of suffering. Since sorrow comes from my own offenses, why should I become angry at anything else? (46) The sword-leaf forest,[2] the birds of hell, they all arise from my own actions, and so does my present suffering; where should I direct my anger?

(47) Moved by my own actions, there arise those who cause me injury. Because of this they will go to the hells. Is it not the case, then, that it is I who do them harm? (48) Because of them, by patiently accepting their offenses, many of my sins will vanish. On the other hand, it is because of me that they will end up in the hells, where they will suffer for a long time. (49) It is I who bring harm to them, they are my benefactors. Why do I turn things around, and, with a violent heart, give rise to anger?

(50) If I do not end up in the hells it will be due to the qualities of my own disposition. What is there for these enemies to gain if I guard myself from impatience? (51) If I were to respond to their offense in this way, they would not be protected, I would lose my conduct, and these wretches would perish.

(52) No one can destroy the mind anywhere and by any means whatsoever, for it is immaterial; yet, by clinging to it the body comes to suffer physical pain. (53) Humiliation, offensive words, and disgrace—these bandits cannot oppress the body. What makes you angry then, oh my mind? (54) Is it because the dislike of others will consume me in this or another birth that I try to avoid it so much? (55) Is it that I try to avoid it because it is an obstacle to the acquisition of my fortune? My fortune will turn to nothing in this very life, but evil will remain the same constantly.

(56) It would be better to die today than to carry for so long this life of falsehood; for, even if I were to live for long, the agony of death would be the same. (57) In dreams a man will enjoy a hundred years of pleasure, only to awaken later; another one enjoys only an instant and then awakens. (58) Doesn't the joy of both end in the same manner upon awakening? It is the same at the time of dying, whether you have lived long or not. (59) Even if you gain numberless acquisitions for a long [time] and enjoy many pleasures for a long time, I will leave with empty hands, naked, as if everything had been suddenly stolen from me.

2. One of the Buddhist hells.

An Objector Interjects: (60ab) But is it not true that as long as I am alive, by means of my fortune and possessions I will be able to cultivate the good and destroy sin?

The Author Replies: (60cd) Do you mean to say that in this way the good would not be lost and evil will not increase, when you get angry, moved by desire for gain? (61) If the one single purpose of my life is lost, then what good is a life that only brings evil?

An Objector Interjects: (62ab) No, what I mean to say is that I feel hatred toward one who denigrates me because his ill will leads many living beings to perdition.

The Author Replies: (62cd) Why are you not angry then in the same way with those who insult others? (63) You are patient with those who show little love to others, when their disfavor has been produced by others, but you are not patient with those who insult you, though this also has been produced by a third factor: the afflictions.

(64) Equally absurd is my hatred toward those who harm or desecrate images and shrines, or disparage the true dharma, for neither buddhas nor their disciples and teachings suffer injury. (65) Put an end to your anger toward those who harm your teachers, relatives, and loved ones, etc., by understanding, as before, that their aggression is born from causes and conditions beyond their control.

(66) Whether it is due to a conscious or an unconscious cause, sorrow is inevitable for all embodied beings; it is found in all sentient beings. Therefore, accept it patiently.

(67) Due to their delusion, some offend, others, equally deluded, become angry at the offense; which of the two will we consider free of guilt? And whom will we declare guilty?

(68) Why did you do what you did in the past, so that now you find yourself tormented by others in this way? All beings act under the influence of their past deeds; who are you to change this? (69) Still, because I understand this, I will devote my efforts to good, so that all of these beings will carry thoughts of mutual amity.

(70) It is like a house on fire—if the flames start spreading to another house, one removes the straw or any other flammable items. (71) In the same way, one should abandon at once all those things that could fuel the fire of hatred in the mind—for fear that the very substance of merit might be burnt.

(72) Wouldn't it be fortunate if a man condemned to death were freed after only cutting his hand? Would it not be equally fortunate if one were to suffer pain in this life instead of ending up in hell? (73) If you are not able to withstand even the insignificant pain of today, why don't you destroy anger, which is after all the cause of suffering in hell? (74) Thus, because of my own anger I have suffered in the hells thousands of times, but I did not achieve anything for myself or others with this suffering. (75) My present pain is nothing comparable to the pains of hell, and it will produce great benefits. It is reasonable that I rejoice in this suffering, which will free the whole world from its suffering.

(76) If others find joy and happiness in praising a person who excels in virtue, why don't you also rejoice, oh mind, in praising him? (77) This practice will bring you an intense delight which is blameless, the source of fur-

ther happiness. The virtuous themselves do not object to it. It is the best way to attract others to the path. (78) If what you do not like about praising others is that only the other person is pleased by it, then you object to all rewards, even that of payment for services, in which case you have also rejected the future reward of your present effort. (79) When your own virtues are being praised, you wish that others may rejoice in them with you. Yet, when the virtues of another are being praised you do not wish joy even for yourself.

(80) If you have given rise to the thought of awakening, by wishing happiness for all sentient beings, how can you now become irritated when sentient beings obtain happiness on their own? (81) You claim that you seek for living beings the state of a buddha, which assures them of the veneration of the three world spheres. Then, how can you burn with envy on seeing that they receive insignificant honors? (82) The person who nourishes those that you are supposed to support is in fact giving only to you. Why do you resent and not enjoy the sustenance your family has received? (83) He who wants awakening for all sentient beings—what will he not want for them? How could the thought of awakening ever occur to one who resents the success of others?

(84) If someone else does not receive the offering you wanted for yourself, it remains in the donor's house. It will not be yours anyway. What does it matter to you whether it is given or not? (85) Should the recipient hinder the transference of merit, the act of virtue in the faithful donor, and his own virtue? Should he not accept, though he receives? Tell me, what would not make you angry? (86) Not only do you fail to regret the evil you yourself have done, you want to compete with others who have done good.

(87) If some calamity came upon your enemy, what in it would give you satisfaction? What has no cause for its occurrence will not occur merely because you desire it. (88) On the other hand, if you could succeed in causing him ill merely by desiring it, why should there be joy in you when there is suffering in him? Even if there is some gain for you in his unhappiness, the resulting loss will be much greater. (89) For this apparent gain is the terrible fishing hook of the fishermen, the afflictions. From their hooks the guardians of hell will purchase you to cook you in their pots.

(90) Praise, fame, honors will not give me merit or long life, strength, health, or bodily comforts. (91) But the latter are the goods desired by a sage who knows what is of benefit. One who seeks only temporary pleasures, on the other hand, can dedicate himself to drinking, gambling, etc. (92) Some will even throw away their fortunes and sacrifice their lives for the sake of fame. But can one eat the syllables in words of praise? Can one enjoy glory after death? (93) Like a child crying in pain when his sand castle is destroyed, my mind weeps when it has lost praise and glory. (94) This praise is nothing more than a sound. It has no thought of its own, therefore it cannot praise me. The only cause for my joy is the idea that someone else is happy for me. (95) What does it matter to me, then, whether someone else's rejoicing arises with respect to me or with respect to another? This joy and happiness belong only to this person. I do not share even a small part of it. (96) If happiness in me is due to his being happy, then I should have the same happiness whenever another is happy. Why is it then that when someone finds joy in the happiness of others I find no happiness myself? (97) Therefore, if I rejoice merely at the thought of receiving praise, there is no connection with this

other person, who is the cause of my happiness, and I am simply playing a childish game.

(98) Praise and honor destroy my serenity and the shock of transmigration. They generate jealousy toward persons of virtue, and resentment of their success. (99) Therefore, those who rise against me to destroy my reputation—are they not dedicated to keeping me from falling into the evil destinies? (100) Wealth and honor are chains for a person who, like myself, seeks liberation. How could I feel any hatred for those who release me from these chains? (101) Since I am rushing toward certain suffering, how could I feel any hatred toward those who stand in my way, like a bolted door, as if the Buddha had placed them there? (102) "But my enemy hinders my good works"—this is no reason for anger. There is no austerity like patience—are they not giving me the opportunity to practice it? (103) If I am not patient with my enemy, the fault is mine: it is I who hinder my own virtue, while he remains the potential cause of my virtue. (104) If the one cannot exist without the other, if when one is present the other is possible, then the first is the cause of the second. Why would you call it a hindrance then?

(105) The mendicant who appears at the proper time is not a hindrance to the exercise of generosity. When one meets a world-renouncer, one does not say that he is a hindrance to renunciation. (106) It is easy to find mendicants in the world, difficult to find offenders; for no one will do me wrong if I have done no wrong myself. (107) It is therefore as if a treasure appeared miraculously in my home. My enemy should be loved, for he is a friend in the path to awakening.

(108) With our joint effort, he offending, I forgiving, I will obtain the fruit of patience. I will first give of this fruit to him, for he is the source of my patience.

(109) If you argue that the enemy does not deserve your consideration because "he has no intention of increasing my patience," then why would you venerate the good dharma? After all, it too becomes a cause for perfection without any intention of doing so. (110) If you think he should not have your respect, thinking "my enemy's intention is to harm me," how would you otherwise practice forgiveness? Would you practice forgiveness toward, say, a physician whose goal is your own good? (111) Therefore, patience is possible only under this condition: that the other harbors an evil intention. Consequently only he who is my enemy is a cause of patience, and, like the good dharma, deserves my veneration.

(112) This is why the Sage has declared that "the field of living beings is one of the fields of merit, the victorious conquerors are another field." For many have reached the highest goal by serving them. (113) If one can find in both sentient beings and victorious conquerors an equal access to the virtues of a buddha, why this distinction of levels that refuses to sentient beings the same respect shown to the victorious conquerors?

(114) The value of the intention is derived not from any intrinsic quality, but from its ultimate effect. Therefore, the value of the intention of sentient beings is the same as that of the victorious conquerors, and they themselves are consequently equal to the victorious conquerors. (115) The exalted character of sentient beings is due only to the fact that one who has benevolent intentions toward them is worthy of veneration. The exalted character of buddhas is due only to the fact that one derives merit from faith in them.

(116) Living beings can be compared to buddhas because they can contribute to and participate in the attainment of buddhahood, but in reality there is not one among them who could be compared to the buddhas, who are oceans of unfathomable virtue. (117) If one could find in a living being even a single atom of the virtue of one of these unique accumulations of virtue called "a buddha," the three world realms would not be enough to offer it its proper veneration. (118) But in living beings is present indeed, and most excellent, a fragment of this faculty of producing the nature of buddhahood. One should offer veneration to living beings in proportion to this partial capacity.

(119) How else could we express our gratitude to our true friends, incomparable benefactors, the buddhas and bodhisattvas, if we did not dedicate ourselves to serving living beings? (120) Buddhas and bodhisattvas will tear their bodies, and descend into the Avichi hell for the sake of these sentient beings. Whatever we do for the sake of these sentient beings is well done. Therefore, I must in every respect behave kindly toward my worst enemies. (121) How could I feel pride instead of humility for these masters, for whose sake my Masters have freely and without regret given even their lives?

(122) When sentient beings are happy, the monarchs among sages rejoice; if they suffer, buddhas are distressed. Buddhas find satisfaction when living beings are satisfied. The sages are hurt when a sentient being is offended or harmed. (123) Just as someone whose body is totally enveloped in flames will find no pleasure in any sense object whatsoever, in the same manner those whose whole being is compassion will find no reason for joy as long as living beings are suffering.

(124) Therefore, since I have caused pain to other human beings, I have brought sorrow to all the compassionate ones. Therefore, I confess today my wrongdoing. May the sages forgive me for having caused them so much distress.

(125) In order to gratify the tathagatas, today I turn my whole being into the slave of the world. May the flood of humanity place their feet on my head. May they strike me, that the world protectors may be satisfied. (126) The compassionate ones have made the whole world their own body, there is no doubt about this. Then, is it not the protectors themselves who appear under the guise of living beings? How could I despise them? (127) Only in this way will I serve the tathagatas, only in this way will I reach my aim, only thus will I quell the suffering of the world; therefore, let this be my vow.

(128) By himself a single member of the royal guard can harass a large crowd; the crowd will not be able to resist him; they will suffer patiently at his hands; (129) because he is not alone, his power is that of the king's army. In the same way do not despise those who offend you because they might seem weak, (130) for they hold the power of both the guardians of hell and the compassionate ones. Therefore, try to please all sentient beings, as a servant a wrathful king.

(131) Could an angry king ever cause pains like those experienced in hell by one who brings grief to sentient beings? (132) Could a satisfied king grant a favor equal to the condition of buddhahood one would enjoy by bringing happiness to sentient beings?

(133–134) Leaving aside this future condition of buddhahood, made possible by service to sentient beings, don't you see that the patient person will attain even here, while still in the cycle of transmigration, good fortune, fame, security, beauty, health, joy, a long life, and the splendid bliss of a world conqueror?

Chapter VII. The Perfection of Fortitude

(1) One who practices patience in the above way should develop fortitude. For awakening depends on fortitude, because without fortitude there is no merit, as there is no movement without wind.

(2ab) What is fortitude? It is persevering effort in the cultivation of virtue.

(2cd) And what are the adversaries of fortitude? They are indolence, a fondness for evil, despondency, and self-deprecation.

(3) Indolence develops when, out of inertia, or due to a taste for pleasure, or due to mental torpor, or because one craves for the comforts of a soft pillow, one is not sensitive to the sufferings of transmigration.

(4) You have been captured by these hunters, the afflictions, and you are now trapped in the net of rebirth. Are you still unaware that you are in the jaws of death? (5) Don't you see how your friends and acquaintances, one after another, fall to death? Still you give yourself to sleep, like a pariah's water buffalo. (6) How can you enjoy eating, sleeping, and sensual pleasures while you are being closely watched by Yama, the King of Death, and all your exits are closed?

(7) Once death has everything prepared for you, it will come swiftly. If you should then abandon your sloth, it would be too late. What will you do then? (8) "This I have not accomplished; that I have just begun; this is half done. Now death has come without warning. Alas, I am lost"—these will be your thoughts, (9) as you see, appearing before you at the same time, on your deathbed, the faces of the messengers of death and your helpless relatives. With the pain of grief their faces have become swollen, the eyes tearful and red. (10) Then as you are tormented by the memory of your sins, and you hear the cries of hell, delirious, from sheer fright your body smeared with feces, what will you do then? (11) "I am like a fish kept alive in a tank." It is only reasonable then that you should fear death, and much more the fearful pains of hell.

(12) When you touch hot water you get burned, my delicate friend. How can you be so indifferent when you have committed acts that will surely lead to hell? (13) Without effort you expect to accomplish something, though you are so delicate, you submit yourself to the tortures of hell. Even when you are in the jaws of death you imagine yourself immortal. You poor wretch, everything you do is for your own harm! (14) You have obtained this human condition, which is like a raft—cross then the river of suffering. You fool, this is no time for sleep, you will not find this craft easily again.

(15) In the higher pleasure of dharma you will find an infinite series of joys; how can you abandon this for the sake of the pleasure of sensual excitement, laughter, and the rest, which will be the cause of your suffering?

(16) The counteragents to the adversaries are confidence and the four "armies" of fortitude: single-mindedness, self-mastery, the identity of self and others, and the substitution of self with others.

(17) I should not become discouraged by thinking, "How could I attain awakening?" For, truly, the Tathagata, who always speaks the truth, has

BUDDHISM

Wheel of existence, Tibet, 1780–1850

The Buddha is said to have advised monks to paint the "wheel of existence" at the entrance of monasteries so that the laity could be instructed about karma and rebirth. Such depictions are particularly popular in Tibetan Buddhism. In this nineteenth-century scroll painting, Yama, the Lord of Death, holds the wheel of existence in his fangs and claws. At its center are a rooster, a snake, and a boar: they represent desire, hatred, and ignorance, which drive the cycle of birth and death. The main part of the painting depicts the six realms of rebirth, with the realms of gods, demigods, and humans in the top half and the realms of animals, ghosts, and the denizens of hell at the bottom.

TIBETAN SCHOOL / © NATIONAL MUSEUMS OF SCOTLAND / THE BRIDGEMAN ART LIBRARY

Seated crowned and bejeweled Buddha, Burma, 1895

Although the Buddha is most commonly depicted in the robes of a monk, in Southeast Asia the Buddha is sometimes shown in royal raiment and adorned with a crown, as in this late nineteenth-century gilded lacquer statue from Burma. The Buddha is represented in his famous "earth-touching" pose, just prior to his enlightenment, when he called on the goddess of the earth to bear witness to his right to sit beneath the Bodhi tree.

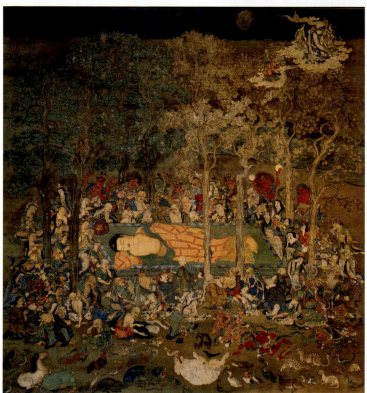

Death of the historical Buddha, Japan, Kamakura period (1185–1333)

The Buddha's passage into nirvana at the age of eighty (described in the *Mahaparinibbana Sutta*) is widely depicted in Buddhist art. In this fourteenth-century Japanese scroll painting of the famous scene, it is not the monks alone who have sorrowfully gathered around their teacher. Also present are gods who have descended from the heavens and the animals of the forest, all lamenting the passing of the enlightened one.

Taizokai mandala, Japan, 13th century

Central to the practice of tantric Buddhism is the mandala (literally, "circle"), representing an enlightened realm populated by buddhas and bodhisattvas, a realm to which the initiate seeks entry. Depicted here is the taizokai or "womb realm" mandala, one of the two chief mandalas of the Shingon sect of esoteric Buddhism in Japan. According to tradition, it was brought from China to Japan by Kukai, the central figure in the history of tantric Buddhism in Japan (see Kukai's *Benkenmitsu Nikyo Ron*).

Virupa, Tibet (Sakya monastery), 13th century

Among the most famous figures in the tantric traditions of India and Tibet are the *mahasiddhas*, or "great adepts"—those who achieve various supernatural powers through tantric practices. The great adepts are depicted here in a thirteenth-century Tibetan scroll painting. The central figure is the great adept Virupa (described in Abhayadatta's *Chaturashitisiddhapravritti*), in the famous scene in which he promises to pay his bar bill when the sun sets, and then stops it in its course across the sky.

JOHN BIGELOW TAYLOR

Tara, central Tibet, 12th century

Perhaps the most famous of the female bodhisattvas of Mahayana Buddhism is Tara, the female savior. She has two forms, white and green, and is depicted in her green form in this twelfth-century Tibetan painting. She is the embodiment of compassion, coming to the aid of those who recite her mantra (see "In Praise of the Twenty-One Taras"). She protects her devotees from eight different dangers, so she appears in eight different forms on the left and right. Above her are five buddhas; below her are protector deities.

THE WALTERS ART MUSEUM, BALTIMORE, PROMISED GIFT OF JOHN AND BERTHE FORD

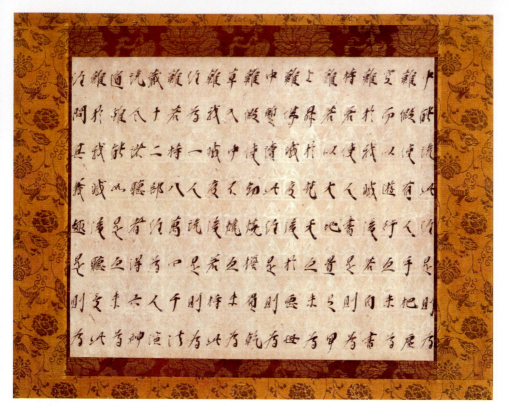

Section of a *Lotus Sutra* scroll, Japan, late Heian period (12th century)

A common element of the Mahayana sutras is advice that the devout should copy the sutra they are reading, and many elaborate copies of sutras are found in East Asia. One of the most copied scriptures is the *Lotus Sutra* (the *Saddharmapundarika*). In the eleventh chapter, a huge jeweled stupa emerges from the earth and floats in the air, revealing a living buddha inside. This twelfth-century Japanese scroll presents a passage from that chapter. It is said that each character of the *Lotus Sutra* is Buddha. Thus, here each character is silhouetted by a small stupa. SYLVAN BARNET AND WILLIAM BURTO COLLECTION / THE ART ARCHIVE AT ART RESOURCE, NY / © ARTRES

Figure of the Penitent Buddha, walking and holding a staff, Burmese school, ca. 1750

During his last days (described in the *Mahaparinibbana Sutta*), the Buddha likened his body to an old cart held together by scraps. Yet depictions of the Buddha, who died at the age of eighty, showing any sign of infirmity are relatively rare. Here, in a Burmese ivory statue formerly owned by Sigmund Freud, the aged Buddha walks with a stick. BURMESE SCHOOL / FREUD MUSEUM, LONDON, UK / THE BRIDGEMAN ART LIBRARY

Buddha's footprint, Burmese, 17th–18th century

The Buddha is said to have left his footprints in stone at a number of locations across Asia. These footprints are revered as signs of the Buddha's former presence in the world, and the image of a wheel on the sole of his foot is counted as one of his auspicious marks. In Southeast Asian Buddhism, the tradition developed of surrounding the wheel with 108 auspicious symbols, as in this sandstone carving. NATIONAL GALLERY OF AUSTRALIA, CANBERRA

Buddhists circumambulating the famous Bodhnath Stupa in Kathmandu, Nepal, 1997

The stupa takes many architectural forms throughout the Buddhist world, including the pagoda in China, Korea, and Japan. A traditional way that Buddhists pay homage to the Buddha is to walk around the stupa in a clockwise direction. PHOTO BY DON FARBER

Buddhist monks in Thailand receiving their daily meal from local villagers

Each monk carries his alms bowl, one of his few possessions. The Sanskrit term translated as "monk" in English literally means "beggar." Monks traditionally beg for their food each morning and, according to the monastic code, are not allowed to eat anything after noon on each day. Offering food to monks is a traditional way that Buddhist laypeople make merit for themselves and their families. PHOTO BY DON FARBER said that (18) those who by their own efforts have attained to supreme awakening—which is so difficult to attain—were previously gnats, flies, mosquitoes, and worms. (19) Then, how would I not attain it, I who have been born a human being, and who am able to distinguish good from evil? Why should I not be able to attain to awakening if I do not neglect the instructions of the all-knowing one?

(20) If what I fear is having to give up my hands, my feet, and my body, it must be that in my lack of judgment I confuse a minor and a greater evil. (21) I will be mutilated, hacked, burnt, cut again and again, for innumerable millions of cosmic ages, and still I will not attain awakening. (22) But the pains I now suffer, which lead to awakening, are limited. They are like the pain caused by the extraction of a thorn from the flesh, which prevents greater pain. (23) All physicians also heal by means of unpleasant treatments. Therefore, in order to get rid of the greater sorrow I should forbear the lesser pain.

(24) The best of physicians, however, does not follow this method of treatment, though it is customary among other physicians. He cures the greatest ailment by means of sweet remedies. (25) At first the Leader only asks us to give small things, such as a leaf of lettuce. Once this has been done, one should thereafter gradually give more until one gives of one's own flesh. (26) When one can think of one's own flesh as a lettuce leaf, then what would be difficult to do for this person who has relinquished flesh and bones? (27) Since he has given up sin he does not suffer any physical pains; because he is wise, he is not distressed in mind: for suffering arises in the mind due to false conceptualizations, and in the body on account of sin. (28ab) With merit the body finds ease, with wisdom the mind finds happiness.

(28cd) What could torment the compassionate one who remains in the cycle of migrations only for the sake of others? (29) As he annihilates his past sins and absorbs oceans of merit, by the sheer force of the thought of awakening the bodhisattva travels more swiftly than those who are mere disciples. (30) How could he be discouraged, this sage who moves in this way from bliss to bliss? I have obtained this chariot of the thought of awakening, which leaves behind all weariness and fatigue.

(31ab) To benefit all sentient beings one needs an army consisting of zeal, pride, joy, and renunciation.

(31cd) Zeal arises from fear of suffering, and by meditation on the benefits of virtue.

(32) Having uprooted in this manner the forces contrary to effort, one should endeavor to increase one's fortitude by using the armies of effort—zeal, pride, joy, renunciation—and by means of single-mindedness and self-mastery.

(33) The faults that I must conquer in myself and others are countless. The destruction of a single fault could take oceans of cosmic ages. (34) Yet, I do not see in myself even a fraction of the fortitude required to destroy these faults. (35) I must master many virtues for my own sake and the benefit of others. For the practice of a single virtue, oceans of cosmic ages would not suffice. (36) I have never practiced even the most insignificant virtue; I have lived in vain this rare birth as a human being, which I obtained with so much difficulty. (37) I have not had the joy of festivals dedicated to the blessed ones; I have not paid my respects to the teaching; I have not realized the hopes of the poor; (38) I have not offered a secure place to those who are in danger;

I have not given happiness to those who suffer. Like a thorn, I came into my mother's womb only to bring suffering. (39) I lacked in past lives the will to practice dharma, therefore now I have been born into such a miserable birth. Seeing this, who would abandon his determination to practice dharma?

(40) The Sage has said that zeal is the root of all virtue; and the root of this zeal is the constant contemplation of the eventual fruit of the ripening of our actions: (41) Wrongdoers will suffer pain, anguish, and fear of all kinds, and the frustration of all their desires. (42) Wherever may go the desires of those who practice what is good, there their own merit will honor them with the prize of its fruit. (43) On the other hand, wherever the evildoer's desire for happiness goes, there his own sins cut his body to pieces with the swords of sorrow. (44) Due to their good works, the sons of the sugatas are reborn before the eyes of the Sugata. Each son is born in the heart of a magnificent, fresh, perfumed lotus, whose splendor grows nourished by the sweet voice of the victorious conquerors. Each one is born with a perfect body when the lotus blooms, awakened by the rays of light emanating from the Buddha. (45) The doer of evil, on the other hand, due to his sins, will fall suddenly on the red-hot iron pavement of hell. He will cry in pain as he is skinned by Yama's henchmen, as his body is bathed in molten copper from the fires of hell, as his flesh is diced by hundreds of flaming swords and spears.

(46) Therefore, I should exercise my will in meritorious activities, having cultivated it zealously in this way. One should cultivate it by adopting pride as it is recommended in the *Vajradhvaja*.[3]

(47) First one should consider the circumstances, and then decide whether to go ahead or not. For it is better not to begin at all than to begin and then give up. (48) The habit will persist in future lives too, and the suffering resulting from sin will increase. Another worthy enterprise will be neglected, time and effort will be lost, and you will have not accomplished the task you had begun.

(49ab) One should show pride in three ways: with regard to action, with regard to the afflictions, and with regard to one's own capacity. (49cd) Pride with respect to action consists of this thought: "I will do it myself." (50) "This world, enslaved by the afflictions, is not capable of attaining its own good. Therefore, I will bring this good to the world; for I am not unable to do it, like the rest." (51) "How can I stand back and see another one performing menial tasks for me? If it is my pride that holds me back from carrying them out myself, then let my pride die!"

(52) A mere crow becomes the great eagle garuda[4] when it lands on a dead lizard. The most insignificant obstacle or lapse will defeat me if my spirit is weak. (53) Is it not easier to fall if you are paralyzed by dejection? But one who raises his spirit and remains active will be invincible even in the most unfavorable conditions. (54) Therefore, with the mind made firm I will bring down every occasion for falling. If I allow myself to be defeated by misfortune, my desire of conquering the three worlds is laughable.

(55) "I must conquer everything, I will not let anything conquer me." This is the only pride I should carry with me, for I am the son of the lion of conquerors. (56) Persons conquered by pride are miserable wretches, not proud

---

3. A Mahayana sutra.   4. A huge bird of Buddhist myth.

persons. The truly proud do not give in to their enemies. Those you regard as proud have given in to pride, their enemy. (57) Pride carries them to evil destinies, and even in this human life takes away all their joy. They live on the crumbs others give them, they behave like slaves, like fools, they become repugnant and emaciated. (58) Everywhere they go they are rejected, they are paralyzed by pride, tortured by it. If you count these among the proud, then tell me, who do you consider pitiful? (59) Truly proud, conquering heroes are only those who carry their pride in order to defeat pride, their enemy; they will attack pride, their enemy, aggressive as he is, and will display to the world the fruit of their conquest.

(60) In the midst of the host of the afflictions he will become a thousand times more arrogant, as invincible by the horde of the afflictions as a lion by a herd of deer. (61) Even in the most desperate situation the eye cannot perceive taste; in the same way, the bodhisattva will not submit to the afflictions no matter how desperate his position.

(62) Like a player desirous to win in his game, one should be completely dedicated to whatever task one has betaken oneself—rejoicing in it, ever insatiate.

(63) Works are carried out for the sake of happiness, whether happiness is finally obtained or not. How could he be happy without acting, he whose happiness is acting itself? (64) In the cycle of transmigration, we are not sated with sense pleasures, though they are like honey on the edge of a razor. Why should anyone ever be sated with the ambrosia of merit, which brings sweet fruits and peace? (65) Therefore, no sooner has one finished a task than he should proceed to the next, as an elephant tortured by the midday sun rushes in as soon as he finds a water hole. (66) If one is not suited to the task, the moment one realizes this, one should abandon it. And once a task has been completed, one should give it up for the one that will follow.

(67) Like someone engaged in a duel with a fierce enemy, one must guard oneself before the sword of the afflictions, with a mind to vanquish that enemy. (68) As one would pick up his sword with great fear, if it was dropped in the midst of battle, so, if one loses the sword of mindfulness, one will pick it up at once fearing the hells. (69) As poison, once it enters the bloodstream, will spread throughout the body, a vice that finds a weak spot will spread through the mind. (70) One who has adopted the vows should be like the man who was forced to carry a bowl filled to the rim with oil under threat of death if he spilled any. As he was watched by sword-bearing guards, he could think of nothing but that bowl, for fear of stumbling and dying. (71) Therefore, if one feels stupor and sloth approaching, one should react swiftly against them, as anyone would jump up if a snake fell on his lap. (72) Every time one stumbles, one should repent, reflecting: "How can I prevent a repetition of this?" (73) One should seek the company of friends in the path, and one should seek the opportunity to act with them, motivated by this reason: "How can I exercise mindfulness under these circumstances?"

(74) In this way one should prepare for action, keeping in mind the *Discourse on Watchfulness*, so that everywhere one will be ready even before the moment for action arises. (75) Like cotton, which in its movements is at the mercy of the wind, the bodhisattva speedily develops psychic powers if his thoughts and actions are subject to his will.

Chapter VIII. The Perfection in Meditation

(1) Having developed fortitude in this way, the bodhisattva should establish his mind in concentration, for a person whose mind is distracted is trapped in the jaws of the afflictions.

(2) Distraction is not possible in one whose body and mind are withdrawn. Therefore, one should renounce the world and abandon the inner discourse of desire.

(3) We are unable to give up the world because of clinging desire, accompanied with our thirst for possessions, fame, and the rest. Therefore, in order to give up this world, and one's ideas about it, the wise reflect as follows: (4) "One who is properly engaged in the cultivation of insight, accompanied by calm, will destroy the afflictions." Knowing this, one should first seek to have calm; and calm arises from equanimity before the delights of the world.

(5) Why should one impermanent being become attached to another impermanent being, since one will not see again one's beloved for a thousand lives? (6) For as long as one does not see the object of one's love, one will find no rest, and thus will not be able to establish concentration. But even if one does see the object of one's love, one is never sated, and thirst continues to oppress him as before. (7) Because of this insatiable desire of possessing the object of one's love, one does not perceive things as they are, one loses the uneasiness that would produce world-weariness, and one is consumed by grief. (8) Moment by moment, one wastes one's brief life in vain, obsessed by the object of one's love. One loses the perennial dharma because of a transient object.

(9) If you follow the conduct of fools, you will surely end in an evil destiny. If you do not behave like them, they will berate you. What do you stand to gain then by associating with fools? (10) In an instant they become your friends; in an instant they become your enemies. They become angry when they should be pleased. It is difficult to win over common people of the world. (11) If I talk to them about what is beneficial for them, they become impatient with me or lead me away from the good. But if I ignore them, they become offended, and by their anger are led to rebirth in evil destinies. (12) Jealous of those who are better than them, contentious with their equals, and arrogant toward their inferiors, praise makes them conceited, and censure makes them hostile. Does good ever come from the fool?

(13) Self-praise, censuring others, and idle talk about the pleasures of the cycle of transmigration, these are some of the demeritorious actions in which a fool who mixes with fools must engage. (14) One fool gets the same from the other. Accordingly, association with fools is association with misfortune. I will therefore live alone, in the open, my mind unaffected by the values of the world.

(15) One should avoid from afar the fool; but if one does meet a person of the world, one should try to please this person with gentle treatment, not in order to establish intimacy but with the neutrality of the sage. (16) As the bee takes only the nectar from flowers, I will take with me only what is essential for the practice of dharma, and I will live everywhere unknown, like the new moon.

(17) "I am a wealthy landowner. People have me in high regard. Many come looking for me." For one who thinks like this, there will be fear of sudden

death. (18) Wherever his mind, crazed by a false sense of happiness, finds enjoyment, there the object itself will become a source of a suffering a thousand times stronger than this pleasure. (19) Therefore, the wise do not want this kind of enjoyment. For fear will come to the person who wants it. But, should the same fear come of itself, the wise would remain firm and wait. (20) There have been many famous and wealthy men; of their wealth and fame we know no more. Where have they gone?

(21) Some despise me; why rejoice then when others praise me? Some praise me; why be dejected when others despise me? (22) Sentient beings have different inclinations. Not even the victorious conquerors could please them all, how much less an ignorant person like myself! Therefore, why should I be concerned with pleasing or displeasing the world? (23) They despise those who have nothing, and resent those who have everything. How can one find pleasure in associating with those whose company is only a source of suffering?

(24) "The fool is nobody's friend," the tathagatas have said, "because the fool gives no love without self-interest." (25) The love that enters through the door of self-interest is love only for one's self. It is like the distress we feel when we lose property, for this distress—like self-interested love—is wrought only by the fear of a loss of pleasure.

(26) Trees do not despise anyone, nor do they demand our devoted attention. When will I be able to live among them, whose company is a true source of happiness? (27) When will I go, free of worries, without looking back, to live under a tree, in an abandoned temple, or in a cave? (28) When will I live without settling anywhere, wandering freely in unclaimed, naturally spacious lands? (29) When will I live without fear, without cares for my body, carrying with me as all of my wealth an earthen bowl, and a robe that would not tempt a thief?

(30) When will I go to the charnel ground, my native land, to compare my own body, destined to decay, with the skeletons of others? (31) For this very body of mine will become so putrid that its stench will keep away even the jackals.

(32) Even these various bones, which are now part of one body, will be scattered; how much faster will be separated from us what is external to us, the object of our love. (33) Because the human being is born and dies alone, no one shares this pain. What good are loved ones, who are only an obstacle in the path? (34) As a traveler on the road stops over and stays as a guest, in the same way the one who travels on the road of existence stops over in various destinies.

(35) It would be better to leave for the forest before four men carry you away to your funeral, as your relatives watch and weep. (36) The renouncer, free from both attraction and revulsion, is nothing but this solitary body. Because he has died to the world long before his physical death, he does not grieve when the time of death arrives. (37) There will be no one around him to upset him with their weeping. There will be no one to distract him from his recollection of the Buddha, the dharma, and the other objects of recollection. (38) Therefore, I should always dedicate myself to this sweet solitude, where there is no anxious striving, where peace is born, where distractions are quelled.

(39) Free from any other concern, the mind having itself as its focus, I will dedicate all my energies to recollection and self-mastery. (40) For desires

bring misfortune in this and the next world—here, with prison, a violent death, or mutilation; there, with hell or another evil destiny.

(41) This is the body for which you repeatedly paid homage to your go-betweens, the body for whose sake you have ignored both sin and disgrace. (42) For it you risked your life and spent your fortune. Here are the bones whose embrace gave you supreme pleasure. (43) These are the same bones, not others. They are now free, without an owner. Why will you not find pleasure in embracing them now that you can do it freely? (44) This is the face you sometimes would see when at great pains you could get her to look up, for her face always looked down bashfully; but sometimes you could not see it, for it was once hidden by a veil. (45) This same face is now unveiled by vultures as if they could not bear your longing. Look at it. Why do you now turn away? (46) The same face you used to protect from the glances of others, now is being devoured by others. Why don't you, who were so jealous before, now come to its rescue?

(47) Upon seeing this mass of flesh devoured by vultures and jackals, you will understand that your gifts of garlands, jewels, and perfumes prepared a feast for others.

(48) If you tremble now like this when you see an unmoving skeleton, why are you not scared when one spirit or another moves the skeleton of a living person? (49) When it is covered by flesh it moves you to passion; why is it unattractive to you once it is uncovered? If you truly did not care for it, why did you caress it when it was covered?

(50) Saliva and feces have the same source—food. If you find feces repugnant, why do you find pleasure in swallowing your own saliva? (51) Lecherous humans, obsessed with impurity, cannot find peace on their cotton pillows, soft though they may be, because they do exude the stench of the human body. (52) If impurity displeases you, why do you embrace someone who is a frame of bones held together by tendons and plastered with the mortar of flesh? (53) You yourself are full of impurities. Be satisfied with these, if you are so eager to enjoy impurity. Forget other bags of filth.

(54) You say you desire this flesh. And you want to see and feel it. Why do you want to touch and feel that whose nature is to be unconscious? (55) The mind in this body you crave for cannot be seen or felt. The body which you can see and feel takes notice of nothing. Why do you embrace it, oh fool? (56) There is nothing surprising in that you cannot see that somebody else's body is made of impurities, but it is amazing that you cannot see that yours is so made. (57) What pleasure can you find in a box of filth, your mind drunk with impurity, that you will even ignore a tender lotus blooming under a sun in cloudless sky?

(58) You refuse to touch the ground or any object tainted by feces; why do you seek to touch the body whence it came? (59) If you feel so much disgust toward impurities, why do you embrace the body, which was conceived and gestated in a bag of impurities? (60) You find repulsive the impure maggot that grows in feces. Is it only because it is so small? After all, you are attracted by a body which is also born from and made of impurities. (61) Lover of filth, not only are you not repulsed by your own impurity, you look for other receptacles of filth.

(62) People think that even things that are otherwise agreeable or savory, such as camphor, rice, and spices, will pollute the ground if they are vomited or spit out.

(63) But if you are still not convinced of the impurity of your own body, evident though it is, contemplate the corpses of others in the charnel ground. (64) Since the body deprived of its skin and flesh gives you such horror, how could you, having seen it in this state, take pleasure in it now that it is alive?

(65) If you sense a pleasant smell on a human body, it must be only sandal,[5] not the body's own odor. Why do you feel passion for one thing because another arouses you? (66) Would it not be more reasonable not to feel passion for what is in itself malodorous? Why is it that human beings will smear it with perfume, so fond of something they really do not like? (67) Is it in any way changed because sandal is inherently aromatic? Why are you made to feel passion for one thing because you like the perfume of another? (68) The body in a natural state would be terrifying: a naked body, covered with mud and dung, with long nails and long hair, the teeth crooked and yellow. (69) Why care for it as one would care for the sword one will use to commit suicide? This earth is full of madmen who work at deceiving themselves. (70) If you see skeletons in the charnel ground they will surely frighten you. Yet, you are aroused by bodies in the village, a charnel ground of moving skeletons.

(71) Though it is so impure the body is not obtained without paying a price. For this body we suffer the anxiety of ambition and the torments of hell. (72) As babies we are not capable of earning and accumulating wealth; how could we then secure happiness in our youth? Youth is spent in acquiring wealth. But once old age arrives, what will we do with the pleasures wealth will buy?

(73) Some men of ambition will wear themselves out in their daily tasks only to return home at nightfall, and collapse in bed like corpses. (74) Others set out with military expeditions, suffering the pains and privations of life away from their homes. For years on end they do not see the wife and children for whom they are sacrificing themselves. (75) They do not even reach the goal for which they have sold themselves, blinded by passion. Their life is spent in vain serving others. (76) Others sell themselves to masters, who impose on them tasks in faraway places; their wives will give birth in the jungle or desert. (77) Others make a living by risking their lives on the battlefield. Their own pride drives them to slavery—fools deceived by their passions. (78) Moved by passion, they end up mutilated, or impaled on spears; one also sees them burnt to death, or pierced by lances. (79) Understand that fortune is nothing but unending misfortune, because of the despair that comes with acquiring, keeping and losing it. Those who cling obsessively to wealth do not allow themselves the opportunity of seeking liberation from the pains of existence. (80) These are the long miseries of passionate humans, but their happiness is brief. They are like the beast of burden hauling a cart for only a mouthful of hay.

(81) For this mouthful of happiness—which even a beast can easily obtain—the human being who is confused by his fate loses the auspicious moment which is so difficult to obtain. (82) These are the struggles one engages in through time for the sake of this insignificant and ephemeral body—which will necessarily fall to hell and the other evil destinies. (83) With one-millionth part of this effort one could obtain the condition of an Awakened One. Though the sufferings of those who are possessed by passion are much greater than the struggles of the path, such suffering will not

5. That is, sandalwood.

bring about awakening. (84) Swords, poison, fire, precipices, and enemies cannot be compared in their capacity to do harm to sensual desire, if one is mindful of the tortures of hell and the other evil destinies.

(85) Therefore, you should fear passions, and should delight in the solitude of a serene forest, free from contentions and strivings. (86) Blessed are those who, concerned only for the welfare of others, stroll on lovely pavements of mountain rock, broad like palace terraces, refreshed by the sandal of the moon's rays, fanned by the gentle, silent blowing of the forest breeze. (87) Dwelling anywhere, for as long as one likes, in a deserted spot, under a tree, in a cave, free from the fatigue of acquiring and keeping property, one wanders at will, even-minded and detached. (88) Even the god Indra[6] would not be able to attain the satisfaction and happiness enjoyed by one who wanders homeless at his own pleasure, bound to no one.

(89) After cultivating the virtues of solitude and mental collectedness in these ways, having brought the discursive mind to calm, one should cultivate the thought of awakening.

(90) First one should cultivate diligently the identification of self and others: "We all are equally subject to pain and pleasure; therefore, I must protect all beings as I protect myself." (91) Just as one should take care of his body as if it were one single entity, though it is made of many separate parts—such as the hands, the feet, etc.—it should be the same toward the whole world, which, though divided into individual beings, is undivided in experiencing suffering and happiness. (92) My suffering is not oppressive to other embodied beings, still it is suffering, made unbearable because of my self-love; (93) in the same way, although I do not feel the suffering of others, it is nevertheless suffering, made unbearable because of their self-love. (94) I should put an end to the suffering of others because it is as much suffering as my own suffering. I should be kind to others because they are living beings like myself. (95) If others and myself find happiness equally desirable, then what makes me so special, that I should eagerly seek happiness only for myself? (96) If others and myself find fear and sorrow equally undesirable, then what makes me so special, that I should protect myself, not others? (97) If you do not try to remove the suffering of others because you reason "this sorrow does not oppress me," then why should you try to avoid the pains that will afflict your body in a future life? (98) You may think, "at that time it will be myself suffering," but these are only vain imaginings, for the person who dies is not the same person who is reborn. (99) If you think that only one's own suffering should be avoided, then given that the foot's pains are not the hand's, how come the latter protects the former? (100) You may claim that your position, though inconsistent, is maintained because of our innate sense of an ego; but this inconsistency should be rejected as much as possible, in oneself as in others.

(101) The chain or aggregate of phenomena that we call "myself" is only deceptively real, like a line of ants or a marching army. There is no one to possess sorrow; therefore, who can call sorrow his own? (102) All sorrow without exception lacks a possessor. It is only because sorrow is sorrow that it should be avoided; why do you imagine then that the sorrow you must allay is limited to your own?

6. King of the gods.

An Objector Interjects: (103ab) Why should one avoid sorrow at all then?

The Author Replies: (103cd) Because all beings agree on wanting to avoid it. If it is to be avoided it should all be avoided in the same way. If it is not to be avoided, then it should not be avoided for oneself also, as much as for other sentient beings.

An Objector Interjects: (104ab) Compassion brings much suffering; why should it be so consciously cultivated?

The Author Replies: (104cd) Compared to the suffering of the world, how could the pain of compassion be regarded as so great? (105) If suffering of the many can be suppressed with the suffering of one individual, then the latter suffering should be fostered by one who feels sympathy for himself and others. (106) This is why Supushpachandra,[7] for the sake of many suffering beings, did not try to prevent his own suffering, though he knew the danger of incurring the king's wrath.

(107) The bodhisattvas, who have cultivated this chain of phenomena that we call "myself," and for whom the most extreme sorrow is the same as pleasure, descend into the Avichi hell like swans diving into a lotus pond. (108) Those who become oceans of joy whenever living beings attain liberation, have they not achieved thereby the highest bliss? Why would they want the tasteless liberation of individual salvation? (109) Then, though they do everything for the sake of others, they feel no pride, show no arrogance, they have no desire for the fruit or maturation of their actions. They act, moved solely by a thirst for the well-being of others.

(110) Therefore, as I would protect myself from all evil, I will think only of care and sympathy toward others.

(111) Although there is no such thing as "myself," by the force of habit I come to perceive a self in these drops of semen and blood, which are other than myself. (112) Why don't I perceive in the same manner my self in the body of another sentient being? It should not be difficult, as it has been established that even my own body is other than myself. (113) By recognizing that I have many faults, while others are oceans of virtue, I should give up completely the self, and practice adopting others as my self. (114) Recognizing one's own faults, and the oceans of virtues possessed by others, one cultivates the practice of giving up one's own self to take the place of another. (115) If by the force of habit the notion of a self is produced with respect to this body, which has no self, then why not produce by the force of habit the notion of a self with respect to other sentient beings?

(116) Thus, even while working to attain the objectives of other sentient beings, there will be no arrogance or pride. It is as if one did not expect any recompense from others, because it is one's self that is already enjoying the fruits. (117) Therefore, in the same way that you seek to protect yourself from pain and grief, you should develop an attitude of care and sympathy toward the world. (118) This is why the protector Avalokiteshvara[8] has established his own name even as a means for people to gain confidence in the public assembly. (119) You should not turn back in the face of obstacles, because the power of practice is such that in the end you will find pleasure only in that loss of self, the mention of which was so terrifying before.

7. A bodhisattva executed by an evil king for teaching the dharma.

8. The bodhisattva who embodies compassion.

(120) Whoever seeks to rapidly rescue himself and others should practice the supreme mystery of placing yourself in the position of another. (121) Due to an excessive attachment to the self, we fear the most insignificant dangers. Who would not hate this self, who, like an enemy, only brings fear to our heart? (122) It is the self who in its attempt to resist weakness, hunger, thirst, and the like brings death to birds, fishes, and land animals, and stands as an enemy against the world. (123) It is the self who for the sake of gain and honor will bring death even to his own parents, who would steal what belongs to the Three Jewels, and thereby become fuel for the fires of the Avichi hell. (124) What wise man would seek to protect or pay his respects to this self and would not see it as an enemy? Who would have a high regard for it? (125) "If I give, what will I eat?"—this selfishness will turn you into an ogre. "If I eat, what will I give?"—this generosity will make you King of the Gods. (126) The one who oppresses another for self-interest will be cooked in the hells. The one who suffers oppression for the sake of others will obtain all perfections. (127) The same desire to exalt oneself that would lead to evil rebirth, low social status, and stupidity can lead to good rebirth, honor, and wisdom, if it is transferred into another. (128) One who makes another work for him without due compensation will suffer slavery and other forms of oppression in his next life. One who works for another will enjoy lordship and other advantages. (129) All those who live in torment in this life suffer only because of their desire for happiness. All those who live in happiness are in such a condition because of their wish to make others happy. (130) But why say more? Simply compare these two: the fool who seeks only his own welfare, and the sage who seeks only to benefit others. (131) Whoever fails to replace his own pleasure with the suffering of others will not reach, of course, the station of the awakened, but neither will he know happiness even in this cycle of transmigration. (132) What is more, even if you leave aside future lives, even in this life if the servant did not carry out his work or if the lord did not pay him the salary that is due to him, no visible results would obtain. (133) Instead of working for the only thing that brings happiness in this and the next world, that is, to give happiness one to another, deluded beings embrace the most horrible pains in order to harm one another.

(134) Whatever calamities, pains, and fears there are in this world, they all are due to grasping at the self. What will I gain by grasping at it in this manner? (135) If one does not abandon the self, one cannot abandon sorrow, as one cannot escape being burned if one does not avoid fire. (136) Therefore, in order to quell my own suffering and that of others, I surrender myself to others, and adopt them as my self. (137) "I belong to others": let this be your conviction, oh my mind. From now on you will have no other concern than the benefit of all sentient beings. (138) Now that I am the other person, my eyes belong to another; they cannot see after my own interests; my hands are his; they cannot possibly work for my own interest. (139) Therefore, being concerned only with other beings, whatever you might see in this your body that may be of value to them, you should take away from yourself and use it to benefit others. (140) If you place yourself in the position of others, even the lowliest, and place them in your self, you may cultivate envy without regret.

(141) "They give him great honors, but I do not receive such honor. He is rich and I am not. He is praised, they despise me. I suffer, he is happy.

(142) I work, but he rests in perfect ease. He is exalted among the people. I am a poor wretch, for I have no virtue of my own. (143) But, is there really someone without virtue? All have some degree of virtue. I am inferior to some, but there are some who are my inferiors. (144) If my moral character and understanding are limited, it is not my fault. It is due to the afflictions. I wish to put an end to this disease. I will accept whatever pains this will require. (145) But if he considers me incurable, why does he still despise me? Why should I then envy his virtue, since his virtue is only selfishness in disguise? (146) He feels no compassion for a human being in the jaws of the wild animals of hell; yet, because of his self-righteousness, he believes he can surpass the wise. (147) If he finds someone he regards as a match for him, he tries to gain some advantage over him, trying to increase fame and fortune through argumentation. (148) Let my own virtues be known in the world. May no one ever hear of his good qualities. (149) Let my defects be hidden from the world, that I may receive all the honor, and he none. Then I will gain wealth easily. I, and not he, will be admired by all. (150) I will enjoy seeing him mistreated, for a change. I will enjoy seeing him despised and insulted. (151) How dare he, this poor wretch, try to compare himself with me. Does he have my erudition, my wisdom, my noble birth, my beauty and wealth? (152) When I hear people praising my virtues everywhere, I will be ecstatic with joy. It will give me the sweetest pleasure. (153) If he has any wealth, I will take it by force, and give him only what he needs to survive, if he agrees to work for me. (154) He should be driven out of his complacency, and forever be placed in charge of my worries. For I have suffered because of him the pains of transmigration hundreds of times."

(155) You have wasted innumerable cosmic cycles in search of your own happiness. Yet, despite this enormous effort, you have achieved nothing but suffering. (156) Follow my advice right away. You will later see the advantages of this practice, for the Sage's words are true. (157) If you had put this into practice before, you would not be in your present predicament—to say nothing of the wasted opportunity of attaining the happiness and virtue of the state of awakening. (158) Therefore, in the same way that you constructed a sense of I with regard to drops of blood and semen that were not really yours, imagine your sense of self in other beings. (159) Becoming a thief for others, steal whatever you see of value in your own body, and use it to benefit others. (160) "He is happy; I suffer. He is exalted; I am rejected. He lives in ease; I have to work hard"—develop in this way your envy against yourself. (161) Drive yourself out of your complacency, and place yourself in charge of his suffering. Observe the devious ways of the self: "When does it do what?" (162) Let this self assume responsibility for the faults of others. Its own transgressions, however insignificant, you should confess to the Great Sage. (163) Cast aspersion on the self's reputation by promoting the reputation of others. Force it to work for the sake of sentient beings, like a poor slave. (164) It is made of defects, so it should not be praised for an occasional virtue. If it should have any virtue, act in such a way that no one finds out about it. (165) In brief, whatever harm you have brought upon others, out of self-interest, now bring it upon yourself in the interest of other living beings.

(166) You should not grant the self any power, because it will want to order you around. Make it act like a newly wed bride: bashful, timid, reserved.

(167) "Do this. Stop. Don't do that"—in this way should you submit it to your will and restrain it if it oversteps its bounds. (168) "If you do not do this when commanded to do so, oh mind, I will force you to do it. You are the reason for all my vices." (169) "Where are you going? I can see you. I will smite your arrogance. We are no more in those former times when I was led to perdition by you." (170) "Give up forthwith all hope that you may still today be of any interest to me. I sold you to others, indifferent to all the fatigue and distress that would be yours." (171) "If out of carelessness I had not delivered you to sentient beings, you would have turned me in to the guardians of hell. I have no doubt of this." (172) "You have done it many times before? For long I have suffered because of you. Remembering our mutual enmity, I will now destroy you, the servant of self-interest."

(173) Therefore, if you want to love yourself, do not love yourself. And, if you want to protect yourself, you should not protect yourself. (174) The more you try to care for your body, the more sensitive it becomes, and the more times it falls in the cycle of transmigration. (175) But no matter how many times it is reborn, the whole earth will not be enough to satisfy its desires. Who then will meet its wishes? (176) By seeking to achieve the impossible—satisfaction in the world—you come to face afflictions and hopelessness. But he who has no expectations with regard to anything will have undecaying happiness. (177) Therefore, one should not cultivate sensual desires. The truly good cannot be grasped in terms of desire.

(178) In the end the body will turn to ashes. Moved by another, it has no movement of its own, this loathsome, impure image. Why do I hold on to it? (179) Of what use to me is this machine, whether it is alive or dead? In what way is it any better than a clod of earth? Why don't you die, oh my sense of self! (180) My partiality toward my body has been to no avail, it has brought me only suffering. What good would it do to love or hate this body, which is only like a dead tree trunk? (181) I have protected it, the vultures and the jackals will devour it, yet it does not love me and it does not hate them. Why should I love it so? (182) I become incensed when it is treated harshly, I am delighted when it is pampered; but if the body itself knows nothing, for whose sake are all my travails? (183) We often think that our true friends are those who care for this body of ours; but everybody cares for their own bodies. Why are they not dear to me? (184) Therefore, I renounce my body without regret, for the benefit of the whole world. If after this I maintain it in spite of its many defects, it is only as an instrument of action.

(185) Enough with the life-paths of the world. I will follow the wise, keeping in mind the *Discourse on Watchfulness*, avoiding sloth and torpor. (186) Therefore, in order to cut through the veils, I will collect my mind, pulling it away from wayward paths, fixing it on the true object.

Chapter IX. The Perfection of Discernment

(1) The Great Muni[9] has taught that one gathers all this equipment of virtues for the sake of wisdom. Therefore, if one seeks nirvana and happiness, one should also develop wisdom.

---

9. Sage (i.e., the Buddha).

(2) Ultimate and conventional truth—truth is thus twofold. The Ultimate does not fall within the scope of intellection. Intellection itself is called "conventional truth."

(3) With respect to these truths the world is divided into two types of persons: yogins and common humans. The vision of yogins invalidates that of common humans.

(4) Yogins in turn can be invalidated by the superior mental faculties of other yogins who have advanced higher in the path. Yet they agree on the similes that describe reality, and therefore do not differ on the goal they seek.

(5) Their dispute with the world stems from the fact that the common human perceives phenomena by reifying them, and not by seeing them as magical creations.

(6) It is well established that perception—of visual objects, etc.—is not a reliable means of knowledge. For instance, the common perception of purity in objects that are impure is clearly false.

(7a–c) The Protector spoke of entities in the process of becoming only as an introduction for the common human into ultimate truth. In reality these entities are not even impermanent.

An Objector Interjects: (7d) But if this is true only from the point of view of conventional reality, then there is a contradiction in presenting impermanence as contradicting the idea of a self-existing entity.

The Author Replies: (8) There is in this no error. According in the yogins' view of conventional reality things are in fact impermanent. Compared to common humans, even the conventional reality of the yogins is a vision of a higher reality. Otherwise, your position with regard to the examination of the impurity of a woman would be contradicted by the common man's perception of her as a pure object.

An Objector Interjects: (9a) Then, buddhas also must be like phantoms. How can one derive merit from worshipping the Victorious Conqueror if he is like a magical creation?

The Author Replies: (9b) In the same manner, how could you derive merit from this even if he were a real entity?

An Objector Interjects: (9cd) If living beings are like magical creations, how can they be reborn after death?

The Author Replies: (10) Magical creations also subsist for as long as there are certain collocations of conditions. Why should you assume that a living being is more real than a magical creation simply because the series of phenomena that you identify with it lasts much longer?

An Objector Interjects: (11ab) There would be no sin in murdering a phantom man, since there is no human mind in it.

The Author Replies: (11cd) But as long as the phantom is associated with the magical illusion of a mind, there will be sin and virtue.

An Objector Interjects: (12ab) A magically generated mind is an impossibility, for there are no magical techniques—formulae, etc.—that can effectively produce a mind.

The Author Replies: (12cd) The magical phenomena we speak of are of a variety of types, and they arise from a variety of causes and conditions. (13ab) One single condition is not sufficient to effectively produce anything under any circumstance.

An Objector Interjects: (13cd) If beings are already in the peace of nirvana, from the absolute point of view, and transmigrate from the point of view of conventional reality only, (14ab) then the Buddha transmigrates too! What is the purpose, then, of the practices that lead to awakening?

The Author Replies: (14cd) Magical creations do not cease while the series of conditions that produce them persists without interruption; (15ab) but once the series of conditions is cut off, the phantom arises no more, even in a conventional sense. . . .

An Objector Interjects: (15cd) But if the mistaken mind does not exist either, then who apprehends the illusion?

The Author Replies: (16ab) If, as you claim, the illusion itself does not exist, what is apprehended by the mind?

The Objector Replies: (16cd) The illusory object is a representation of the errant mind itself, although, in terms of its reality, it is different from the mind.

The Author Replies: (17) If the illusion is nothing but mind, then what is perceived by what? Furthermore, the World Protector has declared that the mind does not perceive the mind. (18ab) "The mind cannot see itself any more than the blade of a sword can cut itself."

* * *

(26) We do not reject things as they are given to us by perception, tradition, or reason. But we do reject the notion that the mind's capacity for generating imagined realities is the cause of sorrow in any substantial sense. (27) If you affirm that illusion is nothing different from the mind, we say it is something totally different from the mind. If you say it is a real entity, we ask "how can it not be a separate reality?" If you say it is the the same as the mind, it can have no reality as an independent entity. (28ab) As the illusion, though unreal, is perceived, so the mind, though unreal, is capable of perceiving. . . .

An Objector Interjects: (31) In the same manner, if you take everything to be like a magical illusion, how will the afflictions ever cease, for even the wonder-worker who creates a phantom woman will feel passion for her.

The Author Replies: (32) In this case, the creator of the phantom has not abandoned the habitual tendency to experience things as real objects and experience afflictive states of mind; consequently, when he perceives the phantom woman, he still has not reached the point where emptiness permeates all his experiences.

(33) If one is infused with the concept of emptiness, the habitual belief in being disappears. Then, by cultivating the idea that neither of these two exists, in the end even the idea of emptiness is abandoned. (34) When one no longer apprehends an entity that one could conceive as not existing, then all being has lost its ground. How could it appear before the mind again? (35) When neither being nor no-being appears any more before the mind, then, having nowhere to go, deprived of its support, the mind is calmed.

* * *

An Objector Interjects: (76ab) If there are no living beings, for whom will we feel compassion?

The Author Replies: (76cd) For sentient beings conceived by a special delusion of mind, which is maintained for the sake of our goal.

An Objector Interjects: (77a) But a goal for whom, if there are no beings?

The Author Replies: (77b–d) It is true that this idea of a goal arises from a delusion; but since it will bring to an end all sorrow, this delusion of the goal should not be rejected. (78) On the other hand, self-centeredness, the cause of sorrow, is intensified by the delusion of selfhood. Since this delusion keeps us from opposing self-centeredness, it is better to cultivate its opposite, selflessness.

(79) The body is not the feet, or the legs, or the thighs, the hips, the abdomen, the back, the chest, or the arms. (80) It is not the hands, nor the sides of the body; nor is it the armpits, the shoulders, the neck, or the head. Which one among these parts is the body? (81) If the body is present in part in all of these, then each part would be in every part, but where then would the whole body itself be? (82) If the body is present in its totality in every part—such as in the hands, etc.—then there would be as many bodies as there are hands and other bodily parts. (83) The body is not internal, nor is it external to the person; how could it be in the various parts of the body? But it does not exist apart from them. How then is it to exist at all? (84) There is no body, but through an illusion one forms the mental representation of a body with respect to the hands and the rest, because of a specific conjunction of conditions, as when one sees a person where there is only a post through the effects of fog or darkness.

(85) As long as there is a certain collocation of conditions, the body is perceived as a person. In the same way, if the hands and other bodily members are in a certain collocation, one sees them as a human body. (86) In the same way, one may ask: in the ensemble of toes and bones, where is the foot? The foot also comes to be by the collocation of joints and bones, and these members in turn can be analyzed into their own minute parts.

(87) Each of these parts can be further broken down into atoms, and each atom can be divided according to the ten directions. But each of these ten sides is empty space, because it is indivisible. Therefore, the atom does not exist. (88) In this way, form is like a dream. Who could feel passion for it, once he has examined it correctly? If the body is not, then who is female, who is male?

(89) If pain exists as a real entity, why is it that it does not afflict us at the same time that we feel pleasure? If pleasure really exists, why is it that one who is tortured by grief finds no pleasure in the most delicious dish? (90) If you propose that the weaker sensation cannot be experienced when it is overpowered by the stronger sensation, why call sensation what cannot be experienced? . . .

(93) . . . This analysis is practiced as a counteragent to habitual misconceptions. For yogins find their sustenance in those states of meditation that grow in the soil of our past misconceptions.

(94) If an interval of space separates the sense organ from its object, then how can there be contact between the two? Again, if there is no interval, they are one thing; how could there be a meeting of the two? (95) It is not that one atom enters into another; for atoms do not occupy space, and are all alike. But without penetration there is no union, and without union there is no contact. (96) Moreover, how can there be any contact between two things that have no parts? If you know of instances of indivisibility in entities that meet in contact, show them to me!

(97) It is also unreasonable to assume that consciousness, which is immaterial, can make contact with the object. Nor is it possible for a collection of atomic particles to have contact among themselves, since their insubstantiality has been demonstrated previously.

(98ab) Therefore, if in this way contact is inexistent, how would sensations be possible?

(98cd) If this is so, why do we persist in suffering? Who is oppressed by what? (99) If there is no experiencer of sensations, and no sensations, then, seeing that such is your nature, oh thirst, why do you not vanish?

*   *   *

(103) Mind does not reside in the sense organs, in their objects, or in the space in between them. Mind is not inside, outside, nor anywhere else. (104) That which is not found in the body, nor elsewhere, nor in both places at the same time or separately, is nothing at all. Therefore, sentient beings are by nature in the state of perfect peace.

(105) If cognition existed before the cognizable object arose, then by depending on what object did the cognition come into existence? If cognition arose simultaneously with its object, by depending on what object did it come into existence? (106ab) But, again, if it appeared after its object, then whence did this cognition arise?

(106cd) In the same manner one cannot apprehend any arising in any thing whatsoever.

An Objector Interjects: (107) If this is so, conventional reality does not exist. Where do you find then a twofold truth? If you claim that conventional reality does exist in the sense that the "reality" contradicted by knowledge of absolute truth is still the object of a conventional cognition of another person, then how could any living being ever attain the peace of nirvana?

The Author Replies: (108) This "living being" is only a conceptual construct in the mind of some other being who is not liberated, but for the one who has attained supreme peace he does not exist even in terms of his own conventional cognitions. For him the only conventional reality there is must be expressed thus: "If this is, that will be; if this is not, that will not be."

(109) Conceptualization and that which is constructed by it are mutually dependent. We present our critique by relying exclusively on things as they are commonly perceived.

An Objector Interjects: (110) But if your critique is based on the same arguments that you criticize, then your conclusion is groundless, insofar as your critique would also be its own critique.

The Author Replies: (111) When the object of our critique has been shown to be false, the discursive faculty has no basis whatsoever. Because it is baseless, it arises no more, and this is called peace, "nirvana." (112) On the other hand, the one who holds that these two, the imagination of discursive thought and its objects, are real, stands on very unstable ground: If the reality of the object depends on the capacity of knowledge to establish it, how does one establish the reality of knowledge? (113) If, on the contrary, knowledge depends on the known object for its reliability, how does one establish the reality of the object to begin with? Finally, if they mutually establish each other's reality, then both would be equally unreal.

* * *

An Objector Interjects: (139) If the validity of all sources of knowledge is denied, then would it not follow that all objects of human knowledge are false? Therefore, in an ultimate sense the emptiness of all entities cannot be established.

The Author Replies: (140) If one does not hold on to the reality of the imagined entity, then one does not grasp at its unreality. Therefore, the nonexistence of an entity that is unreal is itself clearly unreal. (141) If one dreams that one's son has died, the notion that he is no more replaces the notion of his existence. But the new conception, derived from the dream, is also false.

(142) In light of all of the above arguments, we conclude that nothing comes about without a cause, and that nothing is found preexisting in its conditions, whether taken separately or jointly. (143) Nothing comes from elsewhere, nothing remains, nothing goes elsewhere. What difference is there between a magical creation and this that the foolish imagine to be real?

(144) One must carefully examine this matter: what is fashioned by magical trickery and what is fashioned by causes, whence has it arisen, where is it going to? (145) That which we see in the presence of other phenomena, and which we do not see when they are absent, in what sense is this real, since it is artificially created and sustained, like the reflection in a mirror?

(146) What use does the already-existing entity have for causes? But, then, again, what use does the not-yet-existing have for them? (147) No change occurs in what is not existing, even through the agency of hundreds of millions of causes. How could something in such a state become a real entity? Yet, what other thing could come into existence?

(148) If there is no existence at the time of its inexistence, at what point in time does an entity come into existence? For, non-existence cannot be displaced as long as the entity has not come into existence, (149) and it is impossible for the entity to occur as long as non-existence has not been displaced. The existing entity cannot participate in non-existence, because this would lead to the absurd conclusion of two natures in one entity. (150) Thus, nowhere is there cessation, nowhere is there existence. Therefore, all this universe is unborn, without cessation. (151) By extension of this analysis all the stations of sentient beings are like dreams, similar to the stem of the banana plant.[1] In reality there is no difference between those who have attained the peace of nirvana and those who have not.

(152) Thus, among empty phenomena what can be gained, or lost? Who will be honored or despised, by whom? (153) Whence will come pleasure and sorrow? What is pleasure? What is thirst? If one seeks for its intrinsic reality, where will one find thirst? (154) Upon close examination, what is this world of the living? Who dies in it? Who is born? Who existed before? Who has a relative? Who is a friend?

---

1. The banana tree has no heartwood or essence; when its layers are peeled away, nothing is left.

(155ab) Let those who are like myself understand that all this is like empty space. (155cd) Arguments irritate us, joys excite us. (156) With grief, striving, and despondency, we, cutting and poking at each other, go to great pains to consume ourselves with sin while seeking our own pleasure. (157) Upon dying, we fall into the evil destinies, where we undergo long and painful torments. At times we return to good births, only to become used to brief pleasure. (158) In the cycle of becoming there are many falls—yet there is in it nothing real as such. Thus there is only this mutual contradiction. There is nothing real as such.

(159) Still there are endless oceans of sorrow, unimaginable, terrifying. In this world a sentient being's strength is limited, its life brief. (160) Swiftly and in vain life is carried away by one's concern with keeping in health and alive, by hunger, disease, and fatigue, by sleep, by calamities, and by fruitless association with the foolish. (161) Under these circumstances it is difficult to attain a discriminating mind. How is one to gain access to the practice of restraining the habit of distraction? (162) Here also is Mara[2] engaged in bringing about our fall into evil destinies. Here confusion is invincible, for the wrong paths are many.

(163) Moreover, it is difficult to attain the right occasion, extremely difficult to come upon the time of a living buddha, and it is almost impossible to detain the torrent of the afflictions. Thus, alas, comes to be this endless chain of sorrow.

(164) Alas! Only grief is reserved for those who are carried away by this torrent of sorrow—those who fail to perceive their own painful condition, and thus fall into even more painful states. (165) Like a madman who would step on burning coals after every bath to make himself warm, these beings think that they are achieving their own happiness even as they stand in the midst of sorrow. (166) They behave with the concern of someone who is never to age or die. Yet they will come to terrible calamities, beginning with death.

(167) Oh, when will I bring calm to those who are burnt by the fire of suffering, by offering, for the sake of their happiness, my own acts of service, raining down from clouds of merit? (168) When will I avail myself of the language of convention in order to teach emptiness to those who still perceive a real object of clinging? And when will I be able to teach them with dedication how to gather merit without relying on an object of clinging?

Chapter X. Dedication of Merit

(1) May the merit I have obtained by composing this *Introduction to the Practice of the Bodhisattva's Path* transform all sentient beings, adorning them with the conduct of the bodhisattva. (2) Those who in every corner of the universe suffer torments of mind and body, may they find oceans of joy and happiness, through the power of my merit. (3) May these living beings never lose this happiness for as long as they remain in the cycle of transmigration. May the world enjoy without interruption the bliss of the bodhisattvas.

(4) May all embodied beings in the different hells in all the world realms enjoy the happiness and the joys of the Land of Bliss. (5) May those who suffer cold be granted warmth. May those who suffer heat be refreshed by

---

2. The personification of evil and desire.

streams of water that pour down from those prodigious clouds, the bodhisatt-vas. (6) May the forest of sword-leafed trees of hell acquire the splendid qualities of the heavenly Nanda forest, and the thorn brushes of hell turn into Indra's wish-fulfilling trees. (7) May the very center of hell resound with the song of sandpipers, drakes, wild ducks, and wild geese, and be filled with ponds adorned with perfumed lotus blossoms. (8) May the burning coal mounds of hell turn into mounds of jewels, the red-hot pavements into cool crystal, and the grinding mountain millstones of hell become heavenly palaces worthy of adoration, the abode of so many buddhas. (9) Let the rain of red-hot stones, coals, and swords turn into a rain of flowers. Let the sword battles of the asura demons turn into playful jousts with swords of flowers. (10) May the merit I have gained serve those who, as their bodies lose their flesh turning to blanched skeletons, descend into the boiling currents of Vaitarani, the river of Hades. May each one of them gain a celestial body in Mandakini, the Ganges of the heavens, and live there in the company of celestial nymphs.

(11) Let the servants of Yama, and the terrifying jackals and vultures that accompany them, tremble upon seeing that the darkness of the nether world everywhere vanishes miraculously. Let them wonder then, "Whose is this soothing light that brings such bliss and joy?" Then, as they look upward and see, descending from the sky, the flaming Vajrapani, let the force of their joy make them abandon their wickedness, that they may then leave with him. (12) Let a shower of red lotuses, mixed with perfumed water, rain down to extinguish the fires of hell. "What is this?" will say the denizens of hell, sud-denly cooled by joy, as they gain sight of Vajrapani, the one who holds the lotus in his hand.

(13) "Come, come at once, my brothers. Do not fear. We have come back to life. Manjushri,[3] the youth, wearing a triple band, blazing with light, chases all fear away. By his power all sufferings vanish, joy overflows, and one is able to give rise to the thought of awakening, motivated by compassion, which is the mother that rescues all living beings." (14) "Look at him, the crowns of hundreds of gods stoop before the lotus of his feet; his eyes show the tears of compassion; over his head rains a shower of different kinds of flowers, descend-ing from the towered palaces of heaven, where one can hear the praises of hundreds of singing goddesses." May the denizens of hell also praise the bodhisattva Manjushri in this way when he appears before them.

(15) And in this way let them, through the power of my merits, accept and rejoice at the clouds of bodhisattvas that now surround them, with the bodhisattva Samantabhadra[4] at their head. From these clouds descend fresh, perfumed breeze and a rain. (16) Let the intense pains and terrors of hell disappear, and let those who are in evil rebirths become free of them. (17) Let the animals be free from the fear of being devoured by others, and let the hungry ghosts reach satisfaction equal to that of the human beings in the land of Uttarakuru.[5] (18) May the hungry ghosts be sated and may they be able to bathe and refresh themselves in the rivers of milk emanating from the hands of the bodhisattva Avalokiteshvara.

---

3. The bodhisattva of wisdom.
4. A bodhisattva who embodies the practices and vows of the buddhas.

5. In Buddhist cosmology, the continent located to the north of Mount Meru.

(19) May the blind everywhere see shapes and colors, and the deaf be able to hear. Let expectant mothers give birth without pain, like Mayadevi.[6] (20) May all humans have clothing, food, drink, garlands, sandalwood powder, ornaments—may they obtain as much as they desire of everything necessary for their well-being. (21) May those who are afraid lose all their fears. Let the grieving find joy, and the anxious become serene and even-minded. (22) May the sick find health; prisoners, freedom; the weak, strength. May all have loving thoughts toward each other. (23) May all localities be friendly to those who travel through their roads, and may these travelers meet success in the enterprise for which they have set out on their journey. (24) May all those who travel by sea reach their desired destinations, returning safely to shore to rejoicing with their families. (25) Let those who are lost in the jungle find a caravan. Let them continue in their journeys free from fatigue and the fear of bandits and wild beasts. (26) May friendly deities protect from disease, the dangers of the jungle, and other ills all those who are feeble-minded, mad, or drunk, and those who are unprotected, children, and the aged. (27) May all humans be free from conditions unfavorable to following the Path. Let them have faith, wisdom, and compassion, positive attitudes and good conduct, constantly remembering their past lives.

(28) May they come to possess inexhaustible treasures equal to those of the bodhisattva Gaganaganja.[7] Let them not be tied to the pair of duality. Let them be free from coercion, acting in complete freedom. (29) May those hermits who lack fortitude acquire energy, and deformed sentient beings become beautiful. (30) May all women in the world be reborn as men. May those who are small and insignificant achieve greatness, without pride. (31) Let this my merit help all beings, without exception, to stop sin and practice the good. (32) Let no one lack the thought of awakening. Let them be totally devoted to the conduct of the bodhisattva, guided and protected by the awakened ones, having renounced the works of Mara.

(33) Let all sentient beings have a long life. Let them live eternal happiness. Let even the word "death" vanish forever. (34) May all regions of the universe be filled by the presence of the awakened and the sons of the awakened, and may these regions be adorned with parks where wish-fulfilling trees grow, and may the parks be filled with the melody of dharma. (35) Let the earth become soft every where free of roughness, flat like the palm of the hand and covered with beryl. (36) Let there large assemblies of bodhisattvas everywhere sit in circles; and may they adorn the whole earth with their resplendent majesty. (37) May all embodied beings hear incessantly the melody of dharma as it is sung by birds, trees, the sun's rays, and the sky. (38) Let them always walk in the company of the awakened and their sons. Let them worship the Teacher of the World with infinite clouds of adoration. (39) Let the sky god bring rain in proper season, giving abundant crops. May the people prosper, and may the king be just. (40) Let all medicinal herbs and all the curative mantras of the healers effectively heal. May all dakinis, rakshasas, and other demons become compassionate.

(41) Let no sentient being ever be unhappy, and be free of evil, ill, scorned, or rejected—may not one among them be heavyhearted. (42) Let monasteries be a refuge for those devoted to the study of the teaching. Let there be

---

6. The Buddha's mother.   7. A bodhisattva known for his generosity.

harmony in the community, and may the goals of the community be fulfilled. (43) May all monks succeed in keeping their life of solitude, and may they love the precepts. May they practice meditation with alertness and without distractions. (44) May nuns receive abundant offerings. May they avoid quarrels and jealousy. May all sages and hermits observe all the precepts. (45) Let those monks who are careless in their morality become aware of their faults and apply themselves to the destruction of these faults. May they all attain a favorable rebirth, where they will be able to keep their vows. (46) May the truly wise receive honors, offerings, and alms; may the truly pure achieve universal renown. (47) May all beings achieve buddhahood through a single rebirth in the heavens, without further suffering in the unfortunate rebirths, and without having to engage in the difficult practices of the bodhisattvas. (48) May all beings pay homage to the awakened in a variety of ways, and that they may thus become happy many times over by acquiring the inconceivable bliss of awakening. (49) Let the bodhisattvas' wishes for the well-being of the world become reality. May everything that these protectors intend be realized for all sentient beings. (50) May solitary buddhas and mere disciples attain to happiness, venerated with the greatest honors by gods, asuras, and humans.

(51) May I, by the grace of Manjushri, become capable of renunciation and the recollection of past lives, that I may reach the first stage, the Stage of Joy. (52) May I bring to all my enterprises effort and fortitude, and obtain the conditions necessary to lead a life of solitude in all my rebirths. (53) May I be able to see and speak to the protector Manjushri whenever I wish to do so. (54) May I be able to follow by myself the conduct practiced by Manjushri, which effects the goals of all sentient being in the ten directions, to the very end of space. (55) For as long as the vastness of space remains, and as long as the world exists, may I too subsist that long, destroying the suffering of the whole world. (56) Let all the sufferings of the world come to an end in me; and let the whole world achieve happiness through the virtues of the bodhisattvas.

(57) May the teachings of dharma, the only medicine for the world's ills, the cause of all perfection and happiness, long endure in this world, worshipped with offerings and honors. (58) I pay homage to Manjughosha, by whose grace my mind has come to settle on the good. I salute this friend in the path, whose grace increases this thought of the good.

HOW TO MEDITATE ON EMPTINESS

STAGES OF MEDITATION
(The Bhavanakrama)

KAMALASHILA

Despite their reputation for passivity, Buddhist monks have rarely shied away from debate. Polemics have been central to the tradition since the Buddha triumphed over brahmin priests. Over the centuries, all manner of disputation has been pursued: in India, between Buddhist and Hindu logicians; in China, between Buddhist monks and Confucian magistrates; and throughout the Buddhist world, between members of different sects or philosophical schools. But these last cases for the most part have been local. It is rare that Buddhist monks from different countries, and different traditions, have met on the field of verbal battle.

The most famous such confrontation took place at the end of the eighth century in Tibet. Variously referred to in English as the Council of Samye, the Council of Lhasa, and the Samye Debate, it pitted a Chinese monk against an Indian monk, as they argued whether enlightenment was sudden or gradual.

During the reign of Trisong Detsen at the end of the eighth century, there were two Buddhist factions at the Tibetan court. One, favored by the queen, was led by the monk Heshang Moheyan, who was identified with the Northern Chan school (see the *Platform Sutra of the Sixth Patriarch*, p. 531). The other comprised followers of the Bengali monk Shantarakshita, who, together with the king and the great tantric master Padmasambhava, had founded the first Tibetan monastery at Samye. Shantarakshita had recently died, but according to traditional accounts, he foretold the dangers in the Chinese position and left instructions in his will that his student Kamalashila be called from India to counter it.

A conflict seems to have developed between the Indian and Chinese partisans (and their allies in the Tibetan court) over the question of the nature of enlightenment. The Indians held that enlightenment is the culmination of a gradual process, as mental defilements are purified through the three trainings in ethics, meditation, and wisdom. The Chinese argued to the contrary that rather than being a goal of some protracted practice, enlightenment was the intrinsic nature of the mind itself. The only "practice" required was to recognize the presence of this innate nature of enlightenment by entering a state of awareness beyond distinctions. Anything else was superfluous.

Both Chinese and Tibetan records make note of a debate held between Kamalashila and Moheyan at Samye around 797, with the king himself serving as judge. According to Tibetan accounts (contradicted by their Chinese counterparts), Kamalashila was declared the victor: the king proclaimed that thereafter the Madhyamaka school of Nagarjuna (to which both Shantarakshita and Kamalashila belonged) would be followed in Tibet, and Moheyan and his party were banished. The stakes seem to have been high; Kamalashila died shortly after the debate, reportedly assassinated by members of the Chinese faction.

Scholars have accepted the dispute between the Indian and Chinese Buddhists (and their Tibetan partisans) as historical, but suggest that it may have taken the form of an exchange of statements rather than a face-to-face debate. Kamalashila is credited with three works, each titled *Stages of Meditation* (*Bhavanakrama*), composed in defense of gradual enlightenment. Moreover, the Indian triumph was probably less than complete. It is said that when he departed, Moheyan left behind one shoe, indicating that traces of his view would remain in Tibet. Regardless of the merits of the Indian and Chinese philosophical positions, China was Tibet's chief military rival at the time, whereas India posed no military threat. It is thus perhaps significant that from this point on, Tibet largely sought its Buddhism from India.

The second of Kamalashila's *Stages of Meditation* is presented in its entirety here. Like the selection from Buddhaghosa's *Path of Purification* (the *Visuddhimagga*, p. 249), it is a prime example of South Asian Buddhist scholasticism: a systematic work on the practice of the Buddhist path that draws from other works, particularly the sutras, in crafting step-by-step instructions on the practice of the path. Kamalashila's text does not have the personality and poignancy of Shantideva's discussion of the bodhisattva's compassion, and it lacks the relentless philosophical rigor of Nagarjuna's proof that everything is empty. Instead, Kamalashila explains what one does when one sits down on the meditation cushion to cultivate compassion and to understand emptiness.

PRONOUNCING GLOSSARY

Ajatashatru-kaukritya-vinodana: *a-jah-ta-sha-tru-kau-kritya-vih-noh-da-na*

Akashagarbha: *ah-kah-sha-gar-ba*

Akshayamati-nirdesha: *ak-sha-ya-ma-ti nir-de-sha*

Avalokiteshvara: *a-va-loh-ki-taysh-va-ra*

Bhadrachari: *ba-dra-cha-ree*

Bhavanakrama: *ba-va-nah-kruma*

Bodhisattvabhumi: *boh-di-sat-va-boo-mi*

Bodhisattva-Pitaka: *boh-di-sat-va-pi-ta-ka*

Bstan-'gyur: *tehn-gyur*

Chandrapradipa Sutra: *chan-dra-pra-dee-pa soo-tra*

Dashabhumika: *da-sha-boo-mi-ka*

Dashadharmaka Sutra: *da-sha-dar-ma-ka soo-tra*

Dharmasangiti Sutra: *dar-ma-san-gee-ti soo-tra*

Gaganaganja: *ga-ga-na-gan-ja*

Gayashirsha: *gah-ya-sheer-sha*

Gochara-parishuddhi: *goh-cha-ra-pa-ri-shu-di*

Kamalashila: *ka-ma-la-shee-la*

Kashyapa: *kah-shya-pa*

Lankavatara Sutra: *lan-kah-va-tah-ra soo-tra*

Lotsawa Bande Yeshe-de: *loh-tsah-wah bahn-deh yeh-sheh-deh*

Mahaparinirvana Sutra: *ma-hah-pa-ri-nir-vah-na soo-tra*

Mahayana-prasada-bhavana Sutra: *ma-hah-yah-na pra-sah-da bhah-va-nah soo-tra*

Maitreya: *mai-tray-ya*

Manjushri: *man-ju-shree*

Narayana-paripriccha: *nah-rah-ya-na-pa-ri-pri-chah*

Narthang: *nar-tang*

Prajnavarma: *praj-nyah-var-ma*

Ratnachuda-paripriccha: *rat-na-choo-da pa-ri-pri-chah*

Ratnakuta: *rat-na-koo-ta*

Ratnamegha: *rat-na-meh-ga*

Samadhiraja: *sa-mah-di-rah-ja*

Sandhinirmochana Sutra: *san-dih-nir-moh-cha-na soo-tra*

Sarvadharma-sangraha-vaipulya: *sar-va-dar-ma-san-gra-ha-vai-pul-ya*

Sde-dge: *deh-geh*

Shri-paramadya: *shree-pa-ra-mah-dya*

tathagata: *ta-tah-ga-ta*

Udraka Ramaputra: *u-dra-ka rah-ma-pu-tra*

Vairochana: *vai-roh-cha-na*

Vimalakirti-nirdesha: *vi-ma-la-keer-ti-nihr-deh-sha*

Obeisance to Manjushri,[1] True Prince.

I shall describe herein, briefly, the gradual process of cultivation for those who have set out on the path of conduct taught in the sutras of the Great Vehicle.[2]

A person who through this path seeks to attain swiftly the omniscience of a Buddha, if such a person is discerning, should exert himself in order to generate the specific causes and conditions necessary for the obtainment of this state. For, in fact, it cannot be that all-knowledge could arise without causes, as this would entail the absurdity of anyone being able to know all

FROM the Sde-dge, Peking, Cone, and Narthang versions of the Bstan-'gyur; edited and translated from the Tibetan by Luis O. Gómez as *Steps in the Practice of Contemplation*.

1. The bodhisattva of wisdom.   2. Mahayana.

everywhere and at all times. If all-knowledge could arise independently from any conditions, it would not be hindered anywhere, and, under such circumstances, why should it not occur everywhere?

Accordingly, since only some things occur, and only in a certain place and a certain time, every entity must be dependent on causes. The knowledge of all things, likewise, occurs as a particular event in a certain place, at a certain time; it does not occur always, everywhere and all at once; therefore, it too must depend on causes and conditions.

Among the various possible causes and conditions, one should practice only those that are specific and complete. The desired fruit will not be obtained by applying oneself to an inappropriate cause, even if one practices it for a long time. It would be like trying to milk a horn.

Likewise, if the complete cause is not employed, no fruit will be produced; for if one of the appropriate causes (such as the seed, the soil, and the rest) is missing, the effect (the sprout, and the rest) will not arise. Therefore, if one wishes to obtain the fruit, one should practice the appropriate causes and conditions to their full extent.

Which are the causes and conditions that bring about the fruit of all-knowledge? Although I myself am unfit to practice these, for in this regard I am, as it were, a blind man, I will explain them nevertheless using the same words as the Blessed One himself used to explain them to his disciples after he attained full and complete awakening. At that time the Blessed One said:

> Master of Mysteries, the knowledge of the All-knower springs from compassion as its root, from the thought of awakening as its immediate cause, and with the practice of the means to liberate self and others it reaches its culmination.

Therefore, one who would attain to all-knowledge should train in these three: compassion, the thought of awakening, and skill in the means to liberate self and others.

Moved by compassion, the bodhisattvas will surely form the determination to rescue all living beings from transmigration. Thereupon, they will devote themselves reverently to gathering the necessary equipment of merit and wisdom, which is accomplished by practicing the difficult tasks of a bodhisattva unceasingly and for a long time, without regard for themselves. Applying themselves in this way, they will surely accomplish the complete equipment of merit and wisdom. Having gathered the complete equipment, they will hold all-knowledge in the palm of the hand, as it were. Therefore, since compassion is indeed the root of all-knowledge, one should first develop only compassion.

Furthermore, in the *Dharmasangiti*[3] it is said:

> Blessed One, a bodhisattva should not train in too many practices. Blessed One, if a bodhisattva should hold firmly to one practice and understand it fully, he would have all the qualities of a buddha in the palm of his hand. And which one is this one practice? It is great compassion.

---

3. One of the numerous Mahayana works—some of them relatively obscure—that are cited in this text.

Because they have adopted this great compassion as their practice, the awakened blessed ones have attained their own goal in all its perfection; still, moved by this same practice, they remain in the world until the sphere of living beings comes to its end. For, great compassion has taken hold of the blessed ones. They do not enter the peaceful city of final rest as is done by those who are mere disciples.

Out of regard for living beings, the blessed ones keep far away from the peaceful city of final rest, as one would shun a burning iron house. Therefore, only great compassion is the immediate cause for that state of rest in which the blessed ones do not stand still in either the tasks of transmigration or the final peace of nirvana.

I will now begin by explaining the initial steps in the cultivation of compassion. First, one should spend some time cultivating even-mindedness, thus removing both affection and animosity towards all living beings, and accomplishing balance of mind.

One should consider carefully the following thoughts: "All living beings seek happiness and fear suffering. There is no living being who has not been my relative at least a hundred times in this beginningless cycle of transmigration."

If at this point there is any being in particular towards whom he feels affection, or someone towards whom he feels animosity, he should bring to mind this thought: "I should perceive all living beings with the same even-tempered thoughts." Applying his mind in this way, he will develop equanimity first with respect to a neutral subject, then with respect to friends, and lastly with respect to enemies.

Once he succeeds in becoming even-minded towards all living beings, he should cultivate benevolence. When the mind is soaked with the water of benevolence it is made into the most rich soil. If the seed of compassion is then cast on this soil, it will grow quickly.

Thereupon, once the mind has been impregnated by benevolence, one should develop compassion. Compassion is marked by the desire to free all suffering living beings from their misery. Since all living beings in the three world realms[4] suffer intensely on account of at least one of the three types of misery, compassion should be developed with respect to all beings.

For instance, those living beings who inhabit the Hells are, according to the words of the Blessed One, "verily immersed in rivers of various, uninterrupted, long lasting, burning pains."

Likewise, the hungry ghosts also, he has said, "suffer piercing pains, their bodies consumed by the fire of manifold torments such as intolerable hunger and thirst."

Animals too we see suffering numberless torments, because they devour each other, and they are, constantly and furiously, injuring each other.

Humans we also see growing in ill will towards each other and harming each other, because they cannot reach what they seek to obtain. They must part from what is dear to them, and encounter what they loathe, experiencing immeasurable sorrows such as poverty and the rest. And also there are those who are entirely ensnared in their minds by the most diverse afflictions,

4. The Realm of Desire, the Realm of Form, and the Formless Realm; see pp. 54–55.

such as passionate desire, animosity, blind delusion, and the rest, always confused by all kind of mistaken views. They are subject to these causes of misery. Standing at the edge of a cliff, as it were, they too are tormented in the extreme.

The gods too are all tormented by the sorrow of seeing their blissful state gradually come to an end. The gods who inhabit the Realm of Desire, constantly afflicted as they are by the fear of falling from their present state into a lower form of life, how can they be happy?

Moreover, the misery of conditioning encompasses all living beings, because their nature is to be at the mercy of causes external to themselves, that is, at the mercy of action and affliction, and because it is in their nature to arise and perish again and again at every moment.

As one contemplates in this way all beings in the midst of the burning flames of the fires of suffering, two thoughts will arise in his mind: "Just as I do not wish suffering for myself, so is it with all other beings," and "Alas! These beings, who are most dear to me are in pain; how can I free them from this suffering?"

With these thoughts he gives rise to a compassion by which he will aspire to rescue all beings from suffering, acting as if their misery were his own. This compassion can be practiced equally while sitting in meditation or in any other of the postures and movements considered appropriate. It should be developed at all times with respect to all living beings.

At first, this compassion should be developed with respect to one's friends while visualizing them in the process of suffering the various torments described above. Then, one should develop it with respect to those persons towards whom one is indifferent. In terms of the sameness of all beings, and without perceiving any difference among them, one considers the thought that all living beings are indeed one's own kinsmen. When one is able to feel the same compassion for them as one does for his friends, he should develop this compassion with respect to all living beings in the ten directions.[5]

Then, when this compassion becomes like that of a mother towards her own young and beloved suffering child, when it is characterized by a desire to lead all beings out of their misery through one's own effort, when it is motivated only by the taste of compassion, and when it is felt equally towards all living beings, then it is said to be perfect and is given the name "great compassion."

One had first developed benevolence with respect to friends, with a firm desire to bring about their happiness. Then, one gradually came to develop it with respect to evil persons and enemies as well. Developing compassion in the same way, it will grow gradually, by its own nature, into the firm desire to lead all living beings out of the cycle of transmigration.

Thereupon, having developed the root of buddhahood, which is compassion, one should develop the thought of awakening. This thought of awakening is of two kinds: one which is its provisional mode, called "covering," and the other, which is the same as the goal, the ultimate object of the path.

---

5. That is, everywhere (north, south, east, west, northeast, northwest, southeast, southwest, the nadir, and the zenith).

Of these two, the thought of awakening in the mode of covering is the generation of a thought in which, by means of compassion, one makes for the first time the resolution to rescue all living beings from their misery. This initial resolution appears in the mind as a firm desire to attain perfect and unsurpassable awakening, and takes the form "May I become awakened, in order to care for the well-being of the world."

And this thought should be produced according to the rite prescribed in the section on ethical rule and habit in the *Bodhisattvabhumi*, in the presence of someone who is learned and well established in the practice of the precepts of the bodhisattvas—someone who knows them well and is fit to practice them.

Having generated in this way the thought of awakening in the mode of covering, one should endeavor to produce the thought of awakening which is the ultimate object.

The thought of awakening as ultimate object is supramundane, free from all discursive diffusions, and radiant. Its range of action and cognition is ultimate reality; it is stainless, and steady, like the flame of a lamp protected from the wind.

One comes to the realization of this higher thought of awakening by developing the practice of calm and insight, constantly and devoutly, for a long time. As it is said in the noble *Sandhinirmochana*:

> Maitreya, whatever wholesome inner states or virtues, be they worldly or supramundane, are possessed by mere disciples, bodhisattvas, and tathagatas,[6] you should understand that all these are the fruit of calm and insight.

All yogins should practice calm and insight at all times, and by all means, because these two comprise all forms of mental concentration. For the Blessed One has said, in the very same noble *Sandhinirmochana*:

> All the various states of contemplative concentration I have declared to be the practice of mere disciples, bodhisattvas and tathagatas, they all should be understood to be comprised in the practice of calm and insight.

By the sole development of only calm, yogins will not remove all the veils that obscure reality, even though the practice of calm may allow them to achieve a temporary removal of the obscuration produced by the afflictions.

By means of serenity alone one cannot suppress the innate proclivities that underly the obscurations; for, without the dawning of the light of discernment, it is impossible to suppress adequately the innate proclivities. Accordingly, in that same noble *Sandhinirmochana* it is said: "By contemplation one can suppress the afflictions, by discernment one will thoroughly uproot the proclivities."

In the noble *Samadhiraja*, also, it is said:

> Even if he should cultivate this concentration, if he does not bring to an end the perception and conception of a self, the afflictions

6. Buddhas; *tathagata* (literally, "one who has thus come/gone") is the title of a buddha most often used by the historical Buddha to refer to himself. "Maitreya": the next buddha.

will be aroused in him again, as in Udraka Ramaputra's[7] form of cultivating concentration.

If he closely examines the absence of self in all things, growth in this practice will be the cause for obtaining the ultimate fruit, which is final rest in nirvana; any other cause will not bring about peace.

It is also said in the *Bodhisattva-Pitaka*:

> Some do not lend their ears to this dharma discourse of the *Bodhisattva-Pitaka*. Ignoring the noble dharma and vinaya,[8] they are satisfied only by concentration. Overpowered by their own sense of self-worth, they fall into arrogance. They are not liberated from birth, old age, disease, death, grief, lamentation, sorrow, depression and anxiety. They are not liberated from the six destinations in the cycle of rebirth.[9] They are not liberated from this whole mass of sorrow.

Considering this, the Tathagata has said:

> Those who are open to what others teach and lend their ears to it will be liberated from old age and death.

Therefore, he who seeks to produce the most pure wisdom, by giving up all the veils of obscuration will develop discernment while standing firm in calm. As the Buddha also said in the noble *Ratnakuta*:

> By being firm in the precepts and habits of morality, one gains a state of concentration. Then, having obtained concentration, one can develop discernment. By means of discernment one obtains the most pure knowledge. By means of the most pure knowledge one attains to the fulfillment of morality.

It has also been said in the *Mahayana-prasada-bhavana Sutra*:

> Son of a good family, I say that if a bodhisattva does not practice discernment, even if he has faith in the Great Vehicle of the bodhisattvas, there is no way that he will give rise to the wisdom of the Great Vehicle. Son of a good family, conversely, one should know that those who have faith in the Great Vehicle of the bodhisattvas and give rise to wisdom of the Great Vehicle, they all attain to this wisdom by the correct observation of phenomena that is carried out by a mind that is not distracted.

On the other hand, by the sole practice of insight deprived of calm, the yogin's mind becomes distracted with respect to all objects of the mind and the senses. Like the flame of a lamp in the wind, it is never steadfast. Consequently, the light of knowledge cannot shine in its full brilliance.

Therefore, one should practice both equally. In this connection, in the noble *Mahaparinirvana Sutra* it is also said:

> The mere disciples cannot understand the lineage of the tathagatas, because the concentration of disciples is stronger and their

---

7. One of the Buddha's meditation teachers prior to his enlightenment.
8. Rules of monastic discipline.

9. The realms of gods, demigods, humans, animals, ghosts, and the denizens of hell.

discernment is weaker. The bodhisattvas understand it, but not clearly, for in them discernment is much stronger, and concentration is weaker. The tathagatas realize it all, because they possess equally calm and insight.

Due to the power of calm, their mind is not shaken by the wind of discursive thought, as the flame of a lamp is not shaken by the wind. When the impurities of mistaken views are thoroughly removed by the power of insight, the mind's flow cannot be interrupted by other sensory or mental stimuli. As it is said in the *Chandrapradipa Sutra*: "Due to the power of calm he cannot be shaken. Through insight he becomes like a mountain."

Therefore, one should remain engaged in the practice of both of these.

To this end, the yogin who would perfect serenity and insight quickly and easily should first dedicate himself for some time to the gradual gathering of the requisites for calm and insight.

Now, what are the requisites for calm? They are dwelling in a suitable place, few wants, contentment, giving up excessive involvement in worldly affairs, pure moral behavior, and giving up discursive thought rooted in desire, animosity or delusion.

Now, one should know that a suitable place is one provided with five advantages: 1) easy provision, because things like food and clothing can be obtained without difficulty; 2) pleasant habitat, because violent or hostile living beings do not inhabit the area; 3) propitious location, because it is an area without disease; 4) auspicious friend, because there is close by a friend of upright morality and of like views; 5) comfortable, because during the day it is not crowded with many living beings and during the night there are no loud noises.

What is few wants? It is not having a strong desire for expensive or abundant clothing or any other possession.

What is contentment? It is to be always satisfied even if one receives only inferior or cheap clothing and the like.

What is giving up immoderate activities and behaviors? It is giving up completely the evil practices of buying, selling, and the like. Also, whether it be with a layman or with one who has gone forth, you are to give up completely frivolous camaraderie. It also means giving up such practices as medicine and astrology.

What is perfect moral purity? It is not to break the principles of training included in the two kinds of precepts, that is, the precepts prohibiting what is shunned by a natural sense of the right and those that [prohibit transgressions] by prescription of the monastic code.

It also means that if these principles are violated out of negligence, one should repent, and thereafter act according to the dharma. Furthermore, perfect morality also means repenting, with the intention of not repeating the same act in the future, even in the case of those major violations of the precepts of the disciples, about which it is said that they cannot be expiated.

It is also said that one will have perfect moral purity only by examining the absence of self-existence of the very mind which brought about the deed, or by developing an awareness of the absence of self-existence in all things. This can be learned in full from the noble *Ajatashatru-kaukritya-vinodana*. Therefore, one should apply oneself strenuously to contemplative development rather than remorse.

One should also bring the mind to bear on the nature of passionate desires and on the various and abundant torments that will arise from them in this and future lives, and give up all discursive fancies about the objects of these passions. Or, in another way, one should give up all discursive fancies by cultivating this thought: "All things in the cycle of transmigration, whether they are pleasant or unpleasant, are unstable and fleeting conditions, by nature having to end in dissolution. Certainly, all these things and I myself before long will have to part. Why should these things continue to provoke in me clinging, revulsion or delusion?"

And what are the requisites for insight? They are reliance on a saintly teacher, dedication to intense study, and well-centered thought.

On what sort of saintly teacher should one rely? On a person who is well versed in the scriptures, clear worded, compassionate, and patient.

And, what is dedication to intense study? It is to study devoutly and thoroughly the twelve branches of the word of the Blessed One, in their explicit and implicit meanings. As it is said in the noble *Sandhinirmochana*: "Not to listen willingly to the words of the noble ones is a hindrance to insight."

And in the same text it is said: "The cause for the arising of insight is the purified view arising from study and reflection."

It is also said in the noble *Narayana-paripriccha*: "He who is devoted to study will produce discernment. He who is endowed with discernment will bring the afflictions to rest."

And, what is well-centered thought? It is based on a clear determination of which sutras express the ultimate meaning explicitly, and which deliver their meaning only through interpretation. In this way the bodhisattva becomes free from doubts, and is able to fix his mind on a single point during meditation. Otherwise, he would remain in the bondage of doubt, like a man who, having arrived at a road crossing, cannot determine exactly where to go.

The yogin gives up eating fish and meat under all circumstances, consuming only moderate amounts of food, and only of that which is not contrary to the precepts.

Having gathered in this way the requisites for calm and insight, the bodhisattva should thereupon dedicate himself to practicing both in unison. When it is time to practice them, the yogin should first see to it that all his obligatory tasks have been carried out. Then, after relieving bowels and bladder, he should find a pleasant spot, free of loud noises.

There, intent on rescuing all living beings, with the thought, "I will lead and establish all living beings in the very ground of awakening," he should bring to mind great compassion. Then, after bowing low with his whole body to all the buddhas and bodhisattvas in the ten directions, he should place before himself or somewhere else close to himself a painting or other representation of buddhas and bodhisattvas. He should venerate and eulogize them as much as possible. Then he should confess his own sins and rejoice at the merit of all living beings.

Thereupon he should sit on a soft, comfortable seat, assuming the cross-legged posture of Lord Vairochana,[1] or the half-lotus. 1) His eyes should not be either too open nor too closed, aimed at the tip of his nose. 2) He

---

1. An important buddha; see the *Tantra on the Complete Enlightenment of Vairochana* and Kukai's *Treatise Distinguishing the Two Teachings of Exoteric and Esoteric Methods*, pp. 471 and 606.

should keep the body erect, neither bent but nor too rigid. He should sit with all his mindfulness turned inward. 3) He should also keep his shoulders level. 4) The head he should hold neither high nor low. 5) The nose he keeps in line with the navel. 6) Teeth and lips he should hold naturally, the tongue touching the gums of the upper teeth. 7) Exhalation and inhalation should not be audible, neither heavy nor light, the breath should not be at all perceptible, the air should be slowly and effortlessly drawn in and brought out.

Then one first must practice serenity for a while. By serenity is meant that state in which the mind dwells in itself, perfectly pure and satisfied, putting to rest the distractions produced by external objects, constantly and spontaneously moving with the flow of an internal object. When this calm, concentrated state itself becomes the object of meditation, and is then observed and examined, this process is what is called insight. As it is said in the noble *Ratnamegha:* "serenity is one-pointedness of mind. Insight is the examination of the real."

In the *Sandhinirmochana* it is also said:

"Blessed One, how does the bodhisattva seek serenity and how does he become skilled in insight?"

The Blessed One replied, "Maitreya, I have established the various form of expressing the dharma: prose discourses, versified discourses, commentaries, stanzas, utterances, narratives, exploits, anecdotes, past lives, extended discourses, miraculous events, and instructions. These I have taught for the bodhisattvas, who carefully study and duly learn them. They recite them aloud, they ponder them in their minds, and, having examined them thoroughly with insight, they sit alone in a secluded spot, and, inwardly collected, bring their attention to bear on the same aspects of reality they have previously considered with careful reflection. After doing this, they bring their attention to bear on the very mind that produces the act of attention.

"The condition of bodily and mental ease which arises in those who engage in this practice and dwell in it repeatedly is called 'serenity.' In this way a bodhisattva should seek serenity.

"After the bodhisattva has obtained ease of body and ease of mind, he should remain cultivating such a state, and, abandoning mental distraction, he should thoroughly examine all things he had previously considered, but this time he will observe them in the images that appear in the field of his inner concentration. And thus the bodhisattvas produce an intense aspiration to attain a realization of the ultimate reality of all these things. The scrutiny of the object of knowledge as it appears in these images in the field of inner concentration, their thorough scrutiny, thorough understanding, thorough examination, perseverance in this, determination in this, discrimination, perception, and judgments is that which is called 'insight.' In this way the bodhisattva becomes skilled in insight."

In this practice, the yogin who wants to attain calm should at first fix his mind for some time on the discourses in prose, on the discourses in verse, or any other genre of scripture, all of which summarize whatever has been well spoken, that is, what tends towards the reality of all things as they are, what has moved towards this reality as it is, what is moving towards this reality as it is.

Or, in another manner, he may fix his mind in some form of summary of all *dharmas*, such as the five aggregates[2] and the rest.

Or, again, he may fix the mind on an image of the bodily frame of the Buddha as he has seen it or heard about it. As it is said in the noble *Samadhiraja*:

> The World Protector is all pleasing
> with his body, which is the color of gold.
> Focusing his mind on this object of meditation,
> the bodhisattva will be considered "well collected."

Thus, having fixed his mind on whichever object of meditation he wishes to use, he should remain with his mind set on it for some time. With his mind thus fixed he should scrutinize the mind in this way: "Is it grasping the object properly? Is it dull? Or is it being distracted because it is excited by external objects?"

Then, when stiffness and torpor overtake the mind so that it becomes dull, or if one perceives the danger of dullness, then he should bring his mind to bear on a pleasant object, such as the bodily form of the Buddha, or on a mental representation of light, and thus bring to rest the dullness of mind. Thereupon the mind, resting on the object, should come to perceive in all its clarity the object as it really is.

One should know that the mind has become dull whenever it is not able to perceive the object in all its clarity, like a blind man, or like someone in a dark room, or someone with his eyes closed.

When the mind becomes excited, because it is made to run around by the consideration of the properties of external objects, or because the act of attention is directed elsewhere away from the object of meditation, or because there is longing for objects that were enjoyed in the past, or if one sees that there is the possible risk of mental excitement reappearing, then one should produce the thought of an object that will shake the mind from its state of excitement, such as the impermanence or the suffering inherent in all conditioned things.[3] In this way he will bring excitement to rest. In this way, he will tie the elephant of the mind with the rope of awareness to the tree trunk of the meditative object.

When he perceives that the mind, free from dullness and excitement, is coursing evenly on its object, exertion and ease being balanced, he may remain sitting in this way for as long as he wishes. In the body of one who practices serenity in this way, the mind becomes completely pure and it freely moves on the object as it wishes. This should be known to be perfect serenity.

Once serenity has been mastered, one should develop insight. One should reflect thusly: "All the words of the Blessed One have been well spoken. They manifest reality clearly, whether directly or indirectly, they lead to the real. When the real is known, the whole net of views is abandoned, just as darkness is removed when sunlight appears. If one practices only serenity,

2. A standard division of the constituents of mind and body into five groups: form, feeling, discrimination, compositional factors, and con-sciousness. "*Dharmas*": here, "phenomena." 3. That is, conditioned by impermanence.

right discernment will not arise and the veils will not be abandoned. By thoroughly cultivating the correct vision of reality by means of discernment, knowledge will be fully purified.

"Only discernment leads to the understanding of reality. Only discernment leads to the abandonment of the veils. Therefore, standing firmly in serenity, I will seek reality by means of discernment, serenity alone is not enough."

Now, what sort of things is this "reality"? It is the emptiness of a self in all things—persons and dharmas—as seen from the point of view of the ultimate object, and which is understood by discernment and not by any other means. As it has been said in the noble *Sandhinirmochana Sutra*:

"Blessed One, by which perfect virtue does the bodhisattva come
to grasp the absence of an intrinsic nature in all dharmas?"
"Avalokiteshvara,[4] it is by the perfect virtue of discernment that
they come to grasp it."

Therefore, once established in serenity, he should cultivate discernment. To this end the yogin should carry out the examination of the object in the following way: "One does not find a 'person' existing apart from the aggregates, the fields, and the bases.[5] Nor is the person the intrinsic reality of the aggregates and the rest, because they are impermanent and multiple, while others who believe in a 'self' imagine the person to be permanent and one. Likewise, it is not possible to accept a 'person' that exists as a real thing yet is said to be neither identical not different from the aggregates, because two opposite attributes cannot coexist in something real. Therefore, one should examine in this way the worldly notions of 'I' and 'mine' as nothing but delusive errors."

In the same way one should cultivate the perception of the absence of a self in all dharmas, reflecting in this manner: "What we call 'dharmas' can be summarized under the headings of the five aggregates, the twelve fields, and the eighteen bases. Among these, even those aggregates, fields, and bases which are material do not exist in any ultimate sense apart from the modifications of mind. For, if material things are broken into atomic particles, and these particles themselves are analyzed into their parts in order to scrutinize them for their intrinsic nature, no intrinsic reality is ascertained.

"Therefore, it is mind only that from beginningless time has appeared to the foolish as if it were external forms. Owing to the world's persistent grasping at these false images, material forms appear to the mind, as they would if fancied in a dream. Yet, form and the other aggregates, fields, and bases do not exist except as aspects of mind."

With this he understands that "these three world planes are mind only."

Having ascertained that whatever may be called "a dharma" is only of the nature of mind, he will proceed to examine the intrinsic reality of this mind; for by examining mind, he is examining the intrinsic reality of all dharmas. He will examine mind as follows: "The mind also cannot be real

4. The bodhisattva who embodies the compassion of all the buddhas.
5. Two of the groupings of the elements that constitute beings and the world they experience. There are twelve fields (the sense organs—eye, ear, nose, tongue, body, and mind—plus their objects) and eighteen bases (the sense organs, their objects, and the kinds of consciousness associated with each sense).

in an ultimate sense. For, the mind grasps only images of form which have a false intrinsic reality—they are merely the very same mind appearing as the multifarious images of external reality. What sort of reality could mind itself have then? Just as form and the rest are false, in the same way mind also must be false, because it does not exist apart from them.

"Therefore, the intrinsic reality of mind is like that of magical creations or the like. In the same way as in the case of mind, the intrinsic reality of all dharmas also is like that of magical creations, or the like."

When one investigates in this way the intrinsic reality of mind by means of discernment, one does not apprehend a mind inside in any ultimate sense, nor does one apprehend it outside, nor does one apprehend it somewhere in between. Nor does he apprehend mind as past, nor does he apprehend it as future, nor does he apprehend it as present. And mind does not come from somewhere at the time of its arising. And it does not go elsewhere at the time of its ceasing. Mind cannot be grasped, it cannot be held, it is formless.

And what is the intrinsic reality of something that cannot be grasped, cannot be held, and has no form? As it has been said in the noble *Ratnakuta*: "Mind, Kashyapa, even when you look for it, cannot be obtained. What cannot be obtained cannot be apprehended. What cannot be apprehended is not past, future or present . . ."

Investigating in this manner, no beginning of mind is perceived. Nor is any end perceived, nor any middle. He understands that just as mind has no ends or middle, all dharmas also have no ends or middle. Then, having understood in this way that mind has no ends or middle, he does not apprehend anything that could be the intrinsic reality of mind. And the mind by means of which one understands, that too he understands to be empty. So understanding he does not perceive any intrinsic reality whatsoever in those dharmas, form and the rest, whose intrinsic reality is produced by mind.

Thereupon, availing himself of this discernment, he no longer perceives any intrinsic reality in any thing whatsoever, he no longer generates notions of material form being permanent, no notions of it being impermanent, empty or non-empty, defiled or undefiled, produced or non-produced, existing or non-existing. And just as he does not produce any such notions with respect to form, he does not produce them about sensations, perceptions, dispositions, or ideation. If the substantial ground is thus unfounded, all its attributes are also unfounded. On what ground, then, could one build notions about things?

Thereupon, as the yogin examines with discernment in this manner, and when he no longer establishes any intrinsic reality of anything in any ultimate sense, then he enters the non-conceptual concentration. He understands then also the absence of intrinsic reality in all dharmas.

But whoever does not cultivate this mediation in which one examines the intrinsic reality of things by means of discernment, and merely cultivates meditation by abstaining from mental activity, will never be free from conceptual thought, and will never realize the absence of intrinsic reality in all things, for he lacks the light of discernment. As the Blessed One has taught, when by means of this examination one kindles the fire which is knowledge of the real as it is, the wood of discursive thought is consumed, as the fire produced by rubbing two pieces of wood consumes both of them.

It is also taught in the *Ratnamegha*:

He who understands the nature of the most subtle impurities will practice the discipline of cultivating emptiness, in order to become completely free from discursive ideation. As one thoroughly cultivates emptiness, one looks for an intrinsic reality in all things and thus understands the emptiness of whichever object or condition the mind is examining, and of whichever state becomes the mind's resting place. And he also understands that the same mind which is observing is empty. And seeking for the intrinsic nature of this very understanding, he penetrates into its emptiness. Examining in this manner he enters the practice of signless contemplation.

This passage teaches that the entrance into the signless is a relinquishment preceded by examination. It clearly teaches that one cannot enter upon the state without imaginative differentiation by simply giving up mental activity, without investigating the self nature of things by means of discernment. By the same token, one produces this higher state of contemplation only after penetrating into the intrinsic reality of all things, as they are, material form and the rest.

Now, by not dwelling in form and the rest, by not dwelling in this world or the next, one comes to the non-apprehension of form and the rest. This is why this higher contemplation is called the contemplation without dwelling.

It is called the contemplation of the most excellent discernment, because this contemplation without apprehension is produced by means of an examination of the self nature of all things carried out by means of discernment. This is the way it is taught in the noble *Gaganaganja* and in the noble *Ratnachuda-paripriccha*.

When one has penetrated in this fashion into the reality of the absence of self in persons and in all things, since there is nothing else to be examined or viewed, all his mental activity is free from discourse and judgment, without talk and of one taste, moved by its own taste, and he, being free of all predisposition, will then remain cultivating the real object in all its clarity.

Remaining firmly on the object, one should let the mind flow without distraction. If at some later time the mind is distracted by an external object, an object of desire or the like, as soon as he perceives the distraction, he will overcome distraction if he at once focuses the mind on a repulsive image, such as a decaying corpse or the like; thereupon, he will direct the mind back to reality in the object he had been observing.

If he should perceive that the mind is becoming dissatisfied with the meditation, he should cultivate feelings of delight and enthusiasm by contemplating the virtues of concentration. He can also overcome this state of dissatisfaction by contemplating the defects of distraction.

Now, if the mind becomes dull, losing its clarity because it has been carried away by stiffness and torpor, or if he fears that the mind is becoming dull, then, as explained before, he can suppress this dullness by attentively bringing to mind an object that may be a motive for rejoicing. In this way he will be able to apprehend the reality of the object more firmly.

But if at another time he perceives that the mind is excited by the memory of a past moment of laughter or enjoyment, or if he fears that he is becoming excited, then, as explained before, he should suppress this excitement by attentively bringing to mind an object that will shake the mind from its excitement, such as impermanence or the like.

Thereupon he should next strive to make the mind follow only the real without any effort or predisposition. Now, when the mind, because it is free from dullness and excitement, is able to remain aware of reality, proceeding in equilibrium and moved by its own flavor, then the meditator will gain full equanimity, because he has no more need for effort.

But any time that one exerts effort, even when the mind is proceeding in equilibrium, the mind will become distracted. On the other hand, if it becomes dull through lack of effort, then too much dullness may suppress insight, and the mind becomes like a blind man. Therefore, if the mind becomes dull, one should apply effort. If it proceeds in equilibrium there is no need for effort.

But if discernment intensifies due to the cultivation of insight, then calm may become weaker, and the mind then becomes unstable, like the flame of a lamp exposed to the wind. Under these circumstances, reality will not be perceived in its full clarity. Therefore, at that time one should cultivate calm. But if calm becomes stronger, then he should cultivate insight.

When the two are proceeding in equilibrium, the meditator should remain free from conscious effort for as long as he does not feel any bodily or mental discomfort.

If there is any discomfort of body or mind, then he should regard the whole world as one would see a magical creation, a mirage, a dream or the moon reflected in water, and should reflect in this manner: "Living beings have not penetrated a dharma as profound as this; therefore they are affected by the afflictions in this whirlwind of transmigration. I myself will lead every one of them until they are able to understand deeply the nature of all things." With this thought he generates and expresses once more the great compassion and the thought of awakening. Then, after successfully using this technique of rest, he should enter again the concentration which consists in the non-representation of all things. If the mind becomes tired again, he can rest in the same way.

This concentration is a path in which calm and insight are coupled together to work in unison; it includes observing the object with a discursive image and without a discursive image. The yogin may remain in this state, cultivating the contemplation of reality step-by-step, for one hour, or for half a watch, or for a full watch, or for as long as he wishes. And this process, called "Contemplation for Scrutinizing the Object," has been described in the noble *Lankavatara Sutra*.

Thereupon, when he wishes to conclude this exercise in concentration, he should reflect in the following manner, before he separates his legs to stand up from meditation: "All these things and phenomena I now observe, although they are considered to be without any self-existence in any ultimate sense, do subsist in a conventional sense. If they did not exist, how then could there be such phenomena as action, its fruit, and the connection between action and its fruits? And the Blessed One also has taught:

Things arise in the order of the conventional which covers the ultimate.
They have no self-existence from the point of view of the ultimate goal.

"Living beings, who have a childlike intelligence of the world, have their perception of things distorted through the superimposition of being, non-being, and the like on the dharmas, which in fact lack self-subsistence, and they turn around in the wheel of rebirth for a long time. Therefore, I myself will accumulate the unsurpassable equipment of merit and wisdom, to attain the rank of an all-knower, and lead them into the nature of all things."

Then, he slowly separates his legs, and bowing before all the buddhas and bodhisattvas in the ten directions, he offers worship and praise to them all, and utters the solemn vow of the bodhisattva, be it the vow in the noble *Bhadrachari* or any similar ritual text.

Thereafter he should strive to obtain the complete equipment of merit and wisdom, consisting in generous giving and the other perfect virtues, and at the core of which is emptiness together with great compassion.

When the yogin's contemplation proceeds in this fashion it is called "the Contemplation that Achieves Perfect Emptiness Possessed of All the Best Qualities." As it is said in the noble *Ratnachuda*:

> When he has put on the armor of benevolence and stands firmly on great compassion, he practices the contemplation that achieves perfect emptiness possessed of all the highest virtues. Now, what is the emptiness possessed of all the best qualities? It is that emptiness which is not deprived of generous giving, not deprived of morality, not deprived of acceptance, not deprived of fortitude, not deprived of contemplation, not deprived of discernment, not deprived of the means to liberate self and others. . . .

Without question the bodhisattva must dedicate himself to those roots of good such as generous giving and the rest, which are the means to achieve the perfect attainments of a buddha, such as the maturation of all living beings, the buddha-fields,[6] the bodies of a buddha, and the manifestation of his retinue. Otherwise, without these roots, who would gain these perfect attainments taught in the sutras, that is, a buddha-field, a body with the marks and ornaments of the Buddha, and the rest? Therefore, since the knowledge of an all-knower who, possessed of the best qualities, is brought to perfection by these means, generous giving and the rest, the Blessed One has said: "This knowledge of an all-knower culminates with the practice of the means to liberate self and others."

Consequently, the bodhisattva will also dedicate himself to the practice of the means to liberate self and others, that is, generosity and the other virtues, and will not limit himself to the cultivation of mere emptiness. As it is said in the noble *Sarvadharma-sangraha-vaipulya*:

> "If someone, Maitreya, is practicing all of the six perfect virtues of the bodhisattva[7] for the sake of complete awakening, deluded persons will tell him: 'A bodhisattva should train only in the perfect virtue of discernment. What good are the remaining perfect virtues?' Thinking in this way, they will disparage the other perfect virtues. Ajita,[8] what do you think of this? That king of Kashi who gave of his own flesh to a hawk for the sake of a dove,[9] was he a man of little discernment?"
>
> Maitreya said: "In no way, Blessed One."

6. Particular buddhas' spheres of influence and activity. In Buddhist cosmology, each buddha arises in a particular world system.
7. Giving, ethics, patience, effort, concentration, and wisdom.
8. Another name for Maitreya.
9. See the *Shibi Jataka*, p. 100.

The Blessed One said: "Maitreya, those roots of good, closely bound with the six perfect virtues, which I collected while I followed the career of the bodhisattva, are these roots of good counterproductive?"

Maitreya said: "In no way, Blessed One."

The Blessed one said: "You too, Ajita, have carried out the perfect virtue of giving for sixty cosmic ages, you have carried out the perfect virtue of morality for sixty cosmic ages, you have carried out the perfect virtue of acceptance for sixty cosmic ages, you have carried out the perfect virtue or fortitude for sixty cosmic ages, you have carried out the perfect virtue of contemplation for sixty cosmic ages, you have carried out the perfect virtue of discernment for sixty cosmic ages. Deluded persons might still tell you: 'There is only one way to awakening, and that is the way of emptiness.' They will not be able to purify their conduct . . ."

A bodhisattva's discernment alone, without skill in the means for liberating self and others, is very much like the discernment of those who are mere disciples; it is not able to carry out the acts of a buddha. But, possessed of skill in means, he will be able to carry out the acts of a Buddha. As it is said in the noble *Ratnakuta:*

It is as in the case of kings, Kashyapa, who, if they have ministers at their command, are able to perform all their duties. In the same way, a bodhisattva's discernment, if it has skill in means at its command, will also perform all the acts of a Buddha.

The bodhisattvas' view of the path is one thing, another thing is the understanding of those who follow mistaken paths and of the mere disciples. For, in fact, the view of the path of those who follow mistaken paths lacks discernment with respect to everything everywhere, because it is connected with the deceiving distortions of perceiving a self where there is none, and the other three such distortions.[1] Therefore, they will not gain liberation. That of the mere disciples, on the other hand, lacks great compassion and lacks the means to liberate self and others; therefore, they will strive to obtain nirvana only for themselves. The bodhisattvas' path, on the other hand, seeks to obtain both discernment and means; therefore, they will have as their aim a coming to rest in the peace of a nirvana that abides nowhere.

The bodhisattvas seek a path that is possessed of both discernment and means; therefore, they will obtain this nirvana that abides nowhere. Because, by the force of discernment they avoid falling into the whirlwind of transmigration, and by the force of the means of liberation, they avoid falling into a nirvana that is at rest. Therefore, according to the noble *Gayashirsha*, "Two are, in brief, the paths for bodhisattvas. Which two? Means and discernment."

In the noble *Shri-paramadya* it is also said: "The perfect virtue of discernment is the mother. Skill in means is the father."

In the noble *Vimalakirti-nirdesha*[2] it is also said:

---

1. Holding the impermanent to be permanent, the impure to be pure, and suffering to be happiness.

2. See the *Vimalakirti Sutra*, p. 304.

What is bondage for bodhisattvas, what is liberation? To engage in the activities of the world without means is bondage for the bodhisattva. To move about in worldly activity accompanied by means is his liberation. To engage in the activities of the world without discernment is bondage for the bodhisattva. To move about in worldly activity accompanied by discernment is his liberation. Discernment which is not fully possessed of means is bondage. Discernment fully possessed of means is liberation. Means which is not fully possessed of discernment is bondage. Means fully possessed of discernment is liberation. . . .

If a bodhisattva practices only discernment he will end, as it were, in bondage, because he will fall into the complete rest sought by the mere disciples. He will not attain to the liberation found in the peace of a nirvana that abides nowhere. This is why it is said that discernment deprived of means is bondage for the bodhisattvas.

This is why the bodhisattva, making use of discernment coupled with means, resorts to emptiness only in order to avoid the cold wind of erroneous views, just as someone would resort to fire to protect himself from cold winds. But he does not let the fire of emptiness take over, as the mere disciples would do. As it is said in the noble *Dashadharmaka Sutra*:

> Son of good family, it is like the case of a certain man who would light a fire and worship it, venerate it, with the thought: "I should worship fire, I should venerate it." While paying reverence in this way he would not think of holding the fire in his two hands. And why is this so? Because he would realize: "It would cause me bodily pain and mental discomfort." In the same way, the bodhisattva too, although having the aspiration to complete rest, does not bring about complete rest in his own person. And why is this so? Because he would realize: "This would turn me away from awakening."

But if he were to practice only means, the bodhisattva would not go beyond the stage of a common man and he would remain in a state of bondage. Therefore, he should practice means accompanied by discernment. If the bodhisattva, like someone taking poison with the help of mantras, will turn even the afflictions into ambrosia when he perceives them with the power of discernment, how much more will he attain, cultivating in this way generous giving and the other means of liberation, which by themselves bring about the highest results? As it is said in the noble *Ratnakuta*:

> Kashyapa, a poison imbibed with a mantra or an antidote loses its capacity to kill. In the same way, the bodhisattvas will accept the afflictions with discernment, and thus will not slide back.

Consequently, for the very reason that the bodhisattva does not reject the cycle of transmigration, through the power of his practice of the means to liberate self and others, he does not fall into the ultimate rest of nirvana. For the same reason that he has given up all apprehension by the force of discernment, he does not fall into the cycle of transmigration. This is why he attains to the peace of a nirvana that abides nowhere, that is, he attains to buddhahood. This is why it is also said in the noble *Akashagarbha*: "Through skill in discernment, he gives up all the afflictions. Through skill in means, he does not abandon all living beings."

It is also said in the noble *Sandhinirmochana*:

> Someone who does not favor the goals of living beings, who is not well disposed to all the labors pertaining to the compounded, I say that he is not on his way to the unsurpassable full awakening.

Therefore, he who seeks to obtain buddhahood should practice both discernment and means.

Now, it is true that the practice of means, generous giving and the rest, is impossible while one is cultivating supramundane discernment in meditation or during periods of deep concentration; yet, the practice of means is indeed required at the time of the preparatory practices and when practicing the discernment that flows from supramundane knowledge. This is why discernment and means interpenetrate.

Furthermore, this is that path of the bodhisattvas in which discernment and means proceed coupled together: the bodhisattva, having adopted the great compassion, which keeps in view all living beings, practices the supramundane path, but, once he arises from the practice of such meditations, he will practice means free of erroneous views, like the magician of the simile.

As it has been said in the noble *Akshayamati-nirdesha*:

> What is, then, the bodhisattva's means of liberating self and others? What is the perfection of his discernment? That at the time of practicing concentration he is able to collect his mind with great compassion as his object, always keeping in view all sentient beings, this is his skill in means. That his mind proceeds in equilibrium, in perfect serenity and tranquillity, that is his skill in discernment. . . .

It is also said in the *Chapter on the Destruction of Mara*[3]:

> Furthermore, the consummation of the bodhisattvas' practice is a practice in which, by skill in discernment, he acts with no exertion, and by skill in means he gathers all the good qualities and virtues of a buddha. It is a practice in which, by skill in discernment, he is free of the idea of a self, a living being, a soul, a person, or of a human being, and by skill in means he brings all sentient beings to full maturity. . . .

It is also said in the noble *Dharmasangiti Sutra*:

> A magician will exert himself in producing an illusory human being, yet will have no attachment to this magically produced being; for he will know it for what it truly is. In the same way he who is an expert in perfect awakening, having recognized that the triple world is like a magical creation, will put on the armor of the bodhisattva for the sake of the world, knowing the world for what it truly is.

With reference to the bodhisattva's exclusive practice of the method of discernment and means the sutra says: "His activity stands in the cycle of transmigration, while his mind stands in the perfect rest of nirvana."

---

3. Mara is the personification of evil and desire.

Thus, one should cultivate the means to liberate self and others, namely, generous giving and the rest dedicated to the unsurpassable perfect awakening, at the heart of which are emptiness and the great compassion. And in order to produce the thought of awakening in the mode of the ultimate goal, he should, as explained before, repeatedly cultivate as much as possible the practice of both calm and insight.

And one should cultivate skill in means at all times, using as a basis for recollection the benefits that accrue on the bodhisattvas who at all times seek to benefit living beings, as the noble *Gochara-parishuddhi* describes such benefits.

Thus he who cultivates compassion, means, and the thought of awakening, with time he will no doubt come to excel in them. Afterwards, he will constantly see buddhas and bodhisattvas in dreams, and have other auspicious dreams. The gods too, being pleased with him, will protect him. At every moment he will be gathering a vast equipment of merit and wisdom. He will be free of the veil created by the afflictions and by mental obscurations and physical failings. He will always be at ease and with a serene mind. He will be loved by many beings, his body will be free of disease, and he will obtain such superior powers and virtues as the higher forms of knowledge, and the rest. And then, by the force of his psychic powers, he will travel to endless world spheres to render homage to the blessed buddhas, and he will hear the dharma from them. At the time of his death he will surely see buddhas and bodhisattvas. In future lives also he will be born in a noble family in a land not lacking buddhas and bodhisattvas.

Thereafter, he will effortlessly complete the equipment of merit and wisdom; he will obtain the great joy and the vast retinue of buddhas and bodhisattvas; he will also bring to full maturity many living beings using his acute discernment; and he will remember his past lives. One can learn in other sutras as well the immeasurable benefits resulting from this practice.

For, in fact, having developed compassion, means, and the thought of awakening constantly and reverently for a long time in the way described here, the flow of his mind will attain gradually to instants of an ever-increasing purity, and once it is fully mature, when he has reached to the extreme limit of the development of the real object, like fire consuming the two friction sticks that produced it, he will produce a knowledge which is free from the complete network of conceptual thought. With this knowledge he understands clearly the ground of reality which is free from discursive ideation, radiant, stainless, and steady, like the steady flame of a lamp protected from the wind. At that point will have arisen the very essence of the thought of awakening according to the ultimate goal, in conjunction with that path of vision which directly perceives the absence of a self in all dharmas.

When this higher thought of awakening arises, the bodhisattva realizes, as his object of meditation, the limit of the real, and he is born into the family of the tathagatas; he enters the state of assured success of the bodhisattvas. The bodhisattva leaves behind all worldly activity, and stands firmly in the bodhisattvas' understanding of the true nature of all things; he stands firmly in the bodhisattvas' sphere of reality.

These benefits, which arise upon obtaining the first stage of the bodhisattva path, can be understood in detail by consulting the *Dashabhumika* and other sutras. This is the "Contemplation with Suchness as Its Object," as it is taught in the noble *Lankavatara*. This is the bodhisattva's entrance into a condition that is free of both diffuse discursive ideation and conceptual constructs.

The preliminary stage is called the stage of "Practice by Aspiration." It is defined by the fact that in this stage progress is due to the force of aspiration, and not the result of direct realization. Once true knowledge arises, one progresses by means of direct perception, and thus enters the first stage.

Thereafter, in the path of development, one cultivates discernment and the means for liberating self and others by practicing two forms of wisdom: the knowledge that is beyond worldly knowledge and the resultant knowledge as it is applied to the world.

As the bodhisattva with this practice cleanses himself, step-by-step, of ever more subtle veils of those obscurations that are to be cast aside only through cultivation, and as he obtains ever more excellent virtues and good qualities, he purifies the remaining stages of the path until he enters into the wisdom of a tathagata.

Then, entering the ocean of the omniscience of a buddha, he comes to realize fully the meditational object which is the consummation of the task.

The noble *Lankavatara* also has explained in similar fashion how the mind is purified in this gradual fashion. Also in the noble *Sandhinirmochana* it is said: "Step by step, in ever higher stages, the mind is purified, like gold being gradually purified, until one awakens to unsurpassable perfect awakening."

Entering the ocean of all-knowledge, he obtains the accumulation of virtues that heal all living beings, like the wish-fulfilling gem. He attains the fruit of his previous vows; his great compassion acts by its own nature; he becomes possessed of a great variety of means for the liberation of self and others, which carry out their task effortlessly; he carries out all kinds of tasks for the sake of countless living beings using immeasurable apparition bodies. He will perfect incalculable perfect virtues and merit, and remove every single stain of defect, removing even the most subtle traces of stain, yet he will remain until the whole universe of living beings comes to an end. Whosoever understands this will produce faith in the buddhas, the blessed ones, who are the source of all virtues, and, in order to obtain those same virtues, he will exert himself in every way.

This is why the Blessed One has said:

> The knowledge of the All-knower springs from compassion as its root, from the thought of awakening as its immediate cause, and with the practice of the means to liberation it reaches its culmination.

> > Having given up such stains as envy and the rest,
> > Those who practice the good are never satisfied with their
> > own virtue,
> > As the ocean is not sated by its own water.
> > Discerning rightly, they understand what is well spoken,
> > As the wild goose joyfully separates milk from water.
> > Therefore, the truly wise will throw aside all thoughts
> > disturbed by partiality
> > And accept whatever is well spoken even if it comes from the
> > mouth of a child.

By whatever merit I may have gained in explaining the middle
   way,
May all living beings without exception
Obtain this very same middle way.

Thus concludes the *Steps in the Practice of Contemplation* by master Kamalashila. Translated, corrected, and revised by the Indian teacher Prajnavarma
and the Lotsawa Bande Yeshe-de.

BUDDHIST TANTRA

RITUALS FOR A BETTER REBIRTH

TANTRA ON THE COMPLETE PURIFICATION OF ALL NEGATIVE PLACES OF REBIRTH
(*The Sarvadurgatiparishodhana Tantra*)

Buddhist tantra, which began in India in the sixth or seventh century C.E., resists description for a number of reasons. Scholars are unsure of its precise origins, although it shares much with certain Hindu traditions of the same period. What qualifies as "tantric" is also difficult to specify. In the popular imagination, its defining feature is sexual yoga. But this largely misunderstood practice, although present in a number of important tantric texts, is hardly universal. Scholars have pointed to various common elements, such as mandalas, mantras, and mudras (hand gestures), but none of these in and of itself seems able to make a text or practice tantric. Even the meaning of the word *tantra* remains somewhat elusive. Its usual sense, something like "handbook," offers little insight into its use as the name for a hugely influential constituent of Buddhist practice in India, Nepal, Tibet, and East Asia.

Traditional Buddhist exegetes have argued at length about what distinguishes the esoteric, or tantric, path from the exoteric, or sutra, path. There was general consensus, at least among the advocates of tantra, that the tantric path bestowed buddhahood more quickly. However, the reading of almost any of the famous tantras reveals goals far more quotidian than buddhahood, as the tantra provides a handbook for their achievement. Indeed, the means for achieving those goals came to be sorted into four categories: "pacifying activities" (rituals for purifying negativity that appears in such forms as obstacles and illness), "activities of increase" (rituals for increasing prosperity, lengthening life, etc.), "activities of control" (rituals for subjugating the unruly or unwilling), and "violent activities" (rituals for killing both individuals and enemy armies). Nowhere in this schema is enlightenment mentioned.

One work that sets forth such rituals is the *Tantra on the Complete Purification of All Negative Places of Rebirth* (*Sarvadurgatiparishodhana Tantra*). Its earliest translation into Tibetan at the end of the eighth century of the Common Era provides the latest date for the period of its original composition in India. At the beginning of the text, Shakra (another name for Indra), the king of the gods, asks the Buddha about the fate of a deity named Vimalamaniprabha who no longer resides in the Heaven of the Thirty-three atop Mount Meru. The Buddha explains that he has been reborn in the most torturous of the eight hot hells. Alarmed at this news, the gods ask the Buddha how they can avoid rebirth in the three negative places of rebirth (in Sanskrit *durgati*—literally, "bad migrations"): the realms of animals, ghosts, and denizens of hell. In the remainder of the text, the Buddha sets forth a variety of rituals pertaining to the four kinds of activities as well as the dead; examples are included in the selection from the tantra here. The text was widely commented on in Tibet, where it was a major source of rituals for the fortunate rebirth of the dead.

Abhayamdada: *a-ba-yam-da-da*

Akashagarbha: *ah-kah-sha-gar-ba*

Amkusha: *am-ku-sha*

Aparimitayuhpunyajnanasambharatejo-
    raja: *a-pa-ri-mih-tah-yu-pun-ya-jnyah-
    na-sam-bah-ra-te-joh-rah-ja*

Avalokiteshvara: *a-va-loh-ki-tay-shva-ra*

Bhrum: *broom*

Bodhisattva: *boh-dih-sat-tva*

Chakravartin: *cha-kra-var-tin*

Devaputra: *day-va-pu-tra*

Hrih: *hree*

Hrim: *hreem*

Jambudvipa: *jam-bu-dvi-pa*

Kalparaja: *kal-pa-rah-ja*

Karmavishva: *kar-ma-vish-va*

mantrin: *man-trihn*

Mrityu: *mriht-yu*

Padmadhara: *pad-ma-da-ra*

paryanka: *par-yan-ka*

Ratnadhara: *rat-na-da-ra*

sadhana: *sah-da-na*

samayamudra: *sa-ma-ya-mu-drah*

Sarvadurgatiparishodhana Tantra: *sar-
    va-dur-ga-tee-pa-ri-sho-da-na tan-tra*

Svaha: *svah-hah*

Tathagata: *ta-tah-ga-ta*

Trailokyavijayin: *trai-loh-kya-vi-ja-yin*

Vajradhara: *vaj-ra-da-ra*

Vajrapadma: *vaj-ra-pad-ma*

Vajrapani: *vaj-ra-pah-nih*

Vajraratna: *vaj-ra-rat-na*

Vajrasattva Samantabhadra: *vaj-ra-sat-
    tva sa-man-ta-ba-dra*

Vajravajra: *vaj-ra-va-jra*

Vidya: *vi-dyah*

Vishvadhara: *vi-shva-da-ra*

Mandala of the King of Long Life

The Lord *Vajrapani*[1] once more looked at the circle of his assembly and smiled. The *mandala*[2] of the assembly was moved, much moved, animated, much animated, enthused, much enthused, overjoyed, much overjoyed, frolicsome, very frolicsome. Many wonders and marvels were seen in the world. *Brahma* and others, the assembly of gods, overwhelmed with amazement, prostrated themselves before the Lord and said: 'O Lord, what is the reason for your smiling? The Lord Buddhas or *Bodhisattvas* do not smile without reason. Let the Lord explain the reason for his smiling'.

The Lord *Vajrapani* listened to the gods asking for instruction and said: 'O gods, *Brahma* and the rest, listen to what was explained by all the previous Buddhas concerning the formula which destroys *Mrityu*,[3] the mighty power of the formula-*mantra* destroying untimely death'.

The Great Gods, *Brahma* and others, prostrated themselves before the Lord *Vajrapani* greatly rejoicing, their hair tingled and they recited the syllable 'Good'. 'Good good O Lord, good good O *Vajradhara*, please explain the formula having the mighty power and the great force leading to the other shore, and by means of which the living beings of short life gain longevity, those eclipsed by inauspicious *Mrityu* are freed from untimely death, those who are born in misfortune are led away from the path of all evil destinies, and those living beings who are overwhelmed with the fear of *samsara* turn

Translated from the Sanskrit and Tibetan by Tadeusz Skorupski.

1. The bodhisattva who embodies power; also called Vajradhara.
2. Literally, "circle"; the consecrated space for

the performance of a tantric ritual.
3. Literally, "Death."

away from it, by using good methods and quickly understand the supreme and perfect Enlightenment'.

The Lord *Vajrapani*, having listened to the beseeching request of *Brahma* and the others, emitted from the *Vajra* of his Body, Speech, and Mind, this spell-formula of all the *Tathagatas*[4]:

> OM MERIT MERIT, GREAT MERIT, MERIT OF UNLIMITED LIFE. ACCUMULATION OF MASSES OF KNOWLEDGE SVAHA.[5] This is the spell-formula.
> OM HRIH SVAHA. This is the subordinate spell-formula.
> OM BHRUM SVAHA. This is the subordinate spell-formula of the spell.
> OM KRUM SVAHA. This is the spell-impelling formula.
> OM TRAM SVAHA. This is the predominant spell (formula).
> OM HAM SVAHA. This is the secret formula.

This is their *mandala*.

One designs the *mandala* with four spokes. In the centre one should place the *Tathagata* called *Aparimitayuhpunyajnanasambharatejoraja* (Glorious King, the Bestower of Unlimited Life, Merit and Knowledge). The spell is the syllable BHRUM. In front of him is *Vajrapani*. The spell is the syllable HRIH. To the left is *Krodha*.[6] The spell is the syllable KRUM. To the right is *Akashagarbha*.[7] The spell is the syllable TRAM. Behind him is Noble *Avalokiteshvara*[8] known as *Abhayamdada* (The One Bestowing Fearlessness). The spell is the syllable HAM.

The *Vidyas*[9] are to be depicted in this brilliant *Tathagata mandala*. One should place there a set of five or a set of eight vases blessed with the *mantra* of *Chakravartin*,[1] incense and the rest, and other items of worship blessed with the wrathful *mantra* for all the rites, as well as the guardians in all the gates.

The *mantrin*[2] enters himself and summons the Most Blessed One surrounded by the host of his sons and attendants, and together with his *Vidya*. The *Vidya* is to be depicted on the left side of the Blessed One.

He consecrates himself, sits in the *paryanka* posture[3] and makes the recitation one hundred thousand times. In front of him he sees either the *Tathagata* or *Vajrapani* or *Avalokiteshvara*. He receives the boon according to his wish. When he is well concentrating then he is able to perform every act by application of his mind.

He should introduce his pupils by means of *Vajradhara's* gesture. Generating self-confidence he says: OM *VAJRADHARA, RATNADHARA, PADMADHARA, VISHVADHARA,* BY ADHERENCE TO THE *TATHAGATA'S* PLEDGE I HOLD THE *TATHAGATA* PLEDGE. He should have them throw flowers: OM ALL THE *TATHAGATAS* RECEIVE HOH, YOU ARE THE PLEDGE. Putting the garlands on their heads he should give the consecration.

---

4. That is, buddhas; *Tathagata* (literally, "one who has thus come/gone") is the title of a budda most often used by the historical Buddha to refer to himself. "*Vajra*": a kind of mythical thunderbolt, a weapon capable of cutting through anything.
5. An interjection indicating the end of a mantra; *om* marks the beginning.
6. Literally, "Anger."

7. One of the eight great bodhisattvas.
8. The bodhisattva who embodies the compassion of all the buddhas.
9. Consorts.
1. A wheel-turning monarch.
2. A person who recites mantras.
3. Lotus posture.

OM ALL THE *TATHAGATAS* CONSECRATE, *VAJRADHARA*
  COMMAND HUM BHRUM
OM, *VAJRAVAJRA* CONSECRATE HUM HUM
OM, *VAJRARATNA* CONSECRATE HUM TRAM
OM *VAJRAPADMA* CONSECRATE HUM HRIM
OM *KARMAVISHVA* CONSECRATE AH HUM KAM

Then he should bestow the pledge, and the precept-consecration. The pledge is this:

> He will not abandon the Three Jewels,[4] the Thought of Enlighten-
> ment and his good teacher. He will not kill living beings, and he will
> not take what has not been given. He will not say untrue things nor
> approach another man's wife. He will not despise his teacher nor
> cross his shadow. He will not adhere to those who are not true teach-
> ers nor will he pronounce the name of his *vajra*-teacher. He will not
> despise the *mantras*, the *mudras*, nor the divinities ever. If he despises
> them he will certainly die of diseases. He will not tread with his
> feet upon the remainders of the offerings, the shadows of the divin-
> ities, the *mudras* and the signs of the syllables, whether they are of
> this world or of the world above.
>
> The wise one should zealously slay those who are subverted in the
> teaching of Buddha, harmful to the Three Jewels and the rest, and
> intent on abusing the teacher. Out of compassion the *mantrin* by
> means of the *mantra* should destroy those who hate the pledge, who
> do not possess the *Dharma*, who are attached to sin, who always do
> harm to living beings. Taking the wealth of the avaricious ones he
> should give it to those who live in destitution. For the purpose of
> honouring his teacher, likewise for accomplishing the pledge, for
> use in the *mandala*, for the benefit of those belonging to the pledge
> and for worshipping the sons of the Buddhas, if he thinks it to be
> just then he should take the wealth of the avaricious ones. The one
> who delights in acting for the benefit of living beings is permitted
> to speak deceitfully in order to protect those of the pledge, his teach-
> er's possessions and the life of living beings. The one who knows the
> *mantras* may resort to someone else's woman for the sake of his
> *sadhana*,[5] for delighting the Buddhas and for protecting the pledge.
> Abiding in the place of *Vajrasattva*,[6] whether one does everything,
> whether one enjoys everything, one is successful without being in
> fault; so how much the more if one is imbued with compassion.

Then he gives the precept-consecration: OM I GIVE YOU THE PRECEPT OF ALL THE *TATHAGATAS*, ACCEPT IT FOR THE *VAJRA*-SUCCESS. OM *VAJRA* ABIDE HUM. Handing him the *vajra* he should give the *karma* consecration: OM PERFORM ALL THE ACTS OF THE BUDDHAS HUM.

In order to honour the teacher, the pupil should offer his own precious body, belongings, wealth and grain, horses and chariots, best servants and cities, his kingdom and sovereignty, sons, daughters, wife, mother, sister

---

4. The Buddha, the dharma, and the sangha (the   5. Tantric practice.
Buddhist community).   6. A tantric buddha.

and granddaughter. With the thought of gaining benefit he should offer to his teacher everything else he asks for. Then he should ask for an effective method which brings the enlightenment of the Buddhas and for any other worldly prosperity which he desires.

The one who knows the *mantras*, without envy, with faith and loyal disposition should provide the effective method for the benefit of his son. Conceiving in his mind the non-nature of the *dharmas* he envisages a lunar disc (arising) from the syllable. A, and concentrating his thought upon the appropriate seed-syllable in its centre, he should envisage the *samayamudra*[7] and so he transforms it (viz. the seed-syllable) by that process of yoga relating to the divine forms. Then he should empower the *mudra* by means of the appropriate seed-syllable and gesture and give the consecration in due order by means of the Buddhas as previously. Developing a sense of confidence, the wise one should succeed, and if he succeeds in buddhahood, how much the more in other successes.

The Great Gods, *Brahma* and the others, prostrated themselves before the Lord and said: 'O Lord, what is the fruition in the case of the king, his son or minister, warrior, *brahmana*, merchant, member of the fourth class,[8] or someone else, member of the host of low born, one born in a family of border community, who enters this royal mandala?'

The Lord said: 'Good good, O assembly of gods, Great *Brahma* and others, good indeed is this question which you put to me for the benefit of future living beings. Learn the maturation of the fruits in the case of the one who enters this royal *mandala* of the assembly of gods, who is consecrated in it, draws it, and having it drawn rejoices in it, reveres it and worships it. As for me, O gods, in short, I am unable to aspire to tell its benefits. Such merit as I have, although multiplied many hundred thousand times does not come up to its number, is not capable even of its enumeration, does not even bear comparison with it. It cannot be compared even with the merit of all the *Tathagatas*'.

'O Lord, it is wonderful, O Lord *Vajradhara*, it is wonderful, this maturation of the fruits of living beings who enter this *mandala*. We are zealous, O Lord, we are zealous, O *Vajradhara*, in entering this *mandala* and so on'.

The gods prostrated themselves in the same manner and said: 'O Lord, there are living beings in *Jambudvipa*[9] whose life is short and their merit limited. They are subject to evil destinies or they have been reborn in hells, among tormented spirits or among animals. O Lord, how are we to act on their behalf?'.

'O gods, place them here in the mandala. Having placed them in it, consecrate them and recite the *Dharma*-syllable. By means of this action those living beings gain long life. Destitute of merit, they become possessed of merit and they are freed from evil. As for those who have been reborn in evil states, O gods, consecrate their name (card), consecrate their effigy, consecrate their reliquary or the form of their divinity. At least, consecrate their son, someone of their people or of their lineage, someone bearing their name or their servant. Place (their representation) in the *mandala* seven times for seven days and nights; they become freed from the obstructions of evil destinies by means of the consecrations. O gods, recite it with his name

---

7. The visualized deity.
8. A shudra, or servant. "*Brahmana*": priest, a member of the highest caste (brahmin).

9. In Buddhist cosmology, the southern continent, on which ordinary humans dwell.

two hundred thousand times, three hundred thousand times, four hundred thousand times, as many as hundreds of thousands of times. Even those who commit the five deadly offences[1] are liberated; how much more those who commit minor offences'.

'O *Devaputras*,[2] making a hearth for the pacifying rite, round in shape, small, medium or large, one, two or four cubits in size, one should offer a sacrifice one hundred thousand times using the representation of his name and the seeds of white mustard. He is freed from every evil. Should one sacrifice his flesh, bones, hair, ashes or anything else in accordance with this rite, he becomes freed from every sin'.

In the centre (of the hearth) one should draw a circle whose eight spokes blaze forth white light. All around on the circumference he draws five-tipped *vajras* shining with white rays. Next he draws a crossed *vajra*, a *vajra*, a jewel, and a lotus. In order to destroy sins he should make the different *mudras*. On the outside he should draw the *mudras* of the outer *Vajra* Family, the signs of the Planets, Lunar Mansions and the Guardians of the World accordingly. He should place there an image of the Lord painted on a cloth together with the *vajra* entourage, vases and bowls filled with offerings and food for divinities, white in colour. In short, marking with a cord he draws the design in accordance with the rules.

Clad in a white garment, and having the appearance of a Buddha, the fearless one remembering that living being experiencing evil destiny should offer a whole series of *homa* sacrifices[3] in order to eliminate the obstructions of sins, using clarified butter and milk together with honey, parched rice and white mustard mixed together, or using his bones and similar things, or just his name (card).

Once he is born in a happy state, the wise one should perform for him the rite for gaining prosperity. He makes a square hearth, two or four or at the most eight cubits in size, having an edge on all sides. In its centre he should draw a lotus with a jewel radiating rays of golden colour. All around he should draw jewels and on the edges lotuses. On the outside he should mark the seals divided into sets of the Five Families. In the same way he should draw the seals of the outer divinities, *Amkusha*[4] and the others.

Clad in a garment of golden colour, and remembering the one who is experiencing a happy destiny, he should perform on his behalf and for his prosperity the rite for gaining prosperity. He should increase for that embodied creature the length of life, fame, beauty, and good fortune.

Next he should perform for his benefit the rite for subjugation. He makes a hearth shaped like a bow, one or two or four cubits in size. In its centre he draws a red lotus and on the top of it a bow with an arrow attached to it. All around he draws bows and arrows red in colour. The one accomplished in *mantras* should always do the same on the outside of it.

Adorned with a garment red in colour, and remembering that living being, he offers a *homa* sacrifice using saffron mixed with clarified butter, powder of red sandal wood, red flowers or red lotuses together with red fruits. All the divinities and the rest become subdued to his power.

---

1. Killing one's father, killing one's mother, killing an arhat, wounding a buddha, or causing schism in the sangha.

2. Gods.
3. Fire sacrifices.
4. A guardian deity.

In order to destroy the evil ones opposed to him, he should embark on performing the rite for destroying. He makes a hearth two and a half or three or at the most nine cubits in size, triangular in form, with a nine-tipped *vajra* in the centre, with the rim surrounded with tridents and crossed *vajras*, and marked with clubs, heads, tridents and pointed *vajra*-axes. On the outside he should adorn it as before with a threefold series. He places in it vases and bowls for offerings and lots of food for the divinities. He also places everywhere skulls filled with blood and flesh.

The fierce one, *Trailokyavijayin*[5] himself, wearing a black garment, should destroy all the obstructions of sins and so on of that embodied creature. Freed from the obstructions, his sins totally destroyed, he will progress happily to the world of gods or men in the threefold world-spheres.[6]

He should act promptly in the same manner with regard to those who live in this life. It should happen accordingly in the case of those on whose behalf the action is taken.

As for all other rites, he should perform them as previously. In this way the attainment of happiness for living beings is achieved immediately.

The gods, *Brahma* and the others, filled with joy, bowed before the Lord and said: 'With regard to the one who writes this *Kalparaja*[7] or has it written for the benefit, good and happiness of living beings reborn in evil places, we gods, *Brahma* and the rest will protect that son or daughter of (our) lineage like our own subjects, how much more if he follows without false notions its teaching just as it has been explained. We will extend the sovereignty of that king or his son or his minister who expounds the *mantras* in accordance with their invocations. We will promote his sovereignty, protect his country, provinces, people and subjects, his crops and the rest. We will provide wealth and grain in abundance; grant women, men, sons and daughters; bestow prosperity, sustenance, provisions and peace.

Should a believer in this *Kalparaja* put it on the top of the royal banner and enter into cities, trade places and so forth, or should he set out himself mounted on an elephant, wandering through all villages and towns, all deadly calamities will be eliminated. We will recognise the rank of that great being by servitude or with filial submission.

Wherever this should be practiced, we pray that the Lord *Vajrapani* may be present there in the form of *Vajrasattva* with his glorified bodies. We pray that the Lord *Vajrasattva Samantabhadra*,[8] who fulfils all hopes, may abide there in the form of this *Kalparaja*. We pray that all the *Tathagatas* together with their entourage abide there and may that part of the earth become a *chaitya*.[9] We worship, we venerate, we protect. We gods, *Brahma* and the rest, are servants of that great hermit, the *vajra*-teacher who practises *Kalparaja*. We will stand by him like slaves ready to serve and to obey every order. We will grant every benefit, happiness and complete success. O Lord, in short, we will wipe the dust of his feet with our heads. O Lord, we venerate him. O Lord, we worship him and follow behind him.

---

5. "Conqueror of the Three Worlds," a wrathful tantric deity.
6. The Realm of Desire, the Realm of Form, and the Formless Realm; see pp. 54–55.

7. Royal work.
8. The bodhisattva who embodies the practices and vows of the bodhisattva.
9. A shrine.

O Lord, we pray that the living beings who enter and are consecrated in the *mandala* may become our masters. O Lord, we recognise him as *Vajrapani, Vajrasattva, Samantabhadra* the Great Bliss. We recognise him as the *Tathagata.*

The Lord *Vajrapani* addressed the gods, *Brahma* and the others saying: 'It is good that by such a devotion to the *Dharma* you make this true vow. Accomplish it well'.

HOW TO PRACTICE TANTRA

TANTRA ON THE COMPLETE ENLIGHTENMENT OF VAIROCHANA
(*The Vairochanabhisambodhi Tantra*)

Among the elements associated with tantric Buddhism, perhaps none is as recognizable as the mandala, the complex multicolored circular pattern often depicted on Buddhist scrolls. The assumption that a mandala is something for the meditator to gaze at as a means of focusing the mind is fairly widespread, but it is false. The Sanskrit term *mandala* simply means "circle." In early tantric rituals, it was a circle drawn on the ground, meant to designate a consecrated space, a world apart; indeed, initiation into a specific tantric practice was called "entering the mandala." Eventually, the space inside the circle came to be viewed as a buddha's marvelous palace, with doorways in the four cardinal directions and a sacred chamber in the center, where the buddha sat enthroned. Artistic conventions developed to schematically represent this three-dimensional palace in a two-dimensional form. Both the paintings of mandalas placed vertically on walls or scrolls and sand mandalas created horizontally depict these palaces.

Much tantric practice involves visualization; some Tibetan exegetes would argue that the distinguishing feature of tantric practice was to turn the goal into the path by visualizing oneself as the buddha that one seeks to become—imagining oneself with the body of a buddha, adorned with the thirty-two major marks and eighty secondary marks and seated resplendent on the throne at the center of the mandala palace. Thus, mandalas came to be described in great detail, each with a different buddha at its center.

One of the most famous, especially for East Asian Buddhism, is called the mandala of the womb element (*garbhadhatu*): it is set forth in a work titled the *Vairochanabhisambodhi*, the *Enlightenment of Vairochana*. The full Sanskrit title of the work means "The Extensive Sutra on the Enlightenment, Miracles, and Empowerment of Mahavairochana." Vairochana, whose name means "Shining," is one of the five buddhas who appear in many mandalas; he also plays an important role in the *Avatamsaka Sutra*, or *The Flower Garden Discourse*. Here, he is the central buddha.

The text, called a tantra in India and a sutra in China, was likely composed in India sometime between the mid-sixth and seventh centuries. The text is essentially a dialogue between the buddha Vairochana and the bodhisattva Vajrapani ("He Who Holds a Thunderbolt in His Hand"), also known as "Lord of Secrets." The bodhisattva asks the buddha how to gain "the knowledge that knows all," or complete enlightenment (the *abhisambodhi* of the title). Vairochana replies that the aspiration to enlightenment (*bodhichitta*) is its cause, compassion is its root, and skillful means (*upaya*) is its culmination. The remainder of the text expands on these three key concepts, also dealing extensively with initiation, mantra recitation, mudras, visualization, and the description of the mandala.

The selection presented here is the ritual manual appended to the end of the tantra, where specific instructions for daily practice are set forth, including visualization of oneself as the buddha Vajrasattva and as the bodhisattva Avalokiteshvara, the bodhisattva of compassion.

PRONOUNCING GLOSSARY

Achalanatha: *a-cha-la-nah-ta*
anuttara samyaksambodhi: *a-nu-ta-rah sam-yak-sam-boh-di*
argha: *ar-ga*
Avalokiteshvara: *a-va-loh-ki-tay-shva-ra*
Bhadracharyapranidhana: *ba-dra-char yah-pra-ni-dah-na*
bodhisattva: *boh-di-sat-tva*
danapati: *dah-na-pa-ti*
Mahavairochana: *ma-hah-vai-roh-cha-na*
mantrin: *man-trin*
Samantabhadra: *sa-man-ta-ba-dra*
sangha: *san-ga*

siddhi: *si-di*
svaha: *svah-hah*
Tathagata: *ta-tah-ga-ta*
Trailokyavijaya: *trai-loh-kya-vi-ja-ya*
udana: *u-dah-na*
vidya: *vih-dyah*
Vaipulya: *vai-pul-ya*
Vairochana: *vai-roh-cha-na*
Vairochanabhisambodhi Tantra: *vai-ro-cha-nah-bee-sam-bo-dee tan-tra*
vajra: *vaj-ra*
Vajrasattva: *vaj-ra-sat-tva*

Mantra Deeds

Then the mantra practitioner, having finished reciting by the rules as appropriate, should again in accordance with the earlier [ritual] deeds empower himself so that he becomes the person of Vajrasattva,[1] think of the immeasurable merits of multitudes of Buddhas and bodhisattvas, arouse thoughts of great compassion toward inexhaustible realms of beings, and make offerings according to his means. Having made offerings, he should then singlemindedly clasp his palms together and with adamantine chanting and other sublime words extol the true merits of the Tathagata.[2]

Then, with all the good that he has performed, he redirects it and makes a vow, uttering these words: "Just as the Great Awakened World-honored One redirected the merit that he had realized, comprehended, and accumulated toward unsurpassed *bodhi*,[3] so too do I now give my entire mass of merit to beings in the Dharma realm to enable them all to cross the sea of birth-and-death all together, accomplish the path of omniscience, satisfy all the *dharmas* of own-benefit and benefiting others, and abide by the great abode of the Tathagata. It is not that I seek *bodhi* for my own sake alone. As long as I repeat birth-and-death to save beings so that they may similarly obtain all-faceted knowledge, I will always cultivate merit and knowledge

TRANSLATED FROM the Chinese by Rolf W. Giebel. All bracketed additions are the translator's.

1. A buddha.
2. The title of a buddha most often used by the historical Buddha to refer to himself (literally,

"one who has thus come/gone").
3. Enlightenment.

without engaging in any other actions. I pray that we may attain foremost happiness and that the sought-after *siddhis*[4] will be all consummated, free from any obstacles."

In addition, he thinks further: "Let me be quickly endowed with various pure and wondrous jewels, both internal and external, and myself adorned therewith. May they continuously and uninterruptedly flow forth everywhere and by reason of this fulfill every wish of all beings."

Thus has it been explained above in brief. When practicing more extensively, you should do as is explained in *Samantabhadra's Vow of Practice* (*Bhadracharyaprapidhana*) and other sutras of the Great Vehicle,[5] reciting them with resolve. Alternatively, say: "Just as Buddhas and bodhisattvas aroused vows of great compassion [in accordance with] what they themselves had realized, so too do I make a vow."

Next, you should offer up *argha*.[6] Form the hand-clasp of homage, place it on top of your head, think of the true merits of Buddhas and bodhisattvas, make obeisance with utmost sincerity, and speak these verses:

> In all those who have long been free from all faults,
>   whose bodies are adorned with immeasurable merits,
> And who are intent on bringing benefit to beings
>   I now take refuge and make obeisance to them all.

Next, you should address the holy ones, speaking these verses:

> The Buddhas here present, the world-saving bodhisattvas,
> And those who have reached the special stage without
>   discontinuing the teachings of the Great Vehicle—
> I but pray that the multitude of holy divinities will
>   acknowledge me with certainty,
> And may each, according to their abode, later deign to
>   come again out of pity.

Then, using the *samaya* mantra[7] and mystic seal, you should release [the seal] on top of your head and engender the thought that all the protection and empowerment [performed earlier with mantras and seals] has been released. With this expedient means the deities earlier invoked each return to their abode, otherwise [if not released] they will be compelled to remain on account of their unequaled great vows.

Next, use [the mantra and seal of] the essence of the Dharma realm to empower yourself, think of the pure *bodhi*-mind, and dwell in the person of Vairasattva. The *vidyas*[8] and seals for this have already been explained in Chapter II. When you have finished reciting, empower yourself with those three seals, and all the gateways to mantra practices having come to an end, the rules will have all been fulfilled.

Then, in accordance with the earlier expedient means, you should visualize the letter of the Dharma realm (i.e., *Ram*) marking the top of your head with it. Don adamantine armor, and on account of this secret adornment

4. Magical powers.
5. Mahayana Buddhism. Samantabhadra is the bodhisattva who embodies the practices and vows of the bodhisattva.
6. An offering of water mixed with flowers, leaves, and rice.
7. The pledge mantra, used to visualize the deity.
8. Statements of great potency, spells (*vidya* literally means "wisdom").

you will become indestructible, like a *vajra*[9] in nature. All those who hear your voice or see or touch you will most certainly be [established] in *anuttara samyak-sambodhi*,[1] with all merits completely accomplished, and you will be equal to the World-honored One Vairochana,[2] with no difference.

Next, arouse thoughts of advancement and practice special deeds. In a clean place adorned with fragrant flowers first make yourself into the bodhisattva Avalokiteshvara[3] or dwell in the own-nature of the Tathagata and, following the earlier expedient means, empower [yourself] with a mantra and mystic seal. Then, with thoughts of [making] a Dharma gift, read aloud the Vaipulya scriptures[4] of the Great Vehicle or else recite them [silently] in your mind and invite heavenly divinities and so on to listen to them. As is said in these verses:

> In the *Adamantine Pinnacle Sutra* it is taught that
>   Avalokiteshvara, lotus-eyed,
> Is identical with all Buddhas, a body of inexhaustible
>   adornments.
> Alternatively, use the Guiding Teacher of the world,
>   sovereign over all *dharmas*,[5]
> And, taking either of their names, perform empowerment
>   with their original nature.

The seed heart[-mantra] of Avalokiteshvara is: *Namah samantabuddhanam, sah.*

> The true meaning of [this] letter-gateway is that all
>   *dharmas* are undefiled:
> With the enunciation of the sound you should perform
>   such a visualization.
> The appearance of the bodily mystic [seal] for this is the
>   so-called lotus-flower seal,
> Like the seat offered earlier—I have already explained it
>   separately.

Next, the mantra of Avalokiteshvara is: *Namah samantabuddhanam, sarvatathagatavalokita karunamaya ra ra ra hum jah svaha.*

[As] before, place the heart-letter of the Dharma realm (i.e., *Ram*) on top of your head, use this mantra and mystic seal for empowerment, and to the best of your ability read aloud the scriptural Dharma or construct a *chaitya*,[6] *mandala*, and so on. When what has to be done has been completed, next rise from your seat, and with a peaceable countenance you should attend to human affairs.

Then in order to obtain sustenance for your body, next go begging for food, or else it is obtained either through an invitation [to a meal] by a *danapati* (donor) or within the sangha.[7] You should eschew fish, meat, [strong-] smelling vegetables, and leftovers from offerings to your deity and the Bud-

9. A kind of mythical thunderbolt, a weapon capable of cutting through anything.
1. "Unsurpassed complete perfect enlightenment," that is, buddhahood.
2. A buddha.
3. The bodhisattva who embodies the compassion of all the buddhas.
4. "Extensive" scriptures, a class of Mahayana sutras.
5. Here, phenomena.
6. Shrine.
7. The Buddhist community.

dhas, as well as various scraps that are unclean. Nor should you consume any liquor or juices from the fruits of trees which may intoxicate people.

Next, present morsels of food, offering them to your deity, and perform the food rite as you please. If there happen to be any leftovers, then put aside a small amount for the relief of the starving and the needy. You should engender these thoughts: "In order to maintain my physical vessel and practice the path in peace, I accept these morsels of food, just as the linchpin of a cartwheel is greased in order to make it reach the destination without breaking down. I must not on account of the food's taste be swayed in my mind and engender thoughts of pleasure or physical adornment." Then visualize the heart-letter of the Dharma realm, completely purifying the food, and with the action-*vajra* empower your own person: the seed-[-syllable] for this is like the mantra for the letter *Vam* explained [in Chapter III]. Then recite the *vidya* for bestowing the ten powers eight times, and eat the food. This *vidya* is: *Namah sarvabuddhabodhisattvanam, om balamdade tejomalini svaha.* (Homage to all Buddhas and bodhisattvas! *Om*, O you who grant power! you who are wreathed in splendor! *svaha!*[8])

Dwelling thus, first accomplish the *yoga* of your deity. When you have finished eating, you should offer the leftover food that has been touched to those who deserve to eat it with the mantra-heart for accomplishing all deeds. You should use the mantra of the holy one Achala,[9] infallible and most wrathful. You should recite it once, and the recipient will rejoice, constantly follow the practitioner, and think protectively of him. The mantra is: *Namah samantavajranam, trat amoghachandamaharoshana sphotaya hum tramaya tramaya hum trat ham mam.* (Homage to all Vajras! *Trat*, O infallible, violent, and most wrathful one! rend asunder! *hum!* confuse, confuse! *hum trat ham mam!*)

Having finished eating, rest for a short while, and then you should again worship the Buddhas and repent of your sins in order to purify your mind. Cultivate regular actions in this manner, as well as reading the scriptures aloud as before, and always dwell thus. So too is it [done] in the latter part of the day.

In the first watch and final watch of the night think uninterruptedly of the Great Vehicle. On reaching the middle watch of the night, don adamantine armor with the action-*vajra* as before and pay reverence to all the Buddhas and great bodhisattvas. Then you should make offerings with the mind according to the rules and form this thought: "Because I seek after the causes and conditions of the most important thing (i.e., enlightenment) for the sake of all beings, I shall sleep for a short while out of solicitude for this body. It is not because of craving for the pleasures of sleep." First you should arrange your physical posture and lie down on your right side with both feet placed one on top of the other. Should your limbs become tired, you may turn over as you please without offense. In order to make yourself wake up quickly, you should always fix your mind on something bright. Moreover, you should not lie down on a bed.

Next, on other days too practice in this manner. The *mantrin*,[1] by not neglecting the rules and practicing diligently without interruption, gains the

---

8. An interjection indicating the end of a mantra.
9. In tantric Buddhism, a wrathful protector deity.
He is also called Achalanatha.
1. A person who recites mantras.

designation of one who cultivates bodhisattva practices via the gateway of mantras. If, in rites of recitation with the number [of recitations], times, manifestation of signs, and so on [specified], you perform the preliminary expedient means and practice in full the special actions, but are nonetheless unsuccessful, you should admonish yourself and redouble your efforts; do not engender thoughts of inferiority and say, "This method is not suitable for me." In this manner you develop willpower, benefit yourself and benefit others, and never spend your time in vain. Because the practitioner is assiduous and never rests, the holy ones mystically illuminate his mind, whereupon he experiences the establishment of awesome divinity and gains freedom from obstacles.

In this there are two things that you should not forsake. Namely, you should not forsake the Buddhas and bodhisattvas, nor the thought of bringing benefit to inexhaustible beings. Your mind never wavers in its wish for omniscience, and for this reason you will most certainly achieve the appropriate *siddhi*.

> Always rely on internal rites to bathe;
>   you should not be attached to rites for external
>   purification.
> Harbor doubts about food that has been touched and so on:
>   no such [food] should be considered.
> If it is for maintaining the body,
>   bathe at any time to remove grime,
> In a river current and so on according to the ritual
>   instructions
>   and in conjunction with mantras and seals.
> With the heart[-syllable] of the Dharma realm purify the
>   waters
>   and use Achala and Trailokyavijaya² as appropriate,
> Protecting the [four] quarters and so on with their mantras
>   and seals,
>   and dwell in meditation on the own-nature of your deity.
> Then you should mantrify clean earth three times
>   and constantly engage singlemindedly in right thinking.
> Keeping in mind the holy one Achala's mantra and so on,
>   the wise person should bathe in silence.

The heart[-syllable] of the pure Dharma realm and Achalanatha's seed [heart-mantra] and sword seal are all as previously explained. The seed heart[-mantra] of Trailokyavijaya is: *Namah samantavajranam, hah.* (Homage to all Vajras! Hah!)

> The principle behind the sound of the letter-gateway *Ha*
>   here is as explained earlier;
> A slight difference is that it signifies the aspect of
>   purification.
> In the ritual for the bodily mystic [seal] of the honored one
>   Trailokyavijaya
> You should use the five-wisdom *vajra* seal for accomplishing
>   [all] deeds.

---

2. "Conqueror of the Three Worlds," a wrathful tantric deity.

Next, the mantra of Trailokyavijaya is: *Namah samantavajranam, ha ha ha vismaye sarvatathagatavishayasambhava trailokyavijaya hum jah svaha.*

> Having thus bathed and sprinkled [water on yourself] for
> purification,
>> and endowed with the *samaya* [seals], protect [all] parts
>> of your body;
> Think of the inexhaustible multitudes of holy divinities
>> and, thrice taking scoops of water, offer it to them.
> In order to purify your body and mind and benefit others,
>> pay reverence to the Tathagatas and sons born of the
>> Jina,[3]
> And far removed from the differentiation of the three poisons[4]
> and so on,
>> and with your sense organs disciplined, betake yourself
>> to the meditation chamber.
> Alternatively, follow a different expedient means for the
> water chamber,
>> the mind dwelling in accordance with the earlier rules of
>> restraint,
> And make your own three equals the measure
>> for seeking higher, middling, and lower rites.
> When the practitioner performs recitation in this manner,
>> the entire stream of his sins will cease for ever,
> He will most certainly succeed in destroying obstacle's,
>> and the state of omniscience will gather in his person.
> He bases himself on Chapter [V] "Mundane Accomplishment"
>> or on explanations in other sutras,
> And the elements of worship and sundry expedient means
>> are practiced in accordance with their procedures.
> Because he is not yet free from the characteristics of the
> conditioned,
>> this is called mundane *siddhi*.
> Next the most excellent, that without characteristics, is
> explained,
>> observed by those endowed with faith-and-understanding.
> If someone with profound wisdom concerning the Mantra
> Vehicle
>> seeks after the unsurpassed result in this life,
> He should practice contemplation according to his faith-
> and-understanding,
>> as in the earlier rules for mental worship
> And basing himself on the *yoga* rites
>> in Chapter [VI] "The Manifestation of *Siddhi*" and
>> Chapter [XXX] "[Mundane and] Supramundane
>> [Recitation]."
> In the state of truth, of dependent arising,
>> his inner mind with the limbs [of recitation] will be free
>> from objects of cognition,

3. Literally, "Conqueror," a title of buddhas.
4. The three basic mental afflictions: desire, hatred, and ignorance.

And experiencing and practicing on the basis of this
  expedient means,
    he will always gain supramundane accomplishments.

As is said in an *udana*⁵ verse that has been taught:

  The Dharma without [differentiating] characteristics, most
    profound, is unsuitable for those of inferior intelligence.
  In order to cater for them there also exists the teaching of
    that which has [differentiating] characteristics.

The above ritual of worship from the *Scripture of the Enlightenment, Supernatural Transformations, and Empowerment of Mahavairochana*, collected by the *acharya*,⁶ ends herewith. The transmitter is quite satisfied with it. Moreover, out of a desire to reduce its volume, duplicated mantras have been deleted; they are to be transposed and used [as appropriate]. The practitioner should simply combine the meaning of the passages before and after [to determine the omitted mantras].

5. An inspired utterance.   6. Tantric master.

TANTRIC MASTERS

LIVES OF THE EIGHTY-FOUR SIDDHAS
(*The Chaturashitisiddhapravritti*)

ABHAYADATTA

The *mahasiddhas*, or "great adepts" in Sanskrit, are the saints of tantric Buddhism in India and Tibet. Traditionally eighty-four in number (although there are other counts), they are a motley crew drawn largely from the lowest levels of traditional Indian society, including hunters, fishermen, blacksmiths, gamblers, beggars, shoemakers, pimps, and lapsed monks. They are masters of transforming pollution into purity.

This mastery is rooted in their possession of *siddhis*, a Sanskrit term that literally means "accomplishments" but in this context means something closer to "powers," especially magical powers—clairvoyance, clairaudience, telepathy, teleportation, the ability to fly, the ability to walk through walls, the ability to stop the movement of the sun, the ability to transmute base metals into gold, the ability to find buried treasure, the ability to attract a love, the ability to destroy an enemy, and so on. These are sometimes referred to in Buddhist texts as "mundane accomplishments," to distinguish them from the "supramundane accomplishment": buddhahood. Such powers, whether mundane or transcendent, are attained through initiation by a *guru* (the Sanskrit word for "teacher") and the practice of his instructions.

Their stories are widely known and collected in such works as *Lives of the Eighty-Four Siddhas*, composed by Abhayadatta in the late eleventh or early twelfth century, in the final period of Buddhism in India. The biographies he recounts typically begin with the person's name, caste, and place of birth; a brief description of early life culminates in some crisis, at which point the person encounters the guru (whether human or divine), who bestows initiation and offers instruction. The practice of these instructions for a period of time—often twelve years—results in the attainment of magical powers, which the person, now a *mahasiddha*, puts to use in wondrous ways before departing for a heavenly realm. The lives of three of the most famous *mahasiddhas* are presented here.

The first *mahasiddha* is Virupa, whose name in Sanskrit means "deformed" or "misshapen." He begins as a monk devoted to the goddess Vajravarahi, the "diamond sow." But disgusted at his failure to receive *siddhi* from her, he throws his rosary (commonly used by monks for counting mantras) into the latrine. A goddess then appears to him and exhorts him to practice without conceptions. After the customary twelve years, he achieves *siddhi*. Eventually expelled from the monastery for eating meat and drinking alcohol, he wanders through India, defeating Hindus (this was a period of philosophical debate between Buddhists and Hindus), taming witches, and performing miracles, the most famous of which is mentioned by Abhayadatta. Virupa stops in a tavern to drink, and when the tavern keeper demands payment, he offers to pay when the sun has set and then uses his ritual dagger to halt it in its course. While the sun remains fixed for three days, Virupa consumes huge amounts of wine. In order to set the sun in motion again, the king agrees to pay his bill.

The second is Saraha the arrow maker. He was likely a historical figure who lived in Bengal in the eighth century, remembered especially for his enigmatic songs (called *doha*) of spiritual realization. In the story here, he is a wealthy brahmin—a Hindu by day, but a Buddhist by night (Buddhism was persecuted by various Hindu kings). He is accused of drinking, an activity prohibited to brahmins, but denies the charges, passing many tests before his accusers become his disciples. He then retires with his fifteen-year-old wife to the mountains, where he meditates for twelve years. When he rises from his meditation, his wife teaches him an important lesson.

The third is Nagarjuna, already encountered in this volume as the most famous expositor of the doctrine of emptiness (see *Verses on the Middle Way*, p. 366) and as the composer of pious hymns (see the *Chatuhstava*, or Four Hymns, p. 375). Scholars distinguish that Nagarjuna from the tantric alchemist described here; in the Tibetan tradition, they are the same person, who lived for six hundred years. This Nagarjuna, after reciting mantras for twelve years, achieves the power to transform base metals into gold. Later, he grants the wish of a lowly boatman to become a great king. Although he has concocted the elixir of life to extend his life span, when someone asks for his head, he responds as a proper bodhisattva and offers it. But his great powers make it impossible for anyone else to decapitate him. He therefore does it himself, using a sharp blade of grass—an effective method, according to other accounts, because he long ago killed an insect on a blade of grass. It is also related elsewhere that upon his decapitation, his head and body turned to stone; they remain on earth, and his head slowly moves closer toward the body with each passing year. When they reunite, Nagarjuna will again teach the dharma.

PRONOUNCING GLOSSARY

Arya Nagarjuna: *ah-rya nah-gahr-ju-na*

Bhahitana: *ba-hi-ta-na*

Brahmaputra: *bra-ma-poo-tra*

Chaturashitisiddhapravritti: *cha-too-ra-shi-ti-sid-da-pra-vrit-tee*

dakas: *dah-kas*

dakini: *dah-ki-nee*

Devapala: *day-va-pah-la*

Devikota: *day-vee-koh-ta*

Ghadhashila: *ga-da-shee-la*

Kahora: *ka-hoh-ra*

Kanasati: *ka-na-sa-ti*

Kanchi: *kan-chi*

Mahamudra: *ma-hah-mu-drah*

Maheshvara: *ma-haysh-va-ra*

Maitreya: *mai-tray-ya*

Manjushri: *man-ju-shree*

Nagabodhi: *nah-ga-boh-di*

Nagarjuna: *nah-gahr-ju-na*

Rajagriha: *rah-ja-gri-ha*

Rajni: *raj-nyee*

Ratnapala: *rat-na-pah-la*

Shalabhanda: *sha-la-ban da*

Shitavana: *shee-ta-va-na*

Shriparvata: *shree-par-va-ta*
siddhi: *sihd-dhi*
Somapuri: *soh-ma-pu-ree*
Sunandeshvara: *su-nan-daysh va-ra*

Tara: *tah-rah*
Tripura: *tri-pu-ra*
Vajravarahi: *vaj-ra-vah-rah-hee*
Virupa: *vi-roo-pa*

Virupa

Virupa was born in the East, in Tripura, the city of King Devapala.[1] There was, in south India, a vihara[2] called Somapuri, 'the City of the Moon': a Dharma-circle with thousands of monks, a veritable ocean of them. Though he was only a novice, Virupa asked for initiation. In twelve years, Virupa twice-over recited the mantra of Vajravarahi[3] a million times; but not one sign of siddhi[4] came to him even in a dream. He became despondent at this, tore up his rosary, and threw it into the latrine. That evening, when he customarily gave worship, it occurred to him that he was without his rosary. A dakini[5] then appeared, put a rosary in his hand, and gave him these words of encouragement: "O worthy aspirant, do not despair for my blessing. Perform the practice that abandons all names and conceptions."

> This place of the natural mind
> is the essence of Vajravarahi.
> This is so for you as for everyone else;
> you are inexperienced like a child.
> The wishing gem of the mind
> is not polished by conceptualizations.
> To know the best of practice is sufficient.

Virupa then practiced for twelve years, and obtained siddhi. His servant bought meat and wine and brought it to him; Virupa then killed and ate the pigeons in the vihara. When all the pigeons were gone, the monks asked, "Who among us would eat pigeons? Surely no monk would do such a thing." The monks then looked in all the cells, also going to Virupa's room. As they looked in the window, they saw him drinking wine and eating pigeon meat. The monks then assembled and decided to expel Virupa from the vihara. So Virupa offered his monk's robes and begging bowl in front of an image of the Buddha, did reverence, and left. As he was leaving, a monk said to him, "Where will you go now?" And Virupa replied, "You expelled me; why should you care?"

Beside the vihara there was a large lake. Virupa cut off a lotus flower floating on the water and offered it to the Buddha. Then, placing his foot on a lotus leaf at the edge of the lake, he walked across the water to the other shore. Those who were in Somapuri deeply repented; they grasped Virupa's feet, did reverence to him, and asked him, "But why did you kill the pigeons?" "I did not kill them," Virupa said, and he told his servant to bring him the pieces of the pigeon's wings. The master snapped his fingers, and the feathers became pigeons again, which flew off bigger and better than before. This

TRANSLATED FROM the Tibetan by James B. Robinson.

1. A Buddhist emperor (9th century) who ruled the eastern region of the Indian subcontinent.
2. Monastery.

3. "Vajra Sow," a female tantric deity.
4. Accomplishment; magic power.
5. A type of tantric goddess.

was seen by everyone. From then on, Virupa put aside the habit of a monk and took on the ways of a yogin.

When Virupa came to the bank of the Ganges, he begged food and drink from the Ganges goddess, but she did not give him any. The master became angry, parted the waters, and went to the other side.

In the city of Kanasati, Virupa bought wine from a tavern girl; she gave him a glass of wine and a plate of rice which he greatly enjoyed. He continued eating and drinking. For the space of two days and a night, he prevented the sun from moving and the king, amazed, exclaimed: "Who is it who performs such a miracle?" In answer, the goddess of the sun appeared to the king in a dream and said, "A yogin has pledged me as payment to a tavern girl." The king and his subjects paid the price of the wine, which came to a million glasses, and Virupa disappeared.

Virupa then went to the land called Indra in the country of the idolators. In this place, there was an image, eighty-one cubits high, of Shiva as 'the Great Lord' Maheshvara.[6] The inhabitants told Virupa to do reverence to the image, whereupon Virupa replied, "In no system does the older brother do reverence to the younger brother." The king and the others then said to him, "If you do not give reverence we will kill you." But the master replied, "It would be a sin to give reverence to it; so I will not bow down." "Then let the sin fall on me," said the king.

When the master brought his hands together and bowed down, the great statue of Shiva split in half. A voice coming from the sky called forth: "I vow to listen to you." After taking the oath, the statue was restored to its previous condition. The people made the offerings of the statue of Shiva to the master, and were then converted to Buddhism. It is said that the offerings still exist.

After that, the master went to the east of India to Devikota[7] where the entire population of the country had become witches. If anyone stayed in their castle, they put a spell on him.

The master, having arrived at this place of the witches, found food in the town, but no place could he find lodging. He met with a single Buddhist, a young Brahman, who told him that there were no humans left in the land, that all had become witches, and they were doing great harm to everyone. The master and the Brahman boy then proceeded to the temple where the master stayed. There the master initiated the Brahman boy and gave him mantras.

All the witches having gathered, they said among themselves, "What is to be offered: there are all kinds of meat here, but we have no human flesh." One of them spoke up and said, "I have two victims for you!" "Bring them here!" they all cried. But when the witch tried to bring them she was not able to do so, because of the power of the Brahman child. She tried over and over again, but to no avail.

The witches then saw Virupa sitting on a fallen tree. They carried him away together with the tree; but although they planned to cook him, Virupa drank up all the wine they were using as broth. They then thought to kill him another way: all the witches together made a hissing sound, but Virupa just laughed twelve fearful laughs, and all the witches fainted dead away.

Later Virupa bound the witches by oath: that from then on, they would take the Buddhist refuges[8] and would not harm any who had faith in him. They were not to harm any living being, so they could only drink a handful of blood from the bodies of those who had not taken the refuges or who had not produced the thought of enlightenment. If they broke this oath, their necks would be cut off with his discus, and the Yaksha[9] of the North would drink their blood. Even now, the form of that discus and that yaksha can be seen in the sky. He then bound the witches by oath and put them in the retinue of the Dharma-protectors.

Again Virupa returned to Devikota. On the road, Shiva and the goddess Uma[1] created for him a phantom city with 450,000 inhabitants, and the gods of the thirty-three heavens and all the divine realms made him extensive offerings of food. Virupa spoke to them in verse:

> As a novice and monk in Somapuri
> I faithfully carried out the Vinaya,[2]
> and then, by power produced by previous karma,
> I gained full initiation and teachings.
> For twelve years I meditated with conceptions
> and nothing occurred, even in a dream;
> my weary mind cursing, I threw away my rosary.
> After that, a dakini appeared to advise me:
> because of this, I strengthened myself
> and rightly understood the character of samsara.
> From then on I practiced without conceptions,
> although the monks believed I was misbehaving.
> So in order to destroy their misconceptions,
> I walked on water without sinking.
> I reversed the course of the Ganges, and while enjoying myself,
> I put up the sun as a pledge.
> I split the idol of the idolators, breaking its pride,
> and in Devikota, I controlled the witches.
> When Shiva saw my many powers
> he created a city to make me offerings.
> Now, if I did not do these miraculous deeds,
> why would people prefer even the outer Dharma?

Then he went to the realm of the dakas.[3]

Saraha

Saraha, the son of a dakini, was born a Brahman in a city called Roli in a particular part of Rajni, in the east of India. Though he was a Brahman, he had faith in the Dharma of the Buddha, and because he had listened to the Dharma from innumerable masters, he had trust in the Tantric doctrine.

---

8. A Buddhist is traditionally defined as someone who "takes refuge" in the Buddha, the dharma, and the sangha (the Buddhist community).
9. A category of nonhuman beings, a nature spirit.
1. Shiva's wife.
2. Rules of monastic discipline.
3. The male counterparts of *dakinis*.

During the day, he practiced the Hindu system; at night, he practiced the Buddhist system. He also drank wine.

There came a time when this was discovered by the Brahmans, who then attempted to have him banished. They went to King Ratnapala[4] and said to him, "You are the king. Is it proper for you to allow a disreputable system of religion to be practiced in your country? Even though Saraha, 'the Arrow-shooter', is chief of fifteen thousand residences in Roli, he has lowered himself in caste by drinking wine, and therefore must be expelled."

The king, not wanting to expel a man who controlled fifteen thousand households, went to Saraha and said, "You are a Brahman; it is not fit that you drink wine." But Saraha replied, "I do not drink wine. Gather all the men and those Brahmans here, and I will take an oath to that effect." After they had gathered, Saraha stated, "If I have been drinking wine, let my hand burn. If I have not been drinking, may it not burn." He then put his hand in boiling oil, and it was not burnt. "In truth, he does not drink wine," the king said. But the Brahmans said, "But truly he does drink wine."

So Saraha spoke as before. He drank molten copper and was not burnt. "He still drinks," the Brahmans maintained. Saraha then said, "Whosoever sinks when entering the water, he is the one who drinks. If he does not sink, he does not drink." So he and another Brahman both entered the water. Saraha did not sink, but the other one did, so they finally said, "Saraha does not drink."

Similarly, Saraha was weighed on a scale: "Whoever is heavier does not drink," he said. They put three iron weights on the scale, each as heavy as a man, and still Saraha was heavier than the weights. He was heavier than even six of those weights. Finally the king said, "If anyone who has powers like these drinks wine, then let him drink."

The king and the Brahmans bowed to Saraha and asked for his instructions. Saraha then sang to the king, the queen, and all the subjects, of the three cycles of Doha.[5] The Brahmans all abandoned their own system and became Buddhists. The king with all his retinue attained siddhi.

Saraha married a fifteen-year-old house girl, left his home, and went into another land. He settled in a solitary place, where he practiced the Dharma while the girl went out begging for his food. One time, he asked her to prepare some radishes for him. She mixed some radishes in yogurt and took them to him, but he was sitting in meditation, so she went away without disturbing him.

Saraha remained uninterruptedly in meditation for twelve years. When he finally arose, he asked, "Where are my radishes?" The serving girl replied, "How could I keep them? You have not arisen from meditational trance for twelve years. It is now spring, and there are no radishes." Saraha then said to the girl, "I will go to the mountains to meditate." But the girl replied, "A solitary body does not mean solitude. The best solitude is the mind far away from names and conceptions. You have been meditating for twelve years, yet you have not cut off the idea of radishes. What good will it do to go to the mountains?" Saraha thought, "This is true." And so he abandoned names and conceptions.

4. A Hindu king of the late 10th century.
5. A series of songs; one cycle was addressed to each of the recipients named.

By experiencing the essential meaning, he obtained the highest siddhi of Mahamudra,[6] and furthered the aims of living beings. He, together with his woman, entered the realm of the dakas.

Nagarjuna

Nagarjuna lived in a place called Kahora, a section of Kanchi in eastern India. He was of Brahman caste, and he obtained siddhi from Tara.[7] There were 1,500 cities in Kahora, and all of them had been plundered and despoiled. The Brahmans gathered together and decided to leave the strife-torn land and go to another country. The master heard this and sent a messenger to these Brahmans, counseling them not to go to another land, for they would find suffering in those places as well. Then he gave them all his property and wealth. After this, the master left Kahora, and having come to Nalanda,[8] on the other side of the shitavana, he became a monk.

Mastering the five sciences,[9] Nagarjuna arrived at the pinnacle of knowledge. Then, becoming disgusted with just preaching, he set himself to practicing, and saw Tara face to face. He then abandoned the home and sustenance of Nalanda—where abide the hundred assemblies of the Dharma-circle—and begged alms in another city. When again he returned to his home, he thought to himself: "With such a mental attitude as I now have, I will not be able to accomplish the benefit of living beings."

In order to obtain the qualities to benefit living beings, Nagarjuna went to Rajagriha.[1] On the first day of reciting mantras, twelve demonesses of the principal order of demons shook the earth. On the second day, they caused water to flood. Fire appeared on the third day, and on the fourth, a great wind. On the fifth day, a rain of weapons fell, and on the sixth, a rain of stones. On the seventh day, all the demonesses appeared in their own form and threw things around, but they did not frighten the master out of his meditation.

Then these demonesses of the North came to him and said, "What can we do to serve you?" "Serve me enough to sustain me; I need nothing more," Nagarjuna said to them. So every day from then on, they gave him four handfuls of rice and five vegetables. The master ate these and practiced for twelve years. During this time, one hundred and eight demonesses gathered under his power, and his thoughts were on doing benefit for living beings.

Nagarjuna then went to the mountain Ghadhashila and considered transforming that mountain into gold for the benefit of living beings. He made the mountain first into iron, and then into copper. But then the holy Manjushri counseled him that the gold would bring about a great quarrel among the people, and evil would accumulate. Hearing this, Nagarjuna abandoned further effort. Yet to the dull-witted Ghadhashila still appears as a copper-colored lump.

6. Literally, "Great Seal," a form of tantric Buddhist practice as well as its goal.
7. A female bodhisattva believed to be an emanation of the bodhisattva Avalokiteshvara; see the following selection.
8. A Buddhist monastery in the present-day state of Bihar, in eastern India.
9. Language, fine arts and crafts, medicine, logic, and philosophy.
1. The capital of the kingdom of Magadha, in northeast India, where the Buddha lived for many years.

After this, Nagarjuna traveled south toward Shriparvata.[2] Along the way, he came to the shores of the Brahmaputra where he met a group of cowherds. He asked them about a passage across the river, and they showed him an inauspicious way which was filled with ravines and crocodiles. But another cowherd came along who cautioned him about the river and showed him a better place to cross. And the cowherd set out across the river carrying the master on his back.

In the middle of the river, Nagarjuna caused crocodiles and other fearful things to appear, but the herdsman continued on, saying, "You need not be afraid while I am still alive." The master then did away with the apparitions. When they came to the shore, the master said, "I am the Arya[3] Nagarjuna. Do you know me?" "I have indeed heard talk of you," said the herdsman, "but I did not recognize you." "Yet you have saved me from the river. What can I give you as a reward?" The herdsman was elated. "I would like a method to become king," he said. So the master cleared away some ground, sprinkled water on the trunk of a sala tree, and it immediately turned into an elephant. "That will be your vehicle," said Nagarjuna. When the herdsman asked him if he would need an army, the master replied, "If the elephant trumpets, an army will appear." It occurred exactly as was said: the cowherd became King Shalabhanda, his queen was called Sindhi, and he ruled over the extraordinary city of Bhahitana. Under this king there were eight hundred tax-paying cities of 100,000 people.

The master went south to Shriparvata, and he remained there practicing meditation. But King Shalabhanda missed his guru. He went to Shriparvata, gave reverence to Nagarjuna, and circumambulated him. "Since my kingdom has small value and large problems, my unhappiness is increasing. I do not need a kingdom. I ask only to sit before the eyes of the master."

"Do not desert your kingdom," replied Nagarjuna. "Let the precious rosary be your master. Rule the kingdom, and I will give you the elixir which removes fear of death." The king was chagrined. "If it is necessary to rule the kingdom at the same time as I obtain the elixir, then I will do so. But I hope it is not necessary."

Although the king did not want to return to his kingdom, but only wished to remain in that place, the master gave him instructions to practice in his own country. The king then accomplished the alchemical art, and for one hundred years he ruled the kingdom. During that time, the people became wealthy, and even the birds and wild animals in the mountains lived happily.

After one hundred years, the king had reason to go again to Nagarjuna, who was working to extend the teachings of the Buddha. The evil spirit Sunandeshvara had grown jealous and was producing various misfortunes and disruptive omens. The moon and the sun had become dim and without luster; all the fruit was rotting spontaneously; the rain did not fall at the right time; and famine was afflicting the people. Sickness and war increased. The trees and forests were drying up, and various other unfortunate signs were appearing.

King Shalabhanda reflected on this, thinking that these portents were a sign that harm had come to his guru. He gave the kingdom to his son

2. Literally, "Glorious Mountain," a center of tantric worship in modern-day Andhra Pradesh, in southeast India.
3. "Noble."

Chandhikumara and together with only a few of his followers, he went to Shriparvata to the presence of the master, who asked him, "My son, why have you come?" The king replied:

> Either I and the people have exhausted our fortune,
> or the Conqueror's[4] teachings have decayed.
> Or the darker half has become the victor;
> or the great compassion white like the moon,
> has been covered by demons like rainclouds.
> Will the holy guru who is like a diamond
> follow the nature of compounded things?
> I have come because these signs have occurred—
> out of your compassion, please remain in the world.

The master replied, "All that is born must die. All compounded things must disintegrate. All accumulations are spent. Since all compound things are impermanent, why are you unhappy? Take the elixir for yourself and go."

"The elixir is there in front of the guru. If the guru will not remain in the world, what need I of the elixir?" And so the king remained. Then the holy master made gifts of all his property. When the god Brahma appeared as a Brahman and begged for his head, Nagarjuna agreed to give it to him. The king, Shalabhanda, could not bear suffering the death of his teacher, and laying his forehead to the foot of the master, he died. Everyone turned on the Brahman and blamed him for this.

The master then gave his head. However, no one could sever it; so he finally had to cut off his own head, which he did with a stalk of kusha grass. When he then gave his head to the Brahman, all the trees withered, and the people's merit degenerated. Eight of his yakshis[5] were set to guarding the master's body; they are still there.

A light then entered Nagabodhi, the guru's successor, and emanated for about a month during the year in which light emanates. It is said that the body of the master will rise in the future, and will aid living beings when the Buddha Maitreya[6] appears.

---

4. The Buddha.
5. The female counterparts of yakshas.

6. The next buddha.

EVER IN THE FEMALE FORM

IN PRAISE OF THE TWENTY-ONE TARAS

Among the female bodhisattvas in the pantheons of Indian and Tibetan Buddhism, perhaps the most famous, and most propitiated, is Tara. Her name has several meanings in Sanskrit, including "Star" and "Saving." Her historical origins are uncertain; she has both Hindu and Buddhist forms, and begins to appear in Buddhist iconography in India around the seventh century C.E. It is said that Tara was born from a lotus blossom that sprang from a tear shed by the bodhisattva Avalokiteshvara as he surveyed the suffering universe. She is thus the physical manifestation of the compassion of Avalokiteshvara, himself viewed as the quintessence of all the compassion of all the buddhas. Because buddhas are produced from wisdom and compassion, Tara is hailed as "the mother of all buddhas" even though she is most commonly represented as a beautiful sixteen-year-old maiden.

Like all bodhisattvas, she continually appears in the world to benefit suffering sentient beings. According to Tibetan Buddhism, she took human form as the Chinese princess who married King Songtsen Gampo, the first of the Tibetan "dharma kings," bringing with her the Buddha image that would become the most revered in Tibet. Later Tara appeared as the great practitioner of the *chö* tradition (see *Words of My Perfect Teacher*, p. 724), Machig Lapdon (1062–1149). Indeed, it is said that long ago a princess developed the aspiration to enlightenment (*bodhichitta*) for the sake of all sentient beings, thereby beginning the long bodhisattva path. When a group of monks urged her to pray to be reborn as a man, she replied, "I developed bodhichitta as a woman. For all my lifetimes along the path I vow to be born as a woman, and in my final lifetime when I attain buddhahood, I will be a woman." Over the intervening aeons, Tara has therefore always appeared as a female.

She has many iconographic forms in different colors, the most common being Green Tara and White Tara, propitiated especially to bestow long life. Her numerous wrathful forms include Kurukulla—a dancing naked yogini, red in color, who brandishes a bow and arrows in her four hands.

Tara is renowned for her saving powers, appearing the instant that her devotee recites her mantra, *om tare tuttare ture svaha*. She is able to deliver those who call on her from eight fears: the fears of lions, elephants, fire, snakes, bandits, prison, water, and demons. Many tales recount her miraculous interventions. She can appear in peaceful or wrathful forms, depending on the circumstances; her powers extend beyond the subjugation of these worldly frights into the heavens and the hells.

Apart from her mantra, the prayer here is the most common means used in Tibet to invoke Tara. Addressed to twenty-one Taras, it is derived from an Indian tantra devoted to her, the *Source of All Rites to Tara, Mother of All Tathagatas* (*Sarvatathagatamatritara vishvakarmabhavatantra*). According to some traditions of commentary on the prayer, each of the verses refers to a different form of Tara. The prayer is known by heart by Buddhists throughout the Tibetan cultural region, recited by monks each morning, recited especially by travelers to protect them in their long journeys on foot and horseback across mountains and plains, and printed on prayer flags. These colored squares of cloth, imprinted with a prayer or mantra, are attached to poles, and to the rooftops of temples and dwellings, or are strung from the cairns at the summits of mountain passes. The wind is believed to carry the benefits sought by the imprinted prayer not only to the person who flies the flag but to all beings in the region.

PRONOUNCING GLOSSARY

Amitabha: *a-mi-tah-ba*
Avalokiteshvara: *a-va-loh-ki-tay-shva-ra*
gandharva: *gan-dar-va*
kinnara: *ki-na-ra*
Mandara: *man-da-ra*
Meru: *may-ru*
Namo Arya Taraye: *namoh ah-rya tah-ra-yay*
phat: *pat*

svaha: *svah-hah*
Tara: *tah-rah*
Tathagata: *ta-tah-ga-ta*
ture: *tu-ray*
tuttara hum: *tu-tah-ra hoom*
tuttare: *tu-ta-ray*
Vindhya: *vin-dya*
yaksha: *yak-sha*

Homage to the Treasury of Compassion, the Noble Avalokiteshvara Oṃ.
Homage to the Exalted Noble Tara

Homage. Tara, swift heroine, her eyes like a flash of lightening. Born from the blossoming from the tear on the Protector of the Three Worlds'[1] face. (1)

Homage. Her face a hundred full autumn moons amassed, blazing with the light of a thousand gathered stars. (2)

Homage. Her hand adorned with a water-born lotus, blue and gold. Her sphere is giving, effort, austerity, peace, patience, and concentration. (3)

Homage. Crown of the Tathagata,[2] her deeds conquer without end, much accompanied by the children of the Conqueror who have attained perfection. (4)

Homage. She fills desire, direction, and space with the letters *tuttara hum*, pressing down the seven worlds with her feet, able to summon all [beings]. (5)

Homage. She is worshipped by various lords: Indra, Agni, Brahma, Marut;[3] she is praised by hosts of ghosts, risen corpses, gandharvas, and yakshas.[4] (6)

Homage. With *trat* and *phat* she destroys the stratagems of opponents, pressing down with her right foot drawn in and her left foot stretched out, blazing with raging fire. (7)

Homage. *Ture* most horrific, she destroys Mara's[5] hero, with the frown of her lotus face she slays all foes. (8)

Homage. She is adorned at her heart with her fingers in the mudra symbolizing the three jewels,[6] adorned with wheels of all directions, raging with her gathered light. (9)

Homage. She is joyous, her shining crown emits garlands of light, laughing the laugh of *tuttara*, she subdues Mara and the world. (10)

Homage. She is able to summon all the hosts of guardians of the earth; with the letter *hum*, frowning, trembling, she frees the destitute. (11)

Homage. Crowned with a crescent moon, all ornaments blazing; from Amitabha[7] in her piled tresses, light is always created. (12)

Homage. Standing amid a blazing circle, like the aeon-ending fire;[8] surrounded by joy, right leg stretched out, left drawn in, destroying the enemy troops. (13)

TRANSLATED FROM the Tibetan by Donald S. Lopez, Jr. All bracketed additions are the translator's.

1. Here Avolokitesvara, the bodhisattva who embodies the compassion of the buddhas. The "three worlds" are the Realm of Desire, the Realm of Form, and the Formless Realm; see pp. 54–55.
2. The title of a buddha most often used by the historical Buddha to refer to himself (literally, "one who has thus come/gone"); "Conqueror" is another epithet of the Buddha.
3. Vedic deities.
4. Nonhuman beings, nature spirits. "Gandhar-

vas": semidivine beings known as heavenly musicians.
5. The personification of evil and temptation.
6. The Buddha, the dharma, and the sangha (Buddhist community).
7. The buddha ("Infinite Light") who presides over the Pure Land of Sukhavati (see the *Sukhavativyuha Sutra*, p. 316).
8. In Buddhist cosmology, each age ends in all-consuming fire.

Homage. She strikes the surface of the earth with the palm of her hand and beats it with her foot; frowning, with the letter *hum*, she subdues the seven underworlds. (14)

Homage. Blissful, virtuous, peaceful, her sphere is the peace of nirvana; perfectly endowed with *svaha* and *om*,[9] she destroys all sin. (15)

Homage. Surrounded by joy, she vanquishes the body of the enemy; she liberates with the knowledge [mantra] *hum*, arrayed with the ten-syllabled speech [of her mantra]. (16)

Homage. *Ture*, by stamping her foot, her seed is the letter *hum*'s form; trembler of Meru, Mandara, Vindhya[1] and the three worlds. (17)

Homage. Holding in her hand the deer marked [moon] in the form of the lake of the gods; by saying *tara* twice with the syllable *phat*, she dispels all poison. (18)

Homage. She is attended by the king of the hosts of gods, by gods and kinnaras;[2] her joyous splendor dispels the disputes and nightmare of armored ones. (19)

Homage. Her two eyes shine with light of the sun and full moon. By saying *hara* twice with *tuttare*, she dispels the most terrible fever. (20)

Homage. Endowed with pacifying power arrayed with the three realities,[3] she is the supreme *Ture*, destroyer of the hosts of demons, risen corpses, and yaksas. (21)

9. Interjections placed, respectively, at the end and the beginning of mantras.
1. The mountain range that divides the northern and southern portions of the Indian subcontinent. "Meru": in Buddhist cosmology, the mountain at the center of the world. "Mandara": a mountain in Indian mythology.
2. Beings who are half human, half horse, or half bird.
3. The syllables *om ah hum.*

Buddhism in China

According to a traditional account, Buddhism came to China after the emperor had a dream of a golden flying man. The next day, when Emperor Ming described this dream to his ministers, one told him that the man was a sage from the West, called "Buddha." The emperor sent a delegation to find him, and it eventually returned with a scripture (said to have been the *Scripture in Forty-two Sections*) and a statue. Scholars consider the story a myth, and many argue that Buddhism entered China prior to the reign of this emperor (58–75 C.E.). However, it did come from the West—from Central Asia, where Buddhism was flourishing at the time, by way of the Silk Road. The Taliban's demolition in 2001 of the magnificent Buddhas of Bamiyan is a recent reminder that Buddhism was once a powerful presence in what is today Pakistan, Afghanistan, and China's Xinjiang Province (formerly known as Chinese Turkestan).

Buddhism's entry into China was unlike that into other parts of Asia. By the time of its arrival, China had a highly developed culture, boasting a sophisticated written language and a large literature, strong political and social institutions, its own philosophical tradition, and, importantly, a view of itself as the "middle kingdom"—that is, the center of civilization. That Buddhism, a foreign religion, was able to make inroads into China and play such

White-robed Guanyin with Monkey (detail from triptych), by Mu Qi. China, early 13th century.

a powerful role in its history, even to the present day, is one of the most fascinating elements in the larger history of Buddhism, as well as in the history of China. Indeed, China would become the religion's second center, after India, providing the literature, the language, and much of the doctrine and institutional structure for Buddhism in Korea, Japan, and Vietnam.

Buddhism faced immediate barriers in China, beginning with a challenge to the traditional foundation of Buddhism: monastic life. In China, even to shave one's head was considered a desecration of the body given by one's parents. To take a vow of celibacy—thereby putting an end to the family line and the ritual sustenance of the ancestors—was a gross violation of filial piety. To retire from the world was to shirk one's duty to society. Buddhism's doctrine of rebirth seemed incompatible with ancestor worship, and its apparently otherworldly philosophy was at odds with the teachings of the Confucians.

Buddhism would find ways to overcome each of these obstacles by undertaking important adaptations, though what was once called "the Chinese transformation of Buddhism" is perhaps overstated. We should keep in mind that Buddhism gained its initial foothold in China during a period of political disunity called the Six Dynasties (220–589), when northern China came under the control of Central Asian invaders who were patrons of Buddhism. Meanwhile, Chinese literati in the south, already well versed in Daoist texts, were developing an interest in Buddhist philosophy. Also during the Six Dynasties period, a great deal of Buddhist literature, including the recently composed Mahayana sutras, were brought to China from India and Central Asia and translated into Chinese by Kumarajiva—the most famous of the translators—and others. It was not a time of unhindered growth of the dharma, however, as Buddhism suffered the first two of its three major persecutions during this period.

The Sui dynasty (581–618) and Tang dynasty (618–907) are often called the golden age of Buddhism in China; they saw the rise of the major schools of Chinese Buddhism, including the Tiantai (based on the *Lotus Sutra*; see p. 278) and the Huayan (based on the *Flower Garland* or *Avatamsaka Sutra*), and the development of Pure Land practice based on the *Discourse on the Land of Bliss* (see the *Sukhavativyuha Sutra*, p. 316). Indeed, Chinese Buddhism is largely based on Mahayana sutras: its individual schools seek to understand the entire corpus of scriptures in light of a single text that they hold to be the Buddha's highest teaching. Many of these schools took their own distinctive forms as Buddhist doctrine and philosophy was continuing to develop in India; the texts retrieved and translated by Xuanzang (see *The Great Tang Dynasty Record of the Western World*, p. 511), who returned from his famous journey to the West in 645, were among the last Indian works to have measurable influence on the evolution of Chinese Buddhist thought, although Indian Buddhism would continue for another six centuries. That evolution was interrupted during Chinese Buddhism's most serious persecution: between 842 and 845, Emperor Wuzong, a patron of Daoism, ordered that more than four thousand monasteries and forty thousand hermitages be destroyed, and some quarter million monks and nuns returned to lay life.

During the Song dynasty (960–1279), Buddhism slowly recovered, as important developments occurred in the Chan school, including the work of Dahui

(1089–1163; see *Letters from a Zen Master*, p. 557). This was also the period of the rise of Neo-Confucianism and perhaps the most sustained philosophical attack on Buddhism, by the scholar Zhuxi (1130–1200). During the Yuan dynasty (1271–1368) and the Qing dynasty (1644–1911), China was ruled by Mongols and Manchus, respectively; both sets of rulers were patrons of Tibetan Buddhism who also supported Chinese Buddhist schools. With the fall of the Qing and the founding of the Chinese Republic in 1912, Buddhism came under attack as a form of superstition impeding China's entry into the modern world. A new generation of Buddhist teachers tried to respond, representing Buddhism as the religion most suited to the modern world. But China would soon suffer the devastation of Japanese invasion and, after Japan's defeat in World War II, the civil war that ended in the founding of the People's Republic in 1949. Many of the leading Buddhist scholars then fled to Taiwan, where Chinese Buddhism has flourished. The past two decades have seen a revival of Buddhism on the mainland as well.

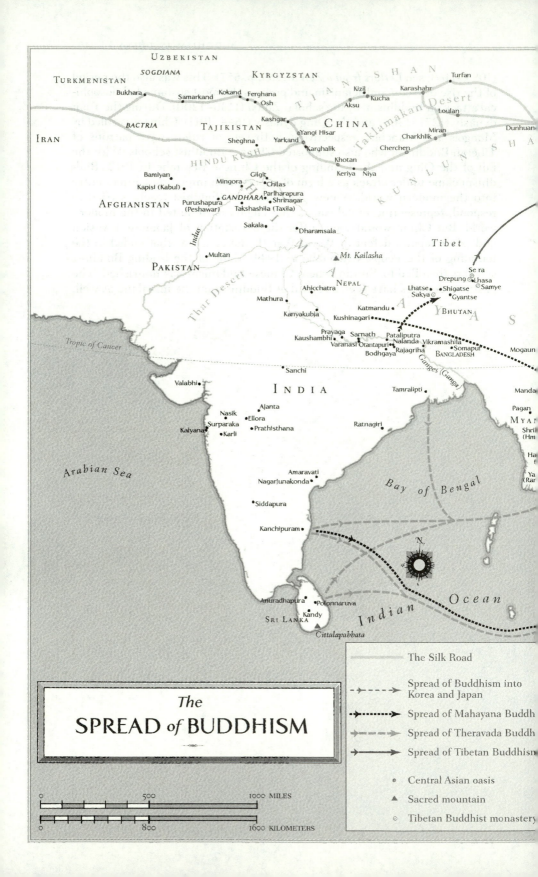

The
SPREAD of BUDDHISM

The Silk Road

Spread of Buddhism into Korea and Japan

Spread of Mahayana Buddh

Spread of Theravada Buddh

Spread of Tibetan Buddhism

• Central Asian oasis

▲ Sacred mountain

◉ Tibetan Buddhist monastery

0   500   1000 MILES
0   800   1600 KILOMETERS

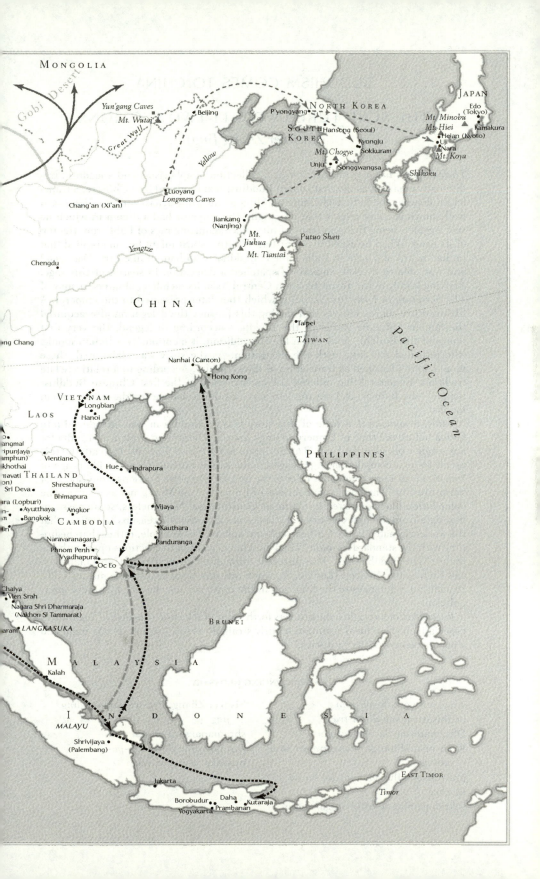

BUDDHISM COMES TO CHINA

THE SCRIPTURE IN FORTY-TWO SECTIONS
(*Sishi'er Zhang Jing*)

The Scripture in Forty-two Sections is a collection of aphorisms and anecdotes traditionally regarded as the first Indian Buddhist text rendered into Chinese, a translation done at the behest of Emperor Ming of the Han dynasty (r. 58–75 C.E.). A well-known account relates that one night, the emperor had a dream in which he saw a golden being flying in front of his palace, emitting rays of light from the top of its head. When he asked his ministers who this spirit might be, one replied that he had heard of a sage in India called "Buddha" who had attained the Way (*dao*) and was able to fly. The emperor dispatched a delegation in search of this sage. Arriving finally in the Tarim Basin in Central Asia, its members obtained a copy of *The Scripture in Forty-two Sections*, which they later presented to the emperor. A fifth-century source reports that during this journey the delegation also acquired the famous Udayana statue of the Buddha—according to legend, the very first image of the Buddha, made from life. In addition, it mentions two Indian monks who returned to China with the delegation. As the story was elaborated, these monks were identified as translators of the scripture. According to a relatively late tradition, Emperor Ming ordered the construction of the first Chinese Buddhist temple—the Baimasi at Luoyang—to serve as the residence for these two Indian monks.

Sadly, it appears that little of this story is true. Buddhism was introduced into China before the time of Emperor Ming's dream. There is no evidence in India for any single work identified with *The Scripture in Forty-two Sections*. Instead, the text seems to be a compilation of passages, some rather famous, from a wide range of Indian sutras. Early catalogues refer to the text as "Forty-two Sections from Buddhist Scriptures" or "The Forty-two Sections of Emperor Xiao Ming," not as a sutra. The compilation likely occurred in China or Central Asia. Nonetheless, some passages may date from the first century C.E.. There are also stylistic reasons to believe that the work originated in the Chinese cultural sphere. For example, rather than beginning with the standard formula "Thus did I hear," most of the sections open with the phrase "The Buddha said." This phrase is immediately evocative of Confucian classics such as the *Analects* (*Lunyu*), in which maxims often begin "The master said." In addition, references to the filial son in the ninth section suggest a Chinese interpolation.

Regardless of its origins, the text sets forth many of the basic concepts of Buddhism, especially in the ethical realm, in a fairly straightforward manner. It has remained a popular text over the centuries.

PRONOUNCING GLOSSARY

anagamin: *a-nah-gah-min*
bodhisattva: *boh-di-sat-tva*
Dharmaratna: *dar-ma-rat-na*
Kashyapa Matanga: *kah-shya-pa mah-tan-ga*
pratyekabuddha: *prat-yay-ka-bu-da*
qi: *chee*
sakridagamin: *sa-krihd-ah-gah-mihn*

Sishi'er Zhang Jing: *see-shieur jahng jing*
shramana: *shra-ma-na*
shrotapanna: *shroh-tah-pa-na*
upasaka: *u-pah-sa-ka*

TRANSLATED IN THE LATER HAN DYNASTY BY
THE *SHRAMANAS* KASHYAPA MATANGA AND DHARMARATNA
OF THE WESTERN REGIONS

1. The Buddha said: "Those who leave their families and go forth from their homes to practice the Way are called *shramanas* (ascetics). Those who constantly follow the 250 precepts in order to [realize] the four noble truths[1] and progressively purify their intentions will become saints (*arhat*).[2] A saint is able to fly and assume different forms; he lives a long life and can move Heaven and Earth. Next is the nonreturner (*anagamin*): at the end of his life the spirit of a nonreturner ascends the nineteen heavens and there attains sainthood. Next is the once-returner (*sakridagamin*): the once-returner ascends [to Heaven] once and returns once and then attains sainthood. Next is the stream-winner (*shrotapanna*): the stream-winner dies and is reborn seven times and then attains sainthood. The severance of passion and desire is like the four limbs severed, they will never be used again."

2. The Buddha said: "Those who shave their heads and faces are *shramanas*. They receive the teaching, abandon worldly wealth and possessions, and beg, seeking only what is necessary. Taking a single meal at midday, and lodging a single night under a tree, they take care not to repeat either. That which makes men ignorant and derelict is passion and desire."

3. The Buddha said: "All beings consider ten things as good and ten things as evil. Three concern the body, four the mouth, and three the mind. The three [evil things] of the body are killing, stealing, and adultery. The four of the mouth are duplicity, slander, lying, and lewd speech. The three of the mind are envy, hatred, and delusion. He who lacks faith in the three honored ones [the Buddha, the teaching, and the community of monks], will mistake falsehood for truth. A lay disciple (*upasaka*) who practices the five precepts [not to kill, to steal, to commit adultery, to speak falsely, or to drink alcohol], without becoming lax and backsliding, will arrive at the ten [good] things [i.e., the antitheses of the ten evil things] and will certainly attain the Way."

4. The Buddha said: "If a man commits multiple transgressions, yet does not repent and quickly quell the [evil] in his heart, his crimes will return to him as water returns to the sea, becoming ever deeper and wider. But should a man come to realize the error of his ways, correct his transgressions, and attain goodness, his days of wrongdoing will come to an end and in time he will attain the Way."

5. The Buddha said: "Should a man malign me and seek to do me harm, I counter with the four virtues of benevolence, [compassion, joy, and equanimity]. The more he approaches me with malice, the more I reach out with

TRANSLATED FROM the Chinese by Robert H. Sharf. All bracketed additions are the translator's.

1. Suffering, origin, cessation, and path; see *Setting the Wheel of the Dharma in Motion*, p. 177, and its introduction.
2. That is, those who will enter nirvana at death.

kindness. The forces (*qi*) of beneficent virtue lie always in this, while harmful forces and repeated misfortune will revert to the other."

6. Once a man heard that the Buddha's Way lies in persevering in benevolence and compassion, and meeting evil with goodness. He then came and cursed the Buddha. The Buddha, remaining silent, did not respond, but rather had pity for one whose ignorance and rage led to such an act. When his cursing abated the Buddha asked him: "If you offer a gift to someone who does not accept it, what happens to the gift?" The man replied: "I would have to take it back." The Buddha said: "Now you have offered me curses but I do not accept them. They return to you, bringing harm to your own person. Like an echo responding to sound, or a shadow following an object, in the end there is no escaping it. Take heed of your evil ways."

7. The Buddha said: "An evil man trying to harm a worthy man is like looking toward Heaven and spitting; the spittle will not befoul Heaven but will return and befoul the one spitting. It is like throwing filth at someone while facing into the wind; the filth will not befoul anyone else but will return and befoul the one throwing. A worthy man cannot be harmed; a man's transgressions will surely destroy only himself."

8. The Buddha said: "The virtue of one who practices universal love, compassion, and generosity for the sake of the Way is not that of great generosity. But if he [further] guards his intentions and honors the Way, his merit is truly great. If you see someone practicing generosity and you joyfully assist him, you too will gain merit in return." Someone asked: "Would not the other person's merit be diminished thereby?" The Buddha said: "It is like the flame of a single torch that is approached by several hundred thousand men each bearing torches. Each lights his torch from the flame and departs, using it to cook food and dispel darkness, yet the original flame is ever the same. Merit is also like this."

9. The Buddha said: "Feeding one hundred common men is not as good as feeding one good man. Feeding one thousand good men is not as good as feeding one who observes the five precepts. Feeding ten thousand men who observe the five precepts is not as good as feeding one stream-winner. Feeding one million stream-winners is not as good as feeding one once-returner. Feeding ten million once-returners is not as good as feeding one nonreturner. Feeding one hundred million nonreturners is not as good as feeding one saint. Feeding one billion saints is not as good as feeding one solitary buddha (*pratyekabuddha*). Feeding ten billion solitary buddhas is not as good as liberating one's parents in this life by means of the teaching of the three honored ones. To teach one hundred billion parents is not as good as feeding one buddha, studying with the desire to attain buddhahood, and aspiring to liberate all beings. But the merit of feeding a good man is [still] very great. It is better for a common man to be filial to his parents than for him to serve the spirits of Heaven and Earth, for one's parents are the supreme spirits."

10. The Buddha said: "There are five difficult things under Heaven. It is difficult for the poor to give alms, it is difficult for the powerful and privileged to cultivate the Way, it is difficult to control fate and avoid death, it is difficult

to attain a glimpse of the Buddha's scriptures, and it is difficult to be born at the time of a buddha."

11. There was a *shramana* who asked the Buddha: "Through what causal factors does one attain the Way, and how does one come to know of one's previous lives?" The Buddha replied: "The Way is without form, and thus to know these things is of no benefit. What is important is to guard your intentions and actions. It is like polishing a mirror: as the dust is removed the underlying luminosity is revealed and you are able to see your own image. Eliminate desire and hold to emptiness and you will come to see the truth of the Way and know your past lives."

12. The Buddha said: "What is goodness? Goodness is the practice of the Way. What is supreme? A mind in accord with the Way is supreme. What has great power? Patience in the face of insult is strongest, for patience and the absence of anger is honored by all. What is supreme enlightenment? When mental impurities are uprooted, when evil conduct has ceased, when one is pure and free of blemish within, when there is nothing that is not known, seen, or heard—from the time when there was yet no Heaven and Earth down to the present day, including everything extant in the ten quarters as well as that which has yet to appear—when omniscience has been attained, this can indeed be called enlightenment."

13. The Buddha said: "A man who holds to passion and desire will not see the Way. It is as if one muddied water by throwing in five colored pigments and vigorously mixed them together. Many might approach the edge of the water, but they would be unable to see their own reflections on the surface. Passion and desire pollute the mind, leaving it murky, and thus the Way goes unseen. If the water is filtered and the filth removed, leaving it pure and free of dirt, one's own reflection will be seen. But if a kettle is placed over a hot flame bringing water to a rapid boil, or if water is covered with a cloth, then those who approach it will similarly not see their own reflections. The three fundamental poisons [of greed, hatred, and delusion] boil and bubble in the mind, while one is cloaked without by the five hindrances [of desire, hatred, sloth, agitation, and doubt]. In the end the Way goes unseen. When mental impurities are exhausted one knows whence the spirit comes and whither life and death go. The Way and its virtue are present in all buddha lands."

14. The Buddha said: "The practice of the Way is like holding a burning torch and entering a dark room: the darkness immediately vanishes and everything is illumined. Cultivate the Way and perceive the truth and evil and ignorance will both vanish, leaving nothing unseen."

15. The Buddha said: "What do I contemplate? I contemplate the Way. What do I practice? I practice the Way. Of what do I speak? I speak of the Way. I contemplate the true Way, never neglecting it for even an instant."

16. The Buddha said: "When gazing at Heaven and Earth contemplate their impermanence. When gazing at mountains and rivers contemplate their impermanence. When gazing at the tremendous variety of shapes and forms of

the myriad things in the world contemplate their impermanence. If you keep your mind thus you will attain the Way in no time."

17. The Buddha said: "If for but a single day you continually contemplate and practice the Way you will attain the foundations of faith. Its blessings are incalculable."

18. The Buddha said: "Ardently contemplate the four primary elements[3] that comprise the body. While each has a name, they are all devoid of self. The [sense of an] 'I' emerges from the aggregate, but it is not long lived and is really but an illusion."

19. The Buddha said: "For a person to follow his desires in search of fame is like putting fire to incense. Many may savor the smell of the incense, but the incense is all the while being consumed by the fire. The foolish, coveting worldly fame, hold not to the truth of the Way. Fame brings misfortune and harm, and one is sure to regret it later."

20. The Buddha said: "Riches and sex are to men what sweet honey on the blade of a knife is to a young child: before he has fully enjoyed a single bite he must suffer the pain of a cut tongue."

21. The Buddha said: "The misery of being shackled to wife, children, wealth, and home is greater than that of being shackled in chains and fetters and thrown in prison. In prison there is the possibility of pardon, but even though the desire for wife and children is as perilous as the mouth of a tiger, men throw themselves into it willingly. For this crime there is no pardon."

22. The Buddha said: "There is no desire more powerful than sex. Sexual desire looms so large that nothing stands outside of it. But luckily there is only one such desire, for were there yet another there would not be a single person in all the world capable of the Way."

23. The Buddha said: "Passion and desire are to man what a flaming torch is to one walking against the wind. Foolish ones who do not let go of the torch are sure to burn their hands. The poisons of craving and lust, anger and hatred, ignorance and delusion all reside in the body. He who does not quickly relinquish these perils by means of the Way will surely meet disaster, just as the foolish one who clings to his torch is sure to burn his hands."

24. A deity presented a woman of pleasure to the Buddha, wanting to test the Buddha's will and examine the Buddha's Way. The Buddha said: "Why have you come here bearing this leather sack of filth? Do you think to deceive me? It is difficult to stir [one possessed of] the six supernatural powers.[4] Begone! I have no use for her." The deity, with increased respect for the Buddha, asked about the Way. The Buddha instructed him, whereupon he attained the stage of a stream-winner.

---

3. That is, earth, air, fire, and water.
4. Clairvoyance, clairaudience, telepathy, mem- ory of one's past lives, yogic power, and knowl- edge of extinction.

25. The Buddha said: "A man practicing the Way is like a piece of wood floating downstream with the current. As long as it avoids catching either the left or the right banks, as long as it is not picked up by someone or obstructed by some spirit, as long as it does not get stuck in a whirlpool or rot away, then I assure you it will eventually reach the sea. As long as a man practicing the Way is not deluded by passion or deceived by falsehood, as long as he energetically advances without doubt, then I assure you he will eventually attain the Way."

26. The Buddha told a *shramana*: "Take care not to place faith in your own intentions. Ultimately intentions cannot be trusted. Take care not to wallow in sensuality, for wallowing in sensuality gives birth to misfortune. Only when you attain sainthood can you place faith in your own intentions."

27. The Buddha told a *shramana*: "Take care not to look at women. If you meet one, look not, and take care not to converse with her. If you must converse, admonish the mind to right conduct by saying to yourself: 'As a *shramana* I must live in this befouled world like a lotus, unsullied by mud.' Treat an old lady as if she were your mother, an elder woman as your elder sister, a younger woman as your younger sister, and a young girl as your own daughter. Show respect for them through your propriety. Remember that you see only the outside, but if you could peer into the body—from head to foot—what then? It is brimming with foulness. By exposing the impure aggregates [that comprise the body] one can free oneself from [impure] thoughts."

28. The Buddha said: "A man practicing the Way must eliminate sentiment and desire. It must be like grass encountering fire; by the time the fire arrives the grass is already gone. In encountering passion and desire the man of the Way must immediately distance himself."

29. The Buddha said: "Once a man was tormented by feelings of lust that would not cease, so he squatted down on the blade of an ax in order to castrate himself. The Buddha said to him: 'Severing the genitals is not as good as severing the mind, for the mind is chief. Put a stop to the chief and all his followers will cease. But if you do not put a stop to your depraved mind, what good will castration do? It will surely result in death.'" The Buddha said: "The vulgar and topsy-turvy views of the world are like those of this foolish man."

30. There was an adulterous young lady who made a pact with another man, but when the scheduled time arrived she did not come. The man repented and said to himself: "Desire, I know you! The initial intent is born with thought. If I did not think of you, you would not come into being." The Buddha was passing by and heard him. He said to the *shramana*: "I recognize those words! It is a verse once uttered by Kashyapa Buddha[5] as he passed through this profane world."

31. The Buddha said: "From passion and desire arises sorrow. From sorrow arises dread. Without passion there is no sorrow, and without sorrow there is no dread."

5. The buddha who preceded the historical Buddha.

32. The Buddha said: "A man practicing the Way is like a lone man in combat against ten thousand. Bearing armor and brandishing weapons, he charges through the gate eager to do battle, but if he is weakhearted and cowardly he will withdraw and flee. Some get halfway down the road before they retreat; some reach the battle and die; some are victorious and return to their kingdoms triumphantly. If a man is able to keep a firm grip on his wits and advance resolutely, without becoming deluded by worldly or deranged talk, then desire will disappear and evil will vanish, and he is certain to attain the Way."

33. There was a *shramana* who mournfully chanted the scriptures at night, his spirit full of remorse as if wanting to return [to lay life]. The Buddha summoned the *shramana* and asked him: "When you were a householder what did you do?" He answered, "I regularly played the lute." The Buddha asked: "What happened when the strings were too loose?" He replied: "It did not sound." "And when the strings were too taut, what then?" [The *shramana*] replied: "The sound was cut short." "And when it was neither too loose nor too taught, what then?" "Then the tones all came into sympathetic accord." The Buddha told the *shramana*: "The cultivation of the Way is just like that; keep the mind in tune and you can attain the Way."

34. The Buddha said: "Practicing the Way is like forging iron: if you gradually but thoroughly cast out impurities, the vessel is sure to come out well. If you cultivate the Way by gradually but thoroughly removing the impurities of mind, your advance will be steady. But when you are too harsh with yourself, the body becomes fatigued, and when the body is fatigued, the mind becomes frustrated. If the mind is frustrated, one's practice will lapse, and when practice lapses, one falls into wrongdoing."

35. The Buddha said: "Whether or not you practice the way you will certainly suffer. From birth to old age, from old age to sickness, from sickness to death, the misery of man is immeasurable. The distressed mind accumulates misdeeds, and life and death know no surcease. Such misery is beyond description."

36. The Buddha said: "It is difficult to free oneself from the three evil realms [the hells, the realm of hungry ghosts, and the realm of animals], and attain human birth. Even if one attains human birth it is difficult to be born a man rather than a woman. Even if one is born a man it is difficult to be born perfect in all six sense faculties. Even if the six faculties are perfect it is difficult to be born in the Middle Kingdom.[6] Even if one lives in the Middle Kingdom it is difficult to be born at a time when the Buddha's Way is honored. Even if born when the Buddha's Way is honored it is difficult to encounter a noble man of the Way. [Moreover,] it is difficult to be born in the family of bodhisattvas. Even if born in the family of bodhisattvas it is difficult to encounter the Buddha's presence in the world with a mind of faith in the three honored ones."

6. The Chinese name for China (Zhongguo). "The six faculties": sight, hearing, taste, smell, touch, and mind.

37. The Buddha asked a group of *shramanas*: "How should one measure the span of a man's life?" [One] replied: "By the span of a few days." The Buddha said: "You are not yet able to practice the Way." He asked another *shramana*: "How should one measure the span of a man's life?" [The *shramana*] replied: "By the space of a single meal." The Buddha said: "You are not yet able to practice the Way." He asked another *shramana*: "How should one measure the span of a man's life?" [The *shramana*] replied: "By the space of a single breath." The Buddha said: "Excellent! You can be called one who practices the Way."

38. The Buddha said: "Should one of my disciples venture several thousand miles from me yet remain mindful of my precepts, he is certain to attain the Way. However, should he stand immediately to my left yet harbor depraved thoughts, in the end he will not attain the Way. The gist lies in one's practice. If one is close to me but does not practice, of what benefit are the myriad divisions [of the path]?"

39. The Buddha said: "Practicing the Way is like eating honey, which is sweet all the way through. My scriptures are also like this: they are all about happiness, and those who practice [in accord with them] will attain the Way."

40. The Buddha said: "A man practicing the Way must be able to pluck up the roots of passion and desire, just as one would pluck a bead from a necklace. One by one they are removed until they are no more. When evil is no more the Way is attained."

41. The Buddha said: "A *shramana* following the Way must be like an ox bearing a heavy burden treading through deep mud, so exhausted that he dares not glance left or right, yearning only to get out of the mud quickly so as to catch his breath. The *shramana* regards his emotions and passions as more formidable than that mud. Mindful of the Way with a one-pointed mind, one is able to escape from myriad sufferings."

42. The Buddha said: "I regard the status of lords as a passing stranger. I regard treasures of gold and jade as gravel. I regard the beauty of fine silks as worn rags."

A BUDDHIST APOCRYPHON

TREATISE ON THE AWAKENING OF FAITH ACCORDING TO THE MAHAYANA
(*The Dasheng Qixin Lun*)

An apocryphon is a text of such questionable authenticity or origin that it has not been included in the canon. Yet apocrypha are also texts that, because they are in a sense outside the law, hold a certain fascination. In the case of Christianity, one thinks immediately of the *Gospel of Thomas*. The decision whether a work should be included in or excluded from the canon rests on a host of factors, perhaps the most important being those who decide the provenance of the work in question.

From an early moment in the tradition, there seems to have been a concern about preserving the Buddha's words. Not long after the Buddha's death, one of his chief disciples overheard a monk expressing relief that the Buddha was no longer around to scold the monks. Aghast at the sentiment, the disciple convened an assembly of five hundred monks in a cave on Vulture Peak outside the city of Rajagriha, the site of many of the Buddha's most famous sermons. The purpose of the assembly was to recite what the Buddha had taught, both his discourses and the code of monastic discipline, so that it would not be forgotten. Ananda, renowned for his prodigious memory, was asked to recite everything he had heard the Buddha teach. He began the recitation of each discourse with his personal testimony, "Thus did I hear."

Unfortunately, this story itself is probably apocryphal. And long after the death of the Buddha, there were those who felt no compunction about composing texts that open with this famous phrase. For example, the Mahayana sutras, which started to appear four centuries after his death, begin this way. As texts of questionable origin, all of the Mahayana sutras can be seen as apocrypha, and over the history of Buddhism in India, many regarded them as spurious. One of the chief dividing lines between the so-called Hinayana (the mainstream schools of Indian Buddhism) and the Mahayana was that only the latter accepted the Mahayana sutras as the word of the Buddha. In the thirteenth century, a Tibetan pilgrim visited Bodh Gaya, the site of the Buddha's enlightenment. As he was walking into the monastery carrying a perfection of wisdom sutra, he was stopped by a Sri Lankan monk who asked him what book it was. When he answered, the monk said, "You are a good monk; the Mahayana text you are carrying on your back is not good. Throw it in the river. This so-called Mahayana was not spoken by the Buddha. It was fabricated by a clever man named Nagarjuna."

As Buddhism spread beyond India, so would the apocrypha, and the meaning of the term changed. For Buddhist cultures outside of India a text that falsely claimed to be of Indian origin is considered an apocryphon. One of the most philosophically influential works in the history of East Asian Buddhism—Buddhism in China, Japan, and Korea—is an apocryphon composed in China. It is known in English as the *Awakening of Faith*. A more literal translation of its title would be "Treatise on the Awakening of Faith according to the Mahayana."

According to tradition, its author is Ashvaghosha, an Indian poet of the second-century C.E. who wrote the famous verse biography of the Buddha, the *Buddhacharita*. But Ashvaghosha was not known as a philosopher, and he was not an adherent of the Mahayana. It is now generally agreed that the *Awakening of Faith* is an indigenous Chinese text composed in the sixth century. The earliest and most widely used "translation" of the work, which dates from 553 C.E., is attributed to the famous Indian scholar Paramartha. Some scholars speculate that Paramartha may in fact have composed the treatise after his arrival in China, perhaps translating his own work from Sanskrit into Chinese.

The work is presented largely from the perspective of the Yogachara school of Buddhist philosophy, to which Paramartha belonged. It addresses a perennial problem for the Mahayana: how to account for the presence of enlightenment and ignorance in a single mind. For it was standard Buddhist doctrine that the mind is defiled by ignorance, an ignorance so profound that it has produced the seeds for an infinite number of rebirths in the realms of samsara. Yet a number of Mahayana sutras had proclaimed the *tathagatagarbha*, the Buddha nature (see the *Tathagatagarbha Sutra*, p. 340) eternally present in the minds of all beings. If the Buddha nature has always been present, how did ignorance ever arise? The solution offered by the *Awakening of Faith* was its famous doctrine of "one mind, two aspects": the true-thusness (*zhenru*), or perhaps "true reality," aspect and the production-and-cessation (*shengmie*) aspect. When seen from the perspective of the buddhas, the mind of the sentient being is in a state of "original enlightenment" (*benjue*); from the internal perspective of the sentient being, it is deluded and in need of purification through a process of "actualizing enlightenment" (*shijue*). Once the process of actualizing enlightenment has been completed, the practitioner realizes that the enlightenment achieved through cultivation is identical to original enlightenment.

Presented here is the fourth chapter of the text, which explains how to undertake the practice of actualizing enlightenment.

PRONOUNCING GLOSSARY

Amitabha: *a-mi-tah-bha*
Avalokiteshvara: *a-va-loh-ki-tay-shva-ra*
Dasheng Qixin Lun: *da-shung chee-shin lun*
dharmadhatu: *dar-ma-dah-tu*
Dharmakaya: *dar-ma-kah-ya*
dharmata: *dar-ma-tah*
dhyana: *dyah-na*
guan: *gwahn*
Hinayana: *hee-na-yah-na*

lakshana: *lak-sha-na*
Manjushri: *man-ju-shree*
samadhi: *sa-mah -di*
Sangha: *san-ga*
shamatha: *sha-ma-ta*
Tathagata: *ta-tah-ga-ta*
Tiantai: *tyehn-tai*
vipashyana: *vih-pash-ya-nah*
zhi: *jer*

Part 4. On Faith and Practice

Having already discussed interpretation, we will now present a discussion of faith and practice. This discussion is intended for those who have not yet joined the group of beings who are determined to attain enlightenment.

Question: What kind of faith [should a man have] and how should he practice it?

Answer: Briefly, there are four kinds of faith. The first is the faith in the *Ultimate Source*. Because [of this faith] a man comes to meditate with joy on the principle of Suchness. The second is the faith in the numberless excellent qualities of the *Buddhas*. Because [of this faith] a man comes to meditate on them always, to draw near to them in fellowship, to honor them, and to respect them, developing his capacity for goodness and seeking after the all-embracing knowledge. The third is the faith in the great benefits of the *Dharma* (Teaching). Because [of this faith] a man comes constantly to remember and practice various disciplines leading to enlightenment. The fourth is the faith in the *Sangha* (Buddhist Community) whose members are able to devote themselves to the practice of benefiting both themselves and others. Because [of this faith] a man comes to approach the assembly of Bodhisattvas constantly and with joy and to seek instruction from them in the correct practice.

> The word "Bodhisattva" does not here refer to beings such as Manjushri, Avalokiteshvara, etc., but to any sentient being who is intrinsically enlightened but who has yet to actualize the original enlightenment, and who is making an effort to this end.

TRANSLATED FROM the Chinese by Yoshito S. Hakeda. All bracketed additions are by the translator, who has also inserted explanatory glosses within the text.

There are five ways of practice which will enable a man to perfect his faith. They are the practices of charity, [observance of] precepts, patience, zeal, and cessation [of illusions] and clear observation.

Question: How should a man practice charity?

Answer: If he sees anyone coming to him begging, he should give him the wealth and other things in his possession in so far as he is able; thus, while freeing himself from greed and avarice, he causes the beggar to be joyful. Or, if he sees one who is in hardship, in fear, or in grave danger, he should give him freedom from fear in so far as he is able. If a man comes to seek instruction in the teaching, he should, according to his ability and understanding, explain it by the use of expedient means. In doing so, however, he should not expect any fame, material gain, or respect, but he should think only of benefiting himself and others alike and of extending the merit [that he gains from the practice of charity] toward the attainment of enlightenment.

Question: How should he practice the [observance of] precepts?

Answer: He is not to kill, to steal, to commit adultery, to be double-tongued, to slander, to lie, or to utter exaggerated speech. He is to free himself from greed, jealousy, cheating, deceit, flattery, crookedness, anger, hatred, and perverse views. If he happens to be a monk [or nun] who has renounced family life, he should also, in order to cut off and suppress defilements, keep himself away from the hustle and bustle of the world and, always residing in solitude, should learn to be content with the least desire and should practice vigorous ascetic disciplines. He should be frightened and filled with awe by any slight fault and should feel shame and repent. He should not take lightly any of the Tathagata's[1] precepts. He should guard himself from slander and from showing dislike so as not to rouse people in their delusion to commit any offense or sin.

Question: How should he practice patience?

Answer: He should be patient with the vexatious acts of others and should not harbor thoughts of vengeance, and he should also be patient in matters of gain or loss, honor or dishonor, praise or blame, suffering or joy, etc.

Question: How should he practice zeal?

Answer: He should not be sluggish in doing good, he should be firm in his resolution, and he should purge himself of cowardice. He should remember that from the far distant past he has been tormented in vain by all of the great sufferings of body and mind. Because of this he should diligently practice various meritorious acts, benefiting himself and others, and liberate himself quickly from suffering. Even if a man practices faith, because he is greatly hindered by the evil karma derived from the grave sins of previous lives, he may be troubled by the evil Tempter (Mara) and his demons, or entangled in all sorts of worldly affairs, or afflicted by the suffering of disease. There are a great many hindrances of this kind. He should, therefore, be courageous and zealous, and at the six four-hour intervals of the day and night should pay homage to the Buddhas, repent with sincere heart, beseech the Buddhas [for their guidance], rejoice in the happiness of others, and direct all the merits [thus acquired] to the attainment of enlightenment. If he never abandons these practices, he will be able to avoid the various hindrances as his capacity for goodness increases.

1. A title of a buddha (literally, "one who has thus come/gone"); it is the one most often used by the historical Buddha to refer to himself.

Question: How should he practice cessation and clear observation?

Answer: What is called "cessation" means to put a stop to all characteristics (*lakshana*) of the world [of sense objects and of the mind], because it means to follow the *shamatha* (tranquility) method of meditation. What is called "clear observation" means to perceive distinctly the characteristics of the causally conditioned phenomena (samsara), because it means to follow the *vipashyana* (discerning) method of meditation.

Question: How should he follow these?

Answer: He should step by step practice these two aspects and not separate one from the other, for only then will both be perfected.

> These two methods of meditation, i.e., *shamatha* (Ch., *zhi*) and *vipashyana* (Ch., *guan*), singly and also as a pair, appear in the scriptures of old Pali sources. Much discussion of them is to be found in the sutras and commentaries. Explanations differ, but the basic notion that *shamatha* implies "tranquilization, stabilization, cessation, etc.," and that *vipashyana* implies "discerning, clear observation, distinct perception, etc." remains unchallenged. The most elaborate descriptions of them are to be found in the Tiantai School of Buddhism in China.

Should there be a man who desires to practice "cessation," he should stay in a quiet place and sit erect in an even temper. [His attention should be focused] neither on breathing nor on any form or color, nor on empty space, earth, water, fire, wind, nor even on what has been seen, heard, remembered, or conceived. All thoughts, as soon as they are conjured up, are to be discarded, and even the thought of discarding them is to be put away, for all things are essentially [in the state of] transcending thoughts, and are not to be created from moment to moment nor to be extinguished from moment to moment; [thus one is to conform to the essential nature of Reality (*dharmata*) through this practice of cessation]. And it is not that he should first meditate on the objects of the senses in the external world and then negate them with his mind, the mind that has meditated on them. If the mind wanders away, it should be brought back and fixed in "correct thought." It should be understood that this "correct thought" is [the thought that] whatever is, is mind only and that there is no external world of objects [as conceived]; even this mind is devoid of any marks of its own [which would indicate its substantiality] and therefore is not substantially conceivable as such at any moment.

Even if he arises from his sitting position and engages in other activities, such as going, coming, advancing, or standing still, he should at all times be mindful [of the application] of expedient means [of perfecting "cessation"], conform [to the immobile principle of the essential nature of Reality], and observe and examine [the resulting experiences]. When this discipline is well mastered after a long period of practice, [the ideations of] his mind will be arrested. Because of this, his power of executing "cessation" will gradually be intensified and become highly effective, so that he will conform himself to, and be able to be absorbed into, the "concentration (*samadhi*) of Suchness." Then his defilements, deep though they may be, will be suppressed and his faith strengthened; he will quickly attain the state in which there will be no retrogression. But those who are skeptical, who lack faith, who speak ill [of the teaching of the Buddha], who have committed grave sins, who are hindered by their evil karma, or who are arrogant or indolent are to be excluded; these people are incapable of being absorbed into [the samadhi of Suchness].

Next, as a result of this samadhi, a man realizes the oneness of the World of Reality (*dharmadhatu*), i.e., the sameness everywhere and nonduality of the Dharmakaya[2] of all the Buddhas and the bodies of sentient beings. This is called "the samadhi of one movement." It should be understood that [the samadhi of] Suchness is the foundation of [all other] samadhi. If a man keeps practicing it, then he will gradually be able to develop countless other kinds of samadhi.

If there is a man who lacks the capacity for goodness, he will be confused by the evil Tempter, by heretics and by demons. Sometimes these beings will appear in dreadful forms while he is sitting in meditation, and at other times they will manifest themselves in the shapes of handsome men and women. [In such a case] he should meditate on [the principle of] "mind only," and then these objects will vanish and will not trouble him any longer. Sometimes they may appear as the images of heavenly beings or Bodhisattvas, and assume also the figure of the Tathagata, furnished with all the major and minor marks; or they may expound the spells or preach charity, the precepts, patience, zeal, meditation, and wisdom; or they may discourse on how the true nirvana is the state of universal emptiness, of the nonexistence of characteristics, vows, hatreds, affections, causes, and effects; and of absolute nothingness. They may also teach him the knowledge of his own past and future states of existence, the method of reading other men's minds, and perfect mastery of speech, causing him to be covetous and attached to worldly fame and profit; or they may cause him to be frequently moved to joy and anger and thus to have unsteadiness of character, being at times very kind-hearted, very drowsy, very ill, or lazy-minded; or at other times becoming suddenly zealous, and then afterward lapsing into negligence; or developing a lack of faith, a great deal of doubt, and a great deal of anxiety; or abandoning his fundamental excellent practices [toward religious perfection] and devoting himself to miscellaneous religious acts, or being attached to worldly affairs which involve him in many ways; or sometimes they may cause him to experience a certain semblance of various kinds of samadhi, which are all the attainments of heretics and are not the true samadhi; or sometimes they may cause him to remain in samadhi for one, two, three, or up to seven days, feeling comfort in his body and joy in his mind, being neither hungry nor thirsty, partaking of natural, fragrant, and delicious drinks and foods, which induce him to increase his attachment to them; or at other times they may cause him to eat without any restraint, now a great deal, now only a little, so that the color of his face changes accordingly.

For these reasons, he who practices ["cessation"] should be discreet and observant, lest his mind fall into the net of evil [doctrine]. He should be diligent in abiding in "correct thought," neither grasping nor attaching himself to [anything]; if he does so, he will be able to keep himself far away from the hindrance of these evil influences.

He should know that the samadhi of the heretics are not free from perverse views, craving, and arrogance, for the heretics are covetously attached

2. Literally, the "truth body" (Sanskrit), which is formless, inconceivable, and unchanging (synonymous with "Suchness").

to fame, profit, and the respect of the world. The samadhi of Suchness is the samadhi in which one is not arrested by the activity of viewing [a subject] nor by the experiencing of objects [in the midst of meditation]; even after concentration one will be neither indolent nor arrogant and one's defilements will gradually decrease. There has never been a case in which an ordinary man, without having practiced this samadhi, was still able to join the group that is entitled to become Tathagatas. Those who practice the various types of dhyana (meditation) and samadhi which are popular in the world will develop much attachment to their flavors and will be bound to the triple world because of their perverse view that atman[3] is real. They are therefore the same as heretics, for as they depart from the protection of their good spiritual friends, they turn to heretical views.

Next, he who practices this samadhi diligently and wholeheartedly will gain ten kinds of advantages in this life. First, he will always be protected by the Buddhas and the Bodhisattvas of the ten directions.[4] Second, he will not be frightened by the Tempter and his evil demons. Third, he will not be deluded or confused by the ninety-five kinds of heretics and wicked spirits. Fourth, he will keep himself far away from slanders of the profound teaching [of the Buddha], and will gradually diminish the hindrances derived from grave sins. Fifth, he will destroy all doubts and wrong views on enlightenment. Sixth, his faith in the Realm of the Tathagata will grow. Seventh, he will be free from sorrow and remorse and in the midst of samsara will be full of vigor and undaunted. Eighth, having a gentle heart and forsaking arrogance, he will not be vexed by others. Ninth, even if he has not yet experienced samadhi, he will be able to decrease his defilements in all places and at all times, and he will not take pleasure in the world. Tenth, if he experiences samadhi, he will not be startled by any sound from without.

Now, if he practices "cessation" only, then his mind will be sunk [in self-complacency] and he will be slothful; he will not delight in performing good acts but will keep himself far away from the exercise of great compassion. It is, therefore, necessary to practice "clear observation" [as well].

He who practices "clear observation" should observe that all conditioned phenomena in the world are unstationary and are subject to instantaneous transformation and destruction; that all activities of the mind arise and are extinguished from moment to moment; and that, therefore, all of these induce suffering. He should observe that all that had been conceived in the past was as hazy as a dream, that all that is being conceived in the present is like a flash of lightning, and that all that will be conceived in the future will be like clouds that rise up suddenly. He should also observe that the physical existences of all living beings in the world are impure and that among these various filthy things there is not a single one that can be sought after with joy.

He should reflect in the following way: all living beings, from the beginningless beginning, because they are permeated by ignorance, have allowed their mind to remain in samsara; they have already suffered all the great miseries of the body and mind, they are at present under incalculable pressure and constraint, and their sufferings in the future will likewise be limitless.

3. A permanent self. "Triple world": the Realm of Desire, the Realm of Form, and the Formless Realm; see pp. 54–55.

4. That is, everywhere: north, south, east, west, northeast, northwest, southeast, southwest, the nadir, and the zenith.

These sufferings are difficult to forsake, difficult to shake off, and yet these beings are unaware [that they are in such a state]; for this, they are greatly to be pitied.

After reflecting in this way, he should pluck up his courage and make a great vow to this effect: may my mind be free from discriminations so that I may practice all of the various meritorious acts everywhere in the ten directions; may I, to the end of the future, by applying limitless expedient means, help all suffering sentient beings so that they may obtain the bliss of nirvana, the ultimate goal.

Having made such a vow, he must, in accordance with his capacity and without faltering, practice every kind of good at all times and at all places and not be slothful in his mind. Except when he sits in concentration in the practice of "cessation," he should at all times reflect upon what should be done and what should not be done.

Whether walking, standing, sitting, lying, or rising, he should practice both "cessation" and "clear observation" side by side. That is to say, he is to meditate upon the fact that things are unborn in their essential nature; but at the same time he is to meditate upon the fact that good and evil karma, produced by the combination of the primary cause and the coordinating causes, and the retributions [of karma] in terms of pleasure, pain, etc., are neither lost nor destroyed. Though he is to meditate on the retribution of good and evil karma produced by the primary and coordinating causes [i.e., he is to practice "clear observation"], he is also to meditate on the fact that the essential nature [of things] is unobtainable [by intellectual analysis]. The practice of "cessation" will enable ordinary men to cure themselves of their attachments to the world, and will enable the followers of the Hinayana[5] to forsake their views, which derive from cowardice. The practice of "clear observation" will cure the followers of the Hinayana of the fault of having narrow and inferior minds which bring forth no great compassion, and will free ordinary men from their failure to cultivate the capacity for goodness. For these reasons, both "cessation" and "clear observation" are complementary and inseparable. If the two are not practiced together, then one cannot enter the path to enlightenment.

Next, suppose there is a man who learns this teaching for the first time and wishes to seek the correct faith but lacks courage and strength. Because he lives in this world of suffering, he fears that he will not always be able to meet the Buddhas and honor them personally, and that, faith being difficult to perfect, he will be inclined to fall back. He should know that the Tathagatas have an excellent expedient means by which they can protect his faith: that is, through the strength of wholehearted meditation on the Buddha, he will in fulfillment of his wishes be able to be born in the Buddha-land beyond, to see the Buddha always, and to be forever separated from the evil states of existence. It is as the sutra says: "If a man meditates wholly on Amitabha Buddha[6] in the world of the Western Paradise and wishes to be born in that world, directing all the goodness he has cultivated [toward that goal], then he will be born there." Because he will see the Buddha at all times, he will never fall back. If he meditates on the Dharmakaya, the Suchness of the Buddha, and with diligence keeps practicing [the meditation], he will be able to be born there in the end because he abides in the correct samadhi.

5. On "the inferior vehicle" (Hinayana), as distinguished from the "great vehicle" (Mahayana); see p. 655.

6. The buddha who presides over the Pure Land (see the *Sukhavativyuha Sutra*, p. 316).

A CHINESE PILGRIM VISITS THE BODHI TREE

THE GREAT TANG DYNASTY RECORD
OF THE WESTERN WORLD
(Da Tang Xiyu Ji)

XUANZANG

In the *Mahaparinibbana Sutta,* or *Great Discourse on the Final Nirvana* (p. 840), the Buddha provides his final instructions to his disciples before he passes into nirvana. Among the most consequential of his pronouncements was that those who visited the places of his birth, enlightenment, first sermon, and death would be reborn in heaven. It ensured—perhaps by encouraging existing practice, as some scholars conjecture— that pilgrimage would be an important element of Buddhism. As the religion spread beyond the borders of India, sacred places came to be identified in the new Buddhist lands of Sri Lanka, China, Japan, Burma, and Tibet. These might commemorate a legendary visit by the Buddha himself, or be the site of a stupa that enshrined a relic, or be a place where a mountain in India on which the Buddha had taught was said to have landed after uprooting itself. Pilgrimage to sacred Buddhist sites thus became common in each Buddhist land.

Yet India remained the most sacred place, and the most stalwart pilgrims made the arduous journey, sometimes by land, sometimes by sea. The pilgrims from China and Korea are the most famous, due largely to the detailed accounts they wrote of their travels; these have proved invaluable to scholars seeking to understand the conditions of Buddhism in particular places at particular times. Perhaps the most famous of these pilgrims, both because of his journey and because of what he brought back, was the Chinese monk Xuanzang (600/602–664).

He was born into a literati family in Henan Province. While still a young boy, in 612, he took part in a state-supported ordination ceremony and entered the monastery of Jingtusi in Luoyang, where his older brother was already a monk. Xuanzang and his brother studied various Mahayana texts, including, perhaps significantly, the *Mahaparinirvana Sutra,* where the benefits of pilgrimage are extolled, and he became a fully ordained monk in 622. Xuanzang grew particularly interested in Buddhist philosophy, especially that of the Yogachara school, but he began to have doubts about the accuracy of the translations from Sanskrit into Chinese of some of the texts he was studying. He concluded that he had to go to India to resolve his uncertainties about the meaning of these texts. Although the emperor had issued an edict forbidding foreign travel, Xuanzang set out for India in 629.

He traveled, often alone and on foot, by the land route, making his way along the Silk Road and into what is today Afghanistan and Pakistan, both of which had rich Buddhist cultures. He visited the famous Buddhist pilgrimage sites and spent a number of years at the great monastery of Nalanda, studying under a renowned Yogachara master. After sixteen years abroad, he came home to China in 645. He was welcomed as a hero by the emperor who, in recognition of his knowledge of the scriptures bestowed upon him the title "Master of the Tripitaka" (*Trepitaka* in Sanskrit, *Sanzang Fashi* in Chinese). Xuanzang returned with a large number of Sanskrit texts, and the emperor established a translation bureau for him in the capital. There, Xuanzang supervised a team of monks; over the next nineteen years, he oversaw the transcription and careful translation into Chinese of some seventy-five sutras and treatises, totaling more than 1,300 rolls.

Xuanzang also wrote *The Great Tang Dynasty Record of the Western World (Da Tang Xiyu Ji)*, a detailed account of these travels that occurred during the Tang dynasty. In the first of two passages from the work presented below, he describes his motives for making the journey and writing his account. The second is his description of the most sacred of all the places of pilgrimage in the Buddhist world: the Bodhi tree, where the Buddha sat on the night of his enlightenment. Xuanzang tells of the place and its history with a mixture of deep piety and ethnographic detail.

PRONOUNCING GLOSSARY

Avalokiteshvara: *a-va-loh-ki-tay-shva-ra*
Bhadrakalpa: *ba-dra-kal-pa*
Bodhimanda: *boh-di-man-da*
Da Tang Xiyu Ji: *da-tang shee-yu jee*
Jambudvipa: *jam-bu-dvee-pa*
Kashyapa: *kah-shya-pa*
li: *lee*
Magadha: *ma-ga-da*
Maheshvara: *ma-haysh-va-ra*
Maitreya: *mai-tray-ya*
Manzhou: *mahn-joh*

Nairanjana: *nai-ran-ja-nah*
Pragbodhi: *prahg-boh-di*
Purnavarman: *poor-na-var-man*
samadhi: *sa-mah-di*
Shashanka: *sha-shahn-ka*
shramana: *shra-ma-na*
Sthavira: *sta-vi-ra*
Tathagata: *ta-tah-ga-ta*
Vaishakha: *vai-shah-ka*
Yumen: *yoo-man*

Though the Buddha was born in the West, his Dharma has spread to the East. In the course of translation, mistakes may have crept into the texts, and idioms may have been misapplied. When the words are wrong, the meaning is lost, and when a phrase is mistaken, the doctrine becomes distorted. Hence the saying, "It is necessary to use correct names." What is valuable is the absence of faults!

Human beings are of different dispositions, stubborn or pliable, and speak different languages. This is caused by climatic conditions and by customary usage. As to the varieties of physical features and natural products of the land of the Lord of Men,[1] and the different customs and temperaments of its people, they are recorded in detail in our national histories. As to the customs of the land of the Lord of Horses and the country of the Lord of Treasure, they are fully described in historical records, and we can give a brief account of them. But as to the country of the Lord of Elephants, it has never been described accurately in our ancient literature. Some said that it was mostly a hot and humid country, and others depicted its people as customarily fond of kindness and compassion. These are mentioned in topographies, but no detailed information can be found. As the Way is sometimes prevalent and sometimes in hiding, do not human affairs also have changes of fortune? Thus we may know that it is difficult to describe all those who predict the right season to pledge allegiance and who come to submit to the benevolence of the Emperor, or who passing one danger after another seek admittance at Yumen Pass[2] and bearing tribute of native rarities, bow before the

---

TRANSLATED FROM the Chinese by Li Rongxi. All bracketed additions are by the translator.

1. That is, the Chinese emperor. Xuanzang has previously explained that there are four rulers in Jambudvipa, the continent on which ordinary humans dwell: the Lord of Men rules the country to the east; the Lord of Horses, to the north; the Lord of Treasures, to the west; and the Lord of Elephants, to the south.
2. The Jade Pass in north-central China, through which the Silk Road ran.

gate of the imperial palace. That is why, in the intervals of my studies during my long journey inquiring for truth, I took notes on the conditions and customs along the way.

* * *

Going southwest from Pragbodhi Mountain for fourteen or fifteen *li*,[3] I reached the Bodhi Tree. The surrounding walls are built high and strong with brick, and they are long from east to west and narrow from south to north, being about five hundred paces in circuit. There are exotic trees and famous flowers, casting continuous shade on the ground, and fine sand and strange plants cover the earth with a green quilt. The main gate opens east toward the Nairanjana River, and the southern gate is close to a large flower pool. The west side is an inaccessible natural barrier, while the northern gate leads to a big monastery. Inside the enclosure the sacred sites are connected with one another. The stupas or shrines were all built by monarchs, ministerial officials, and nobles of various countries of Jambudvipa as memorials to their acceptance of the bequeathed teachings of the Buddha.

At the center of the enclosure of the Bodhi Tree is the Diamond Seat, which came into existence together with the great earth at the beginning of the Bhadrakalpa.[4] It is in the middle of the Three Thousand Great Chiliocosm,[5] reaching down to the golden wheel below the surface of the earth. It is made of diamond and is over one hundred paces in circuit. As the one thousand Buddhas of the Bhadrakalpa all sit on it to enter the Diamond Samadhi,[6] it is called the Diamond Seat, and because it is the place for realizing the Sacred Way, it is also called the *Bodhimanda* (Seat for realizing Buddhahood). When the earth quakes, this spot alone remains stable. Thus when the Tathagata[7] was about to attain enlightenment, all the places where he went at the four corners of this seat trembled, and when he came here, it was calm and quiet, without agitation. Since the commencement of the period of decline at the end of the kalpa[8] when the right dharma started to decline, this site was covered by sand and earth and became lost to sight. After the Buddha's Nirvana, the monarchs of various countries set up two sitting statues of Avalokiteshvara[9] facing the east at the southern and northern limits of the enclosure according to the Buddha's description as they had heard from the tradition. Some old people said that when the statues of the Bodhisattva disappear and become invisible, the Buddha-dharma will come to an end, and now the statue at the south corner has already sunk down up to the chest.

The Bodhi Tree at the Diamond Seat is a pipal tree, which was several hundred feet tall at the time of the Buddha, and although it has been cut down or damaged several times, it still remains forty or fifty feet high. As the Buddha attained full enlightenment while sitting under this tree, it is called the Bodhi Tree (Tree of Enlightenment). The trunk of the tree is yellowish

---

3. One *li* equaled about 1/3 of a mile.
4. Literally, the "Fortunate Aeon" (Sanskrit): the present cosmological period, during which one thousand buddhas will appear.
5. The universe, consisting of one billion worlds.
6. A state of deep meditation.

7. A title of a buddha (literally, "one who has thus come/gone"); it is the one most often used by the historical Buddha to refer to himself.
8. An aeon, or cosmic cycle.
9. The bodhisattva of compassion.

white in color, and its branches and leaves are always green; they never wither away nor change their luster, whether in the winter or in the summer. Each year on the day of the Tathagata's Nirvana, the leaves fade and fall; but they grow out again very soon. On that day the monarchs of various countries and monks and laymen of different places, thousands and myriads in number, gather here by their own will to irrigate and bathe the tree with scented water and milk to the accompaniment of music; with arrays of fragrant flowers and lamps burning uninterruptedly the devotees vie with each other in making offerings to the tree.

After the decease of the Tathagata, when King Ashoka[1] had just ascended the throne, he believed in heretical doctrines and destroyed the sites left by the Buddha. He sent his troops and went in person to cut the tree. He chopped the roots, stalks, branches, and leaves into small pieces and had them heaped up at a spot a few tens of paces to the west, where fire-worshipping Brahmans were ordered to burn the pile as a sacrifice to their god. But before the smoke and flames had vanished, two trees grew out of the furious fire with luxuriant and verdurous leaves; these trees were thus called Ash Bodhi Trees. Upon seeing this strange sight, King Ashoka repented his misdeeds and irrigated the remnant roots with sweet milk. When it was nearly dawn, the tree grew up as before. The king was highly exhilarated to have seen this spiritual wonder and made offerings to the tree in person with so much delight that he forgot to go back home. The queen, being a heretical believer, secretly sent a man to fell the tree after nightfall. When King Ashoka went to worship the tree at dawn, he was very sad to see only the stump of the tree. He prayed earnestly and irrigated the stump with sweet milk, and in a few days the tree grew up once again. With deep respect and astonishment, the king built a stone enclosure to the height of more than ten feet around the tree, which is still in existence. Recently King Shashanka,[2] being a heretical believer, denounced the Buddha-dharma out of jealousy, destroyed monasteries, and cut down the Bodhi Tree. When he dug the ground so deep as to have reached spring water and could not get at the ends of the roots, he set fire to burn it and soaked it with sugarcane juice with the intention of making it rotten, so as to prevent it from sprouting. Several months later, King Purnavarman (known as Manzhou, or Full Armor, in Chinese) of Magadha,[3] the last descendant of King Ashoka, heard about the event and said with a sigh of regret, "The Sun of Wisdom has sunk, and only the Buddha's tree remained in the world; now that the tree has been destroyed, what else is there for living beings to see?" He prostrated himself on the ground and wept touchingly. He irrigated the tree with milk obtained from several thousand cows, and it grew up to some ten feet high in one night. Fearing that people of later times might cut it down, he surrounded it with a stone enclosure to the height of twenty-four feet. Thus the Bodhi Tree at present is behind the stone wall, with over ten feet of its branches growing out above the wall.

To the east of the Bodhi Tree is a shrine one hundred sixty or seventy feet high built on a base of which the front is more than twenty paces broad. It

---

1. An emperor of the Mauryan dynasty (r. ca. 268–238 B.C.E.); see the *Ashokavadana*, or *Legend of Ashoka*, p. 238.
2. Seventh-century king of Gauda (in modern-

day Bengal).
3. In northeast India; its capital was Rajagriha, where the Buddha lived for many years.

was built with brick and plastered with lime. In all the niches arranged in tiers, there are golden images, and on the four walls there are marvellous carvings in the shapes of strings of pearls or figures of fairies. On the top there is installed a gilded copper *amalaka* fruit (it is also said to be a precious bottle or a precious pot). It is connected with a storied pavilion at the east, of which the eaves are in three layers, while the rafters, pillars, ridgepoles, beams, doors, and windows are adorned with gold and silver carvings and studded with pearls and jade in a mixed way. The innermost chamber of the shrine has three doors connecting with the other parts of the structure. On each side of the outer door there is a niche containing an image of Avalokiteshvara Bodhisattva on the left side and that of Maitreya[4] Bodhisattva on the right side, both cast in silver and more than ten feet in height.

Formerly King Ashoka had built a small shrine at the site of the [present] shrine, and later a Brahman extended it. At first there was a Brahman who did not believe in the Buddha-dharma but worshipped the deity Maheshvara.[5] He heard that the deity was living in the Snow Mountains, and so he went with his younger brother to seek the fulfillment of his wishes from the deity. The deity said, "Your wishes can be fulfilled only when you have done meritorious deeds. It is not that you can get things by saying prayers, nor can I make you satisfied." The Brahman said, "What meritorious deed should I do so that my mind can be satisfied?" The deity said, "If you wish to plant the seed of goodness, you should find the Field of Blessedness. As the Bodhi Tree is the place where the Buddha attained Buddhahood, you should quickly go back to the Bodhi Tree to build a great shrine, dig out a large pond, and make various offerings, and then your wishes will be fulfilled." Under the injunction of the deity, the Brahman cherished a mind of great faith and returned with his younger brother. The elder one built the shrine and the younger one excavated a pond. Then they made rich offerings to seek the fulfillment of their wishes. Finally they realized their wishes and became cabinet ministers to the king. Whatever emoluments or rewards they received they gave away as alms.

When the shrine was completed, artists were invited to make an image of the Tathagata as he was at the time of attaining Buddhahood. But for a long time, nobody answered the call for the job. At last a Brahman came and said to the monks, "I am good at making fine images of the Tathagata." The monks said, "What do you need for making the image?" The Brahman said, "I only need some scented clay and a lamp to be placed inside the shrine. When I have entered the shrine, the door should be tightly closed and opened after six months." The monks did as they were told. But when it was four days short of six months, they opened the door out of curiosity to see [what was going on]. They saw that the image inside the shrine was in the posture of sitting cross-legged facing the east, with the right foot upon [the left thigh]; the left hand was drawn back, and the right one pointed downward. It was just as if it were alive. The pedestal was four feet two inches high and twelve feet five inches wide, while the image was eleven feet five inches tall, the two knees being eight feet eight inches apart, and the

4. The future buddha, currently a bodhisattva.   5. Shiva, one of the main deities of Hinduism.

breadth from one shoulder to another measured six feet two inches. All the auspicious physical symbols of a Buddha were complete, and its features of compassion were true to reality, except that a little spot above the right breast was unfinished. As they saw nobody in the shrine, they realized that there was a divine hand at work, and all the monks were filled with amazement and eagerly wished to know about the affair. One of the shramanas,[6] a man of simple and honest mind, had a dream in which he saw the Brahman, who said to him, "I am Maitreya Bodhisattva, and fearing that artists could not imagine the holy features of the Buddha, I came in person to make the image. It is made with the right hand pointing downward, because when the Tathagata was about to attain Buddhahood, Mara[7] came to disturb him, and the earth gods informed him of Mara's arrival. One of the earth gods came out first to assist the Buddha in subjugating Mara, but the Tathagata said to the god, 'Do not worry. I can surely subjugate him with my power of forbearance.' Mara said, 'Who will bear you witness?' The Tathagata then pointed his hand to the earth while saying, 'This one here will bear me witness!' At that moment the second earth god emerged to bear witness. Therefore the image is made with the right hand pointing downward." The monks came to know that it was a divine manifestation, and all of them were moved to tears. The unfinished spot above the breast was made good with various gems, and the image was adorned with a necklace of pearls, crowned with a coronet, and embellished with other valuable ornaments.

When King Shashanka felled the Bodhi Tree, he also wished to destroy this image. But when he looked at the compassionate features of the image, he did not have the heart to do so. At the time of returning home, he told his attendant minister, "You had better remove this image of the Buddha and replace it with that of Maheshvara." Having received the king's edict, the attendant minister was afraid and said with a sigh, "If I destroy the Buddha's image, I shall suffer disaster for many kalpas, but if I disobey the king's order, I shall not only lose my own life but also incur the extermination of my entire family. What shall I do in this awkward plight?" Then he called some Buddhist believers to be his servants and had a brick wall built horizontally in front of the Buddha's image. As he was ashamed to see the image in utter darkness, he lit a lamp for it. On the front of the brick wall he drew a picture of Maheshvara, and when this was done he made a report to the king. Upon hearing the report, the king dreaded the consequences. He suffered from blisters all over his body, and his skin became cracked, and before long he died.

The attendant minister hurriedly went back to the image and demolished the screen wall. After many days the lamp was still burning without extinction. The image is now still in existence, and as it is in a profound chamber, lamps and torches are burning continually. One cannot see the compassionate features clearly unless one reflects sunlight with a big mirror into the chamber to see the divine statue early in the morning. Those who have the chance to see the image are struck with emotion.

---

6. Wandering monks.   7. The personification of evil and temptation.

The Tathagata attained perfect enlightenment on the eighth day of the second half of the month of Vaishakha[8] of the Indian calendar, corresponding to the eighth day of the third month of our calendar, but according to the tradition of the Sthavira school, the event occurred on the fifteenth day of the second half of the month of Vaishakha, corresponding to the fifteenth day of the third month of our calendar. He was then at the age of thirty or thirty-five.

To the north of the Bodhi Tree is a place where the Buddha walked up and down. After achieving perfect enlightenment, the Tathagata did not rise from his seat but sat in meditation for seven days. When he rose to his feet, he went to the north of the Bodhi Tree where he walked to and fro east and west for seven days. When he had walked over ten paces, signs of strange flowers followed his footprints at eighteen points. People of later times built a brick promenade about three feet high at this place. It is said in a previous record that this sacred site can foretell the length of one's life. One should make a sincere vow before taking the measure. The length of the promenade varies with the possible duration of life of those who measure it.

To the north of the promenade, on a huge rock on the right side of the road, is a big shrine in which there is an image of the Buddha with its eyes gazing upward. Formerly the Tathagata looked at the Bodhi Tree from this place for seven days without blinking his eyelids, looking at the tree attentively with a feeling of gratitude.

Not far to the west of the Bodhi Tree there is a great shrine with a brass image of the Buddha in the standing posture facing the east that is adorned with rare jewels. In front of the image is a blue stone with wonderful veins of various hues. This is the place where Brahma built a hall with the seven precious substances and Indra[9] made a seat, also of the seven precious substances, at the time when the Tathagata first attained enlightenment. On this seat he sat in meditation for seven days and emitted an unusual light that shone upon the Bodhi Tree. The precious substances have become stone because the event occurred in the remote past.

Not far to the south of the Bodhi Tree is a stupa more than one hundred feet high built by King Ashoka. After having bathed himself in the Nairanjana River, the Bodhisattva was going to the Bodhi Tree when he pondered what he should use for a seat. Then he got the idea of using some clean grass to make a seat. Meanwhile Indra transformed himself into a grass cutter, carrying a bundle of grass going on his way. The Bodhisattva said to him, "Can you favor me with some of your grass?" The transformed figure respectfully offered him some grass, and after receiving the grass the Bodhisattva proceeded on his way.

Not far to the northeast of the spot of receiving grass is a stupa built at the place where some blue birds (*Eophona personata*) and a drove of deer came as a good omen when the Bodhisattva was about to achieve Buddhahood. Among the signs of auspiciousness in India, their presence is the most lucky symbol. Thus in compliance with the custom of the human world, the celestial

---

8. April-May.
9. The ruler of the Heaven of the Thirty-three.

"Brahma": the god who persuaded the Buddha to teach.

beings of the Pure Abode Heaven made the blue birds fly around the Bodhisattva to signal his spirituality and holiness.

To the east of the Bodhi Tree there are two stupas, one on the left and the other on the right side of the main road. This is the place where the King of Maras disturbed the Bodhisattva. When the Bodhisattva was about to attain Buddhahood, the King of Maras exhorted him to be a supreme ruler [instead of a Buddha]. As this device was ineffective, the King of Maras withdrew in deep sadness. His daughters volunteered to go to seduce the Bodhisattva, who with his divine power changed the beautiful girls into decrepit old dames. They retreated clinging to each other and holding sticks to support their skinny frames.

In a shrine to the northwest of the Bodhi Tree there is an image of Kashyapa Buddha.[1] Well known for its spirituality and sanctity, it often emits a bright light. It is said in a previous record that if a man walks around the image seven times with utmost sincerity, he may gain the wisdom of knowing where he was born in his past life.

To the northwest of the shrine of Kashyapa Buddha, there are two brick chambers, each housing an image of an earth god. One informed the Buddha of the arrival of Mara, and the other one bore witness for the Buddha. People of later times made these images of the gods in memory of their merits.

1. The buddha who immediately preceded Shakyamuni.

BURNING THE BODY FOR THE BUDDHA

ACCOUNTS IN DISSEMINATION AND PRAISE OF THE *LOTUS SUTRA*
(*The Hongzan Fahua Zhuan*)

Buddhist texts, particularly the Mahayana sutras, promise all manner of benefit to those who revere them, with that reverence taking several forms. For example, the *Lotus Sutra* (see the *Saddharmapundarika*, p. 278) recommends five practices for preachers of the dharma: receiving and maintaining the sutra, reading it, reciting it, copying it, and explaining it to others. Reciting, particularly from memory, was considered to be especially potent. Each of these five practices was followed in China, and miraculous tales are told about them. A number of those tales were brought together in the seventh-century Chinese collection excerpted here.

Among the various forms of devotion to the *Lotus Sutra*, the most extreme was self-immolation. Chapter 23 of that text tells of a bodhisattva in the distant past, Bhaishajyaraja ("Medicine King"), who decides to express his dedication to the buddha of that age by transforming himself into a flame. To that end, he ingests a wide variety of oils and fragrances for two hundred thousand years. He then coats his body with oil, dons a jeweled cloak soaked in oil, and sets himself ablaze, creating a light that illumines the universe for two hundred thousand years. Reborn in the presence of that same long-lived buddha he had so honored with his self-immolation, Bhaishayaraja is entrusted with the task of cremating the buddha upon his death, collecting his relics, and erecting stupas. Having completed this task, the bodhisattva immolates his forearm in offering. After recounting this story, the Buddha praises his deed, remarking that burning even a finger or a toe as an offering to a stupa was more meritorious than offering all that is precious in the universe. The Buddha's praise was taken seriously in China, where cases of self-immolation in reverence to the Buddha were documented into the twentieth century. (The Vietnamese monk who famously set himself ablaze in Saigon in 1963 seems to have done so instead as a political protest.) A less extreme and far more common practice was the burning of fingers or the joints of fingers. In the selection below, however, monks and nuns commit their bodies to the flames. Another form of devotion to the *Lotus Sutra* was recitation, less dramatic in form but sometimes producing miraculous results. In the last of the stories reproduced here, a nun recites the *Lotus Sutra* to protect the nunnery from a lecherous man, who loses a different appendage.

PRONOUNCING GLOSSARY

Avatamsaka Sutra: *a-va-tam-sa-ka soo-tra*
Bacheng: *bah-chang*
Bhaisajyaraja: *bai-shaj-ya-rah-ja*
bhikshuni: *bik-shu-nee*
Bingzhou: *beeng-joh*
Chandrasuryavimalaprabhasashri: *chan-dra-soor-ya-vi-ma-la-pra-bah-sa-shree*
Changle: *chahng-la*
Changsha: *chahng-shah*
chang-zhai: *chahng-jai*
Chanjing: *chahn-jeeng*
Cheng: *chang*
Chonggao: *chohng-gau*
Daming: *dah-meeng*
Dashabhumika: *da-sha-boo-mi-ka*
Daye: *dah-yeh*
dharani: *dah-ra-nee*
dhyana: *dyah-na*
Fashang: *fah-shahng*
ganying: *gahn-eeng*
Guangling: *gwahng-leeng*
Guo: *gwo*
Hongzan Fahua Zhuan: *hong-zun fa-hwa-juan*
Huiguo: *hway-gwo*
Huijin: *hway-jeen*
Huiyi: *hway-ee*
Jiangxia: *jyahng-shyah*
Jiangyang: *jyahng-yahng*
Jingzhou: *jeeng-joh*
Linwei: *leen-way*
Liu: *lyoh*
Longmen: *lohng-man*
Prabhutaratna: *pra-boo-ta-rat-na*
qi: *chee*
Qian: *chyehn*

Qianfeng: *chyehn-fang*
Samantabhadra: *sa-man-ta-ba-dra*
Sengding: *sang-deeng*
Shakyamuni: *shah-kya-mu-ni*
sharira: *sha-ree-ra*
Song: *sohng*
Sui: *sway*
Suzhou: *soo-joh*
Tanyou: *tahn-joh*
Trayastrimsha: *trah-yas-trim-sha*
Vimalakirti: *vi-ma-la-keer-ti*
Wang Daozhen: *wahng dau-jan*
Wuxing: *woo-sheeng*
Xian: *shyehn*
Xiaojian: *shyau-jyehn*
Xiaowu: *shyau-woo*
Ximing: *shee-meeng*
Xuzhou: *shoo-joh*
Yangzhou: *yahng-joh*
Yaowangsi: *yau-wahng-su*
Yi Gong: *ee gohng*
ying: *eeng*
Yining: *ee-neeng*
Yongchang: *yohng-chahng*
You: *yoh*
Yueling: *yoo-eh-leeng*
Yuwen Huaji: *yoo-wan hwai-jee*
Yuzhou: *yoo-joh*
Zhang: *jahng*
Zhi: *jer*
Zhiye: *jer-yeh*
Zhong: *johng*
Zhu: *joo*
Zhulin: *joo-leen*
zisu: *tsu-soo*

Sacrificing the Body

The Buddhist monk Huiyi was a native of Guangling. He left home when he was a child and followed his master to Shouzhun. During the Xiaojian reign-period [454–456] of the Song he left the capital and settled at Zhulin Monastery, where he threw himself into the relentless practice of austerities, with the pledge eventually to immolate himself [in offering to the dharma]. When members of the sangha[1] learned of this, some denounced him [in disapproval]; others praised him.

In the fourth year of the Daming era [460] he began to give up coarse grains, eventually taking only hemp [buds] and barley. By the sixth year he had cut these out, too, and consumed only extract of the *zisu* herb. Before long he gave this up as well and took to swallowing nothing but pills of pure aromatic. Although his four vital elements[2] hung by a thread, his spiritual disposition remained as determined and true as ever.

Emperor Xiaowu looked upon Huiyi with deep reverence and awe, and asked after him anxiously. He dispatched the grand steward Yi Gong, king of Jiangxia, to go to the monastery and reason with Huiyi. But Huiyi would not be swayed from his purpose. On the eighth day of the fourth month during the seventh year of the Daming era [463]—the day on which he had chosen to immolate himself—Huiyi set up a cauldron and prepared [a supply of] oil on the south [slope] of Mount Zhong. That morning he mounted an ox-carriage. Pulled along by a crowd of followers, he set out from the temple and proceeded toward the mountain.

Emperors and kings are regarded as the support of the people and the foundation on which the three jewels[3] depend. For this reason [Emperor Xiaowu] personally [thought to] enter the terrace [and watch the event]. But upon reaching Cloud Dragon Gate, he found that [it was thronged with people and that] he could proceed no further. He ordered someone to inquire as to the reason. As it turned out, the man of the way, Huiyi, ready to renounce himself in sacrifice, had come to take his leave of the emperor officially. Being an ardent admirer of the Buddha dharma, the emperor's visage immediately changed, and he personally stepped out of the Cloud Dragon Gate [to show his respect to Huiyi]. Spying the emperor, Huiyi sternly charged him with the protection of the Buddha's dharma. Thereupon he took his leave and departed.

The emperor followed along behind him. Kings and their royal consorts, mendicants and laypersons, knights and rabble alike filled the mountain valley, where they proceeded to cast off garments and jewelry of incalculable value [in offering to the sangha]. Huiyi climbed into the cauldron and seated himself on a small bench. First he wrapped his upper body in bark cloth from the karpasa tree.[4] Over this he wound a single long [strip of cloth] in the form of a turban, which he then sprinkled with oil. As he was getting ready to add the flame, the emperor ordered the grand steward to approach the cauldron and plead with him one last time, saying, "There are many methods for prac-

---

TRANSLATED FROM the Chinese by Daniel B. Stevenson. All bracketed additions are the translator's.

1. The Buddhist community (especially the community of monks).
2. That is, earth, air, fire, and water (the four constituent elements of all matter).
3. The Buddha, the dharma, and the sangha.
4. Cotton tree.

ticing the way. Why must you take your life? I pray that you will think it over three times, and decide upon a different path."

But Huiyi's resolve was firm, and he had no thoughts of regret. Thus he replied, "What is worth preserving in this feeble body and worthless life? Your majesty is sagely and benevolent but shows excessive favoritism toward me. I pray that, instead, you will sponsor twenty persons to leave home [as Buddhist monks or nuns]."

The emperor issued an edict granting his request. Thereupon, taking candle in hand, Huiyi set the turban alight. As the turban caught fire he tossed the candle aside, joined his palms and began to recite the "Medicine King" (Bhaishajyaraja) chapter [of the *Lotus*]. The flame began to creep down over his brow, but the sound of his chanting was still clear and distinct. When it reached his eyes, all was silent. Nobleman and commoner everywhere set up a loud wail, the echo of which reverberated throughout the valley. There wasn't one among them who didn't snap his fingers and praise the name of the Buddha [in admiration], as tears of grief streamed down their sobbing faces.

The fire finally died out at dawn. At that moment the emperor heard strains of flute and pipe and smelled an exceedingly fine aroma wafting through the air around him. Not until the end of the day did he at last return to the palace. That night the emperor dreamt that he saw Huiyi. The master, shaking his mendicant's staff, approached him and charged him again with [protection of] the Buddha's dharma. The next morning the emperor convened a ceremony in order to ordain [the twenty monks, as he had promised]. He ordered the chairman of the vegetarian feast to proclaim and narrate in detail the auspicious wonders [that attended Huiyi's death]. On the site where Huiyi immolated himself, the emperor built Medicine King Monastery (Yaowangsi) in order to commemorate the deed.

In Jingzhou there lived two bhikshunis[5] who were sisters. Their names have been forgotten, but they both recited the *Lotus Sutra*, held a deep loathing for the physical body, and together conceived the desire to give up their lives [in offering to the dharma]. [To this end,] they set restrictions on clothing and diet and prescribed for themselves a regimen of painful austerities. They ingested various perfumed oils and gradually reduced their intake of coarse rice, until they gave up grains altogether and took only fragrant honey. [Even then,] their energy and spiritual determination remained as vigorous and fresh as ever. They announced [widely] to the monks and laity [around them] that at an appointed time in the future they would immolate themselves.

On the evening of the eighth day of the second month during the third year of the Zhenguan era [629], they set up two high seats in the middle of one of the large boulevards of Jingzhou. Then they wrapped their bodies from head to foot in waxed cloth, leaving only their faces exposed. The crowds gathered like a mountain; their songs of praise filled the air like clouds. The two women together began to chant the *Lotus Sutra*. When they reached the "Medicine King" (Bhaishajyaraja) chapter, the older sister first ignited the head of the younger sister, and the younger in turn lit the head of the older sister. Simultaneously the two blazed up, like two torches in the clear night. As the flames crept down over their eyes, the sound of their voices became

5. Buddhist nuns.

even more distinct. But, as it gradually arrived at their noses and mouths, they grew quiet [and their voices were heard no more]. [They remained seated upright] until dawn, linked together on their two seats. Then, all at once, the fire gave out. [As the smoke and flame cleared,] there amidst their charred and desiccated bones lay two tongues, both perfectly intact. The crowd gasped in awe. [A short time later] a tall stupa was constructed for them.

Not far to the west of the city seat of Bingzhou there lived a sutra copyist around twenty-four or twenty-five years of age who recited the *Lotus Sutra*. He made a vow to immolate himself in offering [to the dharma]. Gathering up several bundles of dead stems and brush, he spread them out to sun until they were bone dry. People asked him what he was doing; but he kept his intentions secret, refusing to tell anyone. Sometime later in the middle of the night he set fire [to the pile] and immolated himself. By the time people rushed to his assistance the fire was in full blaze and he was already dead. Thereupon they added more wood to the fire to insure that his body would be completely consumed. A [strange] music and rare fragrance were detected in the air. Many people [as a result] found faith [in the Buddhist teachings].

The Buddhist monk Tanyou had the secular surname of Zhang and was a native of Xuzhou. While traveling abroad to study in Xianyang, he suddenly conceived a profound disgust [for the world]. [Shortly thereafter] he happened to meet the dhyana[6] masters Wuxing and Zhi, as a result of which he left the household life and took up practice of the way on Mount Yueling.

Tanyou concentrated exclusively on recitation of the *Lotus Sutra*. As a rule he would set up a purified altar space (*tan*) of several feet square. Only after hanging out his twenty-one banners and making formal offerings of incense and flowers would he begin to recite the sutra. This he followed as his regular procedure.

Later You moved to Mount Xian, with the intention of reading through the *Avatamsaka Sutra*. Repeatedly he experienced a dream in which someone would come and teach him to recite the verses [of the sutra]. Whenever he reached the point in his recitation [where verses occur], he found that [the verses of the dream] corresponded perfectly with the written text of the scripture.

Later You heard of the numinous Buddha image fashioned by Ashoka[7] that had [miraculously] flown [to China] and been installed in Changsha Monastery. Numerous spiritual manifestations [were said to have been associated with it]. But the subtle sincerity necessary to tap [its supernal potency] will not be present if one is not willing to disregard one's own life and give oneself totally to religious discipline. So thinking, You decided to immolate himself in an offering [to dharma] at this site, [just as the bodhisattva] Medicine King [chose to do in the *Lotus Sutra*].

In the first year of the Qianfeng era [666] he traveled to the spot where the image was enshrined. [Standing in its presence,] he made the solemn vow [to sacrifice himself in offering] and prayed that he might realize his aim with-

---

6. A state of deep concentration achieved through meditation.

7. An emperor of the Mauryan dynasty (r. ca. 268–238 B.C.E.); see the *Ashokavadana*, p. 238.

out impediment. Thereupon, coming from in front of the Buddha hall, he heard the sound of fingers snapping [in approval]. At that moment a heavy downpour began to fall from thick and ominous-looking clouds. As this had been typical of the weather for more than ten days now, those around You sought to dissuade him, fearing that [the rain] might prove an obstacle [to the realization of his aim]. But Tanyou countered, "There is an auspicious omen in this. [My vow] will be realized. Of this I have no doubt."

When the fated night of the fifteenth day of the second month arrived, the sky cleared completely and the light of the full moon streamed forth, illumining everything. Tanyou [wrapped himself in] waxed cotton cloth and set fire simultaneously to his hands and the crown of his head. He wished for the fire to burn slowly, so that he might continue the offering for a long time. He did not want to die quickly. As the fire crept to his two wrists, his countenance showed no change whatsoever. Even as it reached his brow he continued to preach the dharma just as he had at the start. Easeful and single-minded, he kept his gaze fixed on the auspicious image before him. With the light [from the flame] as his offering, he prayed for a vision of the buddha Clear-Radiance-of-Sun-and-Moon (Chandrasuryavimalaprabhasashri), [to whom the bodhisattva Medicine King offered himself in the *Lotus Sutra*].

Those around him [periodically] asked, "How do you feel?" To which he would reply, "My mind is like diamond—unflinching in its resolve. Truly I feel quite cool and pleasant. There is no pain whatsoever." Then, all at once, the blaze flared up brilliantly, consuming him entirely. Still, from the midst of the inferno [one could hear] Tanyou urging those around him to recite the Buddha's name.

When the fire first began to grow in intensity, the monks present all became quite agitated, fearing that without any skeletal remains there would be no evidence to testify to his self-immolation. Hence, they begged that at least a single token [of his saintly deed] be left behind, so that they might display it for [the edification of] the living. When it was finally over and all had been reduced to ashes, only his skull remained. As dawn arrived and word of the event spread through the prefectural seat, the local officials all flocked to the site. They prostrated in obeisance, [ritually] circumambulated the spot, praised You's devotion, and then departed. No sooner had they passed out of the monastery gate than the skull spontaneously burst apart. Some dozen of the faithful [had chosen to] remain in the presence of the sacred skull, where they prayed fervently for sharira [relics] to appear. In all eight or so grains [of relic] descended. Sinking and floating freely [in the air], their miraculous manifestation came in answer to the heartfelt [sincerity of the onlookers]. Today the cremated remains are interred within the temple. The [miraculous] response (*ying*) of the snapping of fingers is regularly heard.

More recently, when he first took up reciting the *Lotus Sutra* from memory, the eremite mendicant Hulun of Ximing Monastery burned one finger [in offering] with completion of each fascicle, so that by the time he reached the eighth and final fascicle, he had burned off eight fingers. Although this is not [the same as] total renunciation, it is next in status to sacrifice of the [entire] body.

Recitation from Memory

The Buddhist monk Puming had the secular surname of Zhang and was a native of Linwei. He left home [to join the sangha] when he was a young boy. Pure by nature, he was never seen to compromise [his vow to] maintain a vegetarian diet and wear cotton robes. He took repentance and recitation [of sutras] as his regular form of practice. The three sets of robes and rope [meditation] couch [of the mendicant] were rarely far from his person. When he wished to rest, he would take a short nap while sitting upright.

He recited the *Lotus* and *Vimalakirti*[8] sutras. Whenever he chanted he would use a special robe and separate seat, which he took great care not to pollute. Upon reaching the "Exhortations" chapter [of the *Lotus*], the bodhisattva Samantabhadra[9] would appear before his very eyes, seated atop a white elephant. When he recited the *Vimalakirti Sutra* he would hear singing and music in the air.

Puming was also skilled in the use of spiritual incantations (*dharani*). Whomever he sought to save was always cured. Once there was a villager known as Wang Daozhen, whose wife came down with a serious illness. He summoned Ming to his house. No sooner did Ming enter the gate than the woman's melancholia departed. Suddenly, running from the dog entrance, they saw a creature several feet in length that looked something like a fox. As a result of this she was cured. Once when Ming was walking near a shrine by the side of the river a shaman[ess] called out, "When the spirits see you they all run away."

Later Ming developed a sudden illness. Sitting in proper meditation posture, he burned incense and quietly passed away. It was the Xiaojian era (454–457) of the Song when he died. He was eighty-five years of age.

The Buddhist monk Huiguo was a native of Yuzhou. When he was a boy he made a vegetarian diet and austerities his regular practice. During the beginning of the Song period [420] he journeyed to the capital and took up residence in Waguan Monastery, where he recited the *Lotus* and *Dashabhumika* sutras. Once in front of the privy he spied a ghost. With utmost reverence [the spirit] approached Guo and said, "Formerly I was a preceptor in this monastic assembly, but I committed a small irregularity and so have fallen among the excrement-eating ghosts. Dharma Master, your [powers of] religious discipline are lofty and illustrious. Moreover, loving-kindness and compassion are your aim. I pray that you may find some method to help alleviate my condition." It went on to say, "Some time ago I had three thousand in cash, which I buried at the foot of the persimmon tree [on the monastery grounds]. Please take it and make meritorious blessings for me."

Guo thereupon informed the assembly of monks and went to dig up [the cash]. Sure enough, the three thousand was there. He used the money to have a copy of the *Lotus Sutra* made and sponsor a noon [dharma] ceremony. Afterward he saw the ghost in a dream, who told him, "I have managed to change my state of existence, and it is vastly superior to that of yesterday." Guo died during the sixth year [425] after the great founding of the [Liu] Song [dynasty], at the age of seventy-six.

8. Excerpted in this anthology; see pp. 278 and 304.   9. The bodhisattva of universal goodness.

There was a certain monk—his name has been forgotten—who lived in a monastery in the eastern section of Qin commandery. [In residence at the monastery] was a young novice who could recite the *Lotus Sutra* with extraordinary fluency, except for the fact that whenever he reached the two words, "cloudy and obscure" (*ai-dai*), in the "Medicinal Herbs" chapter, he would forget them no sooner than he was taught them. This must have happened well over a thousand times. Finally his master scolded him bitterly, saying, "You are able to learn to recite the entire sutra perfectly [from memory]. How is it that you can't muster the concentration to memorize these two words?!"

That night the master dreamt of a Buddhist monk, who told him: "You should not blame this novice. In his previous life he lived in a village on the east side of this monastery, where he had the form of a laywoman. Basically she devoted herself to reciting the single scripture of the *Lotus Sutra*. But at that time, silverfish had eaten away the two characters "cloudy and obscure" in the "Medicinal Herbs" chapter of the household copy of the *Lotus*. Thus the two characters were originally missing from the sutra. [As a result], when in this present life the novice monk tries to learn the words anew, he cannot do it. The surname [of the family] is such and such, and this copy of the sutra may still be found there. If you don't believe my tale, you can go and verify it for yourself."

The very next day the master went to the village and sought out the household. After introducing himself he said to the head of the family, "Do you have a special place for making offerings?" The man replied, "We do." "What scriptures do you keep there?" he asked. To which the man replied, "We have a single copy of the *Lotus Sutra*." The master sent him to fetch it so that he might have a look. Sure enough, the two characters were missing from the "Medicinal Herbs" chapter. [The head of the house] went on to relate, "This is the scripture that the deceased spouse of our elder son kept devotedly while she was alive. Since she passed away it has been seventeen years now."

As it turned out, the dates corresponded perfectly with the month and year of the novice's gestation. . . . No one knows where and when he died.

The Buddhist monk Jingjian. Details of his background are unknown, but he left home as a young boy and for the most part lived on mounts Chonggao and Longmen. He recited the *Lotus Sutra* in its entirety as many as thirteen thousand times. Internally he applied himself zealously to the contemplation of the wondrous [truth], thereby becoming quite skilled in the essentials of dhyana. However, due to having recited [the sutra] for such an extended period of time, his physical strength was exhausted [to the point of] distress.

After [he had suffered from this illness] for more than twenty years, one day children began to gather and chatter raucously on the north side of his hut. This caused him to feel even more stressed and dispirited. Jian could not figure out where they came from. At that time a white-haired codger appeared, dressed in a short coat and skirt of crude white silk. Every day he would come and inquire [of Jian's health], asking: "How are the dhyana master's four elements doing today?" To which Jian would usually reply, "I am feeling progressively more run down. Moreover, I have no idea where all these children are coming from; but daily their disturbance grows worse. I don't think I can bear it much longer."

The old man instructed, "Master, you should go and sit near the spot where they play. Wait for them to take off their clothes and enter the river to bathe. Then take one of the boy's garments and come back [to your hermitage]. When he comes to reclaim it, don't give it back to him. If he curses you, be sure not to respond. I, your disciple, will come to speak with him."

Jian set out to do as the old man instructed. He went and waited for the children to take off their clothes and enter the pool to bathe. Then he snatched up one of the boy's garments and returned promptly to his hut. When the child came after him looking for his robe, Jian recalled the old man's cautions and refused to hand it over. The child bad-mouthed and slandered the dhyana master in the most vile way, even extending his remarks to his ancestors. But the master showed no response. Soon the old man arrived and said to the lad, "[I command you to] enter the master's chest." At first the boy was unwilling to do as he was told. But the old man pressed him repeatedly, until he proceeded to enter Jian's chest and vanish within his belly. The old man asked the master, "How do your four elements feel now?" To which Jian replied, "My vital energy (qi) is far better than ever before." The old man thereupon took his leave [and disappeared].

From that day forward Jian felt physically robust and at ease, and his practice of dhyana and recitation doubled in intensity. Those who understand this sort of thing say that surely this was the work of the bodhisattva Samantabhadra ("Universal Worthy"). The bodhisattva had the [local] mountain spirit compel the seminal essences of different medicinal herbs to transform into the child and become absorbed into [Jian's] body, thereby curing Jian of his illness. Jingjian was the master who instructed dhyana master Mo in the arts of dhyana. We do not know where and how he ended his days.

The Buddhist monk Bacheng left home [and joined the sangha] while a young boy. His faculties were extremely obtuse, yet he faithfully kept the regular post-noon fast (chang-zhai) and a strict vegetarian diet. At age twenty-five he received the full precepts and resolved to learn to recite the *Lotus Sutra* [from memory] in order to obtain rebirth in the western pure land. Daily he would memorize one line, or maybe at most a half a verse. Sometimes he couldn't remember anything. Finally, at the age of eighty, he succeeded in memorizing the entire text.

Sometime after that, while he was taking a nap, Bacheng dreamt that a person wearing a crimson robe and military cap appeared before him with an official scroll of invitation in hand. He opened it and announced to Bacheng: "The lord of heaven, Indra, has dispatched me to extend this summons respectfully to you." Cheng replied, "It is the wish of this humble monk to be reborn in the western [pure land]. Even though the Trayastrimsha Heaven[1] is indeed an excellent place, it does not accord with this humble monk's vow." Thereupon the crimson-robed figure departed.

When he awoke, Cheng related his dream to his disciples. The very next day he dreamt of a stupa of seven stories, with himself dwelling on the fifth. Gazing toward the west he saw a staircase strung with jewels, seemingly endless in length. Two vajra[2] protectors with staves in hand stood guard in

---

1. The Heaven of the Thirty-three, which according to Buddhist cosmology is located on the summit of Meru, the mountain at the center of the world.

2. Usually translated "diamond" or "thunderbolt" (i.e., something unbreakable).

two booths. A handful of azure-clad youths were brushing off the staircase with white whisks. Cheng asked the youths, "Where am I?" They replied, "This is the bejeweled stair that leads to the western [pure land]. We have come to welcome dharma master Cheng."

When Bacheng awoke, he related what had transpired and announced to his disciples: "You may sell my three robes and six items in order to sponsor a maigre feast[3] and offering." They did as he instructed. Just before the maigre feast he asked the assembly, "Do you see the thousand buddhas [gathered here]?" The assembly replied, "We do not." Then again he asked, "Do you smell an unusual fragrance in the air or not?" To which they replied, "We all smell it." At the finish of the feast Cheng bathed himself, shaved his head, sat in perfect [meditation] posture, composed his thoughts, and passed away on the spot.

The Buddhist monk Sengding. Nothing is known of his background, but he lived at Chanjing Monastery in Jiangyang and recited the *Lotus Sutra* [as his regular practice]. He had a particular love of popular song, which he was at an utter loss to restrain. As a result, he was given to the habit of dissipating himself in the dusty and vulgar world [of Jiangyang nightlife]. However, whenever he did so, [his devotion was such that] divine youths would regularly manifest (*gan*) and come to his assistance.

Sometimes when he had passed out blind drunk, his dharma robe cast off [in a heap] from his body, [he would awaken to find that the robe had] spontaneously pleated and folded itself and that covers had been drawn over him, properly concealing his body. If his robe had become soiled with mud when he took it off, in the twinkle of an eye it was washed clean. As he picked it up to put it on, he would find it to be impregnated with a rare and pure fragrance that lingered for a long time [without fading]. On other occasions, the water [in the vessels for offering] automatically replenished itself. Or the floor [of his chamber] always appeared cleanly swept.

One time while Ding was drooling away in a drunken stupor, he awoke suddenly to find divine deva[4] youths standing before him. His whole body was damp with saliva. He felt immediately humbled, and from then on he regarded observance of the precepts with the highest esteem. No one knows where or how he ended his days.

During the era of [Emperor] Wu-cheng of the [Northern] Qi (562–565), a person digging on the slope of Mount Kandong near Bingzhou came upon a patch of soil—yellowish white in color—that stood out in marked contrast from the ground around it. Probing further, he turned up an object that had the appearance of a pair of human lips, with a tongue, fresh red in color, sticking out between them. He reported the matter in a memorial [to the throne]. [The emperor] made inquiries among various learned scholars but could find no one who knew [the meaning of it]. When he heard of this, the mendicant Fashang (495–580), controller-in-chief [of the sangha], memorialized the throne saying, "This is the recompense of nondecay of the sense faculties that is achieved by devotees who [ritually] keep the *Lotus Sutra*. It

---

3. A communal feast that contains no dishes of flesh.

4. A god.

is proof that [this individual] recited [the scripture] more than a thousand times over."

Subsequently, the emperor summoned the secretariat drafter, Gao Chen. "You are one inclined to faith," he ordered, "go personally to look into this matter. Surely [this object] will have some sort of numinous power. Place it in a duly purified place, convene a maigre feast, and make offerings to it."

Chen received the order and went to the site, where he assembled various Buddhist monks renowned for their devotion to the *Lotus*. Holding incense censers in hand and maintaining strict ceremonial purity, they circumambulated [the tongue] and offered prayers saying: "O Bodhisattva! Countless years have passed since you entered into nirvana. As one who has reverently received [the *Lotus* and kept it] flawlessly during this current age of the counterfeit dharma, we beseech you to manifest for us your [marvelous] stimulus and response (*ganying*)."

The instant they raised their voices the tongue and lips began to beat about on the altar top. Although no sound came forth, it looked as though it were chanting. Of those who witnessed it, there was not one whose hair didn't stand on end. Chen reported the phenomenon. The [throne] ordered that it be stored away in a stone casket and moved to a stupa chamber.

The Buddhist monk Lingkan. Details of his background are unknown. [His master] recognized him to be someone who was very bright and compassionate by nature and had him take up regular recitation of the *Lotus Sutra*. However, upon first completing his memorization of the scripture, Lingkan unexpectedly came down with (*gan*) a severe illness. He informed his master of it, saying, "I have heard that if one [ritually] receives and keeps the *Lotus* one will realize purification of the six sense faculties.[5] How is it that my recitation produces (*gan*) illness instead?"

His master replied, "When you recite the sutra how do you go about it?"

Kan said, "Sometimes I do not wash my hands, or bother to clothe myself [with the proper robes]. I may rest the [the sutra] at my feet, or place it at the head of my bed, as the moment moves me."

His teacher said, "In that case it is a beneficent dharma-protecting spirit that has come to inflict punishment on you. If you don't show proper care for the scripture your efforts will bring forth (*gan*) no merits. It is fitting that you repent."

Kan thereupon fashioned a plain wooden case, where he kept the sutra and to which he [regularly] paid obeisance by touching it with the crown of his head. In the [Buddha] hall he ritually circumambulated [the sutra]. Except for eating and relieving himself, he threw himself entirely into this painful penance, chastening himself with such intensity that his head split open and blood flowed.

For three years running he kept up this practice, until one day, just as the light of dawn was beginning to break at the fifth watch, there came a loud pounding at the door of the Buddha hall, and someone called out for it to be opened. At first Kan was reluctant, thinking, "Certainly this must be a criminal. Why else would he want a door to be opened when it is already

---

5. Sight, hearing, taste, smell, touch, and mind.

locked tight?" But the person continued to call without letting up, so Kan finally gave in.

When he opened the door he saw an old man. His beard and temples were a hoary white, and in his hands he clutched a wooden staff. When Kan showed his face the man struck him repeatedly, saying, "Will you dare ever again to make light of the *Lotus Sutra*?" The instant he hit him, the ulcers that covered Kan's body were healed and his four vital elements returned to their normal balance.

When the daylight finally broke Kan inspected the front of the Buddha hall, where he discovered the footprints of an elephant [in the dirt]. Thereupon he realized for the first time that the old man was the bodhisattva Samantabhadra, who had descended to eliminate his sins. From then on he completely reformed his ways and devoted himself unremittingly to the practice of recitation [of the *Lotus*]. We do not know where or when he died.

His old master, Ju, also took the *Lotus* as his main practice. Whenever he recited the scripture he felt as though an ambrosial flavor, unlike anything in the known world, would spread through his mouth. As a result, when he began reciting he never wanted to stop.

The Buddhist monk Zhiye had the secular surname of Yang. He left home as a small boy and took up residence at Changle Monastery in Yangzhou. He kept the monastic precepts assiduously and learned to recite the *Lotus Sutra* with such fluency that the lines flowed from his mouth like a stream of water from a vase. At the end of the Daye era of the Sui [617], Yuwen Huaji committed the heinous act of murdering Emperor Yang in the palace bathhouse. Thereupon the world fell apart and the populace was thrown into famine. Residents scattered and [the region] became a maelstrom [of chaos], with the price of rice soaring to ten thousand cash amidst the tumult. Zhiye at the time was living in a small room of a detached cloister, where he was engaged in uninterrupted recitation of the *Lotus Sutra*. Consequently, he died of starvation in his chamber. There was no one to bury him, and the room itself collapsed around him, trapping his remains beneath it.

When peace was finally restored during the Yining era [617–618], a single stalk of lotus flower suddenly appeared on the spot. Its radiantly colored petals opened forth to display the most extraordinary freshness and beauty. Monks and laity alike were struck with awe, and no one could think of an explanation for it. At that time, an old monk who was a former resident of the monastery realized what was going on and said, "There was once a monk who devoted himself exclusively to recitation of the *Lotus Sutra* on this site. He must have perished here as a result of the turmoil of the times. Since there would have been no one to bury him, his bones are probably still here, and [this lotus has appeared] as a result of the monk's spiritual potency."

They cleared away the debris around the stalk of the flower until they uncovered his skeleton. It turned out that the blue lotus flower had grown up through the skull and was rooted beneath the tongue. The tongue itself was as though still alive, showing no sign of decomposition whatsoever. The monastic assembly took the tongue and blossom to the head of the hall. They rang the bell, gathered the monks, and performed cyclic recitation of the *Lotus*. When the tongue heard the scripture it appeared to be able to move about. Once local monks and laymen heard of it, sightseers gathered around forming a solid human wall. There wasn't one who didn't sigh in admiration. All made the supreme resolution [to seek buddhahood].

The Buddhist monk Huijin had the secular surname of Qian, but no details are known of his background. He left home when he was a young boy and set up a fixed regimen of practice for himself at Lu grotto on Mount Kuang. No matter where he wandered or settled down, he kept up a constant recitation of the *Lotus*. This practice he maintained both day and night, never letting up except to take his meals or lie down to rest.

For reciting the sutra he required a space of several paces in circumference. He would first purify [the ground] by sweeping and sprinkling, gather whatever flowers were in season at the time, and do his best to decorate [the sanctuary] resplendently. In the center, which was some five or six feet in width, he hung banners and offered incense [to the sutra]. In a spot set apart [from the altar itself] he placed a single chair [for recitation]. After putting on a new and clean robe and venerating the buddhas of the ten directions,[6] he would join his palms [in adoration] and assume the formal posture [for seated meditation]. Only then would he begin to recite [the sutra].

One day, after he had completed some ten thousand recitations of the sutra, everything around him suddenly became hazy, like a cloud of mist. In this cloud he saw the three transformations [of the *Lotus* assembly], together with [the stupa of Prabhutaratna], the jeweled thrones [for the manifestation bodies of Shakyamuni[7] Buddha], and their jeweled trees extending throughout the eight directions. Ever so faintly, the buddhas and bodhisattvas [of the assembly] appeared before his eyes. When he reached fifteen thousand recitations, he saw them all with perfect clarity. Where and how he ended his days is not known.

There was a certain bhikshuni, her name [long since] forgotten, who lived on the outskirts of the Kunshan district of Suzhou. She became a nun at an early age and took to constant recitation of the *Lotus Sutra*, which she performed devotedly twice a day for some twenty-odd years. In appearance she was unusually beautiful and refined, so much so that anyone who caught sight of her was struck immediately with affection for her. During the first year of the Yongchang era [689] a certain district office manager named Zhu began to entertain wicked fantasies about her and sought to press her with his less than honorable designs. Yet the bhikshuni remained firm in her chastity and refused to give in to him.

Angered by her rejection, Zhu made a great deal of trouble for the abbey and intentionally sought to disrupt their regular means of livelihood. The bhikshunis were at a total loss as to where to turn to rid themselves of this plight. Whereupon, the nun who kept the *Lotus* said, "How could the *Lotus*

---

6. North, south, east, west, northwest, southeast, southwest, the nadir, and the zenith.
7. Literally, "Sage of the Shakyas"; a title of the

Buddha, who was born into the Shakya clan. "Prabhutaratna": a buddha who plays an important role in the *Lotus Sutra*.

Sutra fail to show its spiritual potency in this matter?" She then donned her purified robe, entered the Buddha hall, burned incense, and professed [solemn] vows.

Not long thereafter the office manager, availing himself of some official pretext, came to the abbey to pass the night. His heart, of course, harbored other intentions. But the very instant he sought to find his way to the nun's quarters, his lower extremities were seized with a burning pain and his male member dropped off. Rivulets of perspiration streamed from his skin, leprous ulcers broke out over his entire body, and his eyebrows, beard, and sideburns all fell out. The office manager grievously recanted, but even after trying a hundred remedies, he still was never completely cured.

ON THE ORIGINS OF ZEN

PLATFORM SUTRA OF THE SIXTH PATRIARCH
(*The Liuzu Tan Jing*)

When Buddhism was first transmitted to China, the monks charged with translating the Sanskrit texts often had trouble finding the right words in Chinese. In some cases, rather than translate a term, they would provide a phonetic equivalent. One such case was *dhyana*, a common term in Buddhism for concentration. The translators rendered this Sanskrit word as *chan na*, which was later abbreviated to *chan*. The Chinese character *chan* is pronounced *zen* in Japanese. Thus, the name of the most famous form of Buddhism is a Japanese pronunciation of a Chinese mispronunciation of a Sanskrit term that means "concentration." And as we will see in the selection below, one of the most important of Zen texts argues that the practice of concentration is unnecessary for enlightenment.

There is no historical evidence of a Zen school in India; it originated instead in China. However, all Buddhist traditions must trace their origins back to the Buddha himself, and the Zen tradition, which will be referred to by its Chinese name *Chan* in what follows, has a particularly powerful story about how it all began.

The Buddha was seated before a large audience on Vulture Peak. Bouquets of flowers, offered by disciples, lay before him. Drawing a single flower from one of the bouquets, he held it up, without saying a word. No one understood except for the monk Mahakashyapa, who simply smiled. The Buddha said to him, "I possess the treasure of the true eye of the dharma, the wondrous mind of nirvana, the subtle entry to the dharma, born from the formlessness of true form, not relying on words and letters, a special transmission outside the teachings. I bequeath it to Mahakashyapa." This mind-to-mind transmission, as it would be called, was passed down from master to disciple in a succession of Indian masters, which included such illustrious figures as Nagarjuna (see *Verses on the Middle Way* and Four Hymns, pp. 366 and 375). Eventually, it was transmitted to the twenty-eighth in this lineage, a prince named Bodhidharma, who in the late fifth century left India and traveled by sea to China. According to a famous story first recorded in 758, Emperor Wu of Liang, a patron of Buddhism, invited the Indian master to his court. The emperor had performed such meritorious deeds as sponsoring the building of monasteries and the printing of sutras. When Bodhidharma arrived, Wu asked him how much merit he had accumulated through these good deeds. Bodhidharma answered, "None." The emperor then asked Bodhidharma who he was. Bodhidharma answered that he did not know. And so the audience ended.

Bodhidharma is said to have retreated into the mountains, where he spent nine years in a form of meditation called "wall gazing." When he was unable to keep his eyes open, he cut off his eyelids and threw them aside, where they grew into the first tea plants in China. According to a story that first appears some four centuries after the event it describes, Bodhidharma was eventually approached by a Chinese scholar who stood silently, waiting for his presence to be acknowledged. But Bodhidharma ignored him, even as snow fell and drifted against his feet. Finally, the man drew his sword, cut off his left arm, and presented it to Bodhidharma, asking the master to calm his mind. Bodhidharma told him that he would calm the scholar's mind if the man would first show it to him. The man said that he had looked for his mind for many years but had not been able to grasp it. Bodhidharma replied, "There, it is calmed." The Chinese scholar became the first Chinese patriarch of the Chan tradition in China. (Chan, as well as other schools of Chinese Buddhism, labeled its lineage of teachers "patriarchs"; the Chinese term is *zushi*, literally "ancestor-teacher.") The Chan tradition became famous for its four tenets: (1) maintaining a special transmission outside the teachings, (2) not relying upon words and letters, (3) pointing directly at the human mind, and (4) seeing one's own nature and becoming a buddha. Despite scholars' best efforts, Bodhidharma remains a nebulous figure, with some question as to whether he actually existed.

The text here is the first and most famous chapter of *The Platform Sutra of the Sixth Patriarch (Liuzu Tan Jing)*, one of the most influential works in the entire Chan/Zen tradition. Composed in the eighth century, it purports to be a collection of sermons by Huineng (638–713), renowned as the sixth Chinese patriarch of the Chan tradition. In the first chapter, he provides a brief biography, telling how, while selling firewood to support his widowed mother, he heard one day a monk reciting the *Diamond Sutra* (see the *Vajracchedika Prajnaparamita*, p. 325) and "my mind opened forth in enlightenment." The story, which includes a famous poetry contest, proceeds from there; that probably none of it is true does not diminish its power.

Elsewhere in this work, Huineng sets forth such seminal Chan notions as the unity of concentration and wisdom, the rejection of all skillful means for realizing the truth, the concept of no thought, and the emphasis on seeing one's own nature. In the ethical realm, he speaks of conferring "formless precepts." Indeed, the "platform" of the title is the ordination platform where he laid out those precepts.

PRONOUNCING GLOSSARY

Baolin si: *bau-leen su*
Bodhidharma: *boh-di-dar-ma*
bodhisattva: *boh-di-sat-va*
Caoqi: *tsau-chee*
Dafan si: *dah-fahn su*
Dayu: *dah-yoo*
Dongchan si: *dohng-chahn su*
Faxing si: *fah-shing su*
Guangdong: *gwahng-dohng*
Guangzhou: *gwahng-joh*
Hongren: *hohng-rehn*
huai: *hwai*
Huangmei xian; *hwahng-may shyehn*
hui: *hway*

Huiming: *hway-meeng*
icchantika: *ich-chan-ti-ka*
Jiangzhou: *jyahng-joh*
Lankavatara Sutra: *lan-kah-va-tah-ra soo-tra*
liang: *lyahng*
Lingnan: *leeng-nahn*
Liuzu Tan Jing: *lee-oo-ju tan jing*
Lu Zhen: *loo jan*
prajna: *praj-nyah*
Qizhou: *chee-joh*
Qizhun: *chee-joon*
Shenxiu; *shan-shyoh*
Sihui: *su-hway*

skandha: *skan-da*
Xinxing xian: *sheen-sheeng shyehn*
Xinzhou: *sheen-joh*
Yangze: *yahng-tsa*

Yinzong: *een-tsong*
Zhang Riyong: *jahng-er-yohng*
Zhouxian: *joh-shyehn*

Number One: Account of Origins

When the Great Master arrived at Baolin [si] ("Treasure Grove Monastery"), Prefect Wei (whose given name was Qu) and his official staff entered the monastery and invited the master to come to the lecture hall at Dafan si ("Great Purity Monastery") within the city, where he could tell his story and preach the Dharma for those assembled. After the master took his seat, the prefect and official staff, more than thirty in number, the Confucian scholars, more than thirty in number, and the monks, nuns, and laypeople, more than a thousand in number, simultaneously did obeisance to him and beseeched him to relate the essentials of the Dharma.

The Great Master told the assembly, "Good friends, *bodhi*[1] is fundamentally pure in its self-nature. You must simply use this mind [that you already have], and you will achieve buddhahood directly and completely. Good friends, listen well! This is the story of how I practiced and attained the Dharma.

"My father was a native of Fanyang (Zhouxian, Hopeh), but he was banished to Lingnan and became a commoner in Xinzhou (Xinxing xian, Guangdong). I have been unfortunate: my father died early, and my aged mother and I, her only child, moved here to Nanhai. Miserably poor, I sold firewood in the marketplace.

"At one time, a customer bought some firewood and had me deliver it to his shop, where he took it and paid me. On my way out the gate I saw someone reciting a sutra, and as soon as I heard the words of the sutra my mind opened forth in enlightenment. I then asked the person what sutra he was reciting, and he said, 'The *Diamond Sutra*.' I also asked, 'Where did you get this sutra?' He said, 'I have come from Dongchan si ("Eastern Meditation Monastery") in Huangmei xian in Qizhou (Qizhun, Hupeh). The Fifth Patriarch, Great Master Hongren, resides at and is in charge of instruction at that monastery. He has over a thousand followers. I went there, did obeisance to him, and received this sutra there. Great Master [Hongren] always exhorts both monks and laymen to simply maintain the *Diamond Sutra*, so that one can see the [self]-nature by oneself and achieve buddhahood directly and completely.'

"My hearing this was through a karmic connection from the past. Someone then gave me ten *liang*[2] of silver to pay for my aged mother's food and clothing and told me to go to Huangmei to do obeisance to the Fifth Patriarch. I then left my mother for the last time and departed. In less than thirty-odd days I arrived at Huangmei, where I did obeisance to the Fifth Patriarch.

TRANSLATED FROM the Chinese by John R. McRae. All bracketed additions are the translator's.

1. Enlightenment.
2. A unit of weight equal to a little more than an ounce.

"The patriarch asked me, 'Where are you from, and what is it you seek?' I replied, 'Your disciple is a commoner from Xinzhou in Lingnan, and I have come this far to pay reverence to you. I wish only to achieve buddhahood and do not seek anything else.' The patriarch said, 'If you're from Lingnan, then you must be a hunter. How could you ever achieve buddhahood?' I said, 'Although people may be from north or south, there is fundamentally no north and south in the Buddha-nature. Although this hunter's body is different from Your Reverence's, how can there be any difference in the Buddha-natures [within]?'

"The Fifth Patriarch wanted to speak further with me, but, seeing that his followers were gathered all around, he told me to go with them to work. I said, 'If I might address Your Reverence, your disciple constantly generates wisdom in my own mind. To not transcend the self-natures is equivalent to the field of blessings. I wonder what work Your Reverence would have me do?' The patriarch said, 'Some Klao[3] barbarian! You're very sharp! Don't say anything else! Go to the work shed.' I then retired to a chapel in the rear [of the monastery].

"A practitioner had me break up kindling and tread the hulling pestle.[4] After more than eight months of this, the patriarch came unexpectedly one day to see me. He said, 'I thought your views might have been of use, but I was afraid there were evil people who might have harmed you. That was why I haven't spoken to you. Do you understand this?' I replied, 'I understood your intentions. I have not dared go by the main hall, so as to not remind people.'

"One day the patriarch called all of his followers together [and addressed them, saying], 'I preach to you that life and death is the great concern for people of this world. But you spend all your time seeking only the fields of blessings, rather than seeking to escape the ocean of suffering of birth and death! If you are deluded as to the self-natures, how can you be saved by blessings? You should each go reflect upon your own wisdom. Taking the essence of *prajna*[5] within your own fundamental minds, you should each compose a verse and come show it to me. If you are enlightened to the great meaning, I will transmit the robe and Dharma to you and make you the patriarch of the sixth generation.

"'Go quickly—this is an emergency, and you must not delay! Thinking is of no use—he who is to see the [self]-nature will see it immediately upon hearing these words! If there is such a one here, he will see it even if encamped on top of a circle of knives!' (*This is a metaphor for one of excellent abilities.*)

"The assembly [of followers] received these instructions and retired, saying to each other, 'We followers do not have to purify our minds and work to compose verses. What advantage would there be in showing anything to His Reverence [Hongren]. The Elder Shenxiu is now our instructor, and he will certainly attain [the rank of sixth patriarch]. If ones such as us tried to compose verses, we would only be wasting our energies.' The others heard these words, and all of them gave up [working on the problem]. They all

3. The native peoples of southern Lu, viewed by the Han as primitive.

4. That is, hull rice.

5. Wisdom.

said, 'Afterward, we will rely on Master Shenxiu. Why trouble to compose verses?'

"Shenxiu thought, 'They are not going to submit verses, thinking that I am their instructor. I must compose a verse and submit it to His Reverence. If I do not submit a verse, how will His Reverence know the profundity of understanding within my mind? If I submit a verse with the intention of seeking the Dharma, it would be good. But if I am seeking to become patriarch, it would be bad. How would that be any different from one with an ordinary mind usurping the sagely status! But if I don't submit a verse, I'll never attain the Dharma. What a problem! What a problem!'

"There was a hallway three bays in length in front of the Fifth Patriarch's hall, where the Auxiliary Lu Zhen was to be asked to paint episodes from the *Lankavatara Sutra* and a diagram of the Fifth Patriarch's lineage, [all for] wider dissemination and offerings. When Shenxiu had finished making up his verse, he tried several times to go to the front of the hall [to offer his verse in person]. But his mind was in a daze and his body covered with sweat, and he was unable to submit [his verse]. Over the space of four days he tried thirteen times to submit his verse but couldn't. He thought, 'It would be better to write it in the hallway. After His Reverence sees it, if he says it is good, I will come forward and bow to him, saying that it was mine. If he says it is unacceptable, I will have wasted several years at this monastery. I will have received the obeisance of others, but what Way will I have cultivated?'

"On that night, in the third watch (about 1:00 A.M.) so that no one else knew, [Shenxiu] took a lamp and wrote his verse on the wall of the south corridor, submitting [to the patriarch] the viewpoint of his mind. The verse read:

> The body is the *bodhi* tree;
> The mind is like a bright mirror's stand.
> Be always diligent in rubbing it—
> Do not let it attract any dust.

"After Shenxiu finished writing his verse, he returned to his room, without anyone knowing. Shenxiu thought, 'Tomorrow, if the Fifth Patriarch sees my verse and is pleased, it will mean I have a karmic connection with the Dharma. If he says it's unacceptable, it will mean I am deluded by the layered barriers of past karma and am not fit to attain the Dharma. The sagely intention is difficult to fathom!' He remained in his room, thinking, but unable to rest either sitting or lying down.

"When it came to be the fifth watch (about 5:00 A.M.), the patriarch knew that Shenxiu had not been able to enter the gate and had been unable to see the self-nature. When morning came, Hongren called the Auxiliary Lu to come paint the lineage and episodes on the wall of the south corridor. Unexpectedly seeing the verse, he announced, 'There is no need for you to paint anything. I am sorry we have troubled you to come so far. The [*Diamond*] *Sutra* says, "All that which has characteristics is false." We should just leave this verse here for people to recite. By cultivating in reliance upon this verse, they will avoid falling into the unfortunate modes of existence. To cultivate according to this verse will be greatly beneficial!'

"[Hongren then] commanded his followers to burn incense and do obeisance [to the verse, saying], 'All who recite this verse will be able to see the nature.' The followers recited it, all of them sighing at how excellent it was.

"But in the third watch [that night] the patriarch called Shenxiu into the hall and asked him, 'Is the verse yours?' Shenxiu said, 'Yes, it is mine, but I am unable to seek the status of patriarch. I seek Your Reverence's compassion. Do I have some small wisdom or not?'

"Hongren said, 'When you composed this verse you had not seen the fundamental nature. You have come only as far as outside the gate; you have not yet come inside. With understanding such as this you will not be able to attain the unsurpassable *bodhi*. The unsurpassable *bodhi* is to be able, at these very words, to recognize your own fundamental mind and to see that your own fundamental nature is neither born nor extinguished. It is to see this naturally in every moment of thought and at all times: the myriad dharmas are without obstruction; the one is true and all are true. The myriad realms are naturally thus-like, and the thus-like mind is the true. If what you see is like this, then it is the self-nature of the unsurpassable bodhisattva.

"'Go now, and meditate upon this for a day or two. Compose another verse and bring it to me. I will see from your verse whether you have been able to enter the gate and whether I should transmit to you the robe and Dharma.' Shenxiu bowed and went out. But even after several days he was unable to create another verse. His mind was in a daze and his spirit was disturbed, as if he were in a dream, and he could take no pleasure in either walking or sitting."

[Huineng continued,] "After a couple of days an acolyte passed by the hulling room reciting the verse. Upon hearing it, I immediately knew that [the author of] the verse had not seen the fundamental nature. Although I had never received any instruction, I had already recognized the great intention [of the sages], so I asked the acolyte, 'What verse is it you're reciting?' The acolyte said, 'What a [disgusting] hunter you are! Don't you know that Great Master [Hongren] has said that life and death is the great concern for people of this world, and, wanting to transmit the robe and bowl, he commanded his followers to compose verses and show them to him? If there were one who was enlightened to the great intention, he would transmit the robe and Dharma and make that one the sixth patriarch. The Elder Shenxiu wrote a formless verse on the wall of the south corridor. Great Master [Hongren] has commanded us all to recite it, [saying that] if we cultivate on the basis of this verse, we will avoid falling into the unfortunate modes of existence, that it will be very beneficial to cultivate on the basis of this verse!'

"I said, (*One text has "I also want to recite this, in order to make certain my conditions for rebirth."*) 'Holy One, I have been treading the pestle here for more than eight months, and I've never even gone past the front of the hall. I would like you to take me to this verse so that I might do obeisance to it.' The acolyte took me to the verse so that I could do obeisance to it. I said, 'I am unable to read. Holy One, would you read it for me?' At the time Zhang Riyong, the Administrative Aide of Jiangzhou, was there, and he read [the verse] to me aloud.

"After hearing it I said, 'I also have a verse, and would like the Administrative Aide to write it for me.' The Administrative Aide said, 'You've composed a verse? How unusual!' I said to the Administrative Aide, 'If you wish to study the unsurpassable *bodhi*, you should not make light of beginners. The lowest of the low may have the most supreme wisdom, and the highest of the high may be without [spiritual] intention or wisdom. To make light of others is a transgression unlimited and infinite.'

"The Administrative Aide said, 'Just recite your verse. I will write it for you. If you attain the Dharma, you must save me first (i.e., before teaching anyone else). Don't forget what I say!'

"My verse went:

> *Bodhi* is fundamentally without any tree;
> The bright mirror is also not a stand.
> Fundamentally there is not a single thing—
> Where could any dust be attracted?

"After I finished this verse everyone around there became agitated and couldn't help sighing with amazement. They all said to each other, 'How strange! You just can't go by looks alone! Why is it always that people like that are living bodhisattvas!' Seeing that they were getting excited and worried that someone might harm me, the patriarch rubbed out the verse with his sandal and said, 'This [person] too has not seen the nature.' Those present accepted this.

"The next day, Hongren secretly came to the hulling room, where he saw me with a rock on my back pounding rice and said, 'He who seeks the Way forgets his body on behalf of the Dharma. Is that how it is [with you]?' He then asked, 'Is the rice ripe yet?' I replied, 'The rice has been ripe for a long time. It only lacks sifting [the hulls from the grain].' The patriarch struck his staff on the pestle three times and left. I understood what he meant— that I should enter his room at the third drum (i.e., the third watch of the night, about 1:00 A.M.).

"The patriarch kept his robe (*kashaya*) hidden and would not let anyone see it. He preached the *Diamond Sutra* for me. When he reached the words 'responding to the nonabiding, yet generating the mind' I experienced a great enlightenment, [realizing that] all the myriad dharmas do not transcend their self-natures. I thereupon informed the patriarch of this, saying, 'No matter when, the self-natures are fundamentally and naturally pure. No matter when, the self-natures are fundamentally neither generated nor extinguished. No matter when, the self-natures are fundamentally and naturally sufficient unto themselves. No matter when, the self-natures are fundamentally without movement. No matter when, the self-natures are able to generate the myriad dharmas.'

"Knowing that I had been enlightened to the fundamental nature, the patriarch said to me, 'If one does not recognize the fundamental mind, studying the Dharma is of no benefit. If one recognizes one's own fundamental mind, one sees one's own fundamental nature. This is to be called a great man, a teacher of men and gods, a Buddha.'

"At the third watch of the night I received the Dharma. No one knew of this. He then transmitted the sudden teaching and the robe and bowl, saying, 'You have become the patriarch of the sixth generation. You should maintain your own mindfulness well, and you should save sentient beings extensively. Do not allow the dissemination [of the Dharma] to be cut off in the future. Listen to my verse:

> Sentient beings cast their seeds;
> Because of the earth the fruits are born.
> Insentient objects have no seeds,
> No natures, and no birth.

"The patriarch went on, 'When Great Master [Bodhi]dharma came to this land long ago, people did not yet come to rely upon him. Therefore he transmitted this robe as the embodiment of reliance [upon him]. It has been handed down for generation after generation. The Dharma, moreover, is the transmission of the mind with the mind. [The mind] must always enlighten itself, emancipate itself. From ancient times, the Buddhas have only transmitted the fundamental essence; the masters have secretly handed on the fundamental mind.

"'The robe [however] has become the focus of conflict, and beginning with you it should not be transmitted. If you transmit this robe, your life expectancy will be like a hanging thread. You should go quickly! I fear people will harm you!' I addressed him, 'Where should I go?' The patriarch said, 'When you encounter destruction (*huai*), you should stop. When you come upon a group (*hui*), you should secret yourself.'

"In the third watch I took the robe and bowl and said, 'I am from south China and do not know the mountainous roads around here. How do I get to the mouth of the [Yangze] River?' The Fifth Patriarch said, 'Do not be disheartened, I will see you off.' The patriarch accompanied me as far as Jiujiang station, where he had us get on a boat. The Fifth Patriarch took the oar and rowed [the boat] himself. I said, 'Your Reverence, please sit. Your disciple should row!' Hongren said, 'I should take you over [to the other shore].' I said, 'When one is deluded, one thinks teachers take [sentient beings over to the other shore], but when one is enlightened, one realizes one crosses over by oneself. Although "cross over" is only a single term, its uses are varied. Since I was born in a border region, my pronunciation is not correct. I have received transmission of the Dharma from you, master, and I have now become enlightened. Can it be anything other than that the self-natures have crossed themselves over?'

"The patriarch said, 'So it is, so it is. In the future, Buddhism will flourish greatly because of you. Three years after you go, I will depart this world. You should go now. Make an effort to go south, and don't be in a hurry to preach [the Dharma]. It is difficult to propagate Buddhism!'

"After I left the patriarch, I started out walking toward the south. In the second month [of traveling] I reached the Dayu Mountains. (*Hongren returned* [to the monastery] *and for several days did not go into the hall. The assembly* [of followers] *was in doubt about this and proceeded to him to ask, "Is Your Reverence ill or discomforted in some small way?" He said, "I am not ill. The robe and Dharma are in the south." They asked, "To whom have you transmitted them?" He said, "One who is able has received them." Thus did the assembly learn of it.*)

"Coming after me were several hundred people, who wanted to take away the robe and bowl. One monk, of the lay surname Chen and named Huiming, had previously been a general of the fourth rank. He was coarse and excitable by nature, and he really wanted to find me. He reached me before the rest of the group chasing me. I threw the robe and bowl down on a rock and said, 'This robe emblematizes reliance [upon the Patriarchs]. How can you struggle for it?' I hid in the underbrush, and Huiming tried to lift it without success. Then he called to me, saying, 'O practitioner, O practitioner! I have come for the Dharma, not for the robe.' I then came out and sat on the rock.

"Huiming bowed to me and said, 'I wish that you would preach the Dharma for me.' I said, 'You say you've come for the Dharma. [If so], you must eliminate the various conditions and not generate a single thought. [If you do], I will preach the Dharma for you.' Huiming was quiet for a time. I said, 'Do not think of good, and do not think of evil. At just such a time, what is Elder Huiming's original face?' At these words, Huiming [experienced] a great enlightenment. He then questioned me again, saying, 'Other than the secret words and secret intention [you expressed] just now, is there any other secret intention?' I said, 'What I have preached to you is not secret. If you counter-illuminate [your own original face you will realize that] the secret was on your side.'

"Huiming said, 'Although I was at [Hongren's monastery in] Huangmei, I actually never thought about my own [original] face. To receive your instructions now is like a man who drinks water knowing [immediately] whether it is cold or warm. Now you are my teacher.'

"I said, 'If this is the case, then we share the same teacher of Huangmei. Well should you protect and maintain [the teaching]!' Huiming asked further, 'Where should I go now?' I said, 'When you encounter ampleness you should stop, when you come upon munificence you should reside.' Huiming bowed and left. (*Huiming returned to the foot of the mountain. He addressed the group that had come after me, saying "I just climbed this mountain of boulders, and there was no trace of him. We should try searching by another road." The group of those chasing [Huineng] all did as he said. Huiming later changed [his name] to Daoming, in order to avoid the first character of his teacher's name.*)

"After this I went to Caoqi. There too I was beset by evil people searching for me and so fled to Sihui [County], where I spent fifteen years in all [living] with a group of hunters. During this time I preached the Dharma to the hunters when the occasion arose. The hunters had always had me guard their nets, but whenever I saw living animals in them I set them free. Whenever it was mealtime, I put vegetables in the pot for boiling the meat. They asked me about this sometimes, and I would answer, 'These are just vegetables to go with the meat.'

"One day I realized that the time had come to disseminate the Dharma, that I could not hide forever. Accordingly, I left [the mountains and] went to Faxing si ("Monastery of the Dharma-nature") in Guangzhou, where I encountered Dharma Master Yinzong lecturing on the *Nirvana Sutra*.

"At that time the wind was blowing and the banner [announcing the lecture] was moving. One monk said that the wind was moving, while another monk said the banner was moving. They argued on and on, so I went forward and said, 'It is not the wind that is moving, and it is not the banner that is moving. It is your minds that are moving.' Everyone listening was amazed. Yinzong had me brought up to the dais, where he examined me on the import of what I had said. Hearing me say that the discrimination of the truth did not depend on written words, Yinzong said, 'You are certainly an extraordinary person. Long ago I heard that the robe and bowl of Huangmei had come south—might you be the one [who received them]?' I said, 'In all modesty, [I am].'

"At this Yinzong bowed to me and asked me to bring forth the robe and bowl to show to the assembly. He questioned me further, saying 'What instructions did you receive, at Huangmei?' I said, 'I received no instructions. [Hongren and I] only discussed seeing the nature, we did not discuss *samadhi*[6] and emancipation.' Yinzong said, 'Why did you not discuss *samadhi* and emancipation?' I said, 'Because the dualistic Dharmas are not Buddhism. Buddhism consists of nondualistic Dharmas.'

"Yinzong also asked, 'How is it that Buddhism consists of nondualistic Dharmas?' I said, 'You lecture on the *Nirvana Sutra*'s elucidation of the Buddha-nature, which is a nondualistic Dharma of Buddhism. Just as when the Bodhisattva King of Lofty Virtue asked the Buddha, 'Do those who break the four major prohibitions and commit the five perverse transgressions, as well as the *icchantikas*,[7] eradicate their good roots and Buddha-natures?' The Buddha said, 'There are two types of good roots. One is permanent and the other is impermanent. The Buddha-nature is not permanent and not impermanent.' Therefore, not to eradicate is said to be nondual. One type [of roots] is said to be the good, and the other is the nongood. The Buddha-nature is not the good and not the nongood. This is called nondual. The *skandhas*[8] and sensory realms are seen as two by ordinary people, but the wise comprehend their natures to be nondual. The nondual nature is none other than the Buddha-nature.'

"When Yinzong heard this explanation, he joyfully held his palms together and said, 'My lecturing on the sutra was like a [worthless piece of] roof tile or rock, while your explanation is like gold.' At this, he administered the tonsure for me and asked to serve me as his teacher.

"Thus did I, under the *bodhi* tree, reveal the East Mountain teaching. After receiving the Dharma at East Mountain, I experienced all kinds of suffering, and my life expectancy was like a dangling thread. Today I have been able to join this assembly of the prefect, government staff members, monks, nuns, and laypeople—could it but be the karmic result of successive eons? Also, that you have been able to hear the sudden teaching just given and have gained the cause for attaining the Dharma can only be because in past lives you cultivated good roots identical to those of the Buddhas. The teaching is that which has been transmitted by the former sages; it is not something known to myself [alone]. I wish you would all listen to this teaching of the former sages: you should all purify your minds, and after hearing it you should all eradicate your doubts. You are no different from the former generations of sages."

The entire assembly, after hearing this Dharma, joyfully did obeisance and dispersed.

---

6. A state of deep meditation.
7. Those unable to gain enlightenment. The translator glosses "the four major prohibitions" as "The four most grave offenses for Buddhist monks and nuns, which result in their expulsion from the order—1) killing, 2) stealing, 3) sexual activity, and 4) lying," and "the five perverse transgressions" as "1) patricide, 2) matricide, 3) killing an arhat, 4) maliciously causing a buddha to bleed, and 5) causing disharmony in the Buddhist order."
8. The "aggregates" (Sanskrit), a standard division of the constituents of mind and body into five groups: form, feeling, discrimination, compositional factors, and consciousness.

INSTRUCTIONS OF A CHAN MASTER

RECORD OF LINJI
(*The Linji Lu*)

"If you meet the Buddha on the road, kill him." This statement—so unexpected, irreverent, and counterintuitive—is often represented as the very essence of Zen. It is attributed to the Tang dynasty monk Linji, who died in 867. Linji has come down through history as the quintessential Chan master, shouting at his students, striking them with his flyswatter, and awakening them to the truth with his iconoclastic statements and witty repartee; all these actions are chronicled in the *Record of Linji* (*Linji Lu*), selections from which appear here. One of the most widely cited of Chan works—in China, Korea, and Japan—it is presented as a verbatim record of his teachings. But Linji himself wrote nothing, and the most popular version of his teaching did not appear until two and half centuries after his death. In the course of those centuries, his followers had become the most powerful of the "Five Houses and Seven Schools" of Chan, enjoying considerable support. They would eventually extend their influence into Korea and then to Japan; indeed, the name of one of the two major Zen sects in Japan, Rinzai, is the Japanese pronunciation of *Linji*.

Thus, although the *Record of Linji* cannot be viewed as accurately documenting what he might have taught, it provides important insights into how one of the most powerful of the Chan traditions wished to represent its founder.

The *Record of Linji* is a relatively short work divided into three sections: (1) formal discourses, some delivered at the request of local officials; (2) Linji's encounters with monks, students, and lay visitors; and (3) a record of his activities. The selections below come from the first section.

PRONOUNCING GLOSSARY

asamkhya kalpa: *a-sam-kya kal-pa*
Chan: *chahn*
Huangbo: *hwahng-boh*

Linji Lu: *lin-jee loo*
pratyekabuddha; *prat-yay-ka-bud-da*
Shakyamuni: *shah-kya-mu-ni*

Constant Attendant Wang, head of the prefecture, and his various officials requested the Master to step up to the lecture seat.

The Master ascended the hall and said, "Today, having found it impossible to refuse, I have complied with people's wishes and stepped up to the lecture seat. If I were to discuss the great concern of Buddhism from the point of view of a follower of the sect of the Chan patriarchs, then I could not even open my mouth, and you would have no place to plant your feet. But today I have been urged to speak by the Constant Attendant, so why should I hide the principles of our sect? Perhaps there are some valiant generals here who would like to draw up their ranks and unfurl their banners. Let them prove to the group what they can do!"

A monk asked, "What is the basic meaning of Buddhism?"

The Master gave a shout.

The monk bowed low.

TRANSLATED FROM the Chinese by Burton Watson.

The Master said, "This fine monk is the kind who's worth talking to!"

Someone asked, "Master, whose style of song do you sing? Whose school of teaching do you carry on?"

The Master said, "When I was at Huangbo's[1] place, I asked a question three times and three times I got hit."

The monk started to say something. The Master gave a shout and then struck the monk, saying, "You don't drive a nail into the empty sky!"

A study director said, "The Three Vehicles[2] and twelve divisions of the teachings make the Buddha-nature clear enough, don't they?"

The Master said, "Wild grass—it's never been cut."

The study director said, "Surely the Buddha wouldn't deceive people!"

The Master said, "Buddha—where is he?"

The study director had no answer.

The Master said, "Are you trying to dupe me right in front of the Constant Attendant? Step aside! You're keeping other people from asking questions!"

The Master resumed, saying, "This religious gathering today is held for the sake of the one great concern of Buddhism. Are there any others who want to ask questions? Come forward quickly and ask them!

"But even if you open your mouths, what you say will have nothing to do with that concern. Why do I say this? Because Shakyamuni[3] said, did he not, that 'the Dharma is separate from words and writings, and is not involved with direct or indirect causes.'

"It's because you don't have enough faith that today you find yourselves tied up in knots. I'm afraid you will trouble the Constant Attendant and the other officials and keep them from realizing their Buddha-nature. It's best for me to withdraw."

With that he gave a shout and then said, "People with so few roots of faith—will the day ever come when they see the end of this? Thank you for standing so long."

* * *

The Master instructed the group, saying: "Those who study the Dharma of the buddhas these days should approach it with a true and proper understanding. If you approach it with a true and proper understanding, you won't be affected by considerations of birth or death, you'll be free to go or stay as you please. You don't have to strive for benefits, benefits will come of themselves.

"Followers of the Way, the outstanding teachers from times past have all had ways of drawing people out. What I myself want to impress on you is that you mustn't be led astray by others. If you want to use this thing, then use it and have no doubts or hesitations!

"When students today fail to make progress, where's the fault? The fault lies in the fact that they don't have faith in themselves! If you don't have faith in yourself, then you'll be forever in a hurry trying to keep up with everything around you, you'll be twisted and turned by whatever environ-

1. Xiyun (d. ca. 850) of Mount Huangbo, a famous Chan master of the time [translator's note].
2. The vehicle of the *shravaka*, or disciple; the vehicle of the *pratyekabuddha*, or individually enlightened one; and the vehicle of the bodhisattva.
3. Literally, "Sage of the Shakyas"; a title of the Buddha, who was born into the Shakya clan.

ment you're in and you can never move freely. But if you can just stop this mind that goes rushing around moment by moment looking for something, then you'll be no different from the patriarchs and buddhas. Do you want to get to know the patriarchs and buddhas? They're none other than you, the people standing in front of me listening to this lecture on the Dharma!

"Students don't have enough faith in themselves, and so they rush around looking for something outside themselves. But even if they get something, all it will be is words and phrases, pretty appearances. They'll never get at the living thought of the patriarchs!

"Make no mistake, you followers of Chan. If you don't find it in this life, then for a thousand lifetimes and ten thousand *kalpas* you'll be reborn again and again in the threefold world,[4] you'll be lured off by what you think are favorable environments and be born in the belly of a donkey or a cow!

"Followers of the Way, as I look at it, we're no different from Shakya-muni. In all our various activities each day, is there anything we lack? The wonderful light of the six faculties[5] has never for a moment ceased to shine. If you could just look at it this way, then you'd be the kind of person who has nothing to do for the rest of his life.

"Fellow believers, 'There is no safety in the threefold world, it is like a burn-ing house.' This is no place for you to linger for long! The deadly demon of impermanence will be on you in an instant, regardless of whether you're rich or poor, old or young.

"If you want to be no different from the patriarchs and buddhas, then never look for something outside yourselves. The clean pure light in a moment of your mind—that is the Essence-body of the Buddha lodged in you. The undifferentiated light in a moment of your mind—that is the Bliss-body of the Buddha lodged in you. The undiscriminating light in a moment of your mind—that is the Transformation-body of the Buddha lodged in you. These three types of bodies are you, the person who stands before me now listening to this lecture on the Dharma! And simply because you do not rush around seeking anything outside yourselves, you can command these fine faculties.

"According to the expounders of the sutras and treatises, the threefold body is to be taken as some kind of ultimate goal. But as I see it, that's not so. This threefold body is nothing but mere names. Or they're three types of dependencies. One man of early times said, 'The body depends on doc-trine for its definition, and the land is discussed in terms of the reality.' This 'body' of the Dharma-realm, or reality, and this 'land' of the Dharma-realm we can see clearly are no more than flickering lights.

"Followers of the Way, you should realize that the person who manipu-lates these flickering lights is the source of the buddhas, the home that all followers of the Way should return to. Your physical body made up of the four great elements[6] doesn't know how to preach the Dharma or listen to the Dharma. Your spleen and stomach, your liver and gall don't know how to preach the Dharma or listen to the Dharma. The empty spaces don't know how to preach the Dharma or listen to the Dharma. What is it, then, that knows how to preach the Dharma or listen to the Dharma? It is you who are right here before my eyes, this lone brightness without fixed shape or form—

4. The Realm of Desire, the Realm of Form, and the Formless Realm; see pp. 54–55. "*Kalpas*": aeons, or cosmic cycles.

5. The five senses plus mind.
6. Earth, air, fire, and water.

this is what knows how to preach the Dharma and listen to the Dharma. If you can see it this way, then you'll be no different from the patriarchs and buddhas.

"But never at any time let go of this even for a moment. Everything that meets your eyes is this. But 'when feelings arise, wisdom is blocked; when thoughts waver, reality departs,' therefore you keep being reborn again and again in the threefold world and undergoing all kinds of misery. But as I see it, there are none of you incapable of profound understanding, none of you incapable of emancipation.

"Followers of the Way, this thing called mind has no fixed form; it penetrates all the ten directions.[7] In the eye we call it sight, in the ear we call it hearing; in the nose it detects odors, in the mouth it speaks discourse; in the hand it grasps, in the feet it runs along. Basically it is a single bright essence, but it divides itself into these six functions. And because this single mind has no fixed form, it is everywhere in a state of emancipation. Why do I tell you this? Because you followers of the Way seem to be incapable of stopping this mind that goes rushing around everywhere looking for something. So you get caught up in those idle devices of the men of old.

"The way I see it, we should cut off the heads of the Bliss-body and Transformation-body buddhas. Those who have fulfilled the ten stages of bodhisattva practice are no better than hired field hands; those who have attained the enlightenment of the fifty-first and fifty-second stages are prisoners shackled and bound; arhats and *pratyekabuddhas* are so much filth in the latrine, *bodhi*[8] and nirvana are hitching posts for donkeys. Why do I speak of them like this? Because you followers of the Way fail to realize that this journey to enlightenment that takes three *asamkhya kalpas*[9] to accomplish is meaningless. So these things become obstacles in your way. If you were truly proper men of the Way, you would never let that happen.

"Just get so you can follow along with circumstances and use up your old karma. When the time comes to do so, put on your clothes. If you want to walk, walk. If you want to sit, sit. But never for a moment set your mind on seeking Buddhahood. Why do this way? A man of old said, 'If you try to create good karma and seek to be a buddha, then Buddha will become a sure sign you will remain in the realm of birth and death.'

"Fellow believers, time is precious! You rush off frantically on side roads, studying Chan, studying the Way, clinging to words, clinging to phrases, seeking Buddha, seeking the patriarchs, seeking a good friend, scheming, planning. But make no mistake. Followers of the Way, you have one set of parents—what more are you looking for? You should stop and take a good look at yourselves. A man of old tells us that Yajnadatta[1] thought he had lost his head and went looking for it, but once he had put a stop to his seeking mind, he found he was perfectly all right.

"Fellow believers, just act ordinary, don't affect some special manner. There's a bunch of old bald-headed fellows who can't tell good from bad but who spy gods here, spy devils there, point to the east, gesture to the west, declare they 'love' clear weather or they 'love' it when it rains. They'll have

---

7. North, south, east, west, northeast, northwest, southeast, southwest, the nadir, and the zenith.
8. Enlightenment. "Arhats": those who enter nirvana at death.

9. Three "countless aeons," the time it takes for a bodhisattva to traverse the path to buddhahood.
1. The so-called madman of Shravasti; this story is told in the *Shurangama Sutra*.

a lot to answer for one day when they stand before old Yama[2] and have to swallow a ball of red-hot iron! Men and women of good family let themselves be taken in by this bunch of wild fox spirits and end up completely bewitched. Blind men, idiots! One day they'll have to pay for all the food wasted on them!"

2. The god of death.

THE TEN KINGS OF HELL

SCRIPTURE ON THE TEN KINGS
(The Shiwang Jing)

The cycle of rebirth called samsara has no beginning, and it has no end except for those who escape it. Countless beings have wandered forever through the six realms of rebirth, as gods, demigods, humans, animals, ghosts, and denizens of hell. Not random, their routes through these realms are determined by their own deeds, their karma. In Buddhism, there are many gods, but there is no God, no creator deity who bestows rewards and metes out punishments. Instead, it is simply the nature of things that virtuous deeds result in happiness in the future and sinful deeds in suffering—perhaps not in this life but in a subsequent lifetime. Thus, though it may appear that the good suffer while the wicked thrive, such a conclusion is shortsighted; in the future, each will reap his or her reward.

Despite the Buddha's admonition to escape entirely from the round of rebirth, and his instruction on how to do so, he also taught the path to rebirth in heaven—and that has been the most trodden of the many Buddhist paths (see also the *Sarva-durgatiparishodhana Tantra*, p. 464). At the same time, Buddhists have long imagined the various fates that await those who commit misdeeds in this life and somehow escape punishment. Heaven is for oneself; hell is for other people. It is perhaps appropriate, therefore, that in the Buddhist cosmology, the most elaborate of the six realms are those at the top and the bottom: there is a system of twenty-seven heavens on the central mountain (Meru), in the skies above it, and in the "Formless Realm." And eight hot hells, eight cold hells, and four neighboring hells are located in the bowels of earth beneath Bodh Gaya, where the Buddha achieved enlightenment.

In scholastic presentations of actions and their effects, there is a mechanistic element—a specific deed bears a specific fruit, a particular action has a particular effect—leading some modern Buddhists to call karma a "natural law." Depending on the circumstances, the deed may be "complete" or "incomplete": complete actions serve as the cause for an entire lifetime (see the *Treasury of Higher Doctrine*, p. 267). The inexorable nature of the law of karma is acknowledged throughout the Buddhist world. Yet much Buddhist practice, in all times and places, has been devoted to somehow subverting that law, especially when dealing with the dead.

As classically construed, there was nothing that could be done for the dead. Each person passed from lifetime to lifetime as a result of his or her own karma. Life is an impermanent process as moments of consciousness move forward through time, sometimes with the physical form of a body and sometimes not. In this regard, the moment between death and rebirth is just another moment of change. A person dies in one moment and is reborn in the next.

But some Buddhist schools argued that for a seed from one village to be planted in another, it needs to be transported, and doing so takes time. They therefore introduced the notion of an "intermediate state" between birth and death while the consciousness of the deceased travels to its next place of rebirth, a journey that might be as brief as an instant or as long as forty-nine days. This period provided an opportunity for the living to benefit the dead, with the aid of Buddhist monks.

Indeed, one of the primary functions of Buddhist monks across the Buddhist world, both in those traditions that assert the existence of an intermediate state and those that do not, is to perform rites for the dead. At funerals in Thailand, Buddhist monks will read summaries of the seven books of the Abhidharma, technical manuals of doctrine. Yet these most scholastic of works are seen to have particular powers of salvation. One of the summaries declares, "Whoever is born or dies on Sunday and hears the *Dhammasangiti* [one of the seven books] will be released from all demerit accrued through the eye. At death this person will not be reborn in hell but will enter heaven." The other six books of the Abhidharma similarly provide salvation to those who are born or die on the other days of the week. In Tibet, a lama will sit with the corpse and read descriptions of what the intermediate state is like, with instructions on how to find liberation there. One manual of such instructions is the so-called *Tibetan Book of the Dead*.

According to standard karmic theory, all intentional deeds of the unenlightened, whether good or evil, produce effects of pleasure and pain. The next place of rebirth is not determined by weighing the accumulated deeds of this life in a balance: instead, each complete deed from any past life is a potential cause of an entire lifetime, and a variety of factors, including one's state of mind at the time of death, determines which particular deed will fructify as the next lifetime. But most Buddhist societies have shown little interest in such doctrinal fine points, while paying great attention to the calculation of karma. In China, for example, hell was transformed into an infernal bureaucracy, where the minions of the Lord of Death consulted ledgers itemizing the deeds of the damned. One of the most important representations of this netherworld is found in a Chinese apocryphon called *The Scripture on the Ten Kings (Shiwang Jing)*, which appears below in its entirety.

Ten times after death (at the end of each of the first seven weeks, at one hundred days, at one year, and at three years) the deceased is escorted into the presence of a king who has before him a precise record of all the person's deeds of the past life. The dead are herded like sheep from court to court, pushed along by ox-headed guards wielding pitchforks. In the fourth court a scale weighs their good deeds against their sins. In the fifth court they are dragged by the hair and made to look into the mirror of karma, where they see their past misdeeds reflected. In the tenth court, reached after three years of suffering, the place of rebirth is decided. Among misdeeds, specific mention is made of the gravity of using money that rightfully belongs to the three jewels (the Buddha, the dharma, and the sangha, or Buddhist community).

In the text, the Buddha explains that if his or her family sends the appropriate offerings at the appropriate time, the deceased individual may be excused from the courts at various points along the journey and be granted a favorable birth. It is particularly efficacious to copy *The Scripture on the Ten Kings* or pictures of the ten kings, or to sponsor the making of such copies or pictures. In testimony to the popularity of this practice, many copies of the scriptures, often with illustrations of the ten courts, have been discovered in manuscript collections.

PRONOUNCING GLOSSARY

Ajitavati: *a-ji-ta-va-tee*

Amitabha Buddha: *a-mi-tah-ba bud-da*

Avichi: *a-vee-chi*

bhikshu: *bik-shu*

bhikshuni: *bik-shu-nee*

Changbei: *chahng-bay*

Chengdu: *chung-doo*
Dashengci si: *dah-shung-tsu su*
Dharani: *dah-ra-nee*
Di: *dee*
Dizang: *dee-tsang*
gatha: *gah-tah*
Guang: *gwahng*
Jambudvipa: *jam-bu-dvee-pa*
Jingang zang: *jin-gahng zahng*
kshana: *ksha-na*
Mahasattva: *ma-hah-sat-tva*

Parinirvana: *pa-ri-nir-vah-na*
Puxian: *poo-shyehn*
Qin: *chin*
samadhi: *sa-mah-di*
Shiwang Jing: *shi-wang jing*
shramana: *shra-ma-na*
Song: *sohng*
upasaka: *u-pah-sa-ka*
upasika: *u-pah-si-kah*
Yama raja: *ya-ma rah-ja*
Zangchuang: *tsang-chwahng*

We reverently open the chanting of *The Scripture of King Yama Raja Concerning the Sevens of Life*[1] *to Be Cultivated in Preparation for Rebirth in the Pure Land*. May our vows and admonitions be lucky. We open the scripture and begin the hymns with the five assemblies. We recite: "A-mi-tabha Buddha."[2]

Recorded by *shramana*[3] Zangchuang of Dashengci si in Chengdu Prefecture.

The Scripture Spoken by the Buddha to the Four Orders[4] *on the Prophecy Given to King Yama Raja Concerning the Sevens of Life to Be Cultivated in Preparation for Rebirth in the Pure Land*.

> The hymn goes:
> When the Thus Come One approached *parinirvana*,[5]
> He widely summoned heavenly dragons and earth spirits.
> For King Yama's sake he made a prophecy,
> And then handed down this rite for the preparatory cultivation
>   of the sevens of life.

Thus have I heard. Once, the Buddha was among the pair of Sala trees on the banks of the Ajitavati River in the city of Kushinagara. As he approached *parinirvana* the Buddha lifted himself up and emitted a ray that universally illuminated the great multitude as well as myriad Bodhisattvas and Mahasattvas;[6] heavenly dragons and spirit kings; Shakra, Emperor and Chief of Heaven; the great kings of the four heavens, Great Brahma, King of Heaven, the *asura*-kings;[7] the various kings of great empires; Yama, Son of Heaven; the Magistrate of Mount Tai; the Officer of Life Spans and Officer of Records; the Great Spirit of the Five Paths;[8] and the officials of the underground prisons. They all came to the gathering, respectfully reverenced the World Honored One, brought their hands together, and stood [to the side].

TRANSLATED FROM the Chinese by Stephen F. Teiser. All bracketed additions are the translator's.

1. Seven feasts that one offers during life in order to ease one's passage from one lifetime to the next. "Yama": in Buddhism, the Lord of Death and the King of Hell. *Raja* means "king" (Sanskrit).
2. The buddha who presides over the Pure Land (see the *Sukhavativyuha Sutra*, p. 316).
3. An ascetic or mendicant monk. (All italicized terms are Sanskrit.)

4. The four categories of the Buddha's disciples: monks, nuns, laymen, and laywomen.
5. The final nirvana.
6. Great beings.
7. *Asuras* are demigods.
8. The paths of a god, human, ghost, animal, or denizen of hell; it is more common to list six paths, adding "demigod" to the list.

The hymn goes:
At that time the Buddha extended a ray of light that filled the Great
    Thousand,
Reaching everywhere to dragons and ghosts, uniting humans and gods.
Indra, Brahma,[9] the various gods and multitudes from the dark,
    hidden world
All came to bow their heads in front of the World Honored One.[1]

The Buddha announced to the entire great multitude that in a world to
come, Yama raja, Son of Heaven, would attain the role of Buddha. He would
be named "King Puxian, Thus Come One," and he would fully possess the
Ten Titles. His land would be ornamented and pure, decorated with a hundred jewels. His country would be named "Flower Ornament," and it would
be completely filled with Bodhisattvas.

The hymn goes:
On this day the World Honored One prophesied that Yama raja
Would before long realize Buddhahood;
His country, decorated with jewels, would always be pure,
With many multitudes cultivating the practice of the Bodhisattva.

At that time Ananda[2] spoke to the Buddha, saying, "World Honored One,
on account of what causes and conditions does Yama raja, Son of Heaven,
settle verdicts in the dark regions? And why, then, in this assembly, has he
received a prophecy of the fruits [he will enjoy] in the future?"
The Buddha said, "There are two causes and conditions for serving as the
various kings in those dark paths. The first involves Bodhisattvas who dwell
on the immovable ground of inconceivable liberation. Desiring to aid in the
transformation of all sentient beings in their extreme suffering, they manifest themselves in the role of those like that King Yama. The second involves
those who have descended to Yama's heaven to play the role of Great King
Mara,[3] because in giving rise to the practice of good they violated the precepts. They keep order over the various ghosts and judge the cases on Jambudvipa[4] involving the ten evils and the five abominations.[5] For all sinners
locked up in prison, day and night undergoing suffering—as the wheel [of
rebirth] turns among them and they receive bodily form in accord with
their actions—[the kings] determine their lives and register their deaths.
Now the causes and conditions of this Yama, Son of Heaven, are already
ripe. For this reason I have prophesied a country of jewels and the realization of great bodhi[6] in a world to come. All of you, men and gods, should
not doubt it."

The hymn goes:
Compassionate toward the hated, he transforms all—that is majestic
    numinosity;
The wheel turns in the six paths, never delaying or stopping.

9. The god who persuaded the Buddha to teach.
"Indra": the ruler of the Heaven of the Thirty-
three.
1. The Buddha.
2. The Buddha's cousin and personal attendant.
3. The Buddhist deity of desire and death.
4. In Buddhist cosmology, the continent on which
all humans live.

5. Killing one's mother, one's father, or an arhat;
maliciously causing a buddha to bleed; and dis-
rupting the sangha (Buddhist community). "Ten
evils": killing, stealing, sexual misconduct, lying,
divisive speech, harsh speech, senseless speech,
covetousness, harmful intent, and wrong views.
6. Enlightenment.

Teaching and transforming, he detests suffering and thinks of joy,
Hence he manifests himself in the form of Yama raja, Son of Heaven.

Now if there is a person who cultivates the commissioning of this scripture, or who receives and upholds or reads and intones it, then after giving up his life he will not be reborn in the three paths,[7] nor will he enter any of the various great underground prisons.

The hymn goes:
If a person believes in the Law and does not doubt it,
And copies the text of this scripture, obeys it, and upholds it,
Then upon giving up his life he will instantly pass over the three evil paths,
And in this body he will always avoid entering Avichi.[8]

For any serious crimes that require serving in the underground prisons for ten *kalpas*[9] or five *kalpas*—killing one's father; injuring one's mother, breaking the fast; breaking the precepts, slaughtering pigs, cattle, sheep, chickens, dogs, or poisonous snakes—a person can during life commission this scripture or the various images of the Honored Ones, and it will be noted in the dark registry. On the day one arrives, King Yama will be delighted and will decide to release the person to be reborn in a rich and noble household, avoiding [punishment for] his crimes and errors.

The hymn goes:
Breaking the fast, damaging the precepts, slaughtering chickens and pigs
Are reflected clearly in the mirror of actions—retribution is never void
If one commissions this scripture together with the painting of images,
King Yama will decide to release you and wipe away your sins.

If there is a good son or good daughter, *bhikshu* or *bhikshuni*, *upasaka*, or *upasika*[1] who cultivates in preparation the seven feasts of life, twice each month offering support to the Three Jewels,[2] then whoever provides for the ten kings will have their names revised and reports will be given; memorials will be sent up to the Six Ministries, the Boys of Good and Evil will send memorials to all the officials of heaven's ministries and earth's prefects, and it will be noted in the register of names. On the day one arrives, one will expediently attain assigned rebirth in a place of happiness. One will not dwell in intermediate darkness for forty-nine days, and one will not have to wait for sons and daughters to attempt posthumous salvation. As one's life span passes before the ten kings, if there is one feast missing, then one is detained before one king, remaining there continuously to undergo suffering, unable to emerge into birth, detained for the length of one year. For this reason you are admonished to perform this crucial service and to pray for the reward of rebirth in the Pure Land.

7. That is, the three lower paths (rebirth as an animal, as a ghost, or in hell).
8. The most painful of the eight hot Buddhist hells.
9. Aeons, or cosmic cycles.
1. Monk or nun, layman, or laywoman.
2. The Buddha, the dharma, and the sangha.

The hymn goes:
The four orders cultivate the feast from time to time:
Two offerings over three-ten days is the standard rite.
Don't miss a chance for good karmic conditions or let your merit
  dwindle,
For then you'll be caught up in the intermediate darkness, detained
  by the dark offices.

At that time Dizang Bodhisattva, Longshu Bodhisattva, Jiuku Guanshiyin
Bodhisattva, Changbei Bodhisattva, Dharani Bodhisattva, and Jingang zang
Bodhisattva each returned in a ray of light from his home path and arrived
at the place of the Thus Come One. From different mouths but with the
same voice, they sang hymns praising how the World Honored One grieves
for the common person and preaches this wondrous Law, which raises the
dead and saves the living. With the crowns of their heads they reverenced
the Buddha's feet.

The hymn goes:
With legs, body, and head,
The Bodhisattvas of the six rays set in motion their profound
  compassion;
With the same voice each one sang hymns in praise
Of how he toils diligently and transforms all creatures, never getting
  weary.

At that time all the wardens of the eighteen prisons, Yama, Son of Heaven,
and the dark officers of the six paths paid their respects and made a vow: "If
there is a member of the four orders—a *bhikshu*, *bhikshuni*, *upasaka*, or
upasika—who commissions this scripture or sings a hymn or intones a single verse, then we shall all exempt him from all of his suffering and pain.
We shall reverse the decision so that he emerges from the underground
prisons and goes to rebirth in the heavenly path. We shall not allow him to
be delayed or to undergo suffering even for one night."

The hymn goes:
The dark officers, the note-takers, as well as King Yama
And all the Buddhas glorified the scripture and reverentially offered
  praise:
If among the four orders someone can uphold a single verse,
We shall all send him off to the halls of heaven.

At that time King Yama, Son of Heaven, spoke to the Buddha, saying a
verse:

"*Namo arhat.*[3]
Many are the evil acts of sentient beings.
The cycle of rebirth has no determinate marks,
Just like waves upon the water."

The hymn goes:
King Yama spoke to the Buddha, saying a *gatha*,[4]

---

3. Homage to the worthy one [translator's note].   4. Verse.

Reciting with sympathy, "Many are the sins and sufferings of all
    sentient beings.
The cycle of rebirth in the six paths has no determinate marks.
Birth and extinction are still the same as waves upon the water."

May the breeze of his wisdom
Drift over the river of the wheel of the Law.
May his ray of brightness illuminate worldly realms,
Making a tour of all past experience.

Universally saving all sentient beings from suffering,
Subduing and gathering together the various demons,
The four kings administer the realm of states,
And transmit the Buddha's *sutras*.

The hymn goes:
May the Buddha bring forth the rising of the wind of wisdom,
Drifting over the sea of the Law, washing away the dust that conceals.
The four kings who protect the world also made a vow
That they would hand down this classic and circulate it
    everywhere.

Common people who cultivate goodness are few;
Those who are confused and who believe in depravity are many.
Uphold the scripture and you will avoid the underground prisons;
Copy it and you will be spared calamity and illness.

You will pass over the difficulties of the three worlds
And never see a *yaksha*.[5]
You will ascend to a high rank in your place of rebirth;
You will be rich, noble, and enjoy a long posterity.

The hymn goes:
Because of evil actions, the power of common people to do good
    is slight;
They believe in falsity, have perverted views, and will enter Avichi.
If you wish to seek riches and nobility and a family with a long life
    span,
You should copy the text of this scripture, obey it, and uphold it.

With utmost mind intone this scripture,
And the kings of heaven will constantly note it in their registers.
Do not take life in sacrificing to the spirits,
Because for this you will enter the underground prisons.

In reciting the Buddha's [name], you can transgress the authentic
    scripture—
You must admonish and exert yourself.
In your hands wield the diamond knife
To wipe out Mara's tribe.

---

5. One of the varieties of nonhuman beings, a kind of nature spirit.

The hymn goes:
Actions of sin and suffering within the three paths are completed
      with ease;
They are all conditioned by taking life while sacrificing to spirits.
You should aspire to wield the diamond sword of authentic wisdom,
To cut off Mara's tribe, and to awaken to the unborn.

The Buddha puts into action an impartial mind,
In which sentient beings are insufficiently endowed.
The cultivation of blessings seems like particles of dust,
The commission of sins like mountain peaks.

You should cultivate the commissioning of this scripture,
And you will be able to endure the sufferings of the underground
      prisons,
Be reborn into a powerful and noble family,
And forever be protected by good spirits.

The hymn goes:
Sins are like mountain peaks, as numerous as sand in the Ganges;
Blessings are few, like particles of dust; they don't amount to much.
But still good spirits will forever protect you,
And you can be reborn into a powerful, rich, and devout family.

Those people who commission the scripture or who read and
      intone it—
When Impermanence suddenly arrives,
The kings of heaven will forever guide and introduce them,
And Bodhisattvas will offer flowers to welcome them.

Dedicate your mind to going to the Pure Land
For eighty trillion lifetimes;
The cultivation of practice will be perfected and achieved,
And diamond *samadhi*[6] will be completed.

The hymn goes:
If a person serves the Buddha by commissioning and upholding this
      scripture,
Then as he approaches the end, Bodhisattvas will personally come
      to welcome him.
After the causes of the cultivation of practice in the Pure Country
      are perfected
He will come to authentic enlightenment and enter the golden city.

   At that time the Buddha announced to Ananda and all of the dragons, gods,
and other members of the eight groups; together with the various great
spirits; Yama raja, Son of Heaven; the Magistrate of Mount Tai; the Officer
of Life Spans and the Officer of Records; the Great Spirit of the Five Paths;
all the officials of the underground prisons; and the great kings who traverse
the path, that they should give rise to compassion: "The Law is broad and

---

6. The state of deep meditation in which buddhahood is achieved.

forgiving. I allow you to be lenient with the compassionate and filial sons and daughters of all sinners. When they cultivate merit and perform sacrifices to raise the dead, repaying the kindness shown in giving birth to them and supporting them, or when during the seven sevens they cultivate feasts and commission statues in order to repay their parents' kindness, then you should allow them to attain rebirth in the heavens."

> The hymn goes:
> The Buddha informed Yama raja and the various great spirits,
> "The actions committed by sentient beings are hard to explain
>   fully.
> You should open up kindness and permit them to make merit,
> And teach the dull how to leave behind suffering and emerge from
>   the stream of delusion."

Yama raja, the King of the Law, spoke to the Buddha, saying, "World Honored One, we, the various kings, will send out messengers riding black horses, holding black banners, and wearing black clothes. They will inspect the homes of deceased people to see what merit is being made. We will allow names to be entered, dispose of warrants, and pluck out sinners. May we not go against our vows."

> The hymn goes:
> The various kings dispatch messengers to inspect the deceased
> And see what causes of merit their sons and daughters are
>   cultivating.
> Depending on one's name, one can be released from the prisons of
>   the three paths,
> And be spared passage through the dark regions and any encounters
>   with suffering and grief.

[King Yama said,] "I humbly vow to the World Honored One that I will listen to the preaching and inspect the feasts for the names of the Ten Kings."

> The hymn goes:
> King Yama went to the Buddha and again explained the situation:
> "I humbly vow to be compassionate in carrying out verification.
> After death, when common people cultivate merit,
> I will inspect the feasts and listen for the preaching of the names
>   of the Ten Kings."

The first. After seven days they pass before King Guang of Qin.

> The hymn goes:
> During the first seven, dead people with bodies of intermediate
>   darkness
> Are herded like sheep, rank after rank, numerous as particles of
>   dust.
> Now they move toward the first king, who inspects each point of the
>   fast;
> Still to come they have not yet crossed the stream of the River Nai.

The second. After seven days they pass before the King of the First River.

The hymn goes:
During the second seven, dead people cross the River Nai;
In hordes of a thousand and groups of ten thousand they step
    through the river's waves.
The ox heads who guide the way clasp cudgels at their shoulders;
The ghost soldiers who press people ahead raise pitchforks in their
    hands.

The third. After seven days they pass before King Di of Song.

The hymn goes:
Dead people during the third seven turn from one annoyance to the
    next,
And begin to be aware how long is the narrow road that winds
    through the dark paths.
One-by-one [the kings] check off names—they know where everyone
    is;
Rank-after-rank [the guards] drive them along to the King of the
    Five Offices.

The fourth. After seven days they pass before the King of the Five Offices.

The hymn goes:
The balance of actions in the five offices is suspended in the air;
To the left and the right the Twin Boys complete the logbook of actions.
The lightness and heaviness [of retribution], alas, is due to what the
    feelings desire;
Whether low or high, one is responsible for past causes and conditions.

The fifth. After seven days they pass before King Yama raja.

The hymn goes:
During the fifth seven, Yama raja puts an end to sounds of dispute,
But in their hearts sinners are resentful and unwilling.
With their hair yanked and their heads pulled up to look in the
    mirror of actions,
They begin to know that affairs from previous lives are rendered
    distinct and clear.

The sixth. After seven days they pass before the King of Transformations.

The hymn goes:
Dead people during the sixth seven clog the dark paths,
Mortally afraid that the living will be stupid in holding to their
    opinions.
Day in and day out all they see is the power of merit,
How the difference between the halls of heaven and the prisons
    underground lies in a *kshana*.[7]

The seventh. After seven days they pass before the King of Mount Tai.

The hymn goes:
During the seventh seven in the dark paths the bodies of
    intermediate darkness

---

7. An instant.

Search for their fathers and mothers, [hoping] to meet with loved
 ones and kin.
Fortunate actions at this time have yet to be determined;
They watch again to see what causes [for merit] sons and daughters
 will perform.

The eighth. After one hundred days they pass before the Impartial King.

The hymn goes:
After one hundred days dead people are subjected to more
 annoyances:
Their bodies meet with cangues[8] and shackles, and they are
 wounded by whips.
If sons and daughters exert themselves in cultivating merit,
Then [the dead] will be spared from dropping into the underground
 prisons, those places of eternal suffering.

The ninth. At one year they pass before the King of the Capital.

The hymn goes:
At one year they pass here, turning about in suffering and grief,
 depending on what merit their sons and daughters have
 cultivated.
The wheel of rebirth in the six paths is revolving, still not settled;
Commission a scripture or commission an image, and they will
 emerge from the stream of delusion.

The tenth. At three years they pass before the King Who Turns the Wheel
of Rebirth in the Five Paths.

The hymn goes:
For the last three, where they pass is an important crossing.
Good and evil [rebirth] depend only on fortunate actions as a cause.
If you don't perform good, there will be still more grief, and within
 a thousand days
They will be reborn into a womb only to die in birth, or to perish at
 a tender age.

[Yama said,] "When the ten feasts are completely fulfilled, we will spare them
from the sins of the ten evils and release them to be reborn in heaven."

The hymn goes:
One body in the six paths suffers without rest;
The ten evils and the three paths are not easy to bear.
But if you exert yourselves to cultivate the feasts, and your merit is
 complete,
Then all sins as numerous as sand in the Ganges will disappear of
 themselves.

[Yama continued,] "I will send the four *yaksha* kings to preserve and protect this scripture and not let it fall into destruction."

The hymn goes:
King Yama upheld the Law and sang a hymn glorifying and praising it,

8. Wooden collars.

Proclaiming to men and gods and to all fields for the practice of the
Way.
"I will send *yakshas* to preserve and protect it;
I will not let it fall into destruction, and will forever have it circulate."

We bow our heads low to the World Honored One. Most of the sinners
in the prisons made use of property belonging to the Three Jewels. With
loud wrangling they suffer punishment for their sins. People with awareness and faith can guard against violating the Three Jewels. Retribution
for actions is hard to endure. Those who see this scripture must cultivate
and study it.

The hymn goes:
If you wish to seek peace and happiness and to dwell among humans
and gods,
Then you must immediately stop appropriating money belonging to
the Three Jewels.
Once you fall into the dark regions and the various underground
prisons,
There will only be crying for the sufferings you endure for I don't
know how many years.

At that time Yama, King of the Law, leapt for joy, reverenced the Buddha's
feet with his head, stepped back, and sat to one side. The Buddha said, "The
name of this scripture is *The Scripture to the Four Orders on the Prophecy
Given to King Yama Raja Concerning the Sevens of Life To Be Cultivated in
Preparation for Rebirth in the Pure Land*. You should circulate it and transmit it
among the states and realms, and uphold practice according to its teachings."

The hymn goes:
King Yama stepped back and sat down and listened with his whole
mind.
Then the Buddha with great care and diligence entrusted him with
this scripture:
"Its name is *The Teaching of the Sevens of Life that Are Cultivated
in Preparation*.
You, together with the four orders, must circulate it widely."

*The Scripture Spoken by the Buddha to the Four Orders on the Prophecy
Given to King Yama Raja Concerning the Sevens of Life To Be Cultivated in
Preparation for Rebirth in the Pure Land*. May our universal admonitions be
lucky. Cultivate merit in preparation. Give rise to the thought [of enlighten-
ment]. Vow to put an end to the wheel of rebirth.
The hymn has two stanzas:

The first hymn:
A single life is perilously brittle, like a lamp in the wind;
Two rats sneak up, gnawing at a creeper in the well.
If within the sea of suffering you don't cultivate a boat or raft for
crossing,
Then what can you hope to depend on to attain deliverance?

The second hymn:
Not to build boats or bridges—this is human ignorance;

You will encounter danger and constant annoyance—this, sir, you
   must begin to know.
If you are aware that one hundred years pass in the snap of the
   fingers,
Then you mustn't delay in cultivating the feasts and listening to
   the Law.

LETTERS FROM A ZEN MASTER

RECORDS OF POINTING AT THE MOON
(*The Zhi Yue Lu*)

DAHUI

The Chan school in China, renowned as "a special transmission outside the scriptures," developed its own sacred texts by collecting and commenting on the statements
of its enlightened teachers. These works, called "recorded saying" and "encounter
dialogues," were works of literature—often brilliant works—presented as verbatim
transcripts of spontaneous conversations between masters and their disciples. The
encounters were frequently marked by non sequiturs. "Q: What is the Buddha? A:
Three pounds of flax." "Q: What is the Buddha? A: A dried shit stick."

These exchanges came to be known as "public cases" (*gong'an*); the term, borrowed from Chinese jurisprudence, literally means "judge's bench" and originally
referred to a legal precedent, a standard of judgment. This Chinese term is pronounced *koan* in Japanese, and it is by this name that these seemingly nonsensical
statements are known in the West. The most famous of all koans, at least in popular culture, is relatively late and of Japanese origin, posed by the eighteenth-century
Zen master Hakuin (see the *O[r]ategama*, p. 668): "What is the sound of one hand
clapping?"

Although koans are commonly represented as logical puzzles designed to break
down conceptual barriers, they have also served as the scriptures of the Chan
tradition; in it, they have been memorized, recited, analyzed, and expounded on
like any other Buddhist text, with their own traditional forms of commentary and
exegesis.

One of the leading proponents of koan practice in China was the monk Dahui
(1089–1163), a member of the Linji school (see *Record of Linji*, p. 541). He studied
with a number of the foremost Chan masters of the day; after winning the favor of
the prime minister, he was appointed abbot of one of the most important monasteries
in China. He was later falsely charged with treason and exiled but was eventually
exonerated, and his position was restored.

Dahui was a harsh critic of what was called "silent illumination Chan," the prolonged sessions of silent seated meditation in which one sought to reveal the original
purity of the mind by ceasing mental activity; he argued that such a practice resulted
only in calluses on the buttocks. He instead advocated what he called "key word
Chan"—that is, the active wrestling with koans—and he strongly condemned the
practice of commenting on those exchanges.

One of the most important koan collections of the day was the *Blue Cliff Record*,
whose one hundred koans had annotations and commentaries by Dahui's revered
teacher, Yuanwu Keqin. In order to discourage his students from intellectualizing
the koans, Dahui reportedly took the woodblocks from which the *Blue Cliff Record*
was printed and burned them.

Within the Chan and Zen traditions of China and Japan, the most famous koan is not about one hand clapping but about a dog. We must keep in mind that in China, dogs traditionally were reviled as scavengers who lived on garbage; moreover, it was standard Buddhist doctrine that all sentient beings have the buddha-nature. When the monk Zhaozhou (Joshu in Japanese) was asked whether a dog had the buddha-nature, he answered, "No" (*wu* in Chinese, *mu* in Japanese). Dahui was particularly committed to Zhaozhou's "no" as means for generating the deep sense of doubt that must precede illumination.

Dahui had a large number of disciples, both monastic and lay, over the course of his life, and he often wrote letters to them with instructions for their practice. Two of those letters are presented here, from a work titled *Zhi Yue Lu*, or "Records of Pointing at the Moon." It is often said in Zen that the Buddhist scriptures are like a finger pointing at the moon, meant to direct one's gaze away from themselves and to what really matters; if one looks only at the finger, one never sees the moon.

PRONOUNCING GLOSSARY

Bo Zhu yi: *boh joo ee*   Qian Tang: *chyehn tahng*
Chan: *chahn*   Vimalakirti: *vi-ma-la-keer-ti*
Dao Lin: *dau lin*   Yong Jia: *yohng jyah*
prajna: *praj-nyah*   Zhi Yue Lu: *jee yu-ay lu*

"Do not grasp another's bow"

"Do not grasp another's bow, do not ride another's horse, do not meddle in another's affairs." Though this is a commonplace saying, it can also be sustenance for entering the Path. Just examine yourself constantly: from morning to night, what do you do to help others and help yourself? If you notice even the slightest partiality or insensitivity, you must admonish yourself. Don't be careless about this!

In the old days Chan Master Dao Lin lived up in a tall pine tree on Chin Wang Mountain; people of the time called him the "Bird's Nest Monk." When Minister Bo Zhu yi was commander of Qian Tang, he made a special trip to the mountain to visit him. Bo said, "It's very dangerous where you're sitting, Chan Master." The Master said, "My danger may be very great, Minister, but yours is even greater." Bo said, "I am commander of Qian Tang: what danger is there?" The Master said, "Fuel and fire are joined, consciousness and identity do not stay: how can you not be in danger?"

Bo also asked, "What is the overall meaning of the Buddhist Teaching?" The Master said, "Don't commit any evils, practice the many virtues." Bo said, "Even a three-year-old child could say this." The Master said, "Though a three-year-old child can say it, an eighty-year-old man cannot carry it out." Bo then bowed and departed.

Now if you want to save mental power, do not be concerned with whether or not a three-year-old child can say it, or whether or not an eighty-year-old man can carry it out. Just don't do any evil and you have mastered

TRANSLATED FROM the Chinese by J. C. Cleary.

these words. They apply whether you believe or not, so please think it over.

If worldly people whose present conduct is without illumination would correct themselves and do good, though the goodness is not yet perfect, isn't this better than depravity and shamelessness? One who does evil on the pretext of doing good is called in the Teachings one whose causal ground is not genuine, bringing on crooked results. If, with a straightforward mind and straightforward conduct, you are able to seize supreme enlightenment directly, this can be called the act of a real man of power. The concerns that have come down from numberless ages are only in the present: if you can understand them right now, then the concerns of numberless ages will instantly disperse, like tiles being scattered or ice melting. If you don't understand right now, you'll pass through countless eons more, and it'll still be just as it is. The truth that is as it is has been continuous since antiquity without ever having varied so much as a hairsbreadth.

Matters of worldly anxieties are like the links of a chain, joining together continuously without a break. If you can do away with them, do away with them immediately! Because you have become habituated to them since beginningless time, to the point where they have become totally familiar, if you don't exert yourself to struggle with them, then as time goes on and on, with you unknowing and unawares, they will have entered deeply into you. Finally, on the last day of your life, you won't be able to do anything about it. If you want to be able to avoid going wrong when you face the end of your life, then from now on whenever you do anything, don't let yourself slip. If you go wrong in your present doings, it will be impossible not to go wrong when you're facing death.

There's a sort of person who reads scriptures, recites the Buddha-name, and repents in the morning, but then in the evening runs off at the mouth, slandering and vilifying other people. The next day he does homage to Buddha and repents as before. All through the years till the end of his life he takes this as daily ritual—this is extreme folly. Such people are far from realizing that the Sanskrit word *kshama* means to repent faults. This is called "cutting off the continuing mind." Once you have cut it off, never continue it again; once you have repented, do not commit (wrongdoings) again—this is the meaning of repentance according to our Buddha, which good people who study the Path should not fail to know.

The mind, discriminating intellect, and consciousness of students of the Path should be quiet and still twenty-four hours a day. When you have nothing to do, you should sit quietly and keep the mind from slackening and the body from wavering. If you practice to perfection over a long long time, naturally body and mind will come to rest at ease, and you will have some direction in the Path. The perfection of quiescence and stillness indeed settles the scattered and confused false consciousness of sentient beings, but if you cling to quiescent stillness and consider it the ultimate, then you're in the grip of perverted "silent illumination" Chan.[1]

The Sanskrit word *prajna* means wisdom. Those who lack clear *prajna* and are greedy, wrathful, stupid, and lustful, those who don't have clear *prajna*

1. See the introduction to this selection.

and harm sentient beings, those who do such things as these—they are running away from *prajna*. How can this be called wisdom?

By keeping mindful of the matter of birth and death, your mental technique is already correct. Once the mental technique is correct, then you won't need to use effort to clear your mind as you respond to circumstances in your daily activities. When you don't actively try to clear out your mind, then you won't go wrong; since you don't go wrong, correct mindfulness stands out alone. When correct mindfulness stands out alone, inner truth adapts to phenomena; when inner truth adapts to events and things, events and things come to fuse in inner truth. When phenomena fuse with their inner truth, you save power; when you feel the saving, this is the empowerment of studying the Path. In gaining power you save unlimited power; in saving power you gain unlimited power.

This matter may be taken up by brilliant quick-witted folks, but if you depend on your brilliance and quick wits, you won't be able to bear up. It is easy for keen and bright people to enter, but hard for them to preserve it. That's because generally their entry is not very deep and the power is meager. With the intelligent and quick-witted, as soon as they hear a spiritual friend mention this matter, their eyes stir immediately and they are already trying to gain understanding through their mind's discriminating intellect. People like this are creating their own hindrances, and will never have a moment of awakening. "When devils from outside wreak calamity, it can still be remedied," but this (reliance on intellectual discrimination) amounts to "When one's own family creates disaster, it cannot be averted." This what Yong Jia[2] meant when he said, "The loss of the wealth of the Dharma and the demise of virtue all stem from mind's discriminating intellect."

Dealing with Situations

Since we parted, I don't know whether or not you can avoid being carried away by external objects in your daily activities as you respond to circumstances, whether or not you can put aside your heap of legal documents as you look through them, whether or not you can act freely when you meet with people, whether or not you engage in vain thinking when you're where it's peaceful and quiet, whether or not you are thoroughly investigating This Matter without any distracted thoughts.

Thus Old Yellow Face (Buddha) has said, "When the mind does not vainly grasp past things, does not long for things in the future, and does not dwell on anything in the present, then you realize fully that the three times are all empty and still." You shouldn't think about past events, whether good or bad; if you think about them, that obstructs the Path. You shouldn't consider future events; to consider them is crazy confusion. Present events are right in front of you: whether they're pleasant or unpleasant, don't fix your mind on them. If you do fix your mind on them, it will disturb your heart. Just take everything in its time, responding according to circumstances, and you will naturally accord with this principle.

Unpleasant situations are easy to handle; pleasant situations are hard to handle. For that which goes against one's will, it boils down to one word:

---

2. Scholar and monk (665–713 C.E.).

patience. Settle down and reflect a moment and in a little while it's gone. It's pleasant situations that truly give you no way to escape: like pairing magnet and iron, unconsciously this and that come together in one place. Even inanimate objects are thus: how much the more so for those acting in ignorance, with their whole beings making a living within it! In this world, if you have no wisdom, you will be dragged unknowing and unawares by that ignorance into a net; once inside the net, won't it be difficult to look for a way out? This is why an early sage said, "Having entered the world, leave the world completely"—this is the same principle. In recent generations there's been a type who lose track of expedient means in their practice. They always consider acting in ignorance to be "entering the world," so then they think of a forced pushing away as the act of "leaving the world completely." Are they not to be pitied? The only exceptions are those who have pledged their commitment, who can see through situations immediately, act the master, and not be dragged in by others.

Hence Vimalakirti[3] said, "For those with the conceit of superiority, falsely claiming attainment, the Buddha just says that detachment from lust, hatred, and ignorance is liberation. For those with no conceit of superiority, the Buddha says that the inherent nature of lust, hatred, and ignorance is identical to liberation." If you can avoid this fault, so that in the midst of situations favorable or adverse there is no aspect of origination or demise, only then can you get away from the name "conceit of superiority" (applied to one who thinks he has attained but hasn't). Only this way can you be considered to have entered the world and be called a man of power.

What I've been talking about thus far is all my personal life experience: even right now I practice just like this. I hope that you will take advantage of your physical strength and health and also enter this stable equilibrium.

3. The central figure in a Mahayana sutra of the same name.

CHINESE PILGRIMS MEET THE BUDDHA

JOURNEY TO THE WEST
(The Xi You Ji)

WU CHENG'EN

Religion and the religious often figure prominently in works of popular literature. In the case of Christianity, *The Decameron* (1350–53) and *The Canterbury Tales* (1386–1400) immediately come to mind. Buddhism is no different. Throughout the Buddhist world, monks and nuns are regularly found among the dramatis personae in all manner of novels and plays, and not always as heroes and heroines. These fictional monks may be lazy, lecherous, or given to drink—sometimes all three. Whether such portrayals are a matter of artistic license or reflect the real world of Buddhist life is a question that requires further research.

But there is no question of how frequently they appear. In *Drunken Games* (*Mattavilasa*), a south Indian play composed around 600 C.E., a Buddhist monk explains that the Buddha instructed monks to live in mansions, to sleep on good beds, to eat good food in the morning, to drink delicious beverages in the afternoon, to chew perfumed leaves, and to wear comfortable clothes. He is puzzled that he has found no instructions requiring that monks marry and drink liquor. He suspects that the Buddha did indeed direct monks to do so, but that old monks, jealous of young monks, had removed these rules from the monastic code. The monk sets out in search of the complete and unedited scripture.

The most famous fictional monk in Asian literature is named Tripitaka, the protagonist of Wu Cheng'en's *Journey to the West*, a Chinese comic novel of the sixteenth century. As in Xuanzang's account of his famous pilgrimage (see *The Great Tang Dynasty Record of the Western World*, p. 511), "the West" is India. Indeed, the novel is inspired by Xuanzang's famous journey. Yet whereas Xuanzang traveled largely alone, heroically facing all manner of obstacles, Tripitaka is hardly heroic. He is well-meaning but weak; though pious and learned, he is inexperienced in the ways of the world, dissolving into tears at the slightest difficulty. He would never have been able to make it to India alone. Fortunately, he is protected by the bodhisattva of compassion, Avalokiteshvara (Guanshiyin), who provides him with a bodyguard, a mischievous monkey endowed with a wide range of magical powers. Along the way, they are joined by three other companions: a pig, a river ogre, and a dragon prince in the form of a white horse. The novel recounts their many adventures as they go to India in search of scriptures. Although not intended for children, the novel is among the most famous children's stories in East Asia; certain chapters in particular have been retold countless times, including in comic books and cartoons.

In the passage below, the pilgrims finally reach India, where they find the Buddha still living. He compassionately allows them to select whichever scriptures they like to take back to China. But this task turns out to be more difficult than they imagined. In the story, the monkey is called Pilgrim, Pilgrim Sun, and Wukong; the pig is called Bajie; and the river ogre is called Sha Monk.

PRONOUNCING GLOSSARY

Avichi: *a-vee-chi*
Bajie: *bah-jyeh*
Dipankara: *dee-pan-ka-ra*
Guanshiyin: *gwahn-sher-een*
Jambudvipa: *jam-bu-dvee-pa*
Kashyapa: *kah-shya-pa*
Sha: *shah*
Shakyamuni: *shah-kya-mu-ni*
shastra: *shah-stra*
Shramana: *shrah-ma-na*
Shravasti: *shrah-va-stee*
Sun: *soon*

Tang: *tahng*
Tathagata: *ta-tah-ga-ta*
upasaka: *u-pah-sa-ka*
upasika: *u-pah-si-kah*
Vairochana: *vai-roh-cha-na*
Wu Cheng 'en: *woo chung-un*
Wujing: *woo-jeeng*
Wukong: *woo-kohng*
Wuneng: *woo-nang*
Xi You Ji: *shee yoo jee*
Xuanzang: *shwehn-tsahng*
Zhao: *jau*

Bending low, Tripitaka said, "Yes, your disciple Xuanzang has arrived." No sooner had he given this reply than he wanted to go inside. "Please wait a moment, Sage Monk," said the Vajra[1] Guardians. "Allow us to announce

TRANSLATED FROM the Chinese by Anthony C. Yu.

1. Usually translated "diamond" or "thunderbolt" (i.e., something unbreakable).

your arrival first before you enter." One of the Vajra Guardians was asked to report to the other Four Great Vajra Guardians stationed at the second gate, and one of those porters passed the news of the Tang monk's arrival to the third gate. Those guarding the third gate happened to be divine monks who served at the great altar. When they heard the news, they quickly went to the Great Hero Hall to announce to Tathagata, the Most Honored One, also named Buddha Shakyamuni,[2] "The sage monk from the Tang court has arrived in this treasure monastery. He has come to fetch the scriptures."

Highly pleased, Holy Father Buddha at once asked the Eight Bodhisattvas, the Four Vajra Guardians, the Five Hundred Arhats,[3] the Three Thousand Guardians, the Eleven Great Orbs, and the Eighteen Guardians of Monasteries to form two rows for the reception. Then he issued the golden decree to summon in the Tang monk. Again the word was passed from section to section, from gate to gate: "Let the sage monk enter." Meticulously observing the rules of ritual propriety, our Tang monk walked through the monastery gate with Wukong, Wuneng, and Wujing, still leading the horse and toting the luggage. Thus it was that

> Commissioned that year, a resolve he made
> To leave with rescript the royal steps of jade.
> The hills he'd climb to face the morning dew
> Or rest on a boulder when the twilight fades.
> He totes his faith to ford three thousand streams,
> His staff trailing o'er endless palisades.
> His every thought's on seeking the right fruit.
> Homage to Buddha will this day be paid.

The four pilgrims, on reaching the Great Hero Treasure Hall, prostrated themselves before Tathagata. Thereafter, they bowed to all the attendants of Buddha on the left and right. This they repeated three times before kneeling again before the Buddhist Patriarch to present their traveling rescript to him. After reading it carefully, Tathagata handed it back to Tripitaka, who touched his head to the ground once more to say, "By the decree of the Great Tang Emperor in the Land of the East, your disciple Xuanzang has come to this treasure monastery to beg you for the true scriptures for the redemption of the multitude. I implore the Buddhist Patriarch to vouchsafe his grace and grant me my wish, so that I may soon return to my country."

To express the compassion of his heart, Tathagata opened his mouth of mercy and said to Tripitaka, "Your Land of the East belongs to the South Jambudvipa Continent.[4] Because of your size and your fertile land, your prosperity and population, there is a great deal of greed and killing, lust and lying, oppression and deceit. People neither honor the teachings of Buddha nor cultivate virtuous karma; they neither revere the three lights nor respect the five grains. They are disloyal and unfilial, unrighteous and unkind, unscrupulous and self-deceiving. Through all manners of injustice and taking of

---

2. Literally, "Sage of the Shakyas"; a title of the Buddha, who was born into the Shakya clan. "Tathagata": a title of a buddha (literally, "one who has thus come/gone"); it is the one most often used by the historical Buddha to refer to himself.
3. Those who will enter nirvana at death.
4. The continent on which ordinary humans dwell.

lives, they have committed boundless transgressions. The fullness of their iniquities therefore has brought on them the ordeal of hell and sent them into eternal darkness and perdition to suffer the pains of pounding and grinding and of being transformed into beasts. Many of them will assume the forms of creatures with fur and horns; in this manner they will repay their debts by having their flesh made for food for mankind. These are the reasons for their eternal perdition in Avichi[5] without deliverance.

"Though Confucius[6] had promoted his teachings of benevolence, righteousness, ritual, and wisdom, and though a succession of kings and emperors had established such penalties as transportation, banishment, hanging, and beheading, these institutions had little effect on the foolish and the blind, the reckless and the antinomian.

"Now, I have here three baskets of scriptures which can deliver humanity from its afflictions and dispel its calamities. There is one basket of vinaya, which speak of Heaven; a basket of shastras,[7] which tell of the Earth; and a basket of sutras, which redeem the damned. Altogether these three baskets of scriptures contain thirty-five titles written in fifteen thousand one hundred and forty-four scrolls. They are truly the pathway to the realization of immortality and the gate to ultimate virtue. Every concern of astronomy, geography, biography, flora and fauna, utensils, and human affairs within the Four Great Continents of this world is recorded therein. Since all of you have traveled such a great distance to come here, I would have liked to give the entire set to you. Unfortunately, the people of your region are both stupid and headstrong. Mocking the true words, they refuse to recognize the profound significance of our teachings of shramana."[8]

Then Buddha turned to call out: "Ananda and Kashyapa,[9] take the four of them to the space beneath the precious tower. Give them a vegetarian meal first. After the maigre,[1] open our treasure loft for them and select a few scrolls from each of the thirty-five divisions of our three canons, so that they may take them back to the Land of the East as a perpetual token of grace."

The two Honored Ones obeyed and took the four pilgrims to the space beneath the tower, where countless rare dainties and exotic treasures were laid out in a seemingly endless spread. Those deities in charge of offerings and sacrifices began to serve a magnificent feast of divine food, tea, and fruit—viands of a hundred flavors completely different from those of the mortal world. After master and disciples had bowed to give thanks to Buddha, they abandoned themselves to enjoyment. In truth

> Treasure flames, gold beams on their eyes have shined;
> Strange fragrance and feed even more refined.
> Boundlessly fair the tow'r of gold appears;
> There's immortal music that clears the ears.
> Such divine fare and flower humans rarely see;

---

5. The most painful of the eight hot Buddhist hells.
6. The Chinese philosopher Kongfuzi (Master Kong, 551–479 B.C.E.); for centuries, the works attributed to him supported the Chinese state ideology.
7. "Treatises": works on Buddhist doctrine, some-

times in the form of a commentary on a sutra. "Vinaya": literally, "discipline" (Sanskrit), the ethical code followed by monks and nuns.
8. Here, the Buddha (an ascetic or mendicant).
9. Two of the Buddha's senior disciples. Ananda was the Buddha's cousin and personal attendant.
1. A meal that contains no dishes of flesh.

Long life's attained through strange food and fragrant tea.
Long have they endured a thousand forms of pain.
This day in glory the Way they're glad to gain.

This time it was Bajie who was in luck and Sha Monk who had the advantage, for what the Buddhist Patriarch had provided for their complete enjoyment was nothing less than such viands as could grant them longevity and health and enable them to transform their mortal substance into immortal flesh and bones.

When the four pilgrims had finished their meal, the two Honored Ones who had kept them company led them up to the treasure loft. The moment the door was opened, they found the room enveloped in a thousand layers of auspicious air and magic beams, in ten thousand folds of colored fog and hallowed clouds. On the sutra cases and jeweled chests red labels were attached, on which the titles of the books were written in clerkly script. After Ananda and Kashyapa had shown all the titles to the Tang monk, they said to him, "Sage Monk, having come all this distance from the Land of the East, what sort of small gifts have you brought for us? Take them out quickly! We'll be pleased to hand over the scriptures to you."

On hearing this, Tripitaka said, "Because of the great distance, your disciple, Xuanzang, has not been able to make such preparation."

"How nice! How nice!" said the two Honored Ones, snickering. "If we imparted the scriptures to you gratis, our posterity would starve to death!"

When Pilgrim saw them fidgeting and fussing, refusing to hand over the scriptures, he could not refrain from yelling, "Master, let's go tell Tathagata about this! Let's make him come himself and hand over the scriptures to old Monkey!"

"Stop shouting!" said Ananda. "Where do you think you are that you dare indulge in such mischief and waggery? Get over here and receive the scriptures!" Controlling their annoyance, Bajie and Sha Monk managed to restrain Pilgrim before they turned to receive the books. Scroll after scroll were wrapped and laid on the horse. Four additional luggage wraps were bundled up for Bajie and Sha Monk to tote, after which the pilgrims went before the jeweled throne again to kowtow and thank Tathagata. As they walked out the gates of the monastery, they bowed twice whenever they came upon a Buddhist Patriarch or a Bodhisattva. When they reached the main gate, they also bowed to take leave of the priests and nuns, the upasakas and upasikas,[2] before descending the mountain. We shall now leave them for the moment.

We tell you now that there was up in the treasure loft the aged Dipankara, also named the Buddha of the Past, who overheard everything and understood immediately that Ananda and Kashyapa had handed over to the pilgrims scrolls of scriptures that were actually wordless. Chuckling to himself, he said, "Most of the priests in the Land of the East are so stupid and blind that they will not recognize the value of these wordless scriptures. When that happens, won't it have made this long trek of our sage monk completely worthless?" Then he asked, "Who is here beside my throne?"

2. Buddhist laymen and laywomen.

The White Heroic Honored One at once stepped forth, and the aged Buddha gave him this instruction: "You must exercise your magic powers and catch up with the Tang monk immediately. Take away those wordless scriptures from him, so that he will be forced to return for the true scriptures with words." Mounting a violent gust of wind, the White Heroic Honored One swept out of the gate of the Thunderclap Monastery. As he called up his vast magic powers, the wind was strong indeed! Truly

> A stalwart Servant of Buddha
> Is not like any common wind god;
> The wrathful cries of an immortal
> Far surpass a young girl's whistle!
> This mighty gust
> Causes fishes and dragons to lose their lairs
> And angry waves in the rivers and seas.
> Black apes find it hard to present their fruits;
> Yellow cranes turn around to seek their nests.
> The phoenix's pure cries have lost their songs;
> The pheasant's callings turn most boisterous.
> Green pine-branches snap;
> Blue lotus-blossoms soar.
> Stalk by stalk, verdant bamboos fall;
> Petal by petal, gold lotus quakes.
> Bell tones drift away to three thousand miles;
> The scripture chants o'er countless gorges fly.
> Beneath the cliff rare flowers' colors fade;
> Fresh, jadelike grasses lie down by the road.
> Phoenixes can't stretch their wings;
> White deer hide on the ledge.
> Vast waves of strange fragrance now fill the world
> As cool, clear breezes penetrate the Heavens.

The elder Tang was walking along when he encountered this churning fragrant wind. Thinking that this was only an auspicious portent sent by the Buddhist Patriarch, he was completely off guard when, with a loud crack in midair, a hand descended. The scriptures that were loaded on the horse were lifted away with no effort at all. The sight left Tripitaka yelling in terror and beating his breast, while Bajie rolled off in pursuit on the ground and Sha Monk stood rigid to guard the empty pannier. Pilgrim Sun vaulted into the air. When that White Heroic Honored One saw him closing in rapidly, he feared that Pilgrim's rod might strike out blindly without regard for good or ill to cause him injury. He therefore ripped the scriptures open and threw them toward the ground. When Pilgrim saw that the scripture wrappers were torn and their contents scattered all over by the fragrant wind, he lowered the direction of his cloud to go after the books instead and stopped his pursuit. The White Heroic Honored One retrieved the wind and fog and returned to report to the Buddha of the Past.

As Bajie sped along, he saw the holy books dropping down from the sky. Soon he was joined by Pilgrim, and the two of them gathered up the scrolls to go back to the Tang monk. His eyes brimming with tears, the Tang monk said, "O Disciples! We are bullied by vicious demons even in this land of ultimate bliss!" When Sha Monk opened up a scroll of scripture which the other two disciples were clutching, his eyes perceived only snow-white paper without a trace of so much as half a letter on it. Hurriedly he presented it to Tripitaka, saying, "Master, this scroll is wordless!" Pilgrim also opened a scroll and it, too, was wordless. Then Bajie opened still another scroll, and it was also wordless. "Open all of them!" cried Tripitaka. Every scroll had only blank paper.

Heaving big sighs, the elder said, "Our people in the Land of the East simply have no luck! What good is it to take back a wordless, empty volume like this? How could I possibly face the Tang emperor? The crime of mocking one's ruler is greater than one punishable by execution!"

Already perceiving the truth of the matter, Pilgrim said to the Tang monk, "Master, there's no need for further talk. This has all come about because we had no gifts for these fellows, Ananda and Kashyapa. That's why we were given these wordless texts. Let's go back quickly to Tathagata and charge them with fraud and solicitation for a bribe."

"Exactly! Exactly!" yelled Bajie. "Let's go and charge them!" The four pilgrims turned and, with painful steps, once more ascended Thunderclap.

In a little while they reached the temple gates, where they were met by the multitude with hands folded in their sleeves. "Has the sage monk returned to ask for an exchange of scriptures?" they asked, laughing. Tripitaka nodded his affirmation, and the Vajra Guardians permitted them to go straight inside. When they arrived before the Great Hero Hall, Pilgrim shouted, "Tathagata, we master and disciples had to experience ten thousand stings and a thousand demons in order to come bowing from the Land of the East. After you had specifically ordered the scriptures to be given to us, Ananda and Kashyapa sought a bribe from us; when they didn't succeed, they conspired in fraud and deliberately handed over wordless texts to us. Even if we took them, what good would they do? Pardon me, Tathagata, but you must deal with this matter!"

"Stop shouting!" said the Buddhist Patriarch with a chuckle. "I knew already that the two of them would ask you for a little present. After all, the holy scriptures are not to be given lightly, nor are they to be received gratis. Some time ago, in fact, a few of our sage priests went down the mountain and recited these scriptures in the house of one Elder Zhao in the Kingdom of Shravasti,[3] so that the living in his family would all be protected from harm and the deceased redeemed from perdition. For all that service they managed to charge him only three pecks and three pints of rice. I told them that they had made far too cheap a sale and that their posterity would have no money to spend. Since you people came with empty hands to acquire scriptures, blank texts were handed over to you. But these blank texts are actually true, wordless scriptures, and they are just as good as those with words. However, those creatures in your Land of the East are so foolish and unenlightened that I have no choice but to impart to you now the texts with words."

"Ananda and Kashyapa," he then called out, "quickly select for them a few scrolls from each of the titles of true scriptures with words, and then come back to me to report the total number."

3. In modern-day Uttar Pradesh.

The two Honored Ones again led the four pilgrims to the treasure loft, where they once more demanded a gift from the Tang monk. Since he had virtually nothing to offer, Tripitaka told Sha Monk to take out the alms bowl of purple gold. With both hands he presented it to the Honored Ones, saying, "Your disciple in truth has not brought with him any gift, owing to the great distance and my own poverty. This alms bowl, however, was bestowed by the Tang emperor in person, in order that I could use it to beg for my maigre, throughout the journey. As the humblest token of my gratitude, I am presenting it to you now, and I beg the Honored Ones to accept it. When I return to the court and make my report to the Tang emperor, a generous reward will certainly be forthcoming. Only grant us the true scriptures with words, so that His Majesty's goodwill will not be thwarted nor the labor of this lengthy journey be wasted." With a gentle smile, Ananda took the alms bowl. All those vira[4] who guarded the precious towers, the kitchen helpers in charge of sacrifices and incense, and the Honored Ones who worked in the treasure loft began to clap one another on the back and tickle one another on the face. Snapping their fingers and curling their lips, every one of them said, "How shameless! How shameless! Asking the scripture seeker for a present!"

After a while, the two Honored Ones became rather embarrassed, though Ananda continued to clutch firmly at the alms bowl. Kashyapa, however, went into the loft to select the scrolls and handed them item by item to Tripitaka. "Disciples," said Tripitaka, "take a good look at these, and make sure that they are not like the earlier ones."

The three disciples examined each scroll as they received it, and this time all the scrolls had words written on them. Altogether they were given five thousand and forty-eight scrolls, making up the number of a single canon. After being properly packed, the scriptures were loaded onto the horse. An additional load was made for Bajie to tote, while their own luggage was toted by Sha Monk. As Pilgrim led the horse, the Tang monk took up his priestly staff and gave his Vairochana hat[5] a press and his brocade cassock a shake. In delight they once more went before our Buddha Tathagata. Thus it is that

> Sweet is the taste of the Great Pitaka,[6]
> Product most refined of Tathagata.
> Note how Xuanzang has climbed the mount with pain.
> Pity Ananda who has but love of gain.
> Their blindness removed by Buddha of the Past,
> The truth now received peace they have at last—
> Glad to bring scriptures back to the East,
> Where all may partake of this gracious feast.

Ananda and Kashyapa led the Tang monk before Tathagata, who ascended the lofty lotus throne. He ordered Dragon-Tamer and Tiger-Subduer, the two arhats, to strike up the cloudy stone-chime to assemble all the divinities, including the three thousand Buddhas, the three thousand guardians, the Eight Vajra Guardians, the five hundred arhats, the eight hundred nuns and

---

4. Retainers.
5. The hat of a head monk (Vairochana was a buddha).
6. Collection of scriptures (lit., "basket"; Sanskrit).

priests, the upasakas and upasikas, the Honored Ones from every Heaven and cave-dwelling, from every blessed land and spirit mountain. Those who ought to be seated were asked to ascend their treasure thrones, while those who should stand were told to make two columns on both sides. In a moment celestial music filled the air as layers of auspicious luminosity and hallowed mist loomed up in the sky. After all the Buddhas had assembled, they bowed to greet Tathagata.

Then Tathagata asked, "Ananda and Kashyapa, how many scrolls of scriptures have you passed on to him? Give me an itemized report."

The two Honored Ones said, "We have turned over to the Tang court the following:

1.	*The Nirvana Sutra*	400 scrolls
2.	*The Akashagarbha-bodhisattva-dharmi Sutra*	20 scrolls
3.	*The Gracious Will Sutra, Major Collection*	40 scrolls
4.	*The Prajnaparamita-samkaya gatha Sutra*	20 scrolls
5.	*The Homage to Bhutatathata Sutra*	20 scrolls
6.	*The Anakshara-granthaka-rochana-garbha Sutra*	50 scrolls
7.	*The Vimalakirti-nirdesha Sutra*	30 scrolls
8.	*The Vajracchedika-prajnaparamita Sutra*	1 scroll
9.	*The Buddha-charita-kavya Sutra*	116 scrolls
10.	*The Bodhisattva-pitaka Sutra*	360 scrolls
11.	*The Surangama-samadhi Sutra*	30 scrolls
12.	*The Arthavinishcaya-dharmaparyaya Sutra*	40 scrolls
13.	*The Avatamsaka Sutra*	81 scrolls
14.	*The Mahaprajna-paramita Sutra*	600 scrolls
15.	*The Abuta-dharma Sutra*	550 scrolls
16.	*The Other Madhyamika Sutra*	42 scrolls
17.	*The Kashyapa-parivarta Sutra*	20 scrolls
18.	*The Pancha-naga Sutra*	20 scrolls
19.	*The Bodhisattva-charya-nirdesha Sutra*	60 scrolls
20.	*The Magadha Sutra*	140 scrolls
21.	*The Maya-dalamahatantra mahayana-gambhira naya-guhya-parashi Sutra*	30 scrolls
22.	*The Western Heaven Shastra*	30 scrolls
23.	*The Buddha-kshetra Sutra*	1,638 scrolls
24.	*The Mahaprajnaparamita Shastra*	90 scrolls
25.	*The Original Loft Sutra*	56 scrolls
26.	*The Mahamayurti-vidyarajni Sutra*	14 scrolls
27.	*The Abhidharma-kosha Shastra*	10 scrolls
28.	*The Mahasamghata Sutra*	30 scrolls
29.	*The Saddharma-pundarika Sutra*	10 scrolls
30.	*The Precious Permanence Sutra*	170 scrolls
31.	*The Sanghika-vinaya Sutra*	110 scrolls
32.	*The Mahayana-shraddhotpada Shastra*	50 scrolls
33.	*The Precious Authority Sutra*	140 scrolls
34.	*The Correct Commandment Sutra*	10 scrolls
35.	*The Vidya-matra-siddhi Shastra*	10 scrolls

From the thirty-five titles of scriptures that are in the treasury, we have selected altogether five thousand and forty-eight scrolls for the sage monk to take back to the Tang in the Land of the East. Most of these have been properly packed and loaded on the horse, and a few have also been arranged in a pannier. The pilgrims now wish to express their thanks to you."

Having tethered the horse and set down the poles, Tripitaka led his three disciples to bow to Buddha, each pressing his palms together in front of him. Tathagata said to the Tang monk, "The efficacy of these scriptures cannot be measured. Not only are they the mirror of our faith, but they are also the source of the Three Religions. They must not be lightly handled, especially when you return to your South Jambudvipa Continent and display them to the multitude. No one should open a scroll without fasting and bathing first. Treasure them! Honor them! Therein will be found the mysteries of gaining immortality and comprehending the Way, the wondrous formulas for the execution of the thousand transformations." Tripitaka kowtowed to thank him and to express his faith and obedience. As before, he prostrated himself in homage three times to the Buddhist Patriarch with all earnestness and sincerity before he took the scriptures and left. As he went through the three monastery gates, he again thanked each of the sages, and we shall speak no more of him for the moment.

After he had sent away the Tang monk, Tathagata dismissed the assembly for the transmission of scriptures. From one side stepped forth the Bodhisattva Guanshiyin,[7] who pressed her palms together to say to the Buddhist Patriarch, "This disciple received your golden decree that year to search for someone in the Land of the East to be a scripture seeker. Today he has succeeded. Altogether, his journey took fourteen years or five thousand and forty days. Eight more days and the perfect canonical number will be attained. Would you permit me to surrender in return your golden decree?"

Highly pleased, Tathagata said, "What you said is most appropriate. You are certainly permitted to surrender my golden decree." He then gave this instruction to the Eight Vajra Guardians: "Quickly exercise your magic powers to lift the sage monk back to the East. As soon as he has imparted the true scriptures to the people there, bring him back here to the West. You must accomplish all this within eight days, so as to fulfill the perfect canonical number of five thousand and forty-eight. Do not delay." The Vajra Guardians at once caught up with the Tang monk, crying, "Scripture seekers, follow us!" The Tang monk and his companions, all with healthy frames and buoyant bodies, followed the Vajra Guardians to rise in the air astride the clouds. Truly

> Their minds enlightened, they bowed to Buddha;
> Merit perfected, they ascended on high.

We do not know how they will pass on the scriptures after they have returned to the Land of the East; let's listen to the explanation in the next chapter.

---

7. See the introduction to the following selection.

THE BODHISATTVA WHO BESTOWS CHILDREN

DHARANI SUTRA OF FIVE MUDRAS OF THE GREAT COMPASSIONATE WHITE-ROBED ONE
(*Baiyi Dabei Wuyinxin Tuoluoni Jing*)

The twenty-fifth chapter of the *Lotus Sutra* (see the *Saddharmapundarika*, p. 278) is devoted to a figure who would become the most famous of all the bodhisattvas in Mahayana Buddhism, Avalokiteshvara. In Sanskrit, his name means the "Lord Who Looks Down." His name was rendered into Chinese as Guanshiyin (shortened to Guanyin), meaning "He Who Observes the Sounds of the World." In Japanese, the Chinese characters *guanyin* are pronounced "Kannon."

Much of the *Lotus Sutra*'s fame in East Asia derives from this brief chapter, likely an interpolation into the earlier text of the sutra. In it, the Buddha explains that if those in distress single-mindedly call his name, this bodhisattva will rescue them from all forms of harm, including fire, flood, shipwreck, murderers, demons, prison, bandits, and wild animals. The chapter became so popular that it often circulated as an independent text, memorized by many. In China, it was considered a great act of piety to copy the sutra, and some even wrote it in their own blood. In the centuries after the sutra was translated into Chinese, miracle stories and testimonials began to circulate about the bodhisattva's wondrous powers; these stories form an important genre of Buddhist literature in East Asia.

In the twenty-fifth chapter of the *Lotus Sutra*, the Buddha declares, "If any woman wanting to have a baby boy pays homage and makes offerings to the bodhisattva Avalokiteshvara, she will bear a baby boy endowed with good merit and wisdom. If she wants to have a baby girl, she will bear a beautiful and handsome baby girl who has planted roots of good merit and will have the love of sentient beings." In the *Lotus Sutra*, and in Tibetan Buddhism to this day, Avalokiteshvara is a male bodhisattva (and is male in the early centuries of Buddhism in China); by the tenth century, however, Guanyin began to take on female characteristics in China and East Asia. By the sixteenth century, Guanyin was a female bodhisattva, described in early and subsequent Western sources as the "Goddess of Mercy." Indeed, the Roman Catholic missionaries to China who encountered images of this deity, wrapped in a flowing hooded robe and holding an infant, wondered whether she was a version of the Virgin Mary. Scholars are still not entirely sure how and why this change in gender took place; that the *Lotus Sutra* lists the bestowal of children among Avalokiteshvara's many powers suggests one reason. But Guanyin does appear to have represented a new kind of deity in the history of China: a universal savior who responded to the prayers of everyone, male and female, rich and poor, educated and uneducated, saint and sinner.

The "White-Robed" Guanyin became an object of particular devotion for her power to grant sons; the appearance of a white placenta around a baby boy was viewed as a sign of her intercession. Apocryphal scriptures began to be composed in her honor. One of these, from the tenth century at the latest, is titled the *Dharani Sutra of Five Mudras of the Great Compassionate White-Robed One (Baiyi Dabei Wuyinxin Tuoluoni Jing)*. Such texts, distributed free of charge as a way of making merit for the donor, were often printed with testimonials to their efficacy appended at the end. Here, the apocryphal scripture from a 1609 printing is provided, followed by some testimonials.

PRONOUNCING GLOSSARY

Amitabha Buddha: *a-mi-tah-ba bud-da*
Amoghavajra: *a-moh-ga-vaj-ra*
Anhui: *ahn-hway*
baiyizi: *bai-ee-tsa*
Baiyi Dabei Wuyinxin Tuoluoni Jing:
  bai-yee da-bay wu-yin-shin tuo-luo-jing
Bao-yue-zhi-yan-guang-yin-zi-zai-wang:
  bau-yooeh-jer-yehn-gwahng-een-tsu-tsai-wahng
bodhisattva: *boh-di-sat-tva*
Changshu: *chahng-shoo*
Chongle: *chohng-la*
Daxing: *dah-sheeng*
Dharani Sutra: *dah-ra-nee soo-tra*
Ding Xian: *deeng shyehn*
Fangyan: *fahng-yehn*
gatha: *gah-tah*
Gengxian: *gang-shyehn*
Guanshiyin: *gwahn-sher-een*
Guanyin: *gwahn-een*
Henan: *ha-nahn*
Hengyang: *hang-yahng*
hou: *hoh*
Hui: *hway*
jiangning: *jyahng-neeng*
Jiangsu: *jyahng-soo*
Jiashan: *jyah-shahn*
Li Boshu: *lee boh-shoo*
Liu: *lyoh*
Longhua: *lohng-hwah*
Maoyuan: *mau-yoo-ehn*

mou: *moh*
Po-lu-jie-di: *poh-loo-jyeh-dee*
Pujiang: *poo-jyahng*
Qingjiang: *cheeng-jyahng*
Qu: *choo*
Qu Ruji: *choo roo-jee*
Shangbei: *shahng-bay*
She: *sha*
shengnu: *shang-noo*
Sheng-sengnu: *shang-sang-noo*
Subhakarasimha: *su-bah-ka-ra-sim-ha*
Tathagata: *ta-tah-ga-ta*
Wang Mengbai: *wahng mang-bai*
Wang Qishan; *wahng chee-shahn*
Wang Xin: *wahng sheen*
Wang Yinlin: *wahng een-leen*
Xing Jian: *sheeng jyehn*
Xu: *shoo*
Xu Wenqing: *shoo wan-cheeng*
Yan Daoche: *yehn dau-cha*
Yibin: *ee-been*
Ying: *eeng*
Yuan Huang: *yoo-ehn hwahng*
Yuansheng; *yoo-ehn-shang*
Yu Muzhai: *yoo moo-jai*
Yungfeng: *yoong-fang*
Yu Zhongpu: *yoo johng-poo*
Zhao: *jau*
Zhao Yungxian: *jau yoong-shyehn*
Zhejiang: *ja-jyahng*
Zheng: *jang*
Zheng Zhili: *jang jer-lee*

The mantra which purifies the karma of the mouth: An-xiu-li, xin-li, mo-ke-xiu-li, xiu-li, xiu-xiu-li, suo-po-ke [svaha[1]].
The mantra which pacifies the earth: Nan-wu-san-man-duo, mo-tuo-nan, an-du-lu-du-lu-di-wei, suo-po-ke.

The sutra-opening gatha:[2]

The subtle and wondrous dharma of utmost profundity
Is difficult to encounter during millions, nay, billions of kalpas.[3]
Now that I have heard it [with my own ears], I will take it securely
  to heart
And hope I can understand the true meaning of the Tathagata.[4]

TRANSLATED FROM the Chinese by Chun-fang Yu. All bracketed additions are the translator's.

1. A capping word in many mantras (similar to the Hebrew *amen*).
2. Verse.
3. Aeons, or cosmic cycles.

4. A title of a buddha (literally, "one who has thus come/gone"); it is the one most often used by the historical Buddha to refer to himself.

Invocation:

> Bowing my head to the Great Compassionate One, Po-lu-jie-di
> Practicing meditation with the sense of hearing, [the bodhisattva]
>   entered samadhi[5]
> Raising the sound of the tide of the ocean,
> Responding to the needs of the world.
> No matter what one wishes to obtain
> [She] will unfailingly grant its fulfillment.

> Homage to the Original Teacher Shakyamuni Buddha[6]
> Homage to the Original Teacher Amitabha Buddha[7]
> Homage to the Bao-yue-zhi-yan-guang-yin-zi-zai-wang (Lord Ishvara[8]
>   Buddha of Precious-Moon Wisdom-Splendor-Light-Sound)
> Homage to Great Compassionate Guanshiyin Bodhisattva
> Homage to White-robed Guanshiyin Bodhisattva
> Front mudra,[9] back mudra, mudra of subduing demons, mind mudra,
>   body mudra.

Dharani[1] I now recite the divine mantra. I beseech the Compassionate One to descend and protect my thought. Here then is the mantra:

> Nan-wu he-la-da-na, shao-la-ye-ye, nan-wu a-li-ye, po-lu-jie-ti,
>   shao-bo-la-ye, pu-ti-sa-duo-po-ye, mo-ke-jie-lu-ni-jia-ye,
>   an-duo-li, duo-li, du-duo-li, du-du-duo-li, suo-po-ke.

When you ask someone else to chant the dharani, the effect is the same as when you chant it yourself.

Evidence Attesting to the Miraculous Responses of the White-robed Guanshiyin Bodhisattva

Formerly a scholar of Hengyang (in present Hunan Province) was already advanced in age but still had no son. He prayed everywhere for an heir. One day he met an old monk who handed him this sutra, saying, "The Buddha preached this sutra. If a person is capable of keeping it, he will receive responses in accordance with his wish and obtain unlimited blessing. If he desires to have a son, a boy of wisdom will be born to him. The baby will show the wonder of being wrapped in a white placenta." The man and his wife chanted this sutra with utmost sincerity for one *canon* (5,048 times), and within several years they had three sons who were all born wrapped in white placenta. The governor saw these events with his own eyes and ordered the printing and distributing of this sutra. He also obtained a son before the year was over.

A scholar named Wang Xin and his wife named Zhao of Jiangning (in present Jiangsu Province) had the misfortune of losing several children. In the spring of 1147 they obtained this sutra and chanted it with faith

---

5. A state of deep meditation.
6. The historical Buddha, who was born into the Shakya clan ("Shakyamuni" means "Sage of the Shakyas").
7. The buddha who presides over the Pure Land

(see the *Sukhavativyuha Sutra*, p. 316).
8. Literally, "Lord" or "Master" (Sanskrit).
9. A symbolic hand gesture.
1. A long mantra.

everyday. On the second day of the fourth month in 1148 a son was born to them.

Zheng Zhili of Pujiang, Mao District (province unspecified), was forty years old and still had no heir. In 1207 he decided to print 5,048 copies of this sutra and distribute the copies for free. On the seventh day of the eighth month in 1208 a son was born to him.

Yu Muzhai and his wife Wang of Danyang Village in Maoyuan County (province unspecified) decided to have one thousand copies of this sutra printed and distributed free. In the eighth month of 1250 when the work of distributing was only half completed, a son arrived.

Fangyan and wife Wang of Yungfeng Village, She County (in present Anhui Province) decided to chant this sutra 5,048 times and print one thousand copies for free distribution in the spring of 1254. They had a son in 1255 and named him Wanggu.

Wang Yinlin, who lived in the 6th ward in Chongle City, south of Hui District (in present Anhui Province), had five hundred copies of this sutra printed and distributed. A son was born to him in the hour of *mou* on the twenty-first day of the fifth month in 1269 and was given the name Yinsun. A pious woman named Zheng who lived in the third ward of the north side of Shangbei City of the same district became seriously ill in the first month of 1274 when she was a young girl. She burned incense and promised to have one thousand copies of the sutra printed and distributed free. At night she dreamt of two monks who came to protect her. She recovered from the illness.

Wang Yuyu lived in Daning ward in Nanjing and was forty years old but still had no son. He prayed to various gods but had no success. One day in the latter half of the tenth month in 1265 he received this sutra from his friend Ma, who kept it enshrined in front of the Guanyin image on his family altar. Wang chanted it every day without interruption. On the night of the fourteenth day in the fourth month, 1267, his wife née Liu dreamt of a person in white who, wearing a golden crown and accompanied by a boy, said to her, "I am delivering to you a holy slave (*shengnu*)." Liu accepted the boy, and upon waking up the next morning she gave birth to a baby boy who was handsome and wrapped in white placenta. They named him Slave of Holy Monk (Sheng-sengnu).

Wang Mengbai, a metropolitan graduate from Qingjiang (in present Jiangxi Province) was born because his parents faithfully chanted this sutra. When he was born, he had the manifestation of the "white robe." He himself also chanted the sutra and in 1214 had a "white-robed son (*baiyizi*)" whom he named Further Manifestation (Gengxian).

Xie Congning, a native of Guangyang (Daxing, the capital) who served as a staffer in the Central Drafting Office, came from a family which had only one son for the past five generations. In 1579 he and his wife, née Gao, started to chant the sutra, which they had also printed and distributed for free. In 1582 they had a son whom they named Gu, in 1585 another son whom they named Lu, and in 1586 twin boys Qu and Ying. All were born with double white placentas.

Ding Xian of Yibin, Nanyang (in present Henan Province), was fifty years old and had no son. So he decided to print this sutra and distribute it for free. He also had a thousand catties of iron melted down in the south garden of the city to make a gilded image of Guanyin. It stood over six feet. At the same time, in order to seek for a son, Xing Jian, the grand commandant, had a shrine dedicated to the White-robed Guanyin erected in the northern part of the city. So the image was moved there to be worshiped. The local official set aside several thousand acres of good farmland to provide for the shrine's upkeep so that people could continue to offer incense in future generations. Not long after this, one night Ding dreamt of a woman who presented him with a white carp. On the next morning, a son was born wrapped in a white placenta. That was the fourth day of the twelfth month, 1583. Earlier, when the image was moved to the White-robed Guanyin Shrine, the gardener had a dream in which the bodhisattva appeared to him looking rather unhappy. When he told Ding about his dream, Ding had another image cast that looked exactly like the first one in the south garden. He invited a monk of repute to stay in the temple to take care of it. He subsequently dreamt of an old man wearing a white gown who came to visit him. The day after he had this dream, while he was relating it to his friend, a man suddenly came to the house seeking to sell the woodblocks of this sutra. Ding bought them and printed a thousand copies for distribution. He also hired a skilled painter to paint several hundred paintings of the White-robed Guanyin to give to the faithful as gifts. In the fourth month of 1586, he had another son. By then, Xing Jian, the grand commandant, had also had a son and a daughter born to him and his wife.

Zhao Yungxian, the son of a grandee of the Tenth Order (the eleventh highest of twenty titles of honorary nobility conferred on meritorious subjects), was a native of Changshu (in Jiangsu Province). His wife née Chen chanted this sutra with great sincerity. On the sixteenth day of the seventh month in 1586, a daughter was born. She was covered with a piece of cloth as white as snow on her face, head, chest, and back. When the midwife peeled it away, the baby's eyes and eyebrows could then be seen. The parents already had sons, but only this daughter had the miraculous evidence of the "white-cloth." It was for this reason that it was written down.

Yuan Huang, the metropolitan graduate who served in the Ministry of Rites, was a native of Jiashan (in Zhejiang Province). He was forty but had no son. After he chanted this sutra, in 1580 a son was born. He named the son Yuansheng (Born from Universal Penetration) because he believed that the boy was a gift from Guanyin, the Universally Penetrating One. The boy had a very distinguished appearance and was unusually intelligent.

A Postscript to the Sutra Written by Qu Ruji

I began to chant this dharani in the second month of 1580 together with my friends Li Boshu and Yan Daoche. Soon afterward Li had a son, and three years later Yan also had a son. I alone failed to experience a divine response. I often blamed myself for my deep karmic obstructions, for I could not match the two gentlemen in their piety. Then one evening in the third month of 1583 I dreamt that I entered a shrine and a monk said to me, "In chanting the dharani, there is one buddha's name you have not chanted. If you chant it, you shall have a son." Upon waking up, I could not understand what he meant by the missing buddha's name, for I had always chanted the various names of Guanyin on the different festival days of her manifestation. In the winter of 1585 I traveled north and was stuck at a government post-house because the river was frozen. On the twelfth day of the twelfth month I entered a small temple and saw this sutra by the side of the *hou* animal mount on which Guanyin sat. It was donated by Wang Qishan, a judicial clerk. When I opened it to read and saw the name of Lord Ishvara Buddha of Precious-Moon Wisdom-Splendor-Light-Sound, a name of which I had never heard up until that time, I had a sudden realization. I knelt down and kowtowed to the seat. I started to chant the name of the buddha upon returning, and after only three days a son was born. It accorded perfectly with my dream.

In 1586 I went to the capital. Xu Wenqing, Yu Zhongpu, and other friends were all chanting the dharani in order to obtain sons. Yu's wife, furthermore, became pregnant after she had a strange dream. So we discussed plans of printing this sutra to promote its circulation. I had earlier consulted the catalogues of the Northern and Southern Tripitakas (two collections of Buddhist scriptures compiled in the Ming) but did not find it listed in either one. I thought this must be a true elixir of life secretly transmitted by foreign monks. Later Yuan Huang told me that this was actually the same dharani as the *Dharani Conforming to Heart's Desire*, two versions of which were included in the Tripitaka. When I learned about this, I rushed to Longhua Monastery to check the Tripitaka kept in the library. Although there were some variations in the sequence of sentences and the exact wordings of the mantra between the text found in the Tripitaka[2] and the popular printed version, the efficacy of chanting the dharani was universally warranted. I could not help but feeling deeply moved by the wonder of Guanyin's universal responsiveness and divinity of the faithful chanters' sincere minds. The text in the Tripitaka did not just promise sons, but the fulfillment of many other desires in accordance with the wishes of sentient beings. According to the instruction given in the sutra contained in the Tripitaka, this dharani should be revealed only to those who were in possession of great compassion. If given to the wrong person, disastrous results would happen, for bad karma caused by hatred might be created if the person used the dharani to subdue enemies or avenge past wrongs. Taking this warning to heart, my friend Xu and I decided that instead of reprinting the version found in the Tripitaka, we would print the dharani alone together with the stories about obtaining sons included in the popular versions of this text that were in circulation. After fasting and bathing, Xu wrote out the sutra and gave it to an engraver to make the woodblocks for printing.

The term "dharani" means to keep all virtues completely. The extended meaning of the term, then, is the keeping of all virtues. For this reason, the merit of keeping the dharani is indeed limitless. With this Guanyin teaches people to do good. Therefore if the practitioners do good, when they chant the words of the dharani, blessings as numerous as the sands of the Ganges will instantly come to them. But if they do not dedicate them-

2. The Buddhist canon (lit., "the three baskets"; Sanskrit).

selves to goodness, they will lose the basis of the dharani. Even if they chant it, the benefit will be slight. I cannot claim to have realized this ideal, but I am willing to work hard toward it together with fellow practitioners. The conventional view of the world says that the ordinary people are totally different from sages and people cannot be transformed into holy persons. Because they narrow their potentiality this way, they cannot keep the dharani. On the other hand, if people fall into the other extreme of nihilism and think that in emptiness there is no law of causality, they also cannot keep the dharani because of their recklessness. When one realizes that the common man and the sage possess the same mind and there is not the slightest difference at all, one has left the conventional view. When one realizes that this one mind can manifest as either ordinary or saintly and this is due to the clear working of the law of causality, one has then left the nihilistic view. Leaving behind these two erroneous views and following the one mind in teaching the world, one can then chant the dharani. Like blowing on the bellows for wind or striking the flint for fire, the effect will be unfailingly efficacious.

A Postscript Written by Yan Daoche after Printing the Sutra

The *Dharani of the White-Robed Guanyin* was not included in the Southern and Northern Tripitaka collections. Its miraculous efficacy in obtaining whatever one wishes, however, and more particularly sons, has been vouchsafed in the world for a long time. Is it because Indian monks such as Subhakarasimha and Amoghavajra (tantric masters active in the eighth century) transmitted this sutra to gentlewomen in China who then kept it secretly, that, although it was not introduced into the canon collection, it has come down to us because of the many miracles connected with it? Or is it because Guanyin revealed her teaching in accordance with the audience and the old monk of Hengyang was actually her transformation? I do not know. I do know that originally I did not have a son, but after my wife and I chanted this sutra for three years, in 1582 we had two sons in quick succession. That is why I am now having the sutra printed and distributed for free in order to fulfill my earlier vow.

The keeping of the dharani is actually not limited to the vocal chanting of the dharani. To believe in the Buddha constantly, to listen to the dharma with pleasure, to serve people, to have a straight mind and a deep mind, to be vigorous in one's practice, to give donations generously, to observe strictly the precepts, to sit in meditation with unperturbed mind, to subdue all evils and cut off all passions, to be patient and gentle in adversities, and to help bad friends but draw near to good friends—all these are meant by "keeping the dharani." I am keenly aware of my own inferior qualities and cannot attain even one iota of the true way of keeping the dharani as I outlined above. Nevertheless, I am trying my best. Since I started to chant the dharani, I have insisted on observing the precept against killing. This precepts heads the list of the perfection of discipline. If you want to have a son of your own, how can you bear to take another life? When you fail to obtain any response by merely mouthing the dharani, you may begin to doubt and want to stop. This then is to commit a blasphemy against the Buddha with your body. I ask all good friends in Buddhism who want to chant this sutra to begin by observing one precept. Gradually you can extend to all precepts. You start with one goodness and extend to all goodness. This will be the real keeping of the dharani. When this is done, not only sons but all kinds of marvelous things will be yours as you wish.

Buddhism in
Korea

The traditional date of Buddhism's arrival in Korea is 372 C.E.; in that year a Chinese monk, bearing Buddhist scriptures and images, reached the court of Koguryo, one of the "Three Kingdoms" of the Korean Peninsula, where a religion usually described as "shamanism" was dominant. Just as was the case in Tibet and regions of Southeast Asia, Buddhism brought with it writing, new artistic and architectural forms, calendrical systems, and healing techniques.

In 668 Silla, the southernmost of the Three Kingdoms, united the Korean Peninsula under its rule and Buddhism became the state religion. Monasteries were founded, and Korean monks traveled to China to study the Buddhist scriptures with the leading Chinese scholars of the day; many Korean monks became distinguished scholars of Buddhism in China. This was the period of Wonhyo, who wrote commentaries on many of the most important texts of Mahayana Buddhism; his commentary on *Treatise on the Awakening of Faith* (*Dasheng Qixin Lun*, p. 503) was particularly influential. In the late eighth century, the Chan school, called Son in Korean, was introduced from China.

Perhaps the golden age of Korean Buddhism was the Koryo dynasty, which began in 918. Inspired in part by the general Buddhist belief that the support of the sangha, or Buddhist community, protects the state, Koryo rulers constructed monasteries

Seokguram Buddha. Gyeongbuk, Korea.

and placed monks in influential positions at court. Chinese Buddhist schools, including Tiantai, continued to be introduced, as Korean monks sought ways to integrate the study of scripture with meditation practice. The most influential figure in this effort was the monk Chinul (1158–1210).

The fortunes of Buddhism in Korea plummeted in 1392 when the Koryo dynasty was replaced by the Choson, a dynasty that turned away from Buddhism and to Neo-Confucianism for its state ideology. Buddhist lands were confiscated, monasteries were closed, and monks and nuns were banned from entering the city walls of Seoul. Buddhism survived largely in mountain retreats far from the cities, although the standing of Buddhist monks rose briefly when monk armies fought bravely in a war with Japan in the last decade of the sixteenth century.

The Choson dynasty fell in 1910 when Korea became a Japanese colony, regaining its independence only with the end of World War II. Because the Japanese lifted many of the restrictions against Buddhism that had existed during the Choson period, some Korean monks welcomed their presence. At the same time, however, the Japanese favored their own forms of Buddhism, sending missionaries of branches previously unknown in Korea, such as Pure Land and Nichiren, and imposed reforms that had occurred in Japan in the previous century—notably, allowing monks to marry. Following independence, a struggle occurred between those monks who had remained celibate and those who had married: the latter eventually carried the day, and the Chogye Order became the dominant school of Buddhism in Korea. Since the Korean War, Buddhism and Christianity have often been at odds in the Republic of Korea, with Buddhism experiencing something of a revival in recent decades. According to surveys, about 47 percent of Koreans have no religion; 29 percent are Christians, and 23 percent are Buddhists.

WHY PRACTICE THE DHARMA

AROUSE YOUR MIND AND PRACTICE
(*Palsim Suhaeng Chang*)

WONHYO

During the seventh century, China was the required destination for Korean monks who sought the highest learning. Thus, in 661 a middle-aged man named Wonhyo (617–686) set out with a fellow monk on the long journey to the Tang capital. Their dream was to study with the great master Xuanzang (see *The Great Tang Dynasty Record of the Western World*, p. 511), recently returned from his journey to the West. Along the way, a storm drove them to seek shelter in a large hole dug in the earth. When Wonhyo became thirsty during the night, he took a drink of pure rainwater from what he thought was a gourd. When they awoke in daylight, the two monks found that they had been sleeping in a tomb and that Wonhyo had drunk from a skull. Wonhyo experienced a flash of insight, realizing that all things are the creation of the mind. Although his companion continued on the journey (eventually returning as a master of the Huayan school of Chinese Buddhism), Wonhyo saw no reason to go to China. He remained in Korea, gave up his monk's vows, and lived the rest of his life as a layman.

A prolific author, Wonhyo was said to have written more than eighty works in Chinese, including commentaries on many of the most important sutras and treatises of Mahayana Buddhism. Among his most influential works is his commentary on *Treatise on the Awakening of Faith* (see *Dasheng Qixin Lun*, p. 503), a text that he regarded as the key to resolving doctrinal controversies.

Despite his great learning, Wonhyo was also a beloved man of the people; as he traveled through the villages, singing and dancing, he carried a gourd that he dubbed "Unhindered." The text presented here is one of his few surviving works intended not for the exegete but for the ordinary Buddhist practitioner.

Within the realm of samsara, rebirth as a human is regarded as something precious and rare, for it is as a human that one can take fullest advantage of the teachings of the Buddha. Yet, this opportunity is regularly squandered in the shortsighted pursuit of the ephemeral pleasures of a brief life. Thus, all traditions of Buddhism urge followers to practice the dharma before death arrives and one is blown by the winds of karma to the next lifetime. Wonhyo's brief work is a particularly poetic exhortation. As he writes, "Today, alas, it is already dusk and we should have been practicing since dawn." This is one of three works read by new postulants in Korean monasteries.

PRONOUNCING GLOSSARY

Palsim Suhaeng Chang: *pahl-sim su-heng chang*
shramana: *shra-ma-na*

Now, all the buddhas adorn the palace of tranquil extinction, nirvana, because they have renounced desires and practiced austerities on the sea of numerous

TRANSLATED FROM the Korean by Robert E. Buswell, Jr.

kalpas.[1] All sentient beings whirl through the door of the burning house of samsara because they have not renounced craving and sensuality during lifetimes without measure. Though the heavenly mansions are unobstructed, few are those who go there; for people take the three poisons (greed, hatred, and delusion) as their family wealth. Though no one entices others to evil destinies, many are those who go there; for people consider the four snakes and the five desires[2] to be precious to their deluded minds.

Who among human beings would not wish to enter the mountains and cultivate the path? But fettered by lust and desires, no one proceeds. But even though people do not return to mountain fastnesses to cultivate the mind, as far as they are able they should not abandon wholesome practices. Those who can abandon their own sensual pleasures will be venerated like saints. Those who practice what is difficult to practice will be revered like buddhas. Those who covet things join Mara's[3] entourage, while those who give with love and compassion are the children of the King of Dharma[4] himself.

High peaks and lofty crags are where the wise dwell. Green pines and deep valleys are where practitioners sojourn. When hungry, they eat tree fruits to satisfy their famished belly. When thirsty, they drink the flowing streams to quench their feeling of thirst. Though one feeds it with sweets and tenderly cares for it, this body is certain to decay. Though one softly clothes it and carefully protects it, this life force must come to an end. Thus the wise regard the grottoes and caves where echoes resound as a hall for recollecting the Buddha's name. They take the wild geese, plaintively calling, as their closest of friends. Though their knees bent in prostration are frozen like ice, they have no longing for warmth. Though their starving bellies feel as if cut by knives, they have no thoughts to search for food.

Suddenly a hundred years will be past; how then can we not practice? How much longer will this life last? Yet still we do not practice, but remain heedless. Those who leave behind the lusts within the mind are called mendicants. Those who do not long for the mundane are called those gone forth into homelessness. A practitioner entangled in the net of the six senses is a dog wearing elephant's hide. A person on the path who still longs for the world is a hedgehog entering a rat's den.

Although talented and wise, if a person dwells in the village, all the buddhas feel pity and sadness for him. Though a person does not practice the path, if he dwells in a mountain hut, all the saints are happy with him. Though talented and learned, if a person does not observe the precepts, it is like being directed to a treasure trove but not even starting out. Though practicing diligently, if a person has no wisdom, it is like one who wishes to go east but instead turns toward the west. The way of the wise is to prepare rice by steaming rice grains; the way of the ignorant is to prepare rice by steaming sand.

Everyone knows that eating food soothes the pangs of hunger, but no one knows that studying the dharma corrects the delusions of the mind. Prac-

---

1. Aeons, or cosmic cycles.
2. The desires associated with the five physical senses (sight, hearing, smell, taste, and touch; the sixth sense is mind). "The four snakes": the

four elements that constitute all matter—earth, air, fire, and water.
3. The personification of evil and desire.
4. That is, the Buddha.

tice and understanding that are both complete are like the two wheels of a cart. Benefiting oneself and benefiting others are like the two wings of a bird. If a person chants prayers when receiving rice gruel but does not understand the meaning, should he not be ashamed before the donors? If one chants when receiving rice but does not tumble to its import, should one not be ashamed before the sages and saints?

Humans despise maggots because they do not discriminate between clean and filthy; saints loathe the *shramanas*[5] who do not differentiate between the pure and impure. The precepts are the skillful ladder for leaving behind the clamor of this world and climbing into the empty sky. Therefore, one who wishes to become a field of merit for others while breaking the precepts is like a bird with broken wings who tries to fly into the sky while bearing a tortoise on its back. A person who is not yet liberated from his own transgressions cannot redeem the transgressions of others. But how could one not cultivating the precepts still accept others' offerings?

There is no benefit in nourishing a useless body that does not practice. Despite clinging to this impermanent, evanescent life, it cannot be preserved. People who hope to achieve the virtue of dragons and elephants—that is, eminent monks—must be able to endure long suffering. Those who aspire to the Lion's Seat of the buddhas must forever turn their backs on desires and pleasures. A cultivator whose mind is pure will be praised by all the gods, while a person on the path who longs for sex will be abandoned by all the wholesome spirits.

The four great elements will suddenly disperse; they cannot be kept together for long. Today, alas, it is already dusk and we should have been practicing since dawn. The pleasures of the world will only bring suffering later, so how can we crave them? One attempt at forbearance conduces to long happiness, so how could we not cultivate? Craving among persons on the path is a disgrace to cultivators. Wealth among those gone forth into homelessness is mocked by the noble. Despite infinite admonitions, craving and clinging are not ended. Despite infinite resolutions, lust and clinging are not eradicated. Though the affairs of this world are limitless, we still cannot forsake worldly events. Though plans are endless, we still do not have a mind to stop them.

For todays without end, our days of doing evil have been rife. For tomorrows without end, our days of doing good have been few. For this years without end, we have not reduced the defilements. For next years without end, we have not progressed toward enlightenment.

Hours after hours continue to pass; swiftly the day and night are gone. Days after days continue to pass; swiftly the end of the month is gone. Months and months continue to pass; suddenly next year has arrived. Years after years continue to pass; unexpectedly we have arrived at the portal of death.

A broken cart cannot move; an old person cannot cultivate. Yet still we humans lie, lazy and indolent; still we humans sit, with minds distracted. How many lives have we not cultivated? Yet still we pass the day and night in vain. How many lives have we spent in our useless bodies? Yet still we do not

---

5. Austere wandering monks, mendicants.

cultivate in this lifetime either. This life must come to an end; but what of the next? Is this not urgent? Is this not urgent?

THE HARMONY OF DOCTRINE AND PRACTICE

SECRETS OF CULTIVATING THE MIND
(Susim Kyeol)

CHINUL

Chinul (1158–1210), the preeminent monk for the Chan tradition in Korea (there called Son) is revered as one of two most important figures in the long history of Korean Buddhism; the other is the seventh-century master Wonhyo (see the previous selection). Ordained as a young boy in 1165, Chinul excelled at his studies, passing the clerical examinations of the Son sect in 1182. Although his ecclesiastical future in the city was bright, he decided to establish a retreat society for some like-minded monks at a monastery in the countryside. There, he experienced the first of his three moments of enlightenment, while studying the *Platform Sutra of the Sixth Patriarch* (p. 531). Three years later, in a mountain monastery, he had his second enlightenment experience—this time while studying an important Chinese commentary on the *Avatamsaka* or *Flower Garland Sutra*.

In 1188, Chinul and a fellow monk founded what they called the Samadhi and Prajna Society (*Chonghye Kyolsa*) at a different mountain monastery, Kojosa on Mount Kong. *Samadhi* (concentration), *prajna* (wisdom), and ethics, were the famous "three trainings" for those seeking enlightenment, set forth in a wide range of works. Yet the *Platform Sutra of the Sixth Patriarch* had declared the unity of *samadhi* and *prajna*. Chinul moved his society to Mount Songgwang and a third monastery, which would eventually become famous and is known today as Songgwangsa. During this period, Chinul is said to have spent a short period at a small mountain hermitage; there he had his third experience of enlightenment, this time while reading the recorded sayings of the Chan master Dahui (see the *Records of Pointing at the Moon*, p. 557).

Painting of the Korean monk Chinul.

Chinul's community was renamed the Son Cultivation Community. Its practice reflected both its founder's experiences of enlightenment and the integrative approach to Buddhist practice that would become the hallmark of Korean Buddhism. The monks recited the *Diamond Sutra* (see p. 325), and they based their practice on three principles: the simultaneous practice of *samadhi* and *prajna* as set forth in the *Platform Sutra*, faith in and understanding of the perfect and sudden teachings according to the *Avatamsaka Sutra*, and the koan method of "observing the keyword" associated with Dahui. The koan method would become the dominant form of Son practice in Korea.

Chinul's approach can be described as harmonizing doctrine and practice, or in his words "the word of the Buddha" and "the mind of the Buddha." On the question of gradual verses sudden enlightenment, he was again integrative, asserting that sudden enlightenment followed by gradual practice was best. This, he said, has been the approach of all of the buddhas.

Among his most famous essays is "Secrets of Cultivating the Mind," which is presented in full here. Composed between 1203 and 1205, the work summarizes many of his central teachings.

PRONOUNCING GLOSSARY

Avalokiteshvara: *a-va-loh-ki-tay-shva-ra*
Bodhidharma: *boh-di-dar-ma*
bodhimanda: *boh-di-man-da*
Caoqi: *tsau-chee*
Chinul: *jee-nool*
Dahui Zonggao: *dah-hway tsohng-gau*
dharmadatu: *dar-ma-dah-tu*
gong'an: *gohng-ahn*
Guifeng: *gway-fang*
Guizong: *gway-tsohng*

Linji: *leen-jee*
Mahayana: *ma-hah-yah-na*
prajna: *praj-nyah*
samadhi: *sa-mah-di*
Son: *san*
Susim Kyeol: *soo-sim kyay-ol*
sutra: *soo-tra*
shravaka: *shrah-va-ka*
tathagata: *ta-tah-ga-ta*
tripitaka: *tri-pi-ta-ka*

The triple world[1] is blazing in defilement as if it were a house on fire. How can you bear to tarry here and complacently undergo such long suffering? If you wish to avoid wandering in *samsara* there is no better way than to seek Buddhahood. If you want to become a Buddha, understand that Buddha is the mind. How can you search for the mind in the far distance? It is not outside the body. The physical body is a phantom, for it is subject to birth and death; the true mind is like space, for it neither ends nor changes. Therefore it is said, "These hundred bones will crumble and return to fire and wind. But One Thing is eternally numinous and covers heaven and earth."

It is tragic. People have been deluded for so long. They do not recognize that their own minds are the true Buddhas. They do not recognize that their own natures are the true dharma. They want to search for the dharma, yet they still look far away for holy ones. They want to search for the Buddha, yet they will not observe their own minds. If they aspire to the path of Buddhahood while obstinately holding to their feeling that the Buddha is outside the mind or the dharma is outside the nature, then, even though they pass through kalpas[2] as numerous as dust motes, burning their bodies, charring their arms, crushing their bones and exposing their marrow, or else write *sutras* with their own blood, never lying down to sleep, eating only one offering a day at the hour of the Hare [5 to 7 A.M.], or even studying through the entire *tripitaka*[3] and cultivating all sorts of ascetic practices, it is like trying to make rice by boiling sand—it will only add to their tribulation. If they would

---

TRANSLATED FROM the Korean by Robert E. Buswell, Jr. All bracketed additions are the translator's.

1. The Realm of Desire, the Realm of Form, and the Formless Realm; see pp. 54–55.
2. Aeons, or cosmic cycles.

3. The Buddhist canon (lit., "three baskets"; Sanskrit).

only understand their own minds, then, without searching, approaches to dharma as numerous as the sands of the Ganges and uncountable sublime meanings would all be understood. As the World Honored One said, "I see that all sentient beings everywhere are endowed with a *tathagata*'s[4] wisdom and virtue." He also said, "All the illusory guises in which sentient beings appear take shape in the sublime mind of the *tathagata*'s complete enlightenment." Consequently, you should know that outside this mind there is no Buddhahood which can be attained. All the Buddhas of the past were merely persons who understood their minds. All the sages and saints of the present are likewise merely persons who have cultivated their minds. All future meditators should rely on this dharma as well.

I hope that you who cultivate the path will never search outside. The nature of the mind is unstained; it is originally whole and complete in itself. If you will only leave behind false conditioning, you will be "such" like the Buddha.

Question: If you say that the Buddha-nature exists in the body right now, then, since it is in the body, it is not separate from us ordinary men. So why can we not see this Buddha-nature now? Please explain this further to enlighten us on this point.

Chinul: It is in your body, but you do not see it. Ultimately, what is that thing which during the twelve periods of the day knows hunger and thirst, cold and heat, anger and joy? This physical body is a synthesis of four conditions: earth, water, fire, and wind. Since matter is passive and insentient, how can it see, hear, sense, and know? That which is able to see, hear, sense, and know is perforce your Buddha-nature. For this reason, Linji[5] said, "The four great elements do not know how to expound dharma or listen to dharma. Empty space does not know how to expound dharma or listen to dharma. It is only that formless thing before your eyes, clear and bright of itself, which knows how to expound dharma or listen to dharma." This "formless thing" is the dharma-seal of all the Buddhas; it is your original mind. Since this Buddha-nature exists in your body right now, why do you vainly search for it outside?

In case you cannot accept this, I will mention some of the events surrounding a few of the ancient saints' entrance onto the path. These should allow you to resolve your doubts. Listen carefully and try to believe.

Once long ago, a king who believed in a heterodox doctrine asked the Venerable Bharati:

> "What is the Buddha?"
> The venerable answered, "Seeing the nature is Buddha."
> The king asked, "Has the master seen the nature yet, or not?"
> The venerable answered, "Yes, I have seen the Buddha-nature."
> "Where is the Buddha-nature?"
> "This nature is present during the performance of actions."
> "During what performance of action? I can't see it now."
> "It appears in this present performance of action; your majesty just doesn't see it."
> "But do I have it too, or not?"

---

4. The title of a buddha (literally, "one who has thus come/gone"); it is the one most often used by the historical Buddha to refer to himself.

"World Honored One": the Buddha.
5. A Chinese Chan master (d. 867); see the *Record of Linji*, p. 541.

"If your majesty performs actions, there are none in which it is not present. If your majesty were not acting, its essence would be very difficult to see."

"But when one acts, at how many places does it appear?"

"It appears in eight different places."

"Would you describe these eight places?"

"In the womb it is called a fetus. On being born it is called a person. In the eyes it is called seeing and in the ears it is called hearing. In the nose it smells, in the tongue it talks, in the hands it grasps, and in the feet it runs. When it is expanded, it contains worlds as numerous as grains of sand. When it is compressed, it exists within one minute particle of dust. Those who have recognized it know that it is the Buddha-nature; those who have not call it soul or spirit."

As the king listened, his mind opened into awakening.

In another case, a monk asked the master Guizong:

"What is the Buddha?"

The master answered, "I will tell you, but I'm afraid you won't believe me."

"How could I dare not believe the sincere words of the master?"

The master said, "It's you!"

"How can you prove it?"

"If there is one eyelash in your eye, flowers in the sky will fall everywhere."

The monk heard this and understood.

These stories I have just told about the saints of old entering the path are clear and simple; they do not strain the powers of comprehension. If you gain some faith and understanding from these two *gong'an*[6] you will walk hand in hand with the saints of old.

Question: You talked about seeing the nature. But when there is true seeing of the nature, the person becomes an enlightened saint and should be able to perform magic and miracles—he would be different from other people. How is it, then, that among those who cultivate the mind nowadays, not one can display these spiritual powers and transformation bodies?

Chinul: You should not utter absurdities lightly; to be unable to differentiate the perverse from the noble is to be deluded and confused. Nowadays, you people who are training on the path chat about truth with your mouth, but in your minds you only shrink from it and end up falling into the error of underestimating yourselves by thinking that you do not share in the Buddha-nature. This is all that you are doubting. You train on the path but do not know the proper sequence of practice. You talk about truth but do not distinguish the root from the branches. This is called wrong view; it is not called cultivation. You are not only deceiving yourselves; you are deceiving others too. How can you not be on your guard against this?

Now, there are many approaches to the path, but essentially they are included in the twofold approach of sudden awakening and gradual cultivation. Although sudden awakening/sudden cultivation has been advocated,

6. Koans.

this is the entrance for people of the highest faculties. If you were to probe their pasts, you would see that their cultivation has been based for many lives on the insights gained in a previous awakening. Now, in this life, after gradual permeation, these people hear the dharma and awaken: in one instant their practice is brought to a sudden conclusion. But if we try to explain this according to the facts, then sudden awakening/sudden cultivation is also the result of an initial awakening and its subsequent cultivation. Consequently, this twofold approach of sudden awakening and gradual cultivation is the track followed by thousands of saints. Hence, of all the saints of old, there were none who did not first have an awakening, subsequently cultivate it, and finally, because of their cultivation, gain realization.

The so-called magic and miracles you mentioned manifest because of the gradual permeation of cultivation based on an initial awakening; it should not be said that they appear simultaneous with that awakening. As it is said in the *sutras*, "The noumenon is awakened to suddenly, and is forged in accordance with this awakening. Phenomena cannot be removed suddenly; they are brought to an end step by step." For this reason, Guifeng,[7] in a profound explanation of the meaning of initial awakening/subsequent cultivation, said:

> Although we know that a frozen pond is entirely water, the sun's heat is necessary to melt it. Although we awaken to the fact that an ordinary man is Buddha, the power of dharma is necessary to make it permeate our cultivation. When that pond has melted, the water flows freely and can be used for irrigation and cleaning. When falsity is extinguished, the mind will be numinous and dynamic and then its function of penetrating brightness will manifest.

These quotations should make it clear that the ability to perform magic and miracles in the phenomenal sphere cannot be perfected in a day: it will manifest only after gradual permeation.

Moreover, in the case of accomplished men, phenomenal spiritual powers are like an eerie apparition; they are only a minor concern of the saints. Although they might perform them, they do not give them undue emphasis. Nowadays, deluded and ignorant people wrongly assume that in the one moment of awakening, incalculable sublime functions, as well as magic and miracles, manifest in tandem. This is the sort of understanding I was referring to when I said that you did not know the proper sequence of practice and did not distinguish the root from the branches. To seek the path to Buddhahood while not knowing the proper sequence of practice or the root and the branches is like trying to put a square peg into a round hole. Can this be anything but a grave mistake? Because such people do not know of any expedients, they hesitate as if they were facing a steep precipice and end up backsliding. Alas, many have broken their ties with the spiritual family of the Buddha in this manner. Since they neither understand for themselves nor believe that others have had an understanding-awakening, when they see someone without spiritual powers they act insolently, ridiculing the sages and insulting the saints. This is really quite pitiful!

Question: You have said that this twofold approach of sudden awakening/ gradual cultivation is the track followed by thousands of saints. But if awak-

---

7. A Chinese scholar-monk (780–841).

ening is really sudden awakening, what need is there for gradual cultivation? And if cultivation means gradual cultivation, how can you speak of sudden awakening? We hope that you will expound further on these two ideas of sudden and gradual and resolve our remaining doubts.

Chinul: First let us take sudden awakening. When the ordinary man is deluded, he assumes that the four great elements are his body and the false thoughts are his mind. He does not know that his own nature is the true dharma-body; he does not know that his own numinous awareness is the true Buddha. He looks for the Buddha outside his mind. While he is thus wandering aimlessly, the entrance to the road might by chance be pointed out by a wise advisor. If in one thought he then follows back the light [of his mind to its source] and sees his own original nature, he will discover that the ground of this nature is innately free of defilement, and that he himself is originally endowed with the non-outflow wisdom-nature which is not a hair's breadth different from that of all the Buddhas. Hence it is called sudden awakening.

Next let us consider gradual cultivation. Although he has awakened to the fact that his original nature is no different from that of the Buddhas, the beginningless habit-energies are extremely difficult to remove suddenly and so he must continue to cultivate while relying on this awakening. Through this gradual permeation, his endeavors reach completion. He constantly nurtures the sacred embryo, and after a long time he becomes a saint. Hence it is called gradual cultivation.

This process can be compared to the maturation of a child. From the day of its birth, a baby is endowed with all the sense organs just like everyone else, but its strength is not yet fully developed. It is only after many months and years that it will finally become an adult.

Question: Through what expedients is it possible to trace back the radiance of one's sense-faculties in one thought and awaken to the self-nature?

Chinul: The self-nature is just your own mind. What other expedients do you need? If you ask for expedients to seek understanding, you are like a person who, because he does not see his own eyes, assumes that he has no eyes and decides to find some way to see. But since he does have eyes, how else is he supposed to see? If he realizes that in fact he has never lost his eyes, this is the same as seeing his eyes, and no longer would he waste his time trying to find a way to see. How then could he have any thoughts that he could not see? Your own numinous awareness is exactly the same. Since this awareness is your own mind, how else are you going to understand? If you seek some other way to understand, you will never understand. Simply by knowing that there is no other way to understand, you are seeing the nature.

Question: When the superior man hears dharma, he understands easily. Average and inferior men, however, are not without doubt and confusion. Could you describe some expedients so that the deluded too can enter into enlightenment?

Chinul: The path is not related to knowing or not knowing. You should get rid of the mind which clings to its delusion and looks forward to enlightenment, and listen to me.

Since all dharmas are like dreams or phantoms, deluded thoughts are originally calm and the sense-spheres are originally void. At the point where all dharmas are void, the numinous awareness is not obscured. That is to say, this mind of void and calm, numinous awareness is your original face. It is also the dharma-seal transmitted without a break by all the Buddhas of the three time periods, the successive generations of patriarchs, and the wise advisors of this world. If you awaken to this mind, then this is truly what is called not following the rungs of a ladder: you climb straight to the stage of Buddhahood, and each step transcends the triple world. Returning home, your doubts will be instantly resolved and you will become the teacher of men and gods. Endowed with compassion and wisdom and complete in the twofold benefit, you will be worthy of receiving the offerings of men and gods. Day after day you can use ten thousand taels of gold without incurring debt. If you can do this, you will be a truly great man who has indeed finished the tasks of this life.

Question: In our case, what is this mind of void and calm, numinous awareness?

Chinul: What has just asked me this question is precisely your mind of void and calm, numinous awareness. Why not trace back its radiance rather than search for it outside? For your benefit I will now point straight to your original mind so that you can awaken to it. Clear your minds and listen to my words.

From morning to evening, throughout the twelve periods of the day, during all your actions and activities—whether seeing, hearing, laughing, talking, whether angry or happy, whether doing good or evil—ultimately who is it that is able to perform all these actions? Speak! If you say that it is the physical body which is acting, then at the moment when a man's life comes to an end, even though the body has not yet decayed, how is it that the eyes cannot see, the ears cannot hear, the nose cannot smell, the tongue cannot talk, the body cannot move, the hands cannot grasp, and the feet cannot run? You should know that what is capable of seeing, hearing, moving, and acting has to be your original mind; it is not your physical body. Furthermore, the four elements which make up the physical body are by nature void; they are like images in a mirror or the moon's reflection in water. How can they be clear and constantly aware, always bright and never obscured—and, upon activation, be able to put into operation sublime functions as numerous as the sands of the Ganges? For this reason it is said, "Drawing water and carrying firewood are spiritual powers and sublime functions."

There are many points at which to enter the noumenon. I will indicate one approach which will allow you to return to the source.

Chinul: Do you hear the sounds of that crow cawing and that magpie calling?
Student: Yes.
Chinul: Trace them back and listen to your hearing-nature. Do you hear any sounds?
Student: At that place, sounds and discriminations do not obtain.
Chinul: Marvelous! Marvelous! This is Avalokiteshvara's[8] method for entering the noumenon. Let me ask you again. You said that sounds and

---

8. The bodhisattva who embodies the compassion of all the buddhas.

discriminations do not obtain at that place. But since they do not obtain, isn't the hearing-nature just empty space at such a time?

Student: Originally it is not empty. It is always bright and never obscured.

Chinul: What is this essence which is not empty?

Student: As it has no former shape, words cannot describe it.

This is the life force of all the Buddhas and patriarchs[9]—have no further doubts about that. Since it has no former shape, how can it be large or small? Since it cannot be large or small, how can it have limitations? Since it has no limitations, it cannot have inside or outside. Since there is no inside or outside, there is no far or near. As there is no far or near, there is no here or there. As there is no here or there, there is no coming or going. As there is no coming or going, there is no birth or death. As there is no birth or death, there is no past or present. As there is no past or present, there is no delusion or awakening. As there is no delusion or awakening, there is no ordinary man or saint. As there is no ordinary man or saint, there is no purity or impurity. Since there is no impurity or purity, there is no right or wrong. Since there is no right or wrong, names and words do not apply to it. Since none of these concepts apply, all sense-bases and sense-objects, all deluded thoughts, even forms and shapes and names and words are all inapplicable. Hence how can it be anything but originally void and calm and originally no-thing?

Nevertheless, at that point where all dharmas are empty, the numinous, awareness is not obscured. It is not the same as insentience, for its nature is spiritually deft. This is your pure mind-essence of void and calm, numinous awareness. This pure, void, and calm mind is that mind of outstanding purity and brilliance of all the Buddhas of the three time periods;[1] it is that enlightened nature which is the original source of all sentient beings. One who awakens to it and safeguards that awakening will then abide in the unitary, "such" and unmoving liberation. One who is deluded and turns his back on it passes between the six destinies,[2] wandering in *samsara* for vast numbers of kalpas. As it is said, "One who is confused about the one mind and passes between the six destinies, goes and takes action. But one who awakens to the *dharmadhatu*[3] and returns to the one mind, arrives and is still." Although there is this distinction between delusion and awakening, in their basic source they are one. As it is said, "The word 'dharma' means the mind of the sentient being." But as there is neither more of this void and calm mind in the saint, nor less of it in the ordinary man, it is also said, "In the wisdom of the saint it is no brighter; hidden in the mind of the ordinary man it is no darker." Since there is neither more of it in the saint nor less of it in the ordinary man, how are the Buddhas and patriarchs any different from other men? The only thing that makes them different is that they can protect their minds and thoughts—nothing more.

If you believe me to the point where you can suddenly extinguish your doubt, show the will of a great man and give rise to authentic vision and understanding, if you know its taste for yourself, arrive at the stage of self-affirmation and gain understanding of your true nature, then this is the understanding-awakening achieved by those who have cultivated the mind.

9. That is, masters in the Chan tradition of Buddhism.
1. The past, the present, and the future.
2. Rebirth as a god, demigod, human, animal,

ghost, or denizen of hell (sometimes numbered at five destinies, omitting the path of the demigod).
3. The ultimate reality (lit., the "element of the dharma" or "sphere of the dharma"; Sanskrit).

Since no further steps are involved, it is called sudden. Therefore it is said, "When in the cause of faith one meshes without the slightest degree of error with all the qualities of the fruition of Buddhahood, faith is achieved."

Question: Once the noumenon is awakened to, no further steps are involved. Why then do you posit subsequent cultivation, gradual permeation, and gradual perfection?

Chinul: Earlier the meaning of gradual cultivation subsequent to awakening was fully explained. But since your feeling of doubt persists, it seems that I will have to explain it again. Clear your minds and listen carefully!

For innumerable kalpas without beginning, up to the present time, ordinary men have passed between the five destinies, coming and going between birth and death. They obstinately cling to "self" and, over a long period of time, their natures have become thoroughly permeated by false thoughts, inverted views, ignorance, and the habit-energies. Although, coming into this life, they might suddenly awaken to the fact that their self-nature is originally void and calm and no different from that of the Buddhas, these old habits are difficult to eliminate completely. Consequently, when they come into contact with either favorable or adverse objects, then anger and happiness or propriety or impropriety blaze forth: their adventitious defilements are no different from before. If they do not increase their efforts and apply their power through the help of *prajna*,[4] how will they ever be able to counteract ignorance and reach the place of great rest and repose? As it is said, "Although the person who has suddenly awakened is the same as the Buddhas, the habit-energies which have built up over many lives are deep-rooted. The wind ceases, but the waves still surge; the noumenon manifests, but thoughts still invade." Son Master Dahui Zonggao[5] said:

> Often gifted people can break through this affair and achieve sudden
> awakening without expending a lot of strength. Then they relax and
> do not try to counteract the habit-energies and deluded thoughts.
> Finally, after the passage of many days and months, they simply
> wander on as before and are unable to avoid *samsara*.

So how could you neglect subsequent cultivation simply because of one moment of awakening? After awakening, you must be constantly on your guard. If deluded thoughts suddenly appear, do not follow after them—reduce them and reduce them again until you reach the unconditioned. Then and only then will your practice reach completion. This is the practice of herding the ox which all wise advisors in the world have practiced after awakening.

Nevertheless, although you must cultivate further, you have already awakened suddenly to the fact that deluded thoughts are originally void and the mind-nature is originally pure. Thus you eliminate evil, but you eliminate without actually eliminating anything; you cultivate the wholesome, but you cultivate without really cultivating anything either. This is true cultivation and true elimination. For this reason it is said, "Although one prepares to cultivate the manifold supplementary practices, thoughtlessness is the origin of them all." Guifeng summed up the distinction between the ideas of initial awakening and subsequent cultivation when he said:

4. Wisdom.
5. A Chinese monk in the Linji school (1089–1163).

He has the sudden awakening to the fact that his nature is originally free of defilement and he is originally in full possession of the non-outflow wisdom-nature which is no different from that of the Buddhas. To cultivate while relying on this awakening is called supreme vehicle Son, or the pure Son of the *tathagatas*. If thought-moment after thought-moment he continues to develop his training, then naturally he will gradually attain to hundreds of thousands of *samadhis*.[6] This the Son which has been transmitted successively in the school of Bodhidharma.[7]

Hence sudden awakening and gradual cultivation are like the two wheels of a cart: neither one can be missing.

Some people do not realize that the nature of good and evil is void; they sit rigidly without moving and, like a rock crushing grass, repress both body and mind. To regard this as cultivation of the mind is a great delusion. For this reason it is said, "*Shravakas*[8] cut off delusion thought after thought, but the thought which does this cutting is a brigand." If they could see that killing, stealing, sexual misconduct, and lying all arise from the nature, then their arising would be the same as their nonarising. At their source they are calm; why must they be cut off? As it is said, "Do not fear the arising of thoughts: only be concerned lest your awareness of them be tardy." It is also said, "If we are aware of a thought at the moment it arises, then through that awareness it will vanish."

In the case of a person who has had an awakening, although he still has adventitious defilements, these have all been purified into cream. If he merely reflects on the fact that confusion is without basis, then all the flowers in the sky of this triple world are like smoke swirling in the wind and the six phantom sense-objects[9] are like ice melting in hot water. If thought-moment after thought-moment he continues to train in this manner, does not neglect to maintain his training, and keeps *samadhi* and *prajna* equally balanced, then lust and hatred will naturally fade away and compassion and wisdom will naturally increase in brightness; unwholesome actions will naturally cease and meritorious practices will naturally multiply. When defilements are exhausted, birth and death cease. When the subtle streams of defilement are forever cut off, the great wisdom of complete enlightenment exists brilliantly of itself. Then he will be able to manifest billions of transformation-bodies in all the worlds of the ten directions[1] following his inspiration and responding to the faculties of sentient beings. Like the moon in the nine empyrean which reflects in ten thousand pools of water, there is no limit to his responsiveness. He will be able to ferry across all sentient beings with whom he has affinities. He will be happy and free of worry. Such a person is called a Great Enlightened World Honored One.

Question: In the approach of subsequent cultivation, we really do not yet understand the meaning of maintaining *samadhi* and *prajna* equally. Could

---

6. States of deep meditation.
7. The Indian prince who is said to have brought Zen Buddhism to China in the late 5th century.
8. Listeners (i.e., disciples who hear the Buddha's teachings and are criticized in Mahayana or Great Vehicle sutras for seeking only their own enlight-

enment, not that of other beings as well).
9. The six sense organs are eye, ear, nose, tongue, body, and mind.
1. That is, everywhere (north, south, east, west, northeast, northwest, southeast, southwest, the nadir, and the zenith).

you expound on this point in detail, so that we can free ourselves of our delusion? Please lead us through the entrance to liberation.

Chinul: Suppose we consider these two dharmas and their attributes. Of the thousands of approaches to enter the noumenon there are none which do not involve *samadhi* and *prajna*. Taking only the essential outline into account, from the standpoint of the self-nature they are characterized as essence and function—what I have called the void and the calm, numinous awareness. *Samadhi* is the essence; *prajna* is the function. Since *prajna* is the functioning of the essence, it is not separate from *samadhi*. Since *samadhi* is the essence of the function, it is not separate from *prajna*. Since in *samadhi* there is *prajna*, *samadhi* is calm yet constantly aware. Since in *prajna* there is *samadhi*, *prajna* is aware yet constantly calm. As Caoqi [the Sixth Patriarch Huineng[2]] said, "The mind-ground which is without disturbance is the *samadhi* of the self-nature. The mind-ground which is without delusion is the *prajna* of the self-nature." If you have this sort of understanding, you can be calm and aware naturally in all situations. When enveloping and reflecting— the characteristics of *samadhi* and *prajna* respectively—are not two, this is the sudden school's cultivation of *samadhi* and *prajna* as a pair.

The practice of *samadhi* and *prajna* intended for those of inferior faculties in the gradual school initially controls the thinking processes with calmness and subsequently controls dullness with alertness; finally, these initial and subsequent counteracting techniques subdue both the dull and the agitated mind in order to enter into stillness. Although this approach also holds that alertness and calmness should be maintained equally, its practice cannot avoid clinging to stillness. Hence how will it allow those who would under-stand the matter of birth and death never to leave the fundamental calm and fundamental awareness and cultivate *samadhi* and *prajna* as a pair naturally in all situations? As Caoqi said, "The practice of self-awakening has noth-ing to do with arguing. If you argue about first and last, you are deluded."

For an accomplished man, maintaining *samadhi* and *prajna* equally does not involve endeavor, for he is always spontaneous and unconcerned about time or place. When seeing forms or hearing sounds, he is "just so." When wearing clothes or eating food, he is "just so." When defecating or urinating, he is "just so." When talking with people, he is "just so." At all times, whether speaking or keeping silent, whether joyful or angry, he is "just so." Like an empty boat riding on the waves which follows the crests and troughs, or like a torrent flowing through the mountains which follows the bends and straights, in his mind he is without intellection. Today, he is at peace naturally in all conditions without destruction or hindrance. Tomorrow, in all situations, he is naturally at peace. He follows all conditions without destruction or hin-drance. He neither eliminates the unwholesome nor cultivates the wholesome. His character is straightforward and without deception. His seeing and hearing return to normal and there are no sense-objects to come in content with [which could cause new defilements to arise]. Why should he have to bother with efforts at effacement? Since he has not a single thought which creates passion, he need not make an effort to forget all conditioning.

But hindrances are formidable and habits are deeply ingrained. Contem-plation is weak and the mind drifts. The power of ignorance is great, but the power of *prajna* is small. He still cannot avoid being alternately unmoved

---

2. On this master of the Chan school (638–713), see *Platform Sutra of the Sixth Patriarch*, p. 531.

and upset when he comes in contact with wholesome and unwholesome sense-objects. When the mind is not tranquil and content, he cannot but work both at forgetting all conditioning and at effacement. As it is said, "When the six sense-bases absorb the sense-spheres and the mind no longer responds to the environment, this is called *samadhi*. When the mind and the sense-spheres are both void and the mirror of the mind shines without obscuration, this is called *prajna*." Even though this is the relative approach to *samadhi* and *prajna* which adapts to signs as practiced by those of inferior faculties in the gradual school, it cannot be neglected as a counteractive technique. If restlessness and agitation are blazing forth, then first, through *samadhi*, use the noumenon to absorb the distraction. For when the mind does not respond to the environment it will be in conformity with original calmness. If dullness and torpor are especially heavy, use *prajna* to investigate dharmas critically and contemplate their voidness, and allow the mirror of the mind to shine without disturbance in conformity with the original awareness. Control distracting thoughts with *samadhi*. Control blankness with *prajna*.

When both activity and stillness disappear, the act of counteraction is no longer necessary. Then, even though there is contact with sense-objects, thought after thought returns to the source; regardless of the conditions he meets, every mental state is in conformity with the path. Naturally *samadhi* and *prajna* are cultivated as a pair in all situations until finally the student becomes a person with no concerns. When this is so, one is truly maintaining *samadhi* and *prajna* equally. One has clearly seen the Buddha-nature.

Question: According to your assessment, there are two types of *samadhi* and *prajna* which are maintained equally during cultivation after awakening: first, the *samadhi* and *prajna* of the self-nature; second, the relative *samadhi* and *prajna* which adapts to signs.

The self-nature type means to be calm yet aware in all circumstances. Since the person who has awakened to the self-nature is always spontaneous and free from attachment to objects, why does he need to trouble with effacing the defilements? Since there is not even one thought which creates passion, there is no need to make vain efforts at forgetting all conditioning. Your assessment was that this approach is the sudden school's equal maintenance of *samadhi* and *prajna* which never leaves the self-nature.

The relative type which follows signs means either to absorb distraction by according with the noumenon or to investigate dharmas critically and contemplate their voidness. One controls both dullness and agitation and thereby enters the unconditioned. But your assessment was that this practice is for those of inferior faculties in the gradual school. We are not yet free of doubts about the *samadhi* and *prajna* of these two different approaches. Would you say that one should first rely on the self-nature type and then, after cultivating *samadhi* and *prajna* concurrently, make further use of the countermeasures or the relative approach? Or should one first rely on the relative type so that after controlling dullness and agitation, he can enter into the self-nature type? If, after initially using the *samadhi* and *prajna* of the self-nature, he is able to remain calm and aware naturally in all situations, thus rendering the counteractive measures unnecessary, why would he subsequently have to apply the relative type of *samadhi* and *prajna*? It is like a piece of white jade: if it is engraved, its natural quality will be destroyed. On the other hand, after the initial application of the relative type of *samadhi* and *prajna*, if the work of counteraction is brought to a close and he then progresses to the self-nature type, this would be merely gradual development prior to awakening as practiced by those of inferior faculties in the gradual school. Then how would you be able to say that the sudden school's approach of initial awakening and subsequent cultivation makes use of the effortless effort?

If these two types can both be practiced in the one time that has no past or future [via sudden awakening/sudden cultivation], there would have to be a difference between the respective suddenness and gradualness of these two types of *samadhi* and *prajna*—so how could they both be cultivated at once? The sudden school adept relies on the self-nature type and eschews effort by remaining natural in all situations. Students of inferior capacity in the gradual school tend toward the relative type and exert themselves applying countermeasures. The suddenness and gradualness of these two types of practices are not identical; their respective superiority and inferiority is obvious. So, in the approach of initial awakening and subsequent cultivation, why is it explained that there are two ways to maintain *samadhi* and *prajna* equally? Could you help us to understand this and eliminate our doubts?

Chinul: The explanation is obvious. Your doubts only come from yourselves! If you try to understand by merely following the words, you will, on the contrary, only give rise to doubt and confusion. It is best to forget the words; do not bother with detailed scrutiny of them. Now let us go on to my assessment of the cultivation of these two types of practice.

Cultivation of the *samadhi* and *prajna* of the self-nature involves the use of the sudden school's effortless effort in which both are put into practice and both are calmed; oneself cultivates the self-nature, and oneself completes the path to Buddhahood. Cultivation of the relative *samadhi* and *prajna* which adapts to signs involves the use of the counteractive measures which are cultivated prior to awakening by those of inferior faculties in the gradual school. Thought-moment after thought-moment, confusion is eliminated; it is a practice which clings to stillness. These two types are different: one is sudden and the other gradual; they should not be combined haphazardly.

Although the approach involving cultivation after awakening does discuss the counteractive measures of the relative approach which adapts to signs, it does not employ the practices of those of inferior faculties in the gradual school in their entirety. It uses its expedients, but only as a temporary measure. And why is this? In the sudden school too there are those whose faculties are superior and those whose faculties are inferior; their "baggage" [their backgrounds and abilities] cannot be weighed according to the same standard.

If a person's defilements are weak and insipid, and his body and mind are light and at ease; if in the good he leaves the good and in the bad he leaves the bad; if he is unmoving In the eight worldly winds;[3] if the three types of feeling[4] are calmed—then he can rely on the *samadhi* and *prajna* of the self-nature and cultivate them concurrently in all situations naturally. He is impeccable and passive; whether in action or at rest he is always absorbed in Son and perfects the principle of naturalness. What need is there for him to borrow the relative approach's counteractive measures? If one is not sick, there is no need to look for medicine.

On the other hand, even though a person might initially have had a sudden awakening, if the defilements are engrossing and the habit-energies deeply

3. Praise, blame, sorrow, happiness, fame, disgrace, gain, and loss. 4. Pleasant, unpleasant, and neutral.

engrained; if the mind becomes passionate whenever it is in contact with sense-objects; if he is always involved in confrontations with the situations he meets; if he is always beset by dullness and agitation; or if he loses the constancy of calmness and awareness—then he should borrow the relative *samadhi* and *prajna* which adapts to signs and not forget the counteractive measures which control both dullness and agitation. Thereby he will enter the unconditioned: this is what is proper here. But even though he borrows the countermeasures in order to bring the habit-energies under temporary control, he has had a sudden awakening to the fact that the mind-nature is fundamentally pure and the defilements fundamentally empty. Hence he does not fall into the corrupt practice of those of inferior faculties in the gradual school. And why is this? Although during cultivation prior to awakening a person following the gradual approach does not forget to be diligent and thought-moment after thought-moment permeates his cultivation, he still gives rise to doubts everywhere and cannot free himself from obstacles. It is as if he had something stuck in his chest: he is always uncomfortable. After many days and months, as the work of counteraction matures, the adventitious defilements of body and mind might then appear to weaken. Although they seem lighter, the root of doubt is not yet severed. He is like a rock which is crushing grass: he still cannot be self-reliant in the realm of birth and death. Therefore, it is said, "Cultivation prior to awakening is not true cultivation."

In the case of a man who has awakened, although he employs expedients, moment to moment he is free of doubts and does not become polluted. After many days and months he naturally conforms with the impeccable, sublime nature. Naturally he is calm and aware in all situations. Moment by moment, as he becomes involved in sensory experience in all the sense-realms, thought after thought he always severs defilements, for he never leaves the self-nature. By maintaining *samadhi* and *prajna* equally, he perfects supreme *bodhi*[5] and is no longer any different from those of superior faculties mentioned previously. Thus, although the relative *samadhi* and *prajna* is a practice for those of inferior faculties in the gradual school, for the man who has had an awakening it can be said that "iron has been transmuted into gold."

If you understand this, how can you have such doubts—doubts like the discriminative view that a sequence or progression is involved in the practice of these two types of *samadhi* and *prajna*? I hope that all cultivators of the path will study these words carefully; extinguish your doubts or you will end up backsliding. If you have the will of a great man and seek supreme *bodhi*, what will you do if you discard this approach? Do not grasp at the words, but try to understand the meaning directly. Stay focused on the definitive teaching, return to yourselves, and merge with the original guiding principle. Then the wisdom which cannot be obtained from any master will naturally manifest. The impeccable noumenon will be clear and unobscured. The perfection of the wisdom-body does not come from any other awakening. And yet, although this sublime truth applies to everyone, unless the omniscient wisdom of *prajna*—the basis of the Mahayana—is started early, you will not be able to produce right faith in a single thought. And how can this merely result in a lack of faith? You will also end up slandering the three treasures[6] and will finally invite punishment in the Interminable Hell. This

5. Enlightenment.
6. That is, the three jewels of Buddhism: the Bud-dha, the dharma, and the sangha (Buddhist community).

happens frequently! But even though you are not yet able to accept this truth in faith, if it passes through your ears just once and you feel affinity with it for even a moment, the merit will be incalculable. As it says in *Secrets on Mind-Only*,[7] "Hearing the dharma but not believing is still cause for the fruition of the seed of Buddhahood. Training on the Buddhist path but not completing it is still merit surpassing that of men and gods." But he who does not lose the right cause for the attainment of Buddhahood and who, moreover, listens and believes, trains and completes his training, and guards his achievement without forgetting it, how can his merit be calculated?

If we consider our actions in our past wanderings in *samsara*, we have no way of knowing for how many thousands of kalpas we have fallen into the darkness or entered the Interminable Hell and endured all kinds of suffering. Nor can we know how many times we have aspired to the path to Buddhahood but, because we did not meet with wise advisors, remained submerged in the sea of birth and death for long kalpas, dark and unenlightened, performing all sorts of evil actions. Though we may reflect on this once in a while, we cannot imagine the duration of our misery. How can we relax and suffer again the same calamities as before? Furthermore, what allowed us to be born this time as human beings—the guiding spirits of all the ten thousand things—who are clear about the right road of cultivation? Truly, a human birth is as difficult to ensure as "a blind turtle putting its head through a hole in a piece of wood floating on the ocean" or "a mustard seed falling onto the point of a needle." How can we possibly express how fortunate we are?

Whenever we become discouraged or indolent, we should always look to the future. In one instant we might happen to lose our lives and fall back into the evil bourns where we would have to undergo unspeakable suffering and pain. At that time, although we might want to hear one phrase of the Buddha-dharma, and would be willing to receive and keep it with faithful devotion to ease our misfortune, how would we ever encounter it there? On the point of death, remorse is of no use whatsoever. I hope that all of you who are cultivating the path will not be heedless and will not indulge in greed and lust. Do not forget to reflect upon this as if you were trying to save your head from burning. Death is fast closing in. The body is like the morning dew. Life is like the twilight in the west. Although we are alive today, there is no assurance about tomorrow. Bear this in mind! You must bear this in mind!

By relying on worldly conditioned, wholesome actions we will avoid the suffering of *samsara* in the three evil bourns. We will obtain the favorable karmic reward of rebirth among gods or men where we will receive abundant joy and happiness. But if we give rise to faith in this most profound approach to dharma of the supreme vehicle for only a moment, no metaphor can describe even the smallest portion of the merit we will achieve. As it is said in the *sutras*:

> If one takes all the seven jewels in all the world systems of this trichiliocosm[8] and offers them to all the sentient beings of those worlds until they are completely satisfied; or, furthermore, if one instructs all the sentient beings of those worlds and causes them to realize the four fruitions, the merit so gained will be immeasurable and boundless. But it is not as great as the merit gained from the first recollection of this dharma for the period of one meal.

7. By the scholar and Chan master Yan-shou (904–975).

8. The universe, consisting of a billion worlds.

Therefore, we should know that our approach to dharma is the holiest and most precious of all; its merit is incomparable. As the *sutras* say:

> One thought of purity of mind is a *bodhimanda*,[9]
> And is better than building seven-jeweled stupas as numerous as
>   the sands of the Ganges.
> Those jeweled stupas will finally be reduced to dust,
> But one thought of purity of mind produces right enlightenment.

I hope that all of you who are cultivating the path will study these words carefully and keep them always in mind. If this body is not ferried across to the other shore in this lifetime, then for which life are you going to wait? If you do not cultivate now, you will go off in the wrong direction for ten thousand kalpas. But if you practice assiduously now, practices which are difficult to cultivate will gradually become easier until, finally, meritorious practice will advance of itself.

Alas! When starving people are given princely delicacies nowadays, they do not even know enough to put them in their mouths. When they are sick they meet the king of doctors but do not even know enough to take the medicine. If no one says, "What shall I do? What shall I do?" then what shall I do for him?

Although the character of mundane, conditioned activities can be seen and its effect experienced, if a person succeeds in one affair, everyone praises the rarity of it. The source of our minds has neither shape to be observed nor form to be seen; the way of words and speech is cut off there. Since the activities of mind are ended, *maras*[1] and heretics have no way to revile us. Even the praises of Indra, Brahma,[2] and all the gods will not reach it; so how can the mind be fathomed by the shallow understanding of ordinary men? How pitiful! How can a frog in a well know the vastness of the sea? How can a fox roar like a lion?

Hence we know that in this degenerate dharma age, a person who is able to hear this approach to dharma, realize its rarity, and receive and keep it with faithful devotion has for innumerable kalpas served all the saints, planted all the roots of goodness, and fully formed the right cause of *prajna*—he has the most proficiency. As the *Diamond Sutra*[3] says, "If there is a person who can have faith in these words, it should be known that this man has planted all the roots of goodness in front of incalculable numbers of Buddhas." It also says, "This is spoken in order to produce the great vehicle; this is spoken in order to produce the supreme vehicle." I hope that those of you who are aspiring to the path will not be cowardly. You must display your ardor. Good causes made in past kalpas cannot be known. If you do not believe in your superiority and, complacently resigning yourself to being inferior, you decide that you will not practice now because it is too difficult, then even though you might have good roots from past lives, you sever them now. The difficulty will keep growing and you will move farther from the goal. Since you have now arrived at the treasure house, how can you return empty-handed? Once you lose a human body, for ten thousand kalpas it will be difficult to recover. Be careful. Knowing that there is a treasure house, how can a wise person turn back and not look for it—and yet continue to resent bitterly his destitution and poverty? If you want the treasure you must throw away this skin-bag.

9. Seat of enlightenment (Sanskrit), specifically, the place where the Buddha sat on the night of his enlightenment.
1. Personifications of evil and temptation.
2. The god who persuaded the Buddha to teach.

"Indra": the king of the gods.
3. See the *Vajracchedika Prajnaparamita*, or *The Perfection of Wisdom That Rends Like a Thunderbolt*, p. 325.

Buddhism in Japan

The history of Buddhism in Japan is generally divided into periods, each taking its name from the place that was then the seat of the ruler. Thus, Japanese Buddhism begins with the Nara period, named after the ancient capital. According to traditional histories, Buddhism was introduced into Japan in 552, when a delegation of monks and nuns from Korea arrived at court, carrying sutras and an image of the Buddha. Over the next two centuries, six schools—known as the Six Nara Schools—developed, including the Ritsu school, which focused on the vinaya, or code of monastic conduct; the Sanron school, derived from a Chinese Madhyamaka school; and the Kusha school, taking its name from the *Kosha*, or *Abhidharmakosha* (p. 267).

The Heian period that followed—after the capital was moved in 794 from Nara to Kyoto (then called Heian-kyo)—saw the development of two important schools. The first was the Tendai school, which established its center on Mount Hiei outside the city. This was the Japanese version of the Chinese Tiantai school, which revered the *Lotus Sutra* (see the *Saddharmapundarika*, p. 278) above all others. The other was the Shingon or "True Word" school, founded by Kukai (p. 606), who argued for the superiority of the esoteric Buddhism taught in the tantras over the exoteric Buddhism of the sutras.

Sculpture of the Japanese priest Kuya reciting "Homage to Amitabha Buddha," by 13th-century sculptor Kosho.

In 1192, the shogun or military dictator of Japan established his capital in Kamakura, marking the beginning of one of the most important periods for the eventual formation of Japanese Buddhism. Each of its three major schools is represented here. It was during this period that Zen Buddhism was introduced from China to Japan in an essay by the Japanese monk Eisai, "Promote Zen to Protect This Kingdom's Rulers." In Japan, however, Eisai is best remembered for something else he brought back from China: tea, which Chinese monks drank to stay awake during their hours of meditation and which he praised in a two-volume treatise, *Drink Tea for Health*. Eisai is credited with founding the Rinzai sect of Zen, which places particular emphasis on koan practice. The other major form of Zen in Japan also arose during the Kamakura period. It is the Soto sect, founded by Dogen, famous for its practice of "just sitting." Also appearing during this period was the Jodo Shinshu, or "True Pure Land School," traced to Shinran, who taught the power of the phrase *namu amida butsu*, "Homage to Amitabha Buddha," and revered the *Discourse on the Land of Bliss* (see the *Sukhavativyuha Sutra*, p. 316) for revealing the presence of Amitabha's pure land. Finally, Nichiren proclaimed that devotion to the *Lotus Sutra* was the sole path to Japan's salvation and promoted the practice of chanting *namu myoho renge kyo*, "Homage to the *Lotus Sutra*." The Nichiren school is named after him.

The Kamakura period ended in 1336 when the shogun moved to Kyoto and settled in the Muromachi district. Contacts between Japan and China continued, with the Zen school bringing various traditions of Chinese painting to Japan. The Muromachi period was also marked by increased Japanese nationalism and nativism, after the successful resistance of invasions by the Mongol rulers of China (themselves Buddhists) in 1274 and 1281; the invaders' fleet was repelled by typhoons that the Japanese dubbed *kamikaze*, "divine winds." This nativism stressed the divine origin of the Japanese people, views that would be central to the emergence of Shinto.

Around the mid-fifteenth century, the Muromachi shogunate fell into political disunity and civil war that came to a close only with the establishment of the Tokugawa shogunate—also known as the Edo period, as the capital moved north from Kyoto to the city of Edo (renamed Tokyo in 1868). A number of important Buddhist figures emerged during this period, including Hakuin (1685–1769), and the major schools of Japanese Buddhism evolved into the forms that they retain today. Institutionally, Buddhism benefited from the compulsory *danka*, or "household registry" system. In 1638, after a Christian rebellion that was brutally suppressed, the state required each household in Japan to register at the nearest Buddhist temple, regardless of the family's prior affiliation, in part to demonstrate that the family was not Christian. The temple kept records and issued a document that served as an identity certificate necessary for travel, marriage, and some professions. In addition to being a form of state surveillance, the system also required that families have funeral rites performed by the local temple; these provided a steady source of income to the temple and aided the rise of what is known as "funerary Buddhism" in Japan.

Throughout the shogunate, the emperor had maintained his ritual role, but in 1868, when Emperor Meiji took the throne, his active political role was restored. Japan undertook a major program of modernization, during which Shinto emerged for the first time as the state religion and Buddhism suffered. The new Meiji government was highly critical of Buddhism as an outmoded institution that did not contribute to the imperial nation. In 1872, the Meiji government denied the special status previously attached to monkhood, thereby subjecting monks to secular education, taxation, and military conscription. It also declared that "From now on Buddhist clerics will be free to eat meat, marry, grow their hair, and so on." Under the laws of the Tokugawa period, all monks had to be celibate and relations with a woman were punishable by death, but monks often had wives and children; indeed, the fate of monks' widows and orphans appears to have been an embarrassment to the state. Although members of the Buddhist sects of Japan were alarmed at the new regulations, especially the freedom to marry, during the twentieth century such marriages became increasingly common. Today, less than 1 percent of male clergy in Japan keep the code of monastic discipline and its vow of celibacy, and thus they are now called "Buddhist priests" rather than "Buddhist monks." The Meiji regulations afforded Japanese nuns the same freedoms, but most have chosen to remain celibate.

During World War II, the schools of Japanese Buddhism were generally supportive of the Japanese imperial project. This support extended beyond sending Buddhist chaplains to the field of battle; some Buddhist leaders argued that Japanese Buddhism was the purest form of Buddhism and needed to be established throughout the "Greater East Asia Co-Prosperity Sphere" (the euphemism used for the expanding Japanese empire). After the war, several Buddhist schools confronted their complicity in the war.

Yet another Buddhist element in modern Japan are the so-called new religions that began to appear after the 1868 Meiji Restoration and had a resurgence after World War II. Numbering in the hundreds, many of these religions combine elements of Buddhism, Shinto, and Japanese folk traditions. The largest of these is Sokka Gakkai, or "Value Creation Society": founded in 1930, it draws its inspiration from Nichiren and the *Lotus Sutra*.

Today, even though 90 percent of the funerals in Japan are conducted by Buddhist priests, only about 25 percent of Japanese identify themselves as Buddhist; the majority of Japanese say that they have no religion.

THE GLORIES OF THE ESOTERIC

TREATISE DISTINGUISHING THE TWO TEACHINGS OF EXOTERIC AND ESOTERIC METHODS
(*The Benkenmitsu Nikyo Ron*)

KUKAI

As Buddhism developed over the centuries, new forms inevitably arose, each claiming authority for itself. Making such claims was fairly easy—the more difficult task was to account for what had come before. One of the Perfection of Wisdom sutras declared itself to be the Buddha's second "turning of the wheel of the dharma," implying that it superseded the first (see *Setting the Wheel of the Dharma in Motion*, p. 177). Not to be outdone, a later Mahayana sutra, appropriately titled *Untying the [Buddha's] Intention* (*Sandhinirmochana*), announced that there were three wheels of the dharma.

The basic argument in defense of new teachings had been given long ago, in the *Lotus Sutra* (see the *Saddharmapundarika*, p. 278), where the Buddha explained his use of "skillful means" (*upayakaushalya*): teaching only what was appropriate for the moment, calibrated to the capacities of a given audience. As new texts proclaimed their supremacy, their advocates could argue that what the Buddha had previously taught was an accommodation for those of lesser capacities; what he taught in their text was his highest teaching.

With the rise of Buddhist tantra, a full millennium after the demise of the Buddha, other strategies came into play. One of them is presented here by the founder of the Shingon or "True Word" school of Esoteric Buddhism in Japan, Kukai (774–835)—affectionately known as Kobo Daishi, "Great Master Who Spread the Dharma." Born into an aristocratic family that had fallen from favor, he studied the Confucian classics before becoming interested in Buddhism. He had a dream in which a man informed him that what he was seeking was found in the *Enlightenment of Vairochana* (see the *Vairochanabhisambodhi Tantra*, p. 471). Kukai acquired a copy of the text but could understand little of it, since it was written in an Indic script. In 804 he sailed to China, where he eventually met a tantric master who gave him both instruction and tantric initiation. Kukai returned to Japan in 806, bringing with him the knowledge he had gained as well as texts and ritual objects. At this time, Buddhism in Japan was dominated by what are called the Six Nara Schools. But when the capital moved from Nara to Kyoto, the emperor did not allow those schools to relocate with the court. Kukai gained the favor of Emperor Saga, who granted him a retreat center on Mount Koya and a temple in Kyoto. He went on to become one of the most powerful monks in Japanese history.

To establish his new tantric school, however, he had to justify its superiority—not just to the Buddhism of the Nara schools but also to the Buddhism taught in many Mahayana sutras then known in Japan. In the essay below, written in 814 and 815, Kukai explains that Esoteric Buddhism is superior to "Exoteric Buddhism" (that is, the Buddhism that was known at the time), because Esoteric Buddhism is taught by a different buddha. He appealed to the classical Mahayana doctrine of the three bodies of the Buddha, which held that Shakyamuni Buddha—the Buddha who appeared in the world—was an "emanation body" (*nirmanakaya*), compassionately dispensing the dharma in a form that benighted sentient beings could understand. The "enjoyment body" (*sambhogakaya*) was a resplendent form of the buddha who appeared only in the pure lands; Amitabha (see the *Sukhavativyuha Sutra*, p. 316) was such a buddha. Finally, there was the "truth body" (*dharmakaya*), generally represented as a kind of cosmic principle of enlightenment in which all buddhas partake. But here, following the *Enlightenment of Vairochana*, Kukai argues that the *dharmakaya* is a specific buddha, the buddha Mahavairochana, and that he teaches the dharma. This dharma is the unadulterated truth, set forth without concessions and intended only for the most advanced of disciples.

PRONOUNCING GLOSSARY

Benkenmitsu Nikyo Ron: *ben-ken-mit-soo nee-kyo rohn*
bodhisattva: *boh-di-sat-tva*
Daizong: *dai-tsong*
Dazhidu lun: *dah-jer-doo loon*
Dashabhumika Sutra: *da-sha-boo-mi-ka soo-tra*
dharani: *dah-ra-ni*
Dharmakaya: *dar-ma-kah-ya*
Hinayana: *hee-na-yah-na*
Kukai: *koo-kai*
Lankavatara Sutra: *lan-kah-va-tah-ra soo-tra*
Madhyamika-karika: *mah-dya-mi-ka-kah-ri-kah*
Mahavairochana: *ma-hah-vai-roh-cha-na*

Mahayana: *ma-hah-yah-na*
Nagarjuna: *nah-gahr-ju-na*
Nirmanakaya: *nir-mah-na-kah-ya*
Qin: *chin*
Sambhogakaya: *sam-boh-ga-kah-ya*
Shakyamuni: *shah-kya-mu-ni*
Shidijing lun: *sher-dee-jeeng loon*
Shimoheyan lun: *sher-moh-ha-yehn loon*
Tang: *tahng*
Tathagata: *ta-tah-ga-ta*
Vajrabodhi: *vaj-ra-boh-di*
Vajrashekhara Sutra: *vaj-ra-sheh-ka-ra soo-tra*
Vasubandhu: *va-su-ban-du*
Xuanzong: *shwen-tsohing*

There are three bodies of the Buddha and two forms of Buddhist doctrine. The doctrine revealed by the Nirmanakaya Buddha [Shakyamuni[1] Buddha] is called Exoteric; it is apparent, simplified, and adapted to the needs of the time and to the capacity of the listeners. The doctrine expounded by the Dharmakaya Buddha [Mahavairochana] is called Esoteric; it is secret and profound and contains the final truth.

The sutras used in Exoteric Buddhism number in the millions. The collection is divided by some into ten and by others into fifty-one parts. They speak of One, Two, Three, Four, and Five Vehicles. In discussing practices, they believe that the Six Paramitas[2] are the most important and explain that in order to attain enlightenment a period of three aeons is needed. The great Sage has explained these matters clearly.

According to the Esoteric *Vajrashekhara Sutra*, the Buddha, manifested in human form, preached the doctrines of the Three Vehicles for the sake of bodhisattvas who were yet to advance to the Ten Stages of Bodhisattvahood, for the followers of Hinayana,[3] and for ordinary people; the Sambhogakaya Buddha taught the doctrine of One Vehicle for the bodhisattvas in the Ten Stages of Bodhisattvahood. Both of these teachings are Exoteric.

TRANSLATED FROM the Japanese by Yoshito S. Hakeda. All bracketed additions are the translator's.

1. Literally, "Sage of the Shakyas"; a title of the Buddha, who was born into the Shakya clan. On the three bodies of the Buddha, see the introduction to this selection.
2. The perfections, or virtues whose practice produces merit (giving, ethics, patience, effort, concentration, and wisdom).
3. On "the inferior vehicle" (Hinayana), as distinguished from the "great vehicle" (Mahayana), see p. 655.

The Dharmakaya Buddha, for his own enjoyment, with his own retinue, preached the doctrine of the Three Mysteries. This is Esoteric. This doctrine of the Three Mysteries is concerned with the innermost spiritual experience of the Dharmakaya Buddha, and the bodhisattvas in the Ten Stages of Bodhisattvahood or even those who are nearly equal to the Buddha cannot penetrate it, much less the Hinayanists and ordinary people, who cannot cross its threshold. It is thus said in the *Shidijing lun* and in the *Shimoheyan lun* that this experience is beyond their capacity. Also the *Cheng weishi lun* and the *Madhyamika-karikas*[4] deplore that it transcends words and thought determinations. Its transcendence is spoken of, however, from the viewpoint of those who have not yet been enlightened and not from the viewpoint of the enlightened ones. I shall give clear evidence for this in the following pages, on the basis of sutras and commentaries. It is hoped that those who aspire to attain enlightenment will understand their meaning clearly.

Being entangled in the net of Exoteric Buddhism, people wear themselves out like male goats dashing themselves against fences; being blocked by the barriers of the Mahayana teachings of provisional nature, they give up advancing further. They are exactly like those who, wishing to rest there, believe in an illusory city,[5] or like children who take a yellow willow leaf to be gold. How can they hope to preserve the glorious treasures which lie within themselves, numberless as the sands of the Ganges? It is as if they were to discard ghee and look for milk, or to throw away precious pearls and pick up fish eyes. They are cut off from their Buddha-seed; they are victims of a mortal disease before which even the King of Medicine would fold his hands in despair, a disease for which even a rain of nectar would be of no avail.

If men and women once grasp the fragrance of this [Esoteric Buddhism], they will have in their minds a clear understanding, as things are reflected in the magic mirror of the Emperor of Qin, and the differences between the provisional and the real doctrines will naturally be resolved. Evidence to this effect is abundant in the sutras and commentaries, and I will reveal part of it in the hope of assisting beginners.

QUESTION: The transmitters of the Dharma in ancient times composed extensive discourses advocating the six schools and expounded the Tripitaka[6] so abundantly that the texts could not be stored even in a large library, and people grew tired of opening them. Why then do you bother to write this book? What is its worth?

ANSWER: There is much to be expressed; therefore, it should be written. Everything transmitted by former masters is Exoteric Buddhist teachings. Here I am concerned with the Esoteric Buddhist teaching about which people have not had an adequate understanding. I should like to compile, therefore, a handy guide book for your reflection, quoting pertinent passages from sutras and commentaries.

---

4. *Verses on the Middle Way*, by Nagarjuna. The other works mentioned are commentaries.
5. An allusion to the *Lotus Sutra* (the *Saddharmapundarika*).

6. The canon of Buddhism. "The six schools": that is, the Six Nara Schools of early Japanese Buddhism.

QUESTION: What are the differences between the Exoteric Buddhist teachings and the Esoteric Buddhist teaching?

ANSWER: The teachings expounded by the Nirmanakaya Buddha in order to help others, responding to the needs of the time, are called Exoteric. What was expounded by the Dharmakaya Buddha for his own enjoyment, on his innermost spiritual experience, is called Esoteric.

QUESTION: The fact that the Nirmanakaya Buddha preached is agreed upon by all schools. As to the Dharmakaya Buddha, however, we understand that he is formless and imageless, that he is totally beyond verbalization and conceptualization, and that therefore there is no way of explaining him or showing him. Sutras and commentaries describe him in this way. Why do you now assert that the Dharmakaya Buddha preaches? What is your evidence for this?

ANSWER: Now and again the sutras and commentaries refer to this preaching. Misled by their biased preconceptions, people overlook these pertinent passages. Indeed, their meanings will be revealed only in accordance with the capacity of the reader: the same water may be seen as emerald by heavenly beings and as burning fire by hungry ghosts; the same darkness may be seen as light by nocturnal birds and as darkness by men.

QUESTION: If what you have said is really true and is given in the teachings of the Buddha, why have the former transmitters of the Dharma not discussed it?

ANSWER: The sermons of the Tathagata[7] were delivered in accordance with the particular diseases in the minds of his audience; manifold remedies were provided, depending on their varied capacities. The sermons thus adapted to the capacity of his listeners were in many cases provisional and seldom final. When the bodhisattvas composed the commentaries, they wrote faithfully on the basis of the sutras which were provisional in nature. It is therefore said in the commentary on the *Dashabhumika Sutra* written by Vasubandhu[8] that "only the way to enlightenment can be talked about [and not the enlightenment itself]," and also in the commentary on *The Awakening of Faith* written by Nagarjuna that "the perfect sea of enlightenment cannot be talked about." These works were based on the [provisional] sutras and were not intended to advocate the final truth.

The masters of the Dharma who transmitted the Exoteric Buddhist teachings interpreted the [passages of] profound significance [appearing in the Exoteric Buddhist texts] in the light of their shallow doctrines and failed to find any Esoteric import in them. Faithfully transmitting the Exoteric Buddhist teachings from master to disciple, they discussed Buddhism according to the tenets of their particular schools. They so eagerly supported their beliefs that they found no time to meditate on those [passages] which might have been disadvantageous to their doctrines. In the meantime, Buddhism had spread eastward in China and gradually gained a significant role there. The Buddhist texts translated from the time of Emperor Ming of the Later

---

7. A title of a buddha (literally, "one who has thus come/gone"); it is the one most often used by the historical Buddha to refer to himself.

8. On this 4th-century scholar, see the *Abhidharmakosha*, p. 267.

Han Dynasty to that of Empress Wu[9] of the Tang Dynasty were all Exoteric. During the reigns of Emperors Xuanzong and Daizong,[1] when Masters Vajrabodhi and Bukong[2] were active, the Esoteric Buddhist teaching flourished and its profound meaning was discussed enthusiastically. The new medicine had not long been in use, and the old disease was not yet cured. [The Chinese masters of Exoteric Buddhism]—even when they came across passages [of Esoteric significance] such as the statement in the *Lankavatara Sutra*[3] that "the Dharmakaya Buddha preaches," or in the *Dazhidu lun* that "the Dharmakaya Buddha is endowed with an exquisite form"—interpreted them according to their imagination or were governed by the professed doctrines of their schools. It was indeed a pity that these wise masters of ancient times failed to appreciate the taste of ghee [the final truth].

QUESTION: If this is the case, in which sutras and commentaries are the differences between the Exoteric and the Esoteric Buddhist teachings given?

[To this question, Kukai gives the titles of six sutras and three commentaries, and then passages from these and other texts with short remarks of his own at the end of a quotation or a group of quotations. These quotations occupy the major part of the work. In the last section, he remarks:]

The foregoing quotations from sutras and commentaries prove that differences exist between Exoteric Buddhism and Esoteric Buddhism and that the latter was preached by the Dharmakaya Buddha himself. It is hoped that learned readers will deliberate on them and remove their misconceptions.

QUESTION: According to your assertion, what the Dharmakaya Buddha preached on his innermost spiritual experience is Esoteric, and all other Buddhist teachings are Exoteric. Then why is the word Esoteric, applied to some sutras preached by the Shakyamuni Buddha [Nirmanakaya]? We also wonder in which group we should include the dharani[4] teachings imparted by that Buddha?

ANSWER: The meanings of exoteric and esoteric are manifold. If the more profound is compared with the less profound, the former is to be called esoteric and the latter, exoteric. This is the reason why we often find the term esoteric introduced in non-Buddhist scriptures as well. Among the teachings given by the Tathagata, various distinctions between exoteric and esoteric have been made. The Hinayana doctrines explained by the Buddha can be called esoteric when compared to the doctrines given by non-Buddhist teachers. In the same way, when the Mahayana doctrines are compared with the Hinayana doctrines, the former are esoteric and the latter, exoteric. Even in the Mahayana itself, the teaching of the One. Vehicle is esoteric in contrast to the teachings of the Three Vehicles.[5] In order to distinguish the dharani section from other lengthy discourses, we call it esoteric. The teaching given by the Dharmakaya Buddha is the most profound, while the teachings of the Nirmanakaya are apparent and simplified; hence, the former is called esoteric.

---

9. That is, from the 1st century C.E. (r. 58–75) to the 7th century (625–705).
1. Two Tang dynasty emperors (r. 712–56; 626–49).
2. The Indian monk Vajrabodhi and his disciple Amoghavajra (Bukong) helped transmit Esoteric Buddhism to China, arriving there in 720.
3. A Mahayana sutra.
4. An extended mantra in tantric Buddhism.
5. On the three vehicles, see the introduction to the *Lotus Sutra*.

The term esoteric is also used in the senses of "conceal" or "hidden," that is, "sentient beings conceal," and "hidden by the Tathagata." Since sentient beings conceal their original nature, that is, true enlightenment, they "conceal" themselves through illusions derived from ignorance. The doctrine revealed by the Nirmanakaya Buddha is adapted to the needs of the time and is, as it were, an effective medicine to cure the diseases of the mind. Thus the Buddha who preaches for the benefit of others keeps his innermost spiritual experience hidden and does not reveal it in his instructions. It is hidden even from those bodhisattvas who are nearly equal to the Buddha; it transcends the range of understanding of those who are in the Ten Stages of Bodhisattvahood. This is the so-called experience "hidden by the Tathagata."

In this way, the meanings of the term esoteric are many, but the term in its proper sense should be applied only to the secret teaching revealing the innermost experience of the ultimate Dharmakaya Buddha. The dharani section preached by the Nirmanakaya is also called esoteric, but when it is compared to the teaching of the Dharmakaya Buddha, it is not final. Among the teachings called esoteric, there are the provisional and the final; they should be classified properly according to the context.

ON THE POWER OF AMITABHA'S VOW

LAMENTING THE DEVIATIONS
(*Tannisho*)

SHINRAN

The claim that there have been buddhas in the past and that there will be buddhas in the future is a standard element of Buddhist doctrine. And it is said that the next buddha does not appear in the world until teachings of the previous buddha have been forgotten. But how long does that forgetting take? Buddhist texts offer a wide range of predictions about the duration of Shakyamuni Buddha's dharma, ranging from five hundred to five thousand years. For example, he himself said that had he not admitted women into his order, his teaching would have lasted for one thousand years; but their inclusion would limit its existence to only five hundred. The Buddha seems to have been wrong about this, since Buddhism has lasted for almost 2,500 years since his passing. But what do we mean by "last"? The predictions of the disappearance of the dharma often speak of a slow but steady process of degeneration— not of the dharma but rather of its practitioners, who increasingly become deficient in intelligence as well as in morality.

Thus, what is one to do if one lives in a period when it is no longer possible to follow the path to its conclusion? One approach is to wait for the next buddha, Maitreya. But his advent is, by common consent, many millions of years in the future. In East Asia, the most important response to this problem was Pure Land practice, first in China and then in Japan, where Pure Land became a major school of Japanese Buddhism.

In the twelfth century, the Japanese monk Honen (1133–1212) read the entire Buddhist canon three times (in Chinese) before concluding that during the degenerate age (which according to the calculations of the day had begun in 1052), faith in chanting the name of the buddha Amitabha (see the *Sukhavativyuha Sutra*, p. 316) was the only possible path to salvation. He is said to have chanted *namu amida butsu*, "Homage to Amitabha Buddha," seventy thousand times a day. He also stressed the importance of ethical practice, saying that if a wicked man can be reborn in the Pure Land, a good man has a far better chance. When two of his monks, known for their beautiful chanting, were invited to court and ended up spending the night in the ladies' quarters, the monks were executed and Honen was sent into exile on the island of Shikoku.

Also exiled (although to a different region) was a disciple of Honen, the monk Shinran (1173–1263), who developed views different from those of his teacher. Like Honen, he believed that any attempt to rely on one's own powers to achieve freedom from rebirth was futile. But he considered the power of Amitabha to be so absolute that even making the effort to silently say *namu amida butsu*—a phrase called "the *nembutsu*" in Japanese—was an act of hubris. Hearing Amitabha's name in one's heart was a sign of his salvific power, not one's own will. It was therefore redundant to say the name more than once in one's life; all subsequent recitation should be regarded as a form of thanksgiving. Shinran therefore reversed Honen's assertion. He said that if the good man can be reborn in the Pure Land, then the wicked man, who had no delusions about his ability to achieve his own salvation, has a far better chance. For once one abandons the conceit that happiness (in this life or the next) can be achieved through one's own willful deeds and instead entrusts oneself to the power of Amitabha, one is instantaneously freed from the bonds of samsara in this life and will be born in his Pure Land at death. Liberation in this sense occurs not at death but at the initial moment of faith in Amitabha, and even that moment of faith is a manifestation of the mind of Amitabha. Thus, for Shinran all other forms of Buddhist practice were pointless. Indeed, he concluded that the sole purpose of Shakyamuni's appearance in the world was to proclaim the existence of Amitabha's Pure Land, as he did in the *Sukhavativyuha Sutra*.

Shinran lived a long life, attracting a large following, but never claimed any particular status for himself; he referred to himself as the "bald-headed idiot." After his death, however, disagreements quickly developed about his theology. In response, one of his disciples wrote down candid conversations that Shinran had had on a wide range of issues. For example, the disciple asks Shinran, "Although I say the nembutsu, I rarely experience joyful happiness, nor do I have the desire to immediately go to the Pure Land. What should be done about this?" Shinran replies that he has the same question. These conversations are found in a small book titled *Tannisho*, or *Lamenting the Deviations*. It is presented here in full.

PRONOUNCING GLOSSARY

Amida: *ah-mee-dah*	Seikan: *say-kahn*
dharmakaya: *dar-ma-kah-ya*	Shandao: *shahn-dau*
Hiei: *hee-ay*	Shingon: *sheen-gohn*
Honen: *hoh-nehn*	Shinran: *sheen-rahn*
Nara: *nah-rah*	Tannisho: *than-nee-shoh*
nembutsu: *nehm-boo-tsoo*	Tathagata: *ta-tah-ga-ta*
Shakyamuni: *shah-kya-mu-ni*	Yuien: *yoo-ee-ehn*

Prologue

In reflecting upon my foolish thoughts and thinking of the past and present, I deeply regret that there are views deviating from the true entrusting which was taught orally by our late master, and I fear that doubts and confusions may arise among the followers who come after us. Unless we rely upon a good teacher with whom, fortunately, our karmic destinies are bound, how can we possibly enter the true gate of effortless practice? Do not violate the fundamentals of Other Power[1] by imposing upon it your own interpretations.

Thus have I committed to writing some words of the late Shinran which still ring clearly in my ears. My sole purpose is to dispel the clouds of doubt in the minds of the practicers with the same aspiration.

I

When the thought of saying the nembutsu[2] emerges decisively from within, having entrusted ourselves to the inconceivable power of Amida's vow[3] which saves us, enabling us to be born in the Pure Land, in that very moment we receive the ultimate benefit of being grasped never to be abandoned.

Amida's Primal Vow does not discriminate between the young and old, good and evil; true entrusting alone is essential. The reason is that the Vow is directed to the being burdened with the weight of karmic evil and burning with the flames of blind passion.

Thus, in entrusting ourselves to the Primal Vow, no other form of good is necessary, for there is no good that surpasses the nembutsu. And evil need not be feared, for there is no evil which can obstruct the working of Amida's Primal Vow.

II

I believe that the reason you have come here, crossing over more than ten provinces at the risk of your lives, is solely to ascertain the path that leads to birth in the Pure Land. But if you suspect that I know ways other than the nembutsu to attain birth, or that I am versed in the scriptures connected with it, you are greatly mistaken. If that be the case, there are many eminent scholars in the monasteries of Nara and Mt. Hiei, so you should go see them and ask them in detail about the way to attain birth in the Pure Land.

As for myself Shinran, I simply receive the words of my dear teacher, Honen,[4] "Just say the nembutsu and be saved by Amida," and entrust myself to the Primal Vow. Besides this, there is nothing else.

I really do not know whether the nembutsu may be the cause for my birth in the Pure Land, or the act that shall condemn me to hell. But I have nothing to regret, even if I should have been deceived by my teacher, and, saying

---

TRANSLATED FROM the Japanese by Taitetsu Unno.

1. The power of Amitabha.
2. See the introduction to this selection.
3. That is, that all who hear his name (Amitabha) and wish to be reborn in his pure land will be

reborn there (see the *Sukhavativyuha Sutra*, p. 316).
4. Founder of the Pure Land school in Japan (1133–1212).

the nembutsu, fall into hell. The reason is that if I were capable of realizing Buddhahood by other religious practices and yet fell into hell for saying the nembutsu, I might have dire regrets for having been deceived. But since I am absolutely incapable of any religious practice, hell is my only home.

If Amida's Primal Vow is true, Shakyamuni's[5] teaching cannot be false. If the Buddha's teaching is true, Shandao's[6] commentaries cannot be false. If Shandao's commentaries are true, how can Honen's words be empty? If Honen's words are true, what I, Shinran, say cannot be meaningless. In essence, such is the true entrusting of this foolish one. Now, whether you accept the nembutsu, entrusting yourself to it, or reject it, that is your own decision.

III

Even a good person attains birth in the Pure Land, how much more so the evil person.

But the peoples of the world constantly say, even the evil person attains birth, how much more so the good person. Although this appears to be sound at first glance, it goes against the intention of the Primal Vow of Other Power. The reason is that since the person of self-power, being conscious of doing good, lacks the thought of entrusting himself completely to Other Power, he is not the focus of the Primal Vow of Amida. But when he turns over self-power and entrusts himself to Other Power, he attains birth in the land of True Fulfillment.

The Primal Vow was established out of deep compassion for us who cannot become freed from the bondage of birth-and-death through any religious practice, due to the abundance of blind passion. Since its basic intention is to effect the enlightenment of such an evil one, the evil person who entrusts himself to Other Power is truly the one who attains birth in the Pure Land. Thus, even the good person attains birth, how much more so the evil person!

IV

There is a difference in compassion between the Path of Sages[7] and the Path of Pure Land. The compassion in the Path of Sages is expressed through pity, sympathy, and care for all beings, but truly rare is it that one can help another as completely as one desires.

The compassion in the Path of Pure Land is to quickly attain Buddhahood, saying the nembutsu, and with the true heart of compassion and love save all beings as we desire.

In this life no matter how much pity and sympathy we may feel for others, it is impossible to help another as we truly wish; thus our compassion is inconsistent and limited. Only the saying of nembutsu manifests the complete and never ending compassion which is true, real, and sincere.

---

5. "Sage of the Shakyas": a title of the Buddha, who was born into the Shakya clan.
6. A Chinese monk (613–681), an important advocate of Pure Land practice.
7. The traditional Mahayana path.

V

I, Shinran, have never even once uttered the nembutsu for the sake of my father and mother. The reason is that all beings have been fathers and mothers, brothers and sisters, in the timeless process of birth-and-death. When I attain Buddahood in the next birth, each and everyone will be saved.

If it were a good accomplished by my own powers, then I could transfer the accumulated merits of nembutsu to save my father and mother. But since this is not the case, when we become free from self-power and quickly attain the enlightenment of the Pure Land, we will save those bound closest to us through transcendental powers, no matter how deeply they are immersed in karmic suffering of the six realms of existence and the four modes of birth.[8]

VI

It is utterly unthinkable that among the followers of single-hearted nembutsu practice there are arguments about "my disciples" and "other's disciples."

As for myself, Shinran, I do not have a single disciple. If I could make others say the nembutsu through my own devices, they would be my disciples. But how arrogant to claim as disciples those who live the nembutsu through the sole working of Amida's compassion.

If the karmic condition is to come together, we shall be together; if the karmic condition is to be separated, we shall be separated. How absurd that some people assert that if one goes against his own teacher and says the nembutsu under another, he cannot attain birth in the Pure Land. Are they saying that they will take back the true entrusting which is a gift from Amida as if it belonged to them? Impossible that such a thing should happen.

When we live according to the reality of "made to become so by itself," we shall know gratitude to the Buddha, as well as to our teachers.

VII

In the person of nembutsu opens up the great path of unobstructed freedom. The reason is that the gods of heaven and earth bow before the practicer of true entrusting, and those of the world of demons and rival paths cannot obstruct his way. The consequences of karmic evil cannot bear fruit, nor does any form of good equal his. Thus, it is called the great path of unobstructed freedom.

VIII

The saying of nembutsu is neither a religious practice nor a good act. Since it is practiced without my calculation, it is "non-practice." Since it is also

8. According to Buddhists, sentient beings are born variously from the womb, from the egg, from warmth and moisture, and from a miracle. "The six realms of existence": the realms of gods, demigods, humans, animals, ghosts, and the denizens of hell.

not a good created by my calculation, it is "non-good." Since it is nothing but Other Power, completely separated from self-power, it is neither a religious practice nor a good act on the part of the practicer.

IX

"Although I say the nembutsu, I rarely experience joyful happiness nor do I have the desire to immediately go to the Pure Land. What should be done about this?," I asked. Then he responded, "I, Shinran, have been having the same question also, and now you, Yuien, have the same thought."

"When I carefully consider the matter, my birth in the Pure Land is settled without doubt for the very reason that I do not rejoice at that which should have me bursting with joy. It is the working of blind passion which suppresses the heart that would rejoice and prevents its fullest expression. All this the Buddha already knew and called us foolish beings filled with blind passion; thus, when we realize that the compassionate Vow of Other Power is for beings like ourselves, the Vow becomes even more reliable and dependable."

"The working of blind passion also causes us not to want to go to the Pure Land and makes us feel uneasy worrying about death when we become even slightly ill. Impossible it seems to leave this old house of agitation where we have wandered aimlessly since the beginning of time, nor can we long for the Pure Land of peace which we have yet to know. This is due to blind passion so truly powerful and overwhelming. But no matter how reluctant we may be, when our life in this world comes to an end, beyond our control, than for the first time we go to the land of Fulfillment. Those who do not want to go immediately are the special concern of true compassion. For this very reason the Vow of true compassion is completely dependable, and our birth in the Pure Land is absolutely certain."

"If our hearts were filled with joyful happiness and we desired to go swiftly to the Pure Land, we might be misled and suspect that perhaps we are free of blind passion."

X

The master Shinran said, in the nembutsu no selfworking is true working; it is beyond description, explanation, and conceivability.

Special Preface

While the master was still living, those who journeyed together with great difficulty to the distant capital with the same aspiration, and who, united in true entrusting, set their hearts on the coming land of Fulfillment, all listened at the same time to his real thoughts. But now I hear that among the countless people young and old who say the nembutsu, following after them, there are some who frequently express erroneous views never taught by the master. Such groundless views call for discussion which follows.

XI

In meeting unlettered people who say the nembutsu some people bother them with such questions as, "Do you say the nembutsu by entrusting yourself to the inconceivable power of the Vow or to the inconceivable power of the Name?" They fail to clarify the two forms of inconceivable powers and their significance. Thus, they confuse the minds of the people. We must turn our attention to this matter and carefully consider the connection between the two.

By virtue of the inconceivable power of the Vow, Amida Buddha devised the Name easy to uphold and pronounce and, thereby, promised to take in all who say the Name. Thus, when we entrust ourselves to the inconceivable power of Amida's compassionate vow which saves us to deliver us from birth-and-death, and when we realize that the saying of nembutsu occurs because of the Tathagata's[9] working, since our own calculation is not involved, we are in accord with the Primal Vow and will be born in the land of True Fulfillment.

When we entrust ourselves to the inconceivable power of the Primal Vow as the heart of the matter, then the inconceivable power of the Name is also naturally found together with it. The inconceivable powers of the Vow and of the Name are therefore one, and not the slightest difference between the two exists.

Next, he who inserts his own calculations into the consideration of good and evil, believing that the former helps and the latter hinders birth in the Pure Land, fails to entrust himself to the inconceivable power of the Vow. Rather, he strives in his own efforts to achieve birth; he claims the nembutsu which he utters as his own practice. Such a person also fails to entrust himself to the inconceivable power of the Name.

However, even though he fails to entrust himself, he will be born in the borderland, the realm of indolence, the castle of doubt, or the palace of womb to be born eventually in the land of Fulfillment by virtue of the Vow which vowed that unless all beings are saved, Amida will not have attained Buddhahood. All this is due to the inconceivable power of the Name. Since this is due to none other than the inconceivable power of the Vow, the Vow and the Name are one and the same.

XII

Some people say that those who do not read and study the sutras and commentaries cannot be certain of birth in the Pure Land. This view is hardly worthy of serious consideration.

All the sutras which reveal the essentials of the truth of Other Power simply state: By saying the nembutsu, entrusting oneself to the Primal Vow, one attains Buddhahood. What further knowledge is required for birth in the Pure Land? Truly, those who are still confused about this should by all means study hard and realize the purpose of the Primal Vow. If the true meaning of the sacred texts is not clearly understood, even though one reads and studies the sutras and commentaries, it is a great pity.

---

9. A title of a buddha (literally, "one who has thus come/gone"); it is the one most often used by the historical Buddha to refer to himself.

Since the Name is devised to be easily said by the unlettered who cannot even grasp the basic meaning of the sutras and commentaries, such utterance is called effortless practice. Learning is a requirement in the Path of Sages; thus, it is called difficult practice. There are some who mistakenly pursue knowledge for the sake of fame and profit; their birth in the next life is doubtful, so reads an attesting passage.

Today, the people of single-hearted nembutsu and those of the Path of Sages fall into dispute, claiming that one school is superior and the other inferior. Thus, enemies of dharma appear, and slandering of dharma occurs. But is this not slandering and destroying one's own dharma?

Even if all the schools together proclaim, "The nembutsu is for those who are foolish; its teaching is shallow and base," do not object. Instead, simply reply, "We are taught that foolish people of inferior capacity like ourselves, unlettered and ignorant, will be saved by entrusting ourselves to Amida. As we accept this and entrust ourselves, it is the supreme dharma for us, regardless of how base it my seem to people of superior capacity. No matter how superb other teachings may be, if they are beyond our realization and mastery, we cannot uphold them. Since it is the basic intention of the Buddhas that we shall all together go beyond birth-and-death, you should not hinder us." In this way, if we have no rancor, who would want to hurt us? Furthermore, an attesting passage states, "Where there are arguments, various kinds of blind passion are awakened; the wise should avoid them."

The late master also said, "The Buddha predicted that there will be people who shall entrust themselves to this dharma and people who shall slander it. I have already entrusted myself to the dharma, and there are those who slander it—by this we know that the Buddha's words are true. In fact, we should realize that our birth is even more firmly settled. If, contrary to this, no one denounced the nembutsu, we might wonder why there are no slanderers, even though there are believers. But this, of course, does not mean that the teaching should necessarily become the object of slander. The Buddha taught this because he knew that both those who entrust themselves and those who slander would exist. His teaching was designed to dispel any doubts that might arise in us."

Is knowledge meant to be no more than a means of defending against criticism and for engaging in arguments and debates? If one truly studies, he will come to see more clearly the intention of the Buddha. Realizing the boundlessness of true compassion, such a student will teach those who are unsure of being born in the Pure Land because of their nature of the Primal Vow does not discriminate between the good and evil, the pure and impure. Only then will learning be meaningful.

People who insist that knowledge is essential frighten those who live the nembutsu in accord with the Primal Vow. Such pedagogues are demons obstructing the dharma and hated enemies of the Buddha. They not only lack the more true entrusting of Other Power, but they wrongly mislead others. They should stand in fear lest they go against the teaching of our late master. And they should be filled with remorse for going against Amida's Primal Vow.

XIII

Some people say that those who do not fear committing evil because of the inconceivable power of Amida's Vow are guilty of taking pride in the Primal

Vow and, therefore, will not attain birth. This betrays doubt in the Primal Vow and shows a lack of understanding of good and evil resulting from past karma.

Good thoughts arise in our minds due to the effect of past good, and we are made to think and do evil due to the working of karmic evil. The late master said, "We should know that even as trifling a thing as the speck of dust on the tip of a rabbit's hair or a sheep's fleece is the product of the evil of past karma." At another time he asked me, "Would you accept anything I say, Yuien?"

"Of course, I will," I replied.

"Are you sure that you won't disobey me?," he repeated, and when I again agreed, he continued, "Go, then, and kill a thousand people and your birth in the Pure Land is settled."

"Even though that is your order," I protested, "and even with all that is in me, I cannot kill even a single person."

"Then why did you just say that you would not disobey what I, Shinran, said?" And then he went on, "By this we know that if we could act according to our thoughts, we could kill a thousand people for the sake of birth in the Pure Land—if so required. We do not kill, not because our thoughts are good but because we do not have the karma to kill even a single person. Yet, even though we do not want to injure anyone, we may be led to kill a hundred or a thousand people."

The gist of this statement is that when we think good thoughts, we think we are good; and when we think evil thoughts, we think we are evil, not realizing fully that it is the inconceivable power of the Vow that makes our salvation possible.

Once there was a man who fell into wrong views proclaiming that he would purposefully do evil as a way for attaining birth, since the Vow is directed to those who commit evil. Thus saying, he performed many evils. When Shinran heard about this, he admonished in a letter, "Do not take poison just because there is an antidote." He made this point to correct such wrong attachments, but not at all to say that evil is an obstacle to attaining birth.

Shinran, furthermore, said, "If upholding the precepts and the disciplines are required for entrusting ourselves to the Primal Vow, how could we ever hope to go beyond birth-and-death? It is only by encountering the Primal Vow that such hopeless beings as ourselves become prideful and haughty. And yet evil can never be committed, unless it is within us."

Again, he said, "People who make a living by casting nets or fishing in the seas and rivers, those who sustain themselves by hunting beasts and catching birds in the moors and mountains, and people who pass their lives by trading and cultivating the fields are all alike." In the words of Shinran, "Under the influence of our karmic past we human beings will do anything."

And yet, in recent years people put on the guise of striving on the nembutsu path. They claim that only the good people should say the nembutsu. Or they post restrictions in the gathering places, proclaiming that those who commit certain acts are prohibited from entering. Are these not the sort of people who show outwardly how wise, virtuous, and diligent they are, while inwardly cherishing vanity and falsehood?

Karmic evil committed because of taking pride in the Vow is also an effect of past karma. Thus, leave everything good and evil to the working of karma and single-heartedly entrust yourself to the Primal Vow. Such is the way of Other Power. In *Essentials of Faith Alone*[1] it is said, "To what extent does one know the power of Amida's compassion when he believes that salvation is impossible because of his karmic evil?" For the very reason that we are guilty of taking pride in the Primal Vow, the true entrusting of Other Power is settled.

We can be free of taking pride in the Primal Vow only after having extinguished karmic evil and blind passion. But if blind passion is extinguished, one is a Buddha, and for a Buddha the Vow realized through five kalpas[2] of profound thought would be of no use.

Since the people who censure others for taking pride in the Primal Vow themselves are filled with blind passion and impurities, are they also not guilty of taking pride in the Primal Vow? If so, what is the evil that takes pride in the Primal Vow, and what is the evil that does not take pride in the Primal Vow? Indeed, all this debate is immature and shallow.

XIV

Some people say that one should believe that heavy evils of eight billion kalpas can be extinguished in the single utterance of nembutsu. This view refers to an evil person, guilty of ten vices and five transgressions,[3] who has never said the nembutsu in his lifetime but who for the first time on his deathbed is told by a good teacher that if he says the nembutsu once, he shall extinguish the evils of eight billion kalpas, and if he says the nembutsu ten times, he shall extinguish the evils of eighty billion kalpas and thus attain birth. Is the single utterance or ten utterances meant to show the relative weights of ten vices and five transgressions? If so, this has to do with the utility of nembutsu in extinguishing evil. This is far from our understanding. The reason is that in the awakening of one thought-moment, having been illuminated by Amida's light, we are endowed with the diamond-like entrusting, and, thus, we are already included in the stage of the truly settled. When our life comes to an end, all the blind passions and evil hindrances are immediately transformed into the realization of the "wisdom of non-origination."

Realizing that without this compassionate vow, wretched and evil beings such as ourselves can never go beyond birth-and-death, we should know that all the nembutsu said throughout our lifetimes simply express gratitude for the benevolence and the virtues of Tathagata's compassion.

To believe that each saying of nembutsu extinguishes evil is to aspire to birth by eliminating evil through one's own efforts. If so, since every thought that we think throughout our life binds us to birth-and-death, we must say the nembutsu, continuously and consistently, until the final moment, for the sake of attaining birth. But karmic consequences being decisive, we may end our life by encountering unforeseen accidents, or be tormented by illness, without ever attaining right-mindedness. Saying the nembutsu in such a state would be, indeed, most difficult. How are we to extinguish evil during such a time? If evil does not disappear, then is attaining birth impossible?

1. A work by Shinran.
2. Aeons, cosmic cycles.
3. The ten vices are killing, stealing, sexual misconduct, lying, divisive speech, harsh speech, senseless speech, covetousness, harmful intent, and wrong views; the five transgressions are killing one's father, killing one's mother, killing an arhat, wounding a buddha, or causing schism in the sangha (Buddhist community).

When we entrust ourselves to the Vow that grasps us never to abandon, we shall quickly attain birth—regardless of whether we commit evils for incomprehensible reasons, and even end our lives without saying the nembutsu. And when we spontaneously say the nembutsu, our trust in Amida becomes stronger and our gratitude to Tathagata deepens as we approach the moment of supreme enlightenment. To desire to extinguish evil is the thought of self-power, the basic intent of those who hope to achieve right-mindedness at the moment of death. This shows the lack of true entrusting to Other Power.

XV

Some people say that enlightenment is already attained in this very body filled with blind passion. This is completely out of the question.

The doctrince of attaining Buddhahood in this very body is the essential teaching of Shingon Esoterism and the ultimate attainment of the three esoteric practices. And the purification of the six sense-organs[4] is the teaching of the One Vehicle Lotus Sutra and the result attained through the four blissful practices.[5] These are all difficult practices performed by those of superior religious capacity, the enlightenment realized through perfecting meditation. In contrast, the enlightenment that unfolds in the next birth is the essence of the Pure Land teaching of Other Power; it is the way of true entrusting which is settled. This is also the effortless practice to be undertaken by those of inferior religious capacity, the dharma in which the discrimination between good and evil is non-existent.

Since it is extremely difficult to sunder blind passion and evil hindrances in this life, the virtuous monks who practice Shingon and Tendai disciplines also pray for enlightenment in the birth to come. How much more so for people like ourselves! Although the observance of precepts and wisdom are lacking, when we have crossed the painful ocean of birth-and-death on the vessel of Amida's Vow and have reached the shore of the land of Fulfillment, the dark clouds of blind passion immediately vanish and the moon of enlightenment of dharma-as-it-is appears instantaneously. Having become one with Unhindered Light that illuminates the ten quarters,[6] we bring benefits to all beings. This is true enlightenment.

Do those who believe that they attain enlightenment in this very body reveal themselves, as did Shakyamuni, in various manifestations of enlightenment, do they possess the thirty-two features and eighty characteristics of an enlightened being, and do they benefit all beings by expounding the dharma? This is what constitutes enlightenment in this life. In a poem Shinran writes:

> When the entrusting of diamond-like firmness
> Is settled, at that very moment
> Amida's light grasps us and protects us
> And we go beyond birth-and-death forever.

4. Eye, ear, nose, tongue, body, and mind.
5. Proper behavior in mind, in body, and in speech and the vow to lead all beings to nirvana.

6. That is, the ten directions, or everywhere (north, south, east, west, northeast, northwest, southeast, southwest, the nadir, and the zenith).

This means that when true entrusting is settled, Amida grasps us never to abandon, and we no longer transmigrate in the six realms of existence. Thus, we go beyond birth-and-death forever.

When we realize this, how can we confuse it with the enlightenment in this life? How sad to have such a misunderstanding! As the late master taught, "In the true teaching of Pure Land I have been taught that in this life we entrust ourselves to the Primal Vow and in that land attain supreme enlightenment."

XVI

Some people say that if a practicer of true entrusting should unexpectedly become angry, act wantonly, or argue with fellow practicers, they should by all means undertake the turning-of-mind. Does this mean that we must sunder evil and practice good?

In the person of single-hearted nembutsu the turning-of-mind occurs only once. The turning-of-mind refers to the transformation of heart of those ignorant of the true teaching of the Primal Vow of Other Power who, being granted Amida's true wisdom and realizing the impossibility of attaining birth with everyday mind, abandons the old mind and entrusts himself to the Primal Vow.

If we had to undertake the turning-of-mind day and night about every deed in order to attain birth, since our lives may come to an end between the moment the exhaled breath is inhaled, we may die before the turning-of-mind or cultivating tenderness and forebearance. Then the Vow which grasps us never to abandon would have been meaningless.

Even though some say that they entrust themselves to the power of the Vow, actually they feel that only the good are saved, no matter how great the inconceivable power of the Vow which saves the evil doer. To that extent they doubt the power of the Vow, lack the thought of entrusting to Other Power, and will be born in the borderland. How lamentable this is!

Once true entrusting is settled, we realize that since our birth is due to the working of Amida, it is not due to our calculation. Even though we do evil, we should even more think of the power of the Vow. Then the thought of tenderness and forebearance will become manifest by virtue of "made to become so by itself."

In all matters regarding birth it is not necessary to contrive or design but always to remember and become enthralled with the deep and profound compassion of Amida. Then we shall be able to say the nembutsu, "made to become so by itself." When I do not contrive, it is called "made to become so by itself." This is none other than Other Power. And yet to my regret I hear that people speak knowingly about "being made so by itself" as though it were something special. How deplorable this is!

XVII

Some people say that those born in the borderland will eventually fall into hell. In what attesting passage is this found?

That this is asserted by those who claim to be scholars is truly deplorable. How do they read the sutras, commentaries, and teachings? I was taught that people who lack true entrusting because they doubt the Primal Vow are born in the borderland where they atone for the evil karma of doubt and ultimately gain enlightenment in the land of Fulfillment.

Since true entrusting is very rare, many people are led to the temporary land. And yet to contend that they are ultimately hopeless is to accuse the Buddha of falsehood.

XVIII

Some people say that the amount of offerings made to the Buddha dharma will determine the size that we will become as Buddhas.

First of all, is it possible to determine the size of Buddha, whether great or small? Even though the size of Buddha in the Pure Land is described in a sutra, it is the manifestation of the dharmakya[7]-as-compassion. When one attains enlightenment of dharma-as-it-is, how can size be a factor, since such shapes as long or short, square or round, do not exist, and it transcends color, whether blue, yellow, red, white, or black?

Some say that they see the transformed Buddha in uttering nembutsu. Could they have based their view on such statements as "In loud utterance one sees a big Buddha, and in quiet utterance one sees a small Buddha" and applied it here?

Furthermore, although offerings can be part of the practice of selfless giving, no matter how many valuables we give to the Buddha or present to our teachers, the deed is meaningless if true entrusting is lacking. If one gives himself up to Other Power and true entrusting is deep, even though one does not give even a single sheet of paper or half a coin to the Buddha dharma, he is in accord with the will of the Vow.

Do people intimidate their fellow practicers, using the dharma as a pretext, to fulfill their own selfish desires?

Epilogue

I feel that the preceding views all arise as the result of differences regarding true entrusting. According to the late master Shinran, it was likewise at the time of his teacher Honen among whose disciples were only a few people who truly entrusted themselves to Amida. Once this caused Shinran to enter into an argument with his fellow disciples. When he said, "Shinran's entrusting and Honen's entrusting are identical," Seikan, Nenbutsu, and others strongly refuted it, saying:

"How can you say that our master's entrusting and your entrusting are identical!" To this Shinran replied,

"Our master's wisdom and learning are truly profound and to claim that ours are identical is preposterous. But as far as the true entrusting which leads to birth is concerned, there is no difference at all. They are one and the same."

Still they continued pressing Shinran, challenging him by saying, "How can that possibly be!" Finally they decided to settle the dispute once and for

7. The dharma body, or "truth."

all, so they related the details to their master Honen. When this was presented to him, Honen said,

"The entrusting of Honen is a gift granted by the Tathagata, and the entrusting of Shinran is also a gift from the Tathagata. Thus, they are the same. People who entrust differently will probably not go to the same Pure Land as I."

Such was the case in earlier times, and it seems that among the followers of single-hearted nembutsu today there are some who do not share the same entrusting as that of Shinran. Although what I have said may be very repetitious, I have put all this down in writing.

Since my life like a dew drop still hangs on this body which is like withered grass, I am able to hear the doubts of my fellow practicers and am able to tell them what I have learned from my master. But I fear and lament that after my eyes close there may arise chaos because of divergent views.

When you are confused by people who advocate such views as the above, you should carefully read the scriptures approved and used by our late master. Generally among scriptures you will find a mixture of teachings which are true and real and which are accommodating and tentative. The master's basic idea was to abandon the teachings accommodating the needs of the people and chose the real, to reject the tentatively presented and select the true. Be very careful to discern such distinctions in the scriptures. I have listed a few passages which attest to true entrusting and have included them into this tract for easy reference.

The master constantly said, "When I ponder on the compassionate vow of Amida, established through five kalpas of profound thought, it was for myself, Shinran, alone. Because I am a being burdened so heavily with karma, I feel even more deeply grateful to the Primal Vow which is decisively made to save me."

As I now reflect upon these words, it is no different from the maxim of Shandao. "Truly know that this self is a foolish being of karmic evil, repeating birth-and-death since beginningless aeons ago, forever drowning and wandering without ever knowing the path of liberation."

How grateful I am that Shinran expressed this in his own person to make us deeply realize that we do not know the depth of karmic evil and that we do not know the height of Tathagata's benevolence, all of which cause us to live in utter confusion.

In reality, all of us, including myself, talk only about what is good and evil without realizing the Tathagata's benevolence. According to the master, he said, "I do not know what the two, good and evil, really mean. I could say that I know what good is, if I knew good as thoroughly and completely as the Tathagata; and I could say I know what evil is, if I knew evil as thoroughly and completely as the Tathagata. But in this foolish being filled with blind passion, living in this impermanent world of burning house, all things are empty and vain; therefore, untrue. Only the nembutsu is true, real, and sincere."

Among the lies we speak to each other, one is truly to be lamented. That is, when people, in saying the nembutsu, talk about true entrusting among themselves or try to explain it to others, they even ascribe words to Shinran never spoken by him in order to silence people or stop further inquiry. How deplorable and regrettable! You should carefully understand this and reflect upon it.

Although the above are by no means my own words, they may sound a little odd, for I am not too well versed in the contents of the sutras and commentaries, and I have yet to clearly perceive the depth of the teaching. But I have tried to recall some fragments, perhaps one one-hundredth, of what the late Shinran taught and have put them down in writing. How sad it is if those who are fortunate enough to say the nembutsu are not immediately born in the land of Fulfillment but must reside in the borderland.

In tears I have dipped my brush in ink and have written this in the hope that conflicting views of true entrusting will not be found among fellow practicers gathered in a single room. Thus, this is called *Tannisho: Lamenting the Deviations*. It should not be shown to outsiders.

TREASURY OF THE TRUE DHARMA EYE
(*The Shobogenzo*)

DOGEN

In 1223, the young Japanese monk Dogen (1200–1253) accompanied his teacher on a voyage to China. He visited a number of monastic centers of the Chan sect, including one on Mount Tiantong, where he met the master Rujing (1162–1227). One day, he overheard the master scolding a monk who was sleeping. Rujing said, "The practice of meditation is the sloughing off of mind and body. What does sleeping accomplish?" There is some question about what was actually said—the phrase "sloughing off mind and body," which would figure prominently in Dogen's later teachings, does not appear in Rujing's surviving writings or in other Chan works of the period, and Dogen likely had a limited understanding of spoken Chinese—but what he heard led to an awakening.

While in China, Dogen apparently had doubts about the efficacy of koan practice, especially when done at the expense of the study of the Indian scriptures, which by that time had been translated into Chinese. Dogen instead preferred the seated meditation of the Caodong lineage, one of the "Five Houses and Seven Schools" of the Chan tradition in China. It was this very lineage that Dahui (see the introduction to *Records of Pointing at the Moon*, p. 557) in the previous century had condemned for its practice of "silent illumination," and Dogen is credited with establishing it in Japan (in Japanese, *Caodong* is pronounced "Soto").

Eiheiji, a Japanese monastery founded by Dogen.

After his return to Japan after four years in China, Dogen slowly developed a following. As a result of sectarian rivalries in Kyoto, in 1243 he moved to a remote region to the north, where he established the monastery of Eiheji; there he would spend the final decade of his life. Like so many of the great teachers of East Asian Buddhism, Dogen was concerned with the relationship between practice and enlightenment, especially in light of the doctrine of the *tathagatagarbha*, or "buddha nature" (see the *Tathagatagarbha Sutra*, p. 340). If all beings are endowed with the buddha nature and thus are originally enlightened, what is the meaning of Buddhist practice? If the buddhas of the past were already buddhas, what does it mean to say that they attained buddhahood? Dogen's conclusion was that practice and attainment are one. He therefore taught what he called "just sitting" (*shikantaza*), a practice not intended to result in any attainment; instead, it is a state of alert attention in which the mind remains free of thought and has no object. For Dogen, this was the meditation practiced by the Buddha: thus, to sit in the meditative posture was to be a buddha.

He was a prolific author whose masterwork is generally considered to be *Shobogenzo*, or *Treasury of the True Dharma Eye*. Dogen presumably took the title from an identically named work written by the Chan master Dahui. Dogen's *Shobogenzo* is a collection of essays composed between 1231 and 1253, the year of his death. It is renowned for its elliptical style, clever wordplay, and mastery of a large literature, which includes both Buddhist texts and Chinese classics. The twenty-eighth chapter— "Paying Obeisance and Getting the Marrow" (Raihai tokuzui), on how to show respect to one's teacher—is presented here in its entirety.

PRONOUNCING GLOSSARY

bhikshu: *bik-shu*
bhikshuni: *bik-shu-nee*
Bodhidharma: *boh-di-dar-ma*
bodhisattva: *boh-di-sat-tva*
deva: *day-va*
Dogen: *doe-gen*
En'o: *ehn-oh*
Gaoan Dayu: *gau-ahn dah-yoo*
Huai: *hwai*
Huangbo: *hwahng-boh*
Kannon Dori Kosho Horinji: *kahn-nohn doh-ree koh-shoh hoh-reen-jee*
kanoe-ne: *ka-noh-eh-neh*
Koshoji: *koh-shoh-jee*
Liaoran: *lyau-rahn*
Linji: *leen-jee*
Mahayana: *ma-hah-yah-na*
Miaoxin: *myau-sheen*
Moshan: *moh-shahn*
Ninji: *neen-jee*

prajna: *praj-nyah*
Raihai tokuzui: *rah-ee-hah-ee toh-koo-zoo-ee*
Seimei: *say-may*
Shakyamuni: *shah-kya-mu-ni*
shobogenzo: *sho-bo-gen-zo*
shravaka: *shrah-va-ka*
Shu: *shoo*
Song: *sohng*
Tang: *tahng*
upasaka: *u-pah-sa-ka*
upasika: *u-pah-si-kah*
Xin: *sheen*
Yang: *yahng*
Yangshan: *yahng-shahn*
Yun: *yoon*
Zhaozhou: *jau-joh*
Zhenji: *jan-jee*
Zhixian: *jer-shyehn*

Book 28. Paying Obeisance and Getting the Marrow
(Raihai tokuzui)

When one practices *anuttara-samyak-sambodhi* ["supreme, perfect awakening"], the most difficult thing is to get a guide. That guide is not in the form of a man or woman but will be a great person, will be "such a person" [who has got "such a thing" as awakening]. It is not a person of past or present; it will likely be a good friend ["teacher"] who is "a fox spirit." This is the face of one who has "got the marrow" [of Bodhidharma's[1] teaching], one who will be our guide and benefactor. It is one who is "not in the dark about cause and effect"; it could be you or I or someone else.

After we have encountered a guide, we should cast off the myriad involvements and, without passing "an inch of shadow" [i.e., a moment of time], devote ourselves vigorously to pursuing the way. We should practice with mind, practice with no mind, practice with half a mind. Thus, we should [make extraordinary efforts, as if to] "brush a fire from our heads," [as if to] study [in the ascetic practice of] "standing on one leg." When we do this, we will not be assaulted by the abusive legions of Mara.[2] The [Zen] Ancestor [Huike][3] who "cut off his arm and got the marrow" [of Bodhidharma] is not someone else; the master who "sloughs off body and mind" is ourselves.

Getting the marrow and receiving transmission of the teachings always depend upon utmost sincerity, upon the believing mind. There are no traces of sincere faith coming from elsewhere, nor are there directions to which it departs from within. It is simply a matter of giving weight to the teachings while taking ourselves lightly. It is to flee the world and regard the way as our abode. If regard for ourselves is even slightly more weighty than the teachings, the teachings will not be passed onto us nor will we gain the way. There is not just one instance [in history] of the determination to give weight to the teachings; and, although we need not rely on the instructions of others, we should present [here] one or two [examples].

To give weight to the teachings means "to make one's body and mind a couch" [for one's master, as did the Buddha in a previous life] and to serve for countless æons whoever maintains the great teaching, whoever has [what Bodhidharma meant when he said,] "you've got" "my marrow"—whether it be a pillar, a lantern, the buddhas, a fox, a spirit, a man, or a woman. Getting a body and mind is easy, as [common as] "rice, hemp, bamboo, and reeds" in the world; to encounter the teachings is rare.

The Buddha Shakyamuni[4] said:

> When you meet teachers who expound the supreme *bodhi*,[5] you must not consider their caste; you must not look at their facial features; you must not scorn their shortcomings; you must not consider their conduct. Simply because we respect and value *prajna* ["wisdom"], we should let them eat [offerings worth] a hundred thousand ounces of gold each day. We should make offerings by presenting heavenly

TRANSLATED FROM the Japanese by Stanley Weinstein. All bracketed additions are the translator's.

1. The Indian Buddhist monk said to have brought Zen to China in the late 5th century C.E.
2. The personification of evil and temptation.
3. Bodhidharma's disciple who became the first Chinese patriarch of the Chan school.
4. Literally, "Sage of the Shakyas"; a title of the Buddha, who was born into the Shakya clan.
5. Enlightenment.

food, make offerings by scattering heavenly flowers. Paying obeisance and venerating them three times a day, do not give rise to
thoughts of vexation. When we behave like this, the way of bodhi will
surely appear. Having practiced like this ever since I produced the
aspiration [to attain bodhi], I have today attained *anuttara-samyak-
sambodhi*.

Thus, we should request to be taught from "trees and rocks" [on which the
Buddha in a previous life once wrote Buddhist verse]; we should seek to be
taught from "fields and villages" [into which the Buddha sent his followers
to preach]. We should, [as the Zen masters say,] "ask the pillars" and investigate "the fences and walls." Long ago, there was the case of Shakra, [the
god Indra,[6]] who took a fox as his teacher, paid it obeisance, and asked it
about the teachings. It became known as a great bodhisattva, without regard
to the status of its karma [as a fox].

However, those imbeciles who do not listen to the Buddhist teachings say:

> I am a great *bhikshu* ["monk"] and should not bow before a younger
> one who has gained the teachings; I am trained in long practice and
> should not bow before a later student who has gained the teachings;
> I have been assigned the title "master" and should not bow before
> one who lacks the title "master"; I hold the office of Buddhist Affairs
> and should not bow before other monks who have gained the teach-
> ings; I hold the office of Ecclesiastical Rectification and should not
> bow before laymen and laywomen who have gained the teachings; I
> am of the three worthy and ten noble [ranks of the bodhisattva path][7]
> and should not pay obeisance to a *bhikshuni* ["nun"] even if she has
> gained the teachings; I belong to the imperial lineage and should not
> bow before the houses of officials or the families of ministers, even
> if they have gained the teachings.

Fools such as these neither see nor listen to the way of the Buddha because
they have vainly left the land of their father to wander the roads of another
land.

Long ago, under the Tang dynasty [in China], Zhaozhou, the Great Master
Zhenji[8] [i.e., Zhaozhou Congshen (778–897)], upon arousing the aspiration
[for awakening] and setting out on a pilgrimage, said, "Even if they are seven
years old, if they are superior to me, I will ask them; even if they are a hundred
years old, if they are inferior to me, I will teach them."

When asking a seven-year-old about the teachings, the old man should
pay obeisance. It is a determination "strange and elusive"; it is the mind-set
of an old buddha. When a bhikshuni who has gained the way and gained the
teachings has emerged in the world [as a teacher], for a member of the bhikshu
community who is studying in search of the teachings to join her community,
pay obeisance, and ask about the teachings is a wonderful example of study.
It is like a thirsty person finding a drink.

6. The king of the gods.
7. Ten stages through which the bodhisattva
passes, beginning with the vow to achieve bud-

dhahood and ending with the achievement of
buddhahood.
8. A Chan master (9th century).

The Chan Master Zhixian [i.e., Guanqi Zhixian (d. 895)], in the land of Cinasthana ["China"] was a venerable under [the famed Zen master] Linji.[9] Once, when Linji saw the master coming, he grabbed hold of him, whereupon the master said, "I understand."

Linji released him, saying, "Well, I'll spare you a blow."

From this time, he became Linji's "child."

When he left Linji and went to [the nun Liaoran, who lived on Mount] Moshan, Moshan asked him, "Where did you just come from?"

The master replied, "The mouth ['entrance'] of the road."

Moshan said, "Why did you come without shutting it?"

The master was without words; paying obeisance, he gave the bow of a disciple to a master.

The master in return put a question to Moshan, "What is Moshan?"

Moshan said, "It doesn't show its peak."

The master said, "What sort of person is on the mountain?"

Moshan said, "One without marks such as male or female."

The master said, "Why don't you change yourself [into a male]?"

Moshan replied, "I'm not a fox spirit. What would I change?"

The master paid obeisance.

Eventually arousing an aspiration, he served as a monastery gardener for fully three years.

Later, when he had emerged in the world [as a teacher], he said to the assembly, "At Papa Linji's place, I got half a ladle; at Mama Moshan's place, I got half a ladle. After putting them together into one ladle and drinking from it, I've been completely full right up till now."

When, hearing these words here, we "admire the ancients" in the traces of yesterday, Moshan was a superior disciple of Gaoan Dayu, with a blood line strong enough to make her Zhixian's "mom"; Linji was the legitimate heir of the master Yun of Huangbo [i.e., Huangbo Xiyun (dates unknown)], with a practice strong enough to make him Zhixian's "pop." ([In Zhixian's words here, the Chinese term] *ye* means "father" and *niang* means "mother.") That the Chan master Zhixian paid obeisance to and sought the dharma from the nun Liaoran of Moshan is an excellent trace of his determination, is integrity to be emulated by later students. It should be called "assaulting the barriers and breaking the knots."

The nun Miaoxin was a disciple of Yangshan[1] [i.e., Yangshan Huiji (803–887)]. When Yangshan was choosing a director of the office for secular affairs, he asked widely among the retired senior and junior officers who the person should be. After an exchange of questions and answers, Yangshan said in the end, "Xin, the disciple from Huai, though she may be female, has the determination of a great person. She's certainly qualified to serve as the director of the office for secular affairs." All in the assembly agreed; and, in the end, Miaoxin was appointed director of the office for secular affairs. At the time, the "dragon elephants" ["senior figures"] in Yangshan's assembly did not resent it. Although this was not really a nontrivial position, the one appointed to it would naturally have cared for it.

---

9. On this Tang dynasty Chan master, see the *Record of Linji*, p. 541.

1. A co-founder of one of the five lineages of Chan.

After she had taken up her position, once, when she was in the office for secular affairs, there were seventeen monks from Shu [modern Sichuan] who had banded together to seek out a teacher and inquire about the way. Thinking to climb Mount Yang, they had taken lodgings at dusk in the office for secular affairs. During the evening talk while they were staying, someone brought up the "wind and banner story" of the Eminent [Sixth] Ancestor [Huineng[2] of] Caoxi [who said to two monks, discussing whether, when the temple banner stirred, it was the wind or the banner that moved or that it was their minds that were moving]. What every one of the seventeen monks had to say [about this story] was wrong. At that time, the director of the office for secular affairs, who could hear from the other side of the wall, said, "Seventeen blind donkeys. How sad! How many pairs of straw sandals have they wasted [in their search for the teachings]? The Buddhist teachings—they've never seen them even in their dreams."

At that time there was a postulant who, hearing the director of the office of secular affair's disapproval of the monks, told the seventeen monks. None of the seventeen monks resented the disapproval of the director of the office for secular affairs. Ashamed that they had been unable to say anything [significant about the story], they straightaway donned proper attire, and offering incense and paying obeisance, requested instruction [from Miaoxin].

The director of the office for secular affairs said, "Come forward!"

As the seventeen monks were still coming forward, the director of the office for secular affairs said, "It's not the wind moving; it's not the flag moving; it's not the mind moving."

Instructed in this way, all seventeen monks had an insight. They expressed their gratitude and established the formal relationship of teacher and disciple. They quickly returned to the Western Shu; in the end, they never climbed Mount Yang. Truly this is not something that could be reached by those on the three worthy and ten noble [stages of the bodhisattva path]; it is the work of the way of successor after successor of buddhas and ancestors.

And so, today too, when the position of abbot or co-seat ["head monk"] falls vacant, a bhikshuni who has gained the teachings should be asked [to fill it]. What would be the use of a bhikshu, even a venerable elder of advanced years, if he has not gained the teachings? A leader of the community should always rely on a clear eye.

However, often they are obstinate and sunk in the body and mind of a villager who would be laughed at even in the secular world; how much less are they deserving of mention in the Buddhist world. Again, there will be some who think they should disapprove of paying obeisance to those teachers transmitting the teachings who are women and nuns. Because they know nothing and do not study, they are close to animals and far from the buddhas and ancestors.

The Buddhist teachings will invariably have compassion for the person who harbors a deep commitment to throw body and mind exclusively into the Buddhist teachings. Even foolish humans and devas ["gods"] have a turn of mind that is moved by sincerity. How could the true teachings of the buddhas lack the compassion that responds sympathetically to sincerity? Even earth, stones, sand, and pebbles have a spirit moved by sincerity.

2. The sixth patriarch (638–713); see *Platform Sutra of the Sixth Patriarch*, p. 531.

At the present time, in the Land of the Great Song [China], if a bhikshuni registered at a monastery has a reputation for having gained the teachings, upon receiving an invitation from the court to fill the post of abbot of a nunnery, she will "ascend to the hall" of that monastery [to deliver a formal lecture]. The monks of the assembly, from the abbot down, will all attend, and when they stand and listen to the teachings, the question words will come from the bhikshu community. This has been the rule since ancient times. Anyone who has gained the teachings is one true old buddha and, therefore, should not be encountered as whoever he or she was in the past. When the person sees us, he or she engages us specifically in the new situation; when we see the person, it should be a relationship in which "today should enter today."

For example, in the case of a bhikshuni who has received and upholds the treasury of the eye of the true teachings, when those possessed of the fourth fruit [i.e., the arhats, who have achieved nirvana], the pratyekabuddhas [those "awakened in solitude"], or those among the three worthy and ten noble [stages of the bodhisattva path] come to pay obeisance and ask about the teachings, the bhikshuni should accept the obeisance. What is so exalted about a male? Space is space; the four primary elements [earth, water, fire, wind] are the four primary elements; the five aggregates [of the psychophysical organism] are the five aggregates. The female is also like this. In gaining the way, all attain the way. All should hold in esteem one who has gained the teachings. Do not make an issue of whether it is man or woman. This is a most wondrous law of the way of the Buddha.

Again, in the Song dynasty, "layman" indicates a gentleman who has not left home [to enter the monastic order]. Some reside in hermitages with their wives; some are solitary and pure. But we can say they are still in "the thicket of afflictions." Nevertheless, when they have some clarity, they [the monastics], "robed in clouds and sleeved in mist," gather to pay obeisance and request benefit, just as they would with a master who had left home. And so it should be whether it be a woman or an animal.

One who has not yet seen the truth of the Buddhist teachings even in his dreams, though he be an old bhikshu of a hundred years, cannot reach the status of a man or woman who has gained the teachings. We should not venerate him but merely treat him according to the etiquette of guest and host.

Those who practice the Buddhist teachings and speak on the Buddhist teachings, though females of but seven years, are guides for the fourfold Buddhist community [of monks, nuns, laymen, and laywomen] and compassionate fathers for all living beings. They are like the dragon girl [in the *Lotus Sutra*] who became a buddha. The offerings and homage to them should be the same as those to the buddhas, the tathagatas ["thus come ones"]. This is an ancient rule in the way of the Buddha. Those who do not know it and have not received its singular transmission are to be pitied.

Treasury of the Eye of the True Teachings
Paying Obeisance and Getting the Marrow
Number 28

Written on the day of Seimei in the *kanoe-ne* year of En'o [April 5, 1240,] at the Kannon Dori Kosho Horinji

Appendix

Furthermore, throughout past and present in both Wa and Kan ["Japan and China"], there have been women who held the rank of emperor. The land of the country was all controlled by these emperors, and the people all became their subjects. They were not venerated as individuals; they were venerated for their rank. Bhikshunis as well from ancient times were not venerated as individuals; it is solely their having gained the teachings that has been venerated.

Also, when there is a bhikshuni who has become an arhat, all the virtues that accompany the fourth fruit[3] will come to her. Given the virtues accompanying it, who among humans or devas surpasses the virtues of the fourth fruit? It is not a place reached by the devas of the three realms [of desire, form, and formlessness]; those who abandon everything are venerated by all the devas. How much more in the case of those who have received the transmission of the true teachings of the tathagatas and aroused the great mind of the bodhisattva—who would not venerate them? Those who fail to venerate them are themselves at fault; one who fails to venerate supreme bodhi is an imbecile who denigrates the teachings.

Again, in our country, there are daughters of emperors or daughters of ministers of state who have served as imperial consorts, as well as empresses, who take the title "cloistered." Some have shaved their heads, and others do not shave their heads. Clergy resembling members of the bhikshu community who are greedy for fame and love profit run to their houses and never fail to [prostrate themselves and] knock their heads at [the ladies'] footwear. They are more degraded than a vassal with his master. Not to mention that there are many who spend years as [such ladies'] servants. How pathetic it is that having been born in a small country and peripheral land [like Japan], they do not realize that this is a corrupt custom. It never existed in India or the land of the Tang ["China"] but only in our country. It is deplorable. Willfully to shave one's head and then destroy the true teachings of the tathagatas must be considered a profoundly serious offense. It is deplorable, that solely because they have forgotten that the paths of this world are dreams, illusions, the "flowers in the sky" [of spots before one's eyes], they are bound as the servants of these women. They are like this for the sake of the worthless paths of the world. Why do they not for the sake of supreme bodhi venerate those who should be venerated for having gained the teachings? It is because their determination to take the teachings seriously is shallow and their determination to seek the teachings is not all-encompassing.

When they covet riches, they do not think that because they are a woman's riches, they should not accept them. When they seek the teachings, this determination should be even stronger. If it is, then grass, trees, fences, and walls will bestow the true teachings; heaven and earth and the myriad things will likewise provide the true teachings. This is a truth we should certainly understand. When we do not seek the teachings with this determination, we will not receive any moisture from the waters of the teachings, even though we encounter a true good friend [to teach us]. We should carefully work on this.

Again, today some people, stupid in the extreme, look at females without revising their sense that they are the objects of lust. A child of the Buddha

---

3. The first three fruits are stream enterer (or stream-winner), once returner, and never returner.

should not be like this. If we despise them because they become the objects of lust, should we also despise all males? In becoming a cause of defilement, men may become the objects, women may become the objects; those neither men nor women may become the objects; dreams, illusions, and "flowers in the sky" may become the objects. There have been impure acts committed with a reflection in the water as the object; there have been impure acts with the sun in the heaven as the object. Spirits may become the objects; demons may become the objects. The objects [of lust] cannot be counted. It is said there are eighty-four thousand objects. Should we discard them all? Should we not look at them?

In [the monastic rules of] the *Vinaya*, it is said, with a man, two places; with a woman, three places: these are all *parajika*, [the gravest offenses] requiring expulsion [from the monastic order].

Since this is the case, if we despise those who become the objects of lust, all men and women will despise each other, and there will be no prospect of deliverance. This truth, we should examine in detail.

Again, there are followers of other [religious] paths who do not have wives. Though they may not have wives, since they have not entered the Buddhist teachings, they are still followers of other paths with false views. Among disciples of the Buddha as well, the two classes of householders have husbands and wives. Though they have husbands and wives, since they are disciples of the Buddha, there are no other types among humans and devas who can stand shoulder to shoulder with them.

Again, in the country of Tang [China], there was an ignorant monk who made a vow saying, "In life after life, through age after age, may I never look upon a woman." On what teachings is this vow based? Is it based on some secular teachings? Is it based on the Buddhist teachings? Is it based on the teachings of some other path? Is it based on the teachings of the god Mara? What fault do women have? What virtue do men have? Among bad people, there are men who are bad people; among good people, there are women who are good people. Desiring to hear the teachings and seeking emancipation certainly do not depend on whether one is a man or a woman. When they have not cut off their delusions, men and women alike have not cut off their delusions; when they have cut off their delusions and verified the principle [of the Buddhist teachings], between men and women there is no distinction. Furthermore, [I ask this monk,] if you vow never to look upon a woman, are you to exclude women when [you recite the bodhisattva vow that says] "living beings are limitless, I vow to deliver them"? If you exclude them, you are not a bodhisattva; do you call this the compassion of the buddhas? These are just the drunken words of someone deeply intoxicated by the wine of the shravaka [the follower of non-Mahayana Buddhist teachings]. Humans and devas should not believe in this as true.

Again, if you despise [women] as having committed offenses in the past, then you should also despise bodhisattvas. If you despise them as likely subsequently to commit offenses, then you should also despise all the bodhisattvas who have aroused the aspiration [for bodhi]. If you are like this, you will be forsaking everyone. How then will the Buddhist teachings be realized? Words like this [vow not to look upon women] are the crazed talk of a fool who does not understand the Buddhist teachings. How sad. According to your vow, would Shakyamuni, the Honored One, as well the bodhisattvas during his lifetime all have committed offenses [by including women in their communities]? And would their aspiration for bodhi have been shallower than yours? You should quietly examine this. If the ancestral masters who succeed to the treasury of the teachings and the bodhisattvas during the lifetime of the Buddha did not make this vow, you should study whether it is something to be learned in the Buddhist teachings. According to your vow, not only would you not save women, but when a woman who has gained the way emerges in the world to preach the teachings for humans and devas, are you not supposed to come to hear her? Should you not come to hear her, you are not a bodhisattva; you are in fact a follower of some other path.

When we look at the Land of the Great Song [China] today, there are clergy resembling those trained in long practice who drift about in the ocean of birth and death while vainly counting the sands of the ocean. Meanwhile, there are those who, although women, inquire of friends ["Buddhist teachers"], make concentrated efforts to pursue the way, and are guides to humans and devas. There are those like the old woman [in the well-known Zen story] who did not sell her cake and threw it away [when a learned monk could not answer her question about Buddhism]. How pitiful it is that a male, while a member of the bhikshu community, would vainly count the sands in the ocean of the teachings and never see the Buddha teachings even in his dreams.

In sum, when we see an object [of lust], we should learn to see it clearly. If we learn only to fear and escape it, this is the teaching and practice of the shravaka of the Lesser Vehicle.[4] If we try to "abandon the east and hide in the west," the west will also not be without objects. Even if we think we have escaped them, when we have not clearly understood them, they are objects [of lust], even if distant, objects [of lust], even if close. This [attempted escape from such objects] is still not a factor conducive to liberation. [Indeed, attraction to] the distant objects will only grow deeper.

Again, there is something laughable in the Land of Japan: called "places of ritually fixed realms" or called "practice sites of the Greater Vehicle," they do not permit bhikshuni or other women to enter. This corrupt custom has been handed down over a long time, and no one ever discerns it as such. Those who investigate the ancient [precedents] do not correct it; gentlemen of broad mastery have given it no thought. It is said to be something established by avatars, or called the heritage of the ancient predecessors. That no one has gone on to take issue with this makes a person laugh till he could bust his gut. Who are these "avatars"? Are they wise men; are they sages? Are they spirits; are they demons? Are they [bodhisattvas on the stages of] the three worthies; are they [bodhisattvas on the stages of] the ten nobles? Are they [bodhisattvas on the final stage of] the virtually awakened? Are they [buddhas, who are] the wondrously awakened? Furthermore, if we should not correct what is old, should we not then abandon our [old state of] drifting about through birth and death?

In addition, the great teacher Shakyamuni, the Honored One, is one who has attained supreme and perfect awakening: all that he should understand he has understood; all that he should do, he has done; all that from which he should be liberated, he has been liberated from. Who today comes close to

---

4. On the "Lesser Vehicle" (Hinayana), as distinguished from the "Greater Vehicle" (Mahayana), see p. 655.

him? Nevertheless, in the assemblies of the Buddha during his lifetime, there were the four classes: bhikshu, bhikshuni, upasaka, and upasika ["monk, nun, layman, and laywoman"]. There was the group of eight [classes of mythical beings]; there was the group of thirty-seven [buddhas and bodhisattvas of the Diamond-realm mandala]; there were eighty-four thousand [types of beings in the assemblies of the Buddha]. The realm of the Buddha ritually fixed by all these is the obvious buddha assembly. In which such assembly are there no bhikshuni, no women, no men, no eight classes [of beings]? We ought not hope for a ritually restricted realm of purity superior to the buddha assembly during the lifetime of the Tathagata; for this would be a realm of the god Mara. The lawful conventions of a buddha assembly do not differ, whether in our own realm or other quarters or among the thousand buddhas of the three ages [of past, present, and future]. If it has a different rule, we can be sure it is not a buddha assembly.

"The fourth fruit" [of an arhat] is the ultimate level [of Buddhist attainment]. Whether in the Greater Vehicle or the Lesser Vehicle, the virtues of the ultimate level are not distinguished. Yet there are many bhikshuni who have realized the fourth fruit. Whether in the three realms, whether in the buddha lands of the ten directions,[5] what realm do they not reach? Who would block their spiritual activities? Again, the wondrous awakening [of a buddha] is the supreme level. Women have become buddhas, so which of the teachings have they not exhaustively mastered? Who would think to obstruct them and prevent them from proceeding [to move about at will]? Since [as buddhas] they have the virtue of "universally illumining the ten directions," what could their boundary be? Again, would a devi [female heavenly being] be blocked and not permitted to proceed? Would a goddess be blocked and not permitted to proceed? The devi and the goddess, not yet being types that have cut off the spiritual afflictions, are still living beings that drift about [in rebirth]. When they have offenses, they have them; when they do not, they do not. Human females and animal females as well, when they have offenses, have them; when they have no offenses, have none. Who would block the paths of the devis and the paths of the goddesses? Since they take part in the assemblies of the buddhas of the three ages, they study at the places of the buddhas. Whatever differs from the places of the buddhas and the assemblies of the buddhas—who would believe it to be the Buddhist teachings? This [practice of creating zones that exclude women] is the extreme of stupidity that only "deceives the people of the world." It is more stupid than the little fox that fears someone will seize its den.

Again, the ranks of the disciples of the Buddha, be they bodhisattvas or shravakas, are as follows: first, bhikshu; second, bhikshuni; third, upasaka; fourth, upasika. These ranks are known in the heavens and among the humans and have long been heard. Thus, the second rank of the disciples of the Buddha must be superior to the wheel-turning sage king [supreme among monarchs], superior to Shakrodevanam Indra [chief among the devas]; there should not be any place she cannot go. How much less, then, should she be lined up amidst the ranks the kings and great ministers of a small country and peripheral land. When we look at the practice places now where bhikshuni

5. That is, everywhere (north, south, east, west, northeast, northwest, southeast, southwest, the nadir, and the zenith).

are not permitted to enter, all manner of country hicks and rustic clods, peasant farmers and old woodcutters enter at will. And, needless to say, who among the kings, great ministers, hundred officials, and prime ministers does not enter? Considering the country hicks and the bhikshuni in terms of their study of the way or their attainment of rank, who in the end would be the superior? Whether we consider them in terms of secular norms or consider them in terms of the Buddhist teachings, country hicks and rustic clods should not be able to go where the bhikshuni cannot. This is confusion in the extreme: our small country is the first to leave this trace [on history]. How sad, that [even senior nuns,] the eldest offspring of [the Buddha,] the compassionate father to [all beings in] the three realms, on coming to a small country, find places where they are prevented from entering.

Again, the sort of fellows who live in those places called "ritually fixed realms" have no fear of the ten evils and violate every one of the ten grave precepts.[6] Do they simply take [these "ritually fixed realms"] as realms for commission of evil and reject those people who do not commit evil? Worse still of course are the heinous offenses [such as patricide, etc.],[7] which are regarded as the most serious. Those living in "places of ritually fixed realms" may also have committed the heinous offenses. We should destroy such a realm of Mara. We should study the instruction of the Buddha; we should enter the realm of the Buddha. This is how we repay the benevolence of the Buddha. You "ancient predecessors," have you understood the significance of a "ritually fixed realm"? From whom have you inherited this? Who granted you the seal [authorizing you to establish your "ritually fixed realms"]?

Whatever enters the great realm ritually fixed by the buddhas—whether buddhas or living beings, earth or space—is liberated from bondage and returns to the source in the wondrous teachings of the buddhas. Therefore, living beings who once set foot in this realm all receive the virtues of a buddha: they have the virtue of not deviating [from the teachings]; they have the virtue of attaining purity. When one area [of such a realm] is ritually fixed, all the realms of the universe are ritually fixed; when one level is ritually fixed, all the realms of the universe are ritually fixed. There are realms ritually fixed by [sprinkling of "ambrosia"] water; there is the ritual fixing of realms by mind; there is the ritual fixing of realms by space. Invariably, [such practices] have a succession and transmission [within the historical Buddhist tradition] through which they can be known.

What is more, at the time of ritually fixing a realm, after the sprinkling of the ambrosia, after the prostrations are finished, and so on, through the purification of the realm, there is a verse saying, "This realm pervades the realms of the universe; its purity is ritually fixed by the unconditioned itself."

Have you "ancient predecessors" and old men who always speak of "ritually fixed realms" understood the meaning of this? I suspect you cannot understand that in the ritual fixing [of an authentic Buddhist realm], the realms of the entire universe are ritually fixed. We know that, drunk on the

6. The five precepts followed by all Buddhists (not to kill, steal, lie, engage in sexual misconduct, or consume intoxicants) plus five that applied only to monks and nuns: not to eat after noon, sleep on high beds, attend musical performances, touch gold or silver, or wear bodily adornments. "The ten evils": killing, stealing, sexual misconduct, lying, divisive speech, harsh speech, senseless speech, covetousness, harmful intent, and wrong views.

7. The five deadly offenses are killing one's father, killing one's mother, killing an arhat, wounding a buddha, and causing schism in the sangha (the Buddhist community).

wine of the shravaka, you think your little realm is a big thing. May you quickly awaken from your current intoxication and no longer deviate from the realm pervaded by the great realm of the buddhas. We should pay obeisance and venerate the virtue that, in delivering them and taking them in, bestows conversion on all living beings. Who would not say that this is "getting the marrow of the way"?

The Treasury of the Eye of the True Teachings
Paying Obeisance and Getting the Marrow

Written the day before winter solstice, first year of
Ninji (*kanoe-ne*) [November 7, 1240,]
at Koshoji

HOW BUDDHISM PROTECTS THE NATION

TREATISE ON THE ESTABLISHMENT OF THE ORTHODOX TEACHING AND THE PEACE OF THE NATION
(*The Rissho Ankokuron*)

NICHIREN

In appealing for acceptance and support by the state, Buddhists have often made the claim that the practice of Buddhism, or the practice of a particular form of Buddhism, has the power to protect the nation from all manner of natural catastrophes, as well as from enemies both foreign and domestic. When the Japanese monk Eisai (1141–1215) returned from China and requested royal approval for the new Zen teachings he had brought back with him, he wrote an essay titled *Promote Zen to Protect This Kingdom's Rulers*.

Perhaps the most adamant advocate of Buddhism for state protection was the Japanese monk Nichiren (1222–1282). As a young monk, he left his rural temple to travel to the capital Kyoto; there he studied at Mount Hiei, the great center of the Tendai sect, which regarded the *Lotus Sutra* (see the *Saddharmapundarika*, p. 278) as the Buddha's highest teaching. Nichiren also studied the works of other Buddhist sects. He took particular exception to the teachings of Honen (see Shinran's *Lamenting the Deviations*, p. 611), who exalted the *Sukhavativyuha Sutra* (p. 316) above all others, including the *Lotus*.

Nichiren eventually came to the conclusion that because the *Lotus Sutra* contained the Buddha's ultimate teaching, all other teachings should be relegated to a provisional status. He asserted that people should place their faith in the *Lotus Sutra* by reciting its "great title" (*daimoku*): *namu myohorengekyo*, or "Homage to the *Lotus Sutra*." Just as Shinran had claimed that a single recitation of *namu amida butsu* ("Homage to Amitabha Buddha") ensured rebirth in the pure land of Amitabha, Nichiren declared that chanting the title of the *Lotus Sutra* was the only way to gain liberation during the time of the decline of the dharma.

Other Japanese sects in Japan, notably the Tendai, had championed the *Lotus* as the Buddha's true and final teaching, regarding other sutras as examples of the

Buddha's skillful methods (that is, provisional teachings tailored for specific audiences). But Nichiren judged all other Buddhist texts to be utterly ineffectual during the degenerate age. For him, it was a heinous sin to promote any text other than the *Lotus*, and such sinners were doomed to hell. He preached this view publicly, attracting the opprobrium of the other Buddhist sects of Japan. Nichiren declared, however, that his harsh rhetoric was required to turn the benighted toward the true teaching and whatever persecution he suffered as a result both confirmed the age's degeneracy—the persecution of its devotees was a sign of degeneration that had been predicted by the sutra itself—and provided an opportunity for him to experience the effects of his own past karma.

In 1260 he wrote *Treatise on the Establishment of the Orthodox Teaching and the Peace of the Nation* (*Rissho Ankokuron*), a tract that encouraged the Kamakura military government of the shogun to rely on the teachings of the *Lotus Sutra* in order to avert disaster and upheaval, and thus to favor Nichiren's school over other Buddhist sects. If it did not do so, Nichiren warned of the conquest of Japan by the same Mongol hordes who had recently overwhelmed China and Korea. The work contained a detailed attack on Honen and his teachings, and implied that the various calamities (pestilence and famine) that had afflicted Japan were the result of the government's patronage of other—in Nichiren's view, heretical—Buddhist sects. The text did not have the desired effect; instead, Nichiren was arrested and exiled in 1261, though he was pardoned two years later. In 1271 a failed assassination plot against Nichiren hardened his resolve. He was arrested again in 1272 and banished to the island of Sado off the northwest coast of Japan, where he wrote many of his most important treatises. Nichiren's followers would eventually form one of the major schools of Japanese Buddhism, named after Nichiren himself. In the twentieth century, a branch of that school, called Soka Gakkai International, would establish centers around the world, all extolling the benefits of chanting *namu myohorengekyo*, "Homage to the *Lotus Sutra*."

Appearing below are the first three chapters of *Treatise on the Establishment of the Orthodox Teaching and the Peace of the Nation*, which take the form of a dialogue between a traveler and a master. Here, the master, who represents Nichiren, displays an impressive command of Buddhist literature on the question of the true causes of natural disasters.

PRONOUNCING GLOSSARY

Amitabha: *a-mi-tah-ba*
Bhaisajyaguru: *bai-sha-jya-gu-ru*
bodhisattva: *boh-di-sat-tva*
Daijikkyo: *dai-jeek-kyoh*
Enryakuji: *ehn-ryah-koo-jee*
Gridhrakuta: *gri-dra-koo-ta*
Haklena: *hak-leh-na*
Hokekyo: *hoh-keh-kyoh*
Jambudvipa: *jam-bu-dvee-pa*
kamadhatu: *kah-ma-dah-tu*
Kan: *kahn*
Konkomyokyo: *kohn-koh-myoh-kyoh*
kshatriya: *ksha-tri-ya*
Kukkutapada: *kuk-ku-ta-pah-da*
Mahakashyapa: *ma-hah-kah-shya-pa*
Meitei: *may-tay*
Mingdi: *meeng-dee*
Mononobe-no-Moriya: *moh-noh-noh-beh-noh-moh-ree-yah*

nayuta: *na-yu-ta*
Nehangyo: *neh-hahn-gyoh*
Nichiren: *nee-chee-ren*
Ninnokyo: *neen-noh-kyoh*
nirvana: *nir-vah-na*
Onjoji: *ohn-joh-jee*
Prasenajit: *pra-say-na-jit*
Rissho Ankokuron: *ree-sho an-ko-koo-rohn*
rupadhatu: *roo-pa-dah-tu*
Shakyamuni: *shah-kya-mu-ni*
Shandao: *shahn-dau*
Shariputra: *shah-ri-pu-tra*
Shingon: *sheen-gohn*
shramana: *shrah-ma-na*
Sumeru: *su-may-ru*
Toji: *toh-jee*
Yakushikyo: *yah-koo-shee-kyoh*

DIALOGUE I

The Cause of the Calamities

The traveler says sorrowfully:

"In recent years there has been much disaster, famine, and pestilence all over the country. Cows and horses lie dead on the roadsides and skeletons are scattered on the streets. Most of the population [of this country] is already dead. I cannot help lamenting all this.

"[In order to avert these calamities] some call the name of the Teacher of the Western World (Amitabha Buddha), believing [the statement of Shandao (Zendo)[1] that calling the name of the Teacher of the Western World] is the sharpest sword [to cut off evil karma]. Some recite the sutra dedicated to the Buddha of the East (Bhaishajyaguru)[2] who vowed that he will cure the diseases [of those who hear his name]. Some treasure the excellent statement in the *Saddharmapundarika-sutra* (*Lotus Sutra; Hokekyo*), [in which] the true teaching [of Shakyamuni[3] Buddha is expounded, that a sick person who hears this sutra] will be cured of his disease and not grow older or die. Some hold the ceremony of giving a hundred lectures [on the *Ninnokyo* (*Karunikarajaprajnaparamita-sutra; Sutra of a Benevolent King*) according to the statement in the sutra that] seven calamities [in a country] will turn into seven felicities [if the king of that country lectures on this sutra]. Some sprinkle water from five vases over offerings in accordance with esoteric Shingon[4] rites. Some practice *zazen*[5] and concentrate their minds in order to see the truth of emptiness as clearly as they see the bright moon. Some write the names of the seven gods and post them on gates. Some make images of the five [bodhisattvas] of great power and hang them on doors. Some practice exorcism at the four corners [of a city] and pray to the gods of heaven and earth.

"Government authorities take various benevolent measures out of compassion for the people. But their painstaking efforts are to no avail. The people have become even more hungry and pestilence more rampant. Beggars and the dead are seen everywhere [on the streets]. Piles of corpses resemble platforms and lined-up bodies look like bridges.

"The sun and the moon shine bright and the five planets make a chain of brilliant gems. The Three Treasures[6] are honored in this country; and the line of a hundred emperors [of this country] has not yet come to the end. But why has this country deteriorated so soon? Why has the Dharma perished? What kind of evil or mistake is responsible for this situation?"

The master says:

"I have long been lamenting over these calamities. Now I know that you have also. Let us talk!

TRANSLATED FROM the Japanese by Murano Senchu. All bracketed additions are the translator's.

1. A Chinese monk and Pure Land master (613–681). "Amitabha": the buddha who presides over the Pure Land (see the *Sukhavativyuha Sutra*, p. 316).
2. The buddha of healing and medicine.
3. Literally, "Sage of the Shakyas"; a title of the Buddha, who was born into the Shakya clan.

4. One of the major schools of Japanese Buddhism, founded by Kukai.
5. Seated meditation.
6. That is, the three jewels of Buddhism: the Buddha, the dharma, and the sangha (the Buddhist community).

"It is to attain Buddhahood through the teaching [of the Buddha] that one renounces his family and becomes a monk. Now I see that no Shinto or Buddhist gods can do anything [to avert these calamities]. Judging from this, I cannot believe that I shall be able to be reborn [in a Buddha land and attain Buddhahood] in a future life [by practicing the teaching of the Buddha]. This may be a result of my ignorance. I cried with regret, looking up to the sky, and thought [about the cause of the calamities], lying with my face on the ground.

"I racked my poor brains and read sutras [to find out the cause of the calamities. At last I have reached the following conclusion]. The people of this country are standing against the Right Dharma. They believe wrong teachings. Thus, the gods have deserted this country. Saints have left us and they will never return. *Maras*[7] and devils have come instead and calamities have taken place. I cannot help saying this. I cannot help but to dread this."

DIALOGUE II

Predictions in the Sutras

The traveler says:

"Not only I but all the people of this country lament over these calamities. Now I have come here and heard from you that these calamities have taken place because the gods and saints have left us. What sutras say so? I want to hear the references [to the cause of such calamities in the sutras], if any."

The master answers:

"There is much evidence in the sutras. In the *Konkomyokyo* (*Suvarnaprabhasa-sutra; Sutra of Golden Light*) [the four great heavenly kings tell the Buddha]:

> [Suppose that] although this sutra exists in a country it is not propagated there yet. The king of that country ignores this sutra and does not wish to hear it, make offerings to it, or respect or praise it. He does not respect or make offerings to the four kinds of devotees (monks, nuns, laymen, and laywomen) who uphold this sutra when he sees them. As a result, we, our attendants, and the other innumerable gods will not be able to hear the profound and wonderful Dharma [expounded in this sutra], nor drink nectar or obtain the Right Dharma. Consequently, we will lose our light and power. Living beings in the evil realms will increase, and those in heavenly and human realms will decrease. Living beings will fall into the river of birth and death (samsara), and depart from the Way to nirvana. World-honored One! If we four [great heavenly] kings and our attendants including *yakshas*[8] see all this, we will leave that country and give up the intention to protect it. Not only we but also the innumerable great gods who are supposed to protect that country will leave that king. After we and those gods depart, that country will suffer from various calamities. The king will be dethroned. The people will not have any good thoughts. There will be arrests, murders,

---

7. Personifications of evil and desire.   8. Nonhuman beings, nature spirits.

quarrels, slander, and flattery. Innocent people will be punished. Pestilence will prevail. Comets will appear from time to time. Two suns will rise at the same time. The darkenings and eclipses of the sun and moon will become irregular. A black rainbow will appear together with a white one and make an ill omen. There will be shooting stars. The earth will quake. Voices will be heard from the bottoms of wells. Rainstorms and windstorms will come unseasonably. Famines will take place one after another. Seedlings will not grow. Plants will not bear fruit. The armies of many other countries will invade the country, and the people will undergo many kinds of suffering. They will lose the places where they might live peacefully.

"The *Daijikkyo* (*Mahasamnipata-sutra*; *Great Collection Sutra*) says:

When the Dharma disappears, [monks] will have long beards, hair, and nails, and my precepts will be forgotten. Loud voices will be heard from the sky, and the earth will quake. All things will shake just as on a waterwheel. The walls of cities will crumble and houses will collapse. The roots, branches, leaves, flowers, fruits, and flavors of the fruits of trees will disappear. The living beings of the whole realm of desire (*kamadhatu*) [and the realm of form (*rupadhatu*)], except those of the Heaven of Pure Abode, will be deprived of food of the seven tastes. Those living beings will also lose the three kinds of energy. All the excellent commentaries on the teaching of liberation will also disappear. Flowers and fruits will be without fragrance and flavor. All the wells, springs, and pools will dry up. Land will be brackish and sterile. Fields will be split into hills and ravines. Mountains will erupt. Dragons in heaven will not send rain. Seedlings will die. . . . Plants will die. Even weeds will not grow. Dust will rain down and obscure the light of the sun and moon. Everything will be dried up all over the land, and many ill omens will be seen from time to time. [The king and monks of that country] will commit the ten evil acts,[9] and their greed, anger, and ignorance (i.e., the three poisons) will increase. The people will ignore their parents just like deer do. They will decrease in number. Their lives will be shortened. Their physical power will be weakened, and their pleasures will diminish. They will be deprived of the pleasures of gods and humans and sent to the evil realms[1] [in their future lives]. When the evil king and monks eliminate my Right Dharma by committing the [ten] evil acts and decrease the worlds of heavenly and human beings, all the gods who are compassionate toward all living beings will abandon that denied country and go to other places.

"The *Ninnokyo* says:

When a country is thrown into disorder, devils will first become active in that country. When they become active, the people [of that country] will be in chaos. That country will be invaded by its enemies, and

---

9. Killing, stealing, sexual misconduct, lying, malicious speech, inconsiderate words, frivolous speech, greed, harmful intent, and wrong views.

1. The hells, the realm of hungry ghosts, and the realm of animals.

many people will be killed. The king, crown prince, other princes, and government officials will quarrel with each other. Disorder will be seen in heaven and on earth. The movements of the twenty-eight constellations, the sun, and the moon will become irregular, and many rebellions will break out.

"The Buddha says in the same sutra:

Seeing [the world] throughout the three periods (past, present, and future) clearly with my five kinds of eyes,[2] I have arrived at the conclusion that all kings have been able to obtain their thrones because they attended five hundred Buddhas in their previous existences. Therefore, all saints [including] arhats[3] will appear in their countries and give great benefits to the kings. When the merit of the kings expires, the saints will leave their countries. Seven calamities will take place [there] after the departure of the saints.

"The *Yakushikyo (Bhaishajyaguruvaiduryaprabhasapurvapranidhanavishe-shavistara; Sutra of Bhaishajyaguru)* says:

The calamities that will trouble the duly inaugurated king and other *kshatriyas*[4] [of a country] are pestilence, foreign invasions, rebellions, disorder in the movements of the constellations, darkenings and eclipses of the sun and the moon, unseasonable windstorms and rainstorms, and famine.

"The Buddha addresses [King Prasenajit][5] in the *Ninnokyo*:

Great king! My teachings extend over ten billion Mount Sumerus[6] and as many suns and moons. Each Mount Sumeru is surrounded by four continents. In the southern continent called Jambudvipa[7] there exist sixteen great countries, five hundred medium-sized countries, and ten thousand small countries. Each country will suffer from seven calamities. [If] a king [reads this sutra] in order to [avert] these calamities, [the seven calamities will turn into seven felicities].

What are the [seven] calamities?

The sun and the moon do not move regularly; the seasons do not follow one another regularly; a red or black sun rises; two, three, four, or five suns rise at the same time; the sun is eclipsed and its light is lost; or the sun is surrounded by one, two, three, four, or five haloes. . . . All this is the first calamity.

The movements of the twenty-eight constellations become irregular; and the gold star, comets, ring star, devil star, fire star, water star, wind star, funnel star, south ladle stars, north ladle stars, largest planet, king star, three minister stars, and a hundred official stars change their appearances from time to time. . . . All this is the second calamity.

The living beings as well as the non-living beings of a country are burned by great fires; or fires are caused by devils, dragons, gods, mountain spirits, humans, trees, or bandits. . . . All this is the third calamity.

Great floods drown people; the seasons do not follow one another regularly; it rains in winter and snows in summer; thunder rolls and lightning flashes in winter; it freezes, frosts, and hails in the sixth month; red, black, or blue rains fall; earth mountains or rock mountains fall from the sky; sand, gravel, or stones fall from the sky; rivers flow upstream, cause mountains to float, or wash away stones. . . . All this is the fourth calamity.

Great winds blow people away to their deaths; mountains, rivers, and trees are blown away at the same time; untimely gales or black, red, or blue winds or the winds of heaven, of the earth, of fire, or of water blow. . . . All this is the fifth calamity.

Everything is dried up; the ground is dry deep down; much grass dies; the five kinds of cereals do not ripen; land looks as if it were burned; and many people die. . . . All this is the sixth calamity.

The country is invaded by the armies of surrounding countries; rebellions break out; bandits take advantage of fires, floods, gales, or devils to torment people; and wars break out. All this is the seventh calamity.

"The *Daijikkyo* says:

Suppose there is a king who practiced almsgiving, kept the precepts, and cultivated wisdom in innumerable previous existences. If he sees that my Dharma is perishing and does not protect it, the innumerable roots of goodness that he planted [in his previous existences] will perish. His country will suffer from three misfortunes: 1) a rise in the price of grain [because of famine], 2) war, and 3) pestilence. The gods will leave his country. The people will not obey his orders. His country will always be invaded by its enemies. Fires will break out everywhere; many windstorms will blow people away; many rainstorms will drown them; and the relatives of the king will revolt against him. The king will soon become seriously ill and he will be sent to a great hell after his death. . . . So too will the queen, crown prince, ministers, headmen of cities and villages, generals, county governors, and prime ministers.

"The meaning of the above quotations from the four sutras is clear and indubitable. The blind and distracted [leaders of this country] believe the wrong teachings and do not understand the Right Dharma. [Misled by them,] the people have deserted all the Buddhas [except those honored by the leaders] and ignore the sutras [other than those chosen by those leaders]. They do not wish to support [other] Buddhas and sutras. [They have eliminated the Three Treasures in the true sense of the word by despising the right teaching of the Buddha.] Therefore, the gods and saints have abandoned this country, and devils and heretics have created calamities."

DIALOGUE III
Priests of Today

The traveler says with anger:

"Emperor Mingdi (Meitei) of the Later Han (Kan) dynasty met a golden man[8] in his dream and obtained sutras [brought by priests mounted] on white horses. Crown Prince Jogu suppressed the anti-Buddhist movement of [Mononobe-no-]Moriya and founded a Buddhist temple. Since then, all the emperors and people [of this country] have been worshiping Buddhist images and reciting Buddhist sutras. Buddhist images and sutras are honored in Enryakuji, the temples of Nara, Onjoji, Toji, and in as many other temples with as many sutras as there are stars and clouds in the sky, built all over this country including the five provinces around Kyoto and the provinces lying along the seven national highways. Some priests as wise as Shariputra[9] are making efforts to obtain wisdom as bright as the moon hanging above [Mount] Gridhrakuta while others as well disciplined as Haklena are practicing meditation [just as Mahakashyapa[1] did] on Mount Kukkutapada.

"You say that the [blind and distracted leaders] have eliminated the Three Treasures [in the true sense of the word] by despising the [right] teaching of the Buddha. Who are they? Tell me about them in detail!"

The master admonishes:

"There are row upon row of temples and sutra storehouses. Priests as numerous as rice plants, hemp plants, bamboo trees, or reeds receive respect day after day, year after year. But they are not good. They flatter [almsgivers] and mislead people. Government officials are too ignorant to know right from wrong.

"The *Ninnokyo* says:

> Suppose bad monks seek fame and gain in a country. A teaching that will destroy both the country and the Buddha-Dharma will be expounded by them to the king, crown prince, and other princes. The king who believes their teaching thoughtlessly will promulgate laws inconsistent with the precepts of the Buddha, and destroy both the country and the Buddha-Dharma.

"In the *Nehangyo* (*Nirvana Sutra*) the Buddha addresses [the bodhisattvas]:

> Bodhisattvas! Do not be afraid of evil elephants! Be afraid of evil friends! . . . When you are killed by an evil elephant, you will not be sent to the three evil realms. But when you are killed by an evil friend, you will go there.

"In the *Saddharmapundarika-sutra* [the eighty billion *nayuta*[2] bodhisattvas address the Buddha]:

8. That is, the Buddha; for this story about Emperor Ming (r. 58–75 c.e.) and the sutras he obtained, see the introduction to the *Scripture in Forty-two Sections*, p. 496.
9. One of the Buddha's chief disciples.
1. Buddha's disciple and the first patriarch in Zen Buddhist tradition (see the introduction to the *Platform Sutra of the Sixth Patriarch*, p. 531). Haklena (2nd century c.e.) was the 23rd Indian Zen patriarch.
2. A large number, assigned various values (Sanskrit).

Some monks in the evil world will be cunning. They will flatter [almsgivers]. Thinking that they have obtained what they have not yet obtained, their minds will be filled with arrogance. They will live in remote places and wear patched pieces of cloth. Believing that they are practicing the True Way, they will despise others. Being attached to worldly profits, they will expound the Dharma to men in white robes. They will be given the same respect by the people of the world as the arhats who have attained the six supernatural powers.[3] . . . In order to speak ill of us in the midst of the great multitude, in order to slander us, in order to say that we are bad, they will say to kings, ministers, brahmans, householders, and monks that we have wrong views and that we are expounding the teaching of heretics. . . . There will be many dreadful things in the evil world of the *kalpa*[4] of defilements. Devils will enter the bodies [of those monks] and cause them to abuse and insult us. . . . Bad monks in the denied world will speak ill of us, grimace at us, or drive us out of our monasteries from time to time without knowing that what you have expounded hitherto is [not the true teaching but only] expedient teachings given according to the capacities of living beings.

"In the *Nehangyo* the Buddha says:

After my nirvana, my right teaching will be preserved for numberless centuries (the Age of the Right Teaching of the Buddha). [In that period there will live] four kinds of saints. After that period the counterfeit of my right teaching will be propagated (the Age of the Counterfeit of the Right Teaching of the Buddha). There will be no saints. The monks in the latter period (the Age of Degeneration) will keep my precepts in form only. They will only partially read and recite sutras. They will be indulgent in eating and drinking and live an easy life. . . . Although they may wear the robes of monks, they will [flatter almsgivers] as carefully as a hunter stalks his game or as a cat watches a rat. They will claim that they have already attained arhatship. . . . They are greedy and jealous but will pretend to be wise and good. They will resemble the brahmans who praise silence. Although they are not *shramanas*[5], they will pretend to be so. They will strongly advocate wrong views and slander the Right Dharma.

"The priests of today are like the monks described in these sutras. How can we hope to accomplish anything without criticizing them?"

---

3. Clairvoyance, clairaudience, telepathy, memory of one's past lives, yogic powers, and knowledge of extinction.

4. An aeon, or cosmic cycle.
5. Austere wandering monks.

NO TALKING IN THE HALL OF SILENCE

FROM SAND AND PEBBLES
(Shasekishu)

MUJU ICHIEN

During the Kamakura period, which lasted from 1185 to 1333, Japan was ruled by a series of shoguns based in the city of Kamakura. It was also one of the most important periods in the history of Japanese Buddhism, producing a number of major figures. The three presented in this volume—Shinran, Dogen, and Nichiren—all denounced the eclectic approach that had characterized Japanese Buddhism to that point, with various practices adopted for various needs and various temperaments. Instead, each proclaimed the exclusive efficacy of a single practice: Shinran advocated the recitation of the homage to Amitabha Buddha; Dogen, the "just sitting" in meditation; and Nichiren, the recitation of the title of the *Lotus Sutra*.

Each of these three figures struggled with the great matter of life and death, as a serious Buddhist should. But everyday existence went on around them, lived by Buddhists who were not always so grave. Some insight into those lives is provided by a book from the period titled *Sand and Pebbles*. It was written by a monk named Muju Ichien (1226–1312), who began, as so many monks of the period did, as a follower of the Tendai school but later became a follower of the Zen master Enni, a rival of Dogen. However, as the following selections make clear, he was not particularly interested in sectarian polemics.

PRONOUNCING GLOSSARY

Amida: *ah-mee-dah*
Bo Juyi: *boh joo-ee*
Churembo: *choo-rehm-boh*
ishi: *ee-shee*
Kenshin: *kehn-sheen*
ki: *kee*
Kofukuji: *koh-foo-koo-jee*
Matsu-no-o: *mah-tsoo-noh-oh*
Muju Ichien: *moo-joo ee-chee-en*

nembutsu: *nehm-boo-tsoo*
Ohara: *oh-hah-rah*
ojoko: *oh-joh-koh*
Rakuten: *rah-koo-tehn*
Shasekishu: *shah-say-kee-shoo*
Takita: *tah-kee-tah*
Todaiji: *toh-dai-jee*
Vimalakirti: *vi-ma-la-keer-ti*
Yamato: *yah-mah-toh*

The Silent Clerics

At a mountain temple were four monks who wished to experience the Reality which is beyond words and practice the silence of Vimalakirti:[1] Vowing their intention, the four adorned the practice hall, and, cutting off the myriad worldly attachments and quieting the activities of body, word, and thought, they entered the hall to begin seven days of silence. A single attendant had access to the room.

It had grown late and the night was dark. Seeing that the lamp was about to go out, the monk in the lowest seat called out: "Attendant. Raise the taper!"

Translated from the Japanese by Robert E. Morrell. All bracketed additions are the translator's.

1. A lay disciple of the Buddha; his "silence" alludes to a famous scene in the *Vimalakirti Sutra*.

"In the hall of silence there is to be no talking," said the monk seated next to him.

The monk in the third seat was extremely annoyed at hearing the two speaking. "You have lost your senses!" he cried.

The old monk in the senior seat thought it shameful and irritating that the others had spoken out, though each had done so for different reasons.

"I alone have said nothing!" he remarked, nodding his head. With his superior air he looked especially foolish.

When we consider this incident, we are reminded that for everyone it is difficult to avoid such attitudes. When we hear people talking about the affairs of others, we find that a person will criticize another mercilessly for something which he himself enjoys doing. Lenient toward his own failings, he excuses himself by saying: "How self-indulgent of me!"—or some such remark, unaware of the fact that he is criticizing others while overlooking his own cherished flaws. Thus it is written: "Censure others bearing in mind your own faults; endanger others considering your own downfall. . . ."

Rakuten (Bo Juyi 772–846) said: "Everyone has one bad habit; my bad habit is literature." Good habits are important.

We all cherish and overlook the shortcomings of that to which we are partial while searching out and condemning the defects of that of which we disapprove. But there are defects in that which pleases me, and I should not become strongly attached to it, taking heed of the fact that others may criticize its shortcomings. Neither should I violently condemn that with which I have no rapport, but recognize that it has its virtues. This will be the attitude of the superior man. Although there are differences in degree, in all things nothing is without its merits and its shortcomings. At no time are the Goddess of Virtue and the Goddess of Darkness apart. This is the heavenly order of things. And so it is said that it is water which bears the boat up, and water which capsizes it; the ruler it is who benefits the people, but he also causes them distress; water, fire, and the like benefit man, but they also harm him—these all illustrate the same point and should be borne in mind. The power of the Buddha's Law is such, that when it is embraced, the benefit is great; when it is rejected, the punishment is likewise great. Compared to this, the profit and loss of things of the world are as nothing; the loss, moreover, is relatively greater than the profit. With Buddhism, on the other hand, the loss is small and the profit great. We ought to abandon our worldly condition of great loss—also inasmuch as it becomes the occasion of our disparaging the Buddha's Law—and enter upon that Path of great profit. But there are many who are attached to the things of the world, having become habituated to them from beginningless time. Those people are rare, who, meeting the Law of the Buddha for the first time, are attracted to it and practice it. What a pity!

A certain lay priest was fond of playing go, and would play on to the end of a winter's night. Because his hands were cold, on top of a rheumatic condition, he played the "stones" (ishi) after heating them first in an earthenware cup. When the oil from the lamp was consumed, he burned reeds and continued to play. When the ashes blew over him, he donned a bamboo hat and kept on going. I heard that this occurred only recently. A man who applied himself to meditation and other religious practices with such zeal would not find the path to enlightenment difficult.

There was a lowly monk who, having a taste for *sake* but not the price of it, tore off one of his sleeves for its purchase. Were he as ungrudging in his support of the Three Treasures,[2] in filial behavior toward his parents, and in almsgiving to the unfortunate, there would be no lack of divine response. If one neglects to perform a good deed with the excuse that there is nothing to be done, it is not that there is really nothing to be done, but only that he lacks the will to do it.

A lay priest, who was also a doctor, loved rice-cakes (*mochi*). Called for his services to a man's home where it happened that they were being prepared, the lay priest, at the sound of the pounding, began moaning in a low voice and ended up gripping the edge of a straw mat.

"You ought to make the rice-cakes somewhere where I can't hear the noise," he remarked. "The sound of the pounding drives me wild with anticipation."

I heard about this incident from the man who owned the house. There can be no doubt that one who would so love the Law and utterly delight in the words of the Buddha would attain the goal of his religious endeavors. Although such cases as this are rare, everyone has that of which he is enamored. Those relatively free of attachments may like to sleep in late, or may be given to fooling around.

There was a monk at a temple in Nara, who, instead of eating his morning gruel, was accustomed to sleep until the sun was high in the sky. When someone asked why he did not eat the gruel, he replied that sleep was far tastier. Had one such a taste for the delights of the Law and of meditation, the path of the Buddha would not be distant.

Similarly, there are those who like poetry and music, those who enjoy gambling and hunting, those given to sensual pleasures, or to food and drink, who are unmindful of the fact that by these things their wealth will be exhausted, their health ruined, and that sickness will arise and misfortune follow. Just as there are differences in the things of the world which men value, so also it is with respect to that which will bring them to the path of the Buddha: the various gates of the Law differ according to people's tastes and the level of their faith and interpretation of the doctrines. For this reason the Buddha, without exhausting the myriad expedients (*ki*), bestows the Accommodated Truths (*hoben*) and sets up the unnumerable (literally, 84,000) gates of the Law. If people would delight in and practice the Buddha's Teaching just as they enjoy *sake* and *go*, they would easily come to an understanding of the Way.

* * *

The Monk Who Was Nursed by His Daughter

The abbot of a mountain temple in the Eastern Provinces was distinguished as a scholar and had many disciples and followers. But in his old age he became paralyzed and lay on his bed passing the years and months barely

2. That is, the "three jewels" of Buddhism: the Buddha, the dharma, and the sangha (the Buddhist community).

alive while his body no longer responded to his wishes. His disciples grew tired of nursing, and finally abandoned him. Then from nowhere appeared a woman who asked if she could take care of the old monk. "As you wish," replied the disciples, and gave their permission. The old monk was unable to speak, but the woman nursed him with a great deal of loving care.

When asked her identity, the woman vaguely replied that she was just a shiftless person not worth knowing about. But as she continued to nurse him with rare solicitude over the days and months, the invalid had to speak to her.

"When I have been abandoned even by my disciples of many years who have both religious and worldly obligations to me, I am extremely grateful for the tender care you have given me. I believe that we surely must have bonds from some previous life to have brought this to pass, and it troubles me that you are so secretive. Who are you, anyhow?"

"Now I will tell you frankly," the woman replied in tears. "I have an unsuspected relationship with you, since I am the daughter of Such-and-such, a person with whom you had a chance affair. Although she said nothing to you, my mother informed me that I was the child of this union. Considering that I am your daughter in body and soul, I have thought over the years that I would like to see you and be recognized by others as your daughter. I considered this for many years, but inasmuch as I was illegitimate, I was hesitant. When I heard that those who nursed you in your illness had tired of it and that you were destitute, I made up my mind that out of filial obligation I would tenderly care for you until your death."

The invalid, impressed by such devotion, was unable to wipe away his tears. "How wondrous are the bonds between parent and child to have brought this to pass."

They were very close to each other. The monk was nursed until the end of his life and died in the woman's tender care. Her extreme sense of filial piety is to be highly esteemed. The saying is indeed true that daughters have a greater sense of filial piety than sons and are more obliging in providing support.

The Monk Who Encouraged Marriage

At a mountain temple called Matsu-no-o in Yamato province lived the monk Churembo, who after having become paralyzed, put up a small hut near the highway in Takita. Whenever monks from the mountain temple passed along the road, he would inquire if they were single; and if they replied that they were, this is how he would encourage them.

"Get yourself a wife right away! It was my lot to be a scholar, and I have been single since my youth. I had a great many disciples and followers, but after I became paralyzed and crippled, these people no longer care about me. I have ended up as a destitute old beggar who has a hard time making ends meet, carrying on barely alive by the side of the road. I feel that if I had a wife and children I might not have come to such a bitter pass. Now, when you are just the right youthful age, get together with someone. As the years go by, the affection between husband and wife deepens. Don't think that such illness as mine just happens to other people."

An unexpected piece of advice to be sure; but since the monk spoke from personal experience, perhaps there was some truth to it.

The Wife Who Was an Impediment in the Final Hour

A priest at a mountain temple fell into the ways of the world and exchanged vows with a certain woman. While they were living together with deep mutual affection, the priest fell gravely ill and was sick for many days. Because his wife had nursed him ever so tenderly, he was very close to her and had few contacts with his disciples or any others. He felt that he had been most wise to have established this mutual relationship and looked forward to a peaceful demise. Finally, in the fullness of time, his original desire to follow the Way returned and he continually repeated the name of the Buddha. Thinking that his end was at hand, he sat up in the posture of meditation and joined his hands. Facing the west, he recited the *nembutsu*.[3]

"Oh no! You are leaving me. Where are you going?" cried his wife, throwing her arms around the monk's neck and pulling him down.

"For heaven's sake, let me die in peace!" pleaded the monk, lifting himself up to recite the *nembutsu*. But again she toppled him over. Although the monk lifted his voice to recite the name of the Buddha, he died on his back, wrestling with his wife. The manner of his passing was most unbecoming. I wonder if it was an obstacle to his obtaining salvation?

Such incidents are rare. But when wife and child are lined up before us and we see their grief and yearning, how could they not be an impediment for those of inferior capacities? Those who truly wish to be freed from illusion should cast off the impediments to the Way which leads to the mountain of Enlightenment, and loosen the mooring lines of the boat which crosses the sea of the passions [to the Other Shore].

The Monk Whose Wife Tried to Kill Him

At a mountain village in the Eastern Provinces was a monk who lived the life of a recluse. Originally he had been a priest of the Kofukuji in Nara and used to tell how in his youth he had witnessed Shunjobo's[4] reconstruction of the Great Buddha Hall at the Todaiji. He remained single until late in life, but when he reached seventy he exchanged vows with a young nun and put her up in his quarters, probably with the thought that she would take care of him.

This nun was about thirty years of age; and, being from the capital, had a witty comment about everything. She held nothing back and discussed the old monk's behavior with others.

"The Lord Abbot of the house calls out to me, 'Well, the passion's up. Heat the water and prepare a bath.' So I hurry and tell him the bath is ready and he says to me: 'All of a sudden my passion has cooled.' It's always the same; and then he gets mad, loses interest, and is in a bad mood." It is amusing that while his temper rises with the temperature of the water, his sexual interest cools along with his passion.

Instead of the nun taking care of the old monk, she secretly carried on an affair with a young ascetic. The old monk's quarters were pleasantly

---

3. The chant *namu amida butsu*, "Homage to Amitabha Buddha," which believers recited to ensure rebirth in the Pure Land.

4. A Japanese monk (1121–1206). "Kofukuji": a Buddhist temple.

appointed and there were also money and provisions for the needs of every season. So the nun decided to get rid of the old monk and live in his quarters after exchanging vows with the young ascetic. At an opportune moment she brought the old monk to the ground; then with all the strength of her vigorous young body in its prime, she twisted the old monk's genitals until he thought he was dead for sure.

"Have pity! Help!" he cried at the top of his voice. "She's killing me!"

The sound of his screaming was heard faintly at a hermitage on the other side of the ridge. The recluse who lived there was startled and ran to the old monk's place to find him already changing color and apparently not breathing. The recluse gave the nun a powerful kick and pulled her away.

The old monk recovered. Since the scandal could not be hushed up, he appealed to the local Land Steward who held a trial by confrontation (*monchu*). The nun was clearly in the wrong and had nothing to say. Her crime was serious and the court could have exacted whatever penalty it wished— the severing of a hand, a foot, or even her neck. But since the monk was already a recluse [and thus somewhat outside the pale of the law] and the Land Steward was a man of compassion, he merely banished her from his territory.

I often saw both the old monk and the nun. I wasn't there when this incident took place, but I heard about it in detail. When we consider such an incident as this, it is hard to follow the advice of the monk with paralysis. We should weigh the options carefully.

One Should Be Wary of Attachment at the Time of Death

In Ohara lived a monk who had religious aspirations, but who was without understanding. Deciding that there was no point in continuing to live in this miserable, floating world,[5] he prepared himself to observe thirty-seven days of silence, and then, on the final day of services, to meet his end by hanging. He discussed his plan with two or three fellow-monks and retired into the practice hall.

News of the affair having spread abroad, the Ohara Superintendant of Priests, moved by admiration and respect, conducted an Expounding-on-Birth-in-the-Pure-Land (*ojoko*) and other services in order to establish karmic affinities with the holy man. As the event was newsworthy, Kenshin wrote to high-ranking prelates in the capital, inviting them to attend, in the hope that the holy man might hear their recitation of Amida's[6] name and his desire for birth in the Pure Land would be reinforced. Then he inaugurated a seven-day service for the continuous repetition of the *nembutsu*.

When word reached the capital, laymen and clerics of both sexes assembled that they might establish a karmic bond with the holy man. They asked to meet with him, and the monk went out to receive them, although this confidants did not approve, considering his behavior unseemly and ostentatious.

The allotted number of days having been fulfilled, the monk's final bath was prepared.

5. A phrase usually applied to the urban plea-sures of the Tokugawa period (1603–1867).

6. That is, Amitabha.

"Now that you have come this far, nothing should be bothering you," said one of his companions. "But the mind of man is fickle; so if there are any attachments standing in your way, speak up. You must face death with no mental blocks. Now is not the time for silence."

"When I first made my decision, I was stout-hearted," replied the monk. "And when I heard about the fellow who died the other day in the bath-house fire, I thought that I should like to go as soon as possible, that I would no longer know such tragedy. But now my resolution fails me and I am no longer in any hurry."

Among the monk's long-standing disciples was a sharp-witted lay priest who lived in the capital and who had come to Ohara for the occasion. Perhaps because he was piqued at not being permitted into the practice hall, he edged up close to the sliding panel and, when he heard the holy man speak, called out in a loud voice.

"Deliberations are in order before the affair has been decided. But having made a noisy announcement of your intentions, and having set the day and the hour, you cannot now come out with sage reasons for changing your mind. This is the work of the devil, so take your bath and get on with it. You're just trying to stall!"

Thus reproached, the monk was silent. Then, making a wry face, he performed his ablutions, hung a rope from a nettle-tree in front of the hall, and hanged himself by the neck. The people venerated and revered him, each taking something which he left behind as a memento.

Some six months after this affair, the Abbot Superintendent fell ill. Signs indicated that a supernatural force was at work, so they protected his body by covering it with mystic formulas. The Abbot babbled, saying many strange things. The ghost of the monk who had hanged himself had taken possession of his faculties.

"Alas! You should have stopped me," said the voice. "It irks me that when I wanted to abandon my plan, you did nothing to help!"

Unable to forget and to cast off his delusive thoughts and attachments, the monk had entered into the path of the demons. What a futile undertaking! We should be well aware and fearful of delusive and binding thoughts.

This is a true story, having been related to me by an Ohara monk of my acquaintance who witnessed it with his own eyes.

The Monk Who Drowned Himself

On a mountain lived a monk with a deep understanding of the Way whose heart was not fixed on this floating world. Wishing to enter quickly into Paradise, he decided to meet his end by drowning. With the support of a fellow-monk, he prepared a boat and rowed out on a lake.

"The moment of death is the most important in one's entire life," said the holy man. "Now even when one is accustomed to a situation, mistakes occur, and he may blunder through carelessness. Since I have never before attained birth in the Pure Land nor experienced death, I am uncertain how I shall behave. If, after I go into the water, delusive and binding thoughts arise so that I begrudge my life, and should extraneous notions distract me from my purpose, my birth in the Pure Land is not assured. Should I want to return after I enter the water, I will jerk the line. Then pull me out."

The monk tied a rope to his side and dived into the water, reciting the name of Amida, but soon felt uncomfortable. So he jerked the line and his companion hauled him out, soaking wet. Although his friend did not know what was going through his mind, he brought him back as promised.

"It was painful in the water and when delusive thoughts arose, I knew that in this state of mind I should never attain birth in the Pure Land. So I came back," explained the monk.

After several days passed, the monk decided that this time he would surely not fail, and again rode out in the boat. But after diving in, he pulled on the line as before, and his companion hauled him back. Two or three unsuccessful attempts later the monk went out again without any high hopes.

But this time after diving in, he did not jerk the rope. In the sky, celestial music was heard and a purple cloud trailed over the waves. When his friend beheld these auspicious signs, tears of gratitude fell with the water dripping from the oars.

Truly, the mind which clings to the thought of self and desires fame cannot be born into the Pure Land. But with genuine faith one can realize his cherished desire. Unlike the monk who hanged himself, wise indeed was this one who kept trying and attained birth in the Pure Land!

CHIDO, WHO HARMS THE NATION, WROTE THIS

DREAMS OF BUDDHISM
(*Buppo Yume Monogatari*)

CHIDO

The title "Buddha" is derived from the Sanskrit verbal root *budh*, which means "to awaken"; it is one of the verbs in Sanskrit for waking up from sleep. In the essay below, composed at a distance of many thousands of miles and hundreds of years from the night when Prince Siddhartha awoke to become the Buddha, a Japanese monk presents the practice of Buddhism in terms of awakening from a dream. Each night we fall asleep and enter a new world, whose truth we do not doubt. Each morning, we wake up to a new reality, learning that the world we knew just moments before was all an illusion. Everyone has this experience each day, yet they do not seek to awaken from the larger dream they inhabit into the reality of enlightenment.

We know little about the author, Chido, who composed this piece in the latter half of the thirteenth century. Some comments in it, and in the few other works by him that survive, suggest that he was a monk of the Shingon school, founded by Kukai (774–835) almost five hundred years before. In Chido's time, the schools of Tendai and Shingon were still powerful: dominance of the Pure Land, Zen, and Nichiren schools—which arose during the thirteenth century—lay in the future. Here, Chido clearly rejects the Pure Land concession that we live in a degenerate age in which enlightenment is no longer possible. Indeed, he recommends meditation on the syllable A, the first syllable of the Sanskrit alphabet and hence the source from which all language and meaning flow.

But this is not a polemical work. Rather, it is a well-composed essay by a highly literate Buddhist monk—one who knows, from example, the story of the Korean monk

Wonhyo (617–686; see *Arouse Your Mind and Practice*, p. 583)—an essay that provides a clear summary of basic Mahayana Buddhist doctrine as understood in Japan. It is the work of a humble author, but one who cannot resist a final dig at those who make grand claims that their Buddhism alone will protect Japan. It ends, "Chido, who harms the nation, wrote this."

PRONOUNCING GLOSSARY

Ajatashatru: *a-jah-ta-sha-tru*
alaya vijnana: *ah-la-ya vij-nyah-na*
bodhisattva: *boh-di-sat-tva*
bonpu: *bohn-poo*
Buppo Yume Monogatari: *boo-po yoo-may mo-no-ga-ta-ree*
Chido: *chee-doh*
Dainichikyo: *dai-nee-chee-kyoh*
Hinayana: *hee-na-yah-na*
Hotsu bodaishin gyoron: *hoh-tsoo boh-dai-sheen gyoh-rohn*
ichinen no shin: *ee-chee-nehn noh sheen*

metsuzai: *meh-tsoo-zah-ee*
musho no sange: *moo-shoh noh sahn-geh*
Namu Amida Butsu: *nah-moo ah-mee-dah boo-tsoo*
nembutsu: *nehm-boo-tsoo*
Risho-bo: *ree-shoh-boh*
Sennyu: *sehn-nyoo*
skandha: *skan-da*
Tathagata: *ta-tah-ga-ta*
Vasubandhu: *va-su-ban-du*
Wonhyo: *wan-hyoh*
Zhuangzi: *jwahng-tsa*

One calm night a guest asked for lodging at a monk's rustic hermitage. In the course of discussing affairs ancient and modern, the guest said, "I have encountered the difficult-to-encounter teachings of the Buddha. Although I have not completely lacked a sincere fear of birth and death (*samsara*, *shoji*), I've been habitually involved in worldly filth. Because I wasted my days hither and thither, only now have I noticed that my limited life span has grown short. I have crossed distant mountains and rivers to come and inquire of you concerning just one issue. What attitude can I adopt so as to attain liberation from birth and death during this life?"

The host replied, "You say that you have spent many years nominally in Buddhist training, yet you have never before given consideration to the single great affair of birth and death? Just regard the dreams you see night after night as your teacher. Then at least you will not deepen your attachments to the world. When people lie down and dream, the things they see do not actually exist. Yet under the conditions of sleep they see all kinds of affairs: different places, living creatures, oneself, and others. Because one's own self is involved, if things go contrary one becomes angry. If things go well one rejoices. It is no different from one's waking reality.

"Liezi[1] dreamed for sixty years. Zhuangzi[2] dreamed that he spent one hundred years as a butterfly. In just one night they saw many months and years come and go. Just imagine how many karmic acts they performed during that time! How many thoughts of good and evil! While dreaming one never thinks that one's imaginary experience is false. Yet if one considers it after awakening, it is obvious that not one of the imaginary objects seen while lying down in bed actually existed. Each living being's entire experience of

TRANSLATED FROM the Japanese by William M. Bodiford. All bracketed additions are the translator's.

1. Chinese Daoist philosopher (4th century B.C.E.).　　2. Chinese Daoist philosopher (ca. 369–286 B.C.E.).

transmigration through birth and death is no different from such dreams. Therefore, again and again the Buddha preached in response to various types of ignorance that we should regard the six courses and four modes of rebirth[3] as dreams.

"'Ignorance' means not knowing that one's own mind is Buddha. Within a single mental instant of this delusion, one leaves the palace of Dharma Nature [i.e., reality as it actually is,] and wanders among the impoverished villages of false thoughts [i.e., our commonsense world of existence]. One might think that the experience of transmigration is real. But if upon encountering the Buddha's teaching that life and death is a dream, one listens with faith, then suddenly one leaves the mistaken beliefs of dreams and awakens on the bed of inherent enlightenment. The fact that one has not yet awakened from dreams is simply because one thinks of them as actually existing. The Buddha appeared in the world to make us become aware of our long night of dreams.

"For those of shallow aptitude, Buddhists first explain the principle of the emptiness of self. This approach is known as the Lesser Vehicle (Hinayana, Shojo). Thoughts of self-existence are what habitually cause infinite sins to arise. If one understands that the self is empty, then the power generated by this understanding transports one out of the three realms of desire, form, and no-form to a land outside of our world system. This approach, however, has the defect of emphasizing the existence of the elements of experience (dharma, ho). Therefore, for those of deeper aptitude, Buddhists explain the emptiness of both self and these elements. This approach is known as the Great Vehicle (Mahayana, Daijo). The emptiness of dharmas teaches that everything seen in dreams, every type of element, are all emptiness: because everything arises from mind, none has reality. Therefore, the knowledge that every type of dharma consists completely of dreams is the doctrine of the Great Vehicle.

"For these reasons, over the course of years in this humble hermitage, during night after night of dreams, I have seen all kinds of things. Sometimes I became upset. Sometimes I became happy. Sometimes I entered the marvelous realm of the immortal sages and became friends with Buddhas and bodhisattvas. Sometimes I tormented myself with the afflictions of demons and poisonous serpents. While viewing these events one thinks they exist. But after awakening they leave no trace. From this experience one should realize that birth and death fundamentally are nonexistent.

"Due to various kinds of causes and conditions, within one's tiny brain one can see ten thousand miles of mountains and rivers. Within the span of a short nap one can experience the passing of many months and years. One should realize, based on this same principle, that a single instant of thought can pervade the Dharma Realm, the entire cosmos. The elements that one sees do not come into existence from the future when one dreams. They do not go out of existence into the past when one awakes. Even while one sees them they do not abide, do not persist in the present anywhere. Based on this experience, one can understand the meaning of the saying that the three periods of past, present, and future cannot be grasped. This being so, any

---

3. According to Buddhist theory, sentient beings are born variously from the womb, from the egg, from warmth and moisture, and from a miracle.

"The six courses": the six destinations—the realms of gods, demigods, humans, animals, ghosts, and the denizens of hell.

sentient being who awakens to this realization can be called a Buddha or a Patriarch.[4]

"The reason I believe there is no teacher better than dreams is that the process of sleeping in bed, resting my head on the pillow of inherent enlightenment, allows me to see how the production of delusions causes birth and death within dreams. My awaking at dawn reveals the similar process of realizing the wisdom of spiritual awakening in all its clarity. Thus living in clear realization of the fundamental nonbeing of birth and death, I know that the sense objects experienced while awake are not different from those experienced in dreams. Joys and sorrows are both forgotten, and my mind is ready to encounter the infinite teachings of the Buddha.

"So long as you do not know that your self exists only as a dream, then no matter how much good karma you cultivate, the best benefit you can attain is rebirth in a human or heavenly realm. You will not realize the salvation of liberation from the cycle of birth and death. But if you know that your self exists only as a dream and that all sights, sounds, sensations, and thoughts exist only as a dream, then even a simple act of good karma, such as reciting one line of scripture or chanting the Buddha's name once, is a powerful enough act to produce Buddhahood.

"You must thoroughly investigate this thing known as our mind of thought (*ichinen no shin*). When the interaction of sense organs and sense objects produces an instant of awareness, it does not come from somewhere in the future. When the awareness stops, it does not go to someplace in the past. If one investigates where this mind abides in the present, it is not inside the body nor outside the body. It cannot be found between the inside and the outside. Yet it is not something nonexistent. Because it is this mind that projects the visions of dreams and waking reality, both consist of elements that are fundamentally nonexistent.

"You must thoroughly investigate what are called 'Buddha' and 'sentient beings.' The scripture says: 'Because of false thoughts, therefore sinking in birth and death; because of knowing reality, therefore realizing *bodhi* [i.e., wisdom].' This means that Buddhas and sentient beings, because both are pure in their fundamental nature, lack the slightest bit of difference. Yet if false thoughts arise, one becomes a sentient being drowning in birth and death. If one knows reality as it is, then one becomes a Buddha who realizes *bodhi*.

"What does the scripture mean by 'false thoughts'? Merely a confused mind. It is like pointing to the east and thinking it is the west. There is a story told about a man, Risho-bo of Sennyu Temple. Once as Risho-bo absentmindedly returned to his temple from Kyoto, he walked across the Fifth Avenue Bridge all the while thinking only that he was traveling west. Then he thought to himself: 'If I am returning from the capital to my temple, then I must be facing east. Why am I thinking that I'm going west?' Although it felt odd, he could not get rid of this thought until he had finished crossing the bridge.

"Your false thoughts of birth and death resemble Risho-bo's confusion. Sentient beings will, because of a single thought of confused discrimination, cling to no-self as a self and construct dreams of birth and death. Just like when Risho-bo later thought to himself, 'Since I must be facing east, why do

4. That is, a master in the Zen tradition of Buddhism.

I think that I am facing west?' the realization that our mind plays tricks on us resembles encountering Buddhism, awakening to the mental origin of reality, and knowing the principle of no-self. His knowing how to distinguish east and west, but not changing his mind while crossing the bridge, resembles the persistence of false thoughts—due to habitual karmic tendencies formed during many previous lives—even though one trusts in the teachings of the Buddha. His regaining his senses after crossing the bridge resembles putting an end to false thoughts by believing in and practicing the teachings of the Buddha.

"Risho-bo realized his mistake in thinking that east is west. Thus he did not stop on the bridge but continued on his way home. If he had been taken in by the false opinion of thinking that east is west, then he would have stopped in midjourney and would not have continued on his way home. Because we know that our false mind is fundamentally empty, we should not be stopped by it. Therefore, [Vasubandhu's[5]] *Treatise on Arousing the Bodhi Mind (Hotsu bodaishin gyoron)* states: 'If the false mind should arise, recognize it and do not follow it.'

"Once a person known as Wonhyo[6] journeyed from the Korean kingdom of Silla to the Tang empire of China in search of the Buddhist Teaching. Encountering rain, he took shelter in a cave. Feeling thirsty, he drank water from a pool in the cavern. The taste of the water resembled sweet nectar. He drank and drank. At dawn he saw a corpse lying in the water. Remembering the water he had drunk, he vomited it up. At that moment he awakened to the fact that all elements of existence (*dharma*) in themselves are neither pure nor impure, but merely coincide to the artifice of the One Mind. Thinking, 'Now there is no further Teaching to seek,' he returned to Silla.

"Not knowing that body and mind are empty with respect to purity and impurity, one performs infinite karmic acts for the sake of the body and thereby randomly engenders suffering. Suppose, for example, there was a crazy person who took a corpse, set it on the side of the road, and decorated it in various ways. Suppose he built a house for it and traveled about getting food and clothing for it. Suppose he became happy when a passerby admired the corpse and became angry when one criticized it. Just for this one corpse he suffered mental and physical exertion. Anyone who saw this would probably say, 'Well, he's crazy!' But our manner of transmigration through birth and death differs not in the slightest. We receive bleached bones from our fathers and obtain red flesh from our mothers. None of this is our own. Yet, what we do every day for ourselves is all just for our corpses, is it not?

"Chinese poets described man's worldly striving as:

> Working late until the stars appear overhead;
> starting early so as to brush off the morning frost:
> Such is one who seeks fame and covets profit.

> Polishing jeweled floors, decorating with embroidered banners,
>   sewing fancy clothes:
> Such is one who is concerned only with outlandish beauty.

---

5. A 4th-century C.E. Indian Buddhist scholar (see the introduction to his *Abhidharmakosha*, or Treasury of Higher Doctrine, p. 267).

6. A Korean monk (617–686); see his *Arouse Your Mind and Practice*, p. 583.

"If one considers these activities thoroughly, it is clear that we are just slaves to our corpses. Our mental and physical toil infects not just this life, but also engenders pleasures and pains for eons to come. How could our craziness be less than that of the crazy person above? Thus, because we cling to no-self as a self and cling to the false and nonexistent as truly real, we have become ordinary unawakened beings (bonpu) caught in birth and death. Therefore, realizing that mind and body absolutely lack any self-sustaining permanent essence and believing that they are just like phantoms and dreams is the event to which the scripture quotation above refers when it says: 'because of knowing reality, therefore realizing wisdom (bodhi).'"

The guest asked, "You say good and evil in reality do not exist. If that is so, then couldn't one perform evil without incurring karmic sins, and couldn't one cultivate good without obtaining karmic benefits?"

The host replied, "If you understand in such a manner, then you would be denying the law of cause and effect, a horrific false view. In fact, it is because of the lack of permanent essence that the performance of evil leads to baleful retributions and that the cultivation of good engenders pleasant benefits. You should understand that the principle of things lacking any fixed nature implies that the karmic connections between good and evil causes and effects are not random.

"Suppose, for example, that in a dream you see someone killed and see a king investigate and judge the crime. While dreaming, the principle of cause and effect cannot be disrupted. Thinking upon this after awaking, however, it is clear that the murderer, the murder victim, the performance of the crime, and the king actually did not exist. Therefore, if one truly believes that both good and evil are dreams, one will transcend cause and effect and realize highest awakening. Because at that time both karmic sin and karmic benefit are totally nonexistent, it is possible even for one who performed the five heinous crimes[7] to attain Buddhahood.

"But as long as one has not attained Buddhahood, the law of cause and effect is completely inviolable. While one is at the level of ordinary unawakened beings, how could the burden of karmic sin not exist? Nonetheless, if one believes that one's sinful heart from its very bottom is fundamentally nonexistent, then there is no doubt that the burden of karmic sin will disappear. Therefore, one should contemplate evil acts before doing them, asking oneself, 'Since these are dreams, how can I do them?' and thereby carefully control body and mind. Because the evil acts that one is about to commit exist only within dreams, they too completely lack any ultimate reality. Even if one seeks throughout, the ten directions and three periods[8] for the mind that commits sins, in the end it cannot be grasped. One should reflect well, thinking: 'Since this mind that commits sins actually does not exist, how can it engender any karmic retribution?' This form of mental reflection is known as repentance of the uncreated (musho no sange).

"King Ajatashatru[9] murdered his father. When he visited the Buddha to repent of his sins, the Buddha told him that all elements of existence are

---

7. Killing one's father, killing one's mother, killing an arhat, wounding a buddha, or causing schism in the sangha (the Buddhist community).
8. The past, the present, and the future. "The ten directions": that is, everywhere (north, south, east,

west, northeast, northwest, southeast, southwest, the nadir, and the zenith).
9. King of Magadha, in northeastern India (5th century B.C.E.).

completely without fixed forms. What is that thing called 'father'? What is that thing called 'son'? The Buddha explained that the idea of father and son result at random from temporary relations between a pair of the five groups[1] ('heaps,' *skandha,* of dharma elements) that constitute sentient beings. By means of the power of this wisdom, in no time at all, Ajatashatru's karmic sins dissolved into the state of fundamental nonbeing. This process is known as the elimination of sins (*metsuzai*).

"Your attempt to rationalize your desire to commit sins by saying, 'Since they are just dreams, how could I suffer consequences?' is a big mistake. You must analyze this distinction well. Just always focus your attention on the situations in which such thoughts arise. Suppose, for example, just when an unexpected thought of dislike toward a person has arisen, you maintain that train of thought in your mind and carefully analyze this occasion of resentment. In the end, you would realize that estrangement characterizes what is called the unawakened being trapped in the currents of life and death. If just when an evil thought is about to arise one asks: 'From where does this thought arise? Who is its subject? Who is its object?' then that train of thought, which initially was hateful, suddenly would disappear without a trace. Suppose, for example, at night one mistakes a post for a demon and runs away in fear. If one asks what kind of demon could be there and goes back to look more carefully, then one would see that the demon fundamentally is a post. All thoughts of fear would vanish. Whenever an instant of false thought is about to arise, carefully return to that instant of arising and ask what is the basis of that instant of thought. Because the fundamental nature of mind is emptiness, ultimately one reaches that state of fundamental nonbeing.

"This attainment is liberation from birth and death. While the mind of an instant of thought has no basis from which to arise, the thought that things actually exist maintains a continuous train of thought that results ultimately in the sea of life and death. Yet if one traces back this thought and analyzes what kind of thing it is, then one realizes that fundamentally it is nothing. Therefore, after reflecting back for awhile, one knows that one is uncreated. Thus, the process of birth and death—heretofore maintained by previous lifetimes of thought—is eliminated.

"The Buddha placed all of the Great Vehicle's doctrines of the uncreated into the one syllable 'A.' Thus, if one unpacks the syllable 'A' it becomes many different doctrines, and if one compresses these, they become the single syllable 'A.' *The Great Sun Sutra* (*Dainichikyo*) states: 'The syllable "A" is itself uncreated, ungraspable, fundamental emptiness. It universally encompasses all Buddhist teachings. By means of mutual empowerment through this emptiness, one is able to embrace all Buddhist teachings and thereby attain Buddhahood.'

"This syllable 'A' consists of color, shape, sound, and meaning. Sometimes one can practice by focusing one's mind on its color and shape. Sometimes one can practice by vocalizing its sound. When one wishes quietude, one can practice by continuous contemplation of its meaning. Because it offers several forms of practice, one's mastery of the highest principle occurs in no time.

---

1. A standard division of the constituents of mind and body (usually called "the five aggregates"): form, feeling, discrimination, compositional factors, and consciousness.

"The Pure Land practice of chanting *Namu Amida Butsu*,[2] by contrast, involves many words and is prone to distraction. Because the breath that comes out when one simply opens one's mouth always is the sound 'A' even when one is distracted, no other practice is as easy as this one. Because all the doctrines preached in the hundreds and thousands of scriptures and treatises in their entirety are encompassed by this one syllable, reciting this one syllable produces the same amount of merit as reading the entire Buddhist canon. Moreover, the doctrines I mentioned above [i.e., no-self, uncreated, and elimination of sins], in their entirety constitute the meaning of this syllable. Therefore, even the merit produced by reciting without any knowledge is no trivial amount. The amount of merit produced by adding to one's recitation of this syllable even one instant of belief in the principle of the uncreated, therefore, could not be explained completely even after infinite eons.

"Thus, at the very last when facing the end in death, one should merely open one's mouth, place one's attention on the 'A' breath, and experience the end. At that moment, because all affairs also come to an end, no matter what one ponders over, it is beyond one's ability to imagine something better. If one tries to contemplate the meaning of 'A' too intently, it will become a hindrance. Merely ending one's life on the single 'A' syllable without any intense contemplation is attainment of self-realization beyond thought [i.e., perfect awakening without delusion or mental effort]."

The guest asked, "The principles of no-self and noncreation probably are, as you say, the foundation of Buddhism. Yet when I reflect on my own mind, there is not even half a moment when I forget about clinging to a self. Never have I been attentive enough to notice the instant when feelings of happiness or joy come over me. Thus, doctrines and practices like these that you've described must be for wise, flawless people only. Some people [e.g., Pure Land leaders] say that during this evil and declining age ordinary unawakened men should not consider such matters. When I evaluate this in my own mind, I think truly there must be reason in their position. Right?"

The host replied, "Because people's aptitudes for Buddhist practice diverge, the Buddha preached the Dharma of a single taste in various ways. One must not necessarily use one version to block all other ways of practice. Because this doctrine of no-self and noncreation is profound, one who lacks affinities from previous lives will not believe it for an instant. But someone who has established many such affinities will, without being able to say why, feel the value of this doctrine upon hearing it. If one arouses even a single instant of faith, then the power of that faith will eliminate the heaviest sins from the beginningless past. One should see that this will plant the seed of Buddhahood in the Storehouse Consciousness (*alaya vijnana*).

"Thus, the class of beings who have aptitude for the Great Vehicle does not even exclude those who violate the precepts and freely perform evil. Merely one instant of faith and understanding qualifies one for inclusion. The reason for this is that even before one thinks that 'the permanent self must be something that really exists,' the Great Vehicle already extends to whatever good or evil karmic nature exists within one's heart. Once one

---

2. Homage to Amitabha Buddha (Japanese); this chant, called the *nembutsu*, was recited by believers to ensure their rebirth in the Pure Land.

believes that birth and death [i.e., *samsara*] and Nirvana are the same as yesterday's dreams, then the power of this faith transports one beyond the distinctions of good and evil. Therefore it matters not in the least if there has been a good or evil determination prior to one's unawakened cognition [i.e., the power of an unawakened person's faith is not limited by his or her moral nature, which has been determined by prior karmic acts]. In this regard, it is because the beginningless cycle of false thoughts and karmic influences has made such a deep impact that people believe only in themselves and distrust the words of the Buddha that promise salvation through the syllable 'A' and think thoughts such as: 'Since I am evil, how could I have the proper aptitude for Buddhism?'

"Examine your lowly self! You are a person within a dream, wherein both good and evil are fundamentally empty. Because everything is fundamentally empty, you are not the slightest bit different from the Buddha. What basis is there for thinking that your aptitude has been fixed at an inferior grade?

"None of the doctrines or practices mentioned above state that one must discard all evil thoughts. Rather they merely encourage one to have faith in the fundamental nonexistence of whatever good or evil thoughts arise. Buddhist tradition has provided the three practices of morality, meditation, and wisdom so that we will attain inner and outer purity, that is, mental insight and physical decorum. Yet even if I were to beg people to practice these, in this latter age they have become too weak to do so. Even if one is unable to manage any kind of multiple practices, I believe that faith in the doctrines of the Great Vehicle for just one instant of thought right now will plant the proper seed of Buddhahood.

"Confused thoughts are characteristic of ordinary unawakened people. Therefore, as long as one is an ordinary person it is impossible for false thoughts not to arise. From this, it is clear that not a single ordinary person who lacks aptitude for the Great Vehicle exists. It is precisely for ordinary unawakened people who lack any foundation in the Buddhist Way that one explains knowledge of the Tathagata's[3] secret treasure of esoteric contemplation of the syllable 'A.'

"I observe that people of this world, in terms of their attitude toward Buddhism, would rather think only of relying on the merit produced by acts such as chanting Amida Buddha's name (*nembutsu*) or chanting scripture to attain transport to Pure Land in their next life. Hardly anyone exists who expends even a single instant of trust in the Buddhist doctrine. Here is what I know. The Buddhist doctrine is difficult to encounter and difficult to believe. Knowing that it is difficult to believe, upon believing it one obtains inconceivable benefits. The saying that the chanting of one line of verse from the Buddhist scripture will destroy infinite eons worth of sins, being the words of the Buddha, could not possibly be a lie. Yet if these sins were really existing things, then their disappearance would take some amount of time. Because these sins are fundamentally empty, upon chanting the name of the Buddha who awakened to this truth, even without understanding anything, they are eliminated. By adding even an instant of faith in this truth to one's chanting, just think how much more merit would be produced! One should reverently

---

3. A title of a buddha (literally, "one who has thus come/gone"); it is the one most often used by the historical Buddha to refer to himself.

arouse one's mind of faith. My speaking like this also is nothing more than words in a dream. . . ."

As these words were spoken the guest disappeared as if erased. Then the host also disappeared. There was just the humble hermitage and the sound of the wind in the pine trees.

Chido, who harms the nation, wrote this.

A CONVERSATION WITH SKELETONS

(Gaikotsu)

IKKYU

Ikkyu (1394–1481), also known as Kyoun shi ("Master Crazy Cloud"), was the quintessential Zen man. His life was legendary, beginning with his parentage: he was said to be the illegitimate son of Emperor Gokomatsu. Orphaned early, at age five he was placed in a Rinzai Zen temple in Kyoto; he left it in 1410 to study with a master of this sect, which traces its lineage back to Linji (see the *Record of Linji*, p. 541). After the death of his teacher—Ikkyu was said to have been so distraught that he almost committed suicide—he continued his studies under Kaso Sodon near Lake Biwa outside the city. Kaso gave him the koan called "Tozan's Sixty Blows."

> Tozan came to study with Ummon and Ummon asked, "Where are you from?" "From Sato," Tozan replied. Ummon asked, "Where were you for the summer?" "A temple at Hozu, south of the lake," Tozan replied. Ummon asked, "When did you leave?" "On the 25th of August," Tozan replied. Ummon said, "You deserve sixty blows with my stick, but I will forgive you today." The next day Tozan bowed to Ummon, saying "Yesterday you spared me sixty blows. I beg you, please tell me my fault." "You bag of rice," shouted Ummon, "you just wander there, wander here." At Ummon's words, Tozan had a realization.

In 1418, during a performance by a troupe of blind singers, Ikkyu understood the koan. Later, while meditating in a boat on the lake, the caw of a crow triggered his awakening. He often lived as a vagabond, frequenting bars and brothels; he apparently felt that the experience of enlightenment was deepened through sexual intercourse. Ikkyu eventually married a blind singer. Despite this irregular behavior (he is said to have torn up his certificate of enlightenment from Kaso), in 1440 Ikkyu was called to serve as the abbot of a monastery, Daitokuji, but he resigned his post the next year. He devoted much of the rest of his life to his poetry, calligraphy, and brushstroke art, achieving great fame. He was also said to be an accomplished flute player. In 1474, Ikkyu was again appointed abbot of Daitokuji, which had suffered a devastating fire during the Onin war. He reluctantly accepted, and devoted himself to its reconstruction until his death.

Among his most famous essays is "A Conversation with Skeletons," for which he himself provided illustrations (not included below). A decaying corpse is said to be one of the forty objects of meditation set forth by the Buddha, and the skeleton has long represented not just impermanence and death but also a kind of bare-bones purity, stripped of pretension. All those themes are at play here. Indeed, in some sense this is a rather conventional Buddhist discourse on the frailty of human birth until its end, when Ikkyu relates the story of the Buddha holding up a flower.

PRONOUNCING GLOSSARY

Bodhidharma: *boh-di-dar-ma*   Kashyapa: *kah-shya-pa*
Daitoku-ji: *dai-toh-koo-jee*   Sojun: *soh-joon*
Gaikotsu: *gai-ko-tsu*   Sumiyoshi: *soo-mee-yoh-shee*
Gautama: *gau-ta-ma*   Toribe: *toh-ree-beh*
Ikkyu: *eek-kyoo*   Xutang: *shoo-tahng*

> In black and white
> One can find written down
> All of Dharma's workings.

The beginner should concentrate wholly on *zazen*.[1] Of the multitudes born into the world, we can speak of no one who does not finally come to naught. Of course, our own time has not yet come. Nor has that of the 'original visage' which manifests itself in every place and time. All things appear out of nothingness. Furthermore, it is because of its very formlessness, that we call this nothingness by terms such as 'Buddha,' 'Buddha-nature,' 'Mind of Buddha,' 'Dharma-mind,' 'Patriarch,' or 'Deity,'—all mere names applied by us from our own limited perspectives. Unless we understand this fact, we are headed straight for Hell.

I had become more and more disgusted with this realm of rebirth, with all its loves and hates, and I longed to entrust myself to the Buddha's teachings which place one at that crossroads where the path to Nirvana splits off from the road to Hades and where one can put an end to this chain of lives. So trusting my feet to lead me, I left home and set out on a journey to nowhere in particular until, at last, I came to an unknown temple in the wilds. As I had on but a thin garment and night was fast approaching, I wanted to lie down for a while, but there seemed to be no place where I could take my rest. Then I looked around and noted that I had made a long detour off the main highway to reach this place by the foot of the mountains. I felt I had come to a 'Plain of Meditation.'

I walked around behind the hall, a pitiful skeleton of a temple, which stood all alone in the midst of a field of graves and spoke these lines aloud:

> An autumnal wind has started across the world,
> Fronds of grass bend as they must.
> Now to the moor, now to the sea.

and:

> Shall I, then,
> Tuck them in my priestly sleeve,
> These dark feelings of life's emptiness?

TRANSLATED FROM the Japanese by James H. Sanford.

1. Seated meditation.

Yet we ought not utter the words 'all things come to naught.' For Death is a return to one's original state. None of the conditioned thoughts that occurred in Bodhidharma's[2] meditations before a blank wall were true. Nor were any of Buddha's fifty-years'-worth of sermons true, for even they did not plumb the depths of other men's souls.

Wondering, thus, if anyone could comprehend my misery, I had come to spend a night in this temple, but I found that I was still very distraught and couldn't sleep well. About daybreak, in a half-waking dream, I went behind the temple and saw there a group of skeletons.

Each of them was doing something different, just as in the world of men. Even as I was wondering at the strangeness of such a scene, one of the skeletons came over to me and said:

> Indeed a passing dream
> of empty recollections.
> What a tasteless role to play.
>
> Cutting the Law up
> Into 'gods' and 'buddhas,'
> How can we follow the true way?
>
> 'I'm still breathing!' we say,
> And corpses in the field
> are viewed without concern.

As I got used to the skeleton, I found myself grateful at having by chance met him. For I could see that this skeleton had left the world to seek the Dharma and to resolve its discriminations, had gone from the shallows to the depths and had brought his feelings to a state of profound clarity.

I lay there with the sound of the pines rustling in my ear and the autumn moonlight playing across my face.

Yet, when are we not lost in dreams? Who among us is more than a skeleton? So we should see ourselves—as skeletons wrapped in a skin of five elements[3] and patterned into two sexes. When breath goes out, the skin will rupture, even sex will be lost, and superior and inferior will be indistinguishable. Beneath the skin of the person we fondle today, there, too, is a skeleton propping the flesh up. One must know this fact and believe it fully. High and low, old and young are all the same. If one but awakens to this one basic truth, he will understand the principle of 'non-birth and non-death.'

> If memorials of the dead
> are going to be slivers of rock,
> Let it be as tea-mortars rather than headstones.

What could be more awe-inspiring than the sight called man?

> Even though the lone moon crosses an unclouded sky,
> We stumble through the darkness;
> Quite lost.

---

2. The Indian Buddhist monk said to have brought Zen to China in the late 5th century C.E.
3. Earth, water, fire, wind, and space.

How else can you see it? Stop the breath, peel off the skin, and everyone looks alike. And no matter how long you keep the body alive, in the end it does no good.

> A long life to our Sovereign.
> May he exemplify the pines of Sumiyoshi.[4]

Cast aside the idea of self-existence, simply entrust yourself to the world's vagrant winds and go where they take you. Those who want to 'live side by side to a ripe old age,' are caught up in a false idea.

> Since the world is but a brief dream,
> Ought we be surprised
> At man's evanescence?

One's span of life is fixed and no fit subject for prayers. Except for the one essential[5] what is there that we should take to heart? That human life is less than secure ought not be something you are hearing now for the first time.

> Though hateful and unreliable,
> the vagaries of the world
> are best enjoyed.
>
> Just why this false world
> should be so gaily decked out is something
> I still can't fathom.
>
> The original man
> must return to his original home.
> Why seek a place that isn't needed?
>
> None of us knows life,
> Or has a home here.
> To go home one must turn to dust.
>
> Numerous paths lead up from the foothills,
> But behold, a single moon above the peak.
>
> If there is no goal at the end of this journey,
> Then no road can lead astray.
>
> The self has neither beginning nor end.
> One ought not think, then,
> Of 'birth,' of 'death.'
>
> Give in to desires, and they are endless.
> Take firm hold of the world, and lay it aside.
>
> Though we distinguish rain and hail,
> Snow and ice,
> With the thaw, it all turns into riverwater.

---

4. Famous old trees in Osaka Bay.   5. The "great matter" of birth and death.

> Though at times the ways of the heart may alter,
> One still sees Heaven's single Law at work.
>
> Fallen pine needles bury the way
> Till one can find no signs of habitation.
>
> A pitiful funeral at Toribe![6]
> How soon before the mourners too,
> give up the ghost?
>
> How long will we stare at Toribe's smoke,
> thinking, 'Life is vanity'
> As if that only meant the dead?
>
> Isn't it pitiful?
> The memory of this morning's friend
> rises as smoke into the evening sky.
>
> See how sad. The smoke at Toribe
> is driven across the sky
> By the evening wind.
>
> Cremated we become ashes, buried, earth.
> I wonder what will remain.
> Our sins . . . ?
>
> With all the sins of the three worlds
> I too will fade away in the end.

This is clearly the way the world is. People who have not realized that this miserable state of affairs obtains even today are surprised and ask 'Does this apply to me?' To which one may reply, 'Nowadays, in contrast to former times, people do not enter the temple life. In the old days a man who felt called on to establish the religious life went into the temple, whereas now they are all leaving. One look shows us priests with no intellect who find *zazen* a bother and who refuse to apply themselves to meditation, men who rather prefer to be connoisseurs of pots, men who ornament their *zazen* with ostentatious pride. These men don priestly garments out of vanity, and though they wear the clothing, they are simply dressed-up laymen. Even as they put on the robe and the cloak, they tell us they are in torment, that the robes bind like cords and the cloaks are heavy as lead.'

If one examines the rules governing the cycle of birth and death, one finds that killing another creature leads to Hell, and stinginess to rebirth as a hungry ghost. Those who persist in ignorance become beasts, the violent become *asuras*.[7] Those who maintain the five precepts[8] are born as men; those who practice the ten virtues become *devas*.[9] Above these are four kinds of saintly beings. Together these make up ten realms. When all ten are grasped in a

---

6. A former cremation ground in Kyoto.
7. Demigods.
8. Not to kill, steal, lie, engage in sexual misconduct, or consume intoxicants.
9. Inhabitants of the heavenly realms. "The ten virtues": not to kill, steal, engage in sexual misconduct, lie, engage in divisive speech, use harsh words, engage in senseless speech, be covetous, have harmful intent, or hold wrong views.

single burst of thought, one sees there is no form, no state between life and death, no realm that is to be hated. Then existence is like the clouds in heaven or the foam on the waters. Without mind to generate things there are no *dharmas* to come into play. Mind and *dharmas* become one and are Void. One no longer knows the doubts of ordinary men.

Let me tell you something. Human birth is analogous to striking up a fire—the father is flint, the mother is stone, and the child is the spark. Once the spark touches a lamp wick it continues to exist through the 'secondary support' of the fuel until that is exhausted. Then it flickers out. The love-making of the parents is the equivalent of striking the spark. Since the parents too have 'no beginning,' in the end they, too, will flicker out. Everything grows out of empty space from which all forms derive. If one lets go the forms, then he reaches what is called the 'original ground.' But since all sentient beings come from nothingness, we can use even the term 'original ground' only as a temporary tag.

> Breaking open cherry trees, they seek,
> Yet to bloom blossoms,
> Which only come in on the Spring breeze.

> Though climbing beyond,
> The endless clouds
> Ask nothing of Gautama's sutras.

When Kashyapa[1] had listened to Gautama's sermons for fifty years and wanted to put those teachings into practice, Gautama gave him a final statement, 'From first to last I preached not a single word,' and he held up a flower. At this. Kashyapa smiled faintly. Gautama gave him the flower and said, 'You have the heart to know my true Dharma.' Kashyapa then asked, 'What do you mean?' and Gautama replied, 'My sermons of fifty years, Kashyapa, were like drawing a child into your arms by telling him you have something hidden in your hand. Just so with my sermons I drew you.'

Thus the Dharma related in words was for the drawing in of children. But the 'flower' cannot be known physically, mentally, or verbally. Think out what 'physical' and 'mental' mean. Though we can speak of men who 'know things' we ought not talk of 'Buddhist philosophers.'

The flower was the universal Dharma that spread through the various Buddha worlds of the three ages[2]—that very flower. It came here to us from the twenty-eight patriarchs in India by way of the six Chinese patriarchs, and besides this 'Original Ground,' nothing else exists. Since all things are without beginning, it is this which we term 'great.' All eight consciousnesses rise out of Nothingness. The forms of the flowers of spring, of summer, of autumn, of winter all evolve out of Nothingness. Too, there are the four great elements, earth, water, fire, and wind, but men understand these least of all. Breath is the equivalent of wind; fire gives warmth; water becomes vital blood flowing through the body. Burn or bury the body, and it turns to earth. But these too are without beginning; nothing really remains.

---

1. One of the Buddha's chief disciples.   2. The past, the present, and the future.

> The whole of the world
> Is but an illusion.
> 'Death' too is a lie.

The false view that holds that though the body dies, the spirit survives, is a very great error. The words of those who have become enlightened tell us that both the body and its seed die together. What we call 'Buddha' is likewise emptiness. The heavens and the earth will all return to that 'original ground.'

I have laid aside the 80,000 volumes of the Scriptures to present in this single chapter the essence of that which can bring man great joy.

> The deep questions we write out
> Are but marks in a dream.
> When we awake, even the questioner is gone.

Fourth month, 8th day of 1457

Written at Daitoku-ji in Japan by Sojun called Ikkyu, 7th in the line of Xutang.[3]

3. A Chinese Chan master (1185–1269).

YOU POOR HOLE-DWELLING DEVIL

ORATEGAMA

HAKUIN

Among the various forms of Chan Buddhism, two became dominant in Japan. The first was the "just sitting" method of Dogen and his Soto school. The other was the koan practice of the Rinzai School. Although he was not the first Japanese master of this practice, Hakuin (1686–1769) revitalized it in the eighteenth century and was largely responsible for the form that would eventually become most famous. It was Hakuin who coined the koan best known in the West: What is the sound of one hand clapping? Like Dahui (see *Records of Pointing at the Moon*, p. 557) in China, Hakuin was a strong advocate of koan practice, or "observing the key word," and a critic of "silent illumination." And also like Dahui, he emphasized the crucial role of doubt as the catalyst of enlightenment. Moreover, he felt that this enlightenment could be deepened and matured through further koan study and contemplation.

All these elements are clear in the piece below, an excerpt from a letter that Hakuin wrote to an old nun of the Nichiren sect (see the *Treatise on the Establishment of the Orthodox Teaching and the Peace of the Nation*, p. 637) when he was in his early sixties. As befits the place of the *Lotus Sutra* (see the *Saddharmapundarika*, p. 278) in the Nichiren sect, the first part of the letter discusses the sutra at some length. The letter ends with the section included here, in which Hakuin recalls his motivation for becoming a monk and his initial disappointment with the *Lotus Sutra*. He goes on to vividly describe his struggles with a number of koans, including the famous "No" (*wu* in Chinese, *mu* in Japanese) in answer to the question of whether a dog has the Buddha nature. At the end of the letter, Hakuin returns to the *Lotus*.

PRONOUNCING GLOSSARY

Biyan lu: *bee-yehn loo*
Cen: *tsan*
Dahui: *dah-hway*
dharani: *dah-ra-nee*
Echigo: *eh-chee-goh*
Eigan-ji: *ay-gahn-jee*
Fozusan jing: *foh-tsoo-sahn jeeng*
Hakuin: *hah-koo-in*
Iyo: *ee-yoh*
Izumi: *ee-zoo-mee*
katsu: *kah-tsoo*
koan: *koh-ahn*
li: *lee*
Linji: *leen-jee*
Mino: *mee-noh*
Mohezhiguan: *moh-ha-jer-gwahn*
Nanquan: *nahn-chwahn*

Orategama: *o-rah-tay-gah-mah*
Reisho-in: *ray-shoh-een*
Samadhi: *sa-mah-di*
Sansheng: *sahn-shang*
Shinano: *shee-nah-noh*
Shinoda: *shee-noh-dah*
Shitou: *sher-toh*
Shoju: *shoh-joo*
Tathagata: *ta-tah-ga-ta*
Wujia zhengzongzan: *woo-jyah jang-tsohng-tsahn*
Xigeng: *shee-gang*
Xiu: *shyoh*
Xutang lu: *shoo-tahng loo*
Yantou: *yehn-toh*
Zhaozhou: *jau-joh*

When I was seven or eight years old my mother took me to a temple for the first time and we listened to a sermon on the hells as described in the *Mohezhiguan*.[1] The priest dwelt eloquently on the torments of the Hells of Wailing, Searing Heat, Incessant Suffering, and the Red Lotus. So vivid was the priest's description that it sent shivers down the spines of both monks and laymen and made their hair stand on end in terror. Returning home, I took stock of the deeds of my short life and felt that there was but little hope for me. I did not know which way to turn and I was gooseflesh all over. In secret I took up the chapter on Kannon from the *Lotus Sutra* and the *dharani*[2] on Great Compassion and recited them day and night.

One day when I was taking a bath with my mother, she asked that the water be made hotter and had the maid add wood to the fire. Gradually my skin began to prickle with the heat and the iron bath-cauldron began to rumble. Suddenly I recalled the descriptions of the hells that I had heard and I let out a cry of terror that resounded through the neighborhood.

From this time on I determined to myself that I would leave home to become a monk. To this my parents would not consent, yet I went constantly to the temple to recite the sutras and to study the works of Confucianism. At fifteen I left home to become a monk and at that time I vowed to myself: "Even if I should die I will not cease my efforts to gain the power of one whom fire will not burn and water will not drown." Day and night I recited the sutras and made obeisance to the Buddhas, but I noticed that when I was ill or

TRANSLATED FROM the Japanese by Philip B. Yampolsky. All bracketed additions are the translator's.

---

1. *The Great Calming and Contemplation*, by the Chinese Buddhist (538–597), founder of the Tiantai school.

2. A long mantra. "Kannon": the Japanese name for Avalokiteshvara, the bodhisattva of compassion.

A painting of Bodhidharma by Hakuin (1685–1768).

taking acupuncture or moxa treatment, the pain I felt was just as it had been before. I was greatly depressed and said to myself: "I became a monk against my parents' wishes and have yet to make the slightest progress. I have heard that the *Lotus* is the king of all sutras, venerated even by ghosts and spirits. People who are suffering in the lower worlds, when they rely on others in their efforts to be saved, always ask that the *Lotus Sutra* be recited for them. When one considers that recitation by others can save a person from suffering, how much more effective must be recitation by oneself! There must indeed be profound and mysterious doctrines in this *Sutra*."

Thereupon I picked up the *Lotus Sutra* and in my study of it found that, other than the passages that explain that there is only One Vehicle[3] and that all phenomena are in the state of Nirvana, the text was concerned with parables relating to cause and effect. If this *Sutra* had all these virtues, then surely the six Confucian classics and the books of all the other schools must be equally effective. Why should this particular sutra be so highly esteemed? My hopes were completely dashed. At this time I was sixteen years of age.

When I was nineteen I happened to read the [*Wujia*] *Zhengzongzan*,[4] in which the story of how the Master *Yantou* was killed by bandits and how his cries at the time resounded for over three *li*[5] is described. I wondered why such an enlightened monk was unable to escape the swords of thieves. If such a thing could happen to a man who was like a unicorn or phoenix among monks, a dragon in the sea of Buddhism, how was I to escape the staves of the demons of hell after I died? What use was there in studying Zen? What a fraud Buddhism! How I regretted that I had cast myself into this band of strange and evil men. What was I to do now? So great was my distress that for three days I could not eat and for a long time my faith in Buddhism was completely lost. Statues of the Buddha and the sacred scriptures looked like

---

3. Mahayana.
4. A collection of 74 biographies of famous monks, with verses in their praise attached. Completed
in 1254 [translator's note].
5. One *li* equals about 1/3 of a mile. Yantou (828–887), Chinese Chan master.

mud and dirt to me. It seemed much better to read lay works, to amuse myself with poetry and prose, and thus to a small degree to alleviate my distress.

When I was twenty-two I went to the province of Wakasa, and while attending lectures on the *Xutang lu*,[6] gained an awakening. Later, when I was in the province of Iyo, I read the *Fozusan jing*[7] and achieved an intense awakening. I concentrated night and day on the *Mu*[8] koan without a moment's rest, but to my great disappointment I was unable to achieve a pure and uninvolved state of undistracted meditation. Equally disappointing to me was the fact that I could not achieve the state where waking and sleeping are the same.

The spring of my twenty-fourth year found me in the monk's quarters of the Eigan-ji in Echigo, pursuing my strenuous studies. Night and day I did not sleep; I forgot both to eat and rest. Suddenly a great doubt manifested itself before me. It was as though I were frozen solid in the midst of an ice sheet extending tens of thousands of miles. A purity filled my breast and I could neither go forward nor retreat. To all intents and purposes I was out of my mind and the *Mu* alone remained. Although I sat in the Lecture Hall and listened to the Master's lecture, it was as though I were hearing a discussion from a distance outside the hall. At times it felt as though I were floating through the air.

This state lasted for several days. Then I chanced to hear the sound of the temple bell and I was suddenly transformed. It was as if a sheet of ice had been smashed or a jade tower had fallen with a crash. Suddenly I returned to my senses. I felt then that I had achieved the status of Yantou, who through the three periods of time[9] encountered not the slightest loss [although he had been murdered by bandits]. All my former doubts vanished as though ice had melted away. In a loud voice I called: "Wonderful, wonderful. There is no cycle of birth and death through which one must pass. There is no enlightenment one must seek. The seventeen hundred koans handed down from the past have not the slightest value whatsoever." My pride soared up like a majestic mountain, my arrogance surged forward like the tide. Smugly I thought to myself: "In the past two or three hundred years no one could have accomplished such a marvelous breakthrough as this."

Shouldering my glorious enlightenment, I set out at once for Shinano. Calling on Master Shoju, I told of my experience and presented him with a verse. The Master, holding my verse up in his left hand, said to me: "This verse is what you have learned from study. Now show me what your intuition has to say," and he held out his right hand.

I replied: "If there were something intuitive that I could show you, I'd vomit it out," and I made a gagging sound.

The Master said: "How do you understand Zhaozhou's *Mu*?"

I replied: "What sort of place does *Mu* have that one can attach arms and legs to it?"

The Master twisted my nose with his fingers and said: "Here's someplace to attach arms and legs." I was nonplussed and the Master gave a hearty

6. The recorded sayings and writings of Xutang Zhiyu [a Chinese monk of the Linji school (1185–1269), called Xigeng on p. 672; translator's note].

7. *Three Teachings of Buddha-Patriarchs*.
8. "No": see the introduction to this selection.
9. The past, the present, and the future.

laugh. "You poor hole-dwelling devil!" he cried. I paid him no attention and he continued: "Do you think somehow that you have sufficient understanding?"

I answered: "What do you think is missing?"

Then the Master began to discuss the koan that tells of Nanquan's[1] death. I clapped my hands over my ears and started out of the room. The Master called after me: "Hey, monk!" and when I turned to him he added: "You poor hole-dwelling devil!" From then on, almost every time he saw me, the Master called me a "poor hole-dwelling devil."

One evening the Master sat cooling himself on the veranda. Again I brought him a verse I had written. "Delusions and fancies," the Master said. I shouted his words back at him in a loud voice, whereupon the Master seized me and rained twenty or thirty blows with his fists on me, and then pushed me off the veranda.

This was on the fourth day of the fifth month after a long spell of rain. I lay stretched out in the mud as though dead, scarcely breathing and almost unconscious. I could not move; meanwhile the Master sat on the veranda roaring with laughter. After a short while I regained consciousness, got up, and bowed to the Master. My body was bathed in perspiration. The Master called out to me in a loud voice: "You poor hole-dwelling devil!"

After this I devoted myself to an intensive study of the koan on the death of Nanquan, not pausing to sleep or eat. One day I had a kind of awakening and went to the Master's room to test my understanding, but he would not approve it. All he did was call me a "poor hole-dwelling devil."

I began to think that I had better leave and go somewhere else. One day when I had gone to town to beg for food I encountered a madman who tried to beat me with a broom. Unexpectedly I found that I had penetrated the koan on the death of Nanquan. Then the other koans that had puzzled me, Sushan's Memorial Tower and Dahui's verse on the Roundness of the Lotus Leaf fell into place of themselves and I penetrated them all. After I returned to the temple I spoke of the understanding I had gained. The Master neither approved nor denied what I said, but only laughed pleasantly. But from this time on he stopped calling me a "poor hole-dwelling devil." Later I experienced enlightenment two or three times, accompanied by a great feeling of joy. At times there are words to express such experiences, but to my regret at other times there are none. It was as though I were walking about in the shadow cast by a lantern. I returned then and attended on my old teacher Nyoka, who had fallen ill.

One day I read in the verse given by Xigeng to his disciple Nampo as they were parting, the passage: "As we go to part a tall bamboo stands by the gate; its leaves stir the clear breeze for you in farewell." I was overcome with a great joy, as though a dark path had suddenly been illumined. Unconsciously I cried aloud: "Today for the first time I have entered into the *samadhi*[2] of words." I arose and bowed in reverence.

After this I set out on a pilgrimage. One day when I was passing through southern Ise I ran into a downpour and the waters reached to my knees. Suddenly I gained an even deeper understanding of the verse on the Roundness

1. A Chinese Chan master (748–834); for the koan, see the end of this letter.
2. A state of deep meditation.

of the Lotus Leaf by Dahui. I was unable to contain my joy. I lost all awareness of my body, fell headlong into the waters, and forgot completely to get up
again. My bundles and clothing were soaked through. Fortunately a passer-by,
seeing my predicament, helped me to get up. I roared with laughter and everyone there thought I was mad. That winter, when I was sitting at night in the
monk's hall at Shinoda in Izumi, I gained an enlightenment from the sound of
snow falling. The next year, while practicing walking meditation at the monk's
hall of the Reisho-in in Mino, I suddenly had an enlightenment experience
greater than any I had had before, and was overcome by a great surge of joy.

I came to this dilapidated temple when I was thirty-two. One night in a
dream my mother came and presented me with a purple robe made of silk.
When I lifted it, both sleeves seemed very heavy, and on examining them I
found an old mirror, five or six inches in diameter, in each sleeve. The reflection from the mirror in the right sleeve penetrated to my heart and vital
organs. My own mind, mountains and rivers, the great earth seemed serene
and bottomless. The mirror in the left sleeve, however, gave off no reflection
whatsoever. Its surface was like that of a new pan that had yet to be touched
by flames. But suddenly I became aware that the luster of the mirror from
the left sleeve was innumerable times brighter than the other. After this, when
I looked at all things, it was as though I were seeing my own face. For the
first time I understood the meaning of the saying, "The Tathagata[3] sees the
Buddha-nature within his eye."

Later I happened to read the *Biyan lu*[4] again, and my understanding of it
differed completely from what it had been before. One night, some time
after, I took up the *Lotus Sutra*. Suddenly I penetrated to the perfect, true,
ultimate meaning of the *Lotus*. The doubts I had held initially were destroyed
and I became aware that the understanding I had obtained up to then was
greatly in error. Unconsciously I uttered a great cry and burst into tears.

I wish that everyone would realize that studying Zen under a teacher is not
such a simple matter after all. Although I am old and dissipated, and have
nothing of which I can be proud, I am aware that at least I have not spent
forty years in vain. Was it not for this reason that Zhang Wu, when he was in
Yangzhou, let go of his gold and engaged in his painful struggles [toward suc-
cess]? As in the example I gave you, if you shoulder the one-sided understanding you have gained and spend your whole life vainly polishing and purifying
it, how are you any different from Zhang Lu, who guarded his piece of gold
throughout his life, starving himself and bringing only harm to his body?

In India such a person is called a poor son of a rich man, [a follower] of
the Two Vehicles.[5] In China he is spoken of as belonging to the group that
practices the heretical silent-illumination Zen. None of these knows the dignity of the bodhisattva, nor does he reach the understanding that illuminates
the cause for entrance to a Buddha land. Nowadays people go about carrying on their shoulders a single empty principle and with it "understand the
Buddha, understand the Patriarchs, understand the old koans." Then they all
say: "Like the stick, like the *dharani*, like the *katsu*."[6] How laughable this is!

---

3. A title of a buddha (literally, "one who has
thus come/gone"); it is the one most often used
by the historical Buddha to refer to himself.
4. *Blue Cliff Records* (1125), a major Chinese collection of koans.

5. The two Hinayana vehicles, that of the *shravaka*, or disciple (lit., "listener"), and that of the
pratyekabuddha, or solitary enlightened one, neither of which lead to buddhahood.
6. Shout.

Exert yourselves, students, for the Buddha Way is deep and far. Let everyone know that the farther you enter the sea the deeper it becomes and the higher you climb a mountain the taller it gets.

If you wish to test the validity of your own powers, you must first study the koan on the death of Nanquan.

A long time ago Sansheng had the head monk Xiu go to the Zen Master Cen of Changsha[7] and ask him: "What happened to Nanquan after he passed away?"

Changsha replied: "When Shitou became a novice monk he was seen by the Sixth Patriarch."

Xiu replied: "I didn't ask you about when Shitou became a novice monk; I asked you what happened to Nanquan after he passed away."

Changsha replied: "If I were you I would let Nanquan worry about it himself."

Xiu replied: "Even though you had a thousand-foot winter pine, there is no bamboo shoot to rise above its branches."

Changsha had nothing to say. Xiu returned and told the story of his conversation to Sansheng. Sanheng unconsciously stuck out his tongue [in surprise] and said: "He has surpassed Linji by seven paces."

If you are able to understand and make clear these words, then I will acknowledge that you have a certain degree of responsiveness to the teachings. Why is this so? If you speak to yourself while no one is around, you behave as meanly as a rat. What can anyone possibly prove [about your understanding]?

I may have been hitting a dangerous animal in the teeth three times. I join my palms together and say: "Let's leave it at that for today."

---

7. A Chinese Chan master (d. 868). Sansheng was a disciple of Linji (d. 867; see the *Record of Linji*, p. 541).

Buddhism in Tibet

B uddhism came to Tibet late, in the seventh century. By that time, it was already well established in regions bordering Tibet, including India (of course) and Nepal to the south, modern Pakistan and Afghanistan to the west, and China to the east and north. Moreover, it had already spread to Sri Lanka, Korea, and Japan. According to traditional histories, the king of Tibet—one of the great military powers of the region—was converted to Buddhism by his wives, one Chinese and one Nepalese. Each princess brought a statue of the Buddha with her, and one of these would become the most sacred Buddha image in the land.

At the end of the eighth century, the first Buddhist monastery was constructed and the first Tibetan monks ordained. But the portents were ominous; and on the advice of the abbot, an Indian monk from Bengal, a tantric master named Padmasambhava was invited from India to subdue the local deities who were impeding the progress of the dharma. Whether or not Padmasambhava was a mythological figure, he was highly mythologized. It is said that because he understood that the Tibetans were not prepared for the most advanced teachings, he buried texts, written in a coded language, all over the country, making prophecies about when they would be unearthed and by whom. These recovered texts, called "treasures" in Tibetan,

The Fifth Dalai Lama, who became ruler of Tibet in 1642.

became an important part of the canon of the Nyingma or "Ancient" sect of Tibetan Buddhism.

However, Tibetans also studied more conventional texts, though they had no written language before Buddhism was introduced. According to what is likely a legend, the king sent a delegation of young men to India to study Sanskrit and then devise a Tibetan alphabet and grammar. Under another of the "dharma kings," a royal translation academy was founded where Tibetan scholars worked with Indian pundits to translate the vast literature of Indian Buddhism, both sutras and tantras, into Tibetan. As a result, more Indian Buddhist works are preserved in Tibetan than in any other language. But that king's support of the dharma drained the treasury and he was deposed by his brother, remembered as an evil suppressor of Buddhism. The usurper's assassination by a Buddhist monk in 842 forever ended the Tibetan monarchy and plunged the country into what is called "the dark period." In the late tenth century, local princes in the far western region of Tibet began a Buddhist revival, sending young men to India to study and inviting Indian masters to come to Tibet. This time is known as "the later spread of the dharma." There are four major sects of Tibetan Buddhism: Nyingma, Kagyu, Sakya, and Geluk (each of which is represented in the selections here). Whereas the Nyingma sect traces its roots to the earlier establishment of Buddhism in Tibet in the late eighth century, the other three sects all trace their roots to the period of revival.

Thus, Tibet not only first received Buddhism later than many other lands where the religion came to flourish, but it maintained direct ties with Indian Buddhism much later than did China, Korea, or Japan. Indeed, Tibetan pilgrims visited India until the demise of Buddhism there in the thirteenth century. As a consequence, many works that were not translated into Chinese or had little importance in China (and hence in Korea or Japan) were highly influential in Tibet. These included writings on Madhyamaka and Yogachara philosophy, as well as a substantial tantric literature. Whereas East Asian Buddhism is largely based on the Mahayana sutras, Tibetan Buddhism is largely based on the Mahayana shastras ("treatises") and tantras. Buddhism became the central religious and cultural element in Tibet; over the centuries, sometimes as many as fifteen percent of men were Buddhist monks and perhaps three percent of women were Buddhist nuns.

With the demise of the Tibetan monarchy, political power devolved to aristocratic families, many of whom were strong patrons of Buddhism. As monasteries were founded across the land, the monasteries and their leading lamas (the Tibetan term for *guru*) also acquired power, both real and symbolic. Since many of these were Buddhist monks who had taken vows of celibacy, the problem of succession eventually arose. In some cases, authority was passed from a monk to his nephew. However, as early as the eleventh century, a form of succession developed in Tibet that is unique in the Buddhist world: the institution of the incarnate lama, or *tulku*. All Buddhist traditions believe in rebirth, and in the Mahayana it is said that buddhas and bodhisattvas intentionally return to the world again and again out of their compassion for all sentient beings. The Tibetans added to this idea the claim that after the death of a great master, his next incarnation could be identified, even when he was a young child. Eventually, some three thousand lines of incarnation developed in Tibet (a few of which are female), the most famous being that of the Dalai Lama. The institution of the incarnate lama would become a central component of Tibetan society, providing the means by which authority and charisma, as well as property, were passed from one generation to another. Indeed, the spread of Tibetan Buddhism is mirrored in the increasingly large geographical areas in which incarnate lamas are discovered, extending today to Europe and North America.

Tibet was not conquered by the Mongols but instead developed a "priest-patron" relationship with the Mongol khans (most famously, with Kublai Khan), in which Tibet provided Buddhist instruction and ritual to the Mongols and the Mongols provided material support and military protection. In 1642, after defeating his rivals with the aid of Mongol forces, the Fifth Dalai Lama, an incarnate lama and monk of the Geluk sect, gained political control of the country. From that time until 1959, Tibet was ruled by a succession of Dalai Lamas, each discovered as a young child after his predecessor had died, and governed by a regent during the child's minority.

During the Qing dynasty (1644–1911) the Manchu rulers of China (who came from Manchuria in the northeast) retained the "priest-patron" relationship and considered Tibet to be part of their empire, though their authority was often nominal. Unlike other Buddhist nations of Asia, Tibet never came under direct or indirect European control (despite British efforts, including a military incursion in 1903), and its storied isolation and snow-peaked setting led to its perception by the West as a place of magic and mystery. In 1950, troops of the People's Liberation Army invaded Tibet. As Chinese control grew, so did popular resistance, until in 1959 a revolt broke out in the capital of Lhasa. While it was underway the Fourteenth Dalai Lama escaped to India, where he has lived ever since. Tibet's incorporation into the People's Republic of China as an "autonomous region" has been accompanied by massive destruction of Buddhist institutions and harsh suppression of Tibetan Buddhism.

HOW TO EXCHANGE SELF AND OTHER

COMMENTARY ON EIGHT VERSES
FOR TRAINING THE MIND
(The Lojong Tsik Gyeme Drelpa)

CHEKAWA

According to Tibetan historians, Buddhism entered their country in two waves: the "early spread of the dharma" and the "later spread of the dharma." The first began in the seventh century when the king, Songtsen Gampo, was converted to Buddhism by his Chinese and Nepalese wives. One of the signal events of this period was the late eighth-century debate over sudden versus gradual enlightenment between the Chinese monk Heshang Moheyan and the Indian monk Kamalashila (see the *Bhavanakrama*, p. 441). Some decades later, an anti-Buddhist king undertook a suppression of Buddhism, bringing the early spread of the dharma to an end. He was assassinated by a Buddhist monk in 842.

The later spread of the dharma began in the first half of the eleventh century. One of the signal events of this period was the arrival in 1042 of the great Bengali monk Atisha, who was renowned for his teachings on compassion. From these teachings, given to monks who came to be known as the "Kadampa geshes," a genre of literature evolved that would prove influential among all the sects of Tibetan Buddhism. It is called *lojong*, literally "mind training." One might feel that all Buddhist practice is "mind training" in one sense or another. However, in this context, "mind" has a specific meaning. It refers to *bodhichitta*, literally the "mind of enlightenment": that is, the aspiration to achieve enlightenment in order to liberate all beings in the universe from suffering. It is this aspiration that makes one a bodhisattva.

A number of techniques for developing this compassionate attitude are found in the Mahayana literature of India. In the *lojong* tradition, the preeminent method is called "the exchange of self and other," which derives from the eighth chapter of Shantideva's *Introduction to the Practice of the Bodhisattva Path* (p. 395). In verse 120 of that chapter, Shantideva declares, "Whoever seeks to rescue rapidly himself and others should practice the supreme mystery of placing yourself in the position of another." His claim is that the source of all suffering in the world is the cherishing of oneself and that the source of all happiness in the world is the cherishing of others. His argument for altruism is not entirely without self-interest, however. He points out that sentient beings have always cherished themselves and yet have continued to suffer in the realms of samsara. The Buddha was himself once an ordinary sentient being but long ago decided to exchange self and other; as a result he achieved the ultimate state of omniscience and bliss.

The literature of mind training is large, but the meditation itself is simple. Its central element is a practice called "giving and taking," in which one imagines that with each inhalation, one takes into oneself all of the sufferings, misfortunes, and negative qualities of all sentient beings, inhaling them in the form of dark clouds of smoke. With each exhalation, one gives away all of one's happiness, good fortune, and positive qualities, exhaling them in the form of luminous clouds; these descend on each being in the universe, entering their bodies and filling them with happiness.

The most famous mind-training texts are two—one only seven verses in length, the other eight. The latter, with commentary, is presented here. The eight verses are attributed to Langri Thangpa (1054–1123) and the commentary is ascribed to Chekawa (1101–1175), both renowned masters of mind training.

PRONOUNCING GLOSSARY

Asanga: *a-san-ga*
Avalokiteshvara: *a-va-loh-ki-taysh-va-ra*
bodhisattva: *boh-di-sat-tva*
Chakshingwa: *chahk-sheeng-wah*
Chekawa Yeshe Dorje: *chay-gah-wah*
  yay-shay dohr-jay
dakini: *dah-ki-nee*
Dromtonpa: *drohm-dun-ba*
Geshe Chekawa: *gay-shay chay-gah-wah*

Kadampa: *kah-dahm-ba*
Langri Thangpa: *lahng-ree tahng-ba*
Lojong Tsik Gyeme Drelpa: *low-jong*
  tsik-gyay-may drel-pa
Longshu Gegong: *lohng-sho geh-gohng*
Meru: *may-ru*
Phen: *pehn*
Shantideva: *shahn-ti-day-va*
Sherapbar: *sheh-rab-bahr*

Herein is contained the *Eight Verses on Mind Training* together with the story of its origin.

I pay homage to the sublime teachers!

Geshe Chekawa once remarked, "My admiration for the Kadampas first arose when I heard the eight verses from Chakshingwa.[1] Thereafter I studied the verses and meticulously memorized the words, repeating them until I arrived at Lungsho Gegong, yet I failed to realize [their meaning] in my heart. For if these verses had entered my heart, things would have been quite different by then. Nonetheless, whenever the fear of being attacked [by bandits and such] appeared in my mind during my journey, I reflected upon these verses and this helped. Also I was often in situations where I had to seek shelter with strangers when my mind turned wild and untamed. During times when I was confronted with seemingly unbearable situations, such as failing to secure a suitable shelter, or when I became the target of others' disparagement, these verses helped me."

What verses are these? They are the following eight verses:

> 1. With the wish to achieve the highest aim,
>   Which surpasses even a wish-fulfilling gem,
>   I shall train myself to at all times
>   Cherish sentient beings as supreme.

In general, in order to train yourself [to view] each sentient being as a wish-fulfilling gem, [you should recall] two [important] points of similarity shared by sentient beings and the precious gem. [First] if you submerge the wish-fulfilling gem in a muddy mire, the gem cannot cleanse itself of the mud; however, if you wash it with scented water on a full-moon day, adorn the tip of a victory banner with it, and make offerings to it, the gem can then become a source of all earthly wishes. In the same way, sentient beings afflicted with the various defects of cyclic existence cannot free themselves from the mire

---

TRANSLATED FROM the Tibetan by Thupten Jinpa. All bracketed additions are the translator's.

1. A monk (ca. mid-12th century) whose teacher was a student of Langri Thangpa (1054–1123), the author of the eight verses. "Geshe": a Tibetan title for a Buddhist master. "The Kadampas": Tibetan followers of Atisha (lit., "Those Bound by Command"; see the introduction to this selection).

of this unenlightened state, nor can they wash away their sufferings and the origins of these sufferings. However, with our help, all the benefits, both immediate and ultimate, can issue from them. Without sentient beings how would you obtain even the immediate benefits—these would cease immediately; even ultimate happiness arises in relation to sentient beings. It is on the basis of sentient beings that you attain the unexcelled state of buddhahood.

Second, in particular:

> 2. Whenever I interact with others,
> I will view myself as inferior to all,
> And I will train myself
> To hold others superior from the depths of my heart.

As stated here, wherever we are and whomever we interact with, we should train to view ourselves, in all possible ways, as lower and to respect others from the depths of our heart. "Others" encompasses those who are higher than us, such as our spiritual teachers; those who are equal to us, such as our fellow monks; and those who are inferior to us, such as beggars. "In all respects" refers to our family lineage, mental capacity, and similar factors. We should reflect upon our own shortcomings in relation to these factors and avoid becoming proud. Thinking "They all belong to the lowly class of butchers," we generate pride on the basis of our physical existence. With skin the color of rusted gold, we are not even worthy of a sentient being's gaze!

With respect to our cognitive capacities, if we feel proud despite our [commonplace] lack of distinction, reflect, "I am ignorant of every one of the five fields of knowledge. Even in those fields where I have listened with care and attention, I fail to discern when I miss certain words and their explanations. In my behavior, too, though I am known to be a monk, there are hardly any negative deeds I have not committed. Even at this very moment, my thoughts embody the three poisons[2] and my actions of body, speech, and mind remain mostly impure. Therefore, in the future, it will be difficult to attain birth in the higher realms,[3] let alone liberation."

Shantideva's *Guide to the Bodhisattva's Way of Life*[4] states:

> By this type of behavior,
> Even the human form will not be obtained;
> If I fail to achieve human existence,
> There is only evil and no virtues.

In this manner we should contemplate all our shortcomings and reflect, "Nothing falls beneath me but this river," and diminish our conceit and learn to respect others. This suggests that whenever we perceive positive qualities in others, or perceive qualities pertaining to family lineage, physical appearance, material resources, or spiritual realizations such as the six perfections,[5]

2. The negative emotions of desire, hatred, and ignorance.
3. The realms of gods, demigods, and humans.
4. See *Introduction to the Practice of the Bod-* *hisattva Path*, p. 395; Shantideva was an 8th-century Indian monk.
5. Giving, ethics, patience, effort, concentration, and wisdom.

we should think, "How wondrous indeed that they possess these qualities despite their flawed natures!" If, instead, they lack these qualities, we should reflect, "Who knows what higher qualities they may actually possess?" [Here] the story of the ugly mendicant is told.[6]

"From the depths or the very bone of my heart" indicates that our thoughts should not remain in our mouth as mere words. Instead, if we have the intention "I shall regard all beings as my family without discriminating on the basis of their family background," even the noble Avalokiteshvara[7] will compliment us with the statement, "O child of noble family, this is excellent!" Just as, when the earth is leveled, oceans form upon it and draw forth the waters, in the same manner, the supramundane qualities flourish in the hearts of those free of pride. Therefore the *Condensed Perfection of Wisdom* states:

> Abide as if you were a servant of all beings.

In essence, the three scriptural collections are a means to vanquish that conceit. When we are conceited, we are unable to live in harmony with others even in this present life. As for its detrimental consequences in the next life, [it is stated]:

> Some ignorant ones, owing to the force of their conceit,
> Take birth in the lower realms[8] and in places bereft of leisure;
> They take birth as paupers or among the lowly castes;
> And they become blind, weak, or possessed of a vile demeanor.

[Because of conceit] our propensities for afflictions will deepen further, and we will generate intense afflictions relative to those we deem inferior to ourselves. There is even a consequence more serious than this: we will fail to attain enlightenment. For it is written:

> The bodhisattva who is conceited
> Remains far away from enlightenment.

So all the states of inferiority, degeneration, and suffering within the bounds of mundane existence arise from grasping at our own self as most precious. In contrast, all the joys—both mundane and supramundane—originate from sentient beings. We should therefore perceive all sentient beings as embodiments of higher qualities and vanquish our pride.

Third, since the afflictions impede us from proceeding in the above manner, eliminate them as follows:

> 3. During all my activities I will probe my mind,
>   And as soon as an affliction arises—
>   Since it endangers myself and others—
>   I will train myself to confront it directly and avert it.

Training ourselves to examine our mental continuum in all our activities and averting the afflictions as soon as they arise is as follows: Whichever of

---

6. The point of the story is that the mendicant, though ugly, was in fact highly learned.
7. The bodhisattva regarded as the embodiment of all the compassion of all the buddhas.
8. The realms of animals, ghosts, and the denizens of hell.

the four everyday activities we engage in,[9] with mindfulness and vigilance, we should analyze whether thoughts such as attachment arise in our mind. With the thought "I will relinquish them the instant they arise," we should level them flat by observing them in this manner. Instead, if we act like an [elderly] couple being robbed by a thief, we procrastinate and then nothing happens. If afflictions proliferate in our mental continuum, emotions like anger will also increase exponentially. A sutra states:

> Likewise, those who place their faith in sleep
> Will procrastinate and fall further into slumber.
> This is true also of those who are lustful,
> And those who crave intoxicants.

Our propensities for afflictions will deepen, and we will experience intense afflictive emotions toward all we perceive to be inferior. A more serious consequence is that we ourselves will experience acute suffering. If we relinquish the afflictions, their propensities too will become lighter. The past propensities will weaken, and only subtle propensities will be created anew toward desirable objects. Since the law of cause and effect is subtle, [the effects] will definitely be realized in our experience. So we should view the afflictions as our enemies and enhance the power of their antidotes.

Shantideva states:

> I may be slain or burned alive;
> Likewise I may be decapitated;
> Under no circumstance shall I
> Bow before my enemy, the afflictions.

As stated here, the conventional enemy can harm us only in this world and not beyond, but the enemy that is our afflictions can injure us throughout all our lives. It has been stated:

> This enemy of mine, the afflictions,
> Is long-lived, with neither beginning nor end;
> No other enemies can endure
> In this manner for so long.

Furthermore, when we concede to our conventional enemies, they no longer harm us and may actually benefit us. If we assuage the afflictions in the same manner, however, they become even more destructive. It has been stated:

> If you relate to your enemies with friendship and gifts,
> These bring benefit and happiness.
> However, if you appease the afflictions,
> It causes ever more suffering and injury.

Furthermore, conventional enemies harm only our body, life, and wealth, whereas the afflictions create immeasurable suffering in this cycle of existence. It has been stated:

> Even were all the gods and demigods
> To rise up against me as my enemies,

---

9. Walking toward a destination, going for a stroll, sleeping, and sitting [translator's note].

They could not drag me and cast me
Into the blazing fire of the eternal hells.

Yet this powerful enemy, my afflictions,
Can fling me instantly
Where even mighty Mount Meru[1]
Would be crushed into dust upon contact.

So we should view the afflictions as our enemy and discard them. While conventional enemies can [return and] cause harm even after they have been banished, the afflictions enemy cannot resurface once they have been eradicated. It is like burnt seeds. The method for eliminating them is through conduct, meditation, and view.

For beginners, given the weakness of their antidotes and their difficulty in countering afflictions that have already arisen, they must relinquish them [first] through their conduct. As for meditation, it is said that each affliction has a corresponding antidote. Since whatever meditative practice we undertake from among the three scopes[2] becomes a remedy against all the afflictions, it is appropriate to engage in this practice. As our mental level advances, since afflictions are devoid of objects, it is sufficient simply to recognize that this is so. Thus there remains nothing to eliminate. [Shantideva] states:

Afflictions! Afflictions! Relinquish them with your eyes of insight.

Fourth, training ourselves to regard beings of unpleasant character and those oppressed by powerful negative karma and suffering with special care and as something rarely found is presented in the following:

4. When I encounter beings of unpleasant character,
   And those oppressed by intense negative karma and suffering,
   As though finding a treasure of precious jewels,
   I will train myself to cherish them, for they are so rarely found.

"Beings of unpleasant character" refers to those like the king Asanga who, not having accumulated merit in the past, experience the arising of afflictions without even a trace of control. It also refers to beings such as the [ill-tempered] person who, while crossing a mountain pass, was given a plate of meat stew. But when the food burned his lips, he tossed the full plate away along with the pan, and then bellowed, "You dare burn me!" "[Intense] negative karma" refers to the five heinous crimes, degeneration of the vows, and [misappropriation of] offerings made to the Three Jewels.[3] "Those oppressed by intense suffering" refers to those who are afflicted by leprosy, other serious illnesses, and so on.

We should not treat them as enemies by saying, "We cannot even look at them, and we must never allow them to come near us." Rather we should feel compassion toward them as though they were being led away by the king's executioners. Even if some among them are morally degenerate, we should

---

1. In Buddhist cosmology, the mountain located at the center of the world.
2. Three types of persons: those who seek a better rebirth within samsara, those who seek liberation from samsara for themselves, and those who seek liberation from samsara for all beings.

3. The Buddha, the dharma, and the sangha (the Buddhist community). "The five heinous crimes": killing one's father, killing one's mother, killing an arhat, wounding a buddha, or causing schism in the sangha.

feel, "What can I do to help them?" until our tears flow freely. This means that we should first console them with words, and if this proves ineffective, we should provide for their material needs and render help to cure their illness. If this, too, is unsuccessful, we should sustain them in our thoughts, and in action we should protect them even with shelter. Some people, thinking, "This will not benefit the other, but it could harm me," cover their noses and walk away from those oppressed by acute suffering. Even so, there is no certainty that such suffering will never befall us. Therefore, in our actions, we should provide others with food, medicine, and the like, while with our thoughts we should contemplate the following and train the mind:

> Whatever sufferings beings have,
> May they all ripen upon me.

The line "I will train myself to cherish them, for they are so rarely found" is explained as follows. Since it is rare to find a precious gem, we do not discard it but rather keep it and cherish it. In the same way, beings of unpleasant character are not so easy to find; yet in dependence upon them compassion arises, and in dependence upon them the awakening mind arises. Without making deliberate efforts, it is rare to encounter such objects as these that allow us to develop the Mahayana[4] paths. Why? Because compassion does not arise toward the noble ones and those with worldly excellence, so they cannot help us enhance the awakening mind. They cannot therefore lead us to the attainment of buddhahood. This is stated in the following:

> Except for the awakening mind,
> The buddhas do not uphold any means.

Fifth, training ourselves to accept the defeat without harboring any resentment, even when faced with misfortunes such as slander and so on, is presented in the following:

> 5. When others out of jealousy
>   Treat me wrongly with abuse and slander,
>   I shall train to take the defeat upon myself
>   And offer the victory to others.

Regardless of whether we are to blame, if others slander us or speak ill of us out of jealousy or other motives, instead of harboring resentment, we should respond with a gentle mind. Free of resentment, we should refrain from claiming, for instance, "I am innocent. Others are to be blamed." Like Langri Thangpa, we should take the defeat upon ourselves. It is said that whenever misfortunes befell another, he would say, "I too am a part of him." When we engage in giving and ethical discipline at present, we do so to purify our negative karma and accumulate merit. If we recognize those who slander us as sources of kindness, although this is not a substitute for the aforementioned two activities, it nevertheless cleanses us of resentment and purifies our negative karma, the master said. Taking the defeat upon ourselves prevents us from adding to our [negative] karma.

Langri Thangpa states, "In regard to purification of negative karma and accumulation of merit, it is more effective to recognize those who baselessly

---

4. On the "great vehicle," as distinguished from the "inferior vehicle" (Hinayana), see p. 655.

slander you as great sources of kindness than it is to offer butter-fried delicacies to each monk of the Phen region." *A Guide to the Bodhisattva's Way
of Life* states:

> Since it is in dependence upon
> His malign intention that forbearance arises,
> It's really he who is the cause of forbearance;
> Like the true Dharma, he is worthy of veneration.

To substantiate this assertion, he [Shantideva] states in the following that
forbearance is more powerful than ethical discipline:

> There is no negativity like anger;
> And there is no fortitude like forbearance. . . .

This presents the forbearance of being unperturbed by harms.

Sixth is the forbearance of voluntarily accepting suffering. When someone
to whom we have rendered help in the past, or in whom we have placed great
hope, betrays or slanders us, we should contemplate them as our teacher with
a sense of gratitude. This is presented in the following:

> 6. Even if one whom I have helped
>   Or in whom I have placed great hope
>   Gravely mistreats me in hurtful ways,
>   I will train myself to view him as my sublime teacher.

As for expectation, [Drom] tonpa[5] once remarked, "In Kham,[6] I went to visit
the teacher Sherapbar, a friend close to my heart. I went knowing he had not
invited me, and he took offense at this and sent me away. He ordered others
to remove all my belongings, and he himself locked me in a dark room. That
was when it became clear whether I had trained my mind in loving-kindness
and compassion, and whether the lines 'May these sufferings ripen upon me;
/ May all my happiness ripen upon them' had remained a lie for me." So we
must never retaliate with resentment.

Furthermore, relating this to our own situation, were it not for inferior
karma, such events would not befall us. For it has been stated:

> Previously I caused harms,
> Such as these, to other sentient beings;
> So it is right that [today] such injuries befall me,
> I who have harmed others.

We should think that we ourselves are to blame [for whatever befalls us]; and
in this manner, by maintaining a warm heart, we remain happy. And because
we do not transfer the blame to others, they too remain happy. We should
reflect, "This is due to my own karma. It is established that no one harms the
noble ones who have eliminated their negative karma." Even from the other's
perspective, it is our own negative karma that caused them to injure us. Reflect,
"Because of me, he will have to go to the lower realms. I am to blame for this."
It has been stated:

---

5. Atisha's main Tibetan disciple (ca. 1004–1064).   6. The southeast region of the Tibetan Plateau.

> Impelled by my own karma,
> [The perpetrators] have brought this harm upon me;
> Because of this they'll be in the pits of hell.
> So is it not I who has destroyed them?

Thus it is appropriate to protect these beings from their suffering. Again, it has been stated:

> Those who falsely accuse me,
> And others who cause me harm,
> Likewise those who insult me:
> May they all share in enlightenment

Also:

> Even if others return kindness with harm,
> I will practice responding with great compassion;
> The most excellent beings of this world
> Answer injury with benevolence.

"To contemplate them gratefully as spiritual teachers" refers to the following: Our spiritual teachers are embodiments of great kindness, for they bestow on us the vows, provide us with the methods of meditative practice, and reveal to us the path to liberation. Of course, if we fail to contemplate this and fail to guard this contemplation, we will not tread the path. So reflect, "What this being has given me helps purify my negative karma and accomplish my accumulations. He has therefore benefited me. So I must view him as my spiritual teacher, no different from the one who has conferred on me the oral transmissions of the meditative practices." In this respect, [Atisha's] *Songs of Blissfulness* states:

> Whether someone is foe or friend—
> These objects that give rise to afflictions—
> He who sees them as spiritual teachers
> Will be joyful wherever he resides.

When such thoughts arise [spontaneously], our mind is trained; then even if we have no other practice, whatever acts we engage in turn into [aspects of the] path to enlightenment. This is like the saying, "One cannot find excrement in a land of gold."

Dharma refers to the transformation of your mind and not to the transformation of the external environment. For a trained person, even were the three worlds—of humans, celestial gods, and demons—to rise up as his enemies, his mind would not be afflicted by nonvirtue and suffering. Since no one can vanquish him, he is called a hero.

Seven, in brief, one must train to offer—both directly and indirectly—all the benefits and joys to our dear mother sentient beings and to take all their hurts and pains into the depths of our hearts. This is presented in the following:

> 7. In brief, I will train myself to offer benefit and joy
> To all my mothers, both directly and indirectly,
> And respectfully take upon myself
> All the hurts and pains of my mothers.

"In brief" refers to condensing all the preceding points. "Respectfully" suggests that we take these into the depths of our hearts while contemplating the kindness of our mothers. In other words, we should practice giving and taking not merely in words but from the depths of our heart. In practice, if we give away such factors of joy as food, medicine, and so on while taking upon ourselves all the hurts and pains of sentient beings, this is a cause for achieving birth in higher realms and attaining definitive goodness. If, however, we are not yet able to actually practice this, we should instead perform the taking mentally by engaging in the meditation of giving and taking and dedicating all the joys of this life. When making aspiration prayers, we should utter from the depth of our hearts the following lines from *A Guide to the Bodhisattva's Way of Life*:

> My own happiness and others' suffering—
> If I do not thoroughly exchange them,
> I will not become fully enlightened;
> In this cyclic existence, too, I'll find no joy.

Eight, since in all these practices it is possible to become defiled, we should make sure that they remain untainted by even the slightest mundane consideration of this life, and with the awareness that recognizes all phenomena as illusionlike, we should train to be utterly free of attachment. This is presented in the following:

> 8. By ensuring that all this remains undefiled
> From the stains of the eight mundane concerns,[7]
> And by understanding all things as illusions,
> I will train myself to be free of the bondage of clinging.

Thus the remedy—the method—is this. When tainted with mundane concerns such as the desire to be perceived by others as praiseworthy, we fall under the influence of the eight mundane concerns, and our pursuits become those of self-interest. When this occurs, then the sacred teachings have been turned into demons. If we understand these [mundane concerns] as illusionlike, later we will relinquish them. Nothing within our present experience possesses substantial reality. [It has been stated:]

> So among these empty phenomena,
> What is there to gain or to lose?
> Who provides you with what service?
> And who subjects you to insults?
>
> From whence do pleasure and pain arise?
> What is there to be sad or joyful about?

And further,

> That all things are just like space,
> I, for one, shall accept.

As for supplicating all [objects of refuge] and reciting this as an aspiration, it is as follows: We should make mandala offering to the teachers and the Three Jewels and make the following supplication:

7. Happiness and sorrow, gain and loss, praise and blame, and fame and disgrace.

"If you—my teachers, the buddhas of the three times,[8] and all the bodhisattvas—possess blessings and compassion; if you—the ten male and ten female wrathful deities—possess power and might; and if you—the wisdom dakinis[9]—possess strength and abilities, bless me so that the meaning of these eight verses will be realized in me. Bless me so that all the suffering and its origin of all sentient beings ripens upon me and that all the fruits of my awakening mind ripen upon all beings." We should relate this [in the same manner] to all four truths[1] and train [our mind].

Whatever virtuous actions, such as these [mind training practices], we may perform, afterward we should recite this aspiration prayer of the eight verses. Making such an aspiration creates propensities for the awakening mind. We should recite the following aspiration prayer: "To such activities of root virtue I will dedicate all my time—all my months and all my years. In the future, too, I will make sure to encounter spiritual teachers and to associate with [virtuous] companions." We should recite these prayers of aspiration repeatedly.

This commentary on the eight verses of the bodhisattva Langri Thangpa was composed by Chekawa Yeshe Dorje. This commentary on the root verses constitutes a profound instruction on mind training. Please strive in this. May [its realization] arise in the hearts [of all].

8. The past, the present, and the future.
9. Tantric goddesses.
1. That is, the four noble truths: suffering, ori-
gin, cessation, and path; see *Setting the Wheel of the Dharma in Motion*, p. 177, and its introduction.

MILAREPA MEDITATES ON HIS MOTHER'S BONES

BIOGRAPHY OF MILAREPA
(*The Mile Namtar*)

TSANGNYON HERUKA

Milarepa (1028/40–1111/23) is the most beloved of all Tibetan saints, admired for his beautiful songs and an inspiration to all for proving by his own example that someone can murder thirty-five people and still become a buddha in one lifetime. Although he was a central figure in the lineage of the Kagyu sect of Tibetan Buddhism, his story is known and his songs are sung across the Tibetan Buddhist world.

Milarepa was born the son of a wealthy landowner who, when dying, asked his brother to take care of his wife and children, as well as his property, until Milarepa was old enough to inherit it. But Milarepa's uncle seized all of the property for himself and forced the young boy, his mother, and his sister to be servants, refusing to give Milarepa his birthright. His mother suffered in disgrace, eventually sending her son to learn the black arts. He excelled at his studies, and during the wedding of his uncle's son, he caused the building to collapse: thirty-five people died, including the bride and groom, but his evil uncle and aunt were spared.

Milarepa in time came to repent his deeds and decided to practice the dharma. He first went to a teacher who taught him a profound meditation practice, but it had no effect whatsoever. Concluding that Milarepa's karmic obstructions were too great for him to benefit from the practice, the teacher suggested that Milarepa seek out Marpa the Translator, a lama who had traveled to India to retrieve tantric teachings. Milarepa found Marpa, who accepted him as his student but treated him cruelly, putting him through horrendous trials. After Milarepa was almost at the point of suicide, Marpa finally revealed that Milarepa was destined to be his great disciple. But in order to succeed on the path to enlightenment, Milarepa needed to be purged of his karmic obscurations. Rather than be reborn in hell for aeons for the sin of murder, he had to experience the effects of those deeds in the present life and so Marpa had treated him cruelly. Milarepa received Marpa's instructions and went into retreat to meditate. During his retreat, he had a dream in which he saw his mother dead and his sister wandering as a beggar. Overcome with emotion, he ended his retreat early and told Marpa that he must go to his mother. The selection below begins with his visit to his home village, where he finds that people do not recognize him. But they have heard the story of the great magician and still fear that he, and the wrathful deities he commands, will return.

After he leaves his village, Milarepa retires to the mountains, where he suffers terrible privations as he meditates, often nearly naked, in cold caves. But he attains his goal, achieving buddhahood in one lifetime.

Although the biography is presented as Milarepa's first-person account to his disciple Rechungpa, it was composed centuries after Milarepa's death by the tantric yogin Tsangnyon Heruka (1452–1507).

PRONOUNCING GLOSSARY

Akshbhya: *a-kshoh-bya*
dakini: *dah-ki-nee*
Drakar Taso: *drah-gahr tah-soh*
Dzese: *dzay-say*
Jetsun lama: *jeh-tsun lah-mah*
Gungtang: *goong-dahng*
Kagyu: *kah-gyoo*
Kazhi Dunggye: *kah-shee doong-gay*
Konchok Lhabum: *kun-chohk lha-boom*
Marpa Lotsawa: *mahr-bah loh-tsah-wah*
Milarepa: *mee-lah-ray-bah*

Mila Shergyal: *mee-lah shehr-gyehl*
Mile Namtar: *mee-lay nam-tar*
Nyangtsa Kargyen: *nyahng-tsah kahr-gyehn*
Orma: *ohr-mah*
Peta Gonkyi: *peh-tah gun-kyi*
Ratnakuta Sutra: *rat-na-koo-ta soo-tra*
Rechungpa: *reh-choong-ba*
Tsangnyon Heruka: *tsang-nyon hey-roo-ka*
Vajradhara: *vaj-ra-da-ra*
Yungyal: *yoon-gyehl*

CHAPTER NINE

[*The Journey Home*]

Again Rechungpa asked, "When the Jetsun lama[1] returned to the land of his birth was it as he had dreamed or did he meet his mother?"

"I did not have the fortune to meet with my mother, just as I had seen in my terrible dream," answered Milarepa.

Rechungpa then said, "In that case, how did the Jetsun arrive at his home? How did he meet with his countrymen when he first arrived?"

Milarepa continued:

When I first arrived in the upper end of the valley, at a spot where I could see my house, there were many herdsmen. I asked them the names of the local places and what the locals were like. They answered in detail. Then I pointed

TRANSLATED FROM the Tibetan by Andrew Quintman.

1. That is, Milarepa; Rechungpa is his disciple.

to my house and asked, "What is that place called? What do they say about the people who live there?"

"That down there is called Kazhi Dunggye. It has no one but ghosts for residents."

Pressing for details, I asked, "Are the people who used to live there dead or have they left the village?"

"At one time, they were among the wealthy people in the region. Then the father, who had just one son, died prematurely and without properly arranging his last will and testament. After the father's death, paternal relatives seized all of his only son's wealth. They were supposed to return it after the son grew up, but refused. Out of revenge, he cast magic and hailstorms, and the region was devastated. Now all of us fear his dharma protectors and we don't dare even to glance in the direction of his house and fields, much less go near them. By that account, the corpse of the only son's mother lies in the house down there, and her ghost still haunts the place. There is a sister who left her mother's corpse and became a beggar, no one knows where. The son himself may now be dead; there's been no news about him at all. It is said that some dharma texts remain in the house down there. Yogin, if you dare go, you should have a look."

"How much time has passed since this happened?"

"Some eight years have passed since she died. Only distant memories of the magic and hail remain. I merely heard about it from others."

I thought that, since they feared my dharma protectors, they would not be able to harm me. I felt certain that my old mother had died and my sister had gone missing. Filled with sorrow, I sat weeping in a hidden spot until the sun went down. When the sun had set I went into the village. Just as in my dream, the fields outside were overrun with weeds and the house, once like a temple, had buckled. Stepping inside, I saw the texts of the precious *Ratnakuta Sutra*[2] damaged by leaking water and falling debris. Birds and mice had made nests in them, covering the books in their droppings. I looked at this scene and took it in, and I was filled with sadness.

Then I walked across the doorstep and found a heap of rags caked with dirt over which many weeds had grown. When I gathered them up, a number of human bones, bleached white, slipped out. When I realized they were the bones of my mother, I was so overcome with grief that I could hardly stand it. I could not think, I could not speak, and an overwhelming sense of longing and sadness swept over me. I was on the verge of fainting. But at that moment I remembered my lama's oral instructions. I then blended my mother's consciousness with my mind and the wisdom mind of the Kagyu[3] lamas. I made a cushion of my mother's bones and rested in a state of luminosity without letting my three gates[4] waver for even an instant. I saw the true possibility of liberating both my mother and my father from the suffering of life's round.

Seven days passed and, emerging from my absorption, I thought things over: "I am convinced that all of life's round is without essence. Thus I shall

2. A Mahayana sutra.
3. One of the major sects of Tibetan Buddhism

that took root in the 11th century.
4. Body, speech, and mind.

make figurines from my mother's bones. As payment for that, I shall make an offering of these *Ratnakuta* texts and then I shall practice at Drakar Taso[5] day and night without regard for my life. If the eight worldly concerns[6] arise in my mind I shall kill myself. If thoughts of a comfortable life come up, may the *dakinis*[7] and dharma protectors strike me down." I repeated this pledge over and over in my mind.

I gathered my mother's bones. Then I took good care of the *Ratnakuta* texts, clearing them of dirt and bird droppings. They were not too damaged by leaking water and the letters were still clear and bright. I loaded the first portion of the texts onto my back and carried my mother's bones in the fold of my cloak. Feeling immeasurable weariness toward the world, I became certain that life's round had no essence. Thus I sang this song of my fervent pledge to carry out the essence of dharma:

> Lord Akshobhya[8] in essence, compassionate one,
> Translator Marpa,[9] in accord with your prophetic command,
> In my homeland, a prison of demons,
> Masters, impermanence and illusion, appeared.
> Bless me to maintain certainty
> In these excellent masters themselves.
>
> In general, all things that exist or appear
> Are impermanent, unstable, they change and they move.
> In particular, the things of life's round have no essence.
> Rather than do things that lack any essence,
> I go to do dharma divine, that's essential.
>
> First when there was a father there was no son.
> Now when there is a son there is no father.
> Though the two come together they've no essence.
> I the son will do dharma divine, that's essential.
> I'm off to meditate at Drakar Taso.
>
> When there was a mother there was no son.
> Before I the son came, the old mother had died.
> Though the two come together they've no essence.
> I the son will do dharma divine, that's essential.
> I'm off to meditate at Drakar Taso.
>
> When there was a sister there was no brother.
> When the brother arrives, the sister is gone.
> Though the two come together they've no essence.
> I the son will do dharma divine, that's essential.
> I'm off to meditate at Drakar Taso.

5. White Rock Horse Tooth, a cave in the Himalayas.
6. Happiness and sorrow, gain and loss, praise and blame, and fame and disgrace.
7. Tantric goddesses.

8. A buddha in Mahayana Buddhism.
9. Milarepa's teacher (1012–1097), a celebrated Tibetan Buddhist who visited India and helped transmit tantric Buddhist practice to Tibet.

When there were holy texts there was no one to tend them.
When the attendant arrives they are damaged by rain.
Though the two come together they've no essence.
I the son will do dharma divine, that's essential.
I'm off to meditate at Drakar Taso.

When there was a house there was no master.
When the master arrives the house is in ruins.
Though the two come together they've no essence.
I the son will do dharma divine, that's essential.
I'm off to meditate at Drakar Taso.

When there were fertile fields there was no owner.
Now the owner arrives they're run over with weeds.
Though the two come together they've no essence.
I the son will do dharma divine, that's essential.
I'm off to meditate at Drakar Taso.

Homeland, house, fields, and the like,
The things of life's round have no essence at all.
Those beings who want things with no essence can have them.
A yogi, I go to achieve liberation.

Kind father Marpa Lotsawa
Bless your son to remain in mountain retreat.

After I had sung a song of my sadness, I first went to the home of the tutor who taught me to read. He had died, so I presented the first portion of the *Ratnakuta* text to his son and said, "I will give you the rest of this religious text. Make figurines from the bones of my old mother."

"Your dharma protectors will follow this book so I don't want it, but I will help you mold the figurines," he replied.

"My protectors will not follow the offerings I make."

"In that case," he said, "it's fine."

With my help, he fashioned the figurines out of my mother's bones and performed the consecration ritual. Then we placed them in a stupa and I prepared to leave.

My tutor's son said, "I will serve you in any way I can, so stay here a few days and talk."

I replied, "I have no time to talk. I am eager to practice."

"Well then, stay tonight. In the morning I shall give you provisions for your practice." I stayed.

He continued, "In the past when you were young, you vanquished your enemies through magic. Now that you are in the prime of your life, you practice the pure dharma—that's amazing. In the future you will become an accomplished master. What sort of lama do you have and what kind of oral instructions did you receive?" He questioned me in detail.

I described how I obtained the Great Perfection and, in particular, how I met Marpa. "How amazing. If that is true, you should repair the house, marry Dzese,[1] and then emulate the life of your lama."

---

1. The village girl to whom Milarepa was betrothed as a child.

"Lama Marpa took a wife for the benefit of beings. I have neither the intention nor the ability to act in that way. To do so would be like a rabbit bounding along in the guise of a lion, it would fall into an abyss and surely die. Broadly speaking, I've become weary of life's round and I have an urgent desire for nothing but the lama's oral instructions and for practice. That I practice in mountain retreat is the very core of the lama's advice. Only in this way can I emulate his life. Through practice I will surely fulfill his wishes. Through practice, I will benefit the teachings and sentient beings. Through practice, my parents will be rescued. Through practice, my own aims will also be realized. I know nothing but practice, I am good for nothing but practice, I think about nothing but practice.

"In particular, witnessing the remains of my parents' estate and the wealth they amassed has given me a fierce intention to practice. I am burning like fire inside. For others, untouched by such misfortune or oblivious to the suffering of death and bad rebirth, a comfortable life is enough. These conditions compel me to practice without regard for food, clothing, or recognition."

Bursting into tears, I sang this song to illustrate these points:

I bow down at the feet of most excellent Marpa.
Bless this beggar to turn away from clinging to things.

Alas, alas. Ay me, ay me. How sad!
People invested in things of life's round—
I reflect and reflect and again and again I despair.
They act and they act and stir up from their depths so much torment.
They spin and they spin and are cast in the depths of life's round.

Those dragged on by karma, afflicted with anguish like this—
What to do? What to do? There's no cure but the dharma.
Lord Akshobhya in essence, Vajradhara,[2]
Bless this beggar to stay in mountain retreat.

In the town of impermanence and illusion
A restless visitor to these ruins is afflicted with anguish.
In the environs of Gungtang, a wondrous landscape,
Grasslands that fed yaks, sheep, cattle, and goats
Are nowadays taken over by harmful spirits.
These too are examples of impermanence and illusion,
Examples that call me, a yogin, to practice.

This home of four pillars and eight beams
Nowadays resembles a lion's upper jaw.
The manor of four corners, four walls, and a roof, making nine
These too are examples of impermanence and illusion,
Examples that call me, a yogin, to practice.

This fertile field Orma Triangle[3]
Nowadays is a tangle of weeds.
My cousins and family relations
Nowadays rise up as an army of foes.

2. A tantric buddha.   3. A plot of land owned by Milarepa's father.

These too are examples of impermanence and illusion,
Examples that call me, a yogin, to practice.

My good father Mila Shergyal
Nowadays, of him no trace remains.
My mother Nyangtsa Kargyen
Nowadays is a pile of bare bones.
These too are examples of impermanence and illusion,
Examples that call me, a yogin, to practice.

My family priest Konchok Lhabum
Nowadays works as a servant.
The sacred text *Ratnakuta*
Nowadays serves as a nest for vermin and birds.
These too are examples of impermanence and illusion,
Examples that call me, a yogin, to practice.

My neighboring uncle Yungyal
Nowadays lives among hostile enemies.
My sister Peta Gonkyi
Has vanished without a trace.
These too are examples of impermanence and illusion,
Examples that call me, a yogin, to practice.

Lord Akshobhya in essence, compassionate one,
Bless this beggar to stay in mountain retreat.

I sang this sad melody of my weariness with the world. The son sighed
deeply and said, "How amazing. That is so very true." His wife was present
and she too sat there with tears streaming from her eyes. Seeing the condition
of my home, I couldn't help but honestly affirm again and again my pledge to
practice. I also kept that pledge continually in mind. Since in reality I fulfilled
that pledge, I have no regrets.
Thus Milarepa spoke.

*This was the sixth of the supreme deeds, the deed in which, having been reminded
once again of the essencelessness of life's round, he vowed to practice.*

THE STAGES OF THE PATH TO ENLIGHTENMENT

GREAT EXPOSITION OF THE STAGES
OF THE PATH
(*The Lam Rim Chen Mo*)

TSONG KHA PA

Each of the sects of Tibetan Buddhism has a text that sets out the entire Buddhist path,
from the initial sense of dissatisfaction with a world beset by suffering to the advanced
meditation on the nature of reality. The most famous of these works on the "stages of

the path" (*lam rim*) is the *Great Exposition of the Stages of the Path to Enlightenment*, completed by Tsong kha pa in 1402. Sometimes called the *Summa Theologica* of Tibetan Buddhism, it is perhaps the second most famous work in the vast Buddhist literature of Tibet, surpassed only by the *Life of Milarepa* (see the previous selection).

Tsong kha pa (1357–1419) is revered as the founder of the Geluk ("System of Virtue") sect of Tibetan Buddhism, the sect of the Dalai Lamas; indeed, one of his disciples would become the First Dalai Lama. His fame is due in part to the later political ascendancy of his sect; in 1642, the Fifth Dalai Lama was placed on the throne of Tibet by the Mongol warlord who was his patron. But Tsong kha pa was also a highly accomplished scholar of all facets of Buddhist thought. Both his originality as a thinker and his skill as a writer have been obscured by his later identification with orthodoxy.

The *Great Exposition of the Stages of the Path* is structured around the notion that there are three types of religious practitioners, distinguished by their capacity: small, intermediate, and great. Those of small capacity are dissatisfied with their present condition and engage in religious practice in order to achieve a better rebirth in their next lifetime. Those of intermediate capacity are dissatisfied with the cycle of rebirth (samsara) at all its levels and seek the peace of nirvana. Those of great capacity also want liberation from rebirth but are moved by compassion to seek the state of buddhahood so that all beings may be freed from suffering. Tsong kha pa proceeds methodically through the practices of the first two that are shared by the last. For example, in order to accumulate the meritorious karma that will lead to a happy rebirth in the next life, one must turn one's attention away from the affairs of this world. Doing so requires contemplating the fact that death is definite and the time of death is indefinite. Because this "mindfulness of death," a practice of beings of small capacity, is likewise crucial to the practices of beings of intermediate and great capacity, Tsong kha pa includes its exposition in his text.

The work is thus presented as a summary of the entire Buddhist path as it would be practiced by a single individual, a kind of "everything you need to know to become enlightened." But even that summary is a massive work, replete with quotations from Indian scriptures; its English translation fills three volumes. The section presented here is Tsong kha pa's final précis of the whole. Dispensing with the more formal style of the main text, he speaks directly to the reader, offering practical instruction. He begins by stressing the importance of relying on a qualified teacher. He then notes a teaching that is crucial to beings of all three capacities: the importance of contemplating "leisure and opportunity." Rebirth as a human who has access to the Buddha's teachings, and who is not too overwhelmed by suffering to benefit from them, is a rare moment in the long history of one's rebirths. Thus the present lifetime is a moment of leisure and opportunity not to be squandered.

To those who have become skilled in the teachings of a being of intermediate capacity, Tsong kha pa says, "Consider the fact that just as you yourself have fallen into the ocean of cyclic existence, so have all beings, your mothers." That it, the beginningless cycle of rebirth, ensures that all beings have been one's human mother in a past life. They are now drowning, and a responsible child must rescue them. He urges the cultivation of the "spirit of enlightenment" (*bodhichitta*), the aspiration to achieve buddhahood for the sake of all beings in the universe. A person endowed with this spirit becomes a bodhisattva, and Tsong kha pa advises that one take the vows of the bodhisattva and strive to keep them. He mentions the "bodhisattva deeds"—the six perfections of giving, ethics, patience, effort, concentration, and wisdom—pausing to discuss the last two, which have been the focus of the final section of his text.

After this summary, he writes, "You have reached a critical point when, while meditating on the lower levels, you increasingly wish to attain the higher levels, and when studying the higher levels, your wish to practice the lower levels becomes stronger and stronger." Such emphasis on the great value of the entire range of practices—elementary to advanced—is a hallmark of Tsong kha pa's thought, and in this section he provides specific advice on how to maintain that balance.

He concludes with a brief discussion of tantric practice, which he calls the Vajra-yana ("Thunderbolt Vehicle") and "mantra path." For Tsong kha pa, it is impossible to achieve buddhahood without entering the tantric path, and he would devote a similarly massive volume to that topic. His emphasis here is on keeping the tantric vows; he states firmly that even in esoteric practice, a commitment to ethics is essential. If you maintain this commitment and go on to practice correctly the two stages of what is called Highest Yoga Tantra (*anuttarayoga tantra*)—the stage of generation and the stage of completion—then "your attainment of leisure in this lifetime will have been worthwhile": that is, you will have made proper use of the precious human form.

PRONOUNCING GLOSSARY

bodhisattva: *boh-di-sat-tva*
Mahayana: *ma-hah-yah-na*

Manjushri-mula-tantra: *man-ju-shri-moo-la-tan-tra*
Vajrayana: *vaj-ra-yah-na*

Now I will give a brief summation of the general meaning of the path. At the outset, the root of the path derives from your reliance upon a teacher, so consider this seriously. Then, once you have developed an uncontrived desire to take advantage of your leisure, this desire will spur you to practice continually. Therefore, in order to develop this, meditate on the topics connected with leisure and opportunity. Unless you then stop the various sentiments which seek the aims of this life, you will not diligently seek the aims of future lives. So work at meditating on how the body you have is impermanent in the sense that it will not last for long, and on how after death you will wander in the miserable realms. At that time, by creating a genuine awareness which is mindful of the frights of the miserable realms, build certainty from the depths of your heart about the qualities of the three refuges.[1] Be constant in the common vow of going for refuge and train in its precepts. Then, from a range of perspectives develop faith, in the sense of conviction, in karma and its effects—this being the great foundation of all positive qualities. Make this faith firm. Strive to cultivate the ten virtues and to turn away from the ten nonvirtues, and always stay within the path of the four powers.[2]

When you have thus trained well in the teachings associated with a person of small capacity and have made this practice firm, you should contemplate often the general and specific faults of cyclic existence, and in general turn your mind away from cyclic existence as much as you can. Then, having identified the nature of karma and the afflictions—the causes from which cyclic existence arises—create an authentic desire to eliminate them. Develop broad certainty about the path that liberates you from cyclic existence, i.e., the three trainings,[3] and particularly make effort at whichever of the vows of individual liberation you have taken.

Translated from the Tibetan by the Lam Rim Chen Mo Translation Committee; Joshua W. C. Cutler, editor-in-chief; Guy Newland, editor.

1. The "three jewels" to which Buddhists go for refuge: the Buddha, the dharma, and the sangha (the Buddhist community).
2. The powers of reliance, regret, the opponent force, and promise. The ten virtues are the oppo-site of the ten nonvirtues (killing, stealing, sexual misconduct, lying, divisive speech, harsh speech, senseless speech, covetousness, harmful intent, and wrong views).
3. In ethics, in meditation, and in wisdom.

When you have thus trained well in the teachings associated with a person of medium capacity and have made this practice firm, consider the fact that just as you yourself have fallen into the ocean of cyclic existence, so have all beings, your mothers. Train in the spirit of enlightenment which is rooted in love and compassion, and strive to develop this as much as you can. Without it, the practices of the six perfections and the two stages[4] are like stories built on a house with no foundation. When you develop a little experience of this spirit of enlightenment, confirm it with the rite. By making effort in this training, make the aspiration as solid as you can. Then study the great waves of the bodhisattva deeds, learning the boundaries of what to discard and what to adopt, and make a strong wish to train in those bodhisattva deeds. After you have developed these attitudes, take the vow of the engaged spirit of enlightenment through its rite. Train in the six perfections that mature your own mind and the four ways of gathering disciples[5] which mature the minds of others. In particular, risk your life in making a great effort to avoid the root infractions. Strive not to be tainted by the small and intermediate contaminants and faults, and even if you are tainted, work to repair it. Then, because you must train specifically in the final two perfections, become knowledgeable in the way to sustain meditative stabilization and then achieve concentration. As much as you can, develop the view of the two selflessnesses, a purity free from permanence and annihilation. After you have found the view and stabilized your the mind upon it, understand the proper way to sustain the view in meditation, and then do so. Such stabilization and wisdom are called serenity and insight, but they are not something separate from the last two perfections. Therefore, after you have taken the bodhisattva vows, they come about in the context of the training in its precepts.

You have reached a critical point when, while meditating on the lower levels, you increasingly wish to attain the higher levels, and when studying the higher levels, your wish to practice the lower levels becomes stronger and stronger. Some say to expend your energy only to stabilize your mind and to understand the view, ignoring all earlier topics, but this makes it very difficult to get the vital points. Therefore, you must develop certainty about the whole course of the path. When you meditate on these topics, train your understanding and then go back to balance your mind. So if it seems that your faith in the teacher who instructs you on the path is decreasing, since this will cut the root of everything good that has come together, work on the methods for relying on the teacher. Similarly, if your joy in your practice loses strength, make meditation on the topics connected with leisure and opportunity your primary focus; if your attachment to this life increases, make meditation on impermanence and the faults of the miserable realms your primary focus. If you seem to be lazy about the proscriptions you have accepted, consider that your certainty about karmic cause and effect is meager and make meditation on karma and its effects your primary focus. If your sense of disenchantment with all of cyclic existence decreases, your desire to seek liberation will become just words. Therefore, contemplate the faults of cyclic existence. If your intention to benefit living beings in whatever you do is not strong, then you will sever the root of the Mahayana. Therefore, frequently cultivate the aspirational spirit of enlightenment together with

4. The stages of generation and completion. "The six perfections": giving, ethics, patience, effort, concentration, and wisdom.

5. Pleasing them by giving them material support, teaching the dharma, encouraging others in their dharma practice, and offering a good example.

its causes. Once you have taken the vows of a conqueror's[6] child and are training in the practices, if the bondage of the reifying conception of signs seems strong, use reasoning consciousnesses to destroy all objects which are apprehended by the mind which conceives of signs, and train your mind in the space-like and illusion-like emptiness. If your mind is enslaved to distraction and does not remain on a virtuous object, you should primarily sustain one-pointed stability, as former teachers have said. From these illustrations, you should understand the cases I have not explained. In brief, without being partial, you have to be able to use the whole spectrum of virtues.

Among the stages of the path of a person of great capacity, I have explained how one who trains in the bodhisattva path practices insight, which is wisdom.

How to Train Specifically in the Vajrayana[7]

After you have trained in this way in the paths common to both sutra and mantra, you must undoubtedly enter the mantra path because it is very much more precious than any other practice and it quickly brings the two collections to completion. If you are to enter it, then as Atisha's[8] *Lamp for the Path to Enlightenment* says, you must first please the guru—even to a greater extent than explained earlier—with deeds such as respect and service and with practice that is in accordance with the guru's words. And you must do this for a guru who meets at least the minimum qualifications of a teacher explained there.

Then, at the outset, your mind should be matured through the ripening initiation as explained in a source tantra. You should then listen to the pledges and vows to be taken, understand them, and maintain them. If you are stricken by root infractions, you may make these commitments again. However, this greatly delays the development of the good qualities of the path in your mind. Make a fierce effort not to be tainted by those root infractions. Strive not to be tainted by the gross infractions, but in the event that you are tainted, use the methods for restoring your vows. Since these are the basis of the practice of the path, without them you will become like a dilapidated house whose foundation has collapsed. The *Root Tantra of Manjushri*[9] (*Manjushri-mula-tantra*) says, "The Master of the Sages does not say that faulty ethical discipline achieves the tantric path," meaning that those with faulty ethical discipline have none of the great, intermediate, or low attainments. And it says in the highest yoga tantra texts that those who do not maintain their vows, those who have inferior initiation, and those who do not understand reality do not achieve anything despite their practice. Therefore someone who talks about practicing the path without maintaining the pledges and vows has completely strayed from the tantric path.

In order to cultivate the mantra path someone who keeps the pledges and vows should at the outset meditate on the stage of generation, the complete divine wheel as explained from a source tantra. The unique object to be eliminated on the tantric path is the conception of ordinariness which regards

6. A buddha.
7. That is, tantric practice (lit., "the Thunderbolt Vehicle"; Sanskrit).
8. A Bengali Buddhist monk (982–1054), who in

1042 arrived in Tibet and helped revive Buddhism.
9. Manjushri is the bodhisattva who embodies wisdom.

the aggregates,[1] constituents, and sensory sources as common. It is the stage of generation itself that eliminates this and transforms the abodes, bodies, and resources so that they appear as special. The conquerors and their children continually bless the person who clears away the conception of ordinariness in this way; such a person easily brings to completion the limitless collections of merit, thereby becoming a suitable vessel for the stage of completion.

This person should then meditate on what appears in the source tantras on the stage of completion. Neither the tantras nor the scholars who explain their intended meanings hold that you should discard the first stage and merely classify it within the latter stage, training only in individual portions of the path. Therefore, you must bear in mind the vital points of the two stages of the complete corpus of the path of highest yoga tantra.

Considering only the terms, I have described a mere fraction of what is involved in entering into the mantra path. Therefore, understand this in detail by using works on the stages of the mantra path. If you train in this way, you will train in the entirely complete corpus of the path, which includes all the vital points of sutra and mantra. As a result, your attainment of leisure in this lifetime will have been worthwhile, and you will be able to extend the Conqueror's precious teaching within both your own and others' minds.

1. A standard division of the constituents of mind and body into five groups: form, feeling, discrimination, compositional factors, and consciousness.

THE PATH AND THE RESULT

HEART OF THE PRACTICE
(*Nyamlen Nyingpo*)

MANGTHO LUDRUP GYATSO

It is sometimes said that Tibet received its Buddhism late. And it is certainly the case that the other major Buddhist traditions beyond India received Buddhism earlier: Sri Lanka in the second century B.C.E., China in the first century C.E., Korea in the fourth century, and Japan in the fifth century. Buddhism was first introduced into the Tibetan court in the seventh century. According to traditional histories, the Tibetan king was converted to the dharma by his foreign wives, both Buddhist—one from China, one from Nepal. But the transmission of Buddhism to Tibet was interrupted in the middle of the ninth century, not resuming for almost two hundred years. Hence, the Buddhism that became established in Tibet represented the Buddhism that was present in India from the eleventh century until its demise there in the thirteenth century.

This late date of transmission had many consequences, one of which is that Tibet received a much larger corpus of Indian literature than any other Buddhist country. In addition to the same sutras that would be so important in East Asia, these texts included a full complement of commentaries and independent treatises on all manner of topics, many of which were not translated into Chinese or, if they were, were of little influence. The texts translated into Tibetan also included a vast tantric literature, which had more influence on Tibetan Buddhism than on any of the other major traditions. The sects of Tibetan Buddhism consider the practice of the Vajrayana, the "Thunderbolt Vehicle," to be the highest form of Buddhist practice and

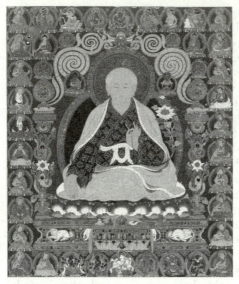

Thangka painting of Kunga Nyingpo, a master of the Sakya tradition, ca. 1600.

the practice essential for the achievement of buddhahood. The different sects of Tibetan Buddhism had different ways of integrating tantric practice into the path. Among the most famous and powerful of these was the Lamdre—literally, "Path-Result"—system of the Sakya sect.

One of the three major sects to emerge during the "later spread of the dharma" that began in the eleventh century C.E., the Sakya traced its teachings to the Indian tantric master Virupa. It takes its name from that of its chief monastery, Sakya (literally, "gray earth"). The sect produced some of the most important scholars and practitioners in the history of Tibetan Buddhism and had great political influence during the thirteenth and fourteenth centuries.

Its central practice might be more accurately rendered as "Taking the Path as the Result." The result is buddhahood, which is to be taken as the path. That is, the ultimate nature of reality, manifested most fully in the enlightenment of a buddha, is not something that is gained after a long path but rather is universal and eternal, and thus always present. The path, then, as in all Buddhist systems, involves the removal of various afflictions and obscurations; but in this system, that process is accomplished by continued focus, through a variety of means, on the omnipresent essence of enlightenment. This element is said to be one of the defining characteristics of tantric practice, enabling the bodhisattva to traverse the path to buddhahood far more quickly than is possible by the practices set forth in the sutras.

The initiations, instructions, and practices required to make this essence fully manifest are complex, and among the various traditions of Tibetan Buddhism the Sakya has been particularly vigilant in maintaining the secrecy so often associated with advanced tantric practice. But an eloquent summary of the entire Sakya path is contained in the work below, presented in its entirety. Titled *Heart of the Practice*, it was composed by Mangtho Ludrup Gyatso (1523–1596) in 1581. Since it summarizes the practice from beginning to end, substantial commentary would be necessary to explain each of its points. Of particular interest are its instructions to anyone unable to achieve buddhahood before dying on how to send one's consciousness at the moment of death to the tantric paradise of Khechara.

PRONOUNCING GLOSSARY

chandali: *chan-dah-lee*
Hevajra: *hay-vaj-ra*
Khechara: *keh-chah-rah*
mahamudra: *ma-hah-mu-drah*
Mangtho Ludrup Gyatso: *mang-ter loo-droop gya-tso*
Nagarjuna: *nah-gahr-ju-na*
Nyamlen Nyingpo: *nyan-len nying-po*

Nyenyo Chagoshong: *nyeh-nyuh chah-go-shohng*
pratyekabuddha: *prat-yay-ka-bud-da*
Samten Lhundrup: *sahm-dehn loon-droop*
shravaka: *shrah-va-ka*
Vairochana: *vai-roh-cha-na*
yogini: *yoh-gi-nee*

With devoted body, speech, and mind, I prostrate at the lotus beneath the feet of my venerable lords and masters.

The heart of the practice, a synopsis of the key points of the esoteric instructions of the Teaching of the Path with the Result, is as follows.

Whatever oral instructions are practiced to achieve the sublime, the mind must turn toward the Dharma. For that purpose, meditation on the faults of samsara is crucial. Therefore, by reflecting on the general and specific sufferings of samsara, draw forth a certainty about the sufferings of samsara that is not mere words. If an uncontrived wish arises to abandon the three poisons, which are the afflictions that cause those sufferings, and to abandon evil actions motivated by them, the mind has turned to the Dharma. So please apply the sufferings of samsara directly to one's own situation, develop an attitude of renunciation from the bottom of one's heart, and create an effective certainty in the mindstream.

> In this samsara that tortures the mind
> with the burning suffering of suffering,
> suffering of change,
> and suffering of conditioned existence,
> no opportunity for happiness exists.
> You must reach the city of liberation—
> my dear disciple!

Then one must meditate on the difficulty of gaining the freedoms and endowments. When one has become mindful of the faults of samsara, the mind has turned toward the Dharma, and the mere wish to practice the Dharma has arisen, one may think that it is enough to practice this Dharma at one's leisure. But it is not. One must intensely begin, starting right now. One must draw forth a certainty that this human body with the freedoms and endowments is as difficult to find as a tiny star in the daytime, that once it is found it is quickly destroyed, and that it is as momentary as the dew on a blade of grass.

> The conditioned existence of this life,
> which is like a streak of lightning in the sky,
> can be destroyed now.
> This self-deception of patiently clinging
> to it as permanent is a great defect.
> Be energetic in the Dharma now—
> my dear disciple!

Even if one has such enthusiastic diligence in the practice of Dharma, if the key points are not understood, that Dharma will not work as a path. So one must then have confidence in the causes and results of actions, primarily abandon nonvirtuous actions, and practice any virtue, even the slightest. Without even roughly understanding rejection and acceptance in regard to the causes and results of actions, with a lofty and high view, hypocritical conduct, and foolish behavior, one will be unable to withstand anything, like a ruined building with a rotten foundation.

TRANSLATED FROM the Tibetan by Cyrus Stearns. All bracketed additions are the translator's.

> Ignoring virtuous and nonvirtuous
> actions and results,
> and then being fanatical about the view,
> having dignified behavior, and so forth,
> may seem so, so profound,
> but like a throne or bridge of grass,
> they will not work as a path—
> my dear disciple!

Then, to remove confusion about the path, the genuine relative enlightenment mind must arise in the mindstream. Without a pristine view in which all phenomena are as ephemeral as a dream or an illusion, one is in danger of taking the wrong path and falling into the abyss of samsara. If this precious enlightenment mind motivated by love and compassion has not arisen in the mindstream, one is in danger of taking a lesser path and falling to the spiritual levels of the shravakas and pratyekabuddhas.[1] Therefore, the perfect enlightenment mind known to have emptiness and compassion as its essence—pervaded by the view, the wisdom that realizes emptiness, and the conduct, compassion—must have arisen in the mindstream.

> If one's mindstream has not been tamed
> by the genuine enlightenment mind,
> the sublime path of combined
> emptiness and compassion,
> one is in danger of falling into the abyss
> of confusion that is not the path.
> Think of altruism that benefits others—
> my dear disciple!

Then, for confusion to arise as primordial awareness, one must meditate on awakening the absolute enlightenment mind. If the exceptional wisdom that realizes the fundamental nature of phenomena has arisen in the mindstream, all appearances of the eight worldly concerns[2] and so forth will dissolve like bubbles into water, and then again appear as friends on the path.

> If one has reached the decisive conclusion
> that all the phenomena of apparent existence
> may arise, but are untrue and confusing,
> like the character of an illusion,
> then, by the play of primordial awareness,
> the eight worldly concerns will appear
> as friends on the path—my dear disciple!

Then the mindstream is ripened by profound initiation. For conceptual elaborations to be eliminated by means of the view, one must meditate on the view of the indivisibility of samsara and nirvana. In this regard, resting serenely, without mentally clinging to this naked clear light of one's mind free from the husk of the dualistic appearances of subject and object, is recogni-

---

1. The disciples (lit., "listeners"; Sanskrit) of Buddha and the solitary enlightened ones, who are two types of Hinayana practioners.

2. Happiness and sorrow, gain and loss, praise and blame, and fame and disgrace.

tion of the natural state of lucidity. Confirming that this lucidity is also not a permanent, stable, eternal thing established forever, but empty of truth like an illusion that is dependent on causes and conditions, is recognition of the natural state of emptiness. Without altering the mind that is understood to be empty while lucid and lucid yet empty, a united lucidity and emptiness, this momentary pure awareness, rest the mind evenly as long as that state remains. This is resolution in unity. Reaching a decisive conclusion about the mind on the basis of these three aspects of coemergence is crucial.

> Clear light free from the filth
> of subject and object is the true nature,
> mind not established as true
> and affected by incidental stains.
> Recognize the natural state
> of united lucidity and emptiness,
> momentary pure awareness—
> my faithful, dear disciple!

Then, to enhance that view, one must be mindful of the three key points of practice. First, to destroy this solid and tenacious attachment to apparent outer objects such as external mountains and fences, apparent phenomena are established to be the mind by means of the eight examples of dreams and so forth, and the pure awareness is fully concentrated and rests upon the lucidity of the mind.

This mind of dualistic appearance, the perceiver of apparent external objects, is also established to be untrue by means of the eight examples of an illusion and so forth. Relax and rest the mind in emptiness, empty of both subject and object.

By means of the eight examples confirming that it is dependently arisen and the eight examples confirming that it is inexpressible, this mind empty of both subject and object is also established to be empty of truth and to be inexpressible and transcendent. One rests evenly in unity, the view of the indivisibility of samsara and nirvana. This is the heart of the practice.

> These external objects
> are like last night's dream,
> and the apprehending mind
> the same as lightning now.
> Rest vividly in this stainless mind,
> as inexpressible as the thoughts of a mute—
> my dear disciple!

Then, of the four paths in connection with the four initiations concerning the method continuum of the body, by means of the outer and inner creation stage, which is the path of the vase initiation, one must first sever the obsession with ordinary attachment to appearances. To purify the stains of the five aggregates, the five afflictions,[3] and so forth, which are the ground

---

3. Desire, hatred, ignorance, pride, jealousy. "The five aggregates": standard division of the constituents of mind and body into five groups: form, feeling, discrimination, compositional factors, consciousness.

of purification, special deities are specifically praised, such as Vairochana[4] for the purification of the aggregate of form. However, in this tradition one single purifying deity is able to purify all ordinary attachment to appearances, which are the ground of purification or what are to be purified. Since this is the heart of the path, clearly imagine oneself as Hevajra,[5] father and mother, with the body mandala. Upholding the firm pride of the deity purifies all ordinary attachment. Practicing by means of vividly transforming whatever appearances arise into the form of the deity, one is able to purify all ordinary appearances.

> One appears as Hevajra,
> father and mother,
> and the environment and its inhabitants
> as the play of the deity and celestial mansion.
> Purify the vulgar stains of ordinary
> attachment to appearances
> and uphold the pride of the creation stage—
> my dear disciple!

When one meditates on the creation stage in this way, the view of the three essences will arise. If one rests lucidly in the state of the creation stage, it is known as "the meditative concentration of the apparent aspect." If the mind rests without anything appearing, like the empty sky, it is known as "the meditative concentration of the empty aspect." If any of the ten signs of clear light appear, such as smoke and mirage, it is known as "the meditative concentration of unity." At that point the view of the vase initiation, mahamudra,[6] has arisen in the mindstream. The appearances of the eight worldly concerns have also thinned out. Even when the eight concerns do arise a bit, if they are apprehended with mindfulness of precisely that view of mahamudra, the eight concerns will be destroyed on the spot and a growing contentment will arise.

To examine whether that view is stable or flimsy, go at night to places where fear arises and in the day to spots where the eight concerns arise. When fears and the eight concerns do arise, relax and rest in the unity of the view of the indivisibility of samsara and nirvana and the mahamudra of the vase initiation. By training again and again in that way, at some point the view will improve and the bliss of refined body and mind will be obtained. The path will gradually be completed by means of the three gatherings of the essential constituents, and the first culmination of attainment—the culmination of attainment as the indivisibility of samsara and nirvana—will be reached without difficulty. Thus my master taught.

> When meditating on the creation stage,
> the ten signs of clear light appear,
> and all appearances are untrue,
> ephemeral, free, and shimmering
> like the smoke of clear light.
> Rest in mahamudra—my dear disciple!

---

4. A buddha.
5. An important tantric deity.

6. Literally, "great seal" (Sanskrit).

To further enhance this view,
in isolated places or in busy spots
of the eight concerns,
practice the three conducts[7]
without losing mindfulness
of the mahamudra view—
my dear disciple!

Then, if the culmination of attainment has not been reached in this lifetime, in order to actualize the clear light of death, the three vase-initiation practices when passing away are crucial. Furthermore, after the definite signs of dying have appeared, this vase initiation practice when passing away is necessary during the arising of the coarse stages of the dissolution of the four elements.[8] Thereafter, during the triad of the white radiance, the red radiance, and the black radiance, it is time for the higher initiation practices when passing away, so one must distinguish these situations.

In that way, when the definite signs of dying appear, receive the initiation from the master or the self-entry from oneself, and mend the sacred commitments. Give away all possessions to virtuous recipients, and totally eliminate all remaining activities of this life. Completely transform all the blurry appearances that arise at the point of death into the appearance of Hevajra, and rest the mind comfortably in that state. That is known as "the transformation of appearances as the practice when passing away."

Another is "the transference with a globe of light as the practice when passing away." This body has nine orifices. When practicing that transference, if this consciousness exits through the anus, one will go to the hells, if through the urethra, one will go to the animal realm, if through the navel, one will be reborn as a god of the desire realm, if through the mouth, as a hungry spirit, if through the two nostrils, as a yaksa, if through the two ears, as a kinnara[9] spirit, if through the two eyes, as a human being, if through the point between the eyebrows, as a god of the form realm, and if through the crown of the head, as a god of the formless realm. So those orifices must be blocked.

Clearly imagining oneself as Hevajra, visualize the central channel straight up the middle of the body, and a drop—a globe of light about the size of a dung pellet—inside the central channel directly at the heart chakra.[1] Clearly imagine that nine globes of light separate from that and block the nine orifices. At the location of the navel is a mandala of the vital wind about the size of the thumb, with the vital wind moving upward. On top of it is a moon mandala, upon which is the essence of one's consciousness, in the form of a blue *hum*. Above the top of the head is the master in the form of Hevajra, surrounded by an assembly of the lineage masters, spiritual heroes, and yoginis.[2]

The key physical point is to sit with the knees raised and both arms wrapped around the knees. The key vocal point is to intensely pronounce *hum* twenty-one times. The key mental point is to indivisibly blend together one's consciousness and the *hum* at the navel. Concentrate single-pointedly

---

7. Three types of tantric conduct.
8. Earth, air, fire and water, believed to constitute all matter.
9. A being that is half human, half horse, or half

bird. "Yaksa": a category of nonhuman beings, a nature spirit.
1. A chakra, or network of energy channels.
2. Female yogins (meditators).

on those three. By long pronunciations of *hum* with the voice, the vital wind of the navel draws up the consciousness in the shape of the *hum*, and at the twentieth pronunciation it arrives at the throat. These three should be done simultaneously: a very intense pronunciation of the twenty-first *hum*, the ejection of the consciousness as the syllable *hum* through the top of the head like a shooting star fired into the heart of the master, and the relaxation of the body and the two arms. Imagine that one's consciousness and the mind of the master as the chosen deity, nondual in the rainbow body of Hevajra, depart for pure Khechara.[3]

When training in this now, train in solitude during the day and at the point of going to sleep at night. Draw the *hum* up to the throat with twenty pronunciations. Drop it to the navel with *ka hi.*

When putting it into action, it is crucial to shoot the consciousness through the crown of the head with the twenty-first *hum.*

> Mend one's essential
> sacred commitments and vows,
> give away to others all that you cherish,
> pray to the sublime master of refuge,
> and sever mental attachments—
> my dear disciple!
>
> By practicing mindfulness
> of the creation stage as the path
> in regard to the forms of clear light
> during the dissolution
> of the four elements of the body,
> transform mental appearance
> into the mandala of the deity Hevajra—
> my dear disciple!
>
> With the nine orifices of the body blocked by light,
> and the mind in the form of a *hum* at the navel,
> fire it with the sound *hum* through the inside
> of the central channel and out the aperture of Brahma[4]—
> my dear disciple!

If the practice when passing away is not successful, it is imperative to remember the practice of the intermediate state. In that intermediate period when the appearances of this life have receded and the next rebirth has not been taken, the seven circumstances of the four frightful sounds and the three terrifying abysses will appear. At that point the five olfactory experiences like forms of light will clearly occur. At that time, these three remembrances should automatically arise: remembrance of one's master, remembrance of the secret name, and remembrance of the chosen deity Hevajra. Whatever olfactory appearances arise, clearly transform them into the deity Hevajra and relax in that state for as long as the mind remains without clinging!

---

3. The tantric paradise.
4. The spot on the top of the head from which consciousness departs the body at death in the case of a favorable rebirth.

When one practices in that way, it is certain that one will be led to a pure land by spiritual heroes and yoginis with parasols, victory banners, streamers, and the sounds of music.

> When suddenly carried friendless
> into the intermediate state,
> the practice of transforming
> the five olfactory lights into the chosen deity
> by means of the three remembrances
> will lead one to the land of Khechara—
> my dear disciple!

Thus, as the preliminaries for stable practice when passing away, and for those of the intermediate state, it is very important to master the instructions of illusory body and dream yoga from this present moment. In a secluded place during the day, inspire one's mindstream with disillusionment and renunciation, and develop expertise in meditative equipoise by resting the mind evenly in a meditative concentration in which all the phenomena of the triad of appearances, sound, and awareness arise, but are without self-nature, like an illusion.

At the point of going to sleep at night, clearly imagine a red lotus with four petals in one's throat. Clearly visualize an *om* in the center and, in a clockwise circle from the front, the four syllables *a nu ta ra* on the four petals. Blending one's mind with the *om* and joining that with sleep, or then blending one's mind with each of the four *a nu ta ra* in sequence and joining that with sleep, recognize the dream. The three remembrances will automatically arise, and various types of clear light will appear, such as a lucid clear light, a blissful clear light, and a nonconceptual clear light. Through developing expertise and so forth by observing pure and impure apparent objects [in dreams], and by multiplication and transformation, a great delight in spiritual practice at night will certainly arise.

> In the mansion of a secluded location
> in the mountain ranges,
> be never apart from disenchantment
> and renunciation.
> With phenomena as ephemeral
> as in an illusion,
> train in the illusory body during the day—
> my dear disciple!
>
> With the practice of *a nu ta ra*
> during the night,
> the three Dharma remembrances
> will easily appear.
>
> Train the mind in multiplication
> and transformation,
> gain control, and cultivate meditative
> concentration while asleep—
> my dear disciple!

Thus the path of the vase initiation, the creation stage with associated practices, is presented as the primary practice of meditative equipoise. In addition to that, if the recitation, sacrificial-cake offering, and so forth are also practiced completely, nowadays one will certainly become a middling yogin.

Then, if one practices the path of the secret initiation, the yoga of the fierce fire of *chandali*,[5] one should purify the body, purify the voice, and purify the mindstream with the guruyoga and so forth. The main practice is the seven yogas of the vital wind, and primarily the practice of the union of the vital winds in the vase retention, which is crucial. Following that the eighteen visualizations of the fierce fire and so forth are extremely profound, but nowadays this *chandali* yoga dependent on four cakras is practiced as the continual practice.

Thus this practice of the three higher initiations can be understood from the presentation of the practical guidance of an excellent lord and master. The meaning cannot be presented through mere writing, so I have not written about it.

Therefore, the essence of the freedoms and endowments of fortunate disciples is made meaningful by purifying the mindstream with the Three Appearances, by removing the chaff of conceptual elaborations with the view of the indivisibility of samsara and nirvana, by how to meditate on the four different paths for the four initiations, by the four different views of mahamudra from meditation on those, by the four different introductions to those and ways to sustain them, by how to practice the four conducts in order to enhance those, by how the four different culminations of attainment are reached through that type of conduct, by the four different practices when passing away if those have not been reached, by the four different practices in the intermediate state if those have not been successful, and by the instructions of illusory body and dream yoga as the evaluation of those paths. This is the Dharma of our amazing and wonderful practice of the Path with the Result in the tradition of the Explication for Disciples.

> Thus this elixir of the heart
> of the Path with the Result,
> the system of the profound lucid path
> of the Explication for Disciples,
> a heart that is not within everyone's range,
> was received by the kindness of the master.

In that way, to benefit knowledgeable people on the occasion of spreading some of the nectar of the Teaching of the Explication for Disciples at the great Dharma institute of Nyenyo Chagoshong in an iron-female-snake year [1581], and especially because of repeated urging from afar by the fully ordained monk, the vajra holder Samten Lhundrup, this practice of the key points of the Path with the Result is sent by Nagarjuna[6] from the Pavilion of Long Life at glorious Nyenyo. May good fortune increase!

---

5. Heat yoga.
6. On Nagarjuna in the Tibetan tradition, see the introduction to the *Lives of the Eighty-Four Sid-* *dhas*, p. 478. "Vajra": an implement used in tantric ritual, said to represent a thunderbolt.

If this skylike mind becomes accustomed
to skylike phenomena as skylike,
it will also reach skylike enlightenment.

If this illusion-like mind becomes accustomed
to illusion-like phenomena as illusion-like,
it will also reach illusion-like enlightenment.

Good fortune!

A TIBETAN BOOK OF THE DEAD

MOONLIGHT BESTOWING THE COOLING COMPLETE BLISS
(Dende Silwa Derje Daser)

JANGGYA

Over the centuries, Buddhists have composed prayers for many purposes. One of the most common is to seek a favorable rebirth, through prayers that are typically recited at the time of death. In Buddhism, the time of death is considered to be of supreme importance, because it is then that the next lifetime, one's future fate, will be determined. According to karmic theory, each person carries a vast store of seeds for future rebirth, any one of which can fructify as an entire lifetime (see the *Abhidharmakosha*, p. 267). There are seeds for favorable rebirths as humans or gods, and there are seeds for horrific rebirths as ghosts or hell beings. One's mental state at the moment of death is believed to determine which of these seeds will create one's next lifetime.

Buddhists therefore go to great lengths to favorably influence the state of mind of the dying person, placing statues of buddhas and bodhisattvas in the room and reading sutras and prayers. However, because the experience of death is so harrowing, it is said that the preparation for it should begin long before the deathbed. In Tibet, many prayers are recited daily in order to review the stages of death so that they will be familiar when they finally arrive. One such work, written by the first Panchen Lama, Losang Chogyi Gyaltsen (1567–1662), appears below. As is common in Buddhist literature, the original work or "root text," here (as often) in verse, is interspersed with a prose commentary by a later scholar. In this case, the commentator is Janggya Rolpe Dorje (1717–1786), a friend and teacher of the Qianlong Emperor of China.

The work begins with a theme found throughout Buddhist literature: death is certain, the time of death is uncertain, and at the time of death nothing is of benefit but the dharma. It then turns to a more specifically tantric view of death, seen as a potent moment in which the most subtle form of consciousness, called the mind of clear light, becomes accessible: for the person with the proper training, death can be "brought to the path" and used for the immediate achievement of buddhahood.

According to an influential tantric system, the process of death occurs over eight dissolutions, as consciousness gradually retreats from the senses toward the heart and as the physical elements of earth, water, fire, and wind lose the capacity to serve as the basis for consciousness. In the first dissolution, the earth constituent dissolves and the individual approaching death no longer can perceive forms clearly. At each stage, a different sign appears to the dying person. Thus, the first dissolution is marked by a mirage, such as the illusion of water in a desert. In the second dissolution, the water constituent dissolves and the dying person is no longer able to hear sounds; its sign is the appearance of smoke. With the third dissolution, that of the fire constituent, the dying person loses the ability to smell and perceives red sparks of light in darkness, "like fireflies." The last of the four elements, the wind constituent, dissolves at the fourth stage, when the individual can no longer taste, experience physical sensation, or move about. At this point, the person stops breathing. The sign that appears to the dying person is "like a burning butter lamp"—that is, a sputtering flame.

In the schema of this tantric physiology, during the process of death the winds or subtle energies that serve as the vehicles for consciousness withdraw from the network of 72,000 channels that course throughout the body. The most important of these is the central channel, which runs from the genitals upward to the crown of the head, then curves down to end in the space between the eyes. Running in parallel are the right and left channels, which wrap around the central channel at several points. At these points of constriction are also networks of smaller channels that radiate throughout the body and are called wheels (chakras).

By the time of the fifth dissolution, the sense consciousnesses have ceased to operate. The winds that course through the channels in the upper part of the body have gathered at the top of the central channel, the crown of the head. When these winds descend through the central channel to the heart wheel, what appears to the mind of the dying person changes from a burning butter lamp to a radiant whiteness. In the sixth cycle the winds from the lower part of the body enter the center channel at the base of the spine and ascend to the heart, producing the appearance of a bright red color. At the seventh stage, the winds that have gathered above and below enter into the heart center, bringing about an appearance of radiant blackness, and the dying person is said to briefly swoon into unconsciousness. Finally, in the last stage, the mind of clear light dawns, with the appearance of the natural color of the sky at dawn. This is death. The mind of clear light then passes into what is called the intermediate state (*bardo*) between death and rebirth, a period that can last up to forty-nine days. At last, impelled by previous actions, the mind finds a place of rebirth.

The tantric yogin is able to make use of these stages of death to shorten the path to buddhahood. The mind of clear light is an elevated form of consciousness that can be employed to understand emptiness (see *Verses on the Middle Way*, p. 366) and destroy the most subtle obstructions to the attainment of perfect enlightenment. The poem and commentary describe this process of death and the means of transforming death into buddhahood.

PRONOUNCING GLOSSARY

Bhairava: *bai-ra-va*

Chakrasamvara: *cha-kra-sam-va-ra*

Choje Losang Sangye: *chur-jay loh-sahng sahng-gyeh*

dakini: *dah-ki-nee*

Dende Silwa Derje Daser: *den-day seel-wa der-jay da-sair*

dhuti: *doo-ti*

gandharva: *gan-dar-va*

geshe: *gay-shay*

Guhyasamaja: *gu-hya-sa-mah-ja*

Guru Manjughosha: *gu-ru man-ju-goh-sha*

Jambudvipa: *jam-bu-dvee-pa*

Janggya: *jahng-gyah*

Losang Chogyi Gyaltsen Bel Zangpo: *loh-sahng chur-gyee gyehl-tsehn behl sahng-boh*

Mahayana: *ma-hah-yah-na*

Manjughosha: *man-ju-goh-sha*

Nagarjuna: *nah-gahr-ju-na*

Panchen lama: *pahn-chen lah-mah*

sangha: *san-ga*

sugata: *su-ga-ta*

tathagata: *ta-tah-ga-ta*

torma: *dohr-mah*

Tshultrim Dargye: *tsul-trim dahr-gyay*

Tsong kha pa: *tsohng kah pah*

Vajradhara: *vaj-ra-da-ra*

Vajrasattva: *vaj-ra-sat-tva*

yi dam: *yee dahm*

Prayers for Deliverance from the Straits of the Bardo, a Hero That Frees from Fear

BY THE FIRST PANCHEN LAMA

Homage to the Guru Manjughosha[1]

I and all transmigrators, equal to space
Go for refuge until the essence of enlightenment
To the sugatas of the three times, together with the doctrine and
 the assembly.
We pray to be delivered from the frights of this [lifetime], future
 [lifetimes], and the bardo.

This auspicious base [the human body], difficult to find and easy
 to destroy,
Is the opportunity to choose profit or loss, joy or sorrow.
Thus, empower us to take the essence, great in meaning,
Without being distracted by the meaningless affairs of this life.

What was joined is parted, all that was accumulated is consumed,
The end of height is sinking, the end of life is death.
Empower us to understand that there is no time;
Not only will we die, but the time of death is uncertain.

Empower us to pacify the suffering in which the body is destroyed
By various causes of death when consciousness is about to leave
The four impure elements and the illusory aggregates
In the city of the mistaken conception of subject and object.

Empower us to pacify the mistaken appearances of nonvirtue
When we are deceived at a time of need by this body lovingly protected,
When the enemies, the frightful lords of death appear,
When we kill ourselves with the weapons of the three poisons.

Empower us to remember the instructions of the lama
When the doctors give up and rites cannot reverse it
And friends have lost the hope that we will live
And we do not know what to do.

TRANSLATED FROM the Tibetan by Donald S. Lopez, Jr. All bracketed additions are the translator's.

1. Another name for Manjushri, the bodhisattva of wisdom.

Empower us to have joy and confidence
When the food and wealth greedily amassed remain behind,
We leave forever friends loved and longed for,
And go alone to a dangerous place.

Empower us to have the strength of a virtuous mind
When the elements of earth, water, fire, and wind gradually dissolve,
The strength of the body is lost, the mouth and nose dry and contract,
The warmth gathers, we gasp for breath, and a wheezing sound
     occurs.

Empower us to realize the deathless mode of being
When the various mistaken appearances, frightful and horrific,
Occur, specifically mirage, smoke, and fireflies,
And the mounts of the eighty conceptions cease.

Empower us to produce strong mindfulness
When the wind constituent begins to dissolve into consciousness,
The outer breath ceases and coarse dualistic appearance disappears
And there dawns an appearance like a blazing butterlamp.

Empower us to know our own nature
Through the yoga that realizes that samsara and nirvana are empty
When appearance, increase, and attainment dissolve, the former into
     the latter
And the experiences like being pervaded by sunlight, moonlight, and
     darkness dawn.

Empower the mother and son clear lights to meet
Upon the dissolution of near-attainment into the all empty,
When all conceptual elaborations are completely pacified
And an experience dawns like an autumn sky free from taint.

Empower us to be placed in one-pointed equipose
On the wisdom of the union of innate bliss and emptiness
As the moon is melted by the lightning-like fire of Brahma
At the time of the four empties.

Empower us to complete the meditative state of illusion
When, rising from that, we ascend to an enjoyment body of the bardo
Blazing with the glorious major and minor marks
[Made] just from the wind and mind of the clear light of death.

If the bardo becomes established due to actions
Empower us so that erroneous appearances appear purely,
Realizing, with immediate analysis, how the sufferings
Of birth, death, and the bardo do not truly exist.

Empower us to be reborn in a pure land
Through the yoga of the transformation of the outer, inner, and
     secret

When the varieties of the four sounds of the reversal of the elements,
The three frightening appearances, the uncertainties, and the signs
    appear.

Empower us to attain quickly the three bodies
Upon assuming a supreme base of a knowledge bearer of the sky
Or the body of one with pure behavior, endowed with the three trainings
Completing the realizations of the two-staged path.

A Commentary on This Prayer, Called "A Moon Bestowing the Coolness of Complete Bliss"

BY JANGGYA

I bow down to the pervasive lord, the lama Vajrasattva[2]
Through relying on whom the great bliss of union
Is bestowed in this very lifetime.
I will comment upon the profound instructions.

Here, I will discuss, for the sake of easy understanding, the stages of practice of this text, *Prayers for Deliverance from the Straits of the Bardo, A Hero That Frees from Fear*, composed by the Panchen, the all-knowing Losang Chogyi Gyaltsen Bel Zangpo (Blo bzang chos kyi rgyal mtshan dpal bzang po), the lord of the complete teaching who has gone to the highest state of attainment, the keeper of the treasury of all the secret instructions of the foremost great being, [Tsong kha pa[3]]. Initially, one should build one's motivation and purify one's continuum by going for refuge and engendering the aspiration to enlightenment. Perform as before the guru yoga that is connected with the *yi dam*[4] of Unexcelled Yoga Tantra, such as Bhairava, Chakrasamvara, or Guhyasamaja, together with the seven-limbed service[5] and the offering of mandala. The prayers are to be [recited] as it appears below with mindfulness of the meaning through strong conviction regarding the inseparability of one's teacher and *yi dam*. In other contexts, when this is connected with meditation in the circle of a mandala, one may conclude with torma offering[6] of self-generation or may conclude with offering and praise of the [deity] generated in front; since either is suitable, it depends on the context.

    The actual prayers are of four [types], the preliminaries, connected with the common path; those connected with the instructions for someone about to die; those connected with instructions for the intermediate state, and those connected with instructions for taking rebirth. The first, [those connected with the common path] comprise the first three stanzas.

Homage to the Guru Manjughosha

This is an obeisance and an expression of worship to the lama and supreme of deities, Manjughosha.

---

2. A tantric form of the Buddha.
3. On Tsong kha pa (1357–1419), see the introduction to the *Great Exposition of the Stages of the Path*, p. 696.
4. Personal deity (Tibetan); in this case, the tantric buddha whom one propitiates in daily practice.
5. Practices to purify negativity and to accumulate merit.
6. A special food offering.

> I and all transmigrators, equal to space
> Go for refuge until the essence of enlightenment
> To the sugatas of the three times,[7] together with the doctrine and the assembly.
> We pray to be delivered from the frights of this [life], future [lives], and the bardo.[8]

[The first stanza] concerns going for refuge. [Going for refuge] is the heartfelt promise that is not broken from now until enlightenment, unwaveringly seeking protection in the place of protection—the tathagatas[9] of the three times, that is, the buddhas, the dharma, and the sangha—for oneself and all transmigrators equal to space from the fears of this life, the next life, and the intermediate state. [Refuge is sought from two perspectives]: a strong awareness fearful of the general and specific sufferings of samsara of myself and all the kind transmigrators, equal to space, and with an authentic awareness that the lama and the three jewels[1] have the capacity to protect us from that [suffering].

> This auspicious base, difficult to find and easy to destroy,
> Is the opportunity to chose profit or loss, joy or sorrow.
> Thus, empower us to take the essence, great in meaning,
> Without being distracted by the meaningless affairs of this life.

The second stanza is concerned with the great meaning of leisure and opportunity and the difficulty of finding them. An auspicious basis endowed with the eighteen qualities of leisure and opportunity,[2] whether [considered] from the viewpoint of cause, entity, or example, is difficult to find and the conditions for its destruction are numerous. Hence, it is easy for it to be destroyed, like the flame of a butterlamp in a strong wind. This [basis], attained merely fortuitously this time, is an opportunity to have the independence to choose joy or sorrow; to acquire the profit of high status [i.e., a good rebirth] and liberation for oneself from now on, or to bring about a loss, such as the sufferings of the bad realms. We pray for empowerment to extract the pure essence through practicing the excellent doctrine of the Mahayana, having the great meaning, practicing daily with determination, never being distracted by the meaningless affairs of this lifetime, such as praise, fame, and resources, which are insignificant because they are not rare; they are even acquired by animals.

> What was joined is parted, all that was accumulated is consumed,
> The end of height is sinking, the end of life is death.
> Empower us to understand that there is no time;
> Not only will we die, but the time of death is uncertain.

The third stanza teaches about impermanence. Like traders at a festival, the happy gatherings of relatives and dear friends in the end powerlessly disperse. Like the honey of a bee, not only is all accumulated wealth consumed in the end; there is no certainty that one will be able to use it oneself. Like

7. The past, the present, and the future. "Sugatas": buddhas (lit., "well gone ones"; Sanskrit).
8. The intermediate state between death and rebirth.
9. "Tathagata" is a title of a buddha (literally, "one

who has thus come/gone"); it is the one most often used by the historical Buddha to refer to himself.
1. The Buddha, the dharma, and the sangha (the Buddhist community).
2. See the *Great Exposition of the Stages of the Path.*

an arrow shot into the sky by a child, one achieves a high rank of glory in the world and in the end one does not escape sinking. This very body that is born complete and is lovingly protected is finally destroyed by the Lord of Death. At that time, being cast as if into an empty wilderness, consciousness must always go on alone. Thus, not only will one die, but the time when one will die—the year, the month, the week—is uncertain. Therefore, there can be no confidence that one will not die even today. Empower us to practice only the excellent doctrine quickly, having understood that there is no time for the limitless affairs which are to be put aside—the appearances of this life—[such as] accumulating and maintaining possessions, subduing enemies and protecting friends.

The preceding has taught the way to train the mind in the prerequisites to the instructions on death. The second group of prayers applies to the instructions for those who are about to die. This has two parts, removing obstacles to the cultivation of the path, that is, engendering the kind of awareness that is concordant with the doctrine, and the actual mode of cultivating the instructions for one about to die. The first is dealt with in four stanzas.

> Empower us to pacify the suffering in which the body is destroyed
> By various causes of death when consciousness is about to leave
> The four impure elements and the illusory aggregates
> In the city of the mistaken conception of subject and object.

If there is a great suffering that destroys the essential [parts of the body] at the time of death, one is prevented from putting the instructions into practice. Therefore, the first stanza is a prayer for empowerment in order that that [suffering] be pacified. This city of the gandharvas,[3] the mundane existence of the mistaken appearances of this life, is produced by dualistic conceptions that perceive the apprehended [objects] and the apprehender [i.e., consciousnesses] to be true. Here, the illusory aggregates are composed of the four elements of earth, water, fire, and wind, which are established from the impure factors of blood and semen from one's parents. These aggregates and one's own consciousness are divided and separated through the divisiveness of the pernicious Lord of Death. As that time draws near, empower us to pacify suffering such that it does not happen that the elements are disturbed by the power of various harmful external and internal causes of death, such as sickness, weapons, and poison, and that a fierce disease ceases and destroys the essential [parts of the] body—the winds, constituents, and the channels that are the basis of the life force.

> Empower us to pacify the mistaken appearances of nonvirtue
> When we are deceived at a time of need by this body lovingly protected,
> When the enemies, the frightful lords of death appear,
> When we kill ourselves with the weapons of the three poisons.

If one conceives the mistaken appearances at the time of death to be true and comes under the power of fear and dread, one is prevented from meditating on the instructions. Therefore, the second stanza is a prayer for empowerment in order to pacify that. Arriving at an inescapable passage, one is deceived at [this] time of need by the body that is cherished and protected with food,

---

3. A standard Buddhist metaphor for something illusory; "gandharvas" are heavenly musicians.

clothing, and wealth, without shunning sin, suffering, or ill-repute, and [mind and body] separate. The enemies, the difficult to withstand and frightening lords of death, that is, the various forms of the lords of death such as the fear of the separation of life from the body and the fear of fear itself appear. At that time, one murders oneself with the weapons of the three poisons—attachment to this body, unbearable hatred of fear and suffering, and the obscuration that conceives whatever appears to be true. We pray that, when we arrive at that point, we be empowered to pacify all the appearances of unpleasant objects created by nonvirtuous misconception and all the mistaken perceptions of subjects that conceive these to be true.

> Empower us to remember the instructions of the lama
> When the doctors give up and rites cannot reverse it
> And friends have lost the hope that we will live
> And we do not know what to do.

Regarding the third, one prays for empowerment in order to have the ability to meditate on the instructions, without being impeded by fear or forgetfulness at that time. The doctors who hope to cure sicknesses give up and various rites do not overcome the fear of death. Relatives, such as one's father and mother, lose hope that one will live; with eyes filled with tears they make arrangements for the funeral ceremonies. One oneself does not know what to do, like someone abandoned by a guide in a frightful place. At that time, abandoning anguish and panic, we pray for empowerment to remember the instructions of the lama, having the confidence to use death on the path.

> Empower us to have joy and confidence
> When the food and wealth greedily amassed remain behind,
> We leave forever friends loved and longed for,
> And go alone to a dangerous place.

Regarding the fourth, all the wealth and possessions, the home and power that one has greedily accumulated and toiled and worried to protect is left as inheritance. Without ever meeting them again, one leaves forever friends loved and longed for, one's father and mother, one's retinue, and students, from whom one cannot bear to be apart from even for a short time. One will be carried powerlessly, alone and without a companion, by the winds of karma to the dangerous place of the bardo where one has never been before and which is unfamiliar, not knowing what frights and sufferings are there. At that time, we pray for empowerment to have a joy and confidence that are agreeable and cheerful, without the slightest panic or anguish, like a child going home, placing confidence in the lama, *yi dam*, and three jewels. That is, one prays for empowerment in order to increase the happiness of the mind, understanding that all of these appearances of the circumstances of death are to be visualized in meditation prior [to death] and are exhortations to the practice of virtue at the time of death.

The second, the actual mode of meditating on the instructions for one about to die, is [dealt with in the next] six stanzas.

> Empower us to have the strength of a virtuous mind
> When the elements of earth, water, fire, and wind gradually dissolve,
> The strength of the body is lost, the mouth and nose dry and contract,
> The warmth gathers, we gasp for breath, and a wheezing sound occurs.

Regarding the first, when the power of the wind that serves as the basis of the physical earth constituent declines and it dissolves into the water constituent, the external sign is that the strength of the body is lost, that is, one says, "I am being pulled down," thinking that one is sinking into the earth. Similarly, when the water constituent dissolves into the fire constituent, the external sign is that the moisture of the mouth and nose dry up and the lips become puckered and so forth. When the fire constituent dissolves into the wind constituent, the external sign is that warmth of the body gathers from the extremities at the heart and one's luster deteriorates. The external sign of the wind constituent dissolving into consciousness is a gasping for breath, and one makes a wheezing sound from [the breath] collecting uneveningly within. Therefore, when those occur, we pray for empowerment not to be moved by nonvirtuous thoughts, but to have the strength of virtuous minds, in general, virtuous minds such as going for refuge and training in the aspiration to enlightenment through giving and taking and, in particular, meditating on one's lama as being inseparable from one's *yi dam* and visualizing oneself and one's environment as the supported and supporting mandala.

> Empower us to realize the deathless mode of being
> When the various mistaken appearances, frightful and horrific,
> Occur, specifically mirage, smoke, and fireflies,
> And the mounts of the eighty conceptions cease.

As the potencies of the physical body begin to disintegrate, appearances occur. There are many frightful and horrific things, such as unpleasant forms and sounds appearing to those who have been nonvirtuous. Various mistaken appearances, such as pleasant forms and sounds, appear to those who have been virtuous. Yogins who have made progress on the path are welcomed by the lama, the *yi dam*, and dakinis,[4] together with amazing visions. Specifically, an appearance like a mirage arises as the internal sign of the dissolution of earth into water, an appearance like smoke as the internal sign of the dissolution of water into fire, and an appearance like fireflies as the internal sign of the dissolution of fire into wind. After that the movements of the karmic winds that serve as the mounts of the eighty thorough conceptions— the forty natural conceptions of appearance, the thirty-three natural conceptions of increase, and the seven natural conceptions of near attainment—grow weaker and weaker and gradually cease. At that time, we pray for empowerment for the ability to sustain the understanding of the profound mode of being, deciding that birth, death, and all of samsara and, specifically, all of these appearance and the mind are mere projections by mistaken conceptions and that ultimately that which is called "death" does not exist even in name.

> Empower us to produce strong mindfulness
> When the wind constituent begins to dissolve into consciousness,
> The outer breath ceases and coarse dualistic appearance disappears
> And there dawns an appearance like a blazing butterlamp.

Regarding the third, then the constituent of the movement of wind becomes very weak and begins to dissolve into the subtle constituent of consciousness.

4. Tantric goddesses.

An external sign of this is that movement of the breath ceases and there is no inhalation. As an internal sign, all coarse dualistic appearances such as the aspect of the external object being distant and cut off from the internal apprehending consciousness disappear and an appearance dawns like a blazing butterlamp unmoved by the wind. At that time, empower us so that the aspect of clarity and knowledge, the conventional entity of the mind, will appear nakedly and so that we will produce a mindfulness that thinks, "I know this sign and that sign," when all of those internal and external signs explained above appear and so that earlier [before death] we will produce an introspection that knows whether or not we are performing the meditation that brings [death] to the path of the two stages.[5]

> Empower us to know our own nature
> Through the yoga that realizes that samsara and nirvana are empty
> When appearance, increase, and attainment dissolve, the former into the latter
> And the experiences like being pervaded by sunlight, moonlight, and darkness dawn.

Regarding the fourth, then, at the time of appearance itself the winds dissolve into the appearance of subtle consciousness and there is the appearance of radiant whiteness in utter vacuity, like a clear autumn sky pervaded by moonlight. At the time of increase itself appearance dissolves into increase and there is the appearance of radiant redness, like a clear autumn sky pervaded by sunlight. At the time of near attainment itself, when increase dissolves into near attainment, there arises the appearance of radiant blackness, like a clear autumn sky pervaded by the thick darkness of evening. When the three appearances, the signs of the gradual dissolution of the former into the latter, appear in that way, empower us to have the ability to understand experientially the entity or mode of being of our own mind exactly as it is through the yoga of the special realization that inseparably joins the entities of the object emptiness—the nonexistence of even a particle of that which is established from its own side among all the phenomena included in cycle of mundane existence and the peace of nirvana—and the subject, the spontaneous great bliss that arises through the method of focusing on important points in the body.

> Empower the mother and son clear lights to meet
> Upon the dissolution of near-attainment into the all empty,
> When all conceptual elaborations are completely pacified
> And an experience dawns like an autumn sky free from taint.

Regarding the fifth, then, upon the dissolution of the subtle mind of near attainment itself into the clear light of the all empty, all the elaborations of thought that conceive various objects such as unity and plurality cease and become pacified and an experience dawns like the utter vacuity of a pure autumn sky free from moonlight, sunlight, and thick darkness, the three tainting conditions that prevent the natural color of the sky from coming out just as it is. The manifestation, just as it is, of the entity of the basic clear light, fundamental and spontaneous, is the mother clear light. That same mind, the

---

5. The stages of generation and completion.

path clear light, which, through meditating on the instructions of the lama, is generated into exalted wisdom that realizes the subtle emptiness with spontaneous great bliss is the son clear light. The union of those in one entity is the meeting of mother and son clear lights. We pray for empowerment to be able to [have them meet when the clear light of death dawns].

> Empower us to be placed in one-pointed equipose
> On the wisdom of the union of innate bliss and emptiness
> As the moon is melted by the lightning-like fire of Brahma[6]
> At the time of the four empties.

Regarding the sixth, at the time of all four empties and specifically of the all empty, the clear light, the fire of Brahma that abides at the triangular junction, that is, the fire of the fierce woman, blazes up like lightning, with the speed of lightning by the yogic power of the basic path. By moving up the central channel it melts the moon, the white mind of enlightenment, at the crown of the head which descends through the *dhuti*,[7] thereby engendering the spontaneous great bliss. We pray for empowerment to be placed in one-pointed equipoise without distraction on the exalted wisdom that inseparably joins in entity that [bliss] and the subtle emptiness.

The foremost great being Tsong kha pa said that the king of instructions for the benefit of those who are about to die is the uninterrupted daily practice that combines three things: mixing in the mind again and again, beginning today, the instructions for one about to die, as they were explained above; forcing oneself to think repeatedly, "At death I should meditate in this way"; and strongly beseeching the lamas and gods for the purpose of that. It is similar with regard to the instruction on the bardo below.

The third group applies to instruction on the bardo and is set forth in three stanzas.

> Empower us to complete the meditative state of illusion
> When, rising from that, we ascend to an enjoyment body of the bardo
> Blazing with the glorious major and minor marks
> [Made] just from the wind and mind of the clear light of death.

Regarding the first, thus, when the wind and mind of the clear light of death are themselves moved by the wind, that is, when one rises from that meditative equipoise, the wind that serves as the mount of the clear light of death acts as the substantial cause of and the mind of clear light acts as the cooperative condition of a body that blazes with the glory of the thirty-two major marks and the eighty minor marks. It is a clear and unobstructed rainbow body, having a nature of mere wind and mind and not a coarse body of physical flesh and bone. The bardo of ordinary sentient beings comes about in the same way, but this yogin who is able to generate the clear light of death, the basis, into the entity of the example clear light on the path rises in an enjoyment body, that is, an impure illusory body. We pray for empowerment to complete the illusion-like meditative stabilization of such an Unexcelled Mantra path. This [discussion] applies to a single yogin who, in this lifetime, has achieved realization of isolated speech, or below, of the stage of completion.

---

6. The god who persuaded the Buddha to teach.   7. The central channel.

> If the bardo becomes established due to actions
> Empower us so that erroneous appearances appear purely,
> Realizing, with immediate analysis, how the sufferings
> Of birth, death, and the bardo do not truly exist.

Regarding the second, if an ordinary body of the mundane bardo becomes established due to actions that did not [permit] the attainment in this lifetime of the realization of the stage of completion such as that [described] above, analyze well immediately and understand that one has established the bardo and then realize that all the appearances of birth, death, and the intermediate state are appearances of a mistaken mind and realize the way in which all of those sufferings are not true, that is, they are not established from their own side even slightly. Empower us so that all of the mistaken appearances that arise will appear purely, as the sport of bliss and emptiness.

> Empower us to be reborn in a pure land
> Through the yoga of the transformation of the outer, inner, and secret
> When the varieties of the four sounds of the reversal of the elements,
> The three frightening appearances, the uncertainties, and the signs
>   appear.

Regarding the third, thus, at the time of the bardo, the signs of the reversal of the elements come. With the reversal of the earth wind there is the sound of an avalanche; with the reversal of the water wind, the sound of a stormy sea; with the reversal of the fire wind, the sound of a forest fire; with the reversal of the wind wind; the sound of the wind storm [at the end of an] aeon. There are four such sounds. The three frightful appearances are the appearance of hell beings, hungry ghosts, and animals or [they are] the form of lords of death carrying weapons, the sound of their saying "I'm going to kill you!" and one becoming sorrowful and terrified because of that. The uncertainties are such things as the uncertainty of abode, because of not abiding in one place and the uncertainty of companions because one is accompanied by a variety of companions. Various signs appear such as being endowed with the power of magical activity and [passing] without obstruction through mountains, walls, buildings, and so forth. At that time, empower us to be born in a pure buddha land, a special place for cultivating the path of Unexcelled Secret Mantra, having closed the door of birth in impure samsara through the force of the three yogas; the transformation of all the appearances of the environment—the outer—into pure divine mansions, the transformation of all the inhabiting sentient beings—the inner—into *yi dams* in the aspect of father and mother, and the transformation of all the movements of mindfulness and thought—the secret—into the meditative state of bliss and emptiness.

The fourth section applies to taking rebirth and is set forth in one stanza.

> Empower us to attain quickly the three bodies
> Upon assuming a supreme base of a knowledge bearer of the sky
> Or the body of one with pure behavior, endowed with the three
>   trainings
> Completing the realizations of the two-staged path.

In dependence upon the instructions of taking the bardo as the path in this way, one takes birth as a supreme knowledge bearer in a special abode caused and assembled by the very forms of outer flying heroes and dakinis. One then completes the remainder of the path and achieves the supreme state. Otherwise, if one takes birth like those endowed with six constituents who are born from a human womb in Jambudvipa,[8] one should stop the mind of desire and hatred for one's father and mother and view them as *yi dams* in the aspect of father and mother. One enters the mother's womb and, upon being born outside, one takes the body of a monk endowed with three trainings of those with pure behavior and enters into the teaching of the Conqueror[9] in accordance with its stages. Then, one's continuum is ripened by the four pure initiations, the doors of entry into Unexcelled Secret Mantra Mahayana. Having kept the pledges and vows correctly, one brings to fulfillment the progression on the paths of the stage of generation and the stage of completion. Having thereby transformed the basic three bodies into the three bodies of the path, one quickly attains, in this very lifetime, the three bodies of a buddha, the effect: the wisdom truth body, the enjoyment body, and the emanation body. Having done that, we pray for empowerment to establish all sentient beings throughout space on the path to ripening and liberation.

Because the meaning of colophon is easy to understand, I will not elaborate. It is said that these instructions should be kept secret from those who are not vessels, such as those without faith, and from those who have not received initiation into Unexcelled Mantra. The explanations above of the instructions on death and the bardo appear to be intended for the profound instructions on the stage of completion. Therefore, regarding the mode of transforming [these instructions] into the king of instructions on death, the practice is to be done daily, as already explained, through causing the meanings of the instructions to appear in meditation, not through merely reciting the words of the prayers but by being mindful of the meaning. If it is practiced in that way, it becomes the supreme method for taking advantage of the basis of leisure and opportunity. I say:

> How wonderful it is to explain clearly with few words
> The essences of the path of the highest vehicle,
> The essentials of the profound thought of Vajradhara,[1]
> The basic promise of the kings of adepts.
>
> By the virtue of striving at this,
> May I and all transmigrators
> Peerlessly uphold and increase
> The path of the highest vehicle in birth after birth
> And become equal to the vajra-bearing Nagarjuna.[2]

The elder lama and monk, Choje Losang Sangye (Chos rje blo bzang sangs rgyas), asked on behalf of one from Mongolia with a youthful mind who is beginning the complete and profound practice that there be made an explanation, condensed and easy to understand, of the meanings of *Prayers for Deliverance from the Straits of the Bardo, A Hero That Frees from Fear* by the

---

8. In Buddhist cosmology, the southern continent, on which all humans live.
9. That is, the Buddha.
1. Vajrapani, the bodhisattva of power.

2. On Nagarjuna in the Tibetan tradition, see the introduction to the *Lives of the Eighty-Four Siddhas*, p. 478. "Vajra": an implement used in tantric ritual, said to represent a thunderbolt.

crown of millions of scholars and adepts, the omniscient Panchen Losang Chogyi Gyaltsen. The scribe of the learned Janggya (Lcang skya rol pa'i rdo rje) was the lama and geshe[3] Tshultrim Dargye (Tshul khrims dar rgyas), for whom billions of texts have been spoken. By [the merit] of having done this, may the teaching of the conqueror Losang [Tsong kha pa] spread and increase in all directions.

3. A title of accomplished Tibetan Buddhist scholars.

SEVERING THE DEMON OF THE SELF

WORDS OF MY PERFECT TEACHER
(Kunzang Lame Shelung)

PATRUL RINPOCHE

Milarepa (p. 1372) was initially unable to benefit from the profound instructions he received because of obstacles caused by his negative deeds. As tantric practice became more systematized in Tibet, each tradition developed what are called "preliminary practices," which served two purposes. First, they developed the student's motivation: the requirement to complete them tested the strength of that motivation for the practice of the path that lay ahead. Second, they purified the most coarse of the mental obstacles to progress.

In the Nyingma sect, those preliminary practices were divided into two groups. The outer practices were designed to turn one's mind away from samsara and toward liberation, as one contemplated four fundamental doctrines of Buddhism: the rarity and preciousness of rebirth as a human, the impermanence of life and inevitability of death, the general and specific sufferings of the realms of samsara, and the cause and effect of actions.

The student would then move to the inner preliminary practices, in which the motivation of the bodhisattva, the purification of sins, and the accumulation of merit were the focus. Here, the student would perform one hundred thousand prostrations while repeating the refuge formula, and would recite the hundred-syllable mantra of the buddha Vajrasattva one hundred thousand times. This was also the context in which the practice often referred to in Western accounts as "exorcism" would be taught.

The bodhisattva must accumulate vast amounts of merit in order to achieve buddhahood; the bodhisattva deeds, known as the six perfections, are the chief vehicle for the accumulation of merit. The first, and most important for creating merit, is the perfection of giving. The bodhisattva must make extravagant gifts. But what if the bodhisattva is a beggar? This practice, called cho (literally "severance" in Tibetan), is also called the "beggar's accumulation of merit."

In the Shibi Jataka (p. 100), the future buddha in his lifetime as King Shibi cut away the flesh of his body to save a dove from a hawk. Here, too, the practitioner gives away his or her body but—as is true of so many tantric practices—in visualization. The practice is described clearly in the passage below. Regardless of actual gender, the practitioner visualizes him- or herself as the Wrathful Black True Mother, a naked dancing goddess brandishing a cleaver and skullcup. In preparing one's own body as an offering to the buddhas and bodhisattvas, the fire below is provided by the red letter a, which melts the white syllable ham (represented as hang in the text) in the space above the skullcup. When these two are combined, they make aham, the

Sanskrit word for "I." Thus, to provide a supreme offering to the buddhas and bodhisattvas, the body and the ego are split apart. Indeed, this practice is connected not only to the perfection of giving but also to the perfection of wisdom, the insight that there is no self.

The instruction excerpted below comes from one of the most widely used works on the preliminary practices: *Words of My Perfect Teacher*, by Patrul Rinpoche (1808–1887), one of the leading figures of the Nyingma renaissance in eastern Tibet in the late nineteenth century. The text is known for its clear and direct style and for its author's willingness to point out how these teachings have sometimes been misused. He makes it clear in this chapter that while the *cho* practice has indeed been used as a form of exorcism, such a use is a gross misunderstanding of its purpose.

PRONOUNCING GLOSSARY

Avalokiteshvara: *a-va-loh-ki-taysh-va-ra*

bodhichitta: *boh-di-chit-ta*

Bodhisattva: *boh-di-sat-tva*

Cho: *chur*

daka: *dah-kah*

dakini: *dah-ki-nee*

gyalgong: *gyahl-gohng*

Jetsun Mila: *jeh-tsoon mee-la*

Kunzang Lame Shelung: *koon-sahng la-may shay-loong*

kushali: *ku-sha-li*

Machik Labdron: *mah-chik lahb-drun*

Meru: *may-ru*

nirmanakaya: *nir-mah-na-kah-ya*

Om Ah Hung: *ohm ah hung*

Padampa Sangye: *pa-dahm-bah sahng-gyay*

Patrul Rinpoche: *pah-ntrool rin-pho-chay*

P'et: *pay*

preta: *pray-ta*

tsen: *tsehn*

Uddiyana: *ud-dee-yah-nah*

yidam: *yee-dahm*

THE KUSHALI'S ACCUMULATION:
DESTROYING THE FOUR DEMONS AT A SINGLE STROKE

Now comes a brief offering of one's own body called the *kushali's* accumulation. Since this practice is linked to the Guru Yoga in *Finding Rest in the Nature of Mind*,[1] it is permissible to combine it with the Guru Yoga. Alternatively, and without any contradiction, it can also be practiced as part of the accumulation of merit along with the mandala offering. That is how it will be explained here, in accordance with an oral tradition that teaches it in that way.

I. The Body as an Offering

The word "kushali" means a beggar. To accumulate merit and wisdom, yogis who have renounced ordinary life—hermits who live in the mountains, for

TRANSLATED FROM the Tibetan by the Padmakara Translation Group.

1. A work by Longchenpa (1308–1364), a Tibetan Nyingma master and scholar.

instance—use visualization to make offerings of their own bodies, having no other possessions to offer.

All the other material things that we gather around us with so much effort and concern are for the care of our bodies, and compared to any other possession it is without doubt our bodies that we cherish most. To sever our infatuation with our own bodies and use them as an offering is therefore far more beneficial than offering any other possession. It is said:

> Offering your horse or bull is worth hundreds of other offerings;
> Offering your child or spouse is worth thousands;
> Offering your own body is worth hundreds of thousands.

Machik Labdron[2] says:

> Not knowing that to give away my body without attachment
> Was to accumulate merit and wisdom,
> I have clung to this dear body of mine.
> This I confess to the nirmanakaya[3] of the Mother.

II. The Practice of Offering the Body

First, if you are used to the visualization you may choose to shoot your consciousness directly into space and visualize it there instantaneously as the Wrathful Black True Mother. If you are not, imagine in your heart the essence of your mental consciousness in the form of the Wrathful Mother. She is dancing and swaying, brandishing a curved knife high in the air with her right hand, and with her left holding a skull-cup full of blood at her heart. The squealing head of a black sow protrudes from behind her right ear. She is wearing the apparel of a wrathful goddess.

As you pronounce the syllable "P'et!" the Wrathful Mother flies up through your central channel. At the exact instant that she shoots up out of the aperture of Brahma[4] on the top of your head, your body becomes a corpse and collapses in a heap. Here, do not think of your body as having its normal appearance. Instead, see it as fat, greasy and huge, as big as the entire cosmos of a billion worlds.

With a single blow of the curved knife in her right hand, the Wrathful Black Mother—the visualized form of your consciousness—slices off the top of the inanimate body's skull at the level of the eyebrows to make a skull cup. Again, meditate that the skull cup is not life-size, but as big as the entire cosmos of a billion worlds. With her left hand the Wrathful Mother picks up the skull cup and places it, with the brow facing her, on a tripod made of three human skulls, each as large as Mount Meru.[5] Then with the hooked knife in her right hand, she lifts the whole corpse and drops it into the skull-cup.

Now visualize in space above the skull a white syllable *hang* with the nature of nectar, and beneath the skull the vertical stroke of a syllable *A*, red, with the nature of fire:

---

2. The disciple (1031–1129) of the Indian Padampa Sangye; she spread his *cho* (cutting, destroying) teachings to Tibet.
3. Emanation body (Sanskrit); one of the three bodies of the Buddha, it is the form of the Buddha that appears in our world.
4. The place from which consciousness departs the body at death in the case of a favorable rebirth.
5. In the Buddhist cosmology, the mountain located at the center of the world.

hang 　ཧཾ　　　vertical stroke of *A* ཨ

As you say "Om Ah Hung," fire blazes up from the stroke of the *A* and heats the skull-cup until the corpse melts into a bubbling nectar, which boils up and fills the whole skull. Everything foul and impure flows off in the form of a frothing scum. Steam rises from the nectar and touches the *hang*, heating it up by the contact. The *hang* exudes streams of red and white nectar, which drip down and blend together in an inseparable unity within the skull. The *hang* itself dissolves into light and melts into the nectar too. Visualizing all this, recite:

P'et! Ridding myself of attachment to the body . . .

and so on. Then, as you repeat "Om Ah Hung," visualize that the *om* purifies the nectar of all imperfections of colour, smell, taste and so on; the *ah* makes it increase many times over; and the *hung* transforms it into everything that could be wished for. It takes on the nature of the immaculate nectar of primal wisdom, manifesting as clouds of offerings that satisfy all possible desires.

Visualize in the sky in front of you a throne piled with silken cushions, on which is seated your gracious root teacher in person. Above him are the lineage teachers, around him are all the yidams,[6] and below in the space above the skull-cup are the Seventy-five Glorious Protectors and all the hosts of other Dharma protectors, both the wisdom protectors and the protectors constrained by the effect of their past actions, along with the deities of the locality and owners of the ground.

Below the skull, visualize all beings of the six realms and the three worlds,[7] among whom your principal guests are the eighty-four thousand types of obstacle makers, the fifteen great demons that prey on children, and, in short, all those who create obstacles and to whom you owe karmic debts, teeming like the countless specks of dust in a sunbeam.

I. THE WHITE FEAST FOR THE GUESTS ABOVE

Now visualize that your root teacher, the lineage teachers and all the assembled Buddhas and Bodhisattvas above his head all imbibe the nectar through their tongues, which have the form of hollow vajra[8] tubes. As a result, you complete the accumulations, you are freed of your obscurations, your violations and breaches of the samaya[9] are purified and you attain both the common and supreme accomplishments.

The yidams and deities of the four and six classes of tantra surrounding the teacher also consume the nectar, absorbing it through hollow tongues whose shapes correspond to the symbol associated with each deity—a vajra, wheel, jewel, lotus, or crossed vajra.[1] As a result you complete the accumulations, clear away your obscurations, purify all violations and breaches of samaya, and attain the common and supreme accomplishments.

---

6. Personal deities.
7. The worlds on, above, and below the earth. "The six realms": the realms of gods, demigods, humans, animals, ghosts, and the denizens of hell.
8. An implement used in tantric ritual, said to represent a thunderbolt.

9. Tantric vows.
1. These are the symbols of the five Buddha families [translator's note; in tantric Buddhism, these "families" are identified with five aspects of body and mind].

The dakas, dakinis,[2] Seventy-five Glorious Protectors and all the other Dharma protectors now also take their share of the nectar through the hollow sunbeams of their tongues. You complete the accumulations and are freed from all obscurations; all obstacles and circumstances unfavourable to the Dharma and the attainment of enlightenment are dispelled. All the favourable Circumstances and good things that you seek are intensified.

2. THE WHITE FEAST FOR THE GUESTS BELOW

Next, if you are experienced in visualization, continue to visualize yourself as the Wrathful Black True Mother and from your heart send out swarms of activity-performing dakinis—white, yellow, red, green and blue, like myriads of specks of dust dancing in the sun's rays. Imagine them satisfying all beings throughout the six realms and the three worlds, as they offer to each a wisdom skull-cup filled with immaculate nectar.

If you are less experienced in visualization, imagine that you yourself— the Wrathful Black Mother—use the skull-cup in your left hand to scoop nectar out of the great skull and scatter it, so that it rains down everywhere in the six realms and the three worlds of existence. All beings drink it and are utterly satisfied.

3. THE VARIEGATED FEAST FOR THE GUESTS ABOVE

Again, steam rises from the boiling nectar, giving rise to inconceivable clouds of offerings. Offer them to the guests above: fresh water for their feet, flowers, incense, lamps, perfumed water, foodstuffs and music, the eight auspicious symbols and seven attributes of royalty, parasols, victory-banners, canopies, golden wheels with a thousand spokes, white conches spiralling to the right, and more. As a result, you and all beings complete the accumulations and are cleansed of all obscurations.

4. THE VARIEGATED FEAST FOR THE GUESTS BELOW

Now come the guests below, namely all the beings of the six realms of existence. Whatever each of them desires pours down on them like rain, satisfying them and filling them with joy.

Think particularly of those beings to whom you have been indebted in all your lives until now in samsara without any beginning. We have all kinds of debts due to past actions: debts that shorten our lives because we have killed; debts that make us poor because we have stolen; debts that plague us with sickness because we have attacked and beaten others; debts for protection given by superiors, for services rendered by inferiors, and for help and support from equals; debts to overlords and underlings, to loved ones, friends, subjects, children and livestock; debts for the food we have eaten and the clothes we have worn, for the money we have borrowed, for the milk we have milked, for the loads we have had carried and for the fields we have ploughed, and for whatever else we may have used.

All of those karmic creditors, whether male or female, want to venge themselves on your flesh and bones, shorten your lifespan and snatch away your life-force. They gather round holding containers, running after you and demanding repayment. The offering is transformed into an inexhaustible

---

2. Tantric gods and goddesses.

treasury of everything desirable, which rains down upon them, bringing each of them whatever they most wish. It brings food for those who want food, clothing for those who want clothing, wealth for those who want wealth, gardens for those who want gardens, horses for those who want horses, houses to live in for those who want houses, and friends and loved ones for those who want friends and loved ones.

When each of them has enjoyed these things you are freed from your karmic obligations. Your debts are repaid. You are delivered from those deadly avengers and purified of all your harmful deeds and obscurations. Everyone is satisfied and happy.

Then imagine that for all those who may have been left behind—the lowly, the weak, the crippled, the blind, the deaf, the dumb and all beings in the six realms who are tortured and worn out by suffering—the offering becomes whatever they may need. It turns into a refuge for those with no refuge, a protector for those who have no protector, friendly assistance for those with no support, loved ones and friends for the lonely, land for the landless, medicines to cure the sick, life-restoring elixirs for the dying, miraculous legs for the crippled, eyes of wisdom for the blind, immaculate ears for the deaf, wisdom tongues for the dumb, and so on. These beings all enjoy the gifts and are satisfied, delivered from all the effects of actions, sufferings and habitual tendencies of each of the six realms. All the males reach the level of sublime Avalokiteshvara, all the females reach the level of noble Tara,[3] and the three worlds of samsara are liberated to their very depths.

Continue to recite "Om Ah Hung" until you have completed this whole visualization. Then recite the passage:

P'et! The guests of the offering above . . .

down to the words:

. . . uncontrived Great Perfection. Ah!

Then rest in the state beyond any concept of an offering, an offerer or a recipient of the offerings.

In the Cho texts there are usually four great feasts: white, red, variegated and black. But in this one there is no red or black feast.

What today's so-called Cho practitioners mean by Cho is a grisly process of destroying malignant spirits by slashing, chopping, chasing and killing them. Their idea of Cho involves being constantly full of anger. Their bravado is nothing more than hatred and pride. They imagine that they have to behave like the henchmen of the Lord of Death. For example, when they practise Cho for a sick person, they work themselves into a furious display of rage, staring with hate-filled eyes as large as saucers, clenching their fists, biting their lower lips, lashing out with blows and grabbing the invalid so hard that they tear the clothes off his back. They call this subduing spirits, but to practise Dharma like that is totally mistaken. Machik Labdron says:

3. On the female bodhisattva Tara, see "In Praise of the Twenty-One Taras," p. 486. "Avalokiteshvara": the bodhisattva regarded as the embodiment of the compassion of all the buddhas.

Since time without beginning, harmful spirits have lived in a cease-less whirl of hallucination and suffering, brought on by their own evil actions and by inauspicious circumstances which drive them like a wind. When they die they inevitably plunge to the very depths of the lower realms. With the hook of compassion I catch those evil spirits. Offering them my warm flesh and warm blood as food, through the kindness and compassion of bodhichitta[4] I transform the way they see everything and make them my disciples. Those malignant spirits are for me the prize that I hold with the hook of compassion—but the great adepts of Cho of the future will boast of killing them, beating them and casting them out. That will be a sign that false doctrines of Cho, the teachings of demons, are spreading.

All the various false Cho practices that she predicted, such as the Ninefold Black Cho, are only the result of thinking that one can subjugate spirits through violence, without the love and compassion of bodhichitta.

A person who uses those practices might just be able to overcome one or two puny little elemental spirits, but if he encounters any really vicious ones, they will attack his life in retaliation—as has been seen to happen on many occasions.

It is particularly difficult for practitioners to tell whether signs of success which occur on the path—the subjugation of a demon, or the experience of some kind of blessing, for instance—are authentic signs of progress, or whether they are in fact obstacles created by demonic forces.

People possessed by malicious spirits usually seem to have clairvoyance and supernatural powers. But as time goes on they get further and further from the genuine Dharma, until not even the tiniest scrap of goodness is left in them. The mountains of offerings that might be heaped upon them are just karmic debts for the future, and even in this life do them no good. In the end they find it hard to scrape together enough to eat or wear. And what they do have, they cannot bear to use up. When they die, they are sure to be reborn in an ephemeral hell or some such realm, as we have already mentioned.

III. The Meaning of Cho

The so-called spirits to be destroyed in Cho practice are not anywhere outside. They are within us. All the hallucinations that we perceive in the form of spirits outside ourselves arise because we have not eradicated the conceit of believing in an "I" and a "self." As Machik says:

> The tangible demon, the intangible demon,
> The demon of exultation and the demon of conceit—
> All of them come down to the demon of conceit.

This thing we call a spirit is in fact the demon of conceit, the belief in a self. Machik also says:

> "The many spirits" means concepts;
> "The powerful spirit" means belief in a self;

---

4. Mind of enlightenment: that is, the desire to achieve enlightenment in order to liberate all beings in the universe from suffering.

"The wild spirits" means thoughts.
To destroy these spirits is to be an adept of Cho.

Jetsun Mila's[5] conversation with the Ogress of the Rock included these words:

Belief in an "I" is more powerful than you are, demoness.
Concepts are more numerous than you are, demoness.
Thoughts are more spoilt by habits than you are, demoness.

He also classified the various kinds of Cho as follows:

Outer Cho is to wander in fearsome places and mountain solitudes;
Inner Cho is to cast away one's body as food;
Absolute Cho is to sever the root once and for all.
I am a yogi who possesses these three kinds of Cho.

All Cho practices are therefore to cut through the belief in a self, which is the root of all ignorance and deluded perceptions. This is what is meant by the line "absolute Cho is to sever the root once and for all." External demons are just deluded perceptions, and as long as you do not destroy your belief in a self, trying to kill them will not put them to death. Beating them will have no effect on them. Trampling them will not crush them. Chasing after them will not make them go away. Unless you sever the root, which is the conceit within you, you will no more be able to annihilate the illusory spirits which are its external manifestation than get rid of smoke without putting out the fire. The Ogress of the Rock told Jetsun Mila:

If you don't know that demons come from your own mind,
There'll be other demons besides myself!
I'm not going to leave just because you tell me to go.

and Jetsun Mila said:

Take a demon as a demon and it'll harm you;
Know a demon's in your mind and you'll be free of it;
Realize a demon to be empty and you'll destroy it.

And again:

You who appear as harmful spirits and yakshas,[6] male or female,
Only when one has no understanding are you demons,
Bringing all your mischief and your obstacles.
But once one understands, even you demons are deities,
And become the source of all accomplishments.

Cho does not mean killing, thrashing, casting out, crushing and destroying demons, but cutting away the root of any belief in them from within. We must understand that the thing to be destroyed is not outside; it is within us.

Generally speaking, most other religious traditions teach an aggressive approach to outer hostile forces and external creators of obstacles, using the sharpness, severity and power of violent methods, the points of arrows and spears, all directed outwards. But our tradition is as Jetsun Mila says:

---

5. That is, Milarepa (1040–1123).   6. Nonhuman beings, nature spirits.

> My system is to cut out the belief in a self at the root, to cast
> the eight ordinary concerns to the winds, and to make the four
> demons feel ashamed.

Direct all your practice inwards and mobilize all your strength, skill and
powers against the belief in a self that dwells within you. To say, "Eat me! Take
me away!" once is a hundred times better than crying, "Protect me! Save me!"
To offer yourself as food to a hundred spirits is better than calling on a hundred protection deities for help.

> We entrust the sick to the demons.
> We rely on our enemies to guide us.
> One "Devour me! Carry me off!"
> Is better than "Protect me! Save me!" hundreds of times.
> This is the venerable Mother's[7] tradition.

If you cut your belief in demons at the root from within, you will perceive
everything as pure, and, as the saying goes:

> Demons change into Dharma protectors, and those protectors'
> faces change into the face of the nirmanakaya.

People today who claim to be practitioners of Cho do not understand any of
this, and persist in thinking of spirits as something outside themselves.
They believe in demons, and keep on perceiving them all the time; in everything that happens they see some ghost or *gyalgong*.[8] They have no peace of
mind themselves, and are always bewildering others with their lies, delivered with much assertive blustering:

"There's a ghost up there! And down there, too, a spirit! That's a ghost!
That's a demon! That's a *tsen*![9] I can see it . . . Ha!—I've got it, I've killed it!
Watch out, there's one lying in wait for you! I've chased it away! There—it
looked back!"

Spirits and pretas know what such people are up to, and follow them around
wherever they go. They might take possession of women who fall easily into
trances, for example, and convincingly proclaim all sorts of things: "I am a
god," "I am a ghost," "I am your old father," "I am your old mother," and so on.
Sometimes they announce, "I am the deity, I am a Dharma protector. I am
Damchen,"[1] and speak of supernatural visions or make false predictions.

Demons fool the lamas and the lamas fool their patrons, or, as the saying
goes, "The son fools his father while enemies fool the son." These are manifest signs of the degenerate age, and show that the demons are taking over.
As the Great Master of Uddiyana[2] prophesied:

> In the decadent age, male spirits will enter men's hearts;
> Female spirits will enter women's hearts;
> Goblins will enter children's hearts;
> Samaya-breakers will enter the clergy's hearts.
> There will be a spirit in every single Tibetan's heart.

---

7. That is, Machik Labdron.
8. A kind of demon.
9. A kind of demon.
1. A deity who protects Buddhism.

2. Padmasambhava, the Indian tantric master
who visited Tibet in the 8th century; he was said
to be from the kingdom of Uddiyana.

And:

> When goblins are taken for gods, a time of suffering will come upon Tibet.

These prophecies have come to pass.

Do not be taken in by that false perception that makes gods, spirits and obstacle-makers appear outside you; that would only reinforce it. Train yourself to see everything as a dream-like display or an illusion. The phenomena of spirits on the one hand and sick people on the other, appearing momentarily as aggressor and victim, both arise from the negative actions and distorted perceptions which link them together in that way. Do not take sides, do not love the one and hate the other. Generate the love and compassion of bodhichitta towards both. Sever at the root all your self-concern and belief in an "I," and give your body and life to the spirits as food without holding back. Pray from the depths of your heart that these beings may take an interest in the true Dharma and pacify their hatred and maliciousness, and then explain the teachings.

When you finally cut through all belief in the duality of aggressor and victim, deities and demons, self and others—and all the resulting concepts of hope and fear, attachment and hatred, good and bad, pleasure and pain—you will find, as it is said:

> Neither deity, nor demon: the confidence of the view.
> Neither distraction, nor fixation: the vital point of the meditation.
> Neither acceptance, nor rejection: the vital point of the action.
> Neither hope, nor fear: the vital point of the result.

When all concepts of anything to be cut and anyone to do the cutting dissolve into the expanse of absolute reality where all things are equal, the inner harmful spirit of conceit is severed at the root. That is the sign that you have realized the absolute and ultimate Cho.

> *I understand that there is no self, but still have gross concepts of "I."*
> *I have decided to renounce duality, but am beset by hopes and fears.*
> *Bless me and all those like me who believe in a self*
> *That we may realize the natural state, the absence of self.*

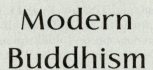

Modern
Buddhism

Unlike the titles of the other sections in this anthology, this one is not a standard term used in the study of Buddhism, nor is it an academic specialty. Unlike the others, this section is named not after a place but a time. The "modern" is always a rather vague label: here, we might say that it denotes the period from the middle of the nineteenth century to the present. What happened during this period to warrant a separate selection of texts?

The nineteenth century was not the first time that Europeans encountered Buddhism. Marco Polo had visited the court of Kublai Khan in the thirteenth century. The Roman Catholic saint Francis Xavier visited Japan in the sixteenth century, and his fellow Jesuit, Matteo Ricci, donned the robes of a Buddhist monk in China some years later. But it was during the nineteenth century that much of Buddhist Asia came under the control, or the threat of control, of the Western powers, especially Britain and France. Among these powers, two attitudes toward Buddhism coexisted: on the one hand, a general denigration of the Buddhist present as a form of superstition and idolatry; on the other hand, a general exaltation of the Buddhist past—especially as it had existed in India—as an ethical philosophy rivaling that of ancient Greece. The former attitude was found largely in the

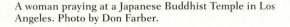

A woman praying at a Japanese Buddhist Temple in Los Angeles. Photo by Don Farber.

Buddhist lands of Asia, where colonial officials and Christian missionaries encountered Buddhism. The latter attitude was common in the universities of Europe, where philologists learned to read Buddhist scriptures in Sanskrit, Pali, Chinese, and Tibetan. In 1844, the French scholar Eugène Burnouf published *Introduction à l'histoire du Buddhisme indien*, regarded as the first European monograph on Buddhism and the foundational text for the academic study of Buddhism in the West.

However, this encounter was not entirely one-sided. Buddhists in Asia learned about Christianity and began to defend themselves against the hostile polemics of missionaries. In 1873, a large public debate took place in Sri Lanka (at that time the British colony of Ceylon) between a Buddhist monk and a Methodist clergyman, as each pointed out the deficiencies in the other's scriptures (e.g., if the Christian God is omniscient, why did the Israelites have to paint blood on their doors to protect their firstborn from his wrath?) and each claimed that his religion was compatible with science. Nineteenth-century philosophies of history and theories of social evolution saw an inevitable advance of humanity upward from the state of primitive superstition to religion, philosophy, and finally science. By asserting that Buddhism was not a religion but a science of the mind, Buddhists, condemned as superstitious idolaters by European missionaries, could jump from the bottom of the evolutionary scale to the top. Indeed, it was during this period that their claims about the compatibility of Buddhism and science were first made— claims that have continued to be voiced, despite the drastic changes in what is meant by both "Buddhism" and "science" over the past century and a half.

In the nineteenth century, scholars in Europe set out on a quest for the historical Buddha, just as they had done for the historical Jesus. Whether they found him or invented him remains an open question, but their representation of the Buddha would become highly influential, not only in the West but in Asia as well. This Buddha was a philosopher who set forth a rational and ethical system by which humans could free themselves from suffering. His philosophy was free of all dogma, ritual, and belief in God. And his was a philosophy that was open to all, regardless of social class or gender. The scholars who painted this portrait were either sons of the French Enlightenment or British or German Protestants, who discerned parallels between what they regarded as the highly mythologized priestcraft of Brahmanism (as Hinduism was then called) and Roman Catholicism. Some went so far as to call the Buddha "the Luther of Asia." This view of the Buddha was accepted by many important Buddhist figures in Asia who were intent on demonstrating the superiority of Buddhism to Christianity, and who adopted a form of "historical criticism" in order to do so. In Thailand, for example, King Mongkut (Rama IV, r. 1851–68), who had spent twenty-seven years as a monk and was a distinguished scholar of Buddhism (unfortunately, remembered in America for little beyond being the historical ruler in *The King and I*), argued that the jatakas or "birth stories," the legends of the Buddha's former lives, should not be included in the canon. Meanwhile, European and American enthusiasts of Buddhism promoted the Buddha in the West and came to the defense of Buddhists in the East; in 1880, Madame Blavatsky and Colonel Olcott, founders of the Theosophical Society, came to Ceylon to lend their support to that island's Buddhists.

Buddhism made a prominent appearance at the World's Parliament of Religions, held in Chicago in 1893, where the Sinhalese activist Anagarika Dharmapala explained the world's debt to the Buddha. Also in attendance was the Zen priest Shaku Soen, who met Paul Carus, the American proponent of the "Religion of Science" and author of *The Gospel of Buddha* (1894). Shaku Soen asked Carus to allow a young student of his, D. T. Suzuki, to work in LaSalle, Illinois, at Carus's Open Court Press. Suzuki would go on to become the leading exponent of Zen Buddhism in English, publishing influential books both before and after World War II. It was largely his work that in the 1950s sparked the interest of Jack Kerouac, Allen Ginsberg, and other artists in Zen. Indeed, in America Zen would remain the primary referent of "Buddhism" until the Vietnam War and its aftermath, which brought a large number of Southeast Asian refugees to the United States. Among them were Buddhist monks, whose performance of the traditional rituals that are the center of Buddhist life drew the attention of Americans fascinated by Buddhism and by a practice rarely performed by Buddhist laypeople in Asia: meditation.

In 1959, the Dalai Lama escaped from Tibet during an uprising against the occupying forces of the People's Liberation Army. Tens of thousands of Tibetans eventually followed him into exile, including prominent monks and lamas of all forms of Tibetan Buddhism. Initially settling in India and Nepal and then moving around the world, they attracted large followings in Europe and America, as well as in Taiwan. The Dalai Lama himself made his first trip to America in 1979; he was awarded the Nobel Peace Prize in 1989 (see his "Nobel Evening Address," p. 781).

Although it was traditionally held that Buddhism could not exist without the presence of an ordained clergy, many of the leaders of modern Buddhism were laypeople and many of the monks who became leaders of Modern Buddhism did not always enjoy the respect, and sometimes not even the recognition, of the monastic establishment. It is one of the characteristics of Modern Buddhism that teachers who gained international celebrity were often marginal figures in their own cultures (the Dalai Lama, Thich Nhat Hanh, and Mahasi Sayadaw being prominent exceptions).

Women have played key roles in the development of Modern Buddhism, which avoids much of the sexism that has traditionally pervaded the Buddhist monastic orders. Yet Modern Buddhism did not reject monastic concerns. Rather, it blurred the boundary between the monk and the layperson, as laypeople took on the vocations of the traditionally elite monks: the study and interpretation of scriptures and the practice of meditation. This focus on silent practice allowed Modern Buddhism generally, and especially in the West, to dismiss the rituals of consecration, purification, expiation, and exorcism so common throughout Asia as extraneous elements. Indeed, the strong emphasis on meditation as the central form of Buddhist practice for all Buddhists, monastic and lay, marked one of the most extreme departures of Modern Buddhism from previous forms; throughout Buddhist history meditation had been the domain of monks, and only one of many vocations within the monastery at that.

It is thus perhaps useful to consider Modern Buddhism not as a universal religion beyond sectarian borders but as itself a Buddhist sect. There is Thai

Buddhism, there is Chinese Buddhism, there is Korean Buddhism, and there is Modern Buddhism. Unlike those national Buddhisms, this new Buddhism is international and does not exclude the embrace of those other forms. Like them, it claims an unbroken connection with the Buddha, especially as a teacher whose message is available to all, regardless of class, ethnicity, or language. And like other Buddhist sects, Modern Buddhism has its own lineage, its own doctrines, its own practices, and its own canon, selections from which appear here.

BUDDHISM COMES TO CHICAGO

THE WORLD'S DEBT TO BUDDHA

ANAGARIKA DHARMAPALA

In 1893, the city of Chicago hosted the World's Columbian Exposition to celebrate, a year late, the four hundredth anniversary of Christopher Columbus's "discovery of America." The event included some two hundred congresses, which drew more than seven hundred thousand people over the course of the year. This was the setting for the World's Parliament of Religions, organized by John Henry Barrows, minister of the First Presbyterian Church of Chicago. Between September 11 and 27, attendees heard 194 papers delivered. The vast majority (152) were by English-speaking Christians, but a number of delegates represented non-Christian religions, in interesting proportions: Buddhism (12); Judaism (11); Hinduism (8); Islam (2); Parsee Religion, that is, Indian Zoroastrians (2); Shinto (2); Confucianism (2); Daoism (1); and Jainism (1).

Among the Buddhist delegates, the most popular speaker was Anagarika Dharmapala (1864–1933). He had been born Don David Hewaviratne in Sri Lanka, then a British colony known as Ceylon, into the English-speaking middle class of Colombo. In Christian schools run by Anglican missionaries, he is said to have memorized large portions of the Bible, but his family remained Buddhist. In 1880, still a teenager, he met Helena Petrovna Blavatksy and Colonel Henry Olcott, founders of the Theosophical Society, when they visited Ceylon in support of Buddhism; he later joined the Theosophical Society and worked closely with Colonel Olcott.

In 1881 Hewaviratne changed his name to Dharmapala, "Protector of the Dharma." He sought to establish a new role for Buddhist laypeople, creating the category of the *anagarika*, or wanderer: a layperson who studies texts and meditates, as monks do, but who remains socially active in the world. He saw himself as the exemplar of this category, calling himself Anagarika Dharmapala. In 1891, he helped found the Maha Bodhi Society. One of the organizations stated goals was to restore Bodh Gaya, the site of the Buddha's enlightenment, to Buddhist control (the temple there was managed by Hindu priests); partial restoration did not occur until 1949, some years after Dharmapala's death.

In 1893 he attended the World's Parliament of Religions. His excellent English and Anglican education made him an effective spokesperson for the dharma, as he sought to demonstrate both its affinities with and alleged superiority to Christianity in an address titled "The World's Debt to Buddha." Several versions of the speech exist; the one reproduced here, from the collection *Return to Righteousness* (1965), is regarded as close to the text that captivated the audience on September 18, 1893. A letter to the *St. Louis Observer* reported, "With his black, curly locks thrown back from his broad brow, his keen, clear eye fixed upon the audience, his long brown fingers emphasizing the utterances of his vibrant voice, he looked the very image of a propagandist, and one trembled to know that such a figure stood at the head of the movement to consolidate all the disciples of Buddha and to spread 'the light of Asia' throughout the civilized world." And indeed, Dharmapala would go on to become one of the founding figures of Modern Buddhism.

PRONOUNCING GLOSSARY

Abhidhamma: *a-bi-dam-ma*
Achiravati: *a-chi-ra-va-tee*
Anagarika Dharmapala: *a-na-gah-ree-ka dar-ma-pah-la*
Anguttara Nikaya: *an-gut-ta-ra ni-kah-ya*
Bhikkhu: *bik-ku*
Brahmajala Sutta: *bra-ma-jah-la soot-ta*
Brahmana: *brah-ma-na*
Brahmanavagga: *brah-ma-na-vag-ga*
Chulavedalla Sutta: *chu-la-vay-dal-la soot-ta*
Dhammika Sutta: *dam-mi-ka-soot-ta*
dhyana: *dyah-na*
Gautama: *gau-ta-ma*
Girnar: *gir-nar*
Kalama Sutta: *kah-lah-ma soot-ta*
Kapilavastu: *ka-pi-la-vas tu*
Kapur-dagiri: *kah-pur-da-gi-ri*
Kshatriya: *ksha-tri-ya*
Kulaputta: *ku-la-put-ta*

Lumbini: *lum-bi-nee*
Mahadhamma Samadana Sutta: *ma-hah-dam-ma sa-mah-dah-na soot-ta*
Mahakarunika: *ma-hah-kah-ru-ni-ka*
Mahaparinibbana Sutta: *ma-hah-pa-ri-nib-bah-na soot-ta*
Mahavagga: *ma-hah-vag-ga*
Shakyamuni: *shah-kya-mu-ni*
Samannaphala Sutta: *sa-man-nya-pa-la soot-ta*
Sarabhu: *sa-ra-bu*
Sariputta: *sah-ri-put-ta*
Sigalovada Sutta: *si-gah-lo-vah-da soot-ta*
Shramana: *shra-ma-na*
Sunaparanta: *su-nah-pa-ran-ta*
Sutta: *soot-ta*
Tathagata: *ta-tah-ga-ta*
Tika Nipata: *ti-ka ni-pah-ta*
Upasaka: *u-pah-sa-ka*
Vaishya: *vai-shya*
Vasala Sutta: *va-sa-la soot-ta*

Ancient India, twenty-five centuries ago, was the scene of a religious revolution, the greatest the world has ever seen. Indian society at this time had two large and distinguished religious foundations—the Shramanas and the Brahmanas.[1] Famous teachers arose and with their disciples went among the people preaching and converting them to their respective views. The air was full of a coming spiritual struggle, hundreds of the most scholarly young men of noble families (Kulaputta) leaving their homes in quest of truth, ascetics undergoing the severest mortifications to discover a panacea for the evils of suffering, young dialecticians wandering from place to place engaged in disputations, some advocating scepticism as the best weapon to fight against the realistic doctrines of the day, some a life of pessimism as the nearest way to get rid of existence, some denying a future life. It was a time of deep and many-sided intellectual movements, which extended from the circles of Brahmanical thinkers far into the people at large. The sacrificial priest was powerful then as he is now. He was the mediator between god and man. Monotheism of the most crude type, from fetishism and animism and anthropomorphic deism to transcendental dualism, was rampant. So was materialism, from sexual epicureanism to transcendental nihilism. In the words of Dr. Oldenberg,[2] "when dialectic scepticism began to attack moral ideas,

---

1. Austere wandering monks and brahmins.
2. Hermann Oldenberg (1854–1920), a German scholar of Indology; the quotation is from his influential study, *Buddha* (1881).

when a painful longing for deliverance from the burden of being was met by the first signs of moral decay, Buddha appeared."

". . . . The Saviour of the World,
Prince Siddhartha styled on earth,
In Earth and Heavens and Hells incomparable,
All honoured, Wisest, Best, most Pitiful
The Teacher of Nirvana and the Law."
—*Sir Edwin Arnold's*[3] Light of Asia

THE DAWN OF A NEW ERA

Oriental scholars, who had begun their researches in the domain of Indian literature, in the beginning of this century, were put to great perplexity of thought at the discovery made of the existence of a religion called after Buddha, in the Indian philosophical books. Sir William Jones, H. H. Wilson, and Colebrooke[4] were embarrassed in being unable to identify him. Dr. Marshman, in 1824, said that Buddha was the Egyptian Apis,[5] and Sir William Jones solved the problem by saying that he was no other than the Scandinavian Woden.[6] But in June, 1837, the whole of the obscure history of India and Buddhism was made clear by the deciphering of the rock-cut edicts of Ashoka the Great, in Girnar and Kapur-dagiri, by that lamented archaeologist, James Prinsep;[7] by the translation of the Pali Ceylon History into English, by Turnour;[8] by the discovery of Buddhist Mss. in the temples of Nepal, Ceylon, and other Buddhist countries. In 1844, the "first rational, scientific and comprehensive account of the Buddhist religion" was published by the eminent scholar Eugene Burnouf.[9] The key to the hidden archives of this great religion was presented to the people of Europe by this great scholar, and the inquiry since begun is being carried on by the most thoughtful men of the day.

Infinite is the wisdom of Buddha; boundless is the love of Buddha to all that lives, say the Buddhist scriptures. Buddha is called the Mahakarunika, which means the "All Merciful Lord who has compassion on all that lives." To the human mind Buddha's wisdom and mercy is incomprehensible. The foremost and greatest of his disciples, the blessed Sariputta, even he has acknowledged that he could not gauge the Buddha's wisdom and mercy. Professor Huxley,[1] in his recent memorable lecture on "Evolution and Ethics",

---

3. English poet (1832–1904); *Light of Asia* (1879), a biography of the Buddha in verse, is his best-known work.
4. Three British Orientalists: Jones (1746–1794), Wilson (1786–1860), and Henry Thomas Colebrooke (1765–1837).
5. A sacred bull deity. Joshua Marshman (1768–1837), a British Baptist missionary and Orientalist.
6. King of the Norse gods (Odin).
7. British Indologist and scientist, "lamented" because of his early death. Ashoka (ca. 300–232 B.C.E.), emperor of the Mauryan dynasty of India; some of the inscriptions specifically

mention the Buddha (the places named are in western India and northwest Pakistan, respectively).
8. George Turnour (1799–1843), the Ceylon-born British Orientalist and translator of Pali texts.
9. French Orientalist (1801–1852); the work referred to is *Introduction to the History of Indian Buddhism.*
1. T. H. Huxley (1825–1895), a biologist and popularizer of science; this lecture was delivered in 1893. He refers to the Anglo-Irish philosopher George Berkeley (1685–1753).

delivered at Oxford, speaking of Buddha says, "Gautama got rid of even that shade of a shadow of permanent existence by a metaphysical *tour de force* of great interest to the student of philosophy, seeing that it supplies the wanting half of Bishop Berkeley's well-known idealist argument. It is a remarkable indication of the subtlety of Indian speculation that Gautama should have seen deeper than the greatest of modern idealists." The tendency of enlightened thought of the day all the world over is not towards theology, but philosophy and psychology. The bark of theological dualism is drifting into danger. The fundamental principles of evolution and monism are being accepted by the thoughtful.

History is repeating itself. Twenty-five centuries ago India witnessed an intellectual and religious revolution which culminated in the overthrow of monotheism, priestly selfishness, and the establishment of a synthetic religion, a system of light and thought which was appropriately called Dhamma—Philosophical Religion. All that was good was collected from every source and embodied therein, and all that was bad discarded. The grand personality who promulgated the Synthetic Religion is known as Buddha. For forty-five years He lived a life of absolute purity and taught a system of life and thought, practical, simple, yet philosophical which, makes man active, intelligent, compassionate and unselfish—to realize the fruits of holiness in this life on this earth. The dream of the visionary, the hope of the theologian, was brought in to objective reality. Speculation in the domain of false philosophy and theology ceased, and active altruism reigned supreme.

Five hundred and forty-three years before the birth of Christ, the great being was born in the Royal Lumbini Garden, near the city of Kapilavastu. His mother was Maya, the queen of Raja Shuddhodana of the Solar Race of India. The story of his conception and birth, and the details of his life up to the twenty-ninth year of his age, his great renunciation, his ascetic life, his enlightenment under the great Bo Tree at Buddha Gaya in Middle India, are embodied in that incomparable epic, "The Light of Asia" by Sir Edwin Arnold. I recommend that beautiful poem to all who appreciate a life of holiness and purity.

Six centuries before Jesus of Nazareth walked over the plains of Galilee preaching a life of holiness and purity, the Tathagata[2] Buddha, the enlightened Messiah of the World, with his retinue of Arhats, or holy men, traversed the whole peninsula of India with the message of peace and holiness to the sin-burdened world. Heart-stirring were the words he spoke to the first five disciples at the Deer Park, the Hermitage of saints at Benares.[3]

HIS FIRST MESSAGE

"Open ye your ears, O Bhikkhus,[4] deliverance from death is found, I teach you, I preach the Law. If ye walk according to my teaching, ye shall be partakers in a short time of that for which sons of noble families leave their homes and go to homelessness—the highest end of religious effort: ye shall even in this present life apprehend the truth itself and see it face to face." And then the exalted Buddha spoke thus: "There are two extremes, O Bhikkhus, which

---

2. A title of a buddha (literally, "one who has thus come/gone"); it is the one most often used by the historical Buddha to refer to himself.

3. That is, Varanasi, in northern India.
4. Fully ordained Buddhist monks (Pali).

the truth seekers ought not to follow: the one a life of sensualism which is low, ignoble, vulgar, unworthy and unprofitable; the other the pessimistic life of extreme asceticism, which is painful, unworthy and unprofitable. There is a Middle Path, discovered by the Tathagata, the Messiah—a path which opens the eyes and bestows understanding, which leads to peace of mind, to the higher wisdom, to full enlightenment, to eternal peace. This Middle Path, which the Tathagata has discovered, is the noble Eight-fold Path, *viz.*, Right Knowledge—the perception of the Law of Cause and Effect, Right Thinking, Right Speech, Right Action, Right Profession, Right Exertion, Right Mindfulness, Right Contemplation. This is the Middle Path which the Tathagata has discovered, and it is the path which opens the eyes, bestows understanding, which leads to peace of mind, to the higher wisdom, to perfect enlightenment, to eternal peace."

Continuing his discourse, he said: "Birth is attended with pain, old age is painful, disease is painful, death is painful, association with the unpleasant is painful, separation from the pleasant is painful, the non-satisfaction of one's desires is painful, in short, the coming into existence is painful. This is the Noble Truth of suffering. Verily it is that clinging to life which causes the renewal of existence, accompanied by several delights, seeking satisfaction now here, now there—that is to say, the craving for the gratification of the passions, or the craving for a continuity of individual existences, or the craving for annihilation. This is the Noble Truth of the origin of suffering. And the Noble Truth of the cessation of suffering consists in the destruction of passions, the destruction of all desires, the laying aside of, the getting rid of, the being free from, the harbouring no longer of this thirst. And the Noble Truth which points the way is the Noble Eightfold Path." This is the foundation of the Kingdom of Righteousness, and from that centre at Benares, this message of peace and love was sent abroad to all humanity: "Go ye, O Bhikkhus, and wander forth for the gain of the many, in compassion for the world, for the good, for the gain, for the welfare of gods and men. Proclaim, O Bhikkhus, the doctrine glorious. Preach ye a life of holiness perfect and pure. Go then through every country, convert those not converted. Go therefore, each one travelling alone filled with compassion. Go, rescue and receive. Proclaim that a blessed Buddha has appeared in the world, and that he is preaching the Law of Holiness."

The essence of the vast teachings of the Buddha is:

> The entire obliteration of all that is evil,
> The perfect consummation of all that is good and pure.
> The complete purification of the mind.

The wisdom of the ages embodied in the three Pitakas[5]—the Sutta, Vinaya, Abhidhamma, comprising 84,000 discourses, were all delivered by Buddha during his ministry of forty-five years. To give an elaborate account of this great system within an hour is not in the power of man.

Buddha, in a discourse called the "Brahmajala Sutta", enumerates sixty-two different religious views held by the sectarians.

---

5. Literally, "baskets"—the canon of Buddhism (the discourses, the rules of discipline, and the "higher dharma," that is, works on doctrinal questions).

After having categorically explained these different systems Buddha continues: Brethren, these believers hold doctrines respecting the past or respecting the future, and meditating on previous events or on those which are in futurity, declare a variety of opinions respecting the past and future in sixty-two modes.

"These doctrines are fully understood by the Tathagata Buddha, he knows the causes of their being held and the experiences upon which they are founded, he also knows other things far more excellent than these; but that knowledge has not been derived from sensual impressions. He with knowledge, not derived from the impressions on the senses, is fully acquainted with that by which both the inpressions and their causes become extinct, and distinctly perceiving the production, the cessation, the advantages, the evils, and the extinctions of the sensations, he is perfectly free having no attachments. Brethren, these doctrines of Buddha are profound, difficult to be perceived, hard to be comprehended, tranquillizing, excellent, not attainable by reason, subtle and worthy of being known by the wise. These the Tathagata (Buddha) has ascertained by his own wisdom and publicly makes them known. But the teachings of the other believers are founded on ignorance, their want of perception, their personal experience, and on the fluctuating emotions of those who are under the influence of their passions.

"Brethren, all these modes of teaching respecting the past or the future originate in the sensations experienced by repeated impressions made on the six organs of sensitiveness,[6] on account of these sensations desire is produced, in consequence of desire and attachment to the desired objects, on account of this attachment, reproduction in an existent state, in consequence of this reproduction of existence, birth; in consequence of birth are produced disease, death, sarrow, weeping, pain, grief and discontent."

A systematic study of Buddha's doctrine has not yet been made by Western scholars, hence the conflicting opinions expressed by them at various times. The notion once held by the scholars that it is a system of materialism has been exploded. The positivists of France found it a Positivism; Buchner[7] and his school of materialists thought it was a materialistic system; agnostics found in Buddha an agnostic, and Dr. Rhys Davids,[8] the eminent Pali scholar, used to call him the agnostic philosopher of India; some scholars have found and expressed monotheism therein; Arthur Lillie,[9] another student of Buddhism, thinks it a theistic system; pessimists identify it with Schopenhauer's pessimism, the late Mr. Buckle identified it with pantheism of Fichte;[1] some have found in it a monism; and the latest dictum of Prof. Huxley is that it is an idealism supplying the wanting half of Bishop Berkeley's well-known idealist argument.

In the religion of Buddha is found a comprehensive system of ethics, and a transcendental metaphysics embracing a sublime psychology. To the simple-minded it offers a code of morality, to the earnest student a system of pure thought. But the basic doctrine is the self-purification of man. Spiritual progress is impossible for him who does not lead a life of purity and compassion.

---

6. Eye, nose, tongue, ear, body, and mind.
7. Ludwig Büchner (1824–1899), a German physician and popularizer of 19th-century scientific materialism.
8. British Orientalist (1843–1922), a prominent scholar of early Buddhism.
9. British author of a number of popular books on Buddhism in the late-19th and early-20th centuries.
1. Arthur Schopenhauer (1788–1860) and Johann Gottlieb Fichte (1762–1814) were German philosophers; Henry Thomas Buckle (1821–1862), a British historian.

The rays of the sunlight of truth enter the mind of him who is fearless to examine truth, who is free from prejudice, who is not tied by the sensual passions and who has reasoning faculties to think. One has to be an atheist in the sense employed by Max Muller:[2] "There is an atheism which is unto death, there is another which is the very life-blood of all truth and faith. It is the power of giving up what, in our best, our most honest moments, we know to be no longer true; it is the readiness to replace the less perfect, however dear, however sacred it may have been to us, by the more perfect, however much it may be detested, as yet by the world. It is the true self surrender, the true self sacrifice, the truest trust in truth, truest faith. Without that atheism, no new religion, no reform, no reformation, no resuscitation would ever have been possible; without that atheism, no new life is possible for any one of us."

The strongest emphasis has been put by Buddha on the supreme importance of having an unprejudiced mind before we start on the road of investigation of truth. Prejudice, passion, fear of expression of one's convictions and ignorance are the four biases that have to be sacrificed at the threshold.

To be born as a human being is a glorious privilege, Man's dignity consists in his capability to reason and think and to live up to the highest ideal of pure life, of calm thought, of wisdom without extraneous intervention. In the Samannaphala Sutta, Buddha says that man can enjoy in this life a glorious existence, a life of undivided freedom, or fearlessness and compassionateness. This dignified ideal of manhood may be attained by the humblest, and this consummation raises him above wealth and royalty. "He that is compassionate and observes the law is my disciple", says Buddha.

HUMAN BROTHERHOOD

This forms the fundamental teaching of Buddha; universal love and sympathy with all mankind and with animal life. Every one is enjoined to love all beings as a mother loves her only child and takes care of it, even at the risk of her life. The realization of the idea of brotherhood is obtained when the first stage of holiness is reached; the idea of separateness is destroyed and the oneness of life is recognized. There is no pessimism in the teaching of Buddha, for he strictly enjoins on his holy disciples not even to suggest to others that life is not worth living. On the contrary, the usefulness of life is emphasized for the sake of doing good to self and to humanity.

RELIGION CHARACTERISTIC OF HUMANITY

From the first worshipping savage to the highest type of humanity, man naturally yearns after something higher, and it is for this reason that Buddha inculcated the necessity of self-reliance and independent thought. To guide humanity in the right path a Tathagata (Messiah) appears from time to time.

THE THEISM OF BUDDHISM

Speaking of deity in the sense of a Supreme Creator, Buddha says that there is no such being. Accepting the doctrine of evolution as the only true one, with its corollary, the law of cause and effect, he condemns the idea of creator and strictly forbids inquiry into it as being useless. But a supreme god of the

2. German scholar of comparative philology and Indian religions (1823–1900); the quotation is from his sixth Hibbert lecture, delivered in 1878 and published in *Lectures on the Origin and Growth of Religion as Illustrated by the Religion of India* (1880).

Brahmans and minor gods are accepted; but they are subject to the law of cause and effect.

EVOLUTION AS TAUGHT BY BUDDHA

The teachings of Buddha on this great subject are clear and expansive. We are asked to look upon the cosmos "as a continuous process unfolding itself in regular order in obedience to natural laws. We see in it all, not a warring chaos restrained by the constant interference from without of a wise and beneficent external power, but a vast aggregate of original elements, perpetually working out their own fresh redistribution in accordance with their own inherent energies. He regards the cosmos as an almost infinite collection of material atoms animated by an infinite sum total of energy"—which is called Akasha. We do not postulate that man's evolution began from the protoplasmic stage; but we are asked not to speculate on the origin of life, on the origin of the law of cause and effect etc. So far as this great law is concerned we say that it controls the phenomena of human life as well as those of external nature. The whole knowable universe forms one undivided whole, a "monon" (see Haeckel: Evolution of Men, Vol II, page 455).

IMPORTANCE OF A SERIOUS STUDY OF ALL SYSTEMS OF RELIGION

Buddha promulgated his system of Philosophy after having studied all religions; and in the Brahmajala Sutta sixty-two creeds are discussed. In the Kalama Sutta, Buddha says: "Do not believe in what ye have heard; do not believe in traditions, because they have been handed down for many generations; do not believe in anything because it is rumoured and spoken of by many; do not believe merely because the written statement of some old sage is produced; do not believe in conjectures; do not believe in that as truth to which you have become attached by habit; do not believe merely on the authority of your teachers and elders; after observation and analysis, when it agrees with reason and is conducive to the good and gain of one and all, then accept it and live up to it" (Anguttara Nikaya).

MORAL TEACHINGS OF BUDDHA

To the ordinary householder whose highest happiness consists in being wealthy here and going to heaven hereafter, Buddha inculcated a simple code of morality. The student of Buddha's religion abstains from destroying life, he lays aside the club and the weapon, he is modest and full of pity, he is compassionate and kind to all creatures that have life. He abstains from theft, and he passes his life in honesty and purity of heart. He lives a life of chastity and purity. He abstains from falsehood and injures not his fellow-men by deceit. Putting away slander he abstains from calumny. He is a peacemaker, a speaker of words that make for peace. Whatever word is humane, pleasant to the ear, lovely, reaching to the heart—such are the words he speaks. He abstains from harsh language. He abstains from foolish talk. He abstains from intoxicants and stupefying drugs.

THE HIGHER MORALITY

The advanced student of the religion of Buddha when he has faith in him thinks: "full of hindrances is household life, a path defiled by passion: free as the air is the life of him who has renounced all wordly things. How difficult it is for the man who dwells at home to live the higher life in all its fullness, in all its purity, in all its perfection! Let me then cut off my hair and beard, let me clothe myself in orange-coloured robes, and let me go forth from a household life into the homeless state.

"Then, before long, forsaking his portion of wealth, forsaking his circle of relatives, he cuts off his hair and beard, he clothes himself in the orange coloured robes and he goes into the homeless state. Then he passes a life self-restrained according to the rules of the order of the Blessed One; uprightness is his delight, and he sees danger in the least of those things he should avoid, he encompasses himself with holiness in word and deed, he sustains his life by means that are quite pure: good is his conduct, guarded the door of his senses, mindful and self-possessed, he is altogether happy."

THE LOW AND LYING ARTS

The student of pure religion abstains from earning a livelihood by the practice of low and lying arts, *viz.*, all divination, interpretation of dreams, palmistry, astrology, crystal-gazing, prophesying, charms of all sorts.

UNIVERSAL PITY

Buddha says: "Just as a mighty trumpeter makes himself heard in all the four directions without difficulty; even so of all things that have life, there is not one that the student passes by or leaves aside, but regards them all with mind set free, and deep-felt pity, sympathy, and equanimity. He lets his mind pervade the whole world with thoughts of Love."

THE REALIZATION OF THE UNSEEN

To realize the unseen is the goal of the student of Buddha's teachings, and such a one has to lead an absolutely pure life. Buddha says: "Let him fulfil all righteousness, let him be devoted to that quietude of heart which springs from within, let him not drive back the ecstacy of contemplation, let him look through things, let him be much alone, fulfil all righteousness for the sake of the living and for the sake of the beloved ones that are dead and gone.

PSYCHIC EXPERIMENTS

Thought transference, thought reading, clair-audience, clairvoyance, projection of the sub-conscious self, and all the higher branches of psychical science that just now engage the thoughtful attention of the psychical researches, are within the reach of him who fulfills all righteousness, who is devoted to solitude and contemplation.

THE COMMON APPANAGE OF ALL GOOD MEN

Charity, observance of moral rules, purifying the mind, making others participate in the good work that one is doing, co-operating with others in doing good, nursing the sick, giving gifts to the deserving ones, hearing all that is good and beautiful, making others learn the rules of morality, accepting the law of cause and effect.

PROHIBITED EMPLOYMENTS

Slave dealing, sale of weapons of warfare, sale of poisons, sale of intoxicants, sale of flesh—these are the lowest of all low professions.

FIVE KINDS OF WEALTH

Faith, pure life, receptivity of the mind to all that is good and beautiful, liberality, wisdom—those who possessed these five kinds of wealth in their past incarnations are influenced by the teaching of Buddha.

UNIVERSALISM OF BUDDHA'S TEACHINGS

Buddha says: "He who is faithful and leads the life of a householder and possesses the following four (Dhammas) virtues: truth, justice, firmness, and liberality—such a one does not grieve when passing away, pray ask other teachers and philosophers far and wide whether there is found anything greater than truth, self-restraint, liberality, and forbearance."

THE PUPIL AND TEACHER

The pupil should minister to his teacher. He should rise up in his presence, wait upon him, listen to all that he says with respectful attention, perform the duties necessary for his personal comfort, and carefully attend to his instruction.

The teacher should show affection to his pupil, he trains him in virtue and good manners, carefully instructs him, imparts unto him a knowledge of the science and wisdom of the ancients, speaks well of him to friends and relations and guards him from danger.

THE HONOURABLE MAN

The honourable man ministers to his friends and relatives by presenting gifts, by courteous language, by promoting them as his equals and by sharing with them his prosperity. They should watch over him when he has negligently exposed himself and guard his property when he is careless, assist him in difficulties, stand by him and help to provide for his family.

THE MASTER AND SERVANT

The master should minister to the wants of his servants and dependents. He assigns them labour suitable to their strength, provides for their comfortable support; he attends to them in sickness, causes them to partake of any extraordinary delicacy he may obtain and makes them occasional presents. And the servants should manifest their attachment to the master. They rise before him in the morning and retire later to rest, they do not purloin his property; do their work cheerfully and actively, and are respectful in their behaviour towards him.

RELIGIOUS TEACHERS AND LAYMEN

The religious teachers should manifest their kind feelings towards them; they should dissuade them for vice, excite them to virtuous acts; being desirous of promoting the welfare of all, they should instruct them in the things they had not previously earned; confirm them in the truths they had received and point out to them the way to heaven.

The laymen should minister to the teachers by respectful attention manifested in their words, actions and thoughts; and by supplying them their temporal wants and by allowing them constant access to themselves.

"In this world, generosity, mildness of speech, public spirit and courteous behaviour are worthy of respect in all circumstances and will be valuable in all places."

If these be not possessed, the mother will receive neither honour nor support from the son, neither will the father receive respect or honour.

THE MISSION OF THE BUDDHA

Buddha says: "Know that from time to time a Tathagata is born into the world, fully enlightened, blessed and worthy, abounding in wisdom and goodness, happy with knowledge of the world, unsurpassed as a guide to erring mortals, a teacher of Gods and men, a blessed Buddha. He by himself thoroughly understands and sees, as it were face to face, this universe, the world below with all its spirits, and the worlds above and all creatures, all religious teachers, gods and men, and he then makes his knowledge known to others, the Truth doth he proclaim both in its letter and its spirit, lovely in its origin, lovely in its progress, lovely in its consummation; the higher life doth he proclaim, in all its purity and in all its perfectness."

THE ATTRIBUTES OF BUDDHA

(1) He is absolutely free from all passions, commits no evil, even in secrecy, and is the embodiment of perfection; he is above doing anything wrong.

(2) Without a teacher by self-introspection he has reached the state of supreme enlightenment.

(3) By means of his divine eye he looks back to the remotest past and future, knows the way of emancipation, is accomplished in the three great branches of divine knowledge and has gained perfect wisdom. He is in possession of all psychic powers, is always willing to listen, full of energy, wisdom and dhyana.[3]

(4) He has realised eternal peace of Nirvana and walks in the perfect Path of Virtue.

(5) He knows the three states of existences.

(6) He is incomparable in purity and holiness.

(7) He is teacher of gods and men.

(8) He exhorts gods and men at the proper time according to their individual temperaments.

(9) He is the supremely enlightened teacher and the perfect embodiment of all the virtues he preaches.

The two characteristics of the Buddha are wisdom and compassion.

BUDDHA'S DISCIPLES

Buddha says: "He who is not generous, who is fond of sensuality, who is distressed at heart, who is of uneven mind, who is not reflective, who is not of calm mind, who is discontented at heart, who has no control over his senses— such a disciple is far from me though he is in body near me."

---

3. A state of deep concentration achieved through meditation.

THE COMPASSIONATENESS SHOWN BY BUDDHIST MISSIONARIES

Actuated by the spirit of compassion, the disciples of Buddha have ever been in the forefront of missionary propaganda. The whole of Asia was brought under the influence of the Buddha's law. Never was the religion propagated by force, not a drop of blood has ever been spilt in the name of Buddha. The shrines of Shakyamuni[4] are stainless. The following story is interesting as it shows the nature of the Buddhist missionaries. Punna, the Bhikkhu, before he was sent in his mission to preach to the people of Sunaparanta[5] was warned by Buddha in the following manner:—

"The people of Sunaparanta are exceedingly violent. If they revile, what will you do?"

"I will make no reply."

"And if they strike you?"

"I will not strike in return."

"And if they try to kill you?"

"Death is no evil in itself, many even desire it, to escape from the vanities of life; but I shall take no step either to hasten or to delay the time of my departure."

THE ULTIMATE GOAL OF MAN

The ultimate goal of the perfected man is eternal peace. To show humanity the path on which to realise this state of eternal peace, Buddha promulgated the Noble Eightfold Path. The Nirvana of Buddha is beyond the conception of the ordinary mind. Only the perfected man realizes it. It transcends all human thought. Caught in the vortex of evolution man undergoes changes and is constantly subject to birth and death. The happiness in the highest heaven comes some day to an end. This change, Buddha declared is sorrowful. And until you realize Nirvana you are subject to birth and death. Eternal changefulness in evolution becomes eternal rest. The constantly dissipating energy is concentrated in Nirvanic life. There is no more birth, no more death. It is eternal peace. On earth the purified, perfected man enjoys Nirvana and after the dissolution of the physical body there is no birth in an objective world. The gods see him not; nor does man.

THE ATTAINMENT OF SALVATION

It is by the perfection of self through charity, purity, self-sacrifice, self-knowledge, dauntless energy, patience, truth, resolution, love, and equanimity, that the goal is realised. The final consummation is Nirvana.

The glorious freedom of self—the last words of Buddha—Be ye lamps unto yourselves. Be ye a refuge to yourselves. Betake yourself to no external refuge. Hold fast to the Truth as a lamp. Hold fast as a refuge to the truth. Look not for refuge to any one besides yourselves. Learn ye then, O Bhikkhus, that knowledge have I attained and have declared unto you, and walk ye in it, practice and increase, in order that this path of holiness may last and long endure, for the blessing of many people, to the relief of the world, to the welfare, the blessing, the joy of gods and men. O Bhikkhus, everything that

---

4. Literally, "Sage of the Shakyas"; a title of the Buddha, who was born into the Shakya clan.

5. A country on the west coast of India.

cometh into being is changeth. Strive on unceasingly for the consummation of the highest ideal."

THE SPREAD OF THE RELIGION OF HUMANITY

Two thousand one hundred years ago the whole of Asia came under the influences of the sceptre of one emperor, and he was truly called Asoka, the delight of the gods. His glory was to spread the teachings of the Buddha throughout the world by the force of love, and indeed nobody could say that he had failed. His only son and daughter were made apostles of the gentle creed, and, clad in the orange-coloured robes, they went to Ceylon, converted the king and established Buddhism there. For the first time in the history of civilization the brotherhood of Humanity is recognised, different nations accept one living truth, virtue is enthroned. It was a proud achievement, unprecedented in history since the dawn of civilization. Pure religion recognizing no Deity finds welcome everywhere. There is a grandeur inherent in it, for it does not want to appeal to the selfishness of man. When the human mind reaches a higher state of development, the conception of a Deity becomes less grand. Nearly three hundred millions of people of the great empire of Asoka embrace a system of pure ethics; a social polity is for the first time enunciated. The king sees much that is sinful in the destruction of animals, and therefore "one must not kill any living animal". He declares that at the time when the edict is engraved "three animals only are killed for the royal table, two peafowls and a gazelle. Even these three animals will not be killed in future." Everywhere in his empire, and in the neighbouring kingdoms such as Greece, etc., the king has provided medicines of two sorts, medicine for men and medicine for animals. Wherever useful plants, either for men or for animals were wanting, they have been imported and planted. And along public roads wells have been dug for the use of animals and men. "It is good and proper to render dutiful service to one's father and mother, to friends, to acquaintances and relations; it is good and proper to bestow alms on religious teachers and students of religion, to respect the life of living beings, to avoid prodigality and violent language."

"Thanks to the instructions of the religion spread by the king, there exist today a respect for living creatures, a tenderness towards them, a regard for relations and for teachers, a dutiful obedience to father and mother and obeisance to aged men, such as have not existed for centuries. The teaching of religion is the most meritorious of acts and there is no practice of religion without virtue."

"The practice of virtue is difficult, and those who practice virtue perform what is difficult. Thus in the past there were no ministers of religion, but I have created ministers of religion. They mix with all sects. They bring comfort to him who is in fetters."

"The king ardently desires that all sects may live in all places. All of them equally purpose the subjection of the senses and the purification of the soul; but man is fickle in his attachments. Those who do not bestow ample gifts may yet possess a control over the senses, purity of soul and gratitude and fidelity in their affections, and this is commendable."

"In past times the kings went out for pastimes. These are my pastimes— visits and gifts to teachers, visits to aged men, the distribution of money, visits to the people of the empire, etc."

"There is no gift comparable with the gift of religion."

"The king honours all sects, he propitiates them by alms. But the beloved of the gods attaches less importance to such gifts and honours than to the endeavour to promote their essential moral virtues. It is true the prevalence of essential virtues differs in different sects. But there is a common basis and that is gentleness and moderation in language. Thus one should not exalt one's own sect and decry the others; one should not deprecate them without cause but should render them on every occasion the honour which they deserve. Striving thus, one promotes the welfare of his own sect while serving the others. Whoever from attachment to his own sect, and with a view to promote it, exalts it and decries others, only deals rude blows to his own sect."

"Hence concord alone is meritorious, so that all bear and love to bear the beliefs of each other. All people, whatever their faith may be, should say that the beloved of the gods attaches less importance to gifts and external observances than to the desire to promote essential moral doctrines and mutual respects for all sects. The result of this is the promotion of my own faith and its advancement in the light of religion."

"The beloved of the gods ardently desires security for all creatures, respect for life, peace and kindliness in behaviour. This is what the beloved of the gods considers as the conquest of religion. . . . I have felt an intense joy—such is the happiness which the conquests of religion procure. It is with this object that this religious inscription has been engraved, in order that our sons and grandsons may not think that a new conquest is necessary; that they may not think that conquest by the sword deserves the name of conquest; that they may see in it nothing but destruction and violence; that they may consider nothing as true conquest as the conquest of religion."

In the Eighth Edict the great Emperor says: "I have also appointed ministers of religion in order that they may exert themselves among all sects, monks as well as wordly men. I have also had in view the interest of the clergy, of Brahmans, of religious mendicants, of religious Nirganthas[6] and of various sects among whom my officers work. The ministers exert themselves, each in his corporation, and the ministers of religion work generally among all sects. In this way acts of religion are promoted in the world as well as the practice of religion, viz., mercy and charity, truth and purity, kindness and goodness. The progress of religion among men is secured in two ways, by positive rules and by religious sentiments. Of these two methods that of positive rules is of poor value, it is the inspiration in the heart which best prevails. It is solely by a change in the sentiments of the heart that religion makes a real advance in inspiring a respect for life, and in the anxiety not to kill living beings." Who shall say that the religion of this humane emperor has not endured, and within the two thousand years which have succeeded, mankind has discovered no nobler religion than to promote in this earth "mercy and charity, truth and purity, kindness and goodness."

To what degree has each religion helped the historic evolution of the Race? When Buddhism flourished in India, the arts, sciences and civilization reached their zenith, as witnessed in the edicts and monuments of Ashoka's reign. Hospitals were first founded for man and beast. Missionaries were sent to all parts of the world. Literature was encouraged. Wherever Buddhism has

6. Jains.

gone, the nations have imbibed its spirit, and the people have become gentler and milder. The slaughter of animals and drunkenness ceased, and wars were almost abolished.

WHAT THE BUDDHIST LITERATURE HAS WROUGHT FOR MANKIND

With the advent of Buddhism into Ceylon, and other Buddhist countries, literature flourished, and wherever it went it helped the development of arts and letters. The monasteries became the seats of learning, and the monks in obedience to their Master's will disseminated knowledge among the people.

RELIGION AND THE FAMILY

The Domestic Education of Children, The Marriage Bond—The Sigalovada Sutta lays down the relations of the members of the household to one another.

Parents should: (1) Restrain their children from vice; (2) Train them in virtue; (3) Have them taught arts and sciences; (4) Provide them with suitable wives and husbands; (5) Endow them with an inheritance.

Children should: (1) Support their parents; (2) Perform the proper family duties; (3) Guard their property; (4) Make themselves worthy to be heirs; (5) Honour their memory; The gift of the whole world with all its wealth would be no adequate return to parents for all that they have done.

The Husband should: (1) Treat his wife with respect; (2) Treat his wife with kindness; (3) Be faithful to her; (4) Cause her to be honoured by others; (5) Give her suitable ornaments and clothes.

The Wife should: (1) Order her household aright; (2) Be hospitable to kinsmen and friends; (3) Be chaste; (4) Be a thrifty house-keeper; (5) Show diligence and skill.

BUDDHIST BROTHERHOOD

Buddha was the first to establish the brotherhood without distinction of caste and race. Twenty-four centuries ago he declared, "As the great streams, O disciples, however many they may be, the Ganges, Yamuna, Achiravati, Sarabhu, when they reach the great ocean, lose their old name and their old descent, and bear only one name—the great ocean, so also do the Brahmans, Kshatriyas, Vaishyas, and Shudras,[7] lose their distinctions when they join the brotherhood." The outcaste as well as the prince was admitted to this order. Virtue was the passport, not wealth and rank.

BUDDHA'S EXALTED TOLERANCE

"Bhikkhus, if others speak against me, or speak against my doctrine, or speak against the order, that is no reason why you should be angry, discontented or displeased with them. . . . If you, in consequence thereof, become angry and dissatisfied, you bring yourself into danger. . . . If you become angry and dissatisfied, will you be able to judge whether they speak correctly or incorrectly? 'We shall not, O Lord, be able. . . . If others speak against me you should repudiate the falsehood as being a falsehood, saying, these things are not so, they are not true, these things are not existing amongst us, they are not in us."

---

7. The four castes in traditional Indian society: priests, warriors, merchants, and servants.

"Bhikkhus, if others speak in praise of me, speak in praise of my doctrine, or speak in praise of the order, that is no reason why you should be pleased, gratified, or elated in mind. . . . If you in consequence thereof, be pleased, gratified, or elated in mind, you bring yourselves thereby into danger. The truth should be received by you as being the truth, knowing that these things exist, that they are true, that they exist among you and are seen in you. . . ."

BUDDHISM AND MODERN SCIENCE

Sir Edwin Arnold says: "I have often said, and I shall say again and again, that between Buddhism and modern Science there exists a close intellectual bond. When Tyndall[8] tells us of sounds we cannot hear, and Norman Lockyer of colours we cannot see, when Sir William Thomson and Prof. Sylvester push mathematical investigation to regions almost beyond the calculus, and others, still bolder, imagine and try to grapple a space of four dimensions, what is all these except the Buddhist Maya? And when Darwin shows us life passing onward and upward through a series of constantly improving forms towards the Better and the Best, each individual starting in new existence with the records of bygone good and evil stamped deep and ineffaceably from the old ones, what is this again but Buddhist Doctrine of Karma and Dharma?" Finally, if we gather up all the results of modern research, and look away from the best literature to the largest discovery in physics and the latest word in biology, what is the conclusion—the high and joyous conclusion—forced upon the mind, if not that which renders true Buddhism so glad and so hopeful?

CAN THE KNOWLEDGE OF THE RELIGION BE SCIENTIFIC?

Buddhism is a scientific religion, in as much as it earnestly enjoins that nothing whatever be accepted on faith. Buddha has said that nothing should be believed merely because it is said. Buddhism is tantamount to a knowledge of other sciences.

RELIGION IN ITS RELATION TO MORALS

The highest morality is inculcated in the system of Buddha since it permits freedom of thought and opinion, sets its face against persecution and cruelty, and recognises the rights of animals. Drink, opium, and all that tend to destroy the composure of the mind are discountenanced.

DIFFERENT SCHEMES FOR THE RESTORATION OF FALLEN MAN

It is the duty of the Bhikkhus and of the religious men (Upasakas) not only to be an example of holy life, but continually to exhort their weaker brethren by pointing out the pernicious effects of an evil life, and the gloriousness of a virtuous life, and urge them to a life of purity. The fallen should on no account be neglected; they are to be treated with sympathy.

RELIGION AND SOCIAL PROBLEMS

The basic doctrine of Buddhism is to relieve human suffering. A life of sensual pleasure is condemned, and the conflicts of labour and capital and

8. All those named by Arnold are prominent British scientists: John Tyndall (1820–1893), a physicist; Joseph Norman Lockyer (1836–1920), an astronomer; Sir William Thomson, Lord Kelvin (1824–1907), and James Sylvester (1814–1897), mathematicians; and Charles Darwin (1809–1882), the naturalist who proposed the theory of evolution by natural selection.

other problems which confront Europe are not to be met with in Buddhistic countries. In the Vasala Sutta he who does not look after the poor is called a vasala or low-born man. In the Sigalovada Sutta, Buddha enjoins on men to devote one-fourth of their wealth in the cause of the relief of the needy. In the Mahadhamma Samadana Sutta, Buddha says the poverty of a man is no excuse for his neglect of religion. As the dropsy patient must take bitter medicine, so the poor, notwithstanding their poverty, must lead the religious life which is hard.

RELIGION AND TEMPERANCE

Buddha said: "Man already drunk with ignorance should not add thereto by the inhibition of alcoholic drinks." One of the vows taken by the Buddhist monks and laity runs thus: "I take the vow to abstain from intoxicating drinks because they hinder progress and virtue." Dhammika Sutta says: "The householder that delights in the Law should not indulge in intoxicating drinks, should not cause others to drink, and should not sanction the acts of those who drink, knowing that it results in insanity. The ignorant commit sins in consequence of drunkenness and also make others drink. You should avoid this. It is the cause of demerit, insanity and ignorance—though it be pleasing to the ignorant."

The dangers of modern life originate chiefly from drink and brutality, and in Buddhist countries the law of Karma, based upon the teaching of Buddhism, prohibits the manufacture, sale and use of liquor, and prevents the slaughter of animals for food.

BENEFITS CONFERRED ON WOMEN BY BUDDHISM

The same rights are given to woman as to man. Not the least difference is shown, and perfect equality has been proclaimed. "Woman", Buddha says in the Chulavedalla Sutta and in the Mahavagga, "may attain the highest path of holiness, Arahatship[9] which is open to man."

The inscriptions of Ashoka and the histories of Ceylon, Burma and other Buddhist countries prove this.

LOVE OF COUNTRY AND OBSERVANCE OF LAW

In the Mahaparinibbana Sutta Buddha enjoined love for one's country. "So long as a people meet together in concord and rise in concord and carry out their undertakings in concord, so long as they enact nothing not already established, abrogate nothing that has been already enacted, and act in accordance with the ancient institutions as established in former days, so long as they esteem and honour and revere the elders, so long as no women or girls are detained among them by force or abduction, so long as they honour and revere the shrines in town and country, so long will they be expected not to decline, but to prosper."

THE FRATERNITY OF PEOPLE

As Buddhism acknowledges no caste system, and admits the perfect equality of all men, it proclaims the universal brotherhood. But peoples should agree in the acceptance of the universal virtues. Buddhism advocates universal

---

9. An arahant or arhat is one who has achieved enlightenment and will enter nirvana at death.

peace amongst nations, and deplore war and bloodshed. The rights of smaller tribes and nations for a separate existence should be protected from aggressive warfare. In the Anguttara Nikaya, Tika Nipata, Brahmanavagga, Buddha advocates arbitration instead of war. Buddhism strongly condemns war on the ground of the great losses it brings on humanity. It says that devastation, famine and other such evils have been brought on by war.

BUDDHISM RETURNS TO INDIA

BUDDHA OR KARL MARX

B. R. AMBEDKAR

In India's caste system those subject to the greatest discrimination are the so-called untouchables, groups outside the fourfold caste system. Also labeled "outcastes," they call themselves Dalit (a term meaning "crushed" or "broken").

Bhimrao Ramji Ambedkar (1891–1956), the son of an Indian officer in the British army, was the fourteenth child in an untouchable family in the Indian state of Maharashtra. Rare among his caste, he received a high school education; eventually he went on to study in London and New York, receiving a doctorate from Columbia University. Upon his return to India he worked both for his country's independence from Britain and for the social and political rights of the Dalits. After independence was gained in 1947, he served in the government of the first prime minister, Jawaharlal Nehru, chairing the committee that drafted the constitution. That constitution abolished the caste system but prejudice, especially against the Dalits, persisted.

Seeking a religious identity for untouchables free from the caste prejudice of Hinduism, he considered Islam, Christianity, Sikhism, and Buddhism before choosing the last. He was not the first Dalit figure to do so; in the nineteenth century, a prominent physician in the southern state of Tamil Nadu had argued that the Tamil Dalits were originally Buddhists who had been persecuted by the Hindus for their beliefs.

On October 14, 1956, six weeks before his death, Ambedkar publicly converted to Buddhism in a traditional ceremony conducted by a Burmese monk, taking refuge in the Three Jewels (the Buddha, dharma, and sangha) and receiving the five precepts of the Buddhist layman (not to kill, steal, lie, engage in sexual misconduct, or use intoxicants). Ambedkar himself then gave the refuge and precepts (plus twenty-two vows of his own design) to an audience of 380,000. Millions of others, mostly from low caste and outcaste groups, would follow his example. Today there are some ten million Buddhists in India, constituting less than 1 percent of the population.

For Ambedkar, the Buddha was above all a social reformer. In the following excerpt from his essay "Buddha or Karl Marx," his summary of the teaching of the Buddha in twenty-five points is also a critique of contemporary Hinduism, at whose hands the untouchables had long suffered. Like the other figures in Modern Buddhism, Ambedkar presents the Buddha as a rationalist philosopher and a social reformer, remaining silent about the supernatural qualities that Buddhists have ascribed to him over the centuries. In his materialist reading, Buddhism is focused on this world and the formation of a just society; he does not mention such central Buddhist doctrines as rebirth and the ultimate goal of liberation from it. For Ambedkar, suffering is caused not by a deep ignorance of the nature of reality but by poverty.

Although Ambedkar cites Buddhist scriptures to support his points, he is far more selective than most Buddhist exegetes, ignoring numerous elements of the tradition that do not conform to his vision of a thoroughly modern dharma—one that is fully compatible with the most modern and egalitarian of European reformers. His Buddhist triumphalism includes a social program designed to materially benefit his people. As Buddhists before him had done in using an ancient text to address a contemporary problem, Ambedkar attacked the bigotry of modern Hinduism and the injustices of Indian society by employing not the common arguments of the day from Christianity or Communism, but an ancient Indian tradition that had been all but forgotten in the land of its birth.

PRONOUNCING GLOSSARY

Ashtanga Marga: *ash-tan-ga mahr-ga*   Potthapada: *pot-ta-pah-da*
Maitri: *mai-tree*   Tripitaka: *tri-pi-ta-ka*
Pancha Sila: *pan-cha see-la*

A comparison between Karl Marx and Buddha may be regarded as a joke. There need be no surprise in this. Marx and Buddha are divided by 2,381 years. Buddha was born in 563 B.C.E. and Karl Marx in 1818 C.E. Karl Marx is supposed to be the architect of a new ideology-polity—a new Economic system. The Buddha on the other hand is believed to be no more than the founder of a religion which has no relation to politics or economics. The heading of this essay 'Buddha or Karl Marx' which suggests either a comparison or a contrast between two such personalities divided by such a lengthy span of time and occupied with different fields of thought is sure to sound odd. The Marxists may easily laugh at it and may ridicule the very idea of treating Marx and Buddha on the same level. Marx so modern and Buddha so ancient! The Marxists may say that the Buddha as compared to their master must be just primitive. What comparison can there be between two such persons? What could a Marxist learn from the Buddha? What can Buddha teach a Marxist? None-the-less a comparison between the two is attractive and instructive. Having read both and being interested in the ideology of both a comparison between them just forces itself on me. If the Marxists keep back their prejudices and study the Buddha and understand what he stood for I feel sure that they will change their attitude. It is of course too much to expect that having been determined to scoff at the Buddha they will remain to pray. But this much can be said that they will realize there is something in the Buddha's teaching which is worth their while to take note of.

I. The Creed of the Buddha

The Buddha is generally associated with the doctrine of Ahimsa.[1] That is taken to be the be-all and end-all of his teachings. Hardly anyone knows that what the Buddha taught is something very vast; far beyond Ahimsa. It is therefore necessary to set out in detail his tenets. I enumerate them below as I have understood them from my reading of the Tripitaka:[2]

-----

1. The doctrine of refraining from doing harm to any living being.

2. The canon of Buddhism.

1. Religion is necessary for a free Society.
2. Not every Religion is worth having.
3. Religion must relate to facts of life and not to theories and speculations about God, or Soul or Heaven or Earth.
4. It is wrong to make God the centre of Religion.
5. It is wrong to make salvation of the soul as the centre of Religion.
6. It is wrong to make animal sacrifices to be the centre of Religion.
7. Real Religion lives in the heart of man and not in the Shastras.
8. Man and mortality must be the centre of Religion. If not, Religion is a cruel superstition.
9. It is not enough for Morality to be the ideal of life. Since there is no God it must become the law of life.
10. The function of Religion is to reconstruct the world and to make it happy and not to explain its origin or its end.
11. That the unhappiness in the world is due to conflict of interest and the only way to solve it is to follow the Ashtanga Marga.[3]
12. That private ownership of property brings power to one class and sorrow to another.
13. That it is necessary for the good of Society that this sorrow be removed by removing its cause.
14. All human beings are equal.
15. Worth and not birth is the measure of man.
16. What is important is high ideals and not noble birth.
17. Maitri or fellowship towards all must never be abandoned. One owes it even to one's enemy.
18. Everyone has a right to learn. Learning is as necessary for man to live as food is.
19. Learning without character is dangerous.
20. Nothing is infallible. Nothing is binding forever. Every thing is subject to inquiry and examination.
21. Nothing is final.
22. Every thing is subject to the law of causation.
23. Nothing is permanent or sanatan. Every thing is subject to change. Being is always Becoming.
24. War is wrong unless it is for truth and justice.
25. The victor has duties towards the vanquished.

This is the creed of the Buddha in a summary form. How ancient but how fresh! How wide and how deep are his teachings!

II. The Original Creed of Karl Marx

Let us now turn to the creed of Karl Marx as originally propounded by him. Karl Marx is no doubt the father of modern socialism or Communism but he was not interested merely in propounding the theory of Socialism. That had been done long before him by others. Marx was more interested in proving that his Socialism was scientific. His crusade was as much against the capitalists as it was against those whom he called the Utopian Socialists. He

---

3. The Eight-Fold Path (Sanskrit), explained later in this essay.

disliked them both. It is necessary to note this point because Marx attached the greatest importance to the scientific character of his Socialism. All the doctrines which Marx propounded had no other purpose than to establish his contention that his brand of Socialism was scientific and not Utopian.

By scientific socialism what Karl Marx meant was that his brand of socialism was *inevitable* and *inescapable* and that society was moving towards it and that nothing could prevent its march. It is to prove this contention of his that Marx principally laboured.

Marx's contention rested on the following theses. They were:

  (i)   That the purpose of philosophy is to reconstruct the world and not to explain the origin of the universe.
  (ii) That the forces which shape the course of history are primarily economic.
  (iii) That society is divided into two classes, owners and workers.
  (iv) That there is always a class conflict going on between the two classes.
  (v)   That the workers are exploited by the owners who misappropriate the surplus value which is the result of the workers' labour.
  (vi) That this exploitation can be put an end to by nationalization of the instruments of production i.e. abolition of private property.
  (vii) That this exploitation is leading to greater and greater impoverishment of the workers.
  (viii) That this growing impoverishment of the workers is resulting in a revolutionary spirit among the workers and the conversion of the class conflict into a class struggle.
  (ix) That as the workers outnumber the owners, the workers are bound to capture the State and establish their rule which he called the dictatorship of the proletariate.
  (x)   These factors are irresistible and therefore socialism is inevitable.

I hope I have reported correctly the propositions which formed the original basis of Marxian Socialism. [. . .]⁴

IV. Comparison Between Buddha and Karl Marx

Taking the points from the Marxian Creed which have survived one may now enter upon a comparison between the Buddha and Karl Marx.

On the first point there is complete agreement between the Buddha and Karl Marx. To show how close is the agreement I quote below a part of the dialogue between Buddha and the Brahmin Potthapada.

'Then, in the same terms, Potthapada asked (the Buddha) each of the following questions:

---

4. The bracketed ellipses here and in sections iv and v are in the 2002 volume from which this text was reprinted.

1. Is the world not eternal?
2. Is the world finite?
3. Is the world infinite?
4. Is the soul the same as the body?
5. Is the soul one thing, and the body another?
6. Does one who has gained the truth live again after death?
7. Does he neither live again, nor not live again, after death?'

And to each question the exalted one made the same reply: It was this.
'That too, Potthapada, is a matter on which I have expressed no opinion.'
'But why has the Exalted One expressed no opinion on that?'
(Because) 'This question is not calculated to profit, it is not concerned with (the Dhamma) it does not rebound even to the elements of right conduct, nor to detachment nor to purification from lust, nor to quietude, nor to tranquillisation of the heart, nor to real knowledge, nor to the insight (of the higher stages of the Path), nor to Nirvana. Therefore it is that I express no opinion about it.' [. . .]

V. The Means

We must now come to the means. The means of bringing about Communism which the Buddha propounded were quite definite. The means can be divided into three parts.

Part I consisted in observing the Pancha Silas.[5]

The Enlightenment gave birth to a new gospel which contains the solution of the problem which was haunting him.

The foundation of the New Gospel is the fact that the world was full of misery and unhappiness. It was a fact not merely to be noted but to be regarded as being the first and foremost in any scheme of salvation. The recognition of this fact the Buddha made the starting point of his gospel.

To remove this misery and unhappiness was to him the aim and object of the gospel if it is to serve any useful purpose.

Asking what could be the causes of this misery the Buddha found that there could be only two.

A part of the misery and unhappiness of man was the result of his own misconduct. To remove this cause of misery he preached the practice of the Panch Sila.

The Panch Sila comprised the following observations: (1) To abstain from destroying or causing destruction to any living thing; (2) To abstain from stealing i.e. acquiring or keeping by fraud or violence, the property of another; (3) To abstain from telling untruth; (4) To abstain from lust; (5) To abstain from intoxicating drinks.

A part of the misery and unhappiness of the world was according to the Buddha the result of man's inequity toward man. How was this inequity to be removed? For the removal of man's inequity towards man the Buddha prescribed the Noble Eight-Fold Path. The elements of the Noble Eight-Fold Path are:

---

5. The five precepts (Pali), explained later in this section.

(1) Right views i.e. freedom from superstition; (2) Right aims, high and worthy of the intelligent and earnest men; (3) Right speech i.e. kindly, open, truthful; (4) Right conduct i.e. peaceful, honest and pure; (5) Right livelihood i.e. causing hurt or injury to no living being; (6) Right perseverance in all other seven; (7) Right mindfulness i.e. with a watchful and active mind; and (8) Right contemplation i.e. earnest thought on the deep mysteries of life.

The aim of the Noble Eight-Fold Path is to establish on earth the kingdom of righteousness, and thereby to banish sorrow and happiness from the face of the world [. . .]

Such is the gospel of the Buddha enunciated as a result of his enlightenment to end the sorrow and misery of the world.

It is clear that the means adopted by the Buddha were to convert a man by changing his moral disposition to follow the path voluntarily.

The means adopted by the Communists are equally clear, short and swift. They are (1) Violence and (2) Dictatorship of the Proletariat.

The Communists say that there are only two means of establishing communism. The first is violence. Nothing short of it will suffice to break up the existing system. The other is dictatorship of the proletariat. Nothing short of it will suffice to continue the new system.

It is now clear what are the similarities and differences between the Buddha and Karl Marx. The differences are about the means. The end is common to both.

HOW TO MEDITATE

PRACTICAL VIPASSANA EXERCISES

MAHASI SAYADAW

In the *Discourse on the Establishment of Mindfulness* or *Satipatthana Sutta*, the Buddha describes a meditation practice that he praises as "a direct path for the purification of beings, for the surmounting of sorrow and lamentation, for the disappearance of pain and grief, for the attainment of the true way, for the realization of nirvana." That practice consists of the four "establishments of mindfulness," and in the twentieth century, it enjoyed a revival in Burma. Since then, known as "the Burmese method" or, more commonly, "insight meditation," it has spread around the world, becoming one of the most popular forms of Buddhist meditation, and one that has been adapted to a wide range of therapeutic practices.

The person most responsible for the international popularity of insight meditation was the distinguished Burmese monk and scholar Mahasi Sayadaw (1904–1982). Born in a village in northern Burma, he began his studies at a local monastery at the age of six; he became a novice monk at twelve and a fully ordained monk at nineteen. He pursued his studies of Buddhist scriptures in Mandalay before returning to the countryside, where he served as a teacher at a small monastery. There, he soon met Mingun Jetavan Sayadaw, a famous meditation master, who instructed him in a technique derived from *The Establishment of Mindfulness*. When Mahasi Sayadaw returned to his native village in 1941, he began to teach this method of insight (*vipassana*) meditation to both monastic and lay disciples. In 1947 he was invited by the prime minister of Burma to serve as chief instructor in a new meditation center in the capital, Rangoon. Centers would eventually be established throughout Burma as well as in Thailand, Sri Lanka, Cambodia, and India (where the method particularly attracted European and North American seekers), providing training to hundreds of thousands of people.

It is often the case in Buddhism that a monk will be renowned as either a practitioner or a scholar, but Mahasi Sayadaw was both. His analyses, critical editions of scriptures, and translations of important texts fill more than sixty volumes. He played a prominent role at the Sixth Buddhist Council in 1954 and later taught in Europe and America.

In the selection below, he lays out the method of meditation in clear and straightforward terms. It is useful to compare the instructions here with those provided by the Buddha himself in *The Establishment of Mindfulness*.

PRONOUNCING GLOSSARY

Mahasi Sayadaw: *ma-ha-see sie-ya-daw*
Satipatthana: *sa-ti-pat-tah-na*
uposatha: *u-poh-sa-ta*

vipassana-bhavana: *vi-pas-sa-nah-bah-va-nah*

Part I. Basic Practice

PREPARATORY STAGE

If you sincerely desire to develop contemplation and attain insight in your present life, you must give up worldly thoughts and actions during training. This course of action is for the purification of conduct, the essential preliminary step towards the proper development of contemplation. You must also observe the rules of discipline prescribed for laymen (or for monks, as the case may be) for they are important in gaining insight. For laypeople, these rules comprise the Eight Precepts which Buddhist devotees observe on Holidays (*uposatha*) and during periods of meditation.[1] An additional rule is not to speak with contempt, in jest, or with malice to or about any of the Noble Ones who have attained states of sanctity. If you have done so, then personally apologize to him or her or make the apology through your meditation instructor. If in the past you have spoken contemptuously to a Noble One who is presently unavailable or deceased, confess this offence to your meditation instructor or introspectively to yourself.

The old masters of the Buddhist tradition suggest that you entrust yourself to the Enlightened One, the Buddha, during the training period, for you may be alarmed if it happens that your own state of mind produces unwholesome or frightening visions during contemplation. Also place yourself under the guidance of your meditation instructor, for then he can talk to you frankly about your work in contemplation and give you the guidance he thinks necessary. These are the advantages of placing trust in the Enlightened One, the Buddha, and practicing under the guidance of your instructor. The aim

---

1. The eight Uposatha precepts are abstention from 1) killing, 2) stealing, 3) all sexual intercourse, 4) lying, 5) intoxicants, 6) partaking of solid food and certain liquids after twelve o'clock, noon, 7) abstension from dance, song, music shows (attendance and performance), from the use of perfumes, ornaments, etc., 8) and from using luxurious beds [Sayadaw's note].

of this practice and its greatest benefit is release from greed, hatred and delusion, which are the roots of all evil and suffering. This intensive course in insight training can lead you to such release. So work ardently with this end in view so that your training will be successfully completed. This kind of training in contemplation, based on the foundations of mindfulness, Sati-patthana has been taken by successive Buddhas and noble ones who attained release. You are to be congratulated on having the opportunity to take the same kind of training they had undergone.

It is also important for you to begin your training with a brief contempla-tion on the "Four Protections" which the Enlightened One, the Buddha, offers you for reflection. It is helpful for your psychological welfare at this stage to reflect on them. The subjects of these four protective reflections are the Bud-dha himself, loving kindness, the loathsome aspects of the body, and death.

First, devote yourself to the Buddha by sincerely appreciating his nine chief qualities in this way:

> Truly, the Buddha is holy, fully enlightened, perfect in knowledge and conduct, a welfarer, world-knower, the incomparable leader of men to be tamed, teacher of gods and mankind, the awakened one and Exalted One.

Second, reflect upon all sentient beings as the receivers of your loving kindness be fortified by your thoughts of loving kindness and identify your-self with sentient beings without distinction, thus:

> May I be free from enmity, disease and grief. As I am, so also may my parents, preceptors, teachers, and intimate, indifferent, and inimical beings be free from enmity, disease and grief. May they be released from suffering.

Third, reflect upon the repulsive nature of the body to assist you in diminishing the unwholesome attachment that so many people have for the body. Dwell upon some of its impurities, such as stomach, intestines, phlegm, pus, blood. Ponder these impurities so that the absurd fondness for the body may be eliminated.

The fourth protection for your psychological benefit is to reflect on the phenomenon of ever-approaching death. Buddhist teachings stress that life is uncertain, but death is certain, life is precarious, but death is sure. Life has death as its goal. There is birth, disease, suffering, old age, and eventual death. These are all aspects of the process of existence.

To begin training, take the sitting posture with the legs crossed. You might feel more comfortable if the legs are not interlocked but evenly placed on the ground, without pressing one against the other. If you find that sitting on the floor interferes with contemplation, then sit in a more comfortable way. Now proceed with each exercise in contemplation as described.

BASIC EXERCISE I

Try to keep your mind (but not your eyes) on the abdomen. You will thereby come to know the movements of rising and falling in this region. If these movements are not clear to you in the beginning, then place both hands on the abdomen to feel these rising and falling movements. After a short time the upward movement of inhalation and the downward movement of exhalation will become clear. Then make a mental note, *rising* for the upward movement, *falling* for the downward movement. Your mental note of each movement must be made while it occurs. From this exercise you learn the actual manner of the upward and downward movements of the abdomen. You are not concerned with the form of the abdomen. What you actually perceive is the bodily sensation of pressure caused by the heaving movement of the abdomen. So do not dwell on the form of the abdomen but proceed with the exercise. For the beginner it is a very effective method of developing the faculties of attention, concentration of mind and insight in contemplation. As practice increases the manner of the movements will be clearer.

The ability to know each successive occurrence of the mental and physical processes at each of the six sense organs[2] is acquired only when insight contemplation is fully developed. Since you are a beginner whose attentiveness and power of concentration are still weak, you may find it difficult to keep the mind on each successive rising movement and falling movement as it occurs. In view of this difficulty, you may be inclined to think: "I just don't know how to keep my mind on each of these movements." Then simply remember that this is a learning process. The rising and falling movements of the abdomen are always present and therefore there is no need to look for them.

Actually it is easy for a beginner to keep his or her mind on these two simple movements. Continue with this exercise in full awareness of the abdomen's rising and falling movements. Never verbally repeat the words rising, falling, and do not think of rising and falling as words. Be aware only of the actual process of the rising and falling movement of the abdomen. Avoid deep or rapid breathing for the purpose of making the abdominal movements more distinct, because this procedure causes fatigue that interferes with the practice. Just be totally aware of the movements of rising and falling as they occur in the course of normal breathing.

BASIC EXERCISE II

While occupied with the exercise of observing each of the abdominal movements, other mental activities may occur between the noting of each rising and falling. Thoughts or other mental functions, such as intentions, ideas, imaginings, etc., are likely to occur between each mental note of rising and falling. They cannot be disregarded. A mental note must be made of each as it occurs.

If you imagine something, you must know that you have done so and make a mental note, *imagining*. If you simply think of something, mentally note, *thinking*. If you reflect, *reflecting*. If you intend to do something, *intending*. When the mind wanders from the object of meditation which is the rising and falling of the abdomen, mentally note, *wandering*. Should you imagine you are going to a certain place, note *going*. When you arrive, *arriving*. When, in your thoughts, you meet a person, note *meeting*. Should you speak to him or her, *speaking*. If you imaginarily argue with that person, *arguing*. If you envision or imagine a light or colour, be sure to note *seeing*. A mental vision must be noted on each occurrence of its appearance until it passes away. After its disappearance, continue with the Basic Exercise I, by knowing, being fully aware of each movement of the rising and falling abdomen.

2. Eye, ear, nose, tongue, body, and mind.

Proceed carefully, without slackening. If you intend to swallow saliva while thus engaged, make a mental note *intending*. While in the act of swallowing, *swallowing*. If you intend to spit, *spitting*. Then return to the exercise of noting rising and falling. Suppose you intend to bend the neck, note *intending*. In the act of bending, *bending*. When you intend to straighten the neck, *intending*. In the act of straightening the neck, *straightening*. The neck movements of bending and straightening must be done slowly. After mentally making a note of each of these actions, proceed in full awareness with noticing the movements of the rising and falling abdomen.

BASIC EXERCISE III

Since you must continue contemplating for a long time while in one position, that of sitting or lying down,[3] you are likely to experience an intense feeling of fatigue, stiffness in the body or in the arms and legs. Should this happen, simply keep the knowing mind on that part of the body where such feelings occur and carry on the contemplation, noting *tired* or *stiff*. Do this naturally; that is, neither too fast nor too slow. These feelings gradually become fainter and finally cease altogether. Should one of these feelings become more intense until the bodily fatigue or stiffness of joints is unbearable, then change your position. However, do not forget to make a mental note of *intending*, before you proceed to change position. Each detailed movement must be contemplated in its respective order.

If you intend to lift the hand or leg, make a mental note *intending*. In the act of lifting the hand or leg, *lifting*. Stretching either the hand or the leg, *stretching*. When you bend it, *bending*. When putting it down, *putting*. Should either the hand or leg touch, *touching*. Perform all of these actions in a slow deliberate manner. As soon as you are settled in the new position, resume contemplation in another position keeping to the procedure outlined in this paragraph.

Should an itching sensation be felt in any part of the body, keep the mind on that part and make a mental note, *itching*. Do this in a regulated manner, neither too fast nor too slow. When the itching sensation disappears in the course of full awareness, continue with the exercise of noticing the rising and falling of the abdomen. Should the itching continue and become too strong and you intend to rub the itchy part, be sure to make a mental note, *intending*. Slowly lift the hand, simultaneously noting the actions of *lifting* and *touching* when the hand touches the part that itches. Rub slowly in complete awareness of *rubbing*. When the itching sensation has disappeared and you intend to discontinue rubbing, be mindful by making the usual mental note of *intending*. Slowly withdraw the hand, concurrently making a mental note of the action, *withdrawing*. When the hand rests in its usual place touching the leg, *touching*. Then again devote yourself to observing the abdominal movements.

If there is pain or discomfort, keep the knowing mind on that part of the body where the sensation arises. Make a mental note of the specific sensation as it occurs, such as *painful, aching, pressing, piercing, tired, giddy*. It must be stressed that the mental note must not be forced nor delayed but

---

3. The meditation instructor will explain the sitting position in detail. See also *The Heart of Buddhist Meditation* by Nyanponika Thera (Rider & Co., London), p. 89.

made in a calm and natural manner. The pain may eventually cease or increase. Do not be alarmed if it increases. Firmly continue the contemplation. If you do so, you will find that the pain will almost always cease. But if after a time, the pain has increased and becomes unbearable, you must ignore the pain and continue with the contemplation of rising and falling.

As you progress in mindfulness you may experience sensations of intense pain, stifling or choking sensations, pain such as from the slash of a knife, the thrust of a sharp-pointed instrument, unpleasant sensations of being pricked by sharp needles, or of small insects crawling over the body. You might experience sensations of itching, biting, intense cold. As soon as you discontinue the contemplation you may also feel that these painful sensations cease. When you resume contemplation you will feel them again as soon as you gain in mindfulness. These painful sensations are not to be considered as something wrong. They are not manifestations of disease but are common factors always present in the body and are usually obscured when the mind is normally occupied with more conspicuous objects. When the mental faculties become keener you are more aware of these sensations. With the continued development of contemplation the time will come when you can overcome them and they will cease altogether. If you continue contemplation, firm in purpose, you will not come to any harm. Should you lose courage, become irresolute in contemplation and discontinue for a time, you may encounter these unpleasant sensations again and again as your contemplation proceeds. If you continue with determination you will most likely overcome these painful sensations and may never again experience them in the course of contemplation.

Should you intend to sway the body, then knowingly note *intending*. While in the act of swaying, *swaying*. When contemplating you may occasionally discover the body swaying back and forth. Do not be alarmed; neither be pleased nor wish to continue to sway. The swaying will cease if you keep the knowing mind on the action of swaying and continue to note *swaying* until the action ceases. If swaying increases in spite of your making a mental note of it, then lean against a wall or post or lie down for a while. Thereafter proceed with contemplation. Follow the same procedure if you find yourself shaking or trembling. When contemplation is developed you may sometimes feel a thrill or chill pass through the back or the entire body. This is a symptom of the feeling of intense interest, enthusiasm or rapture. It occurs naturally in the course of good contemplation. When your mind is fixed in contemplation you may be startled at the slightest sound. This takes place because you feel more intensely the effect of sensory impression while in the state of good concentration.

If you are thirsty while contemplating, notice the feeling, *thirsty*. When you intend to stand, *intending*. Then make a mental note of each movement in preparation for standing. Keep the mind intently on the act of standing up, and mentally note, *standing*. When you look forward after standing up straight, note *looking, seeing*. Should you intend to walk forward, *intending*. When you begin to step forward, mentally note each step as *walking, walking*, or *left, right*. It is important for you to be aware of every moment in each step from beginning to end when you walk. Adhere to the same procedure when strolling or when taking a walking exercise. Try to make a mental note of each step in two sections as follows: *lifting, putting, lifting, putting*. When you have obtained sufficient practice in this manner of walking, then try to make a mental note of each step in three sections; *lifting, pushing, putting*; or *up, forward, down*.

When you look at the water tap, or water-pot, on arriving at the place where you are to take a drink, be sure to make a mental note, *looking, seeing*.

> When you stop walking, *walking*.
> When you stretch the hand, *stretching*.
> When the hand touches the cup, *touching*.
> When the hand takes the cup, *taking*.
> When the hand dips the cup into the water, *dipping*.
> When the hand brings the cup to the lips, *bringing*.
> When the cup touches the lips, *touching*.
> Should you feel cold at the touch, *cold*.
> When you swallow, *swallowing*.
> When returning the cup, *returning*.
> Withdrawing the hand, *withdrawing*.
> When you lower your hand, *lowering*.
> When the hand touches the side of the body, *touching*.
> If you intend to turn back, *intending*.
> When you turn around, *turning*.
> When you walk forward, *walking*.
> On arriving at the place where you intend to stop, *intending*.
> When you stop, *stopping*.

If you remain standing for some time, continue the contemplation of rising and falling. But if you intend to sit down, *intending*. When you go forward to sit down, *walking*. On arriving at the place where you will sit, *arriving*. When you turn to sit, *turning*. While in the act of sitting, *sitting*. Sit down slowly, and keep the mind on the downward movement of the body. You must notice every movement in bringing hands and legs into position. Then resume the prescribed exercise of contemplating the abdominal movements.

Should you intend to lie down, *intending*. Then proceed with the contemplation of every movement in the course of lying down: *lifting, stretching, leaving, touching, lying*. Then make every movement the object of contemplation in bringing hands, legs and body into position. Perform these actions slowly. Thereafter, continue with *rising* and *falling*. Should pain, fatigue, itching, or any other sensation be felt, be sure to notice each of these sensations. Notice all feelings, thoughts, ideas, considerations, reflections; all movements of hands, legs, arms, and body. If there is nothing in particular to note, put the mind on the rising and falling of the abdomen. Make a mental note of *drowsy* when drowsy, and *sleepy* when sleepy. After you have gained sufficient concentration in contemplating, you will be able to overcome drowsiness and sleepiness and feel refreshed as a result. Take up again the usual contemplation of the basic object. Suppose you are unable to overcome a drowsy feeling, you must then continue to contemplate until you fall asleep.

The state of sleep is the continuity of subconsciousness. It is similar to the first state of rebirth consciousness and the last state of consciousness at the moment of death. This state of consciousness is feeble and therefore unable to be aware of an object. When you awake, the continuity of subconsciousness occurs regularly between moments of seeing, hearing, tasting, smelling, touching, and thinking. Because these occurrences are of brief duration, they are usually not clear and therefore not noticeable. Continuity of subconsciousness remains during sleep—a fact which becomes obvious when you wake up; for it is in the state of wakefulness that thoughts and objects become distinct.

Contemplation should start at the moment you wake up. Since you are a beginner, it may not yet be possible for you to start contemplating at the very first moment of wakefulness. But you should start with it from the moment when you remember that you are to contemplate. For example, if on awakening you reflect on something, you should become aware of that fact and begin your contemplation by a mental note, *reflecting*. Then proceed with the contemplation of *rising* and *falling*. When getting up from the bed, mindfulness should be directed to every detail of the body's activity. Each movement of the hands, legs, and back must be performed in complete awareness. Are you thinking of the time of day when awakening? If so, note *thinking*. Do you intend to get out of bed? If so, note *intending*. If you prepare to move the body into position for rising, note *preparing*. As you slowly rise, *rising*. When you are in the sitting position, *sitting*. Should you remain sitting for any length of time, revert to contemplating the abdominal movements of rising and falling.

Perform the acts of washing the face or taking a bath in due order and in complete awareness of every detailed movement; for instance, *looking, seeing, stretching, holding, touching, feeling cold, rubbing*. In the acts of dressing, making the bed, opening and closing doors and windows, handling objects, be occupied with every detail of these actions in their order.

You must attend to the contemplation of every detail in the action of eating.

When you look at the food, *looking, seeing*.
When you arrange the food, *arranging*.
When you bring the food to the mouth, *bringing*.
When you bend the neck forwards, *bending*.
When the food touches the mouth, *touching*.
When placing the food in the mouth, *placing*.
When the mouth closes, *closing*.
When withdrawing the hand, *withdrawing*.
Should the hand touch the plate, *touching*.
When straightening the neck, *straightening*.
When in the act of chewing, *chewing*.
When you are aware of the taste, *knowing*.
When swallowing the food, *swallowing*.
While swallowing the food, should the food be felt touching the sides
    of the gullet, *touching*.

Perform contemplation in this manner each time you partake of a morsel of food until you finish the meal. In the beginning of the practice there will be many omissions. Never mind. Do not waver in your effort. You will make fewer omissions if you persist in your practice. When you reach an advanced stage of the practice, you will also be able to notice more details than those stated here.

ADVANCEMENT IN CONTEMPLATION

After having practiced for a day and a night you may find your contemplation considerably improved and that you are able to prolong the basic exercise of noticing the abdominal rising and falling. At this time you will notice that there is generally a break between the movements of rising and falling. If you are in the sitting posture, fill in this pause with a mental note on the act of sitting in this way: *rising, falling, sitting.* When you make a mental note of sitting, keep your mind on the erect position of the upper body. When you are lying down, you should proceed with full awareness as follows: *rising, falling, lying.* If you find this easy, continue with noticing these three sections. Should you notice that a pause occurs at the end of the rising as well as the falling movement, then continue in this manner: *rising, sitting, falling, sitting.* Or when lying down: *rising, lying, falling, lying.* Suppose you no longer find it easy to make a mental note of three or four objects in the above manner, then revert to the initial procedure of noting only the two sections, *rising* and *falling.*

While engaged in the regular practice of contemplating bodily movements, you need not be concerned with objects of seeing and hearing. As long as you are able to keep your mind on the abdominal movements of rising and falling, it is assumed that the purpose of noticing the acts and objects of seeing is also served. However, you may intentionally look at an object, then simultaneously make a mental note, two or three times, *seeing.* Thereafter return to the awareness of the abdominal movements. Suppose some person comes into your view, make a mental note of *seeing,* two or three times, and then resume attention to the rising and falling movements of the abdomen. Did you happen to hear the sound of a voice? Did you listen to it? If so make a mental note of *hearing, listening,* and having done so, revert to *rising* and *falling.* But suppose you heard loud sounds, such as the barking of dogs, loud talking or singing. If so, immediately make a mental note two or three times, *hearing.* Then return to your basic exercise.

If you fail to note and dismiss such distinctive sights and sounds as they occur, you may inadvertently fall into reflections about them instead of proceeding with intense attention to rising and falling, which may then become less distinct and clear. It is by such weakened attention that mind-defiling passions breed and multiply. If such reflections do occur, make two or three mental notes, *reflecting,* and again take up the contemplation of rising and falling. If you forget to make a mental note of body, leg or arm movements, then mentally note *forgetting,* and resume your usual contemplation of the abdominal movements.

You may feel at times that breathing is slow or that the rising and falling movements of the abdomen are not clearly perceived. When this happens, and you are in the sitting position, simply carry on the attention to *sitting, touching*; if you are lying down, *lying, touching.* While contemplating touching, your mind should not be kept on the same part of the body but on different parts successively. There are several places of touch and at least six or seven should be contemplated.

BASIC EXERCISE IV

Up to this point you have devoted quite some time to the training course. You might begin to feel lazy, thinking that you have made inadequate progress. By no means should you give up. Simply note the fact, *lazy.* Before you gain sufficient strength in attention, concentration and insight, you may doubt the correctness or usefulness of this method of training. In such a case turn to contemplation of the thought, *doubtful*. Do you anticipate or wish for good results? If so, make such thoughts the subject of your contemplation: *anticipating*, or *wishing*. Are you attempting to recall the manner in which this training was conducted up to this point? Yes? Then take up contemplation on *recollecting*. Are there occasions when you examine the object of contemplation in order to determine whether it is mind or matter? If so, then be aware of *examining*. Do you regret that there is no improvement in your contemplation? If so, then attend to that feeling of *regret*. Conversely, are you happy that your contemplation is improving? If you are, then contemplate the feeling of *being happy*.

This is the way in which you make a mental note of every item of mental behaviour as it occurs, and if there are no intervening thoughts or perceptions to note, you should revert to the contemplation of rising and falling. During a strict course of meditation, the time of practice is from the first moment you wake up until you fall asleep. To repeat, you must be constantly occupied either with the basic exercise or with mindful attention throughout the day and during those night hours when you are not asleep. There must be no relaxation. Upon reaching a certain stage of progress in contemplation, you will not feel sleepy in spite of these prolonged hours of practice. On the contrary, you will be able to continue the contemplation day and night.

SUMMARY

It has been emphasized during this brief outline of the training that you must contemplate on each mental occurrence good or bad, on each bodily movement large or small, on every sensation (bodily or mental feeling) pleasant or unpleasant, and so on. If, during the course of training, occasions arise when there is nothing special to contemplate upon, be fully occupied with attention to the rising and falling of the abdomen. When you have to attend to any kind of activity that necessitates walking, then, in complete awareness, each step should be briefly noted as *walking, walking* or *left, right*. But when you are taking a walking exercise, contemplate on each step in three sections *up, forward, down*. The student who thus dedicates himself to the training day and night will be able in not too long a time to develop concentration to the initial stage of the fourth degree of insight (knowledge of arising and passing away) and onward to higher stages of insight meditation (*vipassana-bhavana*).

SAN FRANCISCO ZEN

ZEN MIND, BEGINNER'S MIND

SHUNRYU SUZUKI

Buddhism has come to America by many routes. One mode of transmission has been Buddhist clerics sent from Asia to serve as priests to a local immigrant population, performing funeral rites and officiating at the ceremonies of the ritual year. In some cases, the presence of such clerics is discovered by those outside their community, and the monk (celibate Buddhist cleric) or priest (married cleric) is asked to teach these Americans to do what Buddhist laypeople traditionally do not do: meditate. Perhaps the most influential of these clerics was Shunryu Suzuki (1904–1971), founder of the San Francisco Zen Temple.

He was born in a village near Tokyo, the son of a poor Zen priest. After elementary school, Suzuki went to live at a temple run by a disciple of his father and was ordained as a novice monk in 1917; he later attended Komazawa University in Tokyo, a university of the Soto sect of Zen, graduating in 1930. His training continued at the head temple of the sect, Eiheiji, founded by Dogen (see the *Shobogenzo*, p. 625) in 1246, becoming priest of his father's temple (in 1932) before moving on to the post of head priest at the larger temple of Rinso-in. He married in 1935 and spent the war years at his temple. Unlike many Japanese Buddhist priests, Suzuki did not actively support the war, although his temple was used to house soldiers, Korean laborers, and children displaced by the bombing of Tokyo. When the war ended, he took on the standard duties of the Zen priest in modern Japan: performing services for the dead and running a kindergarten at his temple. In 1952, Suzuki's wife was brutally murdered by a mentally unbalanced Zen priest. After seeing to the education of his children, he accepted an offer by the headquarters of the Soto sect to serve as priest at a Japanese American Zen temple in San Francisco (located in a former synagogue at 1881 Bush Street). He arrived on March 23, 1959, and began performing religious services for a community of some sixty families. His arrival happened to coincide with the Zen craze in San Francisco, especially among members of what has come to be called the "Beat movement." He was invited by American enthusiasts to provide instruction in Zen meditation, and soon a group began gathering at the temple each morning for forty minutes of zazen (seated meditation). In 1963, he ordained an American student as a Zen priest. Suzuki continued to serve as priest to the Japanese community until 1969, when the tensions between his Japanese parishioners and his American disciples became too great: he then resigned from his original position and moved to the newly founded San Francisco Center at 300 Page Street.

The Buddhism of Suzuki Roshi (as his students called him) was very different from that of another more famous Suzuki, D. T. Suzuki (1870–1966), whose more cerebral form of Zen appealed to a number of artists and poets in the middle decades of the twentieth century. His seminars at Columbia University from 1951 to 1957 were attended by Jack Kerouac, Allen Ginsberg, John Cage, and Erich Fromm, among others. Though Suzuki Roshi was a relatively ordinary Zen priest, his simple teachings and emphasis on zazen, not on striving for enlightenment, attracted a devoted following. In 1970, the year before his death, an edited version of some of Suzuki's lectures were published as *Zen Mind, Beginner's Mind*. Some excerpts from that classic of American Zen are provided here.

PRONOUNCING GLOSSARY

Dogen-zenji: *doh-gehn-zehn-jee*

Eiheiji: *ay-hay-jee*

hara-kiri: *hah-rah-kee-ree*

Hideyoshi: *hee-deh-yoh-shee*

Sen no Rikyu: *sehn noh ree-kyoo*

Shunryu Suzuki: *shoon-ree-yu soo-zoo-kee*

Yoshitsune: *yoh-shee-tsoo-neh*

Control

'To give your sheep or cow a large, spacious meadow is the way
to control him.'

To live in the realm of Buddha nature means to die as a small being, moment after moment. When we lose our balance we die, but at the same time we also develop ourselves, we grow. Whatever we see is changing, losing its balance. The reason everything looks beautiful is because it is out of balance, but its background is always in perfect harmony. This is how everything exists in the realm of Buddha nature, losing its balance against a background of perfect balance. So if you see things without realizing the background of Buddha nature, everything appears to be in the form of suffering. But if you understand the background of existence, you realize that suffering itself is how we live, and how we extend our life. So in Zen sometimes we emphasize the imbalance or disorder of life.

Nowadays traditional Japanese painting has become pretty formal and lifeless. That is why modern art has developed. Ancient painters used to practice putting dots on paper in artistic disorder. This is rather difficult. Even though you try to do it, usually what you do is arranged in some order. You think you can control it, but you cannot; it is almost impossible to arrange your dots out of order. It is the same with taking care of your everyday life. Even though you try to put people under some control, it is impossible. You cannot do it. The best way to control people is to encourage them to be mischievous. Then they will be in control in its wider sense. To give your sheep or cow a large, spacious meadow is the way to control him. So it is with people: first let them do what they want, and watch them. This is the best policy. To ignore them is not good; that is the worst policy. The second worst is trying to control them. The best one is to watch them, just to watch them, without trying to control them.

The same way works for you yourself as well. If you want to obtain perfect calmness in your zazen,[1] you should not be bothered by the various images you find in your mind. Let them come, and let them go. Then they will be under control. But this policy is not so easy. It sounds easy, but it requires some special effort. How to make this kind of effort is the secret of practice. Suppose you are sitting under some extraordinary circumstances. If you try to calm your mind you will be unable to sit, and if you try not to be disturbed, your effort will not be the right effort. The only effort that will help you is to count your breathing, or to concentrate on your inhaling and exhaling. We say concentration, but to concentrate your mind on something is not the true purpose of Zen. The true purpose is to see things as they are, to observe things as they are, and to let everything go as it goes. This is to put everything under control in its widest sense. Zen practice is to open up our small mind. So concentrating is just an aid to help you realize 'big mind,' or the mind that is everything. If you want to discover the true meaning of Zen in your everyday life, you have to understand the meaning of keeping your mind on your breathing and your body in the right posture in zazen. You should follow the rules of practice and your study should become more subtle and careful. Only in this way can you experience the vital freedom of Zen.

1. Seated meditation.

Dogen-zenji[2] said, 'Time goes from present to past.' This is absurd, but in our practice sometimes it is true. Instead of time progressing from past to present, it goes backwards from present to past. Yoshitsune was a famous warrior who lived in medieval Japan. Because of the situation of the country at that time, he was sent to the northern provinces, where he was killed. Before he left he bade farewell to his wife, and soon after she wrote in a poem, 'Just as you unreel the thread from a spool, I want the past to become present.' When she said this, actually she made the past time present. In her mind, the past became alive and *was* the present. So as Dogen said, 'Time goes from present to past.' This is not true in our logical mind, but it is in the actual experience of making past time present. There we have poetry, and there we have human life.

When we experience this kind of truth it means we have found the true meaning of time. Time constantly goes from past to present and from present to future. This is true, but it is also true that time goes from future to present and from present to past. A Zen master once said, 'To go eastward one mile is to go westward one mile.' This is vital freedom. We should acquire this kind of perfect freedom.

But perfect freedom is not found without some rules. People, especially young people, think that freedom is to do just what they want, that in Zen there is no need for rules. But it is absolutely necessary for us to have some rules. But this does not mean always to be under control. As long as you have rules, you have a chance for freedom. To try to obtain freedom without being aware of the rules means nothing. It is to acquire this perfect freedom that we practice zazen.

Mind Waves

'Because we enjoy all aspects of life as an unfolding of big mind,
we do not care for any excessive joy. So we have imperturbable composure.'

When you are practicing zazen, do not try to stop your thinking. Let it stop by itself. If something comes into your mind, let it come in, and let it go out. It will not stay long. When you try to stop your thinking, it means you are bothered by it. Do not be bothered by anything. It appears as if something comes from outside your mind, but actually it is only the waves of your mind, and if you are not bothered by the waves, gradually they will become calmer and calmer. In five or at most ten minutes, your mind will be completely serene and calm. At that time your breathing will become quite slow, while your pulse will become a little faster.

It will take quite a long time before you find your calm, serene mind in your practice. Many sensations come, many thoughts or images arise, but they are just waves of your own mind. Nothing comes from outside your mind. Usually we think of our mind as receiving impressions and experiences from outside, but that is not a true understanding of our mind. The true understanding is that the mind includes everything; when you think something comes from outside it means only that something appears in your mind. Nothing outside yourself can cause any trouble. You yourself make the waves

2. The founder of the Soto sect of Japanese Buddhism (1200–1253; see *Treasury of the True Dharma Eye*, p. 625); *zenji* is a title meaning "Zen master."

in your mind. If you leave your mind as it is, it will become calm. This mind is called big mind.

If your mind is related to something outside itself, that mind is a small mind, a limited mind. If your mind is not related to anything else, then there is no dualistic understanding in the activity of your mind. You understand activity as just waves of your mind. Big mind experiences everything within itself. Do you understand the difference between the two minds: the mind which includes everything, and the mind which is related to something? Actually they are the same thing, but the understanding is different, and your attitude towards your life will be different according to which understanding you have.

That everything is included within your mind is the essence of mind. To experience this is to have religious feeling. Even though waves arise, the essence of your mind is pure; it is just like clear water with a few waves. Actually water always has waves. Waves are the practice of the water. To speak of waves apart from water or water apart from waves is a delusion. Water and waves are one. Big mind and small mind are one. When you understand your mind in this way, you have some security in your feeling. As your mind does not expect anything from outside, it is always filled. A mind with waves in it is not a disturbed mind, but actually an amplified one. Whatever you experience is an expression of big mind.

The activity of big mind is to amplify itself through various experiences. In one sense our experiences coming one by one are always fresh and new, but in another sense they are nothing but a continuous or repeated unfolding of the one big mind. For instance, if you have something good for breakfast, you will say, 'This is good.' 'Good' is supplied as something experienced some time long ago, even though you may not remember when. With big mind we accept each of our experiences as if recognizing the face we see in the mirror as our own. For us there is no fear of losing this mind. There is nowhere to come or to go; there is no fear of death, no suffering from old age or sickness. Because we enjoy all aspects of life as an unfolding of big mind, we do not care for any excessive joy. So we have imperturbable composure, and it is with this imperturbable composure of big mind that we practice zazen.

[. . .]³

Bowing

'Bowing is a very serious practice. You should be prepared to bow, even
in your last moment. Even though it is impossible to get rid of our
self-centered desires, we have to do it. Our true nature wants us to.'

After zazen we bow to the floor nine times. By bowing we are giving up ourselves. To give up ourselves means to give up our dualistic ideas. So there is no difference between zazen practice and bowing. Usually to bow means to pay our respects to something which is more worthy of respect than ourselves. But when you bow to Buddha you should have no idea of Buddha, you just become one with Buddha, you are already Buddha himself. When you become

---

3. The bracketed ellipses here and in the following section indicate omitted chapters and are in the 2002 volume from which this text was reprinted.

one with Buddha, one with everything that exists, you find the true meaning of being. When you forget all your dualistic ideas, everything becomes your teacher, and everything can be the object of worship.

When everything exists within your big mind, all dualistic relationships drop away. There is no distinction between heaven and earth, man and woman, teacher and disciple. Sometimes a man bows to a woman; sometimes a woman bows to a man. Sometimes the disciple bows to the master; sometimes the master bows to the disciple. A master who cannot bow to his disciple cannot bow to Buddha. Sometimes we may bow to cats and dogs.

In your big mind, everything has the same value. Everything is Buddha himself. You see something or hear a sound and there you have everything just as it is. In your practice you should accept everything as it is, giving to each thing the same respect given to a Buddha. Here there is Buddhahood. Then Buddha bows to Buddha, and you bow to yourself. This is the true bow.

If you do not have this firm conviction of big mind in your practice, your bow will be dualistic. When you are just yourself, you bow to yourself in its true sense, and you are one with everything. Only when you are you yourself can you bow to everything in its true sense. Bowing is a very serious practice. You should be prepared to bow even in your last moment; when you cannot do anything except bow you should do it. This kind of conviction is necessary. Bow with this spirit and all the precepts, all the teachings are yours, and you will possess everything within your big mind.

Sen no Rikyu, the founder of the Japanese tea ceremony, committed *hara-kiri* (ritual suicide by disembowelment) in 1591 at the order of his lord, Hideyoshi. Just before Rikyu took his own life he said, 'When I have this sword there is no Buddha and no Patriarchs.'[4] He meant that when we have the sword of big mind, there is no dualistic world. The only thing which exists is this spirit. This kind of imperturbable spirit was always present in Rikyu's tea ceremony. He never did anything in just a dualistic way; he was ready to die in each moment. In ceremony after ceremony he died, and he renewed himself. This is the spirit of the tea ceremony. This is how we bow.

My teacher had a callous on his forehead from bowing. He knew he was an obstinate, stubborn fellow, and so he bowed and bowed and bowed. The reason he bowed was that inside himself he always heard his master's scolding voice. He had joined the Soto order when he was thirty, which for a Japanese priest is rather late. When we are young we are less stubborn, and it is easier to get rid of our selfishness. So his master always called my teacher 'You-lately-joined-fellow,' and scolded him for joining so late. Actually his master loved him for his stubborn character. When my teacher was seventy, he said, 'When I was young I was like a tiger, but now I am like a cat!' He was very pleased to be like a cat.

Bowing helps to eliminate our self-centered ideas. This is not so easy. It is difficult to get rid of these ideas, and bowing is a very valuable practice. The result is not the point; it is the effort to improve ourselves that is valuable. There is no end to this practice.

Each bow expresses one of the four Buddhist vows. These vows are: 'Although sentient beings are innumerable, we vow to save them. Although our evil desires are limitless, we vow to be rid of them. Although the teaching is

4. That is, masters in the Zen tradition of Buddhism.

limitless, we vow to learn it all. Although Buddhism is unattainable, we vow to attain it.' If it is unattainable, how can we attain it? But we should! That is Buddhism.

To think, 'Because it is possible we will do it,' is not Buddhism. Even though it is impossible, we have to do it because our true nature wants us to. But actually, whether or not it is possible is not the point. If it is our inmost desire to get rid of our self-centered ideas, we have to do it. When we make this effort, our inmost desire is appeased and Nirvana is there. Before you determine to do it, you have difficulty, but once you start to do it, you have none. Your effort appeases your inmost desire. There is no other way to attain calmness. Calmness of mind does not mean you should stop your activity. Real calmness should be found in activity itself. We say, 'It is easy to have calmness in inactivity, it is hard to have calmness in activity, but calmness in activity is true calmness.'

After you have practiced for a while, you will realize that it is not possible to make rapid, extraordinary progress. Even though you try very hard, the progress you make is always little by little. It is not like going out in a shower in which you know when you get wet. In a fog, you do not know you are getting wet, but as you keep walking you get wet little by little. If your mind has ideas of progress, you may say, 'Oh, this pace is terrible!' But actually it is not. When you get wet in a fog it is very difficult to dry yourself. So there is no need to worry about progress. It is like studying a foreign language; you cannot do it all of a sudden, but by repeating it over and over you will master it. This is the Soto way of practice. We may say either that we make progress little by little, or that we do not even expect to make progress. Just to be sincere and make our full effort in each moment is enough. There is no Nirvana outside our practice.

[. . .]

Zen and Excitement

'Zen is not some kind of excitement, but concentration on
our everyday routine.'

My master died when I was thirty-one. Although I wanted to devote myself just to Zen practice at Eiheiji monastery, I had to succeed my master at his temple. I became quite busy, and being so young I had many difficulties. These difficulties gave me some experience, but it meant nothing compared with the true, calm, serene way of life.

It is necessary for us to keep the constant way. Zen is not some kind of excitement, but concentration on our usual everyday routine. If you become too busy and too excited, your mind becomes rough and ragged. This is not good. If possible, try to be always calm and joyful and keep yourself from excitement. Usually we become busier and busier, day by day, year by year, especially in our modern world. If we revisit old, familiar places after a long time, we are astonished by the changes. It cannot be helped. But if we become interested in some excitement, or in our own change, we will become completely involved in our busy life, and we will be lost. But if your mind is calm and constant, you can keep yourself away from the noisy world even though you are in the midst of it. In the midst of noise and change, your mind will be quiet and stable.

Zen is not something to get excited about. Some people start to practice Zen just out of curiosity, and they only make themselves busier. If your practice makes you worse, it is ridiculous. I think that if you try to do zazen once a week, that will make you busy enough. Do not be too interested in Zen. When young people get excited about Zen they often give up schooling and go to some mountain or forest in order to sit. That kind of interest is not true interest.

Just continue in your calm, ordinary practice and your character will be built up. If your mind is always busy, there will be no time to build, and you will not be successful, particularly if you work too hard on it. Building character is like making bread—you have to mix it little by little, step by step, and moderate temperature is needed. You know yourself quite well, and you know how much temperature you need. You know exactly what you need. But if you get too excited, you will forget how much temperature is good for you, and you will lose your way. This is very dangerous.

Buddha said the same thing about the good ox driver. The driver knows how much load the ox can carry, and he keeps the ox from being overloaded. You know your way and your state of mind. Do not carry too much! Buddha also said that building character is like building a dam. You should be very careful in making the bank. If you try to do it all at once, water will leak from it. Make the bank carefully and you will end up with a fine dam for the reservoir.

Our unexciting way of practice may appear to be very negative. This is not so. It is a wise and effective way to work on ourselves. It is just very plain. I find this point very difficult for people, especially young people, to understand. On the other hand it may seem as if I am speaking about gradual attainment. This is not so either. In fact, this is the sudden way, because when your practice is calm and ordinary, everyday life itself is enlightenment.

AN AMERICAN SUTRA

SMOKEY THE BEAR SUTRA

GARY SNYDER

Scholars of Buddhism apply the label "Buddhist apocrypha" to texts composed outside of India that claim to be the words of Indian Buddhist masters, including the Buddha himself. Some of these writings have become highly influential; *The Awakening of Faith* (p. 503), a Chinese work purportedly by Ashvaghosha, immediately comes to mind. An entire genre central to Tibetan Buddhism is made up of the *terma*, or "treasure texts," which according to tradition were composed by the eighth-century Indian master Padmasambhava and buried in the soil of Tibet, each to be unearthed at the appropriate moment in the future. One might argue, indeed, that a reliable sign that Buddhism has spread to yet another land is that works attributed to the Buddha are composed there. If that be the case, Buddhism has come to America.

Gary Snyder (b. 1930) was born in San Francisco and raised on a farm outside Seattle, Washington; he attended Reed College in Portland, Oregon, where he studied literature and anthropology. Inspired by D. T. Suzuki's *Essays in Zen Buddhism* (3 vols., 1927–34), he taught himself to meditate, finding time to practice Zen meditation while working as a fire lookout in the forests of Washington State. In 1952, he enrolled in the Department of Oriental Languages at the University of California at Berkeley to study Chinese and Japanese. He would later meet Allen Ginsberg and Jack Kerouac in San Francisco, and he participated in the legendary poetry reading at Six Gallery in 1955, when Ginsberg first read his most famous poem, *Howl*. This group of poets, known to history as the Beats, had a strong interest in Zen—and much of that interest was informed by Snyder, who was the model for the character Japhy in Kerouac's 1958 novel *The Dharma Bums*.

Snyder traveled to Japan in 1956, returning again in 1958 to spend seven years practicing meditation at a Zen monastery in Kyoto, Daitokuji. He went back to the United States in 1966 and the following year participated in the first Be-In in Golden Gate Park. Over the course of his long career, his work and his poetry have reflected his commitment both to Buddhism, especially Zen, and to the environment. The two themes unite in this sutra, in which the Buddha predicts that in the future he will appear in the American West in the form of a brown bear wearing a broad-brimmed hat.

Once in the Jurassic about 150 million years ago, the Great Sun Buddha in this corner of the Infinite Void gave a discourse to all the assembled elements and energies: to the standing beings, the walking beings, the flying beings, and the sitting beings—even the grasses, to the number of thirteen billion, each one born from a seed, assembled there: a Discourse concerning Enlightenment on the planet Earth.

"In some future time, there will be a continent called America. It will have great centers of power called such as Pyramid Lake, Walden Pond, Mt. Rainier, Big Sur, Everglades, and so forth; and powerful nerves and channels such as Columbia River, Mississippi River, and Grand Canyon. The human race in that era will get into troubles all over its head, and practically wreck everything in spite of its own strong intelligent Buddha-nature."

"The twisting strata of the great mountains and the pulsings of volcanoes are my love burning deep in the earth. My obstinate compassion is schist and basalt and granite, to be mountains, to bring down the rain. In that future American Era I shall enter a new form; to cure the world of loveless knowledge that seeks with blind hunger: and mindless rage eating food that will not fill it."

And he showed himself in his true form of

SMOKEY THE BEAR

A handsome smokey-colored brown bear standing on his hind legs, showing that he is aroused and watchful.

Bearing in his right paw the Shovel that digs to the truth beneath appearances; cuts the roots of useless attachments, and flings damp sand on the fires of greed and war;

His left paw in the mudra of Comradely Display—indicating that all creatures have the full right to live to their limits and that of deer, rabbits, chipmunks, snakes, dandelions, and lizards all grow in the realm of the Dharma;

Wearing the blue work overalls symbolic of slaves and laborers, the countless men oppressed by a civilization that claims to save but often destroys;

Wearing the broad-brimmed hat of the west, symbolic of the forces that guard the wilderness, which is the Natural State of the Dharma and the true path of man on Earth:

all true paths lead through mountains—

With a halo of smoke and flame behind, the forest fires of the kali-yuga,[1] fires caused by the stupidity of those who think things can be gained and lost whereas in truth all is contained vast and free in the Blue Sky and Green Earth of One Mind;

Round-bellied to show his kind nature and that the great earth has food enough for everyone who loves her and trusts her;

Trampling underfoot wasteful freeways and needless suburbs, smashing the worms of capitalism and totalitarianism;

Indicating the task: his followers, becoming free of cars, houses, canned foods, universities, and shoes, master the Three Mysteries of their own Body, Speech, and Mind; and fearlessly chop down the rotten trees and prune out the sick limbs of this country America and then burn the leftover trash.

Wrathful but calm. Austere but Comic. Smokey the Bear will Illuminate those who would help him; but for those who would hinder or slander him . . .

---

1. In Hindu cosmology, the darkest of the four ages that follow one another in succession.

HE WILL PUT THEM OUT.

Thus his great Mantra:

Namah samanta vajranam chanda maharoshana Sphataya hum traka ham mam

"I DEDICATE MYSELF TO THE UNIVERSAL DIAMOND BE THIS RAGING FURY BE DESTROYED"

And he will protect those who love the woods and rivers, Gods and animals, hobos and madmen, prisoners and sick people, musicians, playful women, and hopeful children:

And if anyone is threatened by advertising, air pollution, television, or the police, they should chant SMOKEY THE BEAR'S WAR SPELL:

DROWN THEIR BUTTS

CRUSH THEIR BUTTS

DROWN THEIR BUTTS

CRUSH THEIR BUTTS

And SMOKEY THE BEAR will surely appear to put the enemy out with his vajra-shovel.[2]

Now those who recite this Sutra and then try to put it in practice will accumulate merit as countless as the sands of Arizona and Nevada.

Will help save the planet Earth from total oil slick.
Will enter the age of harmony of man and nature.
Will win the tender love and caresses of men, women, and beasts.
Will always have ripened blackberries to eat and a sunny spot under a pine tree to sit at.

AND IN THE END WILL WIN HIGHEST PERFECT ENLIGHTENMENT

. . . thus we have heard . . .

(may be reproduced free forever)

---

2. A vajra is a kind of mythical thunderbolt, a weapon capable of cutting through anything.

BUDDHIST MONK WINS NOBEL PEACE PRIZE

THE NOBEL EVENING ADDRESS

THE DALAI LAMA

Among the Buddhist traditions of Asia, the institution of the incarnate lama is unique to Tibetan Buddhism. Yet it is a logical extension of a central tenet of Mahayana Buddhism: that buddhas and bodhisattvas appear in the world in order to benefit suffering sentient beings. Tibet developed systems for identifying such enlightened masters, finding the next incarnations of recently deceased teachers in young boys. Beginning perhaps in the eleventh century, this institution of the incarnate lama became the primary mechanism for passing the power and property, both real and symbolic, of a distinguished monk from one generation to the next. There were eventually several thousand incarnate lamas in Tibet, the most famous of whom is the Dalai Lama.

The first Dalai Lama was identified in the fifteenth century, a disciple of Tsong kha pa. The name *dalai*, a Mongolian word meaning "ocean," was not used until the sixteenth century, when a Tibetan lama named Sonam Gyatso ("Merit Ocean") was called "Dalai Lama" by a Mongol khan. The fifth Dalai Lama assumed political control of Tibet in 1642, with the help of his Mongol patrons, and from then until 1959 the Dalai Lama was the Tibetan head of state (during his minority, the nation was ruled by a regent). Also since that time, the Dalai Lama has been regarded as the human incarnation of the bodhisattva of compassion, Avalokiteshvara, who is said to have vowed to protect the Tibetan people throughout history.

The current Dalai Lama, the fourteenth, was born in 1935. Tibet was invaded by China in 1950 and the Dalai Lama fled to India following an uprising against the Chinese occupation in 1959. He has lived in exile in India ever since, gaining popularity as a Buddhist teacher while working for the freedom of Tibet. He made his first trip to the United States in 1979 and has become an increasingly important figure in Modern Buddhism, often discussing the importance of Buddhist principles for the modern world, exploring the compatibility of Buddhism and science, and working for world peace. In 1989 he was awarded the Nobel Peace Prize for his efforts.

In his Nobel lecture, delivered a day after he accepted the award, the term "Buddhism" rarely appears. Yet his words are imbued with Mahayana teachings of compassion and concern for the welfare of others. His starting point is the common Buddhist belief that all beings seek happiness and avoid suffering, and that all beings equally deserve to find happiness and avoid suffering. Compassion, defined as the wish that others be free from suffering, is therefore not only a requirement for the bodhisattva in his quest for the exalted state of buddhahood but also a real and universal human responsibility beyond any particular religious affiliation, or the lack of one. For the Dalai Lama, compassion is a quality that all humans possess, yet it must be transformed from ordinary affection if it is to form the foundation of human interaction and human society—in particular, policies of nonviolence.

The Dalai Lama closes his 1989 remarks with a discussion of his hopes for a resolution of the Tibetan crisis, envisioning Tibet as a "zone of peace" between India and China. As this anthology is printed, more than two decades later, the Tibetan crisis remains unresolved.

Oslo, Norway

Brothers and Sisters:

It is a great honor to come to this place and to share some of my thoughts with you. Although I have written a speech, it has already been circulated. You know, some of my friends told me it is better to speak in Tibetan and have it translated into English; some say it is better to read my English statement; and some say it is better to speak directly with my broken English. I don't know. Yesterday, I tried my best to be formal but today I feel more free, so I will speak informally. In any case, the main points of my speech are on paper for you to see.

I think it advisable to summarize some of the points that I will consider. I usually discuss three main topics. Firstly, as a human being, as a citizen of the world, every human being has a responsibility for the planet. Secondly, as a Buddhist monk, I have a special connection with the spiritual world. I try to contribute something in that field. Thirdly, as a Tibetan I have a responsibility to the fate of the Tibetan nation. On behalf of these unfortunate people, I will speak briefly about their concerns.

So now, firstly, what is the purpose of life for a human being? I believe that happiness is the purpose of life. Whether or not there is a purpose to the existence of the universe or galaxies, I don't know. In any case, the fact is that we are here on this planet with other human beings. Then, since every human being wants happiness and does not want suffering, it is clear that this desire does not come from training, or from some ideology. It is something natural. Therefore, I consider that the attainment of happiness, peace, and joy is the purpose of life. Therefore, it is very important to investigate what are happiness and satisfaction and what are their causes.

I think that there is a mental factor as well as a physical factor. Both are very important. If we compare these two things, the mental factor is more important, superior to the physical factor. This we can know through our daily life. Since the mental factor is more important, we have to give serious thought to inner qualities.

Then, I believe compassion and love are necessary in order for us to obtain happiness or tranquility. These mental factors are key. I think they are the best source. What is compassion? From the Buddhist viewpoint there are different varieties of compassion. The basic meaning of compassion is not just a feeling of closeness, or just a feeling of pity. Rather, I think that with genuine compassion we not only feel the pains and suffering of others but we also have a feeling of determination to overcome that suffering. One aspect of compassion is some kind of determination and responsibility. Therefore, compassion brings us tranquility and also inner strength. Inner strength is the ultimate source of success.

When we face some problem, a lot depends on the personal attitude towards that problem or tragedy. In some cases, when one faces the difficulty, one loses one's hope and becomes discouraged and then ends up depressed. On the other hand, if one has a certain mental attitude, then tragedy and suffering bring one more energy, more determination.

Usually, I tell our generation we are born during the darkest period in our long history. There is a big challenge. It is very unfortunate. But if there is a challenge then there is an opportunity to face it, an opportunity to demonstrate our will and our determination. So from that viewpoint I think that our generation is fortunate. These things depend on inner qualities, inner strength. Compassion is very gentle, very peaceful, and soft in nature, not harsh. You cannot destroy it easily as it is very powerful. Therefore, compassion is very important and useful.

Then, again, if we look at human nature, love and compassion are the foundation of human existence. According to some scientists, the foetus has feeling in the mother's womb and is affected by the mother's mental state. Then the few weeks after birth are crucial for the enlarging of the brain of the child. During that period, the mother's physical touch is the greatest factor for the healthy development of the brain. This shows that the physical needs some affection to develop properly.

When we are born, our first action is sucking milk from the mother. Of course, the child may not know about compassion and love, but the natural feeling is one of the closeness toward the object that gives milk. If the mother is angry or has ill feeling, the milk may not come fully. This shows that from our first day as human beings the effect of compassion is crucial.

If unpleasant things happen in our daily life, we immediately pay attention to them but do not notice other pleasant things. We experience these as normal or usual. This shows that compassion and affection are part of human nature.

Compassion or love has different levels; some are more mixed than others with desire or attachment. For example, parents' attitudes toward their children contain a mixture of desire and attachment with compassion. The love and compassion between husband and wife—especially at the beginning of marriage when they don't know the deep nature of each other—are on a superficial level. As soon as the attitude of one partner changes, the attitude of the other becomes opposite to what it was. That kind of love and compassion is more of the nature of attachment. Attachment means some kind of feeling of closeness projected by oneself. In reality, the other side may be very negative, but due to one's own mental attachment and projection, it appears as something nice. Furthermore, attachment causes one to exaggerate a small good quality and make it appear 100% beautiful or 100% positive. As soon as the mental attitudes change, that picture completely changes. Therefore, that kind of love and compassion is, rather, attachment.

Another kind of love and compassion is not based on something appearing beautiful or nice, but based on the fact that the other person, just like oneself, wants happiness and does not want suffering and indeed has every right to be happy and to overcome suffering. On such a basis, we feel a sense of responsibility, a sense of closeness towards that being. That is true compassion. This is because the compassion is based on reason, not just on emotional feeling. As a consequence, it does not matter what the other's attitude is, whether negative or positive. What matters is that it is a human being, a sentient being that has the experience of pain and pleasure. There is no reason not to feel compassion so long as it is a sentient being.

The kinds of compassion at the first level are mixed, interrelated. Some people have the view that some individuals have a very negative, cruel attitude towards others. These kinds of individuals appear to have no compassion in their minds. But I feel that these people do have the seed of compassion. The reason for this is that even these people very much appreciate it when someone else shows them affection. A capacity to appreciate other people's affection means that in their deep mind there is the seed of compassion.

Compassion and love are not man-made. Ideology is man-made, but these things are produced by nature. It is important to recognize natural qualities, especially when we face a problem and fail to find a solution. For example, I feel that the Chinese leaders face a problem which is in part due to their own ideology, their own system. But when they try to solve that problem through their own ideology then they fail to tackle that problem. In religious business, sometimes even due to religion, we create a problem. If we try to solve that problem using religious methods, it is quite certain that we will not succeed. So I feel that when we face those kind of problems, it is important to return to our basic human quality. Then I think we will find that solutions come easier. Therefore, I usually say that the best way to solve human problems is with human understanding.

It is very important to recognize the basic nature of humanity and the value of human qualities. Whether one is educated or uneducated, rich or poor, or belongs to this nation or that nation, this religion or that religion, this ideology or that ideology, is secondary and doesn't matter. When we return to this basis, all people are the same. Then we can truly say the words *brother, sister*; then they are not just nice words—they have some meaning. That kind of motivation automatically builds the practice of kindness. This gives us inner strength.

What is my purpose in life, what is my responsibility? Whether I like it or not, I am on this planet, and it is far better to do something for humanity. So you see that compassion is the seed or basis. If we take care to foster compassion, we will see that it brings the other good human qualities. The topic of compassion is not at all religious business; it is very important to know that it is human business, that it is a question of human survival, that it is not a question of human luxury. I might say that religion is a kind of luxury. If you have religion, that is good. But it is clear that even without religion we can manage. However, without these basic human qualities we cannot survive. It is a question of our own peace and mental stability.

Next, let us talk about the human being as a social animal. Even if we do not like other people, we have to live together. Natural law is such that even bees and other animals have to live together in cooperation. I am attracted to bees because I like honey—it is really delicious. Their product is something that we cannot produce, very beautiful, isn't it? I exploit them too much, I think. Even these insects have certain responsibilities, they work together very nicely. They have no constitution, they have no law, no police, nothing, but they work together effectively. This is because of nature. Similarly, each part of a flower is not arranged by humans but by nature. The force of nature is something remarkable. We human beings, we have constitutions, we have law, we have a police force, we have religion, we have many things. But in actual practice, I think that we are behind those small insects.

Sometimes civilization brings good progress, but we become too involved with this progress and neglect or forget about our basic nature. Every development in human society should take place on the basis of the foundation of the human nature. If we lost that basic foundation, there is no point in such developments taking place.

In cooperation, working together, the key thing is the sense of responsibility. But this cannot be developed by force as has been attempted in eastern Europe and in China. There a tremendous effort has to be made to develop in the mind of every individual human being a sense of responsibility, a concern for the common interest rather than the individual interest. They aim their education, their ideology, their efforts to brainwash, at this. But their means are abstract, and the sense of responsibility cannot develop. The genuine sense of responsibility will develop only through compassion and altruism.

The modern economy has no national boundaries. When we talk about ecology, the environment, when we are concerned about the ozone layer, one individual, one society, one country cannot solve these problems. We must work together. Humanity needs more genuine cooperation. The foundation for the development of good relations with one another is altruism, compassion, and forgiveness. For small arguments to remain limited, in the human circle the best method is forgiveness. Altruism and forgiveness are the basis for bringing humanity together. Then no conflict, no matter how serious, will go beyond the bounds of what is truly human.

I will tell you something. I love friends, I want more friends. I love smiles. That is a fact. How to develop smiles? There are a variety of smiles. Some smiles are sarcastic. Some smiles are artificial—diplomatic smiles. These smiles do not produce satisfaction, but rather fear or suspicion. But a genuine smile gives us hope, freshness. If we want a genuine smile, then first we produce the basis for a smile to come. On every level of human life, compassion is the key thing.

Now, on the question of violence and non-violence. There are many different levels of violence and non-violence. On the basis of external action, it is difficult to distinguish whether an action is violent or non-violent. Basically, it depends on the motivation behind the action. If the motivation is negative, even though the external appearance may be very smooth and gentle, in a deeper sense the action is very violent. On the contrary, harsh actions and words done with a sincere, positive motivation are essentially non-violent. In other words, violence is a destructive power. Non-violence is constructive.

When the days become longer and there is more sunshine, the grass becomes fresh and, consequently, we feel very happy. On the other hand, in autumn, one leaf falls down and another leaf falls down. These beautiful plants become as if dead and we do not feel very happy. Why? I think it is because deep down our human nature likes construction, and does not like destruction. Naturally, every action which is destructive is against human nature. Constructiveness is the human way. Therefore, I think that in terms of basic human feeling, violence is not good. Non-violence is the only way.

Practically speaking, through violence we may achieve something, but at the expense of someone else's welfare. That way although we may solve one problem, we simultaneously seed a new problem. The best way to solve problems is through human understanding, mutual respect. On one side make some concessions; on the other side take serious consideration about the problem. There may not be complete satisfaction, but something happens. At least future danger is avoided. Non-violence is very safe.

Before my first visit to Europe in 1973, I had felt the importance of compassion, altruism. On many occasions I expressed the importance of the sense of universal responsibility. Sometimes during this period, some people felt that the Dalai Lama's idea was a bit unrealistic. Unfortunately, in the Western world Gandhian non-violence is seen as passive resistance more suitable to the East. The Westerners are very active, demanding immediate results, even in the course of daily life. But today the actual situation teaches non-violence to people. The movement for freedom is non-violent. These recent events reconfirm to me that non-violence is much closer to human nature.

Again, if there are sound reasons or bases for the points you demand, then there is no need to use violence. On the other hand, when there is no sound reason that concessions should be made to you but mainly your own desire, then reason cannot work and you have to rely on force. Thus, using force is not a sign of strength but rather a sign of weakness. Even in daily human contact, if we talk seriously, using reasons, there is no need to feel anger. We can argue the points. When we fail to prove with reason, then anger comes. When reason ends, then anger begins. Therefore, anger is a sign of weakness.

In this, the second part of my talk, I speak as a Buddhist monk. As a result of more contact with people from other traditions, as time passes I have firmed my conviction that all religions can work together despite fundamental differences in philosophy. Every religion aims at serving humanity. Therefore, it is possible for the various religions to work together to serve humanity and contribute to world peace. So, during these last few years, at every opportunity I try to develop closer relations with other religions.

Buddhism does not accept a theory of god, or a Creator. According to Buddhism, one's own actions are the creator, ultimately. Some people say that, from a certain angle, Buddhism is not a religion but rather a science of mind. Religion has much involvement with faith. Sometimes it seems that there is quite a distance between a way of thinking based on faith and one entirely based on experiment, remaining sceptical. Unless you find something through investigation, you do not want to accept it as fact. From one viewpoint, Buddhism is a religion, from another viewpoint Buddhism is a science of mind and not a religion. Buddhism can be a bridge between these two sides. Therefore, with this conviction I try to have closer ties with scientists, mainly in the fields of cosmology, psychology, neurobiology, physics. In these fields there are insights to share, and to a certain extent we can work together.

Thirdly, I will speak on the Tibetan problem. One of the crucial, serious situations is the Chinese population transfer into Tibet. If the present situation continues for another ten or fifteen years, the Tibetans will be an insignificant minority in their own land, a situation similar to that in inner Mongolia. There the native population is around three million and the Chinese population is around ten million. In East Turkestan, the Chinese population is increasing daily. In Tibet, the native population is six million, whereas the Chinese population is already around seven and one-half million. This is really a serious matter.

In order to develop a closer understanding and harmony between the Chinese and Tibetan—the Chinese call it the unity of the motherland—the first thing necessary to provide the basis for the development of mutual respect is demilitarization, first to limit the number of Chinese soldiers and eventually to remove them altogether. This is crucial. Also, for the purposes of peace in that region, peace and genuine friendship between India and China, the two most populated nations, it is very essential to reduce military forces on both sides of the Himalayan range. For this reason, one point that I have made is that eventually Tibet should be a zone of ahimsa,[1] a zone of non-violence.

Already there are clear indications of nuclear dumping in Tibet and of factories where nuclear weapons are produced. This is a serious matter. Also, there is deforestation, which is very dangerous for the environment. Respect for human rights is also necessary. These are the points I expressed in my Five-Point Peace Plan.[2] These are crucial matters.

We are passing through a most difficult period. I am very encouraged by your warm expression and by the Nobel Peace Prize. I thank you from the depth of my heart.

1. The doctrine of refraining from doing harm to any living being.

2. Proposed by the Dalai Lama in a 1987 address to the U.S. Congressional Human Rights Caucus.

APPENDICES

APPENDICES

Glossary

Words in SMALL CAPS are defined in their own entries.

abhidharma (Sanskrit, "superior doctrine," or perhaps "pertaining to the doctrine"). The genre of Buddhist literature that consists of detailed technical analysis of the constituents of experience and the functions of consciousness (sometimes translated "metaphysics").

aggregates, the. *See* SKANDHAS.

Amitabha (Sanskrit, "Infinite Light"). The BUDDHA who presides over the PURE LAND of Sukhavati, to which he vowed to lead all beings who call upon him. Venerated by all MAHAYANA schools, he is the focus of PURE LAND BUDDHISM.

apocrypha. In Buddhism, texts composed outside of India that are purportedly the words of Indian Buddhist masters, including the BUDDHA himself.

arhat / arahant. (Sanskrit / Pali, "worthy one"). Someone who has destroyed all causes for future rebirth and will enter NIRVANA at death. Because arhats seek only their own liberation from suffering, the MAHAYANA extols the ideal of the BODHISATTVA over that of the arhat.

arya (Sanskrit, "noble one"). Someone who has achieved at least the first of the FOUR STAGES OF THE PATH to NIRVANA.

asura (Sanskrit). A demigod.

atman (Sanskrit). A permanent self; according to the BUDDHA, no such self exists.

Avalokiteshvara (Sanskrit, "the lord who looks down"). The BODHISATTVA regarded as the embodiment of all the compassion of all the BUDDHAS.

avidya (Sanskrit, "ignorance"). A misunderstanding of the true nature of things, especially the nature of the person; one of the afflictions (*KLESHAS*) that cause suffering.

bardo (Tibetan). The intermediate state between death and rebirth; this period can last up to forty-nine days.

bhavana (Sanskrit, "causing to be," "cultivation"). A common term for meditation.

bhikshu / bhikkhu (Sanskrit / Pali, "beggar"). A fully ordained Buddhist monk.

bhikshuni / bhikkhuni (Sanskrit / Pali, "beggar"). A fully ordained Buddhist nun.

Bodh Gaya. The site of the BUDDHA's enlightenment, in the present-day state of Bihar in northeastern India.

bodhi (Sanskrit, "awakening"). Enlightenment.

Bodhi tree. The tree under which the BUDDHA achieved enlightenment.

bodhichitta (Sanskrit, "mind of enlightenment"). The aspiration to enlightenment for the sake of all sentient beings, possessed by the BODHISATTVA.

bodhisattva / bodhisatta (Sanskrit / Pali, "one whose goal is awakening"). A being intent on enlightenment (*BODHI*); one who has vowed to achieve buddhahood for the welfare of all beings.

brahma world. The heaven of the god Brahma, who persuaded the BUDDHA to teach.

brahmaviharas (Sanskrit, "abodes of Brahma," "pure abidings"). Among the most famous of the many objects of meditation in Buddhism: loving-kindness, compassion, sympathetic joy, and equanimity.

Brahmin (Sanskrit, "praise," "worship"). A priest, a member of the highest of the four castes in traditional Indian society (also spelled "Brahman"). *See* KSHATRIYA; SHUDRA; VAISHYA.

buddha (Sanskrit, "awakened one"). The various Buddhist traditions agree that a number of individuals have achieved buddhahood, a state of perfect enlightenment, and that there will be future buddhas. The historical Buddha, known as Shakyamuni Buddha or Gautama Buddha (ca. fifth century B.C.E.), was born an Indian prince, Siddhartha Gautama.

buddha field. A world in which a BUDDHA is present in a given aeon.

buddhadharma (Sanskrit). The teaching of the BUDDHA.

chakra (Sanskrit, "wheel"). In tantric physiology, the network of channels radiating throughout the body that carry the subtle energies that serve as the vehicles for consciousness.

chakravartin (Sanskrit, "one who turns the wheel"). Universal monarch, wheel-turning monarch: in Indian mythology, a figure who possesses a magic wheel that rolls around the world and makes every land it reaches part of his domain; the ideal ruler who upholds the DHARMA in the secular realm.

chan. *See* ZEN.

cho (Tibetan, "severance"). Sometimes called the "beggar's accumulation of merit": a method of practicing the perfection of giving by visualizing giving away one's own body.

Dalit (from Sanskrit, "crushed," "broken"). The so-called untouchables in Indian society: groups outside the fourfold caste system (also called "outcastes"). *See* BRAHMIN; KSHATRIYA; SHUDRA; VAISHYA.

deva (Sanskrit, "shining one"). A god; an inhabitant of the heavenly realms.

dharani (Sanskrit). A kind of extended mantra sometimes considered to be the quintessence of a scripture.

dharma / dhamma (Sanskrit / Pali, "teaching"). A term notoriously difficult to translate, most commonly understood as doctrine or discourses of the BUDDHA. As such, it is one of THE THREE JEWELS. It also often means "phenomenon."

dharmakaya (Sanskrit, "truth body"). One of THE THREE BODIES OF THE BUDDHA: the transcendental and unchanging body, generally represented as a kind of cosmic principle of enlightenment in which all buddhas partake. *See* NIRMANAKAYA; SAMBHOGAKAYA.

dharmavinaya (Sanskrit, "doctrine-discipline"). A generic term for the teachings of the BUDDHA preserved in the monastic community.

dhyana / *jhana* (Sanskrit / Pali). A state of deep concentration achieved through meditation; a place of rebirth in the REALM OF FORM.

Digha Nikaya (Pali, "Long Collection"). A section of the Pali canon consisting of those discourses of the BUDDHA regarded as lengthy.

duhkha / *dukkha* (Sanskrit / Pali, "suffering"). The first of THE FOUR NOBLE TRUTHS.

eightfold path, the. The path to NIRVANA as set forth in the BUDDHA's first sermon: right view, right intention, right speech, right action, right livelihood, right effort, right mindfulness, and right concentration. These elements can be summarized under THE THREE TRAININGS.

Formless Realm. The location of the four highest of the Buddhist heavens, in which the gods have no bodies but exist only as consciousness. It is one of the three realms of the Buddhist universe; *see* REALM OF DESIRE; REALM OF FORM.

four noble truths, the. The four truths for those on the path to enlightenment, set forth in the BUDDHA's first sermon: suffering (*DUKKHA*), origin (*SAMUDAYA*) of suffering, cessation (*nirodha*) of suffering, and the path.

four stages of the path [to NIRVANA], **the.** Stream Enterer (or Stream-Winner), Once Returner, Never Returner, and ARHAT.

gandharva / *gandhabba* (Sankrit / Pali). A kind of musician demigod that subsists on fragrances.

Guanshiyin (Chinese, "He Who Observes the Sounds of the World"). The Chinese name of AVALOKITESHVARA, sometimes shortened to Guanyin.

guru (Sanskrit, "teacher"). Devotion to the guru is especially important in tantric Buddhism.

Hinayana (Sanskrit, "Inferior Vehicle"). The label applied in many MAHAYANA writings to other schools of Buddhism, often called by scholars "mainstream Buddhism." See NIKAYA.

Huayan. A major school of Chinese Buddhism; its central text is the *Avatamsaka Sutra.*

Indra's net. A net said to hang in the palace of the king of the gods: it has a jewel at each knot in the pattern, each jewel reflecting all the others, just as everything in the universe reflects the existence of everything else. It is a common symbol of the interdependence of all things.

Jainism. An ancient religion of India that arose around the time of the BUDDHA; known for its asceticism, it was sometimes a rival of Buddhism.

jataka (Sanskrit / Pali, "birth"). A story of one of the BUDDHA's rebirths before his achievement of buddhahood.

jhana. See DHYANA.

kalpa (Sanskrit). An aeon; a common unit of time in Indian religions.

karma (Sanskrit, "action"). The positive and negative deeds that bear fruit as either happiness or suffering in the future.

kinnara (Sanskrit). In Buddhist cosmology, a demigod that is half-human, half-horse.

klesha (Sanskrit, "affliction"). Negative emotion: the motivation for negative KARMA, and therefore the cause of the cause of suffering.

koan. The Japanese pronunciation of *gong'an* (Chinese, "public cases"), works often presented as verbatim transcripts of spontaneous conversations between masters and their disciples; these verbal puzzles served as objects of meditation in the CHAN and ZEN traditions.

kshatriya / *khattiya* (Sanskrit / Pali, "holder of authority"). A member of the second of the four castes in traditional Indian society, sometimes called the warrior caste. *See* BRAHMIN; SHUDRA; VAISHYA.

lama. The Tibetan term for GURU.

lojong (Tibetan, "mind training"). A genre of literature intended to develop BODHICHITTA, the aspiration to achieve enlightenment in order to liberate all beings in the universe from suffering.

Madhyamaka (Sanskrit, "middle-ist"). A MAHAYANA school that Nagarjuna is credited with founding (second or third century C.E.); renowned for its doctrine of *SHUNYATA*, it stressed the importance of THE MIDDLE WAY between the extremes of existence and nonexistence.

Mahayana (Sanskrit, "Great Vehicle"). A group of SUTRAS that began to appear in India four hundred years after the BUDDHA's death, containing new doctrines, as well as those who accepted those sutras as the word of the Buddha. Among the most important of these doctrines was the claim that all beings would one day achieve buddhahood.

Maitreya (Sanskrit, "kindness"). The next BUDDHA.

mandala (Sanskrit, "circle"). In TANTRA, the palace of a BUDDHA or a deity; its visualization and physical representation became an important part of tantric practice.

mantra (Sanskrit, "instrument of thought," "sacred formula"). A word or phrase used as a focus of meditation or worship.

Mara (Sanskrit, "killer"). The deity who is the personification of evil and desire; in many accounts, Mara seeks to prevent the BUDDHA and his followers from attaining enlightenment.

middle way, the. The way between the extremes of self-indulgence and self-mortification, according to the BUDDHA's first sermon after his enlightenment; in the teaching of Nagarjuna (second or third century C.E.), the middle way between existence and nonexistence. *See* MADHYAMAKA.

mindfulness. The Victorian translation of a term (Sanskrit, *smriti*; Pali, *sati*) that often means "memory," but also has connotations of "awareness" and "attention." In the context of meditation practice, mindfulness is that factor that keeps the mind on its chosen object.

mudra (Sanskrit, "seal," "sign"). A symbolic hand gesture. Such gestures are particularly important in tantric Buddhism.

naga (Sanskrit). A kind of water deity.

***nembutsu*, the** (Japanese). The phrase *namu amida butsu* ("Homage to Amitabha Buddha"): in PURE LAND BUDDHISM, the phrase used to call on the power of AMITABHA for salvation.

Neo-Confucianism. A revival of the ideas of Confucius (551–479 B.C.E.) during the Song dynasty (960–1279); it criticized but was influenced by Buddhism and Daoism.

nikaya (Sanskrit, "school," "group"). The sects of Buddhism that were the majority in India; it is a label applied by scholars to non-MAHAYANA Buddhism in India instead of the pejorative HINAYANA. Also, a group of Buddhist scriptures, such as the *DIGHA NIKAYA*.

nirmanakaya (Sanskrit, "emanation body"). One of THE THREE BODIES OF THE BUDDHA: the visible body manifested by a buddha to benefit ordinary beings. *See SAMBHOGAKAYA; DHARMAKAYA*.

nirvana / nibbana (Sanskrit / Pali, "blown out," "extinguished"). The state of the cessation of the accumulated causes of future suffering and rebirth.

Nyingma (Tibetan, "Ancient"). The oldest of the major sects of Buddhism in Tibet; it traces its roots to the visit there of the tantric master Padmasambhava at the end of the eighth century C.E.

paramita (Sanskrit, "perfections"). The virtues whose practice produces the BODHISATTVA's merit, often numbered as six: giving, ethics, patience, effort, concentration, and wisdom.

parinirvana / parinibbana (Sanskrit / Pali, "final nirvana"). The passage into NIRVANA that occurs at the death of a BUDDHA or an ARHAT.

prajna (Sanskrit). Wisdom; one of THE THREE TRAININGS for those seeking enlightenment.

prajnaparamita (Sanskrit, "perfection of wisdom"). A genre of MAHAYANA texts that began to appear in India in the first century C.E.; this wisdom is often identified as the knowledge of *SHUNYATA*, the knowledge necessary to become a BUDDHA.

pratimoksha / patimokkha (Sanskrit / Pali). The code of monastic conduct.

pratyekabuddha / paccekabuddha (Sanskrit / Pali, "solitary enlightened one"). A follower of the BUDDHA who preferred not to live among the community, but who practiced in solitude, often in silence, achieving enlightenment at a time when no buddhas appeared in the world. As the tradition developed, the *pratyekabuddha* became doctrinally defined in relation to the SHRAVAKA; both seek to become an ARHAT.

preta (Sanskrit, "departed" or "deceased"). A ghost, conventionally portrayed as hungry; one is said to be reborn as a ghost as a result of actions motivated by greed in a former life. One of the six forms of rebirth, together with DEVAS, ASURAS, humans, animals, and denizens of hell.

pure land. A general term for the realm of a BUDDHA that lacks the unfortunate realms of rebirth. It often refers specifically to the BUDDHA FIELD of the buddha named AMITABHA; rebirth in it would become a common goal of Buddhist practice in India, Tibet, and throughout East Asia.

Pure Land Buddhism. The MAHAYANA practice whose primary doctrine is the belief that faith in AMITABHA will lead to rebirth in his PURE LAND. It would become a separate school in Japan.

rains retreat. The period during the monsoon season when the itinerant monks of Buddhism would not wander from place to place.

Realm of Desire. One of the three realms of the Buddhist universe, so named because the beings who inhabit it desire pleasing objects of the senses. It includes the realms of DEVAS (of the Realm of Desire), ASURAS, humans, animals, *PRETAS*, and denizens of hell. *See* REALM OF FORM; FORMLESS REALM.

Realm of Form. One of the three realms of the Buddhist universe, so named because the DEVAS who inhabit it have physical form, unlike the DEVAS of the FORMLESS REALM. Its heavens are divided into four levels, known as DHYANA, which are attained through achieving a particular level of concentration in the previous life as a human. *See* REALM OF DESIRE; FORMLESS REALM.

Rinzai. One of the two major ZEN sects in Japan; it is the Japanese pronunciation of Linji (d. 867), a Chinese monk who founded one of the most important CHAN traditions.

rishi (Sanskrit). Sage.

samadhi (Sanskrit, "concentration"). A state of deep meditation; one of THE THREE TRAININGS for those seeking enlightenment.

sambhogakaya (Sanskrit, "enjoyment body"). One of THE THREE BODIES OF THE BUDDHA: the celestial body, a resplendent form that appears in the PURE LANDS. *See* NIRMANAKAYA; DHARMAKAYA.

samsara (Sanskrit, "wandering"). The endless cycle of birth and death that transpires within the realms of DEVAS, ASURAS, humans, animals, *PRETAS*, and denizens of hell.

samudaya (Sanskrit). Origin, the second of THE FOUR NOBLE TRUTHS.

sangha (Sanskrit, "community"). The Buddhist community, especially the community of monks and nuns; one of THE THREE JEWELS.

Shingon (Japanese, "True Word"). A school of tantric Buddhism founded by Kukai (774–835).

shramana (Sanskrit). A wandering mendicant.

shravaka (Sanskrit, "listener"). A disciple of the BUDDHA who remained in his presence; a follower of non-MAHAYANA Buddhist schools who seeks to become an ARHAT.

shudra / *sudda* (Sanskrit / Pali). A servant, a member of the lowest of the four castes in traditional Indian society. *See* BRAHMIN; KSHATRIYA; VAISHYA.

shunyata (Sanskrit, "emptiness"). In the *PRAJNAPARAMITA* sutras and in the MADHYAMAKA school of Nagarjuna (second or third century C.E.), the nature of reality, often described as the absence of any intrinsic nature in the persons and phenomena of the universe.

siddhi (Sanskrit, "accomplishment"). One of the magical powers possessed by the *mahasiddhas* ("great adepts"), the saints of tantric Buddhism in India and Tibet.

skandhas / *khandhas* (Sanskrit / Pali, "aggregates"). A standard division of the constituents of mind and body into five groups: form, feeling, discrimination, compositional factors, and consciousness.

skillful means (Sanskrit, *upayakaushalya*; also translated "skillful methods," "expedient means"). The BUDDHA's use of various expedient devices to teach only what was appropriate for the moment, calibrated to the capacities of a particular audience. This notion became a central tenet in the MAHAYANA.

stupa. A tomb or reliquary of a BUDDHA, a prominent disciple, or later Buddhist saint.

sutra / *sutta* (Sanskrit / Pali, "discourse"). A discourse of the BUDDHA or one spoken with his sanction, usually presented in the form of a dialogue.

tantra (Sanskrit, "handbook"). Texts setting forth rituals and practices for the attainment of all manner of supernatural powers, including the power to achieve buddhahood, that began to appear in India in the seventh century C.E.; highly influential in India, Nepal, Tibet, and East Asia.

Tathagata (Sanskrit, "one who has thus come/gone"). A title of a BUDDHA; it is often used by the historical Buddha to refer to himself.

tathagatagarbha (Sanskrit, "essence of the TATHAGATA"). The BUDDHA nature, set forth in a number of MAHAYANA SUTRAS: a quality naturally and eternally present in all (or almost all) sentient beings that ensures their eventual enlightenment.

Tendai. *See* TIANTAI.

terma (Tibetan, "treasure texts"). Texts that, according to tradition, were composed by Indian masters, especially the eighth-century master Padmasambhava, and buried in Tibet, to be unearthed at the appropriate moment in the future. This is a genre central to Tibetan Buddhism.

Theravada (Pali, "Way of the Elders"). The Buddhist tradition of modern Sri Lanka and Southeast Asia. A school of mainstream Buddhism, it does not consider the MAHAYANA SUTRAS to be the authentic word of the BUDDHA.

three bodies of the Buddha, the. A MAHAYANA doctrine according to which a BUDDHA has three bodies: see *NIRMANAKAYA*; *SAMBHOGAKAYA*; *DHARMAKAYA*.

three jewels, the. The BUDDHA, the DHARMA, and the SANGHA; by tradition, a Buddhist is anyone who states that he or she takes refuge in them.

three trainings, the. The trainings necessary for liberation from rebirth, which summarize THE EIGHTFOLD PATH: the training in ethics (right speech, right action, right livelihood); in meditation, or SAMADHI (right effort, right mindfulness, right concentration); and in wisdom, or PRAJNA (right view, right intention).

Tiantai. A major Chinese school of Buddhism (named after the mountain where its chief temple was located); it declared that the *Lotus Sutra* represented the fullest exposition of the Buddha's enlightenment. This school would become important in both Japan (as Tendai) and Korea (as Cheontae).

trichiliocosm. The universe, consisting of a billion worlds.

tripitaka (Sanskrit, "three baskets"). The canon of Buddhism: the SUTRAS, the VINAYA, and the *ABHIDHARMA*.

tulku (Tibet). An incarnate LAMA. The idea that the next incarnation of a great master could be identified, even as a young child, became a central component of Tibetan society.

Upanishads, the. One section of the texts that make up the VEDAS, the sacred scriptures of the Hindu tradition.

upayakaushalya. *See* SKILLFUL MEANS.

vaishya / *vessa* (Sanskrit / Pali). A member of the third of the four castes in traditional Indian society, sometimes called the merchant caste. *See* BRAHMIN; KSHATRIYA; SHUDRA.

vajra (Sanskrit). A mythical weapon wielded by the god Indra—a kind of thunderbolt or discus, capable of cutting through anything.

Vajrayana (Sanskrit). The Thunderbolt or Diamond Vehicle; a common term for tantric Buddhism.

Vedas. The sacred texts of Hindus; their authority was rejected by the BUDDHA.

Vedic Hinduism. The dominant religion in India at the time that Buddhism arose; its major texts were the VEDAS.

vihara (Sanskrit). A monastery or nunnery.

vinaya (Sanskrit, "discipline"). The ethical code followed by monks and nuns.

yaksha / yakkha (Sanskrit / Pali). One of the varieties of nonhuman beings, a kind of nature spirit.

Yogachara (Sanskrit, "practitioner of yoga"). A major school of MAHAYANA Buddhist philosophy founded by Asanga (fourth century C.E.). Sometimes called Chittamatra ("mind only"), it provided detailed analyses of consciousness as well as presentations of the structure of the various paths to enlightenment.

yojana (Sanskrit). The standard measurement of distance in ancient India, said to be how far a yoked team of oxen can pull a royal chariot in one day (estimated to be between 5 and 9 miles).

zazen (Japanese). Seated meditation, associated particularly with the CHAN and ZEN schools, which sometimes debated the value of prolonged sessions of silent seated meditation versus the value of KOANS.

zen (Japanese). The Japanese pronunciation of CHAN, a shortened form of *chan na*— the Chinese rendering of a common term in Buddhism for concentration, the Sanskrit word *DHYANA*.

Selected Bibliography

Reference Works, General Introductions, and Anthologies

General English-language reference works on Buddhism include works such as Robert E. Buswell, Jr., ed., *Encyclopedia of Buddhism*, 2004 (2 vols.); Robert E. Buswell, Jr. and Donald S. Lopez, Jr., *The Princeton Dictionary of Buddhism*, 2014; and G. P. Malalasekara, *Dictionary of Pāli Proper Names*, 1937–38 (2 vols.). A large number of Buddhist figures, texts, and topics are also dealt with in the *Encyclopedia of Religion*, ed. Lindsay Jones, 2nd ed., 2005 (15 vols.). The many general introductions and surveys of Buddhism include Heinz Bechert and Richard Gombrich, eds., *The World of Buddhism: Buddhist Monks and Nuns in Society and Culture*, 1984; Rupert Gethin, *The Foundations of Buddhism*, 1998; Donald S. Lopez, Jr., *The Story of Buddhism: A Concise Guide to Its History and Teachings*, 2001; and Richard H. Robinson, Willard L. Johnson, and Thanissaro Bhikkhu, *Buddhist Religions: A Historical Introduction*, 5th ed., 2004. On the origin and development of the Buddhist scriptures, see Kōgen Mizuno, *Buddhist Sutras: Origin, Development, Transmission*, 1982. Other anthologies of Buddhist texts, less extensive than this volume, include John S. Strong, *The Experience of Buddhism: Sources and Interpretations*, 3rd ed., 2007; Donald S. Lopez, Jr., *Buddhism in Practice*, 1995 (abridged ed., 2007); and Donald Lopez, ed., *Buddhist Scriptures*, 2004.

The Life of the Buddha

The most comprehensive study of the life of the Buddha remains the two-volume work by Hajime Nakamura, *Gotama Buddha: A Biography Based on the Most Reliable Texts*, trans. Gaynor Sekimori, 2000–2005. Other useful biographies include John S. Strong, *The Buddha: A Short Biography*, 2001, and Bhikkhu Ñāṇamoli, *The Life of the Buddha, as It Appears in the Pali Canon, the Oldest Authentic Record*, 1972. For translations of two famous traditional biographies of the Buddha, see Patrick Olivelle, *Life of the Buddha by Aśvaghoṣa*, 2008, and Gwendolyn Bays, *Voice of the Buddha, The Beauty of Compassion: The Lalitavistara Sūtra*, 1983 (2 vols.).

Indian Buddhism

For general surveys of the history of Indian Buddhism, see Étienne Lamotte, *History of Indian Buddhism: From the Origins to the Śaka Era*, trans. Sara Webb-Boin under the supervision of Jean Dantinne, 1988; Hajime Nakamura, *Indian Buddhism: A Survey with Bibliographical Notes*, 1980; A. K. Warder, *Indian Buddhism*, 2nd rev. ed., 1980; and Akira Hirakawa, *A History of Indian Buddhism: From Śākyamuni to Early Mahāyāna*, trans. and ed. Paul Groner, 1990. On the earliest Buddhist scriptures, discovered in what is today Pakistan, see Richard Salomon, *Ancient Buddhist Scrolls from Gandhāra: The British Library Kharoṣṭhī Fragments*, 1999. On Indian Buddhist monasticism, see Sukumar Dutt, *Buddhist Monks and Monasteries of India: Their History and Their Contribution to Indian Culture*, 1962. On the social history of Indian Buddhist monasticism, see Gregory Schopen, *Bones, Stones, and Buddhist Monks: Collected Papers on the Archaeology, Epigraphy, and Texts of Monastic Buddhism in India*, 1996, and Gregory Schopen, *Buddhist Monks and Business Matters: Still More Papers on Monastic Buddhism in India*, 2004. On Buddhist cosmology, see Akira Sadakata, *Buddhist Cosmology: Philosophy and Origins*, trans. Gaynor Sekimori, 1997, and Jan Nattier, *Once Upon a Future Time: Studies in a Buddhist Prophecy* of Decline, 1991. On Indian Buddhist abhidharma, see Collett Cox, Disputed Dharmas: Early Buddhist Theories of Existence, 1995. On women in Indian Buddhism, see I. B. Horner, Women under Primitive Buddhism: Laywomen and Almswomen, 1930; Liz Wilson, Charming Cadavers: Horrific Figurations of the Feminine in Indian Buddhist Hagiographic Literature, 1996; and Reiko Ohnuma, Ties That Bind: Maternal Imagery and Discourse in Indian Buddhism, 2012. For a Buddhist account of the life of Emperor Ashoka, see John S. Strong, The Legend of King Aśoka: A Study and Translation of the Aśokāvadāna, 1983. For translations of the many jatakas or "birth stories," stories of the Buddha's former lives, see E. B. Cowell, ed., The Jātaka, or, Stories of the Buddha's Former Births, 1895–1907 (6 vols.), and Justin Meiland, Garland of the Buddha's Past Lives, by Āryaśūra, 2009 (2 vols.). For translations of some of most important Indian avadanas, or "tales," see Andy Rotman, Divine Stories: Divyāvadāna, part 1, 2008, and Joel Tatelman, The Heavenly Exploits: Buddhist Biographies from the Dívyavadána, vol. 1, 2005.

The Pali Canon and the Theravada Tradition
The major works of the Pali canon—that is, the works that form the foundation of Theravada Buddhism in Sri Lanka and Southeast Asia—have been translated into English, in some cases numerous times, beginning with the work of the Pali Text Society, which was launched in the nineteenth century and continues to the present day. Reliable translations of many works are now available online at www.accesstoinsight.org. The four major nikayas or collections of the Pali canon are available in Maurice Walshe, The Long Discourses of the Buddha: A Translation of the Dīgha Nikāya, 1995; Bhikkhu Ñāṇamoli and Bhikkhu Bodhi, The Middle Length Discourses of the Buddha: A New Translation of the Majjhima Nikāya, 2nd ed., 2001; Bhikkhu Bodhi, The Connected Discourses of the Buddha: A New Translation of the Saṃyutta Nikāya, 2000; and Bhikkhu Bodhi, The Numerical Discourses of the Buddha: A Complete Translation of the Aṅguttara Nikāya, 2012. For an anthology of selections from these four collections, see Bhikkhu Bodhi, In the Buddha's Words: An Anthology of Discourses from the Pāli Canon, 2005. For the Pali vinaya or monastic code, see

Thanissaro Bhikkhu, The Buddhist Monastic Code I and II: The Pātimokkha Training Rules, 2nd ed., rev., 2007. On the Pali abhidharma (abhidhamma), see Bhikkhu Bodhi, A Comprehensive Manual of Abhidhamma: The Abhidhammattha Sangaha, 2003. Useful surveys of Pali literature include K. R. Norman, Pāli Literature: Including the Canonical Literature in Prakrit and Sanskrit of All the Hīnayāna Schools of Buddhism, 1983, and Oskar von Hinüber, A Handbook of Pāli Literature, 1996. For a historical survey of Theravada Buddhism, see Richard Gombrich, Theravāda Buddhism: A Social History from Ancient Benares to Modern Colombo, 2nd ed., 2006. On nirvana, see Steven Collins, Nirvana: Concept, Imagery, Narrative, 2010. On the history and meanings of the term "Theravada," see Peter Skilling et al., eds., How Theravāda Is Theravāda? Exploring Buddhist Identities, 2012.

Mahayana Buddhism
Since the translation of the Diamond Sutra from Tibetan into German in 1837, many of the most important of the Mahayana sutras have been translated into European languages. Reliable translations of several of these texts are available online through the Japanese Buddhist organization, Bukkyo Dendo Kyokai (www.bdkamerica.org). For translations of other important sutras, see C. C. Chang, ed., A Treasury of Mahāyāna Sūtras: Selections from the Mahāratnakūṭa Sūtra, 1983; Edward Conze, The Large Sutra of Perfect Wisdom, with the Divisions of the Abhisamayālaṅkāra, 1975; Paul Harrison, The Samādhi of Direct Encounter with the Buddhas of the Present: An Annotated English Translation of the Tibetan Translation of the Pratyupanna-Buddha-Sammukhāvasthita-Samādhi-Sūtra, 1990; and John Powers, Wisdom of the Buddha: The Saṃdhinirmocana Mahāyāna Sūtra, 1995. On the Lotus Sutra, see Stephen F. Teiser and Jacqueline I. Stone, eds., Readings of the Lotus Sūtra, 2009. On the Heart Sutra, see Donald S. Lopez, Jr., Elaborations on Emptiness: Uses of the Heart Sūtra, 1996. On the origins of the Mahayana, see Gregory Schopen, Figments and Fragments of Mahāyāna Buddhism in India: More Collected Papers, 2005; Jan Nattier, A Few Good Men: The Bodhisattva Path According to the Inquiry of Ugra (Ugraparipṛcchā), 2003; and Daniel Boucher, Bodhisattvas of

the Forest and the Formation of the Mahāyāna: A Study and Translation of the Rāṣṭrapālaparipṛcchā-sūtra, 2008. For a general survey of Mahayana doctrine and practice, see Paul Williams, *Mahāyāna Buddhism: The Doctrinal Foundations*, 2nd ed., 2009.

Buddhist Tantra

For an anthology that contains a range of Buddhist tantric texts, see David Gordon White, ed., *Tantra in Practice*, 2000. For studies of tantric Buddhism in India, see Ronald M. Davidson, *Indian Esoteric Buddhism: A Social History of the Tantric Movement*, 2002, and David L. Snellgrove, *Indo-Tibetan Buddhism: Indian Buddhists and Their Tibetan Successors*, 1987, and Christian K. Wedemeyer, *Making Sense of Tantric Buddhism: History, Semiology, and Transgression in the Indian Traditions*, 2013. For translations of important tantric texts, see David L. Snellgrove, *The Hevajra Tantra: A Critical Study*, 1959 (2 vols.); Rolf W. Giebel, *The Vairocanābhisaṃbodhi Sutra*, 2005; and David B. Gray, *The Cakrasamvara Tantra (The Discourse of Śrī Heruka): A Study and Annotated Translation*, 2007. For a detailed description of the initiation process for an influential tantric text, one that remains important in Tibetan Buddhism, see the Dalai Lama and Jeffrey Hopkins, *Kalachakra Tantra: Rite of Initiation: For the Stage of Generation*, new enl. ed., 1999. For an influential exegetical work on the theory and practice of *anuttarayoga tantra*, see Tsongkhapa, *A Lamp to Illuminate the Five Stages: Teachings on the Guhyasamāja Tantra*, trans. Gavin Kilty, 2013. For an extensive sourcebook on Esoteric Buddhism in East Asia, see Charles Orzech, ed., *Esoteric Buddhism and the Tantras in East Asia*, 2010. On Esoteric Buddhism in Japan, see Ryūichi Abé, *The Weaving of Mantra: Kūkai and the Construction of Esoteric Buddhist Discourse*, 1999.

Chinese Buddhism

For a general survey of Chinese Buddhism, see Kenneth Ch'en, *Buddhism in China: A Historical Survey*, 1964. On the introduction and early development of Buddhism in China, see Erik Zürcher, *The Buddhist Conquest of China: The Spread and Adaptation of Buddhism in Early Medieval China*, 3rd ed., 2007. On the role of Buddhism in Chi-

nese society and culture, see Jacques Gernet, *Buddhism in Chinese Society: An Economic History from the Fifth to the Tenth Centuries*, trans. Franciscus Verellen, 1995, and John Kieschnick, *The Impact of Buddhism on Chinese Material Culture*, 2003. For an anthologies that include a wide range of Chinese Buddhist texts, see Donald S. Lopez, Jr., ed., *Religions of China in Practice*, 1996, and Wm. Theodore de Bary et al., eds., *Sources of Chinese Tradition*, 2nd ed., 1999 (2 vols.). On the lives of Chinese "eminent monks," see John Kieschnick, *The Eminent Monk: Buddhist Ideals in Medieval Chinese Hagiography*, 1997. On apocryphal Buddhist texts and their importance in the development of Chinese Buddhism, see Robert E. Buswell, Jr., ed., *Chinese Buddhist Apocrypha*, 1990. On the origins of the Chan school in China, see John R. McRae, *The Northern School and the Formation of Early Ch'an Buddhism*, 1986. On the origins of the famous "ghost festival" of East Asia, see Stephen F. Teiser, *The Ghost Festival in Medieval China*, 1988. On the origins and importance of the "bodhisattva of compassion," Guanyin, see Chün-fang Yü, *Kuanyin: The Chinese Transformation of Avalokiteśvara*, 2001. On the practice of Chinese Buddhism in the twentieth century, see two books by Holmes Welch: *The Practice of Chinese Buddhism: 1900–1950*, 1967, and *Buddhism under Mao*, 1972.

Korean Buddhism

For anthologies that contain a range of Korean Buddhist texts, see Robert E. Buswell, Jr., ed., *Religions of Korea in Practice*, 2007, and Peter Lee and Wm. Theodore de Bary, eds., *Sources of Korean Tradition*, 1997–2000 (2 vols.). On the contemporary monastic life in Korea, see Robert E. Buswell, Jr., *The Zen Monastic Experience: Buddhist Practice in Contemporary Korea*, 1992, and Eun-su Cho, ed., *Korean Buddhist Nuns and Laywomen: Hidden Histories, Enduring Vitality*, 2011.

Japanese Buddhism

For anthologies that contains a range of Japanese Buddhist texts, see George J. Tanabe, Jr., *Religions of Japan in Practice*, 1999, and Wm. Theodore de Bary et al., eds., *Sources of Japanese Tradition*, 2nd ed., 2001–05 (2 vols.). On Soto Zen, see William M. Bodiford, *Sōtō Zen in Medieval*

Japan, 1993. On Dogen, founder of the Soto sect, see Carl Bielefeldt, *Dōgen's Manuals of Zen Meditation*, 1988, and Steven Heine, ed., *Dōgen: Textual and Historical Studies*, 2012. On the Pure Land sects of Japan, see James C. Dobbins, *Jōdo Shinshū: Shin Buddhism in Medieval Japan*, 1989. On debates about the Japanese Buddhist sects, including Tendai and Nichiren, on the question of "original enlightenment," see Jacqueline I. Stone, *Original Enlightenment and the Transformation of Medieval Japanese Buddhism*, 1999. On the transformations of Japanese Buddhism that occurred in the wake of the Meiji Restoration of 1868, see James Edward Ketelaar, *Of Heretics and Martyrs in Japan: Buddhism and Its Persecution*, 1990, and Richard M. Jaffe, *Neither Monk nor Layman: Clerical Marriage in Modern Japanese Buddhism*, 2001. On the "funeral Buddhism" of modern Japan, see Mark Michael Rowe, *Bonds of the Dead: Temples, Burial, and the Transformation of Contemporary Japanese Buddhism*, 2011.

Tibetan Buddhism
For anthologies containing a wide range of Tibetan Buddhist texts, see Donald S. Lopez, Jr., ed., *Religions of Tibet in Practice*, 1997, and Kurtis R. Schaeffer, Matthew T. Kapstein, and Gray Tuttle, eds., *Sources of Tibetan Tradition*, 2013. For overviews of Tibetan culture and history and the important place of Buddhism in both, see Matthew Kapstein, *The Tibetans*, 2006, and Sam van Schaik, *Tibet: A History*, 2011. On the restoration of Buddhism in Tibet that began in the middle of the tenth century, see Ronald M. Davidson, *Tibetan Renaissance: Tantric Buddhism in the Revival of Tibetan Culture*, 2005. On the practice of Tibetan Buddhist pilgrimage, see Toni Huber, *The Cult of Pure Crystal Mountain: Popular Pilgrimage and Visionary Landscape in Southeast Tibet*, 1999. On the role of real and symbolic violence in Tibetan Buddhism, see Jacob P. Dalton, *The Taming of the Demons: Violence and Liberation in Tibetan Buddhism*, 2011. On monastic life in exile, see Georges B. J. Dreyfus, *The Sound of Two Hands Clapping: The Education of a Tibetan Buddhist Monk*, 2003. On the life of the Fourteenth Dalai Lama, see his *Freedom in Exile: The Autobiography of the Dalai Lama*, 1990. On the history of European and American fascination with Tibet and Tibetan Buddhism, see Donald S. Lopez, Jr., *Prisoners of Shangri-La: Tibetan Buddhism and the West*, 1998.

Modern Buddhism
For an English translation of the first European monograph on Buddhism, published in Paris in 1844, see Eugène Burnouf, *Introduction to the History of Indian Buddhism*, trans. Katia Buffetrille and Donald S. Lopez, Jr., 2010. For the history of Buddhism in America, see Rick Fields, *How the Swans Came to the Lake: A Narrative History of Buddhism in America*, 1981, and Thomas A. Tweed, *The American Encounter with Buddhism, 1844–1912: Victorian Culture and the Limits of Dissent*, 1992. On the Japanese delegation to the 1893 World's Parliament of Religions, see Judith Snodgrass, *Presenting Japanese Buddhism to the West: Orientalism, Occidentalism, and the Columbian Exposition*, 2003. On the development of the academic field of Buddhist studies, see Donald S. Lopez, Jr., ed., *Curators of the Buddha: The Study of Buddhism under Colonialism*, 1995. On the formation of Modern Buddhism, see David L. McMahan, *The Making of Buddhist Modernism*, 2008. On the history of the claims for the compatibility of Buddhism and modern science, see Donald S. Lopez, Jr., *Buddhism and Science: A Guide for the Perplexed*, 2008. On the Burmese origins of the modern *vipassana* movement, see Erik Braun, *The Birth of Insight: Meditation, Modern Buddhism, and the Burmese Monk Ledi Sayadaw*, 2013. On Sri Lankan Buddhism during the period of British colonialism, see Anne M. Blackburn, *Locations of Buddhism: Colonialism and Modernity in Sri Lanka*, 2010. For an anthology of texts important to the development of Modern Buddhism, see Donald S. Lopez, Jr., ed., *A Modern Buddhist Bible: Essential Readings from East and West*, 2002.

Permissions Acknowledgments

GENERAL INTRODUCTION

Kay Ryan: "On the Nature of Understanding," from *The New Yorker,* July 25, 2011. Copyright © 2011 by Kay Ryan. Reprinted by permission of the author.

TEXT

Knowledge of Origins, Great Discourse on the Final Nirvana, *and* The Three Knowledges: From THE LONG DISCOURSES OF THE BUDDHA: A TRANSLATION OF THE DIGHA NIKAYA, translated by Maurice Walshe. Copyright © 1987, 1995 by Maurice Walshe. Reprinted with the permission of The Permissions Company, Inc., on behalf of Wisdom Publications.

Prince Vessantara Gives Away His Children: From THE PERFECT GENEROSITY OF PRINCE VESSANTARA, translated by Margaret Cone and Richard F. Gombrich. Reprinted by permission of Richard F. Gombrich.

The Noble Search *and* The Establishment of Mindfulness: From THE MIDDLE LENGTH DISCOURSES OF THE BUDDHA: A NEW TRANSLATION OF THE MAJJHIMA NIKAYA, original translation by Bhikkhu Nanamoli, translation edited and revised by Bhikkhu Bodhi. Copyright © 1995 by Bhikkhu Bodhi. Reprinted with the permission of The Permissions Company, Inc., on behalf of Wisdom Publications.

Account of the Beginning: From THE STORY OF GOTAMA BUDDHA, edited by N. A. Jayawickrama. Copyright © 1990 by Pali Text Society. Reprinted by permission of Pali Text Society.

Setting the Wheel of the Dharma in Motion: From THE CONNECTED DISCOURSES OF THE BUDDHA: A NEW TRANSLATION OF THE SAMYUTTA NIKAYA, VOLUME II, translated by Bhikkhu Bodhi. Copyright © 2000 by Bhikkhu Bodhi. Reprinted with the permission of The Permissions Company, Inc., on behalf of Wisdom Publications.

Verses of the Dharma: From THE DHAMMAPADA, translated by John Ross Carter and Mahinda Palihawadana. Copyright © 1987 by Oxford University Press, Inc. By permission of Oxford University Press, Inc.

The Rhinoceros Horn Sutta, Discourse on Good Fortune, *and* Discourse on Loving-Kindness: From THE GROUP OF DISCOURSES (SUTTA-NIPATA), VOLUME II, translated by K. R. Norman. Copyright © 1992 by the Pali Text Society. Reprinted by permission of the Pali Text Society.

Songs of the Female Elders: From POEMS OF EARLY BUDDHIST NUNS (THERIGATHA), translated by C. A. F. Rhys Davids and K. R. Norman. Copyright © 1989 by the Pali Text Society. Reprinted by permission of the Pali Text Society.

From THE PATH OF PURIFICATION (VISUDDHIMAGGA) by Bhadantācariya Buddhaghosa, translated by Bhikkhu Ñānamoli. Copyright © 1975, 1991 by the Buddhist Publication Society. Reprinted by permission of the Buddhist Publication Society.

Treasury of Higher Doctrine: From ABHIDHARMAKOSHABHASYAM by Vasubandhu. French translation by Louis de la Vallee Poussin; English translation by Leo M. Pruden. Reprinted with permission from Asian Humanities Press, a division of Jain Publishing Company.

White Lotus of the True Dharma: From THE LOTUS SUTRA, translated by Tsugunari Kubo and Akira Yuyama. Copyright © 2007 by Bukkyō Dendō Kyōkai and Numata Center for Buddhist Translation and Research. Reprinted with permission of Bukkyō Dendō Kyōkai and Numata Center for Buddhist Translation and Research.

A Layman Humbles the Monk: From THE VIMALAKĪRTI SUTRA, translated by John R. McRae. Copyright © 2004 by Bukkyō Dendō Kyōkai and Numata Center for Buddhist Translation and Research. Reprinted with permission of Bukkyō Dendō Kyōkai and Numata Center for Buddhist Translation and Research.

Discourse: From LAND OF BLISS: THE PARADISE OF THE BUDDHA OF MEASURELESS LIGHT by Luis O. Gomez. Copyright © 1996 Higashi Honganji Shinshū Ōtani-ha. Reprinted with permission of the University of Hawai'i Press, Honolulu.

The Perfection of Wisdom That Rends Like a Thunderbolt: Originally published as "Vajracchedikā Prajñāpāramitā: A New English Translation of the Sanskrit Text Based on Two Manuscripts from Greater Gandhāra," in Jens Braarvig, gen. ed., *Manuscripts in the Schøyen Collection: Buddhist Manuscripts,* Volume III (Oslo: Hermes Publishing, 2006), pp. 133–59; reprinted here with permission. A revised version is due to appear as THE LIGHTNING BOLT OF INSIGHT: A TRANSLATION AND STUDY OF THE VAJRACCHEDIKĀ PRAJÑĀPĀRAMITĀ (Boston: Wisdom Publications). Reprinted by permission of Hermes Publishing and the translator.

Discourse on the Buddha Nature (The Mahayana Sutra Called a Tathagata Within): From A BUDDHA WITHIN: THE TATHAGATAGARBHASUTRA—THE EARLIEST EXPOSITION OF THE BUDDHA-NATURE TEACHING IN

INDIA by Michael Zimmerman. Reprinted by permission of The International Research Institute for Advanced Buddhology, Soka University, and Michael Zimmerman.

Discourse on the Heart of the Perfection Wisdom (The Heart Sutra): From ELABORATIONS ON EMPTINESS, translated by Donald S. Lopez, Jr. Reprinted by permission of Princeton University Press.

Verses on the Middle Way (On the Meaning of Emptiness): From NGRJUNA'S MIDDLE WAY: THE MLAMADHYMAKAKRIK, translated by Shoryu Katsura and Mark Siderits. Reprinted with the permission of The Permissions Company, Inc., on behalf of Wisdom Publications.

Four Hymns (Nagarjuna's Religious Practices Seen Through the Analysis of His Hymns): Translated by Drasko Mitrikeski. Reprinted by permission of the translator.

Letter to Kanishka: From INVITATION TO ENLIGHTENMENT: LETTER TO THE GREAT KING KANISKA BY MATRCETA AND LETTER TO A DISCIPLE BY CANDRAGOMIN, translated by Michael Hahn. Dharma Publishing, 1999. Reproduced by permission.

Introduction to the Practice of the Bodhisattva Path: From THE BODHICARYAVATARA, translated by Luis Gomez. Reprinted with the permission of The Permissions Company, Inc., on behalf of Wisdom Publications.

Tantra on the Complete Purification of All Negative Places of Rebirth: From THE SARVADURGATIPARISODHANA TANTRA: ELIMINATION OF ALL EVIL DESTINIES, translated by Tadeusz Skorupski. Copyright © 1983 by Motilal Banarsidass Pvt. Ltd. Reprinted by permission of Tadeusz Skorupski.

Tantra on the Complete Enlightenment of Vairochana: From THE VAIROCANĀBHISAMBODHI SUTRA, translated by Rolf W. Giebel. Copyright © 2005 by Bukkyō Dendō Kyōkai and Numata Center for Buddhist Translation and Research. Reprinted with permission of Bukkyō Dendō Kyōkai and Numata Center for Buddhist Translation and Research.

Lives of the Eighty-Four Siddhas: From BUDDHA'S LIONS: THE LIVES OF THE EIGHTY-FOUR SIDDHAS by Abhayadatta, translated by James B. Robinson. Dharma Publishing, 1979. Reproduced by permission.

In Praise of the Twenty-One Taras, Dharma Sutra of Five Mudras, and Moonlight Bestowing the Cooling Complete Bliss: From RELIGIONS OF TIBET IN PRACTICE, edited by Donald S. Lopez, Jr. Copyright © 1997 by Princeton University Press. Reprinted by permission of Princeton University Press.

The Scripture in Forty-Two Sections: From RELIGIONS OF CHINA IN PRACTICE, edited by Donald S. Lopez, Jr. Copyright © 1996 by Princeton University Press. Reprinted by permission of Princeton University Press.

Treatise . . . According to Mahayana: From THE AWAKENING OF FAITH ATTRIBUTED TO ASVAGHOSHA, translated by Yoshito S. Hakeda. Copyright © 1967 by Columbia University Press. Reprinted by permission of Columbia University Press.

From THE GREAT TANG DYNASTY RECORD OF THE WESTERN REGIONS, translated by Li Rongxi. Copyright © 1996 by Bukkyō Dendō Kyōkai and Numata Center for Buddhist Translation and Research. Reprinted with permission of Bukkyō Dendō Kyōkai and Numata Center for Buddhist Translation and Research.

Accounts in Dissemination and Praise of the Lotus Sutra: From BUDDHISM IN PRACTICE, edited by Donald S. Lopez, Jr. Copyright © 1995 by Princeton University Press. Reprinted by permission of Princeton University Press.

From THE PLATFORM SUTRA OF THE SIXTH PATRIARCH, translated by John R. McRae. Copyright © 2000 by Bukkyō Dendō Kyōkai and Numata Center for Buddhist Translation and Research. Reprinted with permission of Bukkyō Dendō Kyōkai and Numata Center for Buddhist Translation and Research.

Record of Linji: From THE ZEN TEACHINGS OF MASTER LIN-CHI, translated by Burton Watson. Copyright © 1999 by Columbia University Press. Reprinted by permission of Columbia University Press.

From THE SCRIPTURE ON THE TEN KINGS: AND THE MAKING OF PURGATORY IN MEDIEVAL CHINESE BUDDHISM by Stephen F. Teiser. Copyright © 1994 by Kuroda Institute. Reprinted with permission of University of Hawai'i Press, Honolulu.

Records of Pointing at the Moon ("Do not grasp another's brow" and "Dealing with situations") by Zen Master Ta Hui from SWAMPLAND FLOWERS: THE LETTERS AND LECTURES OF ZEN MASTER TA HUI, translated by J. C. Cleary. Copyright © 1977 by J. C. Cleary. Reprinted by arrangement with The Permissions Company, Inc., on behalf of Shambhala Publications Inc., Boston, MA. www.shambhala.com.

Journey to the West: From THE MONKEY AND THE MONK: A REVISED ABRIDGMENT OF THE JOURNEY TO THE WEST, translated by Anthony C. Yu. Copyright © 2006 by University of Chicago. Reproduced by permission of University of Chicago Press.

Arouse Your Mind and Practice: From SOURCEBOOK OF KOREAN CIVILIZATION, VOLUME I: FROM EARLY TIMES TO THE SIXTEENTH CENTURY, edited by Peter H. Lee. Copyright © 1999 Columbia University Press. Reprinted by permission of Columbia University Press.

Secrets of Cultivating Your Mind: From TRACING BACK THE RADIANCE: CHINUL'S KOREAN WAY OF ZEN by Robert E. Buswell, Jr. Copyright © 1991by Kuroda Institute. Reprinted with permission of University of Hawai'i Press, Honolulu.

Treatise Distinguishing the Two Teachings of Exoteric and Esoteric Methods: From KUKAI: MAJOR WORKS TRANSLATED, WITH AN ACCOUNT OF HIS LIFE AND A STUDY OF HIS THOUGHT, translated by Yoshito S. Hakeda. Copyright © 1972 by Columbia University Press. Reprinted by permission of Columbia University Press.

Lamenting the Deviations: From TANNISHO: A SHIN BUDDHIST CLASSIC by Taitetsu Unno. Copyright © 1984 by Taitetsu Unno. Reprinted by permission of Taitetsu Unno.

Treasury of the True Dharma Eye: From THE SHOBOGENZO by Dogen, translated by Stanley Weinstein. Reprinted by permission of Sotoshu Shumucho.

Treatise on the Establishment of the Orthodox Teaching and Peace of the Nation: From TWO NICHIREN TEXTS: RISSHŌANKOKURAN & KANJINHONZONSHŌ, translated by Murano Senchu. Copyright © 2003 by Bukkyō Dendō Kyōkai and Numata Center for Buddhist Translation and Research. Reprinted with permission of Bukkyō Dendō Kyōkai and Numata Center for Buddhist Translation and Research.

From SAND AND PEBBLES (SHASEKISHU): THE TALES OF MUJU ICHIEN, A VOICE FOR PLURALISM IN KAMAKURA BUDDHISM, edited by Robert E. Morrell, the State University of New York Press, © 1985, State University of New York. Reprinted by permission. All rights reserved.

Dreams of Buddhism: From RELIGIONS OF JAPAN IN PRACTICE, edited by George J. Tanabe, Jr. Copyright © 1999 by Princeton University Press. Reprinted by permission of Princeton University Press.

A Conversation with Skeletons: From ZEN-MAN IKKYŪ by James H. Sanford. Copyright © 1981 by the President and Fellows of Harvard College. Reprinted by permission of James H. Sanford.

Orategama: From THE ZEN MASTER HAKUIN: SELECTED WRITINGS, translated by Philip B. Yampolsky. Copyright © 1971 by Columbia University Press. Reprinted by permission of Columbia University Press.

Commentary on Eight Verses for Training the Mind: From MIND TRAINING: THE GREAT COLLECTION, compiled by Shonu Gyalchok and Konchock Gyaltsen, translated and edited by Thupten Jinpa. Copyright © 2006 The Institute of Tibetan Classics. Reprinted with the permission of The Permissions Company, Inc., on behalf of Wisdom Publications.

From THE LIFE OF MILAREPA by Tsangnyon Heruka, translated by Andrew Quintman. Copyright © 2010 by Andrew Quintman. Used by permission of Penguin, a division of Penguin Group (USA) Inc., and Andrew Quintman.

Summary and Conclusion by Tsong-Kha-Pa, translated by The Lamrim Chenmo Translation Committee, from THE GREAT TREATISE ON THE STAGES OF THE PATH TO ENLIGHTENMENT, VOLUME THREE. Copyright © 2002 by the Tibetan Buddhist Learning Center. Reprinted with the permission of The Permissions Company, Inc., on behalf of Shambhala Publications Inc. Boston, MA, www.shambhala.com.

Heart of the Practice: From TAKING THE RESULT AS THE PATH: CORE TEACHINGS OF THE SAKYA LAMDRE TRADITION, translated and edited by Cyrus Stearns. Copyright © 2006 The Institute of Tibetan Classics. Reprinted with the permission of The Permissions Company, Inc., on behalf of Wisdom Publications.

From KUNZANG LAMA'I SHELUNG: THE WORDS OF MY PERFECT TEACHER by Patrul Rinpoche, translated by the Padmakara Translation Group. Copyright © 1994 by the Padmakara Translation Group. Reprinted by permission of Yale University Press.

Buddha or Karl Marx, by B. R. Ambedkar: From WRITINGS AND SPEECHES, VOLUME III, compiled by Vasant Moon.

Basic Practice: Preparatory Stage—Basic Exercises IV: From PRACTICAL INSIGHT MEDITATION: BASIC AND PROGRESSIVE STAGES by The Venerable Mahasi Sayadaw, translated by U Pe Thin and Mayanaug U Tin. Copyright © 1971 by The Buddhist Publication Society. Reprinted by permission of Buddhist Publication Society, Kandy Sri Lanka.

Control, Mind Waves, Bowing, and Zen and Excitement: From ZEN MIND, BEGINNER'S MIND by Shunryu Suzuki. Protected under the terms of the International Copyright Union. Reprinted by arrangement with The Permissions Company, Inc., on behalf of Shambhala Publications Inc., Boston, MA. www.shambhala.com.

The Nobel Evening Address: From THE DALAI LAMA, A POLICY OF KINDNESS, edited by Tenzin Gyatso. Address copyright © 1989 by The Nobel Foundation. Reprinted by permission of The Nobel Foundation.

ILLUSTRATIONS

Head of the Buddha (Gandhara): Scala/Art Resource, NY/© Artres

Great Stupa at Sanchi: BOISVIEUX Christophe / hemis.fr/Getty Images

Two young Buddhist monks: Photo by Don Farber

Buddha with his disciples: © The Metropolitan Museum of Art. Image source: Art Resource, NY

Prince Vessantara gives away an elephant: Gift from Doris Duke Charitable Foundation's Southeast Asian Art Collection, 2006.27.81.2 © Asian Art Museum, San Francisco. Used by permission.

Stupa relief (Maya's dream of the elephant): De Agostini Picture Library/G. Nimatallah/The Bridgeman Art Library

Fasting bodhisattva: R. & S. Michaud/akg-images

Buddha turning the wheel of the dharma: © Luca Tettoni/Robert Harding World Imagery/Corbis

Thai nuns: Photo by Don Farber

Cambodian monk, Maha Ghosananda: Photo by Don Farber

Statue of Shariputra: The Avery Brundage Collection, B60S599 © Asian Art Museum, San Francisco. Used by permission.

Buddha Amitabha: Courtesy of Asia Society, New York

Guanyin with Monkey: Photograph courtesy of The Huntington Photographic Archive at The Ohio State University

Seokguram Buddha: © TOPIC PHOTO/Age Fotostock

Painting of Chinul: Courtesy of Hyunho Sunim

Sculpture of Kuya reciting: © The Rokuharamitsu-ji Temple

Japanese monastery: Photo by Don Farber

Painting of Bodhidharma by Hakyin: Indianapolis Museum of Art, James E. Roberts Fund, 65.18

Sculpture of the Fifth Dalai Lama: John Bigelow Taylor

Thangka painting: Photograph courtesy of Sotheby's, Inc. © 2013

Woman praying at Buddhist temple: Photo by Don Farber

Index